Integrated Mathematics 2

TIMOTHY D. KANOLD

EDWARD B. BURGER

JULI K. DIXON

MATTHEW R. LARSON

STEVEN J. LEINWAND

Printed in the U.S.A.

ISBN 978-0-544-38985-4

1 2 3 4 5 6 7 8 9 10 0868 22 21 20 19 18 17 16 15

4500526456 A B C D E F

Authors

Timothy D. Kanold, Ph.D., is an award-winning international educator, author, and consultant. He is a former superintendent and director of mathematics and science at Adlai E. Stevenson High School District 125 in Lincolnshire, Illinois. He is a past president of the National Council of Supervisors of Mathematics (NCSM) and the Council for the Presidential Awardees of Mathematics (CPAM). He has served on several writing and leadership commissions for NCTM during the past decade. He presents motivational professional development seminars with a focus on developing professional learning communities (PLC's) to improve the teaching, assessing, and learning of students. He has recently authored nationally recognized articles, books, and textbooks for mathematics education and school leadership, including *What Every Principal Needs to Know about the Teaching and Learning of Mathematics.*

Edward B. Burger, Ph.D., is the President of Southwestern University, a former Francis Christopher Oakley Third Century Professor of Mathematics at Williams College, and a former vice provost at Baylor University. He has authored or coauthored more than sixty-five articles, books, and video series; delivered over five hundred addresses and workshops throughout the world; and made more than fifty radio and television appearances. He is a Fellow of the American Mathematical Society as well as having earned many national honors, including the Robert Foster Cherry Award for Great Teaching in 2010. In 2012, Microsoft Education named him a "Global Hero in Education."

Juli K. Dixon, Ph.D., is a Professor of Mathematics Education at the University of Central Florida. She has taught mathematics in urban schools at the elementary, middle, secondary, and post-secondary levels. She is an active researcher and speaker with numerous publications and conference presentations. Key areas of focus are deepening teachers' content knowledge and communicating and justifying mathematical ideas. She is a past chair of the NCTM Student Explorations in Mathematics Editorial Panel and member of the Board of Directors for the Association of Mathematics Teacher Educators.

Matthew R. Larson, Ph.D., is the K-12 mathematics curriculum specialist for the Lincoln Public Schools and served on the Board of Directors for the National Council of Teachers of Mathematics from 2010 to 2013. He is a past chair of NCTM's Research Committee and was a member of NCTM's Task Force on Linking Research and Practice. He is the author of several books on implementing the Common Core Standards for Mathematics. He has taught mathematics at the secondary and college levels and held an appointment as an honorary visiting associate professor at Teachers College, Columbia University.

Steven J. Leinwand is a Principal Research Analyst at the American Institutes for Research (AIR) in Washington, D.C., and has over 30 years in leadership positions in mathematics education. He is past president of the National Council of Supervisors of Mathematics and served on the NCTM Board of Directors. He is the author of numerous articles, books, and textbooks and has made countless presentations with topics including student achievement, reasoning, effective assessment, and successful implementation of standards.

Performance Task Consultant

Robert Kaplinsky
Teacher Specialist, Mathematics
Downey Unified School District
Downey, California

STEM Consultants
Science, Technology, Engineering, and Mathematics

Michael A. DiSpezio
Global Educator
North Falmouth, Massachusetts

Michael R. Heithaus
Executive Director, School of Environment, Arts, and Society
Professor, Department of Biological Sciences
Florida International University
North Miami, Florida

Reviewers

Mindy Eden
Richwoods High School
Peoria School District
Peoria, IL

Dustin Johnson
Badger High School Math Teacher
Department Chair
Lake Geneva-Genoa City Union High School District
Lake Geneva, WI

Ashley D. McSwain
Murray High School
Murray City School District
Salt Lake City, UT

Rebecca Quinn
Doherty Memorial High School
Worcester Public Schools District
Worcester, MA

Ted Ryan
Madison LaFollette High School
Madison Metropolitan School District
Madison, WI

Tony Scoles
Fort Zumwalt School District
O'Fallon, MO

Cynthia L. Smith
Higley Unified School District
Gilbert, AZ

Phillip E. Spellane
Doherty Memorial High School
Worcester Public Schools District
Worcester, MA

Mona Toncheff
Math Content Specialist
Phoenix Union High School District
Phoenix, AZ

Characteristics of Functions

UNIT 1

Volume 1

MODULE 1

Analyzing Functions

MODULE 2

Absolute Value Functions, Equations, and Inequalities

UNIT 2

Volume 1

Polynomial Operations

MODULE 3

Rational Exponents and Radicals

MODULE 4

Adding and Subtracting Polynomials

MODULE 5 Multiplying Polynomials

UNIT 3

Volume 1

Quadratic Functions

MODULE 6

Graphing Quadratic Functions

MODULE 7

Connecting Intercepts, Zeros, and Factors

Quadratic Equations and Models

UNIT 4

Volume 1

MODULE 8

Using Factors to Solve Quadratic Equations

MODULE 9

Using Square Roots to Solve Quadratic Equations

MODULE 10

Linear, Exponential, and Quadratic Models

Extending Quadratic Equations

Volume 1

MODULE 11 Quadratic Equations and Complex Numbers

MODULE 12 Quadratic Relations and Systems of Equations

MODULE 13

Functions and Inverses

Geometric Proof

Volume 2

MODULE 14 Proofs with Lines and Angles

MODULE 15

Proofs with Triangles and Quadrilaterals

Similarity and Right Triangles

UNIT 7

Volume 2

MODULE 16 Similarity and Transformations

MODULE 17 Using Similar Triangles

MODULE 18

Trigonometry with Right Triangles

Properties of Circles

UNIT 8

Volume 2

MODULE 19 Angles and Segments in Circles

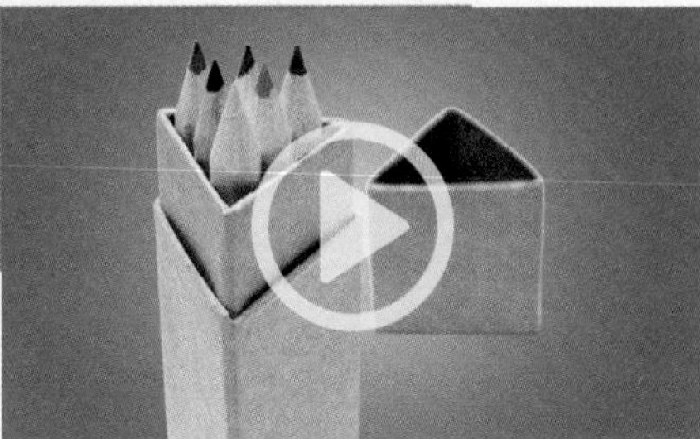

MODULE 20 Arc Length and Sector Area

UNIT 9

Volume 2

Volume

MODULE 21 Volume Formulas

Understanding Probability

UNIT 10

Volume 2

MODULE 22 Introduction to Probability

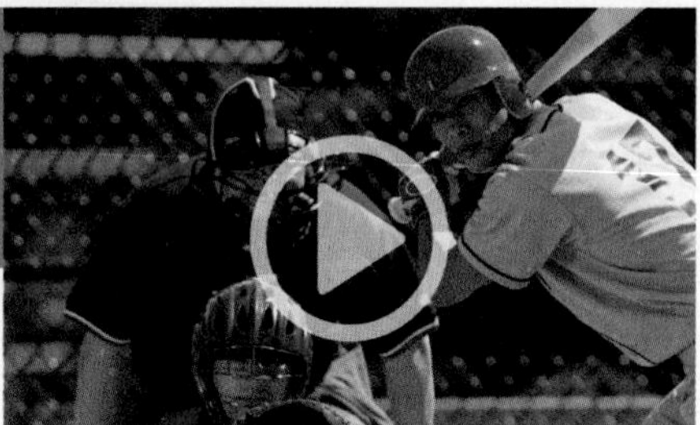

MODULE 23 Conditional Probability and Independence of Events

Probability and Decision Making

HMH Integrated Math 2

Online State Resources

Scan the QR code or visit:
my.hrw.com/nsmedia/osp/2015/ma/hs/tempint
for correlations and other state-specific resources.

Succeeding with HMH Integrated Math 2

HMH Integrated Math 2 is built on the 5E instructional model--Engage, Explore, Explain, Elaborate, Evaluate--to develop strong conceptual understanding and mastery of key mathematics standards.

ENGAGE

Preview the Lesson Performance Task in the Interactive Student Edition.

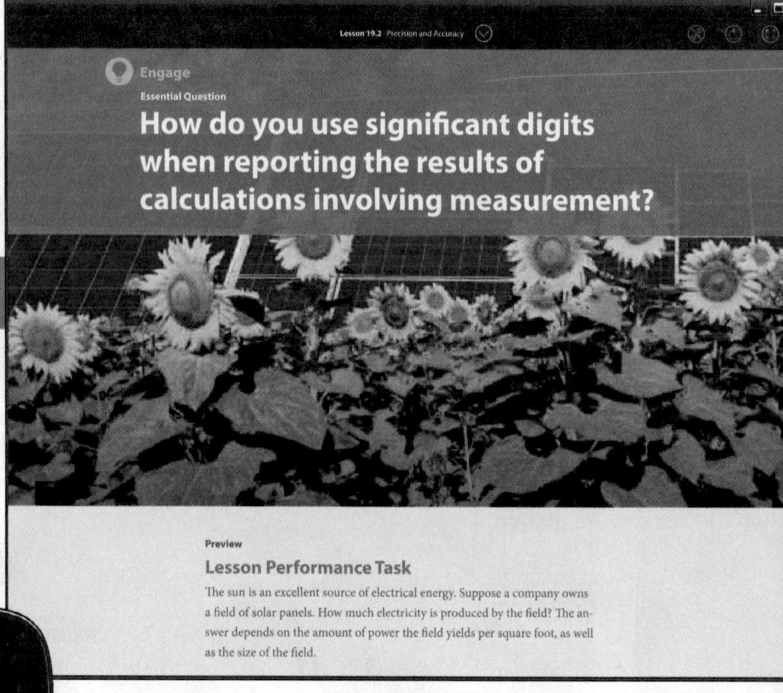

Lesson 19.2 Precision and Accuracy
Engage
Essential Question
How do you use significant digits when reporting the results of calculations involving measurement?
Preview
Lesson Performance Task
The sun is an excellent source of electrical energy. Suppose a company owns a field of solar panels. How much electricity is produced by the field? The answer depends on the amount of power the field yields per square foot, as well as the size of the field.

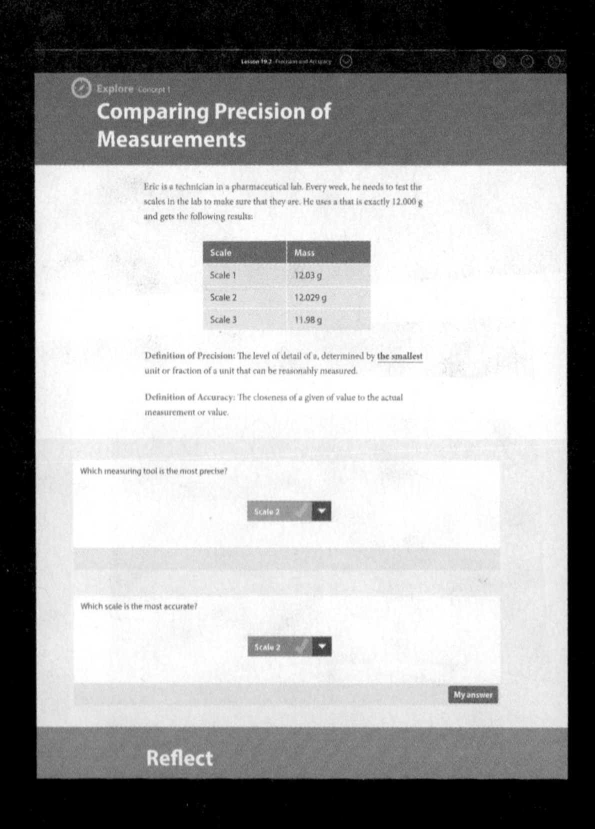

Explore Concept 1

Which measuring tool is the most precise?

Which scale is the most accurate?

My answer

EXPLORE

Explore and interact with new concepts to develop a deeper understanding of mathematics in your book and the Interactive Student Edition.

Scan the QR code to access engaging videos, activities, and more in the Resource Locker for each lesson.

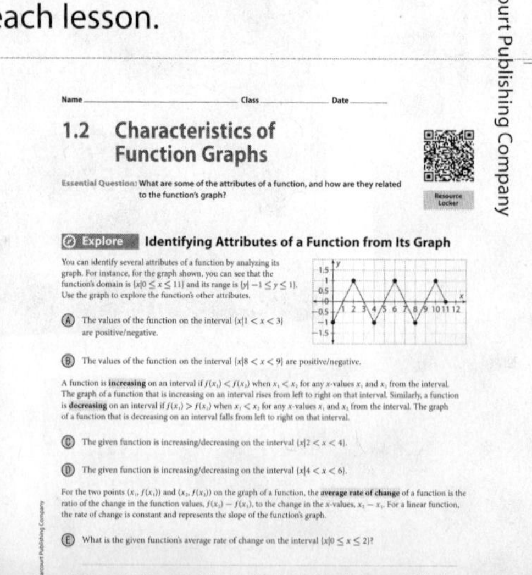

1.2 Characteristics of Function Graphs
Essential Question: What are some of the attributes of a function, and how are they related to the function's graph?
Resource Locker
Explore Identifying Attributes of a Function from Its Graph

Lesson 19.2 Precision and Accuracy

Explain Concept 2

Determining Precision

As you have seen, measurements are given to a certain precision. Therefore, the value reported does not necessarily represent the actual value of the measurement. For example, a measurement of 5 centimeters, which is given to the nearest whole unit, can actually range from 0.5 units below the reported value, 4.5 centimeters, up to, but not including, 0.5 units above it, 5.5 centimeters. The actual length, l, is within a range of possible values: centimeters. Similarly, a length given to the nearest tenth can actually range from 0.05 units below the reported value up to, but not including, 0.05 units above it. So a length reported as 4.5 cm could actually be as low as 4.45 cm or as high as nearly 4.55 cm.

Converting Areas

The area of a yard is 170 ft2. How large is the yard in square meters? Write your answer with the correct number of significant digits. Use 1 m = 3.28 ft.

Conversion factor: $\frac{1\text{ m}}{3.28\text{ ft}}$

EXPLAIN

Learn concepts with step-by-step interactive examples. Every example is also supported by a Math On the Spot video tutorial.

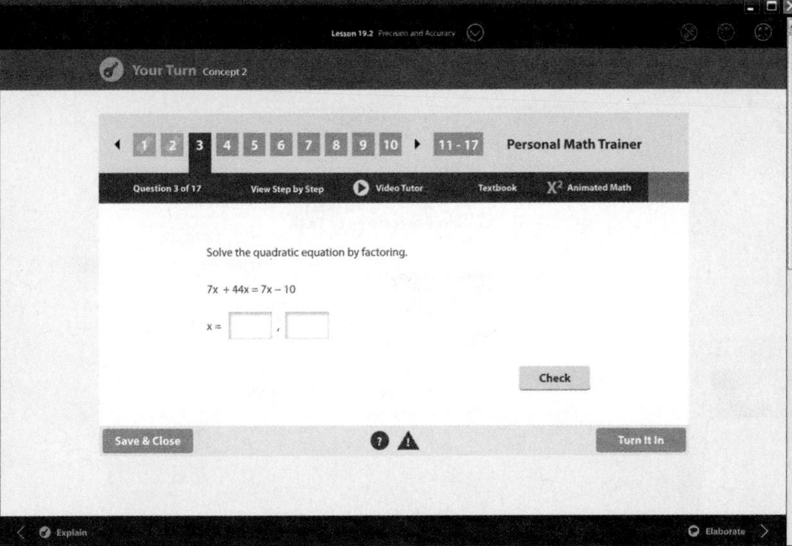

Explain 1 Completing the Square with Expressions

Finding the value of c needed to make an expression such as $x^2 + 6x + c$ into a perfect square trinomial is called **completing the square**.

Using algebra tiles, half of the x-tiles are placed along the right and bottom sides of the x^2-tile. The number of 1-tiles added is the square of the number of x-tiles on either side of the x^2-tile.

To complete the square for the expression $x^2 + bx + c$, replace c with $\left(\frac{b}{2}\right)^2$. The perfect square trinomial is $x^2 + bx + \left(\frac{b}{2}\right)^2$ and factors as $\left(x + \frac{b}{2}\right)^2$.

Example 1 Complete the square to form a perfect trinomial. Then factor the trinomial.

(A) $x^2 + 12x + c$

Identify b.	$b = 12$
Find c.	$c = \left(\frac{b}{2}\right)^2 = \left(\frac{12}{2}\right)^2 = 36$
Write the trinomial.	$x^2 + 12x + 36$
Factor the trinomial.	$x^2 + 12x + 36 = (x + 6)^2$

(B) $z^2 - 26z + c$

Identify b.	$b = \square$
Find c.	$c = \left(\frac{b}{2}\right)^2 = \left(\frac{\square}{2}\right)^2 = \square$
Write the trinomial.	$z^2 + \square z + \square$
Factor the trinomial.	$z^2 + \square z + \square = \square$

Reflect

Complete the square to form a perfect square trinomial. Then factor the trinomial.

3. $a^2 + 18a + \square$ 4. $p^2 - 5p + \square$

Your Turn

5. In Part A, b is positive and in Part B, b is negative. Does this affect the sign of c? Why or why not?

Module 8 460 Lesson 8

Check your understanding of new concepts and skills with Your Turn exercises in your book or online with Personal Math Trainer.

ELABORATE

Show your understanding and reasoning with Reflect and Elaborate questions.

Your Turn

10. The calculator screen shows the graph of $f(x) = 4x^2 - 8x - 5$. Explain how the graph supports the solution in Part B.

Elaborate

11. When solving a quadratic equation in the form $x^2 + bx + c = 0$ by completing the square, what is the purpose of moving the constant to the other side of the equation?

Lesson 19.2 Precision and Accuracy

Elaborate

Given two measurements, is it possible that the more precise measurement may not be the more accurate?

Formula Send to Notebook

What is the relationship between the precision used in the length and width of the rectangle and the precision of the resulting area measurement?

Formula Send to Notebook

How are the significant digits related to the calculations using measurements?

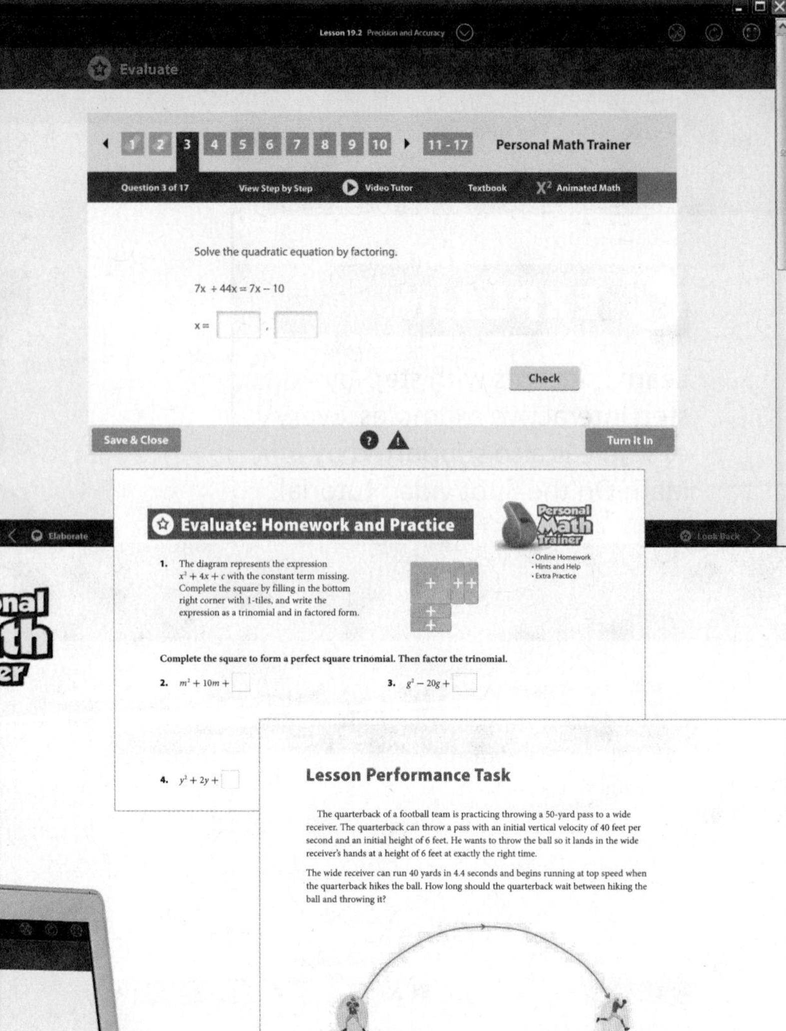

Lesson 19.2 Precision and Accuracy
Evaluate
1 2 3 4 5 6 7 8 9 10 11 - 17 Personal Math Trainer
Question 3 of 17
View Step by Step
Video Tutor
Textbook
Animated Math
Solve the quadratic equation by factoring.
7x + 44x = 7x − 10
x =
Check
Save & Close
Turn It In
Elaborate
Look Back
Evaluate: Homework and Practice
Online Homework
Hints and Help
Extra Practice
1. The diagram represents the expression $x^2 + 4x + c$ with the constant term missing. Complete the square by filling in the bottom right corner with 1-tiles, and write the expression as a trinomial and in factored form.
Complete the square to form a perfect square trinomial. Then factor the trinomial.
2. $m^2 + 10m +$
3. $g^2 - 20g +$
4. $y^2 + 2y +$

EVALUATE

Practice and apply skills and concepts with Evaluate exercises and a Lesson Performance Task in your book with plenty of workspace, or complete these exercises online with Personal Math Trainer.

Personal Math Trainer

Lesson Performance Task

The quarterback of a football team is practicing throwing a 50-yard pass to a wide receiver. The quarterback can throw a pass with an initial vertical velocity of 40 feet per second and an initial height of 6 feet. He wants to throw the ball so it lands in the wide receiver's hands at a height of 6 feet at exactly the right time.

The wide receiver can run 40 yards in 4.4 seconds and begins running at top speed when the quarterback hikes the ball. How long should the quarterback wait between hiking the ball and throwing it?

Journal

Discuss the solution method you used with some of your classmates. Did your thinking change? Summarize anything you learned or shared below.

Formula

Self-Evaluation

This lesson covered the concepts below.

- Using Ratios and Proportions to Solve Problems
- Using Scale Drawings and Models to Solve Problems
- Using Dimensional Analysis to Convert Measurements
- Using Dimensional Analysis to Convert and Compare Rates
- Graphing a Proportional Relationship

LOOK BACK

Review what you have learned and prepare for high-stakes tests with a variety of resources, including Study Guide Reviews, Performance Tasks, and Assessment Readiness test preparation.

STUDY GUIDE REVIEW

Using Square Roots to Solve Quadratic Equations

MODULE 9

Essential Question: How can you use quadratic equations to solve real-world problems?

Key Vocabulary
completing the square (completar el cuadrado)
discriminant (discriminante)
quadratic formula (fórmula cuadrática)
square root (raíz cuadrada)

KEY EXAMPLE (Lesson 9.1)

Solve $(x-8)^2 = 49$ by taking the square root.

$(x-8)^2 = 49$ *Equations in the form $a(x+b)^2 = c$ can be solved by taking square roots.*
$x - 8 = \pm 7$ *Take the square root of both sides.*
$x = \pm 7 + 8$
$x = 7 + 8$ and $x = -7 + 8$ *Solve both cases.*
$x = 15$ and $x = 1$

KEY EXAMPLE (Lesson 9.2)

Solve $9x^2 - 6x = 20$ by completing the square.

$\frac{(-6)^2}{4(9)} = 1$ *Find $\frac{b^2}{4a}$.*
$9x^2 - 6x + 1 = 20 + 1$ *Complete the square.*
$(3x-1)^2 = 21$
$x = \frac{\sqrt{21}+1}{3}$ and $x = \frac{-\sqrt{21}+1}{3}$

KEY EXAMPLE (Lesson 9.3)

Solve $8x^2 - 8x + 2 = 0$ using the quadratic equation.

$a = 8, b = -8, c = 2$ *Identify a, b, and c.*
$x = \frac{-b \pm \sqrt{b^2 - 4ac}}{2a}$ *Use the quadratic formula.*
$x = \frac{8 \pm \sqrt{(-8)^2 - (4)(8)(2)}}{2(8)}$
$x = \frac{8 \pm \sqrt{0}}{16}$ *Since $b^2 - 4ac = 0$, the equation has one real solution.*
$x = \frac{1}{2}$

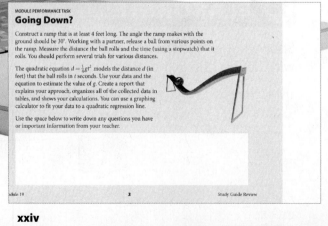

MODULE PERFORMANCE TASK

Going Down?

Construct a ramp that is at least 4 feet long. The angle the ramp makes with the ground should be 30°. Working with a partner, release a ball from various points on the ramp. Measure the distance the ball rolls and the time (using a stopwatch) that it rolls. You should perform several trials for various distances.

The quadratic equation $d = \frac{1}{4}gt^2$ models the distance d (in feet) that the ball rolls in t seconds. Use your data and the equation to estimate the value of g. Create a report that explains your approach, organizes all of the collected data in tables, and shows your calculations. You can use a graphing calculator to fit your data to a quadratic regression line.

Use the space below to write down any questions you have or important information from your teacher.

UNIT 1

Characteristics of Functions

MODULE 1

Analyzing Functions

MODULE 2

Absolute Value Functions, Equations, and Inequalities

MATH IN CAREERS

Community Theater Owner
A community theater owner uses math to determine revenue, profit, and expenses related to operating the theater. Probability and statistical methods are useful for determining the types of performances that will appeal to the public and attract patrons. Community theater owners should also understand the geometry of stage sets, and algebraic formulas for stage lighting, including those used to calculate light beam spread, throw distance, angle, and overall length.

If you are interested in a career as a community theater owner, you should study these mathematical subjects:

- Algebra
- Geometry
- Trigonometry
- Business Math
- Probability
- Statistics

Research other careers that require determining revenue, profit, and expenses. Check out the career activity at the end of the unit to find out how **Community Theater Owners** use math.

Reading Start-Up

Visualize Vocabulary

Copy the graphic and use the ✔ words to complete it. You can put more than one word on each spoke of the information wheel.

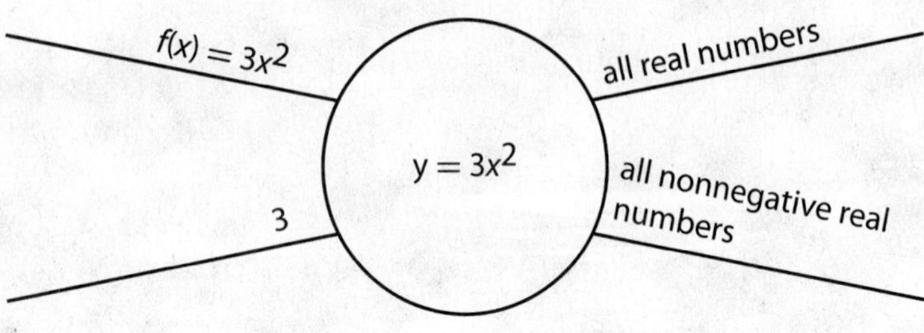

Vocabulary

Review Words

✔ coefficient *(coeficiente)*
✔ domain *(dominio)*
✔ function *(función)*
✔ inequality *(desigualdad)*
✔ interval *(intervalo)*
✔ quadratic function *(función cuadrática)*
✔ range *(rango)*

Preview Words

conjunction *(conjunción)*
disjunction *(disyunción)*
even function *(función par)*
inverse function *(función inversa)*
odd function *(función impar)*
parameter *(parámetro)*

Understand Vocabulary

To become familiar with some of the vocabulary terms in the module, consider the following. You may refer to the module, the glossary, or a dictionary.

1. A __?__ is a constant in the equation of a curve that yields a family of similar curves as it changes.

2. A function $f(x)$ such that $f(x) = f(-x)$ is an __?__ .

3. A compound statement that uses the word *or* is a __?__ .

Active Reading

Three-Panel Flip Chart Before beginning each lesson, create a three-panel flip chart to help you summarize important aspects of the lesson. As you study each lesson, record algebraic examples of functions on the first flap, their graphs on the second flap, and analyses of the functions on the third flap. Add to flip charts from previous lessons by extending the analyses of the functions when possible. For equations and inequalities, record an example on the first flap, a worked out solution on the second flap, and a graph on the third flap.

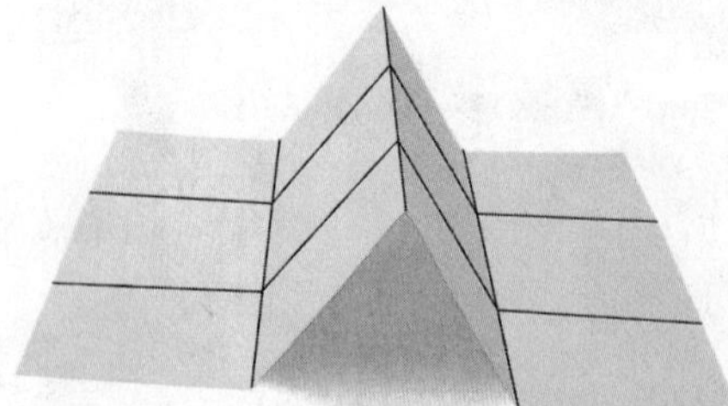

Analyzing Functions

MODULE 1

Essential Question: How can you analyze functions to solve real-world problems?

REAL WORLD VIDEO
Pole vaulting is just one of many track-and-field events that feature a person or object flying through the air. The path of a pole vaulter or of a shot put can be modeled using a quadratic function.

MODULE PERFORMANCE TASK PREVIEW

How High Does a Pole Vaulter Go?

In pole vaulting, a person jumps over a horizontal bar with the assistance of a long fiberglass or carbon-fiber pole. The flexible pole makes it possible for vaulters to achieve much greater heights than jumping without a pole. The goal is to clear the bar without knocking it down. How can mathematics be used to compare the heights of a pole vaulter for two different vaults? Let's jump in and find out!

Complete these exercises to review skills you will need for this module.

- Online Homework
- Hints and Help
- Extra Practice

Algebraic Representations of Transformations

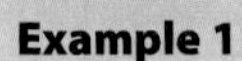

Example 1 Rotate $A(-6,3)$ 90° clockwise.
$(-6(-1), 3) = (6, 3)$ Multiply.
$A(-6, 3) \rightarrow A'(3, 6)$ Switch.

Translate $B(4,7)$ 5 units down.
$(4, 7-5) = (4, 2)$ Subtract.
$B(4, 7) \rightarrow B'(4,2)$

Find the location of A' given that A is (1, 5).

1. Rotate 90° clockwise.

2. Translate 1 unit left.

3. Reflect across the x-axis.

Linear Functions

Example 2 Name the x- and y-intercepts for $y = -2x + 1$.

x-intercept: $0 = -2x + 1$, so $x = 0.5$.

y-intercept: $y = -2(0) + 1 = 1$

Find the x- and y-intercepts for each equation.

4. $y = 8x - 4$

5. $y = -x + 12$

6. $y = 1.2x + 4.8$

7. $3x + 4y = -60$

Rate of Change and Slope

Example 3 Two points on a line are (−3, 3) and (4, 1). Find the slope.

$$\frac{y_1 - y_2}{x_1 - x_2} = \frac{3 - 1}{-3 - 4} = -\frac{2}{7}$$

The slope is $-\frac{2}{7}$.

Find the slope of the line that passes through the two points.

8. (0, 5) and (−9, −4)

9. (6, −2) and (1, −1)

10. (−7, 3) and (−4, −12)

11. (−0.5, 10) and (1.5, 30)

1.1 Domain, Range, and End Behavior

Resource Locker

Essential Question: How can you determine the domain, range, and end behavior of a function?

Explore Representing an Interval on a Number Line

An **interval** is a part of a number line without any breaks. A *finite interval* has two endpoints, which may or may not be included in the interval. An *infinite interval* is unbounded at one or both ends.

Suppose an interval consists of all real numbers greater than or equal to 1. You can use the inequality $x \geq 1$ to represent the interval. You can also use *set notation* and *interval notation*, as shown in the table.

Description of Interval	Type of Interval	Inequality	Set Notation	Interval notation
All real numbers from a to b, including a and b	Finite	$a \leq x \leq b$	$\{x \mid a \leq x \leq b\}$	$[a, b]$
All real numbers greater than a	Infinite	$x > a$	$\{x \mid x > a\}$	$(a, +\infty)$
All real numbers less than or equal to a	Infinite	$x \leq a$	$\{x \mid x \leq a\}$	$(-\infty, a]$

For set notation, the vertical bar means "such that," so you read $\{x \mid x \geq 1\}$ as "the set of real numbers x such that x is greater than or equal to 1."

For interval notation, do the following:

- Use a square bracket to indicate that an interval includes an endpoint and a parenthesis to indicate that an interval doesn't include an endpoint.
- For an interval that is unbounded at its positive end, use the symbol for positive infinity, $+\infty$. For an interval that unbounded at its negative end, use the symbol for negative infinity, $-\infty$. Always use a parenthesis with positive or negative infinity.

So, you can write the interval $x \geq 1$ as $[1, +\infty)$.

(A) Complete the table by writing the finite interval shown on each number line as an inequality, using set notation, and using interval notation.

Finite Interval	−5 −4 −3 −2 −1 0 1 2 3 4 5	−5 −4 −3 −2 −1 0 1 2 3 4 5
Inequality		
Set Notation		
Interval Notation		

Ⓑ Complete the table by writing the infinite interval shown on each number line as an inequality, using set notation, and using interval notation.

Infinite Interval	−5 −4 −3 −2 −1 0 1 2 3 4 5	−5 −4 −3 −2 −1 0 1 2 3 4 5
Inequality		
Set Notation		
Interval Notation		

Reflect

1. Consider the interval shown on the number line.

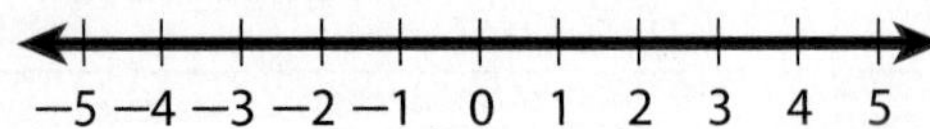

a. Represent the interval using interval notation.

b. What numbers are in this interval?

2. What do the intervals [0, 5], [0, 5), and (0, 5) have in common? What makes them different?

3. **Discussion** The symbol ∪ represents the *union* of two sets. What do you think the notation $(-\infty, 0) \cup (0, +\infty)$ represents?

Explain 1 Identifying a Function's Domain, Range and End Behavior from its Graph

Recall that the *domain* of a function *f* is the set of input values *x*, and the *range* is the set of output values $f(x)$. The **end behavior** of a function describes what happens to the $f(x)$-values as the *x*-values either increase without bound (approach positive infinity) or decrease without bound (approach negative infinity). For instance, consider the graph of a linear function shown. From the graph, you can make the following observations.

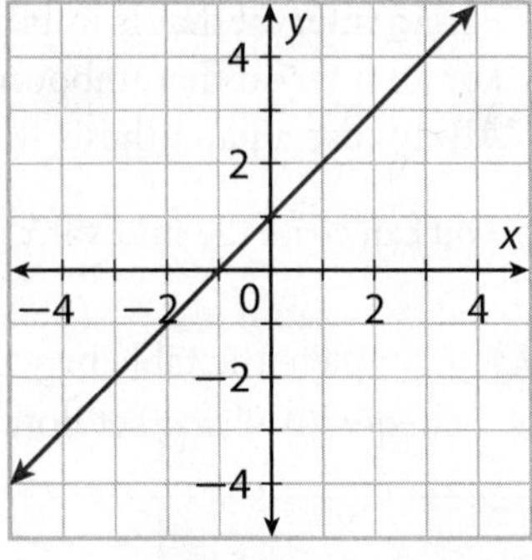

Statement of End Behavior	Symbolic Form of Statement
As the x-values increase without bound, the $f(x)$-values also increase without bound.	As $x \to +\infty$, $f(x) \to +\infty$.
As the x-values decrease without bound, the $f(x)$-values also decrease without bound.	As $x \to -\infty$, $f(x) \to -\infty$.

Example 1 **Write the domain and the range of the function as an inequality, using set notation, and using interval notation. Also describe the end behavior of the function.**

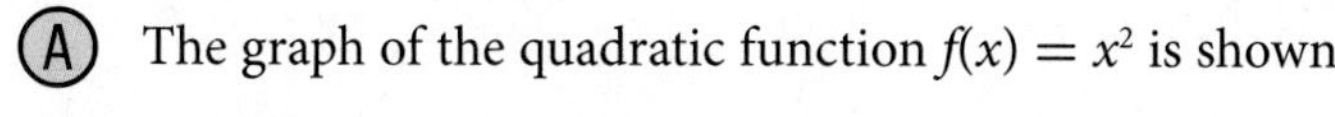

(A) The graph of the quadratic function $f(x) = x^2$ is shown.

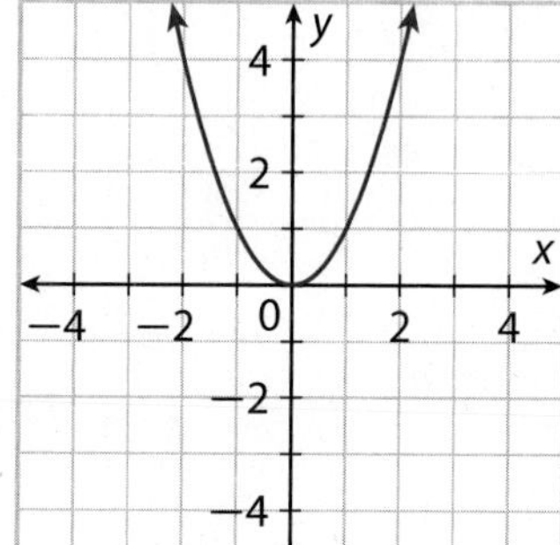

Domain:

Inequality: $-\infty < x < +\infty$

Set notation: $\{x \mid -\infty < x < +\infty\}$

Interval notation: $(-\infty, +\infty)$

Range:

Inequality: $y \geq 0$

Set notation: $\{y \mid y \geq 0\}$

Interval notation: $[0, +\infty)$

End behavior:

As $x \to +\infty$, $f(x) \to +\infty$.

As $x \to -\infty$, $f(x) \to +\infty$.

(B) The graph of the exponential function $f(x) = 2^x$ is shown.

Domain:

Inequality: $-\infty < x < +\infty$

Set notation: $\{x \mid -\infty < x < +\infty\}$

Interval notation: $(-\infty, +\infty)$

Range:

Inequality: $y > 0$

Set notation: $\{y \mid y > 0\}$

Interval notation: $(0, +\infty)$

End behavior:

As $x \to +\infty$, $f(x) \to +\infty$

As $x \to +\infty$, $f(x) \to 0$.

Reflect

4. Why is the end behavior of a quadratic function different from the end behavior of a linear function?
5. In Part B, the $f(x)$-values decrease as the x-values decrease. So, why can't you say that $f(x) \to -\infty$ as $x \to -\infty$?

Your Turn

Write the domain and the range of the function as an inequality, using set notation, and using interval notation. Also describe the end behavior of the function.

6. The graph of the quadratic function $f(x) = -x^2$ is shown.

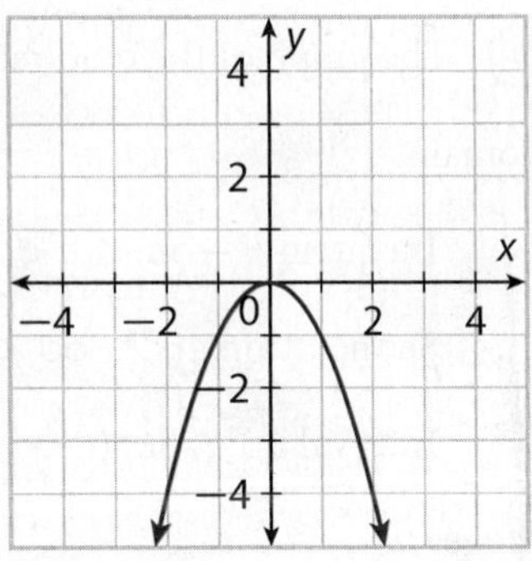

Explain 2 Graphing a Linear Function on a Restricted Domain

Unless otherwise stated, a function is assumed to have a domain consisting of all real numbers for which the function is defined. Many functions—such as linear, quadratic, and exponential functions—are defined for all real numbers, so their domain, when written in interval notation, is $(-\infty, +\infty)$. Another way to write the set of real numbers is $\mathbb{R}$.

Sometimes a function may have a restricted domain. If the rule for a function and its restricted domain are given, you can draw its graph and then identify its range.

Example 2 **For the given function and domain, draw the graph and identify the range using the same notation as the given domain.**

Ⓐ $f(x) = \frac{3}{4}x + 2$ with domain $[-4, 4]$

Since $f(x) = \frac{3}{4}x + 2$ is a linear function, the graph is a line segment with endpoints at $(-4, f(-4))$, or $(-4, -1)$, and $(4, f(4))$, or $(4, 5)$. The endpoints are included in the graph.

The range is $[-1, 5]$.

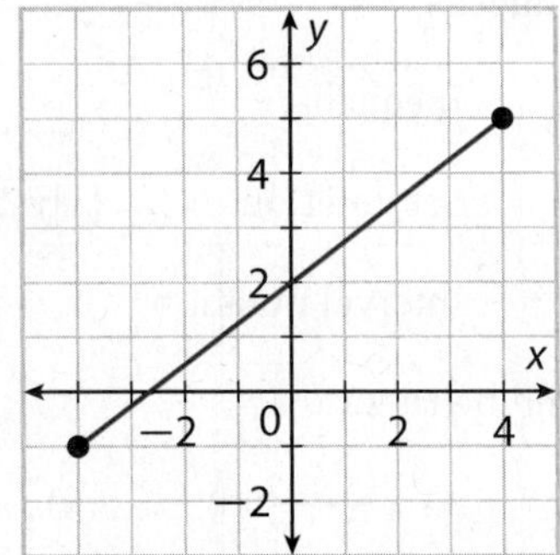

Ⓑ $f(x) = -x - 2$ with domain $\{x|x > -3\}$

Since $f(x) = -x - 2$ is a linear function, the graph is a ray with its endpoint at $(-3, f(-3))$, or $(-3, 1)$. The endpoint is not included in the graph. The range is $\{y|y < 1\}$.

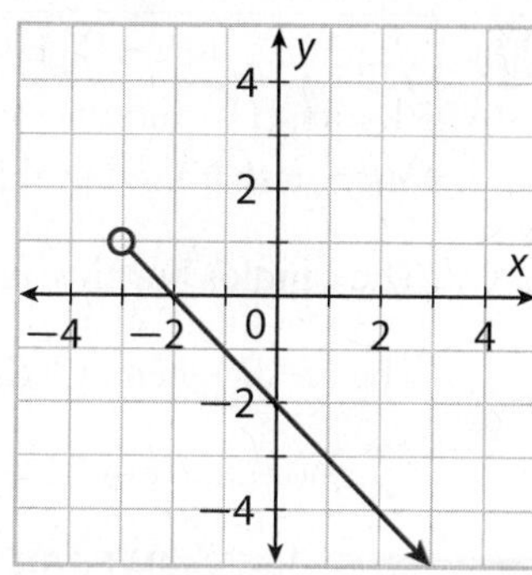

Reflect

7. In Part A, how does the graph change if the domain is $(-4, 4)$ instead of $[-4, 4]$?

8. In Part B, what is the end behavior as x increases without bound? Why can't you talk about the end behavior as x decreases without bound?

Your Turn

For the given function and domain, draw the graph and identify the range using the same notation as the given domain.

9. $f(x) = -\frac{1}{2}x + 2$ with domain $-6 \leq x < 2$

10. $f(x) = \frac{2}{3}x - 1$ with domain $(-\infty, 3]$

Explain 3 Modeling with a Linear Function

Recall that when a real-world situation involves a constant rate of change, a linear function is a reasonable model for the situation. The situation may require restricting the function's domain.

Example 3 **Write a function that models the given situation. Determine a domain from the situation, graph the function using that domain, and identify the range.**

Ⓐ Joyce jogs at a rate of 1 mile every 10 minutes for a total of 40 minutes. (Use inequalities for the domain and range of the function that models this situation.)

Joyce's jogging rate is 0.1 mi/min. Her jogging distance d (in miles) at any time t (in minutes) is modeled by $d(t) = 0.1t$. Since she jogs for 40 minutes, the domain is restricted to the interval $0 \leq t \leq 40$.

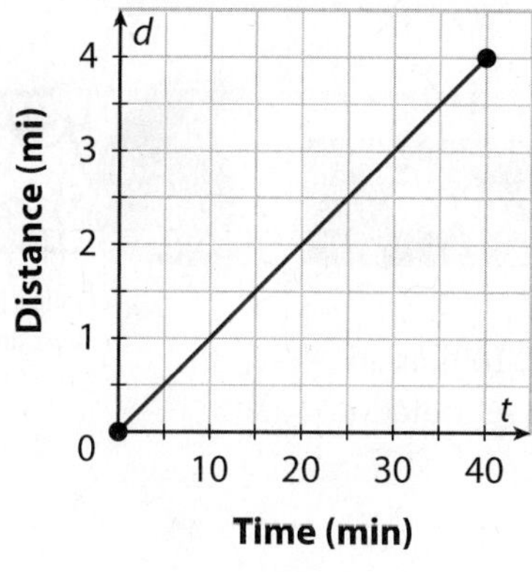

The range is $0 \leq d \leq 4$.

(B) A candle 6 inches high burns at a rate of 1 inch every 2 hours for 5 hours. (Use interval notation for the domain and range of the function that models this situation.)

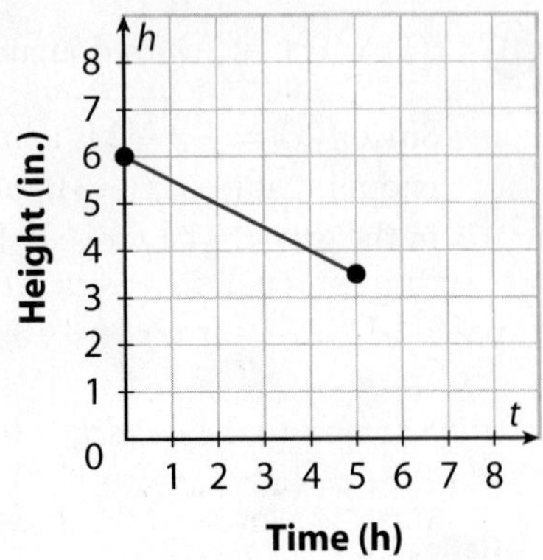

The candle's burning rate is -0.5 in./h.

The candle's height h (in inches) at any time t (in hours) is modeled by $h(t) = 6 - 0.5t$.

Since the candle burns for 5 hours, the domain is restricted to the interval $\left[0, \boxed{5}\right]$.

The range is [3.5, 6].

Reflect

11. In Part A, suppose Joyce jogs for only 30 minutes.

A. How does the domain change?

B. How does the graph change?

C. How does the range change?

Your Turn

12. While standing on a moving walkway at an airport, you are carried forward 25 feet every 15 seconds for 1 minute. Write a function that models this situation. Determine the domain from the situation, graph the function, and identify the range. Use set notation for the domain and range.

Elaborate

13. If a and b are real numbers such that $a < b$, use interval notation to write four different intervals having a and b as endpoints. Describe what numbers each interval includes.

14. What impact does restricting the domain of a linear function have on the graph of the function?

15. **Essential Question Check-In** How does slope determine the end behavior of a linear function with an unrestricted domain?

Evaluate: Homework and Practice

Personal Math Trainer

- Online Homework
- Hints and Help
- Extra Practice

1. Write the interval shown on the number line as an inequality, using set notation, and using interval notation.

3 4 5 6 7 8

2. Write the interval (5, 100] as an inequality and using set notation.

3. Write the interval $-25 \leq x < 30$ using set notation and interval notation.

4. Write the interval $\{x \mid -3 < x < 5\}$ as an inequality and using interval notation.

Write the domain and the range of the function as an inequality, using set notation, and using interval notation. Also describe the end behavior of the function or explain why there is no end behavior.

5. The graph of the quadratic function $f(x) = x^2 + 2$ is shown.

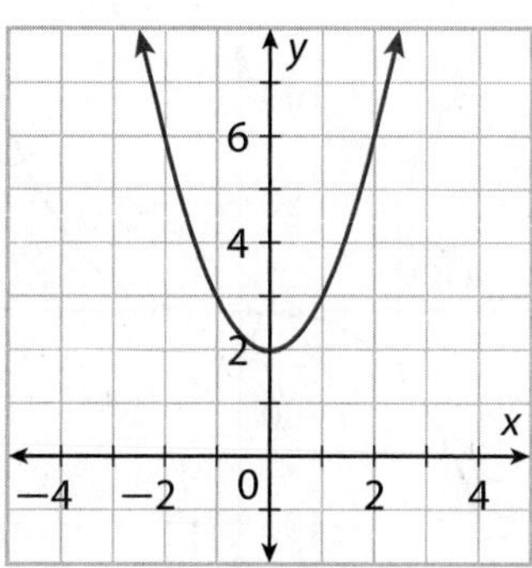

6. The graph of the exponential function $f(x) = 3^x$ is shown.

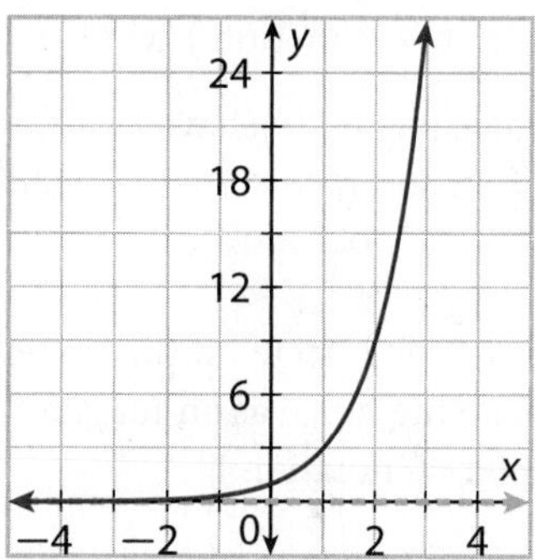

7. The graph of the linear function $g(x) = 2x - 2$ is shown.

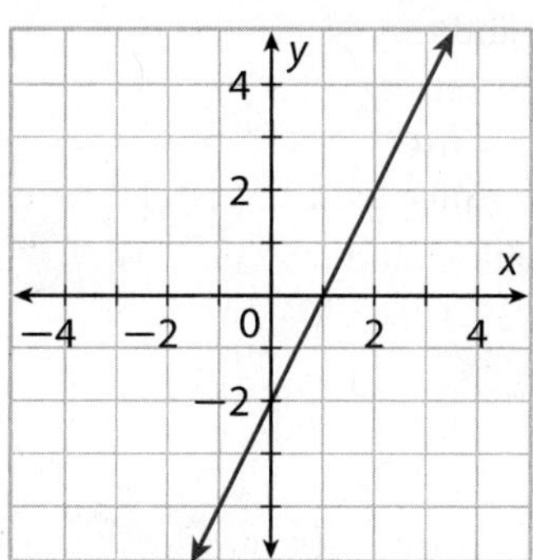

8. The graph of a function is shown.

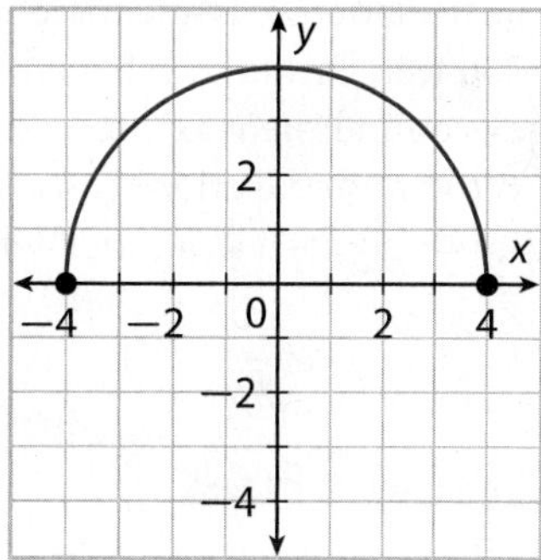

For the given function and domain, draw the graph and identify the range using the same notation as the given domain.

9. $f(x) = -x + 5$ with domain $[-3, 2]$

10. $f(x) = \frac{3}{2}x + 1$ with domain $\{x \mid x > -2\}$

Write a function that models the given situation. Determine the domain from the situation, graph the function using that domain, and identify the range.

11. A bicyclist travels at a constant speed of 12 miles per hour for a total of 45 minutes. (Use set notation for the domain and range of the function that models this situation.)

12. An elevator in a tall building starts at a floor of the building that is 90 meters above the ground. The elevator descends 2 meters every 0.5 second for 6 seconds. (Use an inequality for the domain and range of the function that models this situation.)

H.O.T. Focus on Higher Order Thinking

13. Explain the Error Cameron sells tickets at a movie theater. On Friday night, she worked from 4 p.m. to 10 p.m. and sold about 25 tickets every hour. Cameron says that the number of tickets, n, she has sold at any time t (in hours) can be modeled by the function $n(t) = 25t$, where the domain is $0 \leq t \leq 1$ and the range is $0 \leq n \leq 25$. Is Cameron's function, along with the domain and range, correct? Explain.

14. Multi-Step The graph of the cubic function $f(x) = x^3$ is shown.

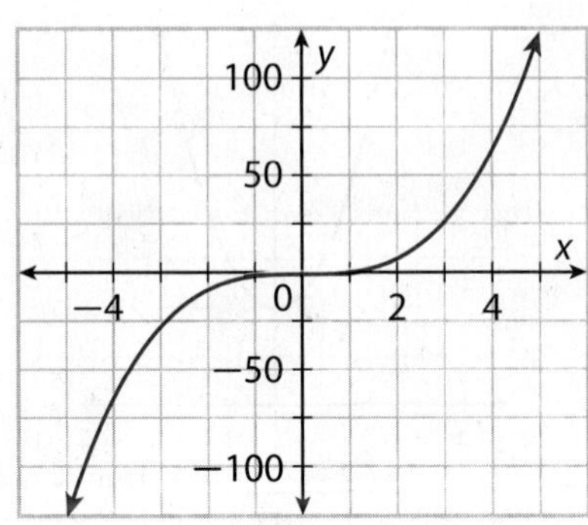

a. What are the domain, range, and end behavior of the function? (Write the domain and range as an inequality, using set notation, and using interval notation.)

b. How is the range of the function affected if the domain is restricted to $[-4, 4]$? (Write the range as an inequality, using set notation, and using interval notation.)

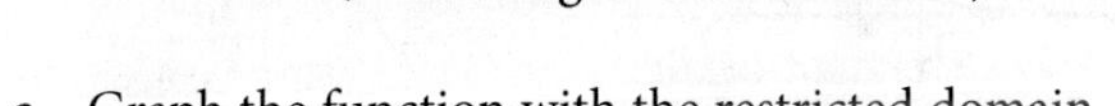

c. Graph the function with the restricted domain.

15. Represent Real-World Situations The John James Audubon Bridge is a cable-stayed bridge in Louisiana that opened in 2011. The height from the bridge deck to the top of the tower where a particular cable is anchored is about 500 feet, and the length of that cable is about 1200 feet. Draw the cable on a coordinate plane, letting the x-axis represent the bridge deck and the y-axis represent the tower. (Only use positive values of x and y.) Write a linear function whose graph models the cable. Identify the domain and range, writing each as an inequality, using set notation, and using interval notation.

Lesson Performance Task

The fuel efficiency for a 2007 passenger car was 31.2 mi/gal. For the same model of car, the fuel efficiency increased to 35.6 mi/gal in 2012. The gas tank for this car holds 16 gallons of gas.

a. Write and graph a linear function that models the distance that each car can travel for a given amount of gas (up to one tankful).

b. Write the domain and range of each function using interval notation.

c. Write and simplify a function $f(g)$ that represents the *difference* in the distance that the 2012 car can travel and the distance that the 2007 car can travel on the same amount of gas. Interpret this function using the graphs of the functions from part a. Also find and interpret $f(16)$.

d. Write the domain and range of the difference function using set notation.

1.2 Characteristics of Function Graphs

Resource Locker

Essential Question: What are some of the attributes of a function, and how are they related to the function's graph?

Explore Identifying Attributes of a Function from Its Graph

You can identify several attributes of a function by analyzing its graph. For instance, for the graph shown, you can see that the function's domain is $\{x|0 \leq x \leq 11\}$ and its range is $\{y|-1 \leq y \leq 1\}$. Use the graph to explore the function's other attributes.

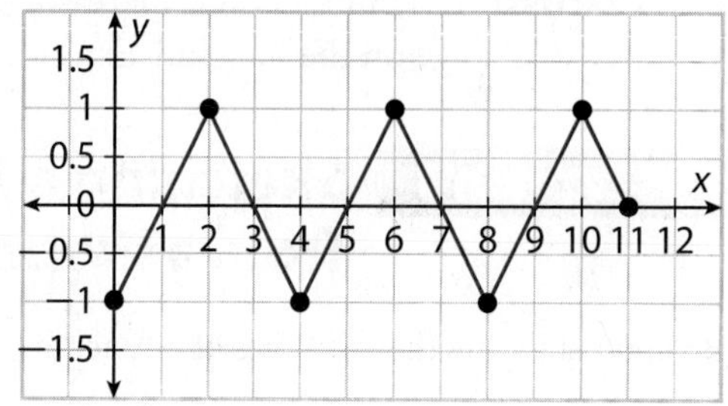

(A) Are the values of the function on the interval $\{x|1 < x < 3\}$ positive or negative?

(B) Are the values of the function on the interval $\{x|8 < x < 9\}$ positive or negative?

A function is **increasing** on an interval if $f(x_1) < f(x_2)$ when $x_1 < x_2$ for any x-values x_1 and x_2 from the interval. The graph of a function that is increasing on an interval rises from left to right on that interval. Similarly, a function is **decreasing** on an interval if $f(x_1) > f(x_2)$ when $x_1 < x_2$ for any x-values x_1 and x_2 from the interval. The graph of a function that is decreasing on an interval falls from left to right on that interval.

(C) Is the given function increasing or decreasing on the interval $\{x|2 < x < 4\}$?

(D) Is the given function increasing or decreasing on the interval $\{x|4 < x < 6\}$?

For the two points $(x_1, f(x_1))$ and $(x_2, f(x_2))$ on the graph of a function, the **average rate of change** of the function is the ratio of the change in the function values, $f(x_2) - f(x_1)$, to the change in the x-values, $x_2 - x_1$. For a linear function, the rate of change is constant and represents the slope of the function's graph.

(E) What is the given function's average rate of change on the interval $\{x|0 \leq x \leq 2\}$?

A function may change from increasing to decreasing or from decreasing to increasing at *turning points.* The value of $f(x)$ at a point where a function changes from increasing to decreasing is a **maximum value**. A maximum value occurs at a point that appears higher than all nearby points on the graph of the function. Similarly, the value of $f(x)$ at a point where a function changes from decreasing to increasing is a **minimum value**. A minimum value occurs at a point that appears lower than all nearby points on the graph of the function.

(F) At how many points does the given function change from increasing to decreasing?

(G) What is the function's value at these points?

(H) At how many points does the given function change from decreasing to increasing?

Ⓘ What is the function's value at these points?

A **zero** of a function is a value of x for which $f(x) = 0$. On a graph of the function, the zeros are the x-intercepts.

Ⓙ How many x-intercepts does the given function's graph have?

Ⓚ Identify the zeros of the function.

Reflect

1. **Discussion** Identify three different intervals that have the same average rate of change, and state what the rate of change is.
2. **Discussion** If a function is increasing on an interval $\{x|a \leq x \leq b\}$, what can you say about its average rate of change on the interval? Explain.

Explain 1 Sketching a Function's Graph from a Verbal Description

By understanding the attributes of a function, you can sketch a graph from a verbal description.

Example 1 **Sketch a graph of the following verbal descriptions.**

Ⓐ Lyme disease is a bacterial infection transmitted to humans by ticks. When an infected tick bites a human, the probability of transmission is a function of the time since the tick attached itself to the skin. During the first 24 hours, the probability is 0%. During the next three 24-hour periods, the rate of change in the probability is always positive, but it is much greater for the middle period than the other two periods. After 96 hours, the probability is almost 100%. Sketch a graph of the function for the probability of transmission.

Probability of Transmission from Infected Tick

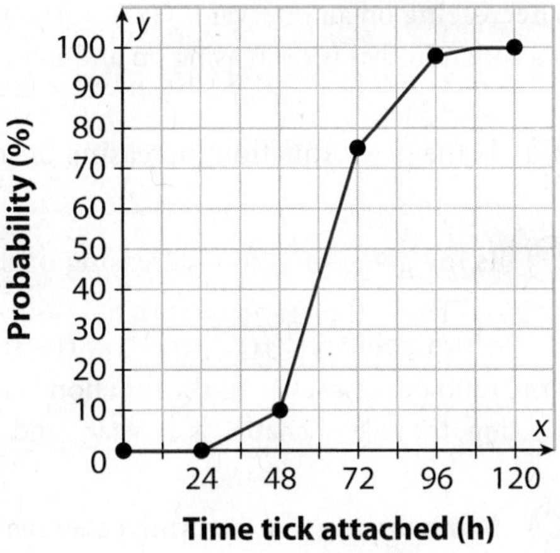

Identify the axes and scales.

The x-axis will be time (in hours) and will run from 0 to at least 96. The y-axis will be the probability of infection (as a percent) from 0 to 100.

Identify key intervals.

The intervals are in increments of 24 hours: 0 to 24, 24 to 48, 48 to 72, 72 to 96, and 96 to 120.

Sketch the graph of the function.

Draw a horizontal segment at $y = 0$ for the first 24-hour interval. The function increases over the next three 24-hour intervals with the middle interval having the greatest increase (the steepest slope). After 96 hours, the graph is nearly horizontal at 100%.

(B) The incidence of a disease is the rate at which a disease occurs in a population. It is calculated by dividing the number of new cases of a disease in a given time period (typically a year) by the size of the population. **To avoid small decimal numbers, the rate is often expressed in terms of a large number of people rather than a single person.** For instance, the incidence of measles in the United States in 1974 was about 10 cases per 100,000 people.

From 1974 to 1980, there were drastic fluctuations in the incidence of measles in the United States. In 1975, there was a slight increase in incidence from 1974. The next two years saw a substantial increase in the incidence, which reached a maximum in 1977 of about 26 cases per 100,000 people. From 1977 to 1979, the incidence fell to about 5 cases per 100,000 people. The incidence fell much faster from 1977 to 1978 than from 1978 to 1979. Finally, from 1979 to 1980, the incidence stayed about the same. **Sketch a graph of the function for the incidence of measles.**

Identify the axes and scales.

The x-axis will represent time given by years and will run from 0 to 6. The y-axis will represent incidence of measles, measured in cases per 100,000 people, and will run from 0 to 30.

Identify key intervals.

The intervals are one-year increments from 0 to 6.

Sketch the graph of the function.

Incidence of Measles in the U.S.

The first point on the graph is (0, 10). The graph slightly rises from $x = 0$ to $x = 1$.

From $x = 1$ to $x = 3$, the graph rises to a maximum y-value of 26. The graph falls steeply from $x = 3$ to $x = 4$ and then falls less steeply from $x = 4$ to $x = 5$. The graph is horizontal from $x = 5$ to $x = 6$.

Reflect

3. In Part B, the graph is horizontal from 1979 to 1980. What can you say about the rate of change for the function on this interval?

Your Turn

4. A grocery store stocks shelves with 100 cartons of strawberries before the store opens. For the first 3 hours the store is open, the store sells 20 cartons per hour. Over the next 2 hours, no cartons of strawberries are sold. The store then restocks 10 cartons each hour for the next 2 hours. In the final hour that the store is open, 30 cartons are sold. Sketch a graph of the function.

Explain 2 Modeling with a Linear Function

When given a set of paired data, you can use a scatter plot to see whether the data show a linear trend. If so, you can use a graphing calculator to perform linear regression and obtain a linear function that models the data. You should treat the least and greatest x-values of the data as the boundaries of the domain of the linear model.

When you perform linear regression, a graphing calculator will report the value of the *correlation coefficient r*. This variable can have a value from -1 to 1. It measures the direction and strength of the relationship between the variables x and y. If the value of r is negative, the y-values tend to decrease as the x-values increase. If the value of r is positive, the y-values tend to increase as the x-values increase. The more linear the relationship between x and y is, the closer the value of r is to -1 or 1 (or the closer the value of r^2 is to 1).

You can use the linear model to make predictions and decisions based on the data. Making a prediction within the domain of the linear model is called *interpolation*. Making a prediction outside the domain is called *extrapolation*.

Example 2 **Perform a linear regression for the given situation and make predictions.**

(A) A photographer hiked through the Grand Canyon. Each day she stored photos on a memory card for her digital camera. When she returned from the trip, she deleted some photos from each memory card, saving only the best. The table shows the number of photos she kept from all those stored on each memory card. Use a graphing calculator to create a scatter plot of the data, find a linear regression model, and graph the model. Then use the model to predict the number of photos the photographer will keep if she takes 150 photos.

Grand Canyon Photos	
Photos Taken	**Photos Kept**
117	25
128	31
140	39
157	52
110	21
188	45
170	42

Step 1: Create a scatter plot of the data.

Let x represent the number of photos taken, and let y represent the number of photos kept. Use a viewing window that shows x-values from 100 to 200 and y-values from 0 to 60.

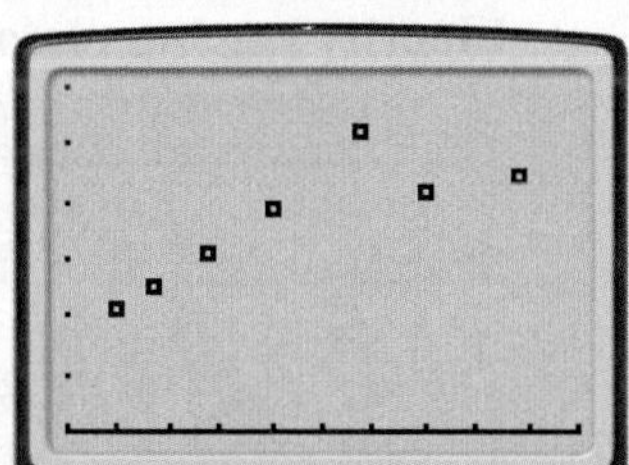

Notice that the trend in the data appears to be roughly linear, with y-values generally increasing as x-values increase.

Step 2: Perform linear regression. Write the linear model and its domain.

The linear regression model is $y = 0.33x - 11.33$. Its domain is $\{x|110 \leq x \leq 188\}$.

Step 3: Graph the model along with the data to obtain a visual check on the goodness of fit.

Notice that one of the data points is much farther from the line than the other data points are. The value of the correlation coefficient r would be closer to 1 without this data point.

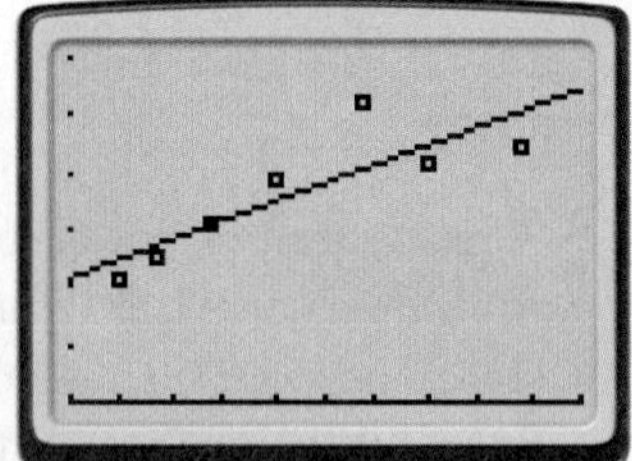

Step 4: Predict the number of photos this photographer will keep if she takes 150 photos.

Evaluate the linear function when $x = 150$: $y = 0.33(150) - 11.33 \approx 38$. So, she will keep about 38 photos if she takes 150 photos.

(B) As a science project, Shelley is studying the relationship of car mileage (in miles per gallon) and speed (in miles per hour). The table shows the data Shelley gathered using her family's vehicle. Use a graphing calculator to create a scatter plot of the data, find a linear regression model, and graph the model. Then use the model to predict the gas mileage of the car at a speed of 20 miles per hour.

Speed (mi/h)	30	40	50	60	70
Mileage (mi/gal)	34.0	33.5	31.5	29.0	27.5

Step 1: Create a scatter plot of the data.

What do x and y represent?

Let x represent the car's speed, and let y represent the car's gas mileage.

What viewing window will you use?

Use a window that shows x-values from 0 to 80 and y-values from 0 to 40.

What trend do you observe?

The trend in the data appears to be quite linear, with y-values generally decreasing as x-values increase.

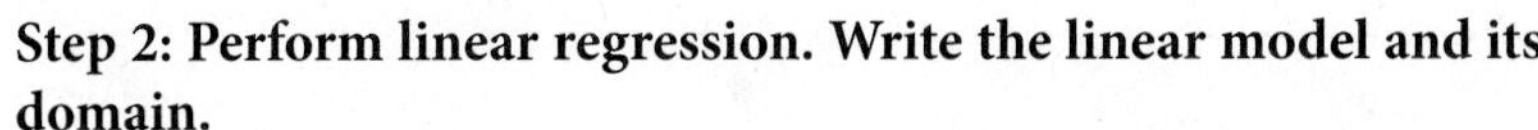

Step 2: Perform linear regression. Write the linear model and its domain.

The linear regression model is $y = -0.175x + 39.85$. Its domain is $\{x|30 \leq x \leq 70\}$.

Step 3: Graph the model along with the data to obtain a visual check on the goodness of fit.

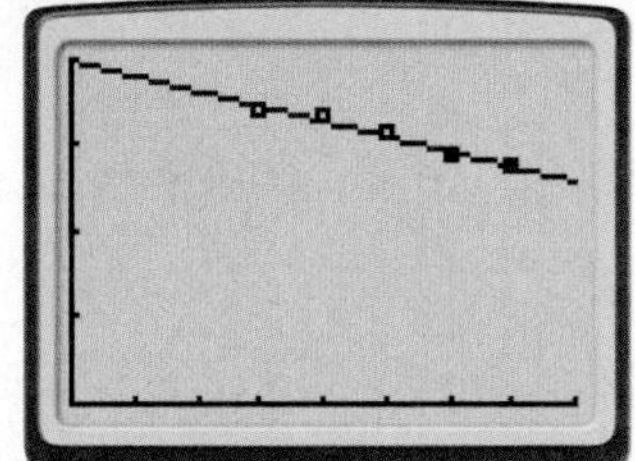

What can you say about the goodness of fit?

As expected from the fact that the value of r from Step 2 is very close to -1, the line passes through or comes close to passing through all the data points.

Step 4: Predict the gas mileage of the car at a speed of 20 miles per hour.

Evaluate the linear function when $x = 20$: $y = -0.175(20) + 39.85 \approx 36.4$. So, the car's gas mileage should be about 36.4 mi/gal at a speed of 20 mi/h.

Reflect

5. Identify whether each prediction in Parts A and B is an interpolation or an extrapolation.

Your Turn

6. Vern created a website for his school's sports teams. He has a hit counter on his site that lets him know how many people have visited the site. The table shows the number of hits the site received each day for the first two weeks. Use a graphing calculator to find the linear regression model. Then predict how many hits there will be on day 15.

Day	1	2	3	4	5	6	7	8	9	10	11	12	13	14
Hits	5	10	21	24	28	36	33	21	27	40	46	50	31	38

Elaborate

7. How are the attributes of increasing and decreasing related to average rate of change? How are the attributes of maximum and minimum values related to the attributes of increasing and decreasing?

8. How can line segments be used to sketch graphs of functions that model real-world situations?

9. When making predictions based on a linear model, would you expect interpolated or extrapolated values to be more accurate? Justify your answer.

10. **Essential Question Check-In** What are some of the attributes of a function?

Evaluate: Homework and Practice

- Online Homework
- Hints and Help
- Extra Practice

The graph shows a function that models the value V (in millions of dollars of a stock portfolio as a function of time t (in months) over an 18-month period.

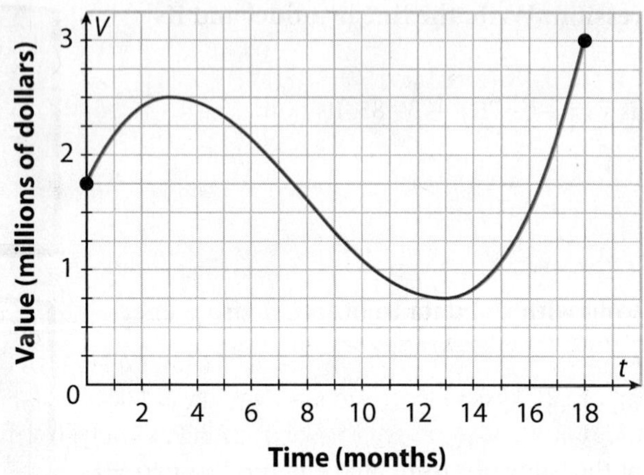

1. On what interval is the function decreasing?
   On what intervals is the function increasing?

2. Identify any maximum values and minimum values.

3. What are the function's domain and range?

The table of values gives the probability $P(n)$ for getting all 5's when rolling a number cube n times.

n	1	2	3	4	5
$P(n)$	$\frac{1}{6}$	$\frac{1}{36}$	$\frac{1}{216}$	$\frac{1}{1296}$	$\frac{1}{7776}$

4. Is $P(n)$ increasing or decreasing? Explain the significance of this.
5. What is the end behavior of $P(n)$? Explain the significance of this.

6. The table shows some values of a function. On which intervals is the function's average rate of change positive? Select all that apply.

x	0	1	2	3
$f(x)$	50	75	40	65

a. From $x = 0$ to $x = 1$
b. From $x = 0$ to $x = 2$
c. From $x = 0$ to $x = 3$
d. From $x = 1$ to $x = 2$
e. From $x = 1$ to $x = 3$
f. From $x = 2$ to $x = 3$

Use the graph of the function $f(x)$ to identify the function's specified attributes.

7. Find the function's average rate of change over each interval.

a. From $x = -3$ to $x = -2$ **b.** From $x = -2$ to $x = 1$

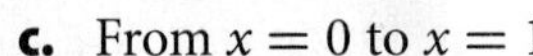

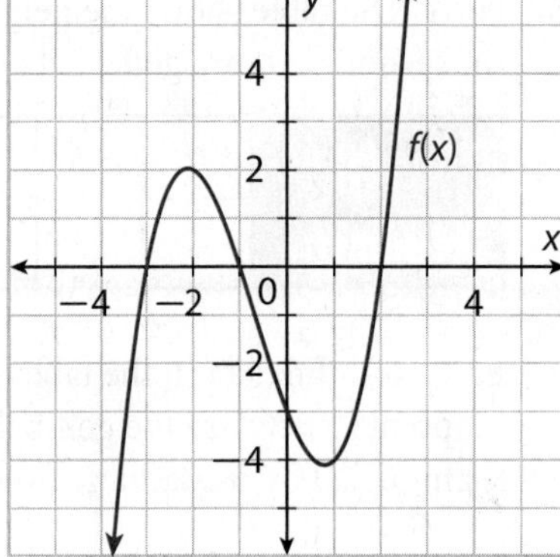

c. From $x = 0$ to $x = 1$ **d.** From $x = 1$ to $x = 2$

e. From $x = -1$ to $x = 0$ **f.** From $x = -1$ to $x = 2$

8. On what intervals are the function's values positive?

9. On what intervals are the function's values negative?

10. What are the zeros of the function?

11. The following describes the United States nuclear stockpile from 1944 to 1974. From 1944 to 1958, there was a gradual increase in the number of warheads from 0 to about 5000. From 1958 to 1966, there was a rapid increase in the number of warheads to a maximum of about 32,000. From 1968 to 1970, there was a decrease in the number of warheads to about 26,000. Finally, from 1970 to 1974, there was a small increase to about 28,000 warheads. Sketch a graph of the function.

12. The following describes the unemployment rate in the United States from 2003 to 2013. In 2003, the unemployment rate was at 6.3%. The unemployment rate began to fall over the years and reached a minimum of about 4.4% in 2007. A recession that began in 2007 caused the unemployment rate to increase over a two-year period and reach a maximum of about 10% in 2009. The unemployment rate then decreased over the next four years to about 7.0% in 2013. Sketch a graph of the function.

13. The following describes the incidence of mumps in the United States from 1984 to 2004. From 1984 to 1985, there was no change in the incidence of mumps, staying at about 1 case per 100,000 people. Then there was a spike in the incidence of mumps, which reached a peak of about 5.5 cases per 100,000 in 1987. Over the next year, there was a sharp decline in the incidence of mumps, to about 2 cases per 100,000 people in 1988. Then, from 1988 to 1989, there was a small increase to about 2.5 cases per 100,000 people. This was followed by a gradual decline, which reached a minimum of about 0.1 case per 100,000 in 1999. For the next five years, there was no change in the incidence of mumps. Sketch a graph of the function.

14. Aviation The table gives the lengths and wingspans of airplanes in an airline's fleet.

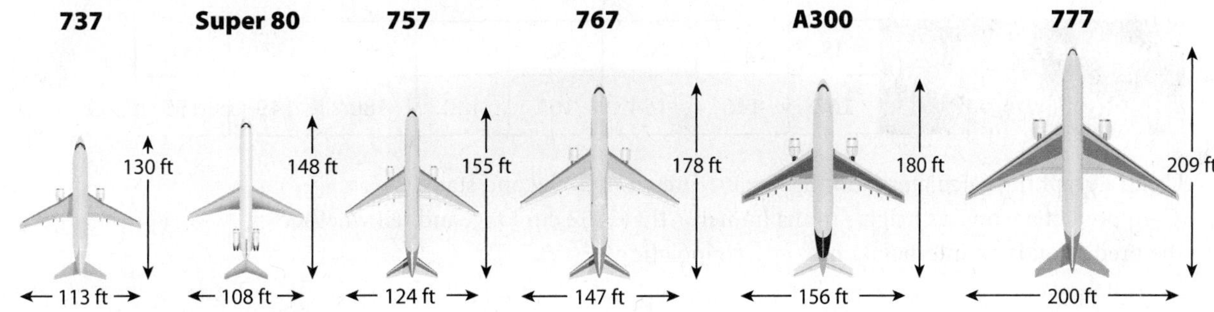

a. Make a scatter plot of the data with x representing length and y representing wingspan.

b. Sketch a line of fit.

c. Use the line of fit to predict the wingspan of an airplane with a length of 220 feet.

15. Golf The table shows the height (in feet) of a golf ball at various times (in seconds) after a golfer hits the ball into the air.

Time (s)	0	0.5	1	1.5	2	2.5	3	3.5	4
Height (ft)	0	28	48	60	64	60	48	28	0

a. Graph the data in the table. Then draw a smooth curve through the data points. (Because the golf ball is a projectile, its height h at time t can be modeled by a quadratic function whose graph is a parabola.)

b. What is the maximum height that the golf ball reaches?

c. On what interval is the golf ball's height increasing?

d. On what interval is the golf ball's height decreasing?

16. The model $a = 0.25t + 29$ represents the median age a of females in the United States as a function of time t (in years since 1970).

a. Predict the median age of females in 1995.

b. Predict the median age of females in 2015 to the nearest tenth.

H.O.T. Focus on Higher Order Thinking

17. Make a Prediction Anthropologists who study skeletal remains can predict a woman's height just from the length of her humerus, the bone between the elbow and the shoulder. The table gives data for humerus length and overall height for various women.

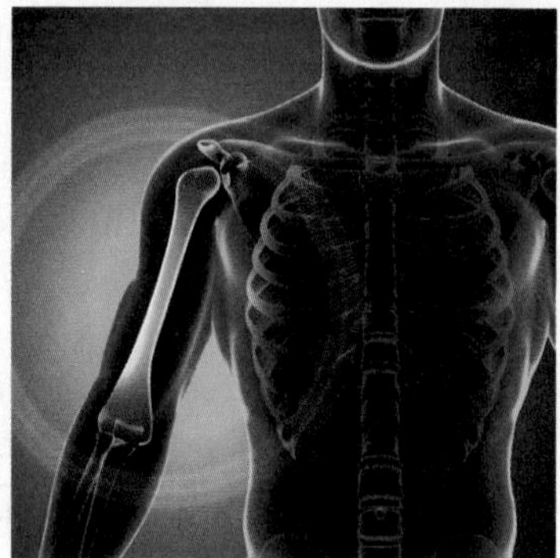

Humerus Length (cm)	35	27	30	33	25	39	27	31
Height (cm)	167	146	154	165	140	180	149	155

Using a graphing calculator, find the linear regression model and state its domain. Then predict a woman's height from a humerus that is 32 cm long, and tell whether the prediction is an interpolation or an extrapolation.

18. Make a Prediction Hummingbird wing beat rates are much higher than those in other birds. The table gives data about the mass and the frequency of wing beats for various species of hummingbirds.

Mass (g)	3.1	2.0	3.2	4.0	3.7	1.9	4.5
Frequency of Wing Beats (beats per second)	60	85	50	45	55	90	40

a. Using a graphing calculator, find the linear regression model and state its domain.

b. Predict the frequency of wing beats for a Giant Hummingbird with a mass of 19 grams.

c. Comment on the reasonableness of the prediction and what, if anything, is wrong with the model.

19. Explain the Error A student calculates a function's average rate of change on an interval and finds that it is 0. The student concludes that the function is constant on the interval. Explain the student's error, and give an example to support your explanation.

20. Communicate Mathematical Ideas Describe a way to obtain a linear model for a set of data without using a graphing calculator.

Lesson Performance Task

Since 1980 scientists have used data from satellite sensors to calculate a daily measure of Arctic sea ice extent. Sea ice extent is calculated as the sum of the areas of sea ice covering the ocean where the ice concentration is greater than 15%. The graph here shows seasonal variations in sea ice extent for 2012, 2013, and the average values for the 1980s.

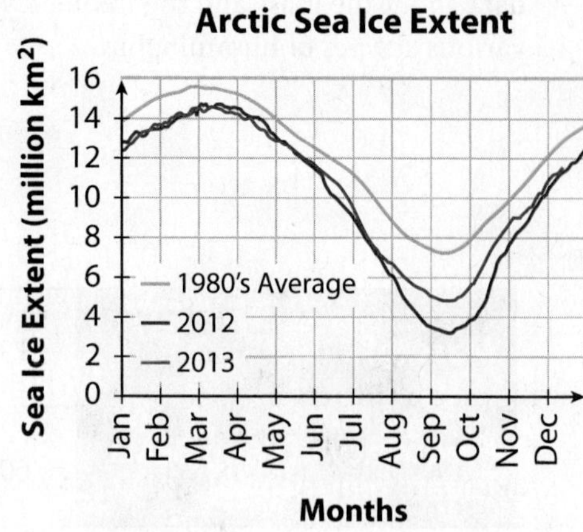

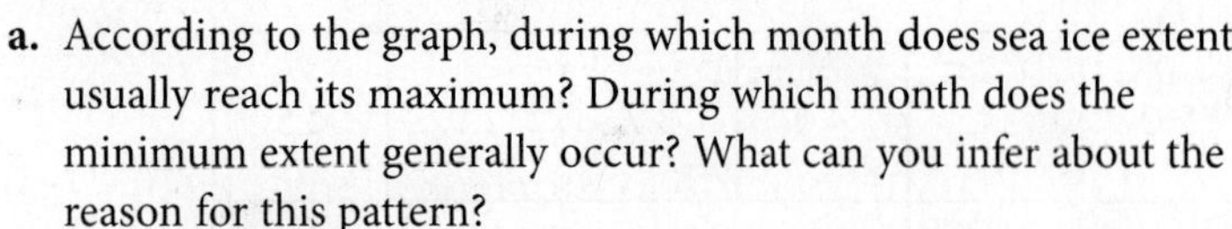

a. According to the graph, during which month does sea ice extent usually reach its maximum? During which month does the minimum extent generally occur? What can you infer about the reason for this pattern?

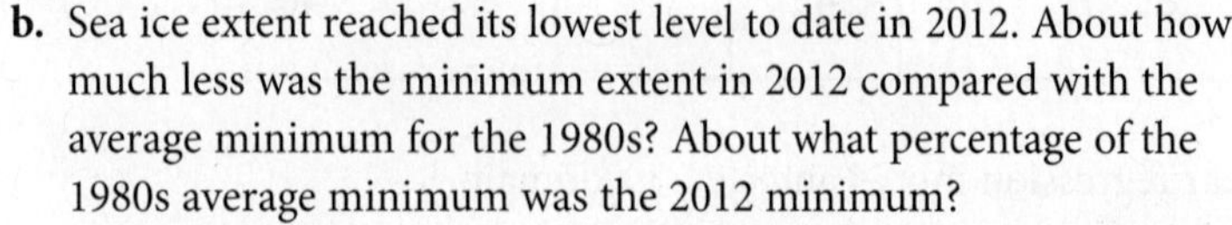

b. Sea ice extent reached its lowest level to date in 2012. About how much less was the minimum extent in 2012 compared with the average minimum for the 1980s? About what percentage of the 1980s average minimum was the 2012 minimum?

c. How does the maximum extent in 2012 compare with the average maximum for the 1980s? About what percentage of the 1980s average maximum was the 2012 maximum?

d. What do the patterns in the maximum and minimum values suggest about how climate change may be affecting sea ice extent?

e. How do the 2013 maximum and minimum values compare with those for 2012? What possible explanation can you suggest for the differences?

1.3 Inverses of Functions

Resource Locker

Essential Question: What is an inverse function, and how do you know it's an inverse function?

Explore Understanding Inverses of Functions

Recall that a *relation* is any pairing of the elements of one set (the domain) with the elements of a second set (the range). The elements of the domain are called inputs, while the elements of the range are called outputs. A function is a special type of relation that pairs every input with exactly one output. In a *one-to-one function*, no output is ever used more than once in the function's pairings. In a *many-to-one function*, at least one output is used more than once.

An **inverse relation** reverses the pairings of a relation. If a relation pairs an input x with an output y, then the inverse relation pairs an input y with an output x. The inverse of a function may or may not be another function. If the inverse of a function $f(x)$ is also a function, it is called the **inverse function** and is written $f^{-1}(x)$. If the inverse of a function is not a function, then it is simply an inverse relation.

Ⓐ The mapping diagrams show a function and its inverse. Complete the diagram for the inverse of the function.

Is the function one-to-one or many-to-one? Explain.

Is the inverse of the function also a function? Explain.

Function

Domain	Range
−4	−2
0	−3
1	2
4	1

Inverse of Function

Domain	Range
−2	−4
−3	
2	
1	4

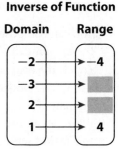

Ⓑ The mapping diagrams show a function and its inverse. Complete the diagram for the inverse of the function.

Is the function one-to-one or many-to-one? Explain.

Is the inverse of the function also a function? Explain.

Function

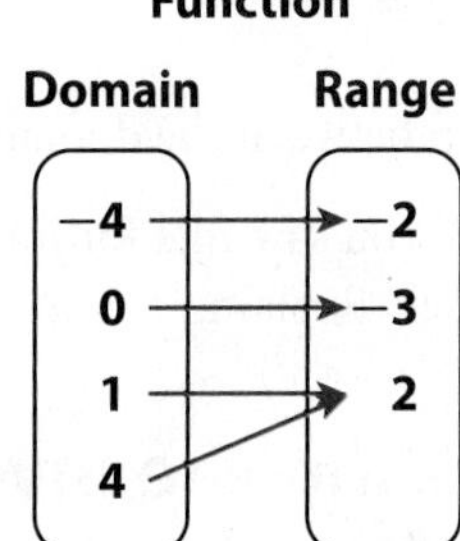

Inverse of Function

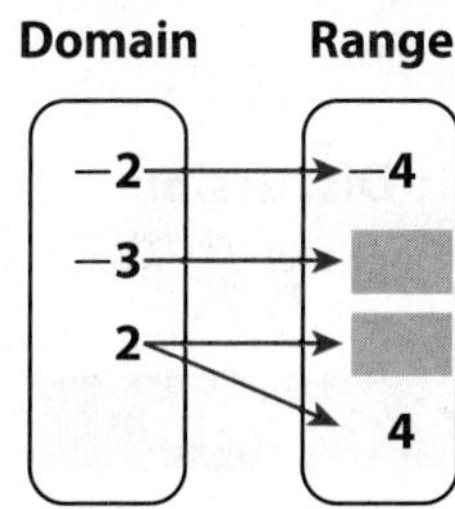

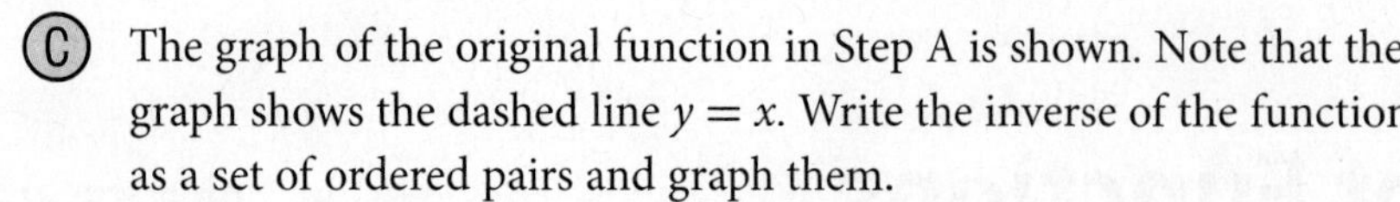

(C) The graph of the original function in Step A is shown. Note that the graph shows the dashed line $y = x$. Write the inverse of the function as a set of ordered pairs and graph them.

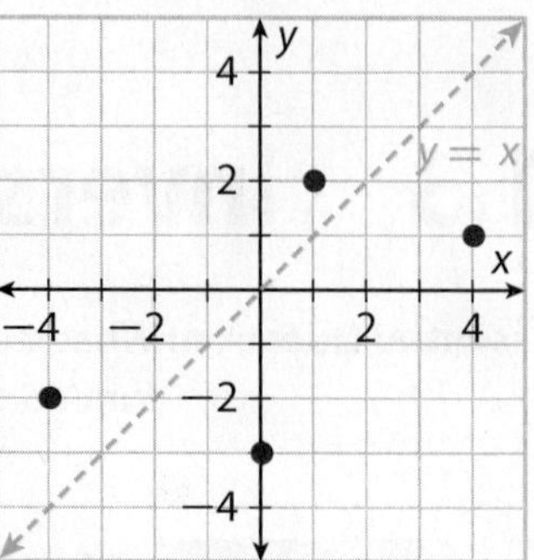

Function: $\{(-4, -2), (0, -3), (1, 2), (4, 1)\}$

Inverse of function:

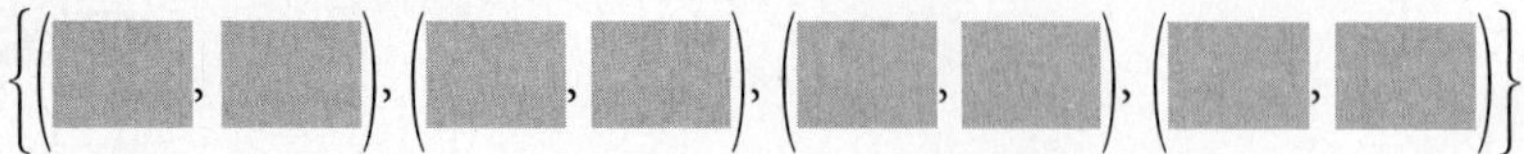

What do you observe about the graphs of the function and its inverse in relationship to the line $y = x$? Why does this make sense?

(D) The **composition of two functions** $f(x)$ and $g(x)$, written $f(g(x))$ and read as "f of g of x," is a new function that uses the output of $g(x)$ as the input of $f(x)$. For example, consider the functions f and g with the following rules.

f: Add 1 to an input. g: Double an input.

Notice that $g(1) = 2(1) = 2$. So, $f(g(1)) = f(2) = 2 + 1 = 3$.

You can also find $g(f(x))$. Notice that $f(1) = 1 + 1 = 2$. So, $g(f(1)) = g(2) = 2(2) = 4$.

For these two functions, you can see that $f(g(1)) \neq g(f(1))$.

You can compose a function and its inverse. For instance, the mapping diagram shown illustrates $f^{-1}(f(x))$ where $f(x)$ is the original function from Step A and $f^{-1}(x)$ is its inverse. Notice that the range of $f(x)$ serves as the domain of $f^{-1}(x)$. Complete the diagram. What do you notice about the outputs of of $f^{-1}(f(x))$? Explain why this makes sense.

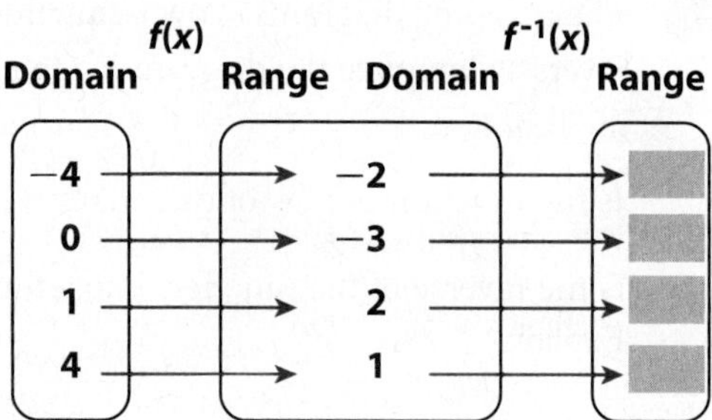

Reflect

1. What is the relationship between the domain and range of a relation and its inverse?

2. **Discussion** In Step D, you saw that for inverse functions, $f^{-1}(f(x)) = x$. What do you expect $f(f^{-1}(x))$ to equal? Explain.

Explain 1 Finding the Inverse of a Linear Function

Every linear function $f(x) = mx + b$ where $m \neq 0$ is a one-to-one function. So, its inverse is also a function. To find the equation of the inverse function, use the fact that inverse functions undo each other's pairings.

To find the inverse of a function $f(x)$:

1. Substitute y for $f(x)$.
2. Solve for x in terms of y.
3. Switch x and y (since the inverse switches inputs and outputs).
4. Replace y with $f^{-1}(x)$.

To check your work and verify that the functions are inverses, show that $f(f^{-1}(x)) = x$ and that $f^{-1}(f(x)) = x$.

Example 1 **Find the inverse function $f^{-1}(x)$ for the given function $f(x)$. Use composition to verify that the functions are inverses. Then graph the function and its inverse.**

(A) $f(x) = 3x + 4$

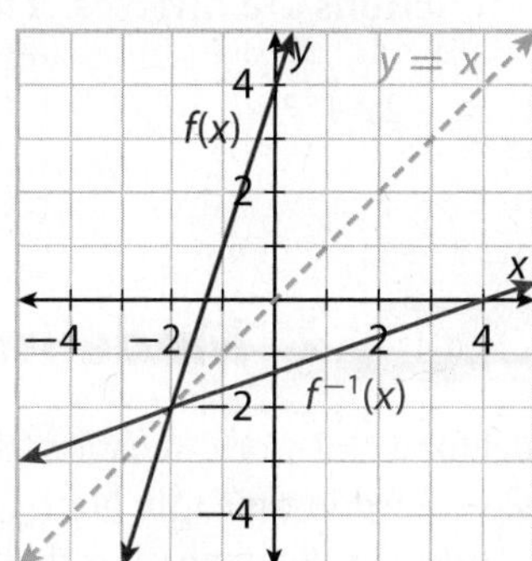

Replace $f(x)$ with y. $\quad y = 3x + 4$

Solve for x. $\quad y - 4 = 3x$

$\frac{y-4}{3} = x$

Interchange x and y. $\quad y = \frac{x-4}{3}$

Replace y with $f^{-1}(x)$. $\quad f^{-1}(x) = \frac{x-4}{3}$

Check: Verify that $f^{-1}(f(x)) = x$ and $f(f^{-1}(x)) = x$.

$$f^{-1}(f(x)) = f^{-1}(3x+4) = \frac{(3x+4)-4}{3} = \frac{3x}{3} = x$$

$$f(f^{-1}(x)) = f\left(\frac{x-4}{3}\right) = 3\left(\frac{x-4}{3}\right) + 4 = (x-4) + 4 = x$$

(B) $f(x) = 2x - 2$

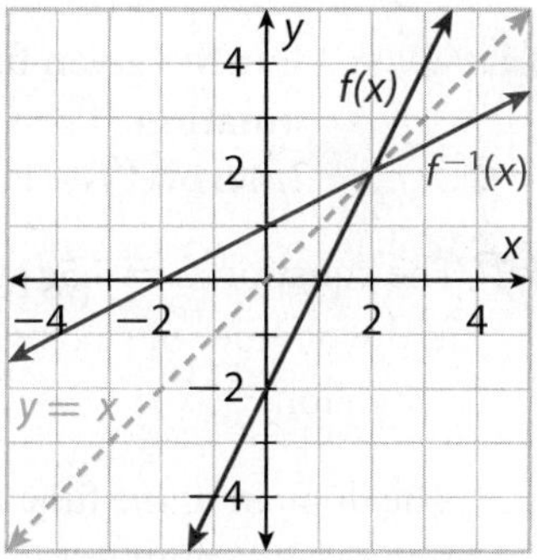

Replace $f(x)$ with y. $\quad y = 2x - 2$

Solve for x. $\quad y + 2 = 2x$

$\frac{y+2}{2} = x$

Interchange x and y. $\quad y = \frac{x+2}{2}$

Replace y with $f^{-1}(x)$. $\quad f^{-1}(x) = \frac{x+2}{2}$

Check: Verify that $f^{-1}(f(x)) = x$ and $f(f^{-1}(x)) = x$.

$$f^{-1}(f(x)) = f^{-1}(2x-2) = \frac{(2x-2)+2}{2} = \frac{2x}{2} = x$$

$$f(f^{-1}(x)) = f\left(\frac{x+2}{2}\right) = 2\left(\frac{x+2}{2}\right) - 2 = (x+2) - 2 = x$$

Reflect

3. What is the significance of the point where the graph of a linear function and its inverse intersect?

4. The graph of a constant function $f(x) = c$ for any constant c is a horizontal line through the point $(0, c)$. Does a constant function have an inverse? Does it have an inverse function? Explain.

Your Turn

Find the inverse function $f^{-1}(x)$ for the given function $f(x)$. Use composition to verify that the functions are inverses. Then graph the function and its inverse.

5. $f(x) = -2x + 3$

Explain 2 Modeling with the Inverse of a Linear Function

In a model for a real-world situation, the variables have specific real-world meanings. For example, the distance d (in miles) traveled in time t (in hours) at a constant speed of 60 miles per hour is $d = 60t$. Writing this in function notation as $d(t) = 60t$ emphasizes that this equation describes distance as a function of time.

You can find the inverse function for $d = 60t$ by solving for the independent variable t in terms of the dependent variable d. This gives the equation $t = \frac{d}{60}$. Writing this in function notation as $t(d) = \frac{d}{60}$ emphasizes that this equation describes time as a function of distance. Because the meanings of the variables can't be interchanged, you do not switch them at the end as you would switch x and y when working with purely mathematical functions. As you work with real-world models, you may have to restrict the domain and range.

Example 2 **For the given function, state the domain of the inverse function using set notation. Then find an equation for the inverse function, and graph it. Interpret the meaning of the inverse function.**

(A) The equation $C = 3.5g$ gives the cost C (in dollars) as a function of the number of gallons of gasoline g when the price is \$3.50 per gallon.

The domain of the function $C = 3.5g$ is restricted to nonnegative numbers to make real-world sense, so the range of the function also consists of nonnegative numbers. This means that the domain of the inverse function is $\{C \mid C \geq 0\}$.

Solve the given equation for g to find the inverse function.

Write the equation. $C = 3.5g$

Divide both sides by 3.5. $\frac{C}{3.5} = g$

So, the inverse function is $g = \frac{C}{3.5}$.

Graph the inverse function.

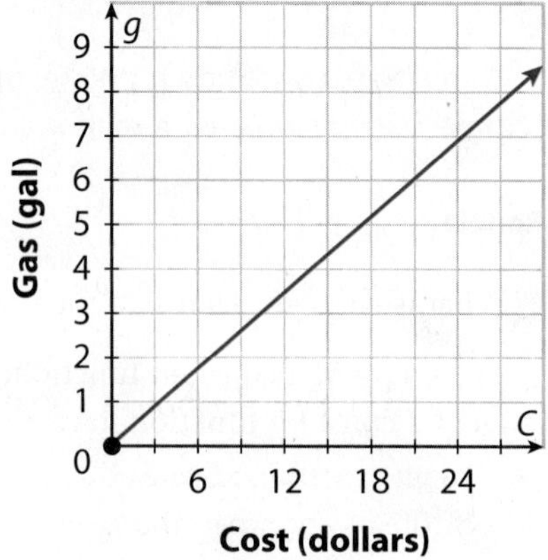

The inverse function gives the number of gallons of gasoline as a function of the cost (in dollars) when the price of gas is \$3.50 per gallon.

Ⓑ A car's gas tank, which can hold 14 gallons of gas, contains 4 gallons of gas when the driver stops at a gas station to fill the tank. The gas pump dispenses gas at a rate of 5 gallons per minute. The equation $g = 5t + 4$ gives the number of gallons of gasoline g in the tank as a function of the pumping time t(in minutes).

The range of the function $g = 5t + 4$ is the number of gallons of gas in the tank, which varies from 4 gallons to 14 gallons. So, the domain of the inverse function is

$\{g \mid \boxed{4} \le g \le \boxed{14}\}$.

Solve the given equation for g to find the inverse function.

Write the equation. $g = \boxed{5}\,t + \boxed{4}$

Solve for t. $\dfrac{\boxed{g-4}}{5} = t$

So, the inverse function is $t = \boxed{\dfrac{g-4}{5}}$.

Graph the inverse function.

The inverse function gives the pumping time (in minutes) as a function of the amount of gas in the tank (in gallons).

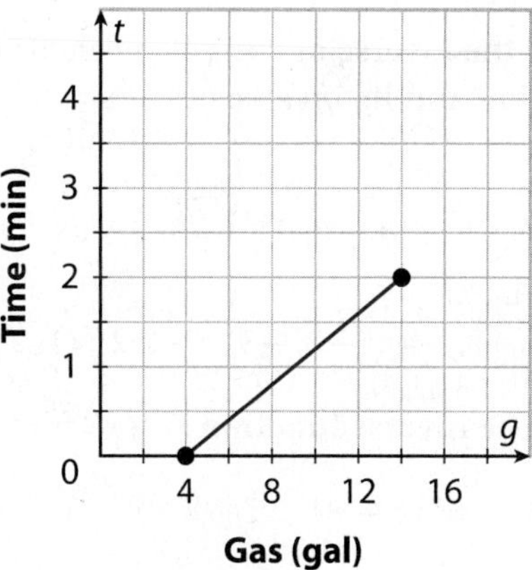

Your Turn

For the given function, determine the domain of the inverse function. Then find an equation for the inverse function, and graph it. Interpret the meaning of the inverse function.

6. A municipal swimming pool containing 600,000 gallons of water is drained. The amount of water w (in thousands of gallons) remaining in the pool at time t (in hours) after the draining begins is $w = 600 - 2t$.

Elaborate

7. What must be true about a function for its inverse to be a function?

8. A function rule indicates the operations to perform on an input to produce an output. What is the relationship between these operations and the operations indicated by the inverse function?

9. How can you use composition to verify that two functions $f(x)$ and $g(x)$ are inverse functions?

10. Describe a real-world situation modeled by a linear function for which it makes sense to find an inverse function. Give an example of how the inverse function might also be useful.

11. **Essential Question Check-In** What is an inverse relation?

Evaluate: Homework and Practice

- Online Homework
- Hints and Help
- Extra Practice

The mapping diagrams show a function and its inverse. Complete the diagram for the inverse of the function. Then tell whether the inverse is a function, and explain your reasoning.

1. Function / Inverse of Function

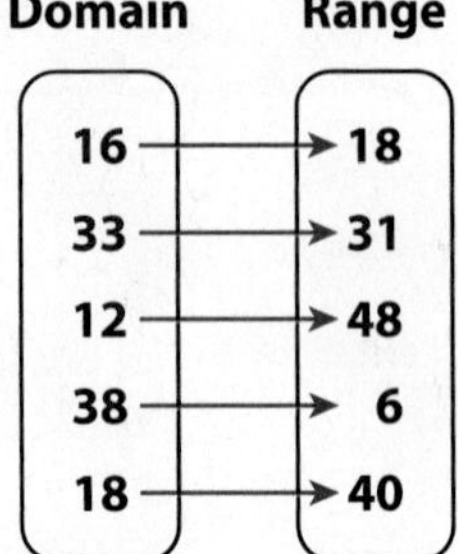

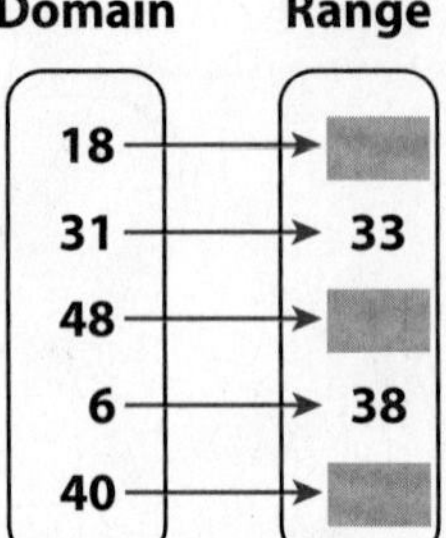

2. Function / Inverse of Function

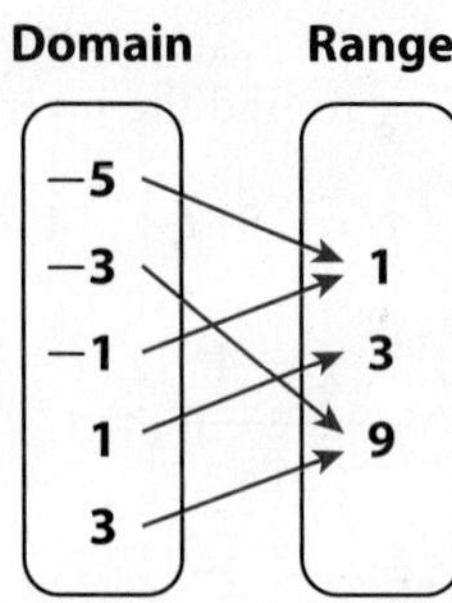

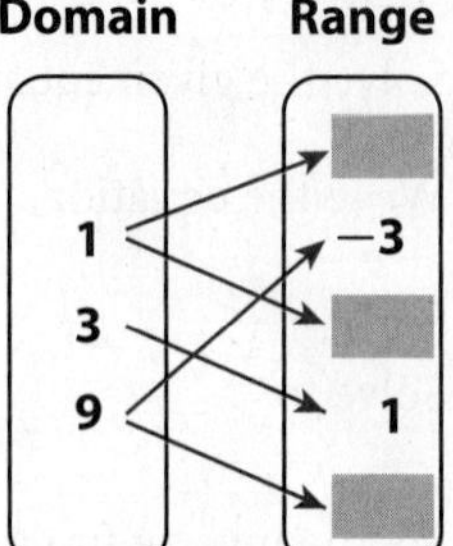

Write the inverse of the given function as a set of ordered pairs and then graph the function and its inverse on a coordinate plane.

3. Function:
$\{(-4, -3), (-2, -4), (0, -2), (1, 0), (2, 3)\}$

4. Function:
$\{(-3, -4), (-2, -3), (-1, 2), (1, 2), (2, 4), (3, 4)\}$

Find the inverse function $f^{-1}(x)$ for the given function $f(x)$.

5. $f(x) = 4x - 8$

6. $f(x) = \dfrac{x}{3}$

7. $f(x) = \dfrac{x+1}{6}$

8. $f(x) = -0.75x$

Find the inverse function $f^{-1}(x)$ for the given function $f(x)$. Use composition to verify that the functions are inverses. Then graph the function and its inverse.

9. $f(x) = -3x + 3$

10. $f(x) = \frac{2}{5}x - 2$

For the given function, determine the domain of the inverse function. Then find an equation for the inverse function, and graph it. Interpret the meaning of the inverse function.

11. Geometry The equation $A = \frac{1}{2}(20)h$ gives the area A (in square inches) of a triangle with a base of 20 inches as a function of its height h (in inches).

12. The label on a gallon of paint says that it will cover from 250 square feet to 450 square feet depending on the surface that is being painted. A painter has 12 gallons of paint on hand. The equation $A = 12c$ gives the area A (in square feet) that the 12 gallons of paint will cover if applied at a coverage rate c (in square feet per gallon).

The graph of a function is given. Tell whether the function's inverse is a function, and explain your reasoning. If the inverse is not a function, tell how can you restrict the domain of the function so that its inverse is a function.

13.

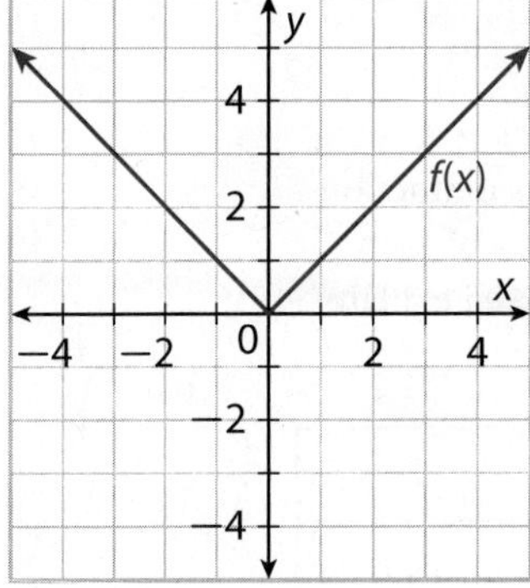

14.

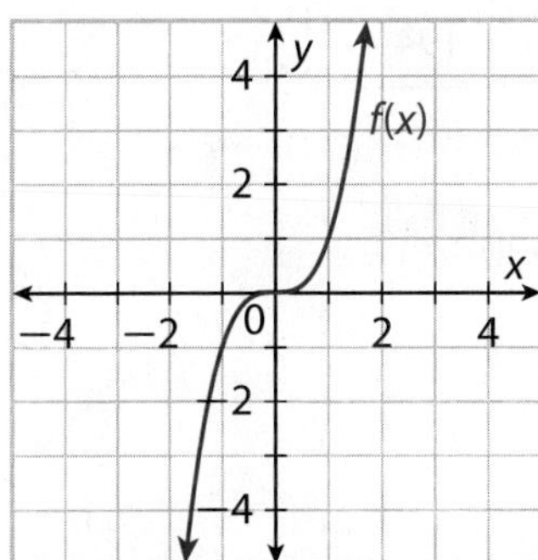

15. Multiple Response Identify the domain intervals over which the inverse of the graphed function is also a function. Select all that apply.

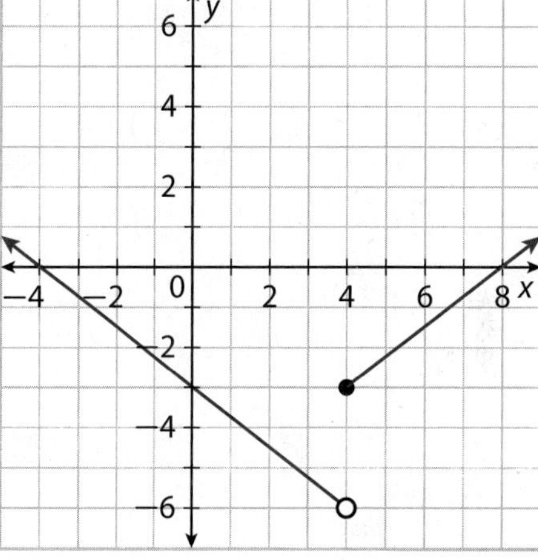

A. $[4, +\infty)$ **D.** $(-\infty, +\infty)$ **G.** $(4, 8)$

B. $(0, +\infty)$ **E.** $(-\infty, 4]$ **H.** $(8, +\infty)$

C. $[-4, +\infty)$ **F.** $(-\infty, 4)$ **I.** $(0, 8]$

H.O.T. Focus on Higher Order Thinking

16. Draw Conclusions Identify all linear functions that are their own inverse.

17. Make a Conjecture Among linear functions (excluding constant functions), quadratic functions, absolute value functions, and exponential functions, which types of function do you have to restrict the domain for the inverse to be a function? Explain.

18. Find the Error A student was asked to find the inverse of $f(x) = 2x + 1$. The student's work is shown. Explain why the student is incorrect and what the student should have done to get the correct answer.

> The function $f(x) = 2x + 1$ involves two operations: multiplying by 2 and adding 1. The inverse operations are dividing by 2 and subtracting 1. So, the inverse function is $f^{-1}(x) = \frac{x}{2} - 1$.

Lesson Performance Task

In an anatomy class, a student measures the femur of an adult male and finds the length of the femur to be 50.0 cm. The student is then asked to estimate the height of the male that the femur came from.

The table shows the femur lengths and heights of some adult males and females. Using a graphing calculator, perform linear regression on the data to obtain femur length as a function of height (one function for adult males, one for adult females). Then find the inverse of each function. Use the appropriate inverse function to find the height of the adult male and explain how the inverse functions would be helpful to a forensic scientist.

Femur Length (cm)	30	38	46	54	62
Male Height (cm)	138	153	168	183	198
Female Height (cm)	132	147	163	179	194

STUDY GUIDE REVIEW

Analyzing Functions

MODULE 1

Essential Question: How can you analyze functions to solve real-world problems?

Key Vocabulary

finite interval *(intervalo finito)*

infinite interval *(intervalo infinito)*

domain *(dominio)*

range *(rango)*

end behavior *(comportamiento final)*

KEY EXAMPLE *(Lesson 1.1)*

Write the domain and range of $f(x) = 3^x$ as an inequality, using set notation, and using interval notation. Then describe the end behavior of the function.

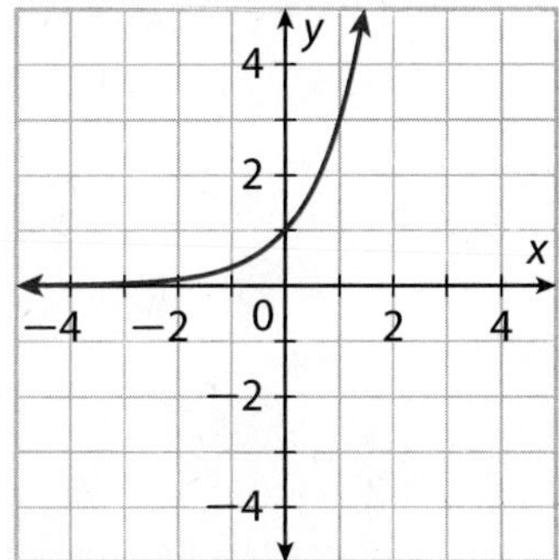

	Domain	Range
Inequality	$\{-\infty < x < +\infty\}$	$y > 0$
Set notation	$\{x \mid -\infty < x < +\infty\}$	$y \mid y > 0$
Interval notation	$(-\infty, +\infty)$	$(0, +\infty)$

End behavior: As $x \to +\infty$, $f(x) \to +\infty$, and as $x \to -\infty$, $f(x) \to 0$.

KEY EXAMPLE *(Lesson 1.3)*

Find the inverse function $f^{-1}(x)$ for $f(x) = -2x + 3$.

$y = -2x + 3$ Replace $f(x)$ with y.

$\frac{y-3}{-2} = x$ Solve for x.

$y = \frac{x-3}{-2}$ Switch x and y.

$f^{-1}(x) = \frac{x-3}{-2}$ Replace y with $f^{-1}(x)$.

Find the inverse function $g^{-1}(x)$ for $g(x) = \frac{(x-3)}{2}$.

$y = \frac{(x-3)}{2}$

$2y + 3 = x$

$g^{-1}(x) = 2x + 3$

EXERCISES

Write the domain and range of the function as an inequality, using set notation, and using interval notation. *(Lesson 1.1)*

1.

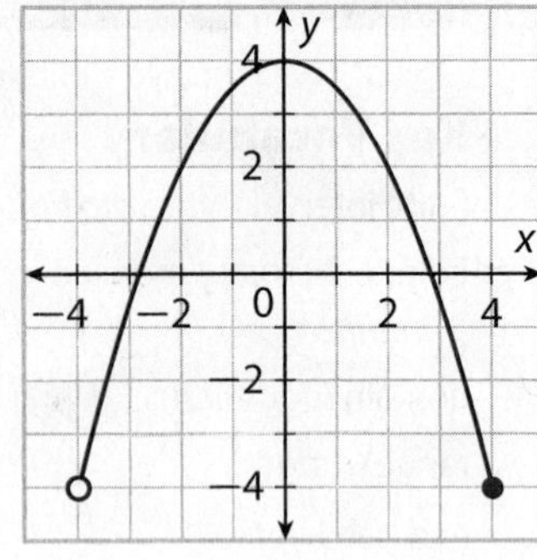

2.

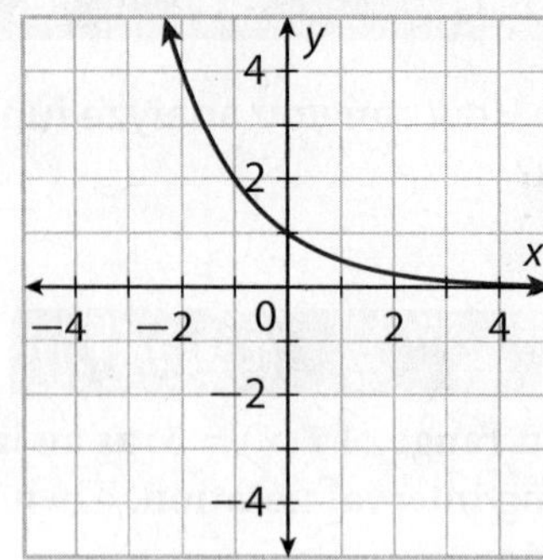

Find the inverse function $f^{-1}(x)$ for the given function $f(x)$. *(Lesson 1.3)*

3. $f(x) = \dfrac{x + 3}{5}$

4. $f(x) = 2x + 6$

MODULE PERFORMANCE TASK

How High Does a Pole-Vaulter Go?

A pole-vaulter performs two vaults, which can be modeled using the functions $h_1(t) = 9.8t - 4.9t^2$ and $h_2(t) = 8.82t - 4.9t^2$ where h is the height in meters at time t in seconds. How do the two vaults compare graphically in terms of the vertices and intercepts, and what do these represent? Which was the higher vault? How do you know?

Be sure to write down all your data and assumptions. Then use graphs, numbers, words, or algebra to explain how you reached your conclusions.

Ready to Go On?

1.1–1.3 Analyzing Functions

- Online Homework
- Hints and Help
- Extra Practice

Write the domain and range of the function $g(x) = 3x^2 - 4$ as an inequality, using set notation, and using interval notation. *(Lesson 1.1)*

1.	Domain	Range
Inequality		
Set notation		
Interval notation		

Find the inverse for each linear function. *(Lesson 1.3)*

2. $f(x) = -2x + 4$

3. $g(x) = \frac{x}{4} - 3$

4. $h(x) = \frac{3}{4}x + 1$

5. $j(x) = 5x - 6$

ESSENTIAL QUESTION

6. What are two ways the graphed function could be used to solve real-world problems? *(Lesson 1.2)*

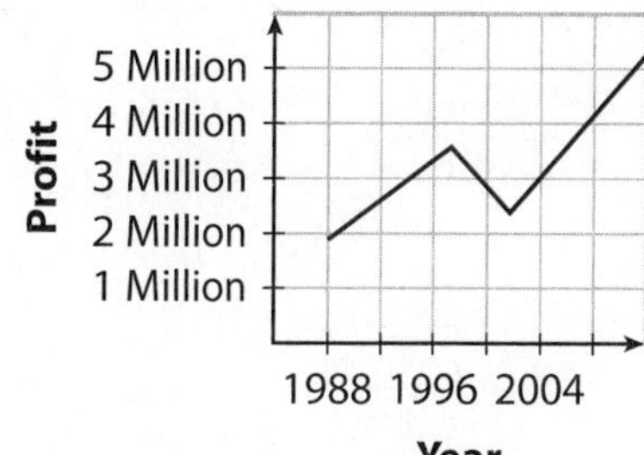

MODULE 1
MIXED REVIEW

Assessment Readiness

1. Look at each equation. Does the graph of the equation have an end behavior that approaches infinity (∞) as $x \to -\infty$?
Write Yes or No for A–C.

A. $y = -2x - 5$
B. $y = 5(x + 2)^2 - 3$
C. $y = -3^x$

2. Consider the function $y = x^2 - 4$. Determine if each statement is True or False.

A. The function has a domain of $(-\infty, \infty)$.
B. The function has a range of $(-\infty, \infty)$.
C. As $x \to -\infty$, $y \to -\infty$.

3. A bike rider starts at a fast pace and rides 40 miles in 2 hours. He gets tired, and slows down, traveling only 20 miles in the next 3 hours. He takes a rest for an hour, then rides back to where he started at a steady pace without stopping for 4 hours. Draw a graph to match the real world situation. Explain your choices.

4. The function to convert Fahrenheit to Celsius is $°C = f(°F) = \frac{5(°F - 32)}{9}$. The inverse function will convert Celsius to Fahrenheit. What is the inverse function? Explain how determining this inverse is different than determining the previous inverses.

Absolute Value Functions, Equations, and Inequalities

MODULE 2

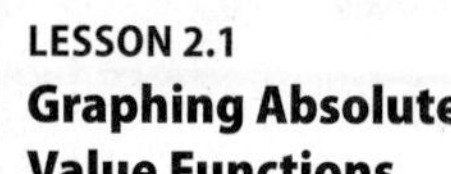

Essential Question: How can you use absolute value functions to solve real-world problems?

REAL WORLD VIDEO
Gold jewelry is sold with a rating for purity. For instance, 18-karat gold is 75% pure by weight. The purity level has to meet tolerances that can be expressed using absolute value inequalities.

MODULE PERFORMANCE TASK PREVIEW

What Is the Purity of Gold?

Because gold is such a soft metal, it is usually mixed with another metal such as copper or silver. Pure gold is 24 karat, and 18 karat indicates a mixture of 18 parts gold and 6 parts of another metal or metals. Imagine someone wants to sell you a ring and claims it is 18 karat. How can you use math to be sure the gold is indeed 18 karat? Let's find out!

Are YOU Ready?

Complete these exercises to review skills you will need for this module.

- Online Homework
- Hints and Help
- Extra Practice

One-Step Equations

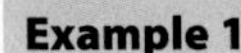

Example 1 Solve $x - 6.8 = 2$ for x.

$x - 6.8 + 6.8 = 2 + 6.8$ Add.

$x = 8.8$ Combine like terms.

Solve each equation.

1. $r + 9 = 7$ **2.** $\frac{w}{4} = -3$ **3.** $10b = 14$

Slope and Slope-Intercept Form

Example 2 Find the slope and y-intercept of $3x - y = 6$.

$-3x + 3x - y = -3x + 6$ Write the equation in $y = mx + b$ form.

$-y(-1) = (-3x + 6)(-1)$

$y = 3x - 6$ The slope is 3 and the y-intercept is -6.

Find the slope and y-intercept for each equation.

4. $y - 8 = 2x + 9$ **5.** $3y = 2(x - 3)$ **6.** $2y + 8x = 1$

Linear Inequalities in Two Variables

Example 3 Graph $y < 2x - 3$.

Graph the y-intercept of $(0, -3)$.

Use the slope of 2 to plot a second point, and draw a dashed line connecting the points. Shade below the line.

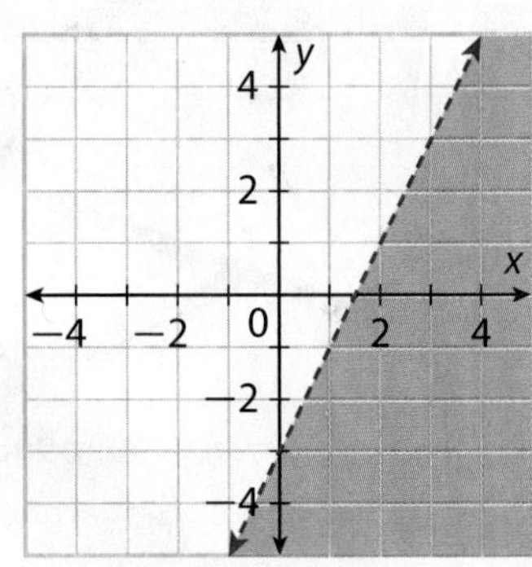

Graph and label each inequality on a coordinate plane.

7. $y \geq -x + 2$ **8.** $y < x - 1$

2.1 Graphing Absolute Value Functions

Essential Question: How can you identify the features of the graph of an absolute value function?

Resource Locker

Explore Graphing and Analyzing the Parent Absolute Value Function

Absolute value, written as $|x|$, represents the distance between x and 0 on a number line. As a distance, absolute value is always positive. For every point on a number line, there is another point on the opposite side of 0 that is the same distance from 0. For example, both 5 and –5 are five units away from 0. Thus, $|-5| = 5$ and $|5| = 5$.

5 units 5 units

–5 0 5

The absolute value function $|x|$, can be defined piecewise as $|x| = \begin{cases} x & x \geq 0 \\ -x & x < 0 \end{cases}$. When x is nonnegative, the function simply returns the number. When x is negative, the function returns the opposite of x.

(A) Complete the input-output table for $f(x)$.

$$f(x) = |x| = \begin{cases} x & x \geq 0 \\ -x & x < 0 \end{cases}$$

x	f(x)
–8	
–4	
0	
4	
8	

(B) Plot the points you found on a coordinate grid. Use the points to complete the graph of the function.

(C) Now, examine your graph of $f(x) = |x|$ and complete the following statements about the function.

$f(x) = |x|$ is symmetric about the ______ and therefore is a(n) ______ function.

The domain of $f(x) = |x|$ is ______.

The range of $f(x) = |x|$ is ______.

Reflect

1. Use the definition of the absolute value function to show that $f(x) = |x|$ is an even function.

Explain 1 Graphing Absolute Value Functions

You can apply general transformations to absolute value functions by changing parameters in the equation $g(x) = a\left|\frac{1}{b}(x-h)\right| + k$.

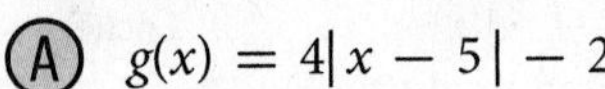

Example 1 **Given the function $g(x) = a\left|\frac{1}{b}(x-h)\right| + k$, find the vertex of the function. Use the vertex and two other points to help you graph $g(x)$.**

(A) $g(x) = 4|x-5| - 2$

The vertex of the parent absolute value function is at (0, 0).

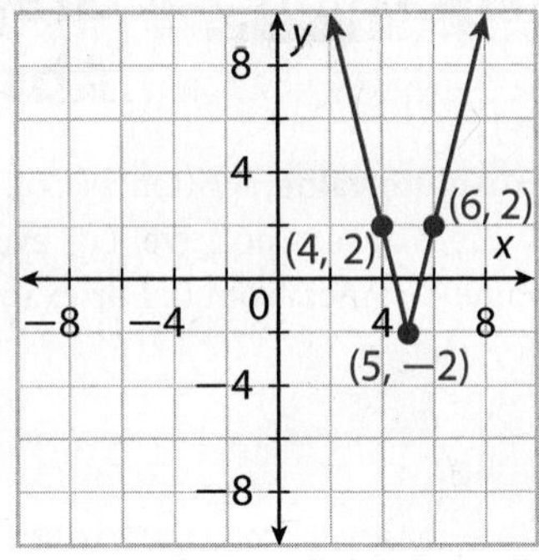

The vertex of $g(x)$ will be the point to which (0, 0) is mapped by $g(x)$.

$g(x)$ involves a translation of $f(x)$ 5 units to the right and 2 units down.

The vertex of $g(x)$ will therefore be at (5, −2).

Next, determine the location to which each of the points (1, 1) and (−1, 1) on $f(x)$ will be mapped.

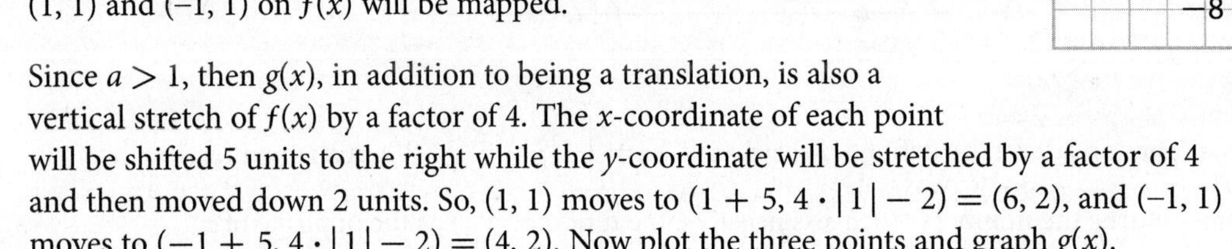

Since $a > 1$, then $g(x)$, in addition to being a translation, is also a vertical stretch of $f(x)$ by a factor of 4. The x-coordinate of each point will be shifted 5 units to the right while the y-coordinate will be stretched by a factor of 4 and then moved down 2 units. So, (1, 1) moves to $(1 + 5, 4 \cdot |1| - 2) = (6, 2)$, and (−1, 1) moves to $(-1 + 5, 4 \cdot |1| - 2) = (4, 2)$. Now plot the three points and graph $g(x)$.

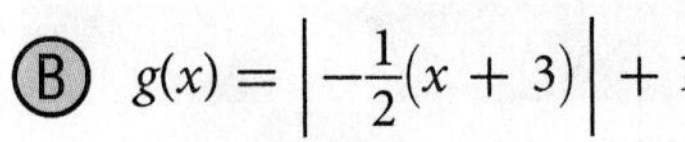

(B) $g(x) = \left|-\frac{1}{2}(x+3)\right| + 1$

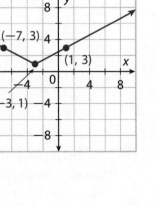

The vertex of the parent absolute value function is at (0, 0).

$g(x)$ is a translation of $f(x)$ 3 units to the left and 1 unit up.

The vertex of $g(x)$ will therefore be at $(-3, 1)$.

Next, determine to where the points (2, 2) and (−2, 2) on $f(x)$ will be mapped. Since $|b| = 2$, $g(x)$ is also a horizontal stretch of $f(x)$ and since b is negative, a reflection across the y-axis.

The x-coordinate will be reflected in the y-axis and stretched by a factor of 2, then moved 3 units to the left.

The y-coordinate will move up 1 unit.

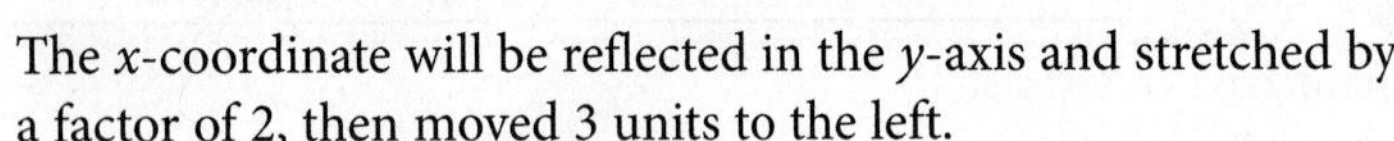

So, (2, 2) becomes $(-2(2) - 3, 2 + 1) = (-7, 3)$, and (−2, 2) becomes $(1, 3)$. Now plot the three points and use them to sketch $g(x)$.

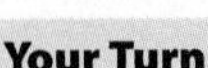

Your Turn

2. Given $g(x) = -\frac{1}{5}|(x+6)| + 4$, find the vertex and two other points and use them to help you graph $g(x)$.

Explain 2 Writing Absolute Value Functions from a Graph

If an absolute value function in the form $g(x) = a\left|\frac{1}{b}(x-h)\right| + k$ has values other than 1 for both a and b, you can rewrite that function so that the value of at least one of a or b is 1.

When a and b are positive: $a\left|\frac{1}{b}(x-h)\right| = \left|\frac{a}{b}(x-h)\right| = \frac{a}{b}\left|(x-h)\right|$.

When a is negative and b is positive, you can move the opposite of a inside the absolute value expression. This leaves −1 outside the absolute value symbol: $-2\left|\frac{1}{b}\right| = -1(2)\left|\frac{1}{b}\right| = -1\left|\frac{2}{b}\right|$.

When b is negative, you can rewrite the equation without a negative sign, because of the properties of absolute value: $a\left|\frac{1}{b}(x-h)\right| = a\left|\frac{1}{-b}(x-h)\right|$. This case has now been reduced to one of the other two cases.

Example 2 **Given the graph of an absolute value function, write the function in the form $g(x) = a\left|\frac{1}{b}(x-h)\right| + k$.**

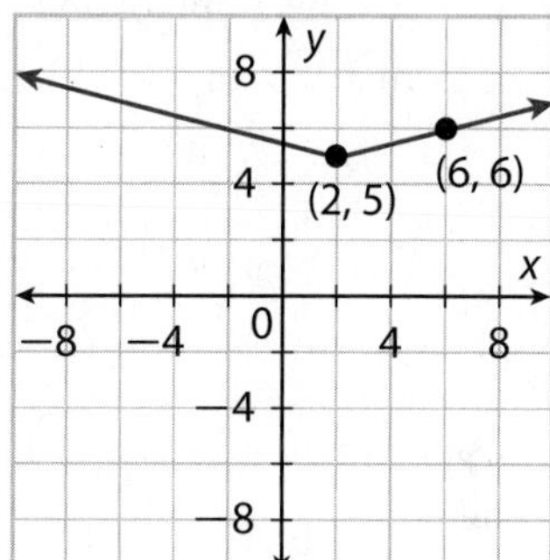

(A) Let $a = 1$.

The vertex of $g(x)$ is at (2, 5). This means that $h = 2$ and $k = 5$.

The value of a is given: $a = 1$.

Substitute these values into $g(x)$, giving $g(x) = \left|\frac{1}{b}(x-2)\right| + 5$.

Choose a point on $g(x)$ like (6, 6), Substitute these values into $g(x)$, and solve for b.

Substitute.	$6 = \left|\frac{1}{b}(6-2)\right| + 5$
Simplify.	$6 = \left|\frac{1}{b}(4)\right| + 5$
Subtract 5 from each side.	$1 = \left|\frac{4}{b}\right|$
Rewrite the absolute value as two equations.	$1 = \frac{4}{b}$ or $1 = -\frac{4}{b}$
Solve for b.	$b = 4$ or $b = -4$

Based on the problem conditions, only consider $b = 4$. Substitute into $g(x)$ to find the equation for the graph.

$g(x) = \left|\frac{1}{4}(x-2)\right| + 5$

(B) Let $b = 1$.

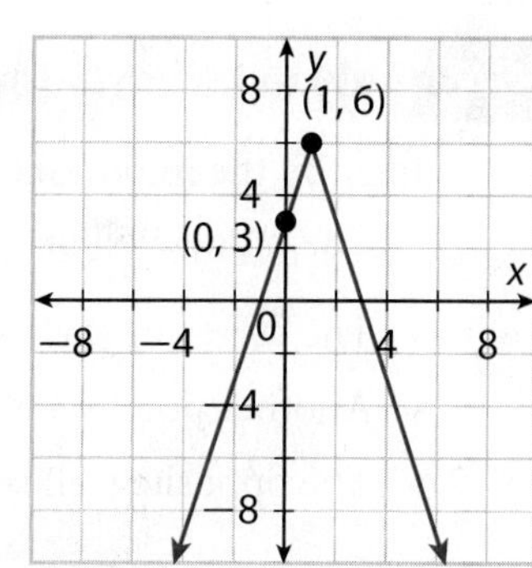

The vertex of $g(x)$ is at (1, 6). This means that $h =$ [1] and $k =$ [6]. The value of b is given: $b = 1$.

Substitute these values into $g(x)$, giving $g(x) = a\left|x - 1\right| + 6$.

Now, choose a point on $g(x)$ with integer coordinates, (0, [3]).

Substitute these values into $g(x)$ and solve for a.

$$g(x) = a\left|x - \boxed{1}\right| + \boxed{6}$$

Substitute. $\boxed{3} = a|0 - 1| + 6$

Simplify. $\boxed{3} = a|-1| + 6$

Solve for a. $\boxed{-3} = a$

Therefore $g(x) = \boxed{-3|x-1| + 6}$.

Your Turn

3. Given the graph of an absolute value function, write the function in the form $g(x) = a\left|\frac{1}{b}(x - h)\right| + k$.

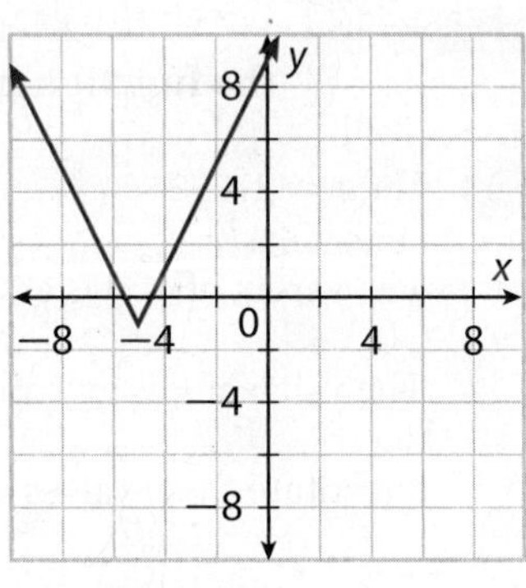

Explain 3 Modeling with Absolute Value Functions

Light travels in a straight line and can be modeled by a linear function. When light is reflected off a mirror, it travels in a straight line in a different direction. From physics, the angle at which the light ray comes in is equal to the angle at which it is reflected away: the angle of incidence is equal to the angle of reflection. You can use an absolute value function to model this situation.

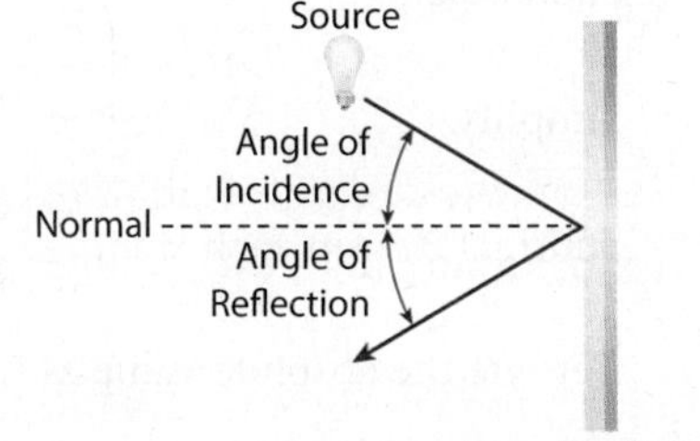

Law of Reflection

Example 3 **Solve the problem by modeling the situation with an absolute value function.**

At a science museum exhibit, a beam of light originates at a point 10 feet off the floor. It is reflected off a mirror on the floor that is 15 feet from the wall the light originates from. How high off the floor on the opposite wall does the light hit if the other wall is 8.5 feet from the mirror?

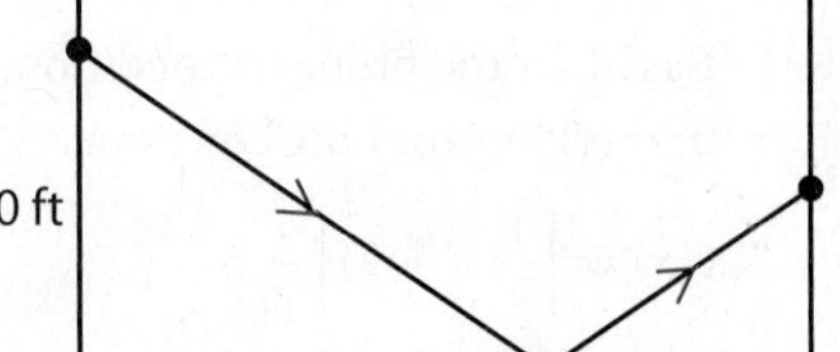

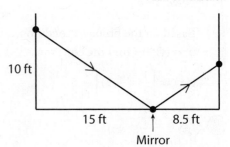

Analyze Information

Identify the important information.

- The model will be of the form $g(x) = a\left|\frac{1}{b}(x - h)\right| + k$.
- The vertex of $g(x)$ is $(15, 0)$
- Another point on $g(x)$ is $(0, 10)$.
- The opposite wall is 23.5 feet from the first wall.

Formulate a Plan

Let the base of the first wall be the origin. You want to find the value of $g(x)$ at $x = \boxed{23.5}$, which will give the height of the beam on the opposite wall. To do so, find the value of the parameters in the transformation of the parent function. In this situation, let $b = 1$. The vertex of $g(x)$ will give you the values of h and k. Use a second point to solve for a. Evaluate $g\left(\boxed{23.5}\right)$.

Solve

The vertex of $g(x)$ is at $\left(\boxed{15}, 0\right)$. Substitute, giving $g(x) = a\left|x - \boxed{15}\right| + \boxed{0}$.

Evaluate $g(x)$ at $(0, 10)$ and solve for a.

Substitute	$10 = a\left\|\boxed{0} - 15\right\| + \boxed{0}$
Simplify.	$\boxed{10} = a\left\|\boxed{-15}\right\|$
Simplify.	$10 = \boxed{15}\,a$
Solve for a.	$a = \boxed{\frac{2}{3}}$

Therefore $g(x) = \frac{2}{3}\left|(x - 15)\right|$. Find $g\left(\boxed{23.5}\right)$. $g(23.5) = \boxed{\frac{17}{3} \approx 5.67}$

Justify and Evaluate

The answer of 5.67 makes sense because the function is symmetric with respect to the line $x = 15$. The distance from this line to the second wall is a little more than half the distance from the line to the beam's origin. Since the beam originates at a height of 10 feet, it should hit the second wall at a height of a little over 5 feet.

Your Turn

4. Two students are passing a ball back and forth, allowing it to bounce once between them. If one student bounce-passes the ball from a height of 1.4 m and it bounces 3 m away from the student, where should the second student stand to catch the ball at a height of 1.2 m? Assume the path of the ball is linear over this short distance.

Elaborate

5. In the general form of the absolute value function, what does each parameter represent?

6. **Discussion** Explain why the vertex of $f(x) = |x|$ remains the same when $f(x)$ is stretched or compressed but not when it is translated.

7. **Essential Question Check-In** What are the features of the graph of an absolute value function?

- Online Homework
- Hints and Help
- Extra Practice

✩ Evaluate: Homework and Practice

Predict what the graph of each given function will look like. Verify your prediction using a graphing calculator. Then sketch the graph of the function.

1. $g(x) = 5|x - 3|$

2. $g(x) = -4|x + 2| + 5$

3. $g(x) = \left|\frac{7}{5}(x - 6)\right| + 4$

4. $g(x) = \left|\frac{3}{7}(x - 4)\right| + 2$

5. $g(x) = \frac{7}{4}|(x - 2)| - 3$

Graph the given function and identify the domain and range.

6. $g(x) = |x|$

7. $g(x) = \frac{4}{3}|(x - 5)| + 7$

8. $g(x) = -\frac{7}{6}|(x - 2)|$

9. $g(x) = \left|\frac{3}{4}(x - 2)\right| - 7$

10. $g(x) = \left|\frac{5}{7}(x - 4)\right|$

11. $g(x) = \left|-\frac{7}{3}(x + 5)\right| - 4$

Write the absolute value function in standard form for the given graph. Use *a* or *b* as directed, $b > 0$.

12. Let $a = 1$.

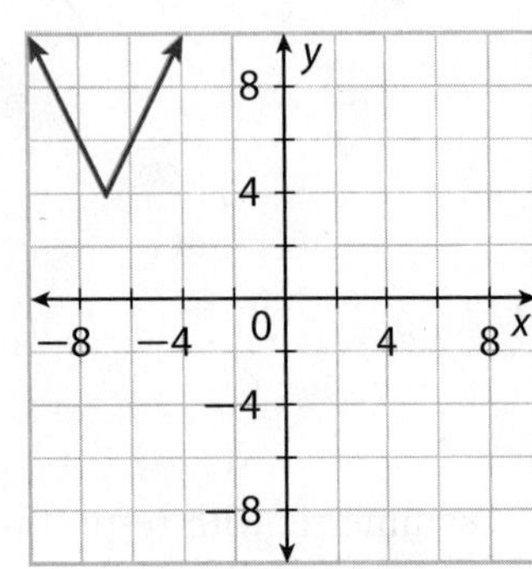

13. Let $b = 1$.

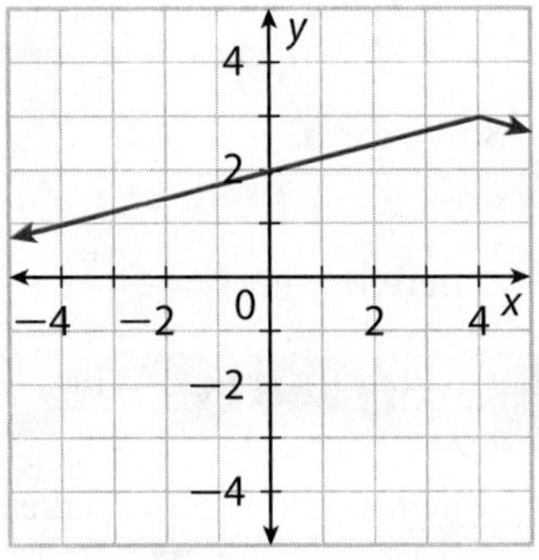

14. A rainstorm begins as a drizzle, builds up to a heavy rain, and then drops back to a drizzle. The rate r (in inches per hour) at which it rains is given by the function $r = -0.5|t - 1| + 0.5$, where t is the time (in hours). Graph the function. Determine for how long it rains and when it rains the hardest.

15. While playing pool, a player tries to shoot the eight ball into the corner pocket as shown. Imagine that a coordinate plane is placed over the pool table. The eight ball is at $\left(5, \frac{5}{4}\right)$ and the pocket they are aiming for is at (10, 5). The player is going to bank the ball off the side at (6, 0).

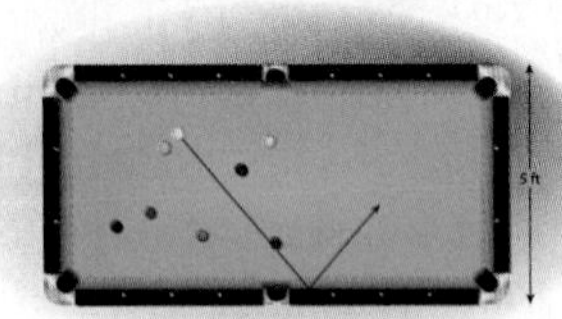

a. Write an equation for the path of the ball.

b. Did the player make the shot? How do you know?

16. Sam is sitting in a boat on a lake. She can get burned by from the sunlight that hits her directly and from sunlight that reflects off the water. Sunlight reflects off the water at the point (2, 0) and hits Sam at the point (3.5, 3). Write and graph the function that shows the path of the sunlight.

17. The Transamerica Pyramid is an office building in San Francisco. It stands 853 feet tall and is 145 feet wide at its base. Imagine that a coordinate plane is placed over a side of the building. In the coordinate plane, each unit represents one foot. Write an absolute value function whose graph is the V-shaped outline of the sides of the building, ignoring the "shoulders" of the building.

18. Match each graph with its function.

a. ___?___ $y = |x + 6| - 4$ b. ___?___ $y = |x - 6| - 4$ c. ___?___ $y = |x - 6| + 4$

A
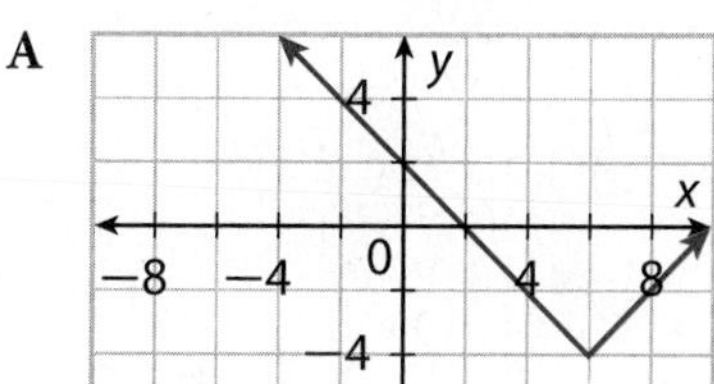

B
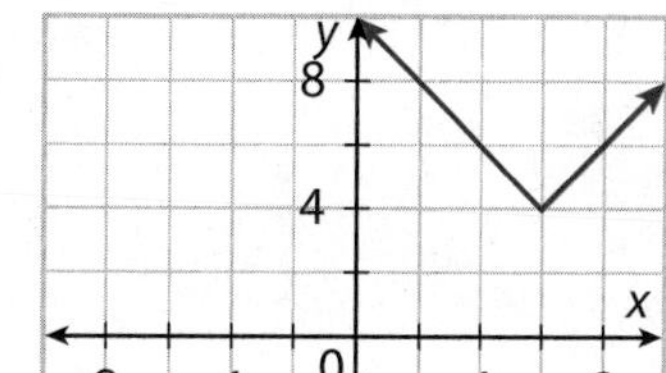

C
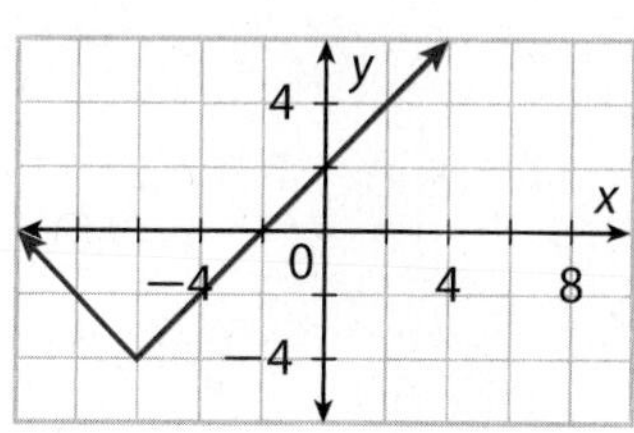

H.O.T. Focus on Higher Order Thinking

19. Explain the Error Explain why the graph shown is not the graph of $y = |x + 3| + 2$. What is the correct equation shown in the graph?

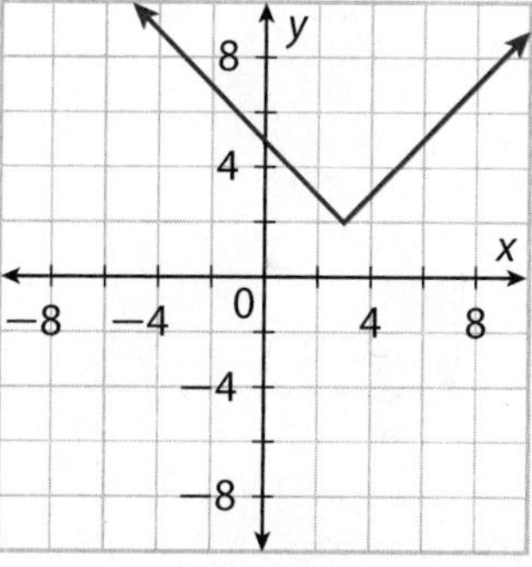

20. Multi-Step A golf player is trying to make a hole-in-one on the miniature golf green shown. Imagine that a coordinate plane is placed over the golf green. The golf ball is at (2.5, 2) and the hole is at (9.5, 2). The player is going to bank the ball off the side wall of the green at (6, 8).

a. Write an equation for the path of the ball.

b. Use the equation in part a to determine if the player makes the shot.

Lesson Performance Task

Suppose a musical piece calls for an orchestra to start at *fortissimo* (about 90 decibels), decrease steadily in loudness to *pianissimo* (about 50 decibels) in four measures, and then increase steadily back to *fortissimo* in another four measures.

a. Write a function to represent the sound level s in decibels as a function of the number of measures m.

b. After how many measures should the orchestra be at the loudness of *mezzo forte* (about 70 decibels)?

c. Describe what the graph of this function would look like.

2.2 Solving Absolute Value Equations

Resource Locker

Essential Question: How can you solve an absolute value equation?

Explore Solving Absolute Value Equations Graphically

Absolute value equations differ from linear equations in that they may have two solutions. This is indicated with a **disjunction**, a mathematical statement created by a connecting two other statements with the word "or." To see why there can be two solutions, you can solve an absolute value equation using graphs.

(A) Solve the equation $2|x - 5| - 4 = 2$.

Plot the function $f(x) = 2|x - 5| - 4$ on a coordinate grid. Then plot the function $g(x) = 2$ as a horizontal line on the same grid, and mark the points where the graphs intersect.

(B) Write the solution to this equation as a disjunction:

$x =$ ☐ or $x =$ ☐

Reflect

1. Why might you expect most absolute value equations to have two solutions? Why not three or four?
2. Is it possible for an absolute value equation to have no solutions? one solution? If so, what would each look like graphically?

Explain 1 Solving Absolute Value Equations Algebraically

To solve absolute value equations algebraically, first isolate the absolute value expression on one side of the equation the same way you would isolate a variable. Then use the rule:

If $|x| = a$ (where a is a positive number), then $x = a$ OR $x = -a$.

Notice the use of a **disjunction** here in the rule for values of x. You cannot know from the original equation whether the expression inside the absolute value bars is positive or negative, so you must work through both possibilities to finish isolating x.

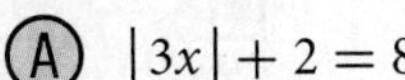 **Solve each absolute value equation algebraically. Graph the solutions on a number line.**

Ⓐ $|3x| + 2 = 8$

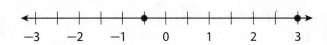

−6 −5 −4 −3 −2 −1 0 1 2 3 4 5 6

Subtract 2 from both sides. $|3x| = 6$

Rewrite as two equations. $3x = 6$ or $3x = -6$

Solve for x. $x = 2$ or $x = -2$

Ⓑ $3|4x - 5| - 2 = 19$

Add 2 to both sides. $3|4x - 5| = 21$

Divide both sides by 3. $|4x - 5| = 7$

Rewrite as two equations. $4x - 5 = 7$ or $4x - 5 = -7$

Add 5 to all four sides. $4x = 12$ or $4x = -2$

Solve for x. $x = 3$ or $x = -\frac{1}{2}$

−3 −2 −1 0 1 2 3

Your Turn

Solve each absolute value equation algebraically. Graph the solutions on a number line.

3. $\frac{1}{2}|x + 2| = 10$

4. $-2|3x - 6| + 5 = 1$

Explain 2 Absolute Value Equations with Fewer than Two Solutions

You have seen that absolute value equations have two solutions when the isolated absolute value expression is equal to a positive number. When the absolute value expression is equal to zero, there is a single solution because zero is its own opposite. When the absolute value is equal to a negative number, there is no solution because absolute value is never negative.

Example 2 **Isolate the absolute value expression in each equation to determine if the equation can be solved. If so, finish the solution. If not, write "no solution."**

Ⓐ $-5|x+1|+2=12$

Subtract 2 from both sides. $-5|x+1|=10$

Divide both sides by -5. $|x+1|=-2$

Absolute values are never negative. No Solution

Ⓑ $\frac{3}{5}|2x-4|-3=-3$

Add 3 to both sides. $\frac{3}{5}|2x-4|=$ 0

Multiply both sides by $\frac{5}{3}$. $|2x-4|=$ 0

Rewrite as one equation. $2x-4=$ 0

Add 4 to both sides. $2x=$ 4

Divide both sides by 2. $x=$ 2

Your Turn

Isolate the absolute value expression in each equation to determine if the equation can be solved. If so, finish the solution. If not, write "no solution."

5. $3\left|\frac{1}{2}x+5\right|+7=5$

6. $9\left|\frac{4}{3}x-2\right|+7=7$

Elaborate

7. Why is important to solve both equations in the disjunction arising from an absolute value equation? Why not just pick one and solve it, knowing the solution for the variable will work when plugged backed into the equation?

8. **Discussion** Discuss how the range of the absolute value function differs from the range of a linear function. Graphically, how does this explain why a linear equation always has exactly one solution while an absolute value equation can have one, two, or no solutions?

9. **Essential Question Check-In** Describe, in your own words, the basic steps to solving absolute value equations and how many solutions to expect.

Evaluate: Homework and Practice

- Online Homework
- Hints and Help
- Extra Practice

Solve the following absolute value equations by graphing.

1. $|x - 3| + 2 = 5$

2. $2|x + 1| + 5 = 9$

3. $-2|x + 5| + 4 = 2$

4. $\left|\frac{3}{2}(x - 2)\right| + 3 = 2$

Solve each absolute value equation algebraically. Graph the solutions on a number line.

5. $|2x| = 3$

6. $\left|\frac{1}{3}x + 4\right| = 3$

7. $3|2x - 3| + 2 = 3$

8. $-8|-x - 6| + 10 = 2$

Isolate the absolute value expressions in the following equations to determine if they can be solved. If so, find and graph the solution(s). If not, write "no solution".

9. $\frac{1}{4}|x + 2| + 7 = 5$

10. $-3|x - 3| + 3 = 6$

11. $2(|x + 4| + 3) = 6$

12. $5|2x + 4| - 3 = -3$

Solve the absolute value equations.

13. $|3x - 4| + 2 = 1$

14. $7\left|\frac{1}{2}x + 3\frac{1}{2}\right| - 2 = 5$

15. $|2(x + 5) - 3| + 2 = 6$

16. $-5|-3x + 2| - 2 = -2$

17. The bottom of a river makes a V-shape that can be modeled with the absolute value function, $d(h) = \frac{1}{5}|h - 240| - 48$, where d is the depth of the river bottom (in feet) and h is the horizontal distance to the left-hand shore (in feet).

A ship risks running aground if the bottom of its keel (its lowest point under the water) reaches down to the river bottom. Suppose you are the harbormaster and you want to place buoys where the river bottom is 30 feet below the surface. How far from the left-hand shore should you place the buoys?

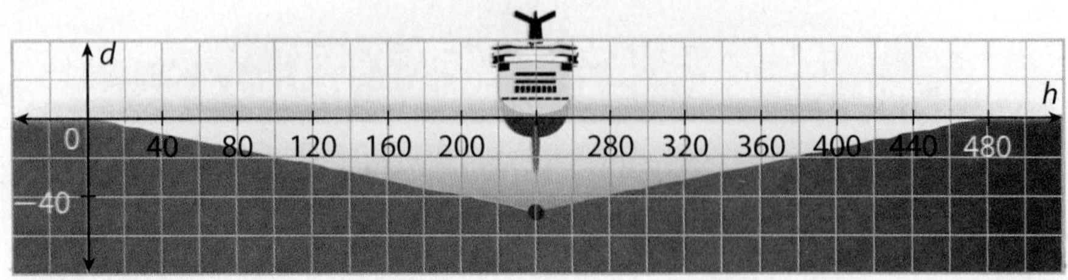

18. A flock of geese is approaching a photographer, flying in formation. The photographer starts taking photographs when the lead goose is 300 feet horizontally from her, and continues taking photographs until it is 100 feet past. The flock is flying at a steady 30 feet per second. Write and solve an equation to find the times after the photographing begins that the lead goose is at a horizontal distance of 75 feet from the photographer.

19. **Geometry** Find the points where a circle centered at (3, 0) with a radius of 5 crosses the x-axis. Use an absolute value equation and the fact that all points on a circle are the same distance (the radius) from the center.

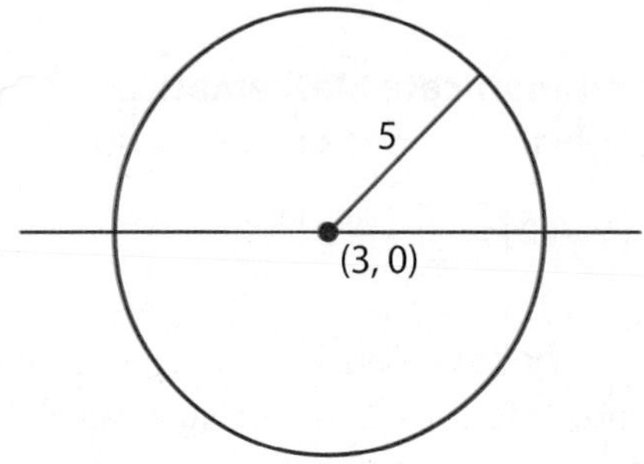

20. Select the value or values of x that satisfy the equation $-\frac{1}{2}|3x - 3| + 2 = 1$.

A. $x = \frac{5}{3}$ B. $x = -\frac{5}{3}$

C. $x = \frac{1}{3}$ D. $x = -\frac{1}{3}$

E. $x = 3$ F. $x = -3$

G. $x = 1$ H. $x = -1$

21. Terry is trying to place a satellite dish on the roof of his house at the recommended height of 30 feet. His house is 32 feet wide, and the height of the roof can be described by the function $h(x) = -\frac{3}{2}|x - 16| + 24$, where x is the distance along the width of the house. Where should Terry place the dish?

H.O.T. Focus on Higher Order Thinking

22. **Explain the Error** While attempting to solve the equation $-3|x - 4| - 4 = 3$, a student came up with the following results. Explain the error and find the correct solution:

$-3|x - 4| - 4 = 3$

$-3|x - 4| = 7$

$|x - 4| = -\frac{7}{3}$

$x - 4 = -\frac{7}{3}$ or $x - 4 = \frac{7}{3}$

$x = \frac{5}{3}$ or $x = \frac{19}{3}$

23. **Communicate Mathematical Ideas** Solve this absolute value equation and explain what algebraic properties make it possible to do so.

$3|x - 2| = 5|x - 2| - 7$

24. **Justify Your Reasoning** This absolute value equation has nested absolute values. Use your knowledge of solving absolute value equations to solve this equation. Justify the number of possible solutions.

$\big||2x + 5| - 3\big| = 10$

25. **Check for Reasonableness** For what type of real-world quantities would the negative answer for an absolute value equation not make sense?

Lesson Performance Task

A snowball comes apart as a child throws it north, resulting in two halves traveling away from the child. The child is standing 12 feet south and 6 feet east of the school door, along an east-west wall. One fragment flies off to the northeast, moving 2 feet east for every 5 feet north of travel, and the other moves 2 feet west for every 5 feet north of travel. Write an absolute value function that describes the northward position, $n(e)$, of both fragments as a function of how far east of the school door they are. How far apart are the fragments when they strike the wall?

2.3 Solving Absolute Value Inequalities

Resource Locker

Essential Question: What are two ways to solve an absolute value inequality?

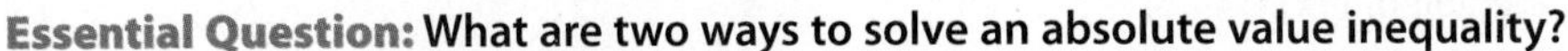

Explore Visualizing the Solution Set of an Absolute Value Inequality

You know that when solving an absolute value equation, it's possible to get two solutions. Here, you will explore what happens when you solve absolute value inequalities.

(A) Determine whether each of the integers from -5 to 5 is a solution of the inequality $|x| + 2 < 5$. If a number is a solution, plot it on a number line.

(B) Determine whether each of the integers from -5 to 5 is a solution of the inequality $|x| + 2 > 5$. If a number is a solution, plot it on a number line.

(C) State the solutions of the equation $|x| + 2 = 5$ and relate them to the solutions you found for the inequalities in Steps A and B.

(D) If x is any real number and not just an integer, graph the solutions of $|x| + 2 < 5$ and $|x| + 2 > 5$.

Reflect

1. It's possible to describe the solutions of $|x| + 2 < 5$ and $|x| + 2 > 5$ using inequalities that don't involve absolute value. For instance, you can write the solutions of $|x| + 2 < 5$ as $x > -3$ and $x < 3$. Notice that the word *and* is used because x must be both greater than -3 and less than 3. How would you write the solutions of $|x| + 2 > 5$? Explain.

2. Describe the solutions of $|x| + 2 \leq 5$ and $|x| + 2 \geq 5$ using inequalities that don't involve absolute value.

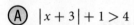

Explain 1 Solving Absolute Value Inequalities Graphically

You can use a graph to solve an absolute value inequality of the form $f(x) > g(x)$ or $f(x) < g(x)$, where $f(x)$ is an absolute value function and $g(x)$ is a constant function. Graph each function separately on the same coordinate plane and determine the intervals on the x-axis where one graph lies above or below the other. For $f(x) > g(x)$, you want to find the x-values for which the graph $f(x)$ is above the graph of $g(x)$. For $f(x) < g(x)$, you want to find the x-values for which the graph of $f(x)$ is below the graph of $g(x)$.

Example 1 **Solve the inequality graphically.**

(A) $|x+3|+1>4$

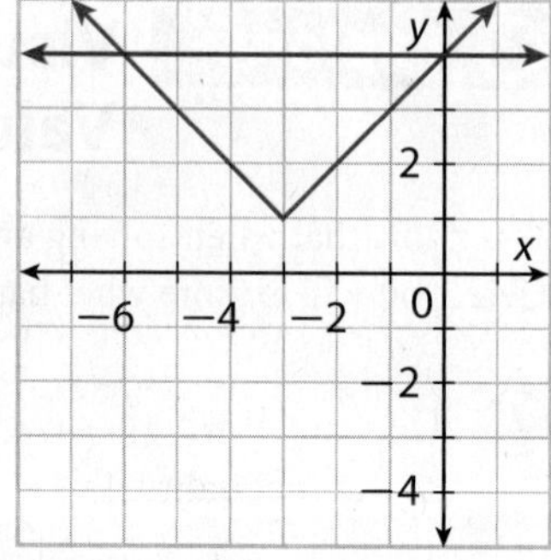

The inequality is of the form $f(x) > g(x)$, so determine the intervals on the x-axis where the graph of $f(x) = |x+3|+1$ lies above the graph of $g(x) = 4$.

The graph of $f(x) = |x+3|+1$ lies above the graph of $g(x) = 4$ to the left of $x = -6$ and to the right of $x = 0$, so the solution of $|x+3|+1>4$ is $x < -6$ or $x > 0$.

(B) $|x-2|-3<1$

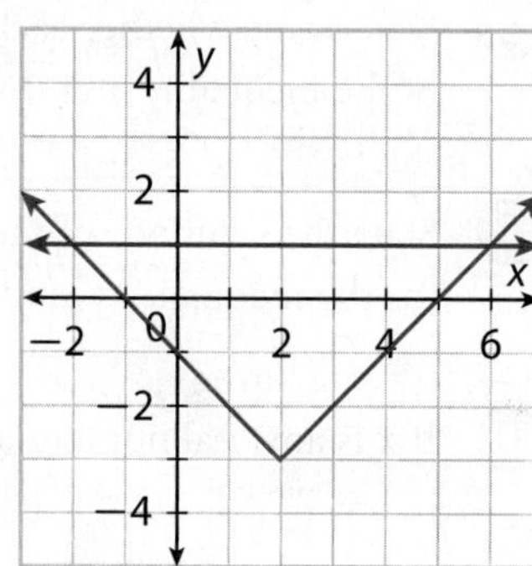

The inequality is of the form $f(x) < g(x)$, so determine the intervals on the x-axis where the graph of $f(x) = |x-2|-3$ lies below the graph of $g(x) = 1$.

The graph of $f(x) = |x-2|-3$ lies below the graph of $g(x) = 1$ between $x =$ [−2] and $x =$ [6], so the solution of $|x-2|-3<1$ is $x >$ [−2] and $x <$ [6].

Reflect

3. Suppose the inequality in Part A is $|x + 3| + 1 \geq 4$ instead of $|x + 3| + 1 > 4$. How does the solution change?

4. In Part B, what is another way to write the solution $x > -2$ and $x < 6$?

5. **Discussion** Suppose the graph of an absolute value function $f(x)$ lies entirely above the graph of the constant function $g(x)$. What is the solution of the inequality $f(x) > g(x)$? What is the solution of the inequality $f(x) < g(x)$?

Your Turn

6. Solve $|x + 1| - 4 \leq -2$ graphically.

Explain 2 Solving Absolute Value Inequalities Algebraically

To solve an absolute value inequality algebraically, start by isolating the absolute value expression. When the absolute value expression is by itself on one side of the inequality, apply one of the following rules to finish solving the inequality for the variable.

Solving Absolute Value Inequalities Algebraically
1. If $|x| > a$ where a is a positive number, then $x < -a$ or $x > a$.
2. If $|x| < a$ where a is a positive number, then $-a < x < a$.

Example 2 **Solve the inequality algebraically. Graph the solution on a number line.**

(A) $|4 - x| + 15 > 21$

$|4 - x| > 6$

$4 - x < -6$ or $4 - x > 6$

$-x < -10$ or $-x > 2$

$x > 10$ or $x < -2$

The solution is $x > 10$ or $x < -2$.

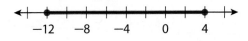

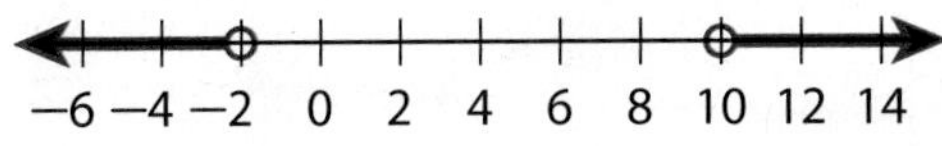

(B) $|x + 4| - 10 \leq -2$

$|x + 4| \leq$ 8

$x + 4 \geq$ −8 and $x + 4 \leq$ 8

$x \geq$ −12 and $x \leq$ 4

The solution is $x \geq$ −12 and $x \leq$ 4, or −12 $\leq x \leq$ 4.

−12 −8 −4 0 4

Reflect

7. In Part A, suppose the inequality were $|4 - x| + 15 > 14$ instead of $|4 - x| + 15 > 21$. How would the solution change? Explain.

8. In Part B, suppose the inequality were $|x + 4| - 10 \leq -11$ instead of $|x + 4| - 10 \leq -2$. How would the solution change? Explain.

Your Turn

Solve the inequality algebraically. Graph the solution on a number line.

9. $3|x-7| \geq 9$

10. $|2x+3| < 5$

Explain 3 Solving a Real-World Problem with Absolute Value Inequalities

Absolute value inequalities are often used to model real-world situations involving a margin of error or *tolerance*. Tolerance is the allowable amount of variation in a quantity.

Example 3

A machine at a lumber mill cuts boards that are 3.25 meters long. It is acceptable for the length to differ from this value by at most 0.02 meters. Write and solve an absolute value inequality to find the range of acceptable lengths.

Analyze Information

Identify the important information.

- The boards being cut are 3.25 meters long.
- The length can differ by at most 0.02 meters.

Formulate a Plan

Let the length of a board be ℓ. Since the sign of the difference between ℓ and 3.25 doesn't matter, take the absolute value of the difference. Since the absolute value of the difference can be at most 0.02, the inequality that models the situation is

$|\ell - 3.25| \leq 0.02$.

Solve

$|\ell - 3.25| \leq 0.02$

$\ell - 3.25 \geq -0.02$ and $\ell - 3.25 \leq 0.02$

$\ell \geq 3.23$ and $\ell \leq 3.27$

So, the range of acceptable lengths is $3.23 \leq \ell \leq 3.27$.

Justify and Evaluate

The bounds of the range are positive and close to 3.25, so this is a reasonable answer.

The answer is correct since $3.23 + 0.02 = 3.25$ and $3.27 - 0.02 = 3.25$.

Your Turn

11. A box of cereal is supposed to weigh 13.8 oz, but it's acceptable for the weight to vary as much as 0.1 oz. Write and solve an absolute value inequality to find the range of acceptable weights.

Elaborate

12. Describe the values of x that satisfy the inequalities $|x| < a$ and $|x| > a$ where a is a positive constant.

13. How do you algebraically solve an absolute value inequality?

14. Explain why the solution of $|x| > a$ is all real numbers if a is a negative number.

15. **Essential Question Check-In** How do you solve an absolute value inequality graphically?

Evaluate: Homework and Practice

- Online Homework
- Hints and Help
- Extra Practice

1. Determine whether each of the integers from −5 to 5 is a solution of the inequality $|x - 1| + 3 \geq 5$. If a number is a solution, plot it on a number line.

2. Determine whether each of the integers from −5 to 5 is a solution of the inequality $|x + 1| - 2 \leq 1$. If a number is a solution, plot it on a number line.

Solve each inequality graphically.

3. $2|x| \leq 6$

4. $|x - 3| - 2 > -1$

5. $\frac{1}{2}|x| + 2 < 3$

6. $|x + 2| - 4 \geq -2$

Match each graph with the corresponding absolute value inequality. Then give the solution of the inequality.

A. $2|x| + 1 > 3$ **B.** $2|x + 1| < 3$ **C.** $2|x| - 1 > 3$ **D.** $2|x - 1| < 3$

7.

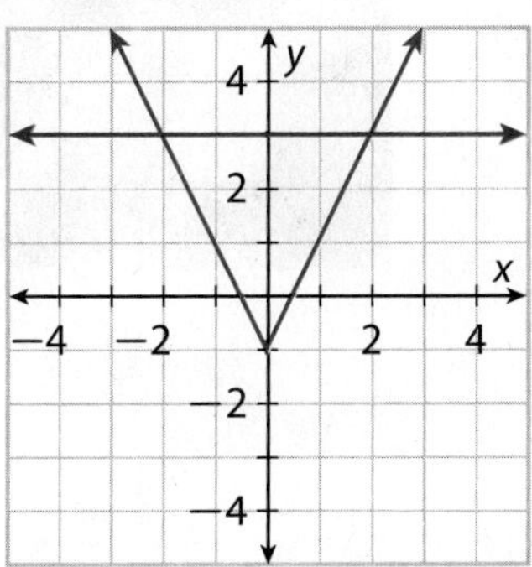

8.

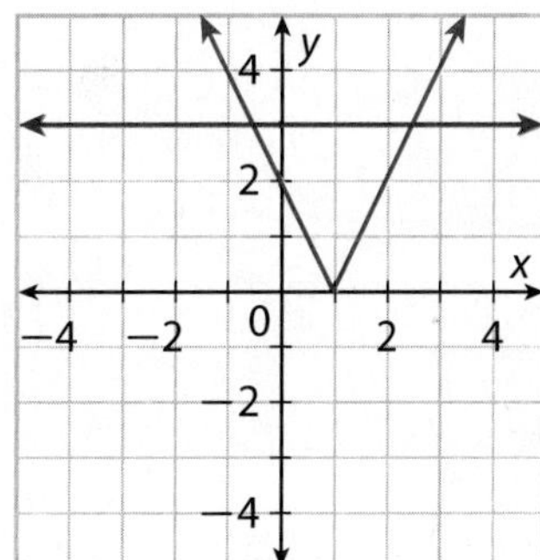

9.

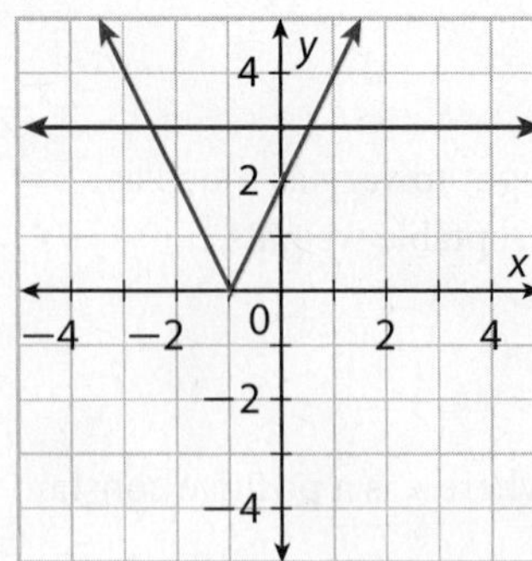

10.

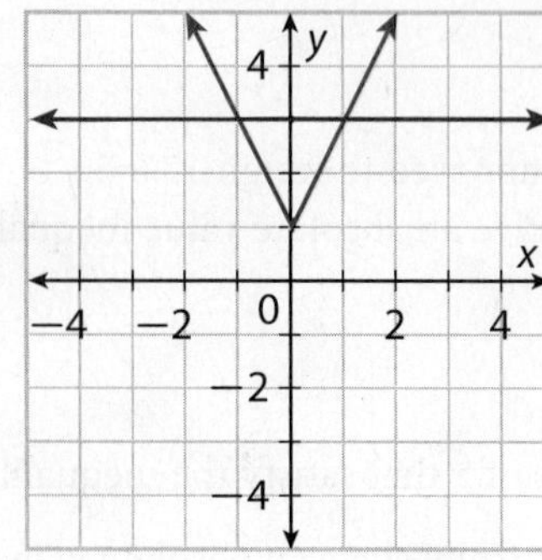

Solve each absolute value inequality algebraically. Graph the solution on a number line.

11. $2\left|x - \frac{7}{2}\right| + 3 > 4$

12. $|2x + 1| - 4 < 5$

13. $3|x + 4| + 2 \geq 5$

14. $|x + 11| - 8 \leq -3$

15. $-5|x - 3| - 5 < 15$

16. $8|x + 4| + 10 < 2$

Solve each problem using an absolute value inequality.

17. The thermostat for a house is set to 68 °F, but the actual temperature may vary by as much as 2 °F. What is the range of possible temperatures?

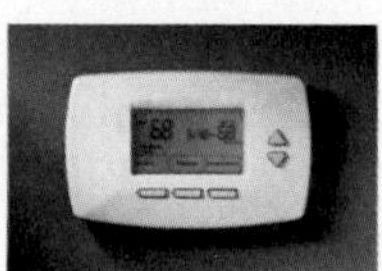

18. The balance of Jason's checking account is $320. The balance varies by as much as $80 each week. What are the possible balances of Jason's account?

19. On average, a squirrel lives to be 6.5 years old. The lifespan of a squirrel may vary by as much as 1.5 years. What is the range of ages that a squirrel lives?

20. You are playing a history quiz game where you must give the years of historical events. In order to score any points at all for a question about the year in which a man first stepped on the moon, your answer must be no more than 3 years away from the correct answer, 1969. What is the range of answers that allow you to score points?

21. The speed limit on a road is 30 miles per hour. Drivers on this road typically vary their speed around the limit by as much as 5 miles per hour. What is the range of typical speeds on this road?

H.O.T. Focus on Higher Order Thinking

22. **Represent Real-World Problems** A poll of likely voters shows that the incumbent will get 51% of the vote in an upcoming election. Based on the number of voters polled, the results of the poll could be off by as much as 3 percentage points. What does this mean for the incumbent?

23. **Explain the Error** A student solved the inequality $|x - 1| - 3 > 1$ graphically. Identify and correct the student's error.

I graphed the functions $f(x) = |x - 1| - 3$ and $g(x) = 1$. Because the graph of $g(x)$ lies above the graph of $f(x)$ between $x = -3$ and $x = 5$, the solution of the inequality is $-3 < x < 5$.

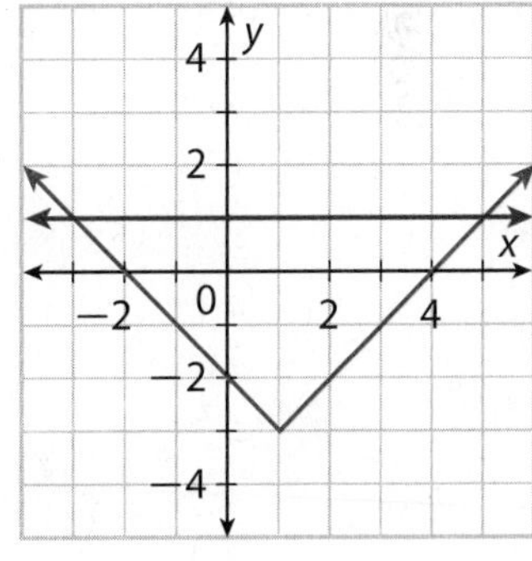

24. **Multi-Step** Recall that a literal equation or inequality is one in which the constants have been replaced by letters.

a. Solve $|ax + b| > c$ for x. Write the solution in terms of a, b, and c. Assume that $a > 0$ and $c \geq 0$.

b. Use the solution of the literal inequality to find the solution of $|10x + 21| > 14$.

c. In Part a, explain how the restrictions $a > 0$ and $c \geq 0$ affect finding the solutions of the inequality.

Lesson Performance Task

The distance between the Sun and each planet in our solar system varies because the planets travel in elliptical orbits around the Sun. Here is a table of the average distance and the variation in the distance for the five innermost planets in our solar system.

	Average Distance	Variation
Mercury	36.0 million miles	7.39 million miles
Venus	67.2 million miles	0.43 million miles
Earth	93.0 million miles	1.55 million miles
Mars	142 million miles	13.2 million miles
Jupiter	484 million miles	23.2 million miles

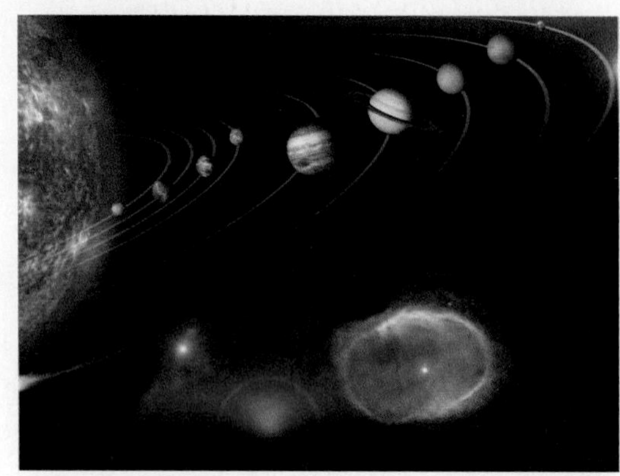

a. Write and solve an inequality to represent the range of distances that can occur between the Sun and each planet.

b. Calculate the percentage variation (variation divided by average distance) in the orbit of each of the planets. Based on these percentages, which planet has the most elliptical orbit?

STUDY GUIDE REVIEW

Absolute Value Functions, Equations, and Inequalities

MODULE 2

Essential Question: How can you use absolute value functions to solve real-world problems?

Key Vocabulary

absolute value *(valor absoluto)*
absolute-value equation *(ecuación de valor absoluto)*
coefficient *(coeficiente)*
disjunction *(disyunción)*
domain *(dominio)*
function *(función)*
inequality *(desigualdad)*
parameter *(parámetro)*
range *(rango)*
symmetry *(simetría)*
vertex *(vértice)*

KEY EXAMPLE (Lesson 2.1)

Given the function $g(x) = \left|\frac{1}{3}(x+6)\right| - 1$, predict what the graph will look like compared to the parent function, $f(x) = |x|$.

The graph of $g(x)$ will be the graph of $f(x)$ translated down 1 unit and left 6 units. There will also be a horizontal stretch of $f(x)$ by a factor of 3.

KEY EXAMPLE (Lesson 2.2)

Solve $6|2x+3| + 1 = 25$ algebraically.

$6|2x+3| = 24$ — Subtract 1 from both sides.

$|2x+3| = 4$ — Divide both sides by 6.

$2x+3 = 4$ or $2x+3 = -4$ — Rewrite as two equations.

$2x = 1$ or $2x = -7$ — Subtract 3 from both sides.

$x = \frac{1}{2}$ or $x = -\frac{7}{2}$ — Solve for x.

So, $x = \frac{1}{2}$ or $-\frac{7}{2}$.

KEY EXAMPLE (Lesson 2.3)

Solve $|x+2| - 4 < 4$ algebraically, then graph the solution on a number line.

$|x+2| - 4 < 4$

$|x+2| < 8$ — Add 4 to both sides.

$x+2 < 8$ and $x+2 > -8$ — Rewrite as two inequalities.

$x < 6$ and $x > -10$ — Subtract 2 from both sides.

The solution is $x < 6$ and $x > -10$.

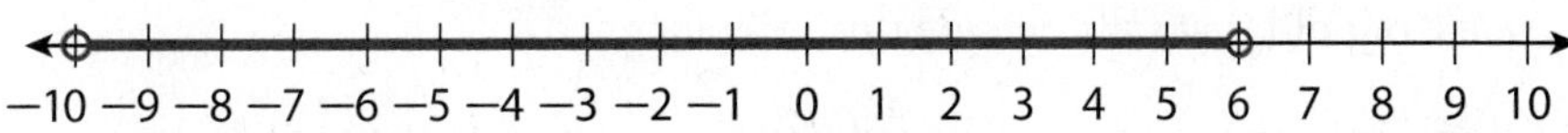

EXERCISES

Solve. *(Lessons 2.2, 2.3)*

1. $-10|x+2| = -70$

2. $|3x+7| = 27$

3. $\frac{1}{7}|8+x| \leq 5$

4. $|x-2| - 5 > 10$

5. Explain how the graph of $g(x) = \left|\frac{3}{7}(x-4)\right| + 2$ compares to the graph of $h(x) = \frac{3}{7}|x-4| + 2$. *(Lesson 2.1)*

6. Leroy wants to place a chimney on his roof. It is recommended that the chimney be set at a height of at least 25 feet. The height of the roof is described by the function $r(x) = -\frac{4}{3}|x-10| + 35$, where x is the width of the roof. Where should Leroy place the chimney if the house is 40 feet wide? *(Lesson 2.3)*

MODULE PERFORMANCE TASK

What Is the Purity of Gold?

You have three gold rings labeled 10 karat, 14 karat, and 18 karat, and would like to know if the rings are correctly labeled. The table shows the results of an analysis of the rings.

Ring Label	Actual Percentage of Gold
10-karat	40.6%
14-karat	59.5%
18-karat	71.2%

In the United States, jewelry manufacturers are legally allowed a half karat tolerance. Determine which of the rings, if any, have an actual percentage of gold that falls outside this tolerance.

List any additional information you will need and then complete the task. Be sure to write down all your data and assumptions. Then use graphs, numbers, words, or algebra to explain how you reached your conclusion.

Ready to Go On?

2.1–2.3 Absolute Value Functions, Equations, and Inequalities

- Online Homework
- Hints and Help
- Extra Practice

Solve. *(Lesson 2.1)*

1. $|-2x - 3| = 6$

2. $\frac{1}{4}|-4 - 3x| = 2$

3. $|3x + 8| = 2$

4. $4|x + 7| + 3 = 59$

Solve each inequality using the method indicated. *(Lesson 2.2)*

5. $|5x + 2| \leq 13$ (algebraically)

6. $|x - 2| + 1 \leq 5$ (graphically)

ESSENTIAL QUESTION

7. Write a real world situation that could be modeled by $|x - 14| = 3$. *(Lesson 2.1)*

MODULE 2
MIXED REVIEW

Assessment Readiness

1. Look at each function. Is the point (−2, −1) on the graph of the function? Write Yes or No for A–C.

A. $g(x) = 3|x - 4|$

B. $h(x) = -\frac{1}{2}|x|$

C. $j(x) = |x + 3| - 2$

2. Consider the absolute value equation $\frac{2}{3}|x - 4| + 2 = 5$. Determine if each statement is True or False.

A. Solving $\frac{2}{3}|x - 4| + 2 = 5$ gives the same x-values as solving $\left|\frac{2}{3}(x - 4)\right| + 2 = 5$.

B. To solve the equation for x, the first step is to add 4 to both sides.

C. Before the step to rewrite as two equations, the equation looks like: $|x - 4| = 3$.

3. Describe the domain, range, and vertex of the function $f(x) = 3|x - 4| + 2$. Explain your answers.

4. Laurie wants to put a portable cellular phone mini-tower on her roof. The tower cannot be placed higher than 30 feet. The slant of her roof can be represented by the equation $r(x) = -\frac{1}{4}|x| + 60$. If her house is 40 feet wide, where could she place the tower? Explain.

UNIT 1 MIXED REVIEW

Assessment Readiness

Personal Math Trainer
- Online Homework
- Hints and Help
- Extra Practice

1. Consider the function $f(x) = 2(x - 1)^2 + 5$. Determine if each statement is True or False.

A. The range is $y \geq 5$.

B. The range is $y \geq 7$.

C. The domain is $-\infty < x < \infty$.

2. Consider the function $g(x) = x^3 + 7$. Determine if each statement is True or False.

A. As $x \to \infty, y \to \infty$.

B. As $x \to -\infty, y \to \infty$.

C. The range is $y \geq 7$.

3. Consider the equation $f(x) = \frac{1}{2}x - 5$. Is the given equation the inverse of $f(x)$? Write Yes or No for A–C.

A. $f^{-1}(x) = 2x - 10$

B. $f^{-1}(x) = -\frac{1}{2}x + 5$

C. $f^{-1}(x) = 2x + 10$

4. Consider the equation $3|x - 2| + 6 = 12$. Determine if each statement is True or False.

A. The equation can be solved using the Pythagorean Theorem.

B. The solutions of the equation are $x = 4$ and $x = 0$.

C. The first step to solving the equation could be subtracting 6 from both sides of the equation.

5. Consider the inequality $|2x - 3| + 1 < 7$. Is the number a solution to the inequality? Write Yes or No for A–C.

A. 0

B. 6

C. -1.5

6. A triathlete is training for her next race and starts by swimming 2 miles in 1 hour. She rests for 1 hour and then rides her bike 100 miles in 5 hours. She rests another hour and runs 20 miles in 5 hours. Draw a graph showing the distance she travels over time. Explain your choice.

7. The maximum number of oranges in a box of volume one cubic foot can be modeled by the inequality $|x - 17| \leq 5$, depending on the size of the oranges. Solve the inequality to find the greatest and least numbers of oranges that could be in a box. Explain your answer.

8. How does the end behavior of $f(x) = (x - 2)^2 + 3$ differ from that of $g(x) = -(3x + 7)^2 - 8$ as $x \to -\infty$? Explain your answer.

Performance Tasks

★ 9. The revenue from an amusement park ride is given by the admission price of \$3 times the number of riders. As part of a promotion, the first 10 riders ride for free.

   A. Write a function for the revenue, R, in terms of the number of riders, n.

   B. Find the inverse of the function found in part A and use it to determine how many riders are needed for the revenue to be \$240.

★★10. A purified water dispenser can be used to fill 5-gallon containers. If the dispenser is functioning properly, the amount of water dispensed is within 4 ounces of 5 gallons.

A. Write and solve an absolute-value equation to find the maximum and minimum volumes of water the machine disperses if it is functioning properly. Your answer should be in terms of ounces. Recall that one gallon is 128 ounces.

B. A technician fills her 5-gallon container using the dispenser and later measures the volume of water to be 2% less than 5 gallons. Is the dispenser working properly? Explain.

★★★11. **Diving** Scuba divers must know that the deeper the dive, the greater the water pressure in pounds per square inch (psi) for fresh water diving, as shown in the table.

Depth (feet)	Pressure (psi)
34	29.4
68	44.1
102	58.8

A. Write the pressure as a function of depth, and identify a reasonable domain and range for this function.

B. Find the inverse of the function from part **A**. What does the inverse function represent?

C. The point (25.9, 25.9) is an approximate solution to both the function from part **A** and its inverse. What does this point mean in the context of the problem?

MATH IN CAREERS

Community Theater Owner A community theater currently sells 200 season tickets at $50 each. In order to increase its season-ticket revenue, the theater surveys its season-ticket holders to see if they would be willing to pay more. The survey finds that for every $5 increase in the price of a season ticket, the theater would lose 10 season-ticket holders. What action, if any, should the theater owner take to increase revenue?

a. Let n be the number of $5 price increases in the cost of a season ticket. Write an expression for the cost of a season ticket after n price increases, and an expression for the number of season-ticket holders after n price increases.

b. Use the expressions from part **a** to create a revenue function, $R(n)$, from the survey information.

c. Determine a constraint on the value of n. That is, write and solve an inequality that represents an upper bound on the value of n, then state a reasonable domain for the revenue function.

d. Graph the revenue function. Be sure to label the axes with the quantities they represent and indicate the axis scales by showing numbers for some grid lines.

e. Write a brief paragraph describing what actions the theater owner should take to maximize revenue. Include what happens to the number of season-ticket holders as well as the season-ticket prices.

UNIT 2

Polynomial Operations

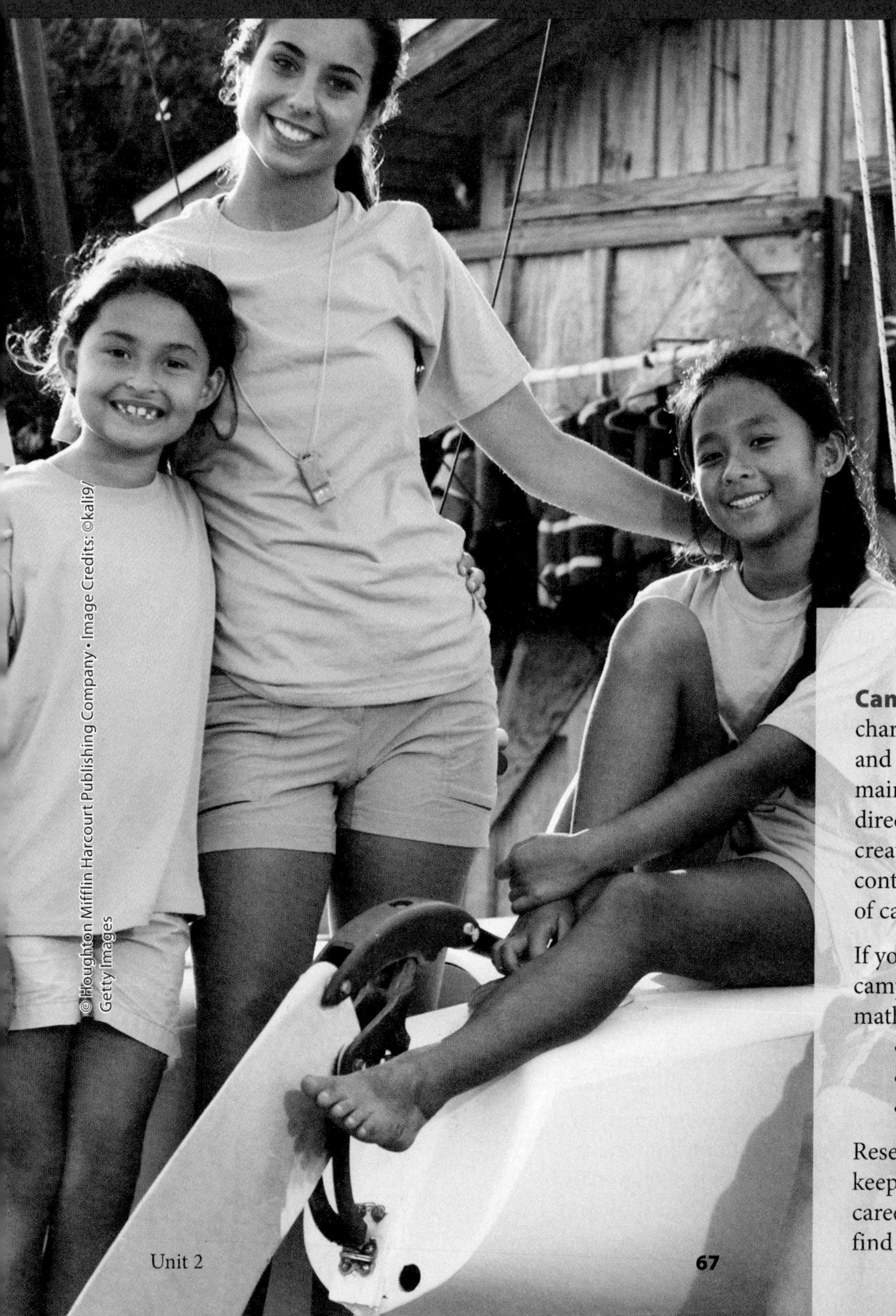

MATH IN CAREERS

Camp Director A camp director is in charge of organizing activities, hiring and supervising staff, and overseeing maintenance of the camp facilities. Camp directors use math for bookkeeping, creating budgets, negotiating vendor contracts, and planning new construction of camp buildings and outdoor spaces.

If you are interested in a career as a camp director, you should study these mathematical subjects:

- Algebra
- Geometry
- Business math

Research other careers that require keeping financial books. Check out the career activity at the end of the unit to find out how **camp directors** use math.

Reading Start-Up

Vocabulary

Review Words

✔ Associative Property (*Propiedad asociativa*)

✔ closure (*cerradura*)

✔ Commutative Property (*Propiedad conmutativa*)

✔ Distributive Property (*Propiedad distributiva*)

✔ like terms (*términos semejantes*)

✔ simplify (*simplificar*)

✔ rational number (*número racional*)

Preview Words

binomial (*binomio*)

FOIL (*FOIL*)

monomial (*monomio*)

perfect-square trinomial (*trinomio cuadrado perfecto*)

polynomial (*polinomio*)

trinomial (*trinomio*)

rational exponent (*exponente racional*)

Visualize Vocabulary

Use the ✔ words to complete the chart. Insert one review word for each section.

The property that states that the sum or product of any two real numbers will equal another real number	The property that states that for all real numbers, the sum is always the same, regardless of their grouping
The property that states that for all real numbers, the sum is always the same, regardless of their ordering	The property that states that if you multiply a sum by a number, you will get the same result if you multiply each addend by that number and then add the products

Properties

Understand Vocabulary

To become familiar with some of the vocabulary terms in this unit, consider the following. You may refer to the module, the glossary, or a dictionary.

1. The prefix *tri-* is used to identify an item that has three parts, such as a *triangle*. What do you think a **trinomial** might be?

?

2. The prefix *poly-* is used to identify an item with many elements, such as a *polygon*. What do you think a **polynomial** might be?

?

Active Reading

Four-Corner Fold Before beginning the unit, create a four-corner fold to help you organize what you learn. Label the flaps "Adding Polynomials," "Subtracting Polynomials," "Multiplying Polynomials," and "Special Products of Binomials." As you study this unit note important ideas and concepts used when performing operations with polynomials under the appropriate flap. You can use your FoldNote later to study for tests and complete assignments.

Rational Exponents and Radicals

MODULE 3

Essential Question: How can you use rational exponents and radicals to solve real-world problems?

REAL WORLD VIDEO
Zoo managers must determine the amount of food needed for a healthy diet for the animals.

How Much Should We Feed the Animals?

You have been selected to be the next reptile chef at the local zoo. This means you are in charge of feeding the reptiles. Reptiles get much of their moisture from the foods they eat, so they need food to stay hydrated as well as to keep from starving. Of course, if they don't get enough food, they starve. If they get too much food, however, they can develop serious health issues that may cause death. So, how much food is enough? How much is too much? Let's find out!

Are YOU Ready?

Complete these exercises to review skills you will need for this module.

Personal Math Trainer

- Online Homework
- Hints and Help
- Extra Practice

Exponents

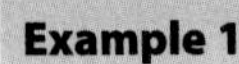

Example 1 Write $(-4)^3$ as a multiplication of factors. Then find its value.

$(-4)^3 = (-4)(-4)(-4)$ Write the base -4 multiplied by itself 3 times.

$(-4)(-4)(-4) = -64$ Multiply.

Write each expression as a multiplication of factors. Then find its value.

1. 13^2

2. $(-5)^4$

3. 9^3

4. 2^5

Algebraic Expressions

Example 2 Evaluate $x^2 + 4$ for $x = -2$.

$x^2 + 4$

$(-2)^2 + 4$ Substitute -2 for x.

$4 + 4$ Evaluate the exponent.

8 Add.

Evaluate each expression for the given value of the variables.

5. $p^3 - 2$ for $p = 3$

6. $5a + b^2$ for $a = -3$ and $b = 4$

7. $6m - n^2$ for $m = 5$ and $n = -7$

8. $x^2 - y^3$ for $x = 6$ and $y = -2$

Real Numbers

Example 3 Tell if 13 is a rational number or an irrational number.

13 can be written as $\frac{13}{1}$, so 13 is a rational number.

A rational number can be expressed in the form $\frac{p}{q}$, where p and q are integers and $q \neq 0$.

An irrational number cannot be written as the quotient of two integers.

Tell if the number is a rational number or irrational number.

9. -23

10. $\sqrt{8}$

11. $\frac{3}{8}$

3.1 Understanding Rational Exponents and Radicals

Resource Locker

Essential Question: How are radicals and rational exponents related?

Explore 1 Understanding Integer Exponents

Recall that powers like 3^2 are evaluated by repeating the base (3) as a factor a number of times equal to the exponent (2). So $3^2 = 3 \cdot 3 = 9$. What about a negative exponent, or an exponent of 0? You cannot write a product with a negative number of factors, but a pattern emerges if you start from a positive exponent and divide repeatedly by the base.

(A) Starting with powers of 3:

$3^3 = $ ☐

$3^2 = $ ☐

$3^1 = $ ☐

(B) Dividing a power of 3 by 3 is equivalent to ☐ the exponent by ☐.

(C) Complete the pattern:

$$3^3 \xrightarrow[\div 3]{} 3^2 \xrightarrow[\div 3]{} 3^1 \xrightarrow[\div 3]{} 3^0 \xrightarrow[\div 3]{} 3^{-1} \xrightarrow[\div 3]{} 3^{-2}$$

$$27 \xrightarrow[\div 3]{} 9 \xrightarrow[\div 3]{} 3 \xrightarrow[\div 3]{} \square \xrightarrow[\div 3]{} \square \xrightarrow[\div 3]{} \square$$

(D) $3^{-1} = \frac{1}{3}, 3^{-2} = \frac{1}{9} = \frac{1}{3^{\square}}$

Integer exponents less than 1 can be summarized as follows:

Words	Numbers	Variables
Any non-zero number raised to the power of 0 is; 0° is undefined.	$3^0 = 1$ $(2.4)^0 = 1$	$x^0 = 1$ for $x \neq 0$
Any non-zero number raised to a negative power is equal to 1 divided by the same number raised to the opposite, positive power.	$3^{-2} = \frac{1}{3^2} = \frac{1}{9}$	$x^{-n} = \frac{1}{x^n}$ for $x \neq 0$, and integer n.

Reflect

1. **Discussion** Why does there need to be an exception in in the second rule for the case of $x = 0$?

Explore 2 Exploring Rational Exponents

A radical expression is an expression that contains the radical symbol, $\sqrt{\ }$.

For $\sqrt[n]{a}$, n is called the **index** and a is called the **radicand**. n must be an integer greater than 1. a can be any real number when n is odd, but must be non-negative when n is even. When $n = 2$, the radical is a square root and the index 2 is usually not shown.

You can write a radical expression as a power. First, note what happens when you raise a power to a power.

$(2^3)^2 = (2 \cdot 2 \cdot 2)^2 = (2 \cdot 2 \cdot 2)(2 \cdot 2 \cdot 2) = 2^6$, so $(2^3)^2 = 2^{3 \cdot 2}$.

In fact, for all real numbers a and all rational numbers m and n, $(a^m)^n = a^{m \cdot n}$. This is called the **Power of a Power Property**.

A radical expression can be written as an exponential expression: $\sqrt[n]{a} = a^k$. Find the value for k when $n = 2$.

(A) Start with the equation. $\sqrt{a} = a^k$

Square both sides. $(\sqrt{a})^{\square} = (a^k)^{\square}$

(B) Definition of square root $\square = (a^k)^2$

(C) Power of a power property $a^1 = a^{\square}$

(D) Equate exponents. $1 = \square$

(E) Solve for k. $k = \square$

Reflect

2. What do you think will be the rule for other values of the radical index n?

Explain 1 Simplifying Numerical Expressions with *n*th Roots

For any integer $n > 1$, the nth root of a is a number that, when multiplied by itself n times, is equal to a.

$$x = \sqrt[n]{a} \Rightarrow x^n = a$$

The nth root can be written as a radical with an index of n, or as a power with an exponent of $\frac{1}{n}$.
An exponent in the form of a fraction is a **rational exponent**.

$$\sqrt[n]{a} = a^{\frac{1}{n}}$$

The expressions are interchangeable, and to evaluate the nth root, it is necessary to find the number, x, that satisfies the equation $x^n = a$.

Example 1 **Find the root and simplify the expression.**

(A) $64^{\frac{1}{3}}$

Convert to radical.	$64^{\frac{1}{3}} = \sqrt[3]{64}$
Rewrite radicand as a power.	$= \sqrt[3]{4^3}$
Definition of nth root	$= 4$

(B) $81^{\frac{1}{4}} + 9^{\frac{1}{2}}$

Convert to radicals.	$81^{\frac{1}{4}} + 9^{\frac{1}{2}} = \sqrt[4]{81} + \sqrt{9}$
Rewrite radicands as powers.	$= \sqrt[4]{3^4} + \sqrt{3^2}$
Apply definition of nth root.	$= 3 + 3$
Simplify.	$= 6$

Your Turn

Find the root and simplify the expression.

3. $8^{\frac{1}{3}}$

4. $16^{\frac{1}{2}} + 27^{\frac{1}{3}}$

 Explain 2

Simplifying Numerical Expressions with Rational Exponents

Given that for an integer n greater than 1, $\sqrt[n]{b} = b^{\frac{1}{n}}$, you can use the Power of a Power Property to define $b^{\frac{m}{n}}$ for any positive integer m.

$$b^{\frac{m}{n}} = b^{\frac{1}{n} \cdot m}$$

$$= \left(b^{\frac{1}{n}}\right)^m \quad \text{Power of a Power Property}$$

$$= \left(\sqrt[n]{b}\right)^m \quad \text{Definition of } b^{\frac{1}{n}}$$

$$b^{\frac{m}{n}} = b^{m \cdot \frac{1}{n}}$$

$$= \left(b^m\right)^{\frac{1}{n}}$$

$$= \sqrt[n]{b^m}$$

The definition of a number raised to the power of $\frac{m}{n}$ is the nth root of the number raised to the mth power. The power of m and the nth root can be evaluated in either order to obtain the same answer, although it is generally easier to find the nth root first when working without a calculator.

Example 2 **Simplify the expressions with rational exponents.**

(A) $27^{\frac{2}{3}}$

Definition of $b^{\frac{m}{n}}$ $\quad 27^{\frac{2}{3}} = \left(\sqrt[3]{27}\right)^2$

Rewrite radicand as a power. $\quad = \left(\sqrt[3]{3^3}\right)^2$

Definition of cube root $\quad = 3^2$

$= 9$

(B) $25^{\frac{3}{2}}$

Definition of $b^{\frac{m}{n}}$ $\quad 25^{\frac{3}{2}} = \left(\sqrt{25}\right)^{3}$

Rewrite radicand as a power. $\quad = \left(\sqrt{5^{2}}\right)^{3}$

Definition of square root $\quad = 5^3$

$= 125$

YourTurn

Simplify the expressions with rational exponents.

5. $32^{\frac{3}{5}}$

6. $4^{\frac{5}{2}} - 4^{\frac{3}{2}}$

Elaborate

7. Why can you evaluate an odd root for any radicand, but even roots require non-negative radicands?

8. In evaluating powers with rational exponents with values like $\frac{2}{3}$, why is it usually better to find the root before the power? Would it change the answer to switch the order?

9. **Essential Question Check-In** How can radicals and rational exponents be used to simplify expressions involving one or the other?

Evaluate: Homework and Practice

- Online Homework
- Hints and Help
- Extra Practice

Evaluate the expressions.

1. 10^{-2}

2. 56^{-1}

3. 2^{-4}

4. $\left(\frac{1}{3}\right)^{-2}$

5. $(-2)^{\circ}$

6. $3 \cdot 6^{-2}$

Find the root(s) and simplify the expression.

7. $81^{\frac{1}{2}}$

8. $125^{\frac{1}{3}}$

9. $49^{\frac{1}{2}} - 4^{\frac{1}{2}}$

10. $16^{\frac{1}{4}} + 32^{\frac{1}{5}}$

Simplify the expressions with rational exponents.

11. $49^{\frac{3}{2}}$

12. $8^{\frac{5}{3}}$

13. $27^{\frac{4}{3}} + 4^{\frac{3}{2}}$

14. $25^{\frac{3}{2}} + 16^{\frac{3}{2}}$

Simplify the expressions.

15. $25^{-\frac{1}{2}}$

16. $8^{-\frac{1}{3}}$

17. $1^{-\frac{2}{3}}$

18. $8^{\frac{2}{3}} + 8^{-\frac{2}{3}}$

19. $\dfrac{25^{\frac{1}{2}}}{27^{\frac{1}{3}}}$

20. $7 \cdot 10^{-3}$

21. $\left(\frac{1}{4}\right)^{-\frac{3}{2}}$

22. $2 \cdot 36^{-\frac{1}{2}} + 6^{-1}$

23. **Geometry** The volume of a cube is related to the area of a face by the formula $V = A^{\frac{3}{2}}$. What is the volume of a cube whose face has an area of 100 cm^2?

24. Biology The approximate number of Calories, C, that an animal needs each day is given by $C = 72m^{\frac{3}{4}}$, where m is the animal's mass in kilograms. Find the number of Calories that a 16 kilogram dog needs each day.

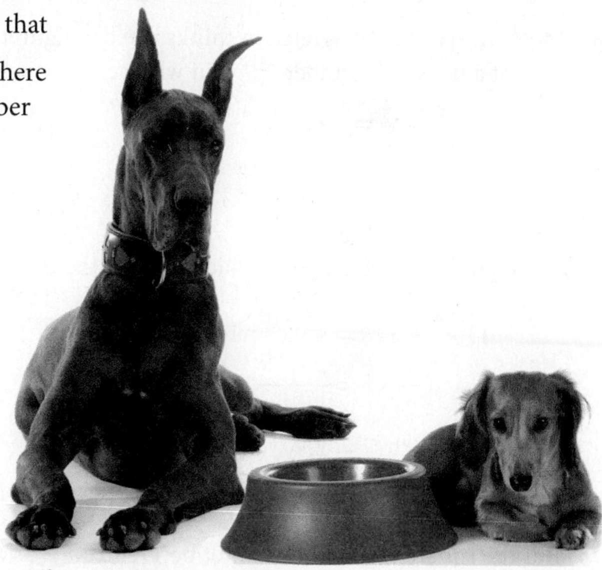

25. Rocket Science Escape velocity is a measure of how fast an object must be moving to escape the gravitational pull of a planet or moon with no further thrust. The escape velocity for the moon is given approximately by the equation $V = 5600 \cdot \left(\frac{d}{1000}\right)^{-\frac{1}{2}}$, where v is the escape velocity in miles per hour and d is the distance from the center of the moon (in miles). If a lunar lander thrusts upwards until it reaches a distance of 16,000 miles from the center of the moon, about how fast must it be going to escape the moon's gravity?

26. Multiple Response Which of the following expressions cannot be evaluated?

a. $4^{\frac{1}{2}}$

b. $(-4)^{-\frac{1}{2}}$

c. 4^{-2}

d. $(-4)^{-2}$

e. $0^{-\frac{1}{2}}$

f. 0^{-2}

H.O.T. Focus on Higher Order Thinking

27. Explain the Error Yuan is asked to evaluate the expression $(-8)^{\frac{2}{3}}$ on his exam, and writes that it is unsolvable because you cannot evaluate a negative number to an even rational power. Is he correct, and if so, why? If he is not correct, what is the correct answer?

28. Communicate Mathematical Ideas Show that the nth root of a number, a, can be expressed with an exponent of $\frac{1}{n}$ for any positive integer, n.

29. **Explain the Error** Gretchen thinks she has figured out how to evaluate the square root of a negative number. Explain why her solution is flawed.

$$(-1)^2\,(-1)^{\frac{1}{2}} = (-1)^{2\cdot\frac{1}{2}}$$
$$= (-1)^0$$
$$= 1$$

Then she solves for $(-1)^{\frac{1}{2}}$ which is the same thing as $\sqrt{-1}$.

$$(-1)^2 \cdot (-1)^{\frac{1}{2}} = 1$$
$$(-1)^{\frac{1}{2}} = \frac{1}{(-1)^2}$$
$$= \frac{1}{1}$$
$$= 1$$

But the square root of -1 cannot be 1, since $1 \cdot 1 = 1$, not -1. What mistake did she make?

Lesson Performance Task

Carbon-14 dating is used to determine the age of archeological artifacts of biological (plant or animal) origin. Items that are dated using carbon-14 include objects made from bone, wood, or plant fibers. This method works by measuring the fraction of carbon-14 remaining in an object. The fraction of the original carbon-14 remaining can be expressed by the function, $f = 2^{\left(-\frac{t}{5700}\right)}$, where t is the length of time since the organism died.

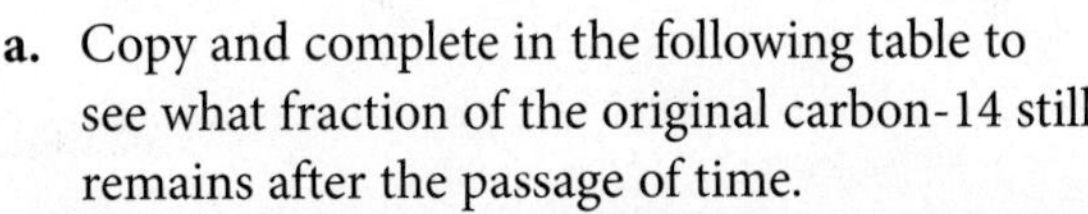

a. Copy and complete in the following table to see what fraction of the original carbon-14 still remains after the passage of time.

t	$\frac{t}{5700}$	Fraction of Carbon-14 Remaining
0		
5700		
11,400		
17,100		

b. The duration of 5700 years is referred to as the "half-life" of carbon-14 because the amount of carbon-14 drops in half 5700 years after any starting point (not just $t = 0$ years). Verify this property by comparing the amount of remaining carbon-14 after 11,400 years and 17,100 years.

c. Write the corresponding expression for the remaining fraction of uranium-234, which has a half-life of about 80,000 years.

3.2 Simplifying Expressions with Rational Exponents and Radicals

Resource Locker

Essential Question: How can you write a radical expression as an expression with a rational exponent?

Explore Exploring Operations with Rational and Irrational Numbers

What happens when you add two rational numbers? Is the result always another rational number or can it be irrational? Will the sum of two irrational numbers always be rational, always be irrational, or can it be either? What about the product of two irrational numbers?

These questions are all used to determine whether a set of numbers is closed under an operation. If the sum of two rational numbers is always rational, the set of rational numbers would be said to be closed under addition. The following tables will combine rational and irrational numbers in various ways. The various sums and products should provide a general idea of which sets are closed under the different operations.

(A) Define rational and irrational numbers.

(B) Complete the following addition table. Note that there are both rational and irrational addends.

$+$	$-\pi$	7	$\frac{1}{4}$	0	$\sqrt{3}$	$-\sqrt{3}$
$-\pi$	-2π					$-\sqrt{3}-\pi$
7						
$\frac{1}{4}$						
0						
$\sqrt{3}$						
$-\sqrt{3}$						

(C) Based on the results in the table, will the sum of two rational numbers sometimes, always, or never be a rational number?

(D) What about the sum of two irrational numbers?

(E) And finally, the sum of a rational number and an irrational number?

(F) Now complete the following multiplication table. Similarly, it has both rational and irrational factors.

$\times$	$-\pi$	7	$\frac{1}{4}$	0	$\sqrt{3}$	$\frac{1}{\sqrt{3}}$
$-\pi$	π^2					
7						
$\frac{1}{4}$						
0						
$\sqrt{3}$	$-\pi\sqrt{3}$					
$\frac{1}{\sqrt{3}}$						

(G) Based on the results in the table, will the product of two rational numbers sometimes, always, or never be a rational number?

(H) What about the product of two irrational numbers?

(I) And finally, the product of a rational number and an irrational number?

Reflect

1. Prove that the product of two rational numbers is a rational number by confirming the general case.
2. **Discussion** Consider the following statement: The product of two rational numbers is an irrational number. Is it a true statement? Justify your answer.

Explain 1 Simplifying Multivariable Expressions Containing Radicals

As you have seen, to simplify expressions containing radicals, you can rewrite the expressions as powers with rational exponents. You can use properties of exponents. You have already seen the Power of a Power Property of exponents. There are additional properties of exponents that are suggested by the following examples.

$2^2 \cdot 2^3 = (2\cdot2)(2\cdot2\cdot2) = 2^5 = 2^{2+3}$

$\frac{2^3}{2^2} = \frac{2\cdot2\cdot2}{2\cdot2} = 2^1 = 2^{3-2}$

$(2\cdot3)^2 = (2\cdot3)(2\cdot3) = (2\cdot2)(3\cdot3) = 2^3\cdot3^2$

$\left(\frac{2}{3}\right)^2 = \frac{2}{3}\cdot\frac{2}{3} = \frac{2\cdot2}{3\cdot3} = \frac{2^2}{3^2}$

$(2^3)^2 = (2\cdot2\cdot2)^2 = (2\cdot2\cdot2)(2\cdot2\cdot2) = 2^6 = 2^{3\cdot2}$

These relationships are formalized in the table below.

Previous lessons have covered the properties of integer exponents. A natural extension of this is to ask if a number can be raised to an exponent that is a rational number. The answer is yes. If we define $a^{\frac{1}{n}} = \sqrt[n]{a}$ where n is an integer and $n \neq 0$, we can demonstrate that $a^{\frac{m}{n}} = (\sqrt[n]{a})^m$ when m and n are integers and $n \neq 0$.

$$a^{\frac{m}{n}} = a^{\frac{1}{n}\cdot m} \qquad = \left(a^{\frac{1}{n}}\right)^m \qquad = (\sqrt[n]{a})^m$$

Notice that $\sqrt[n]{a}$ is not defined if n is even and $a < 0$.

Properties of Exponents	
Let a and b be real numbers and m and n be rational numbers.	
Product of Powers Property	$a^m \cdot a^m = a^{m+n}$
Quotient of Powers Property	$\frac{a^m}{a^n} = a^{m-n}, a \neq 0$
Power of a Product Property	$(a \cdot b)^n = a^n \cdot b^n$
Power of a Quotient Property	$\left(\frac{a}{b}\right)^n = \frac{a^n}{b^n}, b \neq 0$
Power of a Power Property	$(a^m)^n = a^{mn}$

Example 1 **Simplify each expression. Assume all variables are positive.**

Ⓐ $\sqrt[3]{(xy)^9}$

$\sqrt[3]{(xy)^9} = (xy)^{\frac{9}{3}}$ Rewrite using rational exponent.

$= (xy)^3$ Simplify the fraction in the exponent.

$= x^3y^3$ Power of a Product Property

Ⓑ $\sqrt[5]{x}\sqrt{x}$

$\sqrt[5]{x}\sqrt{x} = x^{\frac{1}{5}} x^{\frac{1}{2}}$ Rewrite using rational exponents.

$= x^{\frac{1}{5}+\frac{1}{2}}$ Product of Powers Property

$= x^{\frac{7}{10}}$ Simplify the exponent.

$= \sqrt[10]{x^7}$ Rewrite the expression in radical form.

Reflect

3. **Discussion** Why is $\sqrt[n]{a}$ not defined when n is even and $a < 0$?

4. Rewrite the expression $\sqrt[-n]{a}$ so that n has a coefficient of 1. Then state the conditions under which the expression is undefined.

Your Turn

Simplify each expression. Assume all variables are positive.

5. $\left(x^2y\right)^2 \sqrt[4]{y^4}$

6. $\dfrac{\sqrt[4]{x^8}}{\sqrt[4]{x^6}}$

Explain 2 Simplifying Multivariable Expressions Containing Rational Exponents

Use Properties of Rational Exponents to simplify expressions.

Example 2 **Simplify each expression. Assume all variables are positive.**

Ⓐ $(8x^9)^{\frac{2}{3}}$

$(8x^9)^{\frac{2}{3}} = (2^3)^{\frac{2}{3}}(x^9)^{\frac{2}{3}}$ Power of a Product Property

$= 2^{\left(3 \cdot \frac{2}{3}\right)} x^{\left(9 \cdot \frac{2}{3}\right)}$ Power of a Power Property

$= 2^2 x^6$ Simplify within the parentheses.

$= 4x^6$ Simplify.

Ⓑ $(64x^{12})^{\frac{1}{6}}$

$(64x^{12})^{\frac{1}{6}} = \left(2^{\boxed{6}}\right)^{\boxed{\frac{1}{6}}} (x^{12})^{\boxed{\frac{1}{6}}}$ Power of a Product Property

$= \left(2^{6 \cdot \frac{1}{6}}\right) x^{\left(12 \cdot \frac{1}{6}\right)}$ Power of a Power Property

$= 2^{\boxed{1}} x^{\boxed{2}}$ Simplify within the parentheses.

$= \boxed{2} x^{\boxed{2}}$ Simplify.

Reflect

7. Simplify $(8x^9)^{-\frac{2}{3}}$. How is it related to the simplified form of $(8x^9)^{\frac{2}{3}}$ found in example 2A? Verify the relationship if one exists.

Your Turn

Simplify each expression. Assume all variables are positive.

8. $\left(\dfrac{1}{4x^4} \cdot x^{12}\right)^{-\frac{1}{2}}$

9. $\left(\dfrac{1}{9x^{12}} \cdot x^4\right)^{\frac{1}{2}}$

Explain 3 Simplifying Real-World Expressions with Rational Exponents

The relationship between some real-world quantities can be more complicated than a linear or quadratic model can accurately represent. Sometimes, in the most accurate model, the dependent variable is a function of the independent variable raised to a rational exponent. Use the properties of rational exponents to solve the following real-world scenarios.

Example 3 **Biology Application The approximate number of Calories C that an animal needs each day is given by $C = 72m^{\frac{3}{4}}$, where m is the animal's mass in kilograms.**

(A) Find the number of Calories that a 625 kg bear needs each day.
To solve this, evaluate the equation when $m = 625$.

$C = 72m^{\frac{3}{4}}$

$= 72(625)^{\frac{3}{4}}$ Substitute 625 for m.

$= 72\left(\sqrt[4]{625}\right)^3$

$= 72\left(\sqrt[4]{5^4}\right)^3$

$= 72(5)^3$ Definition of $b^{\frac{m}{n}}$

$= 72(125) = 9000$

A 625 kilogram bear needs 9000 Calories each day.

(B) A particular panda consumes 1944 Calories each day. How much does this panda weigh?

Substitute 1944 for C in the original equation and solve for m.

$C = 72m^{\frac{3}{4}}$ Original equation

$1944 = 72m^{\frac{3}{4}}$ Substitute for C.

$\frac{1944}{72} = m^{\frac{3}{4}}$ Divide each side by 72.

$27 = m^{\frac{3}{4}}$ Simplify.

$3^3 = m^{\frac{3}{4}}$ Rewrite the left side as a power.

$(3^3)^{\frac{4}{3}} = \left(m^{\frac{3}{4}}\right)^{\frac{4}{3}}$ Raise both sides to the $\frac{4}{3}$ power.

$3^{\left(3 \cdot \frac{4}{3}\right)} = m^{\left(\frac{3}{4} \cdot \frac{4}{3}\right)}$ Power of a Power Property

$3^4 = m$ Simplify inside the parentheses.

$m = 81$ Simplify.

The panda weighs 81 kilograms.

Your Turn

Solve each real-world scenario.

10. The speed of light is the product of its frequency f and its wavelength w. In air, the speed of light is 3×10^8 m/s.

a. Write an equation for the relationship described above, and then solve this equation for frequency.

b. Rewrite this equation with w raised to a negative exponent.

c. What is the frequency of violet light when its wavelength is approximately 400 nanometers $\left(1 \text{ nm} = 10^{-9} \text{ m}\right)$?

11. Geometry The formula for the surface area of a sphere S in terms of its volume V is $S = (4\pi)^{\frac{1}{3}}(3V)^{\frac{2}{3}}$. What is the surface area of a sphere that has a volume of 36π cubic centimeters? Leave the answer in terms of π. What do you notice?

Elaborate

12. A set of elements is said to be closed under some operation if performance of that operation on elements of the set always produces an element of the set. Examine the set of integers and the set of rational numbers. Is each set closed under each of the following operations: addition, multiplication, division, and subtraction? Provide a counterexample if the set is not closed under an operation.

13. Why are integers closed under multiplication?

14. Is the set of all numbers of the form a^x, where a is a positive constant and x is a rational number, closed under multiplication? Justify your answer.

15. Essential Question Check-In How can you write a radical expression with a rational exponent?

Evaluate: Homework and Practice

• Online Homework
• Hints and Help
• Extra Practice

1. Why are the tables symmetric about the diagonal from the upper-left corner to the lower-right? For example, why is the entry in the third row of the second column equal to the entry in the second row of the third column? Would a subtraction table be symmetric about the same diagonal?

2. Prove that the rational numbers are closed under addition.

Simplify the given expression.

3. $\sqrt[3]{(27x^3)^4}$

4. $\sqrt[3]{(8x^3)^2}$

5. $\sqrt[3]{(8y^3)^4}\,\sqrt[6]{(8y^3)^4}$

6. $\sqrt[10]{0x}$

7. $\sqrt[\frac{1}{2}]{(2x)^2\sqrt{2x}}$

8. $\sqrt[-\frac{1}{3}]{2x}$

9. $(0x)^{\frac{1}{3}}$

10. $10,000^{\frac{1}{4}} \cdot z + 10,000^{\frac{1}{2}} \cdot z$

11. $\left(\frac{1}{25x} \cdot x^9\right)^{-\frac{1}{2}}$

12. $\left(\frac{1}{125x^3}\right)^{-\frac{1}{3}}$

13. $\left[(2x)^x(2x)^{2x}\right]^{\frac{1}{x}}$

14. $\left[\left(1{,}000{,}000x^6\right)^{-\frac{1}{3}}\right]^{-\frac{1}{2}}$

15. $\left(x^2y\right)^3 \sqrt[2]{y^4}$

16. $\dfrac{\left[\left(x^2y\right)^4\right]^{\frac{1}{2}}}{\left[\left(x^2y\right)^{\frac{1}{2}}\right]^4}$

17. $\left(x^{\frac{1}{8}}y^{\frac{1}{4}}z^{\frac{1}{2}}\right)^8$

18. $\left(\sqrt{z\sqrt{y\sqrt{x}}}\right)^8$

19. $\dfrac{\left(x^{10}\right)^{\frac{1}{5}}}{\sqrt[2]{x^8}}$

20. $\dfrac{\left[\left(x^{-8}\right)^{\frac{1}{4}}\right]^{-1}\sqrt[3]{x^2}}{\sqrt[6]{x^4}}$

21. $\left(x^2y\right)^4\left(\sqrt{y^{\frac{1}{2}}}\right)$

22. $\left(\sqrt{y^{\frac{1}{4}}}\right)^8$

23. **Biology** Biologists use a formula to estimate the mass of a mammal's brain. For a mammal with a mass of m grams, the approximate mass B of the brain, also in grams, is given by $B = \frac{1}{8}m^{\frac{2}{3}}$. Find the approximate mass of the brain of a mouse that has a mass of 64 grams.

24. **Multi-Step** Scientists have found that the life span of a mammal living in captivity is related to the mammal's mass. The life span in years L can be approximated by the formula $L = 12m^{\frac{1}{5}}$, where m is the mammal's mass in kilograms. How much longer is the life span of a lion compared with that of a wolf?

Typical Mass of Mammals	
Mammal	**Mass (kg)**
Koala	8
Wolf	32
Lion	243
Giraffe	1024

Tim and Tom are painters. Use the given information to provide the desired estimate.

25. Tim and Tom use a liters of paint on a large shipping crate. If the next crate they need to paint has a similar shape but twice the volume, how much paint should they plan on buying?

26. Tim and Tom are painting a crate. Tom paints 10 square feet per minute. They painted a particular crate in 1 day. Tim uses a sprayer and is 4.7 times as fast as Tom. How long would it take them to paint a crate with twice the volume and a similar shape?

27. Determine whether each of the following is rational or irrational.

a. The product of $\sqrt{2}$ and $\sqrt{50}$

b. The product of $\sqrt{2}$ and $\sqrt{25}$

c. $C = 2\pi r$ evaluated for $r = \pi^{-1}$

d. $C = 2\pi r$ evaluated for $r = 1$

e. $A = \pi r^2$ evaluated for $r = \pi^{\frac{1}{2}}$

f. The product of $\sqrt{\frac{2}{\pi}}$ and $\sqrt{50\pi}$

g. The product of $\sqrt{2}$ and $\sqrt{\frac{9}{2}}$

H.O.T. Focus on Higher Order Thinking

28. Explain the Error Jim wrote the following derivation in regards to finding the definition of $a^{\frac{1}{n}}$:

$(\sqrt[-n]{a})^n = a$	Definition of root
$(-a^k)^n = a$	Substituting a^k for $\sqrt[n]{a}$
$a^{nk} = a^1$	Power of a power property
$nk = 1$	Equate exponents.
$k = \frac{1}{n}$	Solve for k.

What is his mistake? For what values of n is the proof correct? Correct it.

29. What If? Assume the integers are not closed under addition.

a. Are the rational numbers closed under multiplication?

b. Are the rational numbers closed under addition?

30. Communicate Mathematical Ideas Prove by contradiction that a rational number plus an irrational number is irrational. To do this assume the negation of what you are trying to prove and show how it will logically lead to something contradicting the given. Assume that a rational number plus an irrational number is rational.

$r_1 + i_1 = r_2$	Given
$r_1 + i_1 - r_1 = r_2 - r_1$	Subtract r_1 from both sides.
$i_1 = r_2 - r_1$	Simplify left side.

Provide the contradiction statement to finish the proof.

31. Critical Thinking Show that a number raised to the $\frac{1}{3}$ power is the same as the cube root of that number.

Lesson Performance Task

The balls used in soccer, baseball, basketball, and golf are spheres. How much material is needed to make each of the balls in the table?

The formula for the surface area of a sphere is $S_A = 4\pi r^2$ and the formula for the volume of a sphere is $V = \frac{4}{3}\pi r^3$. Use algebra to find the formula for the surface area of a sphere given its volume.

Complete the table with the surface area of each ball.

Ball	Volume (in cubic inches)	Surface Area (in square inches)
soccer ball	356.8	
baseball	12.8	
basketball	455.9	
golf ball	2.48	

STUDY GUIDE REVIEW

Rational Exponents and Radicals

MODULE 3

Essential Question: How can you use rational exponents and radicals to solve real-world problems?

Key Vocabulary

index *(índice)*
radical expression *(expresión radical)*
radicand *(radicando)*
rational exponent *(exponente racional)*

KEY EXAMPLE *(Lesson 3.1)*

Evaluate the expression 3^{-4}.

$3^{-4} = \frac{1}{3^4}$ — *Definition of negative exponent*

$= \frac{1}{81}$ — *Evaluate.*

KEY EXAMPLE *(Lesson 3.1)*

Simplify $64^{\frac{2}{3}}$.

$64^{\frac{2}{3}} = \left(\sqrt[3]{64}\right)^2$ — *Definition of $b^{\frac{m}{n}}$*

$= \left(\sqrt[3]{4^3}\right)^2$ — *Rewrite radicand as an exponent.*

$= 4^2$ — *Definition of cube root*

$= 16$

Simplify $128^{-\frac{8}{7}}$.

$128^{-\frac{8}{7}} = \frac{1}{\left(\sqrt[7]{128}\right)^8}$ — *Definition of negative exponent and $b^{\frac{m}{n}}$*

$= \frac{1}{\left(\sqrt[7]{2^7}\right)^8}$ — *Rewrite radicand as exponent.*

$= \frac{1}{2^8}$ — *Definition of nth root*

$= \frac{1}{256}$

KEY EXAMPLE *(Lesson 3.2)*

Simplify $\frac{\sqrt[3]{x^8}}{\sqrt[3]{x^6}}$. Assume x is positive.

$$\frac{\sqrt[3]{x^8}}{\sqrt[3]{x^6}} = \frac{x^{\frac{8}{3}}}{x^{\frac{6}{3}}}$$

$$= x^{\frac{8}{3}-\frac{6}{3}}$$

$$= x^{\frac{2}{3}}$$

$$= \sqrt[3]{x^2}$$

EXERCISES

Simplify each expression. *(Lesson 3.1)*

1. $25^{\frac{3}{2}}$

2. $81^{\frac{1}{2}} - 16^{\frac{1}{2}}$

3. $27^{\frac{4}{3}}$

4. $8^{\frac{5}{3}} + 4^{\frac{5}{2}}$

Simplify each expression. *(Lesson 3.2)*

5. $1{,}000{,}000^{\frac{1}{3}} \cdot d + 1{,}000{,}000^{\frac{1}{2}} \cdot d$

6. $\sqrt[3]{(64x^3)^4}$

7. $\sqrt[3]{(27x^3)^2}$

8. $\left(\frac{1}{216x^3}\right)^{-\frac{1}{3}}$

MODULE PERFORMANCE TASK

How Much Should We Feed the Reptiles?

The zoo is expecting a new alligator to arrive in a few days. The previous Reptile Chef fed other species of reptiles currently at the zoo according to the information in the table. You speak with the Mammal Chef, who uses the formula $y = 72m^{\frac{3}{4}}$ to determine the daily calorie intake for mammals, where y is the number of Calories eaten and m is the mammal's mass in kilograms. You wonder if a similar formula might help determine the number of calories for the new alligator. Substitute data pairs from the table into the formula to find a number a so that the expression $y = am^{\left(\frac{3}{4}\right)}$ gives the daily number of Calories required by a reptile with a mass of m kilograms.

Reptile Type	Mass	Daily Calories
Bearded Dragon	0.4 kg	5.0
Spur-thighed Tortoise	4.2 kg	29.3
Spectacled Caiman	34 kg	141
Rhinoceros Iguana	7.4 kg	44.9
Giant Tortoise	250 kg	629

If the alligator has a mass of 400 kilograms, how many calories will it require per day?

Use graphs, numbers, words, or algebra to support your conclusion.

Ready to Go On?

3.1–3.2 Rational Exponents and Radicals

- Online Homework
- Hints and Help
- Extra Practice

Simplify each expression. *(Lesson 3.1)*

1. $216^{\frac{1}{3}} - 125^{\frac{1}{3}}$

2. $3 \cdot 49^{-\frac{1}{2}} + 7^{-1}$

Simplify each expression. *(Lesson 3.2)*

3. $\left(\frac{1}{16x} \cdot x^7\right)^{-\frac{1}{2}}$

4. $(xy^2)^2 \sqrt[2]{y^8}$

5. The volume of a cube is related to the area of a face by the formula $V = A^{\frac{3}{2}}$. What is the volume of a cube whose face has an area of 25 mm²? *(Lesson 3.1)*

6. Biologists use a formula to estimate the mass of a mammal's brain. For a mammal with a mass of m grams, the approximate mass B of the brain, also in grams, is given by $B = \frac{1}{8}m^{\frac{2}{3}}$. Find the approximate mass of the brain of a squirrel that has a mass of 27 grams. *(Lesson 3.2)*

ESSENTIAL QUESTION

7. How are rational exponents and radicals related?

MODULE 3
MIXED REVIEW

Assessment Readiness

1. Consider each expression. Is the expression equivalent to $\frac{512^{\frac{1}{3}}}{64^{\frac{2}{3}}}$? Write Yes or No for each.

   A. $\left(\frac{64^{\frac{2}{3}}}{512^{\frac{1}{3}}}\right)^{-1}$

   B. $\left(64^{\frac{2}{3}} \times 512^{-\frac{1}{3}}\right)^{-1}$

   C. $\frac{64^{-\frac{2}{3}}}{512^{-\frac{1}{3}}}$

2. Consider each set. Does the set represent a function? Write Yes or No for each.

   A. $\{(5, -2), (5, 0), (5, 2), (5, 4),\}$

   B. $\{(3, 4), (4, 4), (5, 2), (6, 4),\}$

   C. $\{(-4, 1), (-2, 3), (0, 4), (2, 3),\}$

3. Consider the graph of $y = \left(\sqrt[3]{8x^3}\right) + 8$. Determine if each of the following statements is True or False.

   A. The slope is 8.

   B. The y-intercept is 8.

   C. The x-intercept is -4.

4. Simplify $216^{\frac{2}{3}}$.

5. Jasmine believes that the sum of two positive irrational numbers can be a rational number. She gives the following example: $\sqrt{2} + \sqrt{2}$. Do you agree with Jasmine? Explain why or why not.

Adding and Subtracting Polynomials

MODULE 4

Essential Question: How can you use adding and subtracting polynomials to solve real-world problems?

REAL WORLD VIDEO
Vehicles, such as planes and cars, are aerodynamically tested in a wind tunnel. The complex factors involved in wind tunnel testing can be modeled with polynomial functions.

MODULE PERFORMANCE TASK PREVIEW

Ozone Levels in the Los Angeles Basin

Ozone in the upper atmosphere helps protect living things from the harmful effects of ultraviolet radiation. However, ozone near the ground is harmful and a major component of air pollution. Suppose you have some data on ozone levels in a community for an entire year. How would you find out the trend in ozone levels for that community? Let's find out!

Are YOU Ready?

Complete these exercises to review skills you will need for this module.

Personal Math Trainer

- Online Homework
- Hints and Help
- Extra Practice

Add and Subtract Integers

Example 1 Add or subtract.

$-9 + (-6)$ Think: Find the sum of 9 and 6.

-15 Same sign, so use the sign of the integers.

$14 + (-17)$ Think: Find the difference of 14 and 17. $17 > 14$, so use the sign of 17.

-3

$3 - (-11)$ Think: Add the opposite of -11.

$3 + 11$ Same sign, so use the sign of the integers.

14

Add or subtract.

1. $-16 + 21$

2. $-13 - 12$

3. $-23 - (-8)$

Algebraic Expressions

Example 2 Simplify $15 + 9x - 6 - 5x$ by combining like terms.

$15 + 9x - 6 - 5x$

$9x - 5x + 15 - 6$ Reorder, grouping like terms together.

$9x - 5x + 9$ Subtract the integers.

$4x + 9$ Combine the like terms.

Simplify by combining like terms.

4. $8a + 5 - 10a - 11$

5. $-7 + d - 6 + 2d$

6. $19z + 14y - y - 3z$

7. $21 - 13p + 12q - 5 + 2p - 15q$

Exponents

Example 3 Find the value of $x^3 + x^2$ when $x = 2$.

$x^3 + x^2$

$2^3 + 2^2$ Substitute 2 for x.

$8 + 4$ Evaluate the exponents.

12 Add.

Find the value.

8. $x^3 + x^2$ when $x = -2$

9. $x^3 - 4$ when $x = 3$

10. $x^3 - 4$ when $x = -3$

4.1 Understanding Polynomial Expressions

Resource Locker

Essential Question: What are polynomial expressions, and how do you simplify them?

Explore Identifying Monomials

A **monomial** is an expression consisting of a number, variable, or product of numbers and variables that have whole number exponents. A monomial cannot have more than one term, and it cannot have a variable in its denominator. (Recall that a term is a product of numbers and variables.) Here are some examples of monomial expressions and expressions that are not monomials.

Monomials					Not Monomials				
4	x	$-4xy$	$0.25x^3$	$\frac{xy}{4}$	$4+x$	$x-1$	$0.7x^{-2}$	$0.25x^{-1}$	$\frac{y}{x^3}$

Use the following process to determine if $5ab^2$ is a monomial.

(A) $5ab^2$ has ____ term(s), so it ____ be a monomial.

(B) Does $5ab^2$ have a denominator?

(C) If possible, split it into a product of numbers and variables.

$5ab^2 = 5 \cdot$ ____ $\cdot$ ____

(D) List the numbers and variables in the product.

Numbers: ____ Variables: ____

(E) Check the exponent of each variable. Complete the following table.

Variable	Exponent
a	
b	

(F) The exponents of the variables in $5ab^2$ are all ____. Therefore, $5ab^2$ ____ a monomial.

(G) Is $\frac{5}{k^2}$ a monomial?

(H) Complete the table below.

Term	Is this a monomial?	Explain your reasoning.
$5ab^2$	yes	$5ab^2$ is the product of a number, 5, and the variables a and b.
x^2		
$\sqrt{y}$	no	
2^2		
$\frac{5}{k^2}$	no	
$5x + 7$		
$x^2 + 4ab$		
$\frac{k^2}{4}$		

Reflect

1. **Discussion** Explain why $16^{\frac{1}{3}}$ is a monomial but $x^{\frac{1}{3}}$ is not a monomial.

2. **Discussion** Is x^0 a monomial? Justify your answer in two ways.

Explain 1 Classifying Polynomials

A **polynomial** can be a monomial or the sum of monomials. Polynomials are classified by the number of terms they contain. A monomial has one term, a **binomial** has two terms, and a **trinomial** has three terms. $8xy^2 - 5x^3y^3z$, for example, is a binomial.

Polynomials are also classified by their degree. The **degree of a polynomial** is the greatest value among the sums of the exponents on the variables in each term.

The binomial $8xy^2 - 5x^3y^3z$ has two terms. The variables in the first term are x and y. The exponent on x is 1, and the exponent on y is 2. The number 8 is not a variable, so it has a degree of 0. The first term has a degree of $0 + 1 + 2 = 3$. The degree of the second term is $0 + 3 + 3 + 1 = 7$. Therefore, $8xy^2 - 5x^3y^3z$ is a 7th degree binomial.

Example 1 **Classify each polynomial by its degree and the number of terms.**

(A) $7x^2 - 5x^3y^3$

Find the degree of each term by adding the exponents of the variables in that term. The greatest degree is the degree of the polynomial. The degree of the term $-5x^3y^3$ is 6, which you obtain by adding the exponents of x and y: $6 = 3 + 3$. Numbers have degree 0.

$7x^2 - 5x^3y^3$

Degree : 6 — $7x^2$ has degree 2, and $-5x^3y^3$ has degree $6 = 3 + 3$.

Binomial — There are two terms.

(B) $3^2 + 2n^3 + 8n$

$3^2 + 2n^3 + 8n$

Degree: 3 — 3^2 has degree 0, $2n^3$ has degree 3, and $8n$ has degree 1.

Trinomial — There are 3 terms.

Reflect

3. What is the degree of $5x^0y^0 + 5$?

4. Is $5x^0y^{0.5} + 5$ a polynomial? Justify your answer.

Your Turn

Classify each polynomial by its degree and the number of terms.

5. $3x^2y^2 + 3xy^2 + 5xy$

6. $8ab^2 - 3a^2b$

Explain 2 Writing Polynomials in Standard Form

The terms of a polynomial may be written in any order, but when a polynomial contains only one variable there is a standard form in which it can be written.

The **standard form of a polynomial** containing only one variable is written with the terms in order of decreasing degree. The first term will have the greatest degree, the next term will have the next greatest degree, and so on, until the final term, which will have the lowest degree.

When written in this form, the coefficient of the first term is called **the leading coefficient**.

$5x^4 + 4x^2 + x - 2$ is a 4th degree polynomial written in standard form. It consists of one variable, and its first term is $5x^4$. The leading coefficient is 5 because it is in front of the highest-degree term.

Example 2 **Write each polynomial in standard form. Then give the leading coefficient.**

Ⓐ $20x - 4x^3 + 1 - 2x^2$

Find the degree of each term and then arrange them in descending order of their degree.

$$\underbrace{20x}_{1}\ \underbrace{-4x^3}_{3}\ \underbrace{+\,1}_{0}\ \underbrace{-2x^2}_{2} = \underbrace{-4x^3}_{3}\ \underbrace{-2x^2}_{2}\ \underbrace{+20x}_{1}\ \underbrace{+\,1}_{0}$$

Degree: 1 3 0 2 = 3 2 1 0

The standard form is $-4x^3 - 2x^2 + 20x + 1$. The leading coefficient is -4.

Ⓑ $z^3 - z^6 + 4z$

Find the degree of each term and then arrange them in descending order of their degree.

$$\underbrace{z^3}_{3}\ \underbrace{-z^6}_{6}\ \underbrace{+4z}_{1} = \underbrace{\boxed{-z^6}}_{6}\ \underbrace{\boxed{+z^3}}_{3}\ \underbrace{\boxed{+4z}}_{1}$$

Degree: 3 6 1 = 6 3 1

The standard form is $-z^6 + z^3 + 4z$. The leading coefficient is $\boxed{-1}$.

Your Turn

Write each polynomial in standard form. Then give the leading coefficient.

7. $10 - 3x^2 + x^5 + 4x^3$

8. $18y^5 - 3y^8 + 10y$

9. $10x + 13 - 15x$

10. $-3b^2 + 2b - 7 + 6b + 12b^2 + 7$

Explain 3 Simplifying Polynomials

Polynomials are simplified by combining like terms. Like terms are monomials that have the same variables raised to the same powers. Unlike terms have different powers.

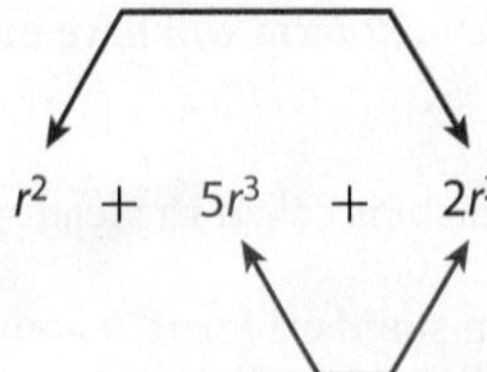

Identify like terms and combine them using the Distributive Property. Simplify.

$r^2 + 5r^3 + 2r^2$

$(r^2 + 2r^2) + 5r^3$	Identify like terms by grouping them together in parentheses.
$r^2(1 + 2) + 5r^3$	Combine using the Distributive Property.
$3r^2 + 5r^3$	Simplify.

Example 3 **Combine like terms to simplify each polynomial.**

(A) $-2y^3 - 8y^2 + y^2 + 2y^3$

$-2y^3 + 2y^3 - 8y^2 + y^2$	Rearrange in descending order of exponents.
$(-2y^3 + 2y^3) + (-8y^2 + y^2)$	Group like terms.
$y^3(-2 + 2) + y^2(-8 + 1)$	Combine using the Distributive Property.
$y^3(0) + y^2(-7)$	Simplify.
$-7y^2$	

(B) $p^2q^3 - 4p^5q^4 - 4p^2q^3 + 3p^5q^4$

$-4p^5q^4 + 3p^5q^4 + p^2q^3 - 4p^2q^3$	Rearrange in descending order of exponents.
$(-4p^5q^4 + 3p^5q^4) + (p^2q^3 - 4p^2q^3)$	Group like terms.
$p^5q^4(\boxed{-4 + 3}) + p^2q^3(\boxed{1 - 4})$	Combine using the Distributive Property.
$p^5q^4(\boxed{-1}) + p^2q^3(\boxed{-3})$	Simplify.
$-p^5q^4 - 3p^2q^3$	

Reflect

11. Can you combine like terms without formally showing the Distributive Property? Explain.

Your Turn

Simplify.

12. $3p^2q^2 - 3p^2q^3 + 4p^2q^3 - 3p^2q^2 + pq$

13. $3(a + b) - 6(b + c) + 8(a - c)$

14. $ab - a^2 + 4^2 - 5ab + 3a^2 + 10$

Explain 4 Evaluating Polynomials

Given a polynomial expression describing a real-world situation and a specific value for the variable(s), evaluate the polynomial by substituting for the variable(s). Then interpret the result.

Example 4 **Evaluate the given polynomial to find the solution in each real-world scenario.**

(A) A skyrocket is launched from a 6-foot-high platform with an initial speed of 200 feet per second. The polynomial $-16t^2 + 200t + 6$ gives the height in feet that the skyrocket will rise in t seconds. How high will the rocket rise if it has a 5-second fuse?

$-16t^2 + 200t + 6$	Write the expression.
$-16(5)^2 + 200(5) + 6$	Substitute 5 for t.
$-16(25) + 200(5) + 6$	Simplify using the order of operations.
$-400 + 1000 + 6$	
606	

The rocket will rise 606 feet.

(B) Lisa wants to measure the depth of an empty well. She drops a ball from a height of 3 feet into the well and measures how long it takes the ball to hit the bottom of the well. She uses a stopwatch, starting when she lets go of the ball and ending when she hears the ball hit the bottom of the well. The polynomial $-16t^2 + 0t + 3$ gives the height of the ball after t seconds where 0 is the initial speed of the ball and 3 is the initial height the ball was dropped from. Her stopwatch measured a time of 2.2 seconds. How deep is the well? (Neglect the speed of sound and air resistance).

$-16t^2 + 0t + 3$	Write the expression.
$-16(2.2)^2 + 3$	Substitute 2.2 for t.
$-16(4.84) + 3$	Simplify using order of operations.
-74.44	

The ball goes [74.44] feet below the ground. The well is [74.44] feet deep.

Your Turn

Solve each real-world scenario.

15. Nate's architectural client said she wanted the width of every room in her house increased by 2 feet and the length decreased by 5 feet. Before the changes, the length of every room is twice the width. The polynomial $2w^2 - w - 10$ gives the area of any room in the house with w representing the room's width. The width of the kitchen is 16 feet. What is the area of the kitchen?

16. A skyrocket is launched from a 20-foot-high platform, with an initial speed of 200 feet per second. If the polynomial $-16t^2 + 200t + 20$ gives the height that the rocket will rise in t seconds, how high will a rocket with a 4-second fuse rise?

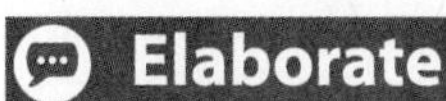

Elaborate

17. What is the degree of the expression $-16t^2 + 200t + 20$, where t is a variable? What is the degree of the expression if $t = 1$? Are the expressions monomials, binomials, or trinomials?

18. Two cars drive toward each other along a straight road at a constant speed. The distance between the cars is $l - (r_1 + r_2)t$, where r_1 and r_2 are their speeds, l is the length of their original separation, and t is a variable representing time. Write the expression in standard form. What is its degree? What is its leading coefficient?

19. The polynomial $-16t^2 + 200t + 20$ gives the height of a projectile launched with an initial speed of 200 feet per second in feet t seconds after launch. A second projectile is launched at the same time but with an initial speed of 300 feet per second, with its height given by the polynomial $-16t^2 + 300t + 20$. How much higher will the second projectile be than the first after 10 seconds?

20. **Essential Question Check-In** What do you have to do to simplify sums of polynomials? What property do you use to accomplish this?

Evaluate: Homework and Practice

- Online Homework
- Hints and Help
- Extra Practice

1. Is $(5 + 4x^0)2x$ a monomial? What about $(5 + 4x^2)2x$?

2. Is the sum of two monomials always a monomial? Is their product always a monomial?

Classify each polynomial by its degree and the number of terms.

3. $x^2 - 5x^3$

4. $x^2 - x^4 + y^2x^3$

5. $a^4b^3 - a^3b^2 + a^2b$

6. $15 + x\sqrt{2}$

7. $x + y + z$

8. $a^5 + b^2 + a^2b^2$

Write each polynomial in standard form. Then give the leading coefficient.

9. $2x - 40x^3 - 2x^2$

10. $3 + c - c^2$

11. $3b^2 - 2b + b^2$

12. $4a - 3a + 21 + 6$

Simplify each polynomial.

13. $-2y^3 - y^2 + y^2 + y^3$

14. $-y^3x - y^2x + y^2 + y^3x + y^2$

15. $xyz\sqrt[3]{2} + 2^5xyz + 2^{10}xy$

16. $a^3 + a^2 + ab$

17. Persevere in Problem Solving Lisa is measuring the depth of a well. She drops a ball from a height of h feet into the well and measures how long it takes the ball to hit the bottom of the well. The polynomial $-16t^2 + 0t + h$ models this situation, where 0 is the initial speed of the ball and h is the height it was dropped from. (This is a different well from the problem you solved before.) She raises her arm very high and drops the ball from a height of 6.0 feet. Her stopwatch measured a time of 3.5 seconds. How deep is the well?

18. Multi-Step Claire and Richard are both artists who use square canvases. Claire and Richard uses the polynomial $40x^2 + 350$ to decide how much to charge for his paintings. In each polynomial, x is the height of the painting in feet.

a. How much does Claire charge for a 6-foot painting?

b. How much does Richard charge for a 5-foot painting?

c. To the nearest tenth, for what height will both Claire and Richard charge the same amount for a painting? Explain how to find the answer.

d. When both Claire and Richard charge the same amount for a painting, how much does each charge?

19. Make a Prediction The number of cells in a bacteria colony increases according to a polynomial expression that depends on the temperature. The expression for the number of bacteria is $t^2 + 4t + 4$ when the temperature of the colony is 20°C and $t^2 + 3t + 4$ when the colony grows at 30 °C. t represents the time in seconds that the colony grows at the given temperature.

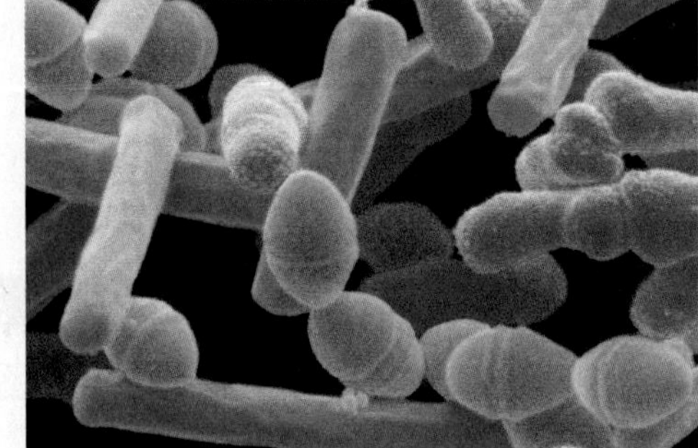

a. After 1 minute, will the population be greater in a colony at 20 °C or 30 °C? Explain.

b. After 10 minutes, how will the colonies compare in size? Explain.

c. After 1000 minutes, how will the colonies compare in size? Will one colony always have more bacteria? Explain.

20. Two cars are driving toward each other along a straight road. Their separation distance is $\ell - (r_1 + r_2)t$, where ℓ is their original separation distance and r_1 and r_2 are their speeds. Will the cars meet? When? What if they are going in the same direction and not driving toward one another? Will they meet then?

H.O.T. Focus on Higher Order Thinking

21. **Explain the Error** Enrique thinks that the polynomial $2^2x^2 + 2^3x + 2^4$ has a degree of 4 since $2 + 2 = 3 + 1 = 4$. Explain his error and determine the correct degree.

22. **Analyze Relationships** Sewell is doing a problem regarding the area of pairs of squares. Sewell says that the expression $(x + 1)^2$ will be greater than $(x - 1)^2$ for all values of x because $x + 1$ will always be greater than $x - 1$. Why is he correct when the expressions are areas of squares? Is he correct for any real x outside this model?

23. **Counterexamples** Prove by counterexample that the sum of monomials is not necessarily a monomial.

24. **Communicate Mathematical Ideas** Polynomials are simplified by combining like terms. When combining like terms, you use the Distributive Property. Prove that the Distributive Property, $a \cdot (b + c) = a \cdot b + a \cdot c$, holds over the positive integers $a, b, c > 0$ from the definition of multiplication: $a \cdot b = a + a + \ldots + a$.

25. **Analyze Relationships** A right triangle has height h and base $h + 8$. Write an expression that represents the area of the triangle. Then calculate the area of a triangle with a height of 16 cm.

Lesson Performance Task

A pyrotechnics specialist is designing a firework spectacular for a company's 75th anniversary celebration. She can vary the launch speed to 200, 250, 300, or 400 feet per second, and can set the fuse on each firework for 3, 4, 5, or 6 seconds. Create a table of the various heights the fireworks can explode at if the height of the firework is modeled by the function $h(t) = -16t^2 + v_0 t$, where t is the time in seconds and v_0 is the initial speed of the firework.

Design a fireworks show using 3 firing heights and at least 30 fireworks. Have some fireworks go off simultaneously at different heights. Describe your display so you will know what needs to be launched and when they will go off.

4.2 Adding Polynomial Expressions

Essential Question: How do you add polynomials?

Resource Locker

Explore Modeling Polynomial Addition Using Algebra Tiles

You have added numbers and variables, which is the same as adding polynomials of degree 0 and degree 1. Adding polynomials of higher degree is similar, but there are more possible like terms to consider.

You can use algebra tiles to model polynomial addition.

Key

+ = 1
− = −1
+ = x
− = $-x$
+ = x^2
− = $-x^2$

As the Key shows, a different-sized tile represents each monomial. Like terms have the same shape and size, but if they are positive, they have a + (plus) sign. If they are negative, they have a − (minus) sign. Use these visual aids to add polynomials.

To add polynomials, start by representing each addend with tiles. Add them by placing the tiles for each polynomial next to each other. Cancel out opposite tiles that are of the same size but have a different symbol. Count the remaining tiles of each size and note the symbol. Translate the tiles to a polynomial. This polynomial represents the simplified sum.

Use algebra tiles to find $(2x^2 - x) + (x^2 + 3x - 1)$.

(A) Which of the two polynomials in the addition expression do these algebra tiles represent?

Model	Algebra
+ + −	

(B) Which polynomial do these algebra tiles represent?

Model	Algebra
+ + + + −	

Ⓒ Place the algebra tiles representing each expression next to each other. This represents addition/subtraction.

Model	Algebra
+ + − + + + + −	

Ⓓ Rearrange tiles so that like tiles are together. ***Like tiles*** are the same size and shape.

Model	Algebra
+ + + − + + + −	

Ⓔ ***Zero pairs*** are like tiles with opposite signs. Together they equal zero.

Simplify the sum by ______ zero pairs.

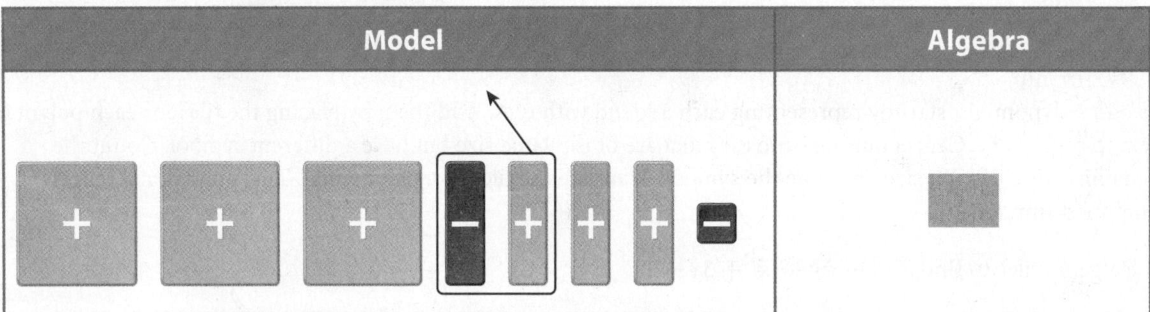

Reflect

1. **Discussion** What properties of addition allow you to rearrange the tiles?

Explain 1 Adding Polynomials Using a Vertical Format

To add polynomials vertically, add like terms in columns. Write the first polynomial in standard form; then write the second polynomial below the first, aligning like terms. Use a monomial with a zero coefficient as a placeholder for missing terms. Add the coefficients of each group and write the sum aligned with the like terms above. Simplify if necessary.

Example 1 **Use the vertical format to find the sum.**

(A) $5x^2 + 2x - 1$ and $4x^2 - x + 2$

$(5x^2 + 2x - 1) + (4x^2 - x + 2)$

Rewrite the problem, vertically aligning the terms.

$$\begin{array}{r} 5x^2 + 2x - 1 \\ +4x^2 - 1x + 2 \\ \hline 9x^2 + 1x + 1 \end{array}$$

Simplify.

$9x^2 + x + 1$

(B) $3y^3 + 2y + 1$ and $y^2 - 1$

$(3y^3 + 2y + 1) + (y^2 - 1)$

Rewrite the problem, vertically aligning the terms.

$$\begin{array}{rrrr} 3y^3 + & \boxed{0}\,y^2 + & 2y + & \boxed{1} \\ +0y^3 + & 1y^2 + & \boxed{0}\,y + & \boxed{-1} \\ \hline 3y^3 + & \boxed{1y^2} + & 2y + & \boxed{0} \end{array}$$

Simplify.

$3y^3 + y^2 + 2y$

Reflect

2. Is the sum of two polynomials always another polynomial? Explain.

Your Turn

Add the given polynomials using the vertical format.

3. $-x^2 - 1$ and $4x^2 - x$

4. $-z^3 - 2z - 1$ and $2z^3 - z^2 + 2z$

5. $x - 1$ and $4x - 6$

Explain 2 Adding Polynomials Using a Horizontal Format

To add polynomials horizontally, combine like terms. Use the Associative and Commutative Properties to regroup. Place all like terms within the same parentheses. Combine like terms by adding their coefficients, simplifying if necessary.

Example 2 **Add the polynomials using the horizontal format.**

Ⓐ $5x^2 + 2x + 1$ and $-4x^2 - x - 2$

$(5x^2 + 2x + 1) + (-4x^2 - x - 2)$ Add.

$= (5x^2 - 4x^2) + (2x - x) + (1 - 2)$ Group like terms by using the Commutative and Associative Properties.

$= x^2 + x - 1$ Combine like terms.

Ⓑ $-ab + b$ and $ab - a$

$(-ab + b) + (ab - a)$ Add.

$= \left(-ab + \boxed{ab}\right) + b + \left(\boxed{-a}\right)$ Group like terms together.

$= \boxed{b - a}$ Combine like terms.

Your Turn

Use the horizontal format to find the sum.

6. $(-6x^2 + 2)$ and $(-4x^2)$

7. $(-x^3 + 2)$ and $(-4x^3 + y + x)$

8. $(y - 7)$ and $(3y + 18)$

Explain 3 Modeling with Polynomials

You can model many situations using polynomials. Sometimes you can model a new situation by adding two or more polynomials.

For example, a company offers two services. The number of people using each service at a given time can be modeled by polynomials that use the same variable. The total number of people using both services can be modeled by adding the two polynomials.

Example 3 **A box company owns two factories in different parts of the country. The profit for each factory is modeled by a polynomial with x representing the number of boxes each produces. Solve by adding the polynomials. The models needed in each situation are provided.**

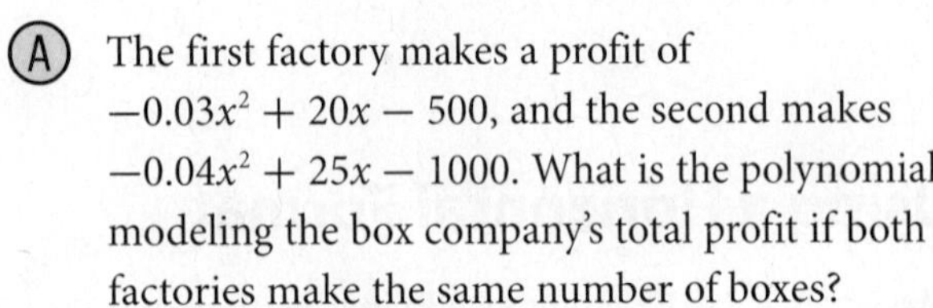

Ⓐ The first factory makes a profit of $-0.03x^2 + 20x - 500$, and the second makes $-0.04x^2 + 25x - 1000$. What is the polynomial modeling the box company's total profit if both factories make the same number of boxes?

$(-0.03x^2 + 20x - 500) + (-0.04x^2 + 25x - 1000)$ Add.

$= (-0.03x^2 - 0.04x^2) + (20x + 25x) + (-500 - 1000)$ Group like terms together.

$= -0.07x^2 + 45x - 1{,}500$ Simplify.

The factories make a total profit of $-0.07x^2 + 45x - 1500$.

(B) The company plans to open a third factory with a projected profit of $-0.03x^2 + 50x - 100$. What will be the total profit of the box company, written as a polynomial, if the projected profit is correct?

The total profit from the first two factories mentioned is $-0.07x^2 + 45x - 1500$. The projected profit from the new factory is $-0.03x^2 + 50x - 100$. Add to solve.

$(-0.07x^2 + 45x - 1{,}500) + (-0.03x^2 + 50x - 100)$	Add.
$= (-0.07x^2 - 0.03x^2) + (45x + 50x) + (-1{,}500 - 100)$	Group like terms together.
$= -0.10x^2 + 95x - 1600$	Simplify.

The total projected profit is $-0.10x^2 + 95x - 1600$.

Reflect

9. **Discussion** How could the polynomials be added if the first factory produced x boxes, the second factory produce y boxes, and the third company z boxes? What kind of polynomial would it be?

Your Turn

Model various situations with the sum of polynomials. Simplify their sum.

10. A scientist is growing cell cultures and examining the effects of various substances on them as part of his research. The culture in one petri dish increases according to the expression $t^2 + 4t + 4$ for time t in minutes. Another increases according to $t^2 + 2t + 4$. He needs to feed all the cells equally, so he needs to know the expression for the total number of cells in both dishes because the food is proportional to the total number of cells. Find the expression.

11. A farmer must add the areas of two plots of land to determine the amount of seed to plant. The area of Plot A can be represented by $3x^2 + 7x - 5$, and the area of Plot B can be represented by $5x^2 - 4x + 11$. Write a polynomial that represents the total area of both plots of land.

Elaborate

12. Is adding polynomials horizontally or vertically equivalent? Explain, describing how the steps are similar or different.

13. A car company is analyzing the profits of two car manufacturing plants. The profit of each plant is modeled by a polynomial. What operation would it use to compute the total profit of both plants? The amount of success of one plant versus the other? The total profit of both plants if the polynomials modeling each plant's profits are the same? Will the results be polynomials?

14. **Essential Question Check-In** What do you have to do to simplify sums of polynomials? What property do you use to accomplish this?

Evaluate: Homework and Practice

- Online Homework
- Hints and Help
- Extra Practice

1. In adding with tiles, one step corresponds to grouping like terms. Do you think this is more similar to the horizontal or vertical method? Explain your reasoning.

2. Show how to add $(x^2 + x)$ and $(-x^2 - 2x)$ with tiles.

Model	Algebra
+ + − − −	?
+ − + − − = −	? = ?

Find each sum vertically.

3. $(x^2 - x^4) + (x^4 - x^2)$

4. $(y^2 - x^4) + (x^4 - x^2)$

5. Add $0.5x + 2$ and $x^2 + 1.5x$.

6. $(2x + y + z) + (-x + y - z)$

7. $(x^2 + y + z) + (-x + y - z) + x - y$

8. $-a^5 + (b^2 + a^2b^2) + (a^5 + b^2 - a^2b^2)$

Find each sum horizontally.

9. $(-x^2 + x) + (x^2 - x - 1)$

10. $(a + b - c^2) + (a + b)$

11. $(ab^2 + b^2) + (-2cab^2 + b^2)$

12. $(2x - x^3 - 2x^2) + (-x^3 - 2x)$

13. $(2^{10}a + ab) + (ab\sqrt[3]{2} + ab - 2^{10}a)$

14. $(7q^3r^2 + 6qr^2 + 21q) + (-6qr^2 - qr^2 - 11q - 3q^3r^2)$

Model various situations using the sum of polynomials. Simplify their sum.

15. A pool is being filled with a large water hose. The height of the water in a pool is determined by $8g^2 + 3g - 4$. Previously, the pool had been filled with a different hose. Then, the height was determined by $6g^2 + 2g - 1$. Write an expression that determines the height of the water in the pool if both hoses are on at the same time. Simplify the expression.

16. The polynomial $-2x^2 + 500x$ represents the budget surplus of the town of Alphaville. Betaville's surplus is represented by $x^2 - 100x + 10{,}000$. If x represents the tax revenue in thousands from both towns, which expression represents the total surplus of both towns together?

17. Geometry The length of a rectangle is represented by $4a + 3b$, and its width is represented by $3a - 2b$. Write a polynomial for the perimeter of the rectangle. What is the minimum perimeter of the rectangle if $a = 12$ and b is a non-zero whole number?

18. Multi-Step Tara plans to put wallpaper on the walls of her room. She will not put the wallpaper across the doorway, which is 3 feet wide and 7 feet tall.

a. Write an expression that represents the number of square feet of wallpaper she will need if the height of her room is x feet, with a length and width that are each 3 times the height of the room. Assume that the walls are four rectangles.

b. Write the expression for the amount of wallpaper in square feet Tara needs for the living room, which is the same height and width as her bedroom, but has a length that is 5 times greater. The living room has 2 doors that are the same size as the door in her bedroom.

c. Tara decides to get the same wallpaper for both rooms. Write the expression for the total amount of wallpaper she needs.

d. If $x = 8$, how much more wallpaper will Tara need for the living room than for the bedroom?

H.O.T. Focus on Higher Order Thinking

19. Critical Thinking Subtracting one polynomial from another is the same as adding the opposite of the polynomial by distributing a -1.

Substitute $n = -1$ in $(x^2 + x) + n(x^2 + 2x)$ and simplify.

20. Multiple Representations Two polynomials model different financial information for a company. The first polynomial, $40{,}000 + 3x^2$ represents the gross monthly income from selling x units, while the second one, $0.05x + 100$ represents the monthly production cost of x units.

Which of the following expressions models gross income less production costs?

a. $40{,}000 + 3x^2 - 0.05x + 100$

b. $(40{,}000 - 100) + 3x^2 - 0.05x$

c. $3x^2 - 0.05x + 39{,}900$

d. $3x^2 - 0.05x + 40{,}100$

e. a and b

f. b and c

21. Explain the Error Jane and Jill were simplifying the expression $(2x^2 + x) + 2(-x^2 + x)$ and obtained different answers. Who is correct and why?

Jane	Jill
$= (2x^2 + x) + 2(-x^2 + x)$	$= (2x^2 + x) + 2(-x^2 + x)$
$= (2x^2 + x) + (-x^2 + x) + (-x^2 + x)$	$= (2x^2 + x) - 2x^2 + x$
$= (2x^2 - x^2 - x^2) + (x + x + x)$	$= 2x$
$= 3x$	

22. Critical Thinking A set is **closed** under an operation if performing that operation on two members of the set results in another member of the set. Is the set of polynomials closed under addition? Is the set of polynomials closed under multiplication by a constant? Explain.

23. Counterexamples You can prove that a statement isn't true by finding a single example that contradicts the statement, which is called a *counterexample.* Show that the set of polynomials is not closed under division by finding a counterexample of division of a polynomial by a polynomial that does not result in a polynomial.

24. Communicate Mathematical Ideas Simplify $(x^2 + x) + n(x^2 + 2x)$ by distributing the n. Show that it is equivalent for $n = 2$ to $(x^2 + x) + (x^2 + 2x) + (x^2 + 2x)$.

25. Multiple Representations Write two polynomials whose sum is $4m^2 + 2m$. Write two polynomials whose difference is $4m^2 + 2m$.

Lesson Performance Task

Swimming pools offer a wide range of activities for both health and leisure. They typically service everyone in the community, from the very young to the elderly. In community pools, the water temperature is often a much debated topic. If the water is too cold, children and older individuals may not be able to use the pool for the length of time they wish. On the other hand, if the pool is too warm, people swimming laps can get overheated.

An architect is working with a health club to design a multi-use aquatics facility that will have two pools. One pool will be primarily used by lap swimmers and local school swim teams. A second pool will be more of a mixed usage pool and have regions of various depths to service the remainder of the community.

Design two swimming pools for the aquatics center and calculate the volume of each pool. The lap pool should be 25 yards long, between 4 and 6 feet deep, and should consist of x lanes, with the width of each lane between 6 and 8 feet. The multi-use pool should have 3 sections. The first section should be a shallow end, where the depth begins between 2.5 and 3.5 feet, and slopes down to a depth equal to one-sixth the width of the pool over about one-third of the pool's length. The last section should slope down to the maximum depth of the pool which should be between 9 and 12 feet. Both pools should have approximately the same width and the multi-use pool should be between 2 and 3 times as long as it is wide.

Produce polynomials representing the volume of each pool and the total volume of water needed by the facility.

4.3 Subtracting Polynomial Expressions

Resource Locker

Essential Question: How do you subtract polynomials?

Explore Modeling Polynomial Subtraction Using Algebra Tiles

You can also use algebra tiles to model polynomial subtraction.

Key
+ $= 1$, − $= -1$; + $= x$; − $= -x$; + $= x^2$; − $= -x^2$

To subtract polynomials, recall that subtraction is equivalent to addition of the opposite.

$5 - 6 = 5 + (-6)$

Polynomial subtraction is the same. To subtract polynomial B from polynomial A, create a new polynomial C that consists of the opposite of each monomial in polynomial B. Add polynomial A and polynomial C.

When using tiles, switch every tile in the polynomial being subtracted for its opposite, the tile of the same size but the opposite sign. Once this is done, place the tiles representing the first polynomial and the new set of tiles next to each other and add like you have done previously. (The opposite of a polynomial is the negative of it. When you add a polynomial to its opposite you get 0.)

 Use algebra tiles to find $(2x^2 + 4) - (4x^2)$. Write the polynomial expression for each set of algebra tiles.

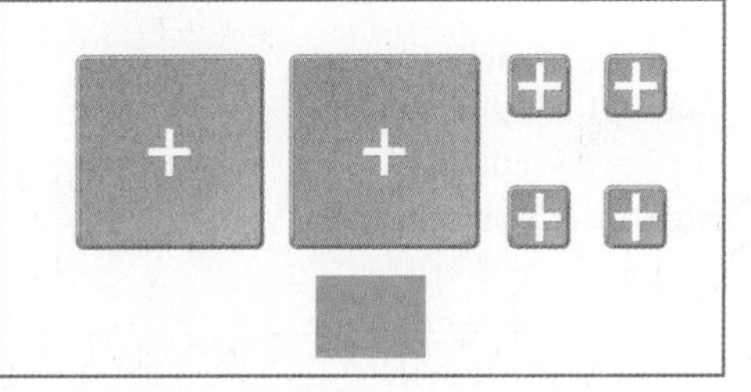

−

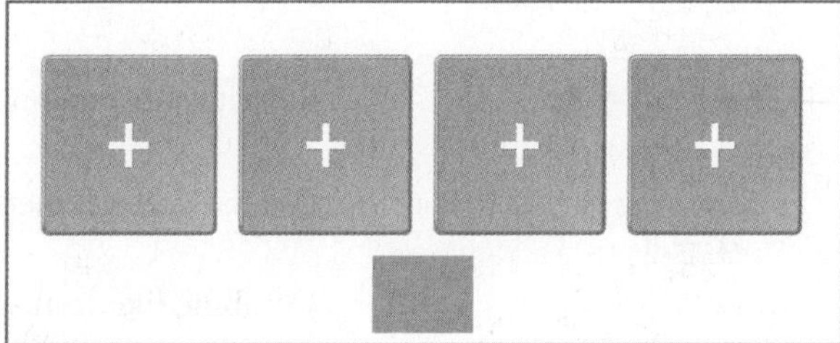

 Write the opposite of $4x^2$.

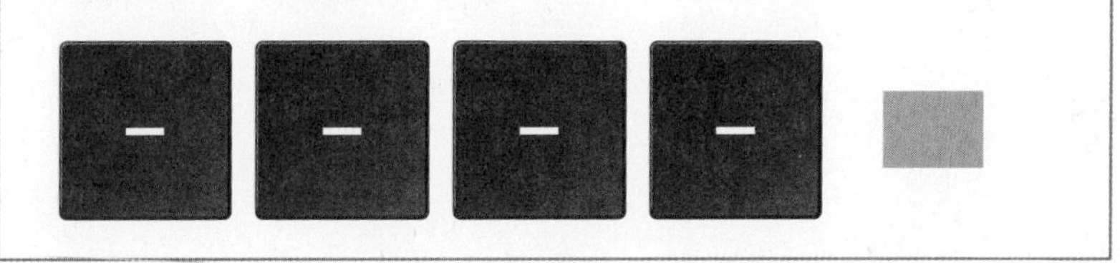

Ⓒ Write the subtraction as addition of the opposite.

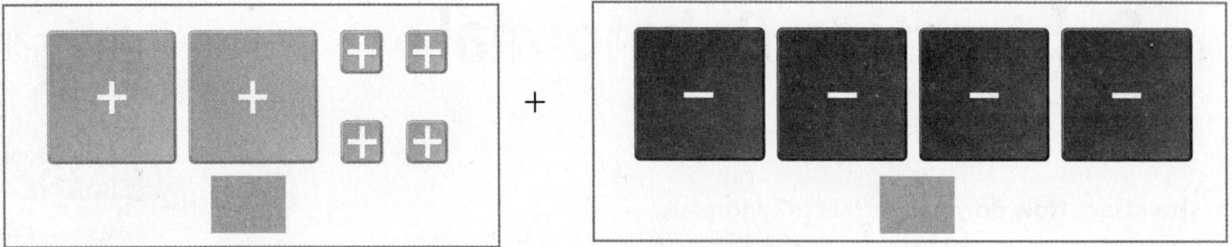

Ⓓ Group like terms and remove zero pairs. Write the resulting expression.

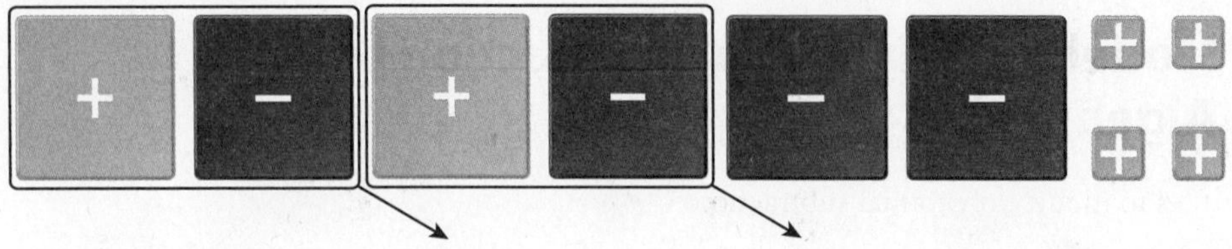

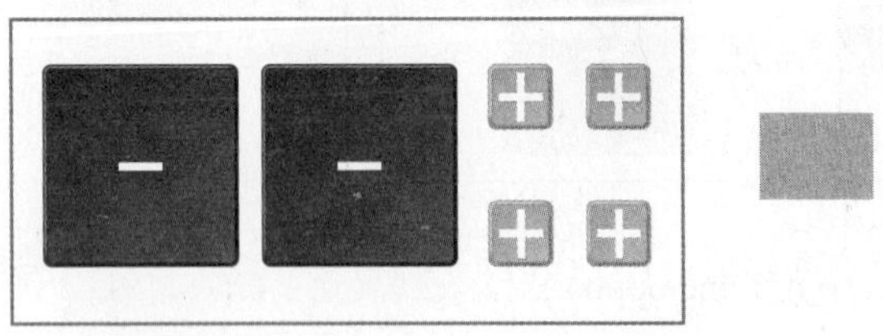

Reflect

1. **Discussion** Explain how removing zero pairs is an application of the additive inverse and the Identity Property of Addition.

Explain 1 Subtracting Polynomials Using a Vertical Format

To subtract polynomials, rewrite the subtraction as addition of the opposite.

Example 1 **Subtract using the vertical method.**

Ⓐ $(5x + 2) - (-2x^2 - 3x + 4)$

$(5x + 2) + (2x^2 + 3x - 4)$ Rewrite subtraction as addition of the opposite.

$$\begin{array}{r} 0x^2 + 5x + 2 \\ + \; 2x^2 + 3x - 4 \\ \hline 2x^2 + 8x - 2 \end{array}$$

Use the vertical method. Write $0x^2$ as a placeholder.

Combine like terms.

(B) $(y^2 + y - 1) - (-2y^2 + y + 1)$

$(y^2 + y - 1) + (\boxed{+}\ 2y^2 \boxed{-}\ y \boxed{-}\ 1)$ Rewrite subtraction as addition of the opposite.

$$\begin{array}{r} y^2 + y - 1 \\ +2y^2 - y - 1 \\ \hline 3y^2 + 0 - 2 \\ 3y^2 - 2 \end{array}$$

Use the vertical method.

Combine like terms and simplify.

Simplify.

Reflect

2. Is the difference of two polynomials always another polynomial? Explain.

Your Turn

Find the difference using a vertical format.

3. $(4x^2 - x) - (-x^2 - 1)$ **4.** $(-z^3 - 2z - 1) - (-z^3 + 2z + 1)$ **5.** $(8y - 7) - (1 - 3y)$

Explain 2 Subtracting Polynomials Using a Horizontal Format

Once the subtraction problem has been rewritten as a sum, the polynomials can be added using the horizontal method. Recall that this method uses the Associative, Commutative, and Distributive properties to group and combine like terms.

Example 2 **Find the difference of the polynomials horizontally.**

(A) $(2q^2 - q - 8) - (2q^2 + q - 4)$

$= (2q^2 - q - 8) + (-2q^2 - q + 4)$ Rewrite subtraction as addition of the opposite.

$= (2q^2 - 2q^2) + (-q - q) + (-8 + 4)$ Group like terms together.

$= -2q - 4$ Simplify.

(B) $(2ab - b + a) - (2b^2 + b + a + 4)$

$= (2ab - b + a) + (-2b^2 - b - a - 4)$ Rewrite subtraction as addition of the opposite.

$= -2b^2 + 2ab + (-b - b) + (a - a) + (-4)$ Group like terms together.

$= -2b^2 + 2ab - 2b - 4$ Simplify.

Your Turn

Find each difference.

6. $(-x^3 + y^2 + y - x) - (-x^3 + y + x)$

7. $(18z + 12) - (11z - 5)$

Explain 3 Modeling with Polynomials

Some scenarios can be modeled by the difference of two polynomials.

Example 3 **Find the difference between two polynomials to solve a real-world problem.**

(A) The cost in dollars of producing x toothbrushes is given by the polynomial $400{,}000 + 3x$, and the revenue generated from sales is given by the polynomial $20x - 0.00004x^2$. Write a polynomial expression for the profit from making and selling x toothbrushes. Then find the profit for selling 200,000 toothbrushes.

Use the formula: Profit = revenue − cost

$(20x - 0.00004x^2) - (400{,}000 + 3x)$

$= (20x - 0.00004x^2) + (-400{,}000 - 3x)$ Add the opposite.

$= -0.00004x^2 + 17x - 400{,}000$ Combine like terms.

To find the profit for selling 200,000 toothbrushes, evaluate the polynomial when $x = 200{,}000$.

$-0.00004x^2 + 17x - 400{,}000$

$= -0.00004(200{,}000)^2 + 17(200{,}000) - 400{,}000 = 1{,}400{,}000$

The company will make $1.4 million from the sale of 200,000 toothbrushes.

(B) The revenue made by a car company from the sale of y cars is given by $0.005y^2 + 10y$. The cost to produce y cars is given by the polynomial $20y + 1{,}000{,}000$. Write a polynomial expression for the profit from making and selling y cars. Find the profit the company will make if it sells 30,000 cars.

$(0.005y^2 + 10y) - (20y + 1{,}000{,}000)$ Profit = revenue − cost

$= (0.005y^2 + 10y) + (-20y - 1{,}000{,}000)$ Add the opposite.

$= 0.005y^2 \boxed{-} 10y - 1{,}000{,}000$ Combine like terms.

To find the profit for selling 30,000 cars, evaluate the polynomial when $x = 30{,}000$.

$0.005y^2 - \boxed{10y} - 1{,}000{,}000$

$= 0.005(30{,}000)^2 - \boxed{10(30{,}000)} - 1{,}000{,}000 = \boxed{3{,}200{,}000}$

The company will make $3.2 million from the sale of 30,000 cars.

Reflect

8. What is the addition problem corresponding to profit = revenue − cost? How do you find revenue if you know profit and cost?

Your Turn

Find the difference between two polynomials to solve a real-world problem.

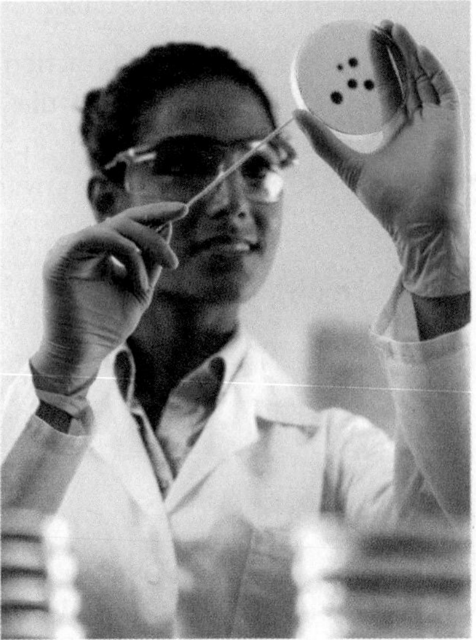

9. Jen, a biologist, is growing bacterial cultures at different temperatures as part of her research. The number of cells in the culture growing at 25 °C is given by the polynomial $t^2 + 4t + 4$, where t is the time elapsed in minutes. The number of cells in the second culture growing at 35 °C is modeled by the polynomial $t^2 + 4$. She needs to measure the success of the 25 °C culture over the 35 °C culture. Find the polynomial representing how many more cells are in the 25 °C culture for time t. How many more cells are there after 15 minutes?

10. The number of gallons of water in a leaking pool is determined by the rate that the water is filling, $8g^2 + 3g - 4$, and the rate that water leaks from the pool, $9g^2 - 2g - 5$, where g represents the number of gallons entering or leaving the pool per minute. Write an expression for the net change in gallons per minute of the water in the pool. Find the change in the amount when the rate, g, is 5 gallons per minute.

Elaborate

11. You can turn a polynomial subtraction problem into an addition problem. Can you turn a polynomial addition problem into a subtraction problem?

12. Discussion Write a pair of polynomials whose sum is $3m^2 + 1$. Write a pair of polynomials whose difference is $3m^2 + 1$. Write a pair of polynomials whose sum and difference are both $3m^2 + 1$.

13. Essential Question Check-In What do you have to do to simplify differences of polynomials? What properties do you use to accomplish this?

Evaluate: Homework and Practice

- Online Homework
- Hints and Help
- Extra Practice

1. Use algebra tiles to model the difference: $(x^2 + x - 3) - (x^2 + 2x + 1)$ and organize the steps in a table.

2. James was solving a subtraction problem using algebra tiles, and he ended with 1 x^2-tile, $2x^2$-tiles, 3 1-tiles, and 1 −1-tile. Model these results with algebra tiles. Assuming James' steps were correct up to that point, explain his mistake. Write the algebraic expression and draw the tiles that should be his result.

Find each difference vertically.

3. $(2x^2 - 2x^4) - (x^4 - x^2)$

4. $(y^2 - x^4) - (-x^4 - x^2)$

5. $(0.75x + 2) - (2.75x + x^2)$

6. $(x^2 + y^2x + z) - (-x + xy^2 - z)$

7. $(m + x + 2z) - (x - y)$

8. $-a^5 - (b^2 + a^2b^2) - (-a^5 - a^2b^2)$

Find each difference horizontally.

9. $(-2x^2 + x + 1) - (2x^2 - x - 1)$

10. $(a + b - 2c) - (a + b + 2c)$

11. $(-2cab^2 + ab^2 + b^2) - (-b^2)$

12. $(-2cab^2 + ab^2 + b^2) - \left[-(-b^2)\right]$

13. $(4^{10}a + ab\sqrt[3]{2}) - (ab\sqrt[3]{2} + ab + 4^{10}a)$

14. $(q^3r^2 - 6qr^2 - 21q) - (-qr^2 - 6qr^2 - 11q - 3q^3r^2)$

Model various situations with the difference of polynomials. Simplify.

15. A bicycle company produces y bicycles at a cost represented by the polynomial $y^2 + 10y + 100{,}000$. The revenue for y bicycles is represented by $2y^2 + 10y + 500$. Find a polynomial that represents the company's profit. If the company only has enough materials to make 300 bicycles, should it make the bicycles?

16. The polynomial $-2x^2 + 500x$ represents the budget surplus of the town of Alphaville for the year 2010. Alphaville's surplus in 2011 can be modeled by $-1.5x^2 + 400x$. If x represents the yearly tax revenue in thousands, by how much did Alphaville's budget surplus increase from 2010 to 2011? If Alphaville took in $750,000 in tax revenue in 2011, what was the budget surplus that year?

Geometry **Mrs. Isabelle is making paper and plastic foam animals for her first-grade class. She is calculating the amount of wasted materials for environmental and financial reasons.**

17. Mrs. Isabelle is cutting circles out of square pieces of paper to make paper animals in her class. Write a polynomial that represents the amount of paper wasted if the class cuts out the biggest circles possible in squares of length ℓ.

18. Mrs. Isabelle's class is making spheres out of plastic foam cubes. Write a polynomial that represents the amount of plastic foam wasted if the class cuts out the biggest spheres possible from cubes with side lengths of l. The volume of a sphere of radius r is $\frac{4}{3}\pi r^3$.

Persevere in Problem Solving **John has yellow, green, and red cubes, each with side length c. Eight yellow cubes are glued together to make a larger cube. An even larger cube is made by gluing on green cubes until no yellow cubes can be seen. After that, John covers the green cubes with red ones so that green also cannot be seen, making an even larger cube. The minimum number of green and red cubes were used to cover previous colors. Use this information for Exercises 19 and 20.**

19. What is the volume of the final big red cube?

20. Write an expression for the volume of the final cube after performing this procedure with n colors of cubes.

21. Suppose you have two polynomials regarding the financial situation of a bicycle company. The first polynomial, $20{,}000 + x^2$, represents revenue from selling x units, and the second, $0.05x + 300$, represents the cost to produce x units.

Which of the following can be the net profit for the company?

a. $20{,}000 + x^2 - (0.05x + 300)$

b. $(20{,}000 + x^2) - (0.05x + 300)$

c. $(20{,}000 + x^2) - 0.05x + 300$

d. $(20{,}000 + x^2) - 0.05x - 300$

e. $(20{,}000 + x^2) - 0.05y - 300$

H.O.T. Focus on Higher Order Thinking

22. Explain the Error Kate performed the following subtraction problem. Explain her error and correct it.

$(5x^2 + x) - (x^3 + 2x)$

$= 5x^2 + x - x^3 + 2x$

$= 5x^2 - x^3 + (1 + 2)x$

$= -x^3 + 5x^2 + 3x$

23. Communicate Mathematical Ideas Hallie subtracted a quantity from the polynomial $3y^2 + 8y - 16$ and produced the expression $y^2 - 4$. What quantity did Hallie subtract? Explain how you got your answer.

24. Counterexamples The Associative Property works for polynomial addition. Does it work for polynomial subtraction? If not, provide a counterexample. Remember, the Associative Property for addition is $(a + b) + c = a + (b + c)$.

25. Draw Conclusions Finish a standard proof that the Associative Property does not work for polynomial subtraction.

To show $(a - b) - c \neq a - (b - c)$, take the right side of the Associative Property and simplify it:

$a - (b - c) = a + \left(\underline{\ ?\ } + \underline{\ ?\ }\right) = a - \underline{\ ?\ } + \underline{\ ?\ }$, which is not generally the same as $a - b - c$ unless $c = 0$.

Lesson Performance Task

The profits of two different manufacturing plants can be modeled as shown, where x is the number of units produced at each plant.

Plant 1: $P_1(x) = -0.03x^2 + 25x - 1500$

Plant 2: $P_2(x) = -0.02x^2 + 21x - 1700$

Find polynomials representing the difference in profits between the companies. Find $P_1(x) - P_2(x)$ and $P_2(x) - P_1(x)$. Compare the two differences and draw conclusions.

STUDY GUIDE REVIEW

Adding and Subtracting Polynomials

MODULE 4

Essential Question: How can you use adding and subtracting polynomials to solve real-world problems?

Key Vocabulary

binomial *(binomio)*
degree of a polynomial *(grado de un polinomio)*
leading coefficient *(coeficiente principal)*
monomial *(monomio)*
polynomial *(polinomio)*
standard form of a polynomial *(forma estándar de un polinomio)*
trinomial *(trinomio)*

KEY EXAMPLE *(Lesson 4.1)*

Combine like terms to simplify the polynomial.

$5y^2 + 12xy + 10 - y^2 + 6xy - 20$	
$5y^2 - y^2 + 12xy + 6xy + 10 - 20$	*Rearrange in descending order of exponents.*
$(5y^2 - y^2) + (12xy + 6xy) + (10 - 20)$	*Group like terms.*
$y^2(5 - 1) + xy(12 + 6) + (10 - 20)$	*Distributive Property*
$y^2(4) + xy(18) + (-10)$	*Simplify.*
$4y^2 + 18xy - 10$	

KEY EXAMPLE *(Lesson 4.2)*

A city planner must add the area of 2 lots to determine the total area of a new park. The area of lot A can be represented by $(2x^2 + 6x + 4)$ ft². The area of lot B can be represented by $(5x^2 - 5x + 10)$ ft². Write an expression that represents the total area of the park.

$(2x^2 + 6x + 4) + (5x^2 - 5x + 10)$	*Add.*
$= (2x^2 + 5x^2) + (6x - 5x) + (4 + 10)$	*Group like terms.*
$= 7x^2 + x + 14$	*Simplify.*

The area of the park is $(7x^2 + x + 14)$ ft².

KEY EXAMPLE *(Lesson 4.3)*

Find the difference.

$(b^2 + 9ab + 15a) - (3b^2 - 25ab + 1)$	
$= (b^2 + 9ab + 15a) + (-3b^2 + 25ab - 1)$	*Rewrite subtraction as addition of the opposite.*
$= (b^2 - 3b^2) + (9ab + 25ab) + 15a - 1$	*Group like terms.*
$= -2b^2 + 34ab + 15a - 1$	*Simplify.*

EXERCISES

Classify each polynomial by degree and number of terms. *(Lesson 4.1)*

1. $z^2 - 12$

2. $r^2 + 8 - 7r^3s$

Combine like terms. *(Lesson 4.1)*

3. $5y - 7y^2 + 10 - 10y^2 + y$

4. $4b(a + b) - 8b^2 + 9ab$

Add or subtract. *(Lessons 4.2, 4.3)*

5. $(7p^2 - 5p + 10) + (p^2 - 8)$

6. $(4r^2 + 9r - 4) - (-2r^2 + 7r + 6)$

7. A student is cutting a square out of a piece of poster board. The area of the poster board can be represented as $(4x^2 + 14x - 8)$ in^2. The area of the square can be represented as $(x^2 + 8x + 16)$ in^2. Write an expression to represent the area of the poster board left after the student cuts out the square. *(Lesson 4.3)*

MODULE PERFORMANCE TASK

Ozone Levels in the Los Angeles Basin

You probably know that ozone in the upper atmosphere protects Earth from ultraviolet radiation, but ozone near the ground is harmful and a major component of air pollution. The table below provides maximum and minimum surface-level ozone concentrations in per parts million (ppm) in the Los Angeles Basin area for several months during 2012.

	Jan	Mar	May	June	Aug	Oct	Dec
Max	0.049	0.078	0.097	0.123	0.098	0.076	0.049
Min	0.020	0.040	0.048	0.054	0.053	0.041	0.038

Use the data to find an equation that models the average ozone level by month and use it to predict the average level for the months of February, April, September, and November of 2012.

Be sure to write down all your data and assumptions. Then use numbers, tables, graphs, or algebra to explain how you reached your conclusion.

Ready to Go On?

4.1–4.3 Adding and Subtracting Polynomials

- Online Homework
- Hints and Help
- Extra Practice

Simplify each expression by combining like terms. Classify the simplified expression by degree and number of terms. *(Lesson 4.1)*

1. $16 - 5x^2 + 6x - 2x^2 + 10$

2. $p^4 - 5p + 3p(p^3 + 4)$

Add or subtract. Write the expression in standard form. *(Lessons 4.1, 4.2, 4.3)*

3. $(9z^2 + 28) - (z^2 + 8z - 8)$

4. $(12y - 8 + 6y^2) + (9 - 4y)$

5. A community swimming pool has a deep end and a shallow end. The volume of water in the deep end can be represented by $(2x^3 + 12x^2 + 10x)$ ft^3, and the volume of water in the shallow end can be represented by $(4x^3 - 100x)$ ft^3. Write an expression that represents the total volume of water in the pool in ft^3. *(Lesson 4.2)*

ESSENTIAL QUESTION

6. What is one way that adding and subtracting polynomials is similar to adding and subtracting whole numbers and integers?

MODULE 4
MIXED REVIEW

Assessment Readiness

1. Is the given polynomial in standard form? Write Yes or No for each polynomial.

A. $-10r^3 + 3r - 18$

B. $-35t^3 - 13t + t^2$

C. $12x^4 - 12x^2 - 5$

2. Consider the sum of $6m^2n + mn - 15$ and $-10mn^2 + mn + 12$. Determine if each statement is True or False.

A. The constant of the sum is -3.

B. $6m^2n$ and $-10mn^2$ are like terms.

C. In simplest form, the sum has 4 terms.

3. A clothing store sells t-shirts and jeans. The store charges customers \$15 per t-shirt and \$35 per pair of jeans. The store pays \$4.50 per t-shirt and \$5.00 per pair of jeans, plus a flat fee of \$150 per order. Write an expression that represents the store's profit for an order if they sell t t-shirts and j pairs of jeans. Show your work.

4. The value of a company, in millions of dollars, during its first 10 years increased by 2% each year. The original valuation of the company was 2.1 million dollars. Write a function to represent the value of the company x years after being founded. How much more was the company worth, in millions of dollars, after 6 years than after 2 years? Explain how you solved this problem.

Multiplying Polynomials

MODULE 5

Essential Question: How can you use multiplying polynomials to solve real-world problems?

REAL WORLD VIDEO
The production of agricultural crops is affected by factors such as weather, pests, and disease. Orange growers can use polynomial expressions to estimate costs, profits, and yield available for consumers.

MODULE PERFORMANCE TASK PREVIEW

Orange Consumption

Do you eat oranges? You probably already know they are high in vitamin C, but they are also good for your skin, eyes, heart, and immune system. Each year the price of oranges increases while the amount consumed varies. In this module, you will explore polynomial operations that will help you model the per capita spending on oranges. So, about how much do Americans spend on oranges each year? Let's find out!

Are YOU Ready?

Complete these exercises to review skills you will need for this module.

Personal Math Trainer

- Online Homework
- Hints and Help
- Extra Practice

Multiply and Divide Integers

Example 1 Multiply or divide.

$-7 \cdot (-3)$ — Think: Multiply 7 and 3.

21 — Same signs, so the product is positive.

$18 \div (-9)$ — Think: Divide 18 by 9.

-2 — Different signs, so the quotient is negative.

Multiply or divide.

1. $-36 \div 4$ **2.** $13 \cdot (-5)$ **3.** $-56 \div -8$

Algebraic Expressions

Example 2 Multiply $3(2x - 5)$.

$3(2x - 5)$

$3(2x) - 3(5)$ — Distributive Property

$6x - 15$ — Multiply.

Multiply.

4. $8(3a + 5)$ **5.** $4(6 - 2d)$ **6.** $9(2x - 7y)$

Exponents

Example 3 Simplify.

$x^4 \cdot x^2 = x^{4+2} = x^6$ — The bases are the same. Add the exponents.

$\frac{x^7}{x^3} = x^{7-3} = x^4$ — The bases are the same. Subtract the exponents.

Simplify.

7. $y^3 \cdot y^6$ **8.** $\frac{n^{10}}{n^2}$

9. $\frac{a^3 \cdot a^9}{a^4}$ **10.** $m^2 \cdot m^5 \cdot m^3$

5.1 Multiplying Polynomial Expressions by Monomials

Resource Locker

Essential Question: How can you multiply polynomials by monomials?

Explore Modeling Polynomial Multiplication

Algebra tiles can be used to model the multiplication of a polynomial by a monomial.

Rules
1. The first factor goes on the left side of the grid, the second factor on the top.
2. Fill in the grid with tiles that have the same height as tiles on the left and the same length as tiles on the top.
3. Follow the key. The product of two tiles of the same color is positive; the product of two tiles of different colors is negative.

(A) Use algebra tiles to find $2(x + 1)$. Then recount the tiles in the grid and write the expression.

First, fill in the factors.

Key

$= x^2$

$= -x^2$

$= x$

$= -x$

$= 1$ $= -1$

Now fill in the table.

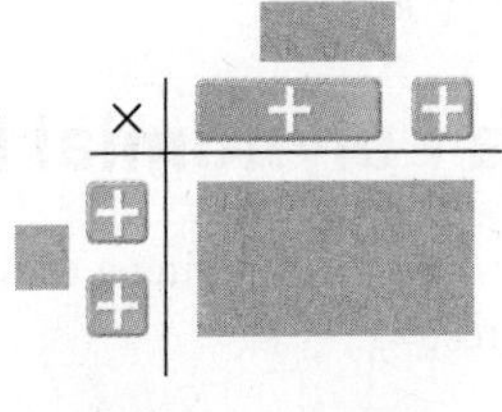

The simplified expression for $2(x + 1) =$ ____ $x +$ ____.

(B) Use algebra tiles to model $2x(x - 3)$. Then write the expression.

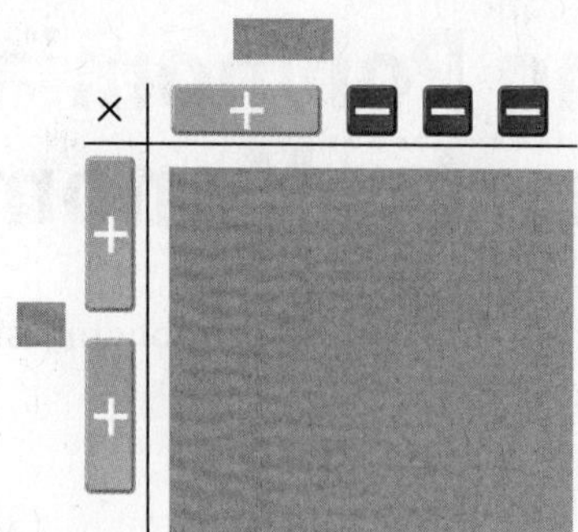

The simplified expression for

$2x(x - 3) =$ ____ $x^2 -$ ____ x.

Reflect

1. **Discussion** How do the tiles illustrate the idea of x^2 geometrically?

2. **Discussion** How does the grid illustrate the Distributive Property?

Explain 1 Multiplying Monomials

When multiplying monomials, variables with exponents may need to be multiplied. Recall the Product of Powers Property, which states that $a^m \cdot a^n = a^{(m+n)}$.

Example 1 Find each product.

(A) $(6x^3)(-4x^4)$

$(6x^3)(-4x^4)$

$= (6 \cdot -4)(x^3 \cdot x^4)$

$= (6 \cdot -4)(x^{3+4})$

$= -24x^7$

(B) $(5xy^2)(7xy)$

$(5xy^2)(7xy)$

$= (5 \cdot \boxed{7})(x \cdot \boxed{x})(\boxed{y^2} \cdot y)$

$= (5 \cdot \boxed{7})(x^{1+\boxed{1}})(y^{\boxed{2}+1})$

$= \boxed{35}\, x^{\boxed{2}} y^{\boxed{3}}$

Reflect

3. In the Product of Powers Property, do the bases need to be the same or can they be different?

Your Turn

Find the product.

4. $(18y^2x^3z)(3x^8y^6z^4)$

Explain 2 Multiplying a Polynomial by a Monomial

Remember that the Distributive Property states that multiplying a term by a sum is the same thing as multiplying the term by each part of the sum then adding the results.

Example 2 **Find each product.**

(A) $3x(3x^2 + 6x - 5)$

$3x(3x^2 + 6x - 5)$ Distribute and simplify.

$= 3x(3x^2) + 3x(6x) + 3x(-5)$

$= 9x^{1+2} + 18x^{1+1} - 15x^1$

$= 9x^3 + 18x^2 - 15x$

(B) $2xy(5x^2y + 3xy^2 + 7xy)$

$2xy(5x^2y + 3xy^2 + 7xy)$ Distribute and simplify.

$= 2xy(5x^2y) + 2xy(\boxed{3xy^2}) + 2xy(\boxed{7xy})$

$= 10x^{1+2}y^{1+1} + \boxed{6}\,x^{1+\boxed{1}}y^{1+\boxed{2}} + \boxed{14}\,x^{1+\boxed{1}}y^{1+\boxed{1}}$

$= 10x^3y^2 + \boxed{6}\,x^{\boxed{2}}y^{\boxed{3}} + \boxed{14}\,x^{\boxed{2}}y^{\boxed{2}}$

Reflect

5. Is the product of a monomial and a polynomial always a polynomial? Explain. If so, how many terms does it have?

Your Turn

Find the product.

6. $2a^2(5b^2 + 3ab + 6a + 1)$

Explain 3 Multiplying a Polynomial by a Monomial to Solve a Real-World Problem

Knowing how to multiply polynomials and monomials is useful when solving real-world problems.

Example 3 **Write a polynomial equation and solve the problem.**

Design Harry is building a fish tank that is a rectangular prism. He wants the height of the tank to be 6 inches longer than the length and width. If he needs the volume to be as close as possible to 3500 in^3, what should be the length of the tank? Round to the nearest inch.

Analyze Information

Identify the important information

- Since the bases are squares, the length and width are equal.
- The height of the tank is 6 more inches than the length.
- The total volume of the model should be as close as possible to 3500 in^3.

Formulate a Plan

Since the desired volume of the model is given, the volume formula should be used to find the answer. The volume formula for a rectangular prism is $V =$ length · width · height. Use this formula and the given information to write and solve an equation.

Solve

Build the equation.

Since the length and width are equal, let s represent these measurements. The volume will be $V = (s \cdot s)\left(s + 6\right) = s^{2}\left(s + 6\right) = s^{3} + 6s^{2}$.

s	$s^3 + 6s^2$
11	2057
12	2592
13	3211
14	3920

Justify and Evaluate

3211 is closer to 3500 than any of the other results, so the length of the fish tank to the nearest whole inch should be 13 inches.

Your Turn

7. **Engineering** Diane needs a piece of paper whose length is 4 more inches than the width, and the area is as close as possible to 50 in². To the nearest whole inch, what should the dimensions of the paper be?

Elaborate

8. What is the power if a monomial is multiplied by a constant?

9. **Essential Question Check-In** What properties and rules are used to multiply a multi-term polynomial by a monomial?

Evaluate: Homework and Practice

- Online Homework
- Hints and Help
- Extra Practice

Find each product.

1. $(3x)(2x^2)$
2. $(19x^5)(8x^3)$
3. $(6x^7)(3x^3)$
4. $(3x^2)(2x^3)$
5. $7xy(3x^2y^3)$
6. $(6xyz^4)(5xy^3)$
7. $(8xy^3)(4y^4z^2)$
8. $(11xy)(x^3y^2)$
9. $(x^2 + x)(x^3)$
10. $(x^3 + 2x^2)(x^4)$
11. $(x^2 + 2x + 5)(x^3)$
12. $(x^4 + 3x^3 + 2x^2 + 11x + 4)(x^2)$
13. $(x^3 + 2y^2 + 3xy)(4x^2y)$
14. $(2x^3 + 5y)(3xy)$
15. $(x^4 + 3x^3y + 3xy^3)(6xy^2)$
16. $(x^4 + 3x^3y^2 + 4x^2y + 8xy + 12x)(11x^2y^3)$

Write a polynomial equation for each situation and then solve the problem.

17. **Design** A bedroom has a length of $x + 3$ feet and a width of x feet. Find the area when $x = 10$.

18. **Engineering** A flat-screen television has a length that is 1 more inch than its width. The area of the television's screen is 1500 in^2. To the nearest whole inch, what are the dimensions of the television?

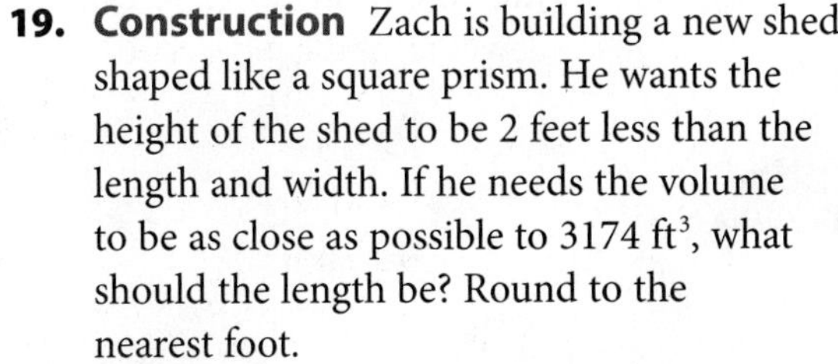

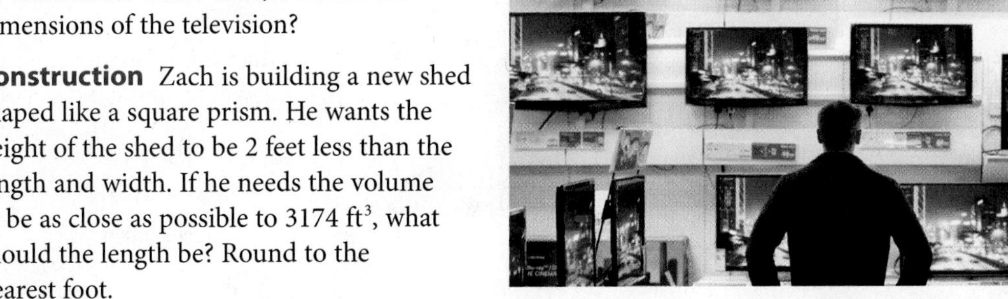

19. **Construction** Zach is building a new shed shaped like a square prism. He wants the height of the shed to be 2 feet less than the length and width. If he needs the volume to be as close as possible to 3174 ft^3, what should the length be? Round to the nearest foot.

20. State whether each polynomial is also a monomial.

    a. x^3

    b. $a^2 + 2a^b + b^c$

    c. $x^3 + 4x^3$

    d. y^{2x^3}

    e. $xyz + txy + tyz + txz$

21. Draw the algebra tiles that model the factors in the multiplication shown. Then determine the simplified product.

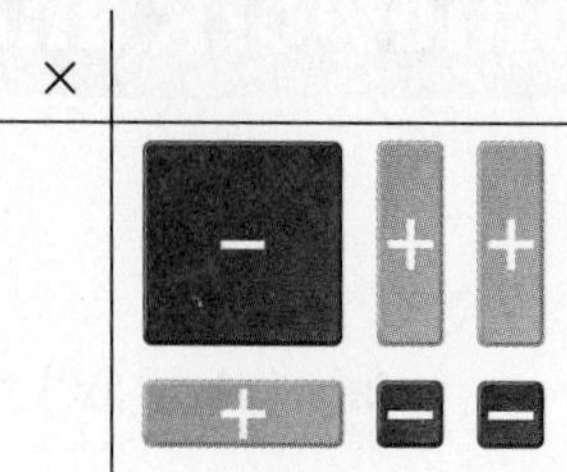

H.O.T. Focus on Higher Order Thinking

22. **Critical Thinking** When finding the product of a monomial and a binomial, how is the degree of the product related to the degree of the monomial and the degree of the binomial?

23. **Explain the Error** Sandy says that the product of x^2 and $x^3 + 5x^2 + 1$ is $x^6 + 5x^4 + x^2$. Explain the error that Sandy made.

24. **Communicate Mathematical Ideas** What is the lowest degree that a polynomial can have? Explain.

Lesson Performance Task

A craftsman is making a dulcimer with the same dimensions as the one shown. The surface shown requires a special, more durable type of finish. Write a polynomial that represents the area to be finished on the dulcimer shown.

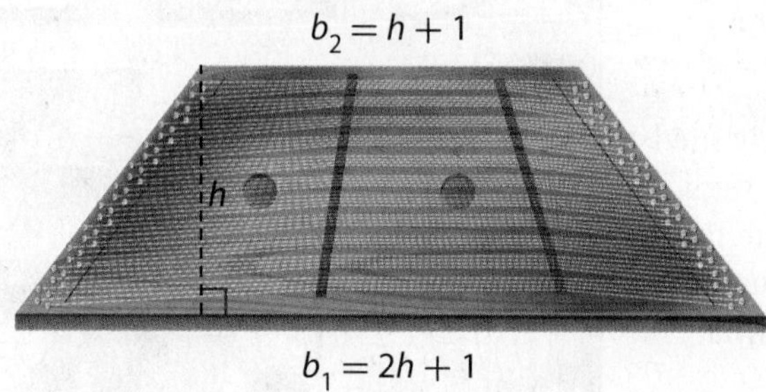

5.2 Multiplying Polynomial Expressions

Essential Question: How do you multiply binomials and polynomials?

Explore Modeling Binomial Multiplication

Using algebra tiles to model the product of two binomials is very similar to using algebra tiles to model the product of a monomial and a polynomial.

Rules

1. The first factor goes on the left side of the grid, and the second factor goes on the top.
2. Fill in the grid with tiles that have the same height as tiles on the left and the same length as tiles on the top.
3. Follow the key. The product of two tiles of the same color is positive; the product of two tiles of different colors is negative.

Use algebra tiles to model $(x + 1)(x - 2)$. Then write the product. First fill in the factors and mat.

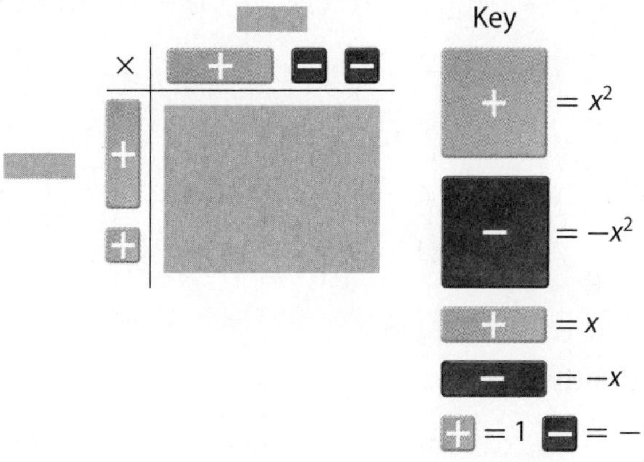

Remove any zero pairs from the mat.

The product $(x + 1)(x - 2)$ in simplest form is ____ x^2 − ____ x − ____.

Reflect

1. **Discussion** Why can zero pairs be removed from the product?
2. **Discussion** Is it possible for more than one pair of tiles to form a zero pair?

Explain 1 Multiplying Binomials Using the Distributive Property

To multiply a binomial by a binomial, the Distributive Property must be applied more than once.

Example 1 **Multiply by using the Distributive Property.**

Ⓐ $(x + 5)(x + 2)$

$(x + 5)(x + 2) = x(x + 2) + 5(x + 2)$ Distribute.

$= x(x + 2) + 5(x + 2)$ Redistribute and simplify.

$= x(x) + x(2) + 5(x) + 5(2)$

$= x^2 + 2x + 5x + 10$

$= x^2 + 7x + 10$

Ⓑ $(2x + 4)(x + 3)$

$(2x + 4)(x + 3) = 2x(x + 3) + \boxed{4}(x + 3)$ Distribute.

$= 2x(x + 3) + \boxed{4}(x + 3)$ Redistribute and simplify.

$= 2x(x) + \boxed{2x}(3) + \boxed{4}(x) + \boxed{4}(3)$

$= \boxed{2}x^{\boxed{2}} + \boxed{6}x + \boxed{4}x + \boxed{12}$

$= \boxed{2}x^{\boxed{2}} + \boxed{10}x + \boxed{12}$

Your Turn

Multiply by using the Distributive Property.

3. $(x + 1)(x - 2)$

Explain 2 Multiplying Binomials Using FOIL

Another way to use the Distributive Property is the *FOIL* method. The **FOIL** method uses the Distributive Property to multiply terms of binomials in this order: First terms, Outer terms, Inner terms, and Last terms.

Example 2 **Multiply by using the FOIL method.**

(A) $(x^2 + 3)(x + 2)$

Use the FOIL method.

$(x^2 + 3)(x + 2) = (x^2 + 3)(x + 2)$	F	Multiply the first terms. Result: x^3
$= (x^2 + 3)(x + 2)$	O	Multiply the outer terms. Result: $2x^2$
$= (x^2 + 3)(x + 2)$	I	Multiply the inner terms. Result: $3x$
$= (x^2 + 3)(x + 2)$	L	Multiply the last terms. Result: 6

Add the result.

$(x^2 + 3)(x + 2) = x^3 + 2x^2 + 3x + 6$

(B) $(3x^2 - 2x)(x + 5)$

Use the FOIL method.

$(3x^2 - 2x)(x + 5) = (3x^2 - 2x)(x + 5)$	F	Multiply the first terms. Result: $3x^3$
$= (3x^2 - 2x)(x + 5)$	O	Multiply the outer terms. Result: $15x^2$
$= (3x^2 - 2x)(x + 5)$	I	Multiply the inner terms. Result: $-2x^2$
$= (3x^2 - 2x)(x + 5)$	L	Multiply the last terms. Result: $-10x$

Add the result.

$(3x^2 - 2x)(x + 5) = 3x^3 + 13x^2 - 10x$

Reflect

4. The FOIL method finds the sum of four partial products. Why does the result from part B only have three terms?

5. Can the FOIL method be used for numeric expressions? Give an example.

Your Turn

Multiply by using the FOIL method.

6. $(x^2 + 3)(x + 6)$

Explain 3 Multiplying Polynomials

To multiply polynomials with more than two terms, the Distributive Property must be used several times.

Example 3 **Multiply the polynomials.**

(A) $(x + 2)(x^2 - 5x + 4)$

$(x + 2)(x^2 - 5x + 4) = x(x^2 - 5x + 4) + 2(x^2 - 5x + 4)$ Distribute.

$= x(x^2 - 5x + 4) + 2(x^2 - 5x + 4)$ Redistribute.

$= x(x^2) + x(-5x) + x(4) + 2(x^2) + 2(-5x) + 2(4)$ Simplify.

$= x^3 - 5x^2 + 4x + 2x^2 - 10x + 8$

$= x^3 - 3x^2 - 6x + 8$

(B) $(3x - 4)(-2x^2 + 5x - 6)$

$(3x - 4)(-2x^2 + 5x - 6) = 3x(-2x^2 + 5x - 6) - 4(-2x^2 + 5x - 6)$ Distribute.

$= 3x(-2x^2 + 5x - 6) - 4(-2x^2 + 5x - 6)$ Redistribute.

$= 3x(-2x^2) + 3x(5x) + 3x(-6) - 4(-2x^2) - 4(5x) - 4(-6)$

Simplify.

$= -6x^3 + 15x^2 - 18x + 8x^2 - 20x + 24$

$= -6x^3 + 23x^2 - 38x + 24$

Reflect

7. **Discussion** Is the product of two polynomials always another polynomial?

8. Can the Distributive Property be used to multiply two trinomials?

9. $(3x + 1)(x^3 + 4x^2 - 7)$

Explain 4 Modeling with Polynomial Multiplication

Polynomial multiplication is sometimes necessary in problem solving.

Example 4

(A) **Gardening** Trina is building a garden. She designs a rectangular garden with length $(x + 4)$ feet and width $(x + 1)$ feet. When $x = 4$, what is the area of the garden?

Let y represent the area of Trina's garden. Then the equation for this situation is $y = (x + 4)(x + 1)$.

$y = (x + 4)(x + 1)$

Use FOIL.

$y = x^2 + x + 4x + 4$

$y = x^2 + 5x + 4$

Now substitute 4 for x to finish the problem.

$y = x^2 + 5x + 4$

$y = (4)^2 + 5(4) + 4$

$y = 16 + 20 + 4$

$y = 40$

The area of Trina's garden is 40 ft^2.

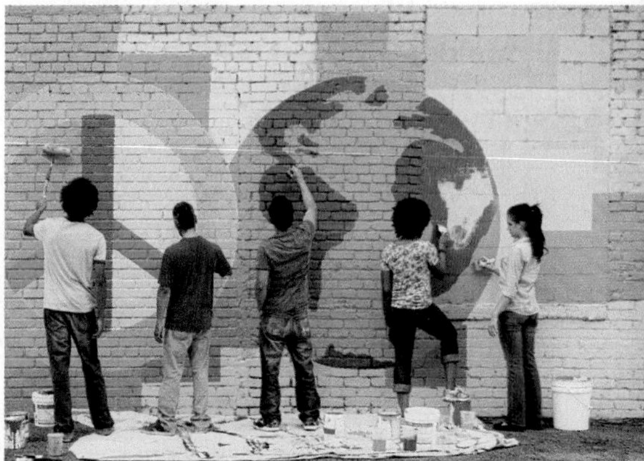

(B) **Design** Orik has designed a rectangular mural that measures 20 feet in width and 30 feet in length. Laura has also designed a rectangular mural, but it measures x feet shorter on each side. When $x = 6$, what is the area of Laura's mural?

Let y represent the area of Laura's mural. Then the equation for this situation is $y = (20 - x)(30 - x)$.

$y = (20 - x)(30 - x)$

Use FOIL.

$y = \boxed{600} - \boxed{20}x - \boxed{30}x + \boxed{1}x^2$

$y = \boxed{1}x^2 - \boxed{50}x + \boxed{600}$

Now substitute $\boxed{6}$ for x to finish the problem.

$y = \boxed{6}^2 - \boxed{50} \cdot \boxed{6} + \boxed{600}$

$y = \boxed{36} - \boxed{300} + \boxed{600}$

$y = \boxed{336}$

The area of Laura's mural is $\boxed{336}$ ft^2.

Your Turn

10. Landscaping A landscape architect is designing a rectangular garden in a local park. The garden will be 20 feet long and 15 feet wide. The architect wants to place a walkway with a uniform width all the way around the garden. What will be the area of the garden, including the walkway?

Elaborate

11. How is the FOIL method different from the Distributive Property? Explain.

12. Why can FOIL not be used for polynomials with three or more terms?

13. Essential Question Check-In How do you multiply two binomials?

Evaluate: Homework and Practice

- Online Homework
- Hints and Help
- Extra Practice

Multiply by using the Distributive Property.

1. $(x + 6)(x - 4)$
2. $(2x + 5)(x - 3)$
3. $(x - 6)(x + 1)$
4. $(x^2 + 3)(x - 4)$
5. $(x^2 + 11)(x + 6)$
6. $(x^2 + 8)(x - 5)$

Multiply by using the FOIL method.

7. $(x + 3)(x + 7)$
8. $(4x + 2)(x - 2)$
9. $(3x + 2)(2x + 5)$
10. $(x^2 - 6)(x - 4)$
11. $(x^2 + 9)(x - 3)$
12. $(4x^2 - 4)(2x + 1)$

Multiply the polynomials.

13. $(x - 3)(x^2 + 2x + 1)$
14. $(x + 5)(x^3 + 6x^2 + 18x)$
15. $(x + 4)(x^4 + x^2 + 1)$
16. $(x - 6)(x^5 + 4x^3 + 6x^2 + 2x)$
17. $(x^2 + x + 3)(x^3 - x^2 + 4)$
18. $(x^3 + x^2 + 2x)(x^4 - x^3 + x^2)$

Write a polynomial equation for each situation.

19. **Gardening** Cameron is creating a garden. He designs a rectangular garden with a length of $(x + 6)$ feet and a width of $(x + 2)$ feet. When $x = 5$, what is the area of the garden?

20. **Design** Sabrina has designed a rectangular painting that measures 50 feet in length and 40 feet in width. Alfred has also designed a rectangular painting, but it measures x feet shorter on each side. When $x = 3$, what is the area of Alfred's painting?

21. **Photography** Karl is putting a frame around a rectangular photograph. The photograph is 12 inches long and 10 inches wide, and the frame is the same width all the way around. What will be the area of the framed photograph?

22. Sports A tennis court is surrounded by a fence so that the distance from each boundary of the tennis court to the fence is the same. If the tennis court is 78 feet long and 36 feet wide, what is the area of the entire surface inside the fence?

23. State the first term of each product.

a. $(2x + 1)(3x + 4)$

b. $(x^4 + x^2)(3x^8 + x^{11})$

c. $x(x + 9)$

d. $(x^2 + 9)(3x + 4)(2x + 6)$

e. $(x^3 + 4)(x^2 + 6)(x + 5)$

24. Draw algebra tiles to model the factors in the polynomial multiplication modeled on the mat. Then write the factors and the product in simplest form.

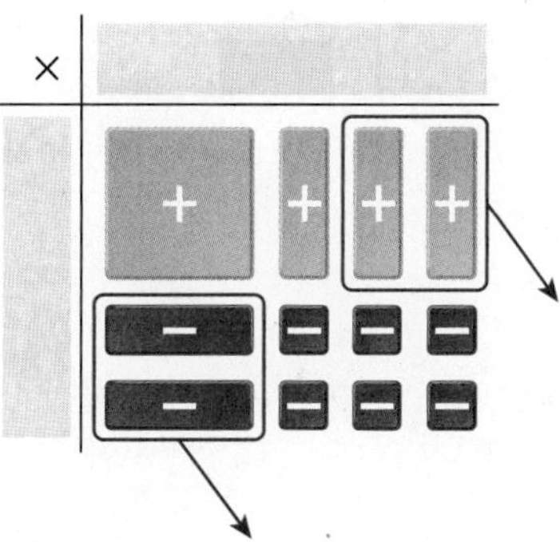

H.O.T. Focus on Higher Order Thinking

25. **Critical Thinking** The product of 3 consecutive odd numbers is 2145. Write an expression for finding the numbers.

26. **Represent Real-World Problems** The town swimming pool is d feet deep. The width of the pool is 10 feet greater than 5 times its depth. The length of the pool is 35 feet greater than 5 times its depth. Write and simplify an expression to represent the volume of the pool.

27. **Explain the Error** Bill argues that $(x + 1)(x + 19)$ simplifies to $x^2 + 20x + 20$. Explain his error.

Lesson Performance Task

Roan is planning a large vegetable garden in her yard. She plans to have at least six x by x regions for rotating crops and some 2 or 3 feet by x strips for fruit bushes like blueberries and raspberries.

Design a rectangular garden for Roan and write a polynomial that will give its area.

5.3 Special Products of Binomials

Essential Question: How can you find special products of binomials?

Explore Modeling Special Products

Use algebra tiles to model the special products of binomials.

(A) Use algebra tiles to model $(2x + 3)^2$. Then write the product in simplest form.

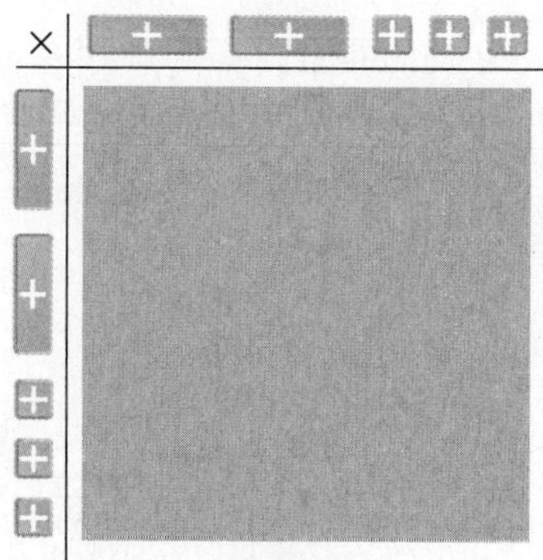

$(2x + 3)^2 =$ ___ $x^2 +$ ___ $x +$ ___.

(B) Use algebra tiles to model $(2x - 3)^2$. Then write the product in simplest form.

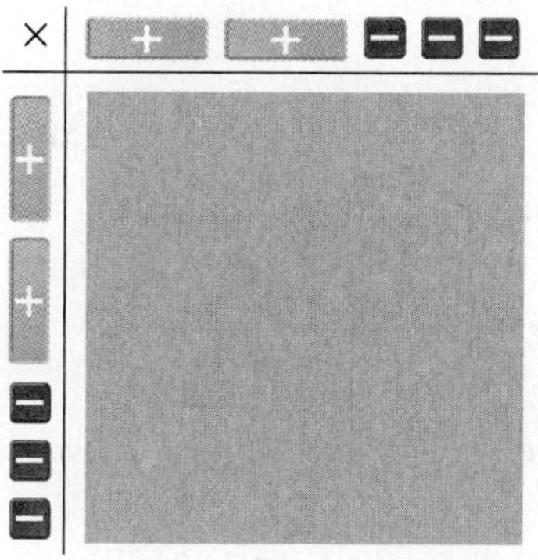

$(2x - 3)^2 =$ ___ $x^2 -$ ___ $x +$ ___.

(C) Use algebra tiles to model $(2x + 3)(2x - 3)$. Then recount the tiles in the grid and write the expression.

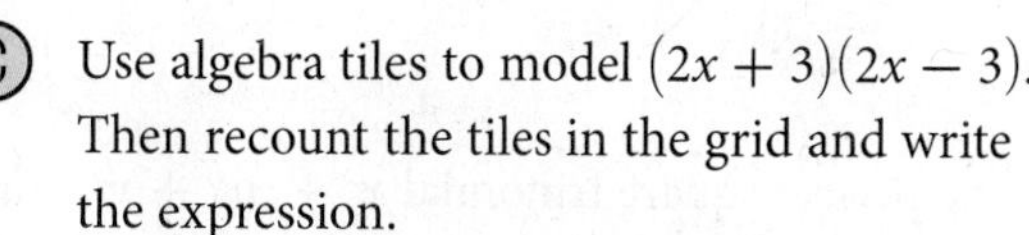

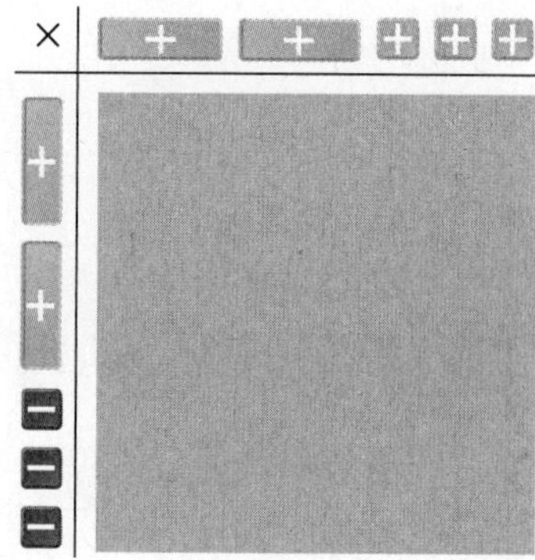

$(2x + 3)(2x - 3) =$ ___ $x^2 +$ ___ $x -$ ___.

Reflect

1. **Discussion** In Step A, which terms of the trinomial are perfect squares? What is the coefficient of x in the product? How can you use the values of a and b in the expression $(2x + 3)^2$ to produce the coefficient of each term in the trinomial? How can you generalize these results to write a rule for the product $(a + b)^2$?

2. **Discussion** In Step B, which terms of the trinomial are perfect squares? What is the coefficient of x in the trinomial? How can you use the values of a and b in the expression $(2x - 3)^2$ to produce the coefficient of each term in the trinomial? How can you generalize these results to write a rule for the product $(a - b)^2$?

3. **Discussion** In Step C, which terms of the product are perfect squares? What is the coefficient of x in the product? How can you use the values of a and b in the expression $(2x + 3)(2x - 3)$ to produce the coefficient of each term in the product? How can you generalize these results to write a rule for the product $(a + b)(a - b)$?

Explain 1 Multiplying $(a + b)^2$

In the Explore, you determined a formula for the square of a binomial sum, $(a + b)^2 = a^2 + 2ab + b^2$. A trinomial of the form $a^2 + 2ab + b^2$ is called a *perfect-square trinomial.* A **perfect-square trinomial** is a trinomial that is the result of squaring a binomial.

Example 1 Multiply.

Ⓐ $(x + 4)^2$

$$a + b = a^2 + 2ab + b^2$$

$$(x + 4)^2 = x^2 + 2(x)(4) + 4^2$$

$$= x^2 + 8x + 16$$

Ⓑ $(3x + 2y)^2$

$$(a + b)^2 = a^2 + 2ab + b^2$$

$$(3x + 2y)^2 = (3x)^2 + 2(\boxed{3}\,x)(\boxed{2}\,y) + (\boxed{2}\,y)^2$$

$$= 9x^2 + \boxed{12}\,xy + \boxed{4}\,y^2$$

Reflect

4. In the perfect square trinomial $x^2 + mx + n$, what is the relationship between m and n? Explain.

Your Turn

Multiply.

5. $(4 + x^2)^2$

6. $(-x + 3)^2$

Explain 2 Multiplying $(a - b)^2$

In the Explore, you determined the square of a binomial difference, $(a - b)^2 = a^2 - 2ab + b^2$. Because $a^2 - 2ab + b^2$ is the result of squaring the binomial $(a - b)$, $a^2 - 2ab + b^2$ is also a perfect-square trinomial.

Example 2 Multiply.

Ⓐ $(x - 5)^2$

$$(a - b)^2 = a^2 - 2ab + b^2$$

$$(x - 5)^2 = x^2 - 2(x)(5) + 5^2$$

$$= x^2 - 10x + 25$$

Ⓑ $(6x - 1)^2$

$$(a - b)^2 = a^2 - 2ab + b^2$$

$$(6x - 1)^2 = (\boxed{6}\,x)^2 - 2(\boxed{6}\,x)(\boxed{1}) + \boxed{1}^2$$

$$= \boxed{36}\,x^2 - \boxed{12}\,x + \boxed{1}$$

Reflect

7. Why is the last term of a perfect square trinomial always positive?

Your Turn

Multiply.

8. $(4x - 3y)^2$

9. $(3 - x^2)^2$

Explain 3 Multiplying $(a + b)(a - b)$

In the Explore, you determined the formula $(a + b)(a - b) = a^2 - b^2$. A binomial of the form $a^2 - b^2$ is called a **difference of two squares**.

Example 3 **Multiply.**

Ⓐ $(x + 6)(x - 6)$

$$(a + b)(a - b) = a^2 - b^2$$

$$(x + 6)(x - 6) = x^2 - 6^2$$

$$= x^2 - 36$$

Ⓑ $(x^2 + 2y)(x^2 - 2y)$

$$(a + b)(a - b) = a^2 - b^2$$

$$(x^2 + 2y)(x^2 - 2y) = \left(\boxed{x^2}\right)^2 - \left(\boxed{2y}\right)^2$$

$$= \boxed{1}\,x^{\boxed{4}} - \boxed{4}\,y^{\boxed{2}}$$

Reflect

10. Why does the product of $a + b$ and $a - b$ always include a minus sign?

Your Turn

Multiply.

11. $(7 + x)(7 - x)$

Explain 4 Modeling with Special Products

Example 4 **Write and simplify an expression to represent the situation.**

Design A designer adds a border with a uniform width to a square rug. The original side length of the rug is $(x - 5)$ feet. The side length of the entire rug including the original rug and the border is $(x + 5)$ feet. What is the area of the border? Evaluate the area of the border if $x = 10$ feet.

Analyze Information

Identify the important information.

The answer will be an expression that represents the area of the border.

List the important information:

- The rug is a square with a side length of $\boxed{x - 5}$ feet.
- The side length of the entire square area including the original rug and the border is $\boxed{x + 5}$ feet.

Formulate a Plan

The area of the rug in square feet is $\left(\boxed{x-5}\right)^2$. The total area of the rug plus the border in square feet is $\left(\boxed{x+5}\right)^2$. The area of the rug can be subtracted from the total area to find the area of the border.

Solve

Find the total area:

$$(x+5)^2 = \boxed{1}x^2 + 2\left(\boxed{x}\right)\left(\boxed{5}\right) + \boxed{5}^2$$

$$= \boxed{1}x^2 + \boxed{10}x + \boxed{25}$$

Find the area of the rug:

$$(x-5)^2 = \boxed{1}x^2 - 2\left(\boxed{x}\right)\left(\boxed{5}\right) + \left(\boxed{5}\right)^2$$

$$= \boxed{1}x^2 - \boxed{10}x + \boxed{25}$$

Find the area of the border:

Area of border = total area – area of rug

$$\text{Area} = \boxed{1}x^2 + \boxed{10}x + \boxed{25} - \left(\boxed{1}x^2 - \boxed{10}x + \boxed{25}\right)$$

$$= \boxed{1}x^2 + \boxed{10}x + \boxed{25} - \boxed{1}x^2 + \boxed{10}x - \boxed{25}$$

$$= \left(\boxed{1}x^2 - \boxed{1}x^2\right) + \left(\boxed{10}x + \boxed{10}x\right) + \left(\boxed{25} - \boxed{25}\right)$$

$$= \boxed{0}x^2 + \boxed{20}x + \boxed{0}$$

$$= \boxed{20}x$$

The area of the border is $\boxed{0}x^2 + \boxed{20}x + \boxed{0} = \boxed{20x}$ square feet.

Justify and Evaluate

Suppose that $x = 10$. The rug is $\boxed{5}$ feet by $\boxed{5}$ feet, so its area is $\boxed{25}$ square feet. The total area is $\left(\boxed{10} + \boxed{5}\right)^2 = \boxed{225}$ square feet, so the area of the border is $\boxed{225} - \boxed{25} = \boxed{200}$ square feet, which is $\boxed{20}(10)$ when $x = 10$. So the answer makes sense.

Reflect

12. Critique Reasoning Estelle solved a problem just like the example, except that the value of b in the two expressions was 8. Her expression for the area of the border was $-32x$. How do you know that she made an error? What do you think her error might have been?

Your Turn

Write and simplify an expression.

13. A square patio has a side length of $(x - 3)$ feet. It is surrounded by a flower garden with a uniform width. The side length of the entire square area including the patio and the flower garden is $(x + 3)$ feet. Write an expression for the area of the flower garden.

Elaborate

14. How can you use the formula for the square of a binomial sum to write a formula for the square of a binomial difference?

15. Can you use the formula for the square of a binomial sum to write a formula for a difference of squares?

16. **Essential Question Check-In** Use one of the special product rules to describe in words how to find the coefficient of xy in the product $(5x - 3y)^2$.

Evaluate: Homework and Practice

- Online Homework
- Hints and Help
- Extra Practice

Multiply.

1. $(x + 8)^2$

2. $(4x + 6y)^2$

3. $(6 + x^2)^2$

4. $(-x + 5)^2$

5. $(x + 11)^2$

6. $(8x + 9y)^2$

7. $(x - 3)^2$

8. $(5x - 2)^2$

9. $(6x - 7y)^2$

10. $(5 - x^2)^2$

11. $(5x - 4y)^2$

12. $(7 - 2x^2)^2$

13. $(x + 4)(x - 4)$

14. $(x^2 + 6y)(x^2 - 6y)$

15. $(9 + x)(9 - x)$

16. $(2x + 5)(2x - 5)$

17. $(3x^2 + 8y)(3x^2 - 8y)$

18. $(7 + 3x)(7 - 3x)$

Write and simplify an expression to represent the situation.

19. **Design** A square swimming pool is surrounded by a cement walkway with a uniform width. The swimming pool has a side length of $(x - 2)$ feet. The side length of the entire square area including the pool and the walkway is $(x + 1)$ feet. Write an expression for the area of the walkway. Then find the area of the cement walkway when $x = 7$ feet.

20. This week Leo worked $(x + 4)$ hours at a pizzeria. He is paid $(x - 4)$ dollars per hour. Leo's friend Frankie worked the same number of hours, but he is paid $(x - 2)$ dollars per hour. Write an expression for the total amount paid to the two workers. Then find the total amount if $x = 12$ dollars.

21. Kyra is framing a square painting with side lengths of $(x + 8)$ inches. The total area of the painting and the frame has a side length of $(2x - 6)$ inches. The material for the frame will cost \$0.08 per square inch. Write an expression for the area of the frame. Then find the cost of the material for the frame if $x = 16$.

22. Geometry Circle A has a radius of $(x + 4)$ units. A larger circle, B, has a radius of $(x + 5)$ units. Use the formula $A = \pi r^2$ to write an expression for the difference in the areas of the circles. Leave your answer in terms of π. Then use 3.14 for π to approximate to the nearest whole number the difference in the areas when $x = 10$.

23. A square has sides with lengths of $(x - 1)$ units. A rectangle has a length of x units and a width of $(x - 2)$ units. Which statements about the situation are true? Select all that apply.

a. The area of the square is $(x^2 - 1)$ square units.

b. The area of the rectangle is $x^2 - 2x$ square units.

c. The area of the square is greater than the area of the rectangle.

d. The value of x must be greater than 2.

e. The difference in the areas is $2x - 1$.

24. Explain the Error Marco wrote the expression $(2x - 7y)^2 = 4x^2 - 49b^2$. Explain and correct his error.

H.O.T. Focus on Higher Order Thinking

25. Critical Thinking Use the FOIL method to justify each special product rule that $(a + b)^2 = a^2 + 2ab + b^2$.

a. $(a + b)^2$

b. $(a - b)^2$

c. $(a + b)(a - b)$

26. Communicate Mathematical Ideas Explain how you can use the special product rules and the Distributive Property to write a general rule for $(a - b)^3$. Then write the rule.

Lesson Performance Task

When building a square-shaped outdoor fireplace, the ground needs to be replaced with stone for an additional two feet on each side. Write a polynomial for the area that needs to be excavated to create an x by x fireplace.

Design your ideal space for sitting around a fire pit and relaxing. Add furniture, flowerbeds, rock gardens, and any other desired features.

Evaluate the polynomial for the size fireplace you are including.

STUDY GUIDE REVIEW

Multiplying Polynomials

MODULE 5

Essential Question: How can you use multiplying polynomials to solve real-world problems?

Key Vocabulary
difference of two squares *(diferencia de dos cuadrados)*
FOIL *(FOIL)*
perfect-square trinomial *(trinomio cuadrado perfecto)*

KEY EXAMPLE (Lesson 5.1)

Multiply.

$\left(-3x^2y^4\right)\left(-6x^3y\right)$

$\left(-3 \cdot -6\right)\left(x^2 \cdot x^3\right)\left(y^4 \cdot y\right)$ *Gather terms with the same base.*

$\left(-3 \cdot -6\right)\left(x^{2+3}\right)\left(y^{4+1}\right)$ *Apply the product of powers rule: $a^m \cdot a^n = a^{m+n}$.*

$18x^5y^5$

KEY EXAMPLE (Lesson 5.2)

Multiply.

$(3x + 7)(x - 1)$ *Multiply using FOIL.*

$= 3x^2 - 3x + 7x - 7$ *First terms $(3x \cdot x)$ Outer terms $(3x \cdot -1)$ Inner terms $(7 \cdot x)$ and Last terms $(7 \cdot -1)$*

$= 3x^2 + 4x - 7$

$(4x - 2)(-2x - 9)$

$= (4x)(-2x) + (4x)(-9) + (-2)(-2x) + (-2)(-9)$

$= -8x^2 - 36x + 4x + 18$

$= -8x^2 - 32x + 18$

KEY EXAMPLE (Lesson 5.3)

Multiply

$(x - 7)(x + 7)$ *The product will be the difference of two squares.*

$= x^2 - 7^2$ $(a + b) = (a - b) = a^2 - b^2$

$= x^2 - 49$

$(2x + 5)^2$ *The product will be a perfect-square trinomial.*

$= (2x)^2 + 2(2x)(5) + 5^2$ $(a + b)^2 = a^2 + 2ab + b^2$

$= 4x^2 + 20x + 25$

EXERCISES

Multiply. *(Lessons 5.1, 5.2)*

1. $(7y^5)(-4y^2)$

2. $(3p^4q)(12p^3q^2)$

3. $(x - 4)(x + 8)$

4. $(4x - 1)(2x + 6)$

Multiply. Identify each product as a perfect-square trinomial or a difference of squares. *(Lesson 5.3)*

5. $(3x + 9)(3x - 9)$

6. $(x - 8)^2$

MODULE PERFORMANCE TASK

Orange Consumption

About how much do Americans spend per capita on oranges each year? The average price of oranges was \$0.57 per pound in 2004 and has been increasing at a rate of \$0.02 per year. The table below shows the per capita orange consumption (in pounds) in the United States from 2004–2012.

Year	2004	2005	2006	2007	2008	2009	2010	2011	2012
Pounds Consumed	83.6	80.3	72.8	65.2	62.3	62.7	61.8	62.3	54.9

How can you use this data to find a model and use it to predict how much money the average American spent on oranges in 2014?

Be sure to write down all your data and assumptions. Then use graphs, numbers, words, or algebra to explain how you reached your conclusion.

Ready to Go On?

5.1–5.3 Multiplying Polynomials

- Online Homework
- Hints and Help
- Extra Practice

Multiply. Identify each product as a perfect-square trinomial, a difference of squares, or neither. *(Lessons 5.1, 5.2, 5.3)*

1. $(2y - 5)(2y + 5)$

2. $(9r^3s^3)(10r^3s^2)$

3. $(4x + 1)^2$

4. $(3x - 4)(x + 8)$

Use the model of the rectangular prism to answer 5 and 6. The width of the prism is $(2x - 2)$ ft, and its height is $(x + 6)$ ft. The area of the base of the prism is $(3x^2 + 2x - 4)$ ft^2.

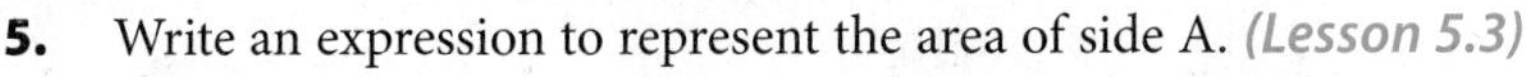

5. Write an expression to represent the area of side A. *(Lesson 5.3)*

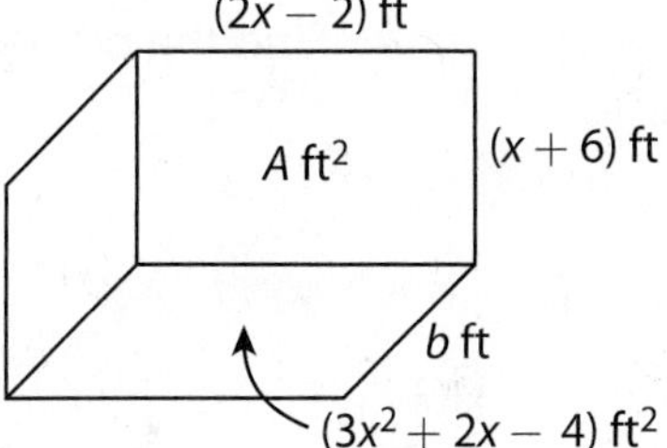

6. Could the length of b be $(3x - 1)$ ft? Explain why or why not. *(Lesson 5.3)*

ESSENTIAL QUESTION

7. Is it necessary to use the formulas for special products of binomials to multiply these binomials? Explain.

MODULE 5
MIXED REVIEW

Assessment Readiness

1. Find the standard form for the product of $(x^2 + 8)$ and $(x^2 - 2)$. Determine if each statement is True or False.
   A. It is a 4th degree polynomial.
   B. The constant term is -16.
   C. It has 3 terms.

2. Multiply $(5x - 9)^2$. Determine if each statement is True or False.
   A. The coefficient of the x-term is -45.
   B. The leading term is $25x^2$.
   C. The constant term is 81.

3. Find the product $(3x + 6)(3x - 6)$. Show your work.

4. Find the product $(x + 10)(4x + 5)$. Show your work.

5. A rectangle has a length $(x + 6)$ m and a width of 7 m. Write expressions to represent the perimeter and area of the rectangle. Explain how you determined your answers.

Assessment Readiness

- Online Homework
- Hints and Help
- Extra Practice

1. Solve each equation. Tell whether each solution is correct.

A. $-4\left(p+3\right)=-3p-7; p=-5$

B. $8r-18=-14; r=\frac{1}{2}$

C. $\frac{t}{5}-2=-5; t=15$

2. Simplify $5x^2\left(\frac{2}{5}-x\right)$. Determine if each statement is True or False.

A. The expression is a trinomial.

B. The expression has a degree of 3.

C. The expression has a constant of -2.

3. Is the given polynomial in standard form?

A. $-5y^2+5y+24$

B. $7x^5-19+x$

C. $15z-3$

4. Simplify $(3x-8)(x+2)$. Determine if each statement is True or False.

A. The coefficient of the x-term is -2.

B. The leading term is $3x^2$.

C. The constant is -16.

5. Is the product of each of the following factors a difference of squares?

A. $3\left(x-3\right)$

B. $4\left(4x^2-1\right)$

C. $\left(5x-2\right)\left(5x+2\right)$

6. Write the difference of the following polynomials in standard form: $\left(11-8y+2y^2\right)-\left(y^2-15\right)$. Classify the difference by its degree and the number of terms.

7. Sandra has been offered two jobs. Job A pays \$25,000 a year with an 8% raise each year. Job B pays \$28,000 a year with a \$2,500 raise each year. Write a function to represent each salary *t* years after being hired. Use a graphing calculator to compare the two salary plans. Will Job A ever have a higher salary than Job B? If so, after how many years will this occur? Explain how you solved this problem.

8.

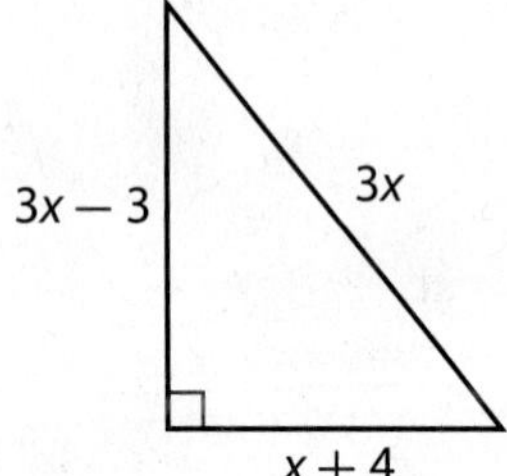

Write an expression that represents the perimeter of the triangle in terms of x and an expression that represents the area of the triangle in terms of x. If the perimeter is 36 cm, what is the area of the triangle? Explain how you solved this problem.

Performance Tasks

★ 9. The profits of two different manufacturing plants can be modeled as shown.

Eastern: $-0.03x^2 + 25x - 1500$

Southern: $-0.02x^2 + 21x - 1700$

A. Write a polynomial that represents the difference of the profits at the Eastern plant and the profits at the Southern plant.

B. Write a polynomial that represents the total profits from both plants.

★★10. A rectangular swimming pool is 25 feet long and 10 feet wide. It is surrounded by a fence that is x feet from each side of the pool.

A. Draw a diagram of the situation.

B. Write expressions for the length, width, and area of the fenced region.

★★★11. Tammy plans to put a wallpaper border around the perimeter of her room. She will not put the border across the doorway, which is 3 feet wide.

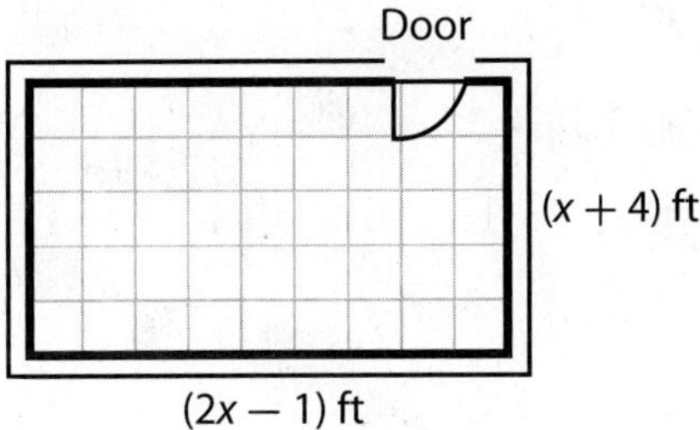

A. Write a polynomial that represents the number of feet of wallpaper border that Tammy will need.

B. A local store has 50 feet of the border that Tammy has chosen. What is the greatest whole-number value of x for which this amount would be enough for Tammy's room? Justify your answer.

C. Determine the dimensions of Tammy's room for the value of x that you found in part **B**.

MATH IN CAREERS

Camp Director For the initial year of a summer camp, 44 girls and 56 boys enrolled. Each year thereafter, 5 more girls and 8 more boys enrolled in the camp.

a. Let t be the time (in years) since the camp opened. Write a rule for each of the following functions:

- $g(t)$, the number of girls enrolled as a function of time t
- $b(t)$, the number of boys enrolled as a function of time t
- $T(t)$, the total enrollment as a function of time t

b. The cost per child each year was $200. Write a rule for each of the following functions:

- $C(t)$, the cost per child as a function of time t
- $R(t)$, the revenue generated by the total enrollment as a function of time t

c. Explain why $C(t)$ is a constant function.

d. What was the initial revenue for the camp? What was the annual rate of change in the revenue?

e. The camp director had initial expenses of $18,000, which increased each year by $2,500. Write a rule for the expenses function $E(t)$. Then write a rule for the profit function $P(t)$ based on the fact that profit is the difference between revenue and expenses.

UNIT 3

Quadratic Functions

MODULE 6

Graphing Quadratic Functions

MODULE 7

Connecting Intercepts, Zeros, and Factors

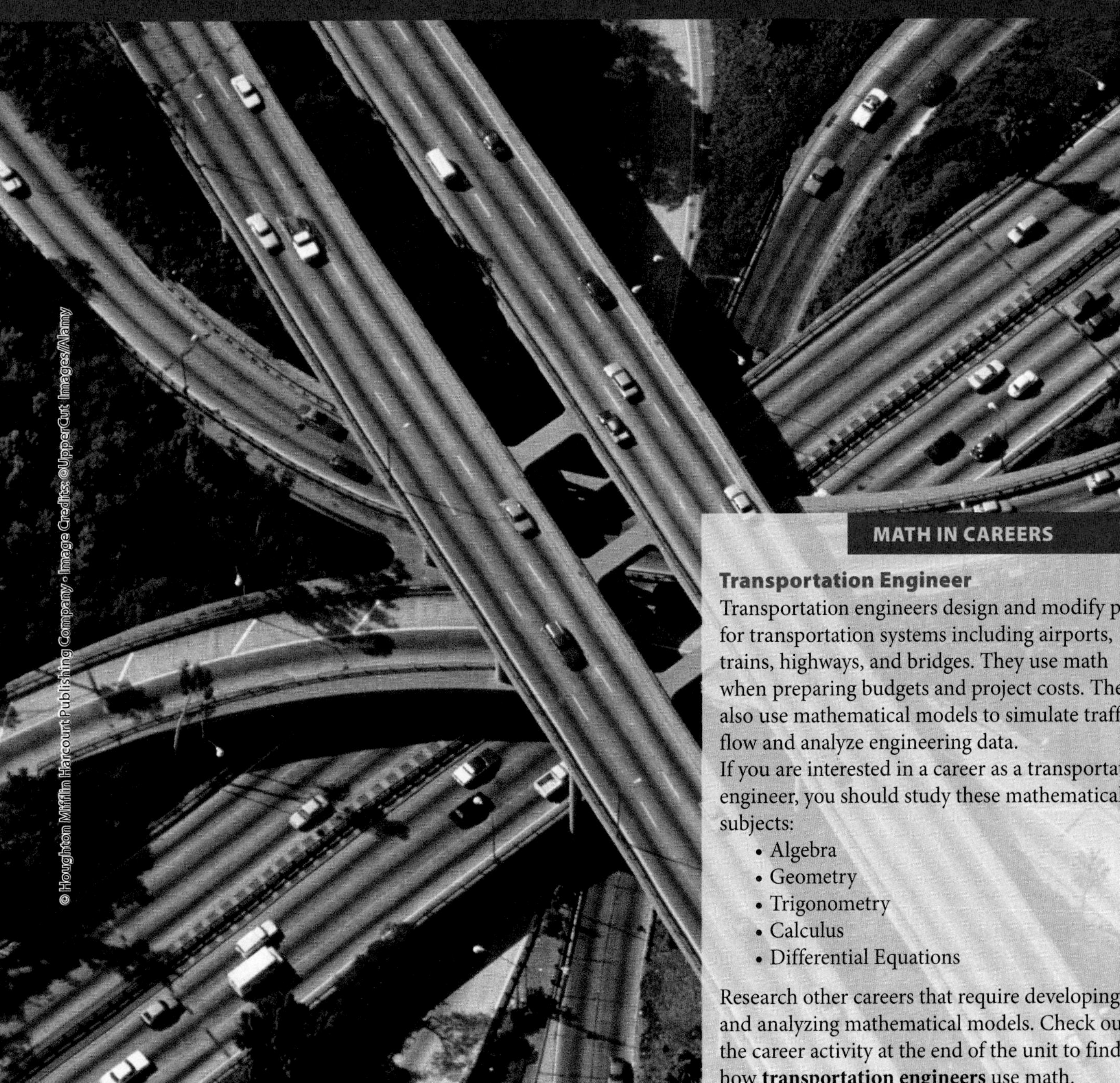

MATH IN CAREERS

Transportation Engineer

Transportation engineers design and modify plans for transportation systems including airports, trains, highways, and bridges. They use math when preparing budgets and project costs. They also use mathematical models to simulate traffic flow and analyze engineering data.

If you are interested in a career as a transportation engineer, you should study these mathematical subjects:

- Algebra
- Geometry
- Trigonometry
- Calculus
- Differential Equations

Research other careers that require developing and analyzing mathematical models. Check out the career activity at the end of the unit to find out how **transportation engineers** use math.

Reading Start-Up

Visualize Vocabulary

Use the ✔ words to complete the graphic. Write the name of a form of linear equation that best fits each equation.

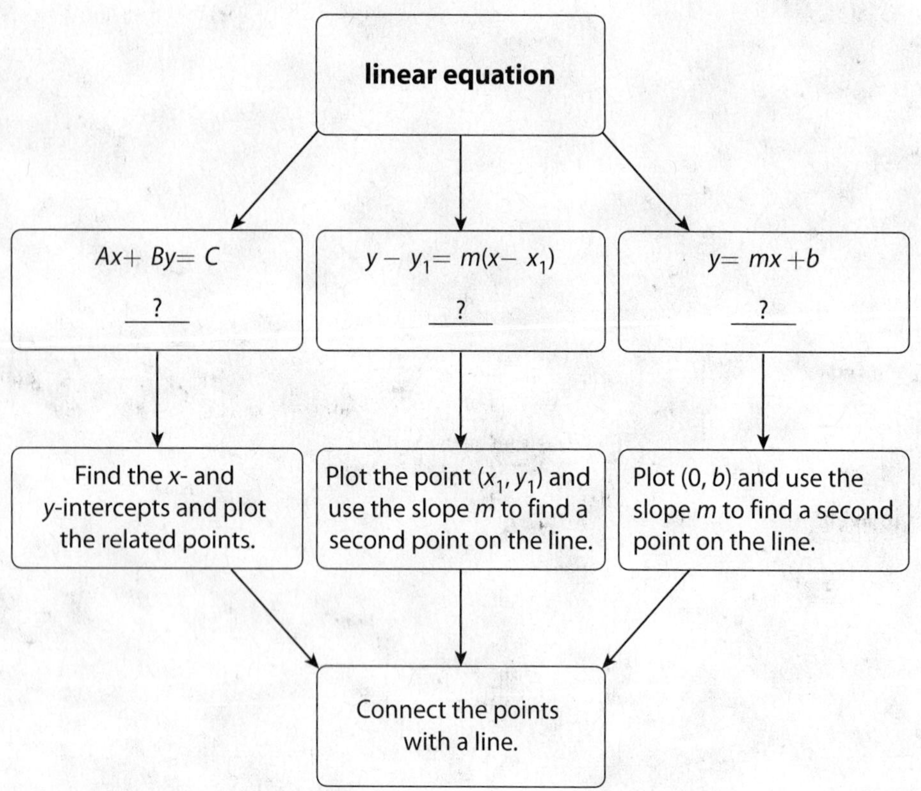
linear equation
$Ax + By = C$
?
$y - y_1 = m(x - x_1)$
?
$y = mx + b$
?
Find the x- and y-intercepts and plot the related points.
Plot the point (x_1, y_1) and use the slope m to find a second point on the line.
Plot (0, b) and use the slope m to find a second point on the line.
Connect the points with a line.

Vocabulary

Review Words

✔ point-slope form *(forma de punto y pendiente)*

✔ slope-intercept form *(forma de pendiente-intersección)*

✔ standard form *(forma estándar)*

x-intercept *(intersección con el eje x)*

y-intercept *(intersección con el eje y)*

Preview Words

intercept form of a quadratic equation *(forma en intersección de una función cuadrática)*

standard form of a quadratic equation *(forma estándar de una ecuación cuadrática)*

vertex form of a quadratic function *(forma en vértice de una función cuadrática)*

Understand Vocabulary

Match the term on the left to the example on the right.

1. __?__ standard form of a quadratic equation A. $y = -(x - 2)^2 + 9$

2. __?__ intercept form of a quadratic equation B. $y = -(x + 1)(x - 5)$

3. __?__ vertex form of a quadratic function C. $y = -x^2 + 4x + 5$

Active Reading

Tri-Fold Before beginning the unit, create a tri-fold to help you learn the concepts and vocabulary in this unit. Fold the paper into three sections. Label the columns "What I Know, "What I Need to Know," and "What I Learned." Complete the first two columns before you read. After studying the unit, complete the third column.

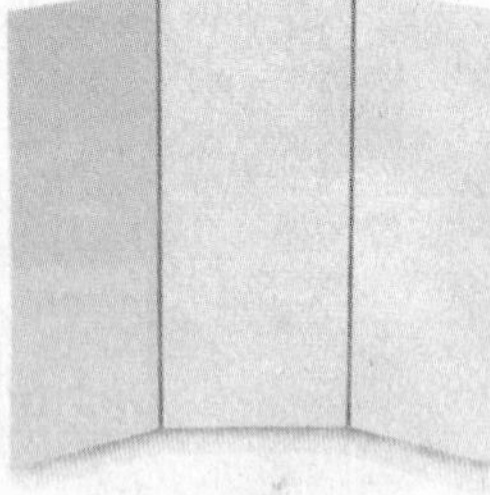

Graphing Quadratic Functions

MODULE 6

Essential Question: How can you use the graph of a quadratic function to solve real-world problems?

REAL WORLD VIDEO
Projectile motion describes the height of an object thrown or fired into the air. The height of a football, volleyball, or any projectile can be modeled by a quadratic equation.

MODULE PERFORMANCE TASK PREVIEW

Throwing for a Completion

Do you wonder how fast a football leaves the hands of a quarterback or how high up it goes? Some professionals can throw approximately 45 miles per hour or faster. The height the ball reaches depends on the initial velocity as well as the angle at which it was thrown. You can use a mathematical model to see how high a football is at different times.

Are YOU Ready?

Complete these exercises to review skills you will need for this module.

Personal Math Trainer

- Online Homework
- Hints and Help
- Extra Practice

Linear Functions

Example 1 Tell whether $6x - 2y = 9$ represents a linear function.

When a linear equation is written in standard form, the following are true.

- x and y both have exponents of 1.
- x and y are not multiplied together.
- x and y do not appear in denominators, exponents, or radicands.

$6x - 2y = 9$ represents a linear function.

Tell whether the equation represents a linear function.

1. $y = 3x^2 + 4x + 1$

2. $3y = 12 - \frac{1}{2}x$

3. $y = 2x + 5$

Algebraic Representations of Transformations

Example 2 The vertices of a triangle are $A(-3, 1)$, $B(0, -2)$, and $C(-4, 2)$. Find the vertices if the figure is translated by the rule $(x, y) \rightarrow (x + 4, y - 3)$.

A $(-3, 1) \rightarrow A'(-3 + 4, 1 - 3)$, so $A'(1, -2)$

B $(0, -2) \rightarrow B'(0 + 4, -2 - 3)$, so $B'(4, -5)$

C $(-4, 2) \rightarrow C'(-4 + 4, 2 - 3)$, so $C'(0, -1)$

Add 4 to each x-coordinate and subtract 3 from each y-coordinate.

The vertices of a triangle are $A(0, 3)$, $B(-2, -4)$, and $C(1, 5)$. Find the new vertices.

4. Use the rule $(x, y) \rightarrow (x - 2, y + 4)$ to translate each vertex.

5. Use the rule $(x, y) \rightarrow (x + 1, y - 2)$ to translate each vertex.

Algebraic Expressions

Example 3 Find the value of $x^2 + 5x - 3$ when $x = 2$.

$x^2 + 5x - 3$

$(2)^2 + 5(2) - 3$ Substitute 2 for x.

$4 + 10 - 3$ Follow the order of operations.

11

Find the value.

6. $x^2 - 7x + 9$ when $x = 6$

7. $2x^2 + 4x - 7$ when $x = -3$

6.1 Understanding Quadratic Functions

Resource Locker

Essential Question: What is the effect of the constant a on the graph of $f(x) = ax^2$?

Explore Understanding the Parent Quadratic Function

A function that can be represented in the form of $f(x) = ax^2 + bx + c$ is called a **quadratic function**. The terms a, b, and c, are constants where $a \neq 0$. The greatest exponent of the variable x is 2. The most basic quadratic function is $f(x) = x^2$, which is the parent quadratic function.

(A) Here is an incomplete table of values for the parent quadratic function. Complete it.

x	$f(x) = x^2$
-3	$f(x) = x^2 = (-3)^2 = 9$
	4
-1	
0	0
1	1
2	
3	

(B) Plot the ordered pairs as points on a graph, and connect the points to sketch a curve.

The curve is called a **parabola**. The point through which the parabola turns direction is called its **vertex**. The vertex occurs at $(0, 0)$ for this function. A vertical line that passes through the vertex and divides the parabola into two symmetrical halves is called the **axis of symmetry**. For this function, the axis of symmetry is the y-axis.

Reflect

1. **Discussion** What is the domain of $f(x) = x^2$?
2. **Discussion** What is the range of $f(x) = x^2$?

Explain 1 Graphing $g(x) = ax^2$ when $a > 0$

The graph $g(x) = ax^2$, is a vertical stretch or compression of its parent function $f(x) = x^2$. The graph opens upward when $a > 0$.

Vertical Stretch

$g(x) = ax^2$ with $|a| > 1$.

The graph of $g(x)$ is narrower than the parent function $f(x)$.

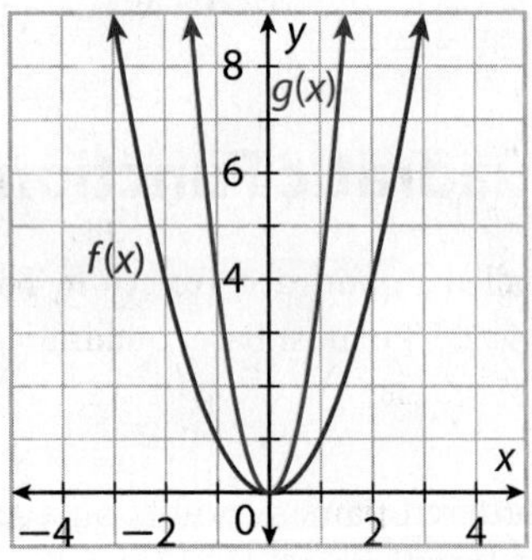

Vertical Compression

$g(x) = ax^2$ with $0 < |a| < 1$.

The graph of $g(x)$ is wider than the parent function $f(x)$.

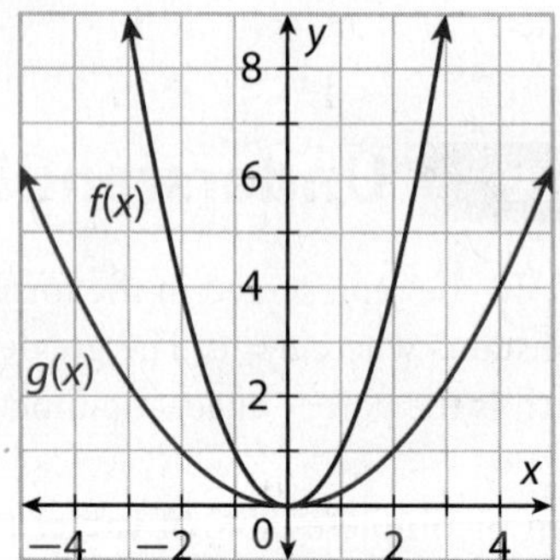

The domain of a quadratic function is all real numbers. When $a > 0$, the graph of $g(x) = ax^2$ opens upward, and the function has a **minimum value** that occurs at the vertex of the parabola. So, the range of $g(x) = ax^2$, where $a > 0$, is the set of real numbers greater than or equal to the minimum value.

Example 1 **Graph each quadratic function by plotting points and sketching the curve. State the domain and range.**

(A) $g(x) = 2x^2$

x	$g(x) = 2x^2$
−3	18
−2	8
−1	2
0	0
1	2
2	8
3	18

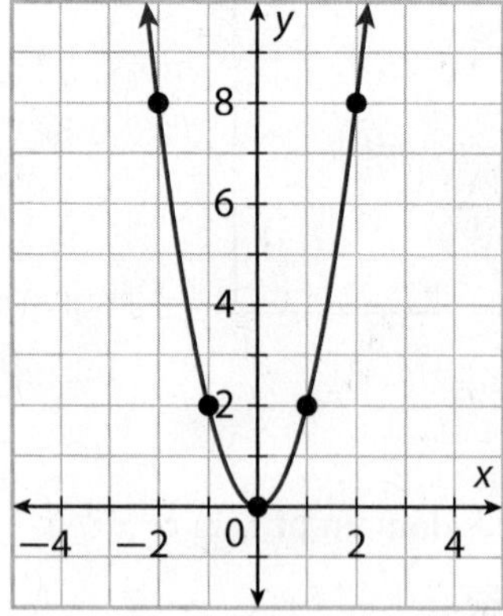

Domain: all real numbers x

Range: $y \geq 0$

Ⓑ $g(x) = \frac{1}{2}x^2$

x	$g(x) = \frac{1}{2}x^2$
−3	$4\frac{1}{2}$
−2	2
0	0
2	2
3	$4\frac{1}{2}$

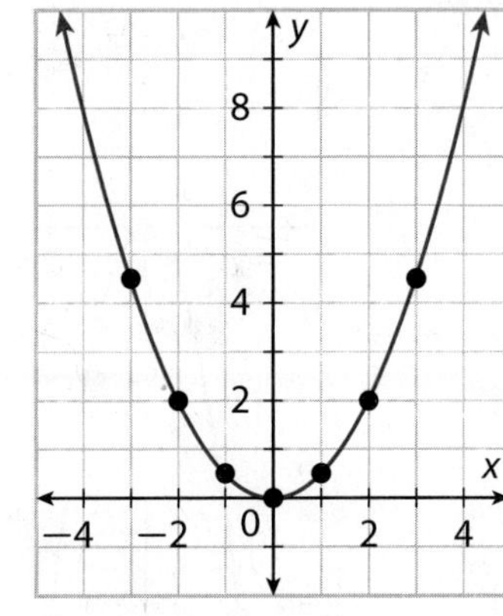

Domain: all real numbers

Range: $y \geq 0$

Reflect

3. For a graph that has a vertical compression or stretch, does the axis of symmetry change?

Your Turn

Graph each quadratic function. State the domain and range.

4. $g(x) = 3x^2$

5. $g(x) = \frac{1}{3}x^2$

Explain 2 Graphing $g(x) = ax^2$ when $a < 0$

The graph of $y = -x^2$ opens downward. It is a reflection of the graph of $y = x^2$ across the x-axis. So, When $a < 0$, the graph of $g(x) = ax^2$ opens downward, and the function has a **maximum value** that occurs at the vertex of the parabola. In this case, the range is the set of real numbers less than or equal to the maximum value.

Vertical Stretch

$g(x) = ax^2$ with $|a| > 1$.

The graph of $g(x)$ is narrower than the parent function $f(x)$.

Vertical Compression

$g(x) = ax^2$ with $0 < |a| < 1$.

The graph of $g(x)$ is wider than the parent function $f(x)$.

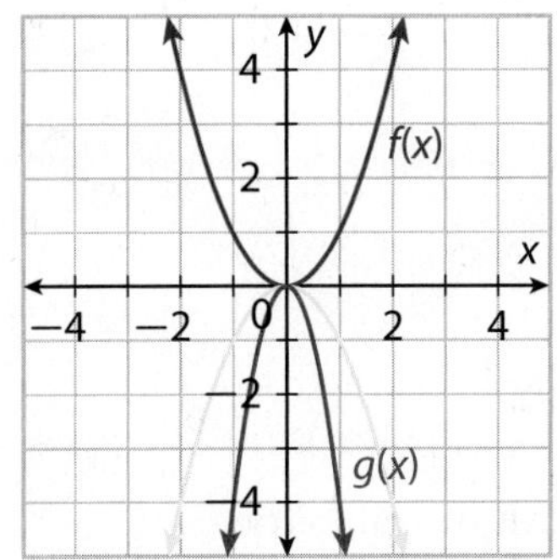

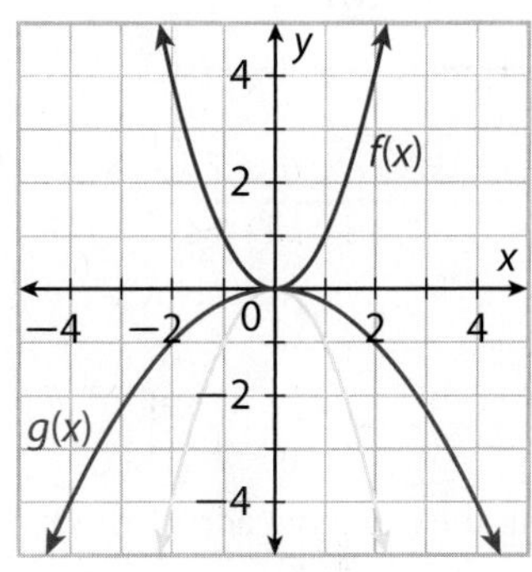

Example 2 **Graph each quadratic function by plotting points and sketching the curve. State the domain and range.**

(A) $g(x) = -2x^2$

x	$g(x) = 2x^2$
−3	−18
−2	−8
−1	−2
0	0
1	−2
2	−8
3	−18

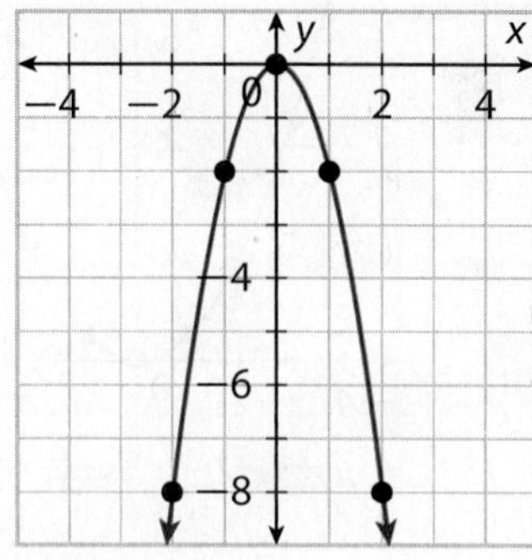

Domain: all real numbers

Range: $y \leq 0$

(B) $g(x) = -\frac{1}{2}x^2$

x	$g(x) = -\frac{1}{2}x^2$
−3	$-4\frac{1}{2}$
−2	−2
−1	$-\frac{1}{2}$
0	−0
1	$-\frac{1}{2}$
2	−2
3	$-4\frac{1}{2}$

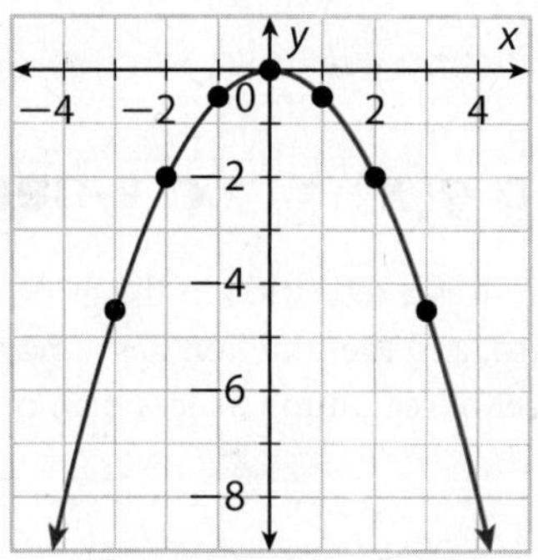

Domain: all real numbers

Range: $y \leq 0$

Reflect

6. Does reflecting the parabola across the x-axis ($a < 0$) change the axis of symmetry?

Your Turn

Graph each function. State the domain and range.

7. $g(x) = -3x^2$

8. $g(x) = -\frac{1}{3}x^2$

Explain 3 Writing a Quadratic Function Given a Graph

You can determine a function rule for a parabola with its vertex at the origin by substituting x and y values for any other point on the parabola into $g(x) = ax^2$ and solving for a.

Example 3 **Write the rule for the quadratic functions shown on the graph.**

(A)

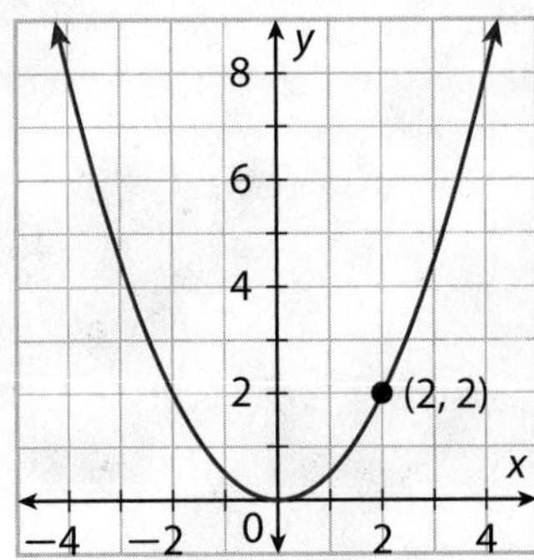

Use the point $(2, 2)$.

Start with the functional form.	$g(x) = ax^2$
Replace x and $g(x)$ with point values.	$2 = a(2)^2$
Evaluate x^2.	$2 = 4a$
Divide both sides by 4 to isolate a.	$\frac{1}{2} = a$
Write the function rule.	$g(x) = \frac{1}{2}x^2$

(B)

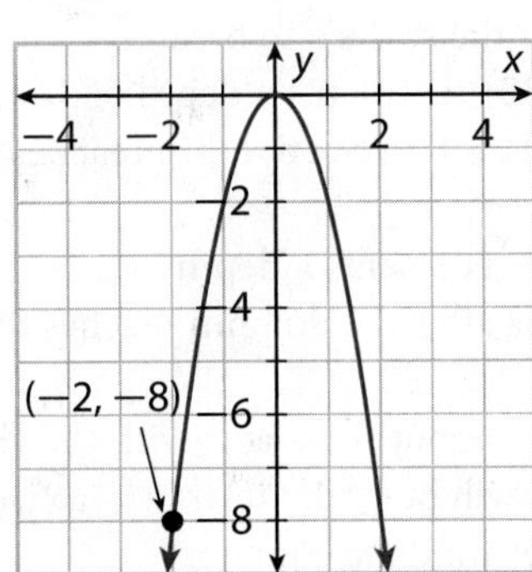

Use the point $(-2, -8)$.

Start with the functional form.	$g(x) = ax^2$
Replace x and $g(x)$ with point values.	$-8 = a(-2)^2$
Evaluate x^2.	$-8 = 4a$
Divide both sides by 4 to isolate a.	$-2 = a$
Write the function rule.	$g(x) = -2x^2$

Your Turn

Write the rule for the quadratic functions shown on the graph.

9.

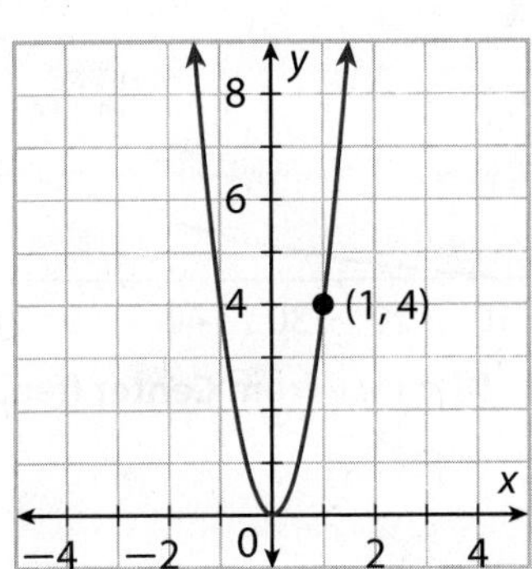

10.

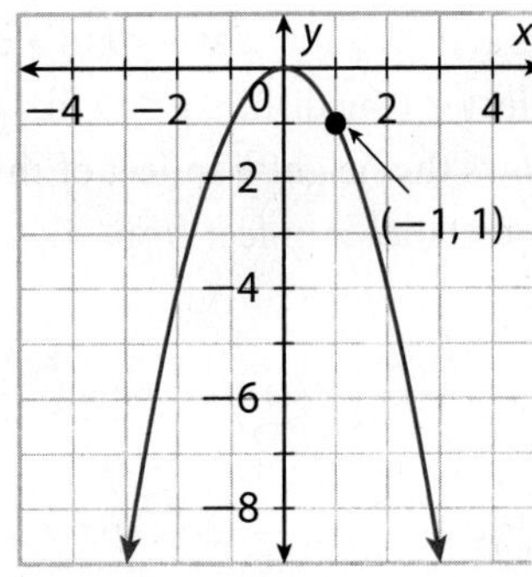

Explain 4 Modeling with a Quadratic Function

Real-world situations can be modeled by parabolas.

Example 4 **For each model, describe what the vertex, y-intercept, and endpoint(s) represent in the situation it models, and then determine the equation of the function.**

(A) This graph models the depth in yards below the water's surface of a dolphin before and after it rises to take a breath and descends again.
The depth d is relative to time t, in seconds, and $t = 0$ is when dolphin reaches a depth of 0 yards at the surface.

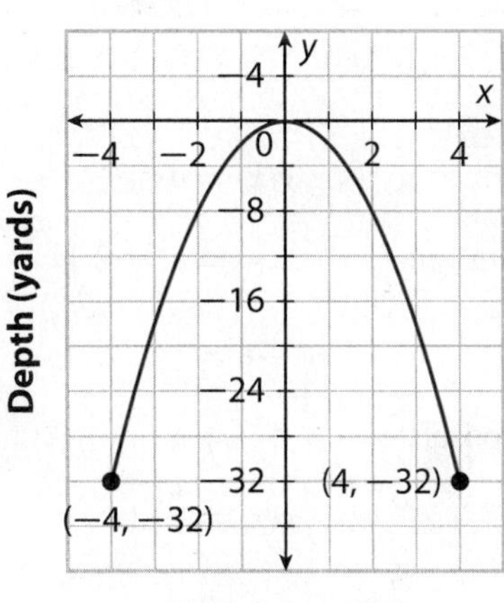

The y-intercept occurs at the vertex of the parabola at $(0, 0)$, where the dolphin is at the surface to breathe.
The endpoint $(-4, -32)$ represents a depth of 32 yards below the surface at 4 seconds before the dolphin reaches the surface to breathe.
The endpoint $(4, -32)$ represents a depth of 32 yards below the surface at 4 seconds after the dolphin reaches the surface to breathe.
The graph is symmetric about the y-axis with the vertex at the origin, so the function will be of the form $y = ax^2$, or $d(t) = at^2$. Use a point to determine the equation.

$d(t) = at^2$

$-32 = a(4)^2$

$-32 = a \cdot 16$

$-2 = a$

The function is $d(t) = -2t^2$.

(B) Satellite dishes reflect radio waves onto a collector by using a reflector (the dish) shaped like a parabola. The graph shows the height h in feet of the reflector relative to the distance x in feet from the center of the satellite dish.

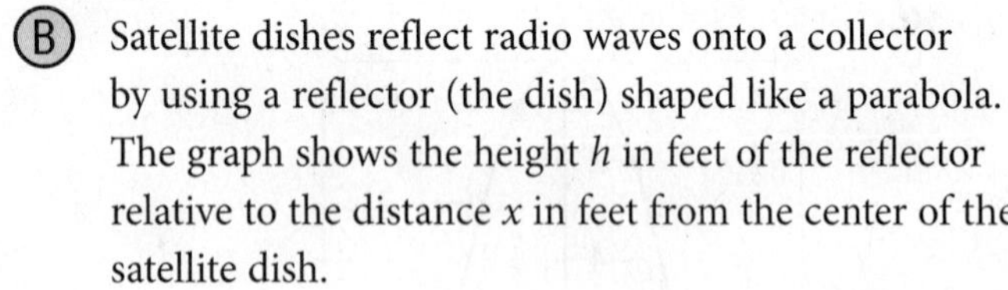

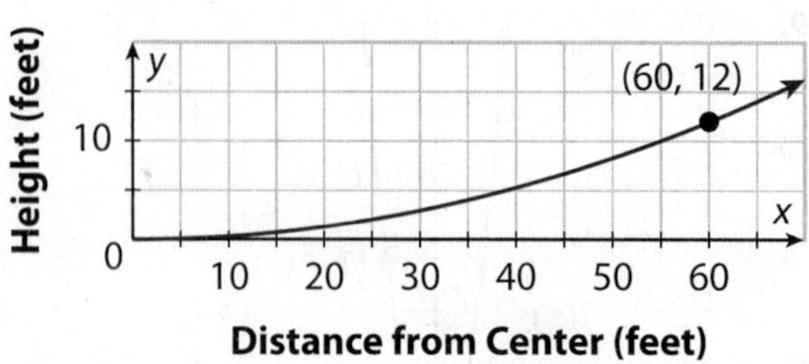

The y-intercept occurs at the vertex, which represents the distance $x = 0$ feet from the center of the dish.
The left end-point represents the height $h = 0$ feet at the center of the dish.
The right end-point represents the height $h = 12$ feet at the distance $x = 60$ feet from the center of the dish.
The function will be of the form $h(x) = ax^2$. Use (60 , 12) to determine the equation.

$h(x) = ax^2$

$12 = a(60)^2$

$12 = 3600a$

$a = \frac{1}{300}$

$h(x) = \frac{1}{300}x^2$

Your Turn

Describe what the vertex, y-intercept, and endpoints represent in the situation, and then determine the equation of the function.

11. The graph shows the height h in feet of a rock dropped down a deep well as a function of time t in seconds.

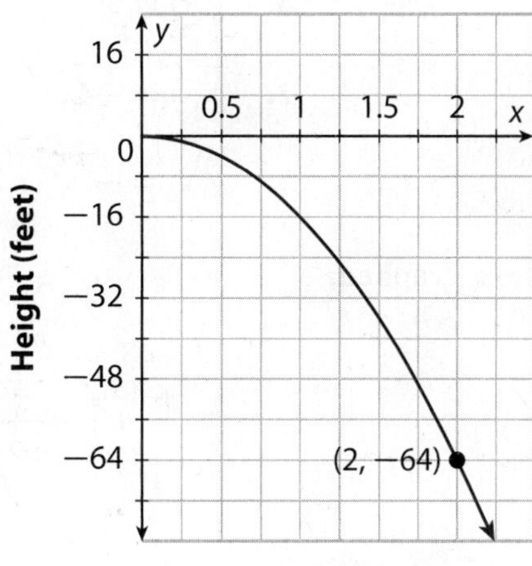

Elaborate

12. Discussion In example 1A the points $(3, 18)$ and $(-3, 18)$ did not fit on the grid. Describe some strategies for selecting points used to guide the shape of the curve.

13. Describe how the axis of symmetry of the parabola sitting on the y-axis can be used to help plot the graph of $f(x) = ax^2$.

14. Essential Question Check-In How can you use the value of a to predict the shape of $f(x) = ax^2$ without plotting points?

Evaluate: Homework and Practice

- Online Homework
- Hints and Help
- Extra Practice

1. Plot the function $f(x) = x^2$ and $g(x) = -x^2$ on a coordinate grid.

Which of the following features are the same and which are different for the two functions?

a. Domain

b. Range

c. Vertex

d. Axis of symmetry

e. Minimum

f. Maximum

Graph each quadratic function. State the domain and range.

2. $g(x) = 4x^2$

3. $g(x) = \frac{1}{4}x^2$

4. $g(x) = \frac{3}{2}x^2$

5. $g(x) = 5x^2$

6. $g(x) = -\frac{1}{4}x^2$

7. $g(x) = -4x^2$

8. $g(x) = -\frac{3}{2}x^2$

9. $g(x) = -5x^2$

Determine the equation of the parabola graphed.

10.

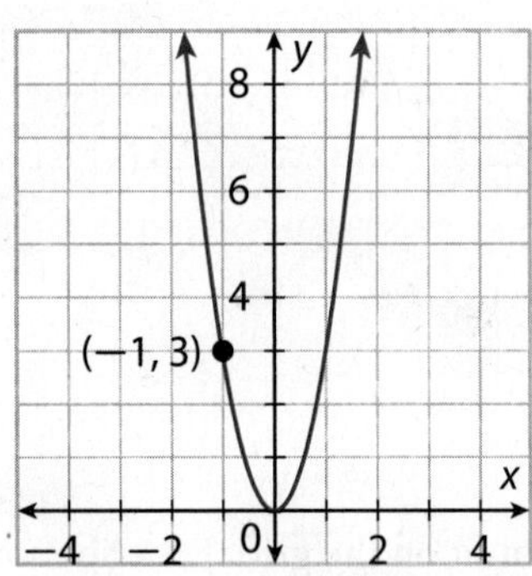

11.

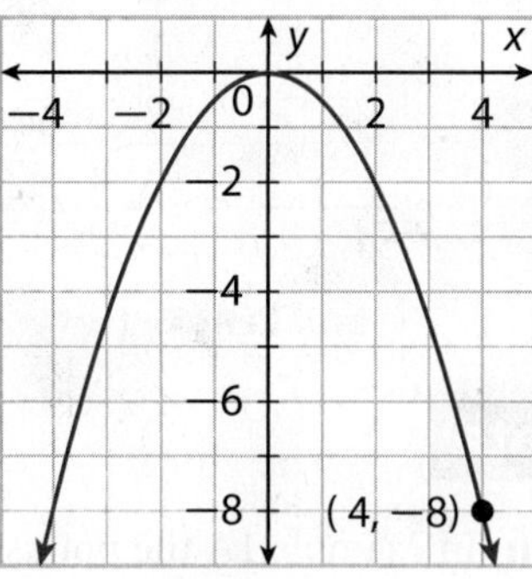

12.

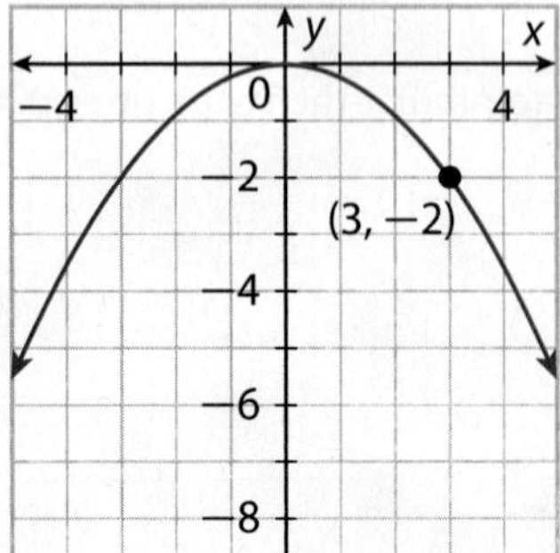

13.

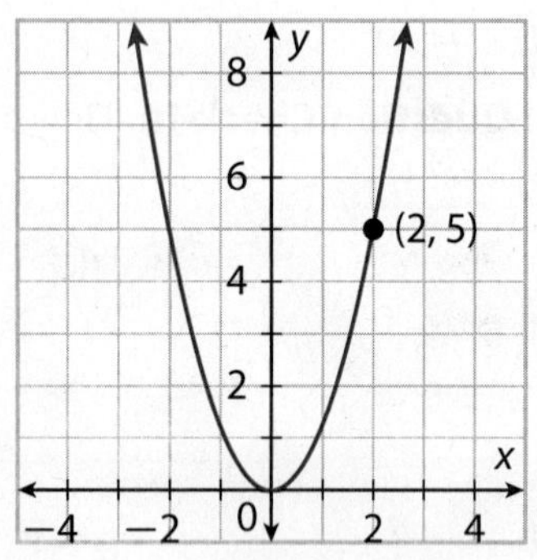

A cannonball fired horizontally appears to travel in a straight line, but drops to earth due to gravity, just like any other object in freefall. The height of the cannonball in freefall is parabolic. The graph shows the change in height of the cannonball (in meters) as a function of distance traveled (in kilometers). Refer to this graph for questions 14 and 15.

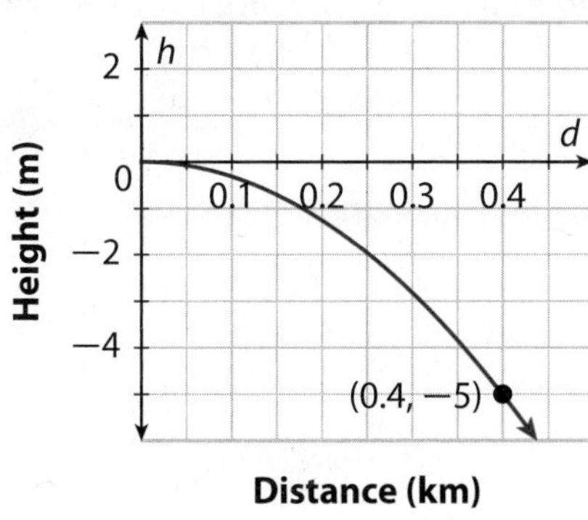

14. Describe what the vertex, y-intercept, and endpoint represent.

15. Find the function $h(d)$ that describes these coordinates.

A slingshot stores energy in the stretched elastic band when it is pulled back. The amount of stored energy versus the pull length is approximately parabolic. Questions 16 and 17 refer to this graph of the stored energy in millijoules versus pull length in centimeters.

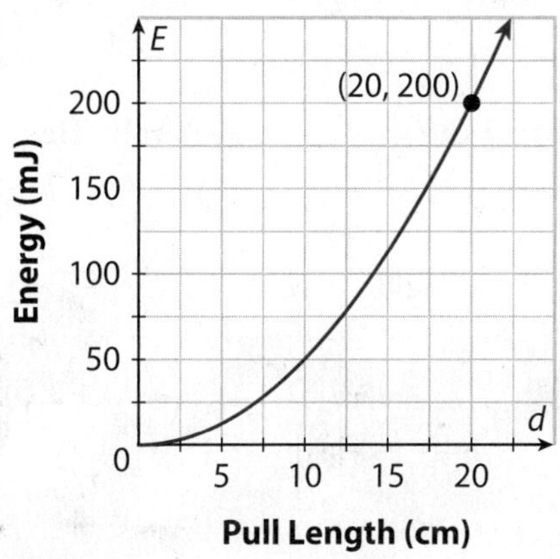

16. Describe what the vertex, y-intercept, and endpoint represent.

17. Determine the function, $E(d)$, that describes this plot.

Newer clean energy sources like solar and wind suffer from unsteady availability of energy. This makes it impractical to eliminate more traditional nuclear and fossil fuel plants without finding a way to store extra energy when it is not available.

One solution being investigated is storing energy in mechanical flywheels. Mechanical flywheels are heavy disks that store energy by spinning rapidly. The graph shows how much energy is in a flywheel, as a function of revolution speed.

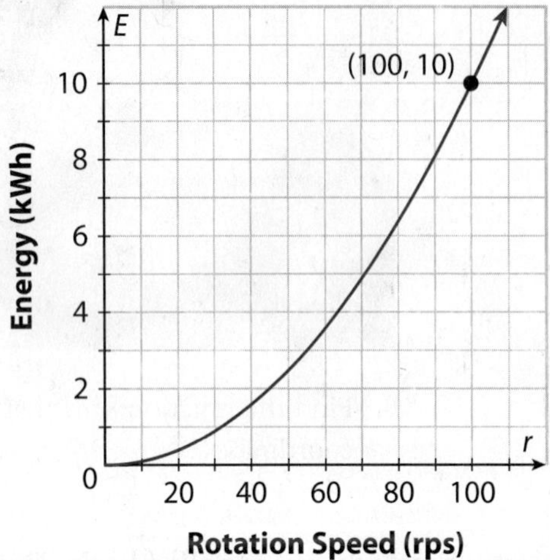

18. Describe what the vertex, y-intercept, and endpoint represent.

19. Determine the function, $E(r)$, that describes this plot.

Phineas is building a homemade skate ramp and wants to model the shape as a parabola. He sketches out a cross section shown in the graph.

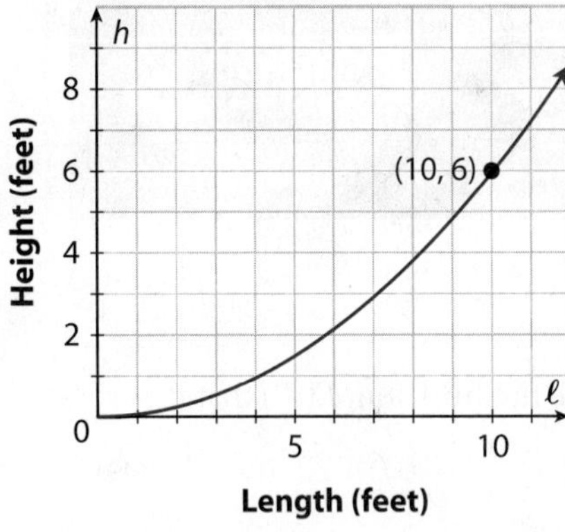

20. Describe what the vertex y-intercept, and endpoint represent.

21. Determine the function, $h(\ell)$, that describes this plot.

H.O.T. Focus on Higher Order Thinking

22. Multipart Classification

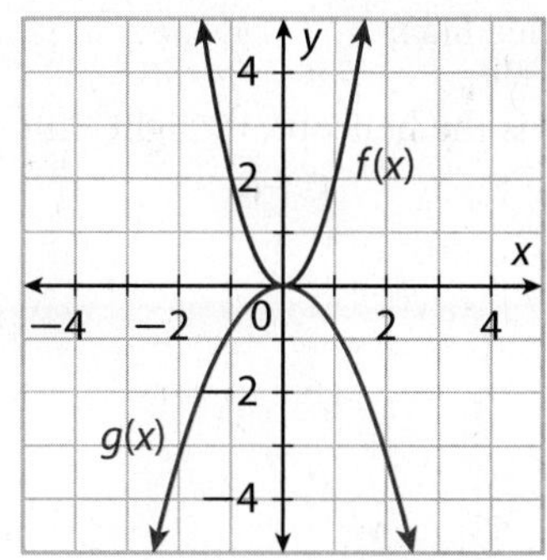

Determine if each statement about $f(x) = x^2$ and $g(x) = ax^2$ is True or False.

a. $a > 1$

b. $a < 0$

c. $a > 0$

d. $|a| < 0$

e. $|a| < 1$

f. The graphs of $f(x)$ and $g(x)$ share a vertex.

g. The graphs share an axis of symmetry.

h. The graphs share a minimum.

i. The graphs share a maximum.

23. Check for Reasonableness The graph of $g(x) = ax^2$ is a parabola that passes through the point $(-2, 2)$. Kyle says the value of a must be $-\frac{1}{2}$. Explain why this value of a is not reasonable.

24. Communicate Mathematical Ideas Explain how you know, without graphing, what the graph of $g(x) = \frac{1}{10}x^2$ looks like.

25. Critical Thinking A quadratic function has a minimum value when the function's graph opens upward, and it has maximum value when the function's graph opens downward. In each case, the minimum or maximum value is the y-coordinate of the vertex of the function's graph. What can you say about a when the function $f(x) = ax^2$ has a minimum value? A maximum value? What is the minimum or maximum value in each case?

Lesson Performance Task

Kylie made a paper helicopter and is testing its flight time from two different heights. The graph compares the height of the helicopter during the two drops. The graph of the first drop is labeled $g(x)$ and the graph of the second drop is labeled $h(x)$.

a. At what heights did Kylie drop the helicopter? What is the helicopter's flight time during each drop?

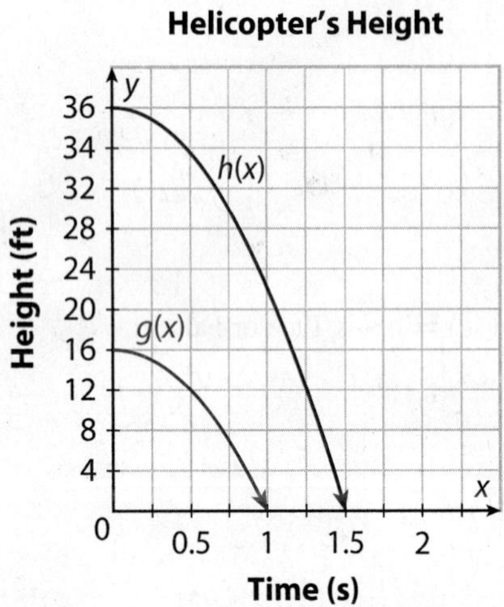

b. If each graph is represented by a function of the form $f(x) = ax^2$, are the coefficients positive or negative? Explain.

c. Estimate the functions for each graph.

6.2 Transforming Quadratic Functions

Resource Locker

Essential Question: How can you obtain the graph of $g(x) = a(x - h)^2 + k$ from the graph of $f(x) = x^2$?

Explore Understanding Quadratic Functions of the Form $g(x) = a(x - h)^2 + k$

Every quadratic function can be represented by an equation of the form $g(x) = a(x - h)^2 + k$. The values of the parameters a, h, and k determine how the graph of the function compares to the graph of the parent function, $y = x^2$. Use the method shown to graph $g(x) = 2(x - 3)^2 + 1$ by transforming the graph of $f(x) = x^2$.

(A) Graph $f(x) = x^2$.

(B) Stretch the graph vertically by a factor of ____ to obtain the graph of $y = 2x^2$. Graph $y = 2x^2$.

Notice that point $(2, 4)$ moves to point ____.

(C) Translate the graph of $y = 2x^2$ right 3 units and up 1 unit to obtain the graph of $g(x) = 2(x - 3)^2 + 1$. Graph $g(x) = 2(x - 3)^2 + 1$.

Notice that point $(2, 8)$ moves to point ____.

(D) The vertex of the graph of $f(x) = x^2$ is ____ while the vertex of the graph of $g(x) = 2(x - 3)^2 + 1$ is ____.

Reflect

1. **Discussion** Compare the minimum values of $f(x) = x^2$ and $g(x) = 2(x - 3)^2 + 1$. How is the minimum value related to the vertex?

2. **Discussion** What is the axis of symmetry of the function $g(x) = 2(x - 3)^2 + 1$? How is the axis of symmetry related to the vertex?

Explain 1 Understanding Vertical Translations

A **vertical translation** of a parabola is a shift of the parabola up or down, with no change in the shape of the parabola.

Vertical Translations of a Parabola
The graph of the function $f(x) = x^2 + k$ is the graph of $f(x) = x^2$ translated vertically.
If $k > 0$, the graph $f(x) = x^2$ is translated k units up.
If $k < 0$, the graph $f(x) = x^2$ is translated $\lvert k \rvert$ units down.

Example 1 **Graph each quadratic function. Give the minimum or maximum value and the axis of symmetry.**

(A) $g(x) = x^2 + 2$

Make a table of values for the parent function $f(x) = x^2$ and for $g(x) = x^2 + 2$. Graph the functions together.

x	$f(x) = x^2$	$g(x) = x^2 + 2$
−3	9	11
−2	4	6
−1	1	3
0	0	2
1	1	3
2	4	6
3	9	11

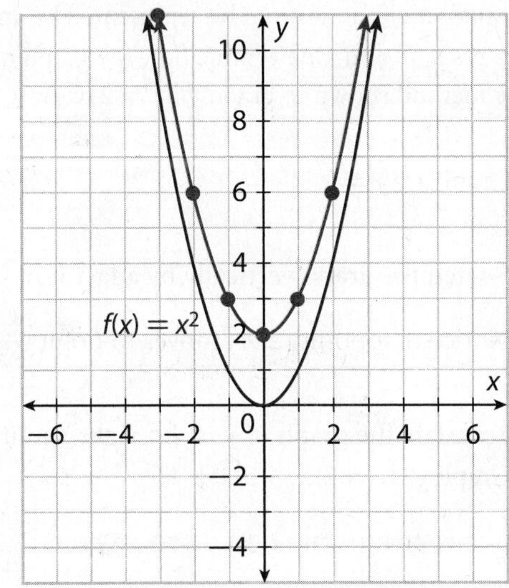

The function $g(x) = x^2 + 2$ has a minimum value of 2.

The axis of symmetry of $g(x) = x^2 + 2$ is $x = 0$.

Ⓑ $g(x) = x^2 - 5$

Make a table of values for the parent function $f(x) = x^2$ and for $g(x) = x^2 - 5$. Graph the functions together.

x	$f(x) = x^2$	$g(x) = x^2 - 5$
−3	9	4
−2	4	−1
−1	1	−4
0	0	−5
1	1	−4
2	4	−1
3	9	4

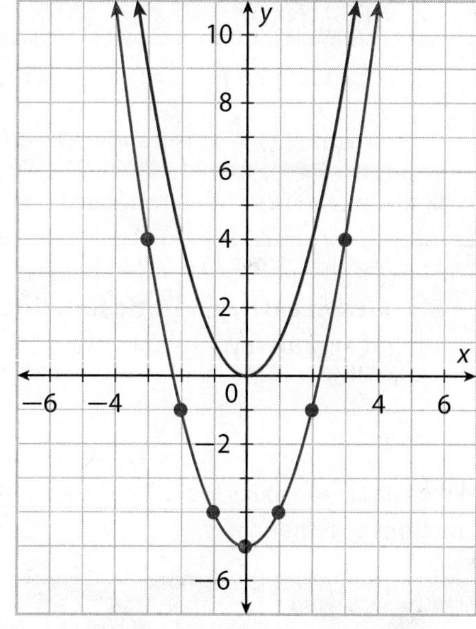

The function $g(x) = x^2 - 5$ has a minimum value of −5.

The axis of symmetry of $g(x) = x^2 - 5$ is $x = 0$.

Reflect

3. How do the values in the table for $g(x) = x^2 + 2$ compare with the values in the table for the parent function $f(x) = x^2$?

4. How do the values in the table for $g(x) = x^2 - 5$ compare with the values in the table for the parent function $f(x) = x^2$?

Your Turn

Graph each quadratic function. Give the minimum or maximum value and the axis of symmetry.

5. $g(x) = x^2 + 4$

6. $g(x) = x^2 - 7$

Explain 2 Understanding Horizontal Translations

A **horizontal translation** of a parabola is a shift of the parabola left or right, with no change in the shape of the parabola.

Horizontal Translations of a Parabola

The graph of the function $f(x) = (x - h)^2$ is the graph of $f(x) = x^2$ translated horizontally.

If $h > 0$, the graph $f(x) = x^2$ is translated h units right.

If $h < 0$, the graph $f(x) = x^2$ is translated h units left.

Example 2 **Graph each quadratic function. Give the minimum or maximum value and the axis of symmetry.**

(A) $g(x) = (x - 1)^2$

Make a table of values for the parent function $f(x) = x^2$ and for $g(x) = (x - 1)^2$. Graph the functions together.

x	$f(x) = x^2$	$g(x) = (x-1)^2$
−3	9	16
−2	4	9
−1	1	4
0	0	1
1	1	0
2	4	1
3	9	4

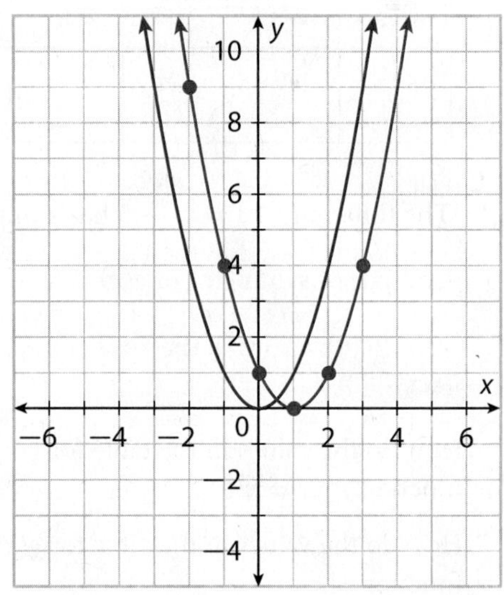

The function $g(x) = (x - 1)^2$ has a minimum value of 0.

The axis of symmetry of $g(x) = (x - 1)^2$ is $x = 1$.

(B) $g(x) = (x + 1)^2$

Make a table of values and graph the functions together.

x	$f(x) = x^2$	$g(x) = (x + 1)^2$
−3	9	4
−2	4	1
−1	1	0
0	0	1
1	1	4
2	4	9
3	9	16

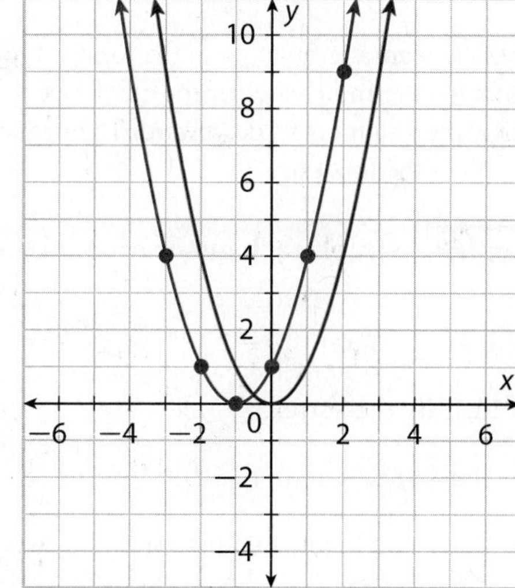

The function $g(x) = (x + 1)^2$ has a minimum value of 0.

The axis of symmetry of $g(x) = (x + 1)^2$ is $x = -1$.

Reflect

7. How do the values in the table for $g(x) = (x - 1)^2$ compare with the values in the table for the parent function $f(x) = x^2$?

8. How do the values in the table for $g(x) = (x + 1)^2$ compare with the values in the table for the parent function $f(x) = x^2$?

Your Turn

Graph each quadratic function. Give the minimum or maximum value and the axis of symmetry.

9. $g(x) = (x - 2)^2$

10. $g(x) = (x + 3)^2$

Explain 3 Graphing $g(x) = a(x - h)^2 + k$

The **vertex form of a quadratic function** is $g(x) = a(x - h)^2 + k$, where the point (h, k) is the vertex. The *axis of symmetry* of a quadratic function in this form is the vertical line $x = h$.

To graph a quadratic function in the form $g(x) = a(x - h)^2 + k$, first identify the vertex (h, k). Next, consider the sign of a to determine whether the graph opens upward or downward. If a is positive, the graph opens upward. If a is negative, the graph opens downward. Then generate two points on each side of the vertex. Using those points, sketch the graph of the function.

Example 3 **Graph each quadratic function.**

Ⓐ $g(x) = -3(x + 1)^2 - 2$

Identify the vertex.

The vertex is at $(-1, -2)$.

Make a table for the function. Find two points on each side of the vertex.

x	−3	−2	−1	0	1
$g(x)$	−14	−5	−2	−5	−14

Plot the points and draw a parabola through them.

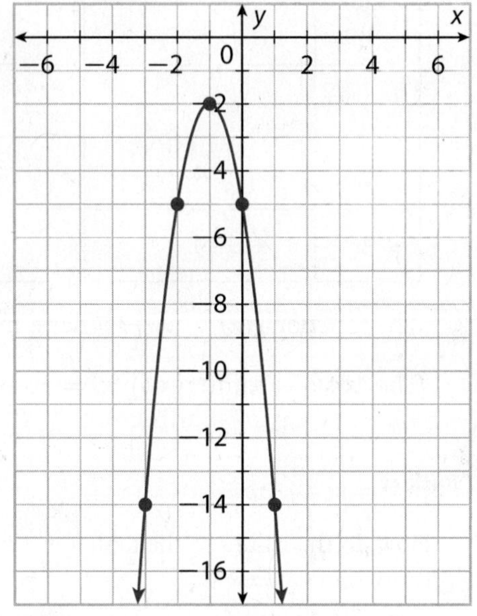

Ⓑ $g(x) = 2(x - 1)^2 - 7$

Identify the vertex.

The vertex is at $(1, -7)$.

Make a table for the function. Find two points on each side of the vertex.

x	−2	0	1	2	4
$g(x)$	11	−5	−7	−5	11

Plot the points and draw a parabola through them.

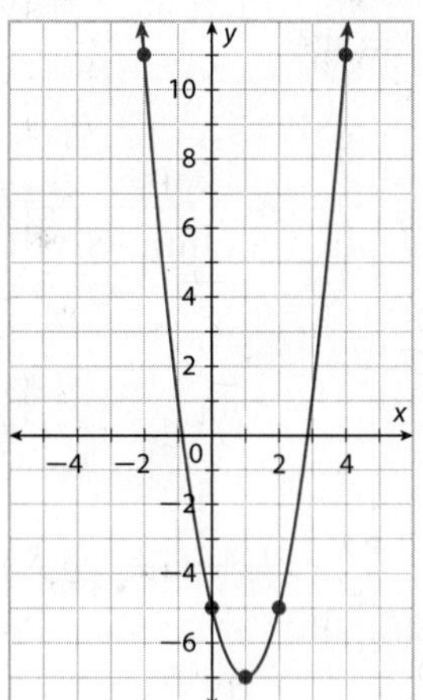

Reflect

11. How do you tell from the equation whether the vertex is a maximum value or a minimum value?

Your Turn

Graph each quadratic function.

12. $g(x) = -(x - 2)^2 + 4$

13. $g(x) = 2(x + 3)^2 - 1$

Elaborate

14. How does the value of k in $g(x) = x^2 + k$ affect the translation of $f(x) = x^2$?

15. How does the value of h in $g(x) = (x - h)^2$ affect the translation of $f(x) = x^2$?

16. In $g(x) = a(x - h)^2 + k$, what are the coordinates of the vertex?

17. **Essential Question Check-In** How can you use the values of a, h, and k, to obtain the graph of $g(x) = a(x - h)^2 + k$ from the graph $f(x) = x^2$?

Evaluate: Homework and Practice

- Online Homework
- Hints and Help
- Extra Practice

Graph each quadratic function by transforming the graph of $f(x) = x^2$. Describe the transformations.

1. $g(x) = 2(x - 2)^2 + 5$

2. $g(x) = 2(x + 3)^2 - 6$

3. $g(x) = \frac{1}{2}(x - 3)^2 - 4$

4. $g(x) = 3(x - 4)^2 - 2$

Graph each quadratic function.

5. $g(x) = x^2 - 2$

6. $g(x) = x^2 + 5$

7. $g(x) = x^2 - 6$

8. $g(x) = x^2 + 3$

9. Graph $g(x) = x^2 - 9$. Give the minimum or maximum value and the axis of symmetry.

10. How is the graph of $g(x) = x^2 + 12$ related to the graph of $f(x) = x^2$?

Graph each quadratic function. Give the minimum or maximum value and the axis of symmetry.

11. $g(x) = (x - 3)^2$

12. $g(x) = (x + 2)^2$

13. How is the graph of $g(x) = (x + 12)^2$ related to the graph of $f(x) = x^2$?

14. How is the graph of $g(x) = (x - 10)^2$ related to the graph of $f(x) = x^2$?

15. Compare the given graph to the graph of the parent function $f(x) = x^2$. Describe how the parent function must be translated to get the graph shown here.

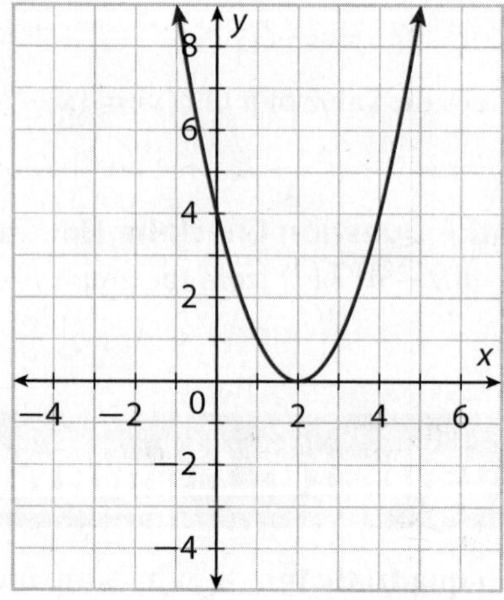

16. For the function $g(x) = (x - 9)^2$ give the minimum or maximum value and the axis of symmetry.

Graph each quadratic function. Give the minimum or maximum value and the axis of symmetry.

17. $g(x) = (x - 1)^2 - 5$

18. $g(x) = -(x + 2)^2 + 5$

19. $g(x) = \frac{1}{4}(x + 1)^2 - 7$

20. $g(x) = -\frac{1}{3}(x + 3)^2 + 8$

21. Compare the given graph to the graph of the parent function $f(x) = x^2$. Describe how the parent function must be translated to get the graph shown here.

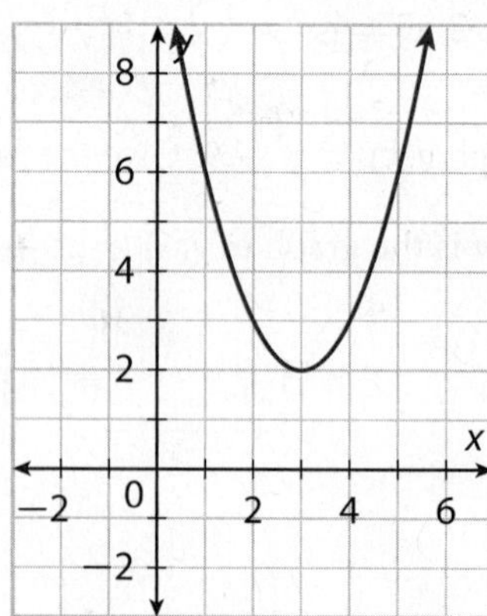

22. **Multiple Representations** If the graph of $f(x) = x^2$ is translated 11 units to the left and 5 units down, which function is represented by the translated graph?

a. $g(x) = (x - 11)^2 - 5$
b. $g(x) = (x + 11)^2 - 5$
c. $g(x) = (x + 11)^2 + 5$
d. $g(x) = (x - 11)^2 + 5$
e. $g(x) = (x - 5)^2 - 11$
f. $g(x) = (x - 5)^2 + 11$
g. $g(x) = (x + 5)^2 - 11$
h. $g(x) = (x + 5)^2 + 11$

H.O.T. Focus on Higher Order Thinking

Critical Thinking Use a graphing calculator to compare the graphs of $y = (2x)^2$, $y = (3x)^2$, and $y = (4x)^2$ with the graph of the parent function $y = x^2$. Then compare the graphs of $y = \left(\frac{1}{2}x\right)^2$, $y = \left(\frac{1}{3}x\right)^2$, and $y = \left(\frac{1}{4}x\right)^2$ with the graph of the parent function $y = x^2$.

23. Explain how the parameter b horizontally stretches or compresses the graph of $y = (bx)^2$ when $b > 1$.

24. Explain how the parameter b horizontally stretches or compresses the graph of $y = (bx)^2$ when $0 < b < 1$.

25. **Explain the Error** Nina is trying to write an equation for the function represented by the graph of a parabola that is a translation of $f(x) = x^2$. The graph has been translated 4 units to the right and 2 units up. She writes the function as $g(x) = (x + 4)^2 + 2$. Explain the error.

26. **Multiple Representations** A group of engineers drop an experimental tennis ball from a catwalk and let it fall to the ground. The tennis ball's height above the ground (in feet) is given by a function of the form $f(t) = a(t - h)^2 + k$ where t is the time (in seconds) after the tennis ball was dropped. Use the graph to find the equation for $f(t)$.

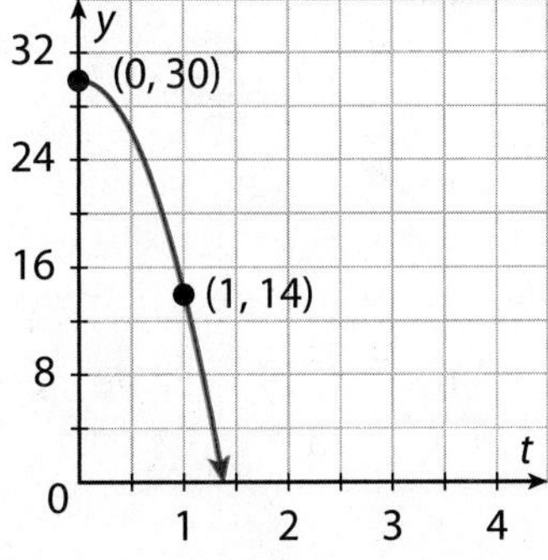

27. **Make a Prediction** For what values of a and c will the graph of $f(x) = ax^2 + c$ have one x-intercept?

Lesson Performance Task

The path a baseball takes after it has been hit is modeled by the graph. The baseball's height above the ground is given by a function of the form $f(t) = a(t - h)^2 + k$, where t is the time in seconds since the baseball was hit.

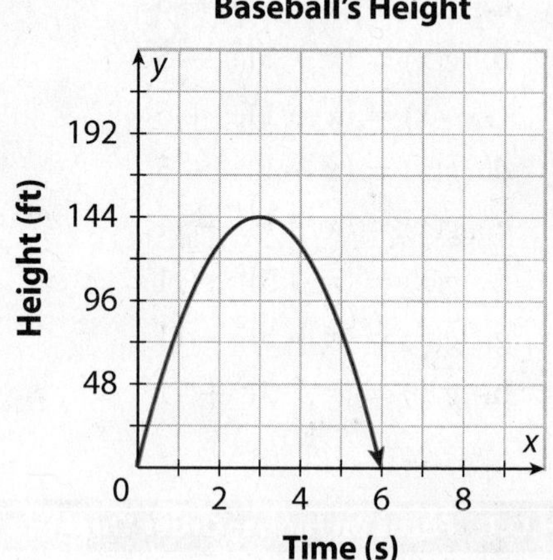

a. What is the baseball's maximum height? At what time was the baseball at its maximum height?

b. When does the baseball hit the ground?

c. Find an equation for $f(t)$.

d. A player hits a second baseball. The second baseball's path is modeled by the function $g(t) = -16(t - 4)^2 + 256$. Which baseball has a greater maximum height? Which baseball is in the air for the longest?

6.3 Interpreting Vertex Form and Standard Form

Resource Locker

Essential Question: How can you change the vertex form of a quadratic function to standard form?

Explore Identifying Quadratic Functions from Their Graphs

Determine whether a function is a quadratic function by looking at its graph. If the graph of a function is a parabola, then the function is a quadratic function. If the graph of a function is not a parabola, then the function is not a quadratic function.

Use a graphing calculator to graph each of the functions. Set the viewing window to show −10 to 10 on both axes. Determine whether each function is a quadratic function.

(A) Use a graphing calculator to graph $f(x) = x + 1$.

(B) Determine whether the function $f(x) = x + 1$ is a quadratic function.

The function $f(x) = x + 1$ ______ a quadratic function.

(C) Use a graphing calculator to graph $f(x) = x^2 + 2x - 6$.

(D) Determine whether the function $f(x) = x^2 + 2x - 6$ is a quadratic function.

The function $f(x) = x^2 + 2x - 6$ ______ a quadratic function.

(E) Use a graphing calculator to graph $f(x) = 2^x$.

(F) Determine whether the function $f(x) = 2^x$ is a quadratic function.

The function $f(x) = 2^x$ ______ a quadratic function.

(G) Use a graphing calculator to graph $f(x) = 2x^2 - 3$.

(H) Determine whether the function $f(x) = 2x^2 - 3$ is a quadratic function.

The function $f(x) = 2x^2 - 3$ ______ a quadratic function.

(I) Use a graphing calculator to graph $f(x) = -(x - 3)^2 + 7$.

(J) Determine whether the function $f(x) = -(x - 3)^2 + 7$ is a quadratic function.

The function $f(x) = -(x - 3)^2 + 7$ ______ a quadratic function.

(K) Use a graphing calculator to graph $f(x) = \sqrt{x}$.

(L) Determine whether the function $f(x) = \sqrt{x}$ is a quadratic function.

The function $f(x) = \sqrt{x}$ ______ a quadratic function.

Reflect

1. How can you determine whether a function is quadratic or not by looking at its graph?
2. **Discussion** How can you tell if a function is a quadratic function by looking at the equation?

Explain 1 Identifying Quadratic Functions in Standard Form

If a function is quadratic, it can be represented by an equation of the form $y = ax^2 + bx + c$, where a, b, and c are real numbers and $a \neq 0$. This is called the **standard form of a quadratic equation**.

The axis of symmetry for a quadratic equation in standard form is given by the equation $x = -\frac{b}{2a}$. The vertex of a quadratic equation in standard form is given by the coordinates $\left(-\frac{b}{2a}, f\left(-\frac{b}{2a}\right)\right)$.

Example 1 **Determine whether the function represented by each equation is quadratic. If so, give the axis of symmetry and the coordinates of the vertex.**

(A) $y = -2x + 20$

$y = -2x + 20$ Compare to $y = ax^2 + bx + c$.

This is not a quadratic function because $a = 0$.

(B) $y + 3x^2 = -4$

Rewrite the function in the form $y = ax^2 + bx + c$.

$y = -3x^2 - 4$

Compare to $y = ax^2 + bx + c$.

This is a quadratic function.

If $y + 3x\ 2 = -4$ is a quadratic function, give the axis of symmetry.

$x = 0$

If $y + 3x\ 2 = -4$ is a quadratic function, give the coordinates of the vertex.

$(0, -4)$.

Reflect

3. Explain why the function represented by the equation $y = ax^2 + bx + c$ is quadratic only when $a \neq 0$.

4. Why might it be easier to determine whether a function is quadratic when it is expressed in function notation?

5. How is the axis of symmetry related to standard form?

Your Turn

Determine whether the function represented by each equation is quadratic.

6. $y - 4x + x^2 = 0$

7. $x + 2y = 14x + 6$

Explain 2 Changing from Vertex Form to Standard Form

It is possible to write quadratic equations in various forms.

Example 2 **Rewrite a quadratic function from vertex form, $y = a(x - h)^2 + k$, to standard form, $y = ax^2 + bx + c$.**

Ⓐ $y = 4(x - 6)^2 + 3$

$y = 4(x^2 - 12x + 36) + 3$ Expand $(x - 6)^2$.

$y = 4x^2 - 48x + 144 + 3$ Multiply.

$y = 4x^2 - 48x + 147$ Simplify.

The standard form of $y = 4(x - 6)^2 + 3$ is $y = 4x^2 - 48x + 147$.

Ⓑ $y = -3(x + 2)^2 - 1$

$y = -3(\boxed{x^2 + 4x + 4}) - 1$ Expand $(x + 2)^2$.

$y = \boxed{-3x^2 - 12x - 12} - 1$ Multiply.

$y = \boxed{-3x^2 - 12x - 13}$ Simplify.

The standard form of $y = -3(x + 2)^2 - 1$ is $y = \boxed{-3x^2 - 12x - 13}$.

Reflect

8. If in $y = a(x - h)^2 + k$, $a = 1$, what is the simplified form of the standard form, $y = ax^2 + bx + c$?

Your Turn

Rewrite a quadratic function from vertex form, $y = a(x - h)^2 + k$, to standard form, $y = ax^2 + bx + c$.

9. $y = 2(x + 5)^2 + 3$

10. $y = -3(x - 7)^2 + 2$

Explain 3 Writing a Quadratic Function Given a Table of Values

You can write a quadratic function from a table of values.

Example 3 **Use each table to write a quadratic function in vertex form, $y = a(x - h)^2 + k$. Then rewrite the function in standard form, $y = ax^2 + bx + c$.**

(A) The minimum value of the function occurs at −3.

x	y
−6	9
−4	1
−3	0
−2	1
0	9

The vertex of the parabola is $(-3, 0)$.

Substitute the values for h and k into $y = a(x - h)^2 + k$.

$y = a(x - (-3))^2 + 0$, or $y = a(x + 3)^2$

Use any point from the table to find a.

$y = a(x + 3)^2$

$1 = a(-2 + 3)^2 = a$

The vertex form of the function is $y = 1(x - (-3))^2 + 0$ or $y = (x + 3)^2$.

Rewrite the function $y = (x + 3)^2$ in standard form, $y = ax^2 + bx + c$.

$y = (x + 3)^2 = x^2 + 6x + 9$

The standard form of the function is $y = x^2 + 6x + 9$.

(B) The minimum value of the function occurs at −3.

x	y
0	13
−1	1
−2	−3
−3	1
−4	13

The vertex of the parabola is is $(-2, -3)$.

Substitute the values for h and k into $y = a(x - h)^2 + k$.

$y =$ $a(x + 2)^2 - 3$

Use any point from the table to find a. $a =$ 4

The vertex form of the function is $y =$ $4(x + 2)^2 - 3$.

Rewrite the resulting function in standard form, $y = ax^2 + bx + c$.

$y =$ $4x^2 + 16x + 13$

Reflect

11. How many points are needed to find an equation of a quadratic function?

Your Turn

Use each table to write a quadratic function in vertex form, $y = a(x - h)^2 + k$. Then rewrite the function in standard form, $y = ax^2 + bx + c$.

12. The vertex of the function is (2, 5).

x	y
−1	59
1	11
2	5
3	11
5	59

13. The vertex of the function is $(-2, -7)$.

x	y
0	−27
−1	−12
−2	−7
−3	−12
−4	−27

Explain 4 Writing a Quadratic Function Given a Graph

The graph of a parabola can be used to determine the corresponding function.

Example 4 **Use each graph to find an equation for $f(t)$.**

(A) A house painter standing on a ladder drops a paintbrush, which falls to the ground. The paintbrush's height above the ground (in feet) is given by a function of the form $f(t) = a(t - h)^2$ where t is the time (in seconds) after the paintbrush is dropped.

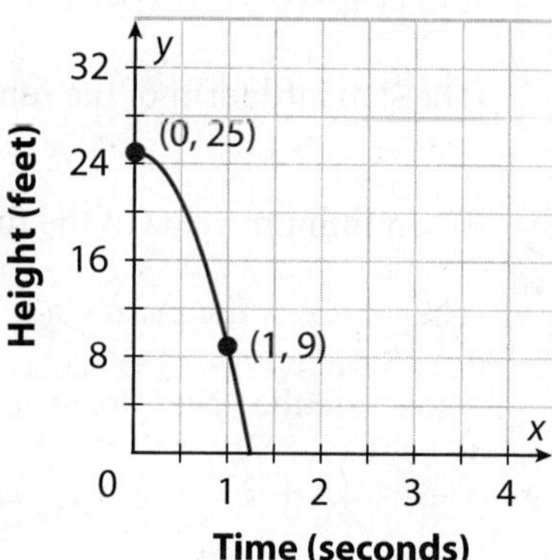

The vertex of the parabola is $(h, k) = (0, 25)$.

$f(t) = a(x - h)^2 + k$

$f(t) = a(t - 0)^2 + 25$

$f(t) = at^2 + 25$

Use the point (1, 9) to find a.

$f(t) = at^2 + 25$

$9 = a(1)^2 + 25$

$-16 = a$

The equation for the function is $f(t) = -16t^2 + 25$.

Ⓑ A rock is knocked off a cliff into the water far below. The falling rock's height above the water (in feet) is given by a function of the form $f(t) = a(t-h)^2 + k$ where t is the time (in seconds) after the rock begins to fall.

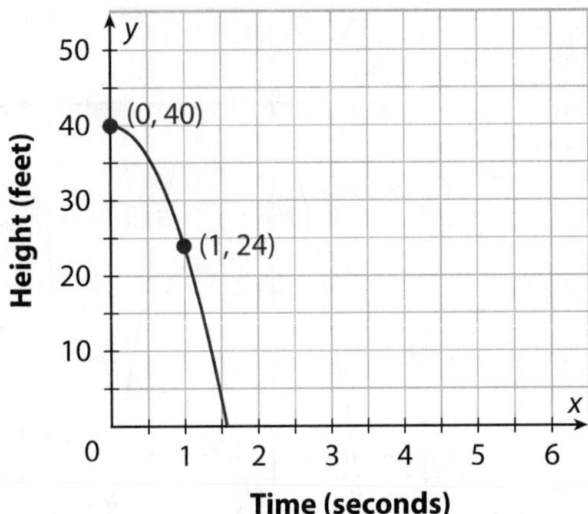

The vertex of the parabola is $(h, k) =$ $(0, 40)$.

$f(t) = a(t-h)^2 + k$

$f(t) = a(t - 0)^2 + 40$.

$f(t) = at^2 + 40$

Use the point $(1, 24)$ to find a.

$f(t) = at^2 + 40$

$24 = a(1)^2 + 40$

$a = -16$

The equation for the function is $f(t) = -16t^2 + 40$.

Reflect

14. Identify the domain and explain why it makes sense for this problem.

15. Identify the range and explain why it makes sense for this problem.

Your Turn

16. The graph of a function in the form $f(x) = a(x - h)^2 + k$, is shown. Use the graph to find an equation for $f(x)$.

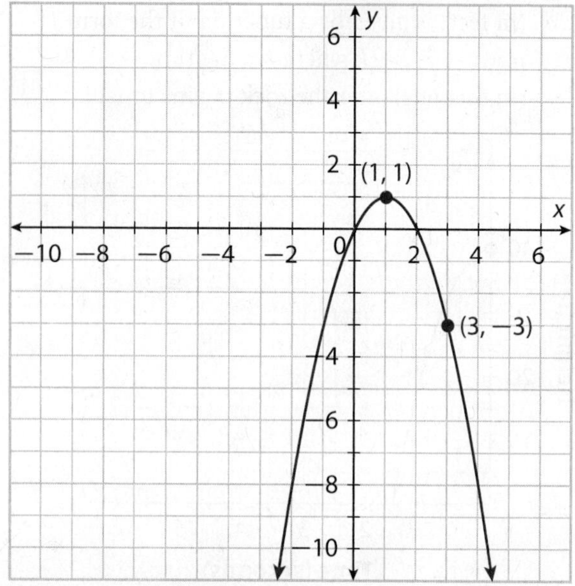

17. A roofer accidentally drops a nail, which falls to the ground. The nail's height above the ground (in feet) is given by a function of the form $f(t) = a(t - h)^2 + k$, where t is the time (in seconds) after the nail drops. Use the graph to find an equation for $f(t)$.

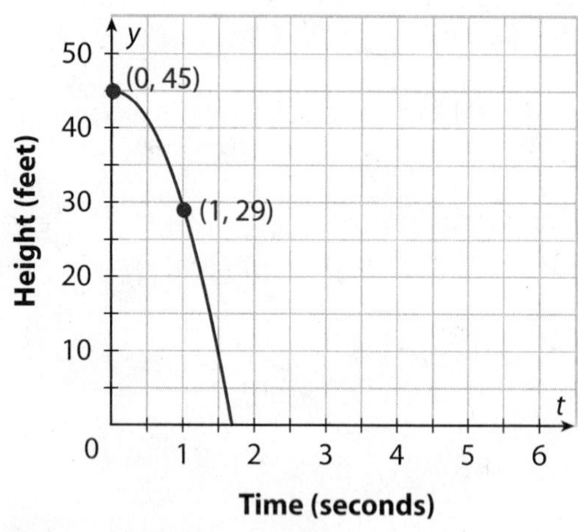

Elaborate

18. Describe the graph of a quadratic function.

19. What is the standard form of the quadratic function?

20. Can any quadratic function in vertex form be written in standard form?

21. How many points are needed to write a quadratic function in vertex form, given the table of values?

22. If a graph of the quadratic function is given, how do you find the vertex?

23. **Essential Question Check-In** What can you do to change the vertex form of a quadratic function to standard form?

Evaluate: Homework and Practice

- Online Homework
- Hints and Help
- Extra Practice

Determine whether each function is a quadratic function by graphing.

1. $f(x) = 0.01 - 0.2x + x^2$
2. $f(x) = \frac{1}{2}x - 4$
3. $f(x) = -4x^2 - 2$
4. $f(x) = 2^{x-3}$

Determine whether the function represented by each equation is quadratic.

5. $y = -3x + 15$
6. $y - 6 = 2x^2$
7. $3 + y + 5x^2 = 6x$
8. $y + 6x = 14$
9. Which of the following functions is a quadratic function? Select all that apply.

   a. $2x = y + 3$

   b. $2x^2 + y = 3x - 1$

   c. $5 = -6x + y$

   d. $6x^2 + y = 0$

   e. $y - x = 4$
10. For $f(x) = x^2 + 8x - 14$, give the axis of symmetry and the coordinates of the vertex.
11. Describe the axis of symmetry of the graph of the quadratic function represented by the equation $y = ax^2 + bx + c$. when $b = 0$.

Rewrite each quadratic function from vertex form, $y = a(x - h)^2 + k$, to standard form, $y = ax^2 + bx + c$.

12. $y = 5(x - 2)^2 + 7$
13. $y = -2(x + 4)^2 - 11$
14. $y = 3(x + 1)^2 + 12$
15. $y = -4(x - 3)^2 - 9$
16. **Explain the Error** Tim wrote $y = -6(x + 2)^2 - 10$ in standard form as $y = 6x^2 + 24x + 14$. Find his error.
17. How do you change from vertex form, $f(x) = a(x - h)^2 + k$, to standard form, $y = ax^2 + bx + c$?

Use each table to write a quadratic function in vertex form, $y = a(x - h)^2 + k$. Then rewrite the function in standard form, $y = ax^2 + bx + c$.

18. The vertex of the function is (6, −8).

x	y
10	24
8	0
6	−8
4	0
2	24

19. The vertex of the function is (4, 7).

x	y
0	−1
2	5
4	7
6	5
8	−1

20. The vertex of the function is (−2, −12).

x	y
2	52
0	4
−2	−11
−4	4
−6	52

21. The vertex of the function is (−3, 10).

x	y
−1	−6
−2	6
−3	10
−4	6
−5	−6

H.O.T. Focus on Higher Order Thinking

22. Make a Prediction A ball was thrown off a bridge. The table relates the height of the ball above the ground in feet to the time in seconds after it was thrown. Use the data to write a quadratic model in vertex form and convert it to standard form. Use the model to find the height of the ball at 1.5 seconds.

Time (seconds)	Height (feet)
0	128
1	144
2	128
3	80
4	0

23. Multiple Representations A performer slips and falls into a safety net below. The function $f(t) = a(t - h)^2 + k$, where t represents time (in seconds), gives the performer's height above the ground (in feet) as he falls. Use the graph to find an equation for $f(t)$.

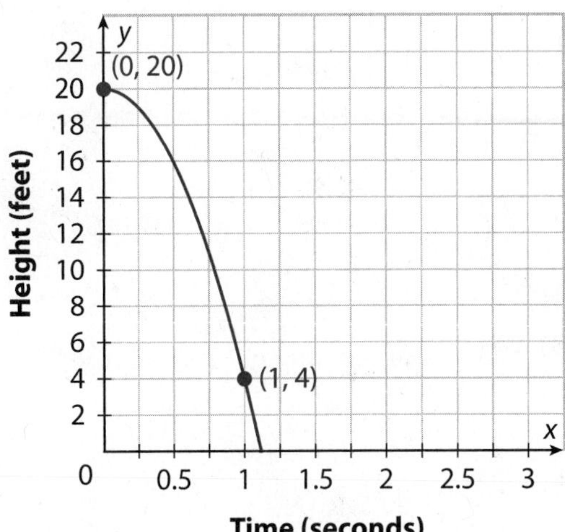

24. Represent Real-World Problems After a heavy snowfall, Ken and Karin made an igloo. The dome of the igloo is in the shape of a parabola, and the height of the igloo in inches is given by the function $f(x) = a(x - h)^2 + k$. Use the graph to find an equation for $f(x)$.

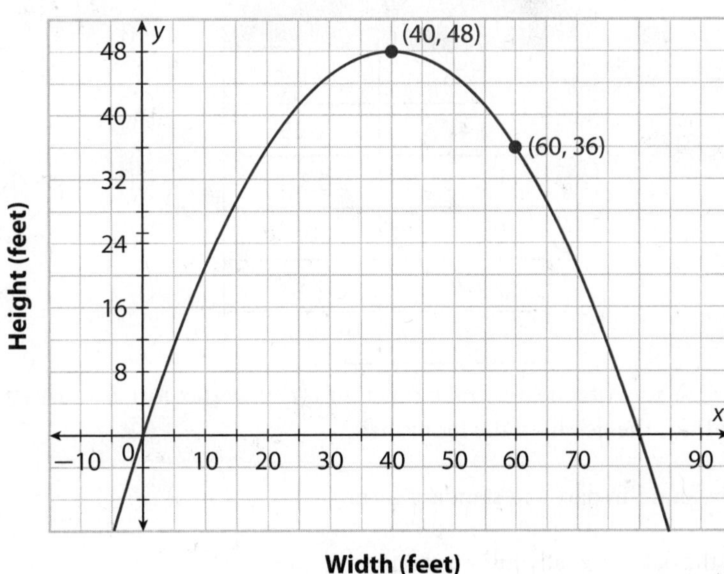

25. Check for Reasonableness Tim hits a softball. The function $f(t) = a(t - h)^2 + k$ describes the height (in feet) of the softball, and t is the time (in seconds). Use the graph to find an equation for $f(t)$. Estimate how much time elapses before the ball hits the ground. Use the equation for the function and your estimate to explain whether the equation is reasonable.

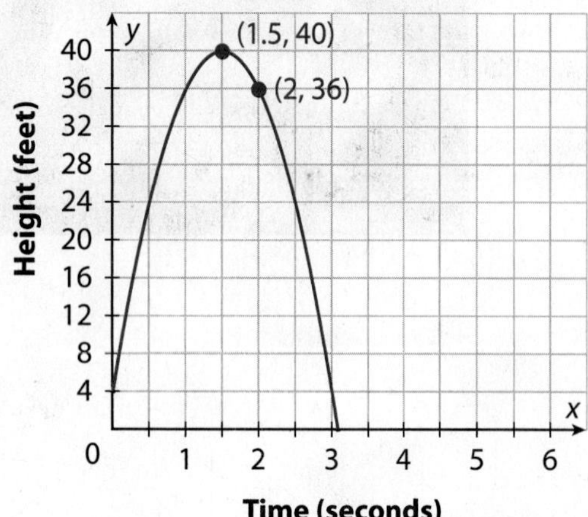

Lesson Performance Task

The table gives the height of a tennis ball t seconds after it has been hit, where the maximum height is 4 feet.

Height (ft)	Time (s)
3.75	0.125
4	0.25
3.75	0.375
3	0.5
1.75	0.625
0	0.75

a. Use the data in the table to write the quadratic function $f(t)$ in vertex form, where t is the time in seconds for the height of the tennis ball.

b. Rewrite the function found in part a in standard form.

c. At what height was the ball originally hit? Explain.

Graphing Quadratic Functions

Essential Question: How can you use the graph of a quadratic function to solve real-world problems?

Key Vocabulary

axis of symmetry *(eje de simetría)*

parabola *(parábola)*

quadratic function *(función cuadrática)*

standard form of a quadratic equation *(forma estándar de una ecuación cuadrática)*

vertex *(vértice)*

KEY EXAMPLE *(Lesson 6.3)*

The graph of a function in the form $f(x) = a(x - h)^2 + k$ is shown. Use the graph to find an equation for $f(x)$.

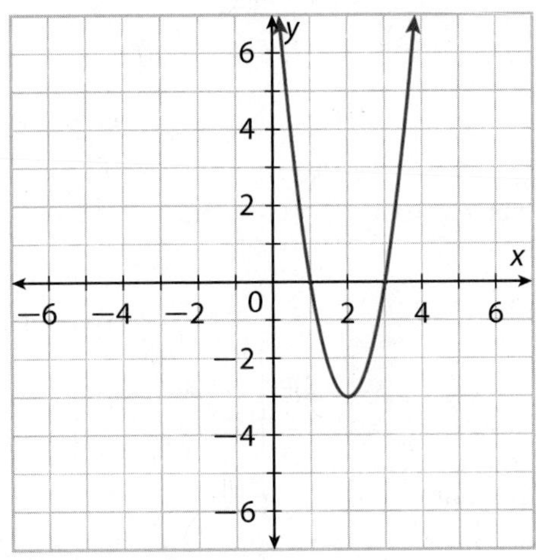

The vertex of the parabola is $(h, k) = (2, -3)$.

$f(x) = a(x - 2)^2 - 3$

From the graph, $f(3) = 0$. Substitute 3 for x and 0 for $f(x)$ and solve for a.

$0 = a(3 - 2)^2 - 3$

$3 = a$

The equation for the function is $f(x) = 3(x - 2)^2 - 3$.

KEY EXAMPLE *(Lesson 6.2)*

Graph $g(x) = -2(x + 2)^2 + 2$.

The vertex is at $(-2, 2)$.

Make a table for the function. Find two points on each side of the vertex.

x	−4	−3	−2	−1	0
$g(x)$	−6	0	2	0	−6

Plot the points and draw a parabola through them.

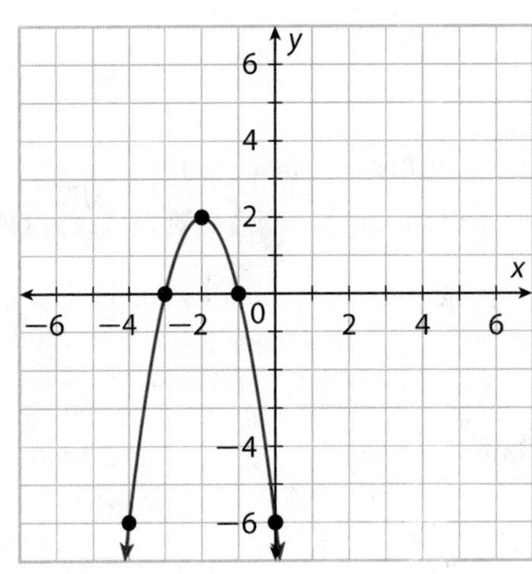

EXERCISES

Graph each quadratic function. Give the minimum or maximum value and the axis of symmetry. *(Lessons 6.1, 6.2)*

1. $f(x) = 2x^2$

2. $g(x) = -(x + 2)^2 + 4$

Write the equation for the function in each graph, in vertex form. *(Lesson 6.3)*

3.

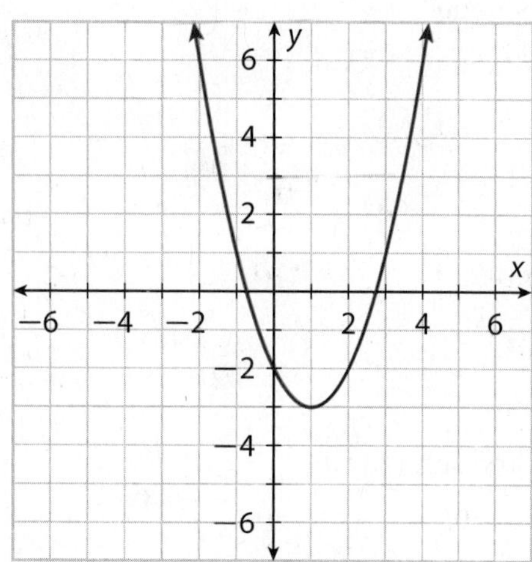

4.

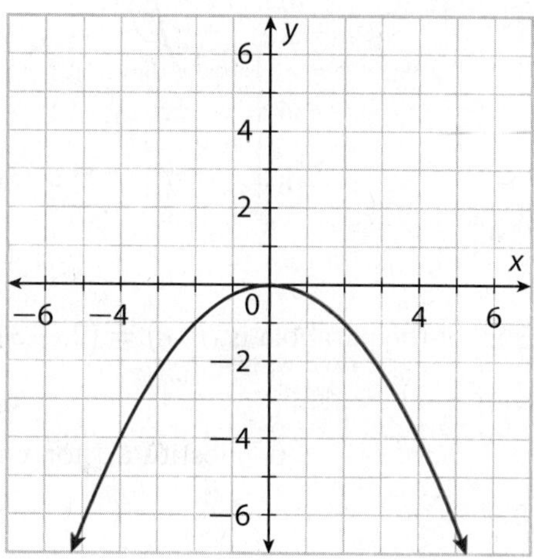

MODULE PERFORMANCE TASK

Throwing for a Completion

Professional quarterbacks can throw a football to a receiver with a velocity of 66 feet per second or greater. If a quarterback throws a pass with that velocity at a 30° angle with the ground, then the initial vertical velocity is 33 feet per second. How can you use the formula $h = -16t^2 + vt + h_0$ to describe the quarterback's pass? Find the maximum height that the football reaches, and then find the total amount of time that the pass is in the air.

Ready to Go On?

6.1–6.3 Graphing Quadratic Functions

- Online Homework
- Hints and Help
- Extra Practice

Graph each quadratic function. *(Lesson 6.1)*

1. $f(x) = -4x^2$

2. $g(x) = \frac{1}{2}x^2$

Describe the transformations necessary to get from the graph of the parent function $f(x) = x^2$ to the graph of each of the given functions. *(Lesson 6.2)*

3. $g(x) = (x + 4)^2 - 7$

4. $g(x) = 5(x - 6)^2 + 9$

Rewrite each function in standard form. *(Lesson 6.3)*

5. $f(x) = 2(x + 3)^2 - 6$

6. $f(x) = 3(x - 2)^2 + 3$

ESSENTIAL QUESTION

7. If the only information you have about a parabola is the location of its vertex, what other characteristics of the graph do you know?

MODULE 6
MIXED REVIEW

Assessment Readiness

1. Consider the graph of $f(x) = \frac{2}{3}(x - 3)^2$.
Determine if each statement is True or False.

A. The vertex is $(3, 0)$.

B. The minimum value is 0.

C. The axis of symmetry is $x = \frac{2}{3}$.

2. Is the given expression equivalent to $16^{\frac{3}{4}} + 32^{\frac{2}{5}}$? Write Yes or No.

A. $\left(16^{\frac{1}{4}}\right)^3 + \left(32^{\frac{1}{5}}\right)^2$

B. $\sqrt[4]{16^3} + \sqrt[5]{32^2}$

C. $2^3 + 2^2$

3. Write the slope-intercept equation of the line that has the same slope as $y - 3 = \frac{1}{2}(x + 3)$ and contains the point $(8, 4)$. Explain how you wrote the equation.

4. Write $f(x) = -2(x - 5)^2 + 3$ in standard form. In which form is it easier to determine the maximum value of the graph? Explain.

Connecting Intercepts, Zeros, and Factors

MODULE 7

Essential Question: How can you use intercepts of a quadratic function to solve real-world problems?

REAL WORLD VIDEO
Skateboard ramps come in many shapes and sizes. The iconic half-pipe ramp has a flat section in the middle and curved, raised sides. Skateboarders can use a half-pipe ramp to perform tricks, turns, and flips.

MODULE PERFORMANCE TASK PREVIEW

Skateboard Ramp

Skateboard riders often use curved ramps to perform difficult tricks and have fun. In this module, you will imagine that you are a design engineer hired by the local government to help construct a new skateboard ramp for the skateboard riders in the area. How do you model the curve of the ramp? Let's find out!

Are YOU Ready?

Complete these exercises to review skills you will need for this module.

- Online Homework
- Hints and Help
- Extra Practice

Exponents

Example 1 Simplify.

$x^5 \cdot x^3 = x^{5+3} = x^8$ The bases are the same. Add the exponents.

$\frac{x^9}{x^4} = x^{9-4} = x^5$ The bases are the same. Subtract the exponents.

Simplify.

1. $b^2 \cdot b^6$

2. $\frac{a^{12}}{a^7}$

3. $\frac{n^4 \cdot n^7}{n^5}$

Algebraic Expressions

Example 2 Find the value of $3x - 6$ when $x = 2$.

$3x - 6$

$3(2) - 6$ Substitute 2 for *x*.

$6 - 6$ Follow the order of operations.

0

Find the value.

4. $6x + 3$ when $x = -\frac{1}{2}$

5. $2x - 5$ when $x = \frac{5}{2}$

6. $9x + 6$ when $x = -\frac{2}{3}$

Linear Functions

Example 3 Tell whether $y = x^2 - 7$ represents a linear function.

$y = x^2 - 7$ does not represent a linear function because x has an exponent of 2.

When a linear equation is written in standard form, the following are true.

- *x* and *y* both have exponents of 1.
- *x* and *y* are not multiplied together.
- *x* and *y* do not appear in denominators, exponents, or radicands.

Tell whether the equation represents a linear function.

7. $y = 3^x + 1$

8. $3x - 2y = 6$

9. $xy + 5 = 8$

7.1 Connecting Intercepts and Zeros

Resource Locker

Essential Question: How can you use the graph of a quadratic function to solve its related quadratic equation?

Explore Graphing Quadratic Functions in Standard Form

A parabola can be graphed using its vertex and axis of symmetry. Use these characteristics, the y-intercept, and symmetry to graph a quadratic function.

Graph $y = x^2 - 4x - 5$ by completing the steps.

(A) Find the axis of symmetry.

$x = -\frac{b}{2a}$

$= -\frac{\square}{2 \cdot \square}$

$= \square$

The axis of symmetry is $x = \square$.

(B) Find the vertex.

$y = x^2 - 4x - 5$

$= \square^2 - 4 \cdot \square - 5$

$= \square - \square - 5$

$= \square$

The vertex is $(\square, \square)$.

(C) Find the y-intercept.

$y = x^2 - 4x - 5$

$y = \square^2 - 4\square + (\square)$

The y-intercept is $\square$; the graph passes through $(0, \square)$.

(D) Find two more points on the same side of the axis of symmetry as the y-intercept.

a. Find y when $x = 1$.

$y = x^2 - 4x - 5$

$= \square^2 - 4 \cdot \square - 5$

$= \square - \square - 5$

$= \square$

The first point is $(\square, \square)$.

b. Find y when $x = -1$.

$y = x^2 - 4x - 5$

$= \square^2 - 4(\square) - 5$

$= \square - (\square) - 5$

$= \square$

The second point is $(\square, \square)$.

(E) Graph the axis of symmetry, the vertex, the y-intercept, and the two extra points on the same coordinate plane. Then reflect the graphed points over the axis of symmetry to create three more points, and sketch the graph.

Reflect

1. **Discussion** Why is it important to find additional points before graphing a quadratic function?

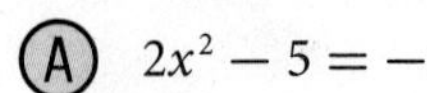

Explain 1 Using Zeros to Solve Quadratic Equations Graphically

A **zero of a function** is an x-value that makes the value of the function 0. The zeros of a function are the x-intercepts of the graph of the function. A quadratic function may have one, two, or no zeros.

Quadratic equations can be solved by graphing the related function of the equation. To write the related function, rewrite the quadratic equation so that it equals zero on one side. Replace the zero with y.

Graph the related function. Find the x-intercepts of the graph, which are the zeros of the function. The zeros of the function are the solutions to the original equation.

Example 1 **Solve by graphing the related function.**

(A) $2x^2 - 5 = -3$

a. Write the related function. Add 3 to both sides to get $2x^2 - 2 = 0$. The related function is $y = 2x^2 - 2$.

b. Make a table of values for the related function.

x	−2	−1	0	1	2
y	6	0	−2	0	6

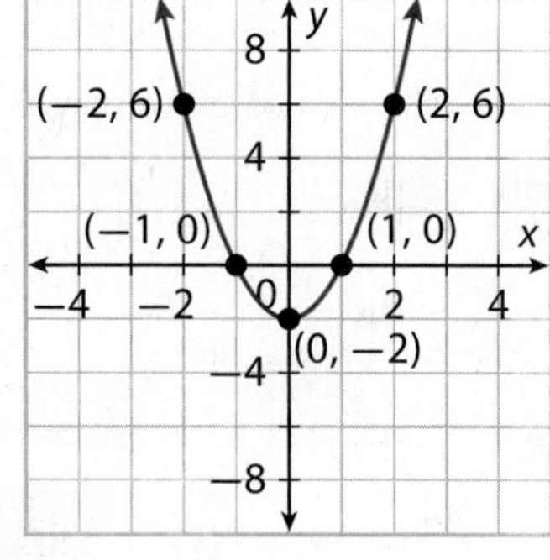

c. Graph the points represented by the table and connect the points.

d. The zeros of the function are −1 and 1, so the solutions of the equation $2x^2 - 5 = -3$ are $x = -1$ and $x = 1$.

(B) $6x + 8 = -x^2$

a. Write the related function. Add x^2 to both sides to get $x^2 + 6x + 8 = 0$.

The related function is $y = x^2 + 6x + 8$.

b. Make a table of values for the related function.

x	−5	−4	−3	−2	−1
y	3	0	−1	0	3

c. Graph the points represented by the table and connect the points.

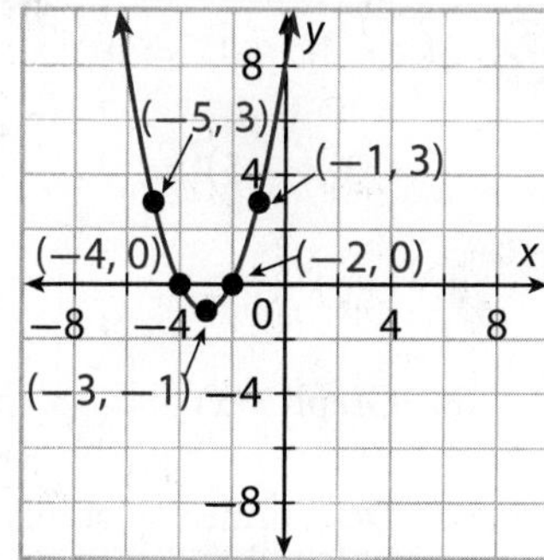

d. The zeros of the function are -4 and -2, so the solutions of the equation

$6x + 8 = -x^2$ are $x = -4$ and $x = -2$.

Reflect

2. How would the graph of a quadratic equation look if the equation has one zero?

Your Turn

Solve by graphing the related function.

3. $x^2 - 4 = -3$

Explain 2 Using Points of Intersection to Solve Quadratic Equations Graphically

You can solve a quadratic equation by rewriting the equation in the form $ax^2 + bx = c$ or $a(x - h)^2 = k$ and then using the expressions on each side of the equal sign to define a function.

Graph both functions and find the points of intersection. The x-coordinates are the points of intersection on the graph. As with using zeros, there may be two, one, or no points of intersection.

Example 2 **Solve each equation by finding points of intersection of two related functions.**

Ⓐ $2(x - 4)^2 - 2 = 0$ Write in vertex form.

$2(x - 4)^2 = 2$ Rewrite as $a(x - h)^2 = k$. Graph each side as related function.

a. Let $f(x) = 2(x - 4)^2$. Let $g(x) = 2$.

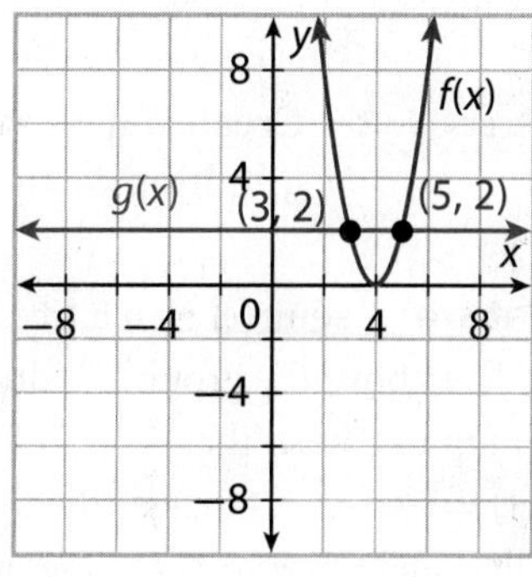

b. Graph $f(x)$ and $g(x)$ on the same graph.

c. Determine the points at which the graphs of $f(x)$ and $g(x)$ intersect.

The graphs intersect at two locations: $(3, 2)$ and $(5, 2)$.

This means $f(x) = g(x)$ when $x = 3$ and $x = 5$.

So the solutions of $2(x - 4)^2 - 2 = 0$ are $x = 3$ and $x = 5$.

(B) $3(x-5)^2 - 12 = 0$

$3(x-5)^2 = 12$

a. Let $f(x) = 3(x-5)^2$. Let $g(x) = 12$.

b. Graph $f(x)$ and $g(x)$ on the same graph.

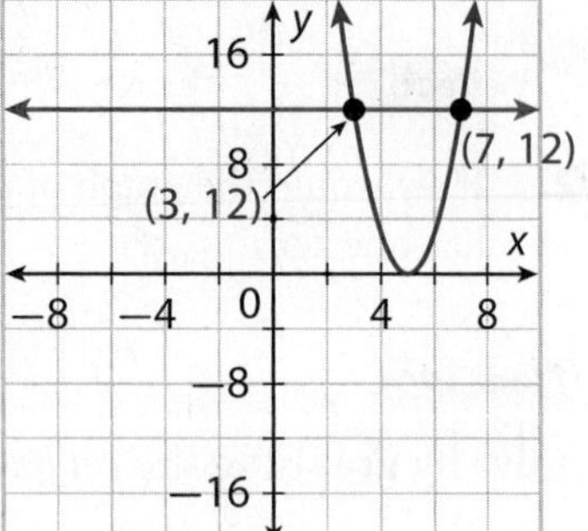

c. Determine the points at which the graphs of $f(x)$ and $g(x)$ intersect.

The graphs intersect at two locations:

$(3, 12)$ and $(7, 12)$.

This means $f(x) = g(x)$ when $x = 3$ and $x = 7$.

Therefore, the solutions of the equation $f(x) = g(x)$ are 3 and 7.

So the solutions of $3(x-5)^2 - 12 = 0$ are $x = 3$ and $x = 7$.

Reflect

4. In Part B above, why is the x-coordinates the answer to the equation and not the y-coordinates?

Your Turn

Solve by finding points of intersection of two related functions.

5. $3(x-2)^2 - 3 = 0$

Explain 3 Modeling a Real-World Problem

Many real-world problems can be modeled by quadratic functions.

Example 3 **Create a quadratic function for each problem and then solve it by using a graphing calculator.**

Nature A squirrel is in a tree holding a chestnut at a height of 46 feet above the ground. It drops the chestnut, which lands on top of a bush that is 36 feet below the squirrel. The function $h(t) = -16t^2 + 46$ gives the height in feet of the chestnut as it falls, where t represents time. When will the chestnut reach the top of the bush?

Analyze Information

Identify the important information.

- The chestnut is 46 feet above the ground, and the top of the bush is 36 feet below the chestnut.
- The chestnut's height as a function of time can be represented by $h(t) = -16t^2 + 46$, where $(h)t$ is the height of the chestnut in feet as it is falling.

Formulate a Plan

Create a related quadratic equation to find the height of the chestnut in relation to time. Use $h(t) = -16t^2 + 46$ and insert the known value for h.

Solve

Write the equation that needs to be solved. Since the top of the bush is 36 feet below the squirrel, it is 10 feet above the ground.

$-16t^2 + 46 = 10$

Separate the function into $y = f(t)$ and $y = g(t)$. $f(t) = -16t^2 + 46$ and $g(t) = 10$.

To graph each function on a graphing calculator, rewrite them in terms of x and y.

$y = -16x^2 + 46$ and $y = 10$

Graph both functions. Use the intersect feature to find the amount of time it takes for the chestnut to hit the top of the bush.

Intersection
X=1.5 Y=10

The chestnut will reach the top of the bush in 1.5 seconds.

Justify and Evaluate

$$-16(1.5)^2 + 46 = 10$$

$$-36 + 46 = 10$$

$$10 = 10$$

When t is replaced by 1.5 in the original equation, $-16t\ 2 + 46 = 10$ is true.

Reflect

6. In Example 3 above, the graphs also intersect to the left of the y-axis. Why is that point irrelevant to the problem?

Your Turn

7. **Nature** An egg falls from a nest in a tree 25 feet off the ground and lands on a potted plant that is 20 feet below the nest. The function $h(t) = -16t^2 + 25$ gives the height in feet of the egg as it drops, where t represents time. When will the egg land on the plant?

Explain 4 Interpreting a Quadratic Model

The solutions of a quadratic equation can be used to find other information about the situation modeled by the related function.

Example 4 **Use the given quadratic function model to answer questions about the situation it models.**

(A) **Nature** A dolphin jumps out of the water. The quadratic function $h(t) = -16t^2 + 20t$ models the dolphin's height above the water in feet after t seconds. How long is the dolphin out of the water?

Use the level of the water as a height of 0 feet. When the dolphin leaves and then reenters the water again, its height is 0 feet.

Solve $0 = -16t^2 + 20t$ to find the times when the dolphin both leaves the water and then reenters. The difference between the times is the amount of time the dolphin is out of the water.

a. Write the related function for $0 = -16x^2 + 20x$.

$y = -16x^2 + 20x$

b. Graph the function on a graphing calculator. Use the trace feature to estimate the zeros.

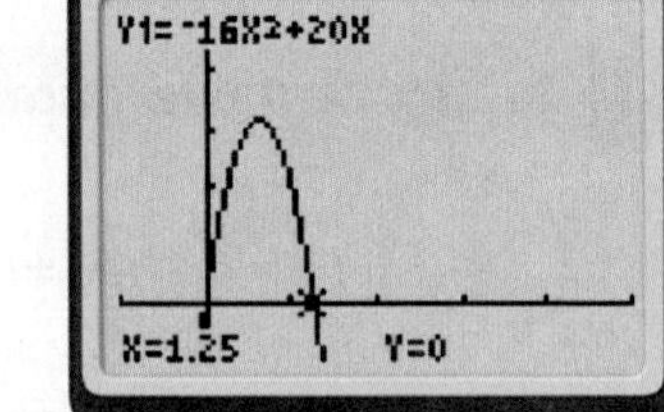

The zeros appear to be 0 and 1.25.

When $x = 0$, the equation reduces to $0 = 0$, which is true. So $x = 0$ is a solution.

Check $x = 1.25$.

$-16(1.25)^2 + 20(1.25) = -16(1.5625) + 25 = -25 + 25 = 0$
so 1.25 is a solution.

Since $1.25 - 0 = 1.25$, the dolphin is out of the water for 1.25 seconds.

(B) **Sports** A baseball coach uses a pitching machine to simulate pop flies during practice. The quadratic function $y = -16t^2 + 80t + 5$ models the height in feet of the baseball after x seconds. The ball leaves the pitching machine and is caught at a height of 5 feet. How long is the baseball in the air?

Solve $0 = -16t^2 + 80t + 5$ to find the times when the baseball enters the air and when it is caught.

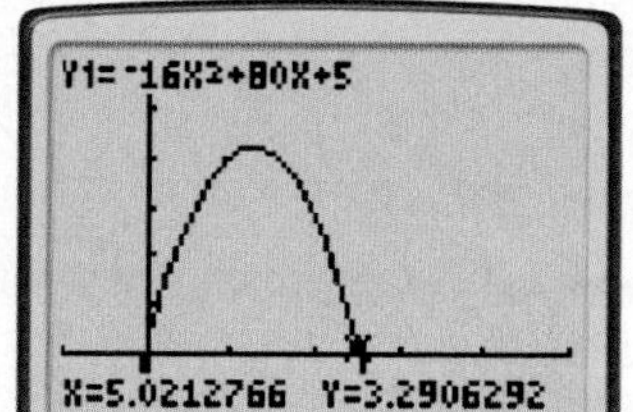

a. Write the related function for $0 = -16t^2 + 80t + 5$.

$y = -16x^2 + 80x + 5$

b. Graph the function on a graphing calculator. Use the trace feature to find the zeros.

The zeros appear to be 0 and 5.

Since $x =$ 0 makes the right side of the equation equal to 5, which is the height of the baseball when it is released by the pitching machine, it is a solution. Check to see if 5 is a solution.

$-16x^2 + 80x + 5 = -16\left(5\right)^2 + 80\left(5\right) + 5 = -400 + 400 + 5 = 5$,

so 5 is a solution.

The ball is in the air for 5 seconds.

Your Turn

8. **Nature** The quadratic function $y = -16x^2 + 5x$ models the height, in feet, of a flying fish above the water after x seconds. How long is the flying fish out of the water?

Elaborate

9. How is graphing quadratic functions in standard form similar to using zeros to solve quadratic equations graphically?

10. How can graphing calculators be used to solve real-world problems represented by quadratic equations?

11. **Essential Question Check-In** How can you use the graph of a quadratic function to solve a related quadratic equation by way of intersection?

Evaluate: Homework and Practice

- Online Homework
- Hints and Help
- Extra Practice

Solve each equation by graphing the related function and finding its zeros.

1. $3x^2 - 9 = -6$

2. $2x^2 - 9 = -1$

3. $4x^2 - 7 = -3$

4. $7x + 10 = -x^2$

5. $2x - 3 = -x^2$

6. $-1 = -x^2$

Solve each equation by finding points of intersection of two functions.

7. $2(x - 3)^2 - 4 = 0$

8. $(x + 2)^2 - 4 = 0$

9. $-(x - 3)^2 + 4 = 0$

10. $-(x + 2)^2 - 2 = 0$

11. $(x + 1)^2 - 1 = 0$

12. $(x + 2)^2 - 2 = 0$

Create a quadratic equation for each problem and then solve the equation with a related function using a graphing calculator.

13. Nature A bird is in a tree 30 feet off the ground and drops a twig that lands on a rosebush 25 feet below. The function $h(t) = -16t^2 + 30$, where t represents the time in seconds, h gives the height, in feet, of the twig above the ground as it falls. When will the twig land on the bush?

14. Nature A monkey is in a tree 50 feet off the ground and drops a banana, which lands on a shrub 30 feet below. The function $h(t) = -16t^2 + 50$, where t represents the time in seconds, h gives the height, in feet, of the banana above the ground as it falls. When will the banana land on the shrub?

15. Sports A trampolinist jumps 60 inches in the air off a trampoline 2 inches off the ground. The function $h(t) = -16t^2 + 60$, where t represents the time in seconds, h gives the height, in inches, of the trampolinist above the ground as he falls. When will the trampolinist land on the trampoline?

16. **Physics** A ball is dropped from 10 feet above the ground. The function $h(t) = -16t^2 + 10$, where t represents the time in seconds, h gives the height, in feet, of the ball above the ground. When will the ball be 4 feet above the ground?

Use the given quadratic function model to answer questions about the situation it models.

17. **Nature** A shark jumps out of the water. The quadratic function $f(x) = -16x^2 + 18x$ models the shark's height, in feet, above the water after x seconds. How long is the shark out of the water?

18. **Sports** A baseball coach uses a pitching machine to simulate pop flies during practice. The quadratic function $f(x) = -16x^2 + 70x + 10$ models the height in feet of the baseball after x seconds. How long is the baseball in the air?

19. The quadratic function $f(x) = -16x^2 + 11x$ models the height, in feet, of a fish above the water after x seconds. How long is the fish out of the water?

20. A football coach uses a passing machine to simulate 50-yard passes during practice. The quadratic function $f(x) = -16x^2 + 60x + 5$ models the height in feet of the football after x seconds. How long is the football in the air?

21. In each polynomial function in standard form, identify *a, b,* and *c.*

    a. $y = 3x^2 + 2x + 4$

    b. $y = 2x + 1$

    c. $y = x^2$

    d. $y = 5$

    e. $y = 3x^2 + 8x + 11$

22. Identify the axis of symmetry, y-intercept, and vertex of the quadratic function $y = x^2 + x - 6$ and then graph the function on a graphing calculator to confirm.

H.O.T. Focus on Higher Order Thinking

23. Counterexamples Pamela says that if the graph of a function opens upward, then the related quadratic equation has two solutions. Provide a counterexample to refute Pamela's claim.

24. Explain the Error Rodney was given the function $h(t) = -16t^2 + 50$ representing the height above the ground (in feet) of a water balloon t seconds after being dropped from a roof 50 feet above the ground. He was asked to find how long it took the balloon to fall 20 feet. Rodney used the equation $-16t^2 + 50 = 20$ to solve the problem. What was his error?

25. Critical Thinking If Jamie is given the graph of a quadratic function with only the x-intercepts and a random point labeled, can she determine an equation for the function Explain?

Lesson Performance Task

Stella is competing in a diving competition. Her height in feet above the water is modeled by the function $f(x) = -16t^2 + 8t + 48$, where t is the time in seconds after she jumps from the diving board. Graph the function and solve. What do the solutions mean in the context of the problem? Are there solutions that do not make sense? Explain.

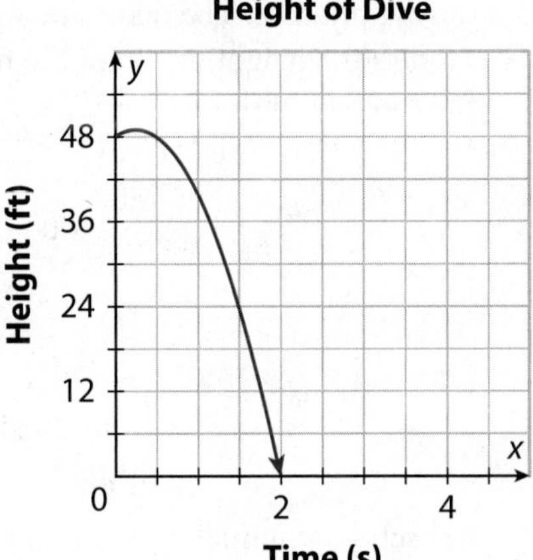

7.2 Connecting Intercepts and Linear Factors

Resource Locker

Essential Question: How are x-intercepts of a quadratic function and its linear factors related?

Explore Connecting Factors and x–Intercepts

Use graphs and linear factors to find the x–intercepts of a parabola.

(A) Graph $y = x + 4$ and $y = x - 2$ using a graphing calculator. Then sketch the graphs on a coordinate grid.

(B) Identify the x-intercept of each line.

The x-intercepts are ____ and ____ .

(C) The quadratic function $y = (x + 4)(x - 2)$ is the product of the two linear factors that have been graphed. Use a graphing calculator to graph the function $y = (x + 4)(x - 2)$. Then sketch a graph of the quadratic function on the same grid with the linear factors that have been graphed.

(D) Identify the x-intercepts of the parabola.

The x-intercepts are ____ and ____.

(E) What do you notice about the x–intercepts of the parabola?

Reflect

1. Use a graph to determine whether $2x^2 + 5x - 12$ is the product of the linear factors $2x - 3$ and $x + 4$.

2. **Discussion** Make a conjecture about the linear factors and x-intercepts of a quadratic function.

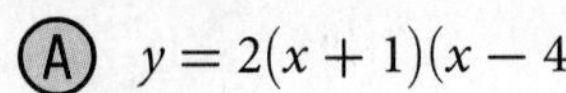 Rewriting from Factored Form to Standard Form

A quadratic function is in **factored form** when it is written as $y = k(x - a)(x - b)$ where $k \neq 0$.

Example 1 **Write each function in standard form.**

(A) $y = 2(x + 1)(x - 4)$

Multiply the two linear factors.

$y = 2(x^2 - 4x + x - 4)$

$y = 2(x^2 - 3x - 4)$

Multiply the resulting trinomial by 2.

$y = 2x^2 - 6x - 8$

The standard form of $y = 2(x + 1)(x - 4)$ is $y = 2x^2 - 6x - 8$.

(B) $y = 3(x - 5)(x - 2)$

Multiply the two linear factors.

$y = 3(\boxed{x - 5})(\boxed{x - 2})$

$y = 3(\boxed{x^2 - 7x + 10})$

Multiply the resulting trinomial by 3.

$y = \boxed{3x^2 - 21x + 30}$

The standard form of $y = 3(x - 5)(x - 2)$ is

$y = 3x^2 - 21x + 30$.

Reflect

3. How do the signs in the factors affect the sign of the x–term in the resulting trinomial?

4. How do the signs in the factors affect the sign of the constant term in the resulting trinomial?

Your Turn

Write each function in standard form.

5. $y = (x - 7)(x - 1)$

6. $y = 4(x - 1)(x + 3)$

Explain 2 Connecting Factors and Zeros

In the Explore you learned that the factors in factored form indicate the x-intercepts of a function. In a previous lesson you learned that the x-intercepts of a graph are the zeros of the function.

Example 2 **Write each function in standard form. Determine x-intercepts and zeros of each function.**

(A) $y = 2(x - 1)(x - 3)$

Write the function in standard form.

$y = 2(x^2 - 3x - x + 3)$

$y = 2(x^2 - 4x + 3)$

$y = 2x^2 - 8x + 6$

The factors indicate the x–intercepts.

* Factor $(x - 1)$ indicates an x–intercept of 1.

* Factor $(x - 3)$ indicates an x–intercept of 3.

The x-intercepts of a graph are the zeros of the function.

* An x–intercept of 1 indicates that the function has a zero of 1.

* An x–intercept of 3 indicates that the function has a zero of 3.

(B) $y = 2(x + 4)(x + 2)$

Write the function in standard form.

$y = 2(\boxed{x+4})(\boxed{x+2})$

$y = 2(\boxed{x^2 + 6x + 8})$

$y = \boxed{2x^2 + 12x + 16}$

The factors indicate the x–intercepts.

* Factor $(x + 4)$ indicates an x–intercept of –4.

* Factor $(x + 2)$ indicates an x–intercept of 2.

The x–intercepts of a graph are the zeros of the function.

* An x–intercept of –4 indicates that the function has a zero of –4.

* An x–intercept of –2 indicates that the function has a zero of –2.

Reflect

7. Discussion What are the zeros of a function?

8. How many x-intercepts can quadratic functions have?

Your Turn

Write each function in standard form. Determine x–intercepts and zeros of each function.

9. $y = -2(x + 5)(x + 1)$

10. $y = 5(x - 3)(x - 1)$

Explain 3 Writing Quadratic Functions Given *x*-Intercepts

Given two quadratic functions $f(x) = (x - a)(x - b)$ and $g(x) = k(x - a)(x - b)$, where k is any non-zero real constant, examine the x–intercepts for each quadratic function.

$f(x) = (x - a)(x - b)$ $0 = (x - a)(x - b)$ $x - a = 0$ or $x - b = 0$ $x = a$ $\quad$ $x = b$	$g(x) = k(x - a)(x - b)$ $0 = k(x - a)(x - b)$ $0 = (x - a)(x - b)$ $x - a = 0$ or $x - b = 0$ $x = a$ $\quad$ $x = b$

Notice that $f(x) = (x - a)(x - b)$ and $g(x) = k(x - a)(x - b)$ have the same x-intercepts. You can use the factored form to construct a quadratic function given the x–intercepts and the value of k.

Example 3 **For the two given intercepts, use the factored form to generate a quadratic function for each given constant k. Write the function in standard form.**

 x-intercepts: 2 and 5; $k = 1$, $k = -2$, $k = 3$

Write the quadratic function with $k = 1$.

$f(x) = k(x - a)(x - b)$

$f(x) = 1(x - 2)(x - 5)$

$f(x) = (x - 2)(x - 5)$

$f(x) = x^2 - 7x + 10$

Write the quadratic function with $k = -2$.

$f(x) = -2(x - 2)(x - 5)$

$f(x) = -2(x^2 - 7x + 10)$

$f(x) = -2x^2 + 14x - 20$

Write the quadratic function with $k = 3$.

$f(x) = 3(x - 2)(x - 5)$

$f(x) = 3(x^2 - 7x + 10)$

$f(x) = 3x^2 - 21x + 30$

(B) x-intercepts: -3 and 4; $k = 1$, $k = -3$, $k = 2$

Write the quadratic function with $k = 1$.

$f(x) =$ $(x + 3)(x - 4)$

$f(x) =$ $x^2 - x - 12$

Write the quadratic function with $k = -3$.

$f(x) =$ $-3(x + 3)(x - 4)$

$f(x) =$ $-3x^2 + 3x + 36$

Write the quadratic function with $k = 2$.

$f(x) =$ $2(x + 3)(x - 4)$

$f(x) =$ $2x^2 - 2x - 24$

Reflect

11. How are the functions with same intercepts but different constant factors the same? How are they different?

Your Turn

For the given two intercepts and three values of k generate three quadratic functions. Write the functions in factored form and standard form.

12. x-intercepts: 1 and 8; $k = 1$, $k = -4$, $k = 5$

13. x-intercepts: -7 and 3; $k = 1$, $k = -5$, $k = 7$

Elaborate

14. If the x–intercepts of a quadratic function are 3 and 8, what can be said about the x–intercepts of its linear factors?

15. If a quadratic function has only one zero, it has to occur at the vertex of the parabola. Using the graph of a quadratic function, explain why.

16. How are x–intercepts and zeros related?

17. What would the factored form look like if there were only one x–intercept?

18. **Essential Question Check-In** How can you find x–intercepts of a quadratic function if its linear factors are known?

Evaluate: Homework and Practice

Personal Math Trainer

- Online Homework
- Hints and Help
- Extra Practice

Graph each quadratic function and each of its linear factors. Then identify the x-intercepts and the axis of symmetry of each parabola.

1. $y = (x - 2)(x - 6)$

2. $y = (x + 3)(x - 1)$

3. $y = (x - 5)(x + 2)$

4. $y = (x - 5)(x - 5)$

Write each function in standard form.

5. $y = 5(x - 2)(x + 1)$

6. $y = 2(x + 6)(x + 3)$

7. $y = -2(x + 4)(x - 5)$

8. $y = -4(x + 2)(x + 3)$

9. Which of the following is the correct standard form of $y = 3(x - 8)(x - 5)$?

a. $y = 3x^2 + 39x - 120$

b. $y = x^2 - 13x + 40$

c. $y = 3x^2 - 39x + 120$

d. $y = x^2 - 39x + 40$

e. $y = 3x^2 + 13x + 120$

10. The area of a Japanese rock garden is $y = 7(x - 3)(x + 1)$. Write $y = 7(x - 3)(x + 1)$ in standard form.

Write each function in standard form. Determine x–intercepts and zeros of each function.

11. $y = -2(x - 4)(x - 2)$

12. $y = 2(x + 4)(x - 2)$

13. $y = -3(x + 1)(x - 3)$

14. $y = 2(x + 2)(x - 1)$

15. A soccer ball is kicked from ground level. The function $y = -16x(x - 2)$ gives the height (in feet) of the ball, where x is time (in seconds). After how many seconds will the ball hit the ground? Use a graphing calculator to verify your answer.

16. A tennis ball is tossed upward from a balcony. The height of the ball in feet can be modeled by the function $y = -4(2x + 1)(2x - 3)$ where x is the time in seconds after the ball is released. Find the maximum height of the ball and the time it takes the ball to reach this height. Graph the function to determine approximately how long it takes the ball to hit the ground.

For the two given intercepts, use the factored form to generate a quadratic function for each given constant k. Write the function in standard form.

17. x-intercepts: -5 and 3; $k = 1, k = -2, k = 5$

18. x-intercepts: 4 and 7; $k = 1, k = -3, k = 5$

H.O.T. Focus on Higher Order Thinking

19. Explain the Error For the given two intercepts, 3 and 9, $k = 4$, Kelly wrote a quadratic function in factored form, $f(x) = 4(x + 3)(x + 9)$, and in standard form, $f(x) = 4x^2 + 48x + 108$. What error did she make?

20. Critical Thinking How is the graph of $f(x) = 7(x + 3)(x - 2)$ similar to and different from the graph of $f(x) = -7x^2 - 7x + 42$?

21. Make a Prediction How could you find an equation of a quadratic function with zeros at -3 and at 1?

Lesson Performance Task

The cross-sectional shape of the archway of a bridge (measured in feet) is modeled by the function $f(x) = -0.5x^2 + 6x$ where $f(x)$ is the height of the arch and x is the horizontal distance from the base of the arch. How wide is the arch at its base? Will a box truck that is 8 feet wide and 13.5 feet tall fit under the arch? If not, what is the maximum height a truck 8 feet wide passing under the bridge can be?

7.3 Applying the Zero Product Property to Solve Equations

Resource Locker

Essential Question: How can you use the Zero Product Property to solve quadratic equations in factored form?

Explore Understanding the Zero Product Property

For all real numbers a and b, if the product of the two quantities equals zero, then at least one of the quantities equals zero.

Zero Product Property

For all real numbers a and b, the following is true.

Words	Sample Numbers	Algebra
If the product of two quantities equals zero, at least one of the quantities equals zero.	$9(\square) = 0$ $0(4) = \square$	If $ab = 0$, then $\square = 0$ or $b = \square$.

(A) Consider the equation $(x-3)(x+8)=0$. Let $a = x - 3$ and $b = \square$.

(B) Since $ab = 0$, you know that $a = 0$ or $b = 0$. $\square = 0$ or $x + 8 = 0$

(C) Solve for x.

$x - 3 = 0$ or $x + 8 = 0$

$x = \square$ $x = \square$

(D) So, the solutions of the equation $(x-3)(x+8)=0$ are $x = \square$ and $x = \square$.

(E) Recall that the solutions of an equation are the zeros of the related function. So, the solutions of the equation $(x-3)(x+8)=0$ are the zeros of the related function $f(x) = \square$ because they satisfy the equation $f(x) = 0$. The solutions of the related function $f(x) = \square$ are $\square$ and $\square$.

Reflect

1. Describe how you can find the solutions of the equation $(x-a)(x-b)=0$ using the Zero Product Property.

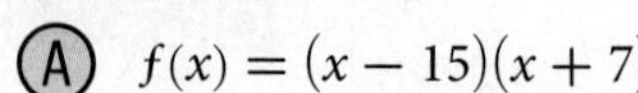 Applying the Zero Product Property to Functions

When given a function of the form $f(x) = (x + a)(x + b)$, you can use the Zero Product Property to find the zeros of the function.

Example 1 **Find the zeros of each function.**

Ⓐ $f(x) = (x - 15)(x + 7)$

Set $f(x)$ equal to zero.	$(x - 15)(x + 7) = 0$		
Apply the Zero Product Property.	$x - 15 = 0$	or	$x + 7 = 0$
Solve each equation for x.	$x = 15$		$x = -7$

The zeros are 15 and −7.

Ⓑ $f(x) = (x + 1)(x + 23)$

Set $f(x)$ equal to zero.	$(x + 1)(x + 23) =$ 0		
Apply the Zero Product Property.	$x +$ 1 $= 0$	or	$x + 23 =$ 0
Solve for x.	$x =$ −1		$x =$ −23

The zeros are −1 and −23.

Reflect

2. **Discussion** Jordie was asked to identify the zeros of the function $f(x) = (x - 5)(x + 3)$. Her answers were $x = -5$ and $x = 3$. Do you agree or disagree? Explain.
3. How would you find the zeros of the function $f(x) = -4(x - 8)$?
4. What are the zeros of the function $f(x) = x(x - 12)$? Explain.

Your Turn

Find the zeros of each function.

5. $f(x) = (x - 10)(x - 6)$

6. $f(x) = 7(x - 13)(x + 12)$

Explain 2 Solving Quadratic Equations Using the Distributive Property and the Zero Product Property

The Distributive Property states that, for real numbers a, b, and c, $a(b + c) = ab + ac$ and $ab + ac = a(b + c)$. The Distributive Property applies to polynomials, as well. For instance, $3x(x - 4) + 5(x - 4) = (3x + 5)(x - 4)$. You can use the Distributive Property along with the Zero Product Property to solve certain equations.

Example 2 **Solve each equation using the Distributive Property and the Zero Product Property.**

Ⓐ $3x(x - 4) + 5(x - 4) = 0$

Use the Distributive Property to rewrite the expression $3x(x - 4) + 5(x - 4)$ as a product. $\quad 3x(x - 4) + 5(x - 4) = (3x + 5)(x - 4)$

Rewrite the equation. $\quad (3x + 5)(x - 4) = 0$

Apply the Zero Product Property. $\quad 3x + 5 = 0 \quad$ or $\quad x - 4 = 0$

Solve each equation for x. $\quad 3x = -5 \qquad x = 4$

$$x = -\frac{5}{3}$$

The solutions are $x = -\frac{5}{3}$ and $x = 4$.

Ⓑ $-9(x + 2) + 3x(x + 2) = 0$

Use the Distributive Property to rewrite the expression $-9(x + 2) + 3x(x + 2)$ as a product. $\quad -9(x + 2) + 3x(x + 2) = (\boxed{-9} + 3x)(x + \boxed{2})$

Rewrite the equation. $\quad (\boxed{-9} + 3x)(x + \boxed{2}) = 0$

Apply the Zero Product Property. $\quad \boxed{-9} + 3x = 0 \quad$ or $\quad x + \boxed{2} = 0$

Solve each equation for x. $\quad 3x = \boxed{9} \qquad x = \boxed{-2}$

$$x = \boxed{3}$$

The solutions are $x = \boxed{3}$ and $x = \boxed{-2}$.

Reflect

7. How can you solve the equation $5x(x - 3) + 4x - 12 = 0$ using the Distributive Property?

Your Turn

Solve each equation using the Distributive Property and the Zero Product Property.

8. $7x(x - 11) - 2(x - 11) = 0$

9. $-8x(x + 6) + 3x + 18 = 0$

Explain 3 Solving Real-World Problems Using the Zero Product Property

Example 3

The height of one diver above the water during a dive can be modeled by the equation $h = -4(4t + 5)(t - 3)$, where h is height in feet and t is time in seconds. Find the time it takes for the diver to reach the water.

Analyze Information

Identify the important information.

- The height of the diver is given by the equation $h = -4(4t + 5)(t - 3)$.
- The diver reaches the water when $h = \boxed{0}$.

Formulate a Plan

To find the time it takes for the diver to reach the water, set the equation equal to $\boxed{0}$ and use the Zero Product Property to solve for t.

Solve

Set the equation equal to zero. $\quad -4(4t + 5)(t - 3) = 0$

Apply the Zero Product Property. Since $-4 \neq 0$, set the other factors equal to 0. $\quad 4t + 5 = 0 \quad$ or $\quad t - 3 = 0$

Solve each equation for x.

$$4t + 5 = 0 \quad \text{or} \quad t - 3 = 0$$

$$4t = \boxed{-5} \qquad t = \boxed{3}$$

$$t = \boxed{-\tfrac{5}{4}}$$

The zeros are $t = \boxed{-\frac{5}{4}}$ and $t = \boxed{3}$. Since time cannot be negative, the time it takes for the diver to reach the the water is $\boxed{3}$ seconds.

Justify and Evaluate

Check to see that the answer is reasonable by substituting 3 for t in the equation $-4(4t + 5)(t - 3) = 0$.

$$-4(4(3) + 5)(3 - 3) = -4(\boxed{12} + 5)(\boxed{3} - 3)$$

$$= -4(\boxed{17})(\boxed{0})$$

$$= \boxed{0}$$

Since the equation is equal to $\boxed{0}$ for $t = 3$, the solution is reasonable. The diver will reach the water after $\boxed{3}$ seconds.

Reflect

10. If you were to graph the function $f(t) = -4(4t + 5)(t - 3)$, what points would be associated with the zeros of the function?

Your Turn

11. The height of a golf ball after it has been hit from the top of a hill can be modeled by the equation $h = -8(2t - 4)(t + 1)$, where h is height in feet and t is time in seconds. How long is the ball in the air?

Elaborate

12. Can you use the Zero Product Property to find the zeros of the function $f(x) = (x - 1) + (2 - 9x)$? Explain.

13. Suppose a and b are the zeros of a function. Name two points on the graph of the function and explain how you know they are on the graph. What are the x-coordinates of the points called?

14. Essential Question Check-In Suppose you are given a quadratic function in factored form that is set equal to 0. Why can you solve it by setting each factor equal to 0?

Evaluate: Homework and Practice

• Online Homework
• Hints and Help
• Extra Practice

Find the solutions of each equation.

1. $(x - 15)(x - 22) = 0$

2. $(x + 2)(x - 18) = 0$

Find the zeros of each function.

3. $f(x) = (x + 15)(x + 17)$

4. $f(x) = \left(x - \frac{2}{9}\right)\left(x + \frac{1}{2}\right)$

5. $f(x) = -0.2(x - 1.9)(x - 3.5)$

6. $f(x) = x(x + 20)$

7. $f(x) = \frac{3}{4}\left(x - \frac{3}{4}\right)$

8. $f(x) = (x + 24)(x + 24)$

Solve each equation using the Distributive Property and the Zero Product Property.

9. $-6x(x + 12) - 15(x + 12) = 0$

10. $10(x - 3) - x(x - 3) = 0$

11. $5x\left(x + \frac{2}{3}\right) + \left(x + \frac{2}{3}\right) = 0$

12. $-(x + 4) + x(x + 4) = 0$

13. $7x(9 - x) + \frac{1}{3}(9 - x) = 0$

14. $-x(x - 3) + 6x - 18 = 0$

Solve using the Zero Product Property.

15. The height of a football after it has been kicked from the top of a hill can be modeled by the equation $h = 2(-2 - 4t)(2t - 5)$, where h is the height of the football in feet and t is the time in seconds. How long is the football in the air?

16. **Archery** Kylie shoots an arrow during an archery lesson at camp. The height of the arrow can be modeled by the equation $h = -8t(2t - 6)$, where h is the height in feet of the arrow and t is the time in seconds. How long is the arrow in the air?

17. **Physics** The height of a flare fired from a platform can be modeled by the equation $h = 8t(-2t + 10) + 4(-2t + 10)$, where h is the height of the flare in feet and t is the time in seconds. Find the time it takes for the flare to reach the ground.

18. **Diving** The depth of a scuba diver can be modeled by the equation $d = 0.5t(3.5t - 28.25)$, where d is the depth in meters of the diver and t is the time in minutes. Find the time it takes for the diver to reach the surface. Give your answer to the nearest minute.

19. A group of friends tries to keep a small beanbag from touching the ground by kicking it. On one kick, the beanbag's height can be modeled by the equation $h = -2(t - 1) - 16t(t - 1)$, where h is the height of the beanbag in feet and t is the time in seconds. Find the time it takes the beanbag to reach the ground.

20. Elizabeth and Markus are playing catch. Elizabeth throws the ball first. The height of the ball can be modeled by the equation $h = -16t(t - 5)$, where h is the height of the ball in feet and t is the time in seconds. Markus is distracted at the last minute and looks away. The ball lands at his feet. If the ball travels horizontally at an average rate of 3.5 feet per second, how far is Markus standing from Elizabeth when the ball hits the ground?

21. Match the function on the left with its zeros on the right.

A. $f(x) = 11(x - 9) + x(x - 9)$	**a.** $x = -11$ and $x = -9$
B. $f(x) = (x + 9)(x - 11)$	**b.** $x = 9$ and $x = -11$
C. $f(x) = 11(x - 9) - x(x - 9)$	**c.** $x = 9$ and $x = 11$
D. $f(x) = (x - 9)(x + 11)$	**d.** $x = -9$ and $x = 11$
E. $f(x) = -x(x + 9) - 11(x + 9)$	

H.O.T. Focus on Higher Order Thinking

22. **Explain the Error** A student found the zeros of the function $f(x) = 2x(x - 5) + 6(x - 5)$. Explain what the student did wrong. Then give the correct answer.

$2x(x - 5) + 6(x - 5) = 0$

$2x(x - 5) = 0$, so $2x = 0$, and $x = 0$, or

$x - 5 = 0$, so $x = 5$, or

$6(x - 5) = 0$, so $x = 5$

Zeros: 0, 5 and 5

23. Draw Conclusions A ball is kicked into the air from ground level. The height h in meters that the ball reaches at a distance d in meters from the point where it was kicked is given by $h = -2d(d - 4)$. The graph of the equation is a parabola.

a. At what distance from the point where it is kicked does the ball reach its maximum height? Explain.

b. Find the maximum height. What is the point $(2, h)$ on the graph of the function called?

24. Justify Reasoning Can you solve $(x - 2)(x + 3) = 5$ by solving $x - 2 = 5$ and $x + 3 = 5$? Explain.

25. Persevere in Problem Solving Write an equation to find three numbers with the following properties. Let x be the first number. The second number is 3 more than the first number. The third number is 4 times the second number. The sum of the third number and the product of the first and second numbers is 0. Solve the equation and give the three numbers.

Lesson Performance Task

The height of a pole vaulter as she jumps over the bar is modeled by the function $f(t) = -1.75(t - 0)(t - 3.5)$, where t is the time at which the pole vaulter leaves the ground.

a. Find the solutions of the function when $t = 0$ using the Zero Product Property. What do these solutions mean in the context of the problem?

b. If the bar is 6 feet high, will the pole vaulter make it over?

STUDY GUIDE REVIEW

Connecting Intercepts, Zeros, and Factors

MODULE 7

Essential Question: How can you use intercepts of a quadratic function to solve real-world problems?

Key Vocabulary

Zero Product Property
(Propiedad del producto cero)

zero of a function
(cero de una función)

KEY EXAMPLE *(Lesson 7.2)*

Generate the quadratic function with x-intercepts 3 and -2 and $k = 3$. Write the function in factored form and standard form.

Write the quadratic function with $k = 3$. Substitute the given values of the x-intercepts and k into $f(x) = k(x - a)(x - b)$ and simplify.

$f(x) = 3(x + 2)(x - 3)$

Write $f(x) = 3(x + 2)(x - 3)$ in standard form.

$$f(x) = 3(x + 2)(x - 3)$$
$$= 3x^2 - 3x - 18$$

KEY EXAMPLE *(Lesson 7.3)*

Solve $2x(x - 2) + 4(x - 2) = 0$ by using the Distributive Property and the Zero Product Property.

Use the Distributive Property to rewrite the expression $2x(x - 2) + 4(x - 2)$ as a product of binomials.	$2x(x - 2) + 4(x - 2) = (2x + 4)(x - 2)$
Rewrite the equation.	$(2x + 4)(x - 2) = 0$
Apply the Zero Product Property.	$2x + 4 = 0$ and $x - 2 = 0$
Solve each equation for x.	$2x = -4$, $x = -2$; $x = 2$

The solutions are $x = -2$ and $x = 2$.

EXERCISES

Solve each equation by graphing. *(Lesson 7.1)*

1. $x^2 - 2x - 1 = 2$

2. $(x + 2)^2 - 4 = 0$

Write a function in factored and standard form for each k and set of x-intercepts. *(Lesson 7.2)*

3. x-intercepts: -3 and 4; $k = -2$

4. x-intercepts: 7 and 2; $k = 3$

Find the zeros of each function. *(Lesson 7.3)*

5. $f(x) = x(x + 17)$

6. $f(x) = -4(x - 2.3)(x - 4.6)$

MODULE PERFORMANCE TASK

Designing a Skateboard Ramp

The local government has made partial plans for the construction of a skateboard ramp, which are shown here. Your task is to complete the plans by modeling the parabolic curve of the ramp itself.

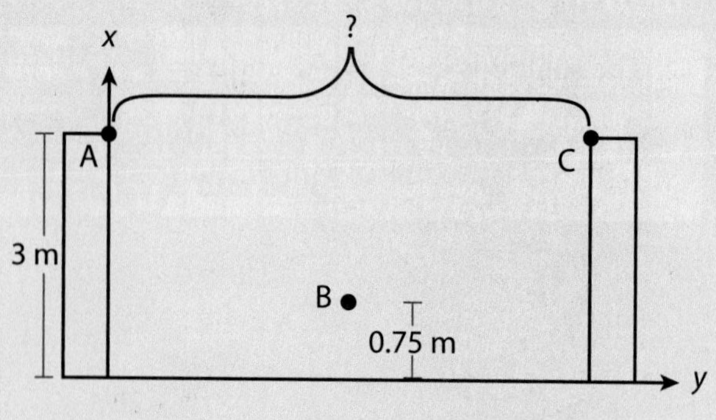

First, choose the total width of the parabola from point A to point C, which should be between 3 meters and 6 meters. Then, create an equation that models the parabola that starts at point A, reaches a minimum at point B, and ends at point C. Note that the x- and y-axes are marked in the diagram. Express your equation in standard form.

Complete the task, using graphs, numbers, or algebra to explain how you reached your conclusion.

Ready to Go On?

7.1–7.3 Connecting Intercepts, Zeros, and Factors

- Online Homework
- Hints and Help
- Extra Practice

Solve each equation by graphing. *(Lesson 7.1)*

1. $-4x + 4 = -x^2$

2. $-x^2 + 1 = 0$

Write a function in factored and standard form for each k and set of x-intercepts. *(Lesson 7.2)*

3. x-intercepts: 5 and -7; $k = -3$

4. x-intercepts: -1 and -8; $k = 4$

Find the zeros of each function. *(Lesson 7.3)*

5. $f(x) = -8(x + 7)(x - 8.6)$

6. $f(x) = x(x - 42)$

7. $f(x) = 9x(x - 4) + 3(x - 4)$

8. $f(x) = -2x(x + 4) + 6x + 24$

ESSENTIAL QUESTION

9. How can you use factoring to solve quadratic equations in standard form?

MODULE 7
MIXED REVIEW

Assessment Readiness

1. Solve $8x(7 - x) + \frac{1}{5}(7 - x) = 0$. Is each of the following a solution of the equation?

A. $x = -7$

B. $x = -\frac{8}{5}$

C. $x = -\frac{1}{40}$

2. For each statement, determine if it is True or False for the graph of $6x - 3y = 21$.

A. The x-intercept is $3\frac{1}{2}$.

B. The y-intercept is -7.

C. The slope is 3.

3. Is the sequence 6, 3, 0, −3, −6, −9, ... arithmetic, geometric, or neither? Explain your answer. Write a recursive rule for the sequence.

4. Graph $f(x) = (x - 2)^2 - 4$. Describe the relationship between the x-intercepts of the graph and the solutions of $(x - 2)^2 - 4 = 0$.

Assessment Readiness

- Online Homework
- Hints and Help
- Extra Practice

1. Consider the graph of $f(x) = -2x^2 - \frac{1}{2}$.
Determine if each statement is True or False.

A. The vertex is $\left(-2, \frac{1}{2}\right)$.

B. The maximum value is $-\frac{1}{2}$.

C. The axis of symmetry is $x = -2$.

2. Does the given statement describe a step in the transformation of the graph of $f(x) = x^2$ that would result in the graph of $g(x) = -5\,(x + 2)^2$?

A. The parent function is reflected across the x-axis.

B. The parent function is stretched by a factor of 5.

C. The parent function is translated 2 units up.

3. Use the graph of $f(x)$ to determine if each statement is True or False.

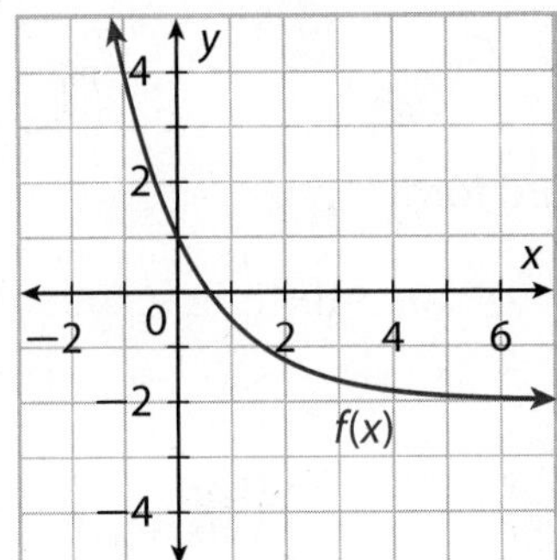

A. As $x \to \infty, y \to -2$.

B. The graph represents a quadratic function.

C. When $f(x) = 1, x = 0$.

4. Solve $\left(2x + \frac{2}{3}\right)(x + 5) = 0$. Is each of the following a solution of the equation?

A. $x = -\frac{1}{3}$

B. $x = -5$

C. $x = \frac{2}{3}$

5. Use the table of values for $h(x)$ to determine if each statement is True or False.

x	−4	−2	0	2	4
$h(x)$	3	0	−3	0	3

A. A zero of the function is −3.

B. A zero of the function is −2.

C. A solution of the equation of the function $h(x) = 0$ is $x = 2$.

6. Graph $y = -2x^2 + 16x - 31$. What is the axis of symmetry of the graph? What is its vertex?

7. Graph $t(x) = \frac{1}{2}(x + 2)(x - 4)$, and write the function in standard form.

Performance Tasks

★ 8. A rectangular picture measuring 6 in. by 10 in. is surrounded by a frame with uniform width x.

A. Write a quadratic function to show the combined area of the picture and frame.

B. Write a quadratic function for the area of the frame.

★★ **9. Estimation** The graph shows the approximate height y in meters of a volleyball x seconds after it is served.

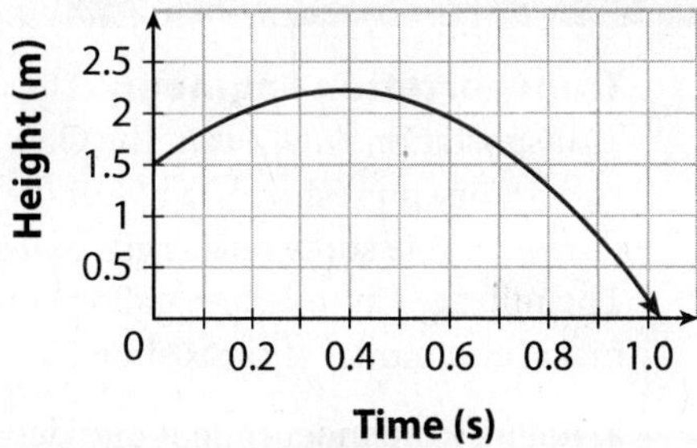

A. Estimate the time it takes for the volleyball to reach its greatest height.

B. Estimate the greatest height that the volleyball reaches.

C. If the domain of a quadratic function is all real numbers, why is the domain of this function limited to nonnegative numbers?

★★★**10.** A rocket team is using simulation software to create and study water bottle rockets. The team begins by simulating the launch of a rocket without a parachute. The table gives data for one rocket design.

A. Show that the data represents a quadratic function.

B. Graph the function.

C. The acceleration due to gravity is 9.8 m/s^2. How is this number related to the data for this water bottle rocket?

Time (s)	Height (m)
0	0
1	34.4
2	58.8
3	73.5
4	78.4
5	73.5
6	58.8
7	34.3
8	0

MATH IN CAREERS

Transportation Engineer The Center for Transportation Analysis in the Oak Ridge National Laboratory publishes data about the transportation industry. One study relates gas mileage and a car's speed. The mileage (in miles per gallon) for a particular year, make, and model of car is shown in the table.

Speed (miles per hour)	Gas Milage (miles per gallon)
40	23.0
50	27.3
55	29.1
60	28.2
70	22.9

a. Identify the independent and dependent variables in this situation. State the units associated with each variable.

b. Sketch a parabola that you think best fits the plotted points. (You will not be able to make the parabola pass through all the points. Instead, you should try to draw the parabola so that some points fall above it and some below it.) Explain why a parabola is a reasonable curve to fit to the data.

c. Write the equation for a function of the form $m(s) = -0.03(s - h)^2 + k$, where s is the speed and m is the gas mileage. Use the coordinates of the vertex of your parabola to determine h and k, and a point on your parabola other than the vertex to solve for the unknown a.

d. Suppose that when the car was driven at a steady speed, its gas mileage was 25 miles per gallon. Describe how you can use your model to find the car's speed. Is only one speed or more than one speed possible? Explain, and then find the speed(s).

UNIT 4

Quadratic Equations and Models

MATH IN CAREERS

Competitive Diver Diving is the sport of jumping into the water from a springboard or platform. Competitive divers should have a strong understanding of the mathematics of projectile motion, including the time spent in the air, the speed at which they hit the water, and the maximum height of a jump.

If you are interested in a career as a competitive diver, you should study these mathematical subjects:

- Algebra
- Business math

Research other careers that require understanding of the mathematics of projectile motion. Check out the career activity at the end of the unit to find out how **competitive divers** use math.

Reading Start-Up

Vocabulary

Review Words

✔ coefficient *(coeficiente)*
✔ greatest common factor *(máximo común divisor (MCD)*
✔ irrational number *(número irracional)*
✔ perfect square *(cuadrado perfecto)*
✔ square root *(raíz cuadrada)*

Preview Words

completing the square *(completar el cuadrado)*
difference of two squares *(diferencia de dos cuadrados)*
Product Property of Square Roots *(Propiedad del producto de raíces cuadradas)*
quadratic formula *(fórmula cuadrática)*
Quotient Property of Square Roots *(Propiedad del cociente de raíces cuadradas)*

Visualize Vocabulary

Use the review words to complete the chart.

?	a square of a whole number
?	one of two equal factors of a number
?	the largest common factor of two or more given numbers
?	a real number that cannot be expressed as the ratio of two integers
?	a number that is multiplied by a variable

Understand Vocabulary

To become familiar with some of the vocabulary terms in this unit, consider the following. You may refer to the module, the glossary, or a dictionary.

1. The __?__ gives the solutions of a quadratic equation.
2. __?__ is a process that forms a perfect square trinomial.
3. By the __?__, $\pm\sqrt{\frac{16}{9}} = \pm\frac{\sqrt{16}}{\sqrt{9}} = \pm\frac{4}{3}$.

Active Reading

Pyramid Before beginning this unit create a pyramid to help you organize what you learn. Label each side with one of the module titles from this unit: "Using Factors to Solve Quadratic Equations," "Using Square Roots to Solve Quadratic Equations," and "Linear, Exponential, and Quadratic Models." As you study each module, write important ideas like vocabulary, properties, and formulas on the appropriate side.

Using Factors to Solve Quadratic Equations

MODULE 8

Essential Question: How can you use factoring a quadratic equation to solve real-world problems?

REAL WORLD VIDEO
Ruling out common elements in a scientific experiment is similar to removing common factors in an equation; logically, whatever is common to two samples can't be the cause of differences between them.

MODULE PERFORMANCE TASK PREVIEW

Fitting Through the Arch

An arched doorway is a strong structure that can usually support more weight than a rectangular doorway. An arched opening is also far less likely than a rectangular opening to topple from vibrations of a train passing through it. However, many man-made objects are rectangular, not curved as an arch is curved. So, how big can a rectangular object be and still pass through an arched door? Let's find out!

Are YOU Ready?

Complete these exercises to review skills you will need for this module.

- Online Homework
- Hints and Help
- Extra Practice

Exponents

Example 1 Simplify $8^5 \cdot 8^{-2}$.

$8^5 \cdot 8^{-2} = 8^{5+(-2)}$ The bases are the same. Add the exponents.

$= 8^3$

$= 512$ Multiply.

Simplify.

1. $3^7 \cdot 3^{-3}$

2. $7^7 \cdot 7^{-5}$

3. $6^9 \cdot 6^{-4} \cdot 6^{-5}$

Algebraic Expressions

Example 2 Simplify $13x + 5 - 9x^2 - 8$.

$13x + 5 - 9x^2 - 8$

$-9x^2 + 13x + 5 - 8$ Reorder in descending order of exponents.

$-9x^2 + 13x - 3$ Combine like terms.

Simplify.

4. $12x + 4x^2 - 3 - 7x$

5. $7x^2 - 6 + 8x - 2x^2$

6. $5 + 7x - 2x^2 - 6$

7. $-4x + 6x^2 - 8 + 9x - 3x^2$

Example 3 Multiply $(x + 7)(x - 3)$.

$(x + 7)(x - 3)$

$x(x) - 3(x) + 7(x) + 7(-3)$ Use FOIL.

$x^2 - 3x + 7x - 21$ Simplify.

$x^2 + 4x - 21$ Combine like terms.

Multiply.

8. $(x - 4)(x + 5)$

9. $(x - 9)(x - 6)$

10. $(2x - 3)(2x + 3)$

11. $(3x - 2)(2x + 5)$

8.1 Solving Equations by Factoring $x^2 + bx + c$

Essential Question: How can you use factoring to solve quadratic equations in standard form for which $a = 1$?

Explore 1 Using Algebra Tiles to Factor $x^2 + bx + c$

In this lesson, multiplying binomials using the FOIL process will be reversed and trinomials will be factored into two binomials. To learn how to factor, let's start with the expression $x^2 + 7x + 6$.

(A) Identify and draw the tiles needed to model the expression $x^2 + 7x + 6$.

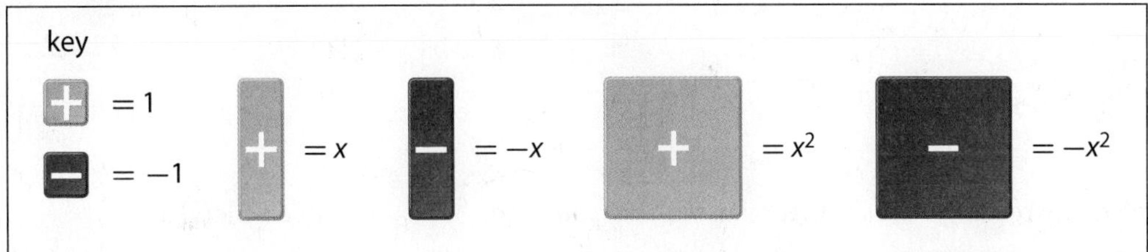

The tiles needed to model the expression $x^2 + 7x + 6$ are:

_____ x^2-tiles(s), _____ x-tile(s), and _____ unit tile(s).

(B) Arrange and draw the algebra tiles on a grid. Place the _____ x^2-tile(s) in the upper left corner and arrange the _____ unit tiles in two rows and three columns in the lower right corner.

(C) Try to complete the rectangle with the x-tiles. Notice that only _____ x-tiles fit on the grid, which leaves out _____ tile(s), so this arrangement is not correct.

(D) Rearrange the unit tiles so that all of the _____ x-tiles fit on the mat.

(E) Complete the multiplication grid by placing the factor tiles on the sides. Then write the factors modeled in this product.

$x^2 + 7x + 6 = (x + \_\_\_)(x + \_\_\_)$

Ⓕ Now let's look at how to factor a quadratic expression with a negative constant term. Use algebra tiles to factor $x^2 + x - 2$. Identify the tiles needed to model the expression.

▭ positive x^2-tile(s), ▭ positive x-tile(s), and ▭ negative unit tile(s)

Ⓖ Arrange the algebra tiles on the grid. Place the ▭ positive x^2-tile(s) in the upper left corner and arrange the ▭ negative unit tiles in the lower right corner.

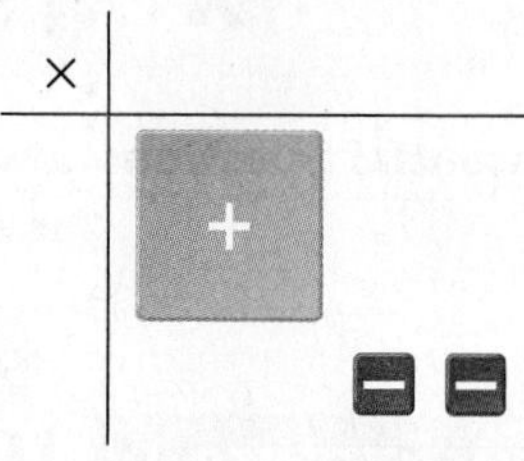

Ⓗ Fill in the empty spaces on the grid with x-tiles. There is/are ▭ positive x-tile(s) to place on the grid, so there will be ▭ empty places for x-tiles.

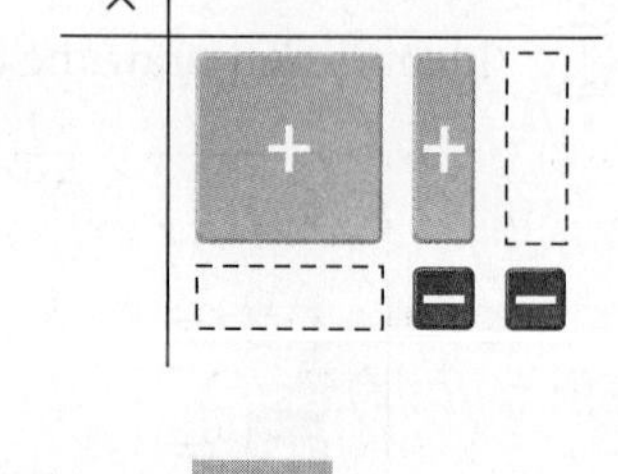

Ⓘ Complete the rectangle on the mat by using *zero pairs*. Add ▭ positive$x$-tile(s) and ▭ negative x-tile(s) to the grid in such a way that the factors work with all the tiles on the mat. Which mat shows the correct position of zero pairs?

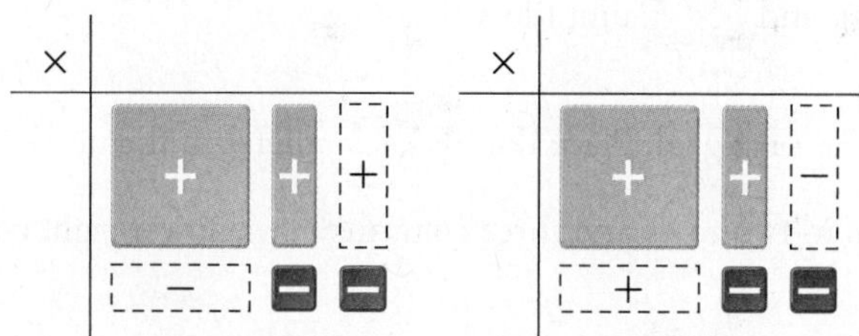

Ⓙ Complete the multiplication grid by placing the factor tiles on the sides. Then write the factors modeled in this product.

$x^2 + x - 2 = (x + \square)(x - \square)$

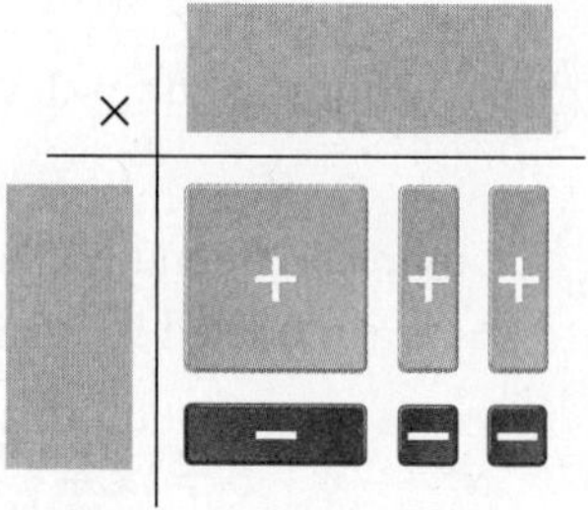

Reflect

1. Are there any other ways to factor the polynomial $x^2 + 7x + 6$ besides $(x + 6)(x + 1)$? Explain.

2. **Discussion** If c is positive in $x^2 + bx + c$, what sign can the constant terms of the factors have? What about when c is negative?

Explore 2 Factoring $x^2 + bx + c$

To factor $x^2 + bx + c$, you need to find two factors of c whose sum is b.

Factoring $x^2 + bx + c$	
WORDS	**EXAMPLE**
To factor a quadratic trinomial of the form $x^2 + bx + c$, find two factors of c whose sum is b. If no such integers exist, the trinomial is not factorable.	To factor $x^2 + 9x + 18$, look for factors of 18 whose sum is 9. Factors of 18 — Sum 1 and 18 — 19 — x 2 and 9 — 11 — x 3 and 6 — 9 — ✓ $x^2 + 9x + 18 = (x + 3)(x + 6)$

If c is positive, the constant terms of the factors have the same sign.

If c is negative, then one constant term of the factors is positive and one is negative.

(A) First, look at $x^2 + 11x + 30$. Find the values of b and c. $b =$ ___ $c =$ ___

(B) c is ___. The sign of the factors will be the ___.

(C) List the factor pairs of c, 30, and find the sum of each pair.

Factors of 30	Sum of Factors
1 and ___	1 + ___ = ___
2 and ___	2 + ___ = ___
3 and ___	3 + ___ = ___
5 and ___	5 + ___ = ___

(D) The factor pair whose sum equals b is ___.

Use this factor pair to factor the polynomial. $x^2 + 11x + 30 = (x + \_\_\_)(x + \_\_\_)$

(E) Now, look at $x^2 + 13x - 30$. Find the values of b and c.

$b =$ ______ $c =$ ______

(F) c is ______. The sign of the factors will be ______.

(G) List the factor pairs of c, -30, and find the sum of each pair.

Factors of −30	Sum of Factors
1 and ______	1 + ______ = ______
2 and ______	2 + ______ = ______
3 and ______	3 + ______ = ______
5 and ______	5 + ______ = ______
−1 and ______	−1 + ______ = ______
−2 and ______	−2 + ______ = ______
−3 and ______	−3 + ______ = ______
−5 and ______	−5 + ______ = ______

(H) The factor pair whose sum equals b is ______.

Use this factor pair to factor the polynomial.

$x^2 + 13x - 30 = (x + \_\_\_)(x - \_\_\_)$

Reflect

3. **Discussion** When factoring a trinomial of the form $x^2 + bx + c$, where c is negative, one binomial factor contains a positive factor of c and one contains a negative factor of c. How do you know which factor of c should be positive and which should be negative?

Explain 1 Solving Equations of the Form $x^2 - bx + c = 0$ by Factoring

As you have learned, the Zero Product Property can be used to solve quadratic equations in factored form.

Example 1 **Solve each equation by factoring. Check your answer by graphing.**

(A) $x^2 - 8x = -12$

First, write the equation in the form $x^2 - bx + c = 0$.

$x^2 - 8x = -12$ Original equation

$x^2 - 8x + 12 = 0$ Add 12 to both sides.

The expression $x^2 - 8x + 12$ is in the form $ax^2 + bx + c$, with $b < 0$ and $c > 0$, so the factors will have the same sign and they both will be negative.

Factors of 12	Sum of Factors
−1 and −12	$-1 + (-12) = -13$
−2 and −6	$-2 + (-6) = -8$
−3 and −4	$-3 + (-4) = -7$

The factor pair whose sum equals −8 is −2 and −6. Factor the equation, and use the Zero Product Property.

$$x^2 - 8x + 12 = 0$$

$$(x - 2)(x - 6) = 0$$

$$x - 2 = 0 \quad \text{or} \quad x - 6 = 0$$

$$x = 2 \qquad\qquad x = 6$$

The zeros of the equation are 2 and 6. Check this by graphing the related function, $f(x) = x^2 - 8x + 12$.

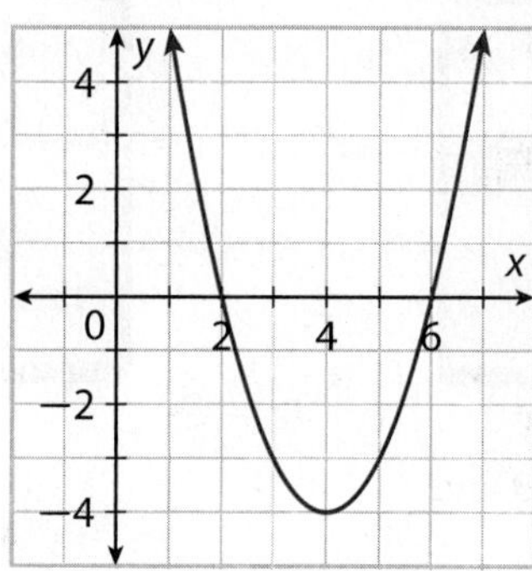

The x-intercepts of the graph are 2 and 6, which are the same as the zeros of the equation. The solutions of the equation are 2 and 6.

(B) $x^2 - 2x = 15$

First, rewrite the expression in the form $x^2 + bx + c = 0$.

$x^2 - 2x = 15$ Original equation

$x^2 - 2x - \boxed{15} = 0$ Subtract 15 both sides.

To find the zeros of the equation, start by factoring. List the factor pairs of c and find the sum of each pair. Since $c < 0$, the factors will have opposite signs. Since $c < 0$ and $b < 0$, the factor with the greater absolute value will be negative.

Factors of −15	Sum of Factors
1 and $\boxed{-15}$	$1 + \boxed{-15} = \boxed{-14}$
3 and $\boxed{-5}$	$3 + \boxed{-5} = \boxed{-2}$
−1 and $\boxed{15}$	$-1 + \boxed{15} = \boxed{14}$
−3 and $\boxed{5}$	$-3 + \boxed{5} = \boxed{2}$

The factor pair whose sum equals −2 is 3 and −5. Factor the equation, and use the Zero Product Property.

$$x^2 - 2x - 15 = 0$$

$$\left(x + \boxed{3}\right)\left(x - \boxed{5}\right) = 0$$

$$x + 3 = 0 \quad \text{or} \quad x - 5 = 0$$

$$x = \boxed{-3} \qquad x = \boxed{5}$$

The zeros of the equation are $\boxed{-3}$ and $\boxed{5}$. Check this by graphing the related function, $f(x) = x^2 - 2x = 15$.

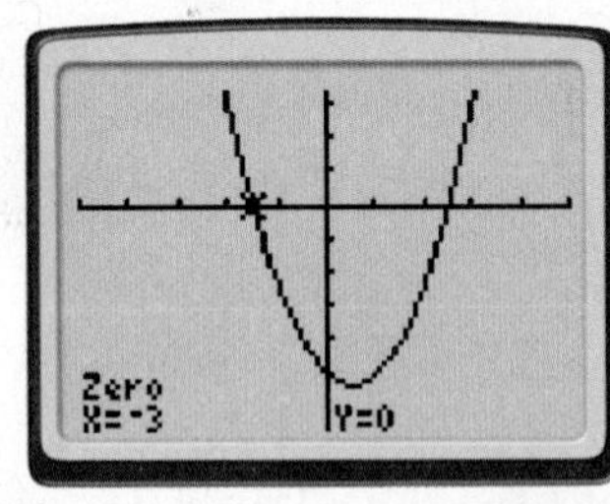

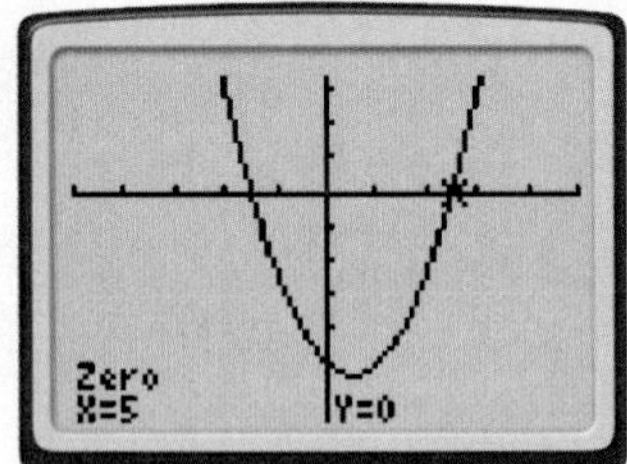

The solutions of the equation are −3 and 5.

Your Turn

Solve each equation.

9. $x^2 + 15x = -54$ **10.** $x^2 - 13x = -12$ **11.** $x^2 - x = 56$

Explain 2 Solving Equation Models of the Form $x^2 + bx + c = 0$ by Factoring

Some real-world problems can be solved by factoring a quadratic equation.

Example 2 **Solve each model by factoring.**

Architecture A rectangular porch has dimensions of $(x + 12)$ and $(x + 5)$ feet. If the area of the porch floor is 120 square feet, what are its length and width?

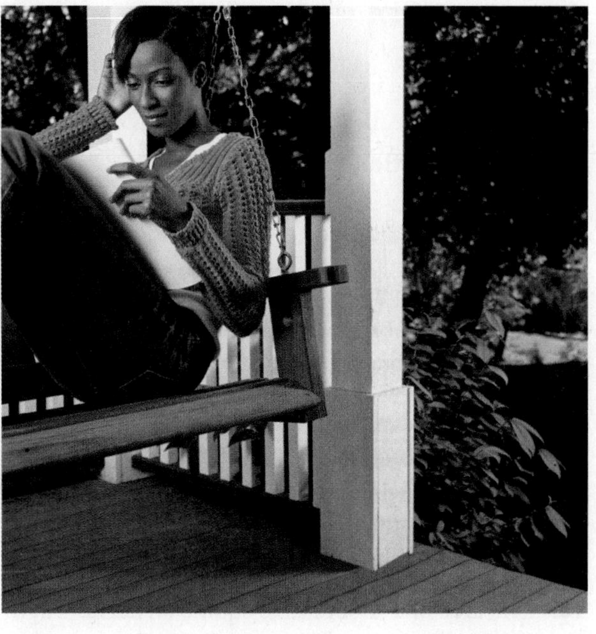

Write an equation for the problem. Substitute 120 for A for the area of the porch.

$$(x + 12)(x + 5) = A$$

$$x^2 + 17x + 60 = A$$

$$x^2 + 17 + 60 = 120$$

$$x^2 + 17x - 60 = 0$$

The factors of -60 that have a sum of 17 are 20 and -3. Use Zero Product Property to find x.

$$(x + 20)(x - 3) = 0$$

$$x + 20 = 0 \quad \text{or} \quad x - 3 = 0$$

$$x = -20 \qquad x = 3$$

Since the area cannot be negative, $x = 3$ feet.

Therefore, the dimensions of the porch are $3 + 12 = 15$ feet long and $3 + 5 = 8$ feet wide.

Elaborate

12. How are the solutions of a quadratic equation related to the zeros of the related function?

13. **Essential Question Check-In** How can you solve a quadratic equation by factoring?

Evaluate: Homework and Practice

- Online Homework
- Hints and Help
- Extra Practice

Use algebra tiles to model the factors of each expression.

1. $x^2 + 6x + 8$

$x^2 + 6x + 8 = (x \quad)(x \quad)$

2. $x^2 + 2x - 3$

$x^2 + 2x - 3 = (x \quad)(x \quad)$

Factor the expressions.

3. $x^2 - 15x + 44$

4. $x^2 + 22x + 120$

5. $x^2 + 14x - 32$

6. $x^2 - 12x - 45$

7. $x^2 + 10x + 24$

8. $x^2 + 7x - 8$

Solve each equation.

9. $x^2 + 19x = -84$

10. $x^2 - 18x = -56$

11. $x^2 - 12x + 27 = 0$

12. $x^2 - 9x - 10 = 0$

13. $x^2 + 6x = 135$

14. $x^2 + 13x = -40$

15. $x^2 + x - 132 = 0$

16. $x^2 - 14x = 32$

17. **Construction** The area of a rectangular fountain is $(x^2 + 12x + 20)$ square feet. A 2-foot walkway is built around the fountain. Find the dimensions of the outside border of the walkway.

18. The area of a room is 396 square feet. The length is $(x + 3)$, and the width is $(x + 7)$ feet. Find the dimensions of the room.

19. A rectangular Persian carpet has an area of $(x^2 + x - 20)$ square feet and a length of $(x + 5)$ feet. The Persian carpet is displayed on a wall. The wall has a width of $(x + 2)$ feet and an area of $(x^2 + 17x + 30)$ square feet. Find the dimensions of the rug and the wall if $x = 20$ feet.

20. The area of a poster board is $x^2 + 3x - 10$ square inches. Find the dimensions of the poster board if $x = 14$.

21. Match the equation to its solutions.

A. $x^2 - 3x - 18 = 0$	a. ___?___	3 and 6
B. $x^2 - 9x + 18 = 0$	b. ___?___	-3 and -6
C. $x^2 + 3x - 18 = 0$	c. ___?___	3 and -6
D. $x^2 + 9x + 18 = 0$	d. ___?___	-3 and 6

H.O.T. Focus on Higher Order Thinking

22. **Explain the Error** Amelie found the solutions of the equation $x^2 - x = 42$ to be 6 and -7. Explain why this answer is incorrect. Then, find the correct solutions.

23. **Communicate Mathematical Ideas** Rico says the expression $x^2 + bx + c$ is factorable when $b = c = 4$. Are there any other values where $b = c$ that make the expression factorable? Explain.

24. **Multi-Step** A homeowner wants to enlarge a rectangular closet that has an area of $(x^2 + 3x + 2)$ square feet. The length of the closet is greater than the width. After construction, the area will be $(x^2 + 8x + 15)$ square feet.

   a. Find the dimensions of the closet before construction.

   b. Find the dimensions of the closet after construction.

   c. By how many feet will the length and width increase after construction?

25. **Critical Thinking** Given $x^2 + bx + 64$, find all the values of b for which the quadratic expression has factors $(x + p)$ and $(x + q)$, where p and q are integers.

Lesson Performance Task

Part of the the roof of a factory is devoted to mechanical support and part to green space. The area of the roof R of a large building can be modeled by the polynomial $2x^2 - 251x + 80{,}000$ and the area M roof that is devoted to mechanical support can be modeled by the polynomial $x^2 + 224x + 31{,}250$. The rest of the area is a rectangular green space. Given that the area G of the green space is 123,750 square feet, write and solve quadratic equations to find the dimensions of the green space.

8.2 Solving Equations by Factoring $ax^2 + bx + c$

Resource Locker

Essential Question: How can you use factoring to solve quadratic equations in standard form for which $a \neq 1$?

Explore Factoring $ax^2 + bx + c$ When $c > 0$

When you factor a quadratic expression in standard form $(ax^2 + bx + c)$, you are looking for two binomials, and possibly a constant numerical factor whose product is the original quadratic expression.

Recall that the product of two binomials is found by applying the Distributive Property, abbreviated sometimes as FOIL:

$$(2x + 5)(3x + 2) = \underbrace{6x^2}_{F} + \underbrace{4x}_{O} + \underbrace{15x}_{I} + \underbrace{10}_{L} = 6x^2 + 19x + 10$$

F The product of the coefficients of the first terms is a.

O, I The sum of the coefficients of the outer and inner products is b.

L The product of the last terms is c.

Because the a and c coefficients each result from a single product of terms from the binomials, the coefficients in the binomial factors will be a combination of the factors of a and c. The trick is to find the combination of factors that results in the correct value of b.

Follow the steps to factor the quadratic $4x^2 + 26x + 42$.

(A) First, factor out the largest common factor of 4, 26, and 42 if it is anything other than 1.

$4x^2 + 26x + 42 = \square(2x^2 + 13x + 21)$

(B) Next, list the factor pairs of 2.

(C) List the factor pairs of 21.

(D) Make a table listing the combinations of the factors of a and c, and find the value of b that results from summing the outer and inner products of the factors.

Factors of 2	Factors of 21	Outer + inner
$\square$ and 2	1 and $\square$	$(\square)(\square) + (2)(1) = 23$
1 and 2	$\square$ and 7	$\square$
1 and 2	7 and 3	$\square$
1 and 2	$\square$ and 1	$\square$

(E) Copy the pair of factors that resulted in an outer + inner sum of 13 into the binomial factors. Be careful to keep the inner and outer factors from the table as inner and outer coefficients in the binomials.

$2x^2 + 13x + 21 = (\square x + \square)(\square x + \square)$

(F) Replace the common factor of the original coefficients to complete the factorization of the original quadratic.

$4x^2 + 26x + 42 = \square(x + 3)(2x + 7)$

Reflect

1. **Critical Thinking** Explain why you should use negative factors of c when factoring a quadratic with $c > 0$ and $b < 0$.
2. **What If?** If none of the factor pairs for a and c result in the correct value for b, what do you know about the quadratic?
3. **Discussion** Why did you have to check each factor pair twice for the factors of c (3 and 7 versus 7 and 3) but only once for the factors of a (1 and 2, but not 2 and 1)? Hint: Compare the outer and inner sums of rows two and three in the table, and also check the outer and inner sums by switching the order of both pairs from row 2 (check 2 and 1 for a with 7 and 3 for c).

Explain 1 Factoring $ax^2 + bx + c$ When $c < 0$

Factoring $x^2 + bx + c$ when $c < 0$ requires one negative and one positive factor of c. The same applies for expressions of the form $ax^2 + bx + c$ as long as $a > 0$. When checking factor pairs, remember to consider factors of c in both orders, **and** consider factor pairs with the negative sign on either member of the pair of c factors.

When you find a combination of factors whose outer and inner product sum is equal to b, you have found the solution. Make sure you fill in the factor table systematically so that you do not skip any combinations.

If $a < 0$, factor out -1 from all three coefficients, or use a negative common factor, so that the factors of a can be left as positive numbers.

Example 1 **Factor the quadratic by checking factor pairs.**

(A) $6x^2 - 21x - 45$

Find the largest common factor of 6, 21, and 45, and factor it out, keeping the coefficient of x^2 positive.

$6x^2 - 21x - 45 = 3(2x^2 - 7x - 15)$

Factors of *a*	Factors of *c*	Outer Product + Inner Product
1 and 2	1 and −15	$(1)(-15) + (2)(1) = -13$
1 and 2	3 and −5	$(1)(-5) + (2)(3) = 1$
1 and 2	5 and −3	$(1)(-3) + (2)(5) = 7$
1 and 2	15 and −1	$(1)(-1) + (2)(15) = 29$
1 and 2	−1 and 15	$(1)(15) + (2)(-1) = 13$
1 and 2	−3 and 5	$(1)(5) + (2)(-3) = -1$
1 and 2	−5 and 3	$(1)(3) + (2)(-5) = -7$
1 and 2	−15 and 1	$(1)(1) + (2)(-15) = -29$

Use the combination of factor pairs that results in a value of −7 for the *b* coefficient.

$2x^2 - 7x - 15 = (x - 5)(2x + 3)$

Replace the common factor of the original coefficients to factor the original quadratic.

$6x^2 - 21x - 45 = 3(x - 5)(2x + 3)$

(B) $20x^2 - 40x - 25$

Factor out common factors of the terms.

$20x^2 - 40x - 25 = \boxed{5}\,(4x^2 - 8x - 5)$

Factors of *a*	Factors of *c*	Outer Product + Inner Product
1 and 4	1 and − 5	$(1)(-5) + (4)(1) = \boxed{-1}$
1 and 4	5 and −1	$\boxed{(1)(-1)} + \boxed{(4)(5)} = \boxed{19}$
1 and 4	−1 and 5	$\boxed{(1)(5)} + \boxed{(4)(-1)} = \boxed{1}$
1 and 4	−5 and 1	$\boxed{(1)(1)} + \boxed{(4)(-5)} = \boxed{-19}$
2 and 2	1 and −5	$\boxed{(2)(-5)} + \boxed{(2)(1)} = \boxed{-8}$
2 and 2	−1 and 5	$\boxed{(2)(-1)} + \boxed{(2)(5)} = \boxed{8}$

Use the combination of factor pairs that results in a value of $\boxed{-8}$ for *b*.

$4x^2 - 8x - 5 = \left(\boxed{2}\,x + \boxed{1}\right)\left(\boxed{2}\,x + \boxed{-5}\right)$

Replace the common factor of the original coefficients to factor the original quadratic.

$20x^2 - 40x - 25 = \boxed{5}\,(2x + 1)(2x - 5)$

Reflect

4. **What If?** Suppose a is a negative number. What would be the first step in factoring $ax^2 + bx + c$?

Your Turn

5. Factor $-5x^2 + 8x + 4$.

Explain 2 Solving Equations of the Form $ax^2 + bx + c = 0$ by Factoring

For a quadratic equation in standard form, $ax^2 + bx + c = 0$, factoring the quadratic expression into binomials lets you use the Zero Product Property to solve the equation, as you have done previously. If the equation is not in standard form, convert it to standard form by moving all terms to one side of the equation and combining like terms.

Example 2 **Change the quadratic equation to standard form if necessary and then solve by factoring.**

(A) $2x^2 + 7x - 2 = 4x^2 + 4$

Convert the equation to standard form:

Subtract $4x^2$ and 4 from both sides. $-2x^2 + 7x - 6 = 0$

Multiply both sides by -1. $2x^2 - 7x + 6 = 0$

Consider factor pairs for 2 and 6. Use negative factors of 6 to get a negative value for b.

Use the combination pair that results in a sum of -7 and write the equation in factored form. Then solve it using the Zero Product Property.

$$(x - 2)(2x - 3) = 0$$

$$x - 2 = 0 \quad \text{or} \quad 2x - 3 = 0$$

$$x = 2 \qquad 2x = 3$$

$$x = \frac{3}{2}$$

The solution is $x = 2$ or $x = \frac{3}{2}$.

The solution can be checked by graphing the related function, $f(x) = 2x^2 - 7x + 6$, and finding the x-intercepts.

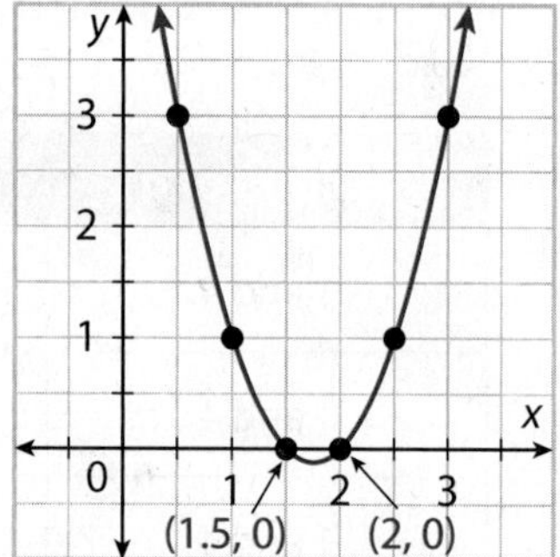

(B) $3(x^2 - 1) = -3x^2 + 2x + 5$

Write the equation in standard form and factor so you can apply the Zero Product Property.

$$3x^2 - 3 = -3x^2 + 2x + 5$$

$$6x^2 - 2x - 8 = 0$$

$$3x^2 - x - 4 = 0$$

Use the combination pair that results in a sum of -1.

$$(x + 1)(3x + -4) = 0$$

$$x + 1 = 0 \quad \text{or} \quad 3x - 4 = 0$$

$$x = -1 \qquad 3x = 4$$

$$x = \frac{4}{3}$$

The solutions are -1 and $\frac{4}{3}$.

Use a graphing calculator to check the solutions.

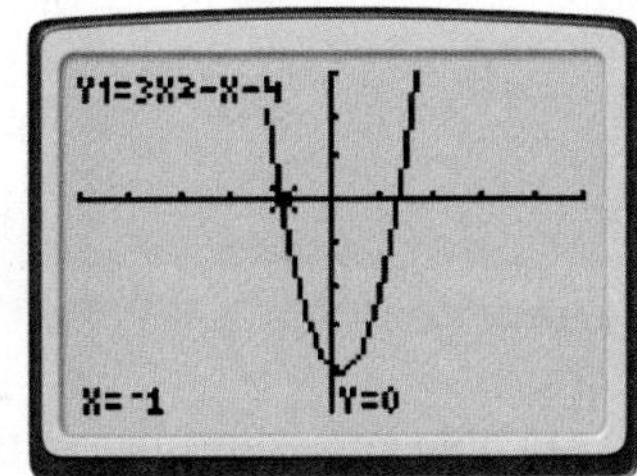

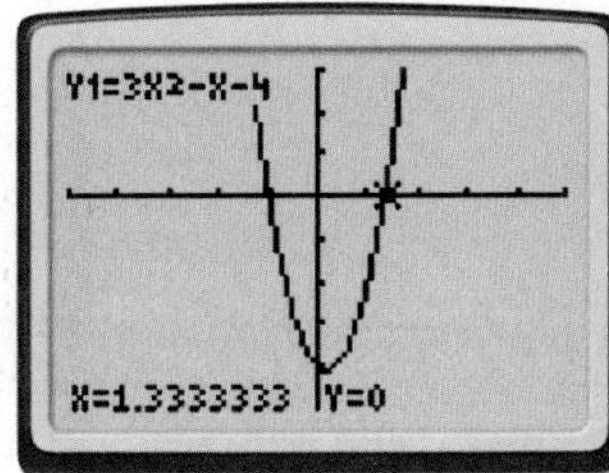

Reflect

6. In the two examples, a common factor was divided out at the beginning of the solution, and it was not used again. Why didn't you include the common term again when solving x for the original quadratic equation?

Your Turn

Solve by factoring.

7. $12x^2 + 48x + 45 = 0$

Explain 3 Solving Equation Models of the Form $ax^2 + bx + c = 0$ by Factoring

A projectile is an object moving through the air without any forces other than gravity acting on it. The height of a projectile at a time in seconds can be found by using the formula $h = -16t^2 + vt + s$, where v is in the initial upwards velocity in feet per second (and can be a negative number if the projectile is launched downwards) and s is starting height in feet. The a term of -16 accounts for the effect of gravity accelerating the projectile downwards and is the only appropriate value when measuring distance with feet and time in seconds.

To use the model to make predictions about the behavior of a projectile, you need to read the description of the situation carefully and identify the initial velocity, the initial height, and the height at time t.

Example 3 **Read the real-world situation and substitute in values for the projectile motion formula. Then solve the resulting quadratic equation by factoring to answer the question.**

(A) When a baseball player hits a baseball into the air, the height of the ball at t seconds after the ball is hit can be modeled with the projectile motion formula. If the ball is hit at 3 feet off the ground with an upward velocity of 47 feet per second, how long will it take for the ball to hit the ground, assuming it is not caught?

Find the parameters v and s from the description of the problem.

$v = 47$ $\quad$ $s = 3$ $\quad$ $h = 0$

Substitute parameter values. $\quad -16t^2 + 47t + 3 = 0$

Divide both sides by -1. $\quad 16t^2 - 47t - 3 = 0$

Use the combination pair that results in a sum of −47.

$$(t-3)(16t+1)=0$$

$$t-3=0 \quad \text{or} \quad 16t+1=0$$

$$t=3 \qquad 16t=-1$$

$$t=-\frac{1}{16}$$

The solutions are 3 and $-\frac{1}{16}$.

The negative time answer can be rejected because it is not a reasonable value for time in this situation. The correct answer is 3 seconds.

(B) A child standing on a river bank ten feet above the river throws a rock toward the river at a speed of 12 feet per second. How long does it take before the rock splashes into the river?

Find the parameters v and s from the description of the provblem.

$v = -12 \qquad s = 10 \qquad h = 0$

Substitute parameter values. $\quad -16t^2 + -12t + 10 = 0$

Divide both sides by -2. $\quad 8t^2 + 6t + -5 = 0$

Use the combination pair that results in a sum of 6.

$$(2t-1)(4t+5)=0$$

$$2t-1=0 \quad \text{or} \quad 4t+5=0$$

$$2t=1 \qquad 4t=-5$$

$$t=\frac{1}{2} \qquad t=-\frac{5}{4}$$

The solutions are $\frac{1}{2}$ and $-\frac{5}{4}$.

The only correct solution to the time it takes the rock to hit the water is $\frac{1}{2}$ second.

Your Turn

8. How long does it take a rock to hit the ground if thrown off the edge of a 72 foot tall building roof with an upward velocity of 24 feet per second?

Elaborate

9. **Discussion** What happens if you do not remove the common factor from the coefficients before trying to factor the quadratic equation?

10. Explain how you can know there are never more than two solutions to a quadratic equation, based on what you know about the graph of a quadratic function.

11. **Essential Question Check-In** Describe the steps it takes to solve a quadratic equation by factoring.

Evaluate: Homework and Practice

- Online Homework
- Hints and Help
- Extra Practice

Factor the following quadratic expressions.

1. $6x^2 + 5x + 1$

2. $9x^2 + 33x + 30$

3. $4x^2 - 8x + 3$

4. $24x^2 - 44x + 12$

5. $3x^2 - 2x - 5$

6. $-10x^2 + 3x + 4$

7. $12x^2 + 22x - 14$

8. $-15x^2 + 21x + 18$

Solve the following quadratic equations.

9. $5x^2 + 18x + 9 = 0$

10. $12x^2 - 36x + 15 = 0$

11. $6x^2 + 28x - 2 = 2x - 10$

12. $-100x^2 + 55x + 3 = 50x^2 - 55x + 23$

13. $8x^2 - 10x - 3 = 0$

14. $-12x^2 = 34x - 28$

15. $(8x + 7)(x + 1) = 9$

16. $3(4x - 1)(4x + 3) = 48x$

Read the real-world situation and substitute in values for the projectile motion formula. Then solve the resulting quadratic equation by factoring to answer the question.

17. A golfer takes a swing from a hill twenty feet above the cup with an initial upwards velocity of 32 feet per second. How long

does it take the ball to land on the ground near the cup?

18. An airplane pilot jumps out of an airplane and has an initial velocity of 60 feet per second downwards. How long does it take to fall from 1000 feet to 900 feet before the parachute opens?

A race car driving under the caution flag at 80 feet per second begins to accelerate at a constant rate after the warning flag. The distance traveled since the warning flag in feet is characterized by $30t^2 + 80t$, where t is the time in seconds after the car starts accelerating again.

19. How long does it take the car to travel 30 feet after it begins accelerating?

20. How long will the car take to travel 160 feet?

Geometry **For each rectangle with area given, determine the binomial factors that describe the dimensions.**

21.

area = $6x^2 + 17x - 3$

22.

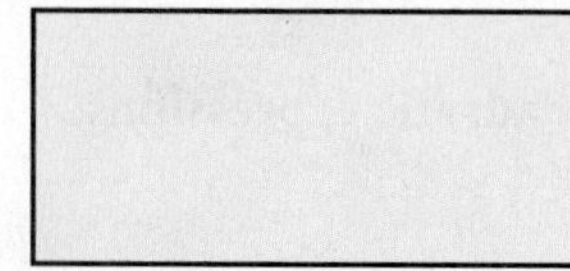

area = $21x^2 + 13x + 2$

23. **Multiple Response** Which of the following expressions in the list describes the complete factorization of the quadratic expression $15x^2 - 25x - 10$?

a. $(3x + 1)(5x - 10)$ **b.** $5(3x + 1)(x - 2)$ **c.** $5(x + 2)(3x - 1)$

d. $5(x - 2)(3x + 1)$ **e.** $5(3x - 1)(x + 2)$ **f.** $(5x - 10)(3x + 1)$

H.O.T. Focus on Higher Order Thinking

24. **Multi-Part Response** A basketball player shoots at the basket from a starting height of 6 feet and an upwards velocity of 20 feet per second. Determine how long it takes for the shot to drop through the basket, which is mounted at a height of 10 feet.

a. Set up the equation for projectile motion to solve for time and convert it to standard form.

b. Solve the equation by factoring.

c. Explain why you got two positive solutions to the equation, and determine how you can rule one of them out to find the answer to the question. Hint: Solving the equation graphically may give you a hint.

25. **Critical Thinking** Find the binomial factors of $4x^2 - 25$.

26. **Communicate Mathematical Ideas** Find all the values of b that make the expression $3x^2 + bx - 4$ factorable.

Lesson Performance Task

The equation for the motion of an object with constant acceleration is $d = d_0 + vt + \frac{1}{2}at^2$, where d is distance from a given point in meters, d_0 is the initial distance from the starting point in meters, v is the starting velocity in meters per second, a is acceleration in meters per second squared, and t is time in seconds.

A car is stopped at a traffic light. When the light turns green, the driver begins to drive, accelerating at a constant rate of 4 meters per second squared. A bus is traveling at a speed of 15 meters per second in another lane. The bus is 7 meters behind the car as it begins to accelerate.

Find when the bus passes the car, when the car passes the bus, and how far each has traveled each time they pass one another.

8.3 Using Special Factors to Solve Equations

Essential Question: How can you use special products to aid in solving quadratic equations by factoring?

Explore Exploring Factors of Perfect Square Trinomials

When you use algebra tiles to factor a polynomial, you must arrange the unit tiles on the grid in a rectangle. Sometimes, you can arrange the unit tiles to form a square. Trinomials of this type are called perfect-square trinomials.

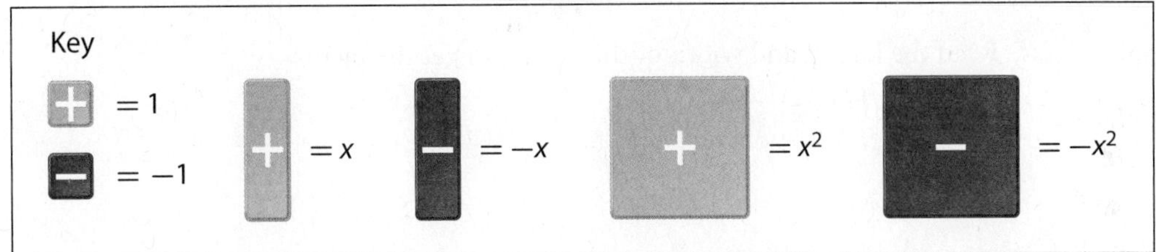

(A) Use algebra tiles to factor $x^2 + 6x + 9$.

Identify the number of tiles you need to model the expression. You need ___ x^2-tiles, ___ x-tiles, and ___ unit tiles.

(B) Arrange the algebra tiles on a grid like the one shown below. Place the ___ x^2-tile in the upper left corner, and arrange the ___ unit tiles in the lower right corner.

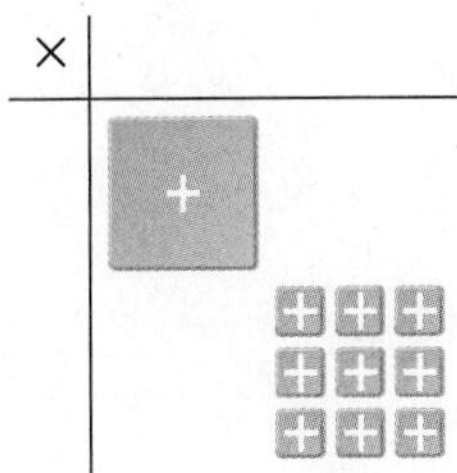

(C) Fill in the empty spaces on the grid with x-tiles.

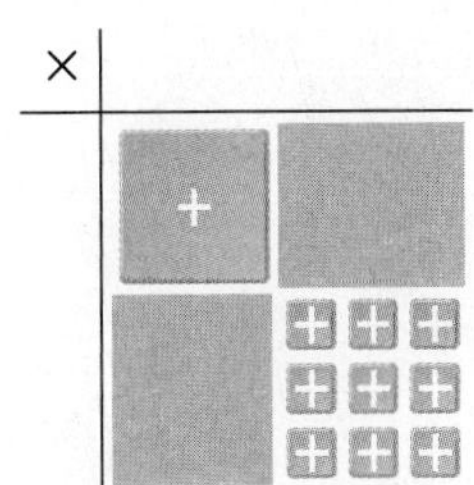

(D) All ___ x-tiles were used, so all the tiles are accounted for and fit in the square with sides of length ___. Read the length and width of the square to get the factors of the trinomial $x^2 + 6x + 9 = (x + \_\_\_)(x + \_\_\_)$.

(E) Now, use algebra tiles to factor $x^2 - 8x + 16$.

You need ___ x^2-tiles, ___ $-x$ -tiles, and ___ unit tiles to model the expression.

(F) Arrange the algebra tiles on a multiplication grid. Place the ___ x^2-tile in the upper left corner, and arrange the ___ unit tiles in the lower right corner.

(G) Fill in the empty spaces on the grid with $-x$-tiles.

(H) All ___ $-x$ -tiles were used, so all the tiles are accounted for and fit in a square with sides of length ___. Read the length and width of the square to get the factors of the trinomial $x^2 - 8x + 16 = (\_\_\_)(\_\_\_)$.

Reflect

1. **What If?** Suppose that the middle term in $x^2 + 6x + 9$ was changed from $6x$ to $10x$. How would this affect the way you factor the polynomial?
2. If the positive unit squares are arranged in a square of unit tiles when factoring with algebra tiles, what will be true about the binomial factors? (The coefficient of the x^2 term is 1 as in the previous problems.)

Explain 1 Factoring $a^2x^2 + 2abx + b^2$ and $a^2x^2 - 2abx + b^2$

Recall that a perfect-square trinomial can be represented algebraically in either the form $a^2 + 2ab + b^2$ or the form $a^2 - 2ab + b^2$.

Perfect-Square Trinomials

Perfect-Square Trinomials	
Perfect-Square Trinomial	**Examples**
$a^2 + 2ab + b^2 = (a+b)(a+b) = (a+b)^2$	$x^2 + 6x + 9 = (x+3)(x+3) = (x+3)^2$
	$c^2x^2 + 2cdx + d^2 = (cx)^2 + 2cdx + d^2 = (cx+d)(cx+d) = (cx+d)^2$
$a^2 - 2ab + b^2 = (a-b)(a-b) = (a-b)^2$	$x^2 - 10x + 25 = (x-5)(x-5) = (x-5)^2$
	$c^2x^2 - 2cdx + d^2 = (cx)^2 - 2cdx + d^2 = (cx-d)(cx-d) = (cx-d)^2$

Example 1 **Factor perfect-square trinomials.**

(A) $4x^3 - 24x^2 + 36x$

$4x^3 - 24x^2 + 36x = 4x(x^2 - 6x + 9)$ Factor out the common monomial factor $4x$.

$= 4x\,[x^2 - 2(1 \cdot 3)x + 3^2]$ Rewrite the perfect square trinomial in the form $a^2x^2 - 2abx + b^2$.

$= 4x(x-3)(x-3)$ Rewrite the perfect square trinomial in the form $(ax-b)(ax-b)$ to obtain factors.

The factored form of $4x^3 - 24x^2 + 36x$ is $4x(x-3)(x-3)$, or $4x(x-3)^2$.

(B) $x^2 + 16x + 64$

$x^2 + 16x + 64 = x^2 + 2(1 \cdot 8)x + 8^2$ Rewrite in the form $a^2x^2 + 2abx + b^2$.

$= (x+8)(x+8)$ Rewrite in the form $(ax+b)(ax+b)$.

The factored form of $x^2 + 16x + 64$ is $(x+8)(x+8)$, or $(x+8)^2$.

Your Turn

Factor perfect-square trinomials.

3. $2y^3 + 12y^2 + 18y$

4. $100z^2 - 20z + 1$

Explain 2 Factoring $a^2x^2 - b^2 = 0$

Recall that a difference of squares can be written algebraically as $a^2 - b^2$ and factored as $(a + b)(a - b)$.

Difference of Squares

Difference of Two Squares	
Perfect-Square Trinomial	**Examples**
$a^2 - b^2 = (a + b)(a - b)$	$x^2 - 9 = (x + 3)(x - 3)$ $4x^2 - 9 = (2x + 3)(2x - 3)$ $9x^2 - 1 = (3x + 1)(3x - 1)$ $c^2x^2 - d^2 = (cx)^2 - d^2$ $= (cx + d)(cx - d)$

Example 2 Factor each difference of squares.

(A) $x^2 - 49$

$x^2 - 49 = x^2 - 7^2$ Rewrite in the form $a^2x^2 - b^2$.

$= (x + 7)(x - 7)$ Rewrite in the form $(ax + b)(ax - b)$.

The factored form of $x^2 - 49$ is $(x + 7)(x - 7)$.

(B) $49q^2 - 4p^2$

$49q^2 - 4p^2 = 7^2 q^2 - (2p)^2$ Rewrite in the form $a^2x^2 - b^2$.

$= (7q + 2p)(7q - 2p)$ Rewrite in the form $(ax + b)(ax - b)$.

The factored form of $49q^2 - 4p^2$ is $(7q + 2p)(7q - 2p)$.

Reflect

5. **Discussion** James was factoring a difference of squares but did not finish his work. What steps is he missing?

$16x^4 - 1 = (4x^2)^2 - 1$

$= (4x^2 + 1)(4x^2 - 1)$

Your Turn

Factor each difference of squares.

6. $x^2 - 144$

7. $81y^4 - 9y^2$

Explain 3 Solving Equations with Special Factors

Equations with special factors can be solved using the Zero Product Property. Remember, the Zero Product Property states that if the product of two factors is zero, then at least one of the factors must be zero. For example, if $(x + 1)(x + 9) = 0$ then $x + 1 = 0$ or $x + 9 = 0$. Consequently, the solutions for the equation are $x = -1$ or $x = -9$.

Example 3 **Solve the following equations with special factors.**

(A) $4x^2 + 12x + 9 = 0$

$4x^2 + 12x + 9 = 0$	
$2^2x^2 + 2(2 \cdot 3)x + 3^2 = 0$	Rewrite in the form $a^2x^2 + 2abx + b^2$.
$(2x + 3)(2x + 3) = 0$	Rewrite in the form $(ax + b)(ax + b)$.
$2x + 3 = 0$	Set factors equal to 0 using Zero Product Property.
$x = -\frac{3}{2}$	Solve equation.

(B) $25x^2 - 1 = 0$

$25x^2 - 1 = 0$	
$\boxed{5}^2 x^2 - \boxed{1}^2 = 0$	Rewrite in the form $a^2x^2 + 2abx + b^2$.
$(\boxed{5x + 1})(\boxed{5x - 1}) = 0$	Rewrite in the form $(ax + b)(ax - b)$.
$\boxed{5x - 1} = 0$ or $\boxed{5x + 1} = 0$	Set factors equal to 0 using Zero Product Property.
$x = \boxed{\frac{1}{5}}$ or $x = \boxed{-\frac{1}{5}}$	Solve equation.

Your Turn

Solve the following equations with special factors.

8. $25x^2 - 10x + 1 = 0$

9. $8x^4 - 2x^2 = 0$

Explain 4 Solving Equation Models with Special Factors

For each real-world scenario, solve the model which involves an equation with special factors.

Example 4 **Write the given information and manipulate into a familiar form. Solve the equation to answer a question about the situation.**

(A) As a satellite falls from outer space onto Mars, its distance in miles from the planet is given by the formula $d = -9t^2 + 776$, where t is the number of hours it has fallen. Find when the satellite will be 200 miles away from Mars.

Analyze Information

Identify the important information

- The satellite's distance in miles is given by the formula $d = -9t^2 + 776$.
- The satellite distance at some time t is $d = 200$.

Formulate a Plan

Substituting the value of the constant $d = 200$ into the equation $d = -9t^2 + 776$ you get the equation $200 = -9t^2 + 776$. Simplify the new equation into a familiar form and solve it.

Solve

Rewrite the equation to be equal to 0.

$\boxed{200} = -9t^2 + 776$ Subtract 200 from both sides.

$0 = -9t^2 + \boxed{576}$ Divide both sides by -1.

$0 = 9t^2 - \boxed{576}$ Factor out 9.

$0 = \boxed{9}\left(t^2 - \boxed{64}\right)$

The equation contains a difference of squares that you can factor.

$0 = 9\left(\boxed{t + 8}\right)\left(\boxed{t - 8}\right)$

Use the Zero Product Property to solve.

$0 = 9\left(t + \boxed{8}\right)\left(t - \boxed{8}\right)$

$\boxed{t + 8} = 0$ or $t - 8 = \boxed{0}$

$t = \boxed{\pm 8}$

The answer is $t = \boxed{8}$ because time must be positive. So, the satellite has fallen for $\boxed{8}$ hours.

Justify and Evaluate

$t =$ 8 makes sense because time must be positive. Check by substituting this value of t into the original equation.

$$-9 \cdot 8^2 + 776 = -9 \cdot 64 + 776$$

$$= 776 - 576$$

$$= 200$$

This is what is expected from the given information.

Your Turn

Write the given information and manipulate it into a familiar form. Solve the equation to answer a question about the situation.

10. A volleyball player sets the ball in the air, and the height of the ball after t seconds is given in feet by $h = -16t^2 + 12t + 6$. A teammate wants to wait until the ball is 8 feet in the air before she spikes it. When should the teammate spike the ball? How many reasonable solutions are there to this problem? Explain.

11. The height of a model rocket is given (in centimeters) by the formula $h = -490t^2$, where t is measured in seconds and $h = 0$ refers to its original height at the top of a mountain. It begins to fly down from the mountain-top at time $t = 0$. When has the rocket descended 490 centimeters?

Elaborate

12. Are the perfect square trinomials $a^2 + 2ab + b^2$ and $a^2 - 2ab + b^2$ very different? How can you get one from the other?

13. How would you go about factoring $a^2 - 2ab + b^2 - 1$?

14. Setting a perfect-square trinomial equal to zero, $a^2x^2 + 2abx + b^2 = 0$, produces how many solutions? How many solutions are produced setting a difference of squares equal to zero, $a^2x^2 - b^2 = 0$?

15. Physical problems involving projectile motion can be modeled using the general equation $h = -16t^2 + v_0t$. Here, h refers to the relative height of the projectile from its initial position, v_0 is its initial vertical velocity, and t is time elapsed from launch. If you are measuring the height of the projectile as it descends from a high place, and it was launched with $v_0 = 0$ (which means it was thrown horizontally or dropped), how would you find the solution using special factors? (Assume that the height the projectile has descended is a square number in this question, although this is not a requirement in real life).

16. Essential Question Check-In How can you use special products to solve quadratic equations?

Evaluate: Homework and Practice

- Online Homework
- Hints and Help
- Extra Practice

For each trinomial, draw algebra tiles to show the factored form. Then, write the factored form.

1. $x^2 - 10x + 25$

2. $x^2 + 8x + 16$

Factor.

3. $4x^2 + 4x + 1$

4. $9x^2 - 18x + 9$

5. $16x^3 + 8x^2 + x$

6. $32x^3 - 16x^2 + 2x$

7. $x^2 - 169$

8. $4p^2 - 9q^4$

9. $32x^4 - 8x^2$

10. $2y^5 - 32z^4y$

Solve the following equations with special factors.

11. $25x^2 + 20x + 4 = 0$

12. $x^3 - 10x^2 + 25x = 0$

13. $4x^4 + 8x^3 + 4x^2 = 0$

14. $4x^2 - 8x + 4 = 0$

15. $x^2 - 81 = 0$

16. $2x^3 - 2x = 0$

17. $16q^2 - 81 = 0$

18. $4p^4 - 25p^2 = -16p^2$

Jivesh is analyzing the flight of a few of his model rockets that he assembled with various equations. In each equation, h is the height of the rocket in centimeters, and the rocket was fired from the ground at time $t = 0$, where t is measured in seconds.

19. For Jivesh's Model A rocket, he uses the equation $h = -490t^2 + 1120t$. When is the height of the Model A rocket 640 centimeters?

20. Jivesh also has a more powerful Model B rocket. For this rocket, he uses the equation $h = -490t^2 + 1260t$. When is the height of the Model B rocket 810 centimeters?

21. Jivesh brought his Model B rocket on a camping trip near the top of a mountain. He wants to model how it descends down the mountain. Here, he uses the equation $h = -490t^2$. When has the rocket descended 1000 centimeters?

22. Geometry Claire is cutting a square out of a bigger square for an art project. She cuts out a square with an area of 9 cm². The leftover area is 16 cm². What is the length of one of the sides of the bigger square? The area of a square is $A = l^2$ where l is the length of one of its sides.

23. The height of a diver during a dive can be modeled by $h = -16t^2$, where h is height in feet relative to the diving platform and t is time in seconds. Find the time it takes for the diver to reach the water if the platform is 49 feet high.

24. Physics Consider a particular baseball player at bat. The height of the ball at time t can be modeled by $h = -16t^2 + v_0t + h_0$. Here, v_0 is the initial upward velocity of the ball, and h_0 is the height at which the ball is hit. If a ball is 4 feet off the ground when it is hit with a negligible upward velocity close to 0 feet per second, when will the ball hit the ground?

25. Explain the Error Jeremy factored $144x^2 - 100$ as follows:

$$144x^2 - 100 = (12x + 10)(12x - 10)$$
$$= 2(6x + 5)(6x - 5)$$

What was his error? Correct his work.

26. Which of the following are solutions to the equation $x^5 - 2x^3 + x = 0$? Select all that apply.

a. $x = -1$

b. $x = 2$

c. $x = 1$

d. $x = 0.5$

e. $x = 0$

H.O.T. Focus on Higher Order Thinking

27. Multi-Step An artist framed a picture. The picture is a square with a side length of $2y$. It is surrounded by a square frame with a side length of $4x$.

a. Find and completely factor the expression for the area of the frame.

b. The frame has an area of 11 square inches and the picture has an area of 25 square inches. Find the width of the frame.

28. Critical Thinking Sinea thinks that the fully factored form of the expression $x^4 - 1$ is $(x^2 - 1)(x^2 + 1)$. Is she correct? Explain.

29. Persevere in Problem Solving Samantha has the equation $x^3 + 2x^2 + x = x^3 - x$. Explain how she can find the solutions of the equation. Then solve the equation.

30. Communicate Mathematical Ideas Explain how to fully factor the expression $x^4 - 2x^2y^2 + y^4$.

Lesson Performance Task

A designer is planning to place a fountain in the lobby of an art museum. Four artists have each designed a fountain to fit the space. Some have designed rectangular fountains and the others designed square fountains. Given a quadratic equation representing the area of the fountain and the actual area of the fountain, find the dimensions of each fountain.

Artist	Artemis	Beatrice	Geoffrey	Daniel
Area equation	$A_A = 9x^2 - 25$	$A_B = 4x^2 - 25$	$A_G = 25x^2 + 80x + 64$	$A_D = 81x^2 + 198x + 121$
Fountain area	39 square feet	$28x - 76$ square feet	$160x$ square feet	$198x + 242$ square feet

STUDY GUIDE REVIEW

Using Factors to Solve Quadratic Equations

MODULE 8

Essential Question: How can you use factoring a quadratic equation to solve real-world problems?

Key Vocabulary
difference of two squares (*diferencia de dos cuadrados*)
perfect-square trinomial (*trinomio cuadrado perfecto*)

KEY EXAMPLE (Lesson 8.1)

Factor $x^2 - 2x - 8$.

Find the factor pair of -8 whose sum is -2.

The factor pair is -4 and 2.

$x^2 - 2x - 8 = (x - 4)(x + 2)$

Factors of −8	Sum of Factors
−1 and 8	7
1 and −8	−7
−2 and 4	2
2 and −4	−2

KEY EXAMPLE (Lesson 8.2)

Solve $4x^2 + 8x + 3 = 0$.

Find the factor pairs of 4 and 3 that result in a sum of 8.

The factor pairs are 2 and 2 and 1 and 3.

Factors of 4	Factors of 3	Outer Product + Inner Product
1 and 4	1 and 3	$(1)(3) + (4)(1) = 7$
1 and 4	3 and 1	$(1)(1) + (4)(3) = 13$
2 and 2	1 and 3	$(2)(3) + (2)(1) = 8$

$$4x^2 + 8x + 3 = 0$$

$$(2x + 1)(2x + 3) = 0$$

$2x + 1 = 0$ and $2x + 3 = 0$

$x = -\frac{1}{2}$ and $x = -\frac{3}{2}$

KEY EXAMPLE (Lesson 8.3)

Solve $16x^2 - 25 = 0$.

$4^2 \cdot x^2 - 5^2 = 0$ *Rewrite in the form $a^2x^2 - b^2$.*

$(4x + 5)(4x - 5) = 0$ *Rewrite in the form $(ax + b)(ax - b)$.*

$4x + 5 = 0$ and $4x - 5 = 0$ *Set factors equal to 0 using Zero Product Property.*

$x = -\frac{5}{4}$ and $x = \frac{5}{4}$

EXERCISES

Solve each equation. *(Lessons 8.1, 8.2, 8.3)*

1. $x^2 - 81 = 0$

2. $2x^2 - 8x - 10 = 0$

3. $x^2 + 7x + 12 = 0$

4. $x^2 - 14x = -49$

5. $16 - 4x^2 = 0$

6. $6x^2 + 5x + 1 = 0$

7. The area of a rectangular pool is $(x^2 + 17x + 72)$ square meters. There is a 3-meter-wide concrete walkway around the pool. Write expressions to represent the dimensions of the outside border of the walkway. *(Lesson 8.1)*

MODULE PERFORMANCE TASK

Fitting Through the Arch

The Ship-Shape Shipping Company ships items in rectangular crates. At one shipping destination, each crate must be able to fit through an arched doorway. The shape of this arched doorway can be modeled by the quadratic equation $y = -x^2 + 16$, where x is the distance in feet from the center of the arch and y is the height of the arch. Find the width of the archway at its base.

The Ship-Shape Shipping Company just unloaded several crates outside the arch ranging in height from 2 feet to 6 feet. Choose a particular crate height. Then, find the maximum width the crate could have and still fit through the arched doorway.

Start by listing how you will tackle this problem. Then complete the task. Be sure to write down all your data and assumptions. Then use graphs, tables, or algebra to explain how you reached your conclusion.

Ready to Go On?

8.1–8.3 Using Factors to Solve Quadratic Equations

- Online Homework
- Hints and Help
- Extra Practice

Identify each expression as a perfect-square trinomial, a difference of squares, or neither. Factor each expression. *(Lessons 8.1, 8.2, 8.3)*

1. $4p^2 + 12p + 9$

2. $a^2 - 9a - 36$

Solve each equation. *(Lessons 8.1, 8.2, 8.3)*

3. $x^2 - 4x - 21 = 0$

4. $49x^2 - 100 = 0$

5. $5x^2 - 33x - 14 = 0$

6. $x^2 + 16x + 64 = 0$

7. A golfer hits a ball from a starting elevation of 4 feet with a vertical velocity of 70 feet per second down to a green with an elevation of -5 feet. The number of seconds t it takes the ball to hit the green can be represented by the equation $-16t^2 + 70t + 4 = -5$. How long does it take the ball to land on the green? *(Lesson 8.2)*

ESSENTIAL QUESTION

8. How can you use factoring to solve quadratic equations in standard form?

MODULE 8
MIXED REVIEW

Assessment Readiness

1. Consider the equation $5x(2x + 1) - 3(2x + 1) = 0$.
   Determine if each statement is True or False.
   A. It is equivalent to $(5x - 3)(2x + 1) = 0$.
   B. A solution of the equation is $x = \frac{1}{2}$.
   C. A zero of the equation is $\frac{3}{5}$.

2. Factor to solve each equation. Does the equation have a solution of $x = 2$? Write Yes or No.
   A. $4x^2 - 16 = 0$
   B. $x^2 - 4x + 4 = 0$
   C. $4x^2 + 16x + 16 = 0$

3. Larry thinks the quotient of $\frac{4x^2 + 7x - 15}{x + 3}$ is $4x - 5$. Explain how you can check his answer using multiplication. Then, check his answer. Is Larry correct?

4. Marcello is replacing a rectangular sliding glass door with dimensions of $(x + 7)$ and $(x + 3)$ feet. The area of the glass door is 45 square feet. What are the length and width of the door? Explain how you got your answer.

Using Square Roots to Solve Quadratic Equations

MODULE 9

Essential Question: How can you use quadratic equations to solve real-world problems?

REAL WORLD VIDEO
The designers of a fireworks display need to make precise timing calculations. An explosion too soon or too late could spell disaster!

MODULE PERFORMANCE TASK PREVIEW

Fireworks Display

As with any other projectile, the relationship between the time since a firework was launched and its height is quadratic. Fireworks must be carefully timed in order to ignite at the most impressive height. In this task, you will figure out how you can use math to launch fireworks that are safe and achieve the maximum possible effect.

Are YOU Ready?

Complete these exercises to review skills you will need for this module.

- Online Homework
- Hints and Help
- Extra Practice

Exponents

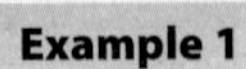

Simplify $25^{\frac{1}{2}}$.

$25^{\frac{1}{2}} = \sqrt{25} = 5$ — A number raised to the $\frac{1}{2}$ power is equal to the square root of the number.

Simplify.

1. $100^{\frac{1}{2}}$
2. $50^{\frac{1}{2}}$
3. $\left(\frac{36}{81}\right)^{\frac{1}{2}}$

Algebraic Expressions

Example 2

Evaluate $\left(\frac{b}{2}\right)^2$ when $b = 18$.

$\left(\frac{b}{2}\right)^2$

$\left(\frac{18}{2}\right)^2 = 9^2 = 81$ — Substitute 18 for ***b*** and evaluate the expression.

Evaluate $\left(\frac{b}{2}\right)^2$ for the given value of *b*.

4. $b = 24$
5. $b = -10$
6. $b = 3$

Example 3

Factor $x^2 + 14x + 49$.

$x^2 + 14x + 49$ — $x^2 + 14x + 49$ is a perfect square.

$x^2 + 2(x)(7) + 7^2$ — Rewrite in the form $a^2 + 2ab + b^2$.

$(x + 7)(x + 7)$ — Rewrite in the form $(a + b)(a + b)$.

$(x + 7)^2$

Factor each perfect square trinomial.

7. $x^2 - 12x + 36$
8. $x^2 + 22x + 121$
9. $4x^2 + 12x + 9$
10. $16x^2 - 40x + 25$

9.1 Solving Equations by Taking Square Roots

Resource Locker

Essential Question: How can you solve quadratic equations using square roots?

Explore Exploring Square Roots

Recall that the **square root** of a non-negative number a is the real number b such that $b^2 = a$. Since $4^2 = 16$ and $(-4)^2 = 16$, the square roots of 16 are 4 and −4. Thus, every positive real number has two square roots, one positive and one negative. The positive square root is given by $\sqrt{a}$ and the negative square root by $-\sqrt{a}$. These can be combined as $\pm\sqrt{a}$.

Properties of Radicals		
Property	**Symbols**	**Example**
Product Property of Radicals	For $a \geq 0$ and $b \geq 0$, $\sqrt{ab} = \sqrt{a} \cdot \sqrt{b}$.	$\sqrt{36} = \sqrt{9 \cdot 4}$ $= \sqrt{9} \cdot \sqrt{4}$ $= 3 \cdot 2$ $= 6$
Quotient Property of Radicals	For $a \geq 0$ and $b > 0$, $\sqrt{\frac{a}{b}} = \frac{\sqrt{a}}{\sqrt{b}}$.	$-\sqrt{0.16} = -\sqrt{\frac{16}{100}}$ $= -\frac{\sqrt{16}}{\sqrt{100}}$ $= -\frac{4}{10}$ $= -0.4$

Find each square root.

(A) $\pm\sqrt{49} = +$ ▢ and $-$ ▢

(B) $\pm\sqrt{25} = +$ ▢ and $-$ ▢

(C) $\pm\sqrt{12} = \pm\sqrt{\square \cdot 3} = \pm\sqrt{\square} \cdot \sqrt{\square}$

$= \pm\square \cdot \sqrt{\square}$

(D) $\pm\sqrt{\frac{16}{9}} = \pm\frac{\sqrt{\square}}{\sqrt{\square}}$

$= \pm\frac{\square}{\square}$

(E) $\pm\sqrt{0.27} = \pm\sqrt{\frac{\square}{100}} = \pm\frac{\sqrt{\square}}{\sqrt{100}} = \pm\frac{\sqrt{\square \cdot 3}}{\square} = \pm\frac{\sqrt{\square} \cdot \sqrt{3}}{\square} = \pm\frac{\square \cdot \sqrt{\square}}{\square}$

Reflect

1. **Discussion** Explain why $\sqrt{6^2}$ and $\sqrt{(-6)^2}$ have the same value.
2. **Discussion** Explain why a must be non-negative when you find $\sqrt{a}$.
3. Does 0 have any square roots? Why or why not?

Explain 1 Solving $ax^2 - c = 0$ by Using Square Roots

Solving a quadratic equation by using square roots may involve either finding square roots of perfect squares or finding square roots of numbers that are not perfect squares. In the latter case, the solution is irrational and can be approximated.

Example 1 **Solve the equation. Give the answer in radical form, and then use a calculator to approximate the solution to two decimal places, if necessary. Use a graphing calculator to graph the related function and compare the roots of the equation to the zeros of the related function.**

(A) $4x^2 - 5 = 2$

Solve the equation for x.

$4x^2 - 5 = 2$	Original equation
$4x^2 - 5 + 5 = 2 + 5$	Add 5 to both sides.
$4x^2 = 7$	Simplify.
$\frac{4x^2}{4} = \frac{7}{4}$	Divide both sides by 4.
$x^2 = 1.75$	Simplify.
$x = \pm\sqrt{1.75}$	Definition of a square root
$x \approx \pm 1.32$	Use a calculator to approximate the square roots.

The approximate solutions of the equation are $x \approx 1.32$ and $x \approx -1.32$.

Use a graphing calculator to graph the related function, $f(x) = 4x^2 - 7$, and find the zeros of the function.

The graph intersects the x-axis at approximately $(1.32, 0)$ and $(-1.32, 0)$. So, the roots of the equation are the zeros of the related function.

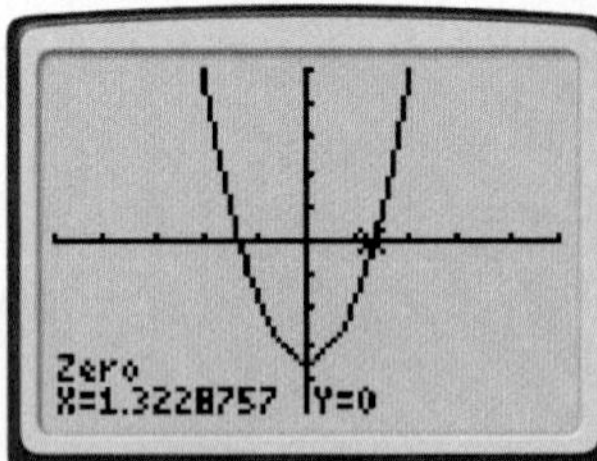

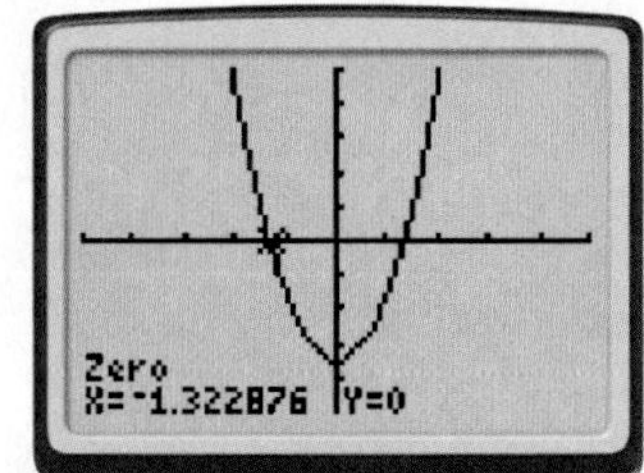

(B) $2x^2 - 8 = 0$

Solve the equation for x.

$2x^2 - 8 = 0$	Original equation
$2x^2 - 8 + \boxed{8} = 0 + \boxed{8}$	Add $\boxed{8}$ to both sides.
$2x^2 = \boxed{8}$	Simplify.
$\dfrac{2x^2}{\boxed{2}} = \dfrac{8}{\boxed{2}}$	Divide both sides by $\boxed{2}$.
$x^2 = \boxed{4}$	Simplify.
$x = \pm\sqrt{\boxed{4}}$	Definition of a square root
$x = \pm\boxed{2}$	Evaluate the square roots.

The solutions of the equation are $x = \boxed{2}$ and $x = \boxed{-2}$.

Use a graphing calculator to graph the related function, $f(x) = 2x^2 - 8$, and find the zeros of the function.

The graph intersects the x-axis at

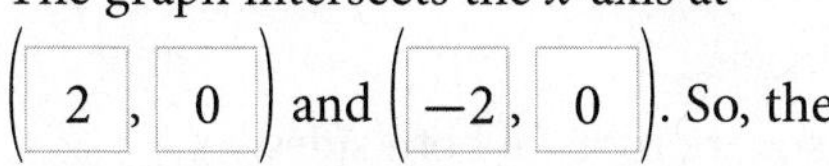

$(\boxed{2}, \boxed{0})$ and $(\boxed{-2}, \boxed{0})$. So, the roots of the equation are the zeros of the related function.

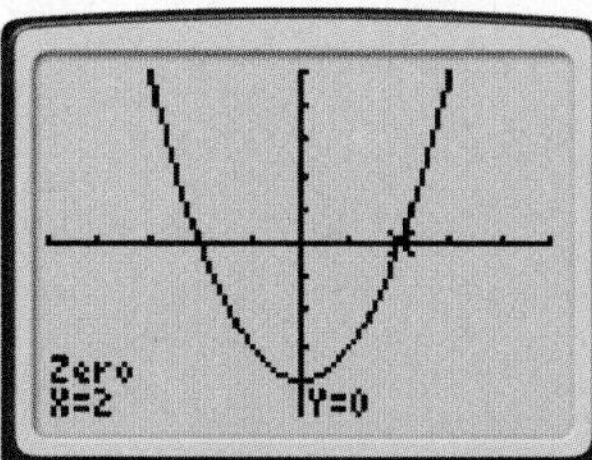

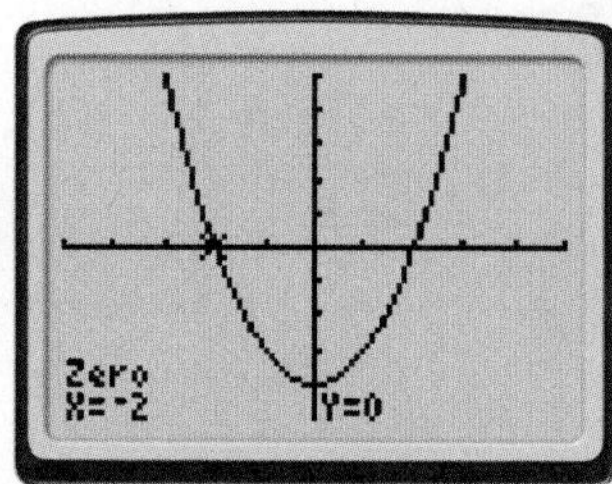

Your Turn

Solve the equation. Give the answer in radical form, and then use a calculator to approximate the solution to two decimal places, if necessary. Use a graphing calculator to graph the related function to check your answer.

4. $3x^2 + 6 = 33$

5. $5x^2 - 9 = 2$

Explain 2 Solving $a(x+b)^2 = c$ by Using Square Roots

Solving a quadratic equation may involve isolating the squared part of a quadratic expression on one side of the equation first.

Example 2 **Solve the equation. Give the answer in radical form, and then use a calculator to approximate the solution to two decimal places, if necessary.**

(A) $(x+5)^2 = 36$

$(x+5)^2 = 36$	Original equation
$x+5 = \pm\sqrt{36}$	Take the square root of both sides.
$x+5 = \pm 6$	Simplify the square root.
$x = \pm 6 - 5$	Subtract 5 from both sides.
$x = -6 - 5$ or $x = 6 - 5$	Solve for both cases.
$x = -11$ $\quad$ $x = 1$	

The solutions are $x = -11$ and $x = 1$.

(B) $3(x-5)^2 = 18$

$3(x-5)^2 = 18$	Original equation
$(x-5)^2 = \boxed{6}$	Divide both sides by $\boxed{3}$.
$x - 5 = \pm\sqrt{\boxed{6}}$	Take the square roots of both sides.
$x = \pm\sqrt{\boxed{6}} + \boxed{5}$	Add $\boxed{5}$ to both sides.
$x = \sqrt{\boxed{6}} + 5$ or $x = -\sqrt{6} + \boxed{5}$	Solve for both cases.
$x \approx \boxed{7.45}$ or $x \approx \boxed{2.55}$	

The approximate solutions are $x \approx \boxed{7.45}$ and $x \approx \boxed{2.55}$.

Reflect

6. Find the solution(s), if any, of $2(x-3)^2 = -32$. Explain your reasoning.

Your Turn

Solve the equation. Give the answer in radical form, and then use a calculator to approximate the solution to two decimal places, if necessary.

7. $4(x + 10)^2 = 24$

8. $(x - 9)^2 = 64$

Explain 3 Solving Equation Models by Using Square Roots

Real-world situations can sometimes be analyzed by solving a quadratic equation using square roots.

Example 3 **Solve the problem.**

(A) A contractor is building a fenced-in playground at a daycare. The playground will be rectangular with its width equal to half its length. The total area will be 5000 square feet. Determine how many feet of fencing the contractor will use.

First, find the dimensions.
Let $A = 5000$, $\ell = x$, and $w = \frac{1}{2}x$.

$$A = \ell w$$

$$5000 = x \cdot \frac{1}{2}x$$

$$5000 = \frac{1}{2}x^2$$

$$10{,}000 = x^2$$

$\pm\sqrt{10{,}000} = x$ Take the square root of both sides.

$\pm 100 = x$ Evaluate the square root.

Since the width of a rectangle cannot be negative, the length of the playground is 100 feet. The width is half the length, or 50 feet.

Find the amount of fencing.

$P = 2\ell + 2w$

$= 2(100) + 2(50)$

$= 200 + 100$ Multiply.

$= 300$ Add.

So, the contractor will use 300 feet of fencing.

(B) A person standing on a second-floor balcony drops keys to a friend standing below the balcony. The keys are dropped from a height of 10 feet. The height in feet of the keys as they fall is given by the function $h(t) = -16t^2 + 10$, where t is the time in seconds since the keys were dropped. The friend catches the keys at a height of 4 feet. Find the elapsed time before the keys are caught.

Let $h(t) = \boxed{4}$. Substitute the value into the equation and solve for t.

$h(t) = -16t^2 + 10$	Original equation
$\boxed{4} = -16t^2 + 10$	Substitute.
$4 - \boxed{10} = -16t^2 + 10 - \boxed{10}$	Subtract 10 from both sides.
$\boxed{-6} = -16t^2$	Simplify.
$\dfrac{-6}{\boxed{-16}} = \dfrac{-16t^2}{\boxed{-16}}$	Divide both sides by -16.
$\boxed{0.375} = t^2$	Simplify.
$\pm\sqrt{\boxed{0.375}} = t$	Take the square root of both sides.
$\pm\boxed{0.61} \approx t$	Use a calculator to approximate the square roots.

Since time cannot be negative, the elapsed time before the keys are caught is approximately $\boxed{0.61}$ second(s).

Your Turn

9. A zookeeper is buying fencing to enclose a pen at the zoo. The pen is an isosceles right triangle. There is already a fence along the hypotenuse, which borders a path. The area of the pen will be 4500 square feet. The zookeeper can buy the fencing in whole feet only. How many feet of fencing should he buy?

Elaborate

10. How many real solutions does $x^2 = -25$ have? Explain.

11. Suppose the function $h(t) = -16t^2 + 20$ models the height in feet of an object after t seconds. If the final height is given as 2 feet, explain why there is only one reasonable solution for the time it takes the object to fall.

12. **Essential Question Check-In** What steps would you take to solve $6x^2 - 54 = 42$?

Evaluate: Homework and Practice

- Online Homework
- Hints and Help
- Extra Practice

Use the Product Property of Radicals, the Quotient Property of Radicals, or both to simplify each expression.

1. $\pm\sqrt{0.0081}$

2. $\pm\sqrt{\dfrac{8}{25}}$

3. $\pm\sqrt{96}$

Solve each equation. Give the answer in radical form, and then use a calculator to approximate the solution to two decimal places, if necessary. Use a graphing calculator to graph the related function to check your answer.

4. $5x^2 - 21 = 39$

5. $0.1x^2 - 1.2 = 8.8$

6. $6x^2 - 21 = 33$

7. $6 - \frac{1}{3}x^2 = -20$

8. $5 - 2x^2 = -3$

9. $7x^2 + 10 = 18$

Solve each equation. Give the answer in radical form, and then use a calculator to approximate the solution to two decimal places, if necessary.

10. $5(x - 9)^2 = 15$

11. $(x + 15)^2 = 81$

12. $3(x + 1)^2 = 27$

13. $\frac{2}{3}(x - 40)^2 = 24$

14. $(x - 12)^2 = 54$

15. $(x + 5.4)^2 = 1.75$

16. The area on a wall covered by a rectangular poster is 320 square inches. The length of the poster is 1.25 times longer than the width of the poster. What are the dimensions of the poster?

17. A circle is graphed with its center on the origin. The area of the circle is 144 square units. What are the coordinates of the x-intercepts of the graph? Round to the nearest tenth.

18. The equation $d = 16t^2$ gives the distance d in feet that a golf ball falls in t seconds. How many seconds will it take a golf ball to drop to the ground from a height of 4 feet? 64 feet?

19. Entertainment For a scene in a movie, a sack of money is dropped from the roof of a 600-foot skyscraper. The height of the sack above the ground in feet is given by $h = -16t^2 + 600$, where t is the time in seconds. How long will it take the sack to reach the ground? Round to the nearest tenth of a second.

20. A lot for sale is shaped like a trapezoid. The bases of the trapezoid represent the widths of the front and back yards. The width of the back yard is twice the width of the front yard. The distance from the front yard to the backyard, or the height of the trapezoid, is equal to the width of the back yard. Find the width of the front and back yards, given that the area is 6000 square feet. Round to the nearest foot.

21. To study how high a ball bounces, students drop the ball from various heights. The function $h(t) = -16t^2 + h_0$ gives the height (in feet) of the ball at time t measured in seconds since the ball was dropped from a height of h_0. If the ball is dropped from a height of 8 feet, find the elapsed time until the ball hits the floor. Round to the nearest tenth.

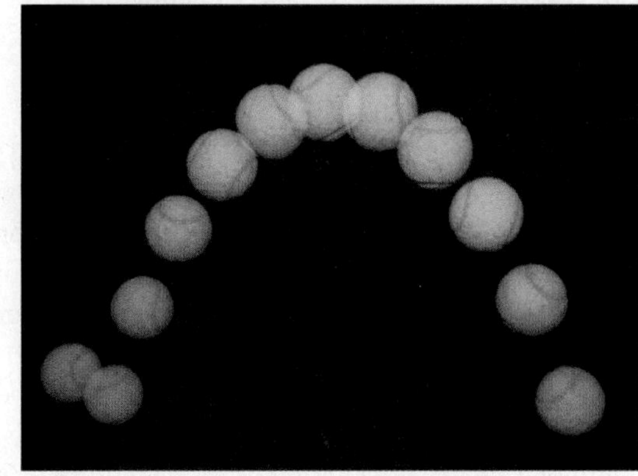

22. Match each equation with its solutions.

A. $2x^2 - 2 = 16$ a. ___?___ $= \pm\frac{2\sqrt{33}}{3}$

B. $2(x-2)^2 = 16$ b. ___?___ $x = \pm 3$

C. $3x^2 + 4 = 48$ c. ___?___ $x = 2 \pm 2\sqrt{2}$

D. $3(x+4)^2 = 48$ d. ___?___ $x = -8$ or $x = 0$

H.O.T. Focus on Higher Order Thinking

23. **Explain the Error** Trent and Lisa solve the same equation, but they disagree on the solution of the equation. Their work is shown. Which solution is correct? Explain.

Trent:	Lisa:
$5x^2 + 1000 = -125$	$5x^2 + 1000 = -125$
$5x^2 = -1125$	$5x^2 = -1125$
$x^2 = -225$	$x^2 = -225$
$x = \pm\sqrt{-225}$	no real solutions
$x = \pm 15$	

24. **Multi-Step** Construction workers are installing a rectangular, in-ground pool. To start, they dig a rectangular hole in the ground where the pool will be. The area of the ground that they will be digging up is 252 square feet. The length of the pool is twice the width of the pool.

a. What are the dimensions of the pool? Round to the nearest tenth.

b. Once the pool is installed, the workers will build a fence, that encloses a rectangular region, around the perimeter of it. The fence will be 10 feet from the edges of the pool, except at the corners. How many feet of fencing will the workers need?

25. **Communicate Mathematical Ideas** Explain why the quadratic equation $x^2 + b = 0$ where $b > 0$, has no real solutions, but the quadratic equation $x^2 - b = 0$ where $b > 0$, has two real solutions.

26. **Justify Reasoning** For the equation $x^2 = a$, describe the values of a that will result in two real solutions, one real solution, and no real solution. Explain your reasoning.

Lesson Performance Task

You have been asked to create a pendulum clock for your classroom. The clock will be placed on one wall of the classroom and go the entire height of the wall. Choose how large you want the face and hands on your clock to be and provide measurements for the body of the clock. The pendulum will start halfway between the center of the clock face and its bottom edge and will initially end 1 foot above the floor. Calculate the period of the pendulum using the formula $L = 9.78t^2$, where L is the length of the pendulum in inches and t is the length of the period in seconds.

Now, adjust the length of your pendulum so the number of periods in 1 minute or 60 seconds is an integer value. How long is your pendulum and how many periods equal one minute?

9.2 Solving Equations by Completing the Square

Essential Question: How can you use completing the square to solve a quadratic equation?

Resource Locker

Explore Modeling Completing the Square

You can use algebra tiles to model a perfect square trinomial.

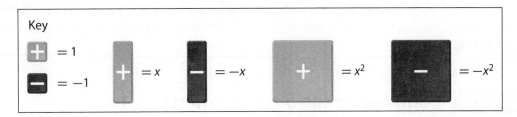

Key

[+] = 1
[−] = −1
[+] = x
[−] = $-x$
[+] = x^2
[−] = $-x^2$

Ⓐ The algebra tiles shown represent the expression $x^2 + 6x$. The expression does not have a constant term, which would be represented with unit tiles. Create a square diagram of algebra tiles by adding the correct number of unit tiles to form a square.

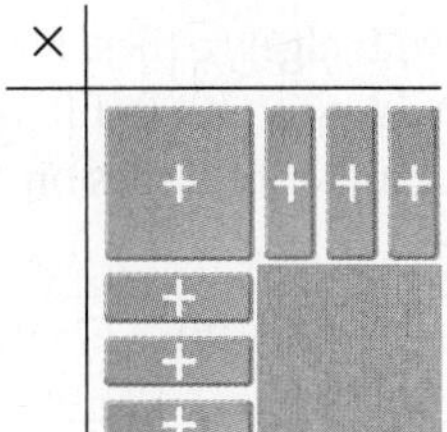

Ⓑ How many unit tiles were added to the expression? ☐

Ⓒ Write the trinomial represented by the algebra tiles for the complete square.

☐ $x^2 +$ ☐ $x +$ ☐

Ⓓ It should be easily recognized that the trinomial ☐ $x^2 +$ ☐ $x +$ ☐ is an example of the special case $(a + b^2) = a^2 + 2ab + b^2$. Recall that trinomials of this form are called perfect-square trinomials. Since the trinomial is a perfect square, it can be factored into two identical binomials.

☐ $x^2 +$ ☐ $x +$ ☐ $= ($ ☐ $x +$ ☐ $)^2$

Ⓔ Refer to the algebra tiles in the diagram. What expression is represented by the tiles?

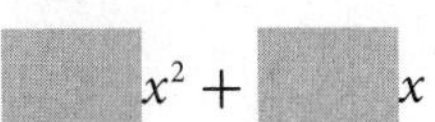

☐ $x^2 +$ ☐ x

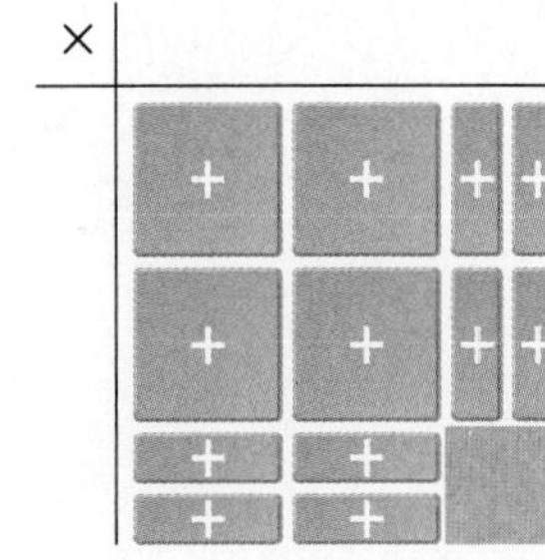

Ⓕ Complete the square in Step E by filling the bottom right corner with unit tiles. How many unit tiles were added to the diagram? ☐

(G) Write the trinomial represented by the algebra tiles for the complete square.

▢ $x^2 +$ ▢ $x +$ ▢

(H) The trinomial is a square of a binomial. Use the algebra tiles to write the trinomial in factored form.

▢ $x^2 +$ ▢ $x +$ ▢ $= ($ ▢ $x +$ ▢ $)^2$

Reflect

1. **Discussion** When using algebra tiles to model the expression $x^2 + 6x + c$, the x-tiles are divided equally, with 3 tiles on the right and bottom sides of the x^2-tile. How does the number 3 relate to the total number of x-tiles? How does the number 3 relate to the total number of unit tiles that were added?

2. In order to form a perfect square trinomial with the expression $x^2 + 8x + c$, how would the algebra tiles be arranged? How many unit tiles must be added? How is the number of unit tiles added related to the total number of x-tiles?

Explain 1 Completing the Square When $a = 1$

Completing the square is a process of rewriting a quadratic expression as a perfect square trinomial so that it can be solved by taking square roots. In the Explore, the method for completing the square when $a = 1$ was modeled with algebra tiles. First, place half of the x-tiles along the right side of the x^2-tile and half underneath the tile. Then add unit tiles to fill in the rectangle started with the x^2- and x-tiles. The number of unit tiles equals the square of the number of x-tiles on either side of the x^2-tile.

In other words, to complete the square for the expression $x^2 + bx + c$, add $\left(\frac{b}{2}\right)^2$. The perfect-square trinomial will then be $x^2 + bx + \left(\frac{b}{2}\right)^2$ and its factored form will be $\left(x + \frac{b}{2}\right)^2$.

Example 1 Complete the square to form a perfect-square trinomial.

(A) $x^2 + 4x$

$x^2 + 4x$

$b = 4$ — Identify b.

$\left(\frac{4}{2}\right)^2 = 2^2 = 4$ — Find $\left(\frac{b}{2}\right)^2$.

$x^2 + 4x + 4$ — Add $\left(\frac{b}{2}\right)^2$ to the expression.

Ⓑ $x^2 - 8x$

$x^2 - 8x$

$b = \boxed{-8}$ Identify b.

$\left(\frac{\boxed{-8}}{2}\right)^2 = \left(\boxed{-4}\right)^2 = \boxed{16}$ Find $\left(\frac{b}{2}\right)^2$.

$x^2 - 8x + \boxed{16}$ Add $\left(\frac{b}{2}\right)^2$ to the expression.

Reflect

3. When b is negative, why is the result added to the expression still positive?

Your Turn

4. Complete the square: $x^2 + 12x$

Explain 2 Solving $x^2 + bx + c = 0$ by Completing the Square

Completing the square can also be used to solve equations in the forms $x^2 + bx + c = 0$ or $x^2 + bx = c$.

Example 2 **Solve each equation by completing the square. Check the answers.**

Ⓐ $x^2 - 4x = 3$

$x^2 - 4x = 3$	
$x^2 - 4x + 4 = 3 + 4$	Add $\left(\frac{b}{2}\right)^2 = \left(\frac{-4}{2}\right)^2 = 4$ to both sides.
$(x-2)^2 = 7$	Factor and simplify.
$x - 2 = \pm\sqrt{7}$	Take the square root of both sides.
$x - 2 = \sqrt{7}$ or $x - 2 = -\sqrt{7}$	Write and solve two equations.
$x = 2 + \sqrt{7}$ $\quad$ $x = 2 - \sqrt{7}$	Add 2 to both sides.

Check the answers.

$(2+\sqrt{7})^2 - 4(2+\sqrt{7})$	$(2-\sqrt{7})^2 - 4(2-\sqrt{7})$
$= 4 + 4\sqrt{7} + 7 - 8 - 4\sqrt{7}$	$= 4 - 4\sqrt{7} + 7 - 8 + 4\sqrt{7}$
$= 4 + 7 - 8 + 4\sqrt{7} - 4\sqrt{7}$	$= 4 + 7 - 8 - 4\sqrt{7} + 4\sqrt{7}$
$= 3$	$= 3$

$2 + \sqrt{7}$ and $2 - \sqrt{7}$ are both solutions of the equation $x^2 - 4x = 3$.

(B) $x^2 + 16x = 36$

$$x^2 + 16x = 36$$

$$\boxed{1}\,x^2 + \boxed{16}\,x + \boxed{64} = \boxed{36} + \boxed{64}$$ Add $\left(\frac{b}{2}\right)^2 = \boxed{64}$ to both sides.

$$\left(\boxed{1}\,x + \boxed{8}\right)^2 = \boxed{100}$$ Factor and simplify.

$$\boxed{1}\,x + \boxed{8} = \pm\boxed{10}$$ Take the square root of both sides.

$$\boxed{1}\,x + \boxed{8} = \boxed{10} \quad \text{or} \quad \boxed{1}\,x + \boxed{8} = -\boxed{10}$$

$$x = \boxed{2} \qquad\qquad x = \boxed{-18}$$

Check the answers.

$$x^2 + 16x = 36$$

$$(-18)^2 + 16 \cdot \boxed{-18} = 36$$

$$\boxed{324} - \boxed{288} = 36$$

$$\boxed{36} = 36$$

$x = -18$ is a solution to the equation $x^2 + 16x = 36$.

$$x^2 + 16x = 36$$

$$2^2 + 16 \cdot \boxed{2} = 36$$

$$\boxed{4} + \boxed{32} = 36$$

$$\boxed{36} = 36$$

$x = 2$ is a solution to the equation $x^2 + 16x = 36$.

Your Turn

Solve each equation by completing the square. Check the answers.

5. $x^2 - 10x = 11$

6. $x^2 + 6x = 2$

Explain 3 Solving $ax^2 + bx + c = 0$ by Completing the Square When a Is a Perfect Square

When a is a perfect square, completing the square is easier than in other cases. Recall that the number of unit tiles needed is equal to the square of b divided by four times a, or $\frac{b^2}{4a}$. This is always the case when a is a perfect square.

Example 3 **Solve each equation by completing the square.**

(A) $4x^2 - 8x = 21$

$4x^2 - 8x = 21$	
$\frac{(-8)^2}{4 \cdot 4} = \frac{64}{16} = 4$	Find $\frac{b^2}{4a}$.
$4x^2 - 8x + 4 = 21 + 4$	Add $\frac{b^2}{4a}$ to both sides.
$(2x - 2)^2 = 25$	Factor and simplify.
$2x - 2 = \pm\sqrt{25}$	Take the square root of the both sides.
$2x - 2 = \pm 5$	Simplify.
$2x - 2 = 5$ or $2x - 2 = -5$	Write and solve 2 equations.
$2x = 7$ or $2x = -3$	Add to both sides.
$x = \frac{7}{2}$ or $x = -\frac{3}{2}$	Divide both sides by 2.

(B) $9x^2 + 6x = 10$

$9x^2 + 6x = 10$	
$\frac{6^2}{4 \cdot 9} = \frac{36}{36} = 1$	Find $\frac{b^2}{4a}$.
$9x^2 + 6x + 1 = 10 + 1$	Add $\frac{b^2}{4a}$ to both sides.
$(3x + 1)^2 = 11$	Factor and simplify.
$3x + 1 = \pm\sqrt{11}$	Take the square root of the both sides.
$3x + 1 = \sqrt{11}$ or $3x + 1 = -\sqrt{-11}$	Write and solve two equations.
$3x = -1 + \sqrt{11}$ $\quad 3x = -1 - \sqrt{11}$	Subtract 1 from both sides.
$x = \frac{-1 + \sqrt{11}}{3}$ $\quad x = \frac{-1 - \sqrt{11}}{3}$	Divide both sides by 3.

Reflect

7. In order for the procedure used in this section to work, why does a have to be a perfect square?

Your Turn

Solve each equation by completing the square.

8. $16x^2 - 16x = 5$

9. $4x^2 + 12x = 5$

Explain 4 Solving $ax^2 + bx + c = 0$ by Completing the Square When a Is Not a Perfect Square

When the leading coefficient a is not a perfect square, the equation can be transformed by multiplying both sides by a value such that a becomes a perfect square.

Example 4 **Solve each equation by completing the square.**

(A) $2x^2 - 6x = 5$

Since the coefficient of x^2 is 2, which is not a perfect square, multiply both sides by a value so the coefficient will have a perfect square. In this case, use 2.

$2x^2 - 6x = 5$

$2(2x^2 - 6x) = 2(5)$ Multiply both sides by 2.

$4x^2 - 12x = 10$ Simplify.

$\frac{(-12)^2}{4 \cdot 4} = \frac{144}{16} = 9$ Find $\frac{b^2}{4a}$.

$4x^2 - 12x + 9 = 10 + 9$ Add $\frac{b^2}{4a}$ to both sides.

$(2x - 3)^2 = 19$ Factor and simplify.

$2x - 3 = \pm\sqrt{19}$ Take the square root of the both sides.

$2x - 3 = \sqrt{19}$ or $2x - 3 = -\sqrt{19}$ Write and solve 2 equations.

$2x = 3 + \sqrt{19}$ $\quad 2x = 3 - \sqrt{19}$ Add to both sides.

$x = \frac{3 + \sqrt{19}}{2}$ $\quad x = \frac{3 - \sqrt{19}}{2}$ Divide both sides by 2.

(B) $3x^2 + 3x = 16$

Since the coefficient of x^2 is 3, which is not a perfect square, multiply both sides by a value so the coefficient will have a perfect square. In this case, use 3.

$$3x^2 + 3x = 16$$

$$3(3x^2 + 2x) = 3(16)$$ Multiply both sides by 3.

$$9x^2 + 6x = 48$$ Simplify.

$$\frac{6^2}{4 \cdot 9} = \frac{36}{36} = 1$$ Find $\frac{b^2}{4a}$.

$$9x^2 + 6x + 1 = 48 + 1$$ Add $\frac{b^2}{4a}$ to both sides.

$$(3x + 1)^2 = 49$$ Factor and simplify.

$$3x + 1 = \pm\sqrt{49} = \pm 7$$ Take the square root of the both sides.

$$3x + 1 = 7 \quad \text{or} \quad 3x + 1 = -7$$ Write and solve two equations.

$$3x = 6 \qquad 3x = -8$$ Subtract 1 from both sides.

$$x = 2 \qquad x = -\frac{8}{3}$$ Divide both sides by 3.

Reflect

10. Consider the equation $2x^2 + 11x = 12$. Why is 2 the best value by which to multiply both sides of the equation before completing the square?

Your Turn

Solve each equation by completing the square.

11. $\frac{1}{2}x^2 + 3x = 14$

12. $2x^2 - 4x = 16$

Explain 5 Modeling Completing the Square for Quadratic Equations

Completing the square can be useful when solving problems involving quadratic functions, especially if the function cannot be factored. In these cases, complete the square to rewrite the function in vertex form: $f(x) = a(x - h)^2 + k$. Completing the square in this situation is similar to solving equations by completing the square, but instead of adding a term to both sides of the equation, you will both add and subtract it from the function's rule.

Recall that the height of an object moving under the force of gravity, with no other forces acting on it, can be modeled by the quadratic function $h = -16t^2 + vt + s$, where t is the time in seconds, v is the initial vertical velocity, and s is the initial height in feet.

Example 5 **Write a function in standard form for each model. Then, rewrite the equation in vertex form and solve the problem. Graph the function on a graphing calculator and find the *x*-intercepts and maximum value of the graph.**

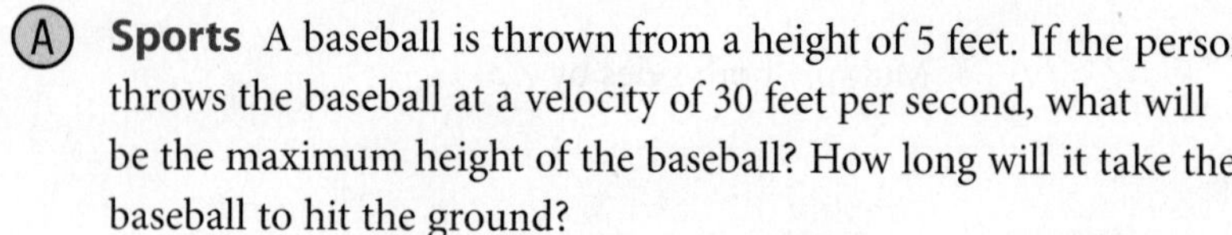

Ⓐ **Sports** A baseball is thrown from a height of 5 feet. If the person throws the baseball at a velocity of 30 feet per second, what will be the maximum height of the baseball? How long will it take the baseball to hit the ground?

The function for this situation is $h = -16t^2 + 30t + 5$.

Complete the square to find the vertex of the function's graph.

$$h = -16t^2 + 30t + 5$$

$$h = -1(16t^2 - 30t) + 5 \qquad \text{Factor out } -1.$$

$$h = -1\left(16t^2 - 30t + \frac{225}{16} - \frac{225}{16}\right) + 5 \qquad \text{Complete the square.}$$

$$h = -1\left(\left(4t - \frac{15}{4}\right)^2 - \frac{225}{16}\right) + 5 \qquad \text{Factor the perfect-square trinomial.}$$

$$h = -\left(4t - \frac{15}{4}\right)^2 + \frac{225}{16} + 5 \qquad \text{Distribute the } -1.$$

$$h = -4\left(t - \frac{15}{4}\right)^2 + \frac{305}{16} \qquad \text{Combine the last two terms.}$$

The coordinates of the vertex are $\left(\frac{15}{4}, \frac{305}{16}\right)$, or about (3.75, 19.06). The maximum height will be about 19 feet.

The graph of the function confirms the vertex at about (3.75, 19.06). The x-intercept at about 2.03 indicates that the ball will hit the ground after about 2 seconds.

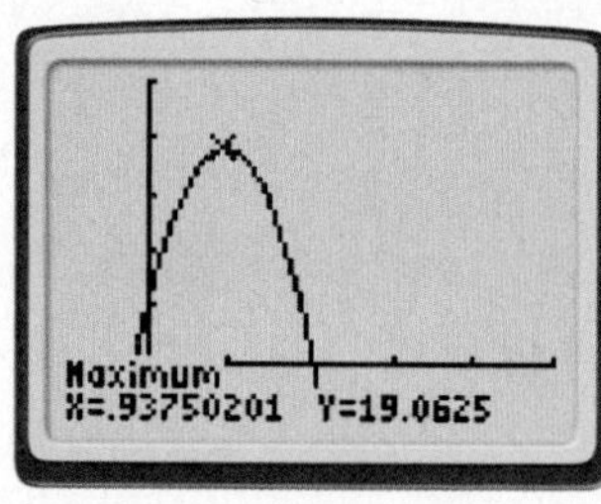

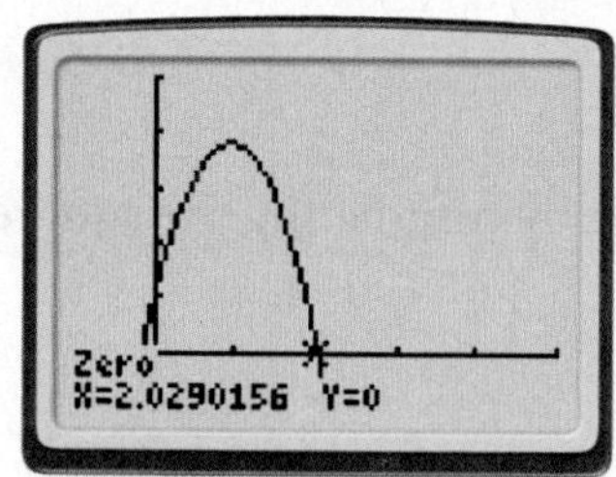

B **Sports** A person kicks a soccer ball with an initial upward velocity of 16 feet per second. What is the maximum height of the soccer ball? When will the soccer ball hit the ground?

An equation for this situation is $h = -16t^2 + \boxed{16}\,t + \boxed{0}$.

Complete the square to find the vertex of the function's graph.

$$h = -16t^2 + \boxed{16}\,t + \boxed{0}$$

$$h = \boxed{-16}\left(\boxed{1}\,t^2 - \boxed{1}\,t\right) + \boxed{0} \qquad \text{Factor out } \boxed{-16}.$$

$$h = \boxed{-16}\left(\boxed{1}\,t^2 - \boxed{1}\,t + \frac{\boxed{1}}{\boxed{4}} - \frac{\boxed{1}}{\boxed{4}}\right) + 0 \qquad \text{Complete the square.}$$

$$h = \boxed{-16}\left(\left(\boxed{1}\,t - \frac{\boxed{1}}{\boxed{2}}\right)^2 - \frac{\boxed{1}}{\boxed{4}}\right) + 0 \qquad \text{Factor the perfect-square trinomial.}$$

$$h = \boxed{-16}\left(\boxed{1}\,t - \frac{\boxed{1}}{\boxed{2}}\right)^2 + \frac{\boxed{16}}{\boxed{4}} + 0 \qquad \text{Distribute the } -16.$$

$$h = \boxed{-16}\left(\boxed{1}\,t - \frac{\boxed{1}}{\boxed{2}}\right)^2 + \boxed{4} \qquad \text{Combine the last two terms.}$$

The coordinates of the vertex are $\left(\frac{\boxed{1}}{\boxed{2}}, \boxed{4}\right)$.

The soccer ball will be at its highest when it is at its vertex, or at $\boxed{4}$ feet.

The graph of the function confirms the vertex at (0.5, 4). The x-intercept at 1 indicates that the ball will hit the ground after 1 second.

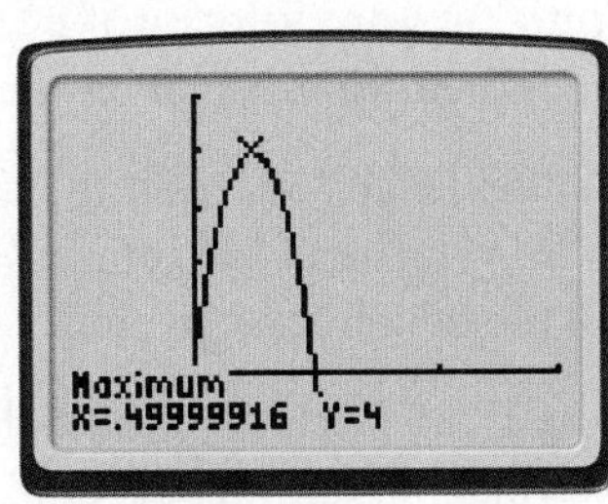

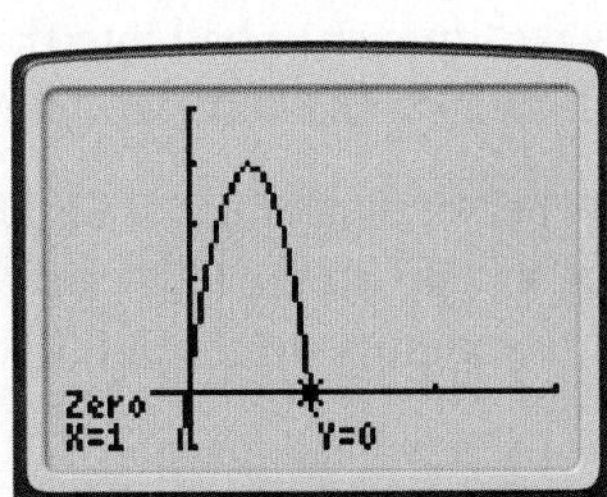

Your Turn

13. **Physics** A person standing at the edge of a cliff 48 feet tall throws a ball up and just off the cliff with an initial upward velocity of 8 feet per second. What is the maximum height of the ball? When will the ball hit the ground?

Elaborate

14. When $b > 0$, the perfect square-trinomial of the expression $x + bx$ is $x^2 + bx + \left(\frac{b}{2}\right)^2$. What is the perfect-square trinomial when $b < 0$? Does the sign of the constant change? Why or why not?

15. **Essential Question Check-In** What is the first step in completing the square to solve a quadratic equation of the form $ax^2 + bx = c$?

Evaluate: Homework and Practice

- Online Homework
- Hints and Help
- Extra Practice

Complete the square to form a perfect-square trinomial.

1. $x^2 + 26x$
2. $x^2 - 18x$
3. $x^2 - 2x$
4. $x^2 - 24x$

Solve each equation by completing the square. Check the answers.

5. $x^2 + 8x = 33$
6. $x^2 - 6x = 8$
7. $x^2 + 12x = 5$
8. $x^2 - 14x = 95$

Solve each equation by completing the square.

9. $9x^2 + 12x = 32$
10. $4x^2 + 20x = 2$
11. $16x^2 - 32x = 65$
12. $9x^2 - 24x = 1$
13. $\frac{1}{2}x^2 + 4x = 10$
14. $3x^2 - 4x = 20$
15. $2x^2 + 14x = 4$
16. $\frac{1}{2}x^2 - 5x = 18$

Projectile Motion Write an equation for each model, rewrite the equation into vertex form, and solve the problem. Then graph the function on a graphing calculator and state the *x*-intercepts of the graph.

17. **Sports** A person kicks a ball into the air with an initial upward velocity of 8 feet per second. What is the maximum height of the ball? When will the ball hit the ground?

18. **Physics** A person reaching out to the edge of a building ledge 85 feet off the ground flicks a twig up and off the ledge with an initial upward velocity of 11 feet per second. What is the maximum height of the twig? When will the twig hit the ground?

19. **Volleyball** A volleyball player hits a ball from a height of 5 feet with an initial vertical velocity of 16 feet per second. What is the maximum height of the volleyball? Assuming it is not hit by another player, when will the volleyball hit the ground?

20. **Lacrosse** A lacrosse player throws a ball into the air from a height of 8 feet with an initial vertical velocity of 32 feet per second. What is the maximum height of the ball? When will the ball hit the ground?

21. Identify the value of a in each equation of the form $ax^2 + bx + c = 0$.

a. $11x^2 + 2x = 4$

b. $4x^2 + 5 = 0$

c. $3x^3 = 7$

d. $5x^2 + 11x = 1$

e. $3x^2 = 5$

22. The diagram represents the expression $x^2 + 8x$. Use algebra tiles to model completing the square. Then write the perfect square trinomial expression.

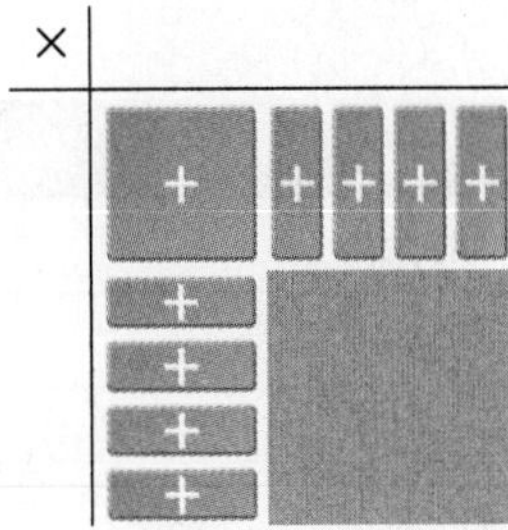

H.O.T. Focus on Higher Order Thinking

23. Explain the Error A student was instructed to solve the equation $x^2 + 4x = 77$ and produced the following work. Explain the student's error. What is the correct solution?

$$x^2 + 4x = 77$$
$$x^2 + 4x + 4 = 77 + 4$$
$$(x + 2)^2 = 81$$
$$x + 2 = 9$$
$$x = 7$$

24. Justify Reasoning Will the equation $x^2 + 6x = -10$ produce an answer that is a real number after the square is completed? Explain.

25. Draw Conclusions When solving a quadratic model, why are some solutions considered extraneous? Is this always the case, or can some quadratic models have two solutions?

Lesson Performance Task

An architect is designing the lobby of a new office building. The company that hired her has reclaimed a large quantity of stone floor tiles from the building previously on the site and wishes to use them to tile the lobby. The lobby needs to be 18 feet longer than it is wide to incorporate an information desk. The table below shows the types of tile available, the general color of the tile, and the area that can be covered by the tile.

Stone	Color	Area in Square Feet
Marble	Cream	175
Marble	Cream with gold flecks	115
Marble	Black	648
Marble	White with black flecks	360
Slate	Gray	280
Slate	Gray with blue gray regions	243
Travertine	Caramel	208
Travertine	Latte	760
Adoquin	Dark gray with black regions	319
Adoquin	Light gray with darker gray regions	403
Limestone	Pewter	448
Limestone	Beige	544

Design the lobby using at least all of one type of tile. You can add additional types of tiles to create patterns in the floor. For this exercise, you can decide on the dimensions of the tiles in order to make any pattern you wish.

9.3 Using the Quadratic Formula to Solve Equations

Resource Locker

Essential Question: What is the quadratic formula, and how can you use it to solve quadratic equations?

Explore Deriving the Quadratic Formula

You can complete the square on the general form of a quadratic equation to derive a formula that can be used to solve any quadratic equation.

(A) Write the standard form of a quadratic equation.

$ax^2 + bx + c = \square$

(B) Subtract c from both sides.

$ax^2 + bx = \square$

(C) Multiply both sides by $4a$ to make the coefficient of x^2 a perfect square.

$4a^2x^2 + \square = \square$

(D) Add b^2 to both sides of the equation to complete the square.

$4a^2x^2 + 4abx + b^2 = -4ac + \square$

(E) Factor the left side to write the trinomial as the square of a binomial.

$\left(\square\right)^2 = b^2 - 4ac$

(F) Take the square roots of both sides.

$\square = \pm\sqrt{\square}$

(G) Subtract b from both sides.

$2ax = \square \pm \sqrt{\square}$

(H) Divide both sides by $2a$ to solve for x.

$x = \dfrac{\square \pm \sqrt{\square}}{\square}$

(I) The formula you just derived, $x = \dfrac{-b \pm \sqrt{b^2 - 4ac}}{2a}$, is called the **quadratic formula**. It gives you the values of x that solve any quadratic equation where $a \neq 0$.

Reflect

1. **What If?** If the derivation had begun by dividing each term by a, what would the resulting binomial of x have been after completing the square? Does one derivation method appear to be simpler than the other? Explain.

Explain 1 Using the Discriminant to Determine the Number of Real Solutions

Recall that a quadratic equation, $ax^2 + bx + c$, can have two, one, or no real solutions. By evaluating the part of the quadratic formula under the radical sign, $b^2 - 4ac$, called the **discriminant**, you can determine the number of real solutions.

Example 1 **Determine how many real solutions each quadratic equation has.**

(A) $x^2 - 4x + 3 = 0$

$a = 1, b = -4, c = 3$	Identify a, b, and c.
$b^2 - 4ac$	Use the discriminant.
$(-4)^2 - 4(1)(3)$	Substitute the identified values into the discriminant.
$16 - 12 = 4$	Simplify.

Since $b^2 - 4ac > 0$, the equation has two real solutions.

(B) $x^2 - 2x + 2 = 0$

$a = \boxed{1}, b = \boxed{-2}, c = \boxed{2}$	Identify a, b, and c.
$b^2 - 4ac$	Use the discriminant.
$\left(\boxed{-2}\right)^2 - 4\left(\boxed{1}\right)\left(\boxed{2}\right)$	Substitute the identified values into the discriminant.
$\boxed{4} - \boxed{8} = \boxed{-4}$	Simplify.

Since $b^2 - 4ac \boxed{<} 0$, the equation has no real solutions.

Reflect

2. When the discriminant is positive, the quadratic equation has two real solutions. When the discriminant is negative, there are no real solutions. How many real solutions does a quadratic equation have if its discriminant equals 0? Explain.

Your Turn

Use the discriminant to determine the number of real solutions for each quadratic equation.

3. $x^2 + 4x + 1 = 0$ **4.** $2x^2 - 6x + 15 = 0$ **5.** $x^2 + 6x + 9 = 0$

Explain 2 Solving Equations by Using the Quadratic Formula

To use the quadratic formula to solve a quadratic equation, check that the equation is in standard form. If not, rewrite it in standard form. Then substitute the values of a, b, and c into the formula.

Example 2 **Solve using the quadratic formula.**

(A) $2x^2 + 3x - 5 = 0$

$a = 2, b = 3, c = -5$	Identify a, b, and c.
$x = \dfrac{-b \pm \sqrt{b^2 - 4ac}}{2a}$	Use the quadratic formula.
$x = \dfrac{-3 \pm \sqrt{(3)^2 - 4(2)(-5)}}{2(2)}$	Substitute the identified values into the quadratic formula.
$x = \dfrac{-3 \pm \sqrt{49}}{4}$	Simplify the radicand and the denominator.
$x = \dfrac{-3 \pm 7}{4}$	Evaluate the square root.
$x = \dfrac{-3 + 7}{4}$ or $x = \dfrac{-3 - 7}{4}$	Write as two equations.
$x = 1$ or $x = -\dfrac{5}{2}$	Simplify both equations.

The solutions are 1 and $-\frac{5}{2}$.

Graph $y = 2x^2 + 3x - 5$ to verify your answers.

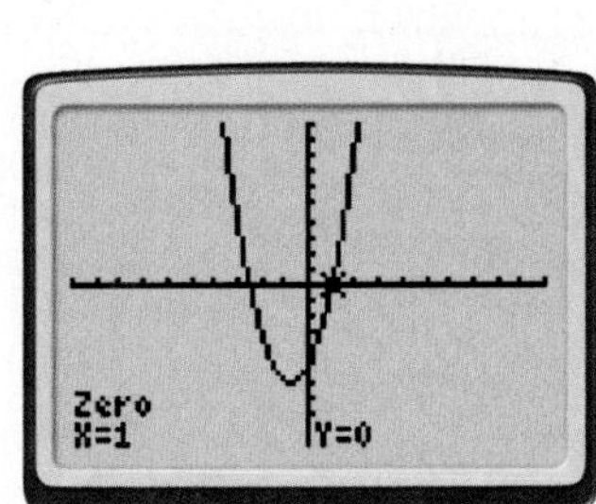
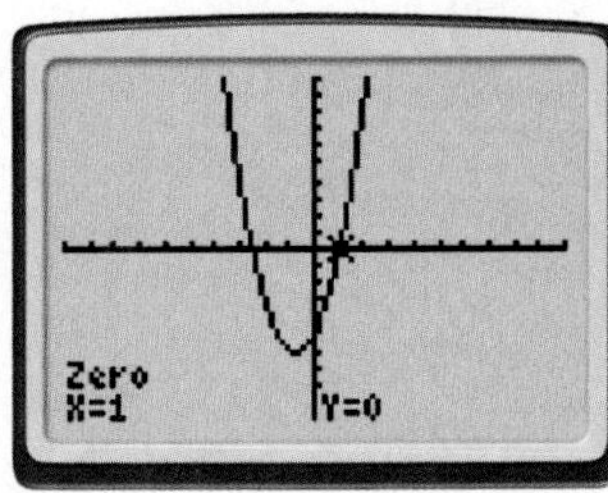

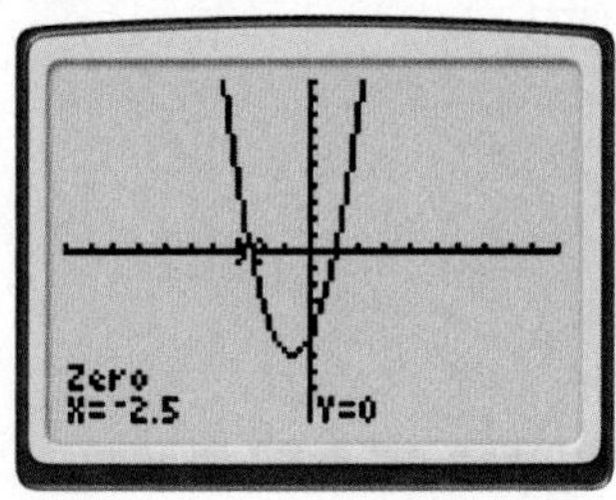

The graph does verify the solutions.

(B) $2x = x^2 - 4$

$x^2 - \boxed{2x} - 4 = 0$ — Write in standard form.

$a = \boxed{1},\ b = \boxed{-2},\ c = \boxed{-4}$ — Identify a, b, and c.

$x = \dfrac{-b \pm \sqrt{b^2 - 4ac}}{2a}$ — Use the quadratic formula.

$x = \dfrac{-\left(\boxed{-2}\right) \pm \sqrt{\left(\boxed{-2}\right)^2 - 4\left(\boxed{1}\right)\left(\boxed{-4}\right)}}{2\left(\boxed{1}\right)}$ — Substitute the identified values into the quadratic formula.

$x = \dfrac{2 \pm \sqrt{\boxed{20}}}{2}$ — Simplify the radicand and the denominator.

$x = \dfrac{2 \pm \sqrt{\boxed{4} \cdot 5}}{2} = \dfrac{2 \pm 2\boxed{\sqrt{5}}}{2} = 1 \pm \boxed{\sqrt{5}}$ — Simplify.

$x = \boxed{1 + \sqrt{5}}$ or $x = \boxed{1 - \sqrt{5}}$ — Write as two equations.

$x \approx \boxed{3.236}$ or $x \approx \boxed{-1.236}$ — Use a calculator to find approximate solutions to three decimal places.

The exact solutions are $\boxed{1 + \sqrt{5}}$ and $\boxed{1 - \sqrt{5}}$. The approximate solutions are $\boxed{3.236}$ and $\boxed{-1.236}$.

Graph $y = x^2 - \boxed{2x} - 4$ and find the zeros using the graphing calculator. The calculator will give approximate values.

The graph does confirm the solutions.

Reflect

6. **Discussion** How can you use substitution to check your solutions?

Your Turn

Solve using the quadratic formula.

6. $x^2 - 6x - 7 = 0$

7. $2x^2 = 8x - 7$

Explain 3 Using the Discriminant with Real-World Models

Given a real-world situation that can be modeled by a quadratic equation, you can find the number of real solutions to the problem using the discriminant, and then apply the quadratic formula to obtain the solutions. After finding the solutions, check to see if they make sense in the context of the problem.

In projectile motion problems where the projectile height h is modeled by the equation $h = -16t^2 + vt + s$, where t is the time in seconds the object has been in the air, v is the initial vertical velocity in feet per second, and s is the initial height in feet. The -16 coefficient in front of the t^2 term refers to the effect of gravity on the object. This equation can be written using metric units as $h = -4.9t^2 + vt + s$, where the units are converted from feet to meters. Time remains in units of seconds.

Example 3 **For each problem, use the discriminant to determine the number of real solutions for the equation. Then, find the solutions and check to see if they make sense in the context of the problem.**

(A) A diver jumps from a platform 10 meters above the surface of the water. The diver's height is given by the equation $h = -4.9t^2 + 3.5t + 10$, where t is the time in seconds after the diver jumps. For what time t is the diver's height 1 meter?

Substitute $h = 1$ into the height equation. Then, write the resulting quadratic equation in standard form to solve for t.

$1 = -4.9t^2 + 3.5t + 10$ $\qquad$ $0 = -4.9t^2 + 3.5t + 9$

First, use the discriminant to find the number of real solutions of the equation.

$b^2 - 4ac$ $\qquad$ Use the discriminant.

$(3.5)^2 - 4(-4.9)(9) = 188.65$

Since $b^2 - 4ac > 0$, the equation has two real solutions.

Next, use the quadratic formula to find the real number solutions.

$a = -4.9,\ b = 3.5,\ c = 9$ $\qquad$ Identify a, b, and c.

$t = \dfrac{-b \pm \sqrt{b^2 - 4ac}}{2a}$ $\qquad$ Use the quadratic formula.

$t = \dfrac{-3.5 \pm \sqrt{188.65}}{2(-4.9)}$ $\qquad$ Substitute the identified values into the quadratic formula and the value of the discriminant.

$t \approx \dfrac{-3.5 \pm 13.73}{-9.8}$ $\qquad$ Simplify.

$t \approx \dfrac{-3.5 + 13.73}{-9.8}$ or $t \approx \dfrac{-3.5 - 13.73}{-9.8}$ $\qquad$ Write as two equations.

$t \approx -1.04$ or $t \approx 1.76$ $\qquad$ Solutions

Disregard the negative solution because t represents the seconds after the diver jumps and a negative value has no meaning in this context. So, the diver is at height 1 meter after a time of $t \approx 1.76$ seconds.

(B) The height in meters of a model rocket on a particular launch can be modeled by the equation $h = -4.9t^2 + 102t + 100$, where t is the time in seconds after its engine burns out 100 meters above the ground. When will the rocket reach a height of 600 meters?

Substitute $h =$ 600 into the height equation. Then, write the resulting quadratic equation in standard form to solve for t.

$$h = -4.9t^2 + 102t + 100$$

$$600 = -4.9t^2 + 102t + 100$$

$$0 = -4.9t^2 + 102t - 500$$

First, use the discriminant to find the number of real solutions of the equation.

$a = -4.9$, $b =$ 102, $c =$ -500 — Identify a, b, and c.

$b^2 - 4ac$ — Use the discriminant.

$(102)^2 - 4(-4.9)(-500)$ — Substitute the identified values into the discriminant.

$10404 - 9800 = 604$ — Simplify.

Since $b^2 - 4ac$ > 0, the equation has 2 real solutions.

Next, use the quadratic formula to find the real number solutions.

$$t = \frac{-102 \pm \sqrt{604}}{2(-4.9)}$$

Substitute the identified values into the quadratic formula and the value of the discriminant.

$$t = \frac{-102 \pm 24.58}{-9.8}$$

Simplify.

$$t \approx \frac{-102 + 24.58}{-9.8} \text{ or } t \approx \frac{-102 - 24.58}{-9.8}$$

Write as two equations.

$t \approx -7.90$ or $t \approx 12.92$ — Solutions

Disregard the negative solution because t represents the seconds after the rocket has launched and a negative value has no meaning in this context. So, the rocket is at height 600 meters after a time of $t \approx$ 12.92 seconds.

Your Turn

For each problem, use the discriminant to determine the number of real solutions for the equation. Then, find the solutions and check to see if they make sense in the context of the problem.

9. A soccer player uses her head to hit a ball up in the air from a height of 2 meters with an initial vertical velocity of 5 meters per second. The height h in meters of the ball is given by $h = -4.9t^2 + 5t + 2$, where t is the time elapsed in seconds. How long will it take the ball to hit the ground if no other players touch it?

10. The quarterback of a football team throws a pass to the team's receiver. The height h in meters of the football can be modeled by $h = -4.9t^2 + 3t + 1.75$, where t is the time elapsed in seconds. The receiver catches the football at a height of 0.25 meters. How long does the ball remain in the air until it is caught by the receiver?

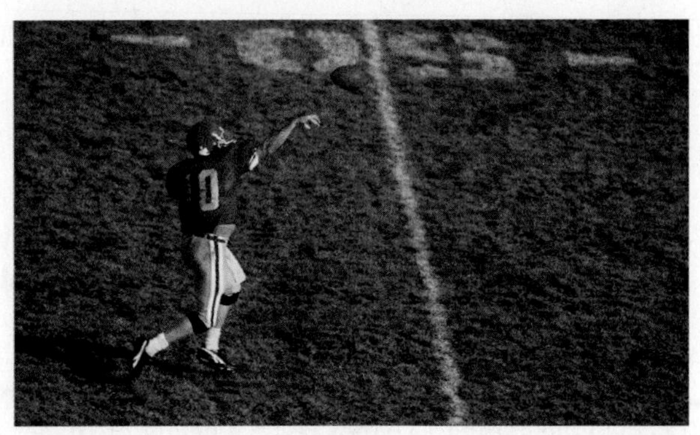

Elaborate

11. How can the discriminant of a quadratic equation be used to determine the number of zeros (x-intercepts) that the graph of the equation will have?

12. What advantage does using the quadratic formula have over other methods of solving quadratic equations?

13. **Essential Question Check-In** How can you derive the quadratic formula?

Evaluate: Homework and Practice

- Online Homework
- Hints and Help
- Extra Practice

Determine how many real solutions each quadratic equation has.

1. $4x^2 + 4x + 1 = 0$
2. $x^2 - x + 3 = 0$
3. $x^2 - 8x^2 - 9 = 0$
4. $2x^2 - x\sqrt{5} + 2 = 0$
5. $\frac{x^2}{2} - x + \frac{1}{4} = 0$
6. $\frac{x^2}{4} - x\sqrt{7} + 7 = 0$
7. $\frac{x^2}{2} - x\sqrt{2} + 1 = 0$
8. $x^2\sqrt{2} - x + \frac{1}{2} = 0$

Solve using the quadratic formula. Leave answers that are not perfect squares in radical form.

9. $10x + 4 = 6x^2$
10. $x^2 + x - 20 = 0$
11. $4x^2 = 4 - x$
12. $9x^2 + 3x - 2 = 0$
13. $14x + 3 = -8x^2$
14. $x^2 + 3x^2 + 1 = 0$

For each problem, use the discriminant to determine the number of real solutions for the equation. Then, find the solutions and check to see if they make sense in the context of the problem.

15. **Sports** A soccer player kicks the ball to a height of 1 meter inside the goal. The equation for the height h of the ball at time t is $h = -4.9t^2 - 5t + 2$. Find the time the ball reached the goal.

16. The length and width of a rectangular patio are, $(x + 8)$ feet and $(x + 6)$ feet, respectively. If the area of the patio is 160 square feet, what are the dimensions of the patio?

17. **Chemistry** A scientist is growing bacteria in a lab for study. One particular type of bacteria grows at a rate of $y = 2t^2 + 3t + 500$. A different bacteria grows at a rate of $y = 3t^2 + t + 300$. In both of these equations, y is the number of bacteria after t minutes. When is there an equal number of both types of bacteria?

Use this information for Exercises 18 and 19. A gymnast, who can stretch her arms up to reach 6 feet, jumps straight up on a trampoline. The height of her feet above the trampoline can be modeled by the equation $h = -16x^2 + 12x$, where x is the time in seconds after her jump.

18. Do the gymnast's hands reach a height of 10 feet above the trampoline? Use the discriminant to explain. (Hint: Since h = height of feet, you must use the difference between the heights of the hands and feet.)

19. Which of the following are possible heights she achieved? Select all that apply.
   a. $h = \frac{9}{4}$
   b. $h = 4$
   c. $h = 3$
   d. $h = 0.5$
   e. $h = \frac{1}{4}$

20. **Explain the Error** Dan said that if a quadratic equation does not have any real solutions, then it does not represent a function. Explain Dan's error.

H.O.T. Focus on Higher Order Thinking

21. **Communicate Mathematical Ideas** Explain why a positive discriminant results in two real solutions.

22. **Multi-Step** A model rocket is launched from the top of a hill 10 meters above ground level. The rocket's initial speed is 10 meters per second. Its height h can be modeled by the equation $h = -4.9t^2 + 10t + 10$, where t is the time in seconds.
   a. When does the rocket achieve a height of 100 meters?
   b. How long does it take the rocket to reach ground level?

Lesson Performance Task

A baseball field is next to a building that is 130 feet tall. A series of batters hit pitched balls into the air with the given initial vertical velocities. (Assume each ball is hit from a height of 3 feet.) After the game, a fan reports that several hits resulted in the ball hitting the roof of the building. How can you use the discriminant to determine whether any of the hits described below could be among them? Explain. If any of the balls hit could have hit the roof, identify them. Can you tell if the ball actually did hit the roof?

Player	Initial Vertical Velocity (ft/s)
Janok	99
Jimenez	91
Serrano	88
Sei	89

9.4 Choosing a Method for Solving Quadratic Equations

Resource Locker

Essential Question: How can you choose a method for solving a given quadratic equation?

Explore Comparing Solution Methods for Quadratic Equations

$7x^2 - 3x - 5 = 0$

Try to solve the equation by factoring.

(A) Find the factors of 7 and −5 to complete the table:

Factors of 7	Factors of −5	Outer Product + Inner Product
1, 7	1, −5	2
1, 7	5, −1	
1, 7	−1, 5	
1, 7	−5, 1	

(B) None of the sums of the inner and outer products of the factor pairs of 7 and −5 equal −3.

Does this mean the equation cannot be solved?

Now, try to solve the equation by completing the square.

(C) The leading coefficient is not a perfect square. Multiply both sides by a value that makes the coefficient a perfect square.

$\square(7x^2 - 3x - 5) = (0)\square$

$\square x^2 - \square x - \square = \square$

(D) Add or subtract to move the constant term to the other side of the equation.

$\square x^2 - \square x = \square$

(E) Find $\frac{b^2}{4a}$ and reduce to simplest form.

$\frac{b^2}{4a} = \frac{\square^2}{4(\square)} = \frac{\square}{\square} = \frac{\square}{\square}$

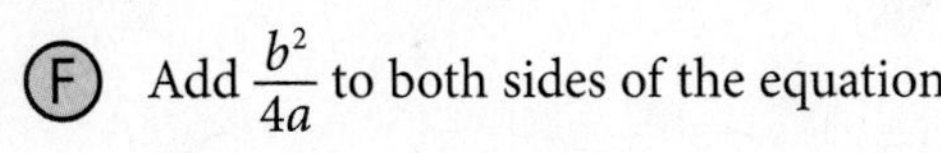

Ⓕ Add $\frac{b^2}{4a}$ to both sides of the equation,

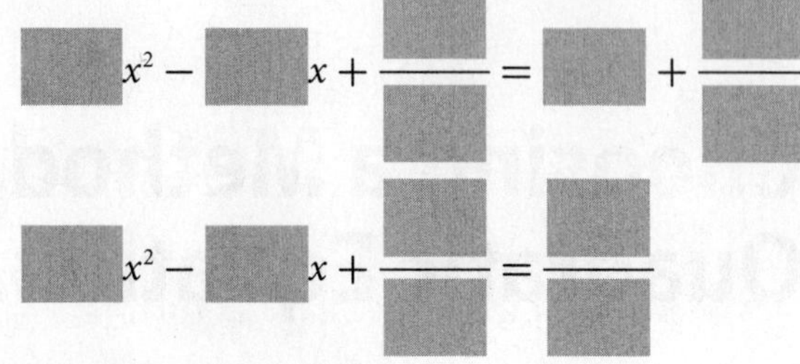

$$\square x^2 - \square x + \frac{\square}{\square} = \square + \frac{\square}{\square}$$

$$\square x^2 - \square x + \frac{\square}{\square} = \frac{\square}{\square}$$

Ⓖ Factor the perfect-square trinomial on the left side of the equation.

$$\left(\square x - \frac{\square}{\square}\right)^2 = \frac{\square}{\square}$$

Ⓗ Take the square root of both sides.

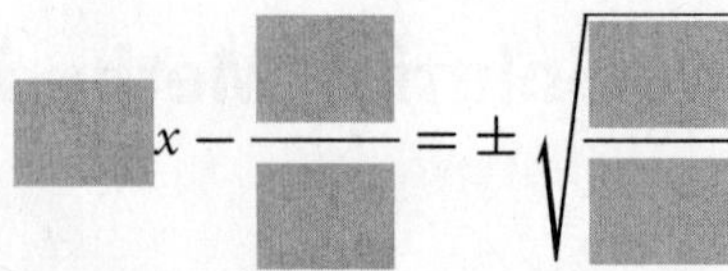

$$\square x - \frac{\square}{\square} = \pm\sqrt{\frac{\square}{\square}}$$

Ⓘ Add the constant to both sides, and then divide by a. Find both solutions for x.

$$\square x - \frac{\square}{\square} + \frac{\square}{\square} = \pm\sqrt{\frac{\square}{\square}} + \frac{\square}{\square}$$

$$\frac{\square x}{\square} = \frac{\pm\sqrt{\frac{\square}{\square}} + \frac{\square}{\square}}{\square}$$

$$x = \frac{\pm\sqrt{\frac{\square}{\square}} + \frac{\square}{\square}}{\square}$$

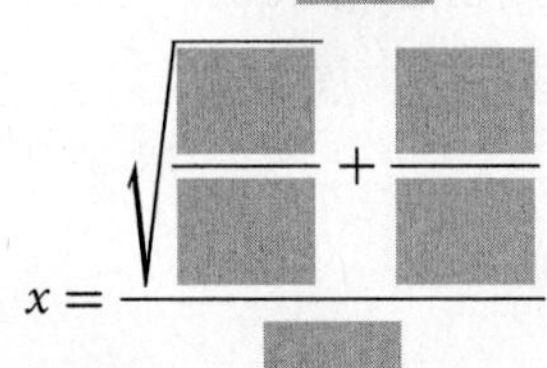

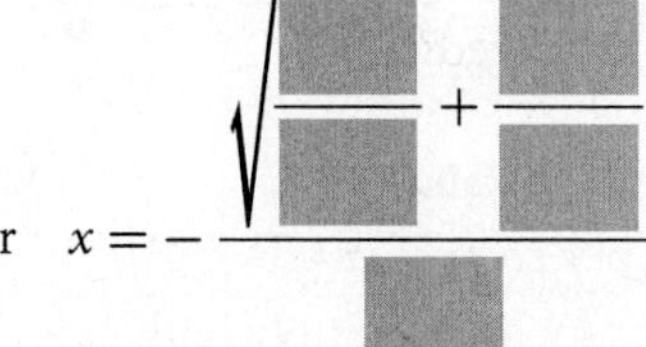

$$x = \frac{\sqrt{\frac{\square}{\square}} + \frac{\square}{\square}}{\square} \quad \text{or} \quad x = -\frac{\sqrt{\frac{\square}{\square}} + \frac{\square}{\square}}{\square}$$

Ⓙ Solve both equations to three decimal places using your calculator.

$x = \square$ or $x = \square$

Now use the quadratic formula to solve the same equation.

Ⓚ Identify the values of a, b, and c. $a = \square$, $b = \square$, $c = \square$

Ⓛ Substitute values into the quadratic formula.

$$x = \frac{-\square \pm \sqrt{\square^2 - 4(7)(\square)}}{2(\square)}$$

(M) Simplify the discriminant and the denominator.

$$x = \frac{3 \pm \sqrt{\square}}{\square}$$

(N) Use your calculator to finish simplifying the expression for x.

$x = \square$ or $x = \square$

Reflect

1. **Discussion** Another method you learned for solving quadratics is taking square roots. Why would that not work in this case?

Explain 1 Solving Quadratic Equations Using Different Methods

You have seen several ways to solve a quadratic equation, but there are reasons why you might choose one method over another.

Factoring is usually the fastest and easiest method. Try factoring first if it seems likely that the equation is factorable.

Both completing the square and using the quadratic formula are more general. Quadratic equations that are solvable can be solved using either method.

Example 1 **Speculate which method is the most appropriate for each equation and explain your answer. Then solve the equation using factoring (if possible), completing the square, and the quadratic formula.**

(A) $x^2 + 7x + 6 = 0$

Factor the quadratic.

Set up a factor table adding factors of c.

Factors of c	Sum of Factors
1, 6	7
2, 3	5

Substitute in factors. $(x + 1)(x + 6) = 0$

Use the Zero Product Property $x + 1 = 0$ or $x + 6 = 0$

Solve both equations for x. $x = -1$ or $x = -6$

Complete the square.

Move the constant term to the right side.	$x^2 + 7x = -6$
Add $\frac{b^2}{4a}$ to both sides.	$x^2 + 7x + \frac{49}{4} = -6 + \frac{49}{4}$
Simplify.	$x^2 + 7x + \frac{49}{4} = \frac{25}{4}$
Factor the perfect-square trimonial on the left.	$\left(x + \frac{7}{2}\right)^2 = \frac{25}{4}$
Take the square root of both sides.	$x + \frac{7}{2} = \pm\frac{5}{2}$
Write two equations.	$x + \frac{7}{2} = \frac{5}{2}$ or $x + \frac{7}{2} = -\frac{5}{2}$
Solve both equations.	$x = -1$ or $x = -6$

Apply the quadratic formula.

Identify the values of a, b, and c.	$a = 1, b = 7, c = 6$
Substitute values into the quadratic formula.	$x = \frac{-7 \pm \sqrt{7^2 - 4(1)(6)}}{2(1)}$
Simplify the discriminant and denominator.	$x = \frac{-7 \pm \sqrt{25}}{2}$
Evaluate the square root and write as two equations.	$x = \frac{-7 + 5}{2}$ or $x = \frac{-7 - 5}{2}$
Simplify.	$x = -1$ or $x = -6$

Because the list of possible factors that needed to be checked was short, it makes sense to try factoring $x^2 + 7x + 6$ first, even if you don't know if you will be able to factor it. Once factored, the remaining steps are fewer and simpler than either completing the square or using the quadratic formula.

 $2x^2 + 8x + 3 = 0$

Factor the quadratic.

Factors of c	Factors of c	Sum of Inner and Outer Products
1, 2	1, 3	5
1, 2	3, 1	7

Can the quadratic be factored? No.

Complete the square.

Move the constant term to the right side.	$2x^2 + 8x = -3$
Multiply both sides by 2 to make a perfect square.	$4x^2 + 16x = -6$
Add $\frac{b^2}{4a}$ to both sides.	$4x^2 + 16x + 16 = 10$
Factor the left side.	$(2x + 4)^2 = 10$

Take the square root of both sides. $2x + 4 = \boxed{\pm\sqrt{10}}$

Write two equations. $2x + 4 = \boxed{\sqrt{10}}$ or $2x + 4 = -\sqrt{10}$

Solve both equations. $x = -2 \boxed{+} \frac{\sqrt{10}}{2}$ or $x = -2 \boxed{-} \frac{\sqrt{10}}{2}$

Apply the quadratic formula.

Identify the values of *a*, *b*, and *c*. $a = \boxed{2}, b = \boxed{8}, c = \boxed{3}$

Substitute values into the quadratic formula. $x = \frac{\boxed{-8} \pm \sqrt{\boxed{8}^2 - 4\left(\boxed{2}\right)\left(\boxed{3}\right)}}{2\left(\boxed{2}\right)}$

Simplify the discriminant and denominator. $x = \frac{-8 \pm \sqrt{\boxed{40}}}{4}$

Evaluate the square root and write as two equations. $x = \frac{-8 \pm \boxed{2}\sqrt{\boxed{10}}}{4}$

Simplify. $x = \boxed{-2} \pm \frac{\sqrt{10}}{\boxed{2}}$

Reflect

2. What are the advantages and disadvantages of solving a quadratic equation by taking square roots?
3. What are the advantages and disadvantages of solving a quadratic equation by factoring?
4. What are the advantages and disadvantages of solving a quadratic equation by completing the square?
5. What are the advantages and disadvantages of solving a quadratic equation by using the quadratic formula?

Your Turn

Solve the quadratic equations by any method you chose. Identify the method and explain why you chose it.

6. $9x^2 - 100 = 0$

7. $x^2 + 4x - 7 = 0$

Explain 2 Choosing Solution Methods for Quadratic Equation Models

Recall that the formula for height, in feet, of a projectile under the influence of gravity is given by $h = -16t^2 + vt + s$, where t is the time in seconds, v is the upward initial velocity (at $t = 0$), and s is the starting height.

Example 2 **Marco is throwing a tennis ball at a kite that is stuck 42 feet up in a tree, trying to knock it loose. He can throw the ball at a velocity of 45 feet per second upward at a height of 4 feet. Will his throw reach the kite? How hard does Marco need to throw the ball to reach the kite?**

Analyze Information

The initial velocity is: 45

The starting height is: 4

The height of the kite is: 42

Formulate a Plan

Use the projectile motion formula to write an equation for the height of the ball t seconds after Marco throws it.

$h = \boxed{-16}\, t^2 + \boxed{45}\, t + \boxed{4}$

To determine if the ball can reach the height of the kite, set up the equation to find the time it takes the ball to reach the height of the kite.

$-16t^2 + 45t + 4 = \boxed{42}$

Convert the equation to standard form.

$-16t^2 + 45t + \boxed{-38} = 0$

This problem will be easiest to solve by using the quadratic formula. To check if the ball reaches the kite, begin by calculating the discriminant. To determine the velocity that Marco must throw the ball to reach the kite, we should find the velocity where the discriminant is equal to 0, which is the exact moment at which the ball changes direction and falls back to earth.

Solve

Identify values of a, b, and c. $a = \boxed{-16}$, $b = \boxed{45}$, $c = \boxed{-38}$

Evaluate the discriminant first. $b^2 - 4ac = \boxed{45}^2 - 4\left(\boxed{-16}\right)\left(\boxed{-38}\right)$

$= \boxed{-407}$

A negative discriminant means that there are 0 solutions to the equation. Marco's throw will not reach as high as the kite.

The velocity with which Marco needs to throw the ball to reach the kite is the coefficient b of the x-term of the quadratic equation.

$b = \boxed{v}$

Substitute v into the discriminant and solve for a discriminant equal to 0 to find the velocity at which Marco needs to throw the ball.

Identify values of a, b, and c. $a = \boxed{-16}$, $b = \boxed{v}$, $c = \boxed{-38}$

Evaluate the discriminant first. $\boxed{v}^2 - 4\left(\boxed{-16}\right)\left(\boxed{-38}\right) = 0$

Simplify. $v^2 - \boxed{2432} = 0$

This quadratic equation should be solved by taking square roots because it has no x-term.

Move the constant term to the right. $v^2 =$ 2432

Take square roots of both sides. Use your calculator. $v \approx \pm$ 49.3

The negative velocity represents a downward throw and will not result in the ball hitting the kite. The tennis ball must have a velocity of at about 49.3 feet per second to reach the kite.

Justify and Evaluate

Plot the graph of Marco's throw on your graphing calculator to see that the conclusion you reached (no solution) makes sense because the graphs do not intersect. Sketch the graph.

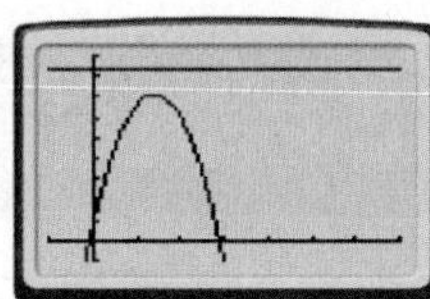

Then plot the height of the ball when the discriminant is equal to zero. The graphs intersect in one point. Sketch the graph.

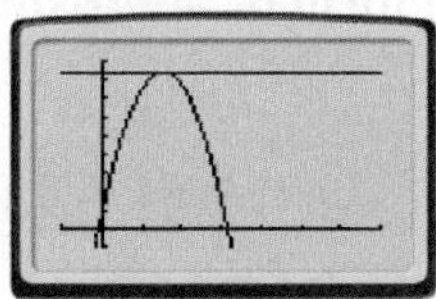

Your Turn

8. The wheel of a remote controlled airplane falls off while the airplane is climbing at 40 feet in the air. The wheel starts with an initial upward velocity of 24 feet per second. How long does it take to fall to the ground? Set up the equation to determine the time and pick one method to solve it. Explain why you chose that method.

9. Marco's brother, Jessie, is helping Marco knock a kite from the tree. He can throw the ball 50 feet per second upwards, from a height of 5 feet. Is he throwing the ball hard enough to reach the kite, and if so, how long does it take the ball to reach the kite?

Elaborate

10. Which method do you think is best if you are going to have to use a calculator?

11. Some factorable quadratic expressions are still quite difficult to solve by factoring rather than using another method. What makes an equation difficult to factor?

12. You are taking a test on quadratic equations and you can't decide which method would be the fastest way to solve a particular problem. How could looking at a graph of the equation on a calculator help you decide which method to use?

13. **Essential Question Check-In** How should you determine a method for solving a quadratic equation?

Evaluate: Homework and Practice

- Online Homework
- Hints and Help
- Extra Practice

1. Look at this quadratic equation and explain what you think will be the best approach to solving it. Do not solve the equation.

$3.38x^2 + 2.72x - 9.31 = 0$

Solve the quadratic equation by any means. Identify the method and explain why you chose it. Irrational answers may be left in radical form or approximated with a calculator (round to two decimal places).

2. $x^2 - 7x + 12 = 0$

3. $36x^2 - 64 = 0$

4. $4x^2 - 4x - 3 = 2$

5. $8x^2 + 9x + 2 = 1$

6. $5x^2 + 0x - 13 = 0$

7. $7x^2 - 5x - 5 = 0$

8. $3x^2 - 6x = 0$

9. $2x^2 + 4x - 3 = 0$

10. $(x - 5)^2 = 16$

11. $(2x - 1)^2 = x$

12. $2(x + 2)^2 - 5 = 3$

13. $(2x - 3)^2 = 4x$

14. $6x^2 - 5x + 12 = 0$

15. $3x^2 + 6x + 2 = 0$

16. $\frac{1}{2}x^2 + 3x + \frac{5}{2} = 0$

17. $(6x + 7)(x + 1) = 26$

Use the projectile motion formula and solve the quadratic equation by any means. Identify the method and explain why you chose it. Irrational answers and fractions should be converted to decimal form and rounded to two places.

18. Gary drops a pair of gloves off of a balcony that is 64 feet high down to his friend on the ground. How long does it take the pair of gloves to hit the ground?

19. A soccer player jumps up and heads the ball while it is 7 feet above the ground. It bounces up at a velocity of 20 feet per second. How long will it take the ball to hit the ground?

20. A stomp rocket is a toy that is launched into the air from the ground by a sudden burst of pressure exerted by stomping on a pedal. If the rocket is launched at 24 feet per second, how long will it be in the air?

21. A dog leaps off of the patio from 2 feet off of the ground with an upward velocity of 15 feet per second. How long will the dog be in the air?

22. **Multipart Classification** Determine whether the following statements about finding solutions to quadratic equations with integer coefficients are True or False.

a. Any quadratic equation with a real solution can be solved by using the quadratic formula.

b. Any quadratic equation with a real solution can be solved by completing the square.

c. Any quadratic equation with a real solution can be solved by factoring.

d. Any quadratic equation with a real solution can be solved by taking the square root of both sides of the equation.

e. If the equation can be factored, it has rational solutions.

f. If the equation has only one real solution, it cannot be factored.

H.O.T. Focus on Higher Order Thinking

23. **Justify Reasoning** Any quadratic equation with a real solution can be solved with the quadratic formula. Describe the kinds of equations where that would not be the best choice, and explain your reasoning.

24. **Critique Reasoning** Marisol decides to solve the quadratic equation by factoring $21x^2 + 47x - 24 = 0$. Do you think she chose the best method? How would you solve this equation?

25. **Communicate Mathematical Ideas** Explain the difference between the statements "The quadratic formula can be used to solve any quadratic equation with a real solution" and "Every quadratic equation has a real solution."

Lesson Performance Task

A landscaper is designing a patio for a customer who has several different ideas about what to make.

Use the given information to set up a quadratic equation modeling the situation and solve it using the quadratic formula. Then determine if another method for solving quadratic equations would have been easier to use and explain why.

a. One of the customer's ideas is to buy bluestone tiles from a home improvement store using several gift cards he has received as presents over the past few years. If the total value of the gift cards is \$6500 and the bluestone costs \$9 per square foot, what are the dimensions of the largest patio that can be made that is 12 feet longer than it is wide?

b. Another of the customer's ideas is simply a quadratic equation scrawled on a napkin.
$x^2 - 54x + 720 = 0$

c. The third idea is also a somewhat random quadratic polynomial.
$x^2 - 40x + 257 = 0$

9.5 Solving Nonlinear Systems

Essential Question: How can you solve a system of equations when one equation is linear and the other is quadratic?

Explore Determining the Possible Number of Solutions of a System of Linear and Quadratic Equations

A system of one linear and one quadratic equation may have zero, one, or two solutions.

(A) Copy the graph of the quadratic function $f(x) = x^2 - 2x - 2$ shown. On the same coordinate plane, graph the following linear functions:

$g(x) = -x - 2$, $h(x) = 2x - 6$, $j(x) = 0.5x - 5$

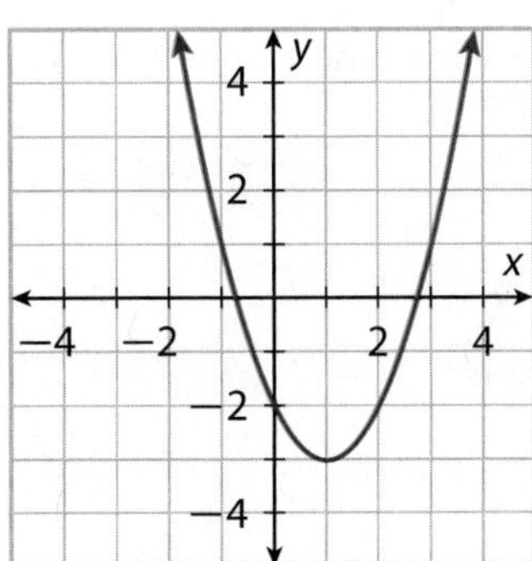

(B) Look at the graph of the system consisting of the quadratic function, $f(x)$, and the linear function, $g(x)$. Based on the intersections of these two graphs, how many solutions exist in a system consisting of these two functions?

(C) Look at the graph of the system consisting of the quadratic function, $f(x)$, and the linear function, $h(x)$. Based on the intersections of these two graphs, how many solutions exist in a system consisting of these two functions?

(D) Look at the graph of the system consisting of the quadratic function, $f(x)$, and the linear function, $j(x)$. Based on the intersections of these two graphs, how many solutions exist in a system consisting of these two functions?

Reflect

1. A system consisting of a quadratic equation and a linear equation can have ____, ____, or  solutions.

Explain 1 Solving a System of Linear and Quadratic Equations Graphically

A system of equations consisting of a linear and quadratic equation can be solved graphically by finding the points where the graphs intersect.

Example 1 **Solve the system of equations graphically.**

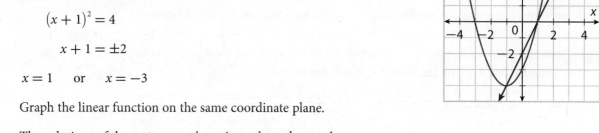

Ⓐ 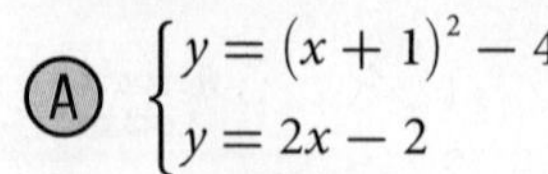

$$\begin{cases} y = (x+1)^2 - 4 \\ y = 2x - 2 \end{cases}$$

Graph the quadratic function. The vertex is the point $(-1, -4)$. The x-intercepts are the points where $y = 0$.

$$(x+1)^2 - 4 = 0$$

$$(x+1)^2 = 4$$

$$x + 1 = \pm 2$$

$$x = 1 \quad \text{or} \quad x = -3$$

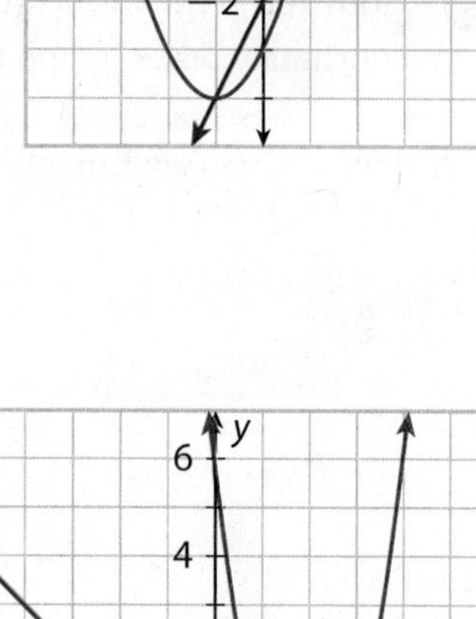

Graph the linear function on the same coordinate plane.

The solutions of the system are the points where the graphs intersect. The solutions are $(-1, -4)$ and $(1, 0)$.

Ⓑ 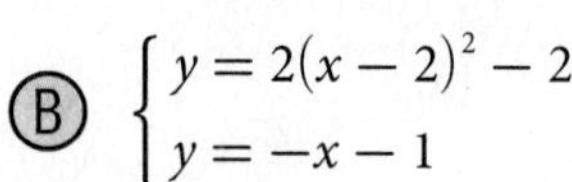

$$\begin{cases} y = 2(x-2)^2 - 2 \\ y = -x - 1 \end{cases}$$

Graph the quadratic function. The vertex is the point $\left(2, \boxed{-2}\right)$.

The x-intercepts are the points where $y = 0$.

$$2(x-2)^2 - 2 = 0$$

$$2(x-2)^2 = \boxed{2}$$

$$(x-2)^2 = \boxed{1}$$

$$\boxed{x - 2} = \pm 1$$

$$x = \boxed{3} \quad \text{or} \quad x = \boxed{1}$$

Graph the linear function on the same coordinate plane.

There are 0 intersection points. This system has 0 solution(s).

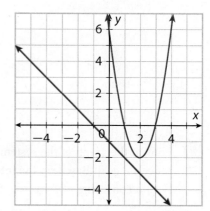

Your Turn

Solve the system of equations graphically.

2. $\begin{cases} y = -2(x+2)^2 + 8 \\ y = 4x + 16 \end{cases}$

3. $\begin{cases} y = (x+1)^2 - 9 \\ y = 6x - 12 \end{cases}$

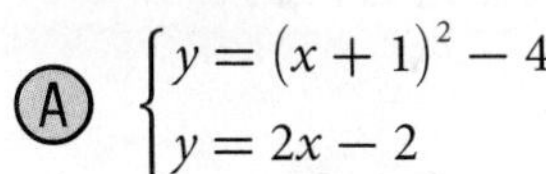

Explain 2 Solving a System of Linear and Quadratic Equations Algebraically

Systems of equations can also be solved algebraically by using the substitution method to eliminate a variable. If the system is one linear and one quadratic equation, the equation resulting after substitution will also be quadratic and can be solved by selecting an appropriate method.

Example 2 **Solve the system of equations algebraically.**

(A) $\begin{cases} y = (x+1)^2 - 4 \\ y = 2x - 2 \end{cases}$

Set the two the expressions for y equal to each other, and solve for x.

$$(x+1)^2 - 4 = 2x - 2$$

$$x^2 + 2x - 3 = 2x - 2$$

$$x^2 - 1 = 0$$

$$x^2 = 1$$

$$x = \pm 1$$

Substitute 1 and -1 for x to find the corresponding y-values.

$y = 2x - 2$	$y = 2x - 2$
$y = 2(1) - 2 = 0$	$y = 2(-1) - 2 = -4$

The solutions are $(1, 0)$ and $(-1, -4)$.

(B) $\begin{cases} y = (x+4)(x+1) \\ y = -x - 5 \end{cases}$

Set the two the expressions for y equal to each other, and solve for x.

$$(x+4)(x+1) = \boxed{-x-5}$$

$$x^2 + \boxed{5}\,x + \boxed{4} = -x - 5$$

$$x^2 + \boxed{6}\,x + \boxed{9} = 0$$

$$\left(x + \boxed{3}\right)(x+3) = 0$$

$$x = \boxed{-3}$$

Substitute -3 for x to find the corresponding y-value.

$$y = -x - 5$$

$$y = -\left(\boxed{-3}\right) - 5 = \boxed{-2}$$

The solution is $\boxed{(-3, -2)}$.

Reflect

4. **Discussion** After finding the x-values of the intersection points, why use the linear equation to find the y-values rather than the quadratic? What if the quadratic equation is used instead?

Your Turn

Solve the system of equations algebraically.

5. $\begin{cases} y = 2x^2 + 9x + 5 \\ y = 3x - 3 \end{cases}$

Explain 3 Solving a Real-World Problem with a System of Linear and Quadratic Equations

Systems of equations can be solved by graphing both equations on a graphing calculator and using the Intersect feature.

Example 3 **Create and solve a system of equations to solve the problem.**

(A) A rock climber is pulling his pack up the side of a cliff that is 175.5 feet tall at a rate of 2 feet per second. The height of the pack in feet after t seconds is given by $h = 2t$. The climber drops a coil of rope from directly above the pack. The height of the coil in feet after t seconds is given by $h = -16t^2 + 175.5$. At what time does the coil of rope hit the pack?

Create the system of equations to solve.

$\begin{cases} h = -16t^2 + 175.5 \\ h = 2t \end{cases}$

Graph the functions together and find any points of intersection.

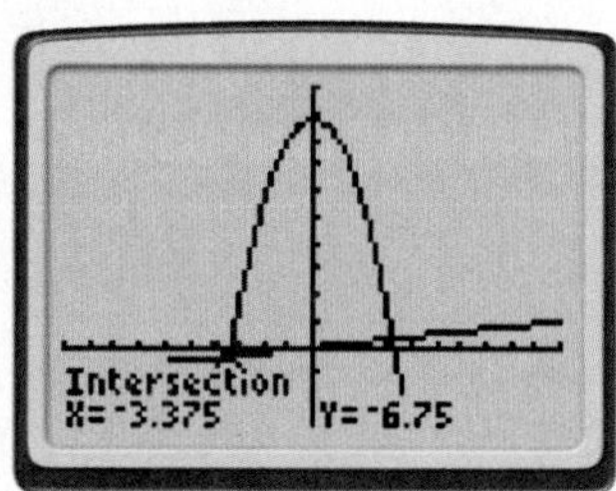

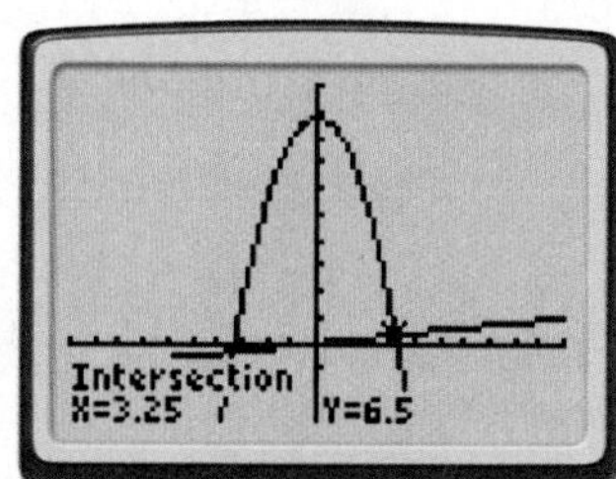

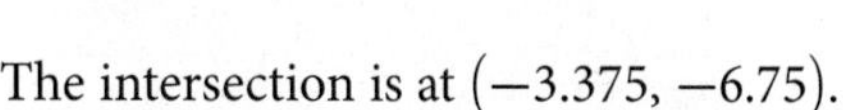

The intersection is at $(-3.375, -6.75)$.

The x-value represents time, so this solution is not reasonable.

The intersection is at $(3.25, 6.5)$.

This solution indicates that the coil hits the pack after 3.25 seconds.

(B) A window washer is ascending the side of a building that is 520 feet tall at a rate of 3 feet per second. The elevation of the window washer after t seconds is given by $h = 3t$. The supplies are lowered to the window washer from the top of the building at the same time that he begins to ascend the building. The height of the supplies in feet after t seconds is given by $h = -2t^2 + 520$. At what time do the supplies reach the window washer?

Create the system of equations to solve.

$\begin{cases} h = \boxed{-2}\,t^2 + \boxed{520} \\ h = \boxed{3}\,t \end{cases}$

Graph the functions together and find any points of intersection.

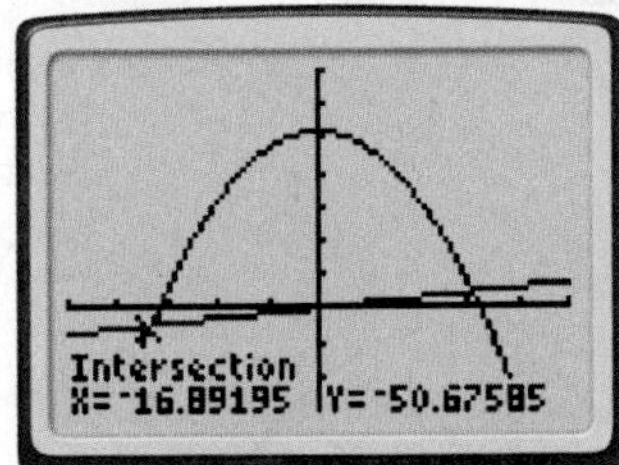

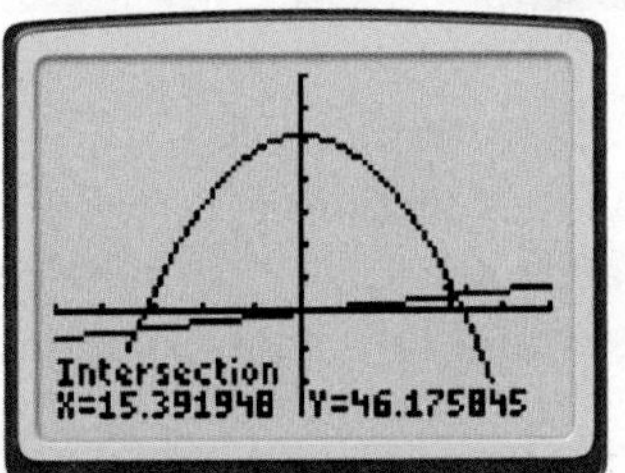

The intersection is at about $\left(-16.9, -50.7 \right)$.

The x-value represents time, so this solution is not reasonable.

The intersection is at about $\left(15.4, 46.2 \right)$.

This solution indicates that the supplies reach the window washer about 15 seconds later.

Reflect

6. How did you know which intersection to use in the example problems?

Your Turn

Write and solve a system of equations to solve the problem.

7. A billboard painter is using a pulley system to hoist a can of paint up to a scaffold at a rate of half a meter per second. The height of the can of paint as a function of time is given by $h(t) = 0.5t$. Five seconds after he starts raising the can of paint, his partner accidentally kicks a paint brush off of the scaffolding, which falls to the ground. The height of the falling paint brush can be represented by $h(t) = -4.9\,(t - 5)^2 + 30$. When does the brush pass the paint can?

Elaborate

8. **Discussion** When solving a system of equations consisting of a quadratic equation and a linear equation by graphing, why is it difficult to be sure there is one solution as opposed to 0 or 2?

9. How can you use the discriminant to determine how many solutions a linear-quadratic system has?

10. **Essential Question Check-in** How can the graphs of two functions be used to solve a system of a quadratic and a linear equation?

Evaluate: Homework and Practice

- Online Homework
- Hints and Help
- Extra Practice

1. The graph of the function $f(x) = -\frac{1}{4}(x-3)^2 + 4$ is shown. Graph the functions $g(x) = x + 1$, $h(x) = x + 2$, and $j(x) = x + 3$ with the graph of $f(x)$, and determine how many solutions each system has.

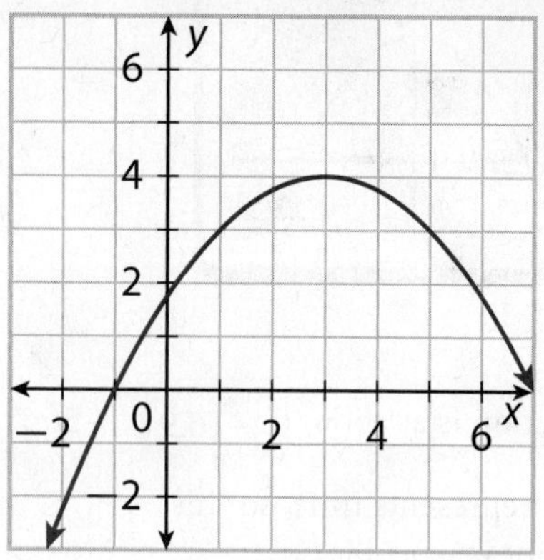

$f(x)$ and $g(x)$

$f(x)$ and $h(x)$

$f(x)$ and $j(x)$

Solve each system of equations graphically.

2. $\begin{cases} y = (x+3)^2 - 4 \\ y = 2x + 2 \end{cases}$

3. $\begin{cases} y = x^2 - 1 \\ y = x - 2 \end{cases}$

4. $\begin{cases} y = (x-4)^2 - 2 \\ y = -2 \end{cases}$

5. $\begin{cases} y = -x^2 + 4 \\ y = -3x + 6 \end{cases}$

6. $\begin{cases} y = -(x-2)^2 + 9 \\ y = 3x + 3 \end{cases}$

7. $\begin{cases} y = 3(x+1)^2 - 1 \\ y = x - 4 \end{cases}$

Solve the system of equations algebraically.

8. $\begin{cases} y = x^2 + 1 \\ y = 5 \end{cases}$

9. $\begin{cases} y = x^2 - 3x + 2 \\ y = 4x - 8 \end{cases}$

10. $\begin{cases} y = (x-3)^2 \\ y = 4 \end{cases}$

11. $\begin{cases} y = -x^2 + 4x \\ y = x + 2 \end{cases}$

12. $\begin{cases} y = 2x^2 - 5x + 6 \\ y = 5x - 6 \end{cases}$

13. $\begin{cases} y = x^2 + 7 \\ y = -9x + 29 \end{cases}$

14. $\begin{cases} y = 4x^2 + 45x + 83 \\ y = 5x - 17 \end{cases}$

15. $\begin{cases} y = (x+2)(x+4) \\ y = 3x + 2 \end{cases}$

Create and solve a linear quadratic system to solve the problem.

16. The height in feet of a skydiver t seconds after deploying her parachute is given by $h(t) = -300t + 1000$. A ball is thrown up toward the skydiver, and after t seconds, the height of the ball in feet is given by $h(t) = -16t^2 + 100t$. When does the ball reach the skydiver?

17. A wildebeest fails to notice a lion that is charging from behind at 65 feet per second until the lion is 40 feet away. The lion's position as a function of time is given by $p(t) = 65t - 40$. The wildebeest has to begin accelerating from a standstill until it is captured or reaches a top speed fast enough to stay ahead of the lion. The wildebeest's position as a function of time is given by $d(t) = 35t^2$. Does the wildebeest escape?

18. An elevator in a hotel moves at 20 feet per second. Leaving from the ground floor, its height in feet after t seconds is given by the formula $h(t) = 20t$. A bolt comes loose in the elevator shaft above, and its height in feet after falling for t seconds is given by $h(t) = -16t^2 + 200$. At what time and at what height does the bolt hit the elevator?

19. A bungee jumper leaps from a bridge 100 meters over a gorge. Before the 40-meter-long bungee begins to slow him down, his height is characterized by $h(t) = -4.9t^2 + 100$. Two seconds after he jumps, a car on the bridge blows out a tire. The sound of the tire blow-out moves down from the top of the bridge at the speed of sound and has a height given by $h(t) = -340(t - 2) + 100$. How high will the bungee jumper be when he hears the sound of the blowout?

20. Explain the Error A student is asked to solve the system of equations $y = x^2 + 2x - 7$ and $y - 2 = x + 1$. For the first step, the student sets the right hand sides equal to each other to get the equation $x^2 + 2x - 7 = x + 1$. Why does this not give the correct solution?

21. Explain the Error After solving the system of equations in Exercise 18 (the elevator and the bolt), a student concludes that there are two different times that the bolt hits the elevator. What is the error in the student's reasoning?

22. Multi-part Classification

The functions listed are graphed here.

$f_1(x) = 2(x + 3)^2 + 1$ and $f_2(x) = -\frac{3}{4}(x - 2)^2 + 3$

$g_1(x) = x + 3$ and $g_2(x) = 3$ and $g_3(x) = -\frac{1}{2}x + 1$

Use the graph to classify each system as having 0, 1, or 2 solutions.

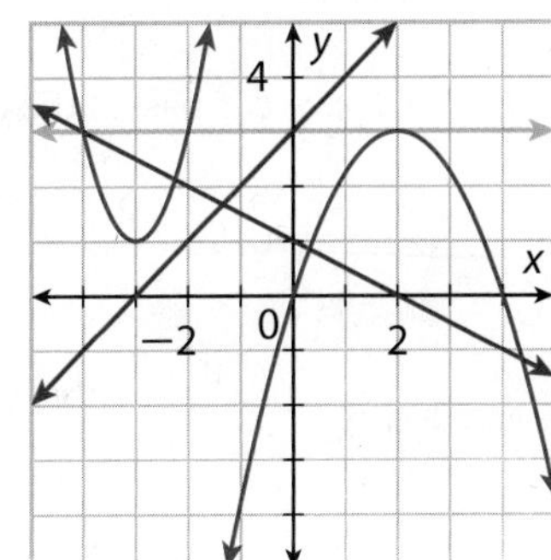

a. 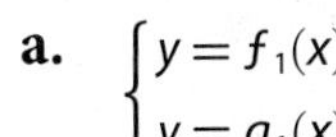 $\begin{cases} y = f_1(x) \\ y = g_1(x) \end{cases}$

b. $\begin{cases} y = f_1(x) \\ y = g_2(x) \end{cases}$

c. $\begin{cases} y = f_1(x) \\ y = g_3(x) \end{cases}$

d. 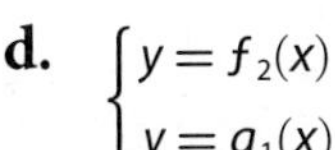 $\begin{cases} y = f_2(x) \\ y = g_1(x) \end{cases}$

e. $\begin{cases} y = f_2(x) \\ y = g_2(x) \end{cases}$

f. $\begin{cases} y = f_2(x) \\ y = g_3(x) \end{cases}$

H.O.T. Focus on Higher Order Thinking

23. Explain the Error After solving the system of equations in Exercise 16 (the skydiver and the ball), a student concludes there are two valid solutions because they both have positive times. The ball must pass by the skydiver twice. What is the error in the student's reasoning?

24. Multi-Part Problem The path of a baseball hit for a home run can be modeled by $y = -\frac{x^2}{484} + x + 3$, where x and y are in feet and home plate is at the origin. The ball lands in the stands, which are modeled by $4y - x = -352$ for $x \geq 400$. Use a graphing calculator to graph the system.

a. What do the variables x and y represent?

b. About how far is the baseball from home plate when it lands?

c. About how high up in the stands does the baseball land?

25. Draw Conclusions A certain system of a linear and a quadratic equation has two solutions, $(2, 7)$ and $(5, 10)$. The quadratic equation is $y = x^2 - 6x + 15$. What is the linear equation? Justify your answer.

26. Justify Reasoning It is possible for a system of two linear equations to have infinitely many solutions. Explain why this is not possible for a system with one linear and one quadratic equation.

Lesson Performance Task

A race car leaves pit row at a speed of 40 feet per second and accelerates at a constant rate of 44 feet per second squared. Its distance from the pit exit is given by the function $d_r(t) = 22t^2 + 40t$. The race car leaves ahead of an approaching pace car traveling at a constant speed of 120 feet per second. In each case, find out if the pace car will catch up to the race car, and if so, how far down the track it will catch up. If there is more than one solution, explain how you know which one to select.

a. The pace car passes by the exit to pit row 1 second after the race car exits.

b. The pace car passes the exit half a second after the race car exits.

STUDY GUIDE REVIEW

Using Square Roots to Solve Quadratic Equations

MODULE 9

Essential Question: How can you use quadratic equations to solve real-world problems?

Key Vocabulary
completing the square *(completar el cuadrado)*
discriminant *(discriminante)*
quadratic formula *(fórmula cuadrática)*
square root *(raíz cuadrada)*

KEY EXAMPLE *(Lesson 9.1)*

Solve $(x - 8)^2 = 49$ by taking the square root.

$(x - 8)^2 = 49$ — *Equations in the form $a(x + b)^2 = c$ can be solved by taking square roots.*

$x - 8 = \pm 7$ — *Take the square root of both sides.*

$x = \pm 7 + 8$

$x = 7 + 8$ and $x = -7 + 8$ — *Solve both cases.*

$x = 15$ and $x = 1$

KEY EXAMPLE *(Lesson 9.2)*

Solve $9x^2 - 6x = 20$ by completing the square.

$\frac{(-6)^2}{4(9)} = 1$ — *Find $\frac{b^2}{4a}$.*

$9x^2 - 6x + 1 = 20 + 1$ — *Complete the square.*

$(3x - 1)^2 = 21$

$x = \frac{\sqrt{21} + 1}{3}$ and $x = \frac{-\sqrt{21} + 1}{3}$

KEY EXAMPLE *(Lesson 9.3)*

Solve $8x^2 - 8x + 2 = 0$ using the quadratic formula.

$a = 8, b = -8, c = 2$ — *Identify a, b, and c.*

$x = \frac{-b \pm \sqrt{b^2 - 4ac}}{2a}$ — *Use the quadratic formula.*

$x = \frac{8 \pm \sqrt{(-8)^2 - (4)(8)(2)}}{2(8)}$

$x = \frac{8 \pm \sqrt{0}}{16}$ — *Since $b^2 - 4ac = 0$, the equation has one real solution.*

$x = \frac{1}{2}$

EXERCISES

Solve each equation. *(Lessons 9.1, 9.2, 9.3, 9.4)*

1. $x^2 + 12x = -17$

2. $(4x - 11)^2 = 100$

3. $4x^2 + 8x = 10$

4. $3x^2 + 17x + 10 = 0$

5. A diver jumps off a high diving board that is 33 feet above the surface of the pool with an initial upward velocity of 6 feet per second. The height of the diver above the surface of the pool can be represented by the equation $-16t^2 + 6t + 33 = 0$. How long will the diver be in the air, to the nearest hundredth of a second? Identify the method you used to solve the quadratic equation, and explain why you chose it. *(Lesson 9.4)*

MODULE PERFORMANCE TASK

Fireworks Display

You are planning a fireworks show for a local Fourth of July celebration. Fire officials require that all fireworks explode at a height greater than 70 meters so that debris has a chance to cool off as it falls.

The firing platform for the fireworks is 1.9 meters off the ground. You have the option of firing your fireworks at an initial velocity of anywhere between 35 and 42 meters/second. If every firework is timed to explode when it reaches its maximum height, find two different initial velocities that are acceptable to the local fire officials. Then, figure out how long to delay the firing of the slower firework so that it will explode at the same time as the faster firework.

Complete the task. Be sure to write down all your data and assumptions. Then use graphs, tables, or algebra to explain how you reached your conclusion.

Ready to Go On?

9.1–9.5 Using Square Roots to Solve Quadratic Equations

- Online Homework
- Hints and Help
- Extra Practice

Find the discriminant of each quadratic equation, and determine the number of real solutions of each equation. *(Lesson 9.4)*

1. $3x^2 + 2x + 6 = 0$

2. $4x^2 + 6x = 8$

Solve each equation using the given method. *(Lessons 9.1, 9.2, 9.3, 9.4)*

3. $8x^2 - 72 = 0$; square root

4. $25x^2 + 20x = 6$; completing the square

5. $2x^2 + 14x + 12 = 0$; factoring

6. $3x^2 + 7x + 8 = 0$; quadratic formula

7. Find the solution or solutions of the system of equations $\begin{cases} y = x^2 + 2 \\ y = x + 4 \end{cases}$. *(Lesson 9.5)*

ESSENTIAL QUESTION

8. What are the methods of solving a quadratic equation without factoring? When can you use each method?

MODULE 9
MIXED REVIEW

Assessment Readiness

1. Is the given expression a perfect-square trinomial? Write Yes or No.

A. $x^2 + 24x + 144$

B. $4x^2 + 36x + 9$

C. $9x^2 - 6x + 1$

2. Consider the following statements. Determine if each statement is True or False.

A. $4x^2 - 64 = 0$ has 2 real solutions.

B. $x^2 - 5x - 9 = 0$ has only 1 real solution.

C. $3x^2 + 4x + 2 = 0$ has no real solutions.

3. Solve $-2x^2 - 9x = -4$. What are the solutions? Explain how you solved the problem.

4. A landscaper is making a garden bed in the shape of a rectangle. The length of the garden bed is 2.5 feet longer than twice the width of the bed. The area of the garden bed is 62.5 square feet. Find the perimeter of the bed. Show your work.

Linear, Exponential, and Quadratic Models

MODULE 10

Essential Question: How can you use linear, exponential, and quadratic models to solve real-world problems?

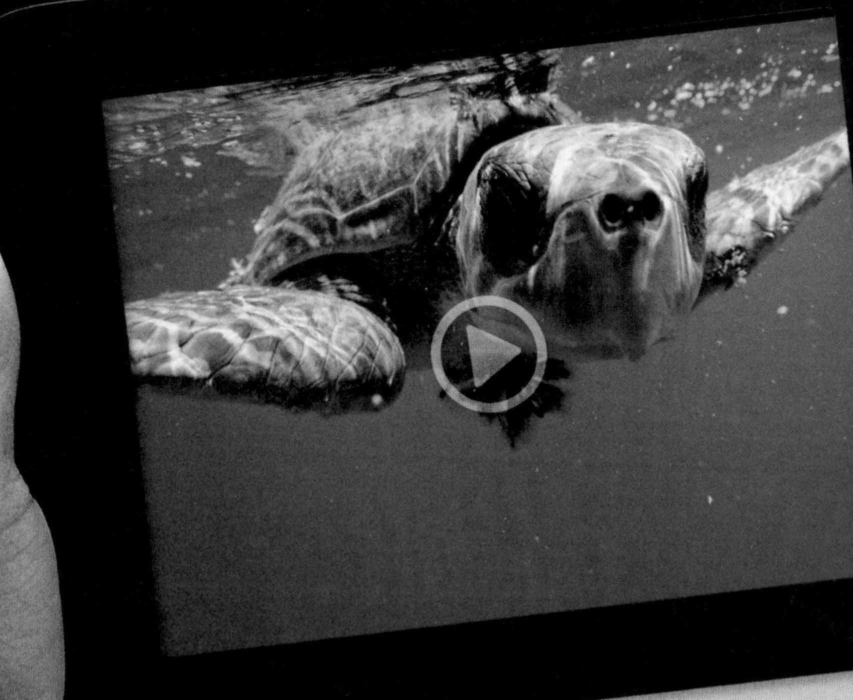

REAL WORLD VIDEO
The Kemp's Ridley sea turtle is an endangered species of turtle that nests along the Texas coast. Functions can be used to model the survivorship curve of the Kemp's Ridley sea turtle.

MODULE PERFORMANCE TASK PREVIEW

What Model Fits a Survivorship Curve?

Survivorship curves are graphs that show the number or proportion of individuals in a particular population that survive over time. Survivorship curves are used in diverse fields such as actuarial science, demography, biology, and epidemiology. How can you determine what mathematical model best fits a certain type of survivorship curve? Let's find out!

Are YOU Ready?

Complete these exercises to review skills you will need for this module.

- Online Homework
- Hints and Help
- Extra Practice

Scatter Plots

Example 1 Tell whether the correlation is positive or negative, or if there is no correlation.

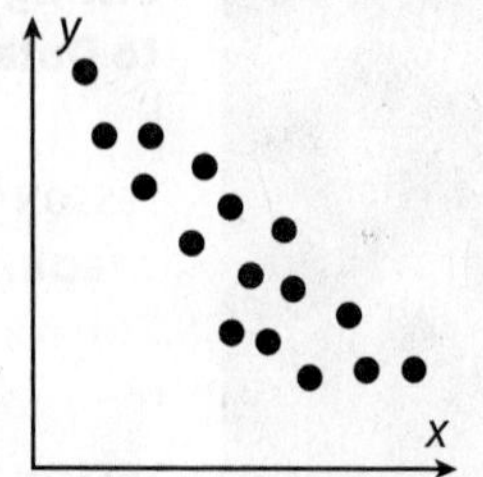

Scatter plots can help you see relationships between two variables.

- In a positive correlation, as the value of one variable increases, the value of the other variable increases.
- In a negative correlation, as the value of one variable decreases, the value of the other variable increases.
- Sometimes there is no correlation, meaning there is no relationship between the variables.

The scatter plot has a negative correlation.

Tell whether the correlation is positive or negative, or if there is no correlation.

1. 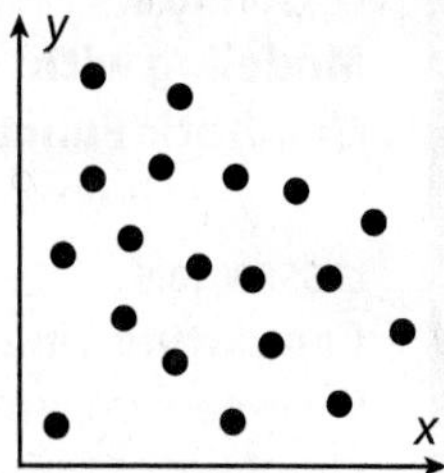

2. 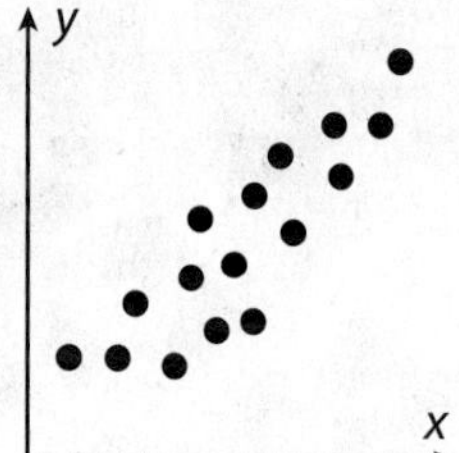

Constant Rate of Change

Example 2 Tell if the rate of change is constant.

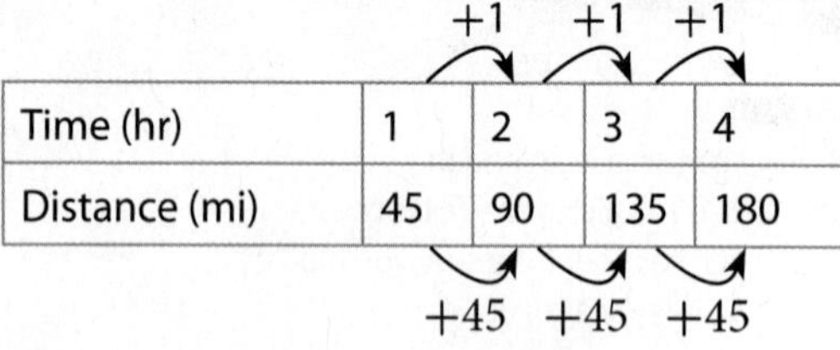

Time (hr)	1	2	3	4
Distance (mi)	45	90	135	180

$$\text{rate of change} = \frac{\text{change in miles}}{\text{change in hours}} = \frac{45}{1}$$

The rate of change is constant.

Tell if the rate of change is constant.

3.

Age (mo)	3	6	9	12
Weight (lb)	12	16	18	20

4.

Hours	2	4	6	8
Pay ($)	16	32	48	64

10.1 Fitting a Linear Model to Data

Essential Question: How can you use the linear regression function on a graphing calculator to find the line of best fit for a two-variable data set?

Resource Locker

Explore 1 Plotting and Analyzing Residuals

For any set of data, different lines of fit can be created. Some of these lines will fit the data better than others. One way to determine how well the line fits the data is by using residuals. A **residual** is the signed vertical distance between a data point and a line of fit.

After calculating residuals, a residual plot can be drawn. A **residual plot** is a graph of points whose x-coordinates are the variables of the independent variable and whose y-coordinates are the corresponding residuals.

Looking at the distribution of residuals can help you determine how well a line of fit describes the data. The plots below illustrate how the residuals may be distributed for three different data sets and lines of fit.

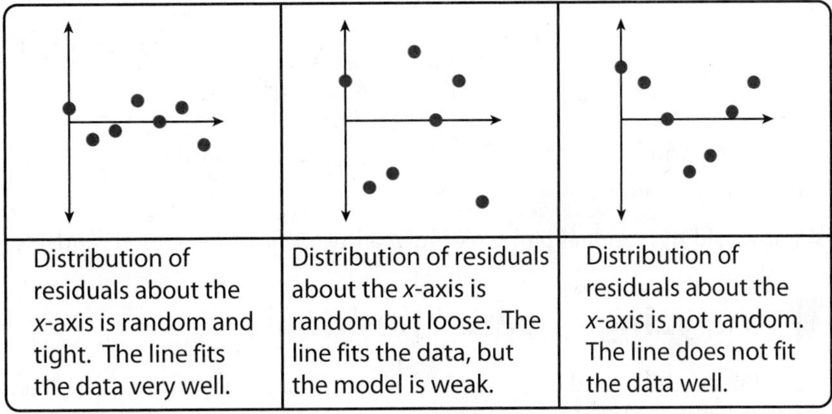

Distribution of residuals about the x-axis is random and tight. The line fits the data very well.	Distribution of residuals about the x-axis is random but loose. The line fits the data, but the model is weak.	Distribution of residuals about the x-axis is not random. The line does not fit the data well.

The table lists the median age of females living in the United States, based on the results of the United States Census over the past few decades. Follow the steps listed to complete the task.

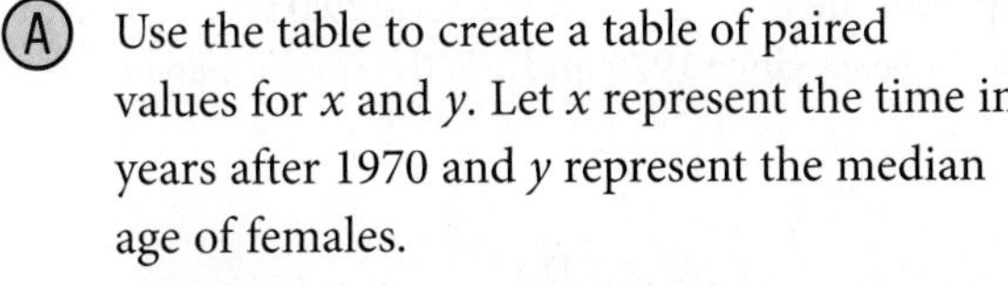

Ⓐ Use the table to create a table of paired values for x and y. Let x represent the time in years after 1970 and y represent the median age of females.

Year	Median Age of Females
1970	29.2
1980	31.3
1990	34.0
2000	36.5
2010	38.2

(B) Use residuals to calculate the quality of fit for the line $y = 0.25x + 29$, where y is median age and x is years since 1970.

x	Actual y	Predicted y based on $y = 0.25x + 29$	Residual *Subtract Predicted from Actual to Find the Residual.*
0	29.2		
10	31.3		
20	34.0		
30	36.5		
40	38.2		

(C) Plot the residuals on a grid like the one shown.

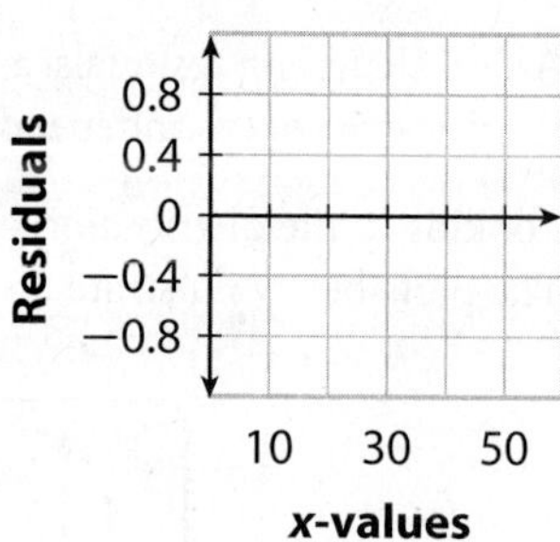

(D) Evaluate the quality of fit to the data for the line $y = 0.25x + 29$.

Reflect

1. **Discussion** When comparing two lines of fit for a single data set, how does the residual size show which line is the best model?

2. **Discussion** What would the residual plot look like if a line of fit is not a good model for a data set?

Explore 2 Analyzing Squared Residuals

When different people fit lines to the same data set, they are likely to choose slightly different lines. Another way to compare the quality of a line of fit is by squaring residuals. In this model, the closer the sum of the squared residuals is to 0, the better the line fits the data.

In the previous section, a line of data was fit for the median age of females over time. After performing this task, two students came up with slightly different results. Student A came up with the equation $y = 0.25x + 29.0$ while Student B came up with the equation $y = 0.25x + 28.8$, where x is the time in years since 1970 and y is the median age of females in both cases.

(A) Complete each table below.

$y = 0.25x + 29.0$				
x	**y (Actual)**	**y (Predicted)**	**Residual**	**Square of Residual**
0	29.2			
10	31.3			
20	34.0			
30	36.5			
40	38.2			

$y = 0.25x + 28.8$				
x	**y (Actual)**	**y (Predicted)**	**Residual**	**Square of Residual**
0	29.2			
10	31.3			
20	34.0			
30	36.5			
40	38.2			

(B) Find the sum of squared residuals for each line of fit.

$y = 0.25x + 29.0$

$y = 0.25x + 28.8$

(C) Which line has the smaller sum of squared residuals?

Reflect

3. How does squaring a residual affect the residual's value?

4. Are the sums of residuals or the sum of the squares of residuals a better measure of quality of fit?

 Explain 1 Assessing the Fit of Linear Functions from Residuals

The quality of a line of fit can be evaluated by finding the sum of the squared residuals. The closer the sum of the squared residuals is to 0, the better the line fits the data.

Example 1 **The data in the tables are given along with two possible lines of fit. Calculate the residuals for both lines of fit and then find the sum of the squared residuals. Identify the lesser sum and the line with better fit.**

(A)

x	2	4	6	8
y	7	8	4	8

$y = x + 2.2$

$y = x + 2.4$

a. Find the residuals of each line.

x	y (Actual)	y Predicted by $y = x + 2.4$	Residual for $y = x + 2.4$	y Predicted by $y = x + 2.2$	Residual for $y = x + 2.2$
2	7	4.4	2.6	4.2	2.8
4	8	6.4	1.6	6.2	1.8
6	4	8.4	−4.4	8.2	−4.2
8	8	10.4	−2.4	10.2	−2.2

b. Square the residuals and find their sum.

$y = x + 2.4 \quad (2.6)^2 + (1.6)^2 + (-4.4)^2 + (-2.4)^2 = 6.76 + 2.56 + 19.36 + 5.76 = 34.44$

$y = x + 2.2 \quad (2.8)^2 + (1.8)^2 + (-4.2)^2 + (-2.2)^2 = 7.84 + 3.24 + 17.64 + 4.84 = 33.56$

The sum of the squared residuals for $y = x + 2.2$ is smaller, so it provides a better fit for the data.

(B)

x	1	2	3	4
y	5	4	6	10

$y = 2x + 3$

$y = 2x + 2.5$

a. Find the residuals of each line.

x	y (Actual)	y Predicted by $y = 2x + 3$	Residual for $y = 2x + 3$	y Predicted by $y = 2x + 2.5$	Residual for $y = 2x + 2.5$
1	5	5	0	4.5	0.5
2	4	7	−3	6.5	−2.5
3	6	9	−3	8.5	−2.5
4	10	11	−1	10.5	−0.5

b. Square the residuals and find their sum.

$y = 2x + 3: (0)^2 + (-3)^2 + (-3)^2 + (-1)^2 = 0 + 9 + 9 + 1 = 19$

$y = 2x + 2.5: (0.5)^2 + (-2.5)^2 + (-2.5)^2 + (-0.5)^2 = 0.25 + 6.25 + 6.25 + 0.25 = 13$

The sum of the squared residuals for $y = 2x + 2.5$ is smaller, so it provides a better fit for the data.

Reflect

5. How do negative signs on residuals affect the sum of squared residuals?

6. Why do small values for residuals mean that a line of best fit has a tight fit to the data?

Your Turn

7. The data in the table are given along with two possible lines of fit. Calculate the residuals for both lines of fit and then find the sum of the squared residuals. Identify the lesser sum and the line with better fit.

x	1	2	3	4
y	4	7	8	6

$y = x + 4$

$y = x + 4.2$

 Explain 2 Performing Linear Regression

The least-squares line for a data set is the line of fit for which the sum of the squared residuals is as small as possible. Therefore the least-squares line is a line of best fit. A **line of best fit** is the line that comes closest to all of the points in the data set, using a given process. **Linear regression** is a method for finding the least-squares line.

Example 2 **Given latitudes and average temperatures in degrees Celsius for several cities, use your calculator to find an equation for the line of best fit. Then interpret the correlation coefficient and use the line of best fit to estimate the average temperature of another city using the given latitude.**

(A)

City	Latitude	Average Temperature (°C)
Barrow, Alaska	71.2°N	−12.7
Yakutsk, Russia	62.1°N	−10.1
London, England	51.3°N	10.4
Chicago, Illinois	41.9°N	10.3
San Francisco, California	37.5°N	13.8
Yuma, Arizona	32.7°N	22.8
Tindouf, Algeria	27.7°N	22.8
Dakar, Senegal	14.0°N	24.5
Mangalore, India	12.5°N	27.1

Estimate the average temperature in Vancouver, Canada at 49.1°N.

Enter the data into data lists on your calculator. Enter the latitudes in column **L1** and the average temperatures in column **L2**.

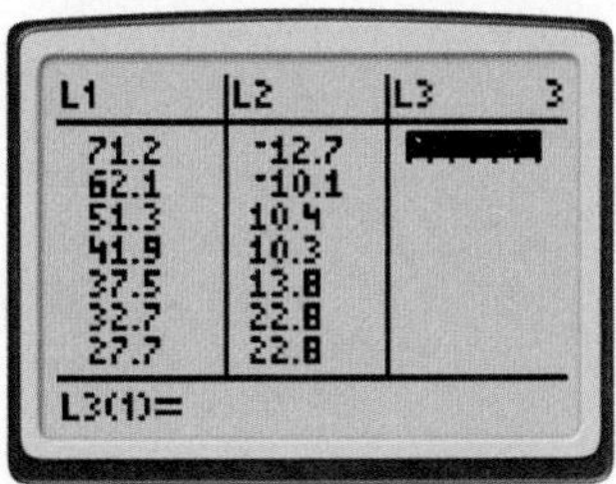

Create a scatter plot of the data.

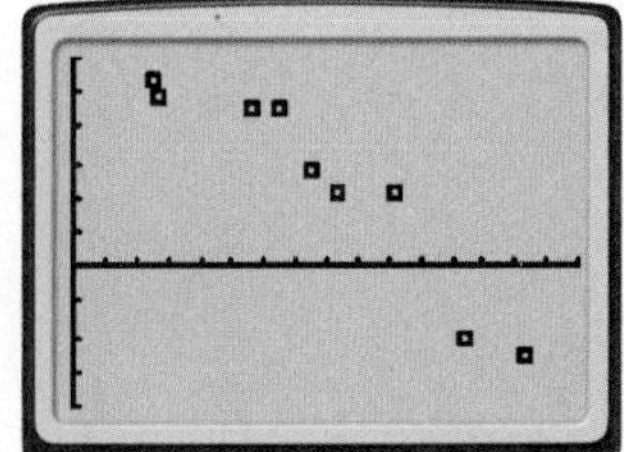

Use the Linear Regression feature to find the equation for the line of best fit using the lists of data you entered. Be sure to have the calculator also display values for the correlation coefficient r and r^2.

The correlation coefficient is about −0.95, which is very strong. This indicates a strong correlation, so we can rely on the line of fit for estimating average temperatures for other locations within the same range of latitudes.

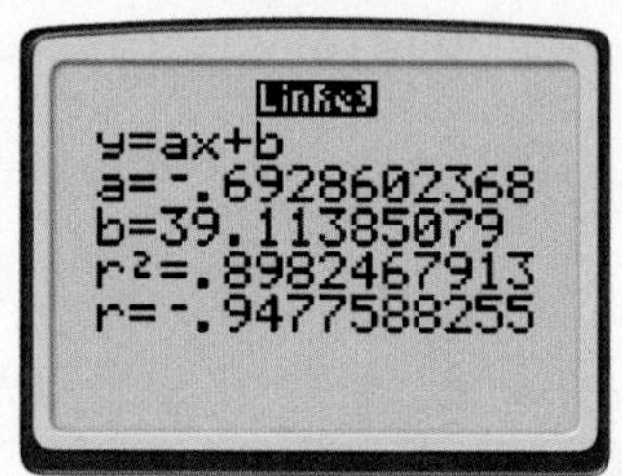

The equation for the line of best fit is $y \approx -0.693x + 39.11$.

Graph the line of best fit with the data points in the scatter plot.

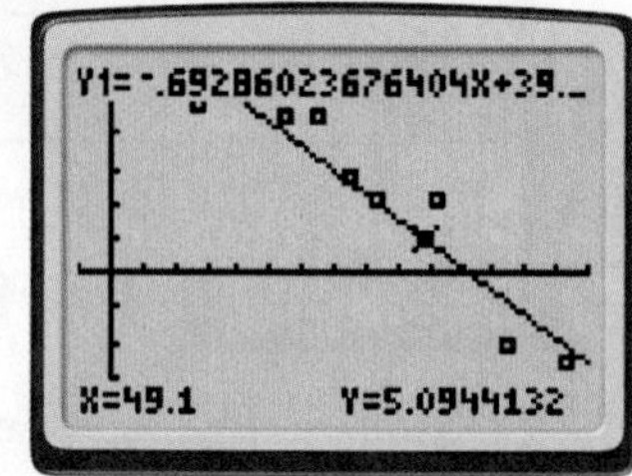

Use the TRACE function to find the approximate average temperature in degrees Celsius for a latitude of 49.1°N.

The average temperature in Vancouver should be around 5°C.

(B)

City	Latitude	Average Temperature (°F)
Fairbanks, Alaska	64.5°N	30
Moscow, Russia	55.5°N	39
Ghent, Belgium	51.0°N	46
Kiev, Ukraine	50.3°N	49
Prague, Czech Republic	50.0°N	50
Winnipeg, Manitobia	49.5°N	52
Luxembourg	49.4°N	53
Vienna, Austria	48.1°N	56
Bern, Switzerland	46.6°N	59

Estimate the average temperature in degrees Fahrenheit in Bath, England, at 51.4°N.

Enter the data into data lists on your calculator.

Use the Linear Regression feature to find the equation for the line of best fit using the lists of data you entered. Be sure to have the calculator also display values for the correlation coefficient r and r^2.

The correlation coefficient is about −0.95, which indicates a very strong correlation. The correlation coefficient indicates that the line of best fit is reliable for estimating temperatures of other locations within the same range of latitudes.

The equation for the line of best fit is $y \approx -$ 1.60 $x +$ 131.05.

Use the equation to estimate the average temperature in Bath, England at 51.4°N.

$y \approx -$ 1.60 $x +$ 131.05

The average temperature in degrees Fahrenheit in Bath, England, should be around 49 °F.

Graph the line of best fit with the data points in the scatter plot. Then use the TRACE function to find the approximate average temperature in degrees Fahrenheit for a latitude of 51.4°N.

Reflect

8. Interpret the slope of the line of best fit in terms of the context for Example 2A.

9. Interpret the y-intercept of the line of best fit in terms of the context for Example 2A.

Your Turn

10. Use the given data and your calculator to find an equation for the line of best fit. Then interpret the correlation coefficient and use the line of best fit to estimate the average temperature of another city using the given latitude.

City	Latitude	Average Temperature (°F)
Anchorage, United States	61.1°N	18
Dublin, Ireland	53.2°N	29
Zurich, Switzerland	47.2°N	34
Florence, Italy	43.5°N	37
Trenton, New Jersey	40.1°N	
Algiers, Algeria	36.5°N	46
El Paso, Texas	31.5°N	49
Dubai, UAE	25.2°N	56
Manila, Philippines	14.4°N	61

Elaborate

11. What type of line does linear regression analysis make?

12. Why are squared residuals better than residuals?

13. **Essential Question Check-In** What four keys are needed on a graphing calculator to perform a linear regression?

Evaluate: Homework and Practice

- Online Homework
- Hints and Help
- Extra Practice

The data in the tables below are shown along with two possible lines of fit. Calculate the residuals for both lines of fit and then find the sum of the squared residuals. Identify the lesser sum and the line with better fit.

1.

x	2	4	6	8
y	1	3	5	7

$y = x + 5$

$y = x + 4.9$

2.

x	1	2	3	4
y	1	7	3	5

$y = 2x + 1$

$y = 2x + 1.1$

3.

x	2	4	6	8
y	2	8	4	6

$y = 3x + 4$

$y = 3x + 4.1$

4.

x	1	2	3	4
y	2	1	4	3

$y = x + 1$

$y = x + 0.9$

5.

x	2	4	6	8
y	1	5	4	3

$y = 3x + 1.2$

$y = 3x + 1$

6.

x	1	2	3	4
y	4	1	3	2

$y = x + 5$

$y = x + 5.3$

7.

x	2	4	6	8
y	3	6	4	5

$y = 2x + 1$

$y = 2x + 1.4$

8.

x	1	2	3	4
y	5	3	6	4

$y = x + 2$

$y = x + 2.2$

9.

x	2	4	6	8
y	1	5	7	3

$y = x + 3$

$y = x + 2.6$

10.

x	1	2	3	4
y	2	5	4	3

$y = x + 1.5$

$y = x + 1.7$

11.

x	1	2	3	4
y	2	9	7	12

$y = 2x + 3.1$

$y = 2x + 3.5$

12.

x	1	3	5	7
y	2	6	8	13

$y = 1.6x + 4$

$y = 1.8x + 4$

13.

x	1	2	3	4
y	7	5	11	8

$y = x + 5$

$y = 1.3x + 5$

14.

x	1	2	3	4
y	4	11	5	15

$y = 2x + 3$

$y = 2.4x + 3$

Use the given data and your calculator to find an equation for the line of best fit. Then interpret the correlation coefficient and use the line of best fit to estimate the average temperature of another city using the given latitude.

15.

City	Latitude	Average Temperature (°F)
Calgary, Alberta	51.0°N	24
Munich, Germany	48.1°N	26
Marseille, France	43.2°N	29
St. Louis, Missouri	38.4°N	34
Seoul, South Korea	37.3°N	36
Tokyo, Japan	35.4°N	38
New Delhi, India	28.4°N	43
Honululu, Hawaii	21.2°N	52
Bangkok, Thailand	14.2°N	58
Panama City, Panama	8.6°N	

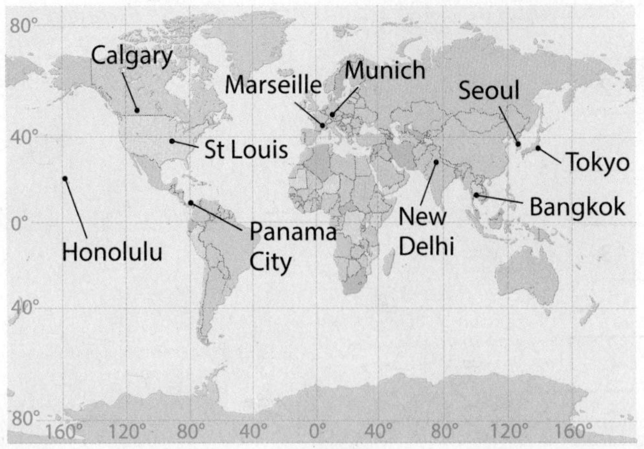

16.

City	Latitude	Average Temperature (°F)
Oslo, Norway	59.6°N	21
Warsaw, Poland	52.1°N	28
Milan, Italy	45.2°N	34
Vatican City, Vatican City	41.5°N	41
Beijing, China	39.5°N	42
Tel Aviv, Israel	32.0°N	48
Kuwait City, Kuwait	29.2°N	
Key West, Florida	24.3°N	55
Bogota, Columbia	4.4°N	64
Mogadishu, Somalia	2.0°N	66

17.

City	Latitude	Average Temperature (°F)
Tornio, Finland	65.5°N	28
Riga, Latvia	56.6°N	36
Minsk, Belarus	53.5°N	39
Quebec City, Quebec	46.5°N	45
Turin, Italy	45.0°N	47
Pittsburgh, Pennsylvania	40.3°N	49
Lisbon, Portugal	38.4°N	52
Jerusalem, Israel	31.5°N	
New Orleans, Louisiana	29.6°N	60
Port-au-Prince, Haiti	18.3°N	69

18.

City	Latitude (°N)	Average Temperature (°F)
Juneau, Alaska	58.2	15
Amsterdam, Netherlands	52.2	24
Salzburg, Austria	47.5	36
Belgrade, Serbia	44.5	38
Philadelphia, Pennsylvania	39.6	41
Tehran, Iran	35.4	44
Nassau, Bahamas	25.0	52
Mecca, Saudi Arabia	21.3	56
Dakar, Senegal	14.4	
Georgetown, Guyana	6.5	65

Demographics **Each table lists the median age of people living in the United States, based on the results of the United States Census over the past few decades. Use residuals to calculate the quality of fit for the line $y = 0.5x + 20$, where y is median age and x is years since 1970.**

19.

Year	Median age of men
1970	25.3
1980	26.8
1990	29.1
2000	31.4
2010	35.6

20.

Year	Median Age of Texans
1970	27.1
1980	29.3
1990	31.1
2000	33.8
2010	37.6

21. State the residuals based on the actual y and predicted y-values.

a. Actual: 23, Predicted: 21

b. Actual: 25.6, Predicted: 23.3

c. Actual: 24.8, Predicted: 27.4

d. Actual: 34.9, Predicted: 31.3

H.O.T. Focus on Higher Order Thinking

22. Critical Thinking The residual plot of an equation has x-values that are close to the x-axis from $x = 0$ to $x = 10$, but has values that are far from the axis from $x = 10$ to $x = 30$. Is this a strong or weak relationship?

23. Communicate Mathematical Ideas In a squared residual plot, the residuals form a horizontal line at $y = 6$. What does this mean?

24. Interpret the Answer Explain one situation other than those in this section where squared residuals are useful.

Lesson Performance Task

The table shows the latitudes and average temperatures for the 10 largest cities in the Southern Hemisphere.

City	Latitude (°S)	Average Temperature (°F)
Sao Paulo, Brazil	23.9	69
Buenos Aires, Argentina	34.8	64
Rio de Janeiro, Brazil	22.8	76
Jakarta, Indonesia	6.3	81
Lodja, DRC	3.5	73
Lima, Peru	12.0	68
Santiago de Chile, Chile	33.2	58
Sydney, Australia	33.4	64
Melbourne, Australia	37.7	58
Johannesburg, South Africa	26.1	61

a. Use a graphing calculator to find a line of best fit for this data set. What is the equation for the best-fit line? Interpret the meaning of the slope of this line.

b. The city of Piggs Peak, Swaziland, is at latitude 26.0 °S. Use the equation of your best-fit line to predict the average temperature in Piggs Peak. The actual average temperature for Piggs Peak is 65.3 °F. How might you account for the difference in predicted and actual values?

c. Assume that you graphed the latitude and average temperature for 10 cities in the Northern Hemisphere. Predict how the line of best fit for that data set might compare with the best-fit line for the Southern Hemisphere cities.

10.2 Graphing Exponential Functions

Resource Locker

Essential Question: How do you graph an exponential function of the form $f(x) = ab^x$?

Explore — Exploring Graphs of Exponential Functions

Exponential functions follow the general shape $y = ab^x$.

(A) Graph the exponential functions on a graphing calculator, and match the graph to the correct function rule.

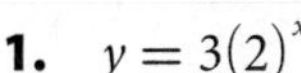

1. $y = 3(2)^x$
2. $y = 0.5(2)^x$
3. $y = 3(0.5)^x$
4. $y = -3(2)^x$

a.

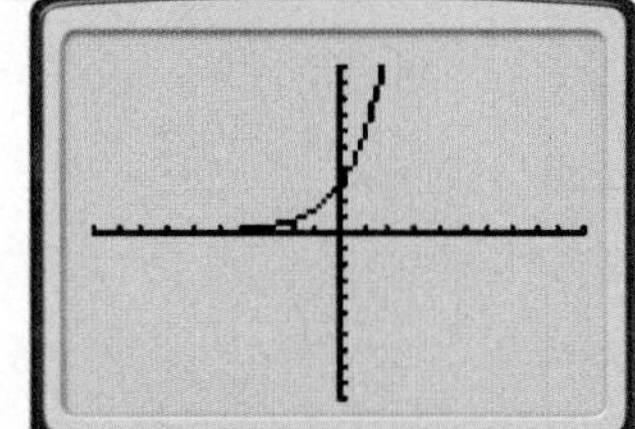

b.

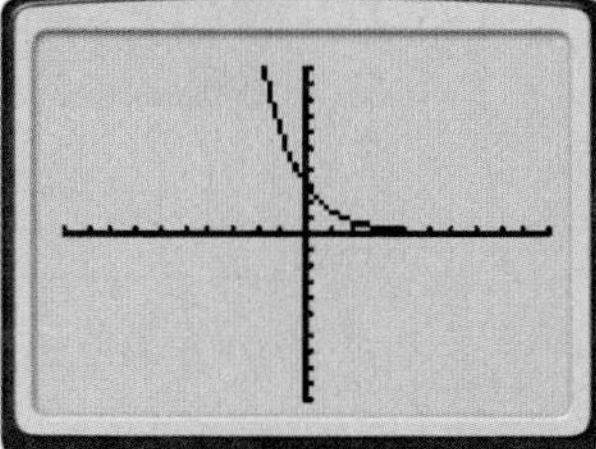

c.

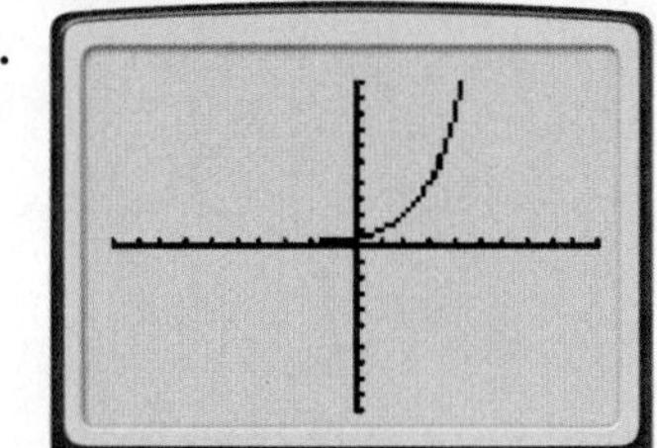

d.

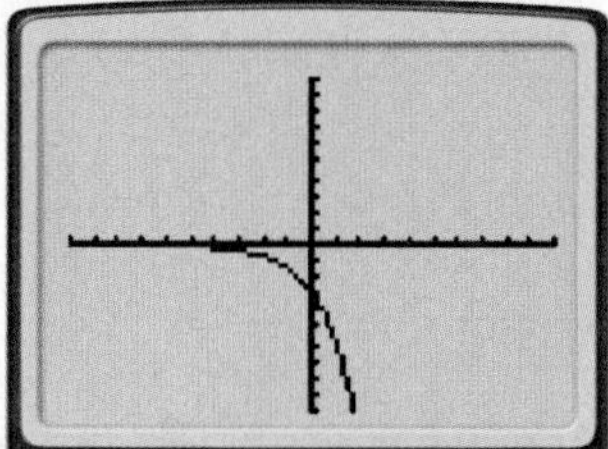

(B) In all the functions 1–4 above, the base $b > 0$.

Use the graphs to make a conjecture. State the domain and range of $y = ab^x$ if $a > 0$.

(C) In all the functions 1–4 above, the base $b > 0$.

Use the graphs to make a conjecture. State the domain and range of $y = ab^x$ if $a < 0$.

(D) What is the y-intercept of $f(x) = 0.5(2)^x$?

(E) Note the similarities between the y-intercept and a. What is their relationship?

Reflect

1. **Discussion** What is the domain for any exponential function $y = ab^x$?
2. **Discussion** Describe the values of b for all functions $y = ab^x$.

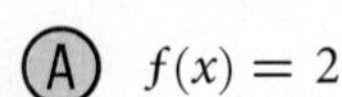

Explain 1 Graphing Increasing Positive Exponential Functions

The symbol ∞ represents *infinity*. We can describe the *end behavior* of a function by describing what happens to the function values as x approaches positive infinity ($x \to \infty$) and as x approaches negative infinity ($x \to -\infty$).

Example 1 **Graph each exponential function. After graphing, identify *a* and *b*, the *y*-intercept, and the end behavior of the graph.**

(A) $f(x) = 2^x$

Choose several values of x and generate ordered pairs.

x	$f(x) = 2^x$
−1	0.5
0	1
1	2
2	4

Graph the ordered pairs and connect them with a smooth curve.

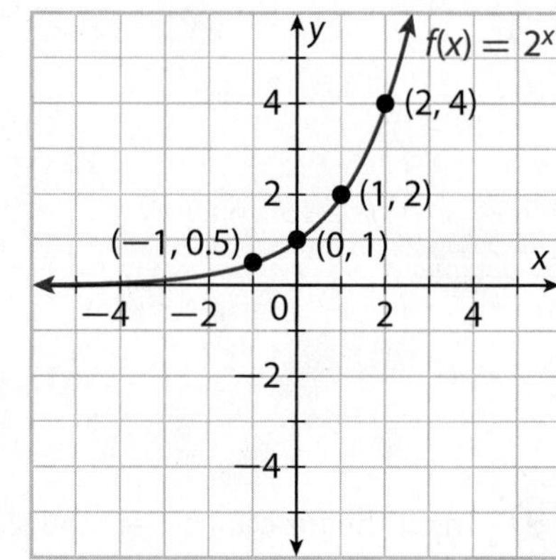

$a = 1$

$b = 2$

y-intercept: $(0, 1)$

End Behavior: As x-values approach positive infinity ($x \to \infty$), y-values approach positive infinity ($y \to \infty$).
As x-values approach negative infinity ($x \to -\infty$), y-values approach zero ($y \to 0$).

Using symbols only, we say: As $x \to \infty$, $y \to \infty$, and as $x \to -\infty$, $y \to 0$.

(B) $f(x) = 3(4)^x$

Choose several values of x and generate ordered pairs.

x	$f(x) = 3(4)^x$
−1	0.75
0	3
1	12
2	48

Graph the ordered pairs and connect them with a smooth curve.

$a = 3$

$b = 4$

y-intercept: $(0, 3)$

End Behavior: As $x \to \infty$, $y \to \infty$ and as $x \to -\infty$, $y \to 0$.

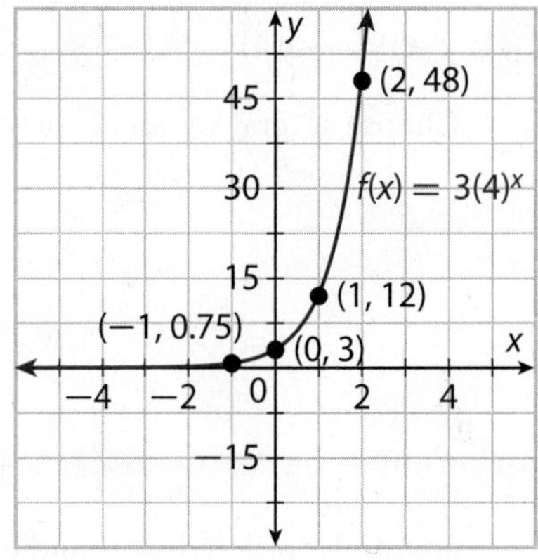

Reflect

3. If $a > 0$ and $b > 1$, what is the end behavior of the graph?
4. Describe the y-intercept of the exponential function $f(x) = ab^x$ in terms of a and b.

Your Turn

5. Graph the exponential function $f(x) = 2(2)^x$
   After graphing, identify a and b, the y-intercept, and the end behavior of the graph.

Explain 2 Graphing Decreasing Negative Exponential Functions

Example 2 **Graph each exponential function. After graphing, identify a and b, the y-intercept, and the end behavior of the graph.**

(A) $f(x) = -2(3)^x$

Choose several values of x and generate ordered pairs.

x	$f(x) = -2(3)^x$
−1	−0.7
0	−2
1	−6
2	−18

Graph the ordered pairs and connect them with a smooth curve.

$a = -2$

$b = 3$

y-intercept: $(0, -2)$

End Behavior: As $x \to \infty$, $y \to -\infty$ and as $x \to -\infty$, $y \to 0$.

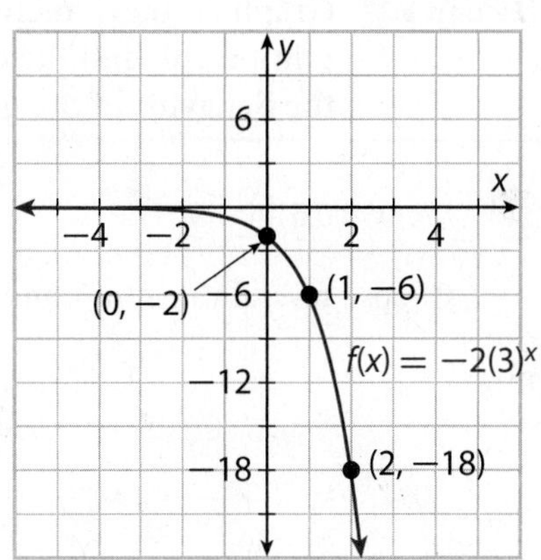

(B) $f(x) = -3(4)^x$

Choose several values of x and generate ordered pairs.

x	$f(x) = -3(4)^x$
−1	−0.75
0	−3
1	−12
2	−48

Graph the ordered pairs and connect them with a smooth curve.

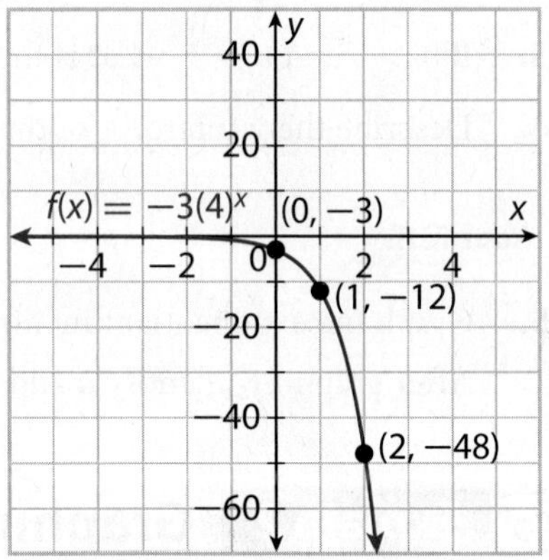

$a =$ −3

$b =$ 4

y-intercept: (0, −3)

End Behavior: As $x \to \infty$, $y \to$ $-\infty$ and as $x \to -\infty$, $y \to$ 0.

Reflect

6. If $a < 0$ and $b > 1$, what is the end behavior of the graph?

Your Turn

7. Graph the exponential function. $f(x) = -3(3)^x$

After graphing, identify a and b, the y-intercept, and the end behavior of the graph.

Explain 3 Graphing Decreasing Positive Exponential Functions

Example 3 **Graph each exponential function. After graphing, identify a and b, the y-intercept, and the end behavior of the graph. Use inequalities to discuss the behavior of the graph.**

(A) $f(x) = (0.5)^x$

Choose several values of x and generate ordered pairs.

x	$f(x) = (0.5)^x$
−1	2
0	1
1	0.5
2	0.25

Graph the ordered pairs and connect them with a smooth curve.

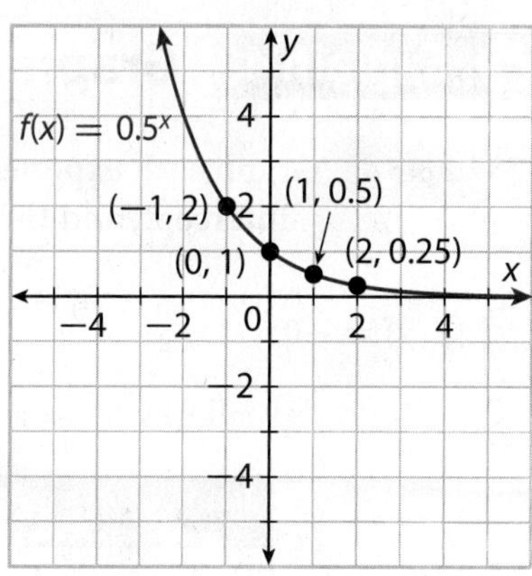

$a = 1$

$b = 0.5$

y-intercept: $(0, 1)$

End Behavior: As $x \to \infty$, $y \to 0$ and as $x \to -\infty$, $y \to \infty$.

(B) $f(x) = 2(0.4)^x$

Choose several values of x and generate ordered pairs.

x	$f(x) = 2(0.4)^x$
−1	5
0	2
1	0.8
2	0.32

Graph the ordered pairs and connect them with a smooth curve.

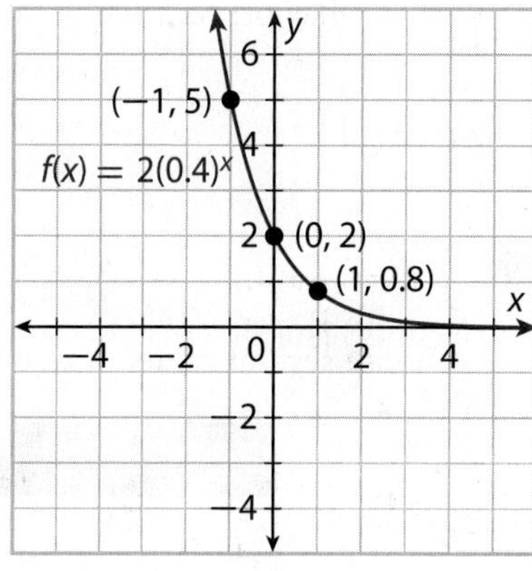

$a =$ 2

$b =$ 0.4

y-intercept: (0, 2)

End Behavior: As $x \to \infty$, $y \to$ 0 and as $x \to -\infty$, $y \to$ ∞.

Reflect

8. If $a > 0$ and $0 < b < 1$, what is the end behavior of the graph?

Your Turn

9. Graph the exponential function. After graphing, identify a and b, the y-intercept, and the end behavior of the graph.

$f(x) = 3(0.5)^x$

Explain 4 Graphing Increasing Negative Exponential Functions

Example 4 **Graph each exponential function. After graphing, identify a and b, the y-intercept, and the end behavior of the graph.**

(A) $f(x) = -0.5^x$

Choose several values of x and generate ordered pairs.

x	$f(x) = -0.5^x$
−1	−2
0	−1
1	−0.5
2	−0.25

Graph the ordered pairs and connect them with a smooth curve.

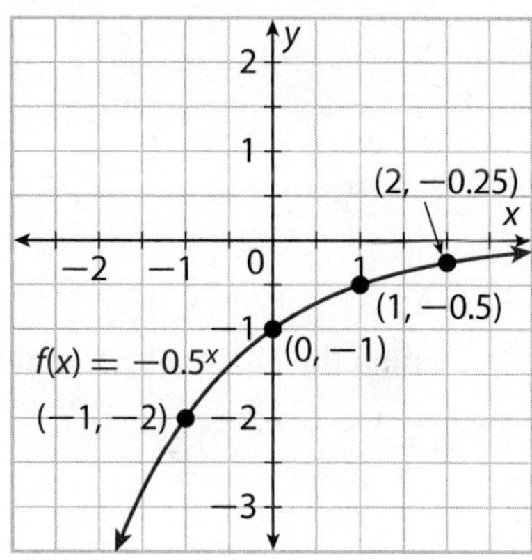

$a = -1$

$b = 0.5$

y-intercept: $(0, -1)$

End Behavior: As $x \to \infty$, $y \to 0$ and as $x \to -\infty$, $y \to -\infty$.

(B) $f(x) = -3(0.4)^x$

Choose several values of x and generate ordered pairs.

x	$f(x) = -3(0.4)^x$
−1	−7.5
0	−3
1	−1.2
2	−0.48

Graph the ordered pairs and connect them with a smooth curve.

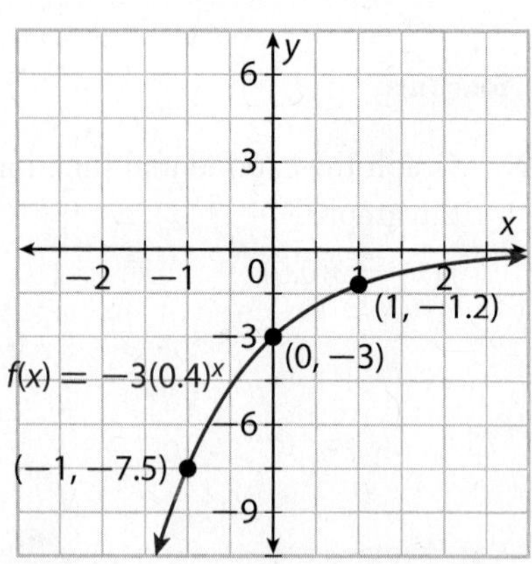

$a =$ −3

$b =$ 0.4

y-intercept: (0 , −3)

End Behavior: As $x \to \infty$, $y \to$ 0 and as $x \to -\infty$, $y \to$ $-\infty$.

Reflect

10. If $a < 0$ and $0 < b < 1$, what is the end behavior of the graph?

Your Turn

11. Graph the exponential function. After graphing, identify a and b, the y-intercept, and the end behavior of the graph. Use inequalities to discuss the behavior of the graph.

$f(x) = -2(0.5)^x$

Elaborate

12. Why is $f(x) = 3(-0.5)^x$ not an exponential function?

13. **Essential Question Check-In** When an exponential function of the form $f(x) = ab^x$ is graphed, what does a represent?

Evaluate: Homework and Practice

- Online Homework
- Hints and Help
- Extra Practice

State a, b, and the y-intercept and then graph the function on a graphing calculator.

1. $f(x) = 2(3)^x$

2. $f(x) = -6(2)^x$

3. $f(x) = -5(0.5)^x$

4. $f(x) = 3(0.8)^x$

5. $f(x) = 6(3)^x$

6. $f(x) = -4(0.2)^x$

7. $f(x) = 7(0.9)^x$

8. $f(x) = -3(2)^x$

State a, b, and the y-intercept and then graph the function and describe the end behavior of the graphs.

9. $f(x) = 3(3)^x$

10. $f(x) = 5(0.6)^x$

11. $f(x) = -6(0.7)^x$

12. $f(x) = -4(3)^x$

13. $f(x) = 5(2)^x$

14. $f(x) = -2(0.8)^x$

15. $f(x) = 9(3)^x$

16. $f(x) = -5(2)^x$

17. $f(x) = 7(0.4)^x$

18. $f(x) = 6(2)^x$

19. Identify the domain and range of each function. Make sure to provide these answers using inequalities.

a. $f(x) = 3(2)^x$

b. $f(x) = 7(0.4)^x$

c. $f(x) = -2(0.6)^x$

d. $f(x) = -3(4)^x$

e. $f(x) = 2(22)^x$

20. **Statistics** In 2000, the population of Massachusetts was 6.3 million people and was growing at a rate of about 0.32% per year. At this growth rate, the function $f(x) = 6.3(1.0032)^x$ gives the population, in millions x years after 2000. Using this model, find the year when the population reaches 7 million people.

21. **Physics** A ball is rolling down a slope and continuously picks up speed. Suppose the function $f(x) = 1.2(1.11)^x$ describes the speed of the ball in inches per minute. How fast will the ball be rolling in 20 minutes? Round the answer to the nearest whole number.

H.O.T. Focus on Higher Order Thinking

22. **Draw Conclusions** Assume that the domain of the function $f(x) = 3(2)^x$ is the set of all real numbers. What is the range of the function?

23. **What If?** If $b = 1$ in an exponential function, what will the graph of b look like?

24. **Critical Thinking** Using the graph of an exponential function, how can b be found?

25. **Critical Thinking** Use the table to write the equation for the exponential function.

x	$f(x)$
−1	$\frac{4}{5}$
0	4
1	20
2	100

Lesson Performance Task

A pumpkin is being grown for a contest at the state fair. Its growth can be modeled by the equation $P = 25(1.56)^n$, where P is the weight of the pumpkin in pounds and n is the number of weeks the pumpkin has been growing. By what percentage does the pumpkin grow every week? After how many weeks will the pumpkin be 80 pounds?

After the pumpkin grows to 80 pounds, it grows more slowly. From then on, its growth can be modeled by $P = 25(1.23)^n$, where n is the number of weeks since the pumpkin reached 80 pounds. Estimate when the pumpkin will reach 150 pounds.

10.3 Modeling Exponential Growth and Decay

Resource Locker

Essential Question: **How can you use exponential functions to model the increase or decrease of a quantity over time?**

Explore 1 Describing End Behavior of a Growth Function

When you graph a function $f(x)$ in a coordinate plane, the x-axis represents the independent variable and the y-axis represents the dependent variable. Therefore, the graph of $f(x)$ is the same as the graph of the equation $y = f(x)$. You will use this form when you use a calculator to graph functions.

(A) Use a graphing calculator to graph the exponential growth function $f(x) = 200(1.10)^x$, using Y_1 for $f(x)$. Use a viewing window from -20 to 20 for x, with a scale of 2, and from -100 to 1000 for y, with a scale of 50. Sketch the curve.

(B) To describe the end behavior of the function, you describe the function values as x increases or decreases without bound. Using the TRACE feature, move the cursor to the right along the curve. Describe the end behavior as x increases without bound.

(C) Using the TRACE feature, move the cursor to the left along the curve. Describe the end behavior as x decreases without bound.

Reflect

1. Describe the domain and range of the function using inequalities.
2. Identify the y-intercept of the graph of the function.
3. An asymptote of a graph is a line the graph approaches more and more closely. Identify an asymptote of this graph.
4. **Discussion** Why is the value of the function always greater than 0?

Explore 2 Describing End Behavior of a Decay Function

Use the form from the first Explore exercise to graph another function on your calculator.

(A) Use a graphing calculator to graph the exponential decay function $f(x) = 500(0.8)^x$, using Y_1 for $f(x)$. Use a viewing window from -10 to 10 for x, with a scale of 1, and from -500 to 5000 for y, with a scale of 500. Sketch the curve.

(B) Using the TRACE feature, move the cursor to the right along the curve. Describe the end behavior as x increases without bound.

(C) Using the TRACE feature, move the cursor to the left along the curve. Describe the end behavior as x decreases without bound.

Reflect

5. **Discussion** Describe the domain and range of the function using inequalities.
6. Identify the y-intercept of the graph of the function.
7. Identify an asymptote of this graph. Why is this line an asymptote?

Explain 1 Modeling Exponential Growth

Recall that a function of the form $y = ab^x$ represents exponential growth when $a > 0$ and $b > 1$. If b is replaced by $1 + r$ and x is replaced by t, then the function is the **exponential growth model** $y = a(1 + r)^t$, where a is the initial amount, the base $(1 + r)$ is the growth factor, r is the growth rate, and t is the time interval. The value of the model increases with time.

Example 1 **Write an exponential growth function for each situation. Graph each function and state its domain, range and an asymptote. What does the y-intercept represent in the context of the problem?**

(A) A painting is sold for \$1800, and its value increases by 11% each year after it is sold. Find the value of the painting in 30 years.

Write the exponential growth function for this situation.

$y = a(1 + r)^t$

$= 1800(1 + 0.11)^t$

$= 1800(1.11)^t$

Find the value in 30 years.

$y = 1800(1.11)^t$

$= 1800(1.11)^{30}$

$\approx 41{,}206.13$

After 30 years, the painting will be worth approximately \$41,206.

Create a table of values to graph the function.

t	y	(t, y)
0	1800	(0, 1800)
8	4148	(8, 4148)
16	9560	(16, 9560)
24	22,030	(24, 22,030)
32	50,770	(32, 50,770)

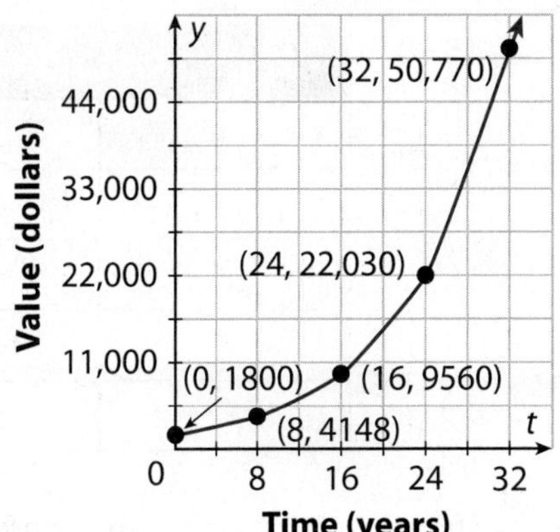

Determine the domain, range and an asymptote of the function.

The domain is the set of real numbers t such that $t \geq 0$.

The range is the set of real numbers y such that $y \geq 1800$.

An asymptote for the function is $y = 0$.

The y-intercept is the value of y when $t = 0$, which is the value of the painting when it was sold.

(B) A baseball trading card is sold for \$2, and its value increases by 8% each year after it is sold. Find the value of the baseball trading card in 10 years.

Write the exponential growth function for this situation.

$y = a(1 + r)^t$

$= \boxed{2}\left(1 + \boxed{0.08}\right)^t$

$= \boxed{2}\left(\boxed{1.08}\right)^t$

Find the value in 10 years.

$y = a(1 + r)^t$

$= \boxed{2}\left(\boxed{1.08}\right)^t$

$= \boxed{2}\left(\boxed{1.08}\right)^{\boxed{10}}$

$\approx \boxed{4.32}$

After 10 years, the baseball trading card will be worth approximately \$4.32.

Create a table of values to graph the function.

t	y	(t, y)
0	2	(0, 2)
3	2.52	(3, 2.52)
6	3.17	(6, 3.17)
9	4.00	(9, 4.00)
12	5.04	(12, 5.04)

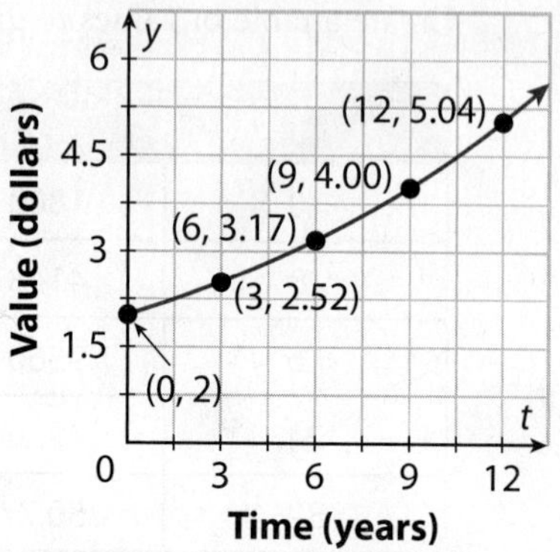

Determine the domain, range, and an asymptote of the function.

The domain is the set of real numbers t such that $t \geq$ 0 .

The range is the set of real numbers y such that $y \geq$ 2 .

An asymptote for the function is $y = 0$.

The y-intercept is the value of y when $t = 0$, which is the value of the card when it was sold.

Reflect

8. Find a recursive rule that models the exponential growth of $y = 1800(1.11)^t$.

9. Find a recursive rule that models the exponential growth of $y = 2(1.08)^t$.

Your Turn

10. Write and graph an exponential growth function, and state the domain and range. Tell what the y-intercept represents. Sara sold a coin for $3, and its value increases by 2% each year after it is sold. Find the value of the coin in 8 years.

Explain 2 Modeling Exponential Decay

Recall that a function of the form $y = ab^x$ represents exponential decay when $a > 0$ and $0 < b < 1$. If b is replaced by $1 - r$ and x is replaced by t, then the function is the **exponential decay model** $y = a(1 - r)^t$, where a is the initial amount, the base $(1 - r)$ is the decay factor, r is the decay rate, and t is the time interval.

Example 2 **Write an exponential decay function for each situation. Graph each function and state its domain and range. What does the y-intercept represent in the context of the problem?**

 The population of a town is decreasing at a rate of 3% per year. In 2005, there were 1600 people. Find the population in 2013.

Write the exponential decay function for this situation.

$y = a(1 - r)^t$

$= 1600(1 - 0.03)^t$

$= 1600(0.97)^t$

Find the value in 8 years.

$y = 1600(0.97)^t$

$= 1600(0.97)^8$

≈ 1254

After 8 years, the town's population will be about 1254 people.

Create a table of values to graph the function.

t	y	(t, y)
0	1600	(0, 1600)
8	1254	(8, 1254)
16	983	(16, 983)
24	770	(24, 770)
32	604	(32, 604)

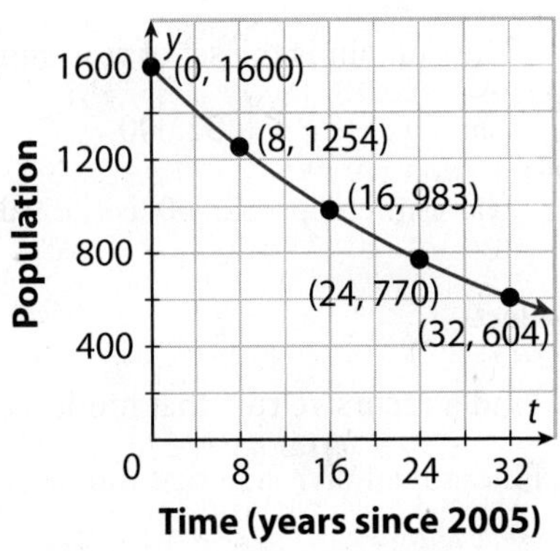

Determine the domain and range of the function.

The domain is the set of real numbers t such that $t \geq 0$. The range is the set of real numbers y such that $0 \leq y \leq 1600$.

The y-intercept is the value of y when $t = 0$, the number of people before it started to lose population.

 The value of a car is depreciating at a rate of 5% per year. In 2010, the car was worth \$32,000. Find the value of the car in 2013.

Write the exponential decay function for this situation.

$y = a(1 - r)^t$

$= \boxed{32{,}000}\left(1 - \boxed{0.05}\right)^t$

$= \boxed{32{,}000}\left(\boxed{0.95}\right)^t$

Find the value in 3 years.

$y = a(1 - r)^t$

$= \boxed{32{,}000}\left(\boxed{0.95}\right)^{t}$

$= \boxed{32{,}000}\left(\boxed{0.95}\right)^{\boxed{3}} \approx \boxed{27{,}436}$

After 3 years, the car's value will be $ 27,436.

Create a table of values to graph the function.

t	y	(t, y)
0	32,000	(0, 32,000)
1	30,400	(1, 30,400)
2	28,880	(2, 28,880)
3	27,436	(3, 27,436)

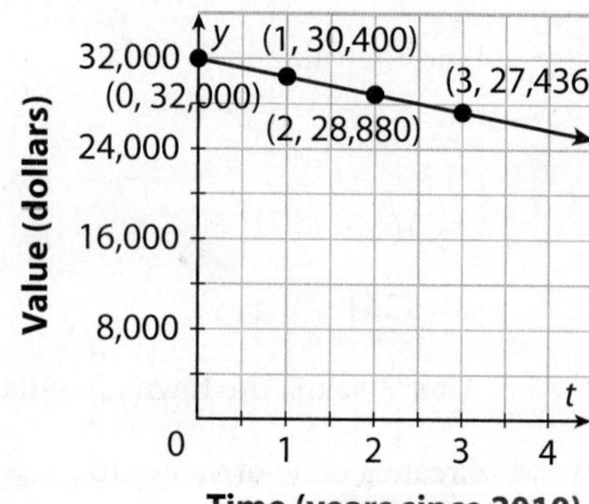

Determine the domain and range of the function.

The domain is the set of real numbers t such that $t \geq$ 0. The range is the set of real numbers y such that 0 $\leq y \leq$ 32,000.

The y-intercept, 32,000, is the value of y when $t = 0$, the original value of the car.

Reflect

11. Find a recursive rule that models the exponential decay of $y = 1600(0.97)^t$.

12. Find a recursive rule that models the exponential decay of $y = 32{,}000(0.95)^t$.

Your Turn

13. The value of a boat is depreciating at a rate of 9% per year. In 2006, the boat was worth $17,800. Find the worth of the boat in 2013. Write an exponential decay function for this situation. Graph the function and state its domain and range. What does the y-intercept represent in the context of the problem?

Explain 3 Comparing Exponential Growth and Decay

Graphs can be used to describe and compare exponential growth and exponential decay models over time.

Example 3 **Use the graphs provided to write the equations of the functions. Then describe and compare the behaviors of both functions.**

(A) The graph shows the value of two different shares of stock over the period of 4 years since they were purchased. The values have been changing exponentially.

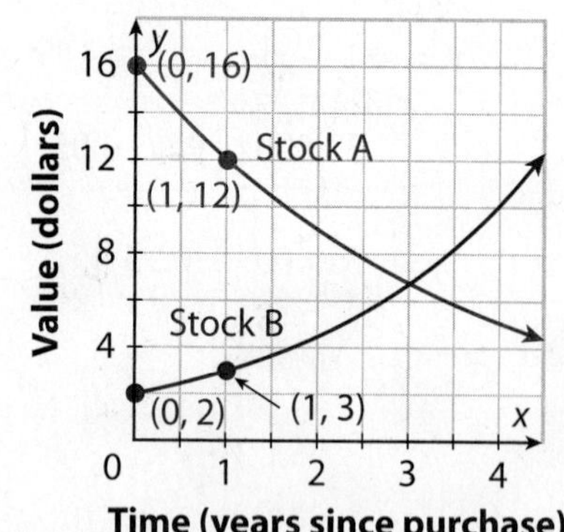

The graph for Stock A shows that the value of the stock is decreasing as time increases.

The initial value, when $t = 0$, is 16. The value when $t = 1$ is 12. Since $12 \div 16 = 0.75$, the function that represents the value of Stock A after t years is $A(t) = 16(0.75)^t$. $A(t)$ is an exponential decay function.

The graph for Stock B shows that the value of the stock is increasing as time increases.

The initial value, when $t = 0$, is 2. The value when $t = 1$ is 3. Since $3 \div 2 = 1.5$, the function that represents the value of Stock B after t years is $B(t) = 2(1.5)^t$. $B(t)$ is an exponential growth function.

The value of Stock A is going down over time. The value of Stock B is going up over time. The initial value of Stock A is greater than the initial value of Stock B. However, after about 3 years, the value of Stock B becomes greater than the value of Stock A.

(B) The graph shows the value of two different shares of stocks over the period of 4 years since they were purchased. The values have been changing exponentially.

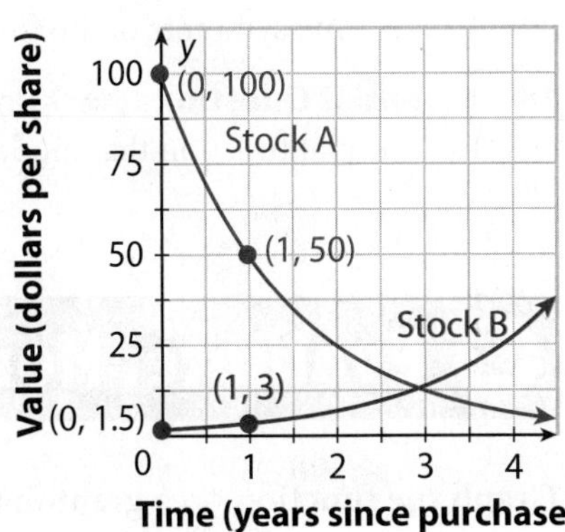

The graph for Stock A shows that the value of the stock is decreasing as time increases.

The initial value, when $t = 0$, is [100]. The value when $t = 1$ is [50]. Since [50] $\div$ [100] $=$ [0.5], the function that represents the value of Stock A after t years is $A(t) =$ [100]([0.5])^t.

$A(t)$ is an exponential decay function.

The graph for Stock B shows that the value of the stock is increasing as time increases.

The initial value, when $t = 0$, is [1.5]. The value when $t = 1$ is [3]. Since [3] $\div$ [1.5] $=$ [2], the function that represents the value of Stock B after t years is $B(t) =$ [1.5]([2])^t. $B(t)$ is an exponential growth function.

The value of Stock A is going down over time. The value of Stock B is going up over time. The initial value of Stock A is greater than the initial value of Stock B. However, after about [3] years, the value of Stock B becomes greater than the value of Stock A.

Reflect

14. **Discussion** In the function $B(t) = 1.5(2)^t$, is it likely that the value of B can be accurately predicted in 50 years?

Your Turn

15. The graph shows the value of two different shares of stocks over the period of 4 years since they were purchased. The values have been changing exponentially. Use the graphs provided to write the equations of the functions. Then describe and compare the behaviors of both functions.

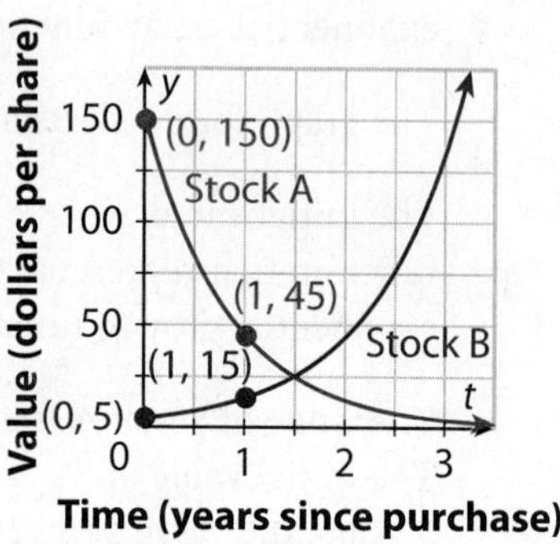

Elaborate

16. If $b > 1$ in a function of the form $y = ab^x$, is the function an example of exponential growth or an example of exponential decay?

17. What is an asymptote of the function $y = 35(1.1)^x$?

18. **Essential Question Check-In** What equation should be used when modeling an exponential function that models a decrease in a quantity over time?

Evaluate: Homework and Practice

- Online Homework
- Hints and Help
- Extra Practice

Graph the function on a graphing calculator, and state its domain, range, end behavior, and an asymptote.

1. $f(x) = 300(1.16)^x$

2. $f(x) = 800(0.85)^x$

3. $f(x) = 65(1.64)^x$

4. $f(x) = 57(0.77)^x$

Write an exponential function to model each situation. Then find the value of the function after the given amount of time.

5. Annual sales for a company are \$155,000 and increases at a rate of 8% per year for 9 years.

6. The value of a textbook is \$69 and decreases at a rate of 15% per year for 11 years.

7. A new savings account is opened with \$300 and gains 3.1% yearly for 5 years.

8. The value of a car is \$7800 and decreases at a rate of 8% yearly for 6 years.

9. The starting salary at a construction company is fixed at \$55,000 and increases at a rate of 1.8% yearly for 4 years.

10. The value of a piece of fine jewelry is \$280 and decreases at a rate of 3% yearly for 7 years.

11. The population of a town is 24,000 and is increasing at a rate of 6% per year for 3 years.

12. The value of a new stadium is \$3.4 million and decreases at a rate of 2.39% yearly for 10 years.

Write an exponential function for each situation. Graph each function and state its domain and range. Determine what the *y*-intercept represents in the context of the problem.

13. The value of a boat is depreciating at a rate of 7% per year. In 2004, the boat was worth \$192,000. Find the value of the boat in 2013.

14. The value of a collectible baseball card is increasing at a rate of 0.5% per year. In 2000, the card was worth \$1350. Find the value of the card in 2013.

15. The value of an airplane is depreciating at a rate of 7% per year. In 2004, the airplane was worth \$51.5 million. Find the value of the airplane in 2013.

16. The value of a movie poster is increasing at a rate of 3.5% per year. In 1990, the poster was worth \$20.25. Find the value of the poster in 2013.

17. The value of a couch is decreasing at a rate of 6.2% per year. In 2007, the couch was worth \$1232. Find the value of the couch in 2014.

18. The population of a town is increasing at a rate of 2.2% per year. In 2001, the town had a population of 34,567. Find the population of the town in 2018.

19. A house is losing value at a rate of 5.4% per year. In 2009, the house was worth \$131,000. Find the value of the house in 2019.

20. An account is gaining value at a rate of 4.94% per year. The account held \$113 in 2005. What will the bank account hold in 2017?

Describe and compare each pair of functions.

21. $A(t) = 13(0.6)^t$ and $B(t) = 4(3.2)^t$

22. $A(t) = 9(0.4)^t$ and $B(t) = 0.6(1.4)^t$

23. $A(t) = 547(0.32)^t$ and $B(t) = 324(3)^t$

24. $A(t) = 2(0.6)^t$ and $B(t) = 0.2(1.4)^t$

25. Identify the *y*-intercept of each of the exponential functions.

    a. $3123(432{,}543)^x$

    b. 0

    c. $45(54)^x$

    d. $76(89{,}047{,}832)^x$

    e. 1

H.O.T. Focus on Higher Order Thinking

26. Explain the Error A student was asked to find the value of a \$2500 item after 4 years. The item was depreciating at a rate of 20% per year. What is wrong with the student's work?

$2500(0.2)^4$

\$4

27. Make a Conjecture The value of a certain car can be modeled by the function $y = 18000(0.76)^t$, where t is time in years. Will the value of the function ever be 0?

28. Communicate Mathematical Ideas Explain how a graph of an exponential function may resemble the graph of a linear function.

Lesson Performance Task

Archeologists have several methods of determining the age of recovered artifacts. One method is radioactive dating.

All matter is made of atoms. Atoms, in turn, are made of protons, neutrons, and electrons. An "element" is defined as an atom with a given number of protons. Carbon, for example, has exactly 6 protons. Carbon atoms can, however, have different numbers of neutrons. These are known as "isotopes" of carbon. Carbon-12 has 6 neutrons, carbon-13 has 7 neutrons, and carbon-14 has 8 neutrons. All carbon-based life forms contain these different isotopes of carbon.

Carbon-12 and carbon-13 account for over 99% of all the carbon in living things. Carbon-14, however, accounts for approximately 1 part per trillion or 0.0000000001% of the total carbon in living things. More importantly, carbon-14 is unstable and has a half-life of approximately 5700 years. This means that, within the span of 5700 years, one-half of any amount of carbon will "decay" into another atom. In other words, if you had 10 g of carbon-14 today, only 5 g would remain after 5700 years.

But, as long as an organism is living, it keeps taking in and releasing carbon-14, so the level of it in the organism, as small as it is, remains constant. Once an organism dies, however, it no longer ingests carbon-14, so the level of carbon-14 in it drops due to radioactive decay. Because we know how much carbon-14 an organism had when it was alive, as well as how long it takes for that amount to become half of what it was, you can determine the age of the organism by comparing these two values.

Use the information presented to create a function that will model the amount of carbon-14 in a sample as a function of its age. Create the model $C(n)$ where C is the amount of carbon-14 in parts per quadrillion (1 part per trillion is 1000 parts per quadrillion) and n is the age of the sample in half-lives. Graph the model.

10.4 Modeling with Quadratic Functions

Resource Locker

Essential Question: How can you use tables to recognize quadratic functions and use technology to create them?

Explore Using Second Differences to Identify Quadratic Functions

A linear function is a straight line, a quadratic function is a parabola, and an exponential function is a curve that approaches a horizontal asymptote in one direction and curves upward to infinity in the other direction.

You can determine if the function is linear or exponential when the values of x and y are presented in a table. For a constant change in x-values, if the difference between the associated y-values is constant, then the function is linear. If the ratio of the associated y-values is constant, then the function is exponential.

What if neither the ratio of successive terms nor the first differences are roughly constant? There is a clue in the method for recognizing a linear function. Find the second difference. The second difference is the value obtained by subtracting consecutive first differences. If this number is non-zero, then the function will be quadratic. Examine the graph of the given quadratic function; then construct a table with values for x, y, and the first and second differences.

(A) Graph the function $f(x) = x^2$ on a coordinate plane.

Use the table to complete Steps B, D, and F.

x	$y = f(x)$	First Difference	Second Difference
1	1	______	______
2	$2^2 =$ ☐	$4 - 1 =$ ☐	______
3	$3^2 =$ ☐	$9 - 4 =$ ☐	$5 - 3 =$ ☐
4	$4^2 =$ ☐	☐ $-$ ☐ $=$	$7 - 5 =$ ☐
5	$5^2 =$ ☐	☐ $-$ ☐ $=$	☐ $-$ ☐ $= 2$

(B) Complete the $y = f(x)$ column of the table with indicated values of $f(x) = x^2$.

Ⓒ Is there a constant difference between x-values?

Ⓓ Recall that the differences between y-values are called the *first differences*. Complete the First Difference column of the table with the indicated first differences.

Ⓔ Are the first differences constant (the same)?

Ⓕ The differences between the first differences are called the **second differences**. Complete the Second Difference column of the table with the indicated second differences.

Ⓖ Are the second differences constant (the same)?

Ⓗ Complete the table for another quadratic function: $f(x) = -3x^2$.

x	$y = f(x)$	First Difference	Second Difference
1	$-3 \cdot 1 =$ ☐	____	____
2	$-3 \cdot 2^2 =$ ☐	$-12 - (-3) =$ ☐	____
3	$-3 \cdot 3^2 =$ ☐	☐ − ☐ = ☐	$-15 - (-9) =$ ☐
4	$-3 \cdot 4^2 =$ ☐	☐ − ☐ = ☐	☐ $- (-15) =$ ☐
5	$-3 \cdot 5^2 =$ ☐	☐ − ☐ = ☐	☐ − ☐ = ☐

Ⓘ Is there a constant difference between x-values?

Are the first differences constant (the same)?

Are the second differences constant (the same)?

Reflect

1. **Discussion** When a table of values with constant x-values leads to constant y-values (*first* differences), what kind of function does that indicate? (linear/quadratic)

2. When a table of values with constant x-values leads to constant *second* differences, what kind of function does that indicate? (linear/quadratic)

Explain 1 Verify Quadratic Relationships Using Quadratic Regression

The second differences for $f(x) = x^2$, the parent quadratic function, are constant for values of y when the corresponding differences between x-values are constant. Now, do the reverse. For a given set of data, verify that the second differences are constant and then use a graphing calculator to find a quadratic model for the data. Enter the independent variable into List 1 and the dependent variable into List 2, and perform a **quadratic regression** on the data. When your calculator performs a quadratic regression, it uses a specific statistical method to fit a quadratic model to the data.

As with linear regression, the data will not be perfect. When finding a model, if the first differences are close but not exactly equal, a linear model will still be a good fit. Likewise, if the second differences aren't exactly the same, a quadratic model will be a good fit if the second differences are close to being the same.

Example 1 **Find a quadratic model for the given situation. Begin by creating a scatter plot of the given data on your graphing calculator, and then find the second differences to verify the data is quadratic. Finally, use a graphing calculator to perform a quadratic regression on the data and graph the regression equation on the scatter plot.**

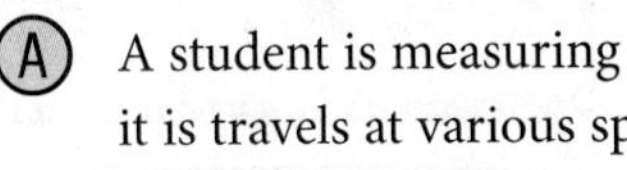

(A) A student is measuring the kinetic energy of a pickup truck as it is travels at various speeds. The speed is given in meters per second, and the kinetic energy is given in kilojoules. Use the given data to find a quadratic model for the data.

Speed x	Kinetic Energy $y = K(x)$	First Difference	Second Difference
20	410	———	———
25	640	230	———
30	922	282	52
35	1256	334	52
40	1640	384	50
45	2076	436	52
50	2563	487	51

Enter the data into a graphing calculator, placing the x-values into List 1 and the y-values into List 2.

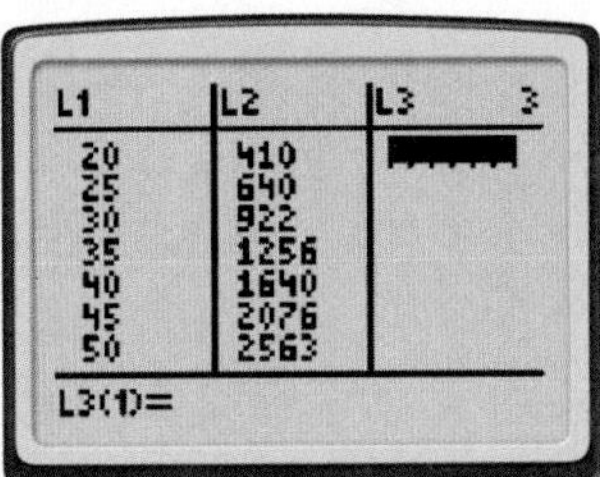

Next view a scatter plot of the data points. The calculator window shown is $15 < x < 55$ with an x-scale of 5 and $0 < y < 3000$ with a y-scale of 500.

Next find the first and second differences and fill in the table.

The first difference of the first and second y-value is found by evaluating the expression below.

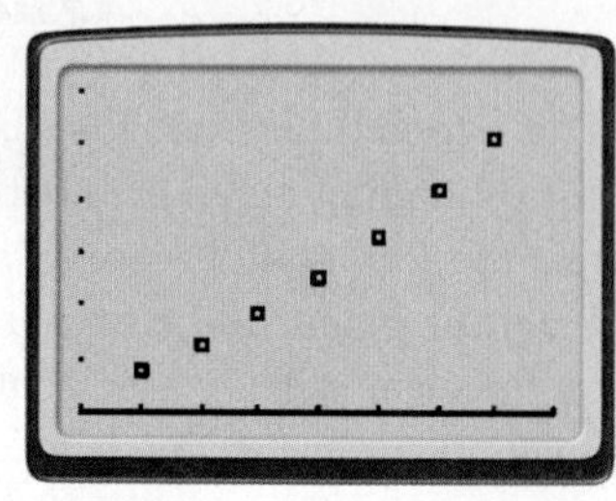

$K(25) - K(20)$

$640 - 410$

230

Find the next first difference in the same manner.

$K(30) - K(25)$

$922 - 640$

282

Find the rest of the first differences and fill in the table.

The first of the second differences is the difference between the values in the third and fourth rows of the first difference column.

$282 - 230 = 52$

Find the rest of the second differences and fill in the rest of the table.

Notice that the second differences are very close to being constant.

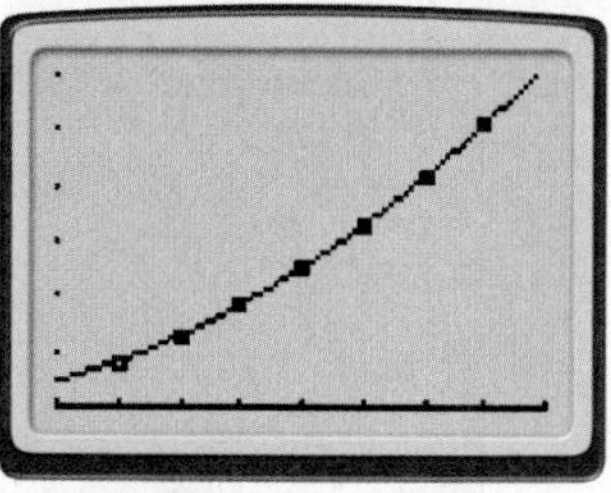

Use a graphing calculator to find the equation for the quadratic regression. $y \approx 1.026x^2 - 0.0548x + 0.3571$

Note that the correlation coefficient is very close to 1, so the model is a good fit.

Plot the regression equation over the scatter plot.

(B) The table shows the speed of a car in meters per second as it accelerates from a stop at a constant rate, measured every 2 seconds.

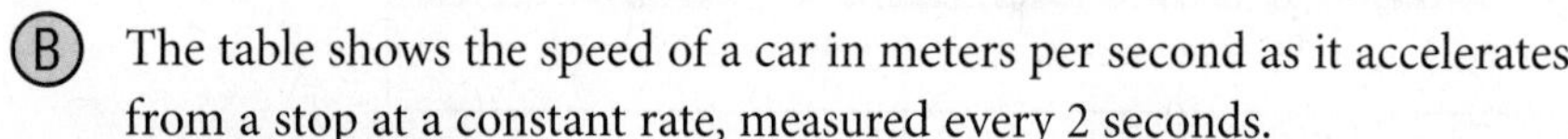

Time	2	4	6	8	10
Speed	5.1	20.4	45.8	81.2	126.1

Create a scatter plot of the data using a graphing calculator.

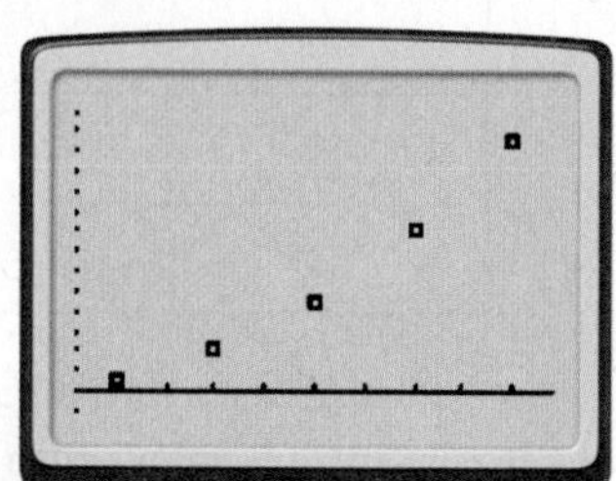

Find the first and second differences and fill out the table.

Time x	Speed y	First Difference	Second Difference
2	5.1	______	______
4	20.4	15.3	______
6	45.8	25.4	10.1
8	81.2	35.4	10
10	126.1	44.9	9.5

Find the regression equation using a graphing calculator. Report the results to 4 significant digits.

$y \approx 1.236x^2 + 0.3114x - 0.52$

Based on the correlation coefficient, the model is a good fit.

Plot the regression equation over the scatter plot.

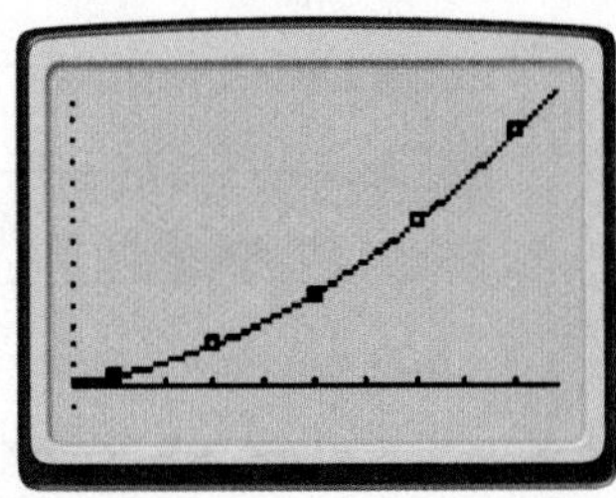

Reflect

3. **Discussion** Give examples of reasons why the second differences in real-world data won't necessarily be equal.

Your Turn

Find a quadratic model for the given situation. Begin by creating a scatter plot of the given data on your graphing calculator, and then find the second differences to verify the data is quadratic. Finally, use a graphing calculator to perform a quadratic regression on the data and graph the regression equation on the scatter plot.

4. The table shows the height of a soccer ball in feet for every half-second after a goalie dropkicks it.

Time	0.5	1.0	1.5	2.0	2.5	3.0	3.5
Height	54	104	142	173	195	208	216

5. A company that makes flying discs to use as promotional materials will produce a flying disc of any size. The table shows the cost of 100 flying discs based on the desired size.

Size	4	4.5	5	5.5	6	6.5	7
Cost	34.99	44.99	54.99	66.99	79.99	92.99	107.99

Explain 2 Using Quadratic Regression to Solve a Real-World Problem

After performing quadratic regression on a given data set, the regression equation can be used to answer questions about the scenario represented by the data.

Example 2 **Use a graphing calculator to perform quadratic regression on the data given. Then solve the problem and identify and interpret the domain and range of the function.**

Ⓐ The height of a model rocket in feet t seconds after it is launched vertically is shown in the following table. Determine the maximum height the rocket attains.

Time	1	2	3	4	5	6	7	8
Height	342	667	902	1163	1335	1459	1584	1864

Enter the data into List 1 and List 2 of a graphing calculator and perform the quadratic regression.

Then plot the regression function over a scatter plot of the data.

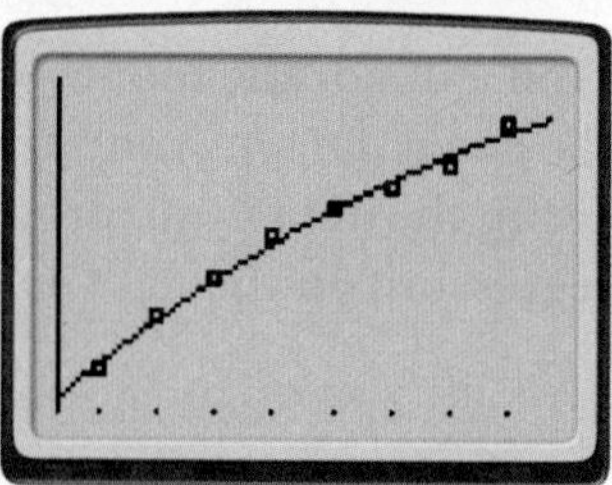

Increase the values of Xmax and Ymax until you can see the maximum value of the function. Then use the maximum function on your graphing calculator to find the maximum height of the rocket.

The model rocket attains a maximum height of approximately 2150 feet 13.5 seconds after launch.

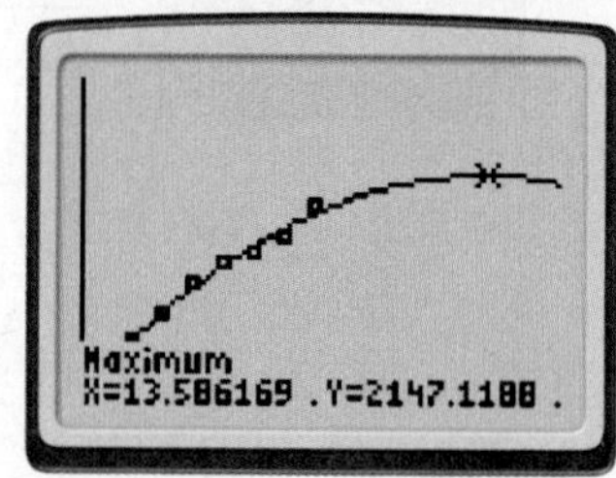

The domain of the function will be $0 \leq t \leq +\infty$. Because the independent variable is time, it doesn't make sense to consider negative time.

The range of the function is $0 \leq y \leq 2150$ because the height of the rocket should never be negative and it will not go higher than its maximum height.

(B) When a rock is thrown into a pond, it makes a series of circular waves. The area enclosed by the first wave is recorded every second and is shown in the table below. If the rock lands 15 meters from shore, when will the first wave reach the shoreline?

Time	1	2	3	4	5	6
Area	9.0	35.8	79.8	145.2	225.1	319.1

Enter the values into List 1 and List 2 of a graphing calculator and use quadratic regression or QuadReg to find the model.

$y \approx$ 8.564 $x^2 +$ 2.444 $x +$ −2.78 $R^2 \approx$ 0.999

$y \approx$ $8.564x^2 + 2.444x - 2.78$

Based on the value of R^2, this function will be a close fit for the data.

The area enclosed by the wave is a circle, so the wave will reach the shore when the radius of the wave is 15 meters.

The area of a circle is given by $A = \pi r^2$.

$A = \pi r^2$

$= \pi (15)^2 = 225\pi \cong 706.858$

Plot the regression equation as Y_1 and let $Y_2 =$ 706.9.

Intersection
X=8.961407 Y=706.9

Find the intersection of the two lines.

The model intersects the line $y = 706.9$ at $x =$ 8.9614. The first wave will reach the shoreline in 9 seconds.

The function only makes sense while the wave is still circular. Once it reaches the shore, the wave will no longer increase in size in the same way. Therefore, the domain of the function is $0 \le x < 9.0$ and the range is $0 \le y \le 706.9$.

Your Turn

Use a graphing calculator to perform quadratic regression on the data given. Then solve the problem and identify and interpret the domain and range of the function.

6. A company needs boxes to package the goods it produces. One product has a standard shape and thickness but comes in a variety of sizes. The sizes are given as integers. The costs of the various sizes in cents are shown in the table. When the packaging cost reaches \$2.00, the company will need to add a surcharge. What is the first size that will have the surcharge added?

Size	1	2	3	4	5	6	7
Cost	7.1	13.8	20.1	29.3	50.1	62.3	86.9

7. A company sells simple circular wall clocks in a variety of sizes. The production cost of each clock is dependent on the diameter of the clock in inches. The costs of making several sizes of clocks in dollars are given in the table. How big would a clock be that costs $4.00 to make? (Round to the nearest eighth.)

Size	8	$8\frac{1}{2}$	9	$9\frac{3}{8}$	$9\frac{1}{2}$	10	12
Cost	1.07	1.16	1.30	1.32	1.36	1.53	2.23

Elaborate

8. Are there any limitations to identifying data that can be modeled by a quadratic function using the method of second differences?

9. A function modeling a situation can be represented as both a function and a graph. Identify some situations where one representation is more helpful than the other.

10. **Essential Question Check-In** When using technology to create a regression model, name two methods for judging the fit of the regression equation.

Evaluate: Homework and Practice

- Online Homework
- Hints and Help
- Extra Practice

Copy the table. Then determine if the function represented in the table is quadratic by finding the second differences.

1.

x	$f(x)$	First Difference	Second Difference
1	2	———	———
2	4		———
3	8		
4	16		
5	32		
6	64		

2.

x	$f(x)$	First Difference	Second Difference
1	3	———	———
2	12		———
3	27		
4	48		
5	75		
6	108		

3.

x	f(x)	First Difference	Second Difference
1	9	———	———
2	13		———
3	17		
4	21		
5	25		
6	29		

4.

x	f(x)	First Difference	Second Difference
1	2	———	———
2	18		———
3	48		
4	92		
5	150		
6	222		

Find the second differences of the given data to verify that the relationship will be quadratic. Then use a graphing calculator to find the quadratic regression equation and R^2 with a precision of 4 digits.

5.

x	1	7	13	19	25	31	37	43	49	55	61	67
y	93	107	125	148	174	203	237	274	316	361	410	462

6.

x	8	11.4	14.8	18.2	21.6	25	28.4	31.8	35.2	38.6	42	45.4
y	24	60	106	161	227	302	387	483	588	703	827	962

7.

x	3.6	17.9	32.2	46.5	60.8	75.1	89.4	103.7	118	132.3	146.6	160.9
y	1946	1684	1442	1219	1012	821	648	494	357	237	133	44

8.

x	9	9.2	9.4	9.6	9.8	10	10.2	10.4	10.6	10.8	11	11.2
y	44	465	844	1180	1475	1728	1941	2117	2255	2355	2409	2416

9.

x	17	20.1	23.2	26.4	29.5	32.7	35.8	38.9	42.1	45.2	48.4	51.5
y	1000	995	974	936	882	814	729	627	510	376	225	58

Find a quadratic model for the given situation. Begin by creating a scatter plot of the given data on your graphing calculator, and then find the second differences to verify the data is quadratic. Finally, use a graphing calculator to perform a quadratic regression on the data.

10. The table shows the height of an arrow in feet x seconds after being released toward a target down range by an archery student.

Time	0.25	0.5	0.75	1.0	1.25	1.5	1.75
Height	12.0	23.7	32.5	39.3	44.6	47.5	47.8

11. The table shows the cost of cleaning a lap pool based on the number of lanes it has.

Number of Lanes	6	8	10	12	14	16
Cleaning Cost	30	95	263	518	875	1299

Use a graphing calculator to find a quadratic model for the given data.

12.

x	2.9	3.9	4.7	5.6	6.9	7.7	8.5
y	8	14	23	29	40	53	70

13.

x	4.7	6.7	8.5	10.1	12.8	14.3	15.9
y	32	17	−27	−94	−193	−321	−499

14.

x	−2.7	−1.9	−0.9	0	0.9	1.9	2.7
y	−13	−8	−6	−4	−5	−8	−13

Use a graphing calculator to perform quadratic regression on the given data. Then solve the problem and identify and interpret the domain and range of the function.

15. The revenue of a company based on the price of its product is in the table below. How much should the company sell the product for to maximize revenue?

Price	1	2	2.75	4	4.5	6	8	8.4	9
Revenue	90	228	303	384	406	396	282	229	135

16. A scuba diver brought an air-filled balloon 150 feet underwater to the bottom of a lake. The diver conducts an experiment to measure the surface area of the balloon while ascending back to the surface. The results of the measurements are shown in the table. How far will the balloon have risen when it has doubled in surface area?

Distance from Bottom	0	20	40	60	80	100	120
Surface Area	28.6	32.2	35.4	39.5	45.0	52.8	65.4

17. The height of a ski jumper with respect to the low point of the ramp in meters is measured every 0.3 seconds. The results are given in the table. If the skier lands at a point 30 meters below the reference point, how long was the skier in the air?

Time	0.3	0.6	0.9	1.2	1.5	1.8	2.1	2.4
Height	11.2	14.06	16.32	18.47	19.48	20.52	21.01	21.01

H.O.T. Focus on Higher Order Thinking

Use the table for Exercises 18 and 19.

x	1	1.25	1.5	1.75	2	3	4	5	6	7	8	9
y	2	2.378	2.828	3.364	4	8	16	32	64	128	256	512

18. What If? If you perform a quadratic regression on the data, will the value of R^2 be close to 1? Justify your answer.

19. Communicate Mathematical Ideas Perform a quadratic regression on the data; then perform a quadratic regression using only the first four data points. Explain the difference in R^2 values between the two models.

20. Multi-Part A trebuchet is a catapult that was used in the Middle Ages to hurl projectiles during a siege. It is now used in various regions of the United States to throw pumpkins. Teams build trebuchets to compete to see who can throw a pumpkin the farthest. On the practice field, one team has measured the height of its pumpkin after it is launched at 1-second intervals. The results are displayed in the table below.

Time	1	2	3	4	5	6	7	8
Height	152	265	377	441	470	450	396	342

a. Find a quadratic function that models the data.

b. Determine the flight time of the pumpkin.

c. If the pumpkin travels horizontally at a speed of 120 feet per second, how far does it travel before it hits the ground?

d. At the official competition, the trebuchet is situated on a slight rise 10 feet above the targeting area. How far will the pumpkin travel in the competition, assuming the height relative to the base of the trebuchet is modeled by the same function and it moves with the same horizontal speed?

Lesson Performance Task

A student stands at the top of a lighthouse that is 200 feet tall. The base of the lighthouse is an additional 300 feet above the ocean below, and the student has a clear shot to the water below to examine the claims made by Galileo. But, this being the 21st century, the student also has a sophisticated laser tracker that continually tracks the exact height of the dropped object from the ground as well as the length of time elapsed from the drop. At the end of the trial, the student gets sample data in the form of a table.

Time	Height above Ground
0	200
0.5	196
1	184
1.5	164
2	136
2.5	100
3	56
3.5	4
4	−56
4.5	−124
5	−200

Examine the data and determine the relationship between time and height. Then find the function that models the data. (Hint: Negative values represent when the object passes the base of the lighthouse.)

10.5 Comparing Linear, Exponential, and Quadratic Models

Resource Locker

Essential Question: How can you determine whether a given data set is best modeled by a linear, quadratic, or exponential function?

Explore Exploring End Behavior of Linear, Quadratic, and Exponential Functions

Recall that you learned to characterize the end behavior of a function by recognizing what the behavior of the function is as x approaches positive or negative infinity. Look at the three graphs to see what the function does as x approaches infinity or negative infinity.

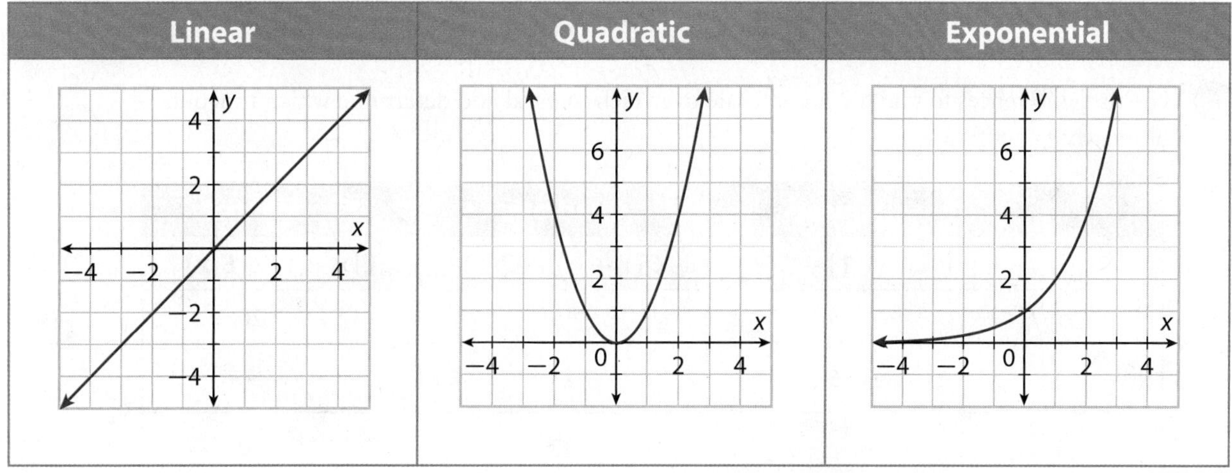

(A) For the linear function, $f(x)$, as x approaches infinity, $f(x)$ ______, and as x approaches negative infinity, $f(x)$ ______.

(B) For the quadratic function, $g(x)$, as x approaches infinity, $g(x)$ ______, and as x approaches negative infinity, $g(x)$ ______.

(C) For the exponential function, $h(x)$, as x approaches infinity, $h(x)$ ______, and as x approaches negative infinity, $h(x)$ ______.

Examine the end behavior and the rate of the change of the three function types by filling in the values of the table.

(D) Fill in the missing values of the table.

	Linear	Quadratic	Exponential
x	$L(x) = 5x - 2$	$Q(x) = 5x^2 - 2$	$E(x) = 5^x - 2$
1	3	3	3
2	8	18	
3	13	43	123
4		78	623
5	23		3123
6	28	178	15,623
7	33	243	
8	38	318	390,623

(E) Use first differences to find the growth rate over each interval and determine which function ultimately grows fastest.

	Linear	Quadratic	Exponential
x	$L(x+1) - L(x)$	$Q(x+1) - Q(x)$	$E(x+1) - E(x)$
1	5	15	20
2	5	25	
3		35	500
4	5		2500
5	5	55	

(F) The fastest growing function of the three is the ______.

Reflect

1. What is the end behavior of $y = 7x + 12$?
2. What is the end behavior of $y = 5x^2 + x + 2$?
3. What is the end behavior of $y = 3^x - 5$?
4. **Make a Conjecture** Does an increasing exponential function always grow faster than an increasing quadratic function? Will the growth rate of an increasing exponential function eventually exceed that of an increasing quadratic function?

Explain 1 Justifying a Quadratic Model as More Appropriate Than a Linear Model

The first step in modeling data is selecting an appropriate functional form. If you are trying to decide between a quadratic and a linear model, for example, you may compare interval rates of change or the end behavior. First and second differences are useful for identifying linear and quadratic functions if the data points have equally spaced x-values.

Example 1 **Examine the data sets provided and determine whether a quadratic or linear model is more appropriate by examining the graph, the end behavior, and the first and second differences.**

Ⓐ

x	$f(x)$
0	3
1	1.5
2	1
3	1.5
4	3
5	5.5
6	9

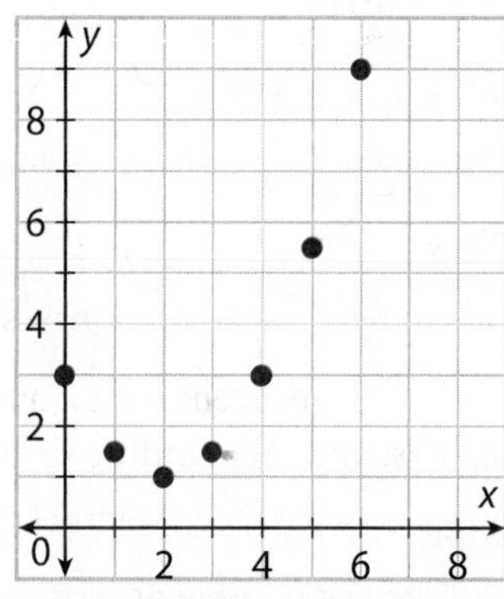

Shape:

The graph of the data appears to follow a curved path that starts downward and turns back upward.

End Behavior:

The path appears to increase without end as x approaches infinity and to increase without end as x approaches negative infinity.

Based on the apparent curvature and end behavior, the function is quadratic.

Interval Behavior:

x	$f(x)$	First Difference	Second Difference
0	3	———	———
1	1.5	−1.5	———
2	1	−0.5	1
3	1.5	0.5	1
4	3	1.5	1
5	5.5	2.5	1
6	9	3.5	1

The first differences increase as x increases, while the second differences are constant, which is characteristic of a quadratic function.

(B)

x	$f(x)$
0	8
1	6.75
2	5
3	2.75
4	0
5	−3.25
6	−7

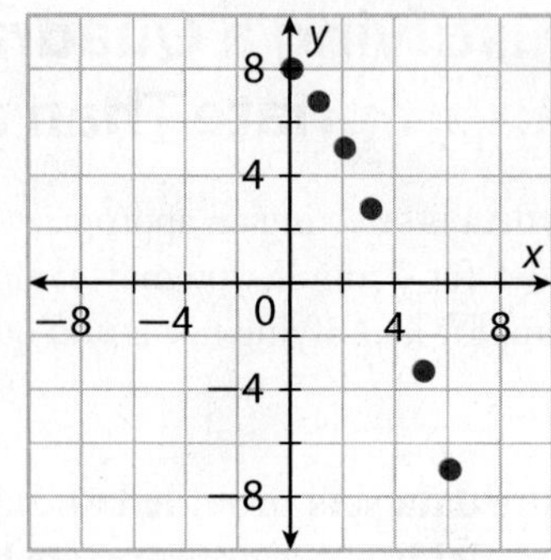

Plot the data on the graph.

Shape:

The graph of the data appears to follow a curved, downward path.

End Behavior:

The path appears to decrease as x increases and to increase as x decreases.

The curvature is more consistent with a quadratic than a line, but the apparent end behavior is not. Fill in the first and second differences to discuss internal behavior.

Interval Behavior:

x	$f(x)$	First Differences	Second Differences
0	8	———	———
1	6.75	−1.25	———
2	5	−1.75	−0.5
3	2.75	−2.25	−0.5
4	0	−2.75	−0.5
5	−3.25	−3.25	−0.5
6	−7	−3.75	−0.5

The absolute values of the first differences increase as x increases, while the second differences are constant, which is characteristic of a quadratic function.

Reflect

5. Was the end behavior helpful in determining that the function in Example 1B was a quadratic? Explain.

6. **Discussion** Can you always tell that a function is quadratic by looking at a graph of it?

Your Turn

7. Plot the data on a graph. Examine the data set and determine whether a quadratic or linear model is more appropriate by examining the graph, the end behavior, and the first and second differences.

x	$f(x)$
0	−4
1	−3.8
2	−3.2
3	−2.2
4	−0.8
5	1
6	3.2

Explain 2 Justifying a Quadratic Model as More Appropriate Than an Exponential Model

Previously, you learned to model data with an exponential function. How do you choose between a quadratic and an exponential function to model a given set of data? Graph the given data points and compare the trend of the data with the general shape and end behavior of the parent quadratic and exponential functions. Use the results to decide if the function appears to be quadratic or exponential. Then examine the first and second differences and the ratios of the function using the function values corresponding to x-values separated by a constant amount.

Properties of $f(x) = x^2$ and $g(x) = b^x$		
	$f(x) = x^2$	$g(x) = b^x$ with $b > 1$
End behavior as:	______	______
x approaches infinity	$f(x)$ approaches infinity	$g(x)$ approaches infinity
x approaches negative infinity	$f(x)$ approaches infinity	$g(x)$ decreases to zero

Example 2 **Determine if the function represented in the given table is quadratic or exponential. Plot the given points and analyze the graph. Draw a conclusion if possible. Then find the first and second differences and ratios and either verify your conclusion or determine the family of the function.**

x	$f(x)$
−3	3
−2	1.5
−1	1
0	1.5
1	3
2	5.5
3	9

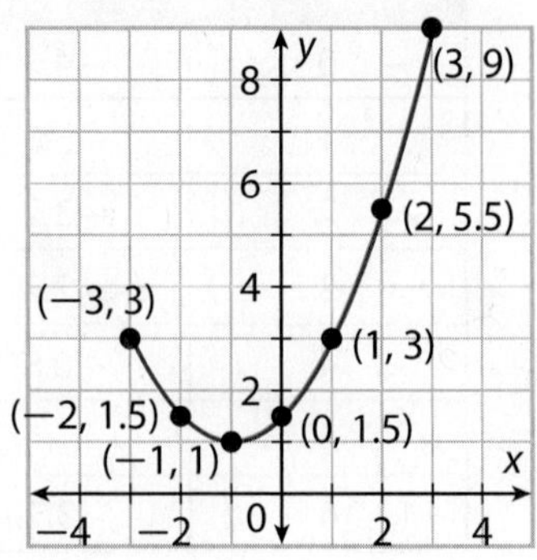

Graph $f(x)$ on the axes provided by plotting the given points and connecting them with a smooth curve.

The data appears to be parabolic.

Also, as x approaches infinity, $f(x)$ appears to increase without end, and as x approaches negative infinity, $f(x)$ appears to increase without end.

It appears that $f(x)$ is a quadratic function.

Now find the first and second differences and the ratio of the values of $f(x)$.

x	$f(x)$	First Difference	Second Difference	Ratio
−3	3	———	———	———
−2	1.5	−1.5	———	0.5
−1	1	−0.5	1	0.67
0	1.5	0.5	1	1.5
1	3	1.5	1	2
2	5.5	2.5	1	1.83
3	9	3.5	1	1.64

The second differences are constant so the function is quadratic as predicted.

Ⓑ

x	$f(x)$	First Difference	Second Difference	Ratio
−2	4	______	______	______
0	3.5	−0.5	______	0.875
2	2	−1.5	−1	0.571
4	−0.5	−2.5	−1	−0.25
6	−4	−3.5	−1	8
8	−8.5	−4.5	−1	2.125

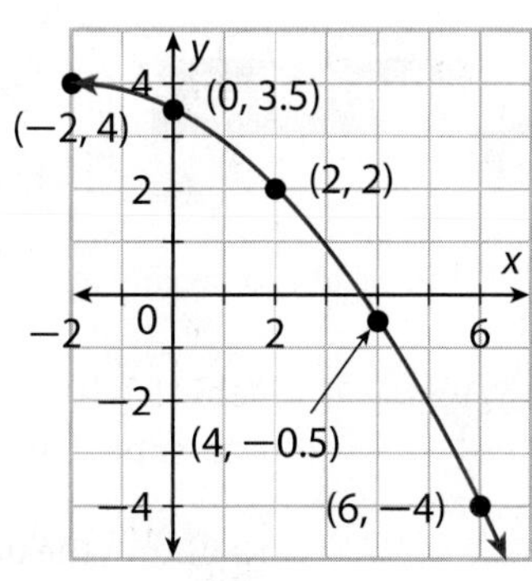

Graph $f(x)$ on the axes provided by plotting the given points and connecting them with a smooth curve. The data appears to be either quadratic or exponential.

As x approaches infinity, $f(x)$ appears to decrease without end.

As x approaches negative infinity, $f(x)$ cannot be determined.

It appears that $f(x)$ could be either quadratic or exponential.

Now find the first and second differences and the ratio of the values of $f(x)$.

The second differences are constant so the function is quadratic.

Your Turn

Determine if the function represented in the given table is quadratic or exponential. Plot the given points and analyze the graph. Draw a conclusion if possible. Then find the first and second differences and ratios and either verify your conclusion or determine the family of the function.

8.

x	$f(x)$	First Difference	Second Difference	Ratio
−3	−5	______	______	______
−2	−3.11		______	
−1	−1.44			
0	0			
1	1.22			
2	2.22			
3	3			
4	3.56			
5	3.89			
6	4			

9.

x	$f(x)$	First Difference	Second Difference	Ratio
−2	8.25	———	———	———
0	6		———	
2	4.25			
4	3			
6	2.25			
8	2			

Explain 3 Selecting an Appropriate Model Given Linear, Exponential, or Quadratic Data

It is important to be able to choose among a variety of models when solving real-world problems.

Example 3 **Decide which type of function is best represented by each of the following data sets. Then perform the following steps:**

1. Graph the data on a scatterplot and draw a fit curve.
2. Identify which function the data appear to represent.
3. Predict the function's end behavior as x approaches infinity.
4. Use a function table to calculate the first differences, second differences, and ratios.
5. Perform the appropriate regression on a graphing calculator. Plot the regression line and data together to evaluate the fit of regression.
6. Answer any additional questions.

(A) **Demographics** The data table describes the average lifespan in the United States over time.

Year	Average Lifespan (years)
1900	47.3
1910	50.0
1920	54.1
1930	59.7
1940	62.9
1950	68.2
1960	69.7
1970	70.8
1980	73.1
1990	75.4

What will be the estimated average lifespan in 2000?

Graph the scatterplot and an approximate line of fit to determine the best function to use for this data set.

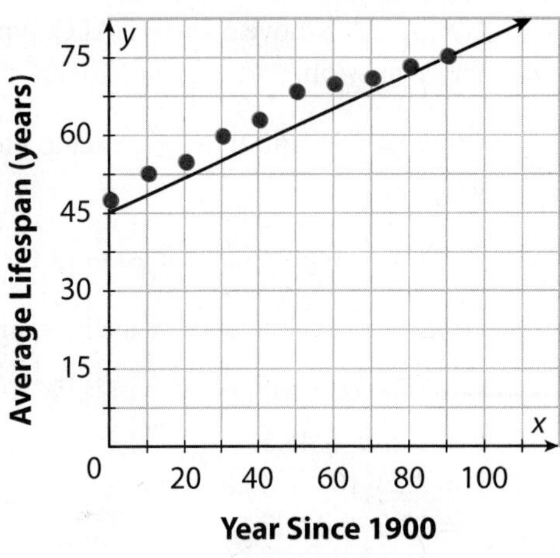

The data set appears to best fit a linear function.

The end behavior of the data is that as x approaches infinity, $f(x)$ approaches infinity.

Complete the function table for first differences, second differences, and ratios.

Year	Average Lifespan (years)	First Difference	Second Difference	Ratio
1900	47.3	___	___	___
1910	50.0	2.7	___	$\frac{50.0}{47.3} = 1.06$
1920	54.1	4.1	1.4	$\frac{54.1}{50.0} = 1.08$
1930	59.7	5.6	1.5	$\frac{59.7}{54.1} = 1.10$
1940	62.9	3.2	−2.4	$\frac{62.9}{59.7} = 1.05$
1950	68.2	5.3	2.1	$\frac{68.2}{62.9} = 1.08$
1960	69.7	1.5	−3.8	$\frac{69.7}{68.2} = 1.02$
1970	70.8	1.1	−0.4	$\frac{70.8}{69.7} = 1.02$
1980	73.1	2.3	1.2	$\frac{73.1}{70.8} = 1.03$
1990	75.4	2.3	0	$\frac{75.4}{73.1} = 1.03$

Since the ratios are dropping, it is possible that the data set can be modeled by an exponential regression. Since the average of the second differences is around 0, however, it is most likely that the data set should be modeled by a linear regression.

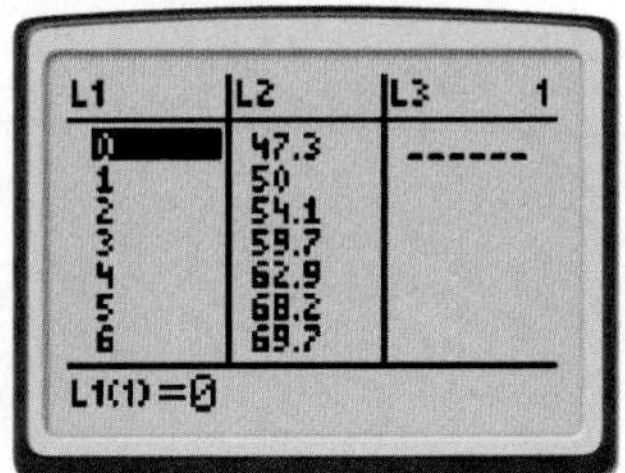

Perform the linear regression by first creating a data table by using the STAT function on a calculator. Use the numbers 0 through 9 to represent the years, starting with 0 for 1900.

Go to STAT, move over to CALC, type 4, and press ENTER to perform the regression.

LinReg
y=ax+b
a=3.232727273
b=48.57272727
r²=.9643984578
r=.9820379105

Press ZOOM and 9 to fit the data. Plot the line from the regression to test its fit.

The linear regression is a good fit for the data set.

To find the estimated average lifespan in 2000, use the equation $y = 3.23x + 48.57$ and substitute 10 for x.

$$y = 3.23x + 48.57$$
$$y = 3.23(10) + 48.57$$
$$= 32.3 + 48.57$$
$$= 80.87$$

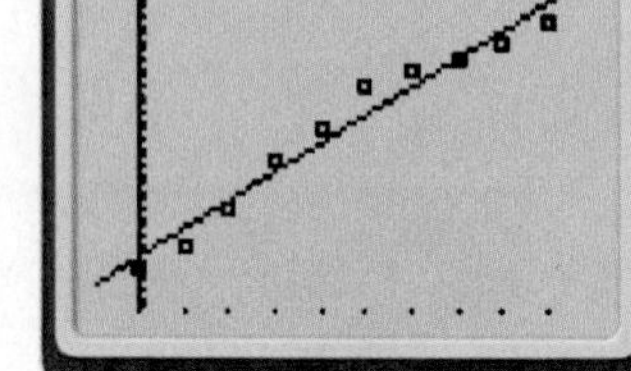

The predicted average lifespan in the year 2000 is 80.87 years.

(B) **Biology** The data table lists the whooping crane population over time.

Whooping Crane	
Year	**Population**
1940	22
1950	34
1960	33
1970	56
1980	76
1990	146
2000	177
2010	281

How many whooping cranes will exist in 2020?

Graph the scatterplot and an approximate line of fit to determine the best function to use for this data set.

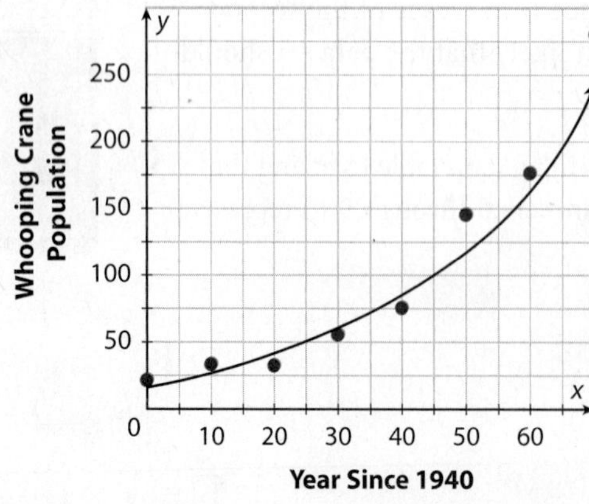

The data set appears to best fit an exponential function.

The end behavior of this data is that as x approaches infinity, $f(x)$, approaches infinity.

Complete the function table for first differences, second differences, and ratios.

Year	Population	First Difference	Second Difference	Ratio
1940	22	———	———	———
1950	34	12	———	$\frac{34}{22} = 1.55$
1960	33	-1	-13	$\frac{33}{34} = 0.97$
1970	56	23	24	$\frac{56}{33} = 1.70$
1980	76	20	-3	$\frac{76}{56} = 1.36$
1990	146	70	50	$\frac{146}{76} = 1.92$
2000	177	31	-39	$\frac{177}{146} = 1.21$
2010	281	104	73	$\frac{281}{177} = 1.59$

Since the ratios are changing and the second difference does not have an average that is close to 0, exponential regression should be used.

Perform the exponential regression by first creating a data table by using the STAT function on a calculator. Use the numbers 0 through 7 to represent the years, starting with 0 for 1940.

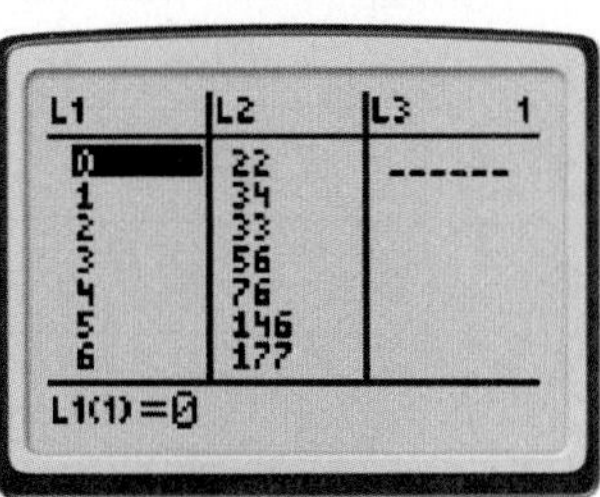

Go to STAT, move over to CALC, type 0, and press ENTER to perform the regression.

Press ZOOM and 9 to fit the data. Plot the line from the regression to test its fit.

The exponential regression is a good fit for the data set.

To find the estimated number of whooping cranes in 2020, use the equation $y =$ $20.05(1.44)^x$ and substitute 8 for x.

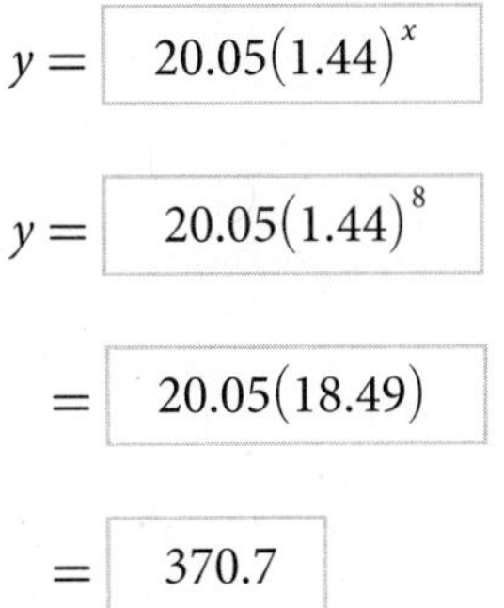

$y = 20.05(1.44)^x$

$y = 20.05(1.44)^8$

$= 20.05(18.49)$

$= 370.7$

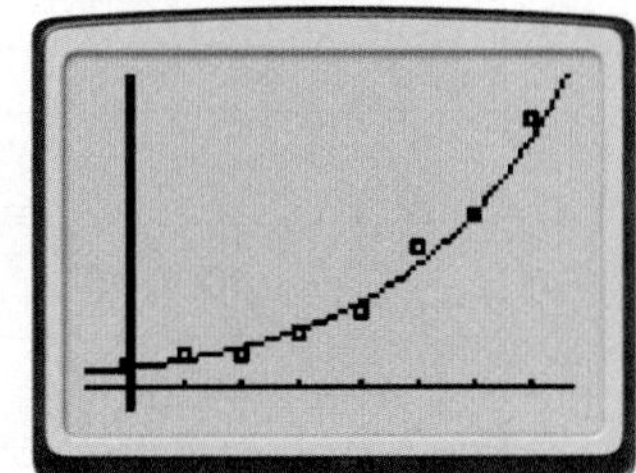

Since it is unrealistic to round up in this situation, the number of whooping cranes in 2020 will be 370.

Your Turn

Decide which type of function is best represented by each of the following data sets. Then perform the following steps:

1. Graph the data on a scatterplot and draw a fit curve.
2. Identify which function the data appear to represent.
3. Predict the function's end behavior as x approaches infinity.
4. Use a function table to calculate the first differences, second differences, and ratios.
5. Perform the appropriate regression on a graphing calculator. Plot the regression line and data together to evaluate the fit of regression.
6. Answer any additional questions.

10. **Population** The data table describes the percentage of people living in central cities in the United States over time. What percentage of people were living in central cities in the United States in 2000?

Year	% of People
1910	21.2
1920	24.2
1930	30.8
1940	32.5
1950	32.8
1960	32.3
1970	31.4
1980	30.0

11. **Automobiles** The data table describes the car weight versus horsepower for automobiles produced in 2012. If a car weighed 6500 pounds in 2012, how much horsepower should the car have?

Car Weight (pounds)	Horsepower in 2012
2000	70
2500	105
3000	145
3500	179
4000	259
4500	338
5000	400
5500	557
6000	556

Elaborate

12. In general, what are three possible end behaviors of exponential, linear, and quadratic graphs as x increases without bound? When do these end behaviors occur?

13. What do function tables tell you that graphs don't ? How can this information be used to help you select a model?

14. When does a graph help determine an appropriate model better than examining first and second differences and ratios?

15. Can two different models be created that represent the same set of data?

16. **Essential Question Check-In** How can a graph be used to determine whether a given data set is best modeled by a linear, quadratic, or exponential function?

Evaluate: Homework and Practice

- Online Homework
- Hints and Help
- Extra Practice

1. For the two function $f(x) = 2x + 1$ and $g(x) = 2^x + 1$ which function has the greatest average rate of change over the interval from 0 to 1? What about the interval from 2 to 3?

2. Plot the data and describe the observed shape and end behavior. Does it appear linear or quadratic? Copy the table, calculate first and second differences, and identify the type of function.

x	$f(x)$	First Difference	Second Difference
0	−0.79	———	———
1	2.81		———
2	4.41		
3	4.01		
4	1.61		
5	−2.79		

3. Plot the data and describe the observed shape and end behavior. Does it appear to be linear or quadratic? Copy the table, calculate first and second differences, and identify the type of function.

x	$f(x)$	First Difference	Second Difference
−2	−4	______	______
−1	−3.3		______
0	−1.2		
1	2.3		
2	7.2		
3	13.5		

4. Plot the data and describe the observed shape and end behavior. Does it appear linear or quadratic? Copy the table, calculate first and second differences, and identify the type of function.

x	$f(x)$	First Difference	Second Difference
0	7.6	______	______
1	6.25		______
2	4.6		
3	2.65		
4	0.4		

5. Plot the data and describe the observed the shape and end behavior. Does it appear linear or quadratic? Copy the table, calculate first and second differences, and identify the type of function?

x	$f(x)$	First Difference	Second Difference
1	−7.2	______	______
2	−3.8		______
3	0		
4	4.2		
5	8.8		

6. Plot the given points. Describe the general shape and end behavior of the graph. Draw a conclusion about the function, if possible. Then copy and complete the table and use the differences to to verify your conclusions.

x	$f(x)$	First Difference	Second Difference	Ratio
−2	−5.75	———	———	———
0	1		———	
2	6.25			
4	10			
6	12.25			
8	13			
10	12.25			
12	10			
14	6.25			

7. Plot the given points. Describe the general shape and end behavior of the graph. Draw a conclusion about the function, if possible. Then copy and complete the table and use the differences to to verify your conclusions.

x	$f(x)$	First Difference	Second Difference	Ratio
−2	9	———	———	———
0	5.5		———	
2	3			
4	1.5			
6	1			

8. Plot the given points. Describe the general shape and end behavior of the graph. Draw a conclusion about the function, if possible. Then copy and complete the table and use the differences to to verify your conclusions.

x	$f(x)$	First Difference	Second Difference	Ratio
−5	−3	———	———	———
−2	−2		———	
1	1			
4	6			
7	13			

H.O.T. Focus on Higher Order Thinking

9. **Critical Thinking** A set of data was modeled by using the quadratic, linear, and exponential forms of regression. Nearly identical statistically significant r^2-values were produced in all three situations. Which type of regression model should be used? Explain.

10. **Explain the Error** To determine if the data represents a linear model, Louise looked at the difference in y-values: 110, 110, 110, 110, 110.

x	7	9	12	14	18
y	150	260	370	480	590

She decided that since the differences between the y-values are all the same, a linear model would be appropriate. Explain her mistake.

11. **Critical Thinking** Suppose that the following r^2-values were produced from an unknown set of data.

r^2-values		
Linear	**Quadratic**	**Exponential**
0.15	0.11	0.13

What type of regression model should be chosen for this data set? Explain.

Lesson Performance Task

The table shows general guidelines for the weight of a Great Dane at various ages. Create a function modeling the ideal weight for a Great Dane at any age. Justify your choice of models. How well do you think your model will do when the puppy is one or two years old?

Age (months)	Weight (kg)
2	12
4	23
6	33
8	40
10	45

STUDY GUIDE REVIEW

MODULE 10

Linear, Exponential, and Quadratic Models

Essential Question: How can you use linear, exponential, and quadratic models to solve real-world problems?

Key Vocabulary

correlation *(correlación)*
exponential function *(función exponencial)*
exponential regression *(regresión exponencial)*
line of best fit *(línea de mejor ajuste)*
linear regression *(regresión lineal)*
quadratic regression *(regresión cuadrática)*

KEY EXAMPLE *(Lesson 10.3)*

A comic book is sold for $3, and its value increases by 6% each year after it is sold. Write an exponential growth function to find the value of the comic book in 25 years.

Write the exponential growth function for this situation.

$$y = a(1 + r)^t$$
$$= 3(1 + 0.06)^t$$
$$= 3(1.06)^t$$

Find the value in 25 years.

$$y = 3(1.06)^t$$
$$= 3(1.06)^{25}$$
$$\approx 12.88$$

After 25 years, the comic book will be worth approximately $12.88.

KEY EXAMPLE *(Lesson 10.4)*

Find the second differences of the given data to verify that the relationship will be quadratic. Use a graphing calculator to find the quadratic regression equation for the data and R^2 to 4 significant digits.

The table below shows the cost of shipping a box that has a volume of x cubic feet.

Volume	Cost ($)	First Difference	Second Difference
1	$6.15		
2	$8.00	8 − 6.15 = 1.85	
3	$13.90	13.9 − 8 = 5.9	5.9 − 1.85 = 4.05
4	$23.75	23.75 − 13.9 = 9.85	9.85 − 5.9 = 3.95
5	$38.25	38.25 − 23.75 = 14.5	14.5 − 9.85 = 4.65

$a \approx 2.09$
$b \approx -4.54$
$c \approx 8.65$
$R^2 \approx 0.9999$

The second differences are close to being constant. Plug the volumes, as the x-values, and the costs, as the y-values, into the graphing calculator and run a quadratic regression.

The quadratic regression equation is $y \approx 2.09x^2 - 4.54x + 8.65$.

EXERCISES

State whether each situation is best represented by an exponential or linear function. Then write an exponential or linear function for the model and state whether the model is increasing or decreasing. *(Lessons 10.1, 10.3)*

1. A customer borrows $950 at 6% interest compounded annually.

2. The population of a town is 8548 people and decreases by 90 people each year.

3. The table below shows the height of a baseball in inches x seconds after it was thrown. Fill in the table with the first differences and second differences. Then, use a graphing calculator to find the quadratic regression equation for the data. *(Lesson 10.4)*

Time	Height	First Difference	Second Difference
0	60	———	———
0.25	59		———
0.5	57		
0.75	52		
1	44		
1.25	35		

MODULE PERFORMANCE TASK

What Model Fits a Survivorship Curve?

A survivorship curve shows the number of surviving members of a population over time from a given set of births. The graph shows the three types of survivorship curves that commonly occur. Which types of functions would appear to best model each type of curve?

The data table presents the results of a survivorship study for a population of 1000 goats. What type of survivorship curve most closely matches the goat data? Can you find a good mathematical model for these data, using either a linear, quadratic, or exponential function, or a combination?

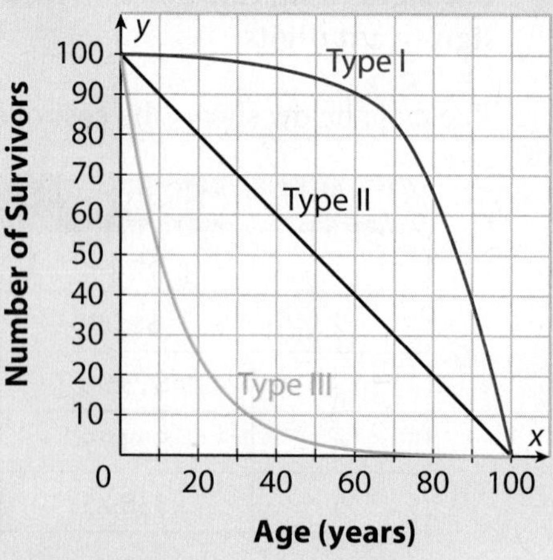

Age (years)	1	2	3	4	5	6	7	8	9	10
Number of Deaths During Year	12	13	9	11	12	11	9	11	11	11
Age (years)	**11**	**12**	**13**	**14**	**15**	**16**	**17**	**18**	**19**	**20**
Number of Deaths During Year	28	14	46	62	52	92	101	133	159	203

Ready to Go On?

10.1–10.5 Linear, Exponential, and Quadratic Models

- Online Homework
- Hints and Help
- Extra Practice

1. The table shows numbers of books read by students in an English class over a summer and the students' grades for the following semester.

Books	0	0	0	0	1	1	1	2	2	3	5	8	10	14	20
Grade	64	68	69	72	71	74	76	75	79	85	86	91	94	99	98

Find an equation for the line of best fit. Calculate and interpret the correlation coefficient. Then use your equation to predict the grade of a student who read 7 books. *(Lesson 10.1)*

2. The height of a plant, in inches, x weeks after it was planted is given in the table below. Use a graphing calculator to write a quadratic regression equation for the data set given. About how many weeks did it take the plant to reach a height of 40 inches? *(Lesson 10.4)*

Weeks	5	10	15	20	25
Height	15	31	55	87	127

3. Graph the data represented in the given table. Determine if the function represented in the given table is best represented by a linear, exponential, or quadratic function. Explain your answer. *(Lesson 10.5)*

x	−3	−2	−1	0	1	2	3
$f(x)$	5.5	3.5	1.5	1	0.6	0.3	0.1

ESSENTIAL QUESTION

4. How can you determine if a function is linear, quadratic, or exponential?

MODULE 10
MIXED REVIEW

Assessment Readiness

1. Consider each data set and if it is best represented by a linear, exponential, or quadratic model. Determine if each statement is True or False.

A. $\{(-5, 2), (-3, 6), (-1, 10), (1, 14), (3, 18)\}$ is best represented by a linear model.

B. $\{(-2, 12), (-1, 6), (0, 3), (1, 1.5), (2, 0.75)\}$ is best represented by a quadratic model.

C. $\{(-5, 4), (-4, 1), (-3, 0), (-2, 1), (-1, 4)\}$ is best represented by an exponential model.

2. Does the given equation have 2 real solutions?

A. $6x^2 + 15 = 0$

B. $8x^2 - 50 = 0$

C. $3x^2 + 4x - 10 = 0$

3. Consider data represented by the following points: $\{(-2, 0.25), (-1, 1.5), (0, 4), (1, 15), (2, 60)\}$. Determine if the data are best represented by a linear, exponential, or quadratic function. Explain your answer.

4. The equation $2x^2 + 8x + c = 0$ has one real solution. What is the value of c? Explain how you found the value of c.

Assessment Readiness

- Online Homework
- Hints and Help
- Extra Practice

1. A quadratic equation has the solutions –3 and 6. Can the quadratic equation be the given equation?

A. $(2x + 6)(x - 6) = 0$

B. $(6x - 1)(x + 3) = 0$

C. $-3x(x - 6) = 0$

2. Factor and solve each equation. Does the equation have a solution of $x = -5$?

A. $3x^2 + 14x - 5 = 0$

B. $x^2 + 3x - 40 = 0$

C. $x^2 - 3x - 40 = 0$

3. Consider the equation $4x^2 - 20 = 0$. Determine if each statement is True or False.

A. The equation has 2 solutions.

B. A solution of the equation is $-\sqrt{20}$.

C. A solution of the equation is $\sqrt{5}$.

4. Solve $\left(2x + \frac{2}{3}\right)(x + 5) = 0$. Is the given value a solution of the equation?

A. $x = -\frac{1}{3}$

B. $x = -5$

C. $x = \frac{2}{3}$

5. The equation $ax^2 + 12x + c = 0$ has one solution. Can a and c equal each of the following values?

A. $a = 4, c = 9$

B. $a = 9, c = 16$

C. $a = 36, c = 1$

6. The table given has been filled out for the function $g(x)$. The values of $g(x)$ are not shown. Is $g(x)$ a linear or quadratic function? Justify your answer.

x	-2		0		2		4		6
$g(x)$									
First difference	—	-4		-4		-4		-4	
Second difference	—	—	0		0		0		

7. The area of a square table top can be represented by $(9x^2 - 30x + 25)$ ft^2. The perimeter of the table top is 34 feet. What is the value of x? Explain how you solved this problem.

8. Solve $4x^2 + 8x = -3$. Which of the following solution methods did you use: factoring, completing the square, or the quadratic formula? Why? Show your work.

Performance Tasks

★ **9.** Abigail has a rectangular quilt with dimensions 36 inches by 48 inches. She decides to sew a border on the quilt, so that the total area of the quilt is 1900 square inches. What will be the width of the border?

★★10. The table shows the average weight of a particular variety of sheep at various ages.

A. None of the three models—linear, quadratic, or exponential—fits the data exactly. Which of these is the best model for the data? Explain your choice.

B. What would you predict for the weight of a sheep who is 1 year old?

C. Do you think you could use your model to find the weight of a sheep at any age? Why or why not?

Sheep	
Age (mo)	**Weight (lb)**
2	36
4	69
6	99
8	120
10	135

★★★11. Examine the two models that represent annual tuition for two colleges.

A. Describe each model as linear, quadratic, or exponential.

B. Write a function rule for each model.

C. Both models have the same values for 2004. What does this mean?

D. Why do both models have the same value for year 1?

Years After 2004	Tuition at College 1 ($)	Tuition at College 2 ($)
0	2000.00	2000.00
1	2200.00	2200.00
2	2400.00	2420.00
3	2600.00	2662.00
4	2800.00	2928.20

Competitive Diver Franco and Grace are competitive divers. Grace dives from a 20-meter cliff into the water, with an initial upward speed of 3.2 m/s. Franco dives from a springboard that is 10 meters above the water surface with an initial upward speed of 4.2 m/s.

The height in meters of an object projected into the air with an initial vertical velocity of v meters per second and initial height of h_0 can be modeled by $h(t) = -4.9t^2 + vt + h_0$.

a. Write a function $h_{\text{Grace}}(t)$ that models the height of Grace's dive.

b. Write a function $h_{\text{Franco}}(t)$ that models the height of Franco's dive.

c. Use a graphing calculator to both functions on the same screen. Label each function.

d. What are the domain and range of each function in terms of the situation? Explain. Round values to the nearest tenth.

e. Compare the maximum heights and the time that elapses before each diver hits the water.

UNIT 5

Extending Quadratic Equations

MODULE 11
Quadratic Equations and Complex Numbers

MODULE 12
Quadratic Relations and Systems of Equations

MODULE 13
Functions and Inverses

MATH IN CAREERS

Ichthyologist An ichthyologist is a biologist who specializes in the study of fish. Ichthyologists work in a variety of disciplines relating to fish and their environment, including ecology, taxonomy, behavior, and conservation. Ichthyologists might perform tasks such as monitoring water quality, designing and conducting experiments, evaluating data using statistics, and publishing results in scientific journals. Ichthyologists utilize mathematical models and collect and analyze experimental and observational data to help them understand fish and their environment.

If you are interested in a career as an ichthyologist, you should study these mathematical subjects:

- Geometry
- Algebra
- Statistics
- Calculus

Research other careers that require using mathematical models to understand an organism and its environment. Check out the career activity at the end of the unit to find out how **ichthyologists** use math.

Reading Start-Up

Visualize Vocabulary

Use the ✔ words to complete the graphic. Place one word in each of the four sections of the frame.

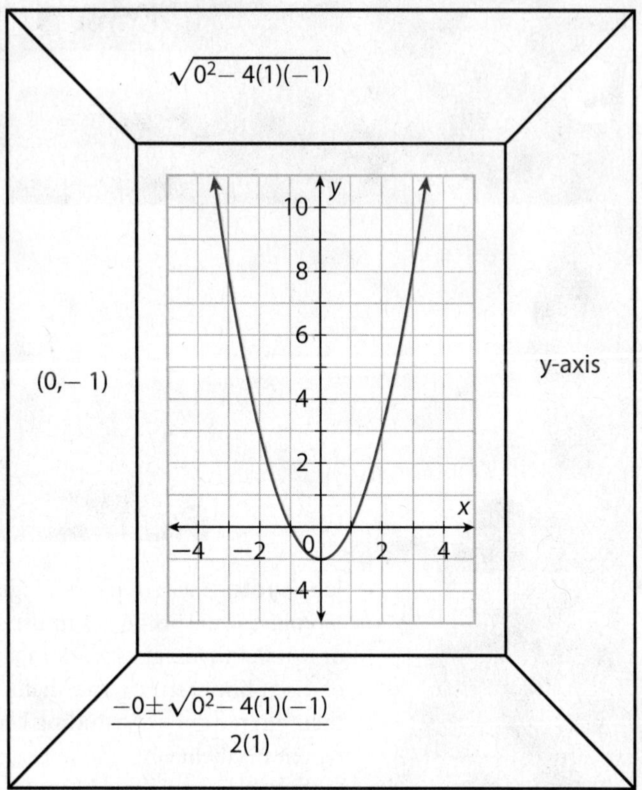

Vocabulary

Review Words

✔ axis of symmetry *(eje de simetría)*
✔ discriminant *(discriminante)*
✔ elimination *(eliminación)*
✔ parabola *(parábola)*
✔ quadratic formula *(fórmula cuadrática)*
✔ substitution *(sustitución)*
✔ vertex *(vértice)*

Preview Words

complex number *(número complejo)*
directrix *(directriz)*
focus *(foco)*
imaginary number *(número imaginario)*
inverse function *(función inversa)*
inverse relation *(relación inversa)*
matrix *(matriz)*
radical function *(función radical)*

Understand Vocabulary

To become familiar with some of the vocabulary terms in the module, consider the following. You may refer to the module, the glossary, or a dictionary.

1. Every point on a parabola is equidistant from a fixed line, called the __?__, and a fixed point, called the __?__.

2. A __?__ is any number that can be written as $a + bi$, where a and b are real numbers and $i = \sqrt{-1}$.

3. A __?__ is a rectangular array of numbers.

Active Reading

Four-Corner Fold Before beginning each lesson, create a four-corner fold to help you organize the characteristics of key concepts. As you study each lesson, define new terms, including an example and a graph or diagram where applicable.

Quadratic Equations and Complex Numbers

MODULE 11

Essential Question: How can you use quadratic equations and complex numbers to solve real-world problems?

REAL WORLD VIDEO
Safe drivers are aware of stopping distances and carefully judge how fast they can travel based on road conditions. Stopping distance is one of many everyday functions that can be modeled with quadratic equations.

MODULE PERFORMANCE TASK PREVIEW

Can You Stop in Time?

When a driver applies the brakes, the car continues to travel for a certain distance until coming to a stop. The stopping distance for a vehicle depends on many factors, including the initial speed of the car and road conditions. How far will a car travel after the brakes are applied? Let's hit the road and find out!

Are YOU Ready?

Complete these exercises to review skills you will need for this module.

- Online Homework
- Hints and Help
- Extra Practice

One-Step Inequalities

Example 1 Solve $-2x \leq 9$ for x.
$x \geq -4.5$

Divide both sides by −2. Because you are dividing by a negative number, flip the inequality symbol.

Solve each inequality.

1. $n - 12 > 9$ **2.** $-3p < -27$ **3.** $\frac{k}{4} \geq -1$

Exponents

Example 2 Simplify $\frac{3a^5b^2}{9a^2b}$.

$$\frac{3a^5b^2}{9a^2b} = \frac{3^1a^5b^2}{3^2a^2b^1} = \frac{a^{5-2}b^{2-1}}{3^{2-1}} = \frac{a^3b}{3}$$

Subtract exponents when dividing.

Simplify each expression.

4. $\frac{16p^2}{2p^4}$ **5.** $5vw^5 \cdot 2v^4$ **6.** $\frac{3x^7y}{6x^4y^2}$

Solving Quadratic Equations by Factoring

Example 3 Factor to solve $x^2 + 2x - 15 = 0$ for x.

Pairs of factors of −15 are:
1 and −15
3 and −5
5 and −3
15 and −1

The pair with the sum of the middle term, 2, is 5 and −3.

$(x + 5)(x - 3) = 0$

Either $x + 5 = 0$ or $x - 3 = 0$, so x-values are −5 and 3.

Factor to solve each equation.

7. $x^2 - 7x + 6 = 0$ **8.** $x^2 - 18x + 81 = 0$ **9.** $x^2 - 16 = 0$

11.1 Solving Quadratic Equations by Taking Square Roots

Resource Locker

Essential Question: What is an imaginary number, and how is it useful in solving quadratic equations?

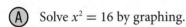

Explore Investigating Ways of Solving Simple Quadratic Equations

There are many ways to solve a quadratic equation. Here, you will use three methods to solve the equation $x^2 = 16$: by graphing, by factoring, and by taking square roots.

(A) Solve $x^2 = 16$ by graphing.

First treat each side of the equation as a function, and graph the two functions, which in this case are $f(x) = x^2$ and $g(x) = 16$, on the same coordinate plane.

Then identify the x-coordinates of the points where two graphs intersect.

$x =$ ____ or $x =$ ____

(B) Solve $x^2 = 16$ by factoring.

This method involves rewriting the equation so that 0 is on one side in order to use the *zero-product property*, which says that the product of two numbers is 0 if and only if at least one of the numbers is 0.

Write the equation.	$x^2 = 16$
Subtract 16 from both sides.	$x^2 -$ ____ $= 0$
Factor the difference of two squares.	$(x +$ ____ $)(x - 4) = 0$
Apply the zero-product property.	$x +$ ____ $= 0$ or $x - 4 = 0$
Solve for x.	$x =$ ____ or $x = 4$

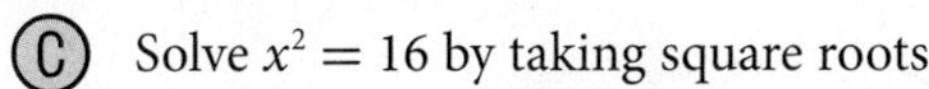

(C) Solve $x^2 = 16$ by taking square roots.

A real number x is a *square root* of a nonnegative real number a provided $x^2 = a$. A square root is written using the radical symbol $\sqrt{}$. Every positive real number a has both a positive square root, written $\sqrt{a}$, and a negative square root, written $-\sqrt{a}$. For instance, the square roots of 9 are $\pm\sqrt{9}$ (read "plus or minus the square root of 9"), or ± 3. The number 0 has only itself as its square root: $\pm\sqrt{0} = 0$.

Write the equation.	$x^2 = 16$
Use the definition of square root.	$x = \pm\sqrt{16}$
Simplify the square roots.	$x =$ ____

Reflect

1. Which of the three methods would you use to solve $x^2 = 5$? Explain, and then use the method to find the solutions.

2. Can the equation $x^2 = -9$ be solved by any of the three methods? Explain.

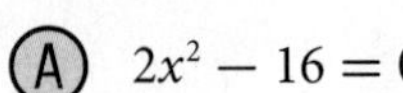

Explain 1 Finding Real Solutions of Simple Quadratic Equations

When solving a quadratic equation of the form $ax^2 + c = 0$ by taking square roots, you may need to use the following properties of square roots to simplify the solutions. (In a later lesson, these properties are stated in a more general form and then proved.)

Property Name	Words	Symbols	Numbers
Product property of square roots	The square root of a product equals the product of the square roots of the factors.	$\sqrt{ab} = \sqrt{a} \cdot \sqrt{b}$ where $a \geq 0$ and $b \geq 0$	$\sqrt{12} = \sqrt{4 \cdot 3}$ $= \sqrt{4} \cdot \sqrt{3}$ $= 2\sqrt{3}$
Quotient property of square roots	The square root of a fraction equals the quotient of the square roots of the numerator and the denominator.	$\sqrt{\frac{a}{b}} = \frac{\sqrt{a}}{\sqrt{b}}$ where $a \geq 0$ and $b > 0$	$\sqrt{\frac{5}{9}} = \frac{\sqrt{5}}{\sqrt{9}}$ $= \frac{\sqrt{5}}{3}$

Using the quotient property of square roots may require an additional step of *rationalizing the denominator* if the denominator is not a rational number. For instance, the quotient property allows you to write $\sqrt{\frac{2}{7}}$ as $\frac{\sqrt{2}}{\sqrt{7}}$, but $\sqrt{7}$ is not a rational number. To rationalize the denominator, multiply $\frac{\sqrt{2}}{\sqrt{7}}$ by $\frac{\sqrt{7}}{\sqrt{7}}$ (a form of 1) and get this result: $\frac{\sqrt{2}}{\sqrt{7}} \cdot \frac{\sqrt{7}}{\sqrt{7}} = \frac{\sqrt{14}}{\sqrt{49}} = \frac{\sqrt{14}}{7}$.

Example 1 **Solve the quadratic equation by taking square roots.**

(A) $2x^2 - 16 = 0$

Add 16 to both sides.	$2x^2 = 16$
Divide both sides by 2.	$x^2 = 8$
Use the definition of square root.	$x = \pm\sqrt{8}$
Use the product property.	$x = \pm\sqrt{4} \cdot \sqrt{2}$
Simplify.	$x = \pm 2\sqrt{2}$

(B) $-5x^2 + 9 = 0$

Subtract 9 from both sides.	$-5x^2 = \boxed{-9}$
Divide both sides by $\boxed{-5}$.	$x^2 = \boxed{\frac{9}{5}}$
Use the definition of square root.	$x = \pm\sqrt{\boxed{\frac{9}{5}}}$
Use the quotient property.	$x = \pm\boxed{\frac{\sqrt{9}}{\sqrt{5}}}$
Simplify the numerator.	$x = \pm\boxed{\frac{3}{\sqrt{5}}}$
Rationalize the denominator.	$x = \pm\boxed{\frac{3\sqrt{5}}{5}}$

Your Turn

Solve the quadratic equation by taking square roots.

3. $x^2 - 24 = 0$

4. $-4x^2 + 13 = 0$

Explain 2 Solving a Real-World Problem Using a Simple Quadratic Equation

Two commonly used quadratic models for falling objects near Earth's surface are the following:

- Distance fallen (in feet) at time t (in seconds): $d(t) = 16t^2$
- Height (in feet) at time t (in seconds): $h(t) = h_0 - 16t^2$ where h_0 is the object's initial height (in feet)

For both models, time is measured from the instant that the object begins to fall. A negative value of t would represent a time before the object began falling, so negative values of t are excluded from the domains of these functions. This means that for any equation of the form $d(t) = c$ or $h(t) = c$ where c is a constant, a negative solution should be rejected.

Example 2 **Write and solve an equation to answer the question. Give the exact answer and, if it's irrational, a decimal approximation (to the nearest tenth of a second).**

(A) If you drop a water balloon, how long does it take to fall 4 feet?

Using the model $d(t) = 16t^2$, solve the equation $d(t) = 4$.

Write the equation.	$16t^2 = 4$
Divide both sides by 16.	$t^2 = \frac{1}{4}$
Use the definition of square root.	$t = \pm\sqrt{\frac{1}{4}}$
Use the quotient property.	$t = \pm\frac{1}{2}$

Reject the negative value of t. The water balloon falls 4 feet in $\frac{1}{2}$ second.

Ⓑ The rooftop of a 5-story building is 50 feet above the ground. How long does it take the water balloon dropped from the rooftop to pass by a third-story window at 24 feet?

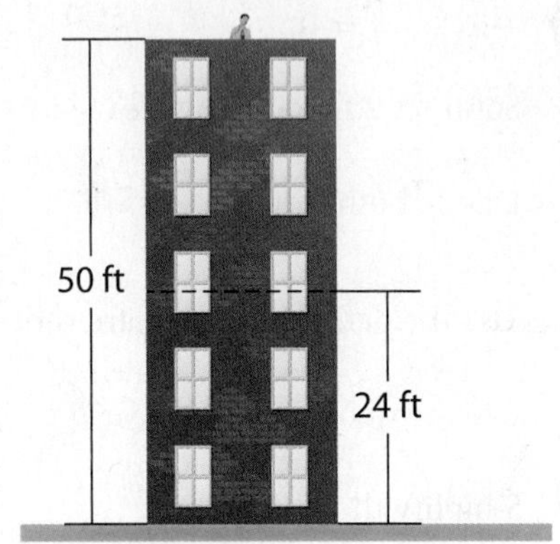

Using the model $h(t) = h_0 - 16t^2$, solve the equation $h(t) = 24$. (When you reach the step at which you divide both sides by -16, leave 16 in the denominator rather than simplifying the fraction because you'll get a rational denominator when you later use the quotient property.)

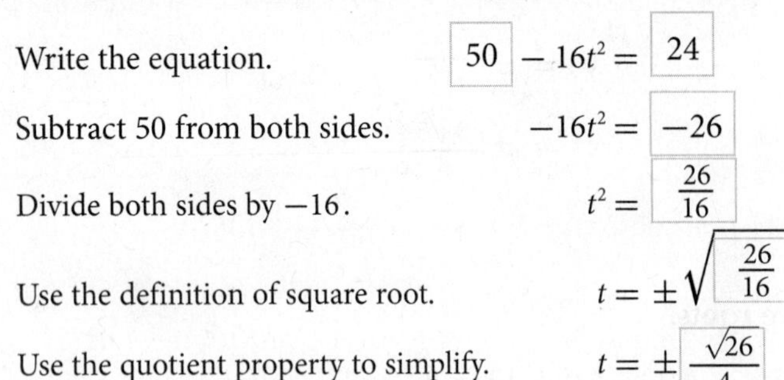

Write the equation. $\boxed{50} - 16t^2 = \boxed{24}$

Subtract 50 from both sides. $-16t^2 = \boxed{-26}$

Divide both sides by -16. $t^2 = \boxed{\frac{26}{16}}$

Use the definition of square root. $t = \pm\sqrt{\boxed{\frac{26}{16}}}$

Use the quotient property to simplify. $t = \pm\boxed{\frac{\sqrt{26}}{4}}$

Reject the negative value of t. The water balloon passes by the third-story window in $\boxed{\frac{\sqrt{26}}{4}} \approx \boxed{1.3}$ seconds.

Reflect

5. Discussion Explain how the model $h(t) = h_0 - 16t^2$ is built from the model $d(t) = 16t^2$.

Your Turn

Write and solve an equation to answer the question. Give the exact answer and, if it's irrational, a decimal approximation (to the nearest tenth of a second).

6. How long does it take the water balloon described in Part B to hit the ground?

7. On the moon, the distance d (in feet) that an object falls in time t (in seconds) is modeled by the function $d(t) = \frac{8}{3}t^2$. Suppose an astronaut on the moon drops a tool. How long does it take the tool to fall 4 feet?

Explain 3 Defining Imaginary Numbers

You know that the quadratic equation $x^2 = 1$ has two real solutions, the equation $x^2 = 0$ has one real solution, and the equation $x^2 = -1$ has no real solutions. By creating a new type of number called *imaginary numbers*, mathematicians allowed for solutions of equations like $x^2 = -1$.

Imaginary numbers are the square roots of negative numbers. These numbers can all be written in the form bi where b is a nonzero real number and i, called the **imaginary unit**, represents $\sqrt{-1}$. Some examples of imaginary numbers are the following:

- $2i$
- $-5i$
- $-\frac{i}{3}$ or $-\frac{1}{3}i$
- $i\sqrt{2}$ (Write the i in front of the radical symbol for clarity.)
- $\frac{i\sqrt{3}}{2}$ or $\frac{\sqrt{3}}{2}i$

Given that $i = \sqrt{-1}$, you can conclude that $i^2 = -1$. This means that the square of any imaginary number is a negative real number. When squaring an imaginary number, use the power of a product property of exponents: $(ab)^m = a^m \cdot b^m$.

Example 3 **Find the square of the imaginary number.**

(A) $5i$

$$(5i)^2 = 5^2 \cdot i^2 = 25(-1) = -25$$

(B) $-i\sqrt{2}$

$$(-i\sqrt{2})^2 = \left(\boxed{-\sqrt{2}}\right)^2 \cdot i^2 = \boxed{2}(-1) = \boxed{-2}$$

Reflect

8. By definition, i is a square root of -1. Does -1 have another square root? Explain.

Your Turn

Find the square of the imaginary number.

9. $-2i$

10. $\frac{\sqrt{3}}{3}i$

Explain 4 Finding Imaginary Solutions of Simple Quadratic Equations

Using imaginary numbers, you can solve simple quadratic equations that do not have real solutions.

Example 4 **Solve the quadratic equation by taking square roots. Allow for imaginary solutions.**

(A) $x^2 + 12 = 0$

Write the equation.	$x^2 + 12 = 0$
Subtract 12 from both sides.	$x^2 = -12$
Use the definition of square root.	$x = \pm\sqrt{-12}$
Use the product property.	$x = \pm\sqrt{(4)(-1)(3)} = \pm 2i\sqrt{3}$

(B) $4x^2 + 11 = 6$

Write the equation.	$4x^2 + 11 = 6$
Subtract 11 from both sides.	$\boxed{4}\,x^2 = \boxed{-5}$
Divide both sides by $\boxed{4}$.	$x^2 = \boxed{-\frac{5}{4}}$
Use the definition of square root.	$x = \pm\sqrt{\boxed{-\frac{5}{4}}}$
Use the qoutient property.	$x = \pm \boxed{\frac{\sqrt{5}}{2}i}$

Your Turn

Solve the quadratic equation by taking square roots. Allow for imaginary solutions.

11. $\frac{1}{4}x^2 + 9 = 0$

12. $-5x^2 + 3 = 10$

Elaborate

13. The quadratic equations $4x^2 + 32 = 0$ and $4x^2 - 32 = 0$ differ only by the sign of the constant term. Without actually solving the equations, what can you say about the relationship between their solutions?

14. What kind of a number is the square of an imaginary number?

15. Why do you reject negative values of t when solving equations based on the models for a falling object near Earth's surface, $d(t) = 16t^2$ for distance fallen and $h(t) = h_0 - 16t^2$ for height during a fall?

16. **Essential Question Check-In** Describe how to find the square roots of a negative number.

☆ Evaluate: Homework and Practice

- Online Homework
- Hints and Help
- Extra Practice

1. Solve the equation $x^2 - 2 = 7$ using the indicated method.
   a. Solve by graphing.
   b. Solve by factoring.
   c. Solve by taking square roots.

2. Solve the equation $2x^2 + 3 = 5$ using the indicated method.
   a. Solve by graphing.
   b. Solve by factoring.
   c. Solve by taking square roots.

Solve the quadratic equation by taking square roots.

3. $4x^2 = 24$

4. $-\frac{x^2}{5} + 15 = 0$

5. $2(5 - 5x^2) = 5$

6. $3x^2 - 8 = 12$

Write and solve an equation to answer the question. Give the exact answer and, if it's irrational, a decimal approximation (to the nearest tenth of a second).

7. A squirrel in a tree drops an acorn. How long does it take the acorn to fall 20 feet?

8. A person washing the windows of an office building drops a squeegee from a height of 60 feet. How long does it take the squeegee to pass by another window washer working at a height of 20 feet?

Geometry **Determine the lengths of the sides of the rectangle using the given area. Give answers both exactly and approximately (to the nearest tenth).**

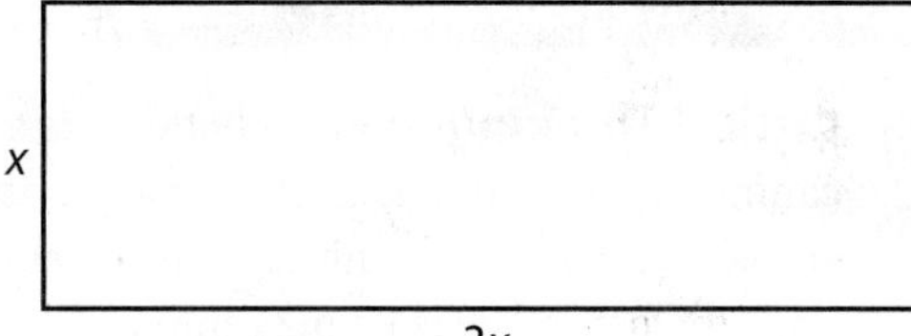

9. The area of the rectangle is 45 cm^2.

10. The area of the rectangle is 54 cm^2.

Find the square of the imaginary number.

11. $3i$

12. $i\sqrt{5}$

13. $-i\frac{\sqrt{2}}{2}$

Determine whether the quadratic equation has real solutions or imaginary solutions by solving the equation.

14. $15x^2 - 10 = 0$

15. $\frac{1}{2}x^2 + 12 = 4$

16. $5(2x^2 - 3) = 4(x^2 - 10)$

Solve the quadratic equation by taking square roots. Allow for imaginary solutions.

17. $x^2 = -81$

18. $x^2 + 64 = 0$

19. $5x^2 - 4 = -8$

20. $7x^2 + 10 = 0$

Geometry **Determine the length of the sides of each square using the given information. Give answers both exactly and approximately (to the nearest tenth).**

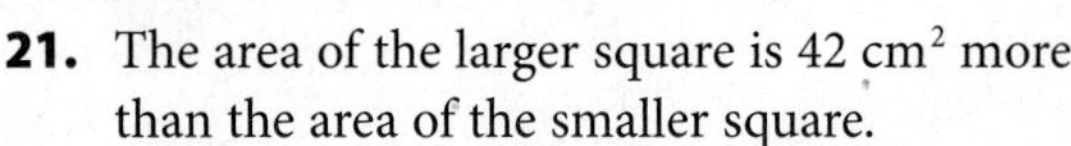

21. The area of the larger square is 42 cm² more than the area of the smaller square.

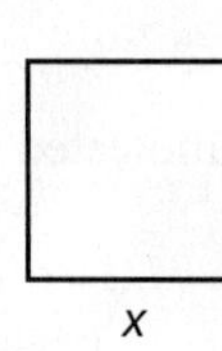

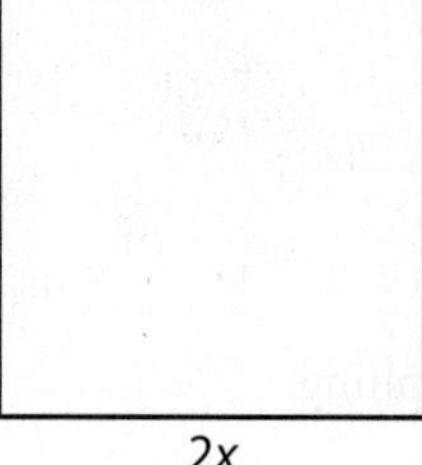

22. If the area of the larger square is decreased by 28 cm², the result is half of the area of the smaller square.

23. Determine whether each of the following numbers is real or imaginary.

a. i

b. A square root of 5

c. $(2i)^2$

d. $(-5)^2$

e. $\sqrt{-3}$

f. $-\sqrt{10}$

H.O.T. Focus on Higher Order Thinking

24. Critical Thinking When a batter hits a baseball, you can model the ball's height using a quadratic function that accounts for the ball's initial vertical velocity. However, once the ball reaches its maximum height, its vertical velocity is momentarily 0 feet per second, and you can use the model $h(t) = h_0 - 16t^2$ to find the ball's height h (in feet) at time t (in seconds) as it falls to the ground.

a. Suppose a fly ball reaches a maximum height of 67 feet and an outfielder catches the ball 3 feet above the ground. How long after the ball begins to descend does the outfielder catch the ball?

b. Can you determine (without writing or solving any equations) the total time the ball was in the air? Explain your reasoning and state any assumptions you make.

25. Represent Real-World Situations The aspect ratio of an image on a screen is the ratio of image width to image height. An HDTV screen shows images with an aspect ratio of 16:9. If the area of an HDTV screen is 864 in^2, what are the dimensions of the screen?

26. Explain the Error Russell wants to calculate the amount of time it takes for a load of dirt to fall from a crane's clamshell bucket at a height of 16 feet to the bottom of a hole that is 32 feet deep. He sets up the following equation and tries to solve it.

$$\begin{aligned} 16 - 16t^2 &= 32 \\ -16t^2 &= 16 \\ t^2 &= -1 \\ t &= \pm\sqrt{-1} \\ t &= \pm i \end{aligned}$$

Does Russell's answer make sense? If not, find and correct Russell's error.

Lesson Performance Task

A suspension bridge uses two thick cables, one on each side of the road, to hold up the road. The cables are suspended between two towers and have a parabolic shape. Smaller vertical cables connect the parabolic cables to the road. The table gives the lengths of the first few vertical cables starting with the shortest one.

Displacement from the Shortest Vertical Cable (m)	Height of Vertical Cable (m)
0	3
1	3.05
2	3.2
3	3.45

Find a quadratic function that describes the height (in meters) of a parabolic cable above the road as a function of the horizontal displacement (in meters) from the cable's lowest point. Use the function to predict the distance between the towers if the parabolic cable reaches a maximum height of 48 m above the road at each tower.

11.2 Complex Numbers

Resource Locker

Essential Question: What is a complex number, and how can you add, subtract, and multiply complex numbers?

Explore Exploring Operations Involving Complex Numbers

In this lesson, you'll learn to perform operations with *complex numbers*, which have a form similar to linear binomials such as $3 + 4x$ and $2 - x$.

(A) Add the binomials $3 + 4x$ and $2 - x$.

Group like terms. $(3 + 4x) + (2 - x) = \left(3 + \square\right) + \left(4x + \square\right)$

Combine like terms. $= \left(\square + \square\right)$

(B) Subtract $2 - x$ from $3 + 4x$.

Rewrite as addition. $(3 + 4x) - (2 - x) = (3 + 4x) + \left(-2 + \square\right)$

Group like terms. $= \left(3 + \square\right) + \left(4x + \square\right)$

Combine like terms. $= \left(\square + \square\right)$

(C) Multiply the binomials $3 + 4x$ and $2 - x$.

Use FOIL. $(3 + 4x)(2 - x) = 6 + (-3x) + \square + \square$

Combine like terms. $= 6 + \square + \square$

Reflect

1. In Step A, you found that $(3 + 4x) + (2 - x) = 5 + 3x$. Suppose $x = i$ (the imaginary unit). What equation do you get?

2. In Step B, you found that $(3 + 4x) + (2 - x) = 1 + 5x$. Suppose $x = i$ (the imaginary unit). What equation do you get?

3. In Step C, you found that $(3 + 4x)(2 - x) = 6 + 5x - 4x^2$. Suppose $x = i$ (the imaginary unit). What equation do you get? How can you further simplify the right side of this equation?

Explain 1 Defining Complex Numbers

A **complex number** is any number that can be written in the form $a + bi$, where a and b are real numbers and $i = \sqrt{-1}$. For a complex number $a + bi$ a is called the *real part* of the number, and b is called the *imaginary part*. (Note that "imaginary part" refers to the real multiplier of i; it does not refer to the imaginary number bi.) The Venn diagram shows some examples of complex numbers.

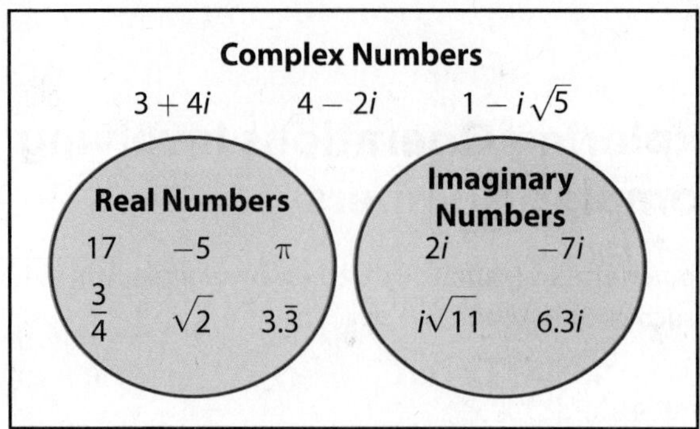

Notice that the set of real numbers is a subset of the set of complex numbers. That's because a real number a can be written in the form $a + 0i$ (whose imaginary part is 0). Likewise, the set of imaginary numbers is also a subset of the set of complex numbers, because an imaginary number bi(where $b \neq 0$) can be written in the form $0 + bi$(whose real part is 0).

Example 1 **Identify the real and imaginary parts of the given number. Then tell which of the following sets the number belongs to: real numbers, imaginary numbers, and complex numbers.**

(A) $9 + 5i$

The real part of $9 + 5i$ is 9, and the imaginary part is 5. Because both the real and imaginary parts of $9 + 5i$ are nonzero, the number belongs only to the set of complex numbers.

(B) $-7i$

The real part of $-7i$ is 0, and the imaginary part is -7. Because the real part is 0, the number belongs to these sets: imaginary numbers and complex numbers.

Your Turn

Identify the real and imaginary parts of the given number. Then tell which of the following sets the number belongs to: real numbers, imaginary numbers, and complex numbers.

4. 11

5. $-1 + i$

Explain 2 Adding and Subtracting Complex Numbers

To add or subtract complex numbers, add or subtract the real parts and the imaginary parts separately.

Example 2 **Add or subtract the complex numbers.**

(A) $(-7 + 2i) + (5 - 11i)$

Group like terms. $(-7 + 2i) + (5 - 11i) = (-7 + 5) + (2i + (-11i))$

Combine like terms. $= -2 + (-9i)$

Write addition as subtraction. $= -2 - 9i$

(B) $(18 + 27i) - (2 + 3i)$

Group like terms. $(18 + 27i) - (2 + 3i) = (18 - \boxed{2}) + (\boxed{27i} - 3i)$

Combine like terms. $= \boxed{16} + \boxed{24}\, i$

Reflect

6. Is the sum $(a + bi) + (a - bi)$ where a and b are real numbers, a real number or an imaginary number? Explain.

Your Turn

Add or subtract the complex numbers.

7. $(17 - 6i) - (9 + 10i)$

8. $(16 + 17i) + (-8 - 12i)$

Explain 3 Multiplying Complex Numbers

To multiply two complex numbers, use the distributive property to multiply each part of one number by each part of the other. Use the fact that $i^2 = -1$ to simplify the result.

Example 3 **Multiply the complex numbers.**

(A) $(4 + 9i)(6 - 2i)$

Use the distributive property. $(4 + 9i)(6 - 2i) = 24 - 8i + 54i - 18i^2$

Substitute -1 for i^2. $= 24 - 8i + 54i - 18(-1)$

Combine like terms. $= 42 + 46i$

Ⓑ $(-3 + 12i)(7 + 4i)$

Use the distributive property. $(-3 + 12i)(7 + 4i) = \boxed{-21} - 12i + \boxed{84i} + 48i^2$

Substitute -1 for i^2. $= \boxed{-21} - 12i + \boxed{84i} + 48(-1)$

Combine like terms. $= \boxed{-69} + \boxed{72}\, i$

Reflect

9. Is the product of $(a + bi)(a - bi)$, where a and b are real numbers, a real number or an imaginary number? Explain.

Your Turn

Multiply the complex numbers.

10. $(6 - 5i)(3 - 10i)$

11. $(8 + 15i)(11 + i)$

Explain 4 Solving a Real-World Problem Using Complex Numbers

Electrical engineers use complex numbers when analyzing electric circuits. An electric circuit can contain three types of components: resistors, inductors, and capacitors. As shown in the table, each type of component has a different symbol in a circuit diagram, and each is represented by a different type of complex number based on the phase angle of the current passing through it.

Circuit Component	Symbol in Circuit Diagram	Phase Angle	Representation as a Complex Number
Resistor	(resistor symbol)	0°	A real number a
Inductor	(inductor symbol)	90°	An imaginary number bi where $b > 0$
Capacitor	(capacitor symbol)	−90°	An imaginary number bi where $b < 0$

A diagram of an alternating current (AC) electric circuit is shown along with the *impedance* (measured in ohms, Ω) of each component in the circuit. An AC power source, which is shown on the left in the diagram and labeled 120 V (for volts), causes electrons to flow through the circuit. Impedance is a measure of each component's opposition to the electron flow.

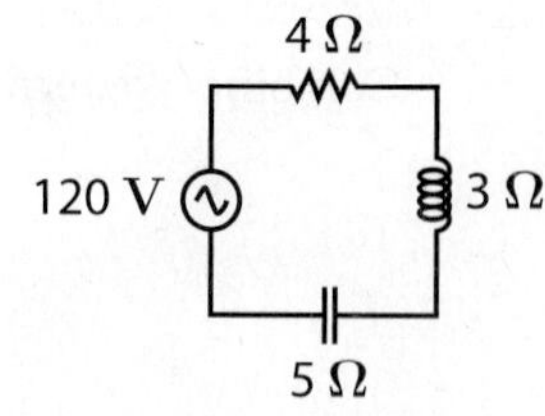

Example 4 **Use the diagram of the electric circuit to answer the following questions.**

(A) The total impedance in the circuit is the sum of the impedances for the individual components. What is the total impedance for the given circuit?

Write the impedance for each component as a complex number.

- Impedance for the resistor: 4
- Impedance for the inductor: $3i$
- Impedance for the capacitor: $-5i$

Then find the sum of the impedances.

Total impedance $= 4 + 3i + (-5i) = 4 - 2i$

(B) Ohm's law for AC electric circuits says that the voltage V (measured in volts) is the product of the current I (measured in amps) and the impedance Z (measured in ohms): $V = I \cdot Z$. For the given circuit, the current I is $24 + 12i$ amps. What is the voltage V for each component in the circuit?

Use Ohm's law, $V = I \cdot Z$, to find the voltage for each component. Remember that Z is the impedance from Part A.

Voltage for the resistor $= I \cdot Z = (24 + 12i)\left(\boxed{4}\right) = 96 + \boxed{48}\, i$

Voltage for the inductor $= I \cdot Z = (24 + 12i)\left(\boxed{3i}\right) = -36 + \boxed{72}\, i$

Voltage for the capacitor $= I \cdot Z = (24 + 12i)\left(\boxed{-5i}\right) = \boxed{60} - 120i$

Reflect

12. Find the sum of the voltages for the three components in Part B. What do you notice?

Your Turn

13. Suppose the circuit analyzed in Example 4 has a second resistor with an impedance of 2 Ω added to it. Find the total impedance. Given that the circuit now has a current of $18 + 6i$ amps, also find the voltage for each component in the circuit.

Elaborate

14. What kind of number is the sum, difference, or product of two complex numbers?

15. When is the sum of two complex numbers a real number? When is the sum of two complex numbers an imaginary number?

16. Discussion What are the similarities and differences between multiplying two complex numbers and multiplying two binomial linear expressions in the same variable?

17. Essential Question Check-In How do you add and subtract complex numbers?

- Online Homework
- Hints and Help
- Extra Practice

Evaluate: Homework and Practice

1. Find the sum of the binomials $3 + 2x$ and $4 - 5x$. Explain how you can use the result to find the sum of the complex numbers $3 + 2i$ and $4 - 5i$.

2. Find the product of the binomials $1 - 3x$ and $2 + x$. Explain how you can use the result to find the product of the complex numbers $1 - 3i$ and $2 + i$.

Identify the real and imaginary parts of the given number. Then tell which of the following sets the number belongs to: real numbers, imaginary numbers, and complex numbers.

3. $5 + i$

4. $7 - 6i$

5. 25

6. $i\sqrt{21}$

Add.

7. $(3 + 4i) + (7 + 11i)$

8. $(2 + 3i) + (6 - 5i)$

9. $(-1 - i) + (-10 + 3i)$

10. $(-9 - 7i) + (6 + 5i)$

Subtract.

11. $(2 + 3i) - (7 + 6i)$

12. $(4 + 5i) - (14 - i)$

13. $(-8 - 3i) - (-9 - 5i)$

14. $(5 + 2i) - (5 - 2i)$

Multiply.

15. $(2 + 3i)(3 + 5i)$

16. $(7 + i)(6 - 9i)$

17. $(-4 + 11i)(-5 - 8i)$

18. $(4 - i)(4 + i)$

Use the diagram of the electric circuit and the given current to find the total impedance for the circuit and the voltage for each component.

19.

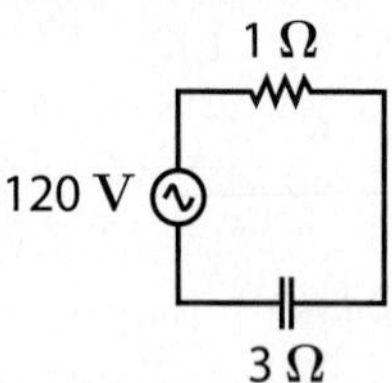

The circuit has a current of $12 + 36i$ amps.

20.

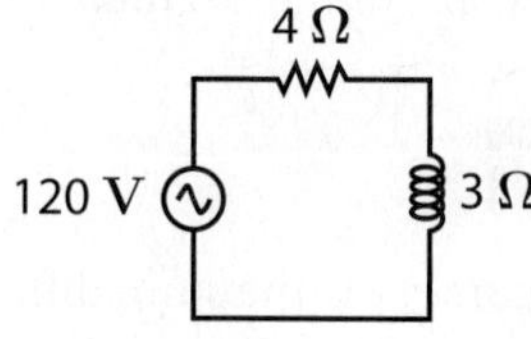

The circuit has a current of $19.2 - 14.4i$ amps.

21.

6 Ω

120 V

2 Ω

10 Ω

The circuit has a current of $7.2 + 9.6i$ amps.

22.

7 Ω

120 V

3 Ω

4 Ω

The circuit has a current of $16.8 + 2.4i$ amps.

23. Match each product on the right with the corresponding expression on the left.

A. $(3 - 5i)(3 + 5i)$ **a.** ___?___ $-16 + 30i$

B. $(3 + 5i)(3 + 5i)$ **b.** ___?___ -34

C. $(-3 - 5i)(3 + 5i)$ **c.** ___?___ 34

D. $(3 - 5i)(-3 - 5i)$ **d.** ___?___ $16 - 30i$

H.O.T. Focus on Higher Order Thinking

41. Explain the Error While attempting to multiply the expression $(2 - 3i)(3 + 2i)$, a student made a mistake. Explain and correct the error.

$$\begin{aligned}(2 - 3i)(3 + 2i) &= 6 - 9i + 4i - 6i^2 \\ &= 6 - 9(-1) + 4(-1) - 6(1) \\ &= 6 + 9 - 4 - 6 \\ &= 5\end{aligned}$$

42. Critical Thinking Show that $\sqrt{3} + i\sqrt{3}$ and $-\sqrt{3} - i\sqrt{3}$ are the square roots of $6i$.

43. Justify Reasoning What type of number is the product of two complex numbers that differ only in the sign of their imaginary parts? Prove your conjecture.

Lesson Performance Task

Just as real numbers can be graphed on a real number line, complex numbers can be graphed on a complex *plane*, which has a horizontal real axis and a vertical imaginary axis. When a set that involves complex numbers is graphed on a complex plane, the result can be an elaborate self-similar figure called a *fractal.* Such a set is called a Julia set.

Consider Julia sets having the quadratic recursive rule $f(n + 1) = (f(n))^2 + c$ for some complex number $f(0)$ and some complex constant c. For a given value of c, a complex number $f(0)$ either belongs or doesn't belong to the "'filled-in" Julia set corresponding to c depending on what happens with the sequence of numbers generated by the recursive rule.

a. Letting $c = i$, generate the first few numbers in the sequence defined by $f(0) = 1$ and $f(n + 1) = (f(n))^2 + i$. Copy the table to record your results.

n	$f(n)$	$f(n+1) = (f(n))^2 + i$
0	$f(0) = 1$	$f(1) = (f(0))^2 + i = (1)^2 + i = 1 + i$
1	$f(1) = 1 + i$	$f(2) = (f(1))^2 + i = (1 + i)^2 + i =$ ▢
2	$f(2) =$ ▢	$f(3) = (f(2))^2 + i = (\ ▢\ )^2 + i =$ ▢
3	$f(3) =$ ▢	$f(4) = (f(3))^2 + i = (\ ▢\ )^2 + i =$ ▢

b. The *magnitude* of a complex number $a + bi$ is the real number $\sqrt{a^2 + b^2}$. In the complex plane, the magnitude of a complex number is the number's distance from the origin. If the magnitudes of the numbers in the sequence generated by a Julia set's recursive rule, where $f(0)$ is the starting value, remain bounded, then $f(0)$ belongs to the "filled-in" Julia set. If the magnitudes increase without bound, then $f(0)$ doesn't belong to the "filled-in" Julia set. Based on your completed table for $f(0) = 1$, would you say that the number belongs to the "filled-in" Julia set corresponding to $c = i$? Explain.

c. Would you say that $f(0) = i$ belongs to the "filled-in" Julia set corresponding to $c = i$? Explain.

11.3 Finding Complex Solutions of Quadratic Equations

Essential Question: How can you find the complex solutions of any quadratic equation?

Explore Investigating Real Solutions of Quadratic Equations

(A) Complete the table.

$ax^2 + bx + c = 0$	$ax^2 + bx = -c$	$f(x) = ax^2 + bx$	$g(x) = -c$
$2x^2 + 4x + 1 = 0$			
$2x^2 + 4x + 2 = 0$			
$2x^2 + 4x + 3 = 0$			

(B) Copy the graph of $f(x) = 2x^2 + 4x$ shown. Graph each $g(x)$. Complete the table.

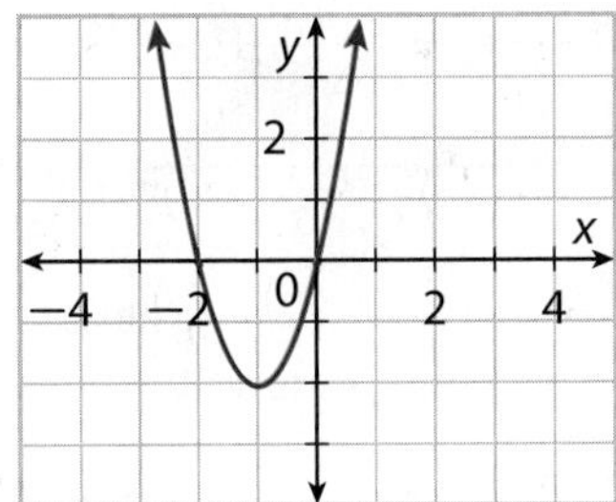

Equation	Number of Real Solutions
$2x^2 + 4x + 1 = 0$	
$2x^2 + 4x + 2 = 0$	
$2x^2 + 4x + 3 = 0$	

(C) Repeat Steps A and B when $f(x) = -2x^2 + 4x$.

$ax^2 + bx + c = 0$	$ax^2 + bx = -c$	$f(x) = ax^2 + bx$	$g(x) = -c$
$-2x^2 + 4x - 1 = 0$			
$-2x^2 + 4x - 2 = 0$			
$-2x^2 + 4x - 3 = 0$			

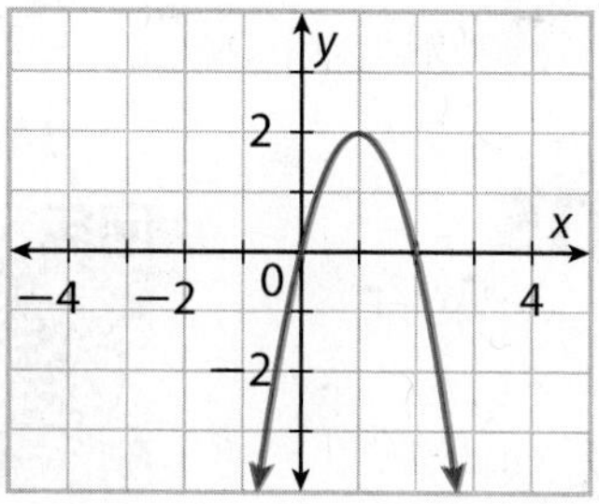

Equation	Number of Real Solutions
$-2x^2 + 4x - 1 = 0$	
$-2x^2 + 4x - 2 = 0$	
$-2x^2 + 4x - 3 = 0$	

Reflect

1. Look back at Steps A and B. Notice that the minimum value of $f(x)$ in Steps A and B is -2. Complete the table by identifying how many real solutions the equation $f(x) = g(x)$ has for the given values of $g(x)$.

Value of $g(x)$	Number of Real Solutions of $f(x) = g(x)$
$g(x) = -2$	
$g(x) > -2$	
$g(x) < -2$	

2. Look back at Step C. Notice that the maximum value of $f(x)$ in Step C is 2. Complete the table by identifying how many real solutions the equation $f(x) = g(x)$ has for the given values of $g(x)$.

Value of $g(x)$	Number of Real Solutions of $f(x) = g(x)$
$g(x) = 2$	
$g(x) > 2$	
$g(x) < 2$	

3. You can generalize Reflect 1: For $f(x) = ax^2 + bx$ where $a > 0$, $f(x) = g(x)$ where $g(x) = -c$ has real solutions when $g(x)$ is greater than or equal to the minimum value of $f(x)$. The minimum value of $f(x)$ is

$$f\left(-\frac{b}{2a}\right) = a\left(-\frac{b}{2a}\right)^2 + b\left(-\frac{b}{2a}\right) = a\left(\frac{b^2}{4a^2}\right) - \frac{b^2}{2a} = \frac{b^2}{4a} - \frac{b^2}{2a} = \frac{b^2}{4a} - \frac{2b^2}{4a} = -\frac{b^2}{4a}.$$

So, $f(x) = g(x)$ has real solutions when $g(x) \geq -\frac{b^2}{4a}$. Since $g(x) = -c$,

Substitute $-c$ for $g(x)$. $\qquad -c \geq -\frac{b^2}{4a}$

Add $\frac{b^2}{4a}$ to both sides. $\qquad \frac{b^2}{4a} - c \geq 0$

Multiply both sides by $4a$, which is positive. $\qquad b^2 - 4ac \geq 0$

In other words, the equation $ax^2 + bx + c = 0$ where $a > 0$ has real solutions when $b^2 - 4ac \geq 0$.

Generalize the results of Reflect 2 in a similar way. What do you notice?

Explain 1 Finding Complex Solutions by Completing the Square

Recall that completing the square for the expression $x^2 + bx$ requires adding $\left(\frac{b}{2}\right)^2$ to it, resulting in the perfect square trinomial $x^2 + bx + \left(\frac{b}{2}\right)^2$, which you can factor as $\left(x + \frac{b}{2}\right)^2$. Don't forget that when $x^2 + bx$ appears on one side of an equation, adding $\left(\frac{b}{2}\right)^2$ to it requires adding $\left(\frac{b}{2}\right)^2$ to the other side as well.

Example 1 **Solve the equation by completing the square. State whether the solutions are real or non-real.**

(A) $3x^2 + 9x - 6 = 0$

1. Write the equation in the form $x^2 + bx = c$.

$$3x^2 + 9x - 6 = 0$$
$$3x^2 + 9x = 6$$
$$x^2 + 3x = 2$$

2. Identify b and $\left(\frac{b}{2}\right)^2$.

$$b = 3$$
$$\left(\frac{b}{2}\right)^2 = \left(\frac{3}{2}\right)^2 = \frac{9}{4}$$

3. Add $\left(\frac{b}{2}\right)^2$ to both sides of the equation.

$$x^2 + 3x + \frac{9}{4} = 2 + \frac{9}{4}$$

4. Solve for x.

$$\left(x + \frac{3}{2}\right)^2 = 2 + \frac{9}{4}$$
$$\left(x + \frac{3}{2}\right)^2 = \frac{17}{4}$$
$$x + \frac{3}{2} = \pm\sqrt{\frac{17}{4}}$$
$$x + \frac{3}{2} = \pm\frac{\sqrt{17}}{2}$$
$$x = -\frac{3}{2} \pm \frac{\sqrt{17}}{2}$$
$$x = \frac{-3 \pm \sqrt{17}}{2}$$

There are two real solutions: $\frac{-3 + \sqrt{17}}{2}$ and $\frac{-3 - \sqrt{17}}{2}$.

(B) $x^2 - 2x + 7 = 0$

1. Write the equation in the form $x^2 + bx = c$.

$$x^2 - 2x = -7$$

2. Identify b and $\left(\frac{b}{2}\right)^2$.

$$b = \boxed{-2}$$
$$\left(\frac{b}{2}\right)^2 = \left(\frac{\boxed{-2}}{2}\right)^2 = \boxed{1}$$

3. Add $\left(\frac{b}{2}\right)^2$ to both sides.

$$x^2 - 2x + \boxed{1} = -7 + \boxed{1}$$

4. Solve for x.

$$x^2 + 2x \boxed{1} = -7 + \boxed{1}$$
$$\left(x - \boxed{1}\right)^2 = \boxed{-6}$$
$$x - \boxed{1} = \pm\sqrt{\boxed{-6}}$$
$$x = 1 \pm \sqrt{\boxed{-6}}$$

There are two non-real solutions: $1 + i\sqrt{6}$ and $1 - i\sqrt{6}$.

Reflect

4. How many complex solutions do the equations in Parts A and B have? Explain.

Your Turn

Solve the equation by completing the square. State whether the solutions are real or non-real.

5. $x^2 + 8x + 17 = 0$

6. $x^2 + 10x - 7 = 0$

Explain 2 Identifying Whether Solutions Are Real or Non-real

By completing the square for the general quadratic equation $ax^2 + bx + c = 0$, you can obtain the *quadratic formula*, $x = \frac{-b \pm \sqrt{b^2 - 4ac}}{2a}$, which gives the solutions of the general quadratic equation. In the quadratic formula, the expression under the radical sign, $b^2 - 4ac$, is called the *discriminant,* and its value determines whether the solutions of the quadratic equation are real or non-real.

Value of Discriminant	Number and Type of Solutions
$b^2 - 4ac > 0$	Two real solutions
$b^2 - 4ac = 0$	One real solution
$b^2 - 4ac < 0$	Two non-real solutions

Example 2 **Answer the question by writing an equation and determining whether the solutions of the equation are real or non-real.**

Ⓐ A ball is thrown in the air with an initial vertical velocity of 14 m/s from an initial height of 2 m. The ball's height h (in meters) at time t (in seconds) can be modeled by the quadratic function $h(t) = -4.9t^2 + 14t + 2$. Does the ball reach a height of 12 m?

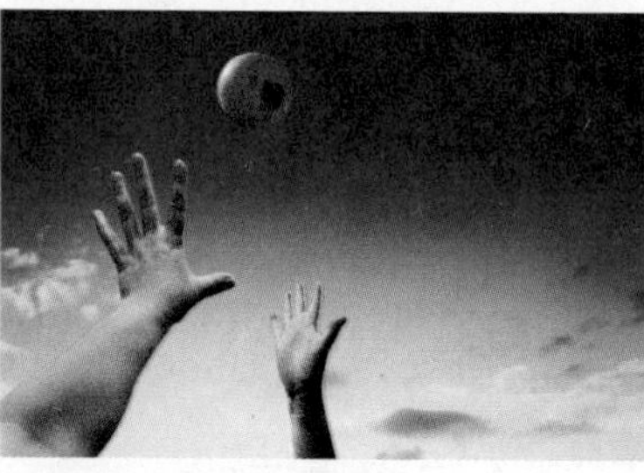

Set $h(t)$ equal to 12. $\quad -4.9t^2 + 14t + 2 = 12$

Subtract 12 from both sides. $\quad -4.9t^2 + 14t + 10 = 0$

Find the value of the discriminant. $\quad 14^2 - 4(-4.9)(-10) = 196 - 196 = 0$

Because the discriminant is zero, the equation as one real solution, so the ballw does reach a height of 12 m.

(B) A person wants to create a vegetable garden and keep the rabbits out by enclosing it with 100 feet of fencing. The area of the garden is given by the function $A(w) = w(50 - w)$ where w is the width (in feet) of the garden. Can the garden have an area of 700 ft^2?

Set $A(w)$ equal to 700. $\qquad w(50 - w) = \boxed{700}$

Multiply on the left side. $\qquad 50w - w^2 = \boxed{700}$

Subtract 700 from both sides. $\qquad -w^2 + 50w - \boxed{700} = 0$

Find the value of the discriminant.

Because the discriminant is negative, the equation has two non-real solutions, so the garden cannot have an area of 700 ft^2.

Your Turn

Answer the question by writing an equation and determining if the solutions are real or non-real.

7. A hobbyist is making a toy sailboat. For the triangular sail, she wants the height h (in inches) to be twice the length of the base b (in inches). Can the area of the sail be 10 in^2?

Explain 3 Finding Complex Solutions Using the Quadratic Formula

When using the quadratic formula to solve a quadratic equation, be sure the equation is in the form $ax^2 + bx + c = 0$.

Example 3 **Solve the equation using the quadratic formula. Check a solution by substitution.**

(A) $-5x^2 - 2x - 8 = 0$

Write the quadratic formula. $\qquad x = \dfrac{-b \pm \sqrt{b^2 - 4ac}}{2a}$

Substitute values. $\qquad = \dfrac{-(-2) \pm \sqrt{(-2)^2 - 4(-5)(-8)}}{2(-5)}$

Simplify. $\qquad = \dfrac{2 \pm \sqrt{-156}}{-10} = \dfrac{1 \pm i\sqrt{39}}{-5}$

So, the two solutions are $-\dfrac{1}{5} - \dfrac{i\sqrt{39}}{5}$ and $-\dfrac{1}{5} + \dfrac{i\sqrt{39}}{5}$.

Check by substituting one of the values.

Substitute. $-5\left(-\frac{1}{5} - \frac{i\sqrt{39}}{5}\right)^2 - 2\left(-\frac{1}{5} - \frac{i\sqrt{39}}{5}\right) - 8 \stackrel{?}{=} 0$

Square. $-5\left(\frac{1}{25} + \frac{2i\sqrt{39}}{25} - \frac{39}{25}\right) - 2\left(-\frac{1}{5} - \frac{i\sqrt{39}}{5}\right) - 8 \stackrel{?}{=} 0$

Distribute. $-\frac{1}{5} - \frac{2i\sqrt{39}}{5} + \frac{39}{5} + \frac{2}{5} + \frac{2i\sqrt{39}}{5} - 8 \stackrel{?}{=} 0$

Simplify. $\frac{40}{5} - 8 \stackrel{?}{=} 0$

$0 = 0$

(B) $7x^2 + 2x + 3 = -1$

Write the equation with 0 on one side. $7x^2 + 2x + \boxed{4} = 0$

Write the quadratic formula. $x = \frac{-b \pm \sqrt{b^2 - 4ac}}{2a}$

Substitute values. $= \frac{-\boxed{2} \pm \sqrt{\left(\boxed{2}\right)^2 - 4\left(\boxed{7}\right)\left(\boxed{4}\right)}}{2\left(\boxed{7}\right)}$

Simplify. $= \frac{-\boxed{2} \pm \sqrt{-\boxed{108}}}{14}$

$= \frac{-\boxed{2} \pm \boxed{6}\, i\sqrt{\boxed{3}}}{14} = \frac{-\boxed{1} \pm \boxed{3}\, i\sqrt{\boxed{3}}}{7}$

So, the two solutions are $-\frac{1}{7} + \frac{3i\sqrt{3}}{7}$ and $-\frac{1}{7} - \frac{3i\sqrt{3}}{7}$.

Check by substituting one of the values.

Substitute. $7\left(-\frac{1}{7} + \frac{3i\sqrt{3}}{7}\right)^2 + 2\left(-\frac{1}{7} + \frac{3i\sqrt{3}}{7}\right)^2 + 4 \stackrel{?}{=} 0$

Square. $7\left(\frac{1}{49} - \frac{6i\sqrt{3}}{49} - \frac{27}{49}\right)^2 + 2\left(-\frac{1}{7} + \frac{3i\sqrt{3}}{7}\right)^2 + 4 \stackrel{?}{=} 0$

Distribute. $\frac{1}{7} - \frac{6i\sqrt{3}}{7} - \frac{27}{7} - \frac{2}{7} + \frac{6i\sqrt{3}}{7} + 4 \stackrel{?}{=} 0$

Simplify. $-\frac{28}{7} + 4 \stackrel{?}{=} 0$

$0 = 0$

Your Turn

Solve the equation using the quadratic formula. Check a solution by substitution.

8. $6x^2 - 5x - 4 = 0$

9. $x^2 + 8x + 12 = 2x$

Elaborate

10. Discussion Suppose that the quadratic equation $ax^2 + bx + c = 0$ has $p + qi$ where $q \neq 0$ as one of its solutions. What must the other solution be? How do you know?

11. Discussion You know that the graph of the quadratic function $f(x) = ax^2 + bx + c$ has the vertical line $x = -\frac{b}{2a}$ as its axis of symmetry. If the graph of $f(x)$ crosses the x-axis, where do the x-intercepts occur relative to the axis of symmetry? Explain.

12. Essential Question Check-In Why is using the quadratic formula to solve a quadratic equation easier than completing the square?

Evaluate: Homework and Practice

- Online Homework
- Hints and Help
- Extra Practice

1. The graph of $f(x) = x^2 + 6x$ is shown. Use the graph to determine how many real solutions the following equations have: $x^2 + 6x + 6 = 0$, $x^2 + 6x + 9 = 0$, and $x^2 + 6x + 12 = 0$. Explain.

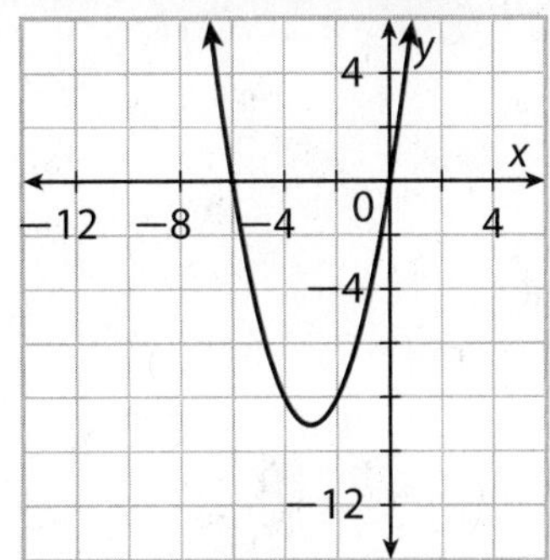

2. The graph of $f(x) = -\frac{1}{2}x^2 + 3x$ is shown. Use the graph to determine how many real solutions the following equations have: $-\frac{1}{2}x^2 + 3x - 3 = 0$, $-\frac{1}{2}x^2 + 3x - \frac{9}{2} = 0$, and $-\frac{1}{2}x^2 + 3x - 6 = 0$. Explain.

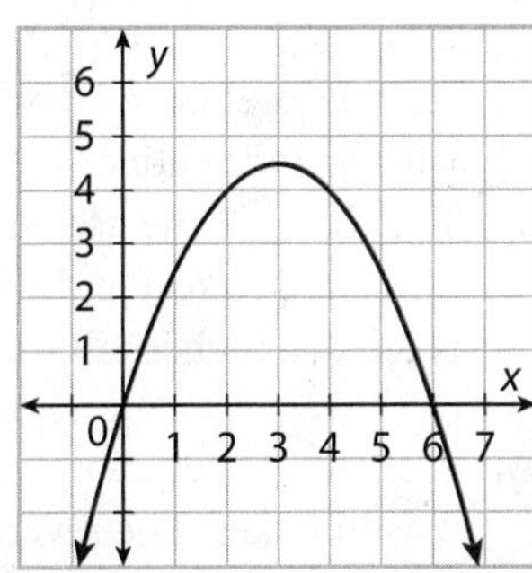

Solve the equation by completing the square. State whether the solutions are real or non-real.

3. $x^2 + 4x + 1 = 0$

4. $x^2 + 2x + 8 = 0$

5. $x^2 - 5x = -20$

6. $5x^2 - 6x = 8$

7. $7x^2 + 13x = 5$

8. $-x^2 - 6x - 11 = 0$

Without solving the equation, state the number of solutions and whether they are real or non-real.

9. $-16x^2 + 4x + 13 = 0$

10. $7x^2 - 11x + 10 = 0$

11. $-x^2 - \frac{2}{5}x = 1$

12. $4x^2 + 9 = 12x$

Answer the question by writing an equation and determining whether the solutions of the equation are real or non-real.

13. A gardener has 140 feet of fencing to put around a rectangular vegetable garden. The function $A(w) = 70w - w^2$ gives the garden's area A (in square feet) for any width w (in feet). Does the gardener have enough fencing for the area of the garden to be 1300 ft^2?

14. A golf ball is hit with an initial vertical velocity of 64 ft/s. The function $h(t) = -16t^2 + 64t$ models the height h (in feet) of the golf ball at time t (in seconds). Does the golf ball reach a height of 60 ft?

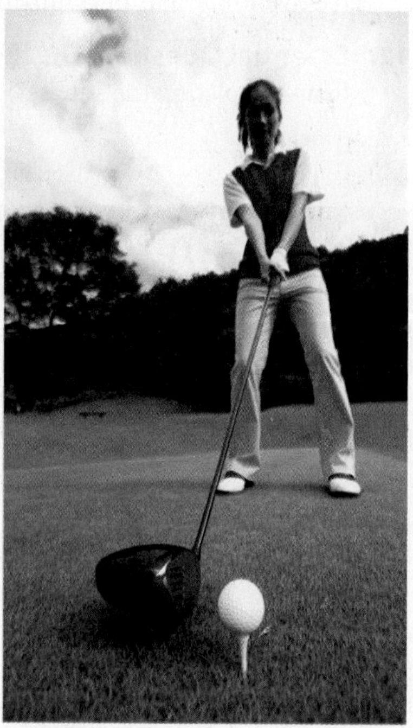

15. As a decoration for a school dance, the student council creates a parabolic arch with balloons attached to it for students to walk through as they enter the dance. The shape of the arch is modeled by the equation $y = x(5 - x)$, where x and y are measured in feet and where the origin is at one end of the arch. Can a student who is 6 feet 6 inches tall walk through the arch without ducking?

16. A small theater company currently has 200 subscribers who each pay \$120 for a season ticket. The revenue from season-ticket subscriptions is \$24,000. Market research indicates that for each \$10 increase in the cost of a season ticket, the theater company will lose 10 subscribers. A model for the projected revenue R (in dollars) from season-ticket subscriptions is $R(p) = (120 + 10p)(200 - 10p)$, where p is the number of \$10 price increases. According to this model, is it possible for the theater company to generate \$25,600 in revenue by increasing the price of a season ticket?

Solve the equation using the quadratic formula. Check a solution by substitution.

17. $x^2 - 8x + 27 = 0$

18. $x^2 - 30x + 50 = 0$

19. $x + 3 = x^2$

20. $2x^2 + 7 = 4x$

21. Copy the table. Place an X in the appropriate column of the table to classify each equation by the number and type of its solutions. Leave the remaining cells of your table blank.

Equation	Two Real Solutions	One Real Solution	Two Non-Real Solutions
$x^2 - 3x + 1 = 0$			
$x^2 - 2x + 1 = 0$			
$x^2 - x + 1 = 0$			
$x^2 + 1 = 0$			
$x^2 + x + 1 = 0$			
$x^2 + 2x + 1 = 0$			
$x^2 + 3x + 1 = 0$			

H.O.T. Focus on Higher Order Thinking

22. Explain the Error A student used the method of completing the square to solve the equation $-x^2 + 2x - 3 = 0$. Describe and correct the error.

$$-x^2 + 2x - 3 = 0$$

$$-x^2 + 2x = 3$$

$$-x^2 + 2x + 1 = 3 + 1$$

$$(x + 1)^2 = 4$$

$$x + 1 = \pm\sqrt{4}$$

$$x + 1 = \pm 2$$

$$x = -1 \pm 2$$

So, the two solutions are $-1 + 2 = 1$ and $-1 - 2 = -3$.

23. Make a Conjecture Describe the values of c for which the equation $x^2 + 8x + c = 0$ has two real solutions, one real solution, and two non-real solutions.

24. Analyze Relationships When you rewrite $y = ax^2 + bx + c$ in vertex form by completing the square, you obtain these coordinates for the vertex: $\left(-\frac{b}{2a}, c - \frac{b^2}{4a}\right)$. Suppose the vertex of the graph of $y = ax^2 + bx + c$ is located on the x-axis. Explain how the coordinates of the vertex and the quadratic formula are in agreement in this situation.

Lesson Performance Task

Matt and his friends are enjoying an afternoon at a baseball game. A batter hits a towering home run, and Matt shouts, "Wow, that must have been 110 feet high!" The ball was 4 feet off the ground when the batter hit it, and the ball came off the bat traveling vertically at 80 feet per second.

a. Model the ball's height h (in feet) at time t (in seconds) using the projectile motion model $h(t) = -16t^2 + v_0t + h$ where v_0 is the projectile's initial vertical velocity (in feet per second) and h_0 is the projectile's initial height (in feet). Use the model to write an equation based on Matt's claim, and then determine whether Matt's claim is correct.

b. Did the ball reach of a height of 100 feet? Explain.

c. Let h_{max} be the ball's maximum height. By setting the projectile motion model equal to h_{max}, show how you can find h_{max} using the discriminant of the quadratic formula.

d. Find the time at which the ball reached its maximum height.

STUDY GUIDE REVIEW

Quadratic Equations and Complex Numbers

MODULE 11

Essential Question: How can you use quadratic equations and complex numbers to solve real-world problems?

Key Vocabulary
complex number
(número complejo)
imaginary number
(número imaginario)
imaginary unit
(unidad imaginaria)
pure imaginary number
(número imaginario puro)

KEY EXAMPLE *(Lessons 11.1, 11.2)*

Take square roots to solve the quadratic equations.

$3x^2 - 27 = 9$

$3x^2 = 36$ Add 27 to both sides.

$x^2 = 12$ Divide both sides by 3.

$x = \pm\sqrt{12}$ Square root

$x = \pm\sqrt{4} \cdot \sqrt{3}$ Product Property

$x = \pm 2\sqrt{3}$ Simplify.

$x^2 + 20 = 0$

$x^2 = -20$ Subtract 20 on both sides.

$x = \pm\sqrt{-20}$ Square root

$x = \pm\sqrt{(-1)(5)(4)}$ Product Property

$x = \pm 2i\sqrt{5}$ Simplify.

KEY EXAMPLE *(Lesson 11.3)*

Solve $2x^2 + 4x - 8 = 0$ by completing the square.

$2x^2 + 4x = 8$ Write the equation in the form $x^2 + bx = c$.

$x^2 + 2x = 4$ Divide both sides by 2.

$x^2 + 2x + 1 = 4 + 1$ Add $\left(\frac{b}{2}\right)^2$ to both sides of the equation.

$(x + 1)^2 = 5$ Solve for x.

$x + 1 = \pm\sqrt{5}$

$x = -1 \pm \sqrt{5}$

EXERCISES

Solve using the method stated. *(Lessons 11.1, 11.3)*

1. $x^2 - 16 = 0$ (square root)

2. $2x^2 - 10 = 0$ (square root)

3. $3x^2 - 6x - 12 = 0$ (completing the square)

4. $x^2 + 6x + 10 = 0$ (completing the square)

5. $x^2 - 4x + 4 = 0$ (factoring)

6. $x^2 - x - 30 = 0$ (factoring)

7. Explain when a quadratic equation can be solved using factoring. *(Lessons 11.1, 11.3)*

8. Can any quadratic equation be solved by completing the square Explain. *(Lessons 11.1, 11.3)*

MODULE PERFORMANCE TASK

Can You Stop in Time?

A driver sees a tree fall across the road 125 feet in front of the car. The driver is barely able to stop the car before hitting the tree. What was the maximum speed in miles per hour that the car could have been traveling when the driver saw the tree fall?

The equation for braking distance is $d = \frac{v^2}{2\mu g}$, where d is braking distance, v is speed of the car, μ is the coefficient of friction between the tires and the road, and g is the acceleration due to gravity, 32.2 ft/s^2.

Start by listing the information you will need and the steps you will take to solve the problem. Then complete the task, using numbers, words, or algebra to explain how you reached your conclusion.

Ready to Go On?

11.1–11.3 Quadratic Equations and Complex Numbers

- Online Homework
- Hints and Help
- Extra Practice

Solve the equations by taking square roots, completing the square, factoring, or using the quadratic formula. *(Lessons 11.1, 11.2, 11.3)*

1. $2x^2 - 16 = 0$

2. $2x^2 - 6x - 20 = 0$

3. $2x^2 + 2x - 2 = 0$

4. $x^2 + x = 30$

5. $x^2 - 5x = 24$

6. $-4x^2 + 8 = 24$

7. $x^2 + 30 = 24$

8. $x^2 + 4x + 3 = 0$

ESSENTIAL QUESTION

9. Write a real world situation that could be modeled by the equation $7m \cdot 5m = 875$. *(Lesson 11.1)*

MODULE 11
MIXED REVIEW

Assessment Readiness

1. Which of the following equations, when graphed, has two x-intercepts?

A. $x^2 + 16 = 0$

B. $2x^2 - 20 = 10$

C. $-3x^2 - 6 = 0$

2. Consider the equation $4x^2 + 4x - 16 = 0$. Determine if each statement is True or False.

A. To solve this equation using complete the square, $\left(\frac{b}{2}\right)^2 = \left(\frac{4}{2}\right)^2 = 4$.

B. If solving this equation using factoring, then $(x + 4)(x - 4) = 0$

C. After completing the square, $x = -\frac{1}{2} \pm \frac{\sqrt{17}}{2}$.

3. Consider the equation $ax^2 + bx = 25$. For what values of a and b would you solve this equation by taking a square root? For what values of a would the square root result in an imaginary number? Explain your answers.

4. Consider the equation $f(x) = ax^2 + bx + c$. For what values of a would the quadratic function open upward? For what values of a would the quadratic function open downward? What would happen to the function if the value of a were 0? Explain.

Quadratic Relations and Systems of Equations

MODULE 12

Essential Question: How can you use systems of equations to solve real-world problems?

REAL WORLD VIDEO
Video game designers need a solid understanding of algebra, including systems of quadratic equations, in order to program realistic interactions within the game environment.

MODULE PERFORMANCE TASK PREVIEW

How Can You Hit a Moving Target with a Laser Beam?

Video games can be a lot of fun. They can also help players to develop and hone skills such as following instructions, using logic in problem solving, hand-eye coordination, and fine motor and spatial abilities. Video game designers often use mathematics to program realistic interactions in the video world. How can math be used to aim a laser beam to hit a virtual clay disk flying through the air? Set your sights on the target and let's get started!

Are YOU Ready?

Complete these exercises to review skills you will need for this module.

- Online Homework
- Hints and Help
- Extra Practice

Graphing Linear Nonproportional Relationships

Example 1 Graph $y = -2x - 3$.

x	0	−2	−3
y	−3	1	3

Make a table of values. Plot the points and draw a line through them.

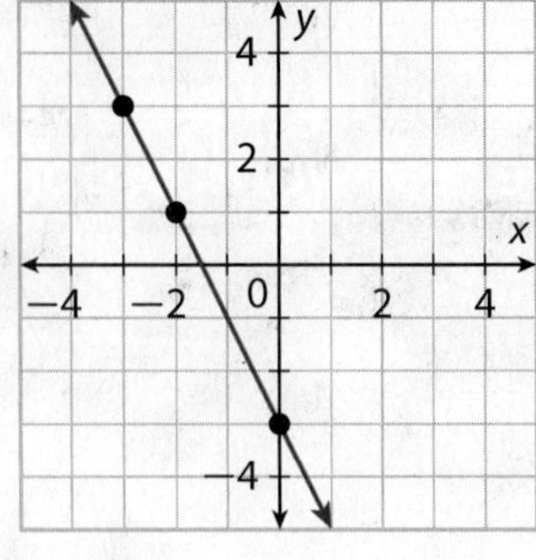

Graph each equation.

1. $y = -x + 5$

2. $y = 3x - 2$

Multi-Step Equations

Example 2 Solve $4(x - 2) = 12$ for x.

$4x - 8 = 12$ Distribute.

$4x = 20$ Add 8 to both sides.

$x = 5$ Divide by 4.

Solve each equation.

3. $5 - 3x = 7(x - 1)$

4. $3x + 2(x - 1) = 28$

5. $2(6 - 5x) = 5x + 9$

Solving Systems of Two Linear Equations

Example 3 Solve the system $\begin{cases} y = 2x + 8 \\ 3x + 2y = 2 \end{cases}$

$3x + 2(2x + 8) = 2$ Substitute.

$x = -2$ Solve for x.

$y = 2(-2) + 8 = 4$ Solve for y.

The solution is $(-2, 4)$.

Solve each system.

6. $\begin{cases} y = 10 - 3x \\ 5x - y = 6 \end{cases}$

7. $\begin{cases} 2x - 3y = 4 \\ -x + 2y = 3 \end{cases}$

8. $\begin{cases} 5x - 2y = 4 \\ 3x + 2y = -12 \end{cases}$

12.1 Circles

Essential Question: What is the standard form for the equation of a circle, and what does the standard form tell you about the circle?

Resource Locker

Explore Deriving the Standard-Form Equation of a Circle

Recall that a circle is the set of points in a plane that are a fixed distance, called the radius, from a given point, called the center.

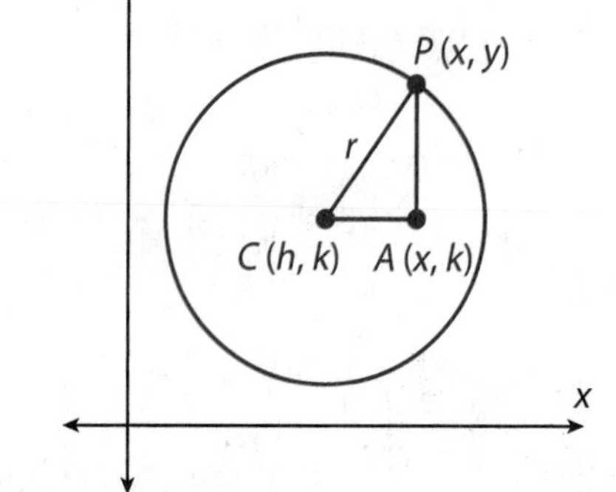

(A) The coordinate plane shows a circle with center $C(h, k)$ and radius r. $P(x, y)$ is an arbitrary point on the circle but is not directly above or below or to the left or right of C. $A(x, k)$ is a point with the same x-coordinate as P and the same y-coordinate as C. Explain why $\triangle CAP$ is a right triangle.

(B) Identify the lengths of the sides of $\triangle CAP$. Remember that point P is arbitrary, so you cannot rely upon the diagram to know whether the x-coordinate of P is greater than or less than h or whether the y-coordinate of P is greater than or less than k, so you must use absolute value for the lengths of the legs of $\triangle CAP$. Also, remember that the length of the hypotenuse of $\triangle CAP$ is just the radius of the circle.

The length of segment AC is $\left| \quad \right|$.

The length of segment AP is $\left| \quad \right|$.

The length of segment CP is ____.

(C) Apply the Pythagorean Theorem to $\triangle CAP$ to obtain an equation of the circle.

$$(x - \quad)^2 + (y - \quad)^2 = \quad^2$$

Reflect

1. **Discussion** Why isn't absolute value used in the equation of the circle?

2. **Discussion** Why does the equation of the circle also apply to the cases in which P has the same x-coordinate as C or the same y-coordinate as C so that $\triangle CAP$ doesn't exist?

Explain 1 Writing the Equation of a Circle

The standard-form equation of a circle with center $C(h, k)$ and radius r is $(x - h)^2 + (y - k)^2 = r^2$. If you solve this equation for r, you obtain the equation $r = \sqrt{(x - h)^2 + (y - k)^2}$, which gives you a means for finding the radius of a circle when the center and a point $P(x, y)$ on the circle are known.

Example 1 **Write the equation of the circle.**

(A) The circle with center $C(-3, 2)$ and radius $r = 4$

Substitute -3 for h, 2 for k, and 4 for r into the general equation and simplify.

$$(x - (-3))^2 + (y - 2)^2 = 4^2$$

$$(x + 3)^2 + (y - 2)^2 = 16$$

(B) The circle with center $C(-4, -3)$ and containing the point $P(2, 5)$

Step 1 Find the radius.

$$r = CP$$

$$= \sqrt{\left(\boxed{2} - (-4)\right)^2 + \left(\boxed{5} - (-3)\right)^2}$$

$$= \sqrt{\left(\boxed{6}\right)^2 + \left(\boxed{8}\right)^2}$$

$$= \sqrt{\boxed{36} + \boxed{64}}$$

$$= \sqrt{\boxed{100}} = \boxed{10}$$

Step 2 Write the equation of the circle.

$$(x - (-4))^2 + (y - (-3))^2 = \boxed{10}^2$$

$$(x + 4)^2 + (y + 3)^2 = \boxed{100}$$

Your Turn

Write the equation of the circle.

3. The circle with center $C(1, -4)$ and radius $r = 2$

4. The circle with center $C(-2, 5)$ and containing the point $P(-2, -1)$

Explain 2 Rewriting an Equation of a Circle to Graph the Circle

Expanding the standard-form equation $(x - h)^2 + (y - k)^2 = r^2$ results in a general second-degree equation in two variables having the form $x^2 + y^2 + cx + dy + e = 0$. In order to graph such an equation or an even more general equation of the form $ax^2 + ay^2 + cx + dy + e = 0$. you must complete the square on both x and y to put the equation in standard form and identify the circle's center and radius.

Example 2 **Graph the circle after writing the equation in standard form.**

(A) $x^2 + y^2 - 10x + 6y + 30 = 0$

Write the equation. $x^2 + y^2 - 10x + 6y + 30 = 0$

Prepare to complete the square on x and y. $(x^2 - 10x + \blacksquare) + (y^2 + 6y + \blacksquare) = -30 + \blacksquare + \blacksquare$

Complete both squares. $(x^2 - 10x + 25) + (y^2 + 6y + 9) = -30 + 25 + 9$

Factor and simplify. $(x - 5)^2 + (y + 3)^2 = 4$

The center of the circle is $C(5, -3)$, and the radius is $r = \sqrt{4} = 2$.

Graph the circle.

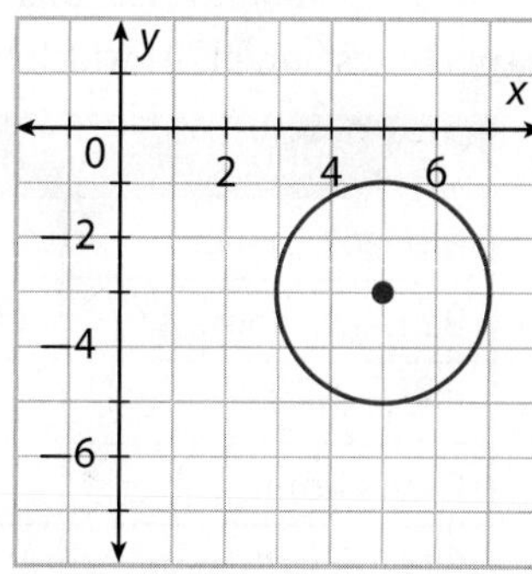

(B) $4x^2 + 4y^2 + 8x - 16y + 11 = 0$

Write the equation. $4x^2 + 4y^2 + 8x - 16y + 11 = 0$

Factor 4 from the x terms and the y terms. $4(x^2 + 2x) + 4(y^2 - 4y) + 11 = 0$

Prepare to complete the square on x and y. $4(x^2 + 2x + \blacksquare) + 4(y^2 - 4y + \blacksquare) = -11 + 4(\blacksquare) + 4(\blacksquare)$

Complete both squares. $4(x^2 + 2x + \boxed{1}) + 4(y^2 - 4y + \boxed{4}) = -11 + 4(\boxed{1}) + 4(\boxed{4})$

Factor and simplify. $4(x + \boxed{1})^2 + 4(y - \boxed{2})^2 = \boxed{9}$

Divide both sides by 4. $(x + \boxed{1})^2 + (y - \boxed{2})^2 = \boxed{\frac{9}{4}}$

The center is $C(\boxed{-1}, \boxed{2})$, and the radius is $r = \sqrt{\boxed{\frac{9}{4}}} = \boxed{\frac{3}{2}}$.

Graph the circle.

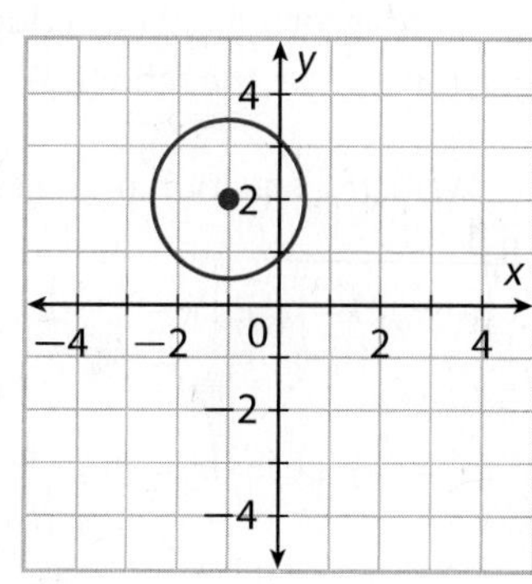

Your Turn

Graph the circle after writing the equation in standard form.

5. $x^2 + y^2 + 4x + 6y + 4 = 0$

6. $9x^2 + 9y^2 - 54x - 72y + 209 = 0$

Explain 3 Solving a Real-World Problem Involving a Circle

A circle in a coordinate plane divides the plane into two regions: points inside the circle and points outside the circle. Points inside the circle satisfy the inequality $(x - h)^2 + (y - k)^2 < r^2$, while points outside the circle satisfy the inequality $(x - h)^2 + (y - k)^2 > r^2$.

Example 3 **Write an inequality representing the given situation, and draw a circle to solve the problem.**

(A) The table lists the locations of the homes of five friends along with the locations of their favorite pizza restaurant and the school they attend. The friends are deciding where to have a pizza party based on the fact that the restaurant offers free delivery to locations within a 3-mile radius of the restaurant. At which homes should the friends hold their pizza party to get free delivery?

Place	Location
Alonzo's home	$A(3, 2)$
Barbara's home	$B(2, 4)$
Constance's home	$C(-2, 3)$
Dion's home	$D(0, -1)$
Eli's home	$E(1, -4)$
Pizza restaurant	$(-1, 1)$
School	$(1, -2)$

Write the equation of the circle with center $(-1, 1)$ and radius 3.

$(x - (-1))^2 + (y - 1)^2 = 3^2$, or $(x + 1)^2 + (y - 1)^2 = 9$

The inequality $(x + 1)^2 + (y - 1)^2 < 9$ represents the situation. Plot the points from the table and graph the circle.

The points inside the circle satisfy the inequality. So, the friends should hold their pizza party at either Constance's home or Dion's home to get free delivery from the restaurant.

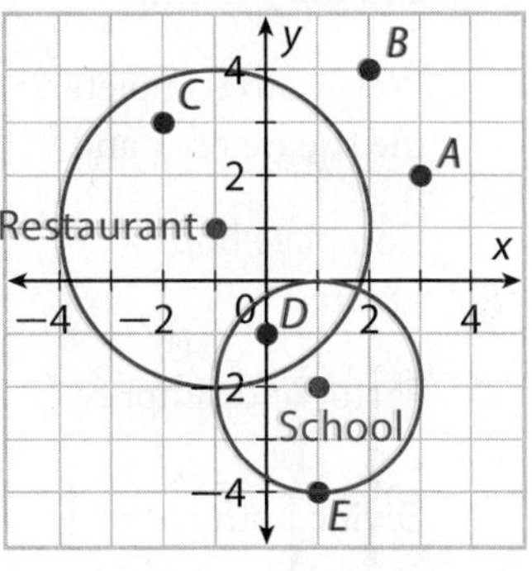

(B) In order for a student to ride the bus to school, the student must live more than 2 miles from the school. Which of the five friends are eligible to ride the bus?

Write the equation of the circle with center $(1, -2)$ and radius 2.

$(x - 1)^2 + (y - (-2))^2 = 2^2$

$(x - 1)^2 + (y + 2)^2 = 4$

The inequality $(x - 1)^2 + (y + 2)^2 > 4$ represents the situation.

Use the coordinate grid in Part A to graph the circle.

The points outside the circle satisfy the inequality. So, Alonzo, Barbara, and Constance are eligible to ride the bus to school.

Reflect

7. For Part B, how do you know that point E isn't outside the circle?

Your Turn

Write an inequality representing the given situation, and draw a circle to solve the problem.

8. Sasha delivers newspapers to subscribers that live within a 4-block radius of her house. Sasha's house is located at point $(0, -1)$. Points A, B, C, D, and E represent the houses of some of the subscribers to the newspaper. To which houses does Sasha deliver newspapers?

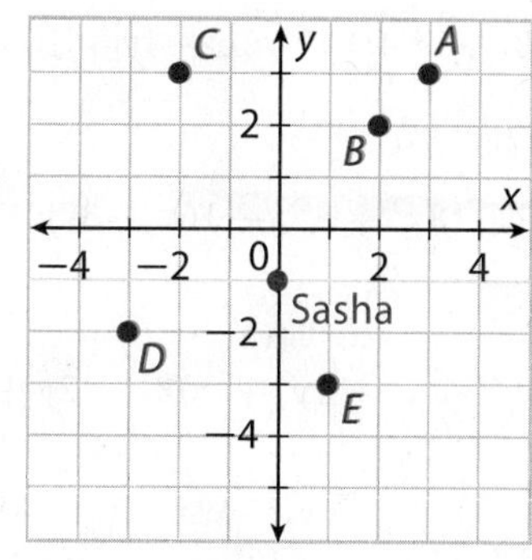

Elaborate

9. Describe the process for deriving the equation of a circle given the coordinates of its center and its radius.

10. What must you do with the equation $ax^2 + ay^2 + cx + dy + e = 0$ in order to graph it?

11. What do the inequalities $(x - h)^2 + (y - k)^2 < r^2$ and $(x - h)^2 + (y - k)^2 > r^2$ represent?

12. **Essential Question Check-In** What information must you know or determine in order to write an equation of a circle in standard form?

Evaluate: Homework and Practice

- Online Homework
- Hints and Help
- Extra Practice

Write the equation of the circle.

1. The circle with $C(4, -11)$ and radius $r = 16$

2. The circle with $C(-7, -1)$ and radius $r = 13$

3. The circle with center $C(-8, 2)$ and containing the point $P(-1, 6)$

4. The circle with center $C(5, 9)$ and containing the point $P(4, 8)$

In Exercises 5–12, graph the circle after writing the equation in standard form.

5. $x^2 + y^2 - 2x - 8y + 13 = 0$

Graph the circle after writing the equation in standard form.

6. $x^2 + y^2 + 6x - 10y + 25 = 0$

7. $x^2 + y^2 + 4x + 12y + 39 = 0$

8. $x^2 + y^2 - 8x + 4y + 16 = 0$

9. $8x^2 + 8y^2 - 16x - 32y - 88 = 0$

10. $2x^2 + 2y^2 + 20x + 12y + 50 = 0$

11. $12x^2 + 12y^2 - 96x - 24y + 201 = 0$

12. $16x^2 + 16y^2 + 64x - 96y + 199 = 0$

In Exercises 13–20, write an inequality representing the problem, and draw a circle to solve the problem.

13. A router for a wireless network on a floor of an office building has a range of 35 feet. The router is located at the point (30, 30). The lettered points in the coordinate diagram represent computers in the office. Which computers will be able to connect to the network through the router?

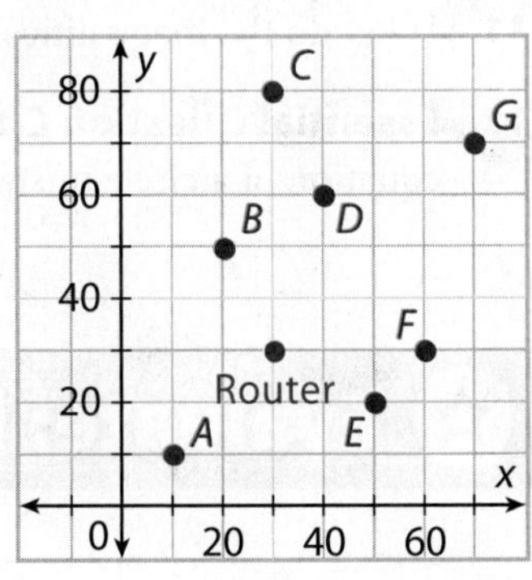

Write an inequality representing the problem, and draw a circle to solve the problem.

14. The epicenter of an earthquake is located at the point (20, −30). The earthquake is felt up to 40 miles away. The labeled points in the coordinate diagram represent towns near the epicenter. In which towns is the earthquake felt?

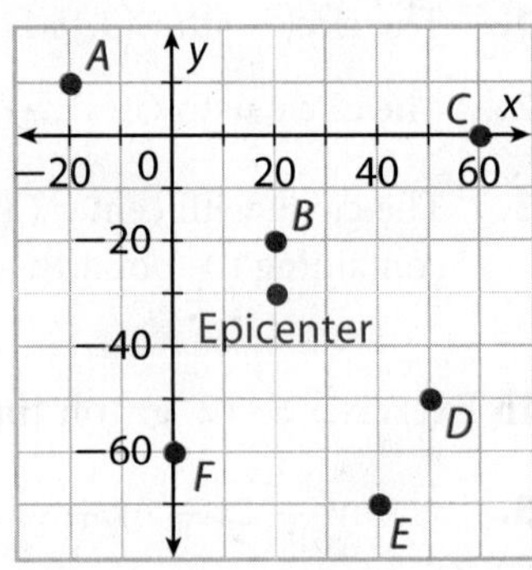

15. Aida's cat has disappeared somewhere in her apartment. The last time she saw the cat, it was located at the point $(30, 40)$. Aida knows all of the cat's hiding places, which are indicated by the lettered points in the coordinate diagram. If she searches for the cat no farther than 25 feet from where she last saw it, which hiding places will she check?

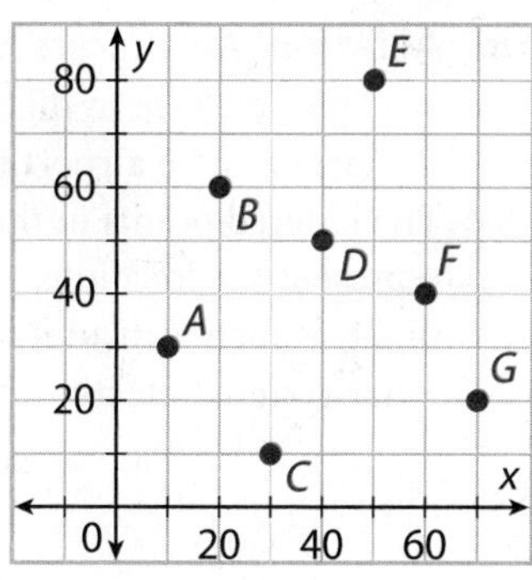

16. A rock concert is held in a large state park. The concert stage is located at the point $(-2, 2)$, and the music can be heard as far as 4 miles away. The lettered points in the coordinate diagram represent campsites within the park. At which campsites can the music be heard?

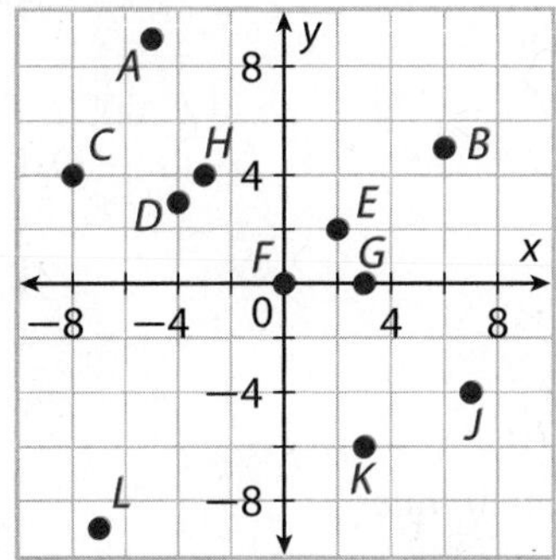

17. **Business** When Claire started her in-home computer service and support business, she decided not to accept clients located more than 10 miles from her home. Claire's home is located at the point (5, 0), and the lettered points in the coordinate diagram represent the homes of her prospective clients. Which prospective clients will Claire not accept?

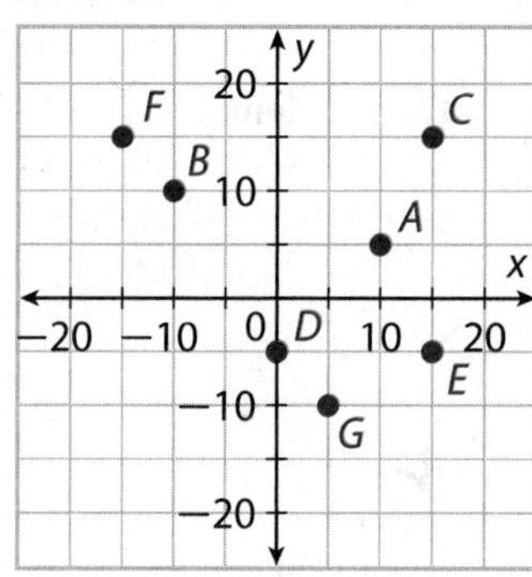

18. Aviation An airport's radar system detects airplanes that are in flight as far as 60 miles from the airport. The airport is located at $(-20, 40)$. The lettered points in the coordinate diagram represent the locations of airplanes currently in flight. Which airplanes does the airport's radar system detect?

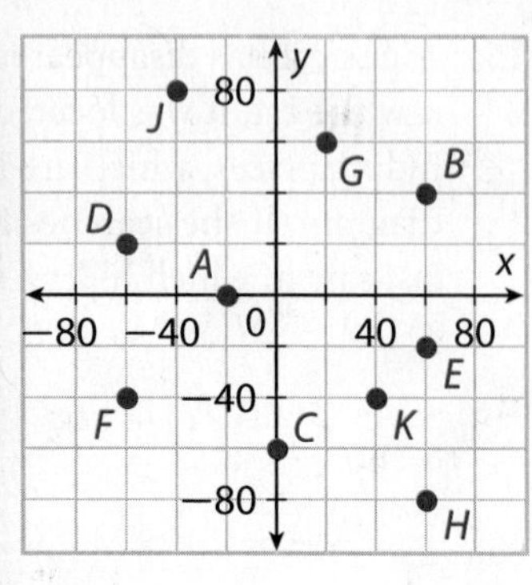

19. Due to a radiation leak at a nuclear power plant, the towns up to a distance of 30 miles from the plant are to be evacuated. The nuclear power plant is located at the point $(-10, -10)$. The lettered points in the coordinate diagram represent the towns in the area. Which towns are in the evacuation zone?

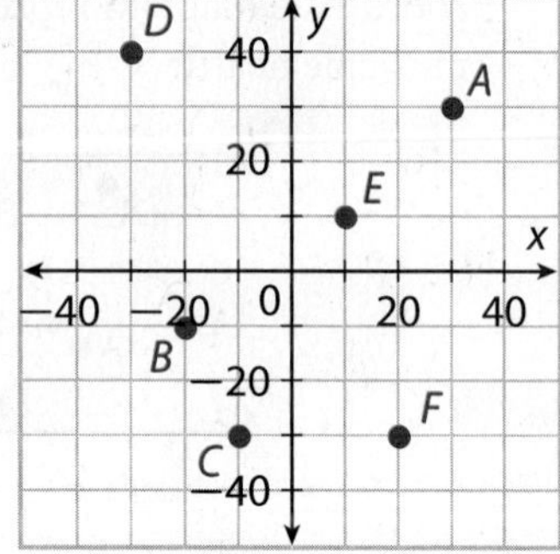

20. Bats that live in a cave at point $(-10, 0)$ have a feeding range of 40 miles. The lettered points in the coordinate diagram represent towns near the cave. In which towns are bats from the cave not likely to be observed? Write an inequality representing the problem, and draw a circle to solve the problem.

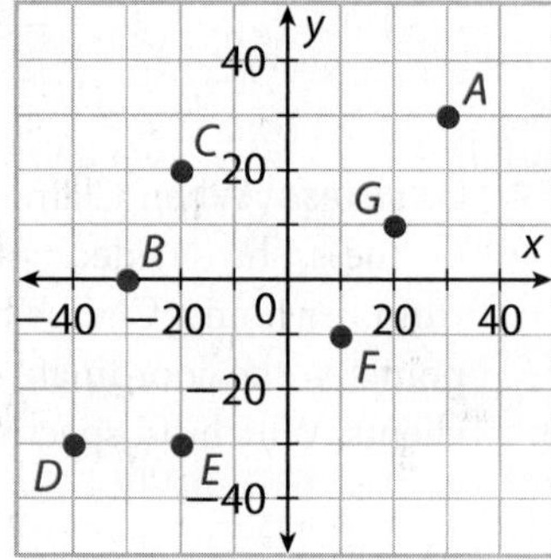

21. Match the equations to the center and radius of the circle each represents. Show your work.

A. $x^2 + y^2 + 18x + 22y - 23 = 0$ **a.** __?__ $C(9, -11); r = 13$

B. $x^2 + y^2 - 18x + 22y + 33 = 0$ **b.** __?__ $C(9, 11); r = 15$

C. $25x^2 + 25y^2 - 450x - 550y - 575 = 0$ **c.** __?__ $C(-9, -11); r = 15$

D. $25x^2 + 25y^2 + 450x - 550y + 825 = 0$ **d.** __?__ $C(-9, 11); r = 13$

H.O.T. Focus on Higher Order Thinking

22. Multi-Step A garden sprinkler waters the plants in a garden within a 12-foot spray radius. The sprinkler is located at the point $(5, -10)$. The lettered points in the coordinate diagram represent the plants. Use the diagram for parts a–c.

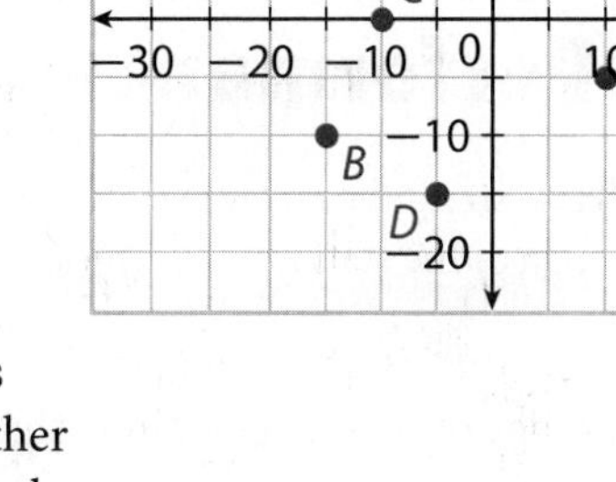

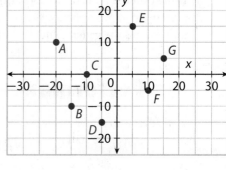

a. Write an inequality that represents the region that does not get water from the sprinkler. Then draw a circle and use it to identify the plants that do not get water from the sprinkler.

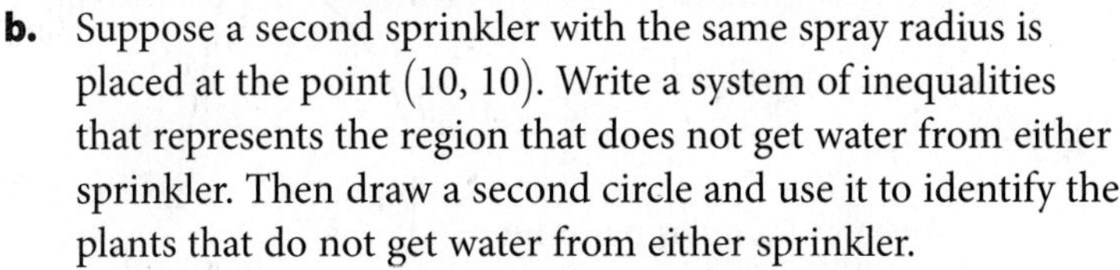

b. Suppose a second sprinkler with the same spray radius is placed at the point $(10, 10)$. Write a system of inequalities that represents the region that does not get water from either sprinkler. Then draw a second circle and use it to identify the plants that do not get water from either sprinkler.

c. Where would you place a third sprinkler with the same spray radius so all the plants get water from a sprinkler? Write a system of inequalities that represents the region that does not get water from any of the sprinklers. Then draw a third circle to show that every plant receives water from a sprinkler.

23. Represent Real-World Situations The orbit of the planet Venus is nearly circular. An astronomer develops a model for the orbit in which the Sun has coordinates $S(0, 0)$, the circular orbit of Venus passes through $V(41, 53)$, and each unit of the coordinate plane represents 1 million miles. Write an equation for the orbit of Venus. How far is Venus from the sun?

24. Draw Conclusions The *unit circle* is defined as the circle with radius 1 centered at the origin. A *Pythagorean triple* is an ordered triple of three positive integers, (a, b, c), that satisfy the relationship $a^2 + b^2 = c^2$. An example of a Pythagorean triple is (3, 4, 5). In parts a–d, you will draw conclusions about Pythagorean triples.

a. Write the equation of the unit circle.

b. Use the Pythagorean triple $(3, 4, 5)$ and the symmetry of a circle to identify the coordinates of two points on the part of the unit circle that lies in Quadrant I. Explain your reasoning.

c. Use your answer from part b and the symmetry of a circle to identify the coordinates of six other points on the unit circle. This time, the points should be in Quadrants II, III, and IV.

d. Find a different Pythagorean triple and use it to identify the coordinates of eight points on the unit circle.

25. Make a Conjecture In a two-dimensional plane, coordinates are given by ordered pairs of the form (x, y). You can generalize coordinates to three-dimensional space by using ordered pairs of the form (x, y, z) where the coordinate z is used to indicate displacement above or below the xy-plane. Generalize the standard-form equation of a circle to find the general equation of a sphere. Explain your reasoning.

Lesson Performance Task

A highway that runs straight east and west passes 6 miles south of a radio tower. The broadcast range of the station is 10 miles.

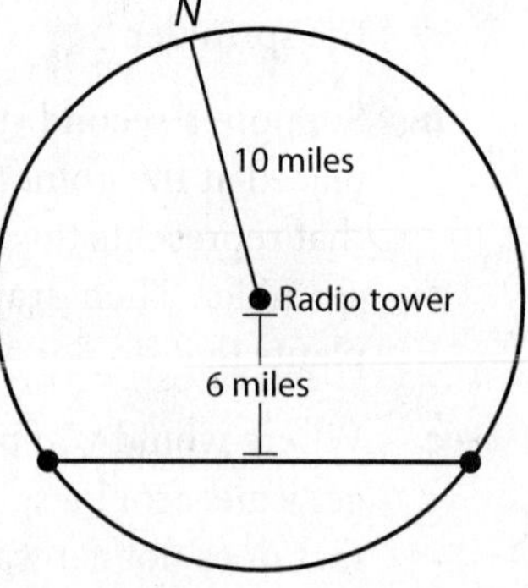

a. Determine the distance along the highway that a car will be within range of the radio station's signal.

b. Given that the car is traveling at a constant speed of 60 miles per hour, determine the amount of time the car is within range of the signal.

12.2 Parabolas

Essential Question: How is the distance formula connected with deriving equations for both vertical and horizontal parabolas?

Resource Locker

Explore Deriving the Standard-Form Equation of a Parabola

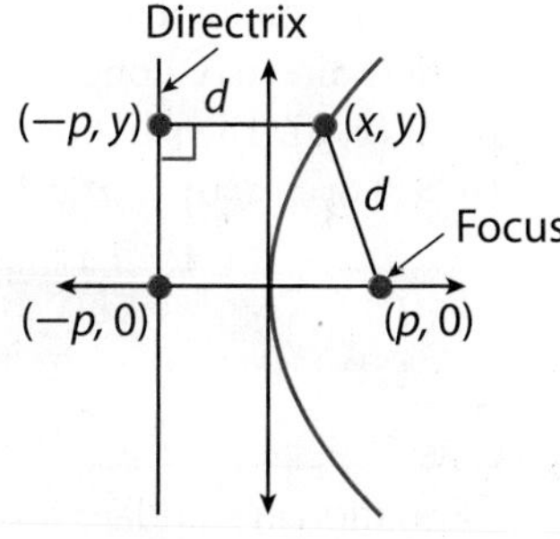

A **parabola** is defined as a set of points equidistant from a line (called the **directrix**) and a point (called the **focus**). The focus will always lie on the axis of symmetry, and the directrix will always be perpendicular to the axis of symmetry. This definition can be used to derive the equation for a horizontal parabola opening to the right with its vertex at the origin using the distance formula. (The derivations of parabolas opening in other directions will be covered later.)

(A) The coordinates for the focus are given by

.

(B) Write down the expression for the distance from a point (x, y) to the coordinates of the focus:

$$d = \sqrt{\left(\square - \square\right)^2 + \left(\square - \square\right)^2}$$

(C) The distance from a point to a line is measured by drawing a perpendicular line segment from the point to the line. Find the point where a horizontal line from (x, y) intersects the directrix (defined by the line $x = -p$ for a parabola with its vertex on the origin).

(D) Write down the expression for the distance from a point, (x, y) to the point from Step C:

$$d = \sqrt{\left(\square - \square\right)^2 + \left(\square - \square\right)^2}$$

(E) Setting the two distances the same and simplifying gives $\sqrt{(x-p)^2 + y^2} = \sqrt{(x+p)^2}$.

To continue solving the problem, square both sides of the equation and expand the squared binomials.

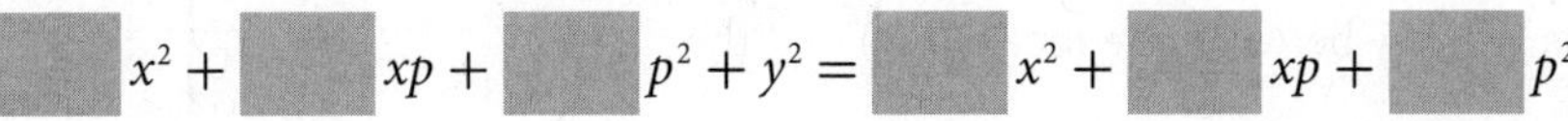

$$\square\, x^2 + \square\, xp + \square\, p^2 + y^2 = \square\, x^2 + \square\, xp + \square\, p^2$$

(F) Collect terms.

$$\square\, x^2 + \square\, px + \square\, p^2 + y^2 = 0$$

(G) Finally, simplify and arrange the equation into the **standard form for a horizontal parabola** (with vertex at (0, 0)):

$$y^2 = \square$$

Reflect

1. Why was the directrix placed on the line $x = -p$?

2. **Discussion** How can the result be generalized to arrive at the standard form for a horizontal parabola with a vertex at (h, k):
$(y - k)^2 = 4p(x - h)$?

Explain 1 Writing the Equation of a Parabola with Vertex at (0, 0)

The equation for a horizontal parabola with vertex at $(0, 0)$ is written in the standard form as $y^2 = 4px$. It has a vertical directrix along the line $x = -p$, a horizontal axis of symmetry along the line $y = 0$, and a focus at the point $(p, 0)$. The parabola opens toward the focus, whether it is on the right or left of the origin $(p > 0$ or $p < 0)$. Vertical parabolas are similar, but with horizontal directrices and vertical axes of symmetry:

Parabolas with Vertices at the Origin		
	Vertical	**Horizontal**
Equation in standard form	$x^2 = 4py$	$y^2 = 4px$
$p > 0$	Opens upward	Opens rightward
$p < 0$	Opens downward	Opens leftward
Focus	$(0, p)$	$(p, 0)$
Directrix	$y = -p$	$x = -p$
Axis of Symmetry	$x = 0$	$y = 0$

Example 1 **Find the equation of the parabola from the description of the focus and directrix. Then make a sketch showing the parabola, the focus, and the directrix.**

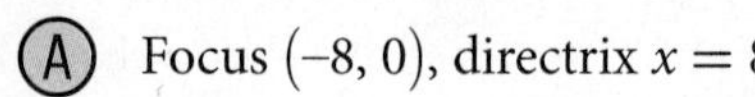

(A) Focus $(-8, 0)$, directrix $x = 8$

A vertical directrix means a horizontal parabola.

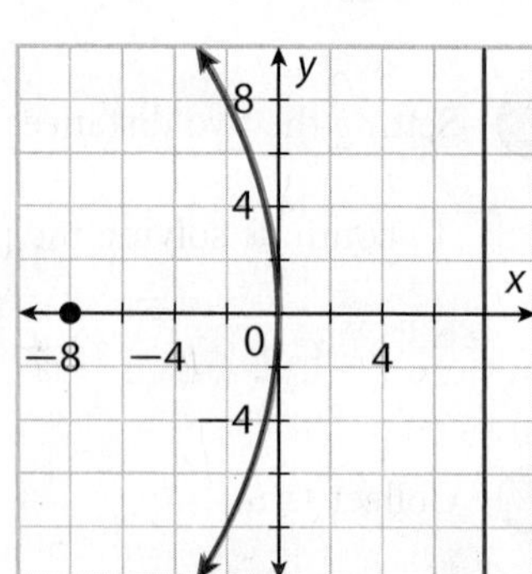

Confirm that the vertex is at $(0, 0)$:

a. The y-coordinate of the vertex is the same as the focus: 0.

b. The x-coordinate is halfway between the focus (-8) and the directrix $(+8)$: 0.

c. The vertex is at $(0, 0)$.

Use the expression for a horizontal parabola, $y^2 = 4px$, and replace p with the x coordinate of the focus: $y^2 = 4(-8)x$

Simplify: $y^2 = -32x$

Plot the focus and directrix and sketch the parabola.

(B) Focus $(0, -2)$, directrix $y = 2$

A horizontal directrix means a vertical parabola.

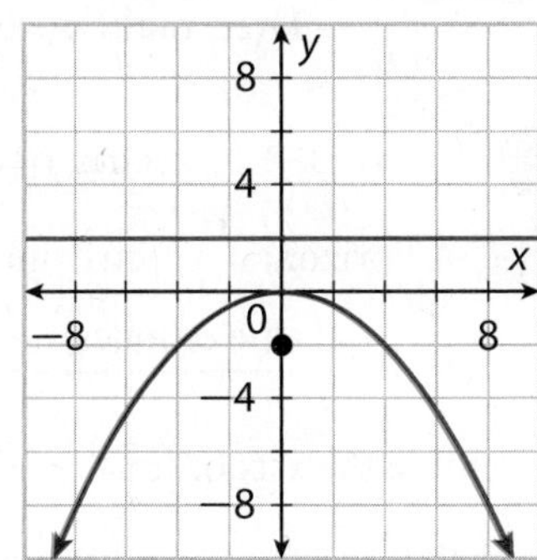

Confirm that the vertex is at $(0, 0)$:

a. The x-coordinate of the vertex is the same as the focus: 0.

b. The y-coordinate is halfway between the focus, -2 and the directrix, 2 : 0

c. The vertex is at $(0, 0)$.

Use the expression for a vertical parabola, $x^2 = 4py$, and replace p with the x coordinate of the focus: $x^2 = 4 \cdot -2 \cdot y$

Simplify: $x^2 = -8y$

Plot the focus, the directrix, and the parabola.

Your Turn

Find the equation of the parabola from the description of the focus and directrix. Then make a sketch showing the parabola, the focus, and the directrix.

3. Focus $(2, 0)$, directrix $x = -2$

4. Focus $\left(0, -\frac{1}{2}\right)$, directrix $y = \frac{1}{2}$

Explain 2 Writing the Equation of a Parabola with Vertex at (h, k)

The standard equation for a parabola with a vertex (h, k) can be found by translating from $(0, 0)$ to (h, k): substitute $(x - h)$ for x and $(y - k)$ for y. This also translates the focus and directrix each by the same amount.

Parabolas with Vertex (h, k)		
	Vertical	**Horizontal**
Equation in standard form	$(x - h)^2 = 4p(y - k)$	$(y - k)^2 = 4p(x - h)$
$p > 0$	Opens upward	Opens rightward
$p < 0$	Opens downward	Opens leftward
Focus	$(h, k + p)$	$(h + p, k)$
Directrix	$y = k - p$	$x = h - p$
Axis of Symmetry	$x = h$	$y = k$

p is found halfway from the directrix to the focus:

- For vertical parabolas: $p = \dfrac{(y \text{ value of focus}) - (y \text{ value of directrix})}{2}$
- For horizontal parabolas: $p = \dfrac{(x \text{ value of focus}) - (x \text{ value of directrix})}{2}$

The vertex can be found from the focus by relating the coordinates of the focus to h, k, and p.

Example 2 **Find the equation of the parabola from the description of the focus and directrix. Then make a sketch showing the parabola, the focus, and the directrix.**

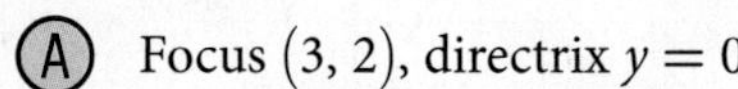

(A) Focus $(3, 2)$, directrix $y = 0$

A horizontal directrix means a vertical parabola.

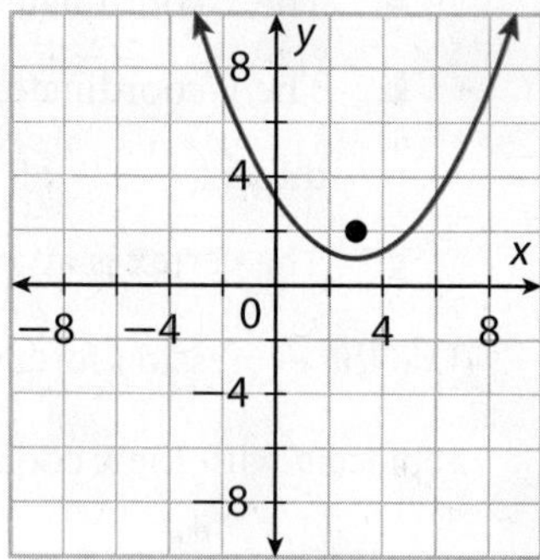

$$p = \frac{(y \text{ value of focus}) - (y \text{ value of directrix})}{2} = \frac{2 - 0}{2} = 1$$

$h =$ the x-coordinate of the focus $= 3$

Solve for k: The y-value of the focus is $k + p$, so
$k + p = 2$

$k + 1 = 2$

$k = 1$

Write the equation: $(x - 3)^2 = 4(y - 1)$

Plot the focus, the directrix, and the parabola.

(B) Focus $(-1, -1)$, directrix $x = 5$

A vertical directrix means a horizontal parabola.

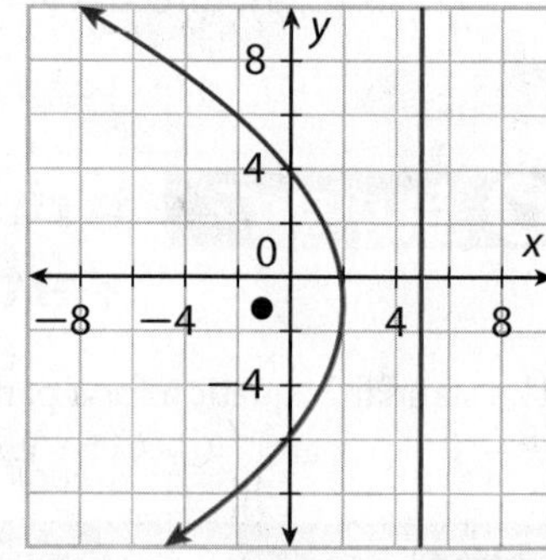

$$p = \frac{(x \text{ value of focus}) - (x \text{ value of directrix})}{2} = \frac{\boxed{-1} - \boxed{5}}{2} = \boxed{-3}$$

$k =$ the y-coordinate of the focus $= \boxed{-1}$

Solve for h: The x-value of the focus is $h + p$, so

$h + p = \boxed{-1}$

$h + (-3) = \boxed{-1}$

$h = \boxed{2}$

Write the equation: $(y + 1)^2 = \boxed{-12}\left(x - \boxed{2}\right)$

Your Turn

Find the equation of the parabola from the description of the focus and directrix. Then make a sketch showing the parabola, the focus, and the directrix.

5. Focus $(5, -1)$, directrix $x = -3$

6. Focus $(-2, 0)$, directrix $y = 4$

Explain 3 Rewriting the Equation of a Parabola to Graph the Parabola

A **second-degree equation in two variables** is an equation constructed by adding terms in two variables with powers no higher than 2. The general form looks like this:

$ax^2 + by^2 + cx + dy + e = 0$

Expanding the standard form of a parabola and grouping like terms results in a second-degree equation with either $a = 0$ or $b = 0$, depending on whether the parabola is vertical or horizontal. To graph an equation in this form requires the opposite conversion, accomplished by completing the square of the squared variable.

Example 3 **Convert the equation to the standard form of a parabola and graph the parabola, the focus, and the directrix.**

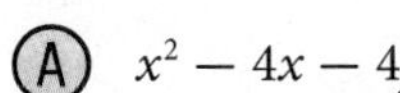

(A) $x^2 - 4x - 4y + 12 = 0$

Isolate the x terms and complete the square on x.

Isolate the x terms.	$x^2 - 4x = 4y - 12$
Add $\left(\frac{-4}{2}\right)^2$ to both sides.	$x^2 - 4x + 4 = 4y - 8$
Factor the perfect square trinomial on the left side.	$(x - 2)^2 = 4y - 8$
Factor out 4 from the right side.	$(x - 2)^2 = 4(y - 2)$

This is the standard form for a vertical parabola. Now find p, h, and k from the standard form $(x - h)^2 = 4p(y - k)$ in order to graph the parabola, focus, and directrix.

$4p = 4$, so $p = 1$ Vertex $= (h, k) = (2, 2)$

$h = 2, k = 2$ Focus $= (h, k + p) = (2, 2 + 1) = (2, 3)$

Directrix: $y = k - p = 2 - 1$, or $y = 1$

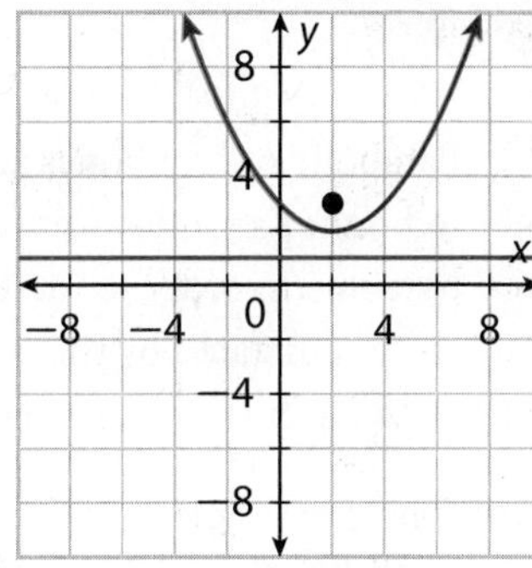

(B) $y^2 + 2x + 8y + 18 = 0$

Isolate the [y] terms.	$y^2 + 8y = -2x - 18$
Add $\left(\frac{[8]}{2}\right)^2$ to both sides.	$y^2 + 8y + [16] = -2x - [2]$
Factor the perfect square trinomial.	$(y + [4])^2 = -2x - [2]$
Factor out [−2] on the right.	$(y + [4])^2 = [-2](x + [1])$

Identify the features of the graph using the standard form of a horizontal parabola, $(y - k)^2 = 4p(x - h)$:

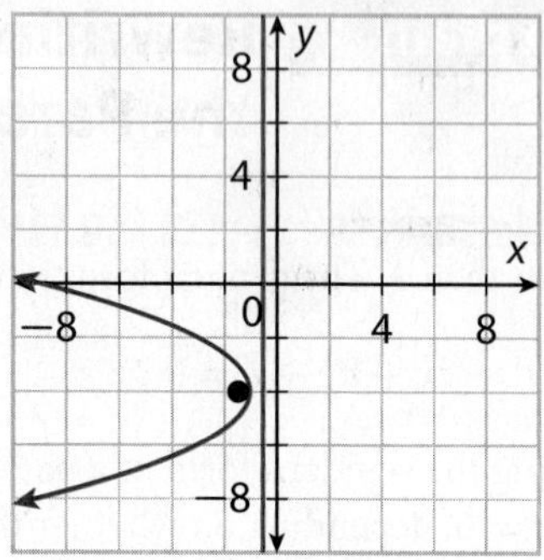

$4p = \boxed{-2}$, so $p = \boxed{-\frac{1}{2}}$

$h = \boxed{-1}$, $k = \boxed{-4}$

Vertex $= (h, k) = \left(\boxed{-1}, \boxed{-4}\right)$

Focus $= (h + p, k) = \left(\boxed{-\frac{3}{2}}, \boxed{-4}\right)$

Directrix: $x = h - p$, or $x = \boxed{-\frac{1}{2}}$

Your Turn

Convert the equation to the standard form of a parabola and graph the parabola, the focus, and the directrix.

7. $y^2 - 12x - 4y + 64 = 0$

8. $x^2 + 8x - 16y - 48 = 0$

Explain 4 Solving a Real-World Problem

Parabolic shapes occur in a variety of applications in science and engineering that take advantage of the concentrating property of reflections from the parabolic surface at the focus.

Example 4

(A) Parabolic microphones are so-named because they use a parabolic dish to bounce sound waves toward a microphone placed at the focus of the parabola in order to increase sensitivity. The dish shown has a cross section dictated by the equation $x = 32y^2$ where x and y are in inches. How far from the center of the dish should the microphone be placed?

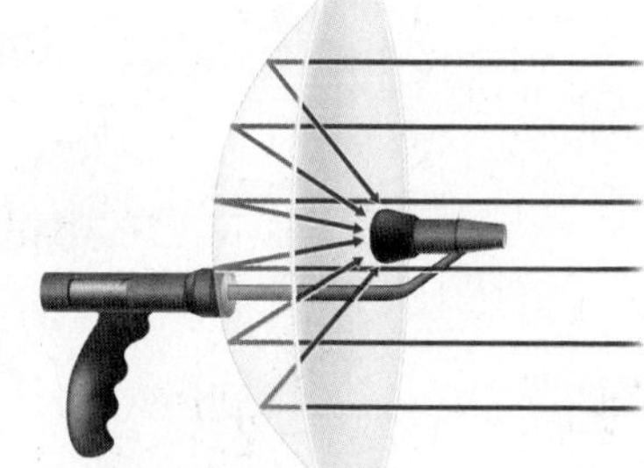

The cross section matches the standard form of a horizontal parabola with $h = 0$, $k = 0$, $p = 8$.

Therefore the vertex, which is the center of the dish, is at $(0, 0)$ and the focus is at $(8, 0)$, 8 inches away.

Ⓑ A reflective telescope uses a parabolic mirror to focus light rays before creating an image with the eyepiece. If the focal length (the distance from the bottom of the mirror's bowl to the focus) is 140 mm and the mirror has a 70 mm diameter (width), what is the depth of the bowl of the mirror?

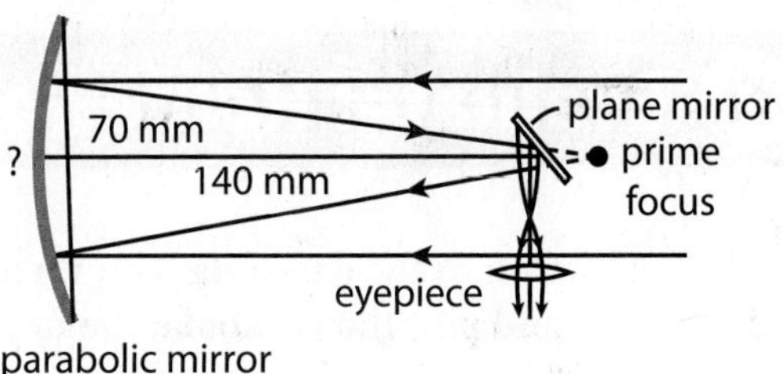

The distance from the bottom of the mirror's bowl to the focus is p. The vertex location is not specified (or needed), so use $(0, 0)$ for simplicity. The equation for the mirror is a horizontal parabola (with x the distance along the telescope and y the position out from the center).

$$\left(y - \boxed{0}\right)^2 = 4p\left(x - \boxed{0}\right)$$

$$y^2 = \boxed{560}\,x$$

Since the diameter of the bowl of the mirror is 70 mm, the points at the rim of the mirror have y-values of 35 mm and −35 mm. The x-value of either point will be the same as the x-value of the point directly above the bottom of the bowl, which equals the depth of the bowl. Since the points on the rim lie on the parabola, use the equation of the parabola to solve for the x-value of either edge of the mirror.

$$\boxed{35}^2 = \boxed{560}\,x$$

$$x \approx \boxed{2.19}\text{ mm}$$

The bowl is approximately 2.19 mm deep.

Your Turn

9. A football team needs one more field goal to win the game. The goalpost that the ball must clear is 10 feet (~3.3 yd) off the ground. The path of the football after it is kicked for a 35-yard field goal is given by the equation $y - 11 = -0.0125\,(x - 20)^2$, in yards. Does the team win?

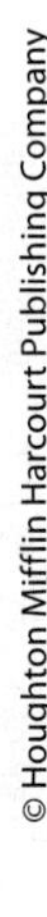

Elaborate

10. Examine the graphs in this lesson and determine a relationship between the separation of the focus and the vertex, and the shape of the parabola. Demonstrate this by finding the relationship between p for a vertical parabola with vertex of $(0, 0)$ and a, the coefficient of the quadratic parent function $y = ax^2$.

11. **Essential Question Check-In** How can you use the distance formula to derive an equation relating x and y from the definition of a parabola based on focus and directrix?

Evaluate: Homework and Practice

- Online Homework
- Hints and Help
- Extra Practice

Find the equation of the parabola with vertex at $(0, 0)$ from the description of the focus and directrix and plot the parabola, the focus, and the directrix.

1. Focus at $(3, 0)$, directrix: $x = -3$

2. Focus at $(0, -5)$, directrix: $y = 5$

3. Focus at $(-1, 0)$, directrix: $x = 1$

4. Focus at $(0, 2)$, directrix: $y = -2$

Find the equation of the parabola with the given information.

5. Vertex: $(-3, 6)$; Directrix: $x = -1.75$

6. Vertex: $(6, 20)$; Focus: $(6, 11)$

Find the equation of the parabola with vertex at (h, k) from the description of the focus and directrix and plot the parabola, the focus, and the directrix.

7. Focus at $(5, 3)$, directrix: $y = 7$

8. Focus at $(-3, 3)$, directrix: $x = 3$

Convert the equation to the standard form of a parabola and graph the parabola, the focus, and the directrix.

9. $y^2 - 20x - 6y - 51 = 0$

10. $x^2 - 14x - 12y + 73 = 0$

11. Communications The equation for the cross section of a parabolic satellite television dish is $y = \frac{1}{50}x^2$, measured in inches. How far is the focus from the vertex of the cross section?

12. Engineering The equation for the cross section of a spotlight is $y + 5 = \frac{1}{12}x^2$, measured in inches. Where is the bulb located with respect to the vertex of the cross section?

13. When a ball is thrown into the air, the path that the ball travels is modeled by the parabola $y - 7 = -0.0175(x - 20)^2$, measured in feet. What is the maximum height the ball reaches? How far does the ball travel before it hits the ground?

14. A cable for a suspension bridge is modeled by $y - 55 = 0.0025x^2$, where x is the horizontal distance, in feet, from the support tower and y is the height, in feet, above the bridge. How far is the lowest point of the cable above the bridge?

15. Match each equation to its graph.

a. __?__ $y + 1 = \frac{1}{16}(x - 2)^2$ b. __?__ $y - 1 = \frac{1}{16}(x + 2)^2$ c. __?__ $x + 1 = -\frac{1}{16}(y - 2)^2$

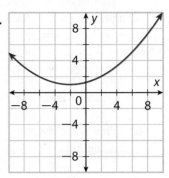

A.

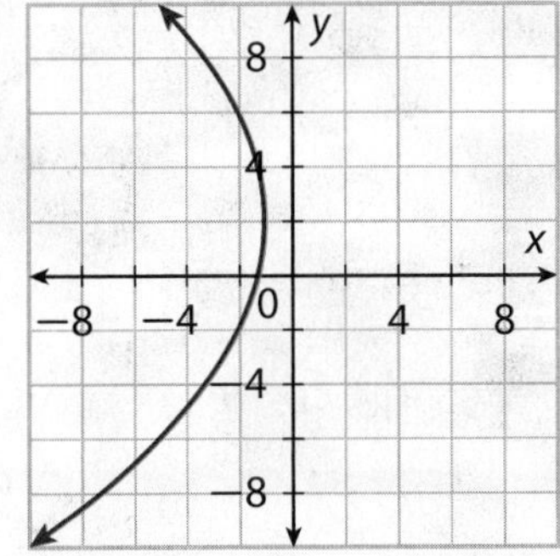

B.

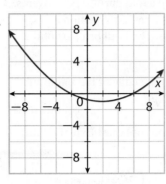

C.

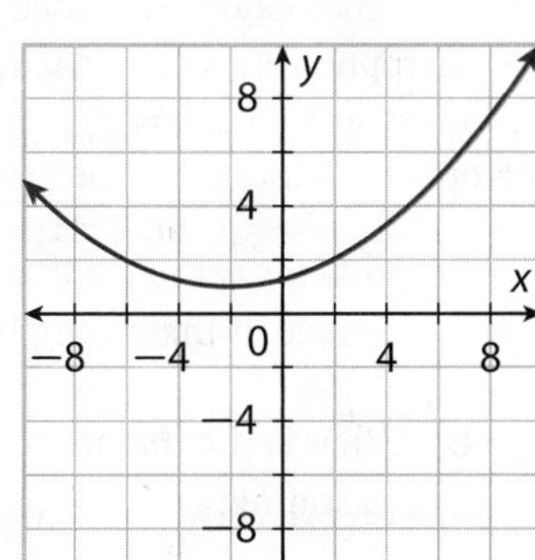

Derive the equation of the parabolas with the given information.

16. An upward-opening parabola with a focus at $(0, p)$ and a directrix $y = -p$.

17. A leftward-opening parabola with a focus at $(-p, 0)$ and directrix at $x = p$.

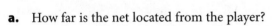

H.O.T. Focus on Higher Order Thinking

18. Multi-Step A tennis player hits a tennis ball just as it hits one end line of the court. The path of the ball is modeled by the equation $y - 4 = -\frac{4}{1521}(x - 39)^2$ where $x = 0$ is at the end line. The tennis net is 3 feet high, and the total length of the court is 78 feet.

a. How far is the net located from the player?

b. Explain why the ball will go over the net.

c. Will the ball land "in," that is, inside the court or on the opposite endline?

19. Critical Thinking The latus rectum of a parabola is the line segment perpendicular to the axis of symmetry through the focus, with endpoints on the parabola. Find the length of the latus rectum of a parabola. Justify your answer. *Hint*: Set the coordinate system such that the vertex is at the origin and the parabola opens rightward with the focus at $(p, 0)$.

20. Explain the Error Lois is finding the focus and directrix of the parabola $y - 8 = -\frac{1}{2}(x + 2)^2$. Her work is shown. Explain what Lois did wrong, and then find the correct answer.

$h = -2, k = 8$

$4p = -\frac{1}{2}$, so $p = -\frac{1}{8}$, or $p = -0.125$

Focus $= (h, k + p) = (-2, 7.875)$

Directrix: $y = k - p$, or $y = 8.125$

Lesson Performance Task

Parabolic microphones are used for field audio during sports events. The microphones are manufactured such that the equation of their cross section is $x = \frac{1}{34}y^2$, in inches. The feedhorn part of the microphone is located at the focus.

a. How far is the feedhorn from the edge of the parabolic surface of the microphone?

b. What is the diameter of the microphone? Explain your reasoning.

c. If the diameter is increased by 5 inches, what is the new equation of the cross section of the microphone?

12.3 Solving Linear-Quadratic Systems

Essential Question: How can you solve a system composed of a linear equation in two variables and a quadratic equation in two variables?

Resource Locker

Explore Investigating Intersections of Lines and Graphs of Quadratic Equations

There are many real-world situations that can be modeled by linear or quadratic functions. What happens when the two situations overlap? Examine graphs of linear functions and quadratic functions and determine the ways they can intersect.

(A) Examine the two graphs below and determine the ways a line could intersect the parabola.

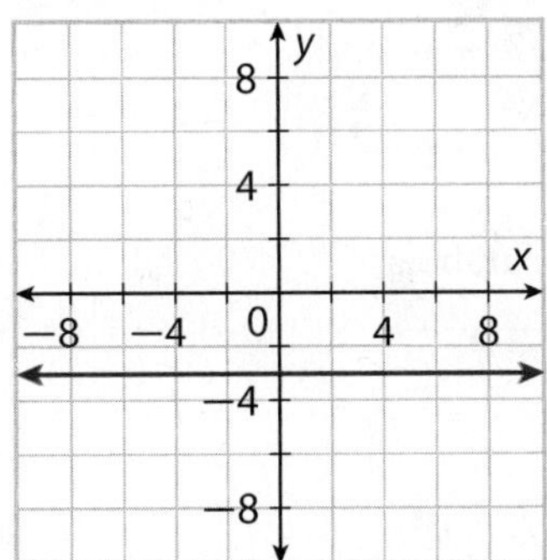

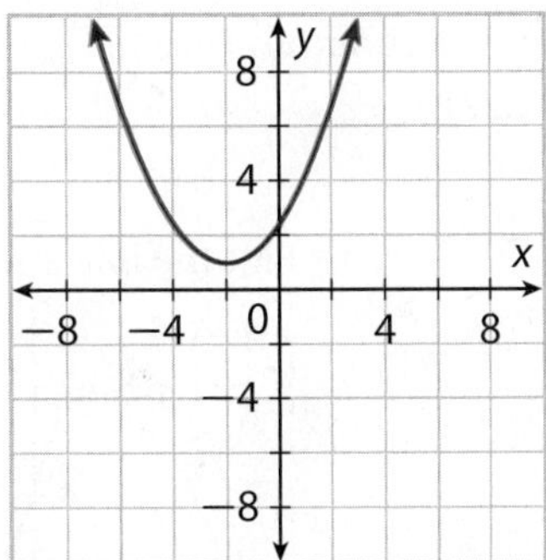

(B) Sketch three graphs of a line and a parabola: one showing intersection in one point, one showing intersection in two points, and one not showing intersection.

(C) So a linear function and a quadratic function can intersect at ______ points.

Reflect

1. If a line intersects a circle at one point, what is the relationship between the line and the radius of the circle at that point?

2. **Discussion** Does a line have to be horizontal to intersect a parabola at exactly one point?

Explain 1 Solving Linear-Quadratic Systems Graphically

Graph each equation by hand and find the set of points where the two graphs intersect.

Example 1 **Solve the given linear-quadratic system graphically.**

Ⓐ 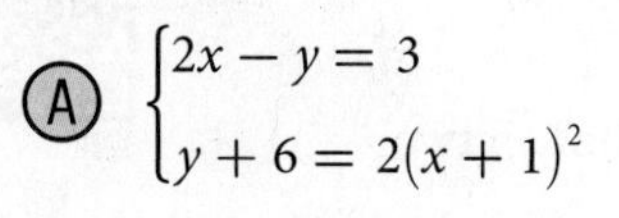

$$\begin{cases} 2x - y = 3 \\ y + 6 = 2(x + 1)^2 \end{cases}$$

Plot the line and the parabola.

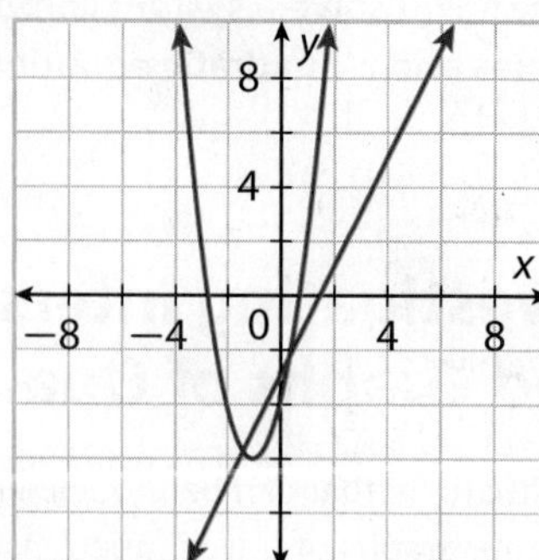

Solve each equation for y.

$$2x - y = 3$$
$$y = 2x - 3$$

$$y + 6 = 2(x + 1)^2$$
$$y = 2(x + 1)^2 - 6$$

Find the approximate points of intersection: Estimating from the graph, the intersection points appear to be near $(-1.5, -5.5)$ and $(0.5, -2.5)$.

The exact solutions (which can be found algebraically) are $\left(\frac{-1 - \sqrt{3}}{2}, -\sqrt{3} - 4\right)$ and $\left(\frac{-1 + \sqrt{3}}{2}, \sqrt{3} - 4\right)$, or about $(-1.37, -5.73)$ and $(0.37, -2.27)$.

Ⓑ $\begin{cases} 3x + y = 4.5 \\ y = \frac{1}{2}(x - 3)^2 \end{cases}$

Plot the line and the parabola.

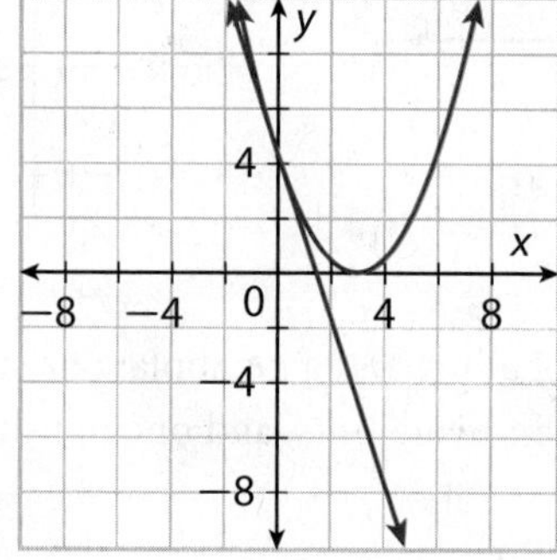

Solve each equation for y.

$$3x + y = 4.5$$

$y =$ $-3x + 4.5$

$y =$ $\frac{1}{2}(x - 3)^2$

Find the approximate point(s) of intersection: $(0, 4.5)$.

Note that checking these coordinates in the original system shows that this is an exact solution.

Your Turn

Solve the given linear-quadratic system graphically.

3. $\begin{cases} y + 3x = 0 \\ y - 6 = -3x^2 \end{cases}$

4. $\begin{cases} y + 1 = \frac{1}{2}(x - 3)^2 \\ x - y = 6 \end{cases}$

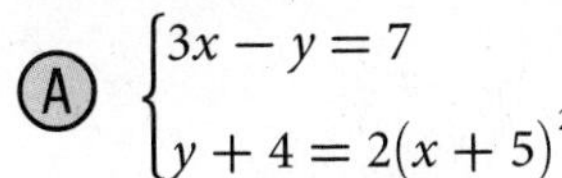

Explain 2 Solving Linear-Quadratic Systems Algebraically

Use algebra to find the solution. Use substitution or elimination.

Example 2 **Solve the given linear-quadratic system algebraically.**

(A) $\begin{cases} 3x - y = 7 \\ y + 4 = 2(x+5)^2 \end{cases}$

Solve this system using elimination. First line up the terms.

$$7 + y = 3x$$
$$4 + y = 2(x+5)^2$$

Subtract the second equation from the first to eliminate the y variable.

$$\begin{array}{r} 7 + y = 3x \\ -\left(4 + y = 2(x + 5^2)\right) \\ \hline 3 = 3x - 2(x+5)^2 \end{array}$$

Solve the resulting equation for x using the quadratic formula.

$$3 = 3x - 2(x+5)^2$$
$$3 = 3x - 2(x^2 + 10x + 25)$$
$$3 = 3x - 2x^2 - 20x - 50$$
$$0 = -2x^2 - 17x - 53$$
$$2x^2 + 17x + 53 = 0$$
$$x = \frac{-17 \pm \sqrt{17^2 - 4 \cdot 2 \cdot 53}}{2 \cdot 2}$$
$$= \frac{-17 \pm \sqrt{289 - 424}}{4}$$
$$= \frac{-17 \pm \sqrt{-135}}{4}$$

There is no real number equivalent to $\sqrt{-135}$, so the system has no solution.

Ⓑ $\begin{cases} y = \frac{1}{4}(x-3)^2 \\ 3x - 2y = 13 \end{cases}$

Solve the system by substitution. The first equation is already solved for y. Substitute the expression $\frac{1}{4}(x-3)^2$ for y in the second equation.

$$3x - 2\left(\frac{1}{4}(x-3)^2\right) = 13$$

Now, solve for x.

$$13 = 3x - 2\left(\frac{1}{4}(x-3)^2\right)$$

$$13 = 3x - \boxed{\frac{1}{2}}(x-3)^2$$

$$13 = 3x - \frac{1}{2}\left(\boxed{x^2 - 6x + 9}\right)$$

$$13 = 3x - \frac{1}{2}x^2 + 3x - \frac{9}{2}$$

$$13 = -\frac{1}{2}x^2 + \boxed{6x} - \frac{9}{2}$$

$$0 = -\frac{1}{2}x^2 + 6x - \frac{35}{2}$$

$$0 = x^2 \boxed{-12x + 35}$$

$$0 = \left(x \boxed{-5}\right)\left(x \boxed{-7}\right)$$

$$x = \left(\boxed{-5}\right) \text{ or } x = \left(\boxed{-7}\right)$$

So the line and the parabola intersect at two points. Use the x-coordinates of the intersections to find the points.

Solve $3x - 2y = 13$ for y.

$$3x - 2y = 13$$

$$-2y = 13 - 3x$$

Find y when $x = 5$ and when $x = 7$.

$$y = \boxed{-\left(\frac{13 - 3x}{2}\right)}$$

$$y = -\frac{13 - 3 \cdot 5}{2} \qquad y = -\frac{13 - 3 \cdot 7}{2}$$

$$= -\frac{13 - 15}{2} \qquad = -\frac{13 - 21}{2}$$

$$= -\frac{-2}{2} \qquad = -\frac{-8}{2}$$

$$= 1 \qquad = 4$$

So the solutions to the system are $(5, 1)$ and $(7, 4)$.

Reflect

5. How can you check algebraic solutions for reasonableness?

Your Turn

Solve the given linear-quadratic system algebraically.

6. $\begin{cases} x - 6 = -\frac{1}{6}y^2 \\ 2x + y = 6 \end{cases}$

7. $\begin{cases} x - y = 7 \\ x^2 - y = 7 \end{cases}$

Explain 3 Solving Real-World Problems

You can use the techniques from the previous examples to solve real-world problems.

Example 3 **Solve each problem.**

(A) A tour boat travels around an island in a pattern that can be modeled by the equation $36x^2 + 25y^2 = 900$. A fishing boat approaches the island on a path that can be modeled by the equation $3x - 2y = -8$. Is there a danger of collision? If so, where?

Write the system of equations.

$$\begin{cases} 36x^2 + 25y^2 = 900 \\ 3x - 2y = -8 \end{cases}$$

Solve the second equation for x.

$$\begin{aligned} 3x - 2y &= -8 \\ 3x &= 2y - 8 \\ x &= \frac{2y - 8}{3} \end{aligned}$$

Substitute for x in the first equation.

$$\begin{aligned} 36x^2 + 25y^2 &= 900 \\ 36\left(\frac{2y - 8}{3}\right)^2 + 25y^2 &= 900 \\ 36\left(\frac{4y^2 - 32y + 64}{9}\right) + 25y^2 &= 900 \\ 4\left(4y^2 - 32y + 64\right) + 25y^2 &= 900 \\ 16y^2 - 128y + 256 + 25y^2 &= 900 \\ 41y^2 - 128y - 644 &= 0 \end{aligned}$$

Solve using the quadratic equation.

$$\begin{aligned} y &= \frac{128 \pm \sqrt{128^2 - 4(41)(-644)}}{2(41)} \\ &= \frac{128 \pm \sqrt{122{,}000}}{82} \\ &\approx -2.70 \text{ or } 5.82 \end{aligned}$$

Collisions can occur when $y \approx -2.70$ or $y \approx 5.82$.

To find the x-values, substitute the y-values into $x = \frac{2y - 8}{3}$.

$$x = \frac{2(-2.70) - 8}{3} \qquad x = \frac{2(5.82) - 8}{3}$$

$$= \frac{-5.40 - 8}{3} \qquad = \frac{11.64 - 8}{3}$$

$$= \frac{-13.40}{3} \qquad = \frac{3.64}{3}$$

$$\approx -4.47 \qquad \approx 1.21$$

So the boats could collide at approximately $(-4.47, -2.70)$ or $(1.21, 5.82)$.

(B) The range of the signal from a radio station is bounded by a circle described by the equation $x^2 + y^2 = 2025$. A stretch of highway near the station is modeled by the equation $y - 15 = \frac{1}{20}x$. At which points, if any, does a car on the highway enter and exit the broadcast range of the station?

Write the system of equations.

$$\begin{cases} x^2 + y^2 = 2025 \\ y - 15 = \frac{1}{20}x \end{cases}$$

Solve the second equation for y.

$$y - 15 = \frac{1}{20}x$$

$$y = \boxed{\frac{1}{20}x + 15}$$

Substitute for x in the first equation.

$$x^2 + y^2 = 2025$$

$$x^2 + \left(\boxed{\frac{1}{20}x + 15}\right)^2 = 2025$$

$$x^2 + \boxed{\frac{1}{400}x^2 + \frac{3}{2}x + 225} = 2025$$

$$\boxed{\frac{401}{400}}x^2 + \frac{3}{2}x + 225 = 2025$$

$$\frac{401}{400}x^2 + \frac{3}{2}x - \boxed{1800} = 0$$

$$401x^2 + 600x - 720000 = 0$$

Solve using the quadratic formula.

$$y = \frac{-600 \pm \sqrt{600^2 - 4(401)(-720000)}}{2(401)}$$

$$= \frac{600 \pm \sqrt{1{,}155{,}240{,}000}}{802}$$

$$\approx \boxed{-41.63} \text{ or } \boxed{43.13} \text{ (rounded to the nearest hundredth)}$$

To find the y-values, substitute the x-values into $y = \frac{1}{20}x + 15$.

$y = \frac{1}{20}(-41.63) + 15$

$= \frac{41.63}{20} + 15$

$= -2.08 + 15$

$= 12.92$

$y = \frac{1}{20}(43.13) + 15$

$= \frac{43.13}{20} + 15$

$= 2.16 + 15$

$= 17.16$

The car will be within the radio station's broadcast area between $(-41.63, 12.92)$ and $(43.13, 17.16)$.

Your Turn

8. An asteroid is traveling toward Earth on a path that can be modeled by the equation $y = \frac{1}{28}x - 7$. It approaches a satellite in orbit on a path that can be modeled by the equation $\frac{x^2}{49} + \frac{y^2}{51} = 1$. What are the approximate coordinates of the points where the satellite and asteroid might collide?

9. The owners of a circus are planning a new act. They want to have a trapeze artist catch another acrobat in mid-air as the second performer comes into the main tent on a zip-line. If the path of the trapeze can be modeled by the parabola $y = \frac{1}{4}x^2 + 16$ and the path of the zip-line can be modeled by $y = 2x + 12$, at what point can the trapeze artist grab the second acrobat?

Elaborate

10. A parabola opens to the left. Identify an infinite set of parallel lines that will intersect the parabola only once.

11. If a parabola can intersect the set of lines $\left\{x = a \middle| a \in R\right\}$ in 0, 1, or 2 points, what do you know about the parabola?

12. **Essential Question Check-In** How can you solve a system composed of a linear equation in two variables and a quadratic equation in two variables?

Evaluate: Homework and Practice

- Online Homework
- Hints and Help
- Extra Practice

1. How many points of intersection are on the graph?

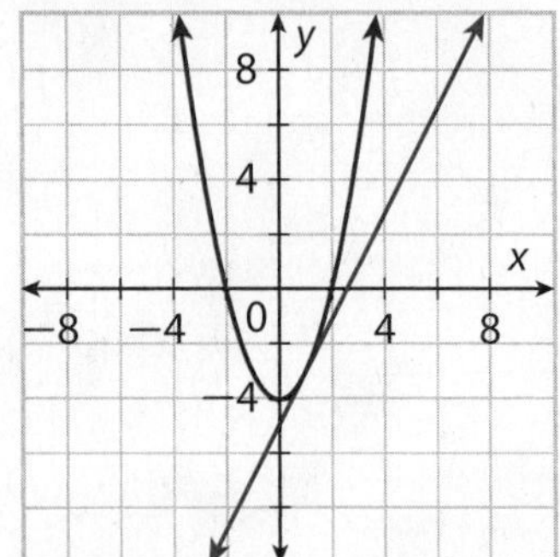

2. How many points of intersection are there on the graph of $\begin{cases} y = x^2 + 3x - 2 \\ y - x = 4 \end{cases}$?

Solve each given linear-quadratic system graphically. If necessary, round to the nearest integer.

3. $\begin{cases} y = -(x-2)^2 + 4 \\ y = -5 \end{cases}$

4. $\begin{cases} y - 3 = (x-1)^2 \\ 2x + y = 5 \end{cases}$

5. $\begin{cases} x = y^2 - 5 \\ -x + 2y = 12 \end{cases}$

6. $\begin{cases} x - 4 = (y+1)^2 \\ 3x - y = 17 \end{cases}$

7. $\begin{cases} (y-4)^2 + x^2 = -12x - 20 \\ x = y \end{cases}$

8. $\begin{cases} 5 - y = x^2 + x \\ y + 1 = \frac{3}{4}x \end{cases}$

Solve each linear-quadratic system algebraically.

9. $\begin{cases} 6x + y = -16 \\ y + 7 = x^2 \end{cases}$

10. $\begin{cases} y - 5 = (x-2)^2 \\ x + 2y = 6 \end{cases}$

11. $\begin{cases} y^2 - 26 = -x^2 \\ x - y = 6 \end{cases}$

12. $\begin{cases} y - 3 = x^2 - 2x \\ 2x + y = 1 \end{cases}$

13. $\begin{cases} y = x^2 + 1 \\ y - 1 = x \end{cases}$

14. $\begin{cases} y = x^2 + 2x + 7 \\ y - 7 = x \end{cases}$

Write and solve a system of equations to find the solutions.

15. Jason is driving his car on a highway at a constant rate of 60 miles per hour when he passes his friend Alan whose car is parked on the side of the road. Alan has been waiting for Jason to pass so that he can follow him to a nearby campground. To catch up to Jason's passing car, Alan accelerates at a constant rate. The distance d, in miles, that Alan's car travels as a function of time t, in hours, since Jason's car has passed is given by $d = 3600t^2$. How long does it takes Alan's car to catch up with Jason's car?

16. The flight of a cannonball toward a hill is described by the parabola $y = 2 + 0.12x - 0.002x^2$.

The hill slopes upward along a path given by $y = 0.15x$.

Where on the hill does the cannonball land?

17. Amy throws a quarter from the top of a building at the same time that a balloon is released from the ground. The equation describing the height y above ground of the quarter in feet is $y = 64 - 2x^2$, where x is the time in seconds. The equation describing the elevation of the balloon in feet is $y = 6x + 8$, where x is the time in seconds. After how many seconds will the balloon and quarter pass each other? Check your solution for reasonableness.

18. The range of an ambulance service is a circular region bounded by the equation $x^2 + y^2 = 400$. A straight road within the service area is represented by $y = 3x + 20$. Find the length of the road, in miles, that lies within the range of the ambulance service (round your answer to the nearest hundredth).

Recall that the distance formula is $d = \sqrt{(x_2 - x_1)^2 + (y_2 - y_1)^2}$.

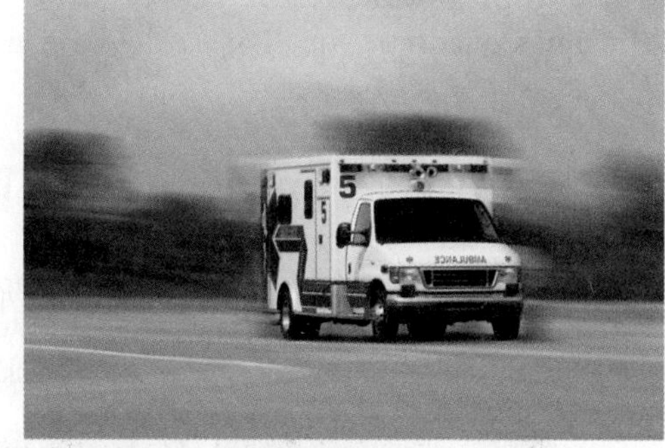

19. Match the equations with their solutions.

a. ___?___ $\begin{cases} y = x - 2 \\ -x^2 + y = 4x - 2 \end{cases}$ **A.** $(4, 3)$ $(-4, -3)$

b. ___?___ $\begin{cases} y = (x - 2)^2 \\ y = -5x - 8 \end{cases}$ **B.** $(0, -2)$ $(5, 3)$

c. ___?___ $\begin{cases} 4y = 3x \\ x^2 + y^2 = 25 \end{cases}$ **C.** $(2, 0)$

d. ___?___ $\begin{cases} y = (x - 2)^2 \\ y = 0 \end{cases}$ **D.** No solution

20. A student solved the system $\begin{cases} y - 7 = x^2 - 5x \\ y - 2x = 1 \end{cases}$ graphically and determined the only solution to be $(1, 3)$. Was this a reasonable answer?

How do you know?

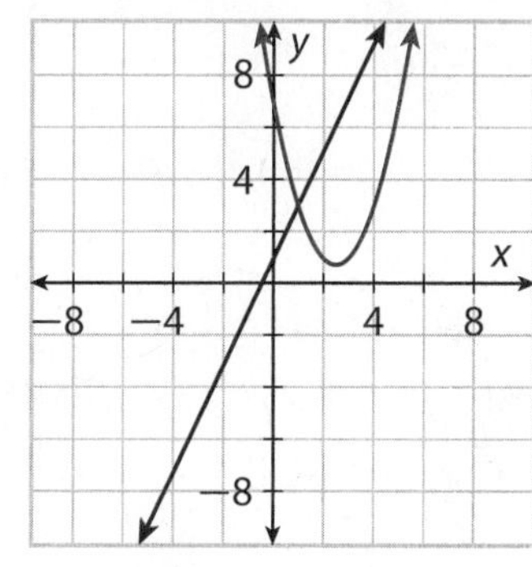

H.O.T. Focus on Higher Order Thinking

21. **Explain the Error** A student was asked to come up with a system of equations, one linear and one quadratic, that has two solutions. The student gave $\begin{cases} y^2 = -(x+1)^2 + 9 \\ y = x^2 - 4x + 3 \end{cases}$ as the answer. What did the student do wrong?

22. **Analyze Relationships** The graph shows a quadratic function and a linear function $y = d$. If the linear function were changed to $y = d + 3$, how many solutions would the new system have? If the linear function were changed to $y = d - 5$, how many solutions would the new system have? Give reasons for your answers.

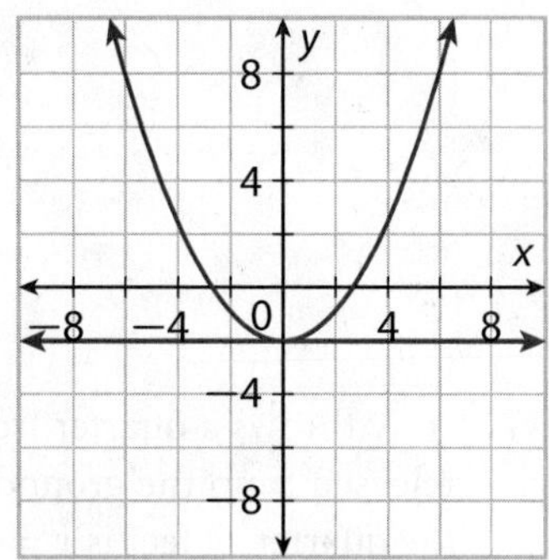

23. **Make a Conjecture** Given $y = 100x^2$ and $y = 0.0001x^2$, what can you say about any line that goes through the vertex of each but is not horizontal or vertical?

24. **Communicate Mathematical Ideas** Explain why a system of a linear equation and a quadratic equation cannot have an infinite number of solutions.

Lesson Performance Task

Suppose an aerial freestyle skier goes off a ramp with her path represented by the equation $y = -0.024(x - 25)^2 + 40$. If the surface of the mountain is represented by the linear equation $y = -0.5x + 25$, find the distance in feet the skier lands from the beginning of the ramp.

STUDY GUIDE REVIEW

Quadratic Relations and Systems of Equations

MODULE 12

Essential Question: How can you use systems of equations to solve real-world problems?

Key Vocabulary

directrix *(directriz)*

focus of a parabola *(foco de una parábola)*

linear equation in three variables *(ecuación lineal en tres variables)*

matrix *(matriz)*

ordered triple *(tripleta ordenada)*

KEY EXAMPLE *(Lesson 12.1)*

Write the equation of a circle that has a center at (–3, 5) and a radius of 9.

$(x-h)^2+(y-k)^2=r^2$ — The standard form of the equation of a circle

$h=-3$ — x-coordinate of center

$k=5$ — y-coordinate of center

$r=9$ — radius

$(x-(-3))^2+(y-5)^2=9^2$ — Substitute.

$(x+3)^2+(y-5)^2=81$ — Simplify.

KEY EXAMPLE *(Lesson 12.3)*

Solve the system using elimination.

$$\begin{cases}-5x+y=10\\ y+2=3(x+4)^2\end{cases}$$

$y-10=5x$ — First, line up the terms.

$y+2=3(x+4)^2$

$\cancel{y}-10=5x$ — Subtract the second equation from the first.

$$\frac{\begin{aligned}-\cancel{y}+(-2)&=-3(x+4)^2\end{aligned}}{-12=5x-3(x+4)^2}$$

$-12=5x-3(x+4)^2$

$-12=5x-3x^2-24x-48$

$0=-3x^2-19x-36$ — Solve the resulting equation for x.

$$x=\frac{19\pm\sqrt{(-19)^2-4(-3)(-36)}}{2(-3)}$$

$$x=\frac{19\pm i\sqrt{71}}{-6}$$

There is no real number equivalent, so the system has no solution.

EXERCISES

Find the equation of the circle with the given characteristics. *(Lessons 12.1)*

1. Center: (3, 4)

Radius: 6

2. Center: (–7.5, 15)

Radius: 1.5

Find the center and radius of the given circle. *(Lessons 12.1)*

3. $(x-5)^2+(y-8)^2=144$

4. $x^2+(y+6)^2=50$

Find the solution to the system of equations using graphing or elimination. *(Lessons 12.2, 12.3)*

5. $\begin{cases} 4x+3y=1 \\ y=x^2-x-1 \end{cases}$

6. $\begin{cases} x-3y=2 \\ y=x^2+2x-34 \end{cases}$

MODULE PERFORMANCE TASK

How Can You Hit a Moving Target with a Laser Beam?

A video game designer is creating a game similar to skeet shooting, where a player will use a laser beam to hit a virtual clay disk launched into the air. The disk is launched from the ground and, if nothing blows it up, it reaches a maximum height of 30 meters and returns to the ground 60 meters away. The laser is fired from a height of 5 meters above the ground. Where should the designer point the laser to hit the disk at its maximum height?

Be sure to write down all your data and assumptions. Then use graphs, numbers, words, or algebra to explain how you reached your conclusion.

Ready to Go On?

12.1–12.3 Quadratic Relations and Systems of Equations

Personal Math Trainer

- Online Homework
- Hints and Help
- Extra Practice

Find the equation of the circle with the given characteristics. *(Lesson 12.1)*

1. Center: (0, –2)

Radius: 1

2. Center: (–4, 4.5)

Radius: 16

Find the center and radius of the given circle. *(Lesson 12.1)*

3. $x^2 + y^2 = 25$

4. $(x - 18)^2 + (y + 18)^2 = 70$

Solve the system of equations using any method. *(Lessons 12.2, 12.3)*

5. $\begin{cases} y + 12 = 4x \\ y - 20 = x^2 - 8x \end{cases}$

6. $\begin{cases} y = x + 2 \\ 2y - 12 = 2x^2 - 8x \end{cases}$

ESSENTIAL QUESTION

7. Describe a real-world situation that might involve a linear equation and a quadratic equation. *(Lesson 12.3)*

MODULE 12
MIXED REVIEW

Assessment Readiness

1. Look at each focus and directrix. Is the resulting parabola horizontal? Write Yes or No for A–C.

A. Focus (−5, 0), Directrix $x = 5$

B. Focus (4, 0), Directrix $x = -4$

C. Focus (0, −3), Directrix $y = 3$

2. Consider the system of equations $\begin{cases} y = x^2 + 6x + 10 \\ y + 6 = 2x \end{cases}$. Tell whether each statement is correct.

A. Another way to write this system is $\begin{cases} y = x^2 + 6x + 10 \\ y = 2x - 6 \end{cases}$.

B. The only way to solve this system is by graphing.

C. There is only one solution to the system, (−4, 2).

3. Is it possible for a system made up of one linear equation and one quadratic equation to have infinitely many solutions? Why or why not?

4. Robin solved a quadratic equation using the process shown. Describe and correct her mistake.

$$0 = \frac{x^2}{4} - 2x + 7$$

$$x = \frac{-(-2) \pm \sqrt{(-2)^2 - 4\left(\frac{1}{4}\right)(7)}}{2(1/4)}$$

$$= \frac{2 \pm \sqrt{-4 - 7}}{\frac{1}{2}}$$

$$= 4 \pm 2\sqrt{-11}$$

$$= 4 \pm 2i\sqrt{11}$$

Functions and Inverses

MODULE 13

Essential Question: How can you use functions and inverses to solve real-world problems?

REAL WORLD VIDEO
Balls of different diameters and volumes can present a variety of packaging challenges for sports equipment manufacturers. Check out how inverse functions can help lead to efficient solutions.

MODULE PERFORMANCE TASK PREVIEW

The Smallest Cube

If you know the dimensions of a box that is shaped like a rectangular prism, you can easily find the volume of the box using the formula $v = l \times w \times h$. But what if you know the volume and want to know the dimensions? That's the problem package designers face when they know the size of a new product and must find the dimensions of the package it will be sold in. You'll do just that after you learn to "unpack" functions in this module—that is, find their inverses.

Are YOU Ready?

Complete these exercises to review skills you will need for this module.

- Online Homework
- Hints and Help
- Extra Practice

Squares and Square Roots

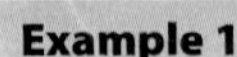

Evaluate $\sqrt{225}$.

Since $15^2 = 15 \cdot 15 = 225$, the square root of 225 is 15.

Evaluate.

1. $\sqrt{144}$ **2.** $\sqrt{256}$ **3.** $\sqrt{\frac{4}{9}}$

Cubes and Cube Roots

Example 2 Evaluate $\sqrt[3]{-27}$.

Since $(-3)^3 = (-3) \cdot (-3) \cdot (-3) = -27$, the cube root of -27 is -3.

Evaluate.

4. $\sqrt[3]{1000}$ **5.** $\sqrt[3]{-125}$ **6.** $\sqrt[3]{-64}$

Linear Functions

Example 3 Write $8x - 2y = 20$ in slope-intercept form.

$-2y = -8x + 20$ Isolate the y-term.

$y = 4x - 10$ Divide both by –2.

Write each equation in slope-intercept form.

7. $2x + 3y = 24$ **8.** $3(2y - x) = -15$ **9.** $3x + 0.4y = -1$

13.1 Graphing Polynomial Functions

Essential Question: How does the value of n affect the behavior of the function $f(x) = x^n$?

Resource Locker

Explore Exploring Graphs of Cubic and Quartic Functions

The **end behavior** of a function is a description of the values of the function as x approaches positive infinity ($x \rightarrow +\infty$) or negative infinity ($x \rightarrow -\infty$). The degree and leading coefficient of a polynomial function determine its end behavior.

(A) Use your graphing calculator to plot each of the cubic functions in the table, and complete the table to describe each function's general shape and end behavior.

Function	Number of Direction Changes	End Behavior as $x \rightarrow +\infty$	End Behavior as $x \rightarrow -\infty$
$f(x) = x^3 - 5x$		$f(x) \rightarrow$	$f(x) \rightarrow$
$f(x) = -2x^3$		$f(x) \rightarrow$	$f(x) \rightarrow$
$f(x) = \frac{3}{2}x^3 + x + 1$		$f(x) \rightarrow$	$f(x) \rightarrow$

(B) All three of these functions are cubic, which means that they have degree ____. Their shapes vary, but one feature they all share is the end behavior. Is it the same or opposite on the two ends?

(C) The graphs show quartic functions. Describe each function's general shape and end behavior.

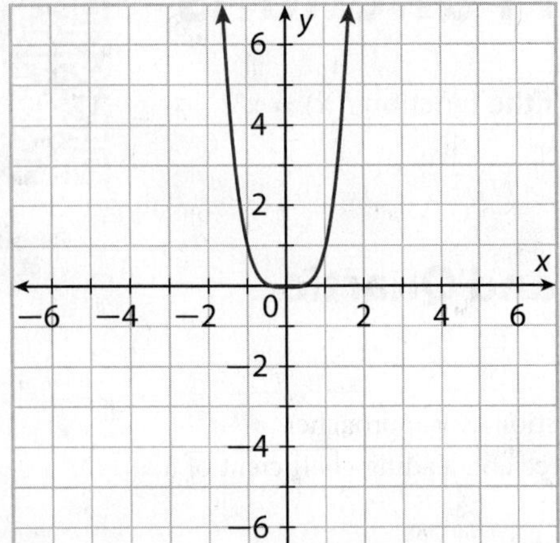

$f(x) = x^4$

▭ direction change(s)

As $x \to +\infty$, $f(x) \to$ ▭.

As $x \to -\infty$, $f(x) \to$ ▭.

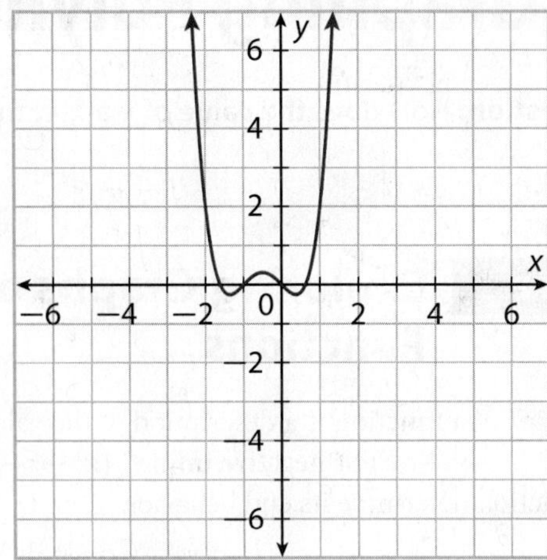

$f(x) = x^4 + 2x^3 - x$

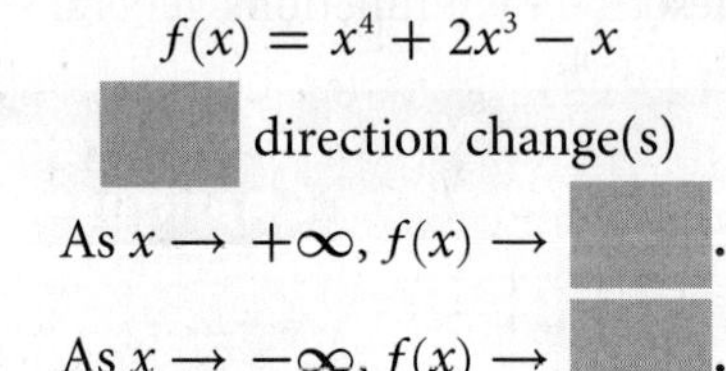

▭ direction change(s)

As $x \to +\infty$, $f(x) \to$ ▭.

As $x \to -\infty$, $f(x) \to$ ▭.

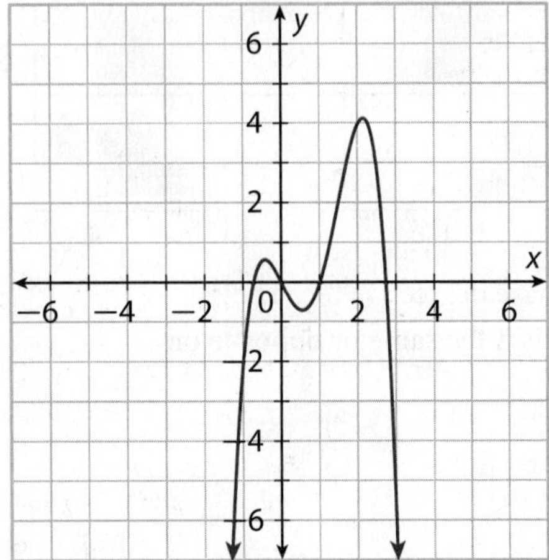

$f(x) = -x^4 + 3x^3 - 2x$

▭ direction change(s)

As $x \to +\infty$, $f(x) \to$ ▭.

As $x \to -\infty$, $f(x) \to$ ▭.

(D) All three of these functions are quartic, which means that they have degree ▭. Their shapes vary, but one feature they all share is the end behavior. Is it the same or opposite on the two ends?

Each of the graphs of the functions in Steps A and C change directions at least once. These direction changes are called **turning points**.

Reflect

1. **Discussion** How many turning points did the cubic functions have? the quartic functions? Do you notice a pattern?

Explain 1 Even and Odd Degree Polynomial Functions

The degree of a polynomial affects the shape of its graph. The table shows representative graphs for polynomial functions with degrees from 1 through 5. A polynomial of degree n can have up to $n - 1$ turning points.

Notice that for functions with odd degrees (1, 3, 5, ...), the end behaviors of graphs are opposite, and for functions with even degrees (2, 4, 6, ...), the end behaviors of graphs are the same.

Graphs of Polynomial Functions

Linear Function Degree 1	Quadratic Function Degree 2	Cubic Function Degree 3	Quartic Function Degree 4	Quintic Function Degree 5
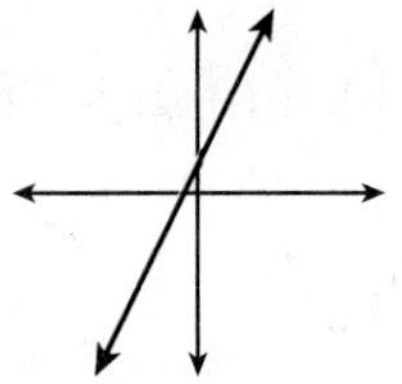	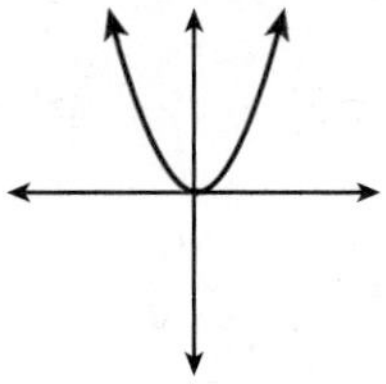	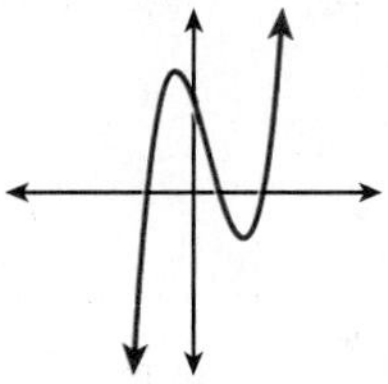	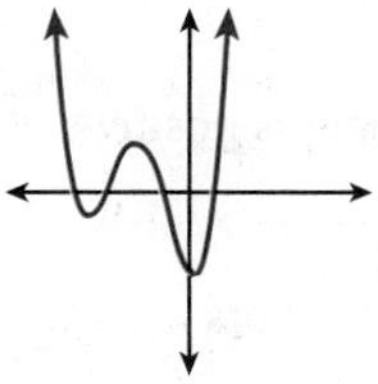	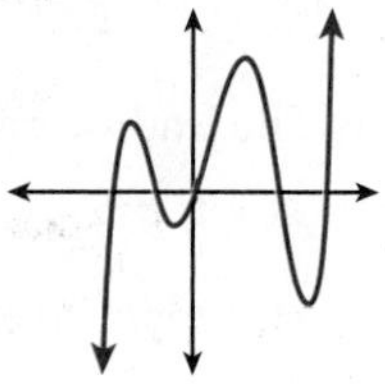

The sign of the leading coefficient determines the end behavior. The table summarizes the end behavior rules for polynomials.

$f(x)$ is a polynomial with...	Odd Degree	Even Degree
Leading coefficient $a > 0$	As $x \to +\infty$, $f(x) \to +\infty$ 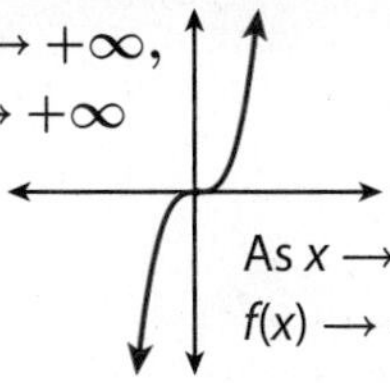 As $x \to -\infty$, $f(x) \to -\infty$	As $x \to -\infty$, $f(x) \to +\infty$ 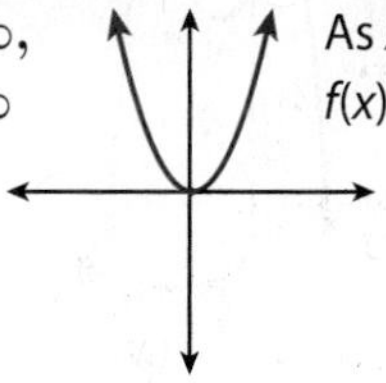 As $x \to +\infty$, $f(x) \to +\infty$
Leading coefficient $a < 0$	As $x \to -\infty$, $f(x) \to +\infty$ 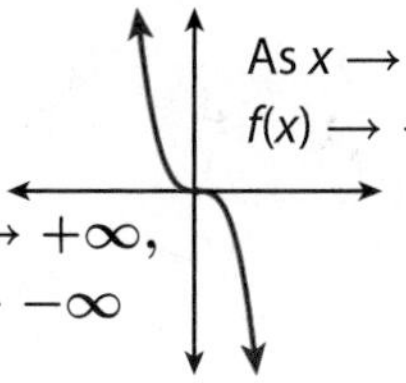 As $x \to +\infty$, $f(x) \to -\infty$	As $x \to -\infty$, $f(x) \to -\infty$ 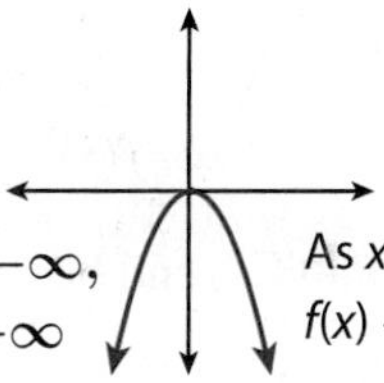 As $x \to +\infty$, $f(x) \to -\infty$

Example 1 **For each graph, identify whether the polynomial $f(x)$ is of odd or even degree, and whether the leading coefficient is positive or negative.**

(A)

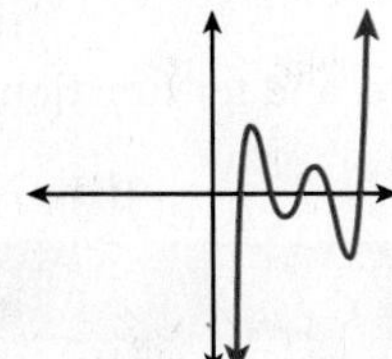

End behavior:

As $x \to +\infty$, $f(x) \to +\infty$.

The leading coefficient is positive.

As $x \to -\infty$, $f(x) \to -\infty$

$\Rightarrow$ Opposite end behaviors

$\Rightarrow$ The polynomial's degree is odd.

(B)

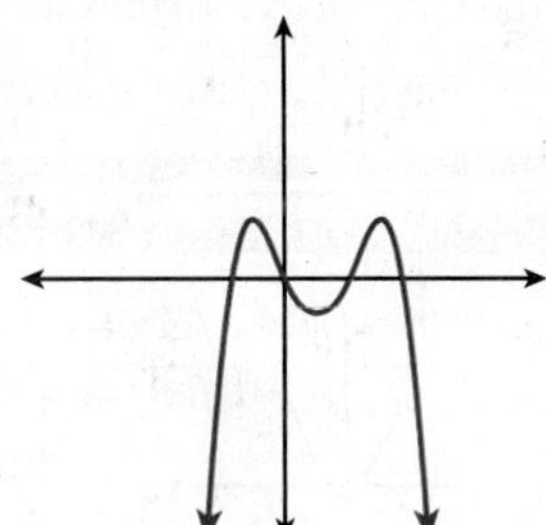

As $x \to +\infty$, $f(x) \to$ $-\infty$.

$\Rightarrow$ The leading coefficient is negative.

As of $x \to -\infty$, $f(x) \to$ $-\infty$.

$\Rightarrow$ Same end behaviors

$\Rightarrow$ The polynomial's degree is even.

Reflect

2. **Discussion** Explain why the leading coefficient is the only polynomial coefficient that determines end-behavior.

Your Turn

For each graph, identify whether the polynomial is of odd or even degree, and whether the leading coefficient is positive or negative.

3.

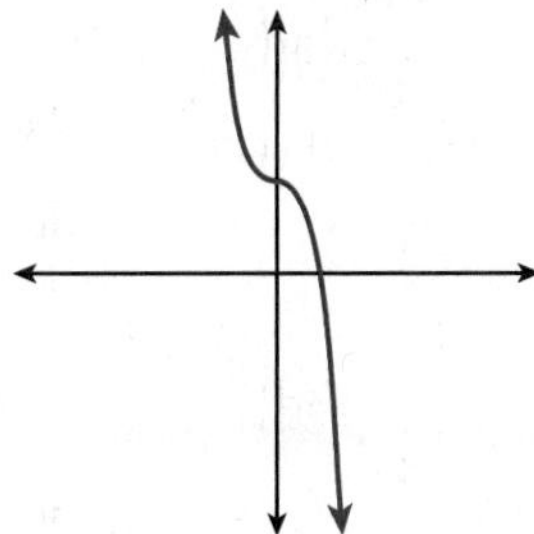

4.

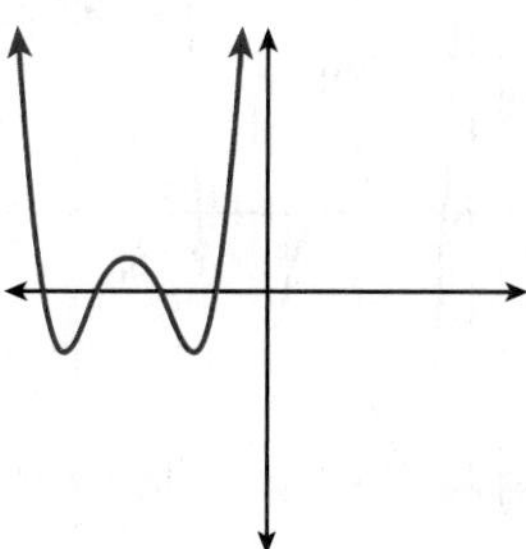

Explain 2 Classifying Even and Odd Functions

A function is an **even function** if $f(-x) = f(x)$ for all values of x. This means that if the point (x, y) is on the graph, then the point $(-x, y)$ is also on the graph.

A function is an **odd function** if $f(-x) = -f(x)$ for all values of x. This means that if the point (x, y) is on the graph, then the point $(-x, -y)$ is also on the graph.

Even Functions	Odd Function

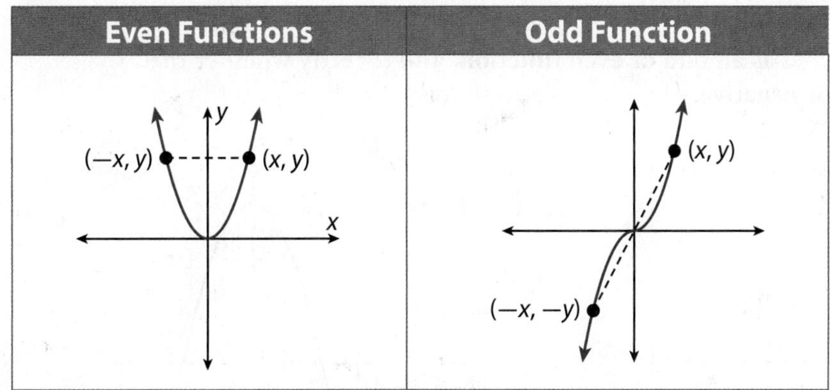

Example 2 **Classify each graphed polynomial as an odd or even function, and identify whether the leading coefficient is positive or negative.**

Ⓐ

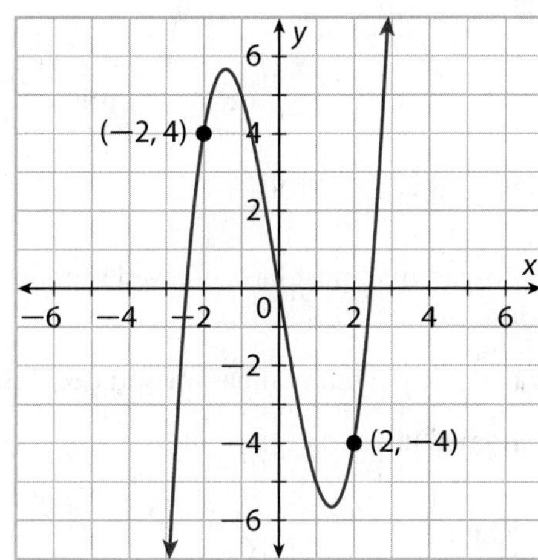

The points (−2, 4) and (2, −4) are on the graph, so the polynomial is an odd function.

End Behavior:

As $x \to +\infty$, $f(x) \to +\infty$, so the leading coefficient is positive.

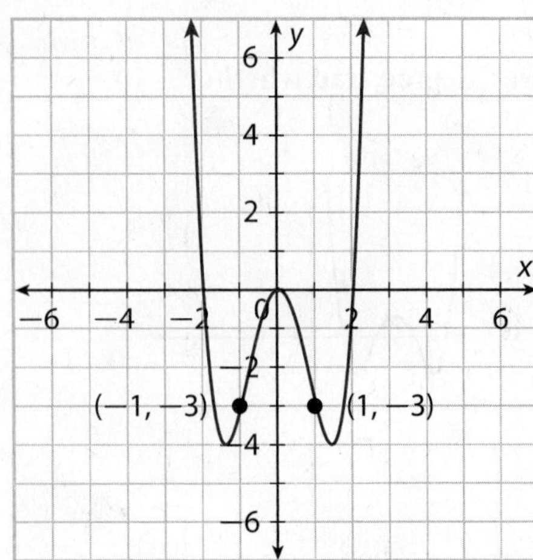

The points $(-1, -3)$ and $(1, -3)$ are on the graph, so the polynomial is an even function.

End Behavior:

As $x \to +\infty$, $f(x) \to$ $+\infty$, so the leading coefficient is positive.

Your Turn

Classify each graphed polynomial as an odd or even function, and identify whether the leading coefficient is positive or negative.

5.

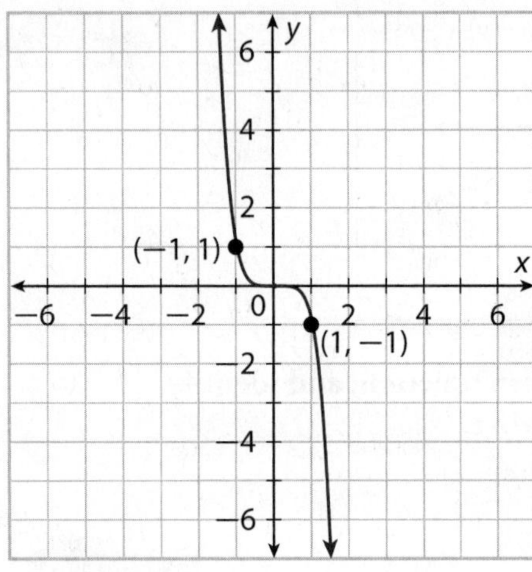

6.

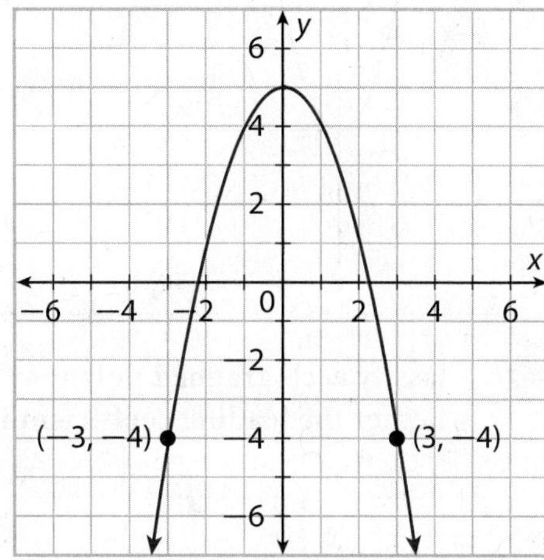

Elaborate

7. How can you tell based on the end behavior that an odd degree polynomial must have an even number of turning points, and an even degree polynomial must have an odd number?

8. If $f(x)$ is a polynomial and $f(-x) = -f(x)$, how do you know that the polynomial has an odd degree?

9. **Essential Question Check-In** How does the degree of a polynomial affect its end behavior?

Evaluate: Homework and Practice

- Online Homework
- Hints and Help
- Extra Practice

1. Use a graphing calculator to plot the function $f(x) = x^3 + 2x^2 - 3x - 4$ and determine how many turning points there are and what the end behavior is.

For each graph, identify whether the polynomial $f(x)$ is of odd or even degree, and whether the leading coefficient is positive or negative.

2.

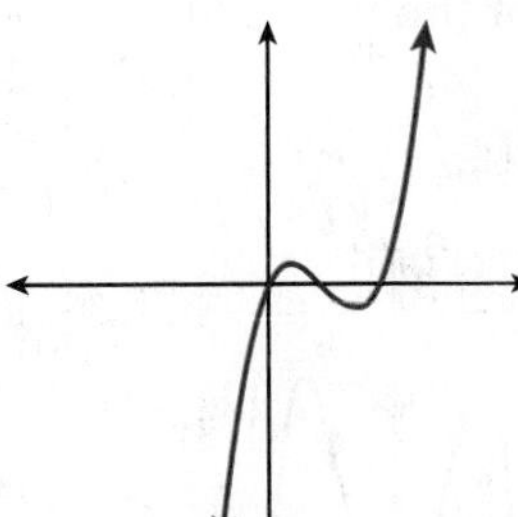

3.

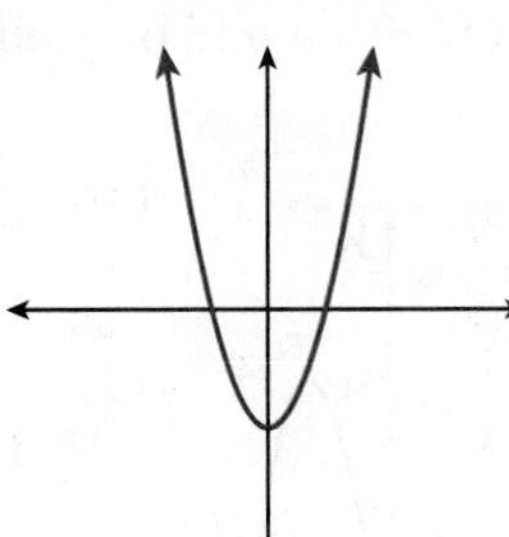

4.

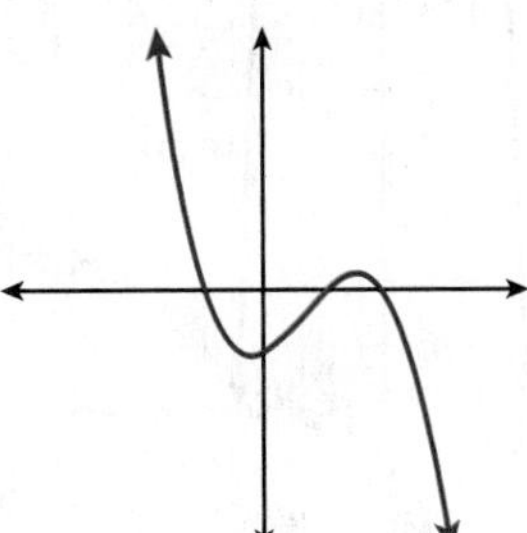

5.

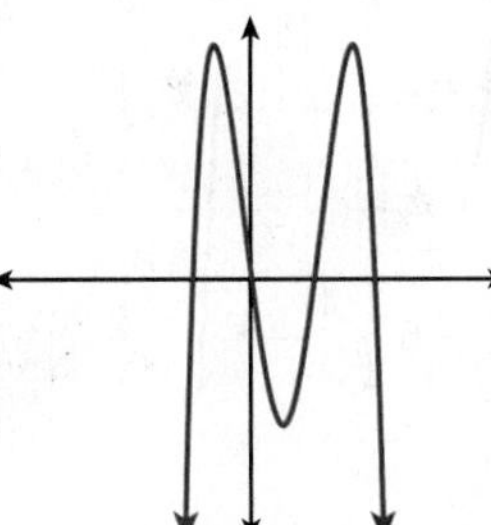

6.

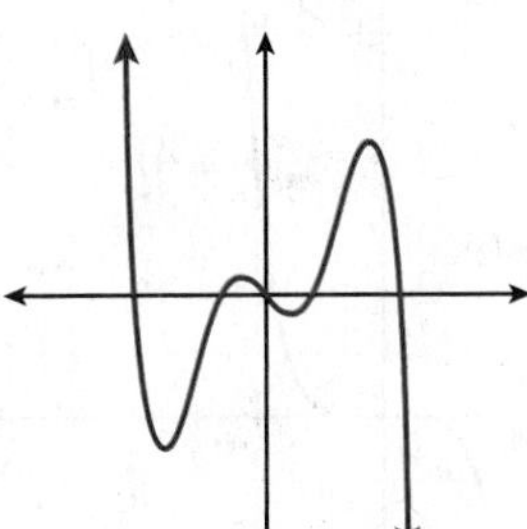

7.

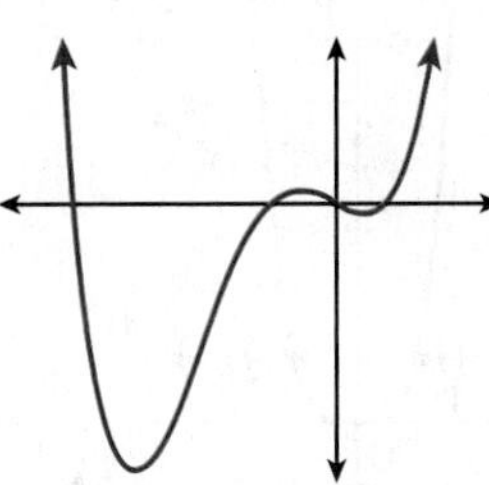

8.

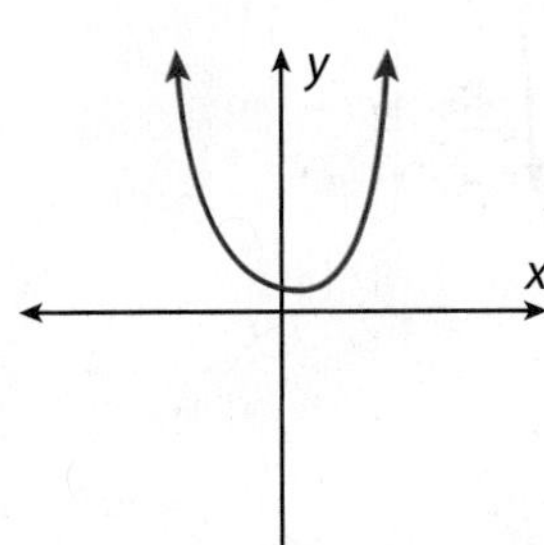

9.

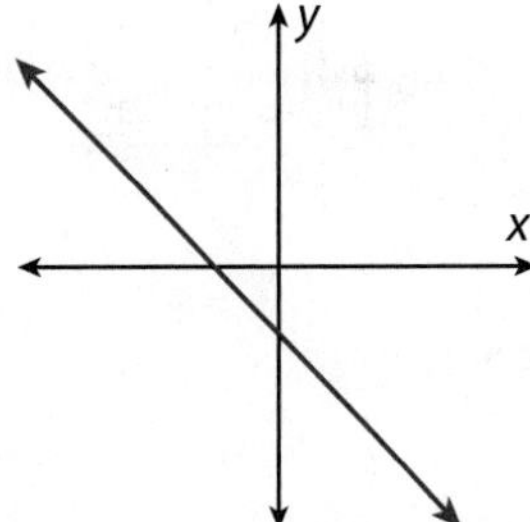

10.

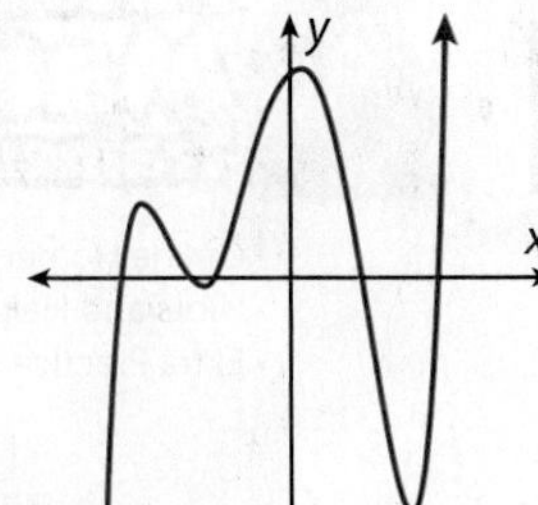

11.

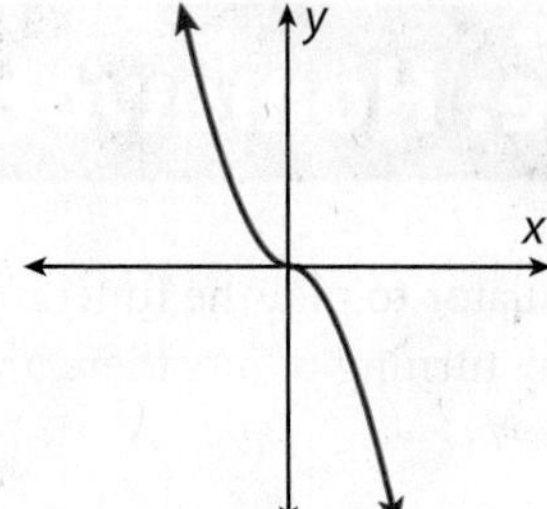

Determine if each function is an odd or even function, and identify the sign of the leading coefficient.

12.

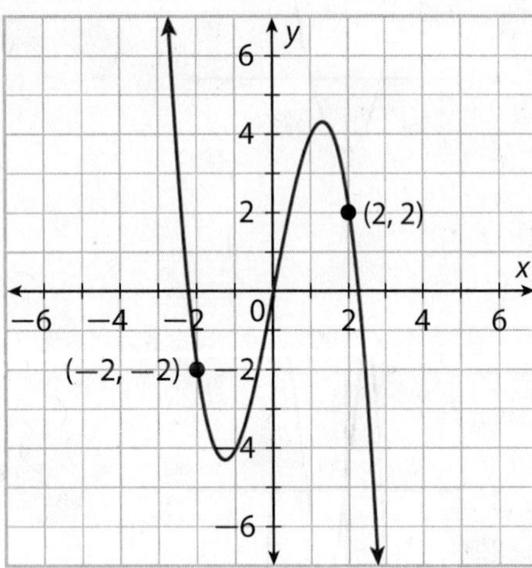

13.

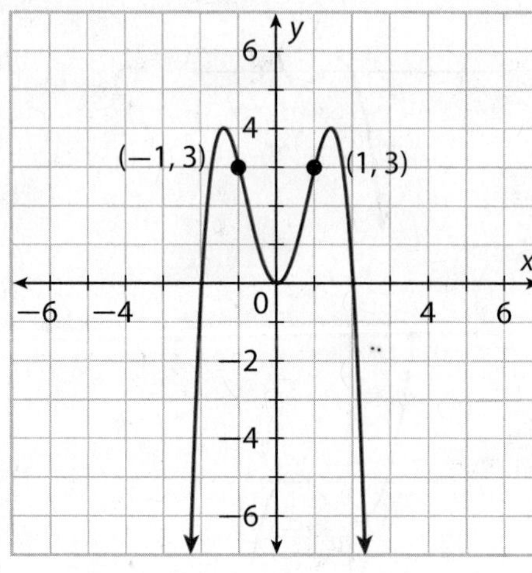

14.

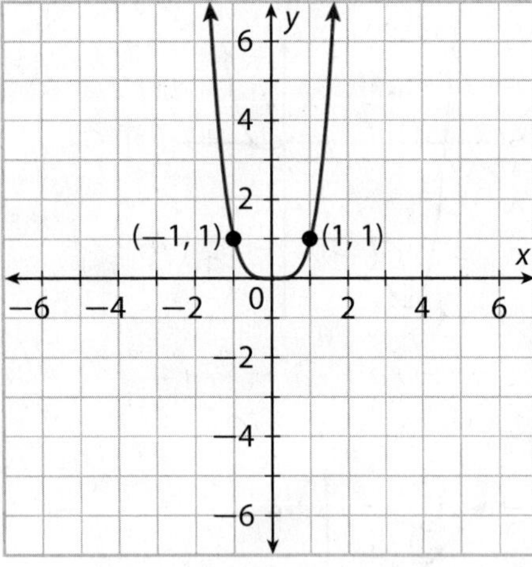

15.

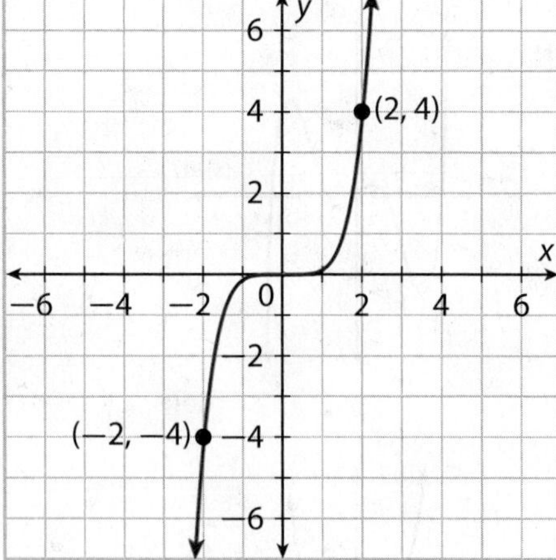

16.

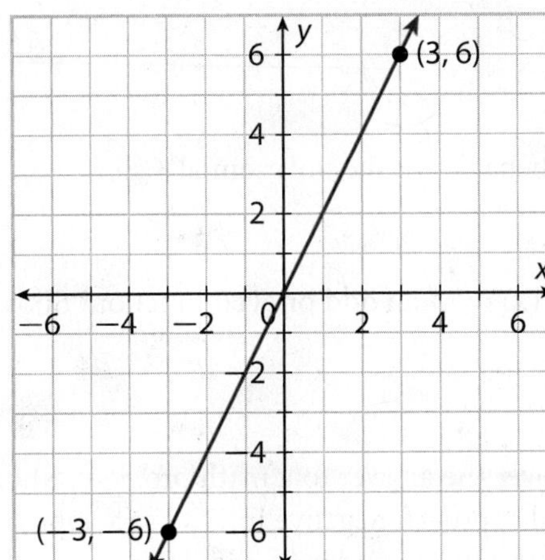

17.

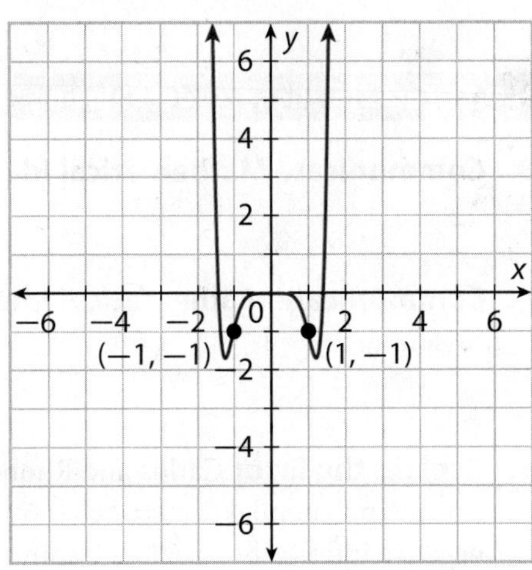

18. Matching Use the end behavior to match each polynomial function to its graph.

A.

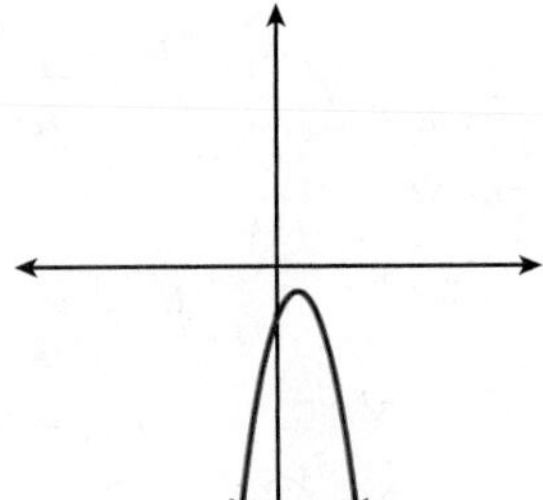

B.

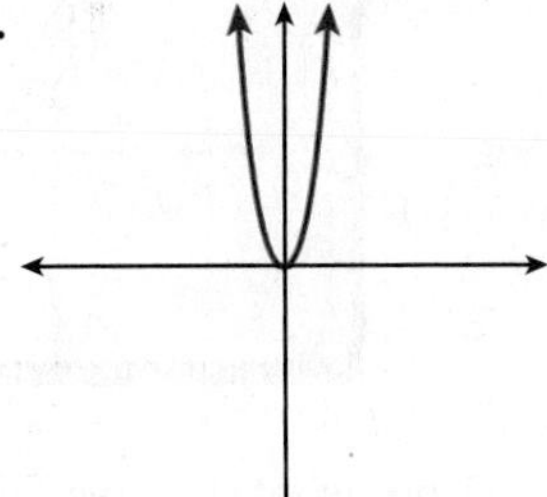

C.

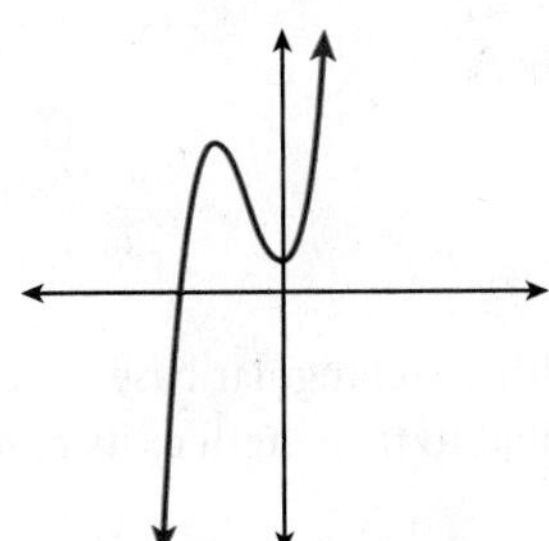

D.

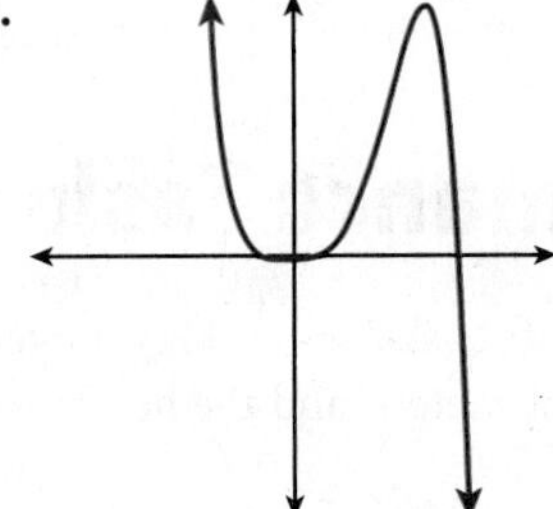

a. ___?___ $f(x) = 5x^3 + 9x^2 + 1$

b. ___?___ $f(x) = 2x^6 + 3x^4 + 5x^2$

c. ___?___ $f(x) = -x^5 + 3x^4 + x$

d. ___?___ $f(x) = -4x^2 + 3x - 1$

H.O.T. Focus on Higher Order Thinking

19. Communicate Mathematical Ideas Predict the end behavior of the polynomial $f(x) = -x^9$.

20. Communicate Mathematical Ideas Is the function $f(x) = x^3$ an odd or even function? Show your reasoning.

21. Explain the Error Carlos and Rhonda are disagreeing over the answer to a math problem. Rhonda claims that the polynomial $f(x) = \frac{1}{3}x^3 + 6x^2 + 21x + 16$ should approach negative infinity as x approaches negative infinity, because the leading term has a positive coefficient and is of odd degree.

Carlos entered the function on his graphing calculator and produced the following graph, which appears to show the function approaching positive infinity as x approaches negative infinity.

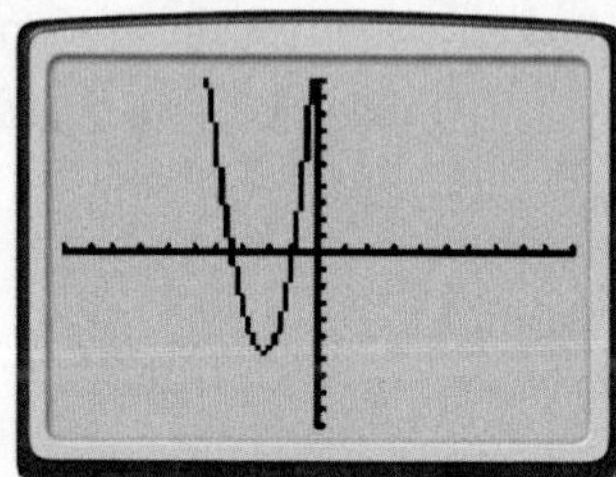

Who is right? Can you figure out what the mistake is?

Lesson Performance Task

A company that specializes in gift baskets is making a pyramid-shaped package with a rectangular base. The base must have a perimeter of 54 centimeters, and the height of the package must be equal to the length of its base.

a. Write a polynomial function, $V(x)$, for the volume of the package, where x is the length of the base. What are the constraints on x for this situation?

b. Use a graphing calculator to find the maximum volume of the package. What value of x corresponds to the maximum volume?

c. What dimensions result in a package with the maximum volume?

13.2 Understanding Inverse Functions

Essential Question: How can you recognize inverses of functions from their graphs and how can you find inverses of functions?

Resource Locker

Explore Exploring Inverses of Functions

You can use a graphing calculator to explore inverse functions and their relationships to the linear function $f(x) = x$.

(A) Using a standard viewing window, graph the function $y = 2^x$ and the linear function $y = x$ on a graphing calculator. Describe the end behavior of $y = 2^x$ as $x \to +\infty$.

(B) Use the DrawInv feature on the calculator to draw the graph of the inverse of $y = 2^x$ along with $y = 2^x$ and $y = x$. How are the graphs of $y = 2^x$ and its inverse related? Is the inverse of $y = 2^x$ a function? Explain your answer.

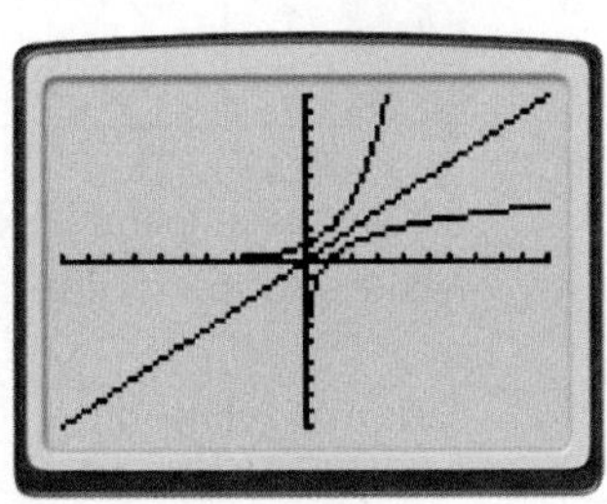

(C) Now graph the function $y = x^2$ and the linear function $y = x$ on a graphing calculator. Use the DrawInv feature to draw the graph of the inverse $y = x^2$ along with $y = x^2$ and $y = x$. How are the graphs of $y = x^2$ and its inverse related? Is the inverse of $y = x^2$ a function? Explain your answer.

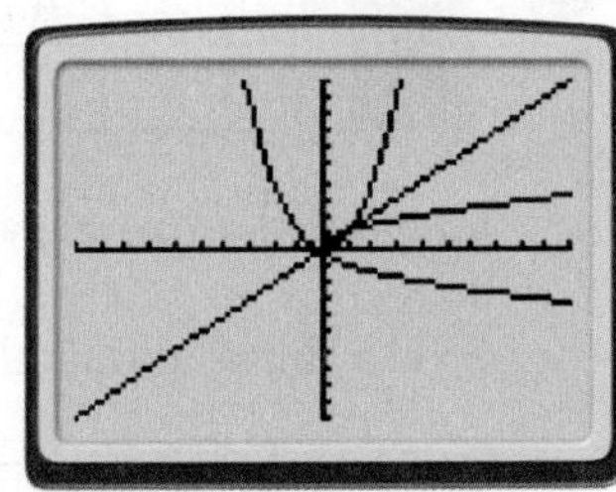

Reflect

1. **Make a Conjecture** Functions and their inverses appear to be reflections across which line?
2. Do you think all inverses of functions are functions? Why or why not?

Explain 1 Graphing Inverse Relations

You have seen the word *inverse* used in various ways.

The additive inverse of 3 is −3.

The multiplicative inverse of 5 is $\frac{1}{5}$.

You can also find and apply inverses to relations, which are sets of ordered pairs, and functions. To graph the **inverse relation**, you can reflect each point across the line $y = x$. This is equivalent to switching the x- and y-values in each ordered pair of the relation.

Example 1 **Graph the relation and connect the points. Then graph the inverse. Identify the domain and range of each relation.**

x	0	1	2	4	8
y	2	4	5	6	7

Graph each ordered pair and connect the points.

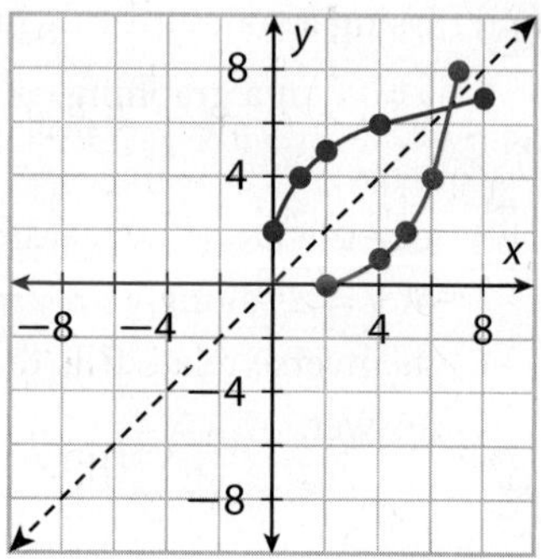

Switch the x- and y-values in each ordered pair.

x	2	4	5	6	7
y	0	1	2	4	8

Reflect each point across $y = x$, and connect the new points. Make sure the points match those in the table.

Original relation: Domain: $0 \le x \le 8$ Range: $2 \le y \le 7$

Inverse relation: Domain: $2 \le x \le 7$ Range: $0 \le y \le 8$

x	1	3	4	5	6
y	0	1	2	3	5

Graph each ordered pair and connect the points.

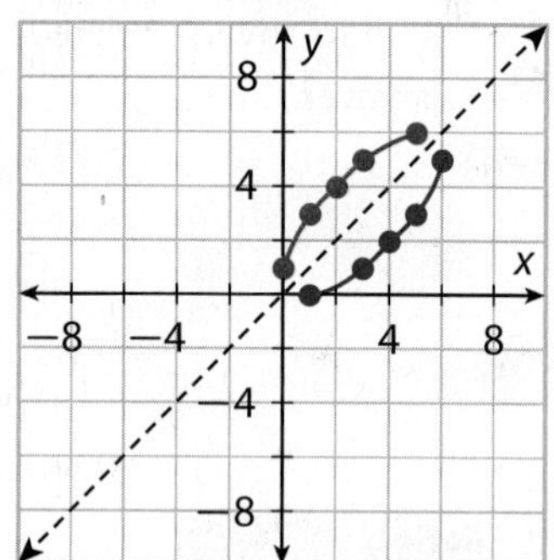

Switch the x- and y-values in each ordered pair.

x	0	1	2	3	5
y	1	3	4	5	6

Reflect each point across $y = x$, and connect the new points. Make sure the points match those in the table.

Original relation: Domain: $1 \le x \le 6$ Range: $0 \le y \le 5$

Inverse relation: Domain: $0 \le x \le 5$ Range: $1 \le y \le 6$

Reflect

3. Discussion How are the domain and range of a relation related to the domain and range of its inverse?

Your Turn

Graph the relation and connect the points. Then graph the inverse. Identify the domain and range of each relation.

4.

x	1	2	3	5	7
y	2	4	6	8	9

Explain 2 Writing Inverse Functions by Using Inverse Operations

When the relation is also a function, you can write the inverse of the function $f(x)$ as $f^{-1}(x)$. This notation does *not* indicate a reciprocal.

Functions that undo each other are called **inverse functions**.

You can find the inverse function by writing the original function with x and y switched and solving for y.

Example 2 **Use inverse operations to find each inverse. Then check your solution.**

(A) $f(x) = 2x$

$y = 2x$ Write y for $f(x)$.

$x = 2y$ Switch x and y.

$y = \frac{x}{2}$ Solve for y.

The inverse is $f^{-1}(x) = \frac{x}{2}$.

Check:

1. Use the input $x = 7$ in $f(x)$.

$f(x) = 2x$

$f(7) = 2(7) = 14$

The output is 14.

2. Verify that the output, 14, gives the input, 7.

$f^{-1}(x) = \frac{x}{2}$

$f^{-1}(14) = \frac{14}{2} = 7$

Since the inverse function *does* undo the original function, $f^{-1}(x) = \frac{x}{2}$ is correct.

(B) $f(x) = \frac{x}{4} - 5$

$y = \frac{x}{4} - 5$ Write y for $f(x)$.

$x = \frac{y}{4} - 5$ Switch x and y.

$y = 4(x + 5)$ Solve for y.

Check:

1. Use the input $x = 40$ in $f(x)$.

$$f(40) = \frac{40}{4} - 5 = 10 - 5 = 5$$

The output is 5.

2. Verify that the output, 5, gives the input, 40.

$$f^{-1}(5) = 4(5 + 5) = 4(10) = 40$$

Since the inverse function does undo the original function, it is correct.

Your Turn

Use inverse operations to find the inverse. Then check your solution.

5. $f(x) = 5x - 7$

Explain 3 Graphing Inverse Functions

A function and its inverse are reflections across the line $y = x$.

Example 3 **Write the inverse of each function. Then graph the function together with its inverse.**

(A) $f(x) = 3x + 6$

$y = 3x + 6$	Write y for $f(x)$.
$x = 3y + 6$	Switch x and y.
$y = \frac{x - 6}{3}$	Solve for y.
$y = \frac{1}{3}x - 2$	Simplify.

The inverse is $f^{-1}(x) = \frac{1}{3}x - 2$.

(B) $f(x) = \frac{2}{3}x + 2$

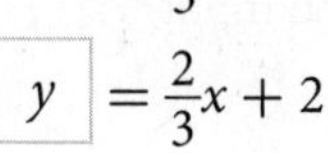

$y = \frac{2}{3}x + 2$ Write y for $f(x)$.

$x = \frac{2}{3}y + 2$ Switch x and y.

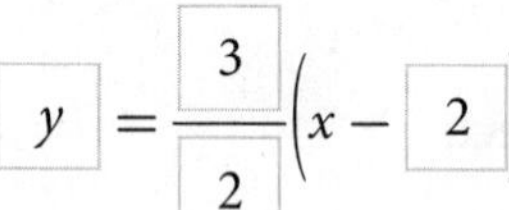

$y = \frac{3}{2}(x - 2)$ Solve for y.

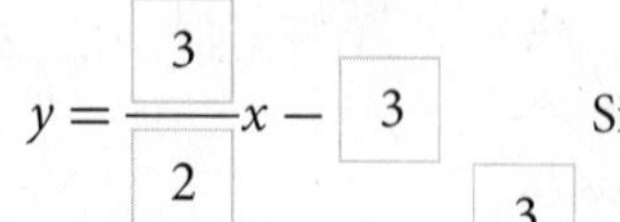

$y = \frac{3}{2}x - 3$ Simplify.

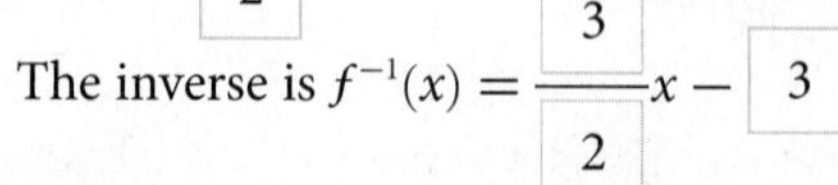

The inverse is $f^{-1}(x) = \frac{3}{2}x - 3$.

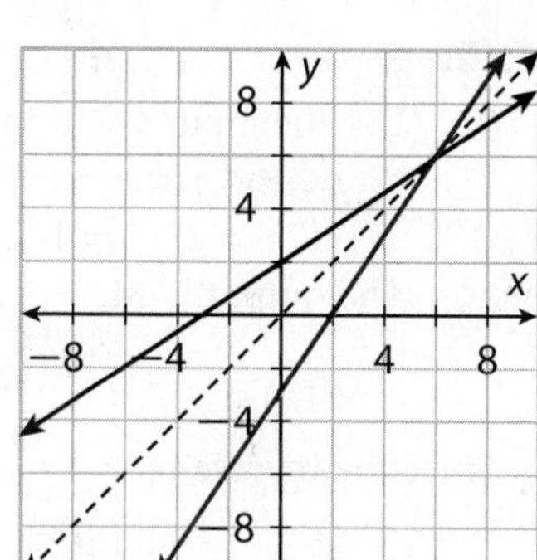

Your Turn

Write the inverse of the function. Then graph the function together with its inverse.

6. $f(x) = 2x - 4$

Explain 4 Using Inverse Functions to Solve Real-World Problems

Any time you need to work backward from a result to the original input, you can apply inverse functions.

Example 4 **Solve each problem by finding and evaluating the inverse function.**

Represent Real-World Problems Lloyd is trying to find the original price of a camera he bought as a gift, but he does not have the store receipt. From the bank transaction, he knows that including a \$3 gift-wrap charge and 8% tax, the total was \$103.14. What was the original price of the camera? Justify your answer.

Analyze Information

Identify the important information.

- Lloyd paid a total of \$ 103.14 for the camera.
- The total includes a gift-wrapping charge of \$ 3 and a sales tax of 8 % of the original price.

Formulate a Plan

Build a function for the total cost t of the camera. Then determine the inverse of the function, and use it to find the original price p.

Solve

total cost = original price + tax + gift-wrapping charge

$$t = p + p \cdot 8\% + 3$$

$$t = p + 0.08p + 3$$

$$t = 1.08p + 3$$

Find the inverse function.

$$t = 1.08p + 3$$

$$t - 3 = 1.08p$$

$$\frac{t - 3}{1.08} = p$$

Use the inverse function to find the original price p for a total price of \$ 103.14.

$$p = \frac{103.14 - 3}{1.08} \approx 92.72$$

The original price of the camera was \$ 92.72.

Justify and Evaluate

Use the original function to check your answer.

$t = \boxed{1.08}\ p + \boxed{3}$

$t = \boxed{1.08} \cdot \left(\boxed{92.72}\right) + \boxed{3} \approx \boxed{103.14}$

Since the inverse function does undo the original function, it is correct.

Reflect

7. What are the domain and range of the function for the total cost and its inverse in Example 4?

Your Turn

8. To make tea, use $\frac{1}{6}$ teaspoon of tea per ounce of water plus a teaspoon for the pot. Use the inverse to find the number of ounces of water needed if 7 teaspoons of tea are used. Check your answer.

Elaborate

9. Explain the result of interchanging x and y to find the inverse function of $f(x) = x$. How could you have predicted this from the graph of $f(x)$?

10. Give an example of a function whose inverse is a function. Give an example of a function whose inverse is not a function.

11. Describe what happens when you take the inverse of the inverse of a function. Is the result necessarily a function? Explain.

12. **Essential Question Check-In** Inverses are reflections of functions across which line?

Evaluate: Homework and Practice

• Online Homework
• Hints and Help
• Extra Practice

Graph the relation and connect the points. Then graph the inverse. Identify the domain and range of each relation.

1.

x	1	2	3	4
y	1	2	4	8

2.

x	3	4	1	−1
y	−1	−2	−4	−4

3.

x	1	3	5	7
y	0	3	6	9

4.

x	−2	0	3	7
y	0	−1	−4	−9

Use inverse operations to find each inverse. Then check your solution.

5. $f(x) = 5x - 1$

6. $f(x) = \frac{x}{2} + 3$

7. $f(x) = 3 - \frac{1}{2}x$

8. $f(x) = \frac{1}{2}(3 - 3x)$

9. $f(x) = 4(x + 1)$

10. $f(x) = \frac{3x - 5}{2}$

Write the inverse of each function. Then graph the function together with its inverse.

11. $f(x) = 5 - 2x$

12. $f(x) = \frac{x}{4} + 2$

13. $f(x) = 10 + 0.6x$

14. $f(x) = 2 + 3x$

Solve each problem using an inverse function.

15. Meteorology The formula $C = \frac{5}{9}(F - 32)$ gives degrees Celsius as a function of degrees Fahrenheit. Find the inverse of this function to convert degrees Celsius to degrees Fahrenheit, and use it to find 16 °C in degrees Fahrenheit.

16. To make coffee using a home drip coffee maker, use $\frac{1}{4}$ tablespoon of coffee grounds per ounce of water plus 2 tablespoons for the coffee pot. Use the inverse to find the number of ounces of water needed if 11 tablespoons of coffee grounds are used.

17. Shopping A shopping attendant needs to price a large jigsaw puzzle returned by a customer. The customer paid a total of \$33.14, including a convenience charge of \$1.50 and 11% sales tax on the subtotal. Use the inverse to find the original price of the puzzle.

18. Education A student wants to figure out her raw score on a test she recently took. Including a 5-point bonus and a 2% increase after the bonus, the student scored a 94. Use the inverse to find the raw score.

19. Currency At one point, the currency exchange rate between the U.S. dollar and the British pound sterling was 0.600 pound per dollar after a 3-dollar exchange fee. Use the inverse to determine how many U.S. dollars 100 British pounds would be worth.

20. Travel A taxi driver charges \$2 for service plus 65¢ per mile. Use the inverse to determine the number of miles driven if the total charge is \$11.75.

21. Identify whether you need to use an additive inverse, multiplicative inverse, or both to find the inverse of the given function.

A. $f(x) = 3x$

B. $f(x) = 3x + 4$

C. $f(x) = \frac{x}{6}$

D. $f(x) = 5x + 6$

E. $f(x) = \frac{x+6}{x+2}$

22. Use a graphing calculator to graph the function $y = 3^x$ on a standard viewing window along with its inverse and the line $y = x$. Is the function's inverse a function? Explain your answer.

H.O.T. Focus on Higher Order Thinking

23. **Critical Thinking** Find the inverse of $f(x) = \frac{x-3}{x+4}$. Then use a sample input and output to check your answer.

24. **Explain the Error** A student produced the following result when attempting to find the inverse of $f(x) = \frac{x}{6} + 5$. Explain the student's error and state the correct answer.

$$y = \frac{x}{6} + 5$$

$$x = \frac{y}{6} + 5$$

$$x - 5 = \frac{y}{6}$$

$$6x - 5 = y$$

Lesson Performance Task

The population p in thousands for the state of Oregon can be modeled by the linear function $p = 39.016t + 1039.614$, where t is the time in years since 1940.

A. Find an equation for the inverse function, rounding the constants and coefficients to three decimal places. What is the meaning of the slope and y-intercept of the inverse function?

B. Use the inverse function to estimate when the population of Oregon was 3,000,000.

C. The population of Oregon was estimated as 3,930,065 in 2013. Use the model to predict when the population of Oregon will be 4,800,000. What would have to be assumed for your answer to be valid?

13.3 Graphing Square Root Functions

Resource Locker

Essential Question: How can you use transformations of the parent square root function to graph functions of the form $f(x) = a\sqrt{x - h} + k$?

Explore 1 Exploring the Inverse of $y = x^2$

Use the steps that follow to explore the inverse of $y = x^2$.

(A) Use a graphing calculator to graph $y = x^2$ and $y = x$. Describe the graph.

(B) Use the DrawInv feature to graph the inverse of $y = x^2$ along with $y = x^2$ and $y = x$. Describe the new graph.

(C) State whether the inverse is a function. Explain your reasoning.

(D) Use inverse operations to write the inverse of $y = x^2$.

Switch x and y in the equation. $x = y^2$

Take the square root of both sides of the equation. $\boxed{} = y$

Reflect

1. **Discussion** Explain why the inverse of $y = x^2$ is not a function.

Explore 2 Graphing the Parent Square Root Function

The graph shows $y = \pm\sqrt{x}$, $y = x^2$, and $y = x$. You have discovered that $y = \pm\sqrt{x}$ is not a function. You will find out how to alter $y = \pm\sqrt{x}$ so that it becomes a function.

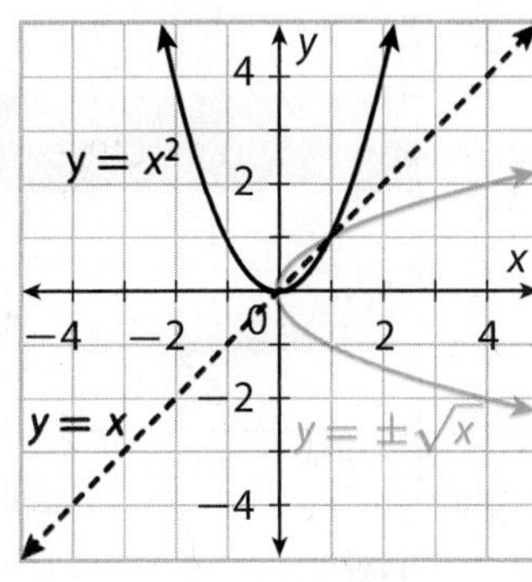

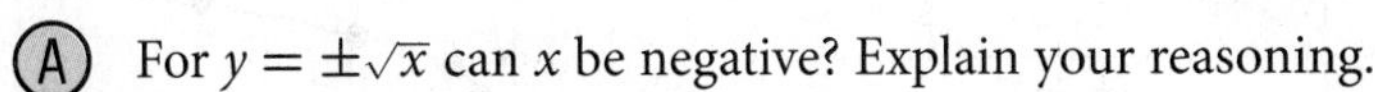
(A) For $y = \pm\sqrt{x}$ can x be negative? Explain your reasoning.

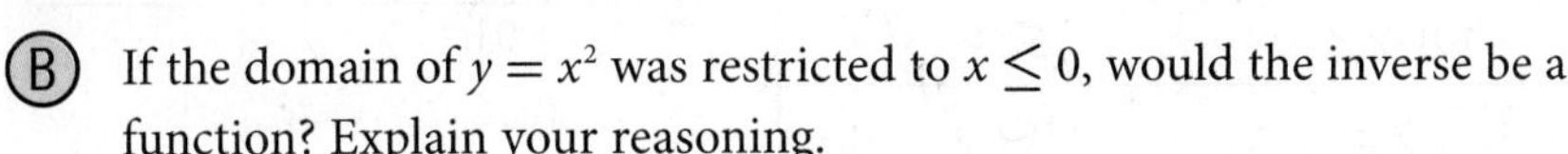
(B) If the domain of $y = x^2$ was restricted to $x \leq 0$, would the inverse be a function? Explain your reasoning.

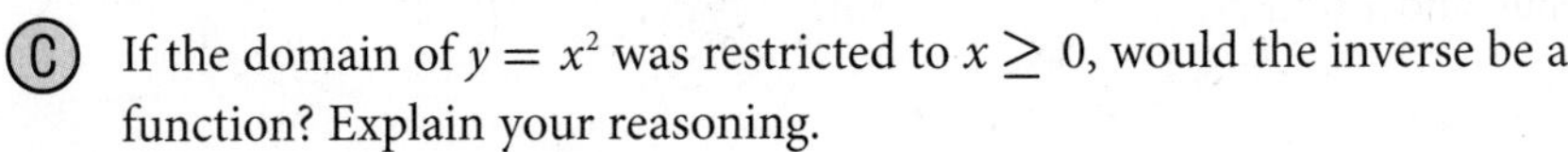
(C) If the domain of $y = x^2$ was restricted to $x \geq 0$, would the inverse be a function? Explain your reasoning.

(D) Typically the domain of $y = x^2$ is restricted to $x \geq 0$ before findng its inverse to create the parent square root function. What is the equation of the parent square root function?

(E) A **radical function** is a function whose rule is a radical expression. A **square root function** is a radical function involving $\sqrt{x}$.

Graph the parent square root function $y = \sqrt{x}$ by first making a table of values.

x	$y = \sqrt{x}$	(x, y)
0	$\sqrt{0}$	(0, 0)
1		(1,)
4		(4,)
9		(9,)

(F) Plot the points and draw a smooth curve through them.

Reflect

2. What are the domain and range of the parent square root function?

Explain 1 Graphing Translations of the Parent Square Root Function

You discovered in Explore 2 that the parent square root function is $y = \sqrt{x}$. The equation $y = \sqrt{x - h} + k$ is the parent square root function with horizontal and vertical translations, where h and k are constants. The constant h will cause a horizontal shift and k will cause a vertical shift.

Example 1 **Graph each function by using a table and plotting the points. State the direction of the shift from the parent square root function, and by how many units. Then state the domain and range. Confirm your graph by graphing with a graphing calculator.**

(A) $y = \sqrt{x - 1} + 2$

x	$y = \sqrt{x - 1} + 2$	(x, y)
1	$\sqrt{1 - 1} + 2$	(1, 2)
2	$\sqrt{2 - 1} + 2$	(2, 3)
5	$\sqrt{5 - 1} + 2$	(5, 4)
10	$\sqrt{10 - 1} + 2$	(10, 5)

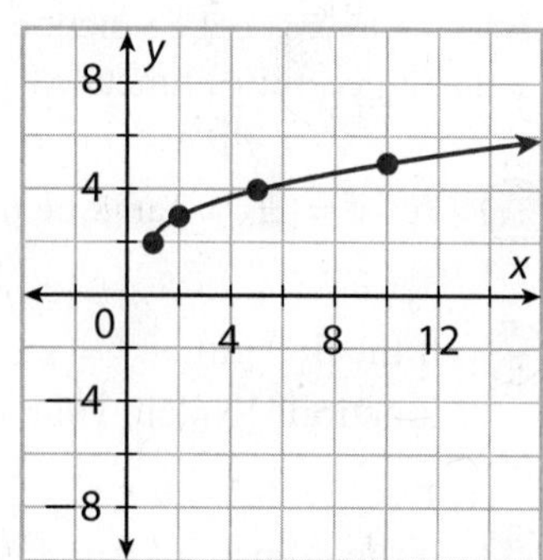

The graph is translated 2 units up and 1 unit right.

Domain: $x \geq 1$ Range: $y \geq 2$

(B) $y = \sqrt{x+3} - 2$

x	$y = \sqrt{x+3} - 2$	(x, y)
-3	$\sqrt{-3+3} - 2$	$(-3, -2)$
-2	$\sqrt{-2+3} - 2$	$(-2, -1)$
1	$\sqrt{1+3} - 2$	$(1, 0)$
6	$\sqrt{6+3} - 2$	$(6, 1)$
13	$\sqrt{13+3} - 2$	$(13, 2)$

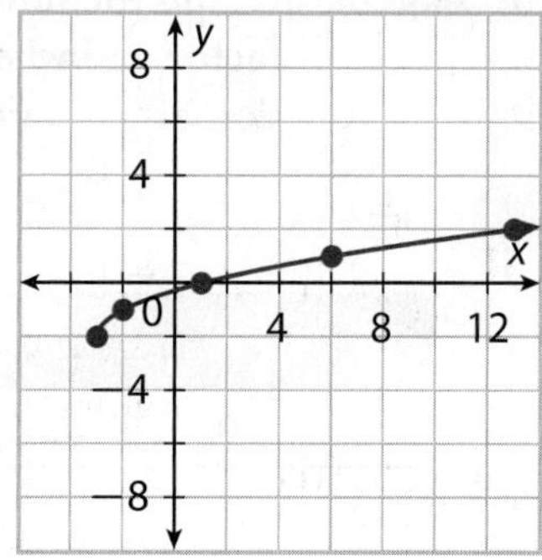

The graph is translated 2 units down and 3 units to the left.

Domain: $x \geq -3$ Range: $y \geq -2$

Your Turn

Graph each function by using a table and plotting the points. State the direction of the shift from the parent square root function, and by how many units. Then state the domain and range. Confirm your graph with a graphing calculator.

3. $y = \sqrt{x+1}$

x	$y = \sqrt{x+1}$	(x, y)
-1	?	?
0	?	?
3	?	?
8	?	?

4. $y = \sqrt{x} - 4$

x	$y = \sqrt{x} - 4$	(x, y)
0	?	?
1	?	?
4	?	?
9	?	?

Explain 2 Graphing Stretches/Compressions and Reflections of the Parent Square Root Function

The equation $y = a\sqrt{x}$, where a is a constant, is the parent square root function with a vertical stretch or compression. If the absolute value of a is less than 1 the graph will be compressed by a factor of $|a|$, and if the absolute value of a is greater than 1 the graph will be stretched by a factor of $|a|$. If a is negative, the graph will be reflected across the x-axis.

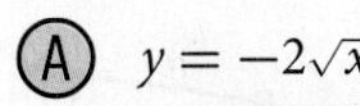

Example 2 **Graph the functions by using a table and plotting the points. State the stretch/compression factor and whether the graph of the parent function was reflected or not. Then state the domain and range. Confirm your graph by graphing with a graphing calculator.**

(A) $y = -2\sqrt{x}$

x	$y = -2\sqrt{x}$	(x, y)
0	$-2\sqrt{0}$	(0, 0)
1	$-2\sqrt{1}$	(1, −2)
4	$-2\sqrt{4}$	(4, −4)
9	$-2\sqrt{9}$	(9, −6)

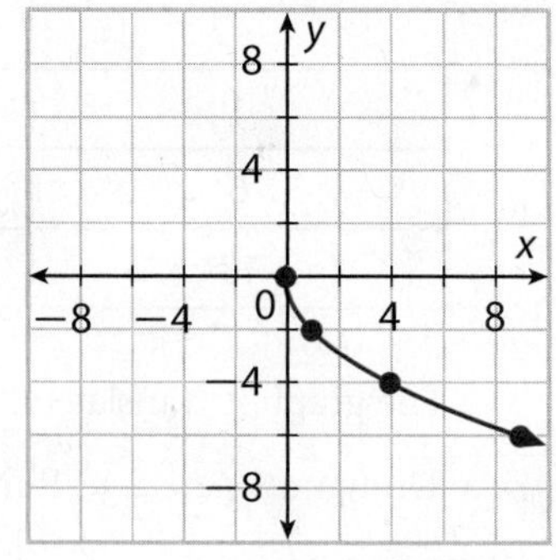

There is a vertical stretch by a factor of 2, and the graph is reflected across the x-axis.

Domain: $x \geq 0$ Range: $y \leq 0$

(B) $y = \frac{1}{2}\sqrt{x}$

x	$y = \frac{1}{2}\sqrt{x}$	(x, y)
0	$\frac{1}{2}\sqrt{0}$	(0, 0)
1	$\frac{1}{2}\sqrt{1}$	$\left(1, \frac{1}{2}\right)$
4	$\frac{1}{2}\sqrt{4}$	(4, 1)
9	$\frac{1}{2}\sqrt{9}$	$\left(9, \frac{3}{2}\right)$

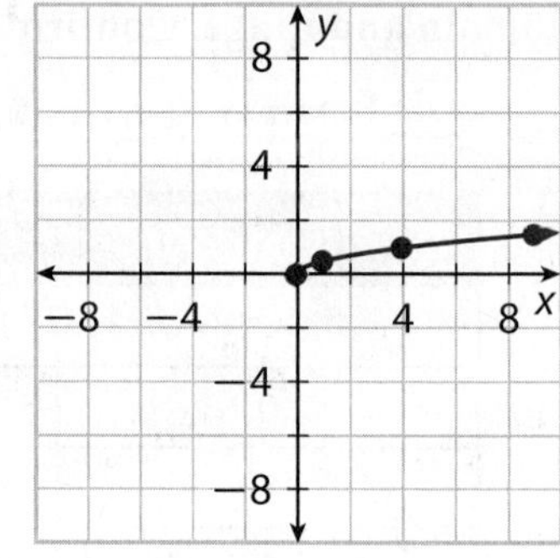

There is a vertical compression by a factor of $\frac{1}{2}$, and the graph is not reflected across the x–axis.

Domain: $x \geq 0$ Range: $y \geq 0$

Your Turn

Graph the functions by using a table and plotting the points. State the stretch/compression factor and whether the graph of the parent function was reflected or not. Then state the domain and range. Confirm your graph by graphing with a graphing calculator.

5. $y = 3\sqrt{x}$

x	$y = 3\sqrt{x}$	(x, y)
0	$3\sqrt{0}$	(0, 0)
1	?	?
4	?	?
9	?	?

6. $y = -\frac{1}{4}\sqrt{x}$

x	$y = -\frac{1}{4}\sqrt{x}$	(x, y)
0	$-\frac{1}{4}\sqrt{0}$	$(0, 0)$
1	?	?
4	?	?
9	?	?

Explain 3 Modeling Real-World Situations with Square Root Functions

You can use transformations of square root functions to model real-world situations.

Example 3 **Construct a square root function to solve each problem.**

(A) On Earth, the function $f(x) = \frac{6}{5}\sqrt{x}$ approximates the distance in miles to the horizon observed by a person whose eye level is x feet above the ground. Use the function to estimate the distance to the horizon for someone whose eyes are 6.5 ft above Earth's surface, rounding to one decimal place.

$f(x) = \frac{6}{5}\sqrt{x}$

$f(6.5) = \frac{6}{5}\sqrt{6.5}$ Substitute 6.5 for x.

$f(6.5) \approx 3.1$ miles Simplify.

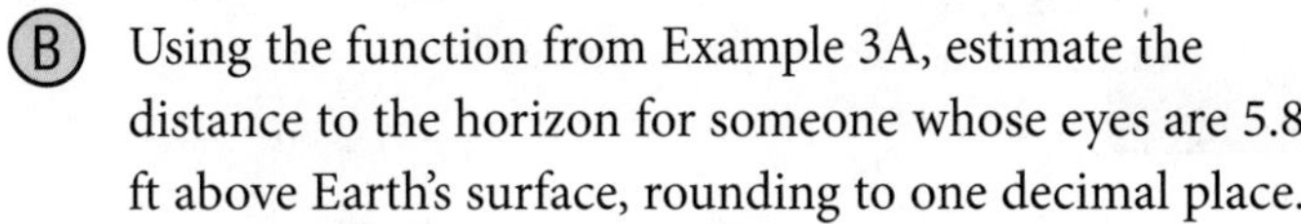

(B) Using the function from Example 3A, estimate the distance to the horizon for someone whose eyes are 5.8 ft above Earth's surface, rounding to one decimal place.

$f(x) = \frac{6}{5}\sqrt{x}$

$f(5.8) = \frac{6}{5}\sqrt{5.8}$ Substitute 5.8 for x.

$f(5.8) \approx 2.9$ miles Simplify.

Your Turn

7. On Earth, the function $f(x) = \frac{6}{5}\sqrt{x}$ approximates the distance in miles to the horizon observed by a person whose eye level is x feet above the ground. The graph of the corresponding function for Mars has a vertical stretch relative to $f(x)$ of $\frac{\sqrt{5}}{3}$. Write the corresponding function $g(x)$ for Mars and use it to estimate the distance to the horizon for an astronaut whose eyes are 6.2 ft above Mars's surface, rounding to one decimal place.

8. Using the function from the previous question, estimate the distance to the horizon for an astronaut whose eyes are 5.5 ft above Mars's surface, rounding to one decimal place.

Elaborate

9. What can be said about the inverse of $y = x^2$ when the domain isn't restricted?

10. Are there any square root functions that do not have a restricted domain? Explain.

11. **Essential Question Check-In** What is the domain and range of the function $f(x) = \sqrt{x - h} + k$?

Evaluate: Homework and Practice

- Online Homework
- Hints and Help
- Extra Practice

1. What is the inverse of $y = x^2$? Select the correct answer.

A. $y = \sqrt{x}$ B. $y = \pm\sqrt{x}$ C. $y = -\sqrt{x}$ D. $y = x$

2. What is the parent square root function? What is its domain and range?

For Exercises 3–14, copy and complete the table, graph each function, describe any transformation from the parent function, and state the domain and range.

3. $y = \sqrt{x + 1} - 4$

x	$y = \sqrt{x+1} - 4$	(x, y)
−1	$\sqrt{-1+1} - 4$	(−1, −4)
0	?	?
3	?	?
8	?	?

4. $y = \sqrt{x} + 6$

x	$y = \sqrt{x} + 6$	(x, y)
0	$\sqrt{0} + 6$	(0, 6)
1	?	?
4	?	?
9	?	?

5. $y = \sqrt{x + 8}$

x	$y = \sqrt{x+8}$	(x, y)
−8	$\sqrt{-8+8}$	(−8, 0)
−7	?	?
−4	?	?
1	?	?
8	?	?

6. $y = \sqrt{x - 4} + 3$

x	$y = \sqrt{x - 4} + 3$	(x, y)
4	$\sqrt{4 - 4} + 3$	$(4, 3)$
5	?	?
8	?	?

7. $y = \sqrt{x + 5} - 7$

x	$y = \sqrt{x + 5} - 7$	(x, y)
−5	$\sqrt{-5 + 5} - 7$	$(-5, -7)$
−4	?	?
−1	?	?
4	?	?

8. $y = \sqrt{x + 4} + 7$

x	$y = \sqrt{x + 4} + 7$	(x, y)
−4	$\sqrt{-4 + 4} + 7$	$(-4, 7)$
−3	?	?
0	?	?
5	?	?

9. $y = -\sqrt{x}$

x	$y = -\sqrt{x}$	(x, y)
0	$-\sqrt{0}$	$(0, 0)$
1	?	?
4	?	?
9	?	?

10. $y = \frac{1}{10}\sqrt{x}$

x	$y = \frac{1}{10}\sqrt{x}$	(x, y)
0	$\frac{1}{10}\sqrt{0}$	$(0, 0)$
1	?	?
4	?	?
9	?	?

11. $y = -5\sqrt{x}$

x	$y = -5\sqrt{x}$	(x, y)
0	$-5\sqrt{0}$	$(0, 0)$
1	?	?
4	?	?
9	?	?

12. $y = \frac{1}{3}\sqrt{x}$

x	$y = \frac{1}{3}\sqrt{x}$	(x, y)
0	$\frac{1}{3}\sqrt{0}$	$(0, 0)$
1	?	?
4	?	?
9	?	?

13. $y = 6\sqrt{x}$

x	$y = 6\sqrt{x}$	(x, y)
0	$6\sqrt{0}$	$(0, 0)$
1	?	?
4	?	?
9	?	?
16	?	?

14. $y = -\frac{1}{2}\sqrt{x}$

x	$y = -\frac{1}{2}\sqrt{x}$	(x, y)
0	$-\frac{1}{2}\sqrt{0}$	$(0, 0)$
1	?	?
4	?	?
9	?	?

Construct a square root function to solve the problem.

15. The speed in miles per hour of a tsunami can be modeled by the function $s(d) = 3.86\sqrt{d}$, where d is the average depth in feet of the water over which the tsunami travels. Predict the speed of a tsunami over water with a depth of 1500 feet, rounding to the nearest tenth.

16. Pilots use the function $D(A) = 3.56\sqrt{A}$ to approximate the distance D in kilometers to the horizon from an altitude A in meters. What is the approximate distance to the horizon observed by a pilot flying at an altitude of 11,000 meters? (Round to the nearest tenth of a kilometer.)

17. A pharmaceutical company samples the raw materials it receives before they are used in the manufacture of drugs. For inactive ingredients, the company uses the function $s(x) = \sqrt{x} + 1$ to determine the number of samples s that should be taken from a shipment of x containers. How many samples should be taken from a shipment of 45 containers of an inactive ingredient? (Round to the nearest whole number.)

18. Copy and complete the table. Graph the equation $y = 2\sqrt{x+2} + 2$. Then state the domain and range.

x	$y = 2\sqrt{x+2} + 2$	(x, y)
−2	$2\sqrt{-2+2}+2$	(−2, 2)
−1	?	?
2	?	?
7	?	?

Write an equation for each graph. Explain your reasoning.

19.

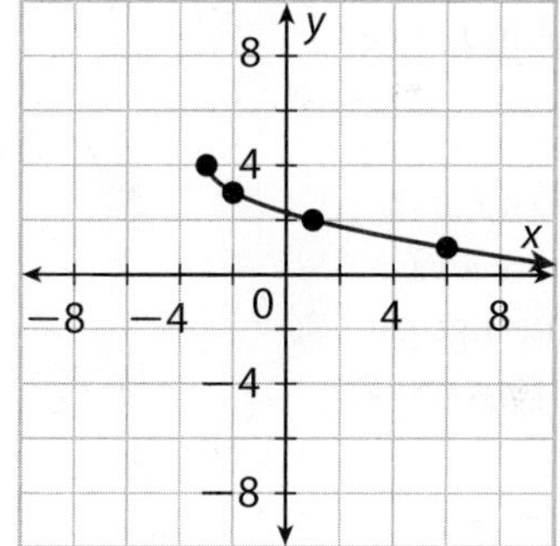

20.

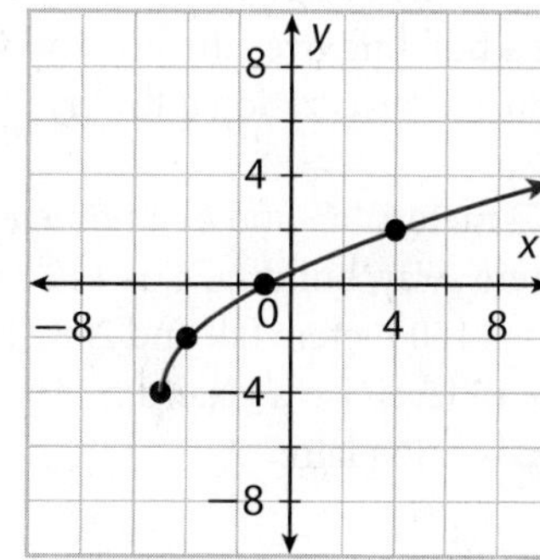

H.O.T. Focus on Higher Order Thinking

21. Explain the Error A student said the domain and range for the equation $y = \frac{1}{2}\sqrt{x + 10} - 7$ was $x \leq -10$ and $y \geq 7$. Is the student correct? If not, give the mistake and the correct answer.

22. Multi-Step The time t in seconds required for an object to fall from a certain height can be modeled by the function $t(h) = \frac{1}{4}\sqrt{h}$, where h is the initial height of the object in feet. How much longer will it take for a piece of an iceberg to fall into the ocean from a height of 240 ft than from a height of 100 ft? (Round to the nearest hundredth of a second.)

23. Analyze Relationships Describe how a horizontal translation and a vertical translation of the function $f(x) = \sqrt{x}$ each affect the function's domain and range.

24. Represent Real-World Problems Pilots use the function $D(A) = 3.56\sqrt{A}$ to approximate the distance D in kilometers to the horizon from an altitude A in meters on a clear day.

a. A vertical compression of $D(A)$ by a factor of $\frac{1}{4}$ can be used to model the distance to the horizon on a partly cloudy day. Write the new function and approximate the distance to the horizon observed by a pilot flying at an altitude of 5000 m. (Round to the nearest whole kilometer.)

b. How will the distance to the horizon on a partly cloudy day change if the pilot descends by 1500 m?

Lesson Performance Task

On a clear day, the ability to see a faraway unobstructed object on flat land is limited by the curvature of Earth. For an object with a height H in meters being observed by a person at height h in meters above the ground, the approximate distance d, in kilometers, at which the object falls below the horizon is given by the function $d(H) = 3.57\sqrt{H} + 3.57\sqrt{h}$.

A. What is the effect of the observer's height h on the graph of $d(H)$?

B. An observational tower has two levels, one at 100 meters and the second at 200 meters, so more visitors are able to visit the tower and the visitors have two different perspectives. Several tall buildings are in different directions and are all unobstructed from the observational tower. Plot two functions for the distance required to see a building over the horizon versus the height of the building, one for each level on the observational tower.

C. Building A is 40 meters tall and 60 kilometers away, building B is 80 meters tall and 62 kilometers away, building C is 110 meters tall and is 68 kilometers away, and building D is 150 meters tall and is 80 kilometers away. Which buildings can be seen from both levels on a clear day? Which buildings can be seen from the top level on a clear day? Explain.

13.4 Graphing Cube Root Functions

Resource Locker

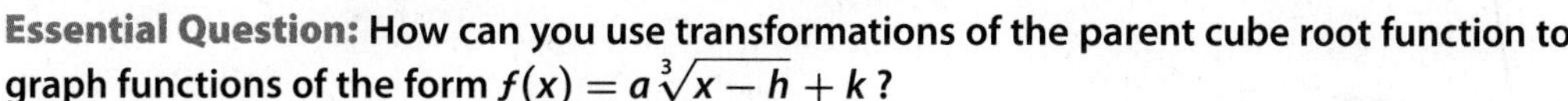

Essential Question: How can you use transformations of the parent cube root function to graph functions of the form $f(x) = a\sqrt[3]{x - h} + k$?

Explore 1 Exploring the Inverse of $y = x^3$

The inverse of a function can be found both algebraically and graphically. Explore the graph of the inverse of $y = x^3$ first and then find the functional form.

(A) Use your graphing calculator to plot the functions $y = x^3$ and $y = x$, with the standard window settings. The graph of ______ produces a diagonal line across the screen.

(B) Use the DrawInv feature to draw the graph of the inverse of $y = x^3$ along with $y = x^2$ and $y = x$.

The newly drawn inverse should look like a ______ of the parent function across the line, $y = x$.

(C) The inverse graph drawn by the calculator passes the ______ line test, indicating that it is a function.

(D) Cube roots are the inverse operation of cubing. Use inverse operations to write the inverse of $y = x^3$.

Switch x and y in the equation. $x = y^3$

Take the cube roots of both sides of the equation. ______ $= y$

Reflect

1. **Discussion** When you take the cube root of a number or variable, do you have to consider both positive and negative cases? Explain why or why not.

Explore 2 Graphing the Parent Cube Root Function

The graph shows and $y = x^3$ and $y = \sqrt[3]{x}$.

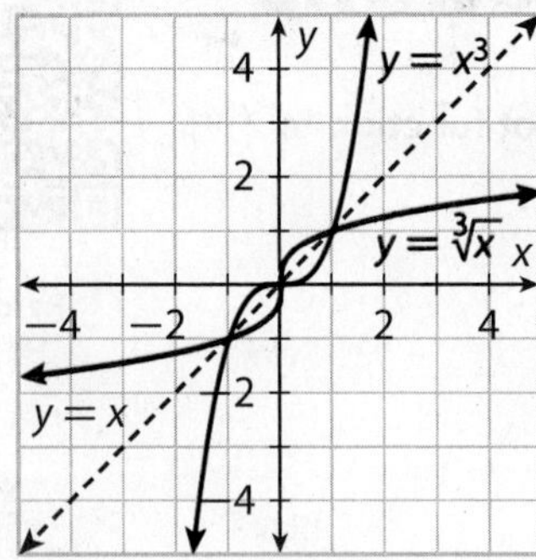

(A) What is the range of $y = x^3$?

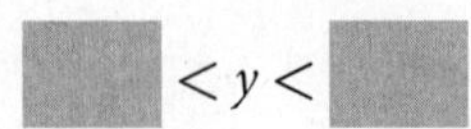

$\square < y < \square$

(B) What values of y cannot result from evaluating the cubic function, $y = x^3$?

(C) If any value of y can result from evaluating the cubic function, $y = x^3$, then $\square$ value of x can be used to evaluate the function, $y = \sqrt[3]{x}$.

(D) The domain of $y = \sqrt[3]{x}$ is $\square < x < \square$.

(E) Is there any need to restrict the domain of $y = \sqrt[3]{x}$?

(F) A **cube root function** is a function whose rule is a cube root expression. $y = \sqrt[3]{x}$ is the parent cube root function. Plot the function for yourself by completing the table of values, and plotting the points.

x	$y = \sqrt[3]{x}$
−8	−2
−1	
0	
1	
8	

Reflect

2. Why is it that x can be a negative number in the cube root function, but not the square root function?

Explain 1 Graphing Translations of the Parent Cube Root Function

Functions of the form $y = \sqrt[3]{x - h} + k$ are translations of the cube root parent function $y = \sqrt[3]{x}$. For example, the graph of $y = \sqrt[3]{x - h} + k$ looks like the graph of $y = \sqrt[3]{x}$ shifted to the right by h units and up by k units. Positive values of h would result in a shift to the left, and negative values of k would result in a downward shift.

Example 1 **Use a table of values to add the graph of the transformed function to the parent function provided. Describe how the parent function was shifted. State the domain and range. Check your graphs on a graphing calculator.**

Ⓐ $y = \sqrt[3]{x - 3} - 4$

x	y
−5	−6
2	−5
3	−4
4	−3
11	−2

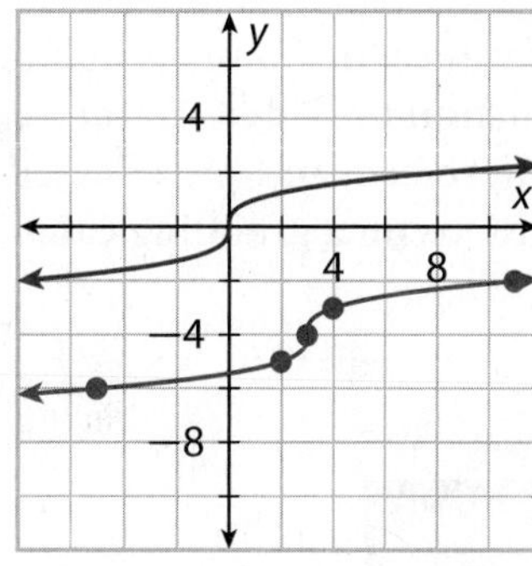

The transformed function was shifted right by 3 units and down by 4 units.

Domain: $-\infty < x < \infty$

Range: $-\infty < y < \infty$

Ⓑ $y = \sqrt[3]{x + 2} + 8$

x	y
−10	6
−3	7
−2	8
−1	9
6	10

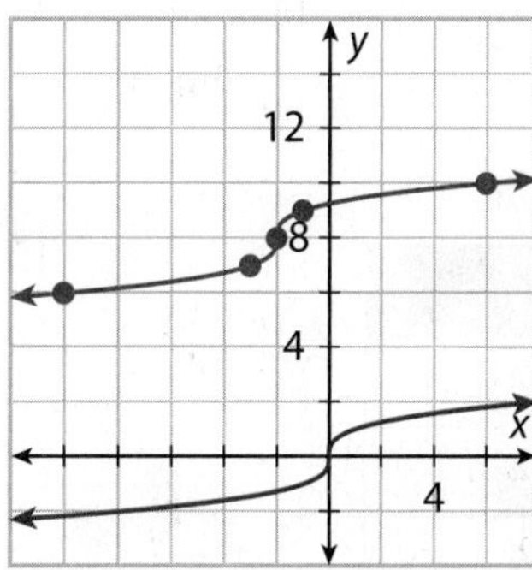

The transformed function was shifted left by 2 units and up by 8 units.

Domain: $-\infty$ $< x <$ ∞

Range: $-\infty$ $< y <$ ∞

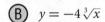

Your Turn

Graph the function and compare it to the parent cube root function. State the shift in direction and by how many units. Then state the domain and range.

3. $y = \sqrt[3]{x + 3} - 6$

Explain 2 Graphing Stretches/Compressions and Reflections of the Parent Cube Root Function

Functions of the form $y = a\sqrt[3]{x}$ with $a \neq 0$ are vertical stretches and compressions of the cube root parent function. The graph of $y = a\sqrt[3]{x}$ looks like the graph of $y = \sqrt[3]{x}$ but will be stretched vertically by a factor of $|a|$ if $|a| > 1$ or compressed vertically by a factor of $\left|\frac{1}{a}\right|$ if $|a| < 1$. If $a < 0$, the graph will also be reflected across the x-axis.

Example 2 **Use a table of values to add the graph of the transformed function to the parent function provided. Describe how the parent function was stretched, compressed, and/or reflected. State the domain and range. Check your graphs on a graphing calculator.**

(A) $y = \frac{1}{2}\sqrt[3]{x}$

x	y
−1	−0.5
0	0
1	0.5

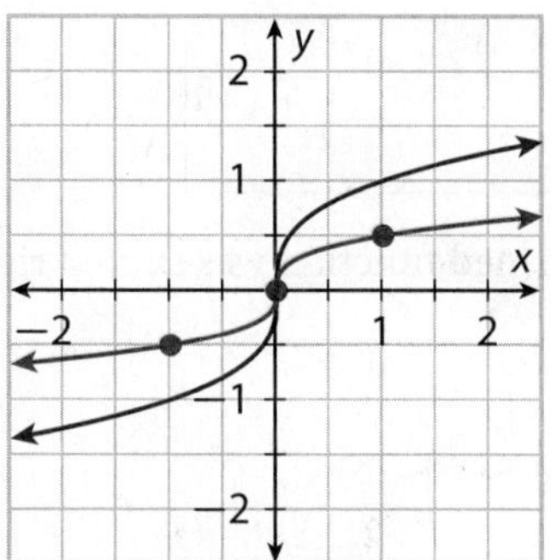

The transformed plot was compressed by a factor of $\frac{1}{2}$ and is not reflected across the x-axis.

Domain: $-\infty < x < \infty$

Range: $-\infty < y < \infty$

(B) $y = -4\sqrt[3]{x}$

x	y
−8	8
−1	4
0	0
1	−4
8	−8

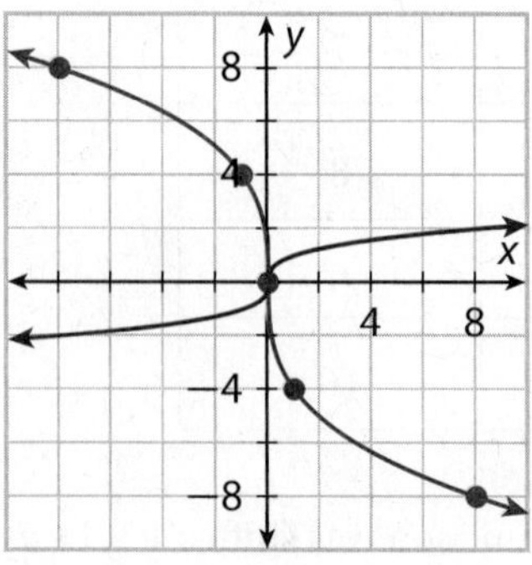

The transformed plot was stretched by a factor of 4 and reflected across the x-axis.

Domain: $-\infty$ $< x <$ ∞

Range: $-\infty$ $< y <$ ∞

Your Turn

Graph the function and compare it to the parent cube root function. State the stretch/compression factor and whether it was reflected or not. Then state the domain and range.

4. $y = 2\sqrt[3]{x}$

Elaborate

5. Does the domain of $y = x^3$ need to be restricted in order for its inverse to be a function? Explain why or why not.

6. How do the transformation parameters, a, h, and k affect the domain and range of $y = a\sqrt[3]{x - h} + k$?

7. **Essential Question Check-In** Describe how the parameters a, h, and k affect the graph of $y = a\sqrt[3]{x - h} + k$ as they are changed.

Evaluate: Homework and Practice

- Online Homework
- Hints and Help
- Extra Practice

1. Use inverse operations to find the inverse of $y = 8x^3$.

2. Graph $y = \sqrt[3]{x}$ together with $y = \sqrt{x}$ from 0 to 10. What for what positive values of x is the cube root of x greater than the square root of x? What for what positive values of x is the square root of x greater than the cube root of x?

Graph each function along with the parent function by making a table of values.

3. $y = \sqrt[3]{x - 4}$

4. $y = \sqrt[3]{x} - 5$

5. $y = \sqrt[3]{x - 2} - 2$

6. $y = \sqrt[3]{x + 3} + 7$

7. $y = -2\sqrt[3]{x}$

8. $y = \frac{1}{4}\sqrt[3]{x}$

9. $y = 5\sqrt[3]{x}$

10. $y = -\frac{1}{2}\sqrt[3]{x}$

Describe the transformation or transformations of each function from the parent cube root function, $y = \sqrt[3]{x}$.

11. $y = \sqrt[3]{x - 1} + 5$

12. $y = \sqrt[3]{x + 5} + 5$

13. $y = \sqrt[3]{x - 3} - 3$

14. $y = \sqrt[3]{x + 7} - 2\frac{1}{2}$

15. $y = 3\sqrt[3]{x}$

16. $y = -\frac{3}{2}\sqrt[3]{x}$

17. $y = -\frac{1}{5}\sqrt[3]{x}$

18. $y = \frac{1}{10}\sqrt[3]{x}$

19. A cylindrical water holding tank with a height equal to its diameter has a height of $h = \sqrt[3]{\frac{4}{\pi}}\sqrt[3]{V}$, where V is the volume of the tank. Graph the height function.

20. Geometry The Louvre Palace in Paris has a large glass pyramid in the main court. For a square pyramid with height equal to length, the height is related to the volume by $h = \sqrt[3]{3}\sqrt[3]{V}$. Graph the height of a pyramid as a function of volume.

21. Geometry The diameter of a ball as a function of its volume is given by $d = 2\sqrt[3]{\frac{3}{4\pi}}\sqrt[3]{V} \approx 1.24\sqrt[3]{V}$. Describe the transformations of a graph of the radius of a sphere compared to parent cube root function, $r = \sqrt[3]{V}$, and graph the function.

22. The function, $y = \frac{1}{3}\sqrt[3]{x+2} - 5$, has been transformed from the parent function, $y = \sqrt[3]{x}$, by which of the following transformations? Select all that apply.

A. vertical stretch by $\frac{1}{3}$

B. vertical compression by $\frac{1}{3}$

C. reflection across the y-axis

D. reflection across the x-axis

E. shifted up by 5

F. shifted down by 5

G. shifted right by 2

H. shifted left by 2

H.O.T. Focus on Higher Order Thinking

23. Critical Thinking If the graph of $y = \frac{1}{2}\sqrt[3]{x}$ is shifted left 2 units, what is the equation of the translated graph?

24. Communicate Mathematical Ideas Mitchio says that cube root functions of the form $y = a\sqrt[3]{x}$ should be considered to have a limited domain, because a cannot equal 0. Explain why you do or do not agree with Mitchio.

25. Multi-step The length of a cube as a function of total volume is given by $\ell = \sqrt[3]{V_t}$.

a. Write the function for the length of a cubic box needed to hold a cube-shaped glass vase that has a volume of 125 cubic inches and the packing material that surrounds the vase V_p.

b. What are the domain and range of this function?

c. Graph the function.

Lesson Performance Task

A manufacturer wants to make a ball bearing that is made of a mixture of zinc, iron, and copper and has come down to two alloys. Alloy A has a density of $7.5\ \frac{g}{cm^3}$ and alloy B has a density of $8.5\ \frac{g}{cm^3}$.

A. Use the formula for the volume of a sphere, $V = \frac{4}{3}\pi r^3$ and the formula for density, $D = \frac{m}{V}$, to write an equation for m as a function of r for each alloy.

B. Find the inverse of each function. Write the function in terms of $r = a\sqrt{m}$, where a is rounded to three decimal places.

C. How does the graph of each inverse function compare to the parent cube root function? For a given mass, which alloy would have a greater radius?

D. The manufacturer wants the ball bearings to have a mass of 12 grams and to have a radius as close to 0.7 cm as possible. Which alloy would be closer to the manufacturer's desired specifications? Explain.

STUDY GUIDE REVIEW

Functions and Inverses

MODULE 13

Essential Question: How can you use functions and inverses to solve real-world problems?

Key Vocabulary
cube root function
(función de raíz cubo)
inverse function
(inverso de una function)
radical function
(radical de una function)
square root function
(función de raíz cuadrada)

KEY EXAMPLE *(Lessons 13.1, 13.2, 13.3)*

Graph $f(x) = x^2 + 1$ and its inverse.

$$y = x^2 - 1$$
$$x = y^2 - 1$$
$$x - 1 = y^2$$
$$\pm\sqrt{x-1} = y$$

To find the inverse of $f(x)$, or $f^{-1}(x)$, switch x and y, and solve for y.

For the inverse to be a function, restrict it to nonnegative numbers, $f^{-1}(x) = \sqrt{x-1}$.

Fill in a table of values for $f(x)$ and $f^{-1}(x)$.

x	$f(x)$	$f^{-1}(x)$
−2	$(-2)^2 + 1 = 5$	not a real number
−1	$(-1)^2 + 1 = 2$	not a real number
0	$(0)^2 + 1 = 1$	not a real number
1	$(1)^2 + 1 = 2$	$\sqrt{1-1} = 0$
2	$(2)^2 + 1 = 5$	$\sqrt{2-1} = 0$
3	$(3)^2 + 1 = 10$	$\sqrt{3-1} \approx 1.41$
4	$(4)^2 + 1 = 17$	$\sqrt{4-1} \approx 1.73$

Graph the ordered pairs.

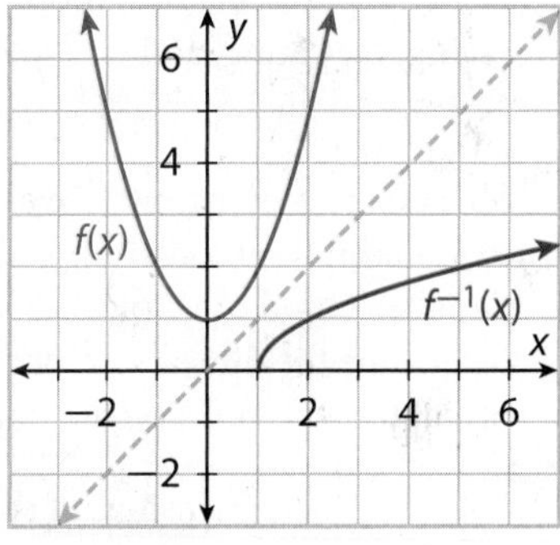

$f^{-1}(x)$ is a reflection of $f(x)$ over $y = x$ for nonnegative values of x.

The domain of $f(x)$ is all real numbers, and the range of $f(x)$ is $y \geq 1$.

The domain of $f^{-1}(x)$ is $x \geq 1$, and the range of $f^{-1}(x)$ is $y \geq 0$.

EXERCISES

1. Graph $f(x) = \frac{1}{2}(x + 2)^3$. *(Lesson 13.1)*

Write the inverse of each function. *(Lesson 13.2)*

2. $g(x) = 4x^2 + 7$

3. $t(x) = (x + 15)^3 - 4$

4. Graph $h(x) = \sqrt[3]{x} - 2$. Find the domain and range of $h(x)$. *(Lesson 13.4)*

MODULE PERFORMANCE TASK

The Smallest Cube

Foolish Sports makes sporting equipment for people who play unusual sports like lawnmower racing, pie eating, and cheese rolling. For some reason, companies that make footballs, roller skates, and hockey sticks make a lot more money.

So, Foolish is going into the ordinary-sports business. Its first project is to make and sell baseballs, basketballs, and golf balls. The company's package designer found the typical volumes of the three products and now must determine the dimensions of the boxes they will be sold in. Each box must be cubical and must be the smallest box that can contain the ball.

Basketball	448 cu in.
Baseball	14.1 cu in.
Golf ball	2.48 cu in

What are the dimensions of the three boxes? Explain how you found the dimensions.

Start by listing the information you will need to solve the problem. Use numbers, words, or algebra to explain how you reached your conclusion.

Ready to Go On?

13.1–13.4 Functions and Inverses

- Online Homework
- Hints and Help
- Extra Practice

Graph each function. *(Lesson 13.1)*

1. Graph $g(x) = \frac{1}{4}(x + 1)^3 - 4$.

2. Find and graph the inverse of $f(x) = 2x^2 - 4$. *(Lessons 13.2, 13.3)*

3. Graph $h(x) = 2\sqrt[3]{x + 6} + 4$. *(Lesson 13.4)*

ESSENTIAL QUESTION

4. How could you sketch the inverse of an exponential function?

MODULE 13
MIXED REVIEW

Assessment Readiness

1. Find the solutions of $-2x(x+1)(3x+5)=0$. Is the given value of x a solution? Write Yes or No for each possible solution.

A. $x=-\frac{5}{3}$

B. $x=0$

C. $x=1$

2. Find the inverse of $f(x)=\frac{1}{3}x-2$.

Use the inverse to determine if each of the following equations is True or False.

A. $f^{-1}(-2)=0$

B. $f^{-1}(0)=2$

C. $f^{-1}(3)=15$

3. Factor $8x^2-50$ completely. Is the following expression a factor of this expression? Write Yes or No for each possible factor.

A. $(x-10)$

B. $(x+5)$

C. 2

4. Graph $f(x)=\frac{1}{2}x^3+2$. Describe the end behavior of the graph.

UNIT 5 MIXED REVIEW

Assessment Readiness

- Online Homework
- Hints and Help
- Extra Practice

1. Consider the system $\begin{cases} y \leq \frac{1}{2}x + 3 \\ y \geq 2x \end{cases}$.

Tell whether each of the following is a solution to the system.

A. $(-2, -5)$

B. $(2, 4)$

C. $(3, -1)$

2. Factor and solve each of the following equations. Is –4 a solution of the equation? Write Yes or No for each equation.

A. $x^2 + 4x + 16 = 0$

B. $2x^2 - 8x + 32 = 0$

C. $5x^2 - 80 = 0$

3. Find the inverse of $f(x) = x^2 - 2$. Determine if each statement is True of False.

A. $f^{-1}(x)$ is a square root function.

B. The domain of is $f^{-1}(x)$ is $x \geq -2$.

C. The range of $f^{-1}(x)$ is all real numbers.

4. Look at each focus and directrix. Is the resulting parabola vertical? Write Yes or No for A–C.

A. Focus $(6, -3)$, Directrix $x = 2$

B. Focus $(-4, -2)$, Directrix $y = -3$

C. Focus $(0, 1)$, Directrix $y = 2$

5. The graph of $f(x) = \frac{1}{3}x + 1$ is shown. Find and graph the inverse of $f(x)$.

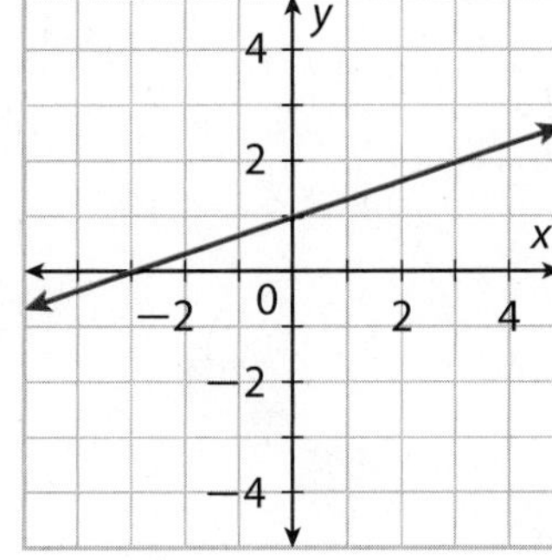

6. Consider the equation $-4x^2 + x = 3$. What method should be used to most easily solve the equation if you have a choice between taking the square root, completing the square, using the quadratic formula, or factoring? Explain your reasoning, and then solve the equation.

7. Graph $f(x) = (x + 2)^3$. Use the graph to solve $-8 = (x + 2)^3$.

Performance Tasks

★ **8.** The relationship between the radius r, in centimeters, of a solid gold sphere and its mass m, in grams, is given by $r = 0.23\sqrt[3]{m}$. Graph this relationship for the interval $0 \leq m \leq 10$.

★★ **9.** The spittlebug is the world's highest-jumping animal relative to its body length of about 6 millimeters. The height h of a spittlebug's jump in millimeters can be model by the function $h(t) = -4000t^2 + 3000t$, where t is the time in seconds.

A. What is the maximum height that the spittlebug will reach? Explain how you found your answer.

B. What is the ratio of a spittlebug's maximum jumping height to its body length? In the best human jumpers, this ratio is about 1.38 to 1. Compare the ratio for spittlebugs with the ratio for the best human jumpers.

★★★**10.** The distance, d, in meters, an object falls after time t, in seconds, is given by $d = 4.9t^2$.

A. Find the inverse of this function.

B. How much time does it take for a stone dropped from the edge of a cliff to hit the ground 80 meters below? Round your answer to the nearest tenth of a second.

C. The relationship between the temperature in degrees Fahrenheit and Kelvin is given by $F = \frac{9}{5}(K - 273) + 32$. Find the inverse of this function

D. If the speed of sound in air is given by $s = 20.1\sqrt{K}$, where s is in meters per second, how long after dropping the stone can the sound of the stone striking the ground be heard at the edge of the cliff, if the temperature is 77°F? Explain how you got your answer.

MATH IN CAREERS

Ichthyologist A pike is a type of freshwater fish. An ichthyologist uses the function $W(L) = \frac{L^3}{3500}$ to find the approximate weight W in pounds of a pike with length L inches.

a. Write the inverse function $L(W)$.

b. Graph the inverse function.

c. What is the significance in the context of the problem of the point at approximately (6, 28) on the graph of $L(W)$?

d. What are the reasonable domain and range of the function $L(W)$?

UNIT 6

Geometric Proof

MODULE 14

Proofs with Lines and Angles

MODULE 15

Proofs with Triangles and Quadrilaterals

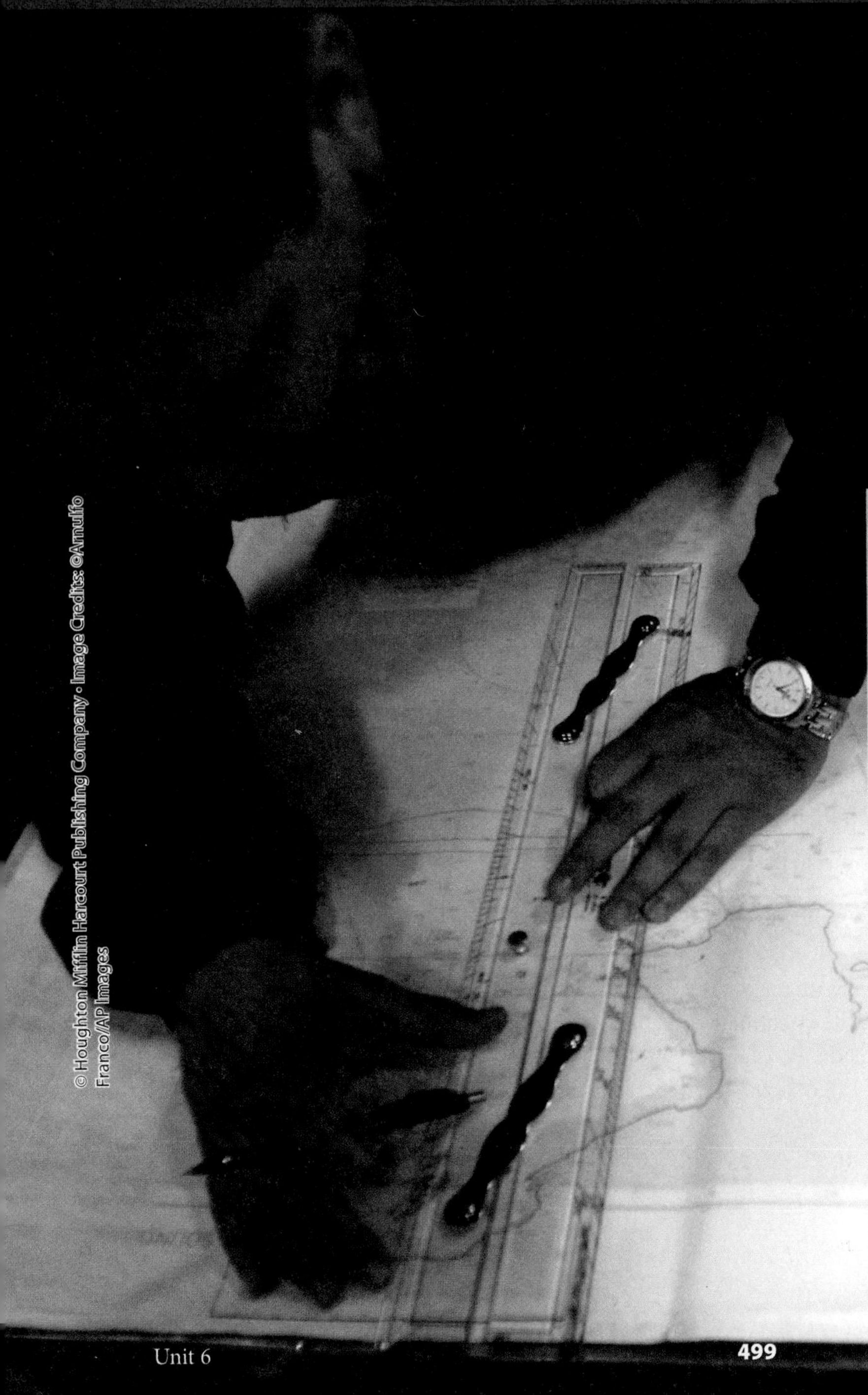

MATH IN CAREERS

Cartographer A cartographer creates and updates maps, which can include roads, buildings, geographic features, and landmarks. Cartographers often use tools such as a computer-aided drafting (CAD) program, satellite images, and a geographic information system (GIS). Cartographers must understand mathematical concepts such as measurement, geometry, and trigonometry.

If you are interested in a career as a cartographer, you should study these mathematical subjects:

- Algebra
- Geometry
- Trigonometry

Research other careers that require understanding geometry. Check out the career activity at the end of the unit to find out how **cartographers** use math.

Reading Start-Up

Vocabulary

Review Words

✔ adjacent angles *(ángulos adyacentes)*

✔ parallel lines *(líneas paralelas)*

✔ congruence *(congruencia)*

✔ vertical angles *(ángulos verticales)*

✔ complementary angles *(ángulos complementarios)*

✔ supplementary angles *(ángulos suplementarios)*

✔ transversal *(transversal)*

Preview Words

indirect proof *(demostración indirecta)*

interior angle *(ángulo interior)*

exterior angle *(ángulo exterior)*

isosceles triangle *(triángulo isósceles)*

equilateral triangle *(triángulo equilátero)*

parallelogram *(paralelogramo)*

quadrilateral *(cuadrilátero)*

rhombus *(rombo)*

Visualize Vocabulary

Copy the case diagram and use the ✔ words to complete the diagram. Write the review words in the bubbles and draw a picture to illustrate each case.

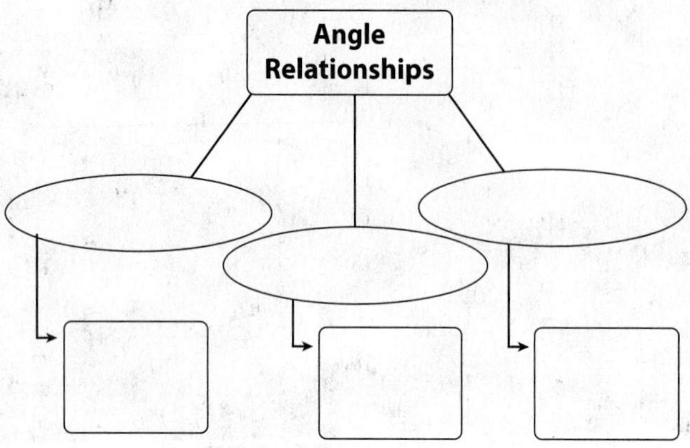

Understand Vocabulary

Complete the sentences using the preview words.

1. A(n) __?__ has three sides with the same length.
2. Any polygon with four sides is called a __?__. If opposite pairs of sides are parallel, the shape is a __?__. If all four sides are congruent, the shape is a __?__.

Active Reading

Key-Term Fold While reading each module, create a Key-Term Fold to help you organize vocabulary words. Write vocabulary terms on one side and definitions on the other side. Place a special emphasis on learning and speaking the English word while discussing the unit.

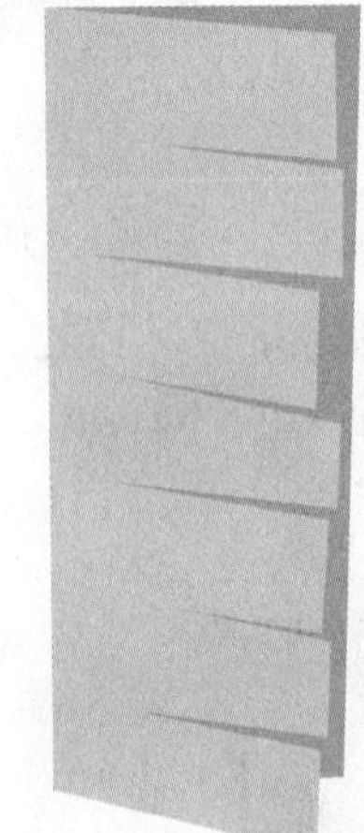

Proofs with Lines and Angles

MODULE 14

Essential Question: How can you use parallel and perpendicular lines to solve real-world problems?

REAL WORLD VIDEO
Check out how properties of parallel and perpendicular lines and angles can be used to create real-world illusions in a mystery spot building.

MODULE PERFORMANCE TASK PREVIEW

Mystery Spot Building

In this module, you will use properties of parallel lines and angles to analyze the strange happenings in a mystery spot building. With a little bit of geometry, you'll be able to figure out whether mystery spot buildings are "on the up-and-up!"

Are YOU Ready?

Complete these exercises to review skills you will need for this module.

Personal Math Trainer
- Online Homework
- Hints and Help
- Extra Practice

Angle Relationships

Example 1

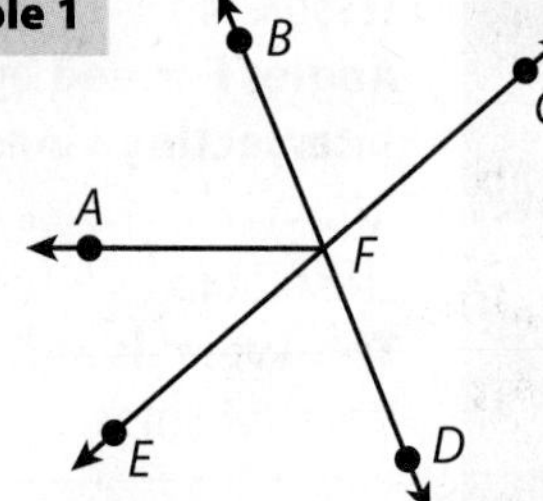

The measure of $\angle AFB$ is 70° and the measure of $\angle AFE$ is 40°. Find the measure of angle $\angle BFE$.

$m\angle BFE = m\angle AFB + m\angle AFE$ Angle Addition Postulate

$m\angle BFE = 70° + 40°$ Substitute.

$m\angle BFE = 110°$ Solve for $m\angle BFE$.

Find the measure of the angle in the image from the example.

1. The measure of $\angle BFE$ is 110°. Find $m\angle EFD$.

2. The measure of $\angle BFE$ is 110°. Find $m\angle BFC$.

Parallel Lines Cut by a Transversal

Example 2 The measure of $\angle 7$ is 110°. Find $m\angle 3$. Assume $p \parallel q$.

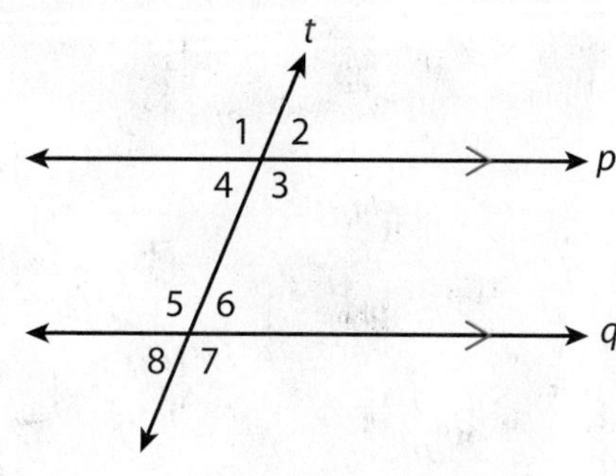

$m\angle 3 = m\angle 7$ Corresponding Angles Theorem

$m\angle 3 = 110°$ Substitute.

Find the measure of the angle in the image from the example. Assume $p \parallel q$.

3. The measure of $\angle 3$ is 110°. Find $m\angle 1$.

4. The measure of $\angle 3$ is 110°. Find $m\angle 6$.

Writing Equations of Parallel, Perpendicular, Vertical, and Horizontal Lines

Example 3 Find the line parallel to $y = 2x + 7$ that passes through the point (3, 6).

$(y - y_1) = m(x - x_1)$ Use point-slope form.

$(y - 6) = 2(x - 3)$ Substitute for m, x_1, y_1. Parallel lines have the same slope, so $m = 2$.

$y - 6 = 2x - 6$ Simplify.

$y = 2x$ Solve for y.

Find the equation of the line described.

5. Perpendicular to $y = 3x + 5$; passing through the point $(-6, -4)$

6. Parallel to the x-axis; passing through the point $(4, 1)$

14.1 Angles Formed by Intersecting Lines

Essential Question: How can you find the measures of angles formed by intersecting lines?

Resource Locker

Explore 1 Exploring Angle Pairs Formed by Intersecting Lines

When two lines intersect, like the blades of a pair of scissors, a number of angle pairs are formed. You can find relationships between the measures of the angles in each pair.

(A) Using a straightedge, draw a pair of intersecting lines like the open scissors. Label the angles formed as 1, 2, 3, and 4.

(B) Use a protractor to find each measure.

Angle	Measure of Angle
$m\angle 1$	
$m\angle 2$	
$m\angle 3$	
$m\angle 4$	
$m\angle 1 + m\angle 2$	
$m\angle 2 + m\angle 3$	
$m\angle 3 + m\angle 4$	
$m\angle 1 + m\angle 4$	

You have been measuring *vertical angles* and *linear pairs* of angles. When two lines intersect, the angles that are opposite each other are **vertical angles**. Recall that a *linear pair* is a pair of adjacent angles whose non-common sides are opposite rays. So, when two lines intersect, the angles that are on the same side of a line form a linear pair.

Reflect

1. Name a pair of vertical angles and a linear pair of angles in your diagram in Step A.
2. Make a conjecture about the measures of a pair of vertical angles.
3. Use the Linear Pair Theorem to tell what you know about the measures of angles that form a linear pair.

Explore 2 Proving the Vertical Angles Theorem

The conjecture from the Explore about vertical angles can be proven so it can be stated as a theorem.

The Vertical Angles Theorem

If two angles are vertical angles, then the angles are congruent.

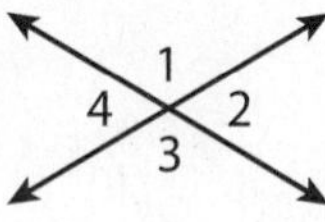

$\angle 1 \cong \angle 3$ and $\angle 2 \cong \angle 4$

You have written proofs in two-column and paragraph proof formats. Another type of proof is called a *flow proof.* A **flow proof** uses boxes and arrows to show the structure of the proof. The steps in a flow proof move from left to right or from top to bottom, shown by the arrows connecting each box. The justification for each step is written below the box. You can use a flow proof to prove the Vertical Angles Theorem.

Follow the steps to write a Plan for Proof and a flow proof to prove the Vertical Angles Theorem.

Given: $\angle 1$ and $\angle 3$ are vertical angles.

Prove: $\angle 1 \cong \angle 3$

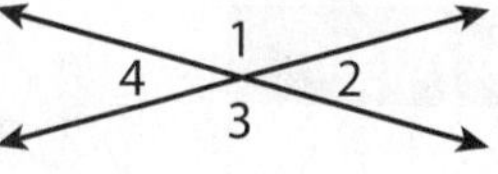

(A) Write the final steps of a Plan for Proof:

Because $\angle 1$ and $\angle 2$ are a linear pair and $\angle 2$ and $\angle 3$ are a linear pair, these pairs of angles are supplementary. This means that $m\angle 1 + m\angle 2 = 180°$ and $m\angle 2 + m\angle 3 = 180°$. By the Transitive Property, $m\angle 1 + m\angle 2 = m\angle 2 + m\angle 3$.

Next:

Ⓑ Copy the flow proof diagram. Use the Plan for Proof to complete the flow proof. Begin with what you know is true from the Given or the diagram. Use arrows to show the path of the reasoning. Write the missing statement or reason in each step.

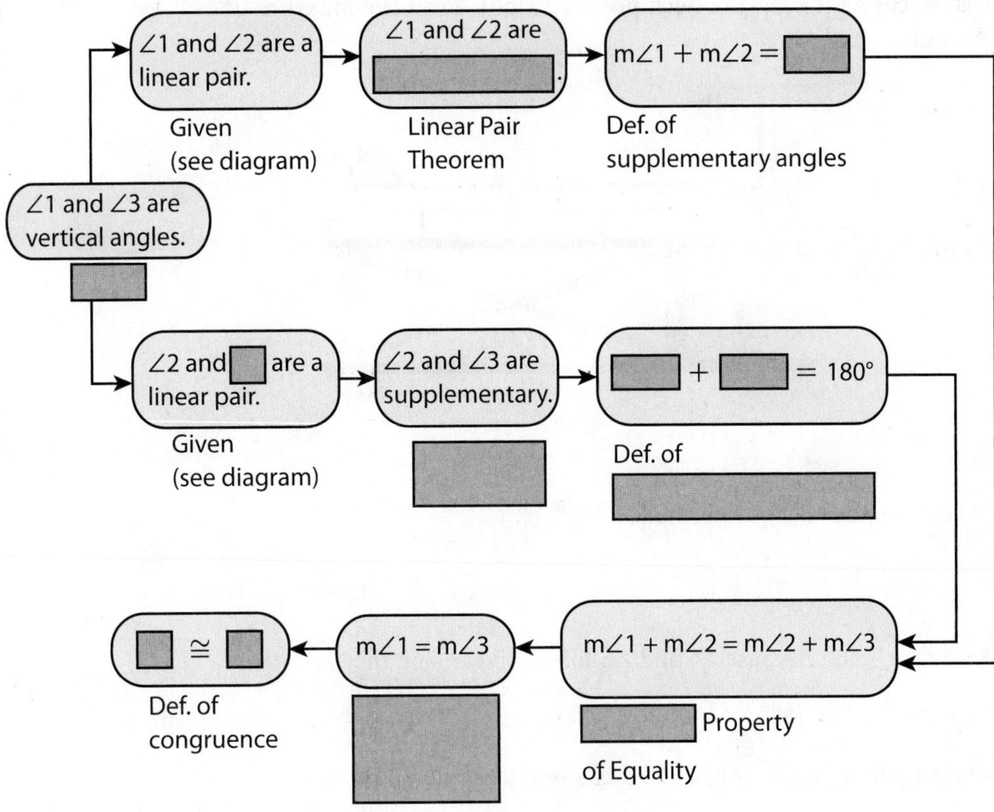

∠1 and ∠2 are a linear pair.
Given (see diagram)
∠1 and ∠2 are ___.
Linear Pair Theorem
m∠1 + m∠2 = ___
Def. of supplementary angles
∠1 and ∠3 are vertical angles.
∠2 and ___ are a linear pair.
Given (see diagram)
∠2 and ∠3 are supplementary.
___ + ___ = 180°
Def. of ___
m∠1 + m∠2 = m∠2 + m∠3
___ Property of Equality
m∠1 = m∠3
___ ≅ ___
Def. of congruence

Reflect

4. **Discussion** Using the other pair of angles in the diagram, ∠2 and ∠4, would a proof that ∠2 ≅ ∠4 also show that the Vertical Angles Theorem is true? Explain why or why not.

5. Draw two intersecting lines to form vertical angles. Label your lines and tell which angles are congruent. Measure the angles to check that they are congruent.

Explain 1 Using Vertical Angles

You can use the Vertical Angles Theorem to find missing angle measures in situations involving intersecting lines.

Example 1 **Cross braces help keep the deck posts straight. Find the measure of each angle.**

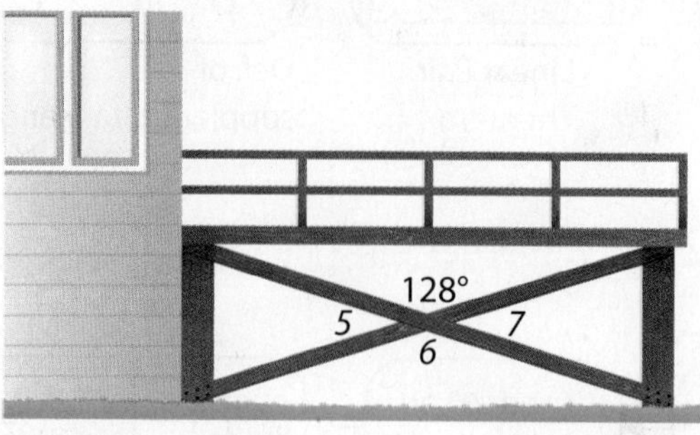

(A) $\angle 6$

Because vertical angles are congruent, $m\angle 6 = 146°$.

(B) $\angle 5$ and $\angle 7$

From Part A, $m\angle 6 = 146°$. Because $\angle 5$ and $\angle 6$ form a linear pair, they are

supplementary and $m\angle 5 = 180° - 146° =$ 34° . $m\angle$ 7 $=$ 34° because $\angle$ 7

also forms a linear pair with $\angle 6$, or because it is a vertical angle with $\angle 5$.

Your Turn

6. The measures of two vertical angles are 58° and $(3x + 4)°$. Find the value of x.

7. The measures of two vertical angles are given by the expressions $(x + 3)°$ and $(2x - 7)°$. Find the value of x. What is the measure of each angle?

Explain 2 Using Supplementary and Complementary Angles

Recall what you know about complementary and supplementary angles. **Complementary angles** are two angles whose measures have a sum of 90°. **Supplementary angles** are two angles whose measures have a sum of 180°. You have seen that two angles that form a linear pair are supplementary.

Example 2 **Use the diagram below to find the missing angle measures. Explain your reasoning.**

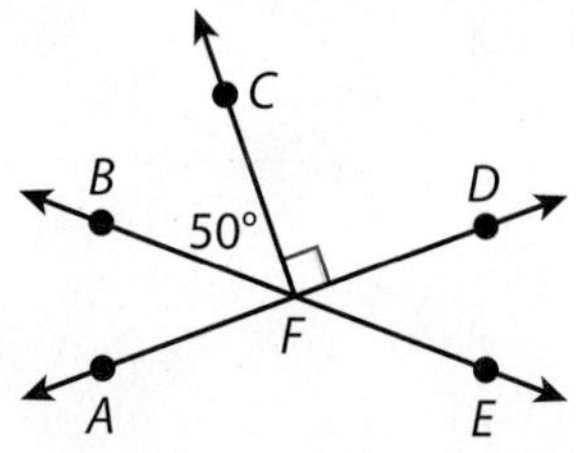

Ⓐ Find the measures of $\angle AFC$ and $\angle AFB$.

$\angle AFC$ and $\angle CFD$ are a linear pair formed by an intersecting line and ray, $\overleftrightarrow{AD}$ and $\overrightarrow{FC}$, so they are supplementary and the sum of their measures is 180°. By the diagram, $m\angle CFD = 90°$, so $m\angle AFC = 180° - 90° = 90°$ and $\angle AFC$ is also a right angle.

Because together they form the right angle $\angle AFC$, $\angle AFB$ and $\angle BFC$ are complementary and the sum of their measures is 90°. So, $m\angle AFB = 90° - m\angle BFC = 90° - 50° = 40°$.

Ⓑ Find the measures of $\angle DFE$ and $\angle AFE$.

$\angle BFA$ and $\angle DFE$ are formed by two intersecting lines and are opposite each other,

so the angles are vertical angles. So, the angles are congruent. From Part A

$m\angle AFB = 40°$, so $m\angle DFE =$ 40° also.

Because $\angle BFA$ and $\angle AFE$ form a linear pair, the angles are supplementary and the sum

of their measures is 180°. So, $m\angle AFE =$ 180° $- m\angle BFA =$ 180° $-$ 40° $=$ 140°.

Reflect

8. In Part A, what do you notice about right angles $\angle AFC$ and $\angle CFD$? Make a conjecture about right angles.

Your Turn

You can represent the measures of an angle and its complement as $x°$ and $(90 - x)°$. Similarly, you can represent the measures of an angle and its supplement as $x°$ and $(180 - x)°$. Use these expressions to find the measures of the angles described.

9. The measure of an angle is equal to the measure of its complement.

10. The measure of an angle is twice the measure of its supplement.

Elaborate

11. Describe how proving a theorem is different than solving a problem and describe how they are the same.

12. **Discussion** The proof of the Vertical Angles Theorem in the lesson includes a Plan for Proof. How are a Plan for Proof and the proof itself the same and how are they different?

13. Draw two intersecting lines. Label points on the lines and tell what angles you know are congruent and which are supplementary.

14. **Essential Question Check-In** If you know that the measure of one angle in a linear pair is 75°, how can you find the measure of the other angle?

Evaluate: Homework and Practice

- Online Homework
- Hints and Help
- Extra Practice

Use this diagram and information for Exercises 1–4.

Given: $m\angle AFB = m\angle EFD = 50°$

Points *B*, *F*, *D* and points *E*, *F*, *C* are collinear.

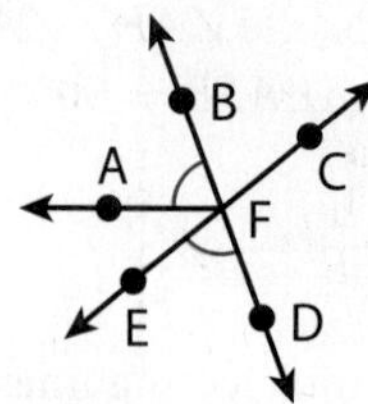

1. Determine whether each pair of angles is a pair of vertical angles, a linear pair of angles, or neither.

A. $\angle BFC$ and $\angle DFE$

B. $\angle BFA$ and $\angle DFE$

C. $\angle BFC$ and $\angle CFD$

D. $\angle AFE$ and $\angle AFC$

E. $\angle BFE$ and $\angle CFD$

F. $\angle AFE$ and $\angle BFC$

2. Find $m\angle AFE$.

3. Find $m\angle DFC$.

4. Find $m\angle BFC$.

5. Represent Real-World Problems A sprinkler swings back and forth between *A* and *B* in such a way that $\angle 1 \cong \angle 2$, $\angle 1$ and $\angle 3$ are complementary, and $\angle 2$ and $\angle 4$ are complementary. If $m\angle 1 = 47.5°$, find $m\angle 2$, $m\angle 3$, and $m\angle 4$.

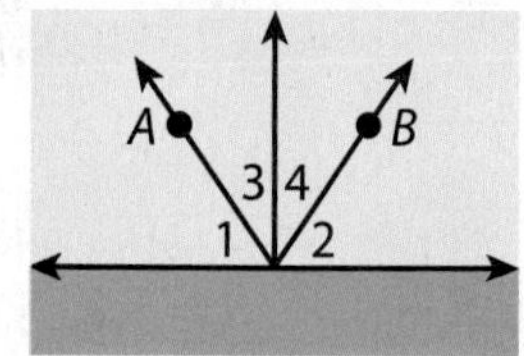

Determine whether each statement is true or false. If false, explain why.

6. If an angle is acute, then the measure of its complement must be greater than the measure of its supplement.

7. A pair of vertical angles may also form a linear pair.

8. If two angles are supplementary and congruent, the measure of each angle is 90°.

9. If a ray divides an angle into two complementary angles, then the original angle is a right angle.

You can represent the measures of an angle and its complement as $x°$ and $(90 - x)°$. Similarly, you can represent the measures of an angle and its supplement as $x°$ and $(180 - x)°$. Use these expressions to find the measures of the angles described.

10. The measure of an angle is three times the measure of its supplement.

11. The measure of the supplement of an angle is three times the measure of its complement.

12. The measure of an angle increased by 20° is equal to the measure of its complement.

Write a plan for a proof for each theorem.

13. If two angles are congruent, then their complements are congruent.

Given: $\angle ABC \cong \angle DEF$

Prove: The complement of $\angle ABC \cong$ the complement of $\angle DEF$.

14. If two angles are congruent, then their supplements are congruent.

Given: $\angle ABC \cong \angle DEF$

Prove: The supplement of $\angle ABC \cong$ the supplement of $\angle DEF$.

15. Justify Reasoning Complete the two-column proof for the theorem "If two angles are congruent, then their supplements are congruent."

Statements	Reasons
1. $\angle ABC \cong \angle DEF$	1. Given
2. The measure of the supplement of $\angle ABC = 180° - m\angle ABC$.	2. Definition of the ___?___ of an angle
3. The measure of the supplement of $\angle DEF = 180° - m\angle DEF$.	3. ___?___
4. ___?___	4. If two angles are congruent, their measures are equal.
5. The measure of the supplement of $\angle DEF = 180° - m\angle ABC$.	5. Substitution Property of ___?___
6. The measure of the supplement of $\angle ABC$ = the measure of the supplement of $\angle DEF$.	6. ___?___
7. The supplement of $\angle ABC \cong$ the supplement of ___?___.	7. If the measures of the supplements of two angles are equal, then supplements of the angles are congruent.

16. Probability The probability P of choosing an object at random from a group of objects is found by the fraction $P(\text{event}) = \frac{\text{Number of favorable outcomes}}{\text{Total number of outcomes}}$. Suppose the angle measures 30°, 60°, 120°, and 150° are written on slips of paper. You choose two slips of paper at random.

a. What is the probability that the measures you choose are complementary?

b. What is the probability that the measures you choose are supplementary?

H.O.T. Focus on Higher Order Thinking

17. Communicate Mathematical Ideas Write a proof of the Vertical Angles Theorem in paragraph proof form.

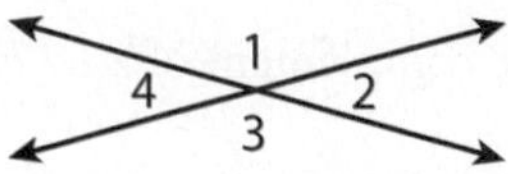

Given: $\angle 2$ and $\angle 4$ are vertical angles.

Prove: $\angle 2 \cong \angle 4$

18. Analyze Relationships If one angle of a linear pair is acute, then the other angle must be obtuse. Explain why.

19. Critique Reasoning Your friend says that there is an angle whose measure is the same as the measure of the sum of its supplement and its complement. Is your friend correct? What is the measure of the angle? Explain your friend's reasoning.

20. Critical Thinking Two statements in a proof are:

$$m\angle A = m\angle B$$

$$m\angle B = m\angle C$$

What reason could you give for the statement $m\angle A = m\angle C$? Explain your reasoning.

Lesson Performance Task

The image shows the angles formed by a pair of scissors. When the scissors are closed, $m\angle 1 = 0°$. As the scissors are opened, the measures of all four angles change in relation to each other. Describe how the measures change as $m\angle 1$ increases from 0° to 180°.

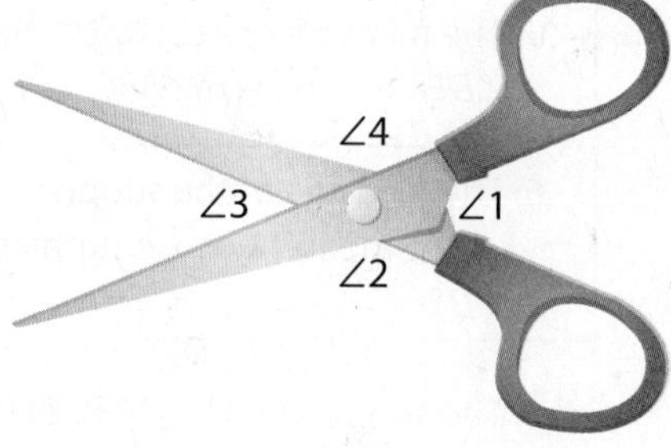

14.2 Transversals and Parallel Lines

Resource Locker

Essential Question: How can you prove and use theorems about angles formed by transversals that intersect parallel lines?

Explore Exploring Parallel Lines and Transversals

A **transversal** is a line that intersects two coplanar lines at two different points. In the figure, line t is a transversal. The table summarizes the names of angle pairs formed by a transversal.

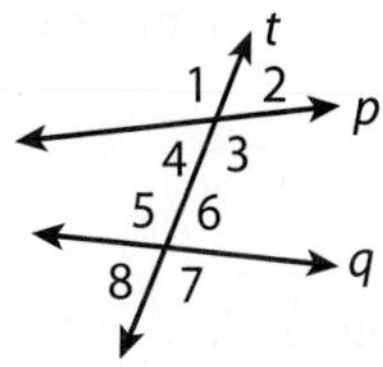

Angle Pair	Example
Corresponding angles lie on the same side of the transversal and on the same sides of the intersected lines.	$\angle 1$ and $\angle 5$
Same-side interior angles lie on the same side of the transversal and between the intersected lines.	$\angle 3$ and $\angle 6$
Alternate interior angles are nonadjacent angles that lie on opposite sides of the transversal between the intersected lines.	$\angle 3$ and $\angle 5$

Recall that parallel lines lie in the same plane and never intersect. In the figure, line ℓ is parallel to line m, written $\ell \| m$. The arrows on the lines also indicate that they are parallel.

ℓ

m

$\ell \| m$

When parallel lines are cut by a transversal, the angle pairs formed are either congruent or supplementary. The following postulate is the starting point for proving theorems about parallel lines that are intersected by a transversal.

Same-Side Interior Angles Postulate

If two parallel lines are cut by a transversal, then the pairs of same-side interior angles are supplementary.

Follow the steps to illustrate the postulate and use it to find angle measures.

(A) Draw two parallel lines and a transversal, and number the angles formed from 1 to 8.

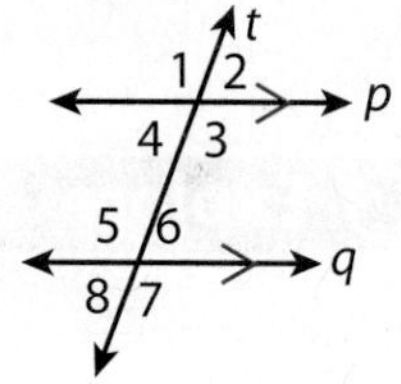

(B) Identify the pairs of same-side interior angles.

(C) What does the postulate tell you about these same-side interior angle pairs?

(D) If $m\angle 4 = 70°$, what is $m\angle 5$? Explain.

Reflect

1. Explain how you can find $m\angle 3$ in the diagram if $p \parallel q$ and $m\angle 6 = 61°$.

2. **What If?** If $m \parallel n$, how many pairs of same-side interior angles are shown in the figure? What are the pairs?

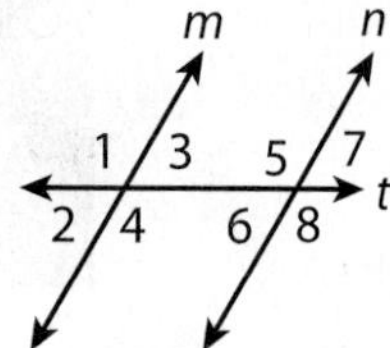

Explain 1 Proving that Alternate Interior Angles are Congruent

Other pairs of angles formed by parallel lines cut by a transversal are alternate interior angles.

Alternate Interior Angles Theorem

If two parallel lines are cut by a transversal, then the pairs of alternate interior angles have the same measure.

To prove something to be true, you use definitions, properties, postulates, and theorems that you already know.

Example 1 **Prove the Alternate Interior Angles Theorem.**

Given: $p \parallel q$

Prove: $m\angle 3 = m\angle 5$

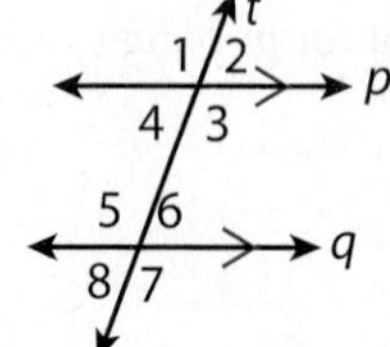

Complete the proof by writing the missing reasons. Choose from the following reasons. You may use a reason more than once.

- Same-Side Interior Angles Postulate
- Given
- Definition of supplementary angles
- Subtraction Property of Equality
- Substitution Property of Equality
- Linear Pair Theorem

Statements	Reasons
1. $p \parallel q$	**1.** Given
2. $\angle 3$ and $\angle 6$ are supplementary.	**2.** Same-Side Interior Angles Postulate
3. $m\angle 3 + m\angle 6 = 180°$	**3.** Definition of supplementary angles
4. $\angle 5$ and $\angle 6$ are a linear pair.	**4.** Given
5. $\angle 5$ and $\angle 6$ are supplementary.	**5.** Linear Pair Theorem
6. $m\angle 5 + m\angle 6 = 180°$	**6.** Definition of supplementary angles
7. $m\angle 3 + m\angle 6 = m\angle 5 + m\angle 6$	**7.** Substitution Property of Equality
8. $m\angle 3 = m\angle 5$	**8.** Subtraction Property of Equality

Reflect

3. In the figure, explain why $\angle 1$, $\angle 3$, $\angle 5$, and $\angle 7$ all have the same measure.

4. Suppose $m\angle 4 = 57°$ in the figure shown. Describe two different ways to determine $m\angle 6$.

Explain 2 Proving that Corresponding Angles are Congruent

Two parallel lines cut by a transversal also form angle pairs called corresponding angles.

Corresponding Angles Theorem

If two parallel lines are cut by a transversal, then the pairs of corresponding angles have the same measure.

Example 2 Complete a proof in paragraph form for the Corresponding Angles Theorem.

Given: $p \parallel q$

Prove: $m\angle 4 = m\angle 8$

t
1 2 p
4 3
5 6 q
8 7

By the given statement, $p \| q$. $\angle 4$ and $\angle 6$ form a pair of alternate interior angles.

So, using the Alternate Interior Angles Theorem, $m\angle 4 = m\angle 6$.

$\angle 6$ and $\angle 8$ form a pair of vertical angles. So, using the Vertical Angles Theorem,

$m\angle 6 = m\angle 8$. Using the Substitution Property of Equality

in $m\angle 4 = m\angle 6$, substitute $m\angle 4$ for $m\angle 6$. The result is $m\angle 4 = m\angle 8$.

Reflect

5. Use the diagram in Example 2 to explain how you can prove the Corresponding Angles Theorem using the Same-Side Interior Angles Postulate and a linear pair of angles.

6. Suppose $m\angle 4 = 36°$. Find $m\angle 5$. Explain.

Explain 3 Using Parallel Lines to Find Angle Pair Relationships

You can apply the theorems and postulates about parallel lines cut by a transversal to solve problems.

Example 3 **Find each value. Explain how to find the values using postulates, theorems, and algebraic reasoning.**

(A) In the diagram, roads a and b are parallel. Explain how to find the measure of $\angle VTU$.

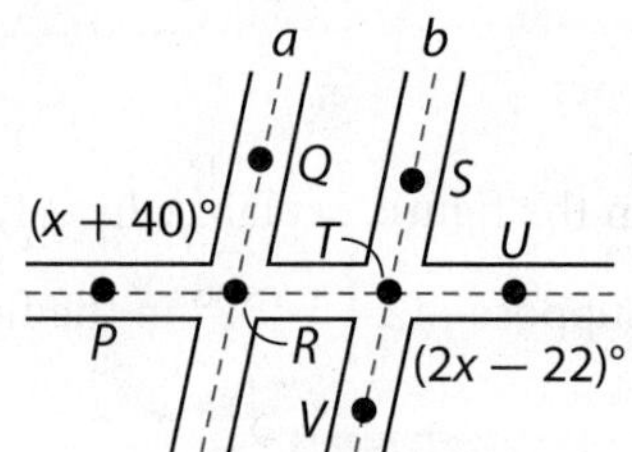

It is given that $m\angle PRQ = (x + 40)°$ and $m\angle VTU = (2x - 22)°$.

$m\angle PRQ = m\angle RTS$ by the Corresponding Angles Theorem and

$m\angle RTS = m\angle VTU$ by the Vertical Angles Theorem.

So, $m\angle PRQ = m\angle VTU$, and $x + 40 = 2x - 22$. Solving for x,

$x + 62 = 2x$, and $x = 62$. Substitute the value of x to find $m\angle VTU$:

$m\angle VTU = \left(2(62) - 22\right)° = 102°$.

(B) In the diagram, roads a and b are parallel. Explain how to find the measure of $m\angle WUV$.

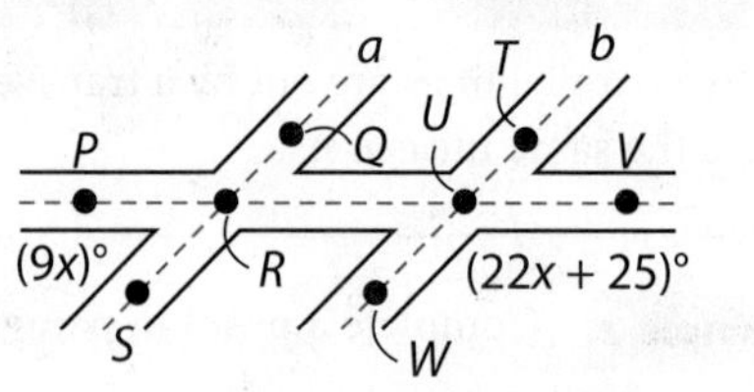

It is given that $m\angle PRS = (9x)°$ and $m\angle WUV = (22x + 25)°$.

$m\angle PRS = m\angle RUW$ by the Corresponding Angles Theorem.

$\angle RUW$ and $\angle WUV$ are supplementary angles.

So, $m\angle RUW + m\angle WUV = 180°$. Solving for x, $31x + 25 = 180$,

and $x = 5$. Substitute the value of x to find $m\angle WUV$;

$m\angle WUV = (22(5) + 25)° = 135°$.

Your Turn

7. In the diagram of a gate, the horizontal bars are parallel and the vertical bars are parallel. Find x and y. Name the postulates and/or theorems that you used to find the values.

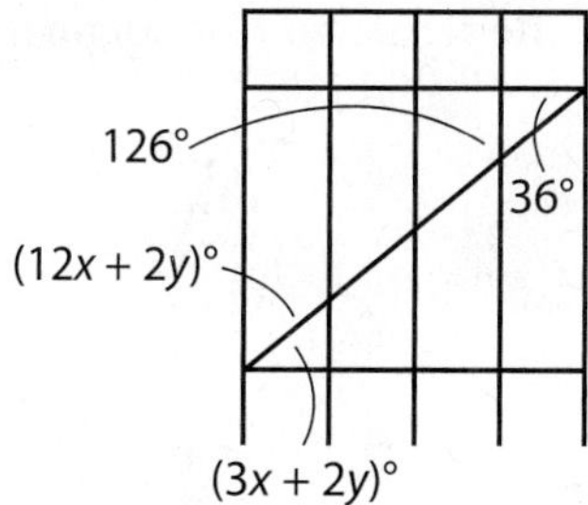

Elaborate

8. How is the Same-Side Interior Angles Postulate different from the two theorems in the lesson (Alternate Interior Angles Theorem and Corresponding Angles Theorem)?

9. **Discussion** For the given figure, if you know that p and q are parallel, and are given one angle measure, can you find all the other angle measures? Explain.

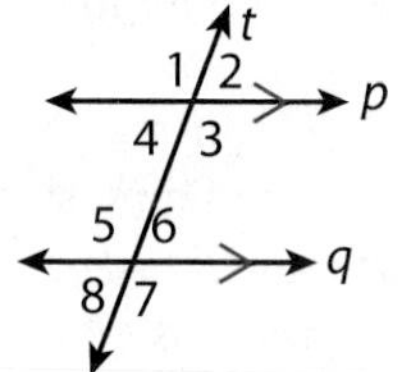

10. **Essential Question Check-In** Why is it important to establish the Same-Side Interior Angles Postulate before proving the other theorems?

Evaluate: Homework and Practice

- Online Homework
- Hints and Help
- Extra Practice

1. In the figure below, $m \| n$. Match the angle pairs with the correct label for the pairs.

A. $\angle 4$ and $\angle 6$ **a.** __?__ Corresponding Angles

B. $\angle 5$ and $\angle 8$ **b.** __?__ Same-Side Interior Angles

C. $\angle 2$ and $\angle 6$ **c.** __?__ Alternate Interior Angles

D. $\angle 4$ and $\angle 5$ **d.** __?__ Vertical Angles

2. Complete the definition: A __?__ is a line that intersects two coplanar lines at two different points.

Use the figure to find angle measures. In the figure, $p \| q$.

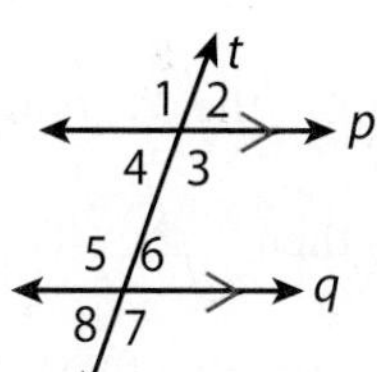

3. Suppose $m\angle 4 = 82°$. Find $m\angle 5$.

4. Suppose $m\angle 3 = 105°$. Find $m\angle 6$.

5. Suppose $m\angle 3 = 122°$. Find $m\angle 5$.

6. Suppose $m\angle 4 = 76°$. Find $m\angle 6$.

7. Suppose $m\angle 5 = 109°$. Find $m\angle 1$.

8. Suppose $m\angle 6 = 74°$. Find $m\angle 2$.

Use the figure to find angle measures. In the figure, *m* || *n* and *x* || *y*.

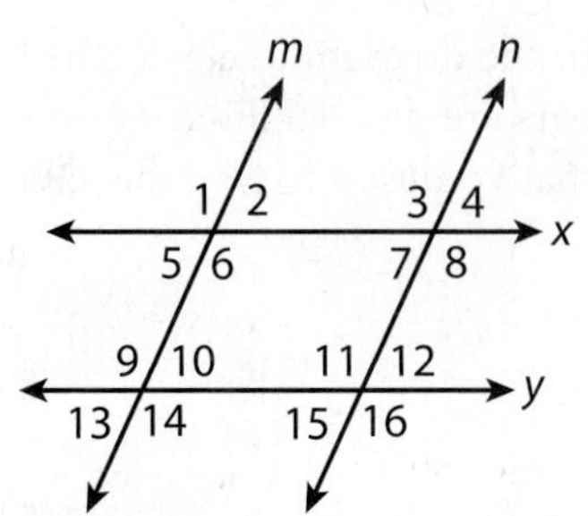

9. Suppose $m\angle 5 = 69°$. Find $m\angle 10$.

10. Suppose $m\angle 9 = 115°$. Find $m\angle 6$.

11. Suppose $m\angle 12 = 118°$. Find $m\angle 7$.

12. Suppose $m\angle 4 = 72°$. Find $m\angle 11$.

13. Suppose $m\angle 4 = 114°$. Find $m\angle 14$.

14. Suppose $m\angle 5 = 86°$. Find $m\angle 12$.

15. Ocean waves move in parallel lines toward the shore. The figure shows the path that a windsurfer takes across several waves. For this exercise, think of the windsurfer's wake as a line. If $m\angle 1 = (2x + 2y)°$ and $m\angle 2 = (2x + y)°$, find x and y. Explain your reasoning.

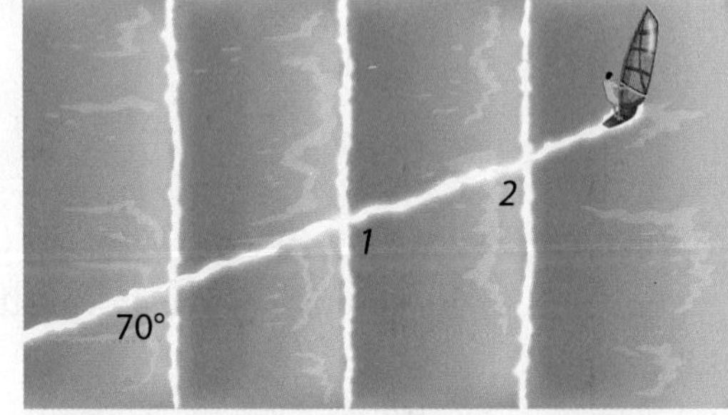

In the diagram of movie theater seats, the incline of the floor, *f*, is parallel to the seats, *s*.

16. If $m\angle 1 = 60°$, what is x?

17. If $m\angle 1 = 68°$, what is y?

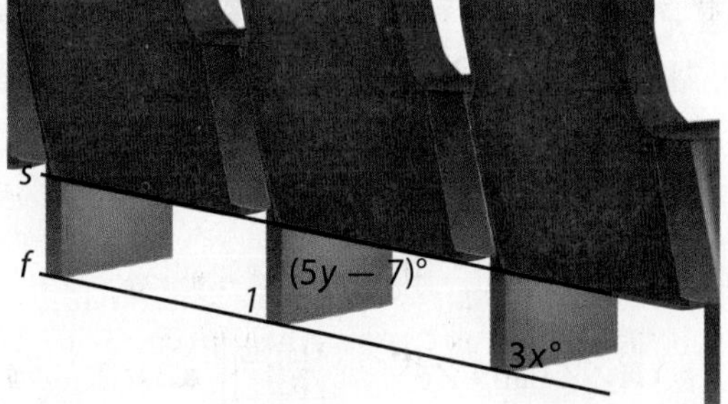

18. Complete a proof in paragraph form for the Alternate Interior Angles Theorem.

Given: $p \parallel q$

Prove: $m\angle 3 = m\angle 5$

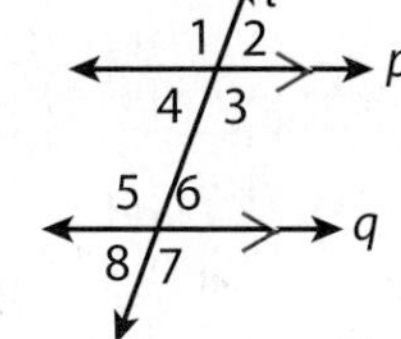

It is given that $p \parallel q$, so using the Same-Side Interior Angles Postulate, $\angle 3$ and $\angle 6$ are __?__. So, the sum of their measures is __?__ and $m\angle 3 + m\angle 6 = 180°$. You can see from the diagram that $\angle 5$ and $\angle 6$ form a line, so they are a __?__, which makes them __?__. Then $m\angle 5 + m\angle 6 = 180°$. Using the Substitution Property of Equality, you can substitute __?__ in $m\angle 3 + m\angle 6 = 180°$ with $m\angle 5 + m\angle 6$. This results in $m\angle 3 + m\angle 6 = m\angle 5 + m\angle 6$. Using the Subtraction Property of Equality, you can subtract __?__ from both sides. So, __?__.

19. Write a proof in two-column form for the Corresponding Angles Theorem.

Given: $p \parallel q$

Prove: $m\angle 1 = m\angle 5$

20. Explain the Error Angelina wrote a proof in paragraph form to prove that the measures of corresponding angles are congruent. Identify her error, and describe how to fix the error.

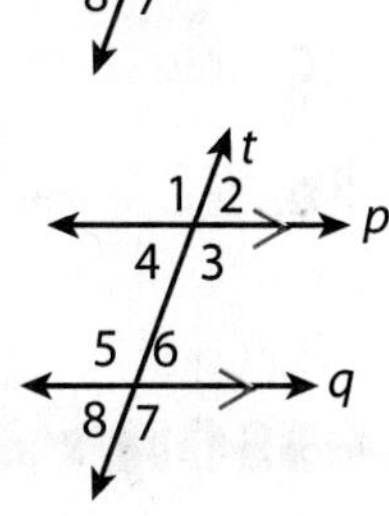

Angelina's proof:

I am given that $p \parallel q$. $\angle 1$ and $\angle 4$ are supplementary angles because they form a linear pair, so $m\angle 1 + m\angle 4 = 180°$. $\angle 4$ and $\angle 8$ are also supplementary because of the Same-Side Interior Angles Postulate, so $m\angle 4 + m\angle 8 = 180°$. You can substitute $m\angle 4 + m\angle 8$ for $180°$ in the first equation above. The result is $m\angle 1 + m\angle 4 = m\angle 4 + m\angle 8$. After subtracting $m\angle 4$ from each side, I see that $\angle 1$ and $\angle 8$ are corresponding angles and $m\angle 1 = m\angle 8$.

21. Counterexample Ellen thinks that when two lines that are not parallel are cut by a transversal, the measures of the alternate interior angles are the same. Write a proof to show that she is correct or use a counterexample to show that she is incorrect.

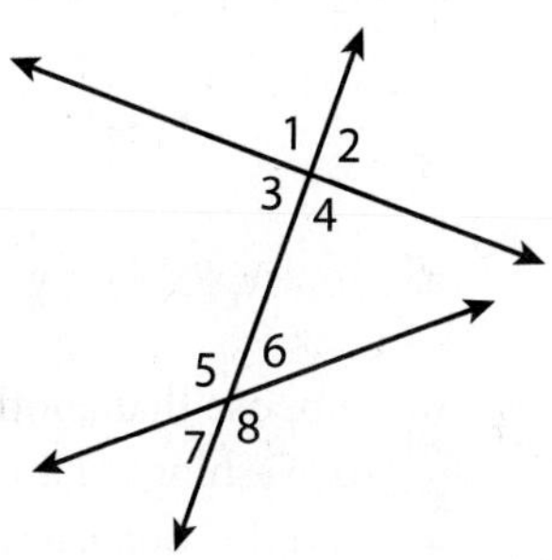

H.O.T. Focus on Higher Order Thinking

Analyzing Mathematical Relationships Use the diagram of a staircase railing for Exercises 22 and 23. $\overline{AG} \parallel \overline{CJ}$ and $\overline{AD} \parallel \overline{FJ}$. Choose the best answer.

22. Which is a true statement about the measure of $\angle DCJ$?

A. It is 30°, by the Alternate Interior Angles Theorem.

B. It is 30°, by the Corresponding Angles Theorem.

C. It is 50°, by the Alternate Interior Angles Theorem.

D. It is 50°, by the Corresponding Angles Theorem.

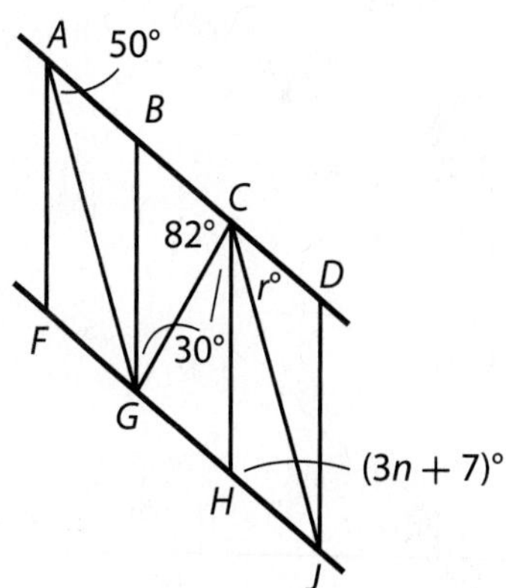

23. Which is a true statement about the value of n?

A. It is 25, by the Alternate Interior Angles Theorem.

B. It is 25, by the Same-Side Interior Angles Postulate.

C. It is 35, by Alternate Interior Angles Theorem.

D. It is 35, by the Same-Side Interior Angles Postulate.

Lesson Performance Task

Washington Street is parallel to Lincoln Street. The Apex Company's headquarters is located between the streets. From headquarters, a straight road leads to Washington Street, intersecting it at a 51° angle. Another straight road leads to Lincoln Street, intersecting it at a 37° angle.

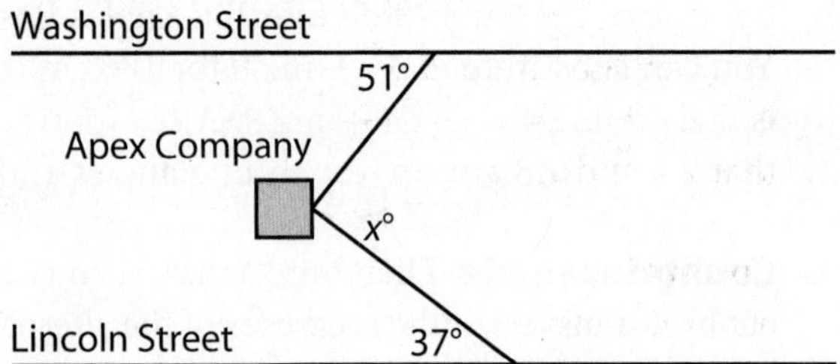

a. Find x. Explain your method.

b. Suppose that another straight road leads from the opposite side of headquarters to Washington Street, intersecting it at a y° angle, and another straight road leads from headquarters to Lincoln Street, intersecting it at a z° angle. Find w, the measure of the angle formed by the two roads. Explain how you found w.

14.3 Proving Lines are Parallel

Resource Locker

Essential Question: How can you prove that two lines are parallel?

Explore Writing Converses of Parallel Line Theorems

You form the **converse** of and if-then statement "if p, then q" by swapping p and q. The converses of the postulate and theorems you have learned about lines cut by a transversal are true statements. In the Explore, you will write specific cases of each of these converses.

The diagram shows two lines cut by a transversal t. Use the diagram and the given statements in Steps A–D. You will complete the statements based on your work in Steps A–D.

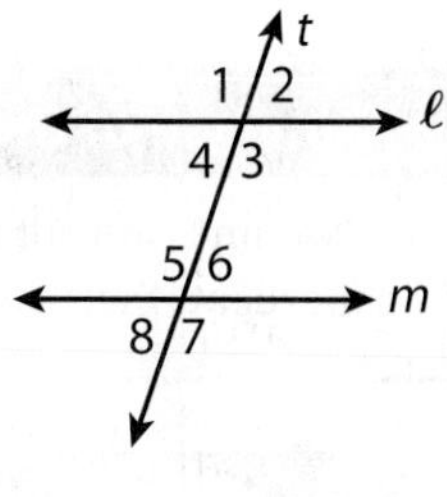

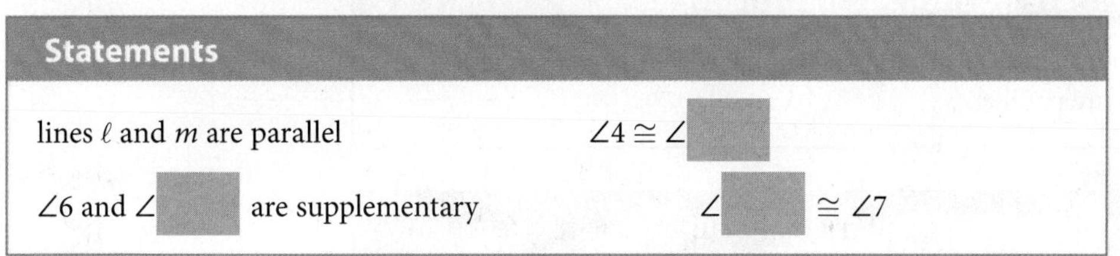

Statements	
lines ℓ and m are parallel	$\angle 4 \cong \angle$ ___
$\angle 6$ and $\angle$ ___ are supplementary	$\angle$ ___ $\cong \angle 7$

(A) Use two of the given statements together to complete a statement about the diagram using the Same-Side Interior Angles Postulate.

By the postulate: If , ___ then $\angle 6$ and $\angle$ ___ are supplementary.

(B) Now write the converse of the Same-Side Interior Angles Postulate using the diagram and your statement in Step A.

By its converse: If , ___ then lines ℓ and m are parallel.

(C) Repeat to illustrate the Alternate Interior Angles Theorem and its converse using the diagram and the given statements.

By the theorem: If ___, then $\angle 4 \cong \angle$ ___.

By its converse: If , ___

then ___.

(D) Use the diagram and the given statements to illustrate the Corresponding Angles Theorem and its converse.

By the theorem: If , ___ then $\angle$ ___ $\cong \angle 7$.

By its converse: ___.

Reflect

1. How do you form the converse of a statement?
2. What kind of angles are ∠4 and ∠6 in Step C? What does the converse you wrote in Step C mean?

Explain 1 Proving that Two Lines are Parallel

The converses from the Explore can be stated formally as a postulate and two theorems. (You will prove the converses of the theorems in the exercises.)

Converse of the Same-Side Interior Angles Postulate

If two lines are cut by a transversal so that a pair of same-side interior angles are supplementary, then the lines are parallel.

Converse of the Alternate Interior Angles Theorem

If two lines are cut by a transversal so that any pair of alternate interior angles are congruent, then the lines are parallel.

Converse of the Corresponding Angles Theorem

If two lines are cut by a transversal so that any pair of corresponding angles are congruent, then the lines are parallel.

You can use these converses to decide whether two lines are parallel.

Example 1 **A mosaic designer is using quadrilateral-shaped colored tiles to make an ornamental design. Each tile is congruent to the one shown here.**

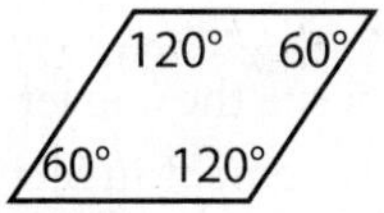

120° 60° 60° 120°

The designer uses the colored tiles to create the pattern shown here.

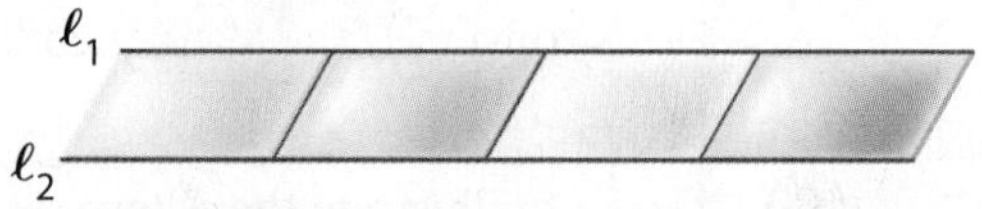

ℓ_1 ℓ_2

ℓ_1 1 ℓ_2 2

(A) Use the values of the marked angles to show that the two lines ℓ_1 and ℓ_2 are parallel.

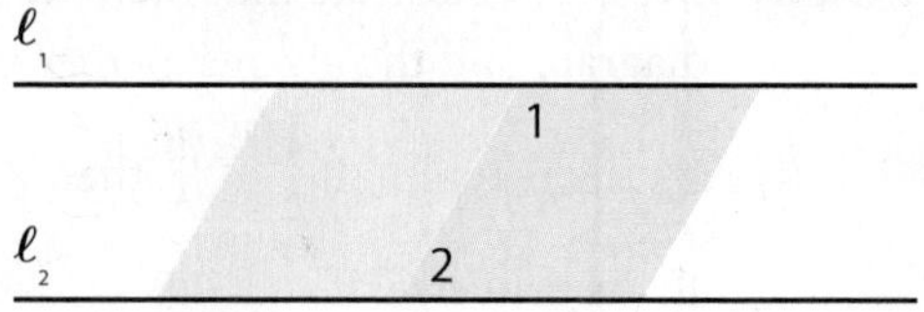

Measure of ∠1: 120° Measure of ∠2: 60°

Relationship between the two angles: They are supplementary.

Conclusion: $\ell_1 \parallel \ell_2$ by the Converse of the Same-Side Interior Angles Postulate.

Ⓑ Now look at this situation. Use the values of the marked angles to show that the two lines are parallel.

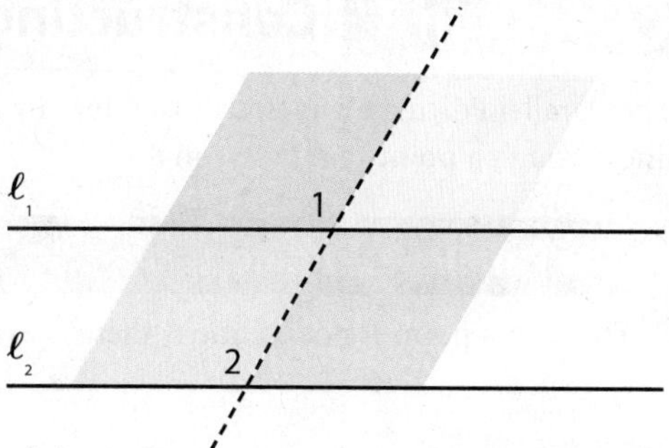

Measure of ∠1: 120° Measure of ∠2: 120°

Relationship between the two angles: They are congruent corresponding angles.

Conclusion:

ℓ 1 || ℓ 2 by the Converse of the Corresponding Angles Theorem.

Reflect

3. **What If?** Suppose the designer had been working with this basic shape instead. Do you think the conclusions in Parts A and B would have been different? Why or why not?

110° 70°
70° 110°

Your Turn

Explain why the lines are parallel given the angles shown. Assume that all tile patterns use this basic shape.

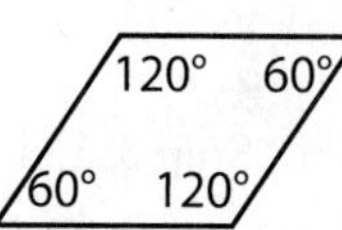

4.

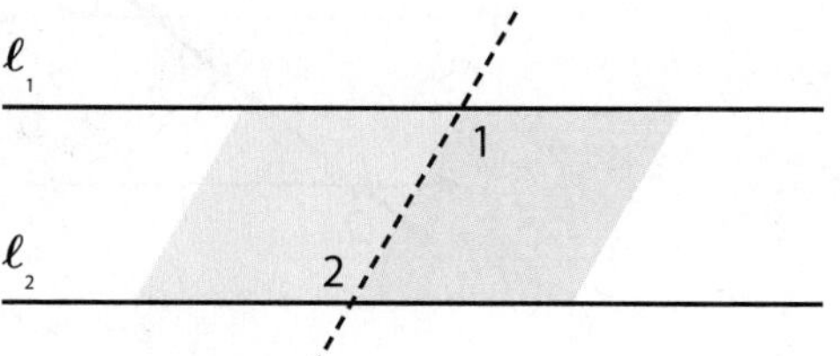

5.

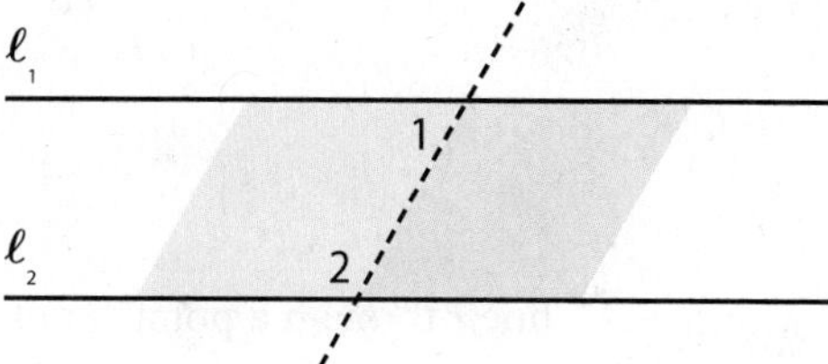

Explain 2 Constructing Parallel Lines

The Parallel Postulate guarantees that for any line ℓ, you can always construct a parallel line through a point that is not on ℓ.

The Parallel Postulate

Through a point P not on line ℓ, there is exactly one line parallel to ℓ.

Example 2 **Use a compass and straightedge to construct parallel lines.**

(A) Construct a line m through a point P not on a line ℓ so that m is parallel to ℓ.

Step 1 Draw a line ℓ and a point P not on ℓ.

Step 2 Choose two points on ℓ and label them Q and R. Use a straightedge to draw $\overleftrightarrow{PQ}$.

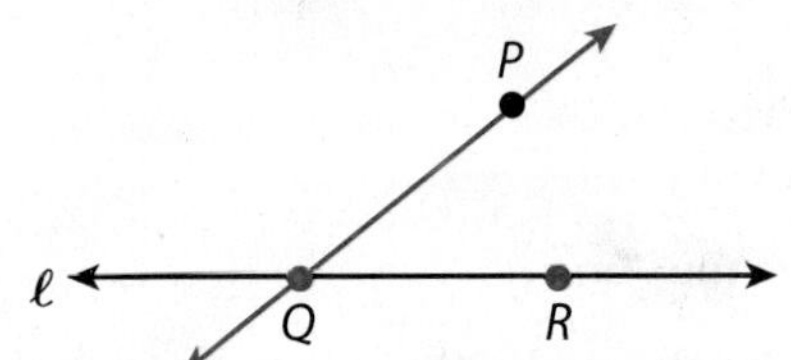

Step 3 Use a compass to copy $\angle PQR$ at point P, as shown, to construct line m. Line $m \parallel$ line ℓ.

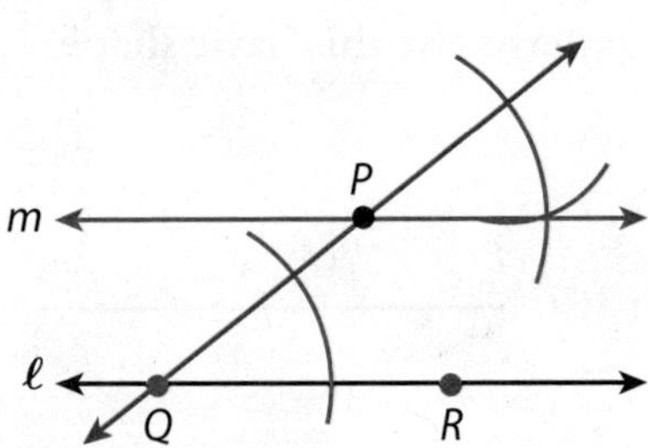

(B) Construct a line r through a point G not on a line s so that r is parallel to s.

Step 1 Draw a line s and a point G not on s.

Step 2 Choose two points on s and label them E and F. Use a straightedge to draw $\overleftrightarrow{GE}$.

Step 3 Use a compass to copy $\angle GEF$ at point G. Label the side of the angle as line r. Line $r \parallel$ line s.

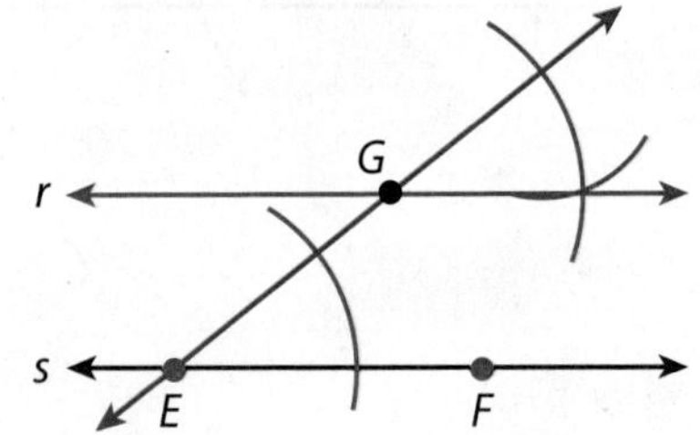

Reflect

6. **Discussion** Explain how you know that the construction in Part A or Part B produces a line passing through the given point that is parallel to the given line.

Your Turn

7. Draw a line ℓ and a point P not on ℓ. Construct a line m through P parallel to line ℓ.

Explain 3 Using Angle Pair Relationships to Verify Lines are Parallel

When two lines are cut by a transversal, you can use relationships of pairs of angles to decide if the lines are parallel.

Example 3 **Use the given angle relationships to decide whether the lines are parallel. Explain your reasoning.**

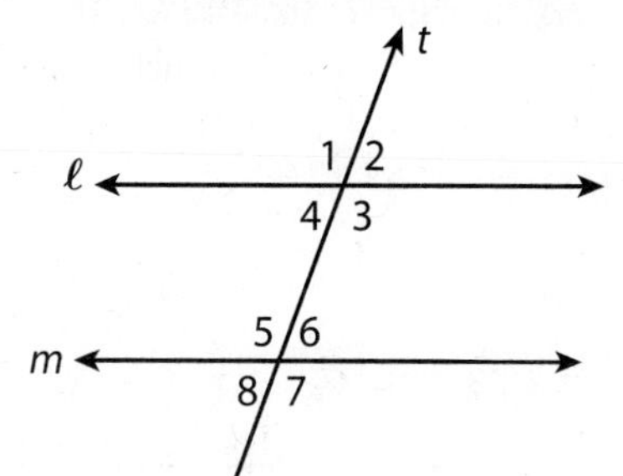

(A) $\angle 3 \cong \angle 5$

Step 1 Identify the relationship between the two angles.
$\angle 3$ and $\angle 5$ are congruent alternate interior angles.

Step 2 Are the lines parallel? Explain.
Yes, the lines are parallel by the Converse of the Alternate Interior Angles Theorem.

(B) $m\angle 4 = (x + 20)°$, $m\angle 8 = (2x + 5)°$, and $x = 15$.

Step 1 Identify the relationship between the two angles.

$m\angle 4 = (x + 20)°$ $= \left(\boxed{15} + 20\right)° = \boxed{35°}$

$m\angle 8 = (2x + 5)°$ $= \left(2 \cdot \boxed{15} + 5\right)° = \boxed{35°}$

So, $\angle 4$ and $\angle 8$ are congruent corresponding angles.

Step 2 Are the lines parallel? Explain.

Yes, the lines are parallel by the Converse of the Corresponding Angles Theorem.

Your Turn

Identify the type of angle pair described in the given condition. How do you know that lines ℓ and m are parallel?

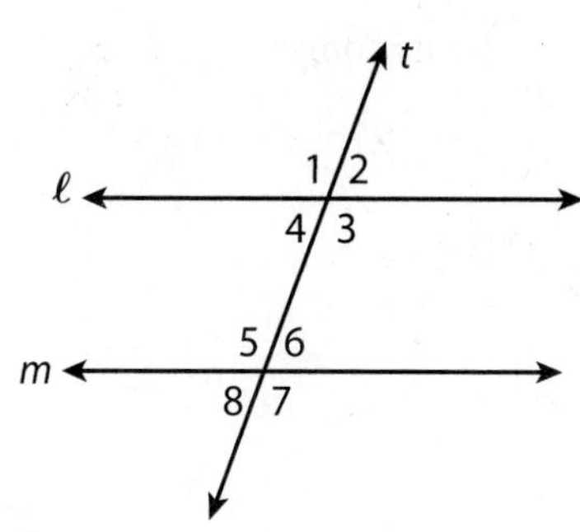

8. $m\angle 3 + m\angle 6 = 180°$

9. $\angle 2 \cong \angle 6$

Elaborate

10. How are the converses in this lesson different from the postulate/theorems in the previous lesson?

11. What If? Suppose two lines are cut by a transversal such that alternate interior angles are both congruent and supplementary. Describe the lines.

12. Essential Question Check-In Name two ways to test if a pair of lines is parallel, using the interior angles formed by a transversal crossing the two lines.

- Online Homework
- Hints and Help
- Extra Practice

Evaluate: Homework and Practice

Complete the statements below. Then use the statements and the diagram in Exercises 1–3.

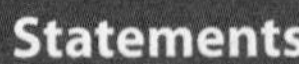

Statements
lines ℓ and m are parallel
$m\angle$ __?__ $+ m\angle 3 = 180°$
$\angle 1 \cong \angle$ __?__
$\angle$ __?__ $\cong \angle 6$

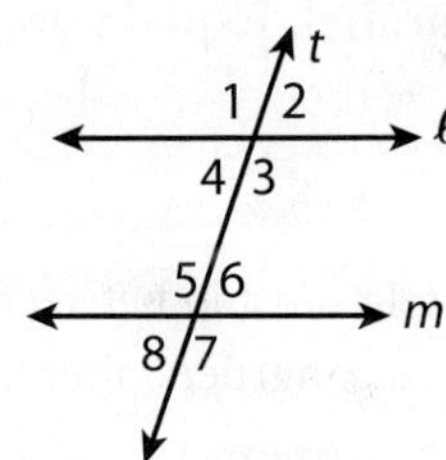

1. Use two of the given statements together to complete statements about the diagram to illustrate the Corresponding Angles Theorem. Then write its converse.

By the theorem: If __?__, then $\angle 1 \cong \angle$ __?__.

By its converse: __?__

2. Use two of the given statements together to complete statements about the diagram to illustrate the Same-Side Interior Angles Postulate. Then write its converse.

By the postulate: If __?__, then $m\angle$ __?__ $+ m\angle 3 = 180°$.

By its converse: __?__

3. Use two of the given statements together to complete statements about the diagram to illustrate the Alternate Interior Angles Theorem. Then write its converse.

By the theorem: If __?__, then $\angle$ __?__ $\cong \angle 6$.

By its converse: __?__

4. **Matching** Justify each angle pair relationship with the name of a postulate or theorem that you could use to prove that lines ℓ and m in the diagram are parallel. Several angle pairs may use the same postulate or theorem.

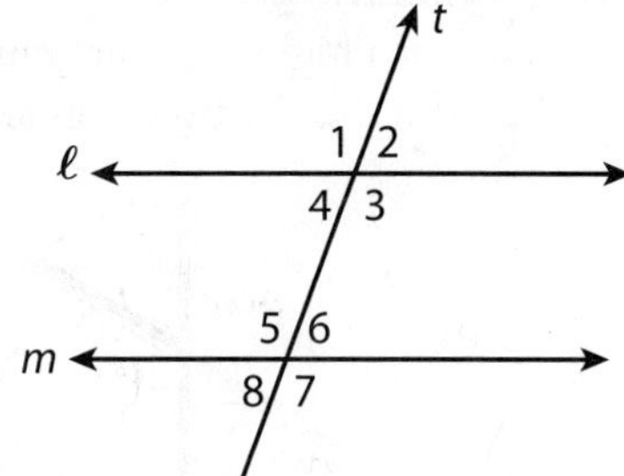

A. $\angle 2 \cong \angle 6$

B. $\angle 3 \cong \angle 5$

C. $\angle 4$ and $\angle 5$ are supplementary.

D. $\angle 4 \cong \angle 8$

E. $m\angle 3 + m\angle 6 = 180°$

F. $\angle 4 \cong \angle 6$

a. ___?___ Converse of the Corresponding Angles Theorem

b. ___?___ Converse of the Same-Side Interior Angles Postulate

c. ___?___ Converse of the Alternate Interior Angles Theorem

Use the diagram for Exercises 5–8.

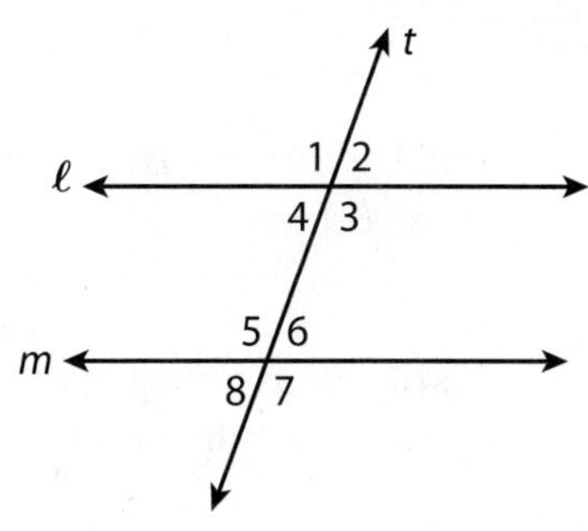

5. What must be true about $\angle 7$ and $\angle 3$ for the lines to be parallel? Name the postulate or theorem.

6. What must be true about $\angle 6$ and $\angle 3$ for the lines to be parallel? Name the postulate or theorem.

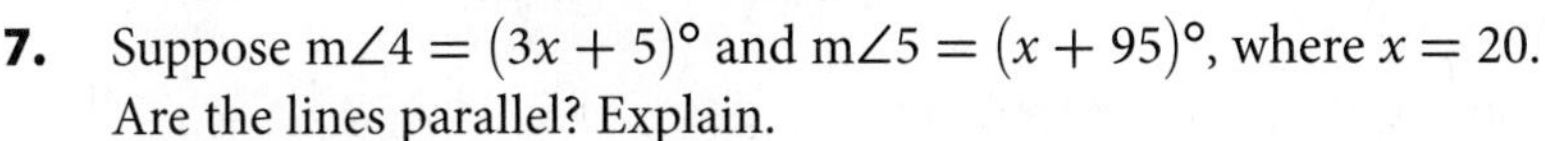

7. Suppose $m\angle 4 = (3x + 5)°$ and $m\angle 5 = (x + 95)°$, where $x = 20$. Are the lines parallel? Explain.

8. Suppose $m\angle 3 = (4x + 12)°$ and $m\angle 7 = (80 - x)°$, where $x = 15$. Are the lines parallel? Explain.

Use a converse to answer each question.

9. What value of x makes the horizontal parts of the letter Z parallel?

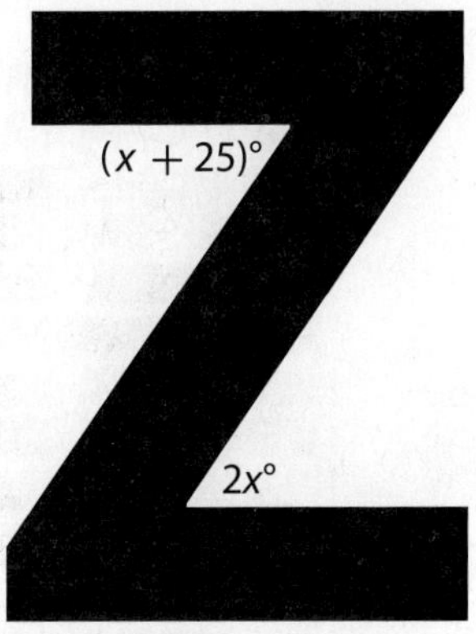

10. What value of x makes the vertical parts of the letter N parallel?

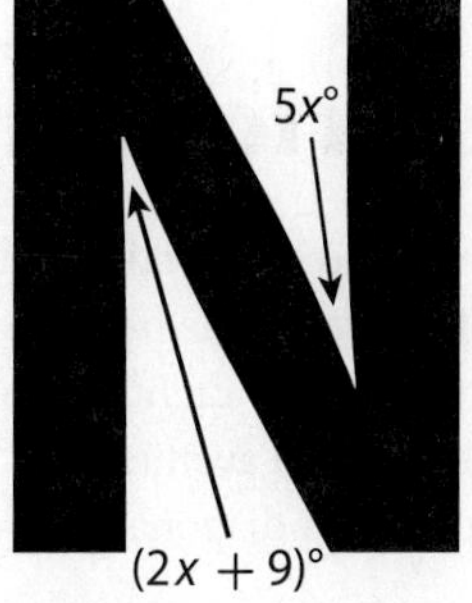

11. Engineering An overpass intersects two lanes of a highway. What must the value of x be to ensure the two lanes are parallel?

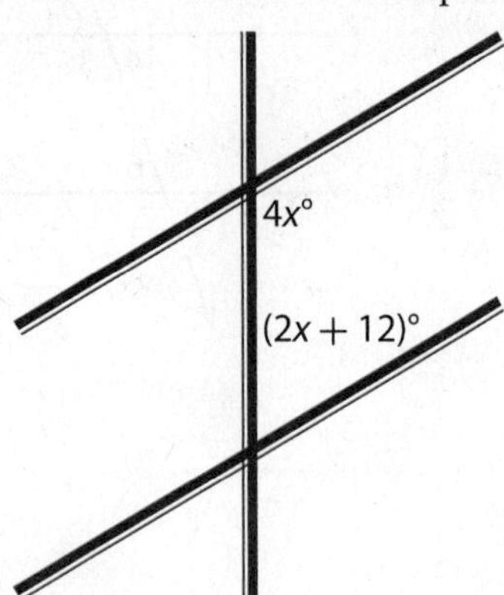

12. A trellis consists of overlapping wooden slats. What must the value of x be in order for the two slats to be parallel?

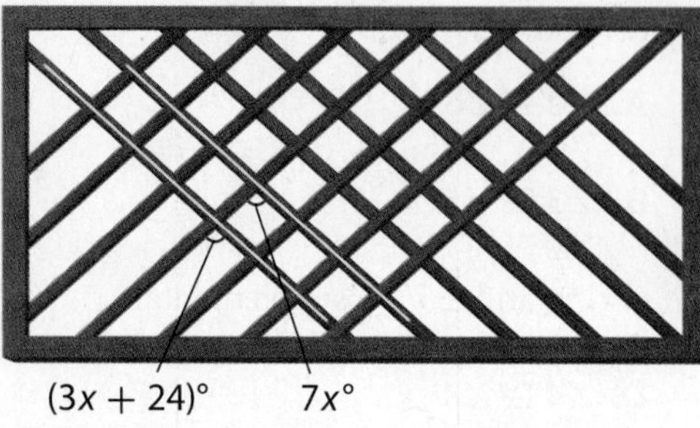

13. Draw a line ℓ and a point P not on ℓ. Construct a line parallel to ℓ that passes through P.

14. Communicate Mathematical Ideas In Exercise 13, how many parallel lines can you draw through P that are parallel to ℓ? Explain.

H.O.T. Focus on Higher Order Thinking

15. Justify Reasoning Write a two-column proof of the Converse of the Alternate Interior Angles Theorem.

Given: lines ℓ and m are cut by a transversal t; $\angle 1 \cong \angle 2$

Prove: $\ell \parallel m$

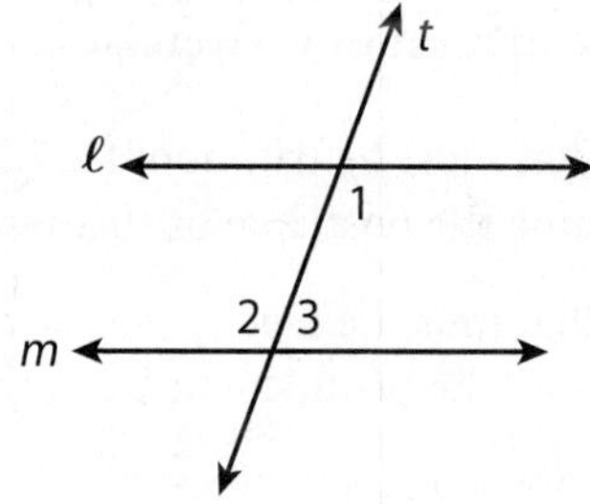

16. Justify Reasoning Write a two-column proof of the Converse of the Corresponding Angles Theorem.

Given: lines ℓ and m are cut by a transversal t; $\angle 1 \cong \angle 2$

Prove: $\ell \parallel m$

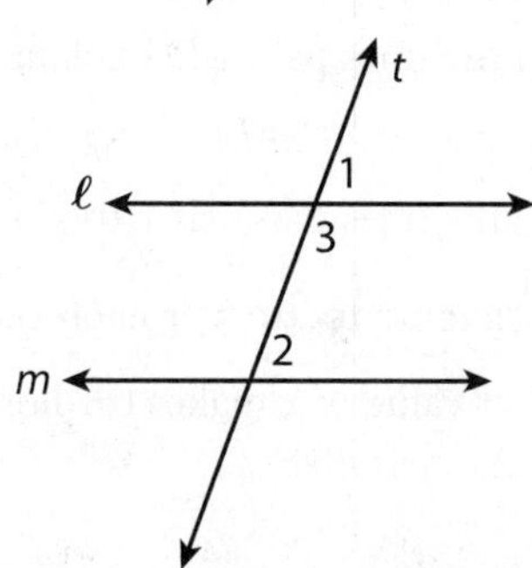

Lesson Performance Task

A simplified street map of a section of Harlem in New York City is shown here. Draw a sketch of the rectangle bounded by West 110 Street and West 121st Street in one direction and Eighth Avenue and Lenox Avenue in the other. Include all the streets and avenues that run between sides of the rectangle. Show St. Nicholas Avenue as a diagonal of the rectangle.

Now imagine that you have been given the job of laying out these streets and avenues on a bare plot of land. Explain in detail how you would do it.

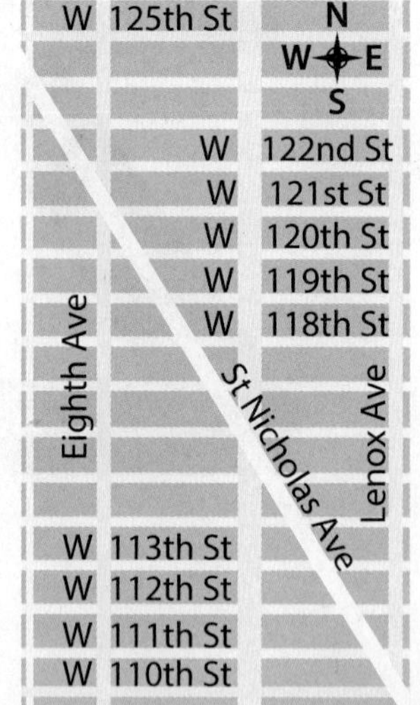

14.4 Perpendicular Lines

Essential Question: What are the key ideas about perpendicular bisectors of a segment?

Resource Locker

Constructing Perpendicular Bisectors and Perpendicular Lines

You can construct geometric figures without using measurement tools like a ruler or a protractor. By using geometric relationships and a compass and a straightedge, you can construct geometric figures with greater precision than figures drawn with standard measurement tools.

In Steps A–C, construct the perpendicular bisector of $\overline{AB}$.

Ⓐ Place the point of the compass at point A. Using a compass setting that is greater than half the length of $\overline{AB}$, draw an arc.

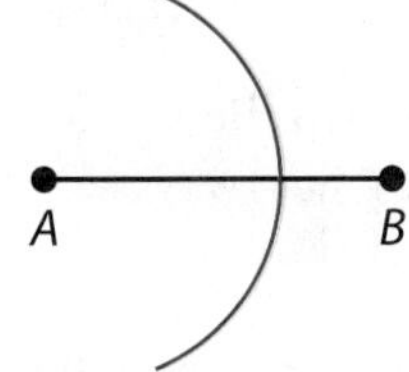

Ⓑ Without adjusting the compass, place the point of the compass at point B and draw an arc intersecting the first arc in two places. Label the points of intersection C and D.

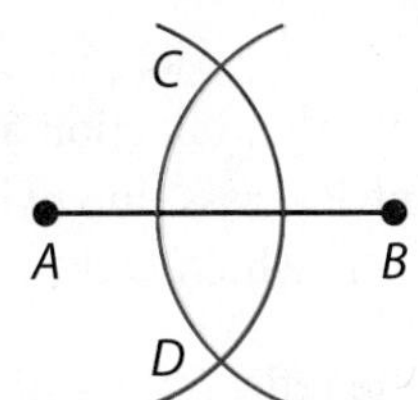

Ⓒ Use a straightedge to draw $\overleftrightarrow{CD}$, which is the perpendicular bisector of $\overline{AB}$.

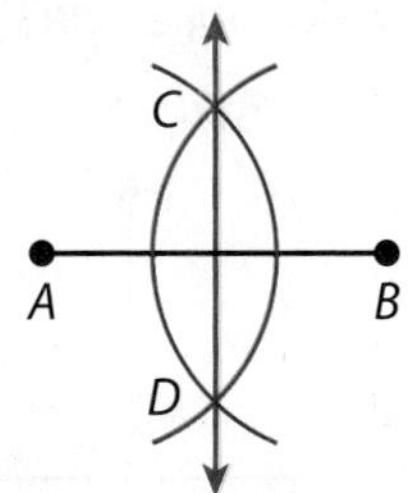

In Steps D–E, construct a line perpendicular to a line ℓ that passes through some point P that is not on ℓ.

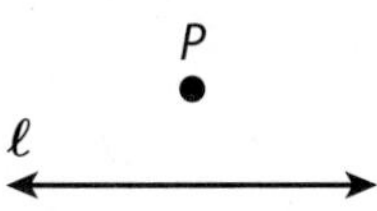

Ⓓ Place the point of the compass at P. Draw an arc that intersects line ℓ at two points, A and B.

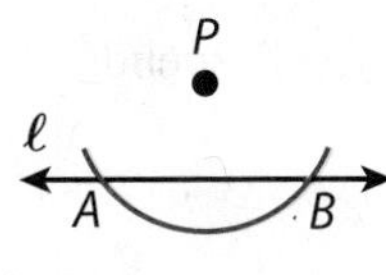

Ⓔ Use the methods in Steps A–C to construct the perpendicular bisector of $\overline{AB}$.

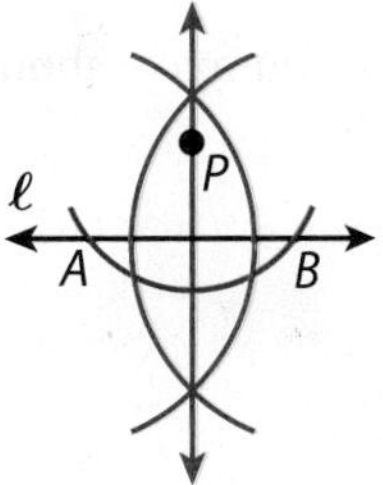

Because it is the perpendicular bisector of $\overline{AB}$, then the constructed line through P is perpendicular to line ℓ.

Reflect

1. In Step A of the first construction, why do you open the compass to a setting that is greater than half the length of $\overline{AB}$?

2. **What If?** Suppose Q is a point *on* line ℓ. Is the construction of a line perpendicular to ℓ through Q any different than constructing a perpendicular line through a point P *not* on the line, as in Steps D and E?

Explain 1 Proving the Perpendicular Bisector Theorem Using Reflections

You can use reflections and their properties to prove a theorem about perpendicular bisectors. These theorems will be useful in proofs later on.

Perpendicular Bisector Theorem

If a point is on the perpendicular bisector of a segment, then it is equidistant from the endpoints of the segment.

Example 1 **Prove the Perpendicular Bisector Theorem.**

Given: P is on the perpendicular bisector m of $\overline{AB}$.

Prove: $PA = PB$

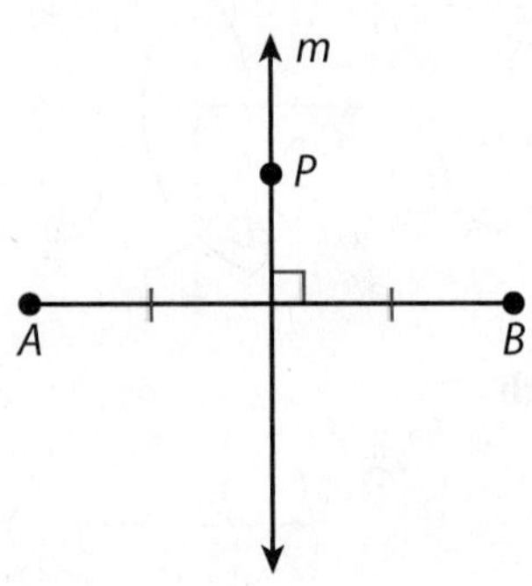

Consider the reflection across line m. Then the reflection of point P across line m is also P because point P lies on line m, which is the line of reflection.

Also, the reflection of point A across line m is B by the definition of reflection.

Therefore, $PA = PB$ because reflection preserves distance.v

Reflect

3. **Discussion** What conclusion can you make about $\triangle KLJ$ in the diagram using the Perpendicular Bisector Theorem?

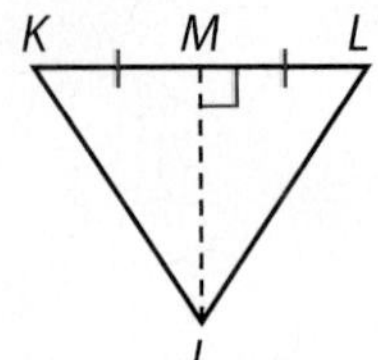

Your Turn

Use the diagram shown. $\overline{BD}$ is the perpendicular bisector of $\overline{AC}$.

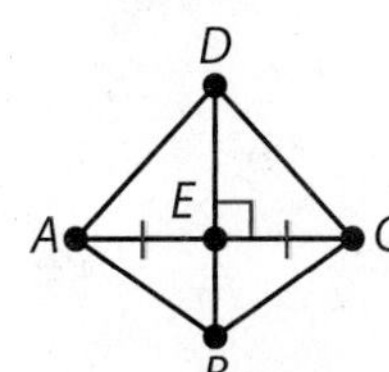

4. Suppose $ED = 16$ cm and $DA = 20$ cm. Find DC.

5. Suppose $EC = 15$ cm and $BA = 25$ cm. Find BC.

Explain 2 Proving the Converse of the Perpendicular Bisector Theorem

The converse of the Perpendicular Bisector Theorem is also true. In order to prove the converse, you will use an *indirect proof* and the *Pythagorean Theorem.*

In an **indirect proof**, you assume that the statement you are trying to prove is false. Then you use logic to lead to a contradiction of given information, a definition, a postulate, or a previously proven theorem. You can then conclude that the assumption was false and the original statement is true.

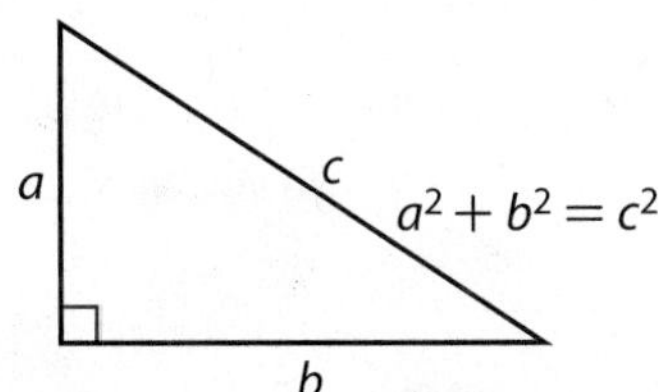

Recall that the Pythagorean Theorem states that for a right triangle with legs of length a and b and a hypotenuse of length c, $a^2 + b^2 = c^2$.

Converse of the Perpendicular Bisector Theorem

If a point is equidistant from the endpoints of a segment, then it lies on the perpendicular bisector of the segment.

Example 2 **Prove the Converse of the Perpendicular Bisector Theorem**

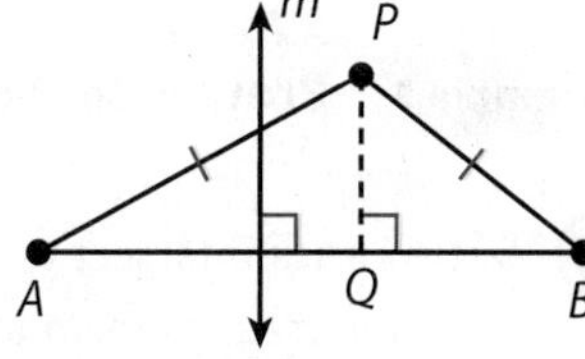

Given: $PA = PB$

Prove: P is on the perpendicular bisector m of $\overline{AB}$.

Step A: Assume what you are trying to prove is false.

Assume that P is *not* on the perpendicular bisector m of $\overline{AB}$.
Then, when you draw a perpendicular line from P to the line containing A and B, it intersects $\overline{AB}$ at point Q, which is not the midpoint of $\overline{AB}$.

Step B: Complete the following to show that this assumption leads to a contradiction.

$\overline{PQ}$ forms two right triangles, $\triangle AQP$ and $\triangle BQP$.

So, $AQ^2 + QP^2 = PA^2$ and $BQ^2 + QP^2 =$ PB^2 by the Pythagorean Theorem.

Subtract these equations:

$$\begin{array}{l} AQ^2 + QP^2 = PA^2 \\ BQ^2 + QP^2 = PB^2 \\ \hline AQ^2 - BQ^2 = PA^2 - PB^2 \end{array}$$

However, $PA^2 - PB^2 = 0$ because $PA = PB$.

Therefore, $AQ^2 - BQ^2 = 0$. This means that $AQ^2 = BQ^2$ and $AQ = BQ$. This contradicts the fact that Q is not the midpoint of $\overline{AB}$. Thus, the initial assumption must be incorrect, and P must lie on the perpendicular bisector of $\overline{AB}$.

Reflect

6. In the proof, once you know $AQ^2 = BQ^2$, why can you conclude that $AQ = BQ$?

Your Turn

7. $\overline{AD}$ is 10 inches long. $\overline{BD}$ is 6 inches long. Find the length of $\overline{AC}$.

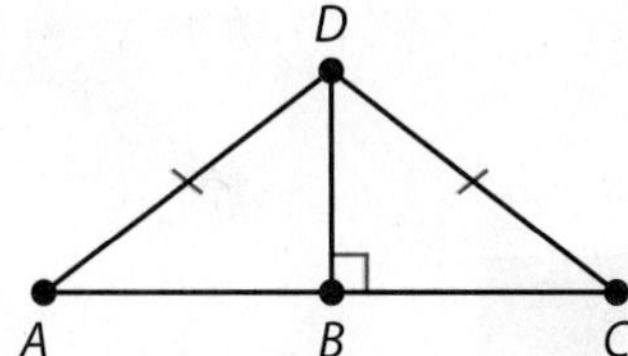

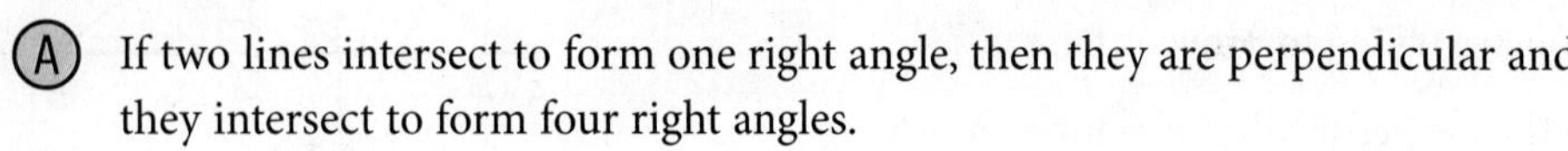

Explain 3 Proving Theorems about Right Angles

The symbol $\perp$ means that two figures are perpendicular. For example, $\ell \perp m$ or $\overleftrightarrow{XY} \perp \overline{AB}$.

Example 3 **Prove each theorem about right angles.**

(A) If two lines intersect to form one right angle, then they are perpendicular and they intersect to form four right angles.

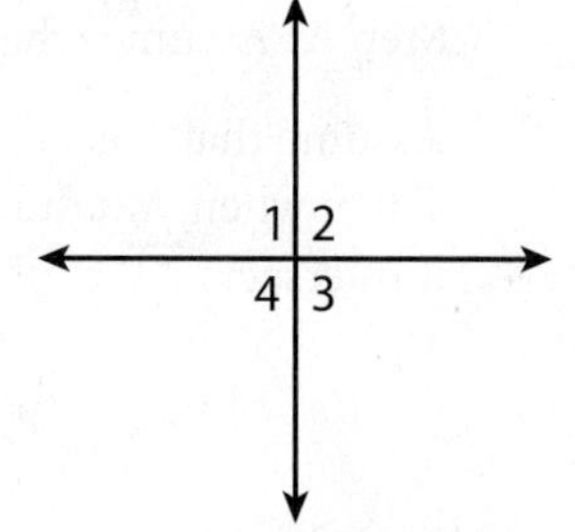

Given: $m\angle 1 = 90°$ **Prove:** $m\angle 2 = 90°$, $m\angle 3 = 90°$, $m\angle 4 = 90°$

Statement	Reason
1. $m\angle 1 = 90°$	**1.** Given
2. $\angle 1$ and $\angle 2$ are a linear pair.	**2.** Given
3. $\angle 1$ and $\angle 2$ are supplementary.	**3.** Linear Pair Theorem
4. $m\angle 1 + m\angle 2 = 180°$	**4.** Definition of supplementary angles
5. $90° + m\angle 2 = 180°$	**5.** Substitution Property of Equality
6. $m\angle 2 = 90°$	**6.** Subtraction Property of Equality
7. $m\angle 2 = m\angle 4$	**7.** Vertical Angles Theorem
8. $m\angle 4 = 90°$	**8.** Substitution Property of Equality
9. $m\angle 1 = m\angle 3$	**9.** Vertical Angles Theorem
10. $m\angle 3 = 90°$	**10.** Substitution Property of Equality

(B) If two intersecting lines form a linear pair of angles with equal measures, then the lines are perpendicular.

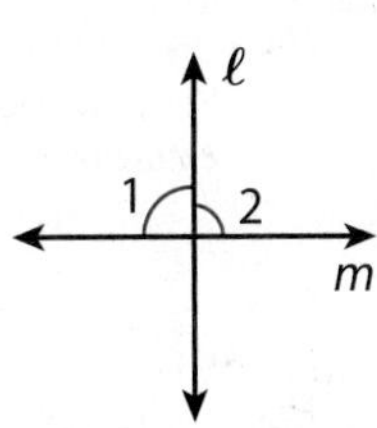

Given: $m\angle 1 = m\angle 2$ **Prove:** $\ell \perp m$

By the diagram, $\angle 1$ and $\angle 2$ form a linear pair so $\angle 1$ and $\angle 2$ are supplementary by the Linear Pair Theorem. By the definition of supplementary angles, $m\angle 1 + m\angle 2 = 180°$. It is also given that $m\angle 1 = m\angle 2$, so $m\angle 1 + m\angle 1 = 180°$ by the Substitution Property of Equality. Adding gives $2 \cdot m\angle 1 = 180°$, and $m\angle 1 = 90°$ by the Division Property of Equality. Therefore, $\angle 1$ is a right angle and $\ell \perp m$ by the definition of perpendicular lines.

Reflect

8. State the converse of the theorem in Part B. Is the converse true?

Your Turn

9. Given: $b \parallel d$, $c \parallel e$, $m\angle 1 = 50°$, and $m\angle 5 = 90°$. Use the diagram to find $m\angle 4$.

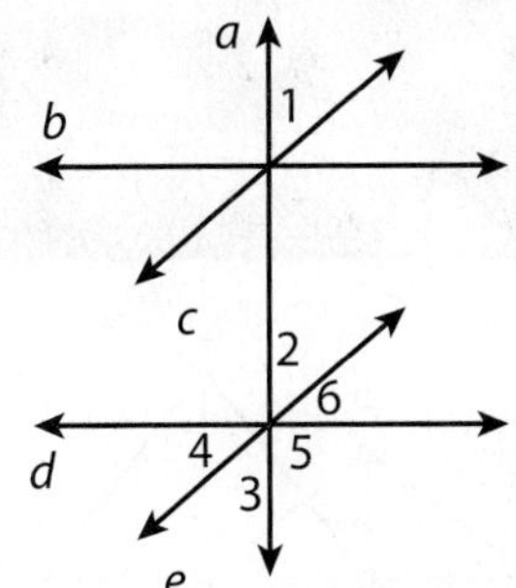

Elaborate

10. **Discussion** Explain how the converse of the Perpendicular Bisector Theorem justifies the compass-and-straightedge construction of the perpendicular bisector of a segment.

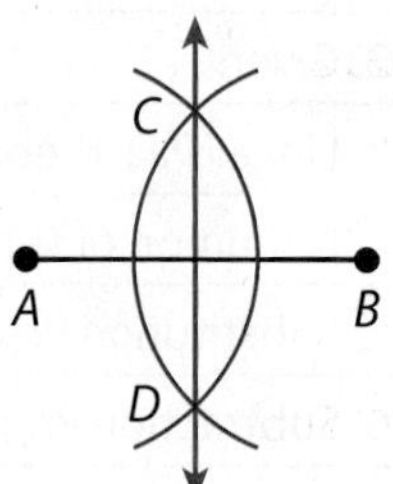

11. **Essential Question Check-In** How can you construct perpendicular lines and prove theorems about perpendicular bisectors?

Evaluate: Homework and Practice

- Online Homework
- Hints and Help
- Extra Practice

1. How can you construct a line perpendicular to line ℓ that passes through point P using paper folding?

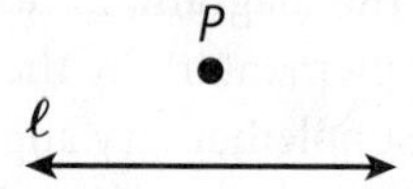

2. **Check for Reasonableness** How can you use a ruler and a protractor to check the construction in Elaborate Exercise 10?

3. Describe the point on the perpendicular bisector of a segment that is closest to the endpoints of the segment.

4. **Represent Real-World Problems** A field of soybeans is watered by a rotating irrigation system. The watering arm, $\overline{CD}$, rotates around its center point. To show the area of the crop of soybeans that will be watered, construct a circle with diameter CD.

Use the diagram to find the lengths. $\overline{BP}$ is the perpendicular bisector of $\overline{AC}$. $\overline{CQ}$ is the perpendicular bisector of $\overline{BD}$. $AB = BC = CD$.

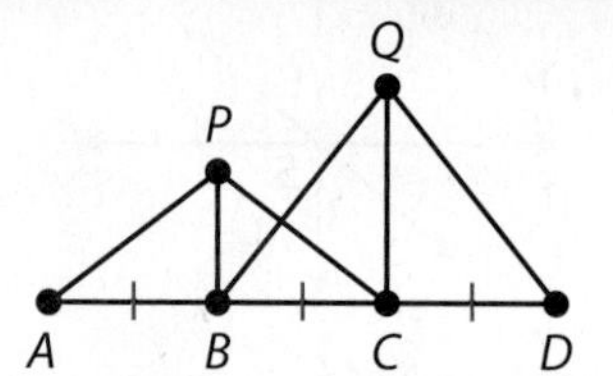

5. Suppose $AP = 5$ cm. What is the length of $\overline{PC}$?

6. Suppose $AP = 5$ cm and $BQ = 8$ cm. What is the length of $\overline{QD}$?

7. Suppose $AC = 12$ cm and $QD = 10$ cm. What is the length of $\overline{QC}$?

8. Suppose $PB = 3$ cm and $AD = 12$ cm . What is the length of $\overline{PC}$?

Given: $PA = PC$ and $BA = BC$. Use the diagram to find the lengths or angle measures described.

9. Suppose $m\angle 2 = 38°$. Find $m\angle 1$.

10. Suppose $PA = 10$ cm and $PB = 6$ cm. What is the length of $\overline{AC}$?

11. Find $m\angle 3 + m\angle 4$.

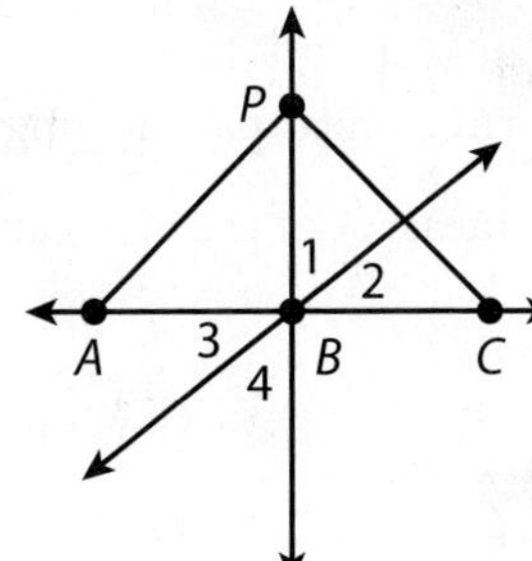

Given: $m \parallel n$, $x \parallel y$, and $y \perp m$. Use the diagram to find the angle measures.

12. Suppose $m\angle 7 = 30°$. Find $m\angle 3$.

13. Suppose $m\angle 1 = 90°$. What is $m\angle 2 + m\angle 3 + m\angle 5 + m\angle 6$?

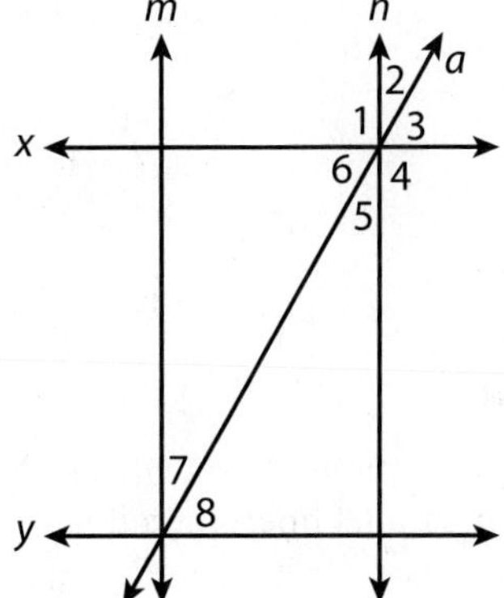

Use this diagram of trusses for a railroad bridge in Exercise 14.

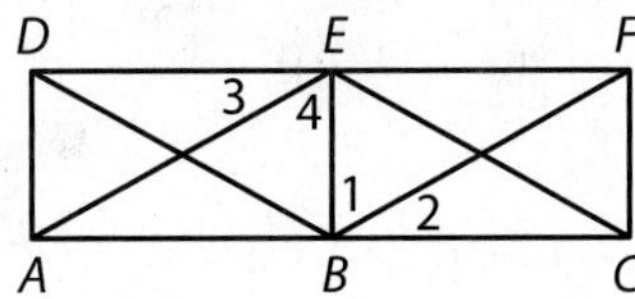

14. Suppose $\overline{BE}$ is the perpendicular bisector of $\overline{DF}$. Which of the following statements do you know are true? Determine all that apply. Explain your reasoning.

A. $BD = BF$

B. $m\angle 1 + m\angle 2 = 90°$

C. E is the midpoint of $\overline{DF}$.

D. $m\angle 3 + m\angle 4 = 90°$

E. $\overline{DA} \perp \overline{AC}$

15. Algebra Two lines intersect to form a linear pair with equal measures. One angle has the measure $2x°$ and the other angle has the measure $(20y - 10)°$. Find the values of x and y. Explain your reasoning.

16. Algebra Two lines intersect to form a linear pair of congruent angles. The measure of one angle is $(8x + 10)°$ and the measure of the other angle is $\left(\frac{15y}{2}\right)°$. Find the values of x and y. Explain your reasoning.

H.O.T. Focus on Higher Order Thinking

17. Communicate Mathematical Ideas The valve pistons on a trumpet are all perpendicular to the lead pipe. Explain why the valve pistons must be parallel to each other.

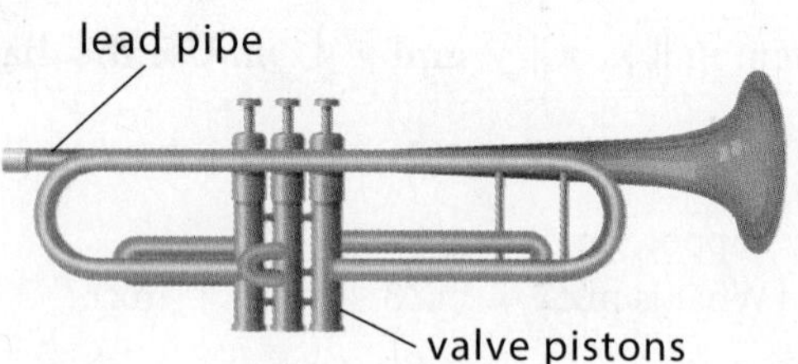

18. Justify Reasoning Prove the theorem: In a plane, if a transversal is perpendicular to one of two parallel lines, then it is perpendicular to the other.

Given: $\overline{RS} \perp \overline{CD}$ and $\overline{AB} \parallel \overline{CD}$ Prove: $\overline{RS} \perp \overline{AB}$

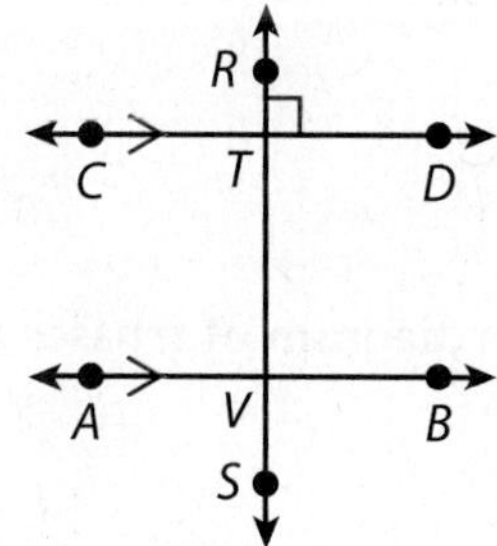

19. Analyze Mathematical Relationships Complete the indirect proof to show that two supplementary angles cannot both be obtuse angles.

Given: $\angle 1$ and $\angle 2$ are supplementary.

Prove: $\angle 1$ and $\angle 2$ cannot both be obtuse.

Assume that two supplementary angles *can* both be obtuse angles. So, assume that

$\angle 1$ and $\angle 2$ __?__. Then $m\angle 1 > 90°$ and $m\angle 2 >$ ☐

by __?__. Adding the two inequalities,

$m\angle 1 + m\angle 2 >$ ☐. However, by the definition of supplementary angles,

__?__. So $m\angle 1 + m\angle 2 > 180°$ contradicts the given information.

This means the assumption is __?__, and therefore __?__.

Lesson Performance Task

A utility company wants to build a wind farm to provide electricity to the towns of Acton, Baxter, and Coleville. Because of concerns about noise from the turbines, the residents of all three towns do not want the wind farm built close to where they live. The company comes to an agreement with the residents to build the wind farm at a location that is equally distant from all three towns.

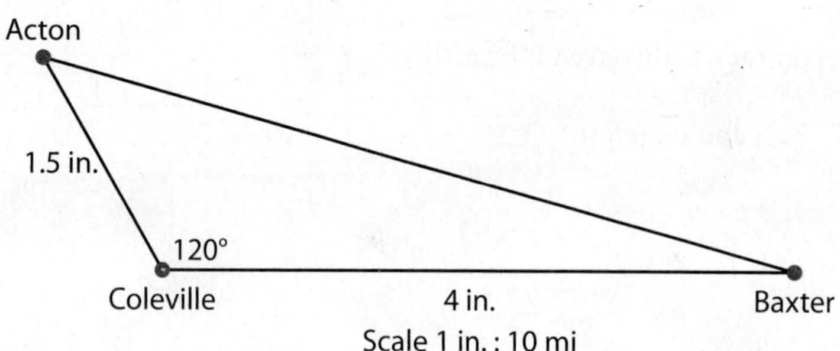

a. Use the drawing to draw a diagram of the locations of the towns using a scale of 1 in. : 10 mi. Draw the 4-inch and 1.5-inch lines with a 120° angle between them. Write the actual distances between the towns on your diagram.

b. Estimate where you think the wind farm will be located.

c. Use what you have learned in this lesson to find the exact location of the wind farm. What is the approximate distance from the wind farm to each of the three towns?

STUDY GUIDE REVIEW

Proofs with Lines and Angles

MODULE 14

Essential Question: How can you use parallel and perpendicular lines to solve real-world problems?

Key Vocabulary
vertical angles
(ángulos verticales)
complementary angles
(ángulos complementarios)
supplementary angles
(ángulos suplementarios)
transversal *(transversal)*
indirect proof *(prueba indirecta)*

KEY EXAMPLE *(Lesson 14.1)*

Find $m\angle ABD$ given that $m\angle CBE = 40°$ and the angles are formed by the intersection of the lines $\overleftrightarrow{AC}$ and $\overleftrightarrow{DE}$.

When two lines intersect, they form two pairs of vertical angles at their intersection. Note that $\angle ABD$ and $\angle CBE$ are vertical angles and $\angle DBC$ and $\angle ABE$ are vertical angles.

$\angle ABD \cong \angle CBE$	Vertical Angles Theorem
$m\angle ABD = m\angle CBE = 40°$	Definition of congruence of angles

KEY EXAMPLE *(Lesson 14.2)*

Find $m\angle APD$ given that $\overleftrightarrow{AB}$ intersects the parallel lines $\overleftrightarrow{DE}$ and $\overleftrightarrow{FG}$ at the points P and Q, respectively, and $m\angle AQF = 70°$.

When a transversal intersects two parallel lines, it forms a series of angle pairs. Note that $\angle APD$ and $\angle AQF$ are a pair of corresponding angles.

$m\angle APD = m\angle AQF$	Corresponding Angles Theorem
$m\angle APD = 70°$	Substitute the known angle measure.

KEY EXAMPLE *(Lesson 14.3)*

Determine whether the lines $\overleftrightarrow{DE}$ and $\overleftrightarrow{FG}$ are parallel given that $\overleftrightarrow{AB}$ intersects them at the points P and Q, respectively, $m\angle APE = 60°$, and $m\angle BQF = 60°$.

Lines $\overleftrightarrow{AB}$ and $\overleftrightarrow{DE}$ intersect, so they create two pairs of vertical angles. The angle which is the opposite of $\angle APE$ is $\angle DPB$, so they are called vertical angles.

$\angle APE \cong \angle DPB$	Vertical Angles Theorem
$m\angle APE = m\angle DPB$	Definition of congruence
$m\angle DPB = 60°$	Substitute the known angle measure.
$m\angle BQF = m\angle DPB = 60°$	
$\angle BQF \cong \angle DPB$	Definition of congruence

Thus, the lines $\overleftrightarrow{DE}$ and $\overleftrightarrow{FG}$ are parallel by the converse of the Corresponding Angles Theorem because their corresponding angles are congruent.

EXERCISES

Find the angle measure.

1. m$\angle ABD$ given that m$\angle CBD = 40°$ and the angles are formed by the intersection of the lines $\overleftrightarrow{AC}$ and $\overleftrightarrow{DE}$. *(Lesson 14.1)*

2. m$\angle BPE$ given that $\overleftrightarrow{AB}$ intersects the parallel lines $\overleftrightarrow{DE}$ and $\overleftrightarrow{FG}$ at the points P and Q, respectively, and m$\angle AQF = 45°$. *(Lesson 14.2)*

Determine whether the lines are parallel. *(Lesson 14.3)*

3. $\overleftrightarrow{DE}$ and $\overleftrightarrow{FG}$, given that $\overleftrightarrow{AB}$ intersects them at the points P and Q, respectively, m$\angle APD = 60°$, and m$\angle BQG = 120°$.

Find the distance and angle formed from the perpendicular bisector. *(Lesson 14.4)*

4. Find the distance of point D from B given that D is the point at the perpendicular bisector of the line segment $\overline{AB}$, $\overleftrightarrow{DE}$ intersects $\overline{AB}$, and $AD = 3$. Find m$\angle ADE$.

MODULE PERFORMANCE TASK

Mystery Spot Geometry

Inside mystery spot buildings, some odd things can appear to occur. Water can appear to flow uphill, and people can look as if they are standing at impossible angles. That is because there is no view of the outside, so the room appears to be normal.

The illustration shows a mystery spot building constructed so that the floor is at a 25° angle with the ground.

View from outside

View from inside

- A table is placed in the room with its legs perpendicular to the floor and the tabletop perpendicular to the legs. Sketch or describe the relationship of the tabletop to the floor, walls, and ceiling of the room. What would happen if a ball were placed on the table?
- A chandelier hangs from the ceiling of the room. How does it appear to someone inside? How does it appear to someone standing outside of the room?

Use sketches, words, or geometry to explain how you reached your conclusions.

Ready to Go On?

14.1–14.4 Proofs with Lines and Angles

- Online Homework
- Hints and Help
- Extra Practice

Find the measure of each angle. Assume lines $\overleftrightarrow{GB}$ and $\overleftrightarrow{FC}$ are parallel. *(Lessons 14.1, 14.2)*

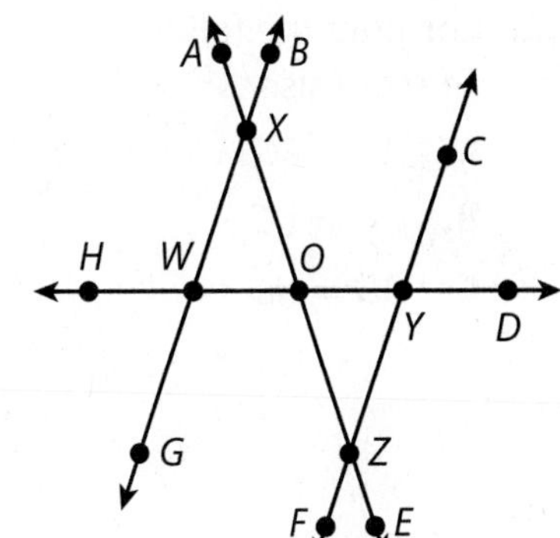

1. The measure of $\angle WOX$ is 70°. Find $m\angle YOZ$.

2. The measure of $\angle AXB$ is 40°. Find $m\angle FZE$.

3. The measure of $\angle XWO$ is 70°. Find $m\angle OYC$.

4. The measure of $\angle BXO$ is 110°. Find $m\angle OZF$.

Use the diagram to find lengths. $\overline{PB}$ is the perpendicular bisector of $\overline{AC}$. $\overline{QC}$ is the perpendicular bisector of $\overline{BD}$. $AB = BC = CD$. *(Lesson 14.4)*

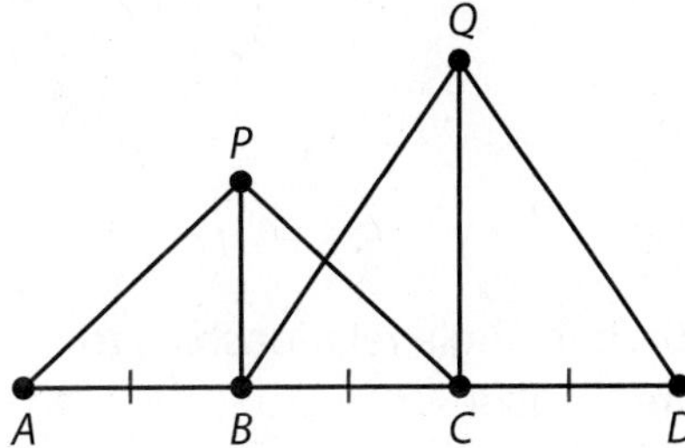

5. Given $BD = 24$ and $PC = 13$, find PB.

6. Given $QB = 23$ and $BC = 12$, find QD.

ESSENTIAL QUESTION

7. Say you want to create a ladder. Which lines should be parallel or perpendicular to each other?

MODULE 14
MIXED REVIEW

Assessment Readiness

1. Consider each equation. Is it the equation of a line that is either parallel or perpendicular to $y = 3x + 2$?
Write Yes or No for A–C.

A. $y = -\frac{1}{3}x - 8$

B. $y = 3x - 10$

C. $y = 2x + 4$

2. Consider the following statements about $\triangle ABC$. Determine if each statement is True or False.

A. $AC = BC$

B. $CD = BC$

C. $AD = BD$

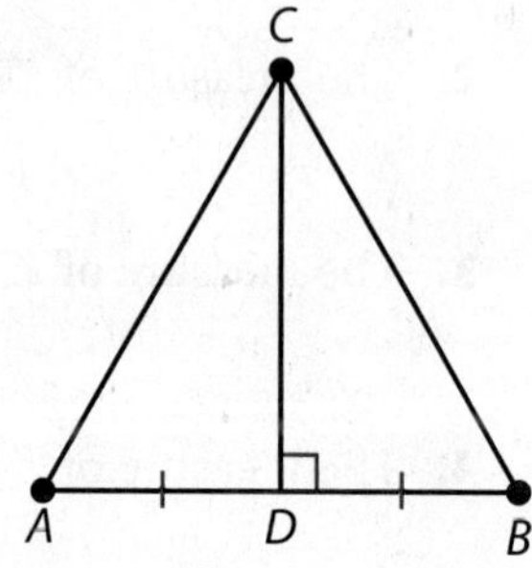

3. The measure of angle 3 is 130° and the measure of angle 4 is 50°. State two different relationships that can be used to prove $m\angle 1 = 130°$.

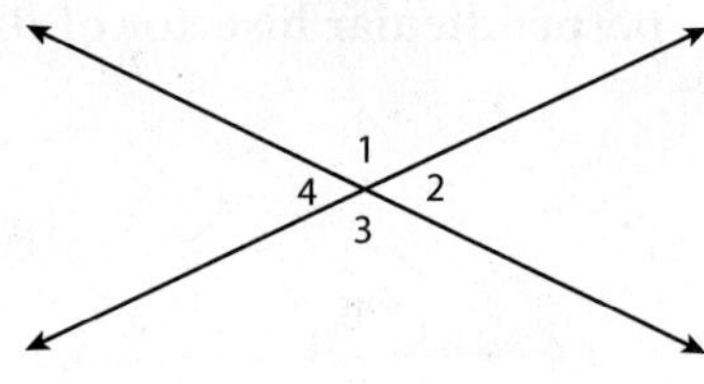

4. $m\angle 1 = 110°$ and $m\angle 6 = 70°$. Use angle relationships to explain why lines m and n are parallel.

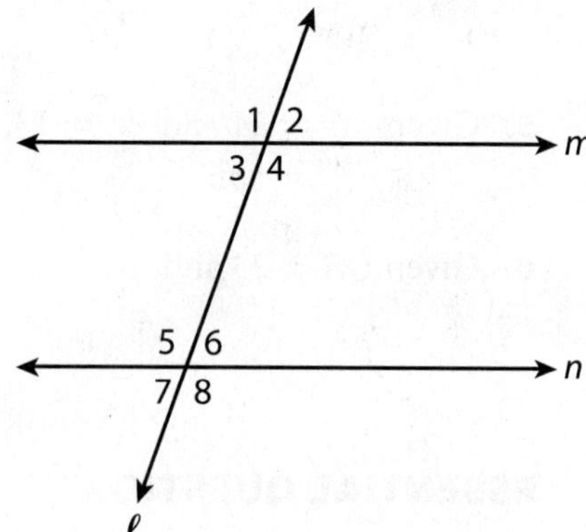

Proofs with Triangles and Quadrilaterals

MODULE 15

Essential Question: How can you use proofs with triangles and quadrilaterals to solve real-world problems?

REAL WORLD VIDEO
Check out how architects use properties of quadrilaterals to design unusual buildings, such as the Seattle Central Library.

MODULE PERFORMANCE TASK PREVIEW

How Big Is That Face?

In this module, you will use the geometry of trapezoids and other quadrilaterals to solve a problem related to the external dimensions of the Seattle Central Library. Let's get started and explore this interesting "slant" on architecture!

Are YOU Ready?

Complete these exercises to review the skills you will need for this chapter.

Personal Math Trainer
- Online Homework
- Hints and Help
- Extra Practice

Parallelograms

Example 1 **Determine if the figure is a parallelogram.**

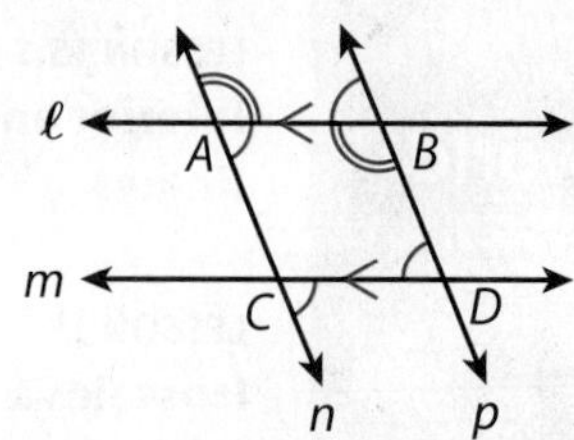

It is given that lines ℓ and m are parallel. Lines n and p are also parallel because of the Converse of the Corresponding Angles Theorem. Therefore, $ABCD$ is a parallelogram.

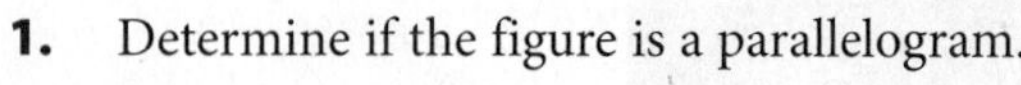

1. Determine if the figure is a parallelogram.

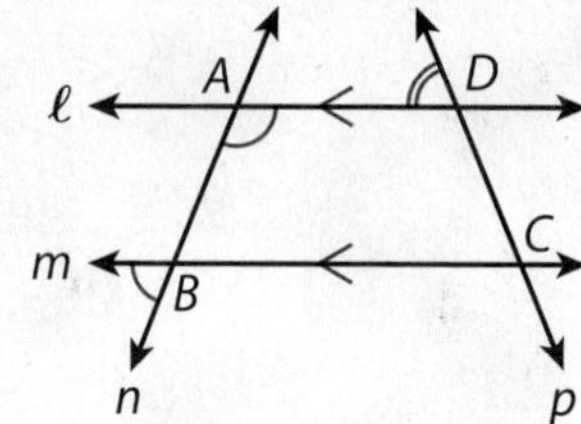

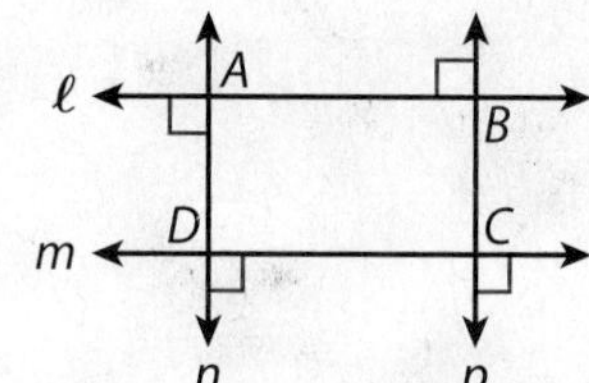

Angle Relationships

Example 2 Find the measure of $\angle x$.

$m\angle x + 72° = 180°$ Definition of supplementary angles

$m\angle x = 180° - 72°$ Solve for $m\angle x$.

$m\angle x = 108°$ Simplify.

Find the measure of each angle in the image from the example.

2. $m\angle y =$ ___?___

3. $m\angle z =$ ___?___

Angle Theorems for Triangles

Example 3 Find the missing angle.

$62° + 62° + m\angle x = 180°$ Triangle Sum Theorem

$m\angle x = 180° - 62° - 62°$ Solve for $m\angle x$.

$m\angle x = 56°$ Simplify.

Find the missing angle measures in the given triangles.

4.

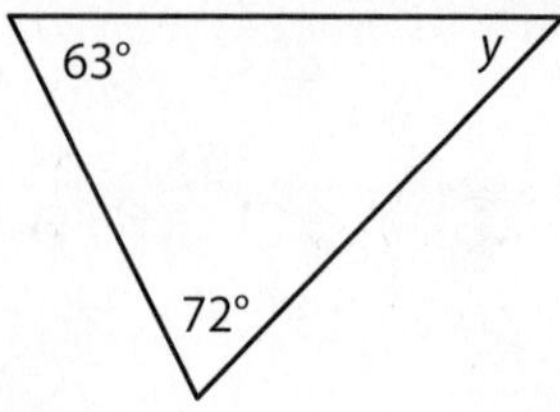

$m\angle y =$ ___?___

5.

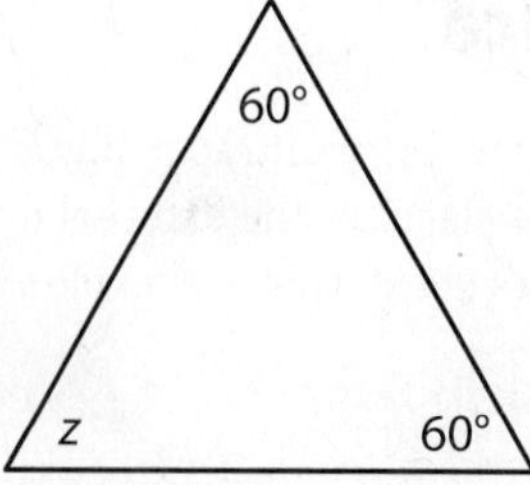

$m\angle z =$ ___?___

15.1 Interior and Exterior Angles

Resource Locker

Essential Question: What can you say about the interior and exterior angles of a triangle and other polygons?

Explore 1 Exploring Interior Angles in Triangles

You can find a relationship between the measures of the three angles of a triangle. An **interior angle** is an angle formed by two sides of a polygon with a common vertex. So, a triangle has three interior angles.

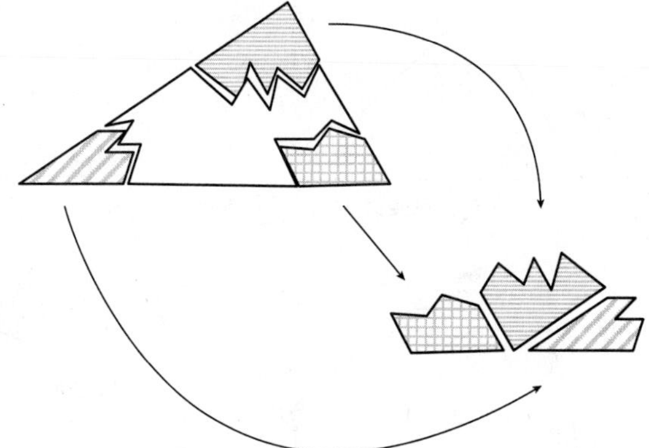

(A) Use a straightedge to draw a large triangle on a sheet of paper and cut it out. Tear off the three corners and rearrange the angles so their sides are adjacent and their vertices meet at a point.

(B) What seems to be true about placing the three interior angles of a triangle together?

(C) Make a conjecture about the sum of the measures of the interior angles of a triangle.

The conjecture about the sum of the interior angles of a triangle can be proven so it can be stated as a theorem. In the proof, you will add an *auxiliary line* to the triangle figure. An **auxiliary line** is a line that is added to a figure to aid in a proof.

The Triangle Sum Theorem
The sum of the angle measures of a triangle is 180°.

(D) Complete the proof of the Triangle Sum Theorem.

Given: $\triangle ABC$

Prove: $m\angle 1 + m\angle 2 + m\angle 3 = 180°$

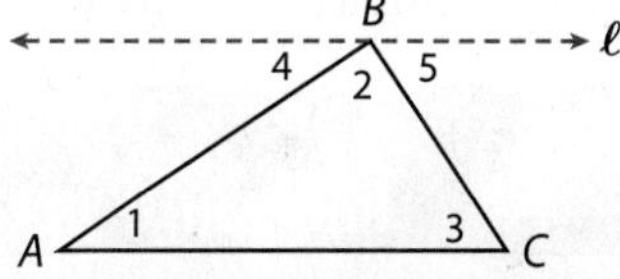

Statements	Reasons
1. Draw line ℓ through point B parallel to $\overline{AC}$.	1. Parallel Postulate
2. $m\angle 1 = m\angle$ ____ and $m\angle 3 = m\angle$ ____	2. ____
3. $m\angle 4 + m\angle 2 + m\angle 5 = 180°$	3. Angle Addition Postulate and definition of straight angle
4. $m\angle$ ____ $+ m\angle 2 + m\angle$ ____ $= 180°$	4. ____

Reflect

1. Explain how the Parallel Postulate allows you to add the auxiliary line into the triangle figure.
2. What does the Triangle Sum Theorem indicate about the angles of a triangle that has three angles of equal measure? How do you know?

Explore 2 Exploring Interior Angles in Polygons

To determine the sum of the interior angles for any polygon, you can use what you know about the Triangle Sum Theorem by considering how many triangles there are in other polygons. For example, by drawing the diagonal from a vertex of a quadrilateral, you can form two triangles. Since each triangle has an angle sum of 180°, the quadrilateral must have an angle sum of 180° + 180° = 360°.

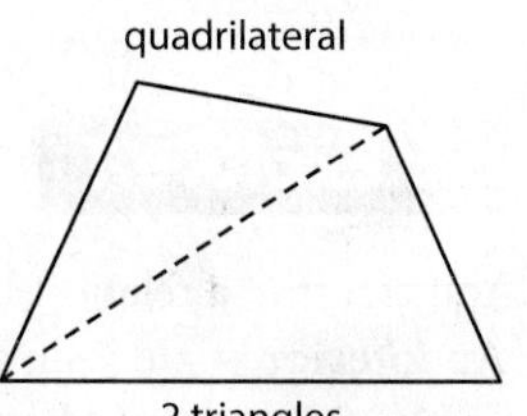

(A) Sketch each polygon. Draw the diagonals from any one vertex for each. Then state the number of triangles that are formed. The first two have already been completed.

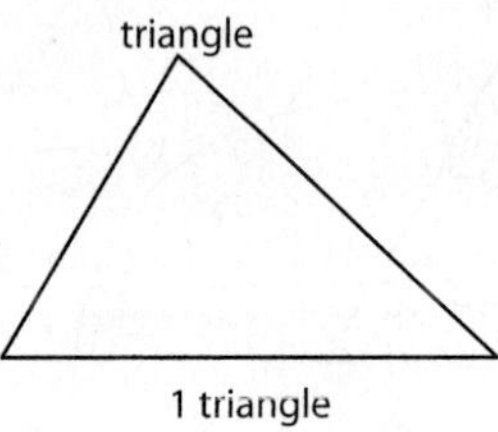

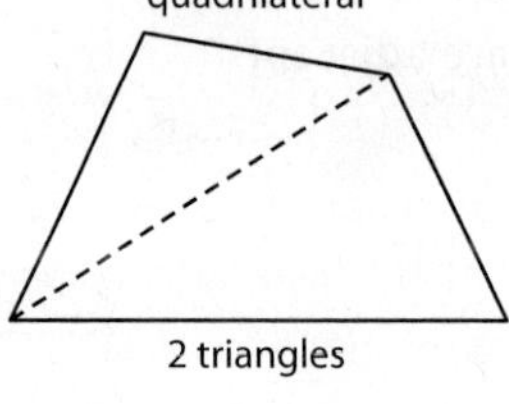

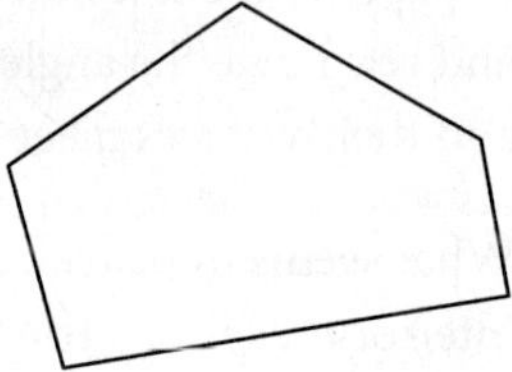

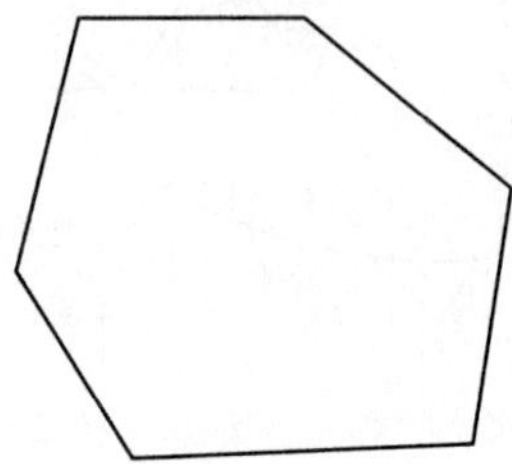

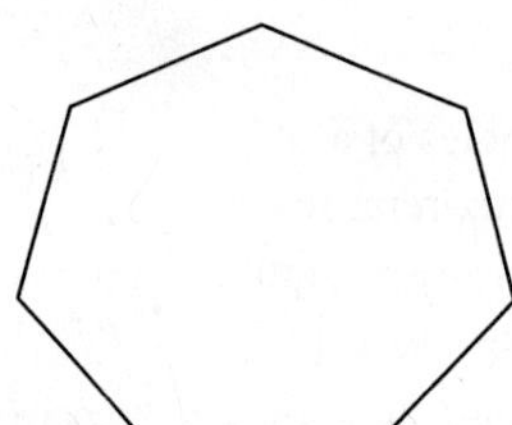

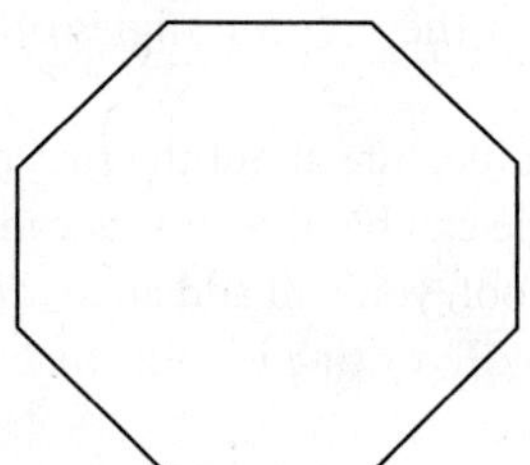

(B) For each polygon, identify the number of sides and triangles, and determine the angle sums. Then complete the chart. The first two have already been done for you.

Polygon	Number of Sides	Number of Triangles	Sum of Interior Angle Measures
Triangle	3	1	(1)180° = 180°
Quadrilateral	4	2	(2)180° = 360°
Pentagon			( ) 180° =
Hexagon			( ) 180° =
Decagon			( ) 180° =

Ⓒ Do you notice a pattern between the number of sides and the number of triangles? If n represents the number of sides for any polygon, how can you represent the number of triangles?

Ⓓ Make a conjecture for a rule that would give the sum of the interior angles for any n-gon.

Sum of interior angle measures = ______

Reflect

3. In a regular hexagon, how could you use the sum of the interior angles to determine the measure of each interior angle?

4. How might you determine the number of sides for a polygon whose interior angle sum is 3240°?

Explain 1 Using Interior Angles

You can use the angle sum to determine the unknown measure of an angle of a polygon when you know the measures of the other angles.

Polygon Angle Sum Theorem

The sum of the measures of the interior angles of a convex polygon with n sides is $(n - 2)180°$.

Example 1 **Determine the unknown angle measures.**

Ⓐ For the nonagon shown, find the unknown angle measure $x°$.

First, use the Polygon Angle Sum Theorem to find the sum of the interior angles:

$n = 9$

$(n - 2)180° = (9 - 2)180° = (7)180° = 1260°$

Then solve for the unknown angle measure, $x°$:

$125 + 130 + 172 + 98 + 200 + 102 + 140 + 135 + x = 1260$

$x = 158$

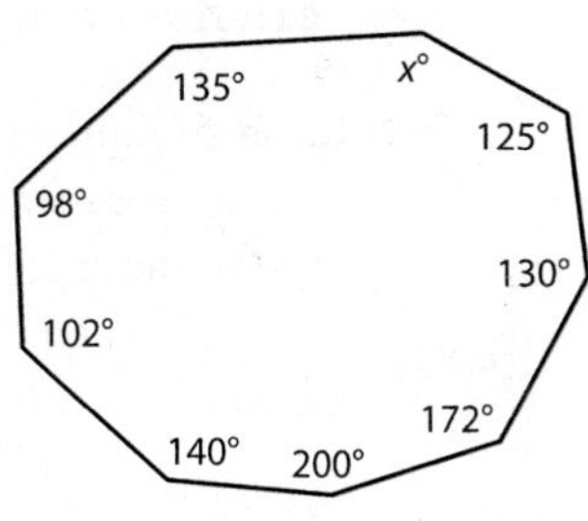

The unknown angle measure is 158°.

Ⓑ Determine the unknown interior angle measure of a convex octagon in which the measures of the seven other angles have a sum of 940°.

$n = 8$

$\text{Sum} = (8 - 2)180° = (6)180° = 1080°$

$940 + x = 1080$

$x = 140$

The unknown angle measure is 140°.

Reflect

5. How might you use the Polygon Angle Sum Theorem to write a rule for determining the measure of each interior angle of any regular convex polygon with n sides?

Your Turn

6. Determine the unknown angle measures in this pentagon.

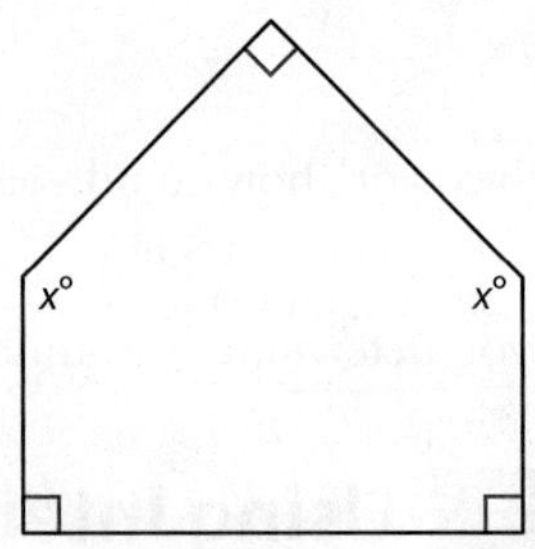

7. Determine the measure of the fourth interior angle of a quadrilateral if you know the other three measures are 89°, 80°, and 104°.

8. Determine the unknown angle measures in a hexagon whose six angles measure 69°, 108°, 135°, 204°, b°, and $2b$°.

Explain 2 Proving the Exterior Angle Theorem

An **exterior angle** is an angle formed by one side of a polygon and the extension of an adjacent side. Exterior angles form linear pairs with the interior angles.

A **remote interior angle** is an interior angle that is not adjacent to the exterior angle.

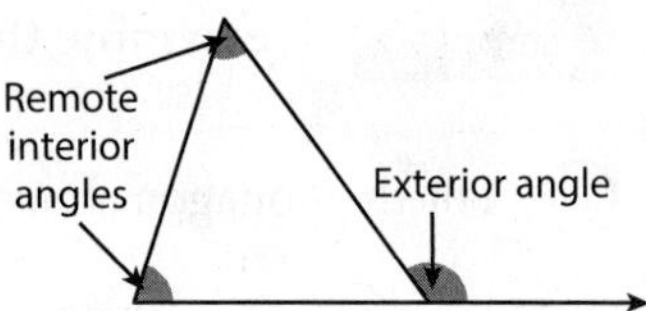

Example 2 **Follow the steps to investigate the relationship between each exterior angle of a triangle and its remote interior angles.**

Step 1 Use a straightedge to draw a triangle with angles 1, 2, and 3. Line up your straightedge along the side opposite angle 2. Extend the side from the vertex at angle 3. You have just constructed an exterior angle. The exterior angle is drawn *supplementary* to its adjacent interior angle.

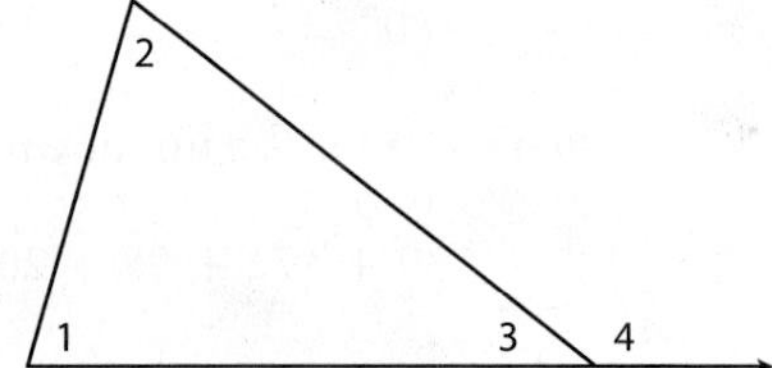

Step 2 You know the sum of the measures of the interior angles of a triangle.

$m\angle 1 + m\angle 2 + m\angle 3 =$ 180 °

Since an exterior angle is supplementary to its adjacent interior angle, you also know:

$m\angle 3 + m\angle 4 =$ 180 °

So, $m\angle 1 + m\angle 2 + m\angle 3 = m\angle 3 + m\angle 4$

$m\angle 1 + m\angle 2 = m\angle 4$

Make a conjecture: What can you say about the measure of the exterior angle and the measures of its remote interior angles?

Conjecture: The measure of the exterior angle is the same as the sum of the measures of its two remote interior angles.

The conjecture you made in Step 2 can be formally stated as a theorem.

Exterior Angle Theorem

The measure of an exterior angle of a triangle is equal to the sum of the measures of its remote interior angles.

Step 3 Complete the proof of the Exterior Angle Theorem.

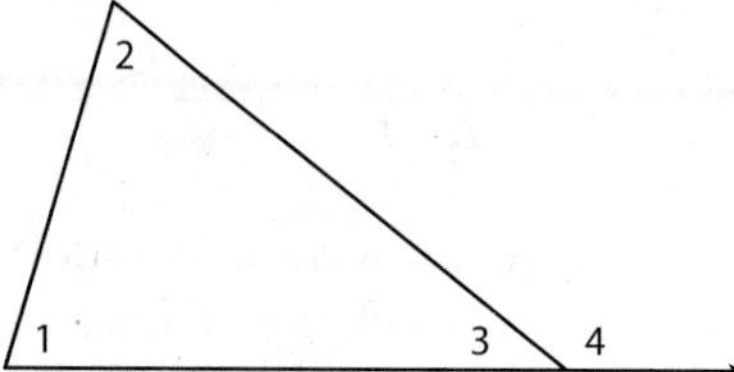

$\angle 4$ is an exterior angle. It forms a linear pair with interior angle $\angle 3$. Its remote interior angles are $\angle 1$ and $\angle 2$.

By the Triangle Sum Theorem, $m\angle 1 + m\angle 2 + m\angle 3 = 180°$.

Also, $m\angle 3 + m\angle 4 = 180°$ because they are supplementary and make a straight angle.

By the Substitution Property of Equality, then, $m\angle 1 + m\angle 2 + m\angle 3 = m\angle 3 + m\angle 4$.

Subtracting $m\angle 3$ from each side of this equation leaves $m\angle 1 + m\angle 2 = m\angle 4$.

This means that the measure of an exterior angle of a triangle is equal to the sum of the measures of the remote interior angles.

Reflect

9. **Discussion** Determine the measure of each exterior angle. Add them together. What can you say about their sum? Explain.

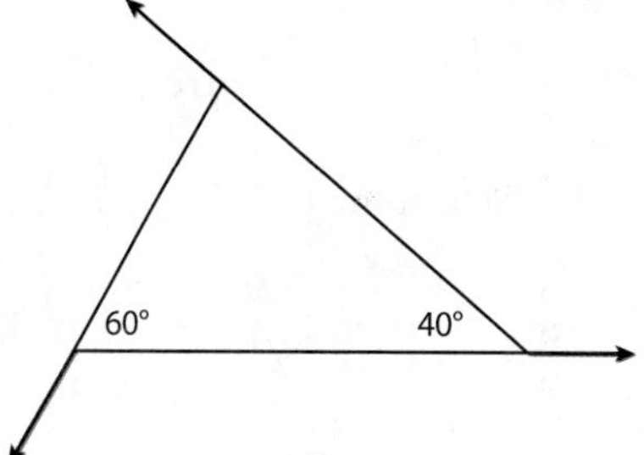

10. According to the definition of an exterior angle, one of the sides of the triangle must be extended in order to see it. How many ways can this be done for any vertex? How many exterior angles is it possible to draw for a triangle? for a hexagon?

Explain 3 Using Exterior Angles

You can apply the Exterior Angle Theorem to solve problems with unknown angle measures by writing and solving equations.

 Determine the measure of the specified angle.

(A) Find $m\angle B$.

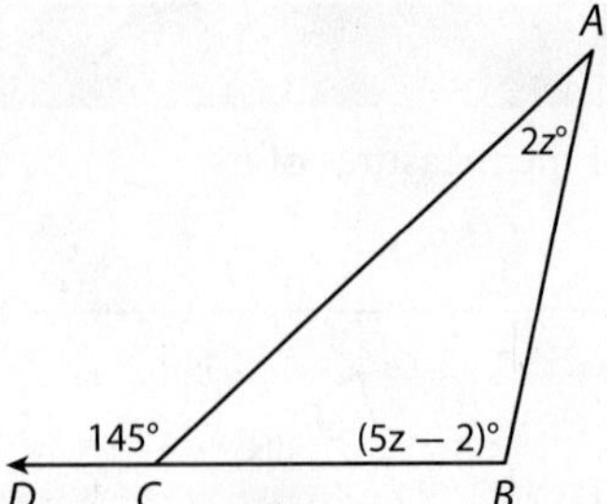

Write and solve an equation relating the exterior and remote interior angles.

$145 = 2z + 5z - 2$

$145 = 7z - 2$

$z = 21$

Now use this value for the unknown to evaluate the expression for the required angle.

$m\angle B = (5z - 2)° = (5(21) - 2)°$

$= (105 - 2)°$

$= 103°$

 Find $m\angle PRS$.

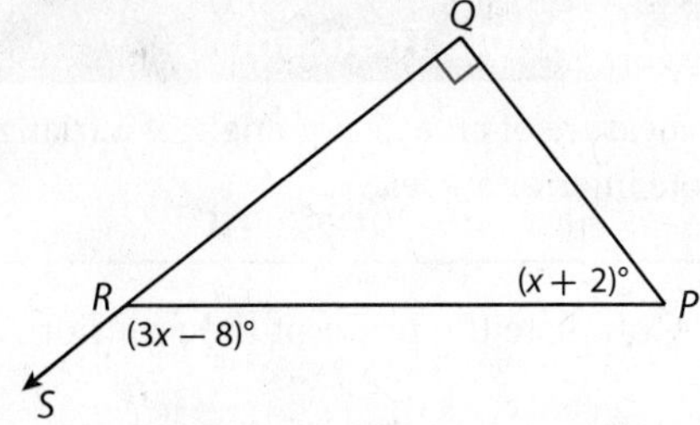

Write an equation relating the exterior and remote interior angles.

$3x - 8 = (x + 2) + 90$

Solve for the unknown. $3x - 8 = x + 92$

$2x = 100$

$x = 50$

Use the value for the unknown to evaluate the expression for the required angle.

$m\angle PRS = (3x - 8)° = (3(50) - 8)° = 142°$

Your Turn

Determine the measure of the specified angle.

11. Determine $m\angle N$ in $\triangle MNP$.

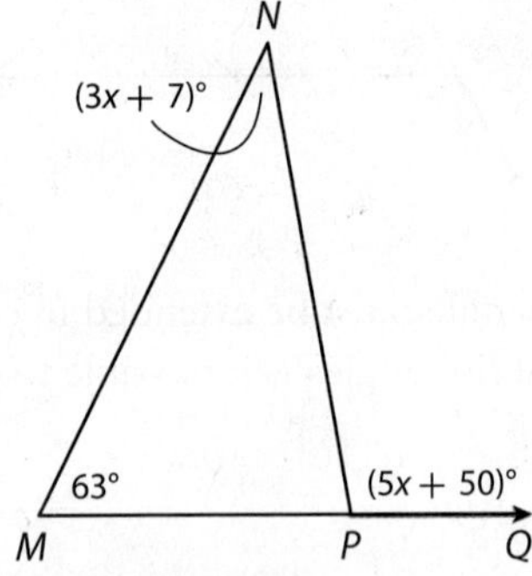

12. If the exterior angle drawn measures 150°, and the measure of $\angle D$ is twice that of $\angle E$, find the measure of the two remote interior angles.

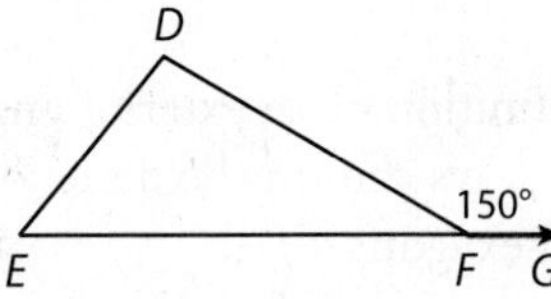

Elaborate

13. In your own words, state the Polygon Angle Sum Theorem. How does it help you find unknown angle measures in polygons?

14. When will an exterior angle be acute? Can a triangle have more than one acute exterior angle? Describe the triangle that tests this.

15. **Essential Question Check-In** Summarize the rules you have discovered about the interior and exterior angles of triangles and polygons.

Evaluate: Homework and Practice

- Online Homework
- Hints and Help
- Extra Practice

1. Consider the Triangle Sum Theorem in relation to a right triangle. What conjecture can you make about the two acute angles of a right triangle? Explain your reasoning.

2. Copy and complete a flow proof for the Triangle Sum Theorem.

   Given $\triangle ABC$

   Prove $m\angle 1 + m\angle 2 + m\angle 3 = 180°$

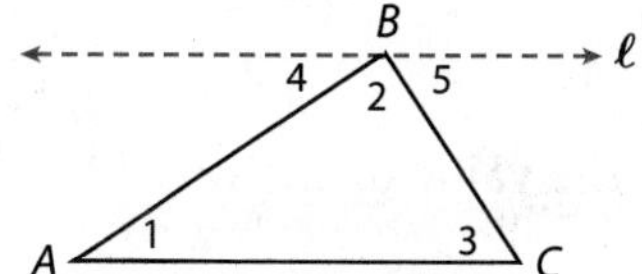

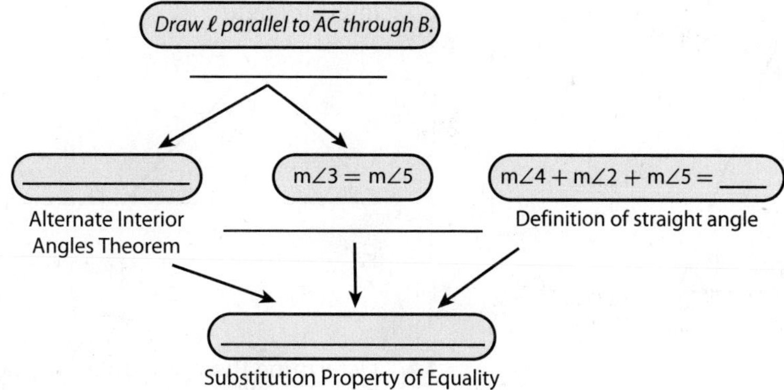

3. Given a polygon with 13 sides, find the sum of the measures of its interior angles.

4. A polygon has an interior angle sum of 3060°. How many sides must the polygon have?

5. Two of the angles in a triangle measure 50° and 27°. Find the measure of the third angle.

Solve for the unknown angle measures of the polygon.

6. A pentagon has angle measures of 100°, 105°, 110° and 115°. Find the fifth angle measure.

7. The measures of 13 angles of a 14-gon add up to 2014°. Find the fourteenth angle measure?

8. Determine the unknown angle measures for the quadrilateral in the diagram.

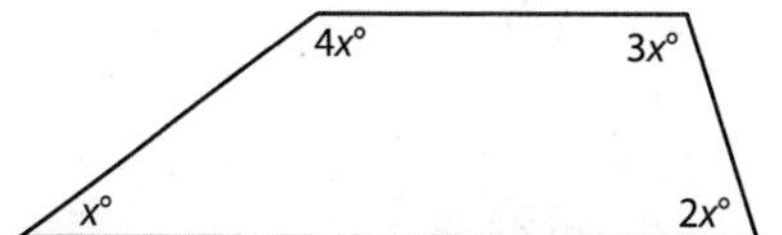

9. The cross-section of a beehive reveals it is made of regular hexagons. What is the measure of each angle in the regular hexagon?

10. Create a flow proof for the Exterior Angle Theorem.

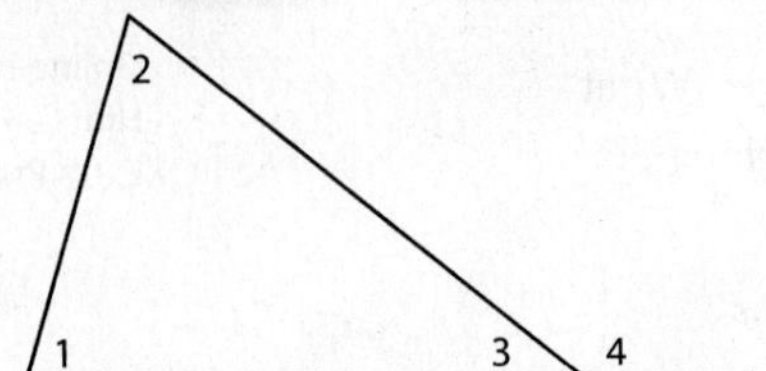

Find the value of the variable to find the unknown angle measure(s).

11. Find w to find the measure of the exterior angle.

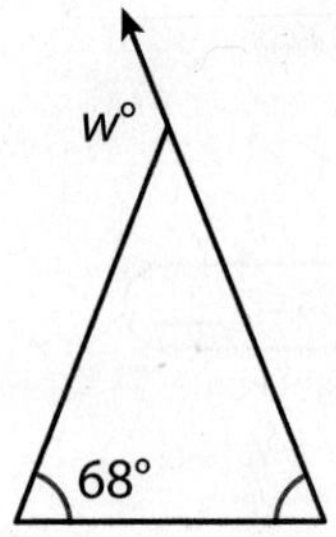

12. Find x to find the measure of the remote interior angle.

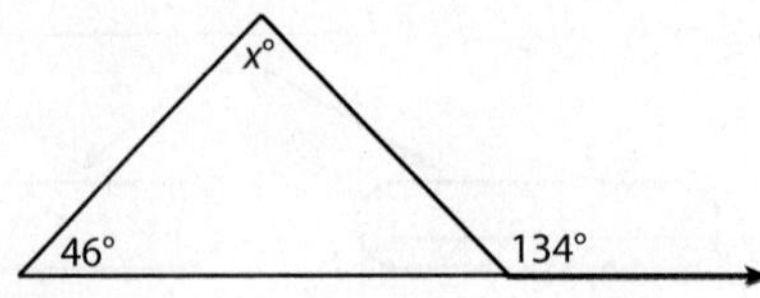

13. Find $m\angle H$.

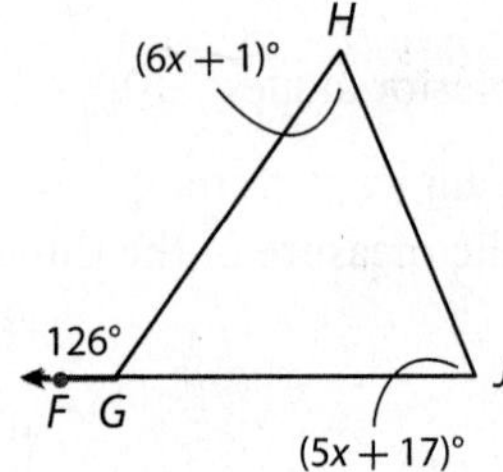

14. Determine the measure of the indicated exterior angle in the diagram.

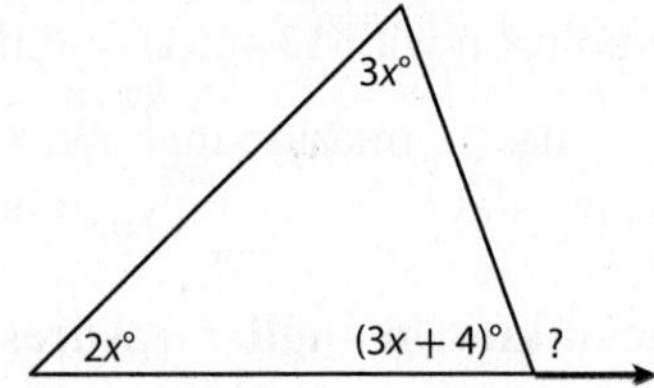

15. Match each angle with its corresponding measure, given $m\angle 1 = 130°$ and $m\angle 7 = 70°$.

A. $m\angle 2$ **a.** ___?___ 50°

B. $m\angle 3$ **b.** ___?___ 60°

C. $m\angle 4$ **c.** ___?___ 70°

D. $m\angle 5$ **d.** ___?___ 110°

E. $m\angle 6$ **e.** ___?___ 120°

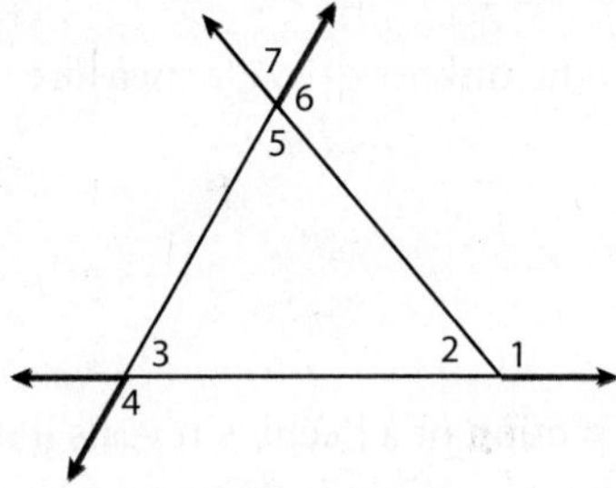

16. The map of France commonly used in the 1600s was significantly revised as a result of a triangulation survey. The diagram shows part of the survey map. Use the diagram to find the measure of $\angle KMJ$.

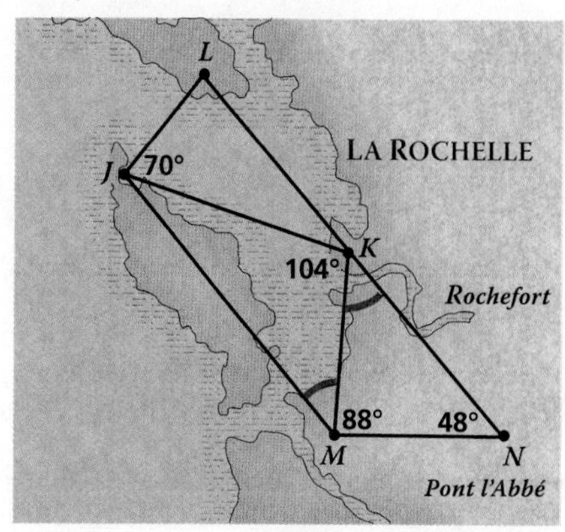

17. An artistic quilt is being designed using computer software. The designer wants to use regular octagons in her design. What interior angle measures should she set in the computer software to create a regular octagon?

18. A ladder propped up against a house makes a 20° angle with the wall. What would be the ladder's angle measure with the ground facing away from the house?

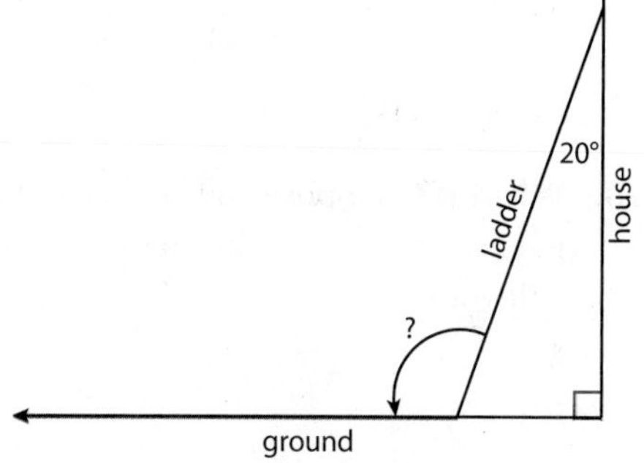

19. Photography The aperture of a camera is made by overlapping blades that form a regular decagon.

a. What is the sum of the measures of the interior angles of the decagon?

b. What would be the measure of each interior angle? each exterior angle?

c. Find the sum of all ten exterior angles.

20. Determine the measure of $\angle UXW$ in the diagram.

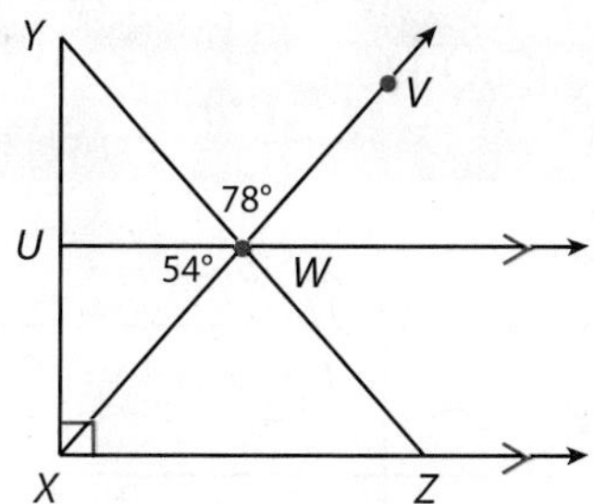

21. Determine the measures of angles x, y, and z.

80°
100°
55°
$x°$
$z°$
$y°$
60°

22. Given the diagram in which $\overrightarrow{BD}$ bisects $\angle ABC$ and $\overrightarrow{CD}$ bisects $\angle ACB$, what is $m\angle BDC$?

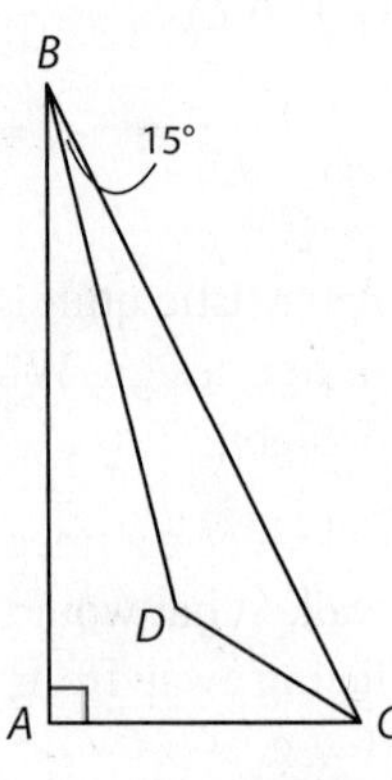

23. What If? Suppose you continue the congruent angle construction shown here. What polygon will you construct? Explain.

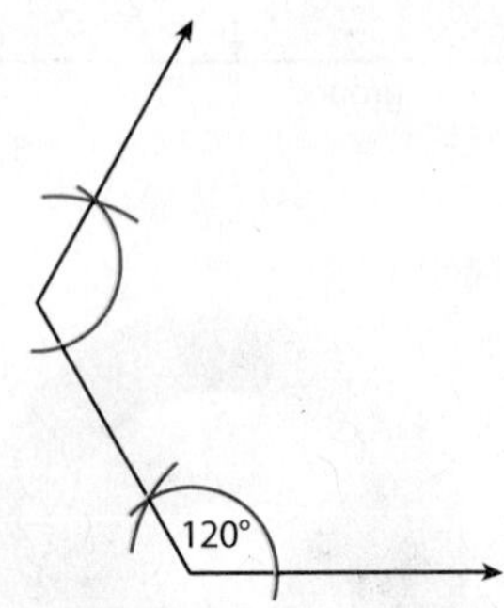

24. Algebra Draw a triangle ABC and label the measures of its angles $a°$, $b°$, and $c°$. Draw ray BD that bisects the exterior angle at vertex B. Write an expression for the measure of angle CBD.

25. Look for a Pattern Find patterns within this table of data and extend the patterns to complete the remainder of the table. What conjecture can you make about polygon exterior angles from Column 5?

Column 1 Number of Sides	Column 2 Sum of the Measures of the Interior Angles	Column 3 Average Measure of an Interior Angle	Column 4 Average Measure of an Exterior Angle	Column 5 Sum of the Measures of the Exterior Angles
3	180°	60°	120°	120°(3) =
4	360°	90°	90°	90°(4) =
5	540°	108°		
6		120°		

26. Explain the Error Find and explain what this student did incorrectly when solving the following problem.

What type of polygon would have an interior angle sum of 1260°?

$$1260 = (n - 2)180$$
$$7 = n - 2$$
$$5 = n$$

The polygon is a pentagon.

H.O.T. Focus on Higher Order Thinking

27. Communicate Mathematical Ideas Explain why if two angles of one triangle are congruent to two angles of another triangle, then the third pair of angles are also congruent.

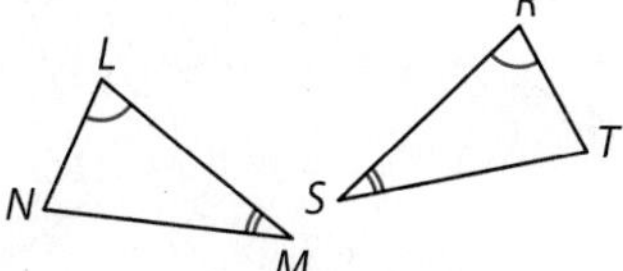

Given: $\angle L \cong \angle R$, $\angle M \cong \angle S$

Prove: $\angle N \cong \angle T$

28. Analyze Relationships Consider a right triangle. How would you describe the measures of its exterior angles? Explain.

29. Look for a Pattern In investigating different polygons, diagonals were drawn from a vertex to break the polygon into triangles. Recall that the number of triangles is always two less than the number of sides. But diagonals can be drawn from all vertices. Make a table where you compare the number of sides of a polygon with how many diagonals can be drawn (from all the vertices). Can you find a pattern in this table?

Lesson Performance Task

You've been asked to design the board for a new game called Pentagons. The board consists of a repeating pattern of regular pentagons, a portion of which is shown in the illustration. When you write the specifications for the company that will make the board, you include the measurements of $\angle BAD$, $\angle ABC$, $\angle BCD$ and $\angle ADC$. Find the measures of those angles and explain how you found them.

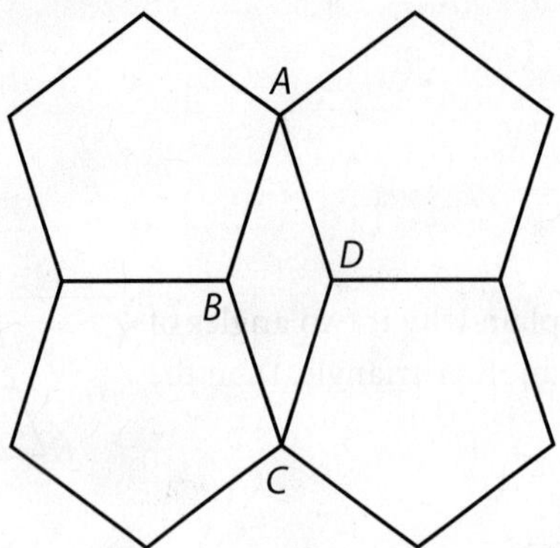

15.2 Isosceles and Equilateral Triangles

Resource Locker

Essential Question: **What are the special relationships among angles and sides in isosceles and equilateral triangles?**

Explore Investigating Isosceles Triangles

An **isosceles triangle** is a triangle with at least two congruent sides.

The congruent sides are called the **legs** of the triangle.

The angle formed by the legs is the **vertex angle**.

The side opposite the vertex angle is the **base**.

The angles that have the base as a side are the **base angles**.

Vertex angle
Legs
Base
Base angles

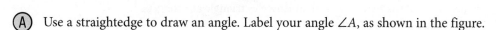

In this activity, you will construct isosceles triangles and investigate other potential characteristics/properties of these special triangles.

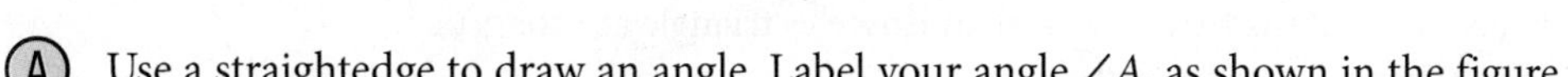

(A) Use a straightedge to draw an angle. Label your angle $\angle A$, as shown in the figure.

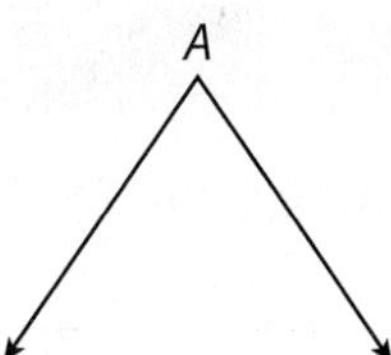

(B) Using a compass, place the point on the vertex and draw an arc that intersects the sides of the angle. Label the points B and C.

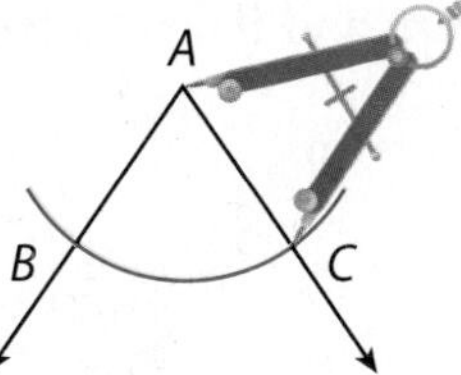

(C) Use the straightedge to draw line segment $\overline{BC}$.

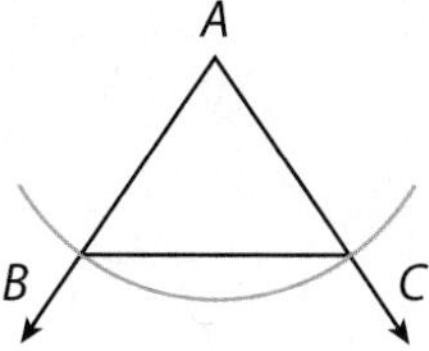

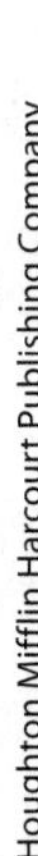

Ⓓ Use a protractor to measure each angle. Copy the table and record the angle measures under the column for Triangle 1.

	Triangle 1	Triangle 2	Triangle 3	Triangle 4
m∠A				
m∠B				
m∠C				

Ⓔ Repeat steps A–D at least two more times and record the results in the table. Make sure ∠A is a different size each time.

Reflect

1. How do you know the triangles you constructed are isosceles triangles?

2. **Make a Conjecture** Looking at your results, what conjecture can be made about the base angles, ∠B and ∠C?

Explain 1 Proving the Isosceles Triangle Theorem and Its Converse

In the Explore, you made a conjecture that the base angles of an isosceles triangle are congruent. This conjecture can be proven so it can be stated as a theorem.

Isosceles Triangle Theorem

If two sides of a triangle are congruent, then the two angles opposite the sides are congruent.

This theorem is sometimes called the Base Angles Theorem and can also be stated as "Base angles of an isosceles triangle are congruent."

Example 1 **Prove the Isosceles Triangle Theorem and its converse.**

Step 1 Complete the proof of the Isosceles Triangle Theorem.

Given: $\overline{AB} \cong \overline{AC}$

Prove: $\angle B \cong \angle C$

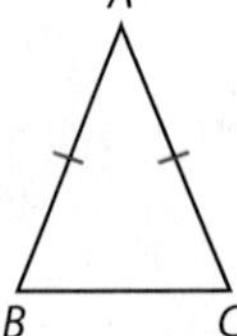

Statements	Reasons
1. $\overline{BA} \cong \overline{CA}$	1. Given
2. $\angle A \cong \angle A$	2. Reflexive Property of Congruence
3. $\overline{CA} \cong \overline{BA}$	3. Symmetric Property of Equality
4. $\triangle BAC \cong \triangle CAB$	4. SAS Triangle Congruence Theorem
5. $\angle B \cong \angle C$	5. CPCTC

Step 2 Complete the statement of the Converse of the Isosceles Triangle Theorem.
If two angles of a triangle are congruent, then the two sides opposite those angles are congruent.

Step 3 Complete the proof of the Converse of the Isosceles Triangle Theorem.

Given: $\angle B \cong \angle C$

Prove: $\overline{AB} \cong \overline{AC}$

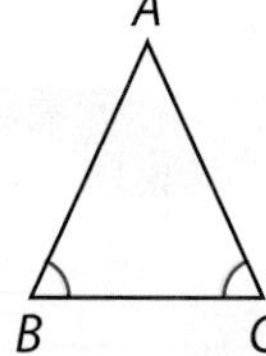

Statements	Reasons
1. $\angle ABC \cong \angle ACB$	1. Given
2. $\overline{BC} \cong \overline{CB}$	2. Reflexive Property of Congruence
3. $\angle ACB \cong \angle ABC$	3. Symmetric Property of Equality
4. $\triangle ABC \cong \triangle ACB$	4. ASA Triangle Congruence Theorem
5. $\overline{AB} \cong \overline{AC}$	5. CPCTC

Reflect

3. **Discussion** In the proofs of the Isosceles Triangle Theorem and its converse, how might it help to sketch a reflection of the given triangle next to the original triangle, so that vertex B is on the right?

Explain 2 Proving the Equilateral Triangle Theorem and Its Converse

An **equilateral triangle** is a triangle with three congruent sides.

An **equiangular triangle** is a triangle with three congruent angles.

Equilateral Triangle Theorem
If a triangle is equilateral, then it is equiangular.

Example 2 **Prove the Equilateral Triangle Theorem and its converse.**

Step 1 Complete the proof of the Equilateral Triangle Theorem.

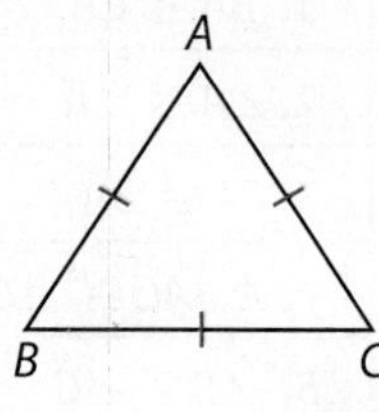

Given: $\overline{AB} \cong \overline{AC} \cong \overline{BC}$
Prove: $\angle A \cong \angle B \cong \angle C$

Given that $\overline{AB} \cong \overline{AC}$ we know that $\angle B \cong \angle C$ by the Isosceles Triangle Theorem.

It is also known that $\angle A \cong \angle B$ by the Isosceles Triangle Theorem, since $\overline{AC} \cong \overline{BC}$

Therefore, $\angle A \cong \angle C$ by substitution.

Finally, $\angle A \cong \angle B \cong \angle C$ by the Transitive Property of Congruence.

The converse of the Equilateral Triangle Theorem is also true.

Converse of the Equilateral Triangle Theorem

If a triangle is equiangular, then it is equilateral.

Step 2 Complete the proof of the Converse of the Equilateral Triangle Theorem.

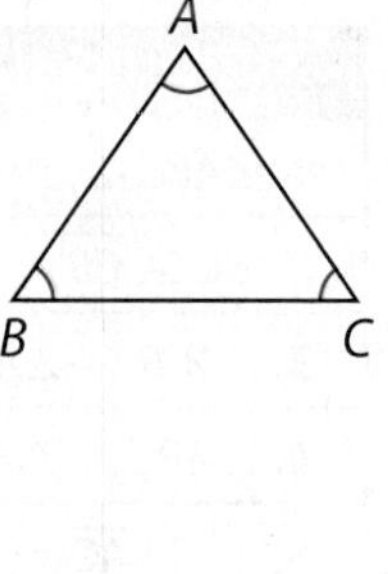

Given: $\angle A \cong \angle B \cong \angle C$

Prove: $\overline{AB} \cong \overline{AC} \cong \overline{BC}$

Because $\angle B \cong \angle C$, $\overline{AB} \cong$ $\overline{AC}$ by the Converse of the Isosceles Triangle Theorem.

$\overline{AC} \cong \overline{BC}$ by the Converse of the Isosceles Triangle Theorem because

$\angle A$ $\cong \angle B$.

Thus, by the Transitive Property of Congruence, $\overline{AB} \cong \overline{BC}$, and therefore, $\overline{AB} \cong \overline{AC} \cong \overline{BC}$.

Reflect

4. To prove the Equilateral Triangle Theorem, you applied the theorems of isosceles triangles. What can be concluded about the relationship between equilateral triangles and isosceles triangles?

Explain 3 Using Properties of Isosceles and Equilateral Triangles

You can use the properties of isosceles and equilateral triangles to solve problems involving these theorems.

Example 3 **Find the indicated measure.**

(A) Katie is stitching the center inlay onto a banner that she created to represent her new tutorial service. It is an equilateral triangle with the following dimensions in centimeters. What is the length of each side of the triangle?

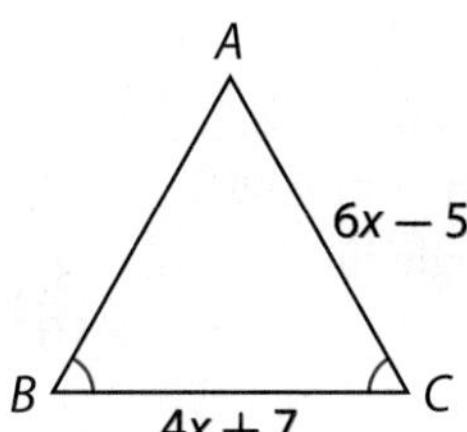

To find the length of each side of the triangle, first find the value of x.

$\overline{AC} \cong \overline{BC}$	Converse of the Equilateral Triangle Theorem
$AC = BC$	Definition of congruence
$6x - 5 = 4x + 7$	Substitution Property of Equality
$x = 6$	Solve for x.

Substitute 6 for x into either $6x - 5$ or $4x + 7$.

$6(6) - 5 = 36 - 5 = 31$ or $4(6) + 7 = 24 + 7 = 31$

So, the length of each side of the triangle is 31 cm.

 $m\angle T$

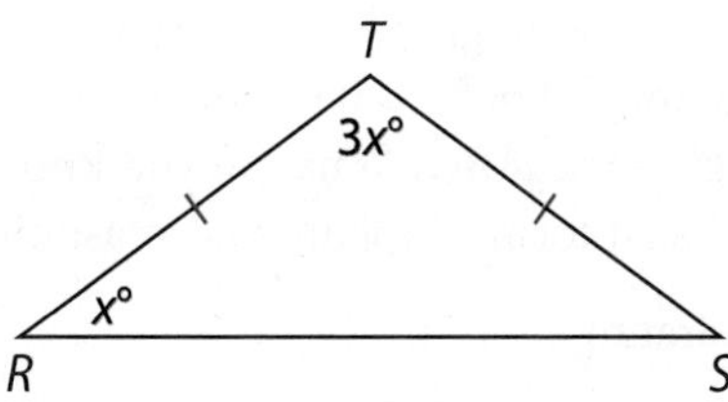

To find the measure of the vertex angle of the triangle, first find the value of x.

$m\angle R = m\angle S = x°$	Isosceles Triangle Theorem
$m\angle R + m\angle S + m\angle T = 180°$	Triangle Sum Theorem
$x + x + 3x = 180$	Substitution Property of Equality
$5x = 180$	Addition Property of Equality
$x = 36$	Division Property of Equality

So, $m\angle T = 3x° = 3(36)° = 108°$.

Your Turn

5. Find m$\angle P$.

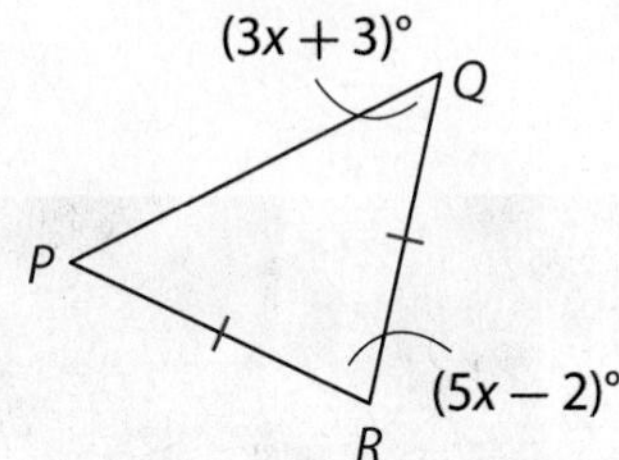

6. Katie's tutorial service is going so well that she is having shirts made with the equilateral triangle emblem. She has given the t-shirt company these dimensions. What is the length of each side of the triangle in centimeters?

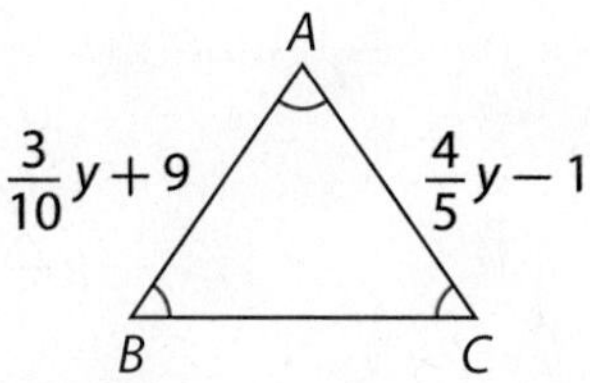

Elaborate

7. **Discussion** Consider the vertex and base angles of an isosceles triangle. Can they be right angles? Can they be obtuse? Explain.

8. **Essential Question Check-In** Discuss how the sides of an isosceles triangle relate to its angles.

Evaluate: Homework and Practice

- Online Homework
- Hints and Help
- Extra Practice

1. Use a straightedge. Draw a line. Draw an acute angle with vertex A along the line. Then use a compass to copy the angle. Place the compass point at another point B along the line and draw the copied angle so that the angle faces the original angle. Label the intersection of the angle sides as point C. Look at the triangle you have formed. What is true about the two base angles of $\triangle ABC$? What do you know about $\overline{CA}$ and $\overline{CB}$? What kind of triangle did you form? Explain your reasoning.

2. Prove the Isosceles Triangle Theorem as a paragraph proof.

Given: $\overline{AB} \cong \overline{AC}$

Prove: $\angle B \cong \angle C$

3. Copy and complete the flow proof of the Equilateral Triangle Theorem.

Given: $\overline{AB} \cong \overline{AC} \cong \overline{BC}$

Prove: $\angle A \cong \angle B \cong \angle C$

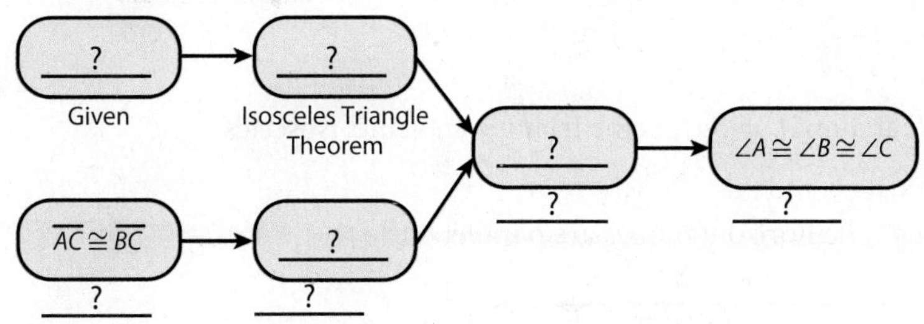

Find the measure of the indicated angle.

4. $m\angle A$

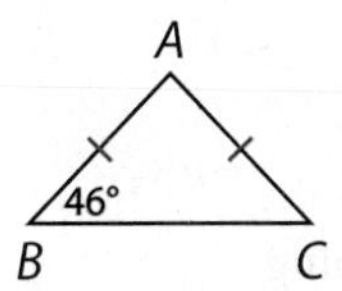

5. $m\angle R$

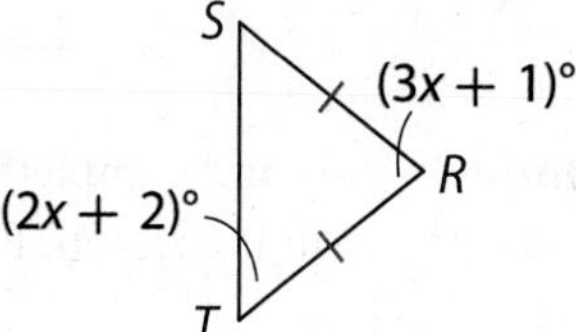

6. $m\angle O$

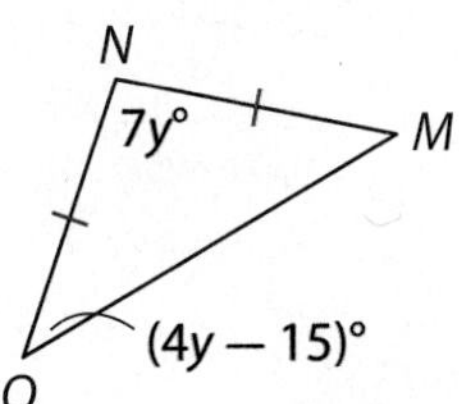

7. $m\angle E$

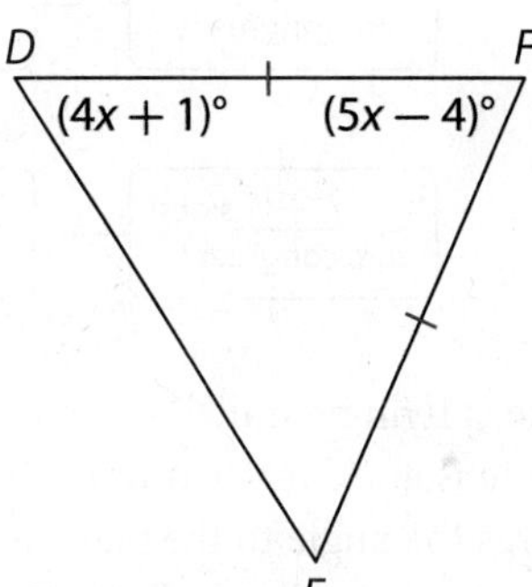

Find the length of the indicated side.

8. $\overline{DE}$

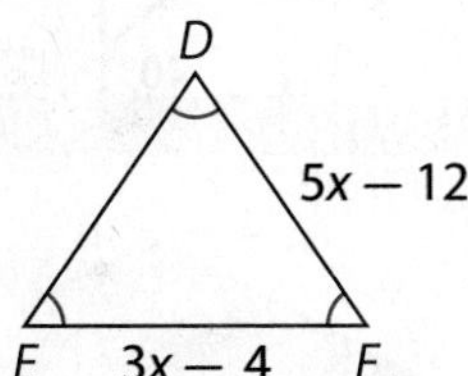

9. $\overline{KL}$

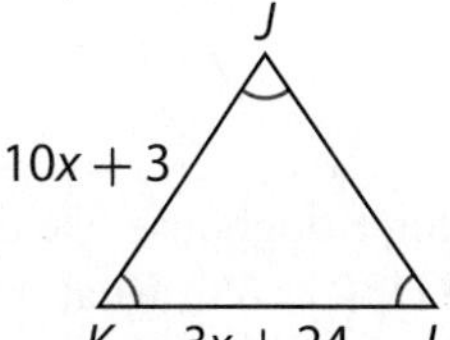

10. $\overline{AB}$

11. $\overline{BC}$

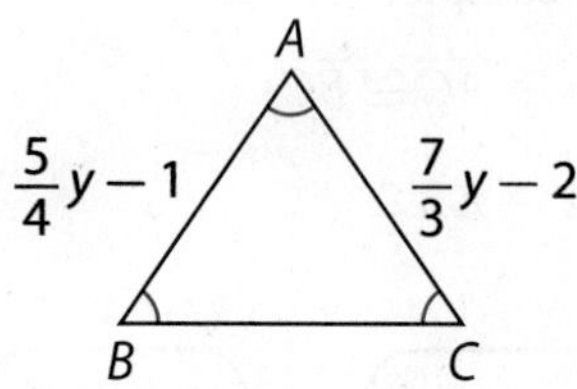

12. Given $\triangle JKL$ with $m\angle J = 63°$ and $m\angle L = 54°$, is the triangle an acute, isosceles, obtuse, or right triangle?

13. Find x. Explain your reasoning. The horizontal lines are parallel.

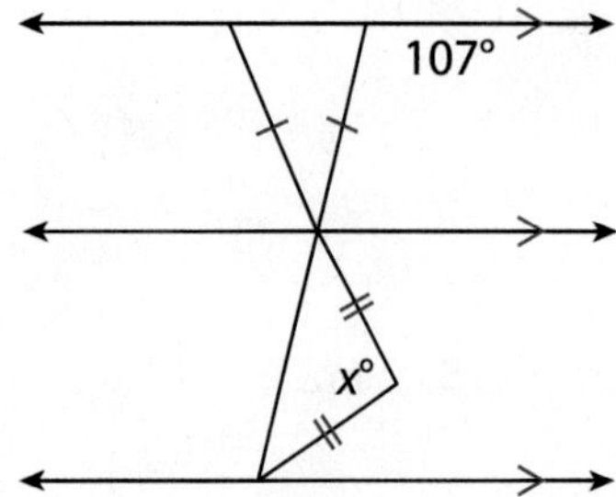

14. Summarize Copy and complete the diagram to show the cause and effect of the theorems covered in the lesson. Explain why the arrows show the direction going both ways.

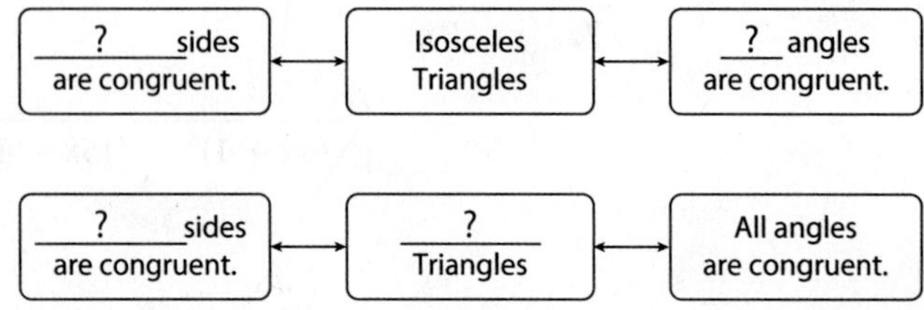

15. A plane is flying parallel to the ground along $\overrightarrow{AC}$. When the plane is at A, an air-traffic controller in tower T measures the angle to the plane as 40°. After the plane has traveled 2.4 miles to B, the angle to the plane is 80°. How can you find BT?

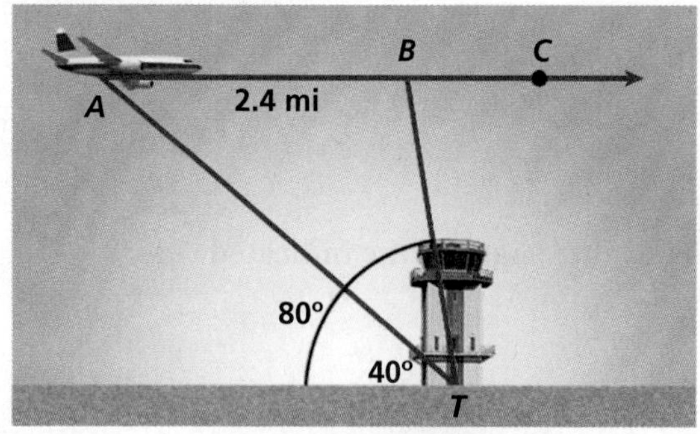

16. John is building a doghouse. He decides to use the roof truss design shown. If $m\angle DBF = 35°$, what is the measure of the vertex angle of the isosceles triangle?

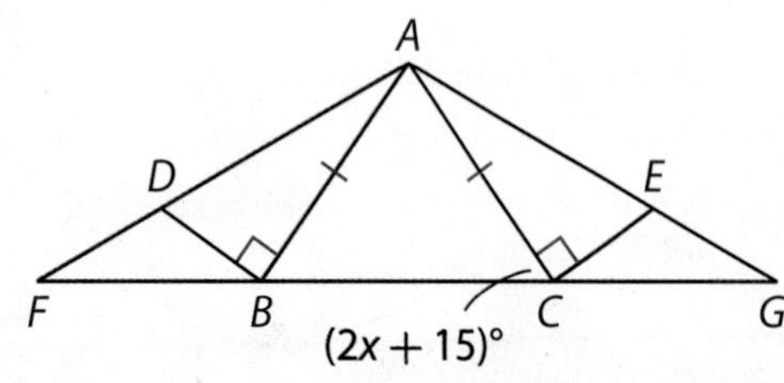

17. The measure of the vertex angle of an isosceles triangle is 12 more than 5 times the measure of a base angle. Determine the sum of the measures of the base angles.

18. Justify Reasoning Determine whether each of the following statements is true or false. Explain your reasoning.

a. All isosceles triangles have at least two acute angles.

b. If the perimeter of an equilateral triangle is P, then the length of each of its sides is $\frac{P}{3}$.

c. All isosceles triangles are equilateral triangles.

d. If you know the length of one of the legs of an isosceles triangle, you can determine its perimeter.

e. The exterior angle of an equilateral triangle is obtuse.

19. Critical Thinking Prove $\angle B \cong \angle C$, given point M is the midpoint of $\overline{BC}$.

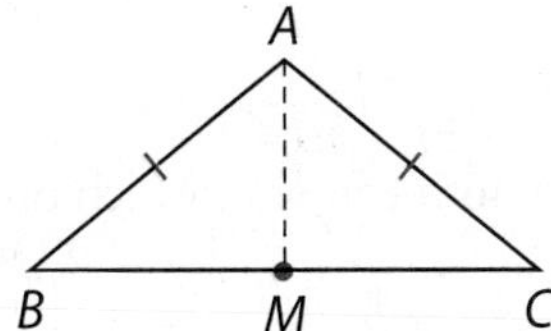

20. Given that $\triangle ABC$ is an isosceles triangle and $\overline{AD}$ and $\overline{CD}$ are angle bisectors, what is $m\angle ADC$?

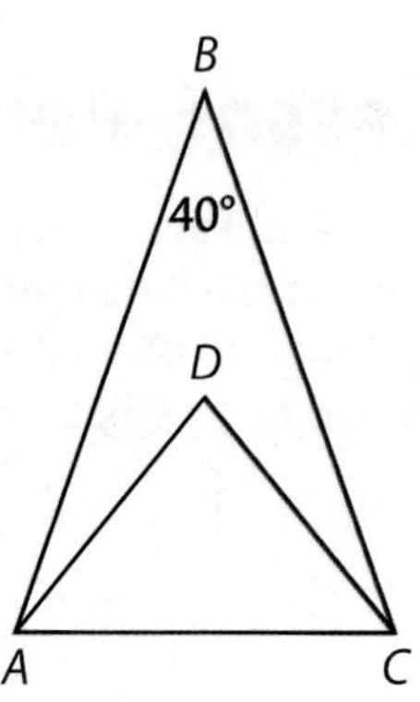

H.O.T. Focus on Higher Order Thinking

21. Analyze Relationships Isosceles right triangle ABC has a right angle at B and $\overline{AB} \cong \overline{CB}$. $\overline{BD}$ bisects angle B, and point D is on $\overline{AC}$. If $\overline{BD} \perp \overline{AC}$, describe triangles ABD and CBD. Explain. HINT: Draw a diagram.

Communicate Mathematical Ideas Follow the method to construct a triangle. Then use what you know about the radius of a circle to explain the congruence of the sides.

22. Construct an isosceles triangle. Explain how you know that two sides are congruent.

- Use a compass to draw a circle. Mark two different points on the circle.
- Use a straightedge to draw a line segment from the center of the circle to each of the two points on the circle (radii).
- Draw a line segment (chord) between the two points on the circle.

I know two sides are congruent because ___?___.

23. Construct an equilateral triangle. Explain how you know the three sides are congruent.

- Use a compass to draw a circle.
- Draw another circle of the same size that goes through the center of the first circle. (Both should have the same radius length.)
- Mark one point where the circles intersect.
- Use a straightedge to draw line segments connecting both centers to each other and to the intersection point.

I know the three sides are congruent because ___?___.

Lesson Performance Task

The control tower at airport *A* is in contact with an airplane flying at point *P*, when it is 5 miles from the airport, and 30 seconds later when it is at point *Q*, 4 miles from the airport. The diagram shows the angles the plane makes with the ground at both times. If the plane flies parallel to the ground from *P* to *Q* at constant speed, how fast is it traveling?

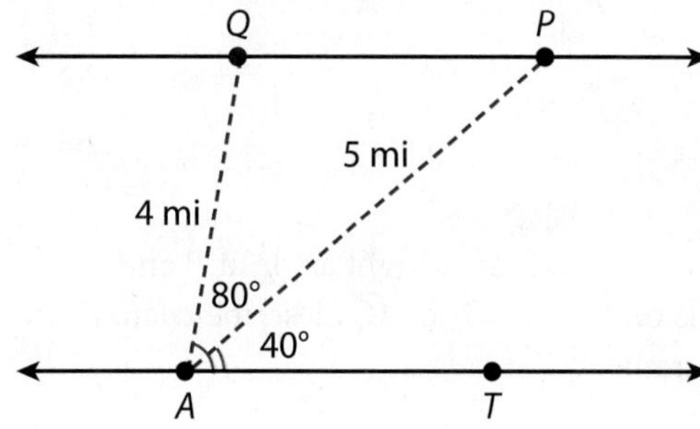

15.3 Triangle Inequalities

Essential Question: How can you use inequalities to describe the relationships among side lengths and angle measures in a triangle?

Explore Exploring Triangle Inequalities

A triangle can have sides of different lengths, but are there limits to the lengths of any of the sides?

Ⓐ Consider a $\triangle ABC$ where you know two side lengths, $AB = 4$ inches and $BC = 2$ inches. On a separate piece of paper, draw $\overline{AB}$ so that it is 4 inches long.

Ⓑ To determine all possible locations for C with $\overline{BC} = 2$ inches, set your compass to 2 inches. Draw a circle with center at B.

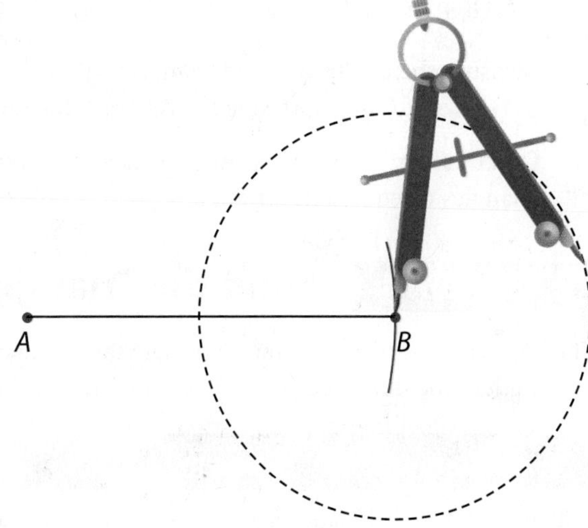

Ⓒ Choose and label a final vertex point C so it is located on the circle. Using a straightedge, draw the segments to form a triangle.

Are there any places on the circle where point C cannot lie? Explain.

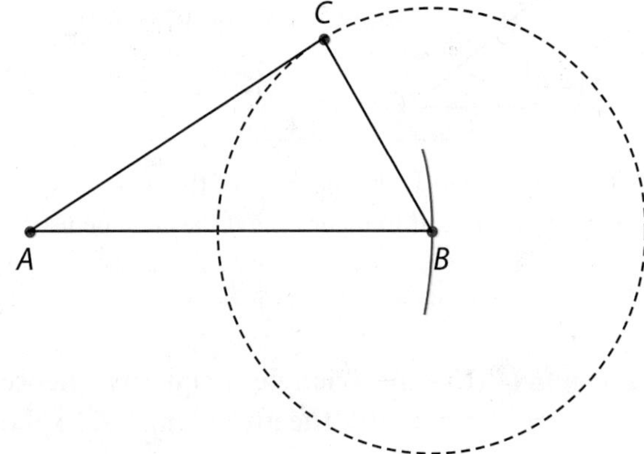

Ⓓ Measure and record the lengths of the three sides of your triangle.

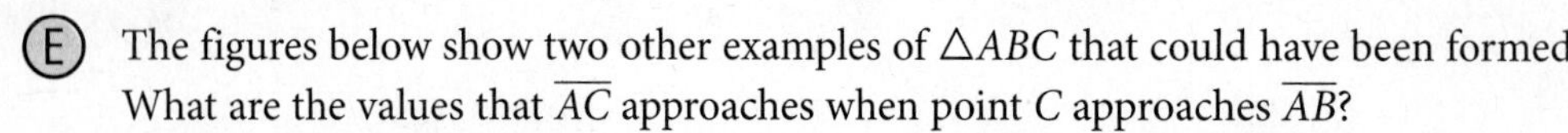

Ⓔ The figures below show two other examples of $\triangle ABC$ that could have been formed. What are the values that $\overline{AC}$ approaches when point C approaches $\overline{AB}$?

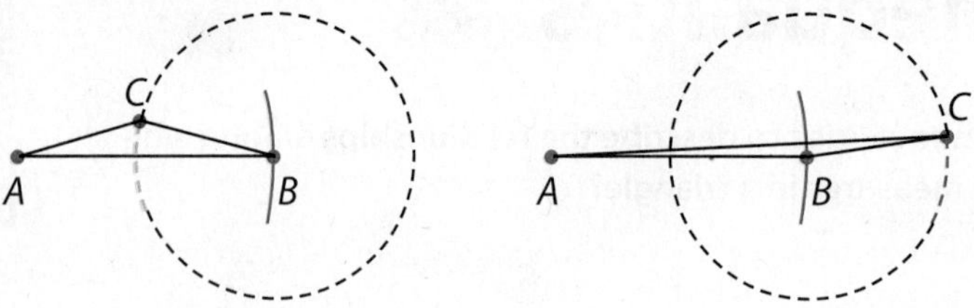

Reflect

1. Use the side lengths from your table to make the following comparisons. What do you notice?

$AB + BC \ ? \ AC \qquad BC + AC \ ? \ AB \qquad AC + AB \ ? \ BC$

2. Measure the angles of some triangles with a protractor. Where is the smallest angle in relation to the shortest side? Where is the largest angle in relation to the longest side?

3. **Discussion** How does your answer to the previous question relate to isosceles triangles or equilateral triangles?

Explain 1 Using the Triangle Inequality Theorem

The Explore shows that the sum of the lengths of any two sides of a triangle is greater than the length of the third side. This can be summarized in the following theorem.

Triangle Inequality Theorem

The sum of any two side lengths of a triangle is greater than the third side length.

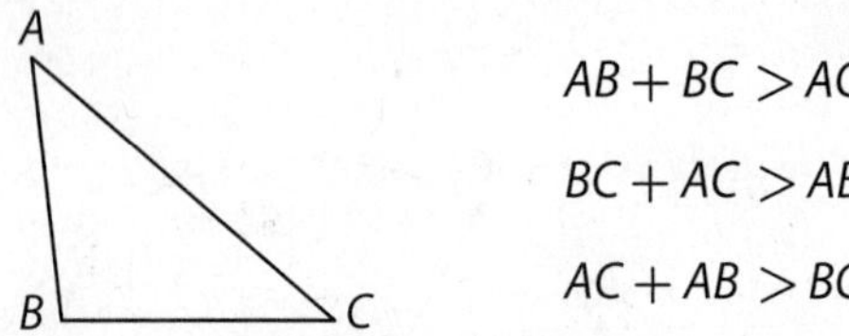

$AB + BC > AC$

$BC + AC > AB$

$AC + AB > BC$

To be able to form a triangle, each of the three inequalities must be true. So, given three side lengths, you can test to determine if they can be used as segments to form a triangle. To show that three lengths cannot be the side lengths of a triangle, you only need to show that one of the three triangle inequalities is false.

Example 1 **Use the Triangle Inequality Theorem to tell whether a triangle can have sides with the given lengths. Explain.**

Ⓐ 4, 8, 10

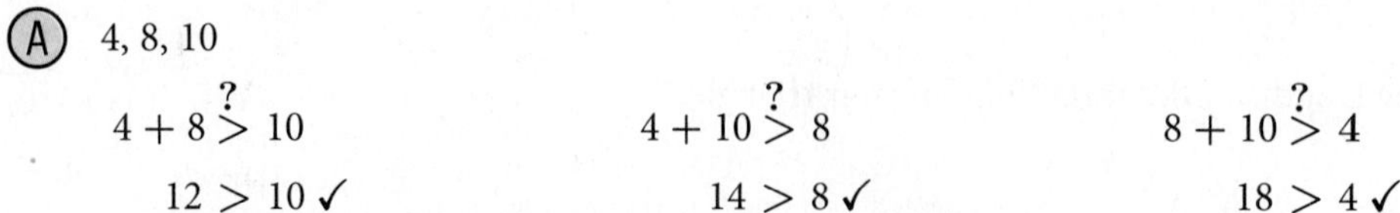

$4 + 8 \stackrel{?}{>} 10 \qquad 4 + 10 \stackrel{?}{>} 8 \qquad 8 + 10 \stackrel{?}{>} 4$

$12 > 10$ ✓ $\qquad 14 > 8$ ✓ $\qquad 18 > 4$ ✓

Conclusion: The sum of each pair of side lengths is greater than the third length. So, a triangle can have side lengths of 4, 8, and 10.

(B) 7, 9, 18

7 + 9 $\overset{?}{>}$ 18	7 + 18 $\overset{?}{>}$ 9	9 + 18 $\overset{?}{>}$ 7
16 > 18 ✗	25 > 9 ✓	27 > 7 ✓

Conclusion:
Not all three inequalities are true. So, a triangle cannot have these three side lengths.

Reflect

4. Can an isosceles triangle have these side lengths? Explain. 5, 5, 10

5. How do you know that the Triangle Inequality Theorem applies to all equilateral triangles?

Your Turn

Determine if a triangle can be formed with the given side lengths. Explain your reasoning.

6. 12 units, 4 units, 17 units

7. 24 cm, 8 cm, 30 cm

Explain 2 Finding Possible Side Lengths in a Triangle

From the Explore, you have seen that if given two side lengths for a triangle, there are an infinite number of side lengths available for the third side. But the third side is also restricted to values determined by the Triangle Inequality Theorem.

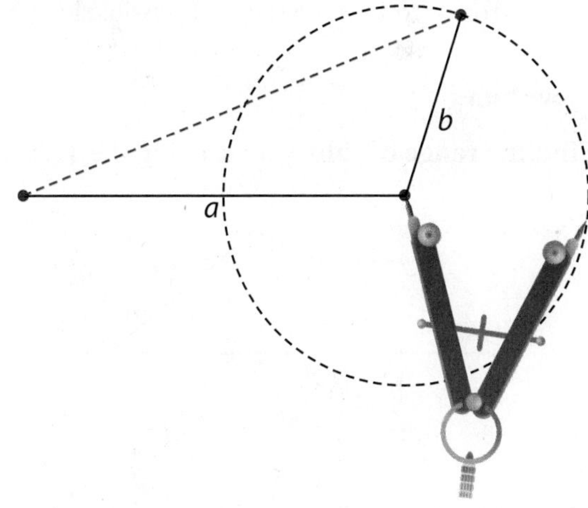

Example 2 **Find the range of values for *x* using the Triangle Inequality Theorem.**

(A) Find possible values for the length of the third side using the Triangle Inequality Theorem.

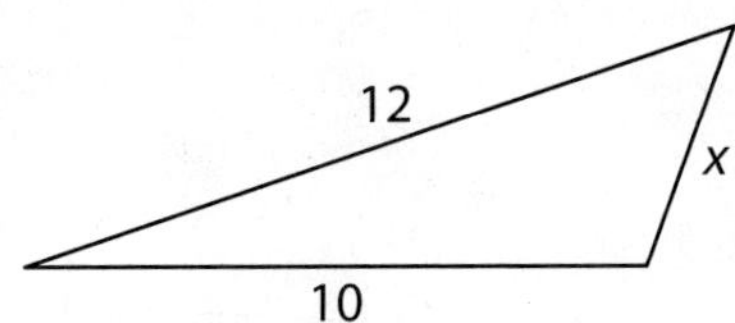

$x + 10 > 12$
$x > 2$

$x + 12 > 10$
$x > -2$

$10 + 12 > x$
$22 > x$

$2 < x < 22$

Ignore the inequality with a negative value, since a triangle cannot have a negative side length. Combine the other two inequalities to find the possible values for x.

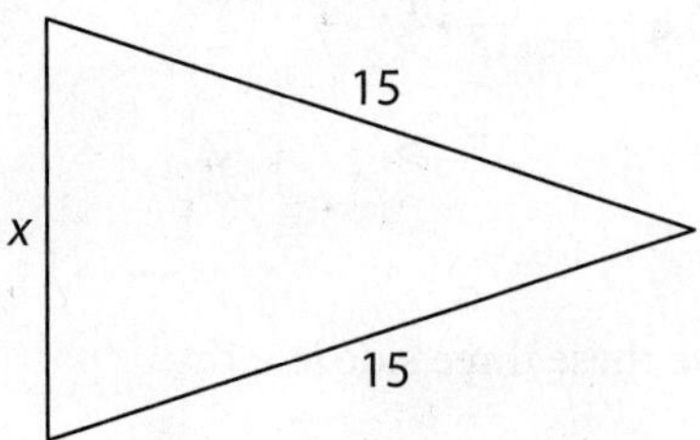

x + 15 > 15 $\quad$ x + 15 > 15 $\quad$ 15 + 15 > x

x > 0 $\quad$ x > 0 $\quad$ 30 > x

$0 < x < 30$

Reflect

8. **Discussion** Suppose you know that the length of the base of an isosceles triangle is 10, but you do not know the lengths of its legs. How could you use the Triangle Inequality Theorem to find the range of possible lengths for each leg? Explain.

Your Turn

Find the range of values for x using the Triangle Inequality Theorem.

9.

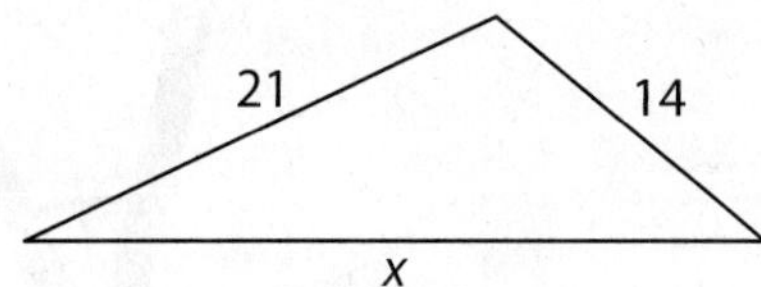

10.

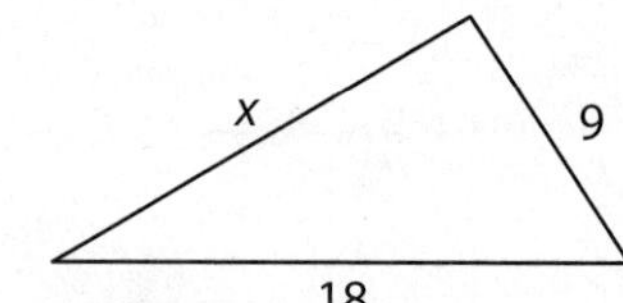

Explain 3 Ordering a Triangle's Angle Measures Given Its Side Lengths

From the Explore Step D, you can see that changing the length of $\overline{AC}$ also changes the measure of $\angle B$ in a predictable way.

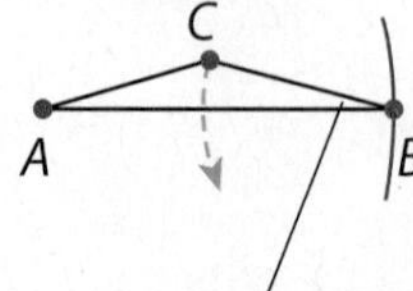

As side AC gets shorter, m$\angle B$ approaches 0°.

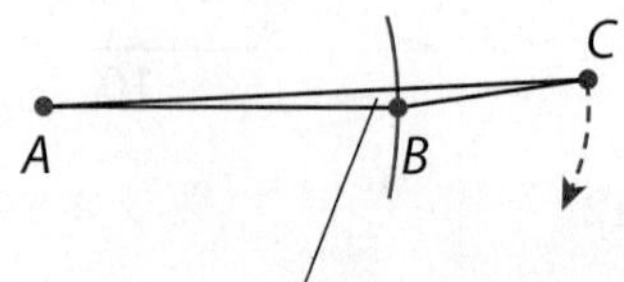

As side AC gets longer, m$\angle B$ approaches 180°.

Side-Angle Relationships in Triangles

If two sides of a triangle are not congruent, then the larger angle is opposite the longer side.

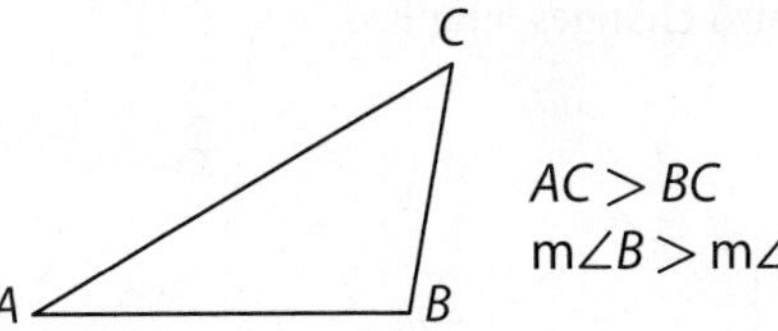

$AC > BC$
$m\angle B > m\angle A$

Example 3 **For each triangle, order its angle measures from least to greatest.**

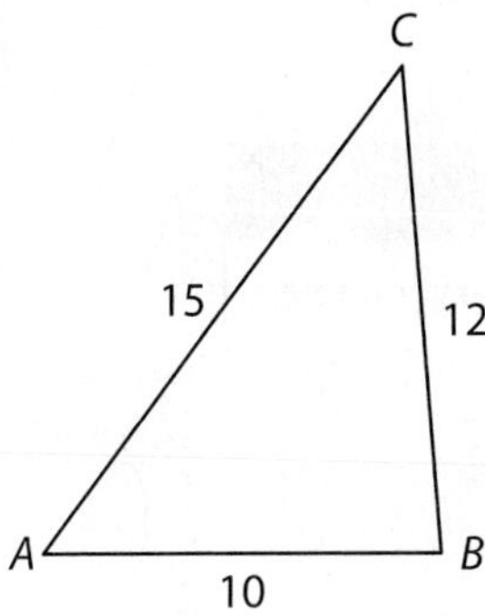

Longest side length: AC

Greatest angle measure: $m\angle B$

Shortest side length: AB

Least angle measure: $m\angle C$

Order of angle measures from least to greatest: $m\angle C$, $m\angle A$, $m\angle B$

Ⓑ

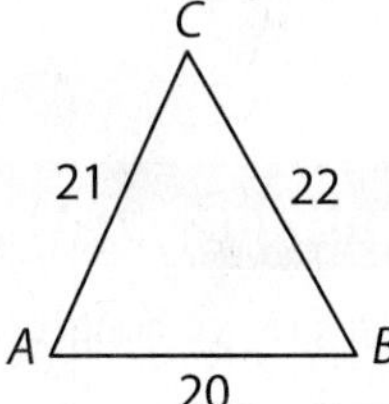

Longest side length: BC

Greatest angle measure: $m\angle A$

Shortest side length: AB

Least angle measure: $m\angle C$

Order of angle measures from least to greatest: $m\angle C$, $m\angle B$, $m\angle A$

Your Turn

For each triangle, order its angle measures from least to greatest.

11.

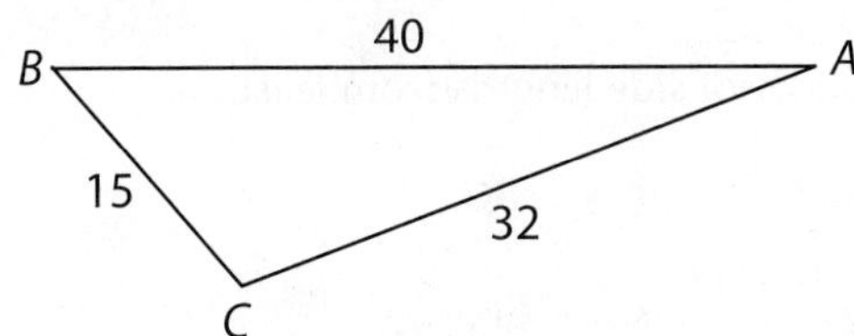

12.

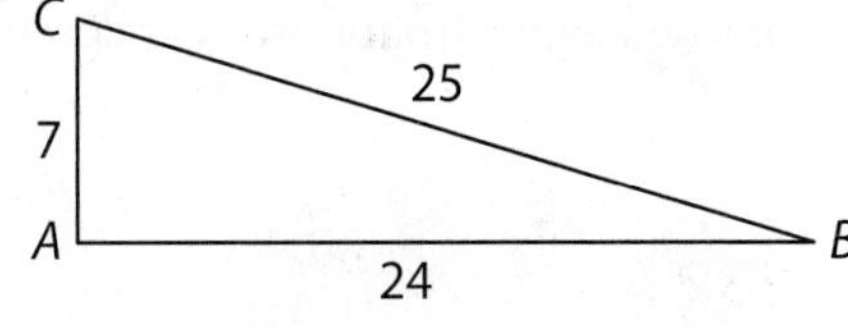

Explain 4 Ordering a Triangle's Side Lengths Given Its Angle Measures

From the Explore Step D, you can see that changing the the measure of $\angle B$ also changes length of $\overline{AC}$ in a predictable way.

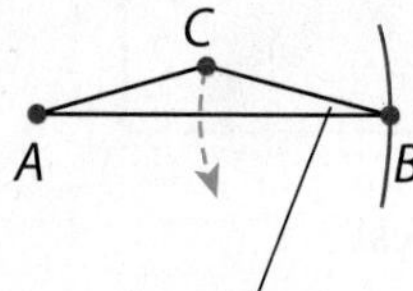

As m$\angle B$ approaches 0°, side *AC* gets shorter.

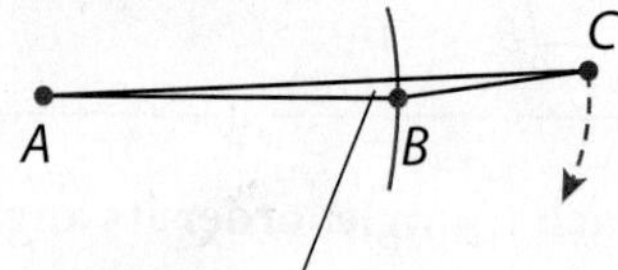

As m$\angle B$ approaches 180°, side *AC* gets longer.

Angle-Side Relationships in Triangles

If two angles of a triangle are not congruent, then the longer side is opposite the larger angle.

Example 4 **For each triangle, order the side lengths from least to greatest.**

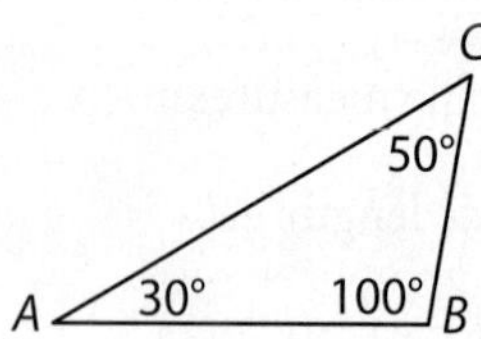

Greatest angle measure: m$\angle B$

Longest side length: *AC*

Least angle measure: m$\angle A$

Shortest side length: *BC*

Order of side lengths from least to greatest: *BC, AB, AC*

(B)

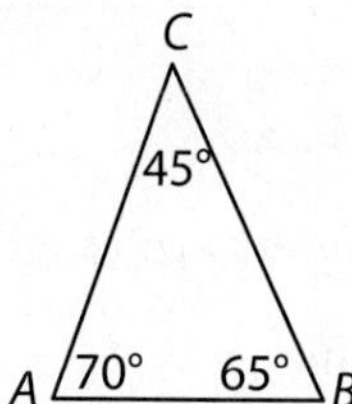

Greatest angle measure: m$\angle A$

Longest side length *BC*

Least angle measure: m$\angle C$

Shortest side length: *AB*

Order of side lengths from least to great: *AB, AC, BC*

Your Turn

For each triangle, order the side lengths from least to greatest.

13. 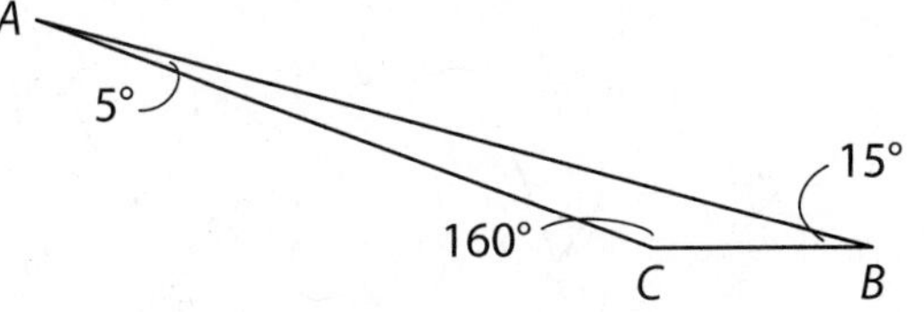

14. 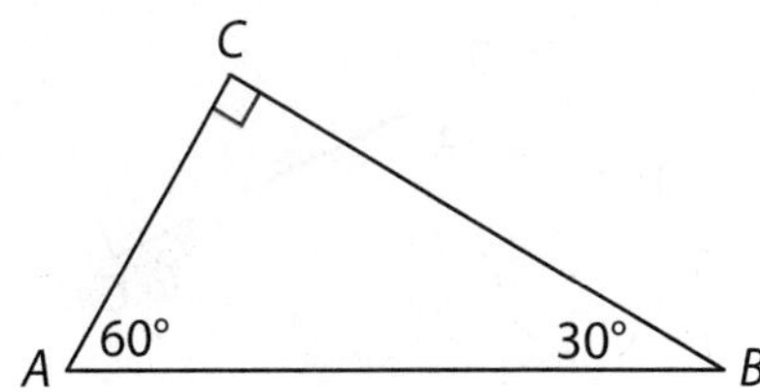

Elaborate

15. When two sides of a triangle are congruent, what can you conclude about the angles opposite those sides?

16. What can you conclude about the side opposite the obtuse angle in an obtuse triangle?

17. **Essential Question Check-In** Suppose you are given three values that could represent the side lengths of a triangle. How can you use one inequality to determine if the triangle exists?

Evaluate: Homework and Practice

Use a compass and straightedge to decide whether each set of lengths can form a triangle.

1. 7 cm, 9 cm, 18 cm

2. 2 in., 4 in., 5 in.

3. 1 in., 2 in., 10 in.

4. 9 cm, 10 cm, 11 cm

Determine whether a triangle can be formed with the given side lengths.

5. 10 ft, 3 ft, 15 ft

6. 12 in., 4 in., 15 in.

7. 9 in., 12 in., and 18 in.

8. 29 m, 59 m, and 89 m

Find the range of possible values for *x* using the Triangle Inequality Theorem.

9. 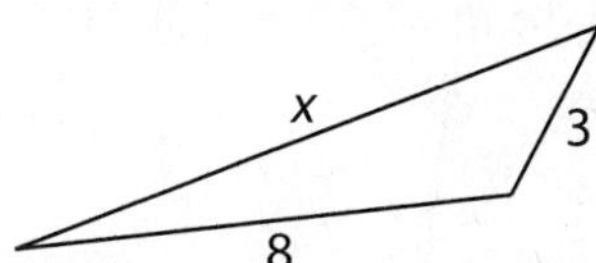

10. 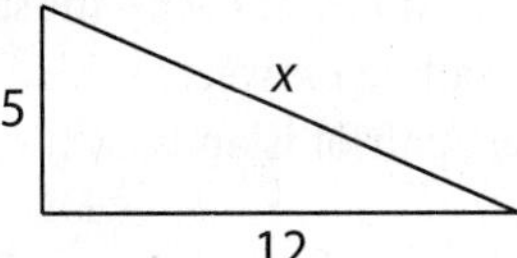

11. A triangle with side lengths 22.3, 27.6, and x

12. **Analyze Relationships** Suppose a triangle has side lengths AB, BC, and x, where $AB = 2 \cdot BC$. Find the possible range for x in terms of BC.

For each triangle, write the order of the angle measures from least to greatest.

13.

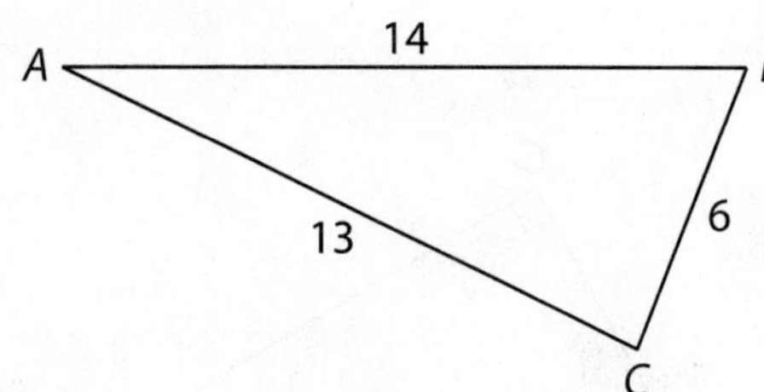

14.

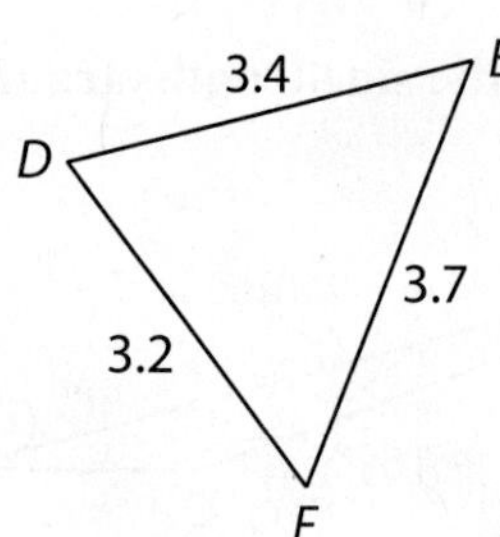

15. Analyze Relationships Suppose a triangle has side lengths *PQ*, *QR*, and *PR*, where $PR = 2PQ = 3QR$. Write the angle measures in order from least to greatest.

For each triangle, write the side lengths in order from least to greatest.

16.

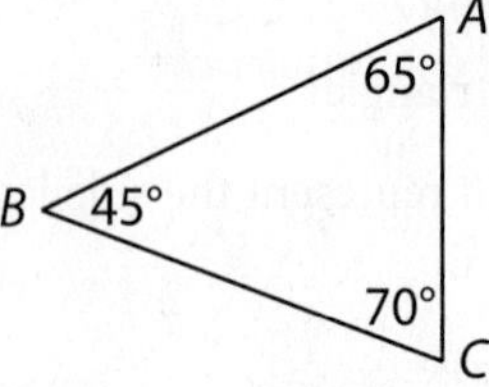

17.

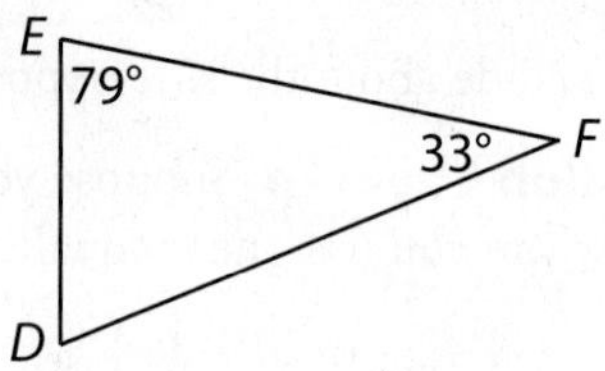

18. In $\triangle JKL$, $m\angle J = 53°$, $m\angle K = 68°$, and $m\angle L = 59°$.

19. In $\triangle PQR$, $m\angle P = 102°$ and $m\angle Q = 25°$.

20. Represent Real-World Problems Rhonda is traveling from New York City to Paris and is trying to decide whether to fly via Frankfurt or to get a more expensive direct flight. Given that it is 3,857 miles from New York City to Frankfurt and another 278 miles from Frankfurt to Paris, what is the range of possible values for the direct distance from New York City to Paris?

21. Represent Real-World Problems A large ship is sailing between three small islands. To do so, the ship must sail between two pairs of islands, avoiding sailing between a third pair. The safest route is to avoid the closest pair of islands. Which is the safest route for the ship?

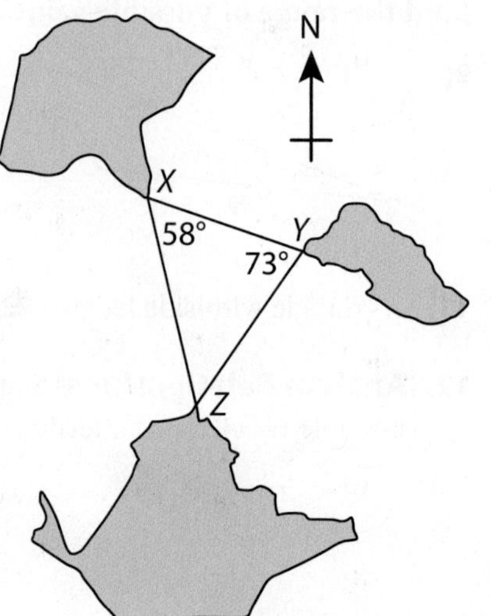

22. Represent Real-World Problems A hole on a golf course is a dogleg, meaning that it bends in the middle. A golfer will usually start by driving for the bend in the dogleg (from A to B), and then using a second shot to get the ball to the green (from B to C). Sandy believes she may be able to drive the ball far enough to reach the green in one shot, avoiding the bend (from A direct to C). Sandy knows she can accurately drive a distance of 250 yd. Should she attempt to drive for the green on her first shot? Explain.

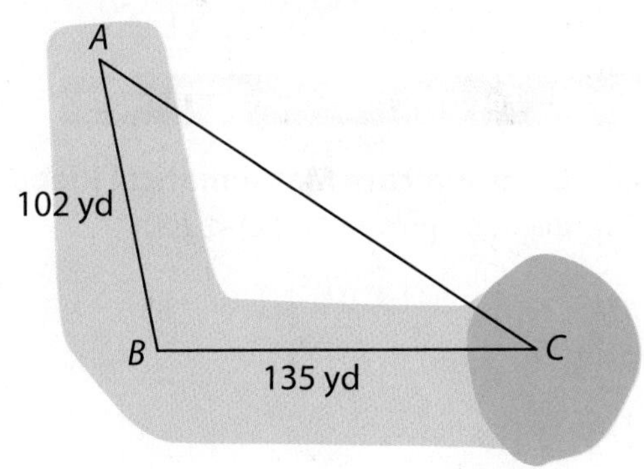

23. Represent Real-World Problems Three cell phone towers form a triangle, $\triangle PQR$. The measure of $\angle Q$ is 10° less than the measure of $\angle P$. The measure of $\angle R$ is 5° greater than the measure of $\angle Q$. Which two towers are closest together?

24. Algebra In $\triangle PQR$, $PQ = 3x + 1$, $QR = 2x - 2$, and $PR = x + 7$. Determine the range of possible values of x.

25. In any triangle ABC, suppose you know the lengths of $\overline{AB}$ and $\overline{BC}$, and suppose that $AB > BC$. If x is the length of the third side, $\overline{AC}$, use the Triangle Inequality Theorem to prove that $AB - BC < x < AB + BC$. That is, x must be between the difference and the sum of the other two side lengths. Explain why this result makes sense in terms of the constructions shown in the figure.

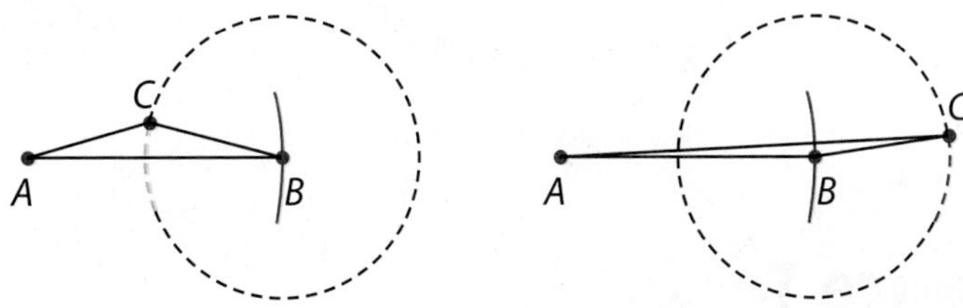

26. Given the information in the diagram, prove that $m\angle DEA < m\angle ABC$.

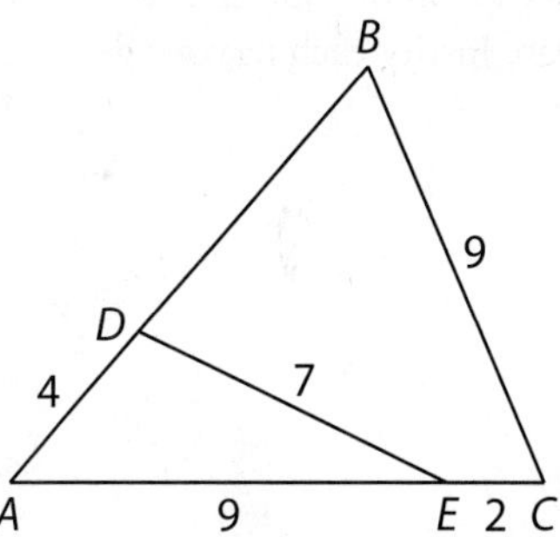

27. An isosceles triangle has legs with length 11 units. Which of the following could be the perimeter of the triangle? Determine all that apply. Explain your reasoning.

a. 22 units

b. 24 units

c. 34 units

d. 43 units

e. 44 units

H.O.T. Focus on Higher Order Thinking

28. Communicate Mathematical Ideas Given the information in the diagram, prove that $PQ < PS$.

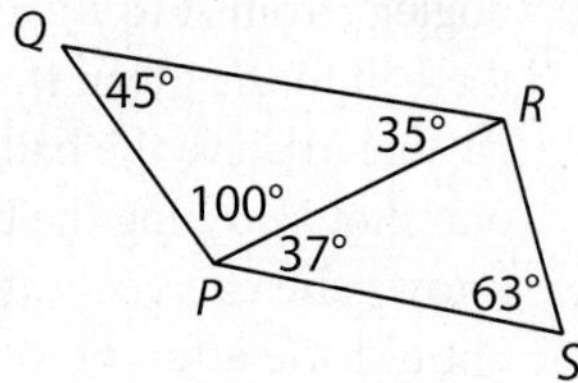

29. Justify Reasoning In obtuse $\triangle ABC$, $m\angle A < m\angle B$. The auxiliary line segment $\overline{CD}$ perpendicular to $\overrightarrow{AB}$ (extended beyond B) creates right triangles ADC and BDC. Describe how you could use the Pythagorean Theorem to prove that $BC < AC$.

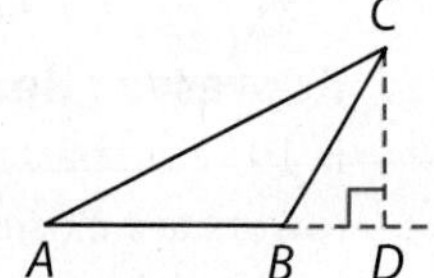

30. Make a Conjecture In acute $\triangle DEF$, $m\angle D < m\angle E$. The auxiliary line segment $\overline{FG}$ creates $\triangle EFG$, where $EF = FG$. What would you need to prove about the points D, G, and E to prove that $\angle DGF$ is obtuse, and therefore that $EF < DF$? Explain.

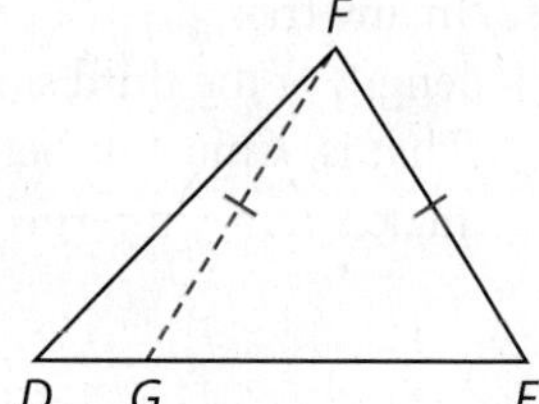

Lesson Performance Task

As captain of your orienteering team, it's your job to map out the shortest distance from point A to point H on the map. Justify each of your decisions.

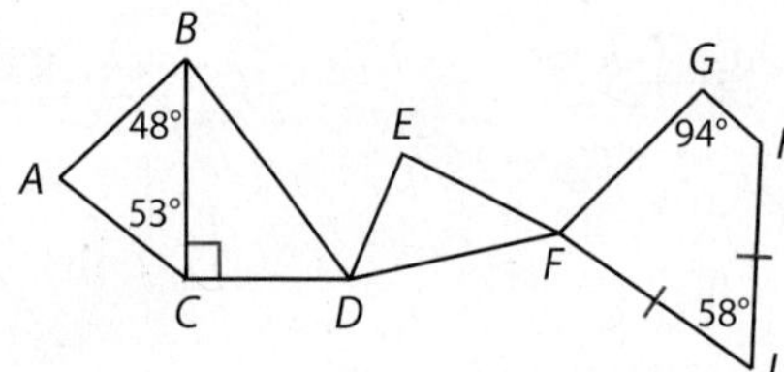

15.4 Perpendicular Bisectors of Triangles

Resource Locker

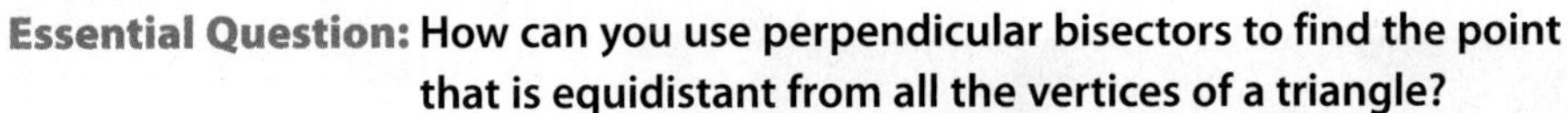

Essential Question: How can you use perpendicular bisectors to find the point that is equidistant from all the vertices of a triangle?

Explore Constructing a Circumscribed Circle

A circle that contains all the vertices of a polygon is **circumscribed** about the polygon. In the figure, circle C is circumscribed about $\triangle XYZ$, and circle C is called the **circumcircle** of $\triangle XYZ$. The center of the circumcircle is called the **circumcenter** of the triangle.

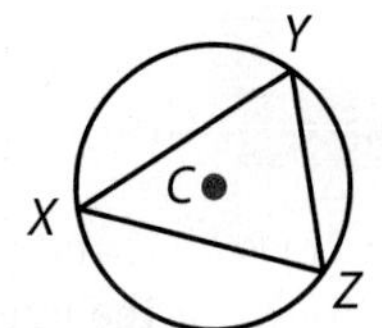

In the following activity, you will construct the circumcircle of $\triangle PQR$. Copy the triangle onto a separate piece of paper.

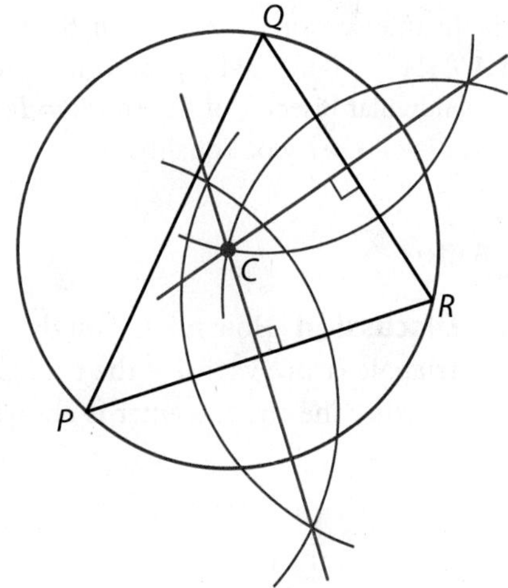

(A) The circumcircle will pass through P, Q, and R. So, the center of the circle must be equidistant from all three points. In particular, the center must be equidistant from Q and R.

The set of points that are equidistant from Q and R is called the ________ of $\overline{QR}$. Use a compass and straightedge to construct the set of points.

(B) The center must also be equidistant from P and R. The set of points that are equidistant from P and R is called the ________ of $\overline{PR}$. Use a compass and straightedge to construct the set of points.

(C) The center must lie at the intersection of the two sets of points you constructed. Label the point C. Then place the point of your compass at C and open it to distance CP. Draw the circumcircle.

Reflect

1. **Make a Prediction** Suppose you started by constructing the set of points equidistant from P and Q and then constructed the set of points equidistant from Q and R. Would you have found the same center? Check by doing this construction.

2. Can you locate the circumcenter of a triangle without using a compass and straightedge? Explain.

Explain 1 Proving the Concurrency of a Triangle's Perpendicular Bisectors

Three or more lines are **concurrent** if they intersect at the same point. The point of intersection is called the **point of concurrency**. You saw in the Explore that the three perpendicular bisectors of a triangle are concurrent. Now you will prove that the point of concurrency is the circumcenter of the triangle. That is, the point of concurrency is equidistant from the vertices of the triangle.

Circumcenter Theorem

The perpendicular bisectors of the sides of a triangle intersect at a point that is equidistant from the vertices of the triangle.

$PA = PB = PC$

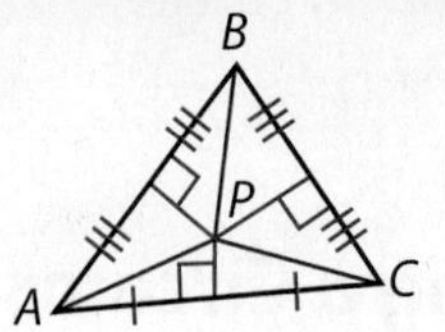

Example 1 **Prove the Circumcenter Theorem.**

Given: Lines ℓ, *m*, and *n* are the perpendicular bisectors of $\overline{AB}$, $\overline{BC}$, and $\overline{AC}$, respectively. *P* is the intersection of ℓ, *m*, and *n*.

Prove: $PA = PB = PC$

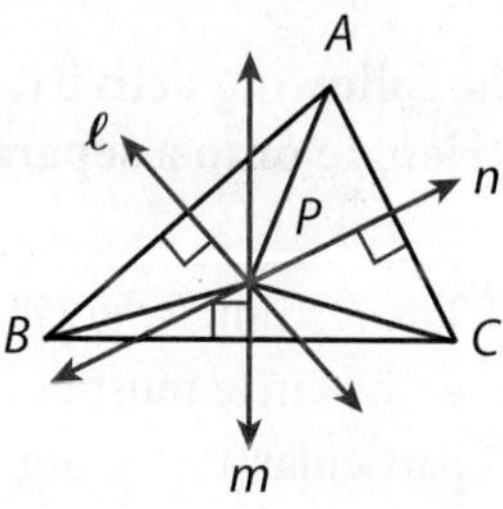

P is the intersection of ℓ, *m*, and *n*. Since *P* lies on the perpendicular bisector of $\overline{AB}$, $PA = PB$ by the Perpendicular Bisector Theorem. Similarly, *P* lies on the perpendicular bisector of $\overline{BC}$, so $PB = PC$. Therefore, $PA = PB = PC$ by the Transitive Property of Equality.

Reflect

3. **Discussion** How might you determine whether the circumcenter of a triangle is always inside the triangle? Make a plan and then determine whether the circumcenter is always inside the triangle.

Explain 2 Using Properties of Perpendicular Bisectors

You can use the Circumcenter Theorem to find segment lengths in a triangle.

Example 2 **$\overline{KZ}$, $\overline{LZ}$, and $\overline{MZ}$ are the perpendicular bisectors of $\triangle GHJ$. Use the given information to find the length of each segment. Note that the figure is not drawn to scale.**

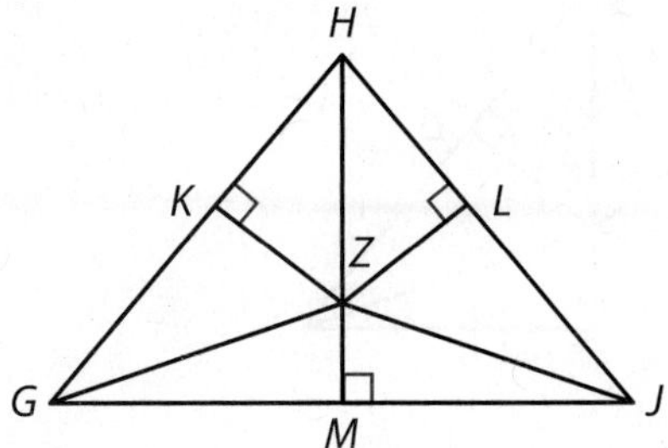

(A) Given: $ZM = 7$, $ZJ = 25$, $HK = 20$

Find: ZH and HG

Z is the circumcenter of $\triangle GHJ$, so $ZG = ZH = ZJ$.

$ZJ = 25$, so $ZH = 25$.

K is the midpoint of $\overline{GH}$, so $HG = 2 \cdot KH = 2 \cdot 20 = 40$.

(B) Given: $ZH = 85$, $MZ = 13$, $HG = 136$

Find: KG and ZJ

K is the midpoint of $\overline{HG}$, so $KG = \boxed{\frac{1}{2}} HG = \boxed{\frac{1}{2}} \cdot \boxed{136} = \boxed{68}$.

Z is the circumcenter of $\triangle GHJ$, so $ZG = ZH = ZJ$.

$ZH = 85$, so $ZJ = 85$.

Reflect

4. In $\triangle ABC$, $\angle ACB$ is a right angle and D is the circumcenter of the triangle. If $CD = 6.5$, what is AB? Explain your reasoning.

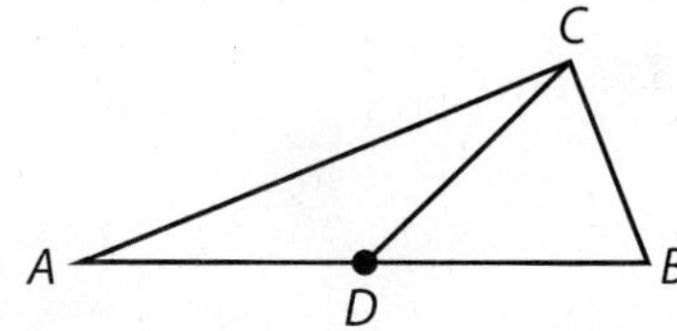

Your Turn

$\overline{KZ}$, $\overline{LZ}$, and $\overline{MZ}$ are the perpendicular bisectors of $\triangle GHJ$. Copy the sketch and label the given information. Use that information to find the length of each segment. Note that the figure is not drawn to scale.

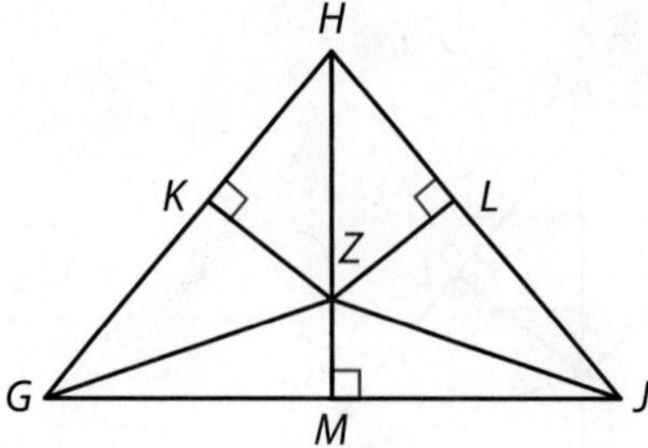

5. Given: $ZG = 65$, $HL = 63$, $ZL = 16$
Find: HJ and ZJ

6. Given: $ZM = 25$, $ZH = 65$, $GJ = 120$
Find: GM and ZG

Explain 3 Finding a Circumcenter on a Coordinate Plane

Given the vertices of a triangle, you can graph the triangle and use the graph to find the circumcenter of the triangle.

Example 3 **Graph the triangle with the given vertices and find the circumcenter of the triangle.**

(A) $R(-6, 0)$, $S(0, 4)$, $O(0, 0)$

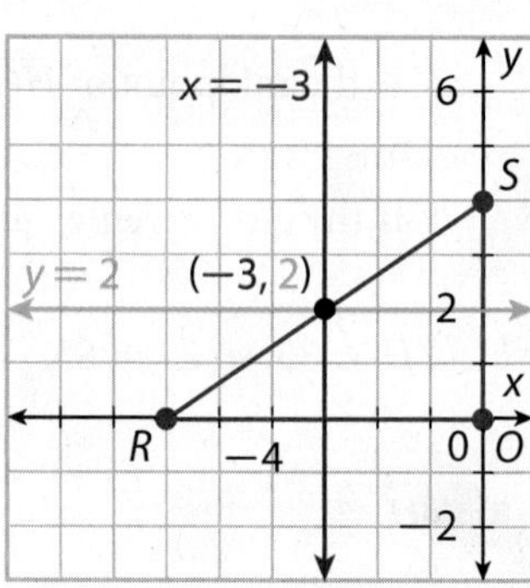

Step 1: Graph the triangle.

Step 2: Find equations for two perpendicular bisectors.

Side $\overline{RO}$ is on the x-axis, so its perpendicular bisector is vertical: the line $x = -3$.

Side $\overline{SO}$ is on the y-axis, so its perpendicular bisector is horizontal: the line $y = 2$.

Step 3: Find the intersection of the perpendicular bisectors.

The lines $x = -3$ and $y = 2$ intersect at $(-3, 2)$.

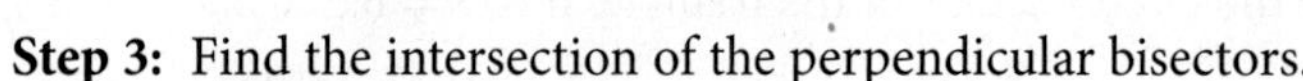

$(-3, 2)$ is the circumcenter of $\triangle ROS$.

(B) $A(-1, 5), B(5, 5), C(5, -1)$

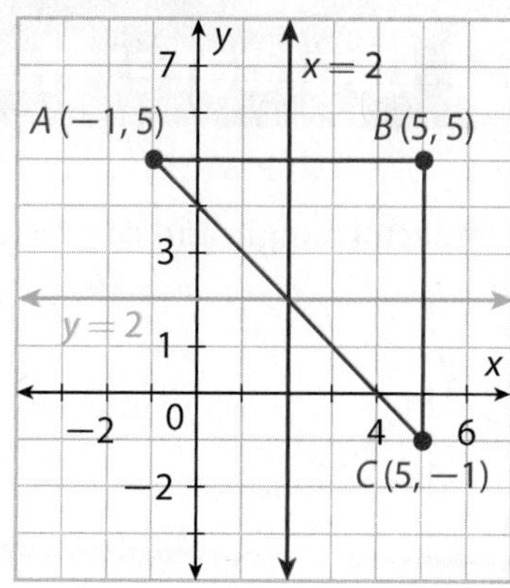

Step 1 Graph the triangle.

Step 2 Find equations for two perpendicular bisectors.

Side $\overline{AB}$ is horizontal, so its perpendicular bisector is vertical.

The perpendicular bisector of $\overline{AB}$ is the line $x = 2$.

Side $\overline{BC}$ is vertical, so the perpendicular bisector of $\overline{BC}$ is horizontal, the line $y = 2$.

Step 3 Find the intersection of the perpendicular bisectors.

The lines $x = 2$ and $y = 2$ intersect at $(2, 2)$.

$(2, 2)$ is the circumcenter of $\triangle ABC$.

Reflect

7. **Draw Conclusions** Could a vertex of a triangle also be its circumcenter? If so, provide an example. If not, explain why not.

Your Turn

Graph the triangle with the given vertices and find the circumcenter of the triangle.

8. $Q(-4, 0), R(0, 0), S(0, 6)$

9. $K(1, 1), L(1, 7), M(6, 1)$

Elaborate

10. A company that makes and sells bicycles has its largest stores in three cities. The company wants to build a new factory that is equidistant from each of the stores. Given a map, how could you identify the location for the new factory?

11. A sculptor builds a mobile in which a triangle rotates around its circumcenter. Each vertex traces the shape of a circle as it rotates. What circle does it trace? Explain.

12. **What If?** Suppose you are given the vertices of a triangle PQR. You plot the points in a coordinate plane and notice that $\overline{PQ}$ is horizontal but neither of the other sides is vertical. How can you identify the circumcenter of the triangle? Justify your reasoning.

13. **Essential Question Check-In** How is the point that is equidistant from the three vertices of a triangle related to the circumcircle of the triangle?

Evaluate: Homework and Practice

- Online Homework
- Hints and Help
- Extra Practice

Copy each triangle and construct its circumcircle. Label the circumcenter *P*.

1.

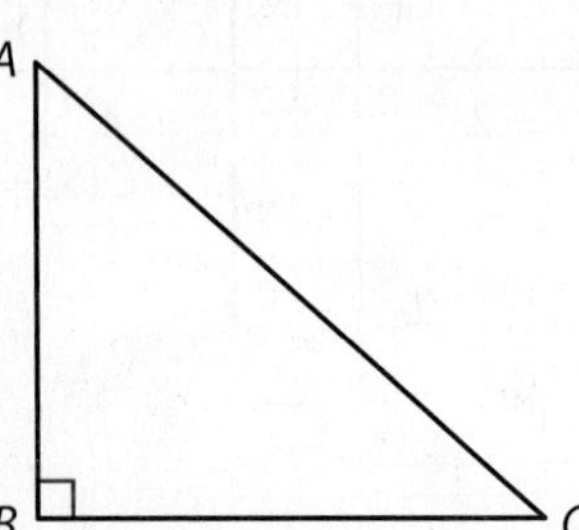

2.

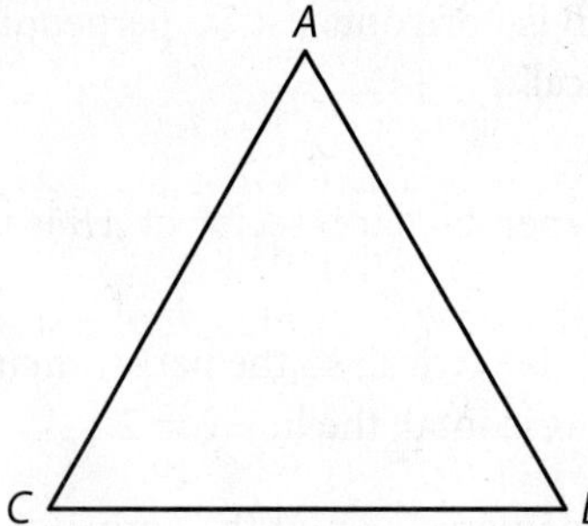

3.

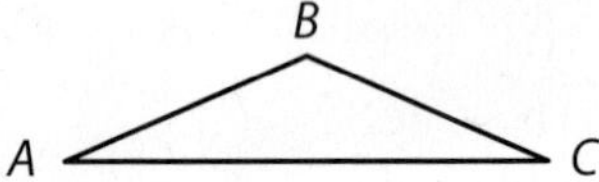

4.

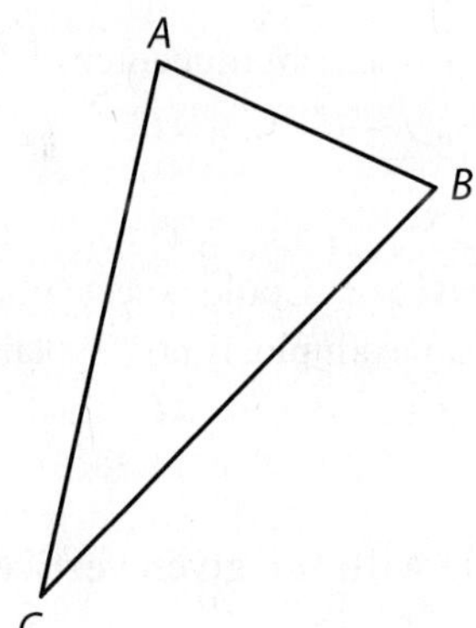

Use the diagram for Exercise 5–8. $\overline{ZD}$, $\overline{ZE}$, and $\overline{ZF}$ are the perpendicular bisectors of $\triangle ABC$. Use the given information to find the length of each segment. Note that the figure is not drawn to scale.

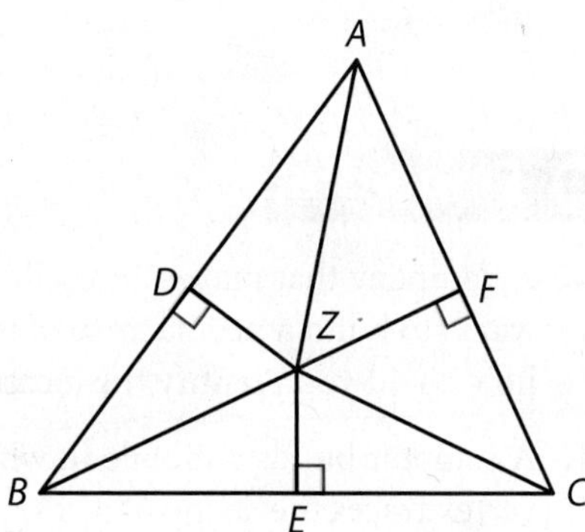

5. Given: $DZ = 40$, $ZA = 85$, $FC = 77$

Find: ZC and AC

6. Given: $FZ = 36$, $ZA = 85$, $AB = 150$

Find: AD and ZB

7. Given: $AZ = 85$, $ZE = 51$

Find: BC

(*Hint*: Use the Pythagorean Theorem.)

8. Analyze Relationships How can you write an algebraic expression for the radius of the circumcircle of $\triangle ABC$ in Exercises 5–7? Explain.

Copy and complete the proof of the Circumcenter Theorem.

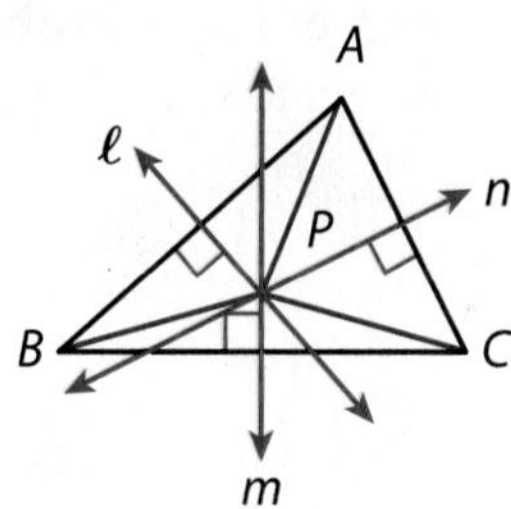

9. **Given:** Lines ℓ, m, and n are the perpendicular bisectors of $\overline{AB}$, $\overline{BC}$, and $\overline{AC}$, respectively. P is the intersection of ℓ, m, and n.

Prove: $PA = PB = PC$

Statements	Reasons
1. Lines ℓ, m, and n are the perpendicular bisectors of $\overline{AB}$, $\overline{BC}$, and $\overline{AC}$.	1. ▇
2. P is the intersection of ℓ, m, and n.	2. ▇
3. $PA =$ ▇	3. P lies on the perpendicular bisector of $\overline{AB}$.
4. ▇ $= PC$	4. P lies on the perpendicular bisector of $\overline{BC}$.
5. $PA =$ ▇ $=$ ▇	5. ▇

10. $\overline{PK}$, $\overline{PL}$, and $\overline{PM}$ are the perpendicular bisectors of sides $\overline{AB}$, $\overline{BC}$, and $\overline{AC}$. Tell whether the given statement is justified or not justified by the figure.

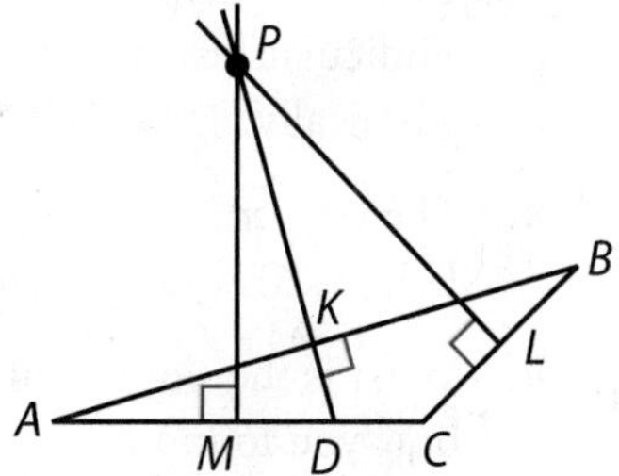

a. $AK = KB$

b. $PA = PB$

c. $PM = PL$

d. $BL = \frac{1}{2}BC$

e. $PK = KD$

Graph the triangle with the given vertices and find the circumcenter of the triangle.

11. $D(-5, 0), E(0, 0), F(0, 7)$

12. $Q(3, 4), R(7, 4), S(3, -2)$

13. Represent Real-World Problems For the next Fourth of July, the towns of Ashton, Bradford, and Clearview will launch a fireworks display from a boat in the lake. Draw a sketch to show where the boat should be positioned so that it is the same distance from all three towns. Justify your sketch.

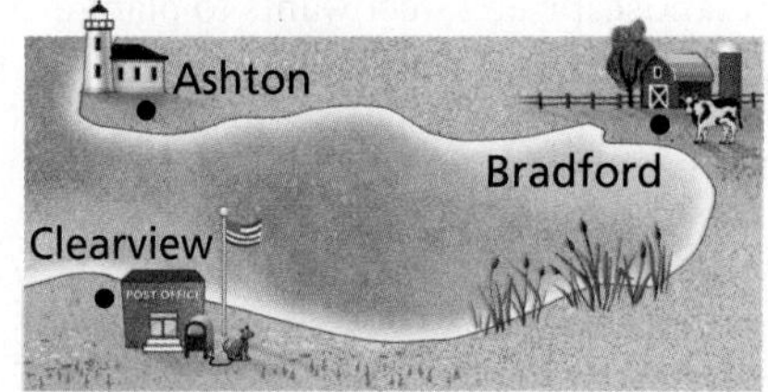

H.O.T. Focus on Higher Order Thinking

14. Analyze Relationships Explain how can you draw a triangle JKL whose circumcircle has a radius of 8 centimeters.

15. Persevere in Problem Solving $\overline{ZD}$, $\overline{ZE}$, and $\overline{ZF}$ are the perpendicular bisectors of $\triangle ABC$, which is not drawn to scale.

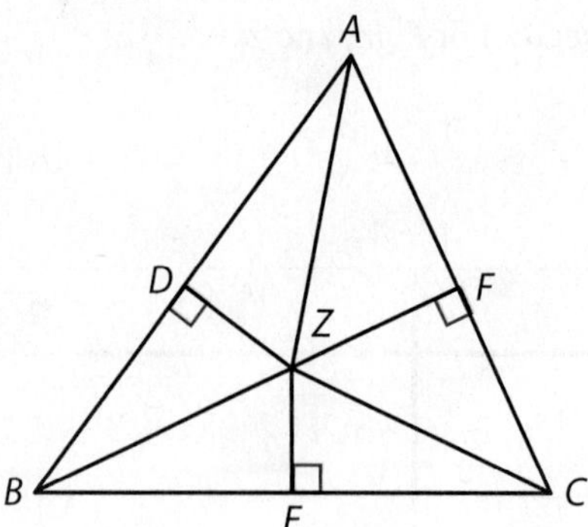

a. Suppose that $ZB = 145$, $ZD = 100$, and $ZF = 17$. How can you find AB and AC?

b. Find AB and AC.

c. Can you find BC? If so, explain how and find BC. If not, explain why not.

16. Multiple Representations Given the vertices $A(-2, -2)$, $B(4, 0)$, and $C(4, 4)$ of a triangle, the graph shows how you can use a graph and construction to locate the circumcenter P of the triangle. You can draw the perpendicular bisector of $\overline{CB}$ and construct the perpendicular bisector of $\overline{AB}$. Consider how you could identify P algebraically.

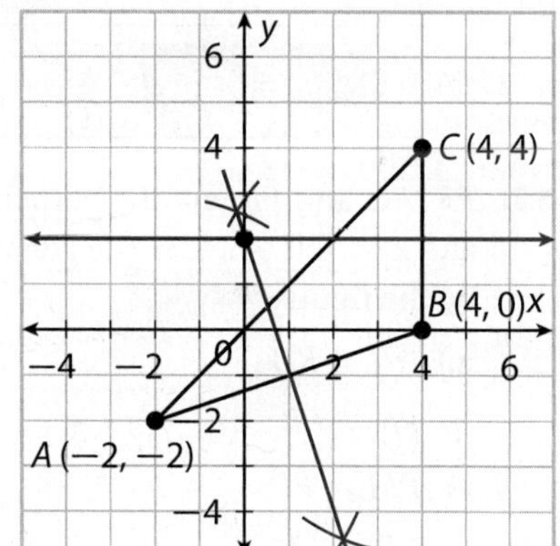

a. The perpendicular bisector of $\overline{AB}$ passes through its midpoint. Use the Midpoint Formula to find the midpoint of $\overline{AB}$.

b. What is the slope m of the perpendicular bisector of $\overline{AB}$? Explain how you found it.

c. Write an equation of the perpendicular bisector of $\overline{AB}$ and explain how you can use it find P.

Lesson Performance Task

A landscape architect wants to plant a circle of flowers around a triangular garden. She has sketched the triangle on a coordinate grid with vertices at $A(0, 0)$, $B(8, 12)$, and $C(18, 0)$.

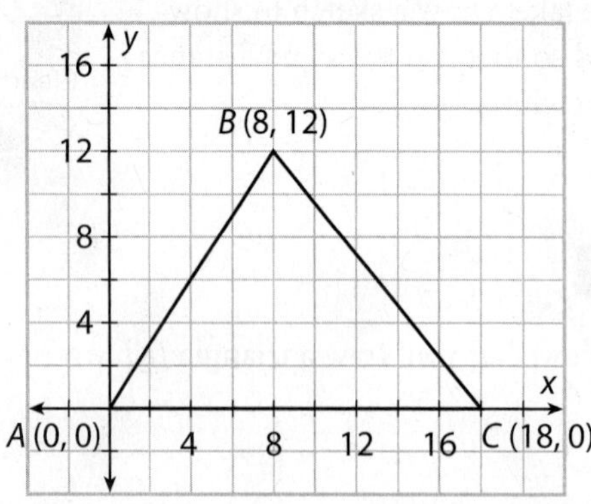

Explain how the architect can find the center of the circle that will circumscribe triangle ABC. Then find the radius of the circumscribed circle.

15.5 Angle Bisectors of Triangles

Essential Question: How can you use angle bisectors to find the point that is equidistant from all the sides of a triangle?

Explore Investigating Distance from a Point to a Line

Use a ruler, a protractor, and a piece of tracing paper to investigate points on the bisector of an angle.

(A) Use the ruler to draw a large angle on tracing paper. Label it $\angle ABC$. Fold the paper so that $\overrightarrow{BC}$ coincides with $\overrightarrow{BA}$. Open the paper. The crease is the bisector of $\angle ABC$. Plot a point P on the bisector.

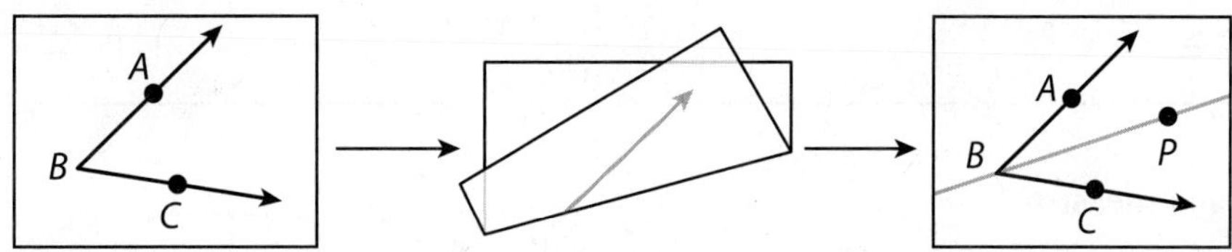

(B) Use the ruler to draw several different segments from point P to $\overrightarrow{BA}$. Measure the lengths of the segments. Then measure the angle each segment makes with $\overrightarrow{BA}$. What do you notice about the shortest segment you can draw from point P to $\overrightarrow{BA}$?

(C) Draw the shortest segment you can from point P to $\overrightarrow{BC}$. Measure its length. How does its length compare with the length of the shortest segment you drew from point P to $\overrightarrow{BA}$?

Reflect

1. Suppose you choose a point Q on the bisector of $\angle XYZ$ and you draw the perpendicular segment from Q to $\overrightarrow{YX}$ and the perpendicular segment from Q to $\overrightarrow{YZ}$. What do you think will be true about these segments?

2. **Discussion** What do you think is the best way to measure the distance from a point to a line? Why?

Explain 1 Applying the Angle Bisector Theorem and Its Converse

The **distance from a point to a line** is the length of the perpendicular segment from the point to the line. You will prove the following theorems about angle bisectors and the sides of the angle they bisect in Exercises 16 and 17.

Angle Bisector Theorem

If a point is on the bisector an of angle, then it is equidistant from the sides of the angle.

$\angle APC \cong \angle BPC$, so $AC = BC$.

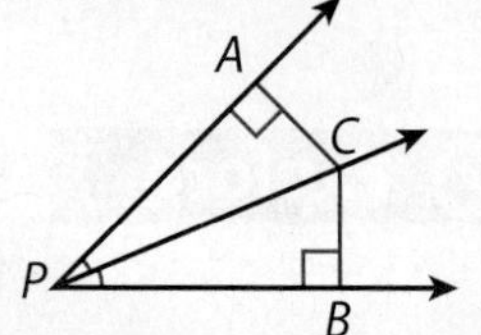

Converse of the Angle Bisector Theorem

If a point in the interior of an angle is equidistant from the sides of the angle, then it is on the bisector of the angle.

$AC = BC$, so $\angle APC \cong \angle BPC$

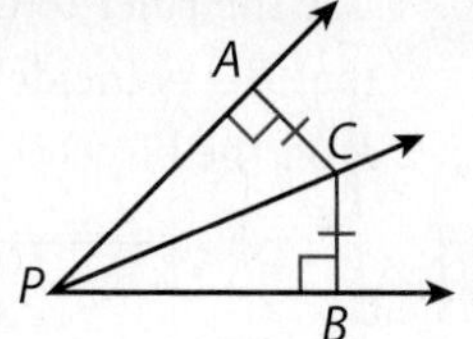

Example 1 Find each measure.

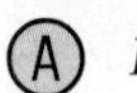 LM

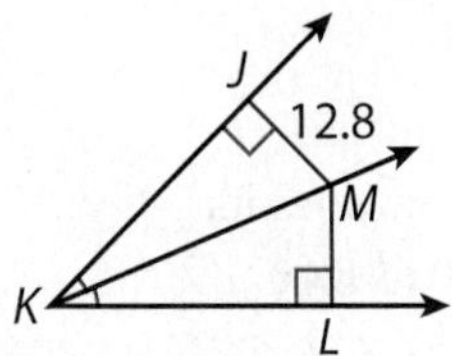

$\overrightarrow{KM}$ is the bisector of $\angle JKL$, so $LM = JM = 12.8$.

(B) m$\angle ABD$, given that m$\angle ABC = 112°$

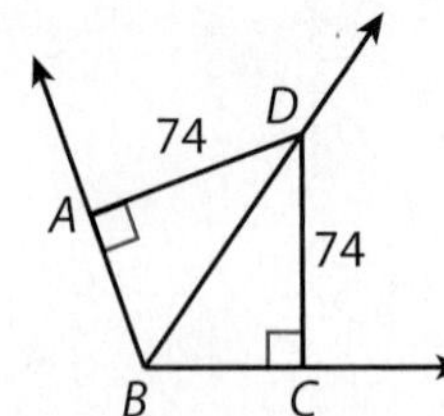

Since $AD = DC$, $\overline{AD} \perp \overrightarrow{BA}$, and $\overline{DC} \perp \overrightarrow{BC}$, you know that $\overrightarrow{BD}$ bisects $\angle ABC$ by the Converse of the Angle Bisector Theorem.

So, $m\angle ABD = \frac{1}{2} m\angle ABC =$ 56 °.

Reflect

3. In the Converse of the Angle Bisector Theorem, why is it important to say that the point must be in the *interior* of the angle?

Your Turn

Find each measure.

4. QS

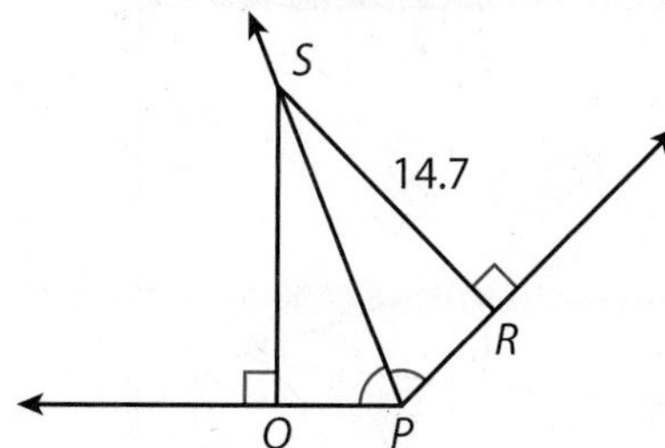

5. $m\angle LJM$, given that $m\angle KJM = 29°$

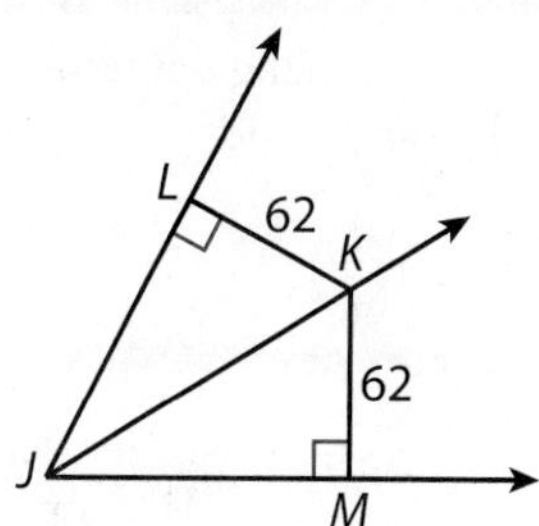

Explain 2 Constructing an Inscribed Circle

A circle is **inscribed** in a polygon if each side of the polygon is tangent to the circle. In the figure, circle C is inscribed in quadrilateral $WXYZ$ and this circle is called the **incircle (inscribed circle)** of the quadrilateral.

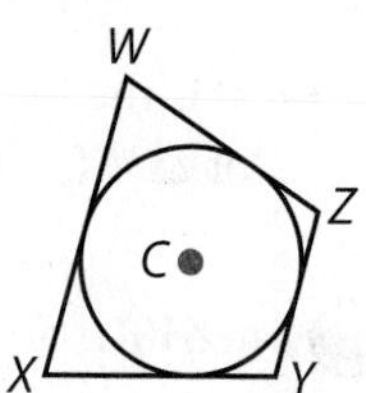

In order to construct the incircle of a triangle, you need to find the center of the circle. This point is called the **incenter** of the triangle.

Example 2 **Use a compass and straightedge to construct the inscribed circle of $\triangle PQR$.**

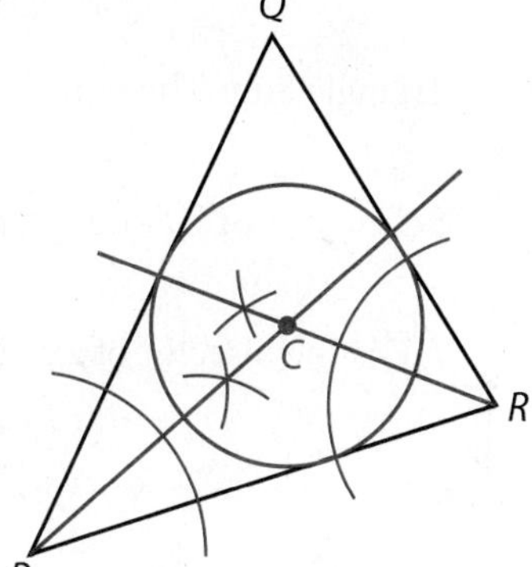

Step 1 The center of the inscribed circle must be equidistant from $\overline{PQ}$ and $\overline{PR}$. The set of points equidistant from $\overline{PQ}$ and $\overline{PR}$ is the bisector of $\angle P$. Construct this set of points.

Step 2 The center must also be equidistant from $\overline{PR}$ and $\overline{QR}$. The set of points equidistant from $\overline{PR}$ and $\overline{QR}$ is the bisector of $\angle R$ Construct this set of points.

Step 3 The center must lie at the intersection of the two sets of points you constructed. Label this point C.

Step 4 Place the point of your compass at C and open the compass until the pencil just touches a side of $\triangle PQR$. Then draw the inscribed circle.

Reflect

6. Suppose you started by constructing the set of points equidistant from $\overline{PR}$ and $\overline{QR}$, and then constructed the set of points equidistant from $\overline{QR}$ and $\overline{QP}$. Would you have found the same center point? Check by doing this construction.

Explain 3 Using Properties of Angle Bisectors

As you have seen, the angle bisectors of a triangle are concurrent. The point of concurrency is the incenter of the triangle.

Incenter Theorem

The angle bisectors of a triangle intersect at a point that is equidistant from the sides of the triangle.

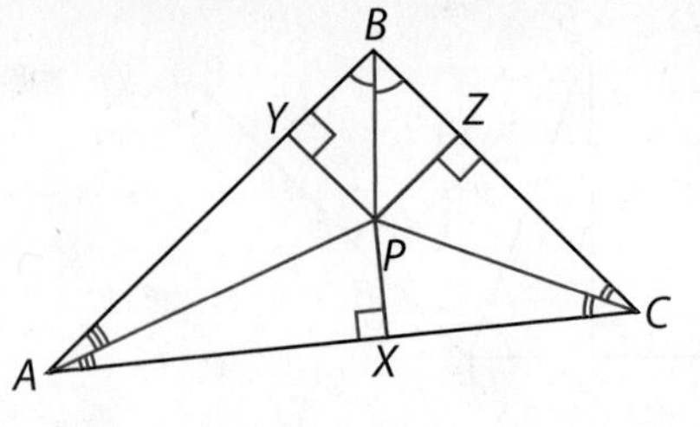

$PX = PY = PZ$

Example 3 $\overline{JV}$ **and** $\overline{KV}$ **are angle bisectors of** $\triangle JKL$**. Find each measure.**

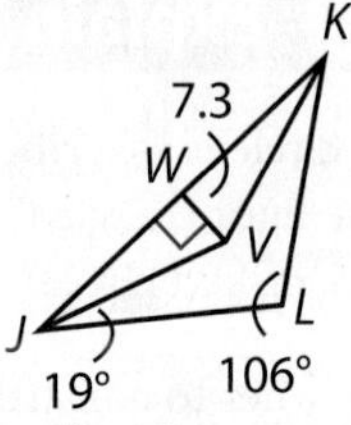

(A) the distance from V to $\overline{KL}$

V is the incenter of $\triangle JKL$. By the Incenter Theorem, V is equidistant from the sides of $\triangle JKL$. The distance from V to $\overline{JK}$ is 7.3. So the distance from V to $\overline{KL}$ is also 7.3.

(B) $m\angle VKL$

$\overline{JV}$ is the bisector of $\angle$ KJL.	$m\angle KJL = 2(19°) = 38°$
Triangle Sum Theorem	$38° + 106° + m\angle JKL = 180°$
Subtract 144° from each side.	$m\angle JKL = 36°$
$\overline{KV}$ is the bisector of $\angle JKL$.	$m\angle VKL = \frac{1}{2}(36°) = 18°$

Reflect

7. In Part A, is there another distance you can determine? Explain.

Your Turn

$\overline{QX}$ **and** $\overline{RX}$ **are angle bisectors of** $\triangle PQR$**. Find each measure.**

8. the distance from X to $\overline{PQ}$

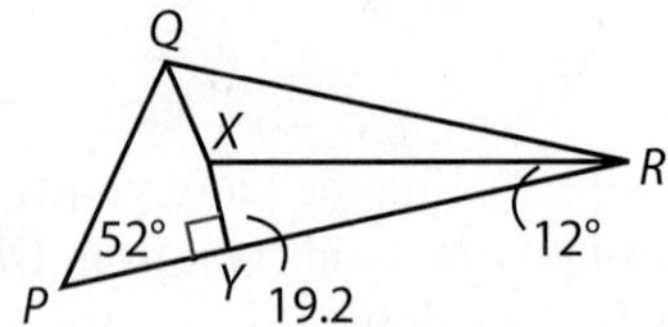

9. $m\angle PQX$

Elaborate

10. P and Q are the circumcenter and incenter of $\triangle RST$, but not necessarily in that order. Which point is the circumcenter? Which point is the incenter? Explain how you can tell without constructing any bisectors.

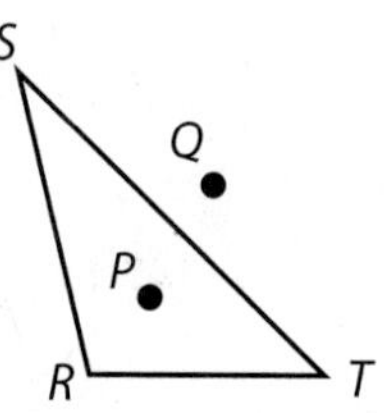

11. Write the word or phrase that makes each statement true.

	Circumcenter	Incenter
Definition	The point of concurrency of the ___?___	The point of concurrency of the ___?___
Distance	Equidistant from the ___?___	Equidistant from the ___?___
Location (Inside, Outside, On)	Can be ___?___ the triangle	Always ___?___ the triangle

12. **Essential Question Check-In** How do you know that the intersection of the bisectors of the angles of a triangle is equidistant from the sides of the triangle?

Evaluate: Homework and Practice

- Online Homework
- Hints and Help
- Extra Practice

1. Use a compass and straightedge to investigate points on the bisector of an angle. On a separate piece of paper, draw a large angle A.

a. Construct the bisector of $\angle A$.

b. Choose a point on the angle bisector you constructed. Label it P. Construct a perpendicular through P to each side of $\angle A$.

c. Explain how to use a compass to show that P is equidistant from the sides of $\angle A$.

For Exericses 2–5, find each measure.

2. VP

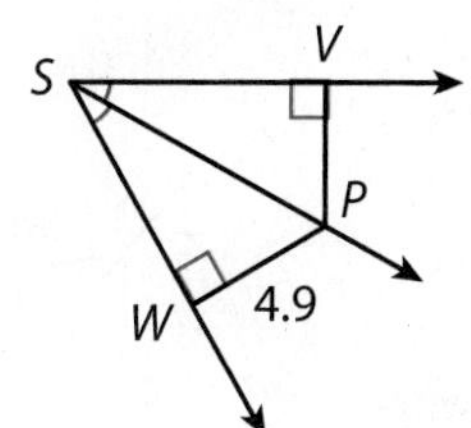

3. $m\angle LKM$, given that $m\angle JKL = 63°$

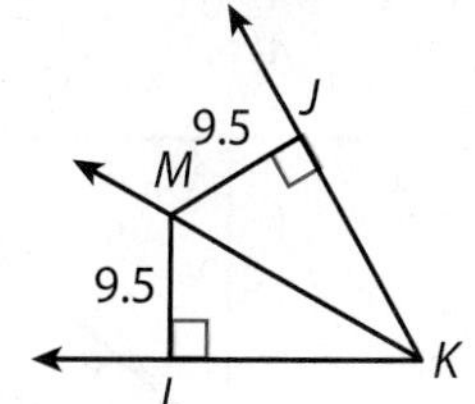

4. AD

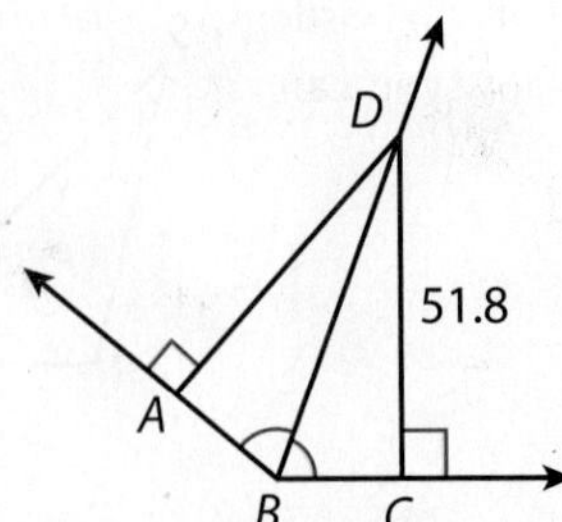

5. $m\angle HFJ$, given that $m\angle GFJ = 45°$

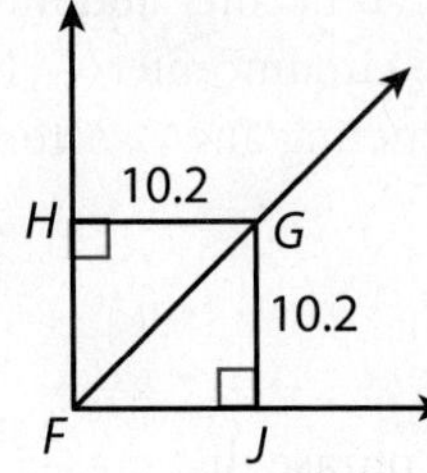

Copy each triangle. Then construct an inscribed circle for each triangle.

6.

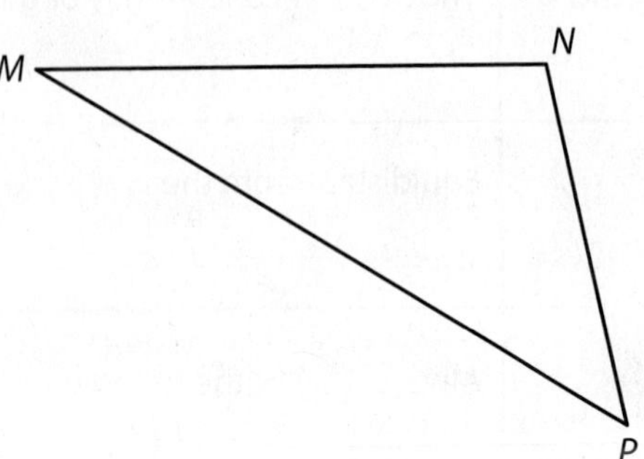

7.

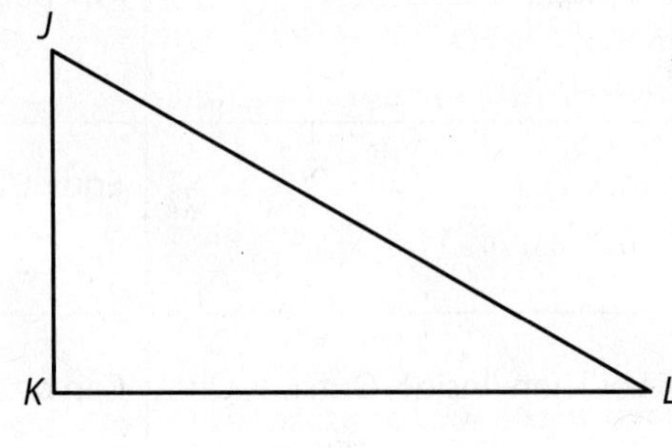

$\overline{CF}$ and $\overline{EF}$ are angle bisectors of $\triangle CDE$. Find each measure.

8. the distance from F to $\overline{CD}$

9. $m\angle FED$

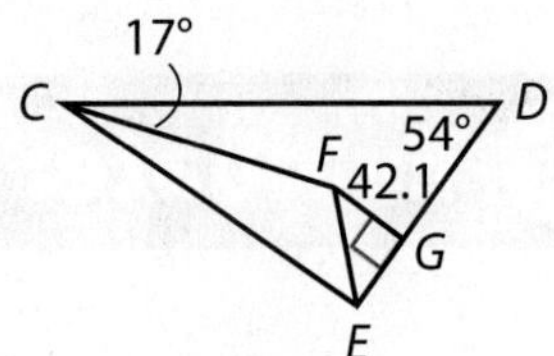

$\overline{TJ}$ and $\overline{SJ}$ are angle bisectors of $\triangle RST$. Find each measure.

10. the distance from J to $\overline{RS}$

11. $m\angle RTJ$

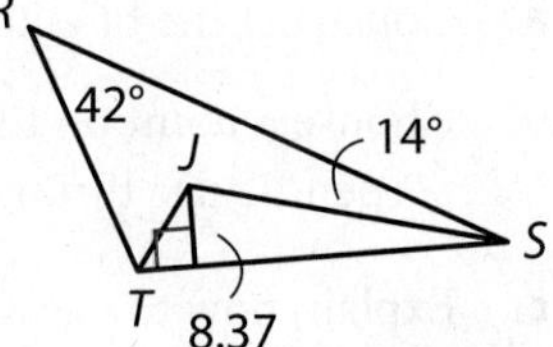

Find each measure.

12. BC

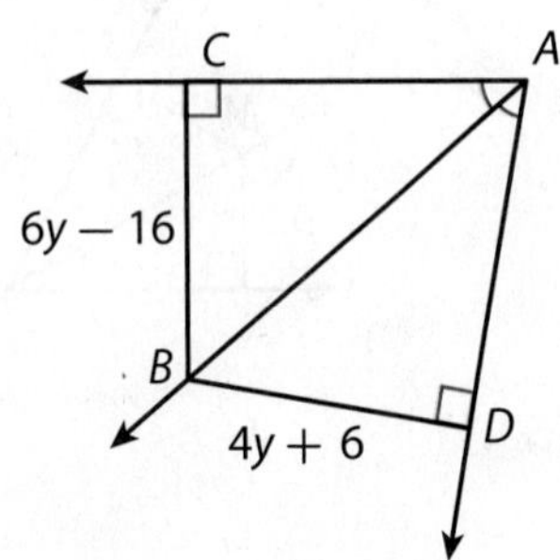

13. VY

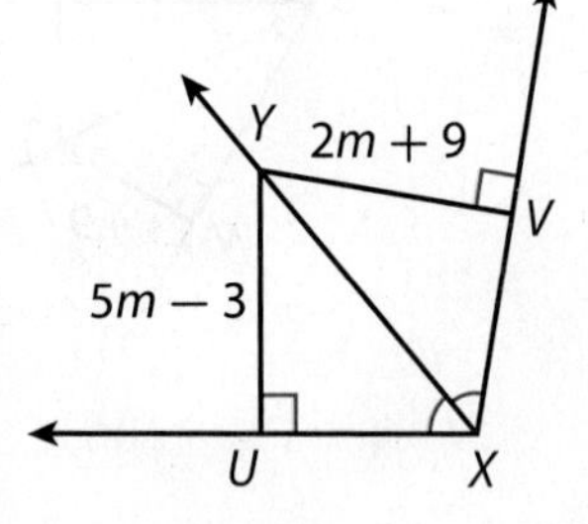

14. $m\angle JKL$

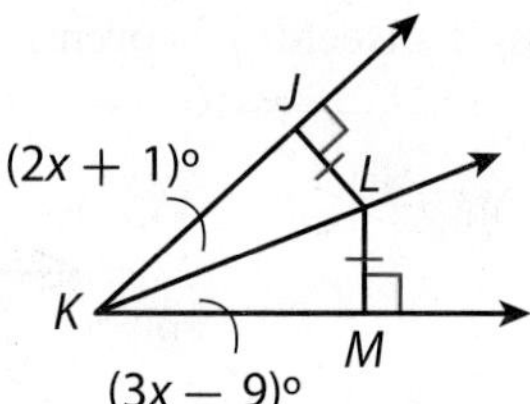

15. $m\angle GDF$

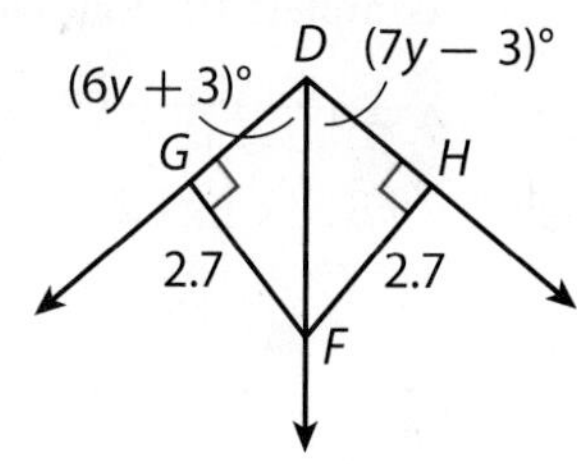

16. Copy and complete the following proof of the Angle Bisector Theorem.

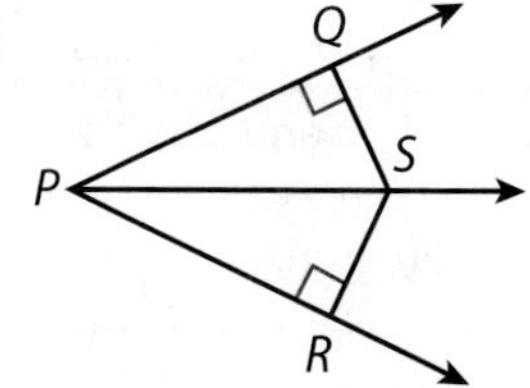

Given: $\overrightarrow{PS}$ bisects $\angle QPR$.

$\overline{SQ} \perp \overrightarrow{PQ}$, $\overline{SR} \perp \overrightarrow{PR}$

Prove: $SQ = SR$

Statements	Reasons
1. $\overrightarrow{PS}$ bisects $\angle QPR$. $\overline{SQ} \perp \overrightarrow{PQ}$, $\overline{SR} \perp \overrightarrow{PR}$	1.
2. $\angle QPS \cong \angle RPS$	2.
3. $\angle SQP$ and $\angle SRP$ are right angles.	3. Definition of perpendicular
4. $\angle SQP \cong \angle SRP$	4. All right angles are congruent.
5.	5. Reflexive Property of Congruence
6.	6. AAS Triangle Congruence Theorem
7. $\overline{SQ} \cong \overline{SR}$	7.
8. $SQ = SR$	8. Congruent segments have the same length.

17. Copy and complete the following proof of the Converse of the Angle Bisector Theorem.

Given: $\overline{VX} \perp \overrightarrow{YX}$, $\overline{VZ} \perp \overrightarrow{YZ}$, $VX = VZ$.

Prove: $\overrightarrow{YV}$ bisects $\angle XYZ$.

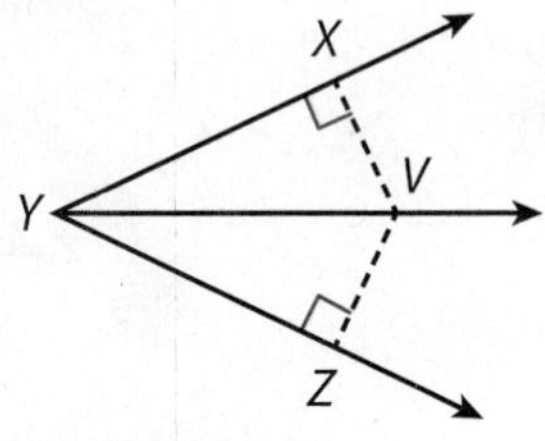

Statements	Reasons
1. $\overline{VX} \perp \overrightarrow{YX}$, $\overline{VZ} \perp \overrightarrow{YZ}$, $VX = VZ$	1.
2. $\angle VXY$ and $\angle VZY$ are right angles.	2.
3. $\overline{YV} \cong \overline{YV}$	3.
4. $\triangle YXV \cong \triangle YZV$	4.
5. $\angle XYV \cong \angle ZYV$	5.
6.	6.

18. Complete the following proof of the Incenter Theorem.

Given: $\overrightarrow{AP}$, $\overrightarrow{BP}$, and $\overrightarrow{CP}$ bisect $\angle A$, $\angle B$ and $\angle C$, respectively.
$\overline{PX} \perp \overline{AC}$, $\overline{PY} \perp \overline{AB}$, $\overline{PZ} \perp \overline{BC}$

Prove: $PX = PY = PZ$

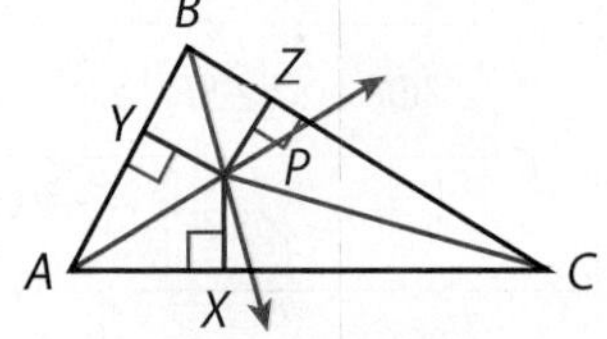

Let P be the incenter of $\triangle ABC$. Since P lies on the bisector of $\angle A$, $PX = PY$ by the Angle Bisector Theorem. Similarly, P also lies on the bisector of $\angle B$, so $PY = PZ$. Therefore, $PX = PY = PZ$, by the Transitive Property of Equality.

19. A city plans to build a firefighter's monument in a triangular park between three streets. Copy the figure. Then draw a sketch on the figure to show where the city should place the monument so that it is the same distance from all three streets. Justify your sketch.

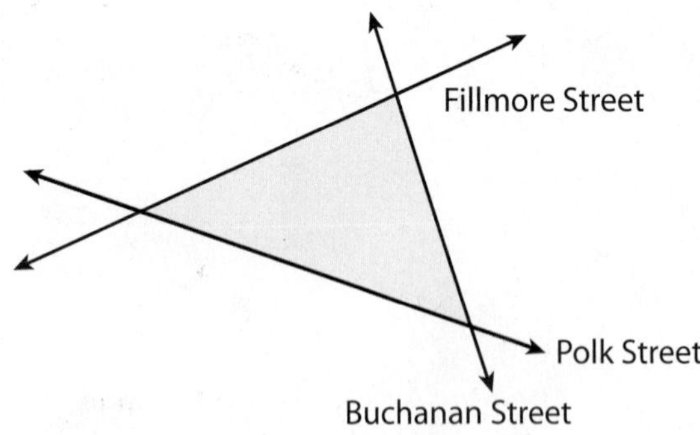

20. A school plans to place a flagpole on the lawn so that it is equidistant from Mercer Street and Houston Street. They also want the flagpole to be equidistant from a water fountain at W and a bench at B. Copy the figure. Then find the point F where the school should place the flagpole. Mark the point on the figure and explain your answer.

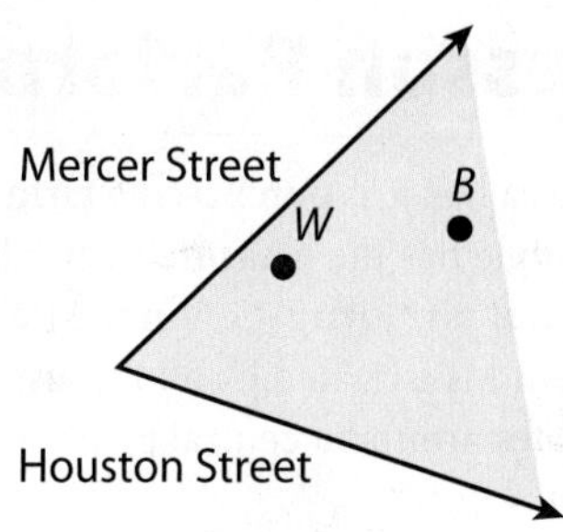

21. P is the incenter of $\triangle ABC$. Determine whether each statement is true or false.

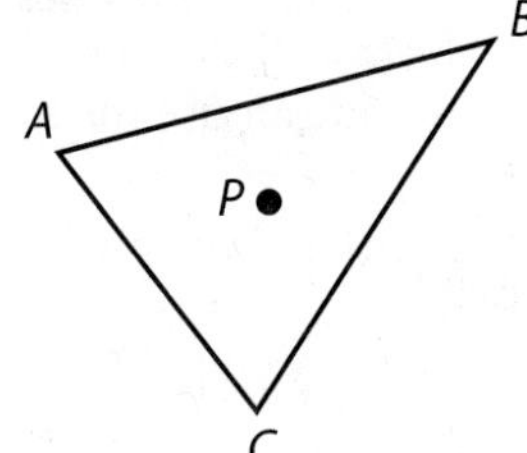

a. Point P must lie on the perpendicular bisector of $\overline{BC}$.

b. Point P must lie on the angle bisector of $\angle C$.

c. If AP is 23 mm long, then CP must be 23 mm long.

d. If the distance from point P to $\overline{AB}$ is x, then the distance from point P to $\overline{BC}$ must be x.

e. The perpendicular segment from point P to $\overline{AC}$ is longer than the perpendicular segment from point P to $\overline{BC}$.

H.O.T. Focus on Higher Order Thinking

22. **What If?** In the Explore, you constructed the angle bisector of acute $\angle ABC$ and found that if a point is on the bisector, then it is equidistant from the sides of the angle. Would you get the same results if $\angle ABC$ were a straight angle? Explain.

23. **Explain the Error** A student was asked to draw the incircle for $\triangle PQR$. He constructed angle bisectors as shown. Then he drew a circle through points J, K, and L. Describe the student's error.

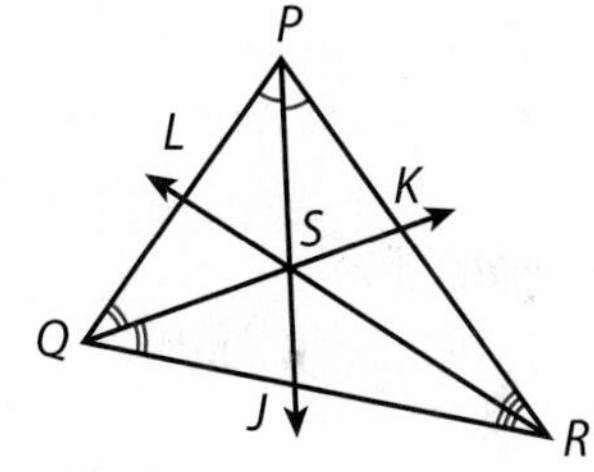

Lesson Performance Task

Teresa has just purchased a farm with a field shaped like a right triangle. The triangle has the measurements shown in the diagram. Teresa plans to install central pivot irrigation in the field. In this type of irrigation, a circular region of land is irrigated by a long arm of sprinklers—the radius of the circle—that rotates around a central pivot point like the hands of a clock, dispensing water as it moves.

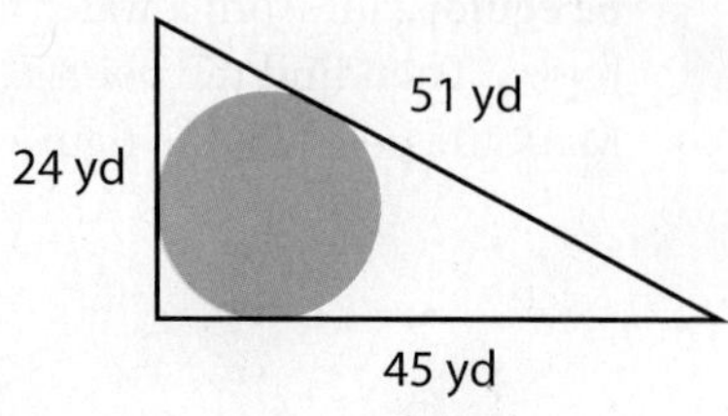

a. Describe how she can find where to locate the pivot.

b. Find the area of the irrigation circle. To find the radius, r, of a circle inscribed in a triangle with sides of length a, b, and c,

you can use the formula $r = \frac{\sqrt{k(k-a)(k-b)(k-c)}}{k}$, where $k = \frac{1}{2}(a+b+c)$.

c. About how much of the field that *not* be irrigated?

15.6 Properties of Parallelograms

Resource Locker

Essential Question: **What can you conclude about the sides, angles, and diagonals of a parallelogram?**

Explore Investigating Parallelograms

A **quadrilateral** is a polygon with four sides. A **parallelogram** is a quadrilateral that has two pairs of parallel sides. You can use geometry software to investigate properties of parallelograms.

(A) Draw a straight line. Then plot a point that is not on the line. Construct a line through the point that is parallel to the line. This gives you a pair of parallel lines.

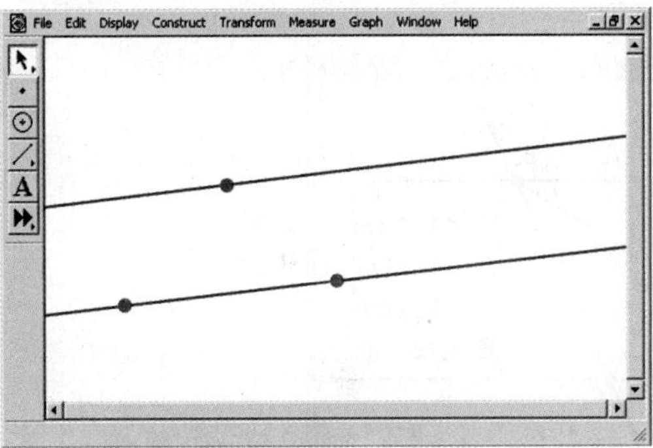

(B) Repeat Step A to construct a second pair of parallel lines that intersect those from Step A.

(C) The intersections of the parallel lines create a parallelogram. Plot points at these intersections. Label the points A, B, C, and D.

Identify the *opposite sides* and *opposite angles* of the parallelogram.

Opposite sides: 

Opposite angles:

(D) Measure each angle of the parallelogram.

Measure the length of each side of the parallelogram. You can do this by measuring the distance between consecutive vertices.

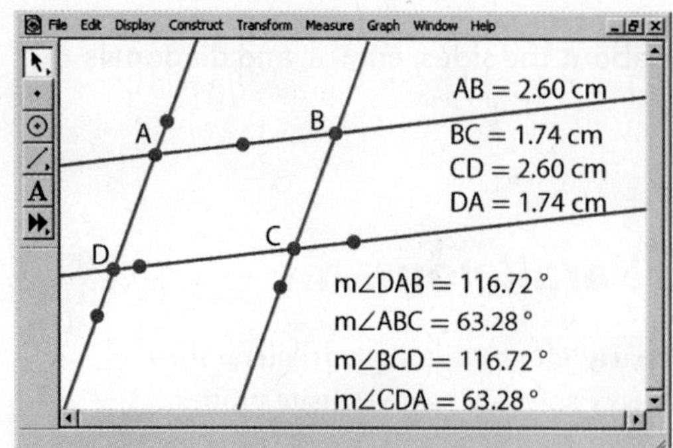

(E) Then drag the points and lines in your construction to change the shape of the parallelogram. As you do so, look for relationships in the measurements. Make a conjecture about the sides and angles of a parallelogram.

Conjecture:

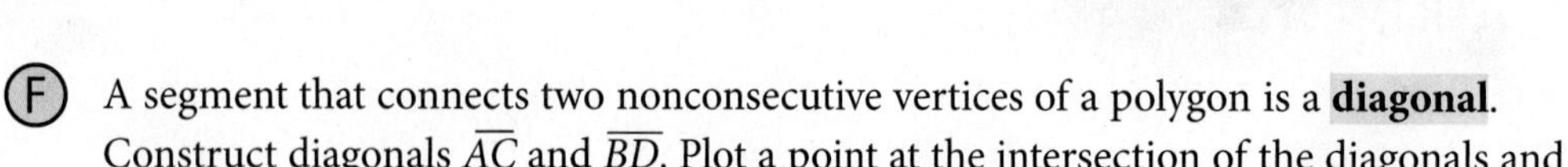

(F) A segment that connects two nonconsecutive vertices of a polygon is a **diagonal**. Construct diagonals $\overline{AC}$ and $\overline{BD}$. Plot a point at the intersection of the diagonals and label it *E*.

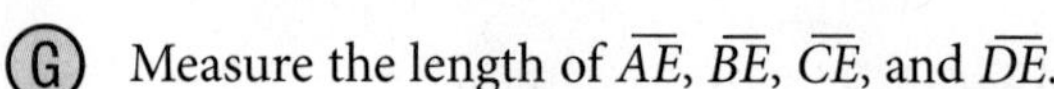

(G) Measure the length of $\overline{AE}$, $\overline{BE}$, $\overline{CE}$, and $\overline{DE}$.

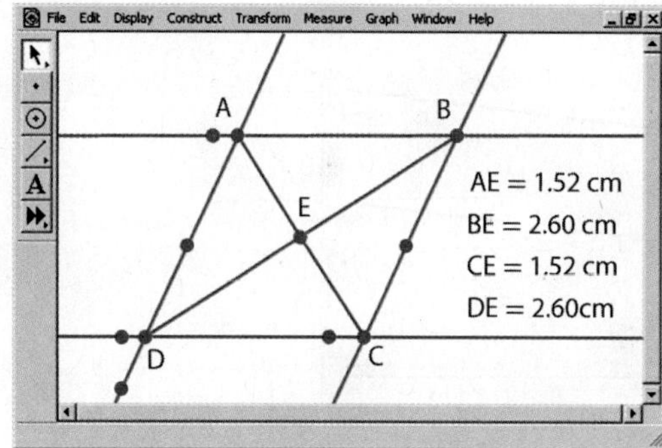

(H) Drag the points and lines in your construction to change the shape of the parallelogram. As you do so, look for relationships in the measurements in Step G. Make a conjecture about the diagonals of a parallelogram.

Conjecture:

Reflect

1. *Consecutive angles* are the angles at consecutive vertices, such as $\angle A$ and $\angle B$, or $\angle A$ and $\angle D$. Use your construction to make a conjecture about consecutive angles of a parallelogram.

   Conjecture:

2. **Critique Reasoning** A student claims that the perimeter of $\triangle AEB$ in the construction is always equal to the perimeter of $\triangle CED$. Without doing any further measurements in your construction, explain whether or not you agree with the student's statement.

Explain 1 Proving Opposite Sides Are Congruent

The conjecture you made in the Explore about opposite sides of a parallelogram can be stated as a theorem. The proof involves drawing an *auxiliary line* in the figure.

Theorem
If a quadrilateral is a parallelogram, then its opposite sides are congruent.

Example 1 **Prove that the opposite sides of a parallelogram are congruent.**

Given: *ABCD* is a parallelogram.

Prove: $\overline{AB} \cong \overline{CD}$ and $\overline{AD} \cong \overline{CB}$

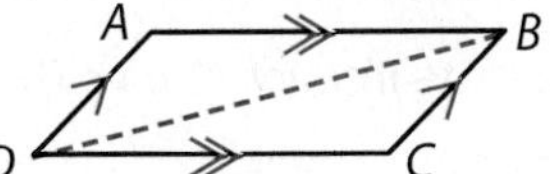

Statements	Reasons
1. *ABCD* is a parallelogram.	1. Given
2. Draw $\overline{DB}$.	2. Through any two points, there is exactly one line.
3. $\overline{AB} \parallel \overline{DC}$, $\overline{AD} \parallel \overline{BC}$	3. Definition of parallelogram
4. $\angle ADB \cong \angle CBD$ $\angle ABD \cong \angle CDB$	4. Alternate Interior Angles Theorem
5. $\overline{DB} \cong \overline{DB}$	5. Reflexive Property of Congruence
6. $\triangle ABD \cong \triangle CDB$	6. ASA Triangle Congruence Theorem
7. $\overline{AB} \cong \overline{CD}$ and $\overline{AD} \cong \overline{CB}$	7. CPCTC

Reflect

3. Explain how you can use the rotational symmetry of a parallelogram to give an argument that supports the above theorem.

Explain 2 Proving Opposite Angles Are Congruent

The conjecture from the Explore about opposite angles of a parallelogram can also be proven and stated as a theorem.

Theorem

If a quadrilateral is a parallelogram, then its opposite angles are congruent.

Example 2 **Prove that the opposite angles of a parallelogram are congruent.**

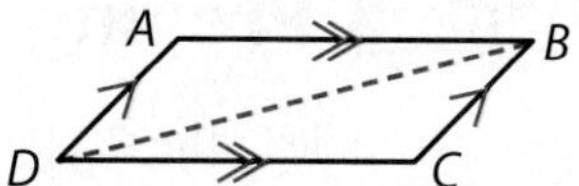

Given: *ABCD* is a parallelogram.

Prove: $\angle A \cong \angle C$ (A similar proof shows that $\angle B \cong \angle D$.)

Statements	Reasons
1. *ABCD* is a parallelogram.	1. Given
2. Draw $\overline{DB}$.	2. Through any two points, there is exactly one line
3. $\overline{AB} \parallel \overline{DC}$, $\overline{AD} \parallel \overline{BC}$	3. Definition of parallelogram
4. $\angle ADB \cong \angle CBD$, $\angle ABD \cong \angle CDB$	4. Alternate Interior Angles Theorem
5. $\overline{DB} \cong \overline{DB}$	5. Reflexive Property of Congruence
6. $\triangle ABD \cong \triangle CDB$	6. ASA Triangle Congruence Theorem
7. $\angle A \cong \angle C$	7. CPCTC

Reflect

4. Explain how the proof would change in order to prove $\angle B \cong \angle D$.

5. In Reflect 1, you noticed that the consecutive angles of a parallelogram are supplementary. This can be stated as the theorem, *If a quadrilateral is a parallelogram, then its consecutive angles are supplementary.* Explain why this theorem is true.

Explain 3 Proving Diagonals Bisect Each Other

The conjecture from the Explore about diagonals of a parallelogram can also be proven and stated as a theorem. One proof is shown on the facing page.

Theorem

If a quadrilateral is a parallelogram, then its diagonals bisect each other.

Example 3 **Complete the flow proof that the diagonals of a parallelogram bisect each other.**

Given: $ABCD$ is a parallelogram.

Prove: $\overline{AE} \cong \overline{CE}$ and $\overline{BE} \cong \overline{DE}$

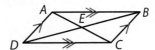

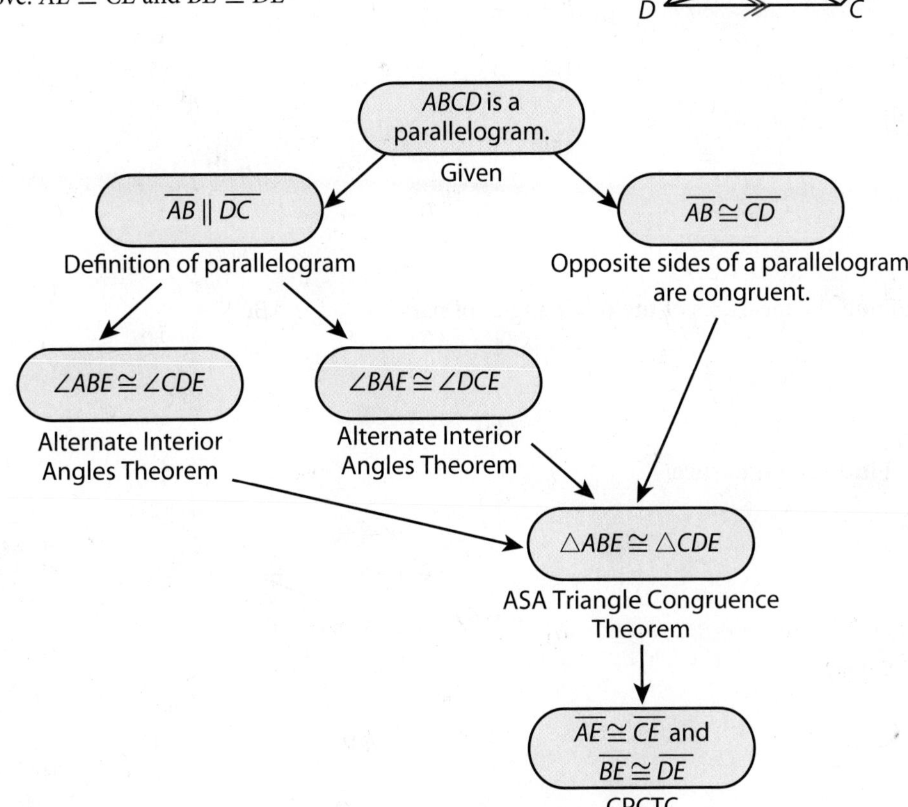

ABCD is a parallelogram.
Given
AB || DC
Definition of parallelogram
AB ≅ CD
Opposite sides of a parallelogram are congruent.
∠ABE ≅ ∠CDE
Alternate Interior Angles Theorem
∠BAE ≅ ∠DCE
Alternate Interior Angles Theorem
△ABE ≅ △CDE
ASA Triangle Congruence Theorem
AE ≅ CE and BE ≅ DE
CPCTC

Reflect

6. **Discussion** Is it possible to prove the theorem using a different triangle congruence theorem? Explain.

Explain 4 Using Properties of Parallelograms

You can use the properties of parallelograms to find unknown lengths or angle measures in a figure.

Example 4 ***ABCD* is a parallelogram. Find each measure.**

 AD

Use the fact that opposite sides of a parallelogram are congruent, so $\overline{AD} \cong \overline{CB}$ and therefore $AD = CB$.

Write an equation. $7x = 5x + 19$

Solve for x. $x = 9.5$

$AD = 7x = 7(9.5) = 66.5$

Ⓑ m∠B

Use the fact that opposite angles of a parallelogram are congruent,

so $\angle B \cong \angle$ D and therefore $m\angle B = m\angle$ D .

Write an equation. $6y + 5 = 8y - 17$

Solve for y. $11 = y$

$$m\angle B = (6y + 5)^\circ = \left(6\left(11\right) + 5\right)^\circ = 71^\circ$$

Reflect

7. Suppose you wanted to find the measures of the other angles of parallelogram *ABCD*. Explain your steps.

Your Turn

***PQRS* is a parallelogram. Find each measure.**

8. *QR*

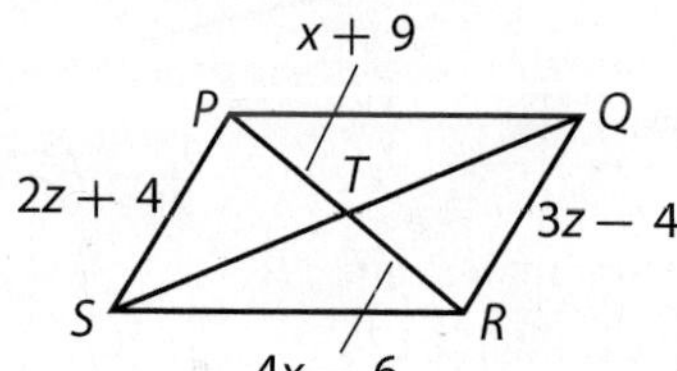

9. *PR*

Elaborate

10. What do you need to know first in order to apply any of the theorems of this lesson?

11. In parallelogram *ABCD*, point *P* lies on $\overline{DC}$, as shown in the figure. Explain why it must be the case that $DC = 2AD$. Use what you know about base angles of an isosceles triangle.

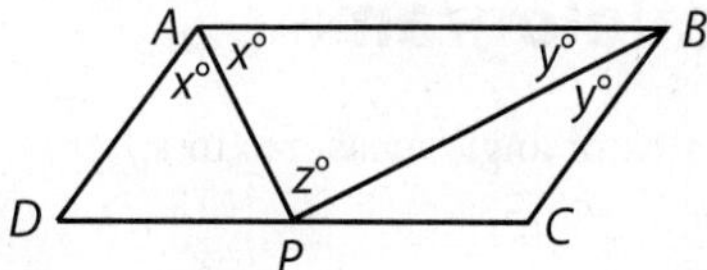

12. Essential Question Check-In *JKLM* is a parallelogram. Name all of the congruent segments and angles in the figure.

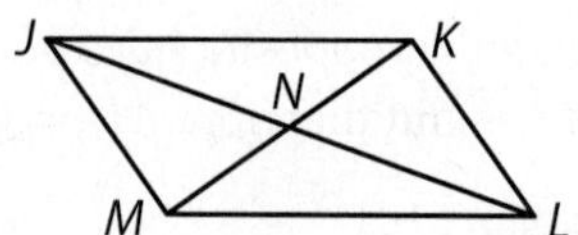

Evaluate: Homework and Practice

- Online Homework
- Hints and Help
- Extra Practice

1. Pablo traced along both edges of a ruler to draw two pairs of parallel lines, as shown. Explain the next steps he could take in order to make a conjecture about the diagonals of a parallelogram.

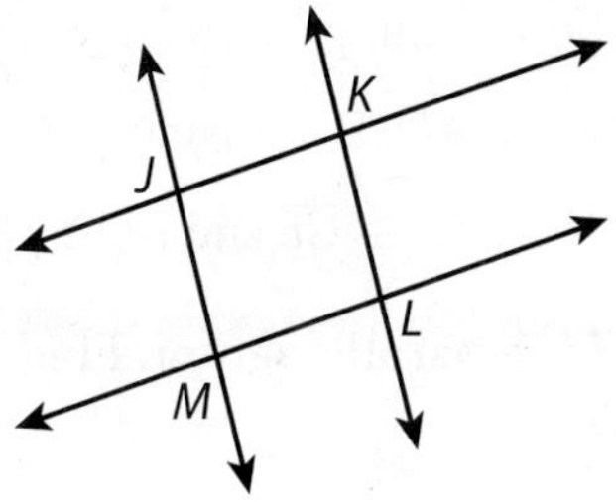

2. Sabina has tiles in the shape of a parallelogram. She labels the angles of each tile as $\angle A$, $\angle B$, $\angle C$, and $\angle D$. Then she arranges the tiles to make the pattern shown here and uses the pattern to make a conjecture about opposite angles of a parallelogram. What conjecture does she make? How does the pattern help her make the conjecture?

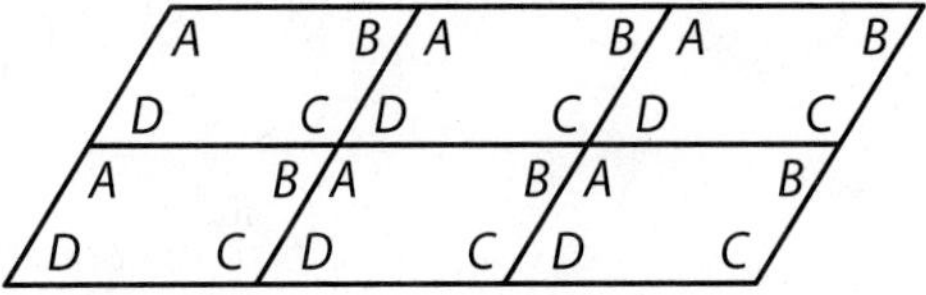

3. Copy the diagram. Then complete the flow proof that the opposite sides of a parallelogram are congruent.
Given: *ABCD* is a parallelogram.
Prove: $\overline{AB} \cong \overline{CD}$ and $\overline{AD} \cong \overline{CB}$

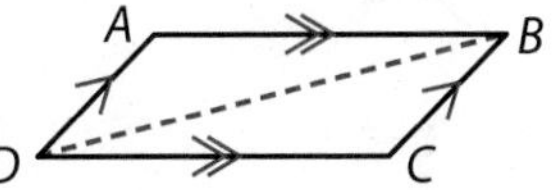

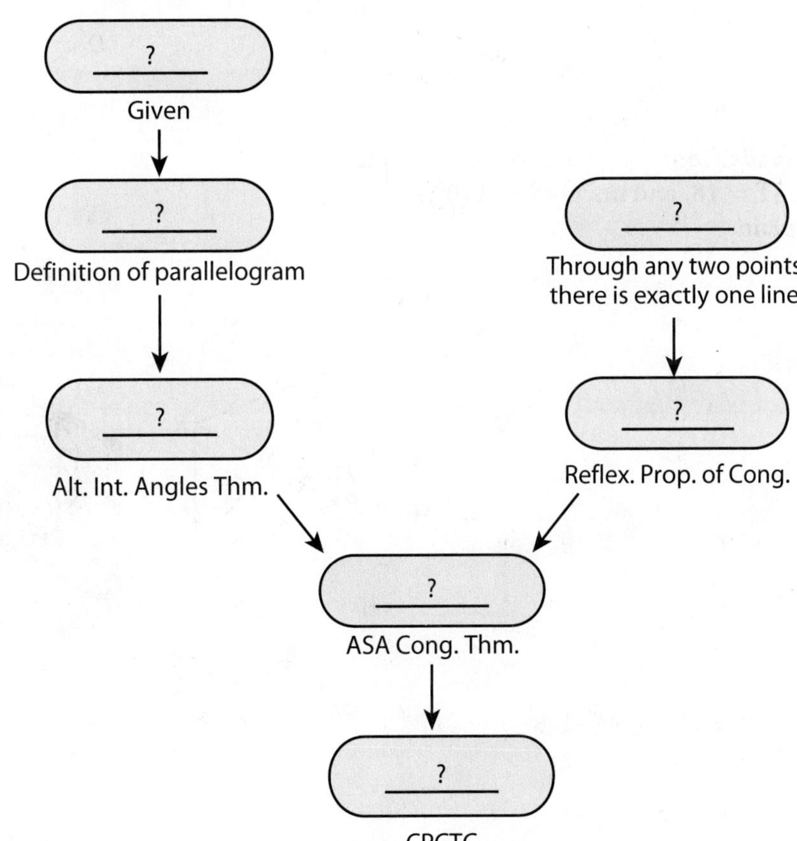

4. Write the proof that the opposite angles of a parallelogram are congruent as a paragraph proof.

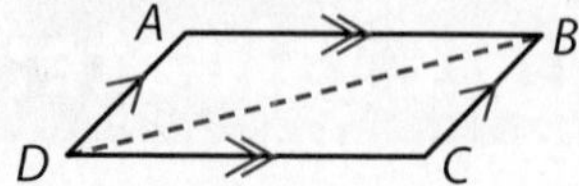

Given: *ABCD* is a parallelogram.

Prove: $\angle A \cong \angle C$ (A similar proof shows that $\angle B \cong \angle D$.)

5. Write the proof that the diagonals of a parallelogram bisect each other as a two-column proof.

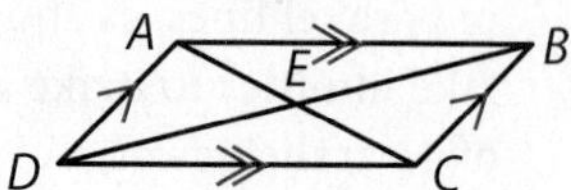

Given: *ABCD* is a parallelogram.

Prove: $\overline{AE} \cong \overline{CE}$ and $\overline{BE} \cong \overline{DE}$

***EFGH* is a parallelogram. Find each measure.**

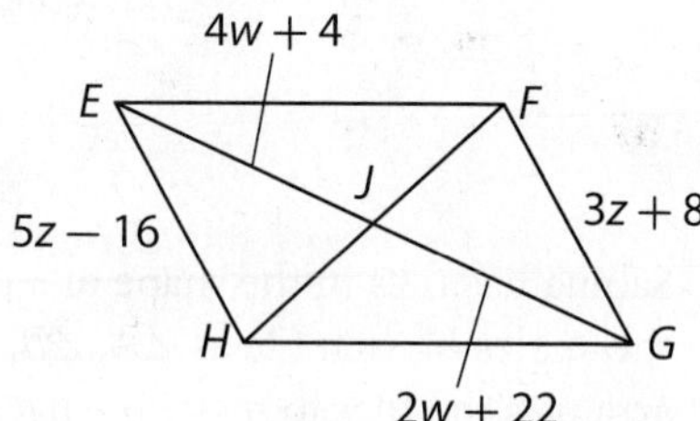

6. *FG*

7. *EG*

***ABCD* is a parallelogram. Find each measure.**

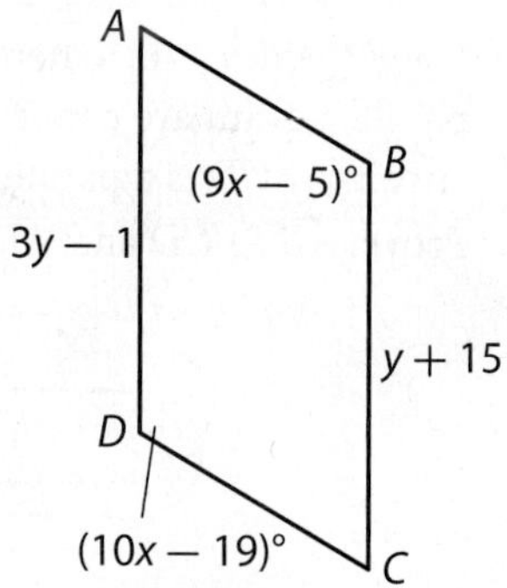

8. $m\angle B$

9. *AD*

A staircase handrail is made from congruent parallelograms.
In $\square PQRS$, $PQ = 17.5$, $ST = 18$, and $m\angle QRS = 110°$.
Find each measure. Explain.

10. *RS*

11. *QT*

12. $m\angle PQR$

13. $m\angle SPQ$

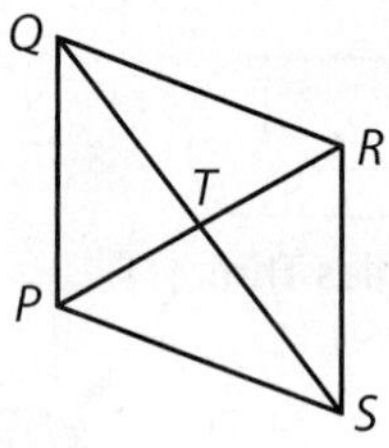

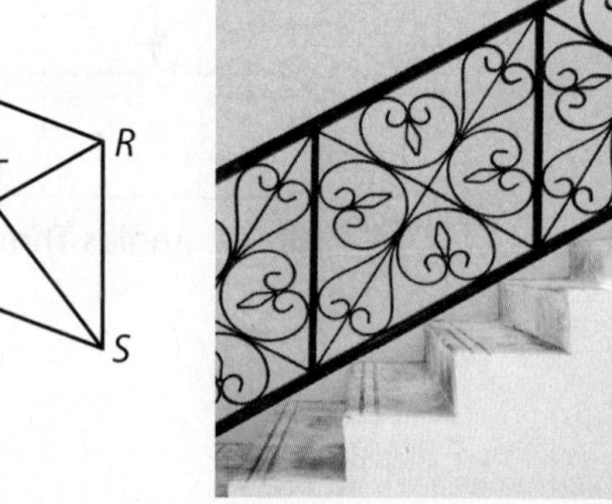

Write each proof as a two-column proof.

14. Given: *GHJN* and *JKLM* are parallelograms.
Prove: $\angle G \cong \angle L$

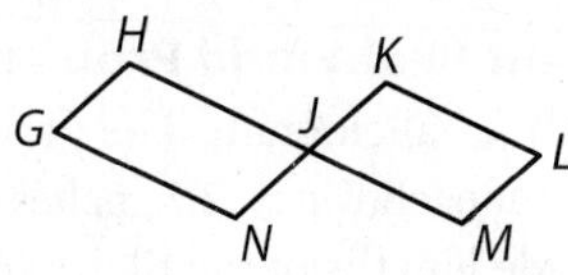

15. Given: *PSTV* is a parallelogram. $\overline{PQ} \cong \overline{RQ}$
Prove: $\angle STV \cong \angle R$

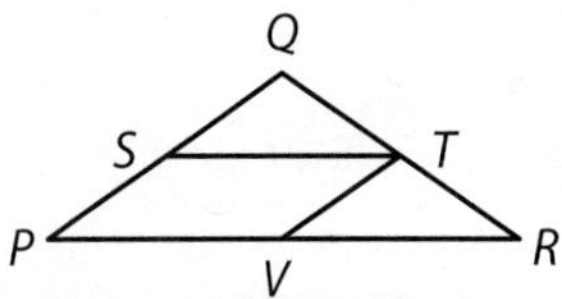

16. Given: *ABCD* and *AFGH* are parallelograms.
Prove: $\angle C \cong \angle G$

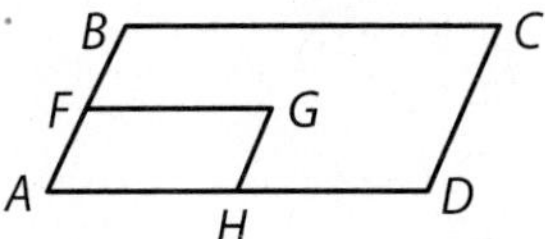

Justify Reasoning **Determine whether each statement is always, sometimes, or never true. Explain your reasoning.**

17. If quadrilateral *RSTU* is a parallelogram, then $\overline{RS} \cong \overline{ST}$.

18. If a parallelogram has a 30° angle, then it also has a 150° angle.

19. If quadrilateral *GHJK* is a parallelogram, then $\overline{GH}$ is congruent to $\overline{JK}$.

20. In parallelogram *ABCD*, $\angle A$ is acute and $\angle C$ is obtuse.

21. In parallelogram *MNPQ*, the diagonals $\overline{MP}$ and $\overline{NQ}$ meet at *R* with $MR = 7$ cm and $RP = 5$ cm.

22. **Communicate Mathematical Ideas** Explain how you can use the rotational symmetry of a parallelogram to give an argument that supports the fact that opposite angles of a parallelogram are congruent.

23. To repair a large truck or bus, a mechanic might use a parallelogram lift. The figure shows a side view of the lift. *FGKL*, *GHJK*, and *FHJL* are parallelograms.

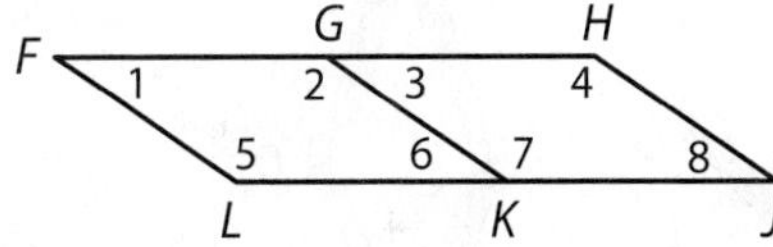

a. Which angles are congruent to $\angle 1$? Explain.

b. What is the relationship between $\angle 1$ and each of the remaining labeled angles? Explain.

24. **Justify Reasoning** *ABCD* is a parallelogram. Determine whether each statement must be true. Explain your reasoning.

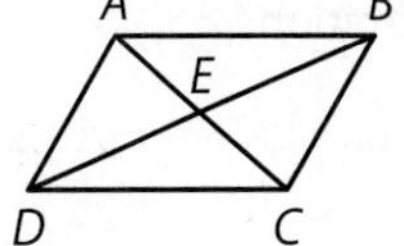

A. The perimeter of *ABCD* is $2AB + 2BC$.

B. $DE = \frac{1}{2}DB$

C. $\overline{BC} \cong \overline{DC}$

D. $\angle DAC \cong \angle BCA$

E. $\triangle AED \cong \triangle CEB$

F. $\angle DAC \cong \angle BAC$

H.O.T. Focus on Higher Order Thinking

25. Represent Real-World Problems A store sells tiles in the shape of a parallelogram. The perimeter of each tile is 29 inches. One side of each tile is 2.5 inches longer than another side. What are the side lengths of the tile? Explain your steps.

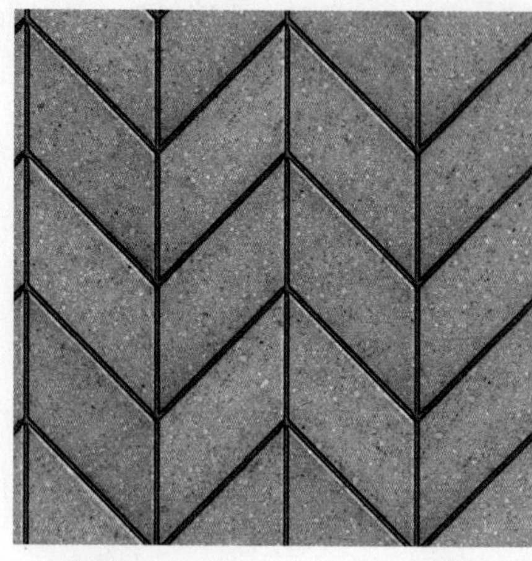

26. Critique Reasoning A student claims that there is an SSSS congruence criterion for parallelograms. That is, if all four sides of one parallelogram are congruent to the four sides of another parallelogram, then the parallelograms are congruent. Do you agree? If so, explain why. If not, give a counterexample. Hint: Draw a picture.

27. Analyze Relationships The figure shows two congruent parallelograms. How are x and y related? Write an equation that expresses the relationship. Explain your reasoning.

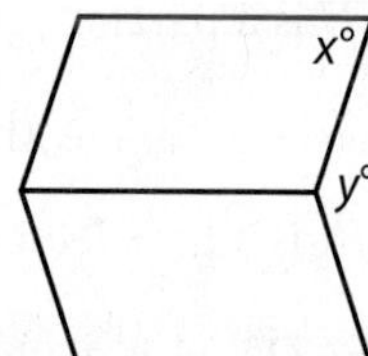

Lesson Performance Task

The principle that allows a scissor lift to raise the platform on top of it to a considerable height can be illustrated with four freezer pop sticks attached at the corners.

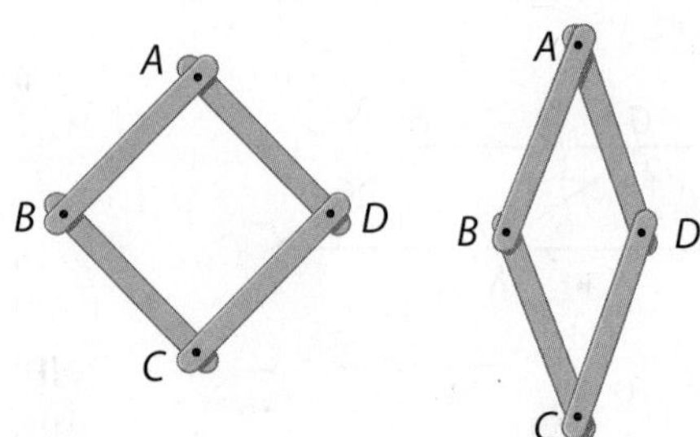

Answer these questions about what happens to parallelogram *ABCD* when you change its shape as in the illustration.

a. Is it still a parallelogram? Explain.

b. Is its area the same? Explain.

c. Compare the lengths of the diagonals in the two figures as you change them.

d. Describe a process that might be used to raise the platform on a scissor lift.

15.7 Conditions for Rectangles, Rhombuses, and Squares

Resource Locker

Essential Question: How can you use given conditions to show that a quadrilateral is a rectangle, a rhombus, or a square?

Explore Properties of Rectangles, Rhombuses, and Squares

In this lesson we will start with given properties and use them to prove which special parallelogram it could be.

(A) Start by drawing two line segments of the same length that bisect each other but are not perpendicular. They will form an X shape, as shown.

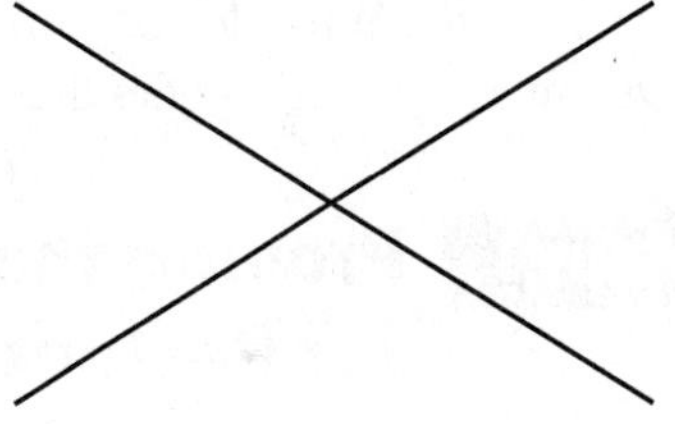

(B) Connect the ends of the line segments to form a quadrilateral.

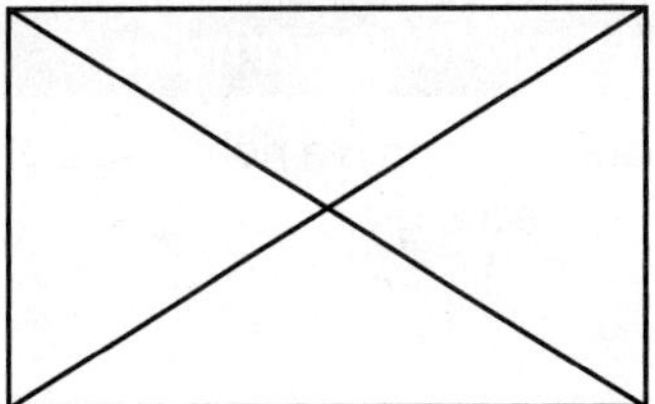

(C) Measure each of the four angles of the quadrilateral, and use those measurements to name the shape.

Ⓓ Now, draw two line segments that are perpendicular and bisect each other but that are not the same length.

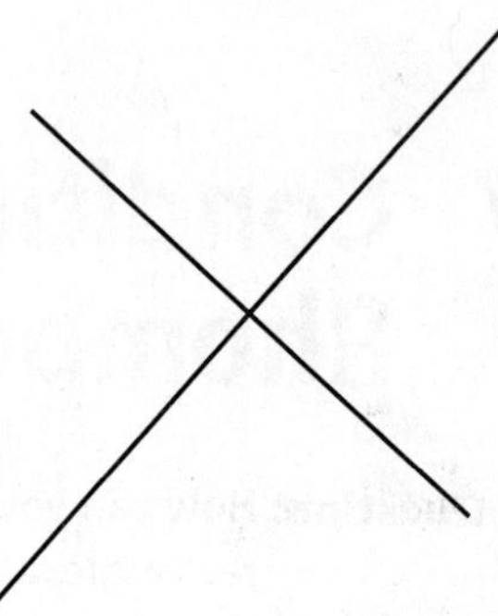

Ⓔ Connect the ends of the line segments to form a quadrilateral.

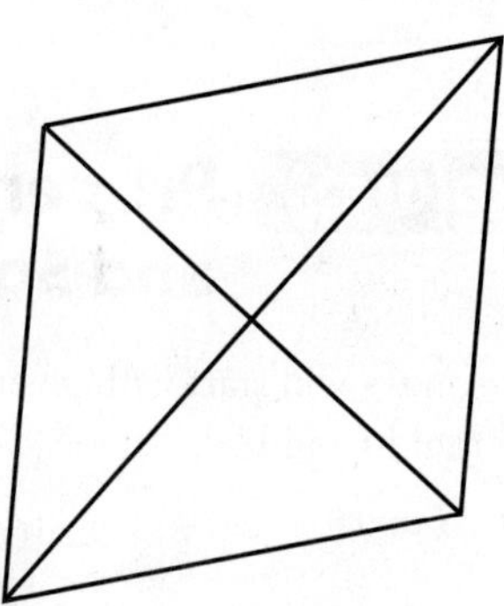

Ⓕ Measure each side length of the quadrilateral. Then use those measurements to name the shape.

Reflect

1. **Discussion** How are the diagonals of your rectangle in Step B different from the diagonals of your rhombus in Step E?

2. Draw a line segment. At each endpoint draw line segments so that four congruent angles are formed as shown. Then extend the segments so that they intersect to form a quadrilateral. Measure the sides. What do you notice? What kind of quadrilateral is it? How does the line segment relate to the angles drawn on either end of it?

Explain 1 Proving that Congruent Diagonals Is a Condition for Rectangles

When you are given a parallelogram with certain properties, you can use the properties to determine whether the parallelogram is a rectangle.

Theorems: Conditions for Rectangles	
If one angle of a parallelogram is a right angle, then the parallelogram is a rectangle.	B C A D
If the diagonals of a parallelogram are congruent, then the parallelogram is a rectangle.	B C A D $\overline{AC} \cong \overline{BD}$

Example 1 **Prove that if the diagonals of a parallelogram are congruent, then the parallelogram is a rectangle.**

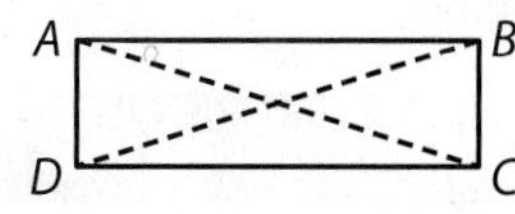

Given: $ABCD$ is a parallelogram; $\overline{AC} \cong \overline{BD}$.

Prove: $ABCD$ is a rectangle.

Because opposite sides of a parallelogram are congruent, $\overline{AB} \cong \overline{CD}$.

It is given that $\overline{AC} \cong \overline{BD}$, and $\overline{AD} \cong \overline{AD}$ by the Reflexive Property of Congruence.

So, $\triangle ABD \cong \triangle DCA$ by the SSS Triangle Congruence Theorem, and

$\angle BAD \cong \angle CDA$ by CPCTC. But these angles are supplementary

since $\overline{AB} \parallel$ $\overline{DC}$. Therefore, $m\angle BAD + m\angle CDA =$ $180°$. So

$m\angle BAD +$ $m\angle BAD$ $=$ $180°$ by substitution, $2 \cdot m\angle BAD = 180°$,

and $m\angle BAD = 90°$. A similar argument shows that the other angles

of $ABCD$ are also right angles, so $ABCD$ is a rectangle.

Reflect

3. **Discussion** Explain why this is a true condition for rectangles: *If one angle of a parallelogram is a right angle, then the parallelogram is a rectangle.*

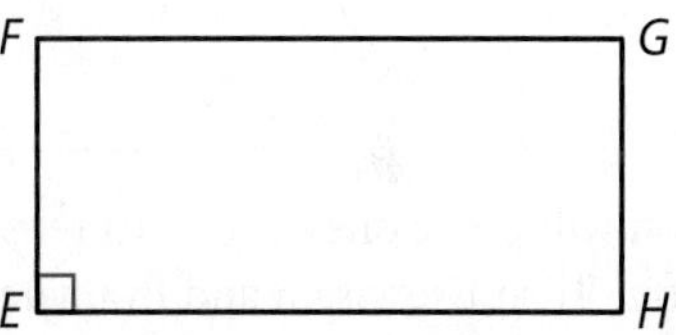

Your Turn

Use the given information to determine whether the quadrilateral is necessarily a rectangle. Explain your reasoning.

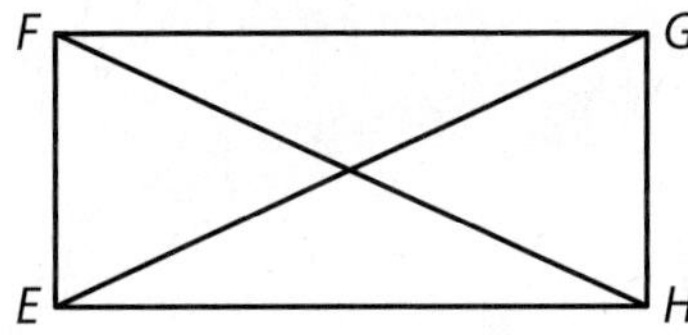

4. Given: $\overline{EF} \cong \overline{GF}$, $\overline{FG} \cong \overline{HE}$, $\overline{FH} \cong \overline{GE}$

5. Given: $m\angle FEG = 45°$, $m\angle GEH = 50°$

Explain 2 Proving Conditions for Rhombuses

You can also use given properties of a parallelogram to determine whether the parallelogram is a rhombus.

Theorems: Conditions for Rhombuses	
If one pair of consecutive sides of a parallelogram are congruent, then the parallelogram is a rhombus.	
If the diagonals of a parallelogram are perpendicular, then the parallelogram is a rhombus.	
If one diagonal of a parallelogram bisects a pair of opposite angles, then the parallelogram is a rhombus.	

You will prove one of the theorems about rhombuses in Example 2 and the other theorems in Your Turn Exercise 6 and Evaluate Exercise 22.

Example 2 **Complete the flow proof that if one diagonal of a parallelogram bisects a pair of opposite angles, then the parallelogram is a rhombus.**

Given: *ABCD* is a parallelogram; $\angle BCA \cong \angle DCA$; $\angle BAC \cong \angle DAC$

Prove: *ABCD* is a rhombus.

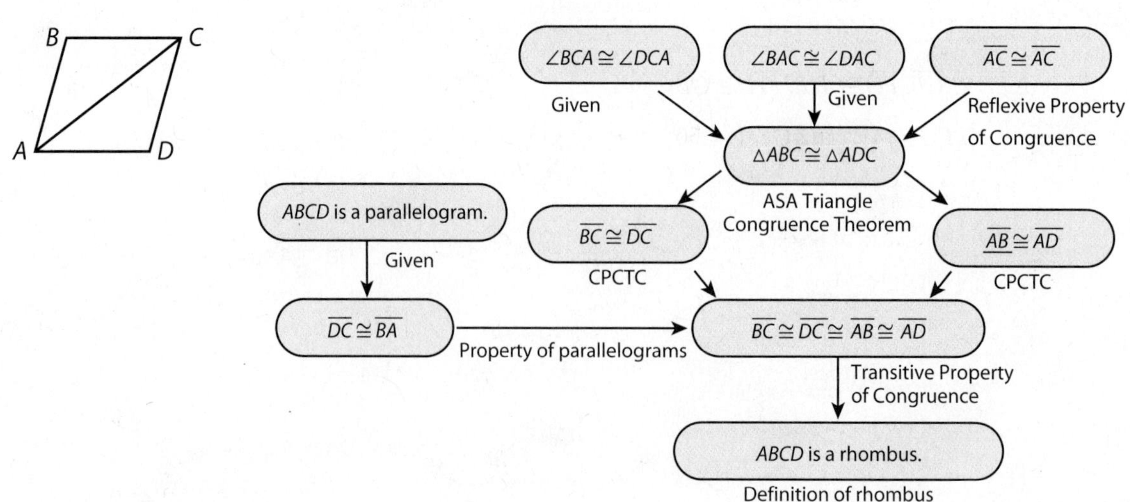

Your Turn

6. Prove that If one pair of consecutive sides of a parallelogram are congruent, then it is a rhombus.

Given: $JKLM$ is a parallelogram. $\overline{JK} \cong \overline{KL}$

Prove: $JKLM$ is a rhombus.

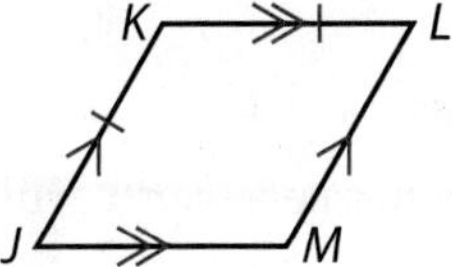

Explain 3 Applying Conditions for Special Parallelograms

In Example 3, you will decide whether you are given enough information to conclude that a figure is a particular type of special parallelogram.

Example 3 **Determine if the conclusion is valid. If not, tell what additional information is needed to make it valid.**

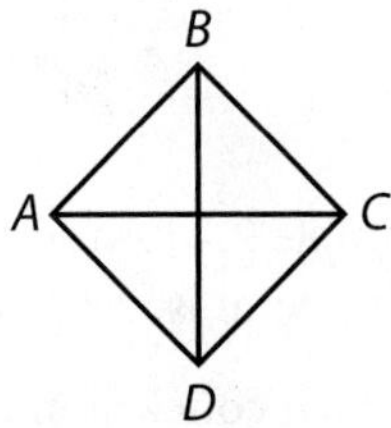

(A) **Given:** $\overline{AB} \cong \overline{CD}$; $\overline{BC} \cong \overline{DA}$; $\overline{AD} \perp \overline{DC}$; $\overline{AC} \perp \overline{BD}$

Conclusion: $ABCD$ is a square.

To prove that a given quadrilateral is a square, it is sufficient to show that the figure is both a rectangle and a rhombus.

Step 1: Determine if $ABCD$ is a parallelogram.

$\overline{AB} \cong \overline{CD}$ and $\overline{BC} \cong \overline{DA}$ are given. Since a quadrilateral with opposite sides congruent is a parallelogram, we know that $ABCD$ is a parallelogram.

Step 2: Determine if $ABCD$ is a rectangle.

Since $\overline{AD} \perp \overline{DC}$, by definition of perpendicular lines, $\angle ADC$ is a right angle. A parallelogram with one right angle is a rectangle, so $ABCD$ is a rectangle.

Step 3: Determine if $ABCD$ is a rhombus.

$\overline{AC} \perp \overline{BD}$. A parallelogram with perpendicular diagonals is a rhombus. So $ABCD$ is a rhombus.

Step 4: Determine if $ABCD$ is a square.

Since $ABCD$ is a rectangle and a rhombus, it has four right angles and four congruent sides. So $ABCD$ is a square by definition.

So, the conclusion is valid.

Ⓑ **Given:** $\overline{AB} \cong \overline{BC}$

Conclusion: *ABCD* is a rhombus.

The conclusion is not valid. It is true that if two consecutive sides of a parallelogram are congruent, then the parallelogram is a rhombus. To apply this theorem, however, you need to know that *ABCD* is a parallelogram. The given information is not sufficient to conclude that the figure is a parallelogram.

Reflect

7. Draw a figure that shows why this statement is not necessarily true: If one angle of a quadrilateral is a right angle, then the quadrilateral is a rectangle.

Your Turn

Determine if the conclusion is valid. If not, tell what additional information is needed to make it valid.

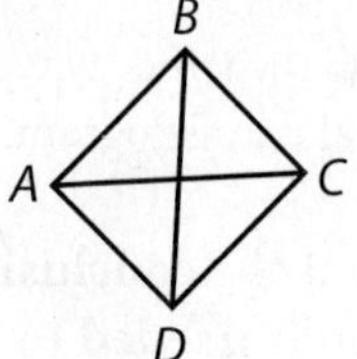

8. **Given:** ∠*ABC* is a right angle.

Conclusion: *ABCD* is a rectangle.

Elaborate

9. Look at the theorem boxes in Example 1 and Example 2. How do the diagrams help you remember the conditions for proving a quadrilateral is a special parallelogram?

10. *EFGH* is a parallelogram. In *EFGH*, $\overline{EG} \cong \overline{FH}$. Which conclusion is incorrect?

A. *EFGH* is a rectangle.

B. *EFGH* is a square.

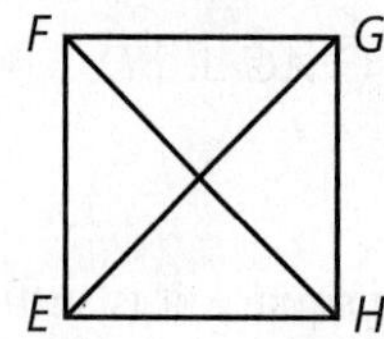

11. Essential Question Check-In How are theorems about conditions for parallelograms different from the theorems regarding parallelograms used in the previous lesson?

Evaluate: Homework and Practice

- Online Homework
- Hints and Help
- Extra Practice

1. Suppose Anna draws two line segments, $\overline{AB}$ and $\overline{CD}$ that intersect at point E. She draws them in such a way that $\overline{AB} \cong \overline{CD}$, $\overline{AB} \perp \overline{CD}$, and $\angle CAD$ is a right angle. What is the best name to describe $ACBD$? Explain.

2. Write a two-column proof that if the diagonals of a parallelogram are congruent, then the parallelogram is a rectangle.

Given: $EFGH$ is a parallelogram; $\overline{EG} \cong \overline{HF}$.

Prove: $EFGH$ is a rectangle.

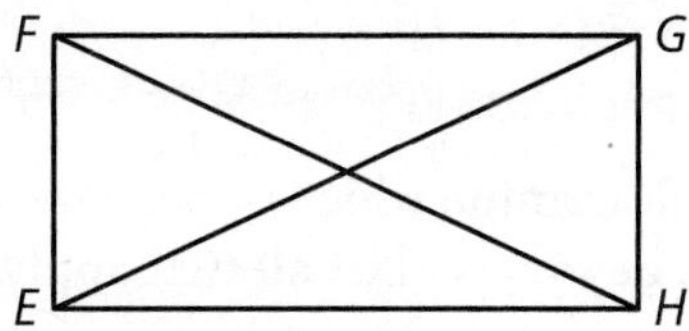

Determine whether each quadrilateral must be a rectangle. Explain.

3. 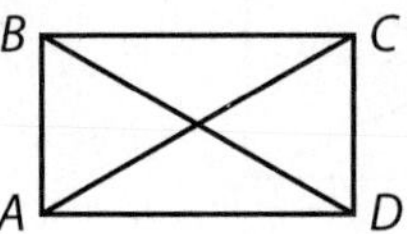

Given: $BD = AC$

4. 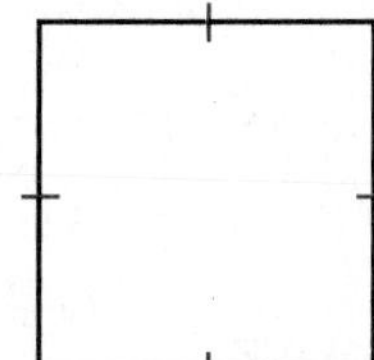

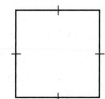

Each quadrilateral is a parallelogram. Determine whether each parallelogram is a rhombus or not.

5. 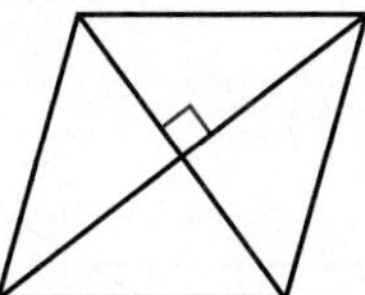

6. 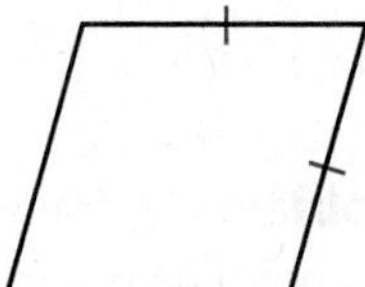

Give one characteristic about each figure that would make the conclusion valid.

7. Conclusion: $JKLM$ is a rhombus.

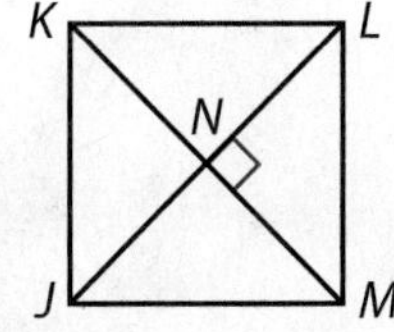

8. Conclusion: $PQRS$ is a square.

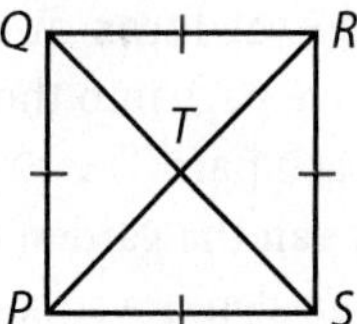

Determine if the conclusion is valid. If not, tell what additional information is needed to make it valid.

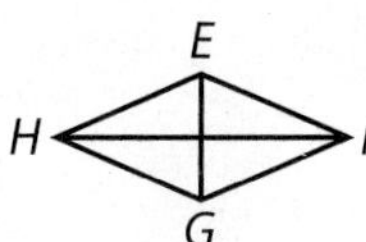

9. Given: $\overline{EG}$ and $\overline{FH}$ bisect each other. $\overline{EG} \perp \overline{FH}$

Conclusion: $EFGH$ is a rhombus.

10. $\overline{FH}$ bisects $\angle EFG$ and $\angle EHG$.

Conclusion: $EFGH$ is a rhombus.

Find the value of *x* that makes each parallelogram the given type.

11. square

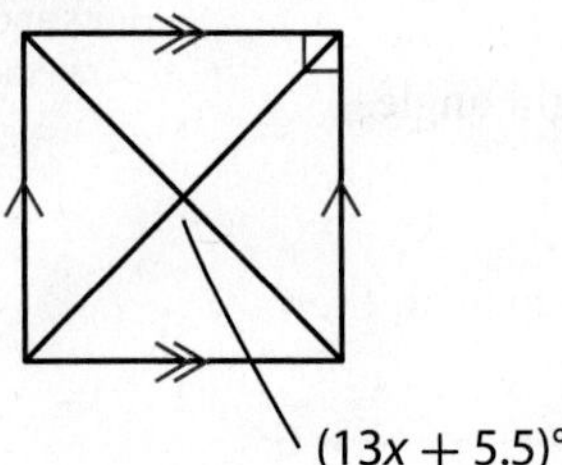

12. rhombus

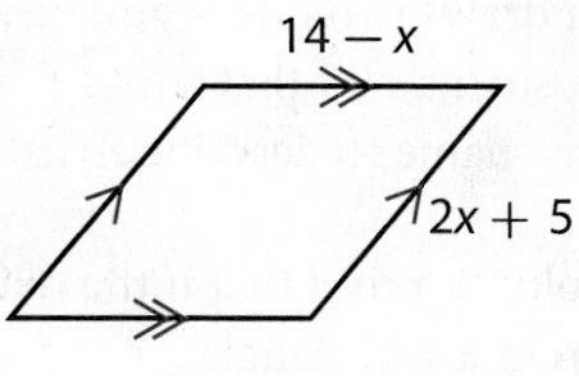

In Exercises 13–16, determine which quadrilaterals match the figure: parallelogram, rhombus, rectangle, or square. List all that apply.

13. Given: $\overline{WY} \cong \overline{XZ}$, $\overline{WY} \perp \overline{XZ}$, $\overline{XY} \cong \overline{ZW}$

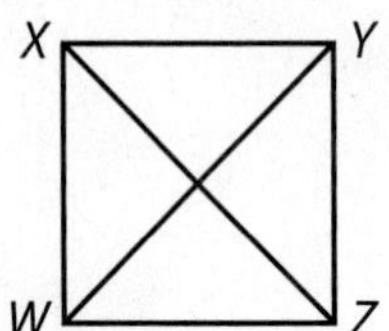

14. Given: $\overline{XY} \cong \overline{ZW}$, $\overline{WY} \cong \overline{ZX}$

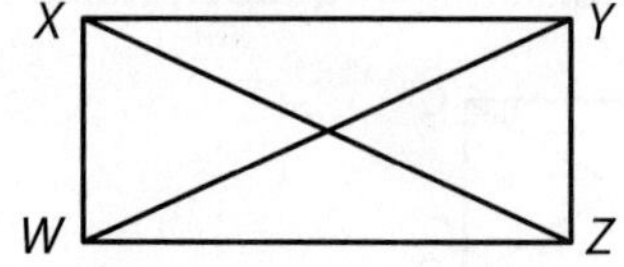

15. Given: $\overline{XY} \cong \overline{ZW}$, $\angle XWY \cong \angle YWZ$, $\angle XYW \cong \angle ZYW$

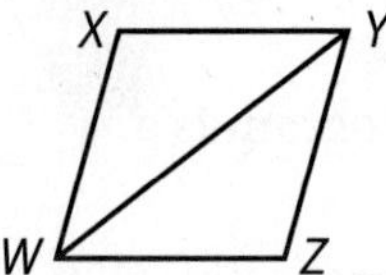

16. Given: $m\angle WXY = 130°$, $m\angle XWZ = 50°$, $m\angle WZY = 130°$

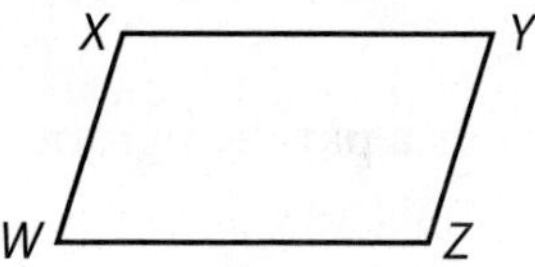

17. Represent Real-World Problems A framer uses a clamp to hold together pieces of a picture frame. The pieces are cut so that $\overline{PQ} \cong \overline{RS}$ and $\overline{QR} \cong \overline{SP}$. The clamp is adjusted so that *PZ*, *QZ*, *RZ*, and *SZ* are all equal lengths. Why must the frame be a rectangle?

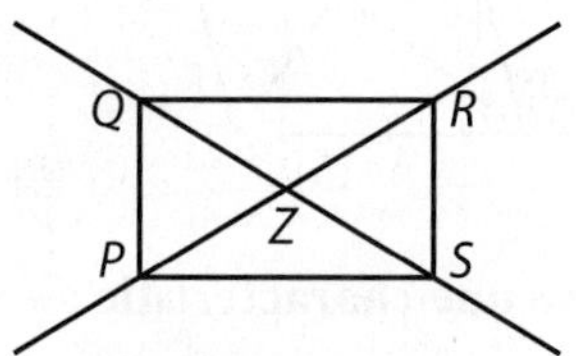

18. Represent Real-World Problems A city garden club is planting a square garden. They drive pegs into the ground at each corner and tie strings between each pair. The pegs are spaced so that $\overline{WX} \cong \overline{XY} \cong \overline{YZ} \cong \overline{ZW}$. How can the garden club use the diagonal strings to verify that the garden is a square?

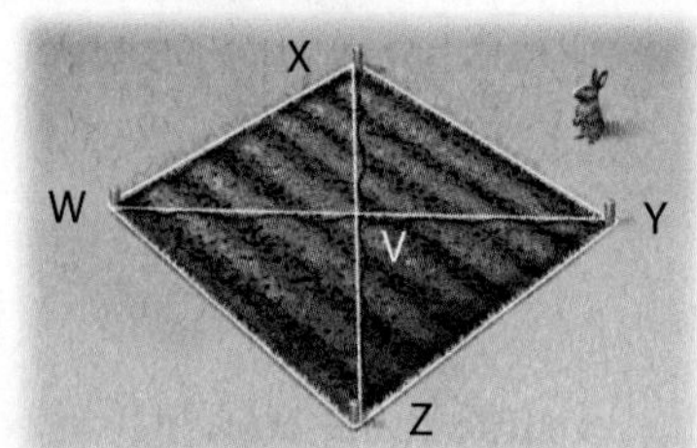

19. A quadrilateral is formed by connecting the midpoints of a rectangle. Which of the following could be the resulting figure? Select all that apply.

A. parallelogram　　**C.** rectangle

B. rhombus　　**D.** square

H.O.T. Focus on Higher Order Thinking

20. Critical Thinking The diagonals of a quadrilateral are perpendicular bisectors of each other. What is the best name for this quadrilateral? Explain your answer.

21. Draw Conclusions Think about the relationships between angles and sides in this triangular prism to decide if the given face is a rectangle.

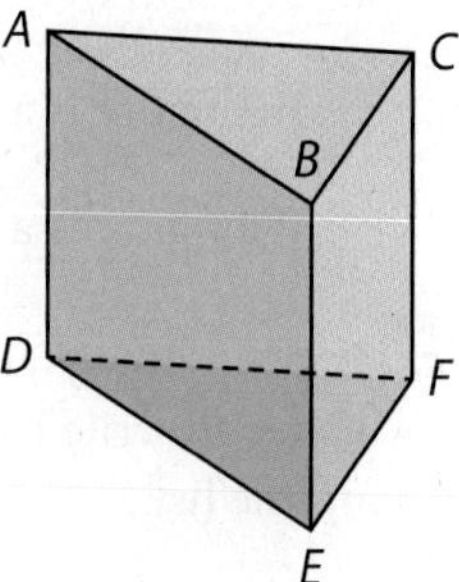

Given: $\overline{AC} \cong \overline{DF}$, $\overline{AB} \cong \overline{DE}$, $\overline{AB} \perp \overline{BC}$, $\overline{DE} \perp \overline{EF}$, $\overline{BE} \perp \overline{EF}$, $\overline{BC} \parallel \overline{EF}$

Prove: *EBCF* is a rectangle.

22. Justify Reasoning Copy and complete the table. Use one of the other rhombus theorems to prove that if the diagonals of a parallelogram are perpendicular,
then the parallelogram is a rhombus.

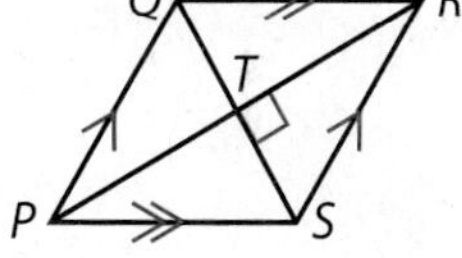

Given: *PQRS* is a parallelogram. $\overline{PR} \perp \overline{QS}$

Prove: *PQRS* is a rhombus.

Statements	Reasons
1. *PQRS* is a parallelogram.	1. Given
2. $\overline{PT} \cong$ __?__	2. Diagonals of a parallelogram bisect each other.
3. $\overline{QT} \cong$ __?__	3. Reflexive Property of Congruence
4. $\overline{PR} \perp \overline{QS}$	4. Given
5. $\angle QTP$ and $\angle QTR$ are right angles.	5. __?__
6. $\angle QTP \cong \angle QTR$	6. __?__
7. $\triangle QTP \cong \triangle QTR$	7. __?__
8. $\overline{QP} \cong$ __?__	8. CPCTC
9. *PQRS* is a rhombus.	9. __?__

Lesson Performance Task

The diagram shows the organizational ladder of groups to which tigers belong.

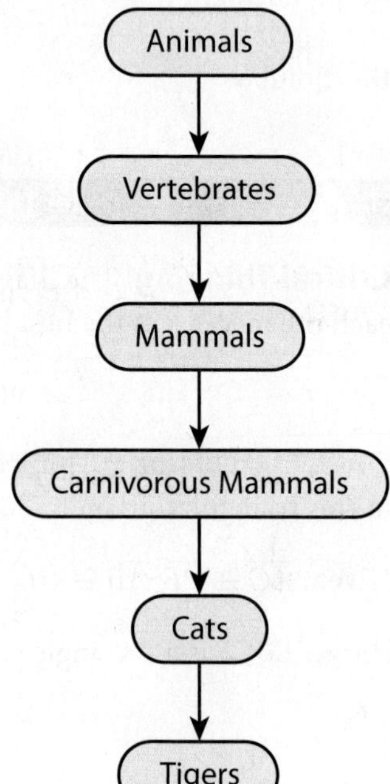

a. Use the terms below to create a similar ladder in which each term is a subset of the term above it.

Parallelogram	Geometric figures	Squares
Quadrilaterals	Figures	Rhombuses

b. Decide which of the following statements is true. Then write three more statements like it, using terms from the list in part (a).

If a figure is a rhombus, then it is a parallelogram.

If a figure is a parallelogram, then it is a rhombus.

c. Explain how you can use the ladder you created above to write if-then statements involving the terms on the list.

STUDY GUIDE REVIEW

Proofs with Triangles and Quadrilaterals

MODULE 15

Essential Question: How can you use the properties of triangles and quadrilaterals to solve real-world problems?

Key Vocabulary

auxiliary line *(línea auxiliar)*
circumcenter of a triangle *(circuncentro de un triángulo)*
circumscribed circle *(círculo circunscrito)*
concurrent *(concurrente)*
equiangular triangle *(triángulo equiangular)*
equilateral triangle *(triángulo equilátero)*
exterior angle *(ángulo exterior)*
incenter of a triangle *(incentro de un triángulo)*
inscribed circle *(círculo inscrito)*
interior angle *(ángulo interior)*
isosceles triangle *(triángulo isósceles)*
kite *(el deltoide)*
parallelogram *(paralelogramo)*
point of concurrency *(punto de concurrencia)*
quadrilateral *(cuadrilátero)*
rectangle *(rectángulo)*
remote interior angle *(ángulo interior remoto)*
rhombus *(rombo)*
square *(cuadrado)*
trapezoid *(trapecio)*

KEY EXAMPLE (Lesson 15.1)

Determine the measure of the fifth interior angle of a pentagon if you know the other four measures are 100°, 50°, 158°, and 147°.

$\text{Sum} = (5 - 2)180° = 540°$ — Apply the Polygon Angle Sum Theorem.

$100 + 50 + 158 + 147 + x = 540$ — Set the sum of the angle measures equal to 540.

$455 + x = 540$

$x = 85$ — Solve for *x*.

KEY EXAMPLE (Lesson 15.4)

Find the coordinates of the circumcenter of the triangle.

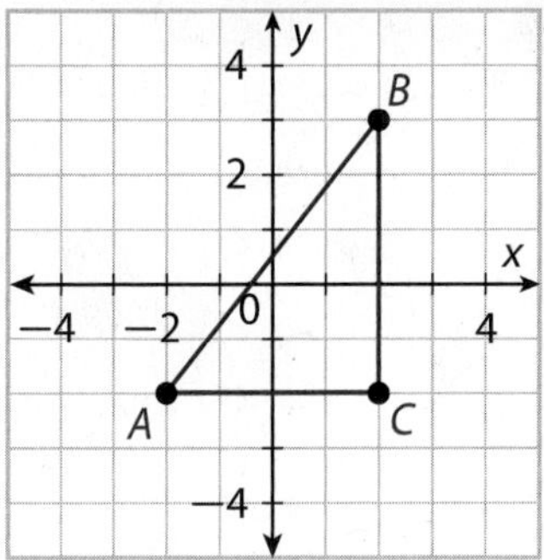

Coordinates: $A(-2, -2)$, $B(2, 3)$, $C(2, -2)$

$M_{AC} = \left(\dfrac{-2+2}{2}, \dfrac{-2+(-2)}{2}\right) = (0, -2)$ — Midpoint of $\overline{AC}$

$\overline{AC}$ is horizontal, so the line perpendicular to it is vertical and passes through the midpoint. The equation is $x = 0$. — Find the equation of the line perpendicular to $\overline{AC}$.

$M_{BC} = \left(\dfrac{2+2}{2}, \dfrac{3+(-2)}{2}\right) = \left(2, \dfrac{1}{2}\right)$ — Midpoint of $\overline{BC}$

$\overline{BC}$ is vertical, so the line perpendicular to it is horizontal and passes through the midpoint. The equation is $y = \dfrac{1}{2}$. — Find the equation of the line perpendicular to $\overline{BC}$.

The coordinates of the circumcenter are $\left(0, \dfrac{1}{2}\right)$.

KEY EXAMPLE (Lesson 15.5)

$\overline{AP}$ and $\overline{CP}$ are angle bisectors of $\triangle ABC$, where P is the incenter of the triangle. The measure of $\angle BAC$ is 56°. The measure of $\angle BCA$ is 42°.

Find the measures of $\angle PAC$ and $\angle PCB$.

Since $\overline{AP}$ is an angle bisector of $\angle BAC$, the measures of $\angle PAC$ and $\angle PAB$ are equal. Since the measure of $\angle BAC$ is 56°, the measure of $\angle PAC$ is 28°.

Since $\overline{CP}$ is an angle bisector of $\angle BCA$, the measures of $\angle PCB$ and $\angle PCA$ are equal. Since the measure of $\angle BCA$ is 42°, the measure of $\angle PCA$ is 21°.

KEY EXAMPLE (Lesson 15.6)

Given: $ABCD$ and $EDGF$ are parallelograms.

Prove: $\angle A \cong \angle G$

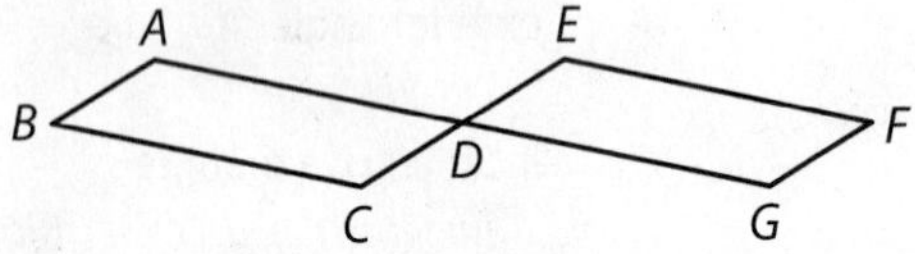

Proof	Reason
$ABCD$ and $EDGF$ are parallelograms.	Given
$\angle A \cong \angle C$	Opposite angles of a parallelogram are congruent.
$\overline{AB} \parallel \overline{CE}$	Definition of a parallelogram
$\overline{CE} \parallel \overline{FG}$	Definition of a parallelogram
$\angle C \cong \angle CDG$	Interior angle theorem
$\angle CDG \cong \angle G$	Interior angle theorem
$\angle A \cong \angle G$	Transitive property of congruence

KEY EXAMPLE (Lesson 15.7)

Determine which quadrilaterals match the figure: parallelogram, rhombus, rectangle, or square.

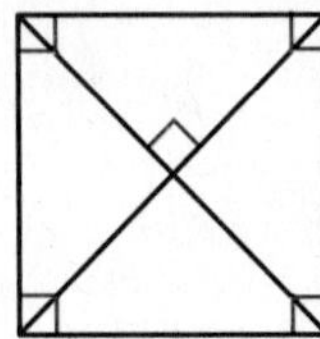

Since the figure has four 90° angles and a perpendicular bisector, then the figure is a square. Since the figure is a square, then it is also a rectangle, rhombus, and parallelogram.

EXERCISES

Find how many sides a polygon has with the given interior angle sum. *(Lesson 15.1)*

1. 2700°

2. 1800°

Find the sum of interior angles a polygon has with the given number of sides. *(Lesson 15.1)*

3. 3

4. 19

Given an isosceles triangle $\triangle DEF$ with $\overline{DE} \cong \overline{DF}$, $DE = 26$, and $m\angle F = 45°$, find the desired measurements. *(Lesson 15.2)*

5. DF

6. $m\angle D$

7. Find the coordinates of the circumcenter. *(Lesson 15.4)*

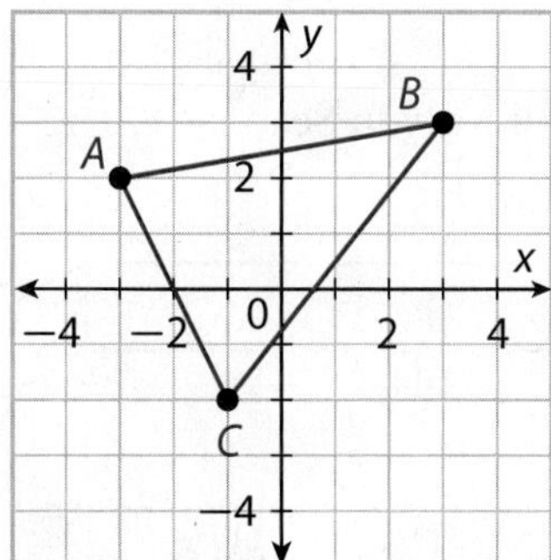

$\overline{AP}$, $\overline{BP}$, and $\overline{CP}$ are angle bisectors of $\triangle ABC$, where P is the incenter of the triangle. The measure of $\angle BAC$ is 24°. The measure of $\triangle BCA$ is 91°. Find the measures of the angles. *(Lesson 15.5)*

8. $\angle BAP$

9. $\angle ABP$

10. $\angle BCP$

***EFGH* is a parallelogram. Find the given side length.** *(Lesson 15.6)*

11. EF

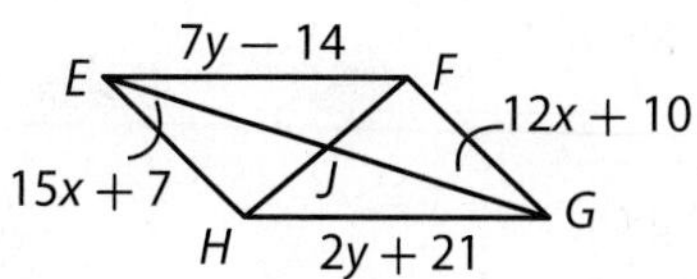

12. EG

Find the value of x that makes each parallelogram the given type. *(Lesson 15.7)*

13. Rectangle

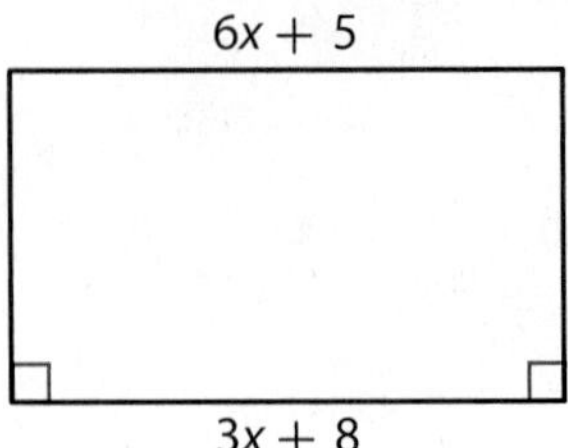

14. Square

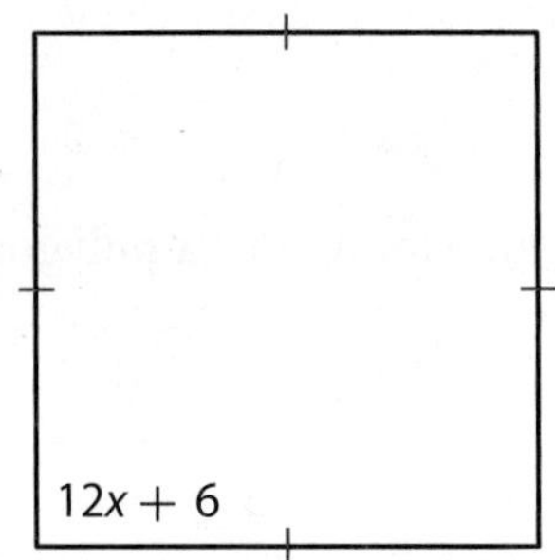

MODULE PERFORMANCE TASK

How Big Is That Face?

This strange image is the flattened east façade of the central library in Seattle, WA, designed by architect Rem Koolhaas. The faces of this unusual and striking building take the form of triangles, trapezoids, and other quadrilaterals.

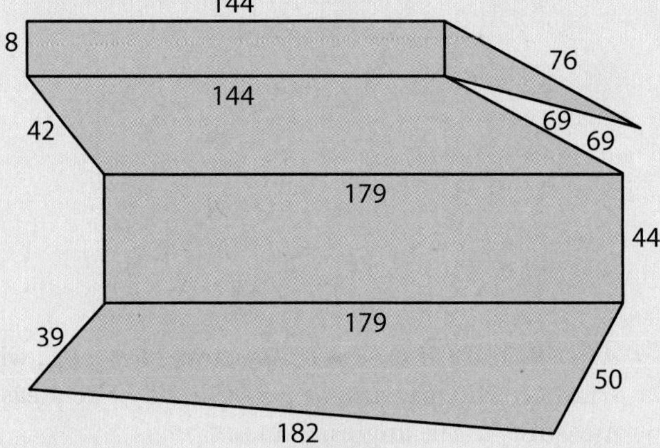

The diagram shows the dimensions of the faces labeled in feet. What is the total surface area of the east façade?

Write down any questions you have and describe how you would find the area. Then complete the task. Be sure to write down all your data and assumptions. Then use numbers, words, or algebra to explain how you reached your conclusion.

Ready to Go On?

15.1–15.7 Proofs with Triangles and Quadrilaterals

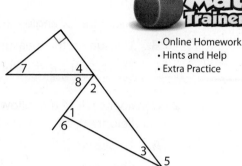

Personal Math Trainer
- Online Homework
- Hints and Help
- Extra Practice

Use the figure to answer the following. *(Lesson 15.1)*

1. Given m∠2 = 76°, m∠1 = 3 · m∠3, and ∠4 ≅ ∠8, find m∠1, m∠3, m∠4, m∠5, m∠6, m∠7, and m∠8.

2. Locate the circumcenter and incenter of △*ABC*. *(Lessons 15.4, 15.5)*

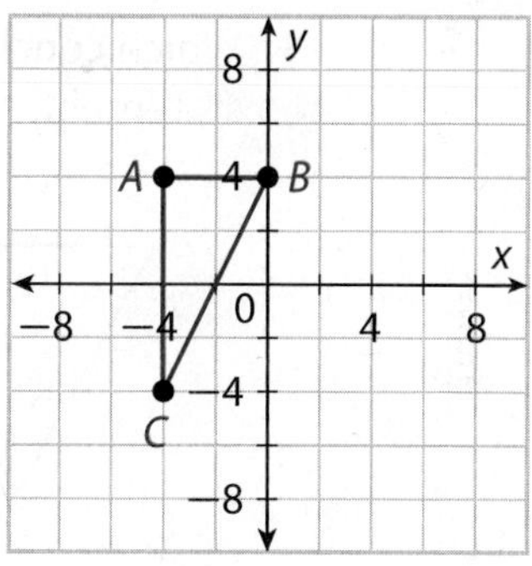

   a. Determine the coordinates of the circumcenter of △*ABC*.

   b. In what quadrant or on what axis does the incenter of △*ABC* lie?

3. A parallelogram has two pairs of congruent sides. Is any quadrilateral with two pairs of congruent sides necessarily a parallelogram? Explain. *(Lesson 15.6)*

ESSENTIAL QUESTION

4. Is it possible for one angle of a triangle to be 180°? If so, demonstrate with an example. If not, explain why not.

MODULE 15
MIXED REVIEW

Assessment Readiness

1. Consider the following statements about a seven-sided polygon. Determine if each statement is True or False.

A. Each interior angle measures 135°.

B. The sum of the measures of the interior angles is 1260°.

C. The sum of the measures of the interior angles is 900°.

2. Consider each of the following quadrilaterals. Decide whether each is also a parallelogram. Write Yes or No for A–C.

A. Trapezoid

B. Rhombus

C. Square

3. Which conclusions are valid given that *ABCD* is a parallelogram? Determine if each statement is True or False.

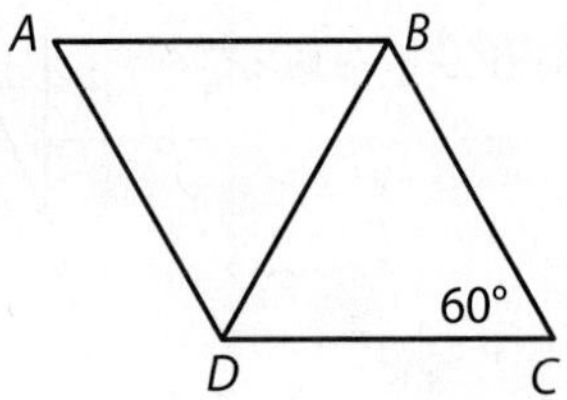

A. $\angle A \cong \angle C$

B. $\angle A$ and $\angle B$ are complimentary.

C. $\overline{AD} \parallel \overline{BC}$

4. What is the solution of $|4x + 1| = 14$? Show your work.

5. The graph of $y = 3x^2 + 4x + c$ has one *x*-intercept. What is the value of *c*? Explain how you found your answer.

Assessment Readiness

Personal Math Trainer

- Online Homework
- Hints and Help
- Extra Practice

1. Determine whether each pair of angles is a pair of vertical angles, a linear pair of angles, or neither.

A. $\angle AFC$ and $\angle CFD$

B. $\angle AFB$ and $\angle CFD$

C. $\angle BFD$ and $\angle AFE$

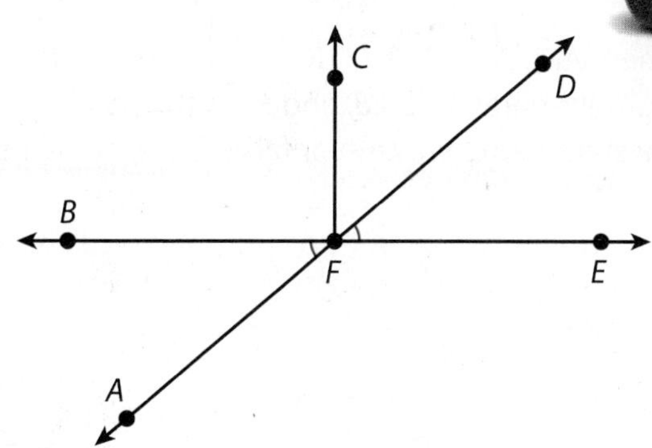

2. Determine if each statement is True or False.

A. If one pair of consecutive sides of a parallelogram is congruent, then the parallelogram is a rectangle.

B. If one pair of consecutive sides of a rhombus is perpendicular then the rhombus is a square.

C. If a quadrilateral has four right angles then it is a square.

3. Are the triangles congruent?

Write Yes or No for each statement.

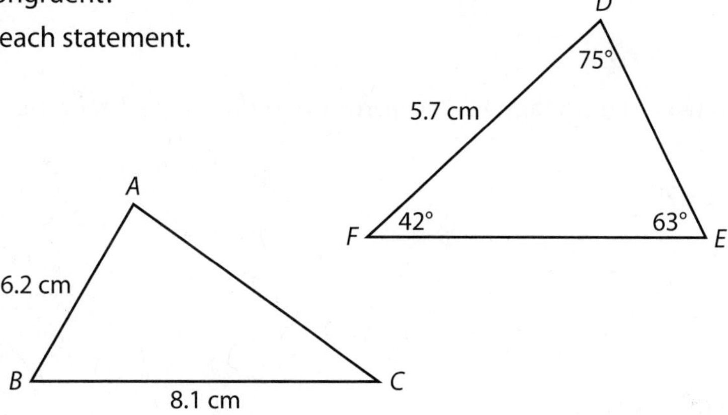

A. $AC = 5.7$ cm

B. $m\angle BAC = 75°$, $m\angle ABC = 63°$, and $DE = 6.2$ cm

C. $m\angle ACB = 42°$, $m\angle ABC = 63°$, and $FE = 8.2$ cm

4. Triangle $\triangle ABC$ is in the second quadrant and translated along $(-3, 2)$ and reflected across the y-axis. Determine if the translation will be in the given quadrant. Write Yes or No for each statement.

A. In the first quadrant after the first transformation

B. In the second quadrant after the first transformation

C. In the third quadrant after the second transformation

5. Given $\triangle ABC$ where $A(2, 3)$, $B(5, 8)$, $C(8, 3)$, $\overline{RS}$ is the midsegment parallel to $\overline{AC}$, $\overline{ST}$ is the midsegment parallel to $\overline{AB}$, and $\overline{RT}$ is the midsegment parallel to $\overline{BC}$, determine if the statements are true or false. Determine if each statement is True or False.

A. $ST = 4$

B. $RT = 5$

C. $RS = 3$

6. Find each angle measure.

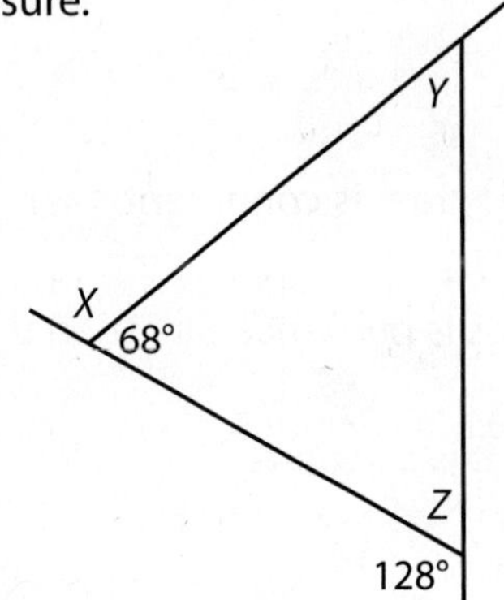

7. Write a proof in two-column form for the Corresponding Angles Theorem.

Given: $\ell \parallel m$

Prove: $m\angle 3 = m\angle 7$

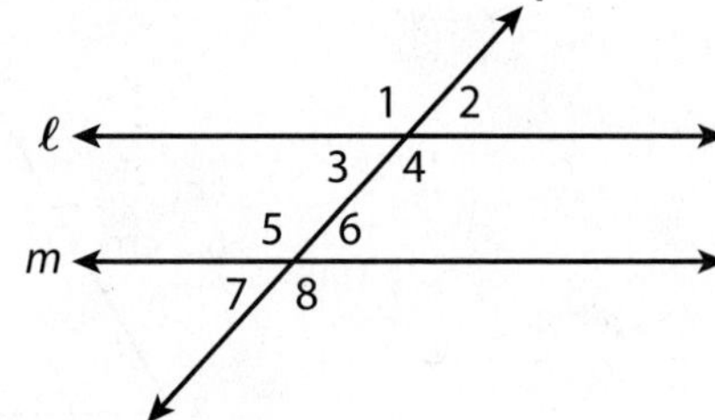

Performance Tasks

★ **8.** Lines L_1 and L_2 are parallel, and line L_3 is a transversal. What is the value of y? Show your work.

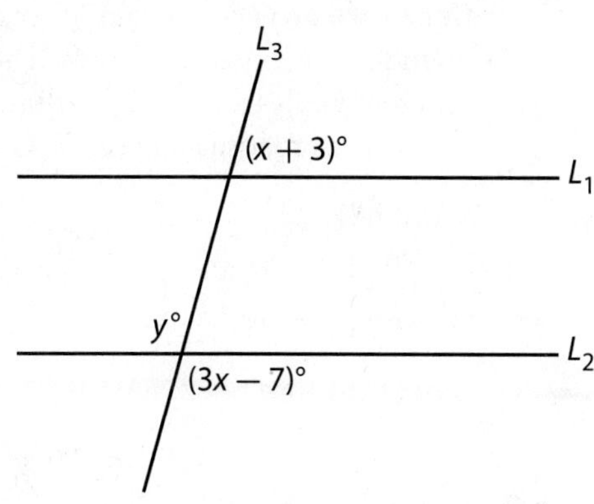

★★ **9.** Consider the figure shown, where $\angle A \cong \angle D$ and $\overline{AB} \cong \overline{DB}$. Prove $\overline{EB} \cong \overline{CB}$. Explain your reasoning.

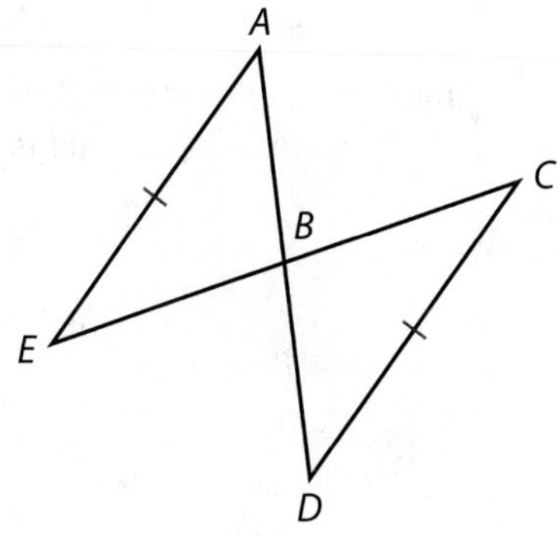

★★★ **10.** Triangle ABC is equilateral, $\overline{AD}$ is an angle bisector of $\angle ABC$, and $\overline{EF}$ is parallel to $\overline{AC}$. Find the measures of angles x, y, and z, and explain how you found each one.

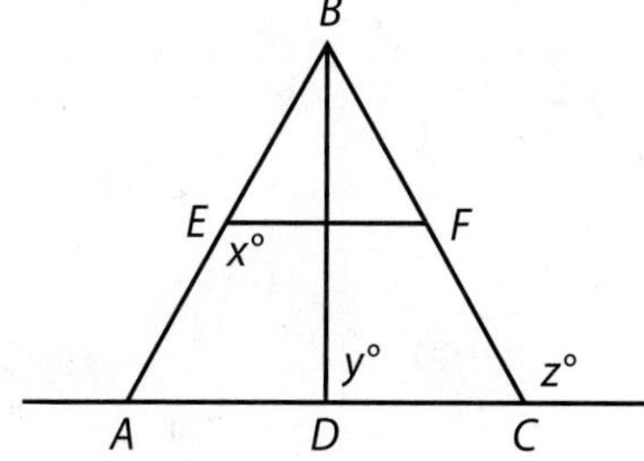

MATH IN CAREERS

Cartographer A cartographer is working on a map of an area which includes a park bounded on all sides by roads. The cartographer knows the measurements of several different angles formed by the intersection of the surrounding streets, as shown on the figure, with roads labeled A, B, C, D, and E.

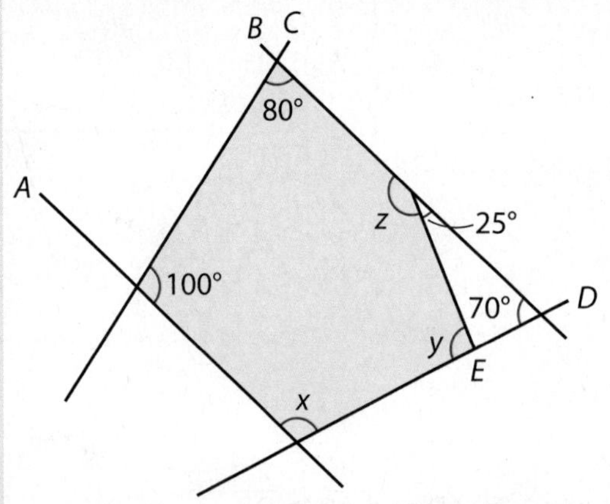

Find the remaining angle measurements. Assume all roads are straight. Explain in detail using geometric arguments how you determined your answers.

UNIT 7

Similarity and Right Triangles

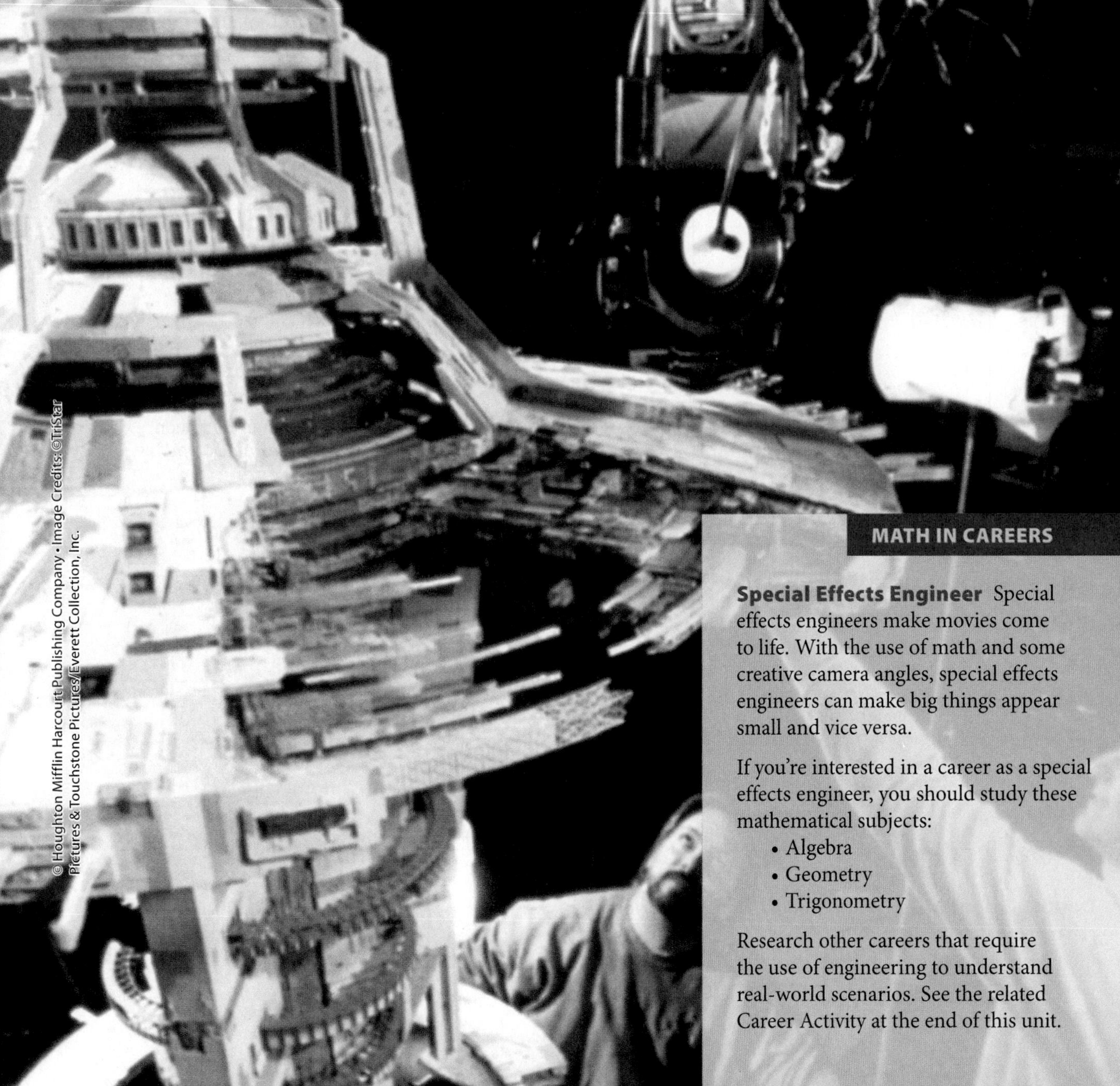

MATH IN CAREERS

Special Effects Engineer Special effects engineers make movies come to life. With the use of math and some creative camera angles, special effects engineers can make big things appear small and vice versa.

If you're interested in a career as a special effects engineer, you should study these mathematical subjects:

- Algebra
- Geometry
- Trigonometry

Research other careers that require the use of engineering to understand real-world scenarios. See the related Career Activity at the end of this unit.

Reading Start-Up

Visualize Vocabulary

Copy the main idea web and use the ✔ words to complete it. Write the review words in the squares and include definitions.

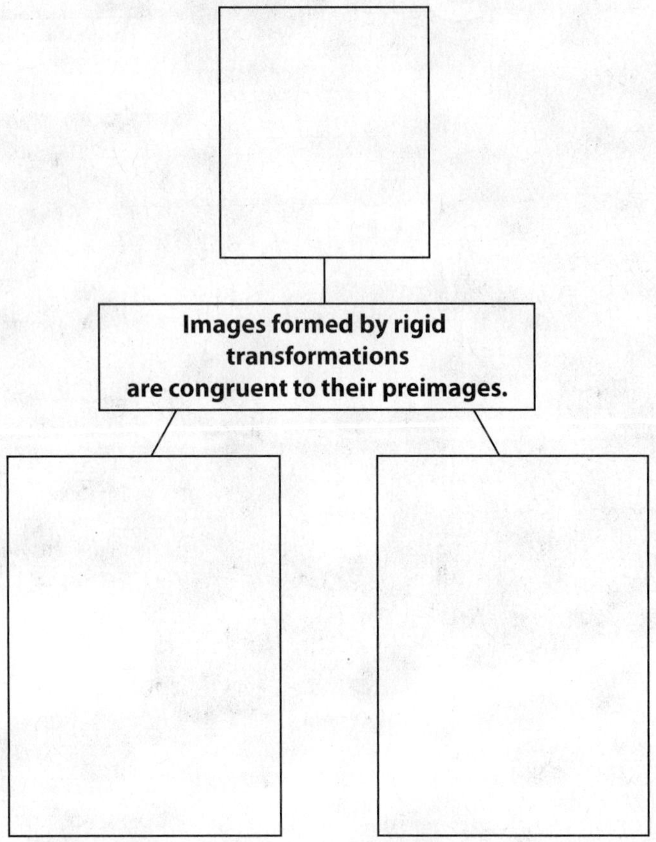
Images formed by rigid transformations are congruent to their preimages.

Understand Vocabulary

Complete the sentences using the preview words.

1. The image formed by a(n) __?__ has the same shape as its pre-image.

2. The __?__ indicates the ratio of the lengths of corresponding sides of two similar figures.

3. In the proportion $\frac{a}{x} = \frac{x}{b}$, x is called the __?__.

Vocabulary

Review Words

- ✔ betweenness (*intermediación*)
- ✔ collinearity (*colinealidad*)
- ✔ congruent (*congruente*)
- ✔ hypotenuse (*hipotenusa*)
- ✔ legs (*catetos*)
- ✔ orientation (*orientación*)
- ✔ parallel (*paralelo*)
- ✔ reflection (*reflejo*)
- ✔ rotation (*rotación*)
- ✔ transformation (*transformación*)
- ✔ translation (*traslación*)

Preview Words

center of dilation (*centro de la dilatación*)
cosine (*coseno*)
dilation (*dilatación*)
geometric mean (*media geométrica*)
indirect measurement (*medición indirecta*)
scale factor (*factor de escala*)
similar (*similar*)
similarity transformation (*transformación de semejanza*)
sine (*seno*)
tangent (*tangente*)
trigonometric ratio (*razón trigonométrica*)

Active Reading

Double-Door Fold Create a Double-Door Fold prior to starting the unit. Write characteristics of congruency under one flap. Fill out the other flap with corresponding characteristics of similarity so that the two topics can be compared more easily.

Similarity and Transformations

MODULE 16

Essential Question: How can you use similarity and transformations to solve real-world problems?

REAL WORLD VIDEO
Check out how properties of similarity and transformations can be used to create scale models of large, real-world structures like monuments.

MODULE PERFORMANCE TASK PREVIEW

Modeling the Washington Monument

In this module, you will be challenged to create a plan for a scale model of the Washington Monument. How can you use similarity and dilations to help you produce an accurate model? Let's find out.

Are YOU Ready?

Complete these exercises to review skills you will need for this module.

Personal Math Trainer

- Online Homework
- Hints and Help
- Extra Practice

Properties of Transformations

Example 1 Stretch $\triangle ABC$ with points $A(1, 2)$, $B(3, 2)$, and $C(3, -1)$ horizontally and vertically by a factor of 4.

$(x, y) \rightarrow (4x, 4y)$ Write the transformation rule.

$A'(4, 8)$, $B'(12, 8)$, $C'(12, -4)$ Use the transformation to write each transformed point.

Describe the transformation.

1. Stretch $\triangle DEF$ with points $D(-2, 1)$, $E(-1, -1)$, and $F(-2, -2)$ horizontally and vertically by a factor of -3.

2. Is the stretch a rigid motion?

3. Is it true that $\triangle DEF \cong \triangle D'E'F'$?

Similar Figures

Example 2 Transform $\triangle ABC$ with points $A(3, 4)$, $B(-1, 6)$, and $C(0, 1)$ by shifting it 2 units to the right and 1 unit up.

$(x, y) \rightarrow (x + 2, y + 1)$ Write the transformation rule.

$A'(5, 5)$, $B'(1, 7)$, $C'(2, 2)$ Write each transformed point.

Describe the transformation shown in the graph.

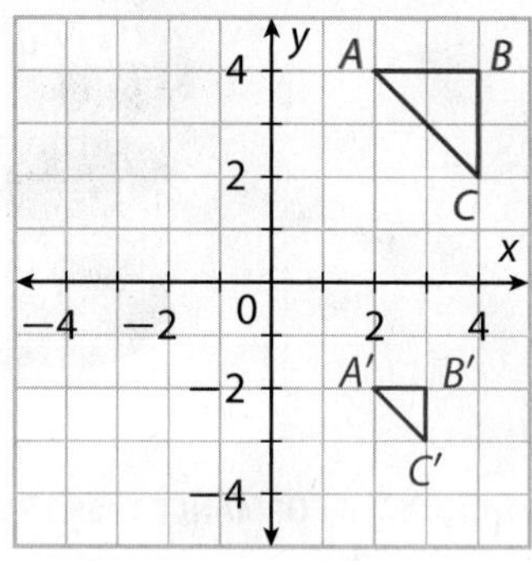

4. Write the rule used to transform $\triangle ABC$.

5. Describe in words the transformation shown in the figure.

16.1 Dilations

Essential Question: How does a dilation transform a figure?

Resource Locker

Explore 1 Investigating Properties of Dilations

A **dilation** is a transformation that can change the size of a polygon but leaves the shape unchanged. A dilation has a *center of dilation* and a *scale factor* which together determine the position and size of the image of a figure after the dilation.

Use $\triangle ABC$ and its image $\triangle A'B'C'$ after a dilation to answer the following questions.

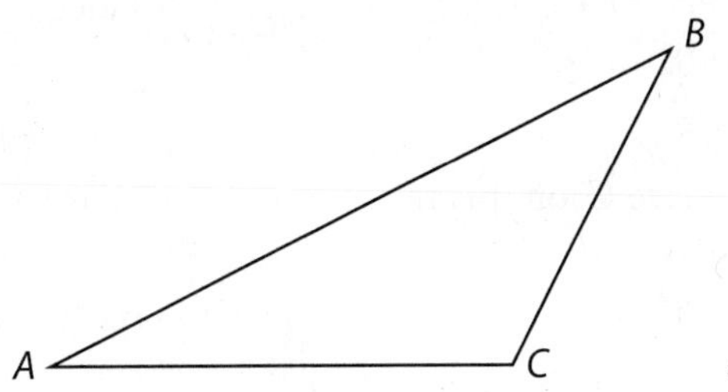

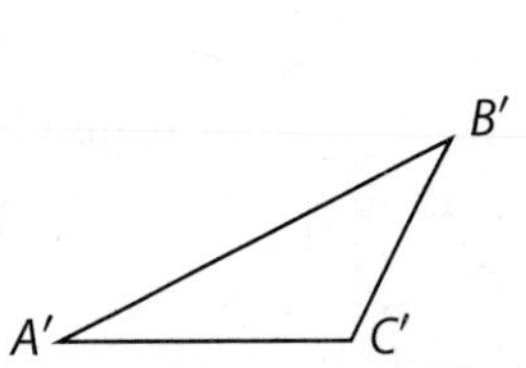

(A) Use a ruler to measure the following lengths. Measure to the nearest tenth of a centimeter.

$AB =$ cm $A'B' =$ cm

$AC =$ cm $A'C' =$ cm

$BC =$ cm $B'C' =$ cm

(B) Use a protractor to measure the corresponding angles.

$m\angle A =$ $m\angle A' =$

$m\angle B =$ $m\angle B' =$

$m\angle C =$ $m\angle C' =$

(C) Complete the following ratios

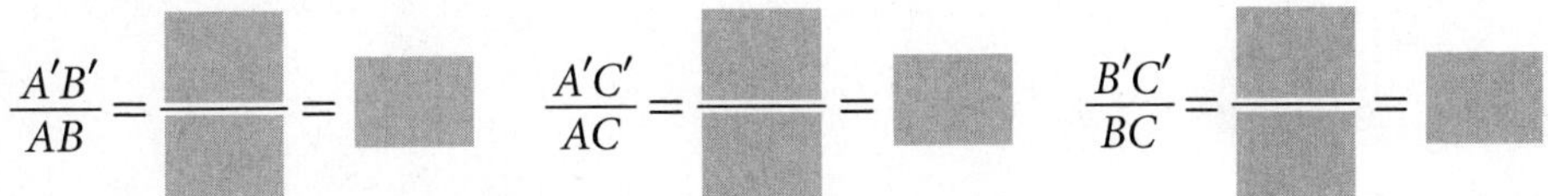

Reflect

1. What do you notice about the corresponding sides of the figures? What do you notice about the corresponding angles?

2. **Discussion** What similarities are there between reflections, translations, rotations, and dilations? What is the difference?

Explore 2 Dilating a Line Segment

The dilation of a line segment (the pre-image) is a line segment whose length is the product of the scale factor and the length of the pre-image.

Copy the figure on a sheet of paper. Then use the following steps to apply a dilation by a factor of 3, with center at the point O, to $\overleftrightarrow{AC}$.

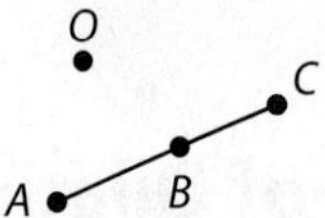

(A) To locate the point A', draw a ray from O through A. Place A' on this ray so that the distance from O to A' is three times the distance from O to A.

(B) To locate point B', draw a ray from O through B. Place B' on this ray so that the distance from O to B' is three times the distance from O to B.

(C) To locate point C', draw a ray from O through C. Place C' on this ray so that the distance from O to C' is three times the distance from O to C.

(D) Draw a line through A', B', and C'.

(E) Measure $\overline{AB}$, $\overline{AC}$, and $\overline{BC}$. Measure $\overline{A'B'}$, $\overline{A'C'}$, and $\overline{B'C'}$. Make a conjecture about the lengths of segments that have been dilated.

Reflect

3. Make a conjecture about the length of the image of a 4 cm segment after a dilation with scale factor k. Can the image ever be shorter than the preimage?

4. What can you say about the image of a segment under a dilation? Does your answer depend upon the location of the segment? Explain

Explain 1 Applying Properties of Dilations

The **center of dilation** is the fixed point about which all other points are transformed by a dilation. The ratio of the lengths of corresponding sides in the image and the preimage is called the **scale factor**.

Properties of Dilations

- Dilations preserve angle measure.
- Dilations preserve betweenness.
- Dilations preserve collinearity.
- Dilations preserve orientation.
- Dilations map a line segment (the pre-image) to another line segment whose length is the product of the scale factor and the length of the pre-image.
- Dilations map a line not passing through the center of dilation to a parallel line and leave a line passing through the center unchanged.

Example 1 **Determine if the transformation on the coordinate plane is a dilation. If it is, give the scale factor.**

 Preserves angle measure: yes

Preserves betweenness: yes

Preserves collinearity: yes

Preserves orientation: no

Ratio of corresponding sides: 1 : 1

Is this transformation a dilation? No, it does not preserve orientation.

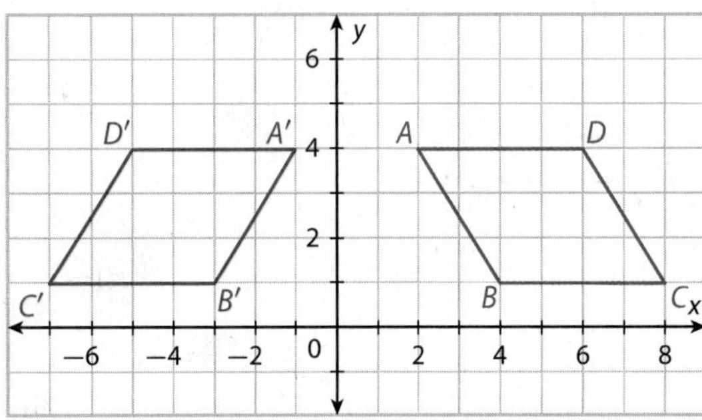

 Preserves angle measure: yes

Preserves betweenness: yes

Preserves collinearity: yes

Preserves orientation: yes

Scale Factor: 2

Is this transformation a dilation? yes

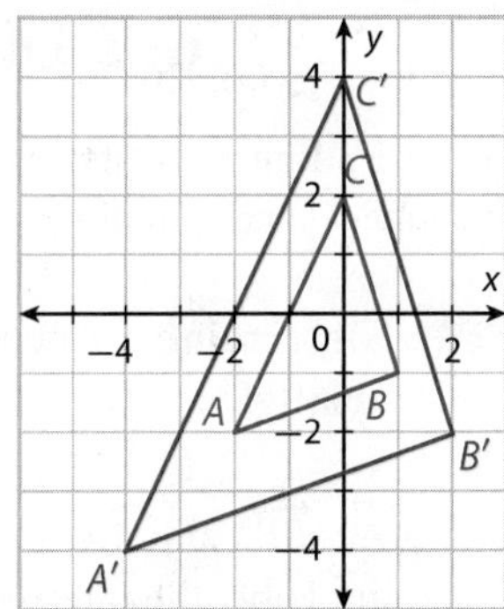

Your Turn

Determine if the transformations are dilations. Explain why or why not.

5.

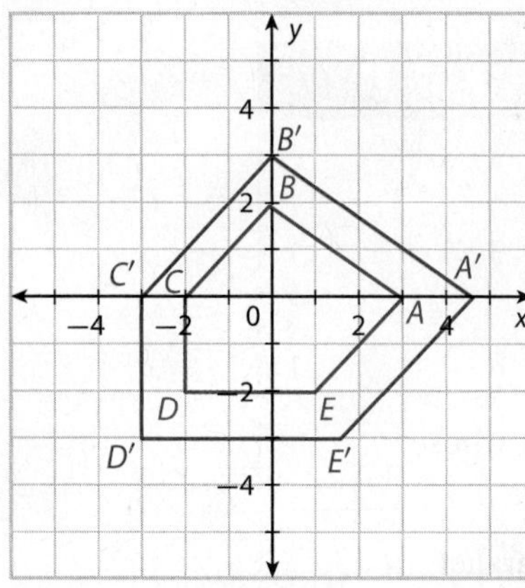

6.

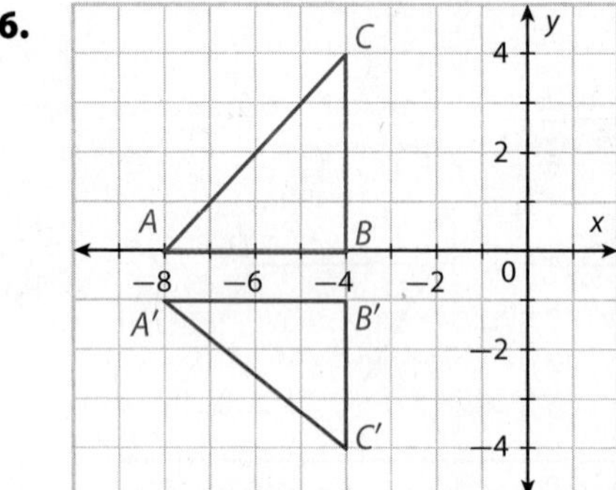

Explain 2 Determining the Center and Scale of a Dilation

When you have a figure and its image after dilation, you can find the center of dilation by drawing lines that connect corresponding vertices. These lines will intersect at the center of dilation.

Example 2 **Determine the center of dilation and the scale factor of the dilation of the triangles.**

(A) Draw $\overleftrightarrow{AA'}$, $\overleftrightarrow{BB'}$, and $\overleftrightarrow{CC'}$. The point where the lines cross is the center of dilation. Label the intersection O. Measure to find the scale factor.

$OA = 25$ mm $\quad$ $OB = 13$ mm $\quad$ $OC = 19$ mm

$OA' = 50$ mm $\quad$ $OB' = 26$ mm $\quad$ $OC' = 38$ mm

The scale factor is 2 to 1.

A′
C′
B′
A
C
B
O

(B) Draw $\overleftrightarrow{AA'}$, $\overleftrightarrow{BB'}$, and $\overleftrightarrow{CC'}$. Measure from each point to the intersection O to the nearest millimeter.

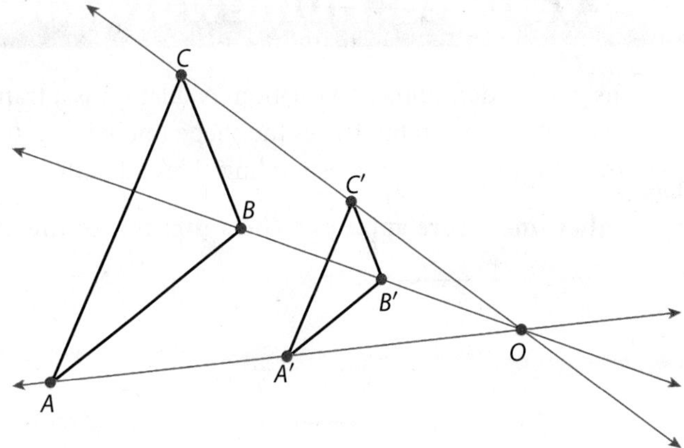

$OA = 60$ mm

$OA' = 30$ mm

$OB = 38$ mm

$OB' = 19$ mm

$OC = 52$ mm

$OC' = 26$ mm

The scale factor is 1 to 2.

Reflect

7. For the dilation in Your Turn 5, what is the center of dilation? Explain how you can tell without drawing lines.

Your Turn

8. Copy the triangles on a sheet of paper. Then find the center of dilation, the scale factor of the dilation, OA', and OA.

$OA' =$ , $OA =$ ▭

The scale factor of the dilation is ▭.

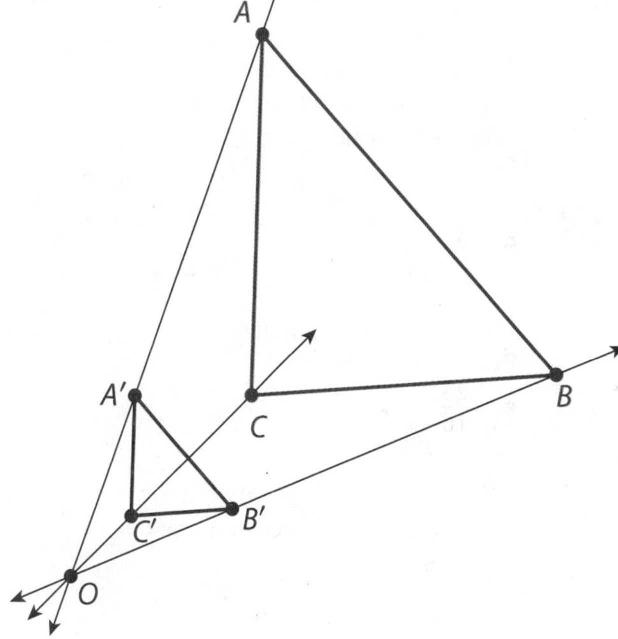

Elaborate

9. How is the length of the image of a line segment under a dilation related to the length of its preimage?

10. **Discussion** What is the result of dilating a figure using a scale factor of 1? For this dilation, does the center of dilation affect the position of the image relative to the preimage? Explain.

11. **Essential Question Check-In** In general how does a dilation transform a figure?

Evaluate: Homework and Practice

- Online Homework
- Hints and Help
- Extra Practice

1. Consider the definition of a dilation. A dilation is a transformation that can change the size of a polygon but leaves the shape unchanged. In a dilation, how are the ratios of the measures of the corresponding sides related?

Tell whether one figure appears to be a dilation of the other figure Explain.

2.

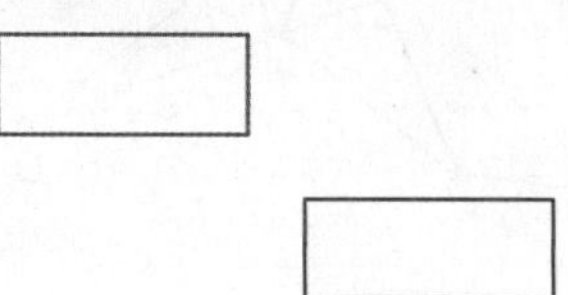

3.

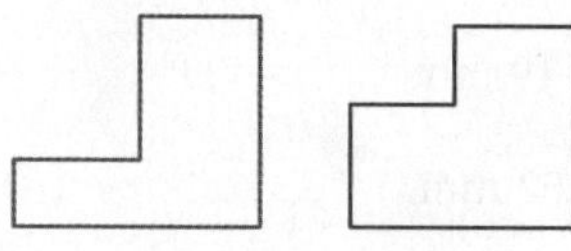

4. Is the scale factor of the dilation of $\triangle ABC$ equal to $\frac{1}{2}$? Explain.

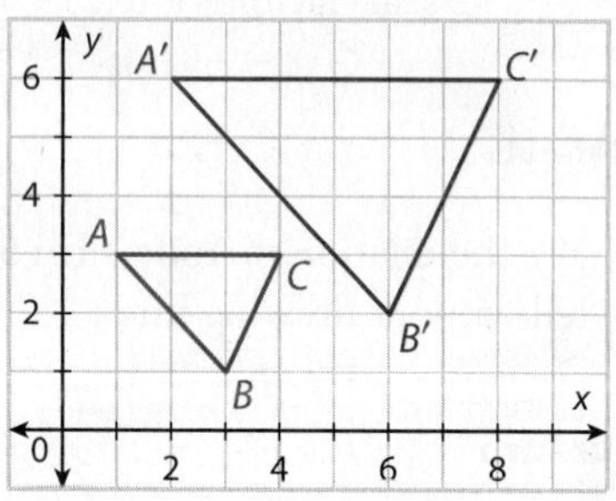

5. Square A is a dilation of square B. What is the scale factor?

a. $\frac{1}{7}$

b. $\frac{4}{5}$

c. $\frac{5}{4}$

d. 7

e. $\frac{25}{16}$

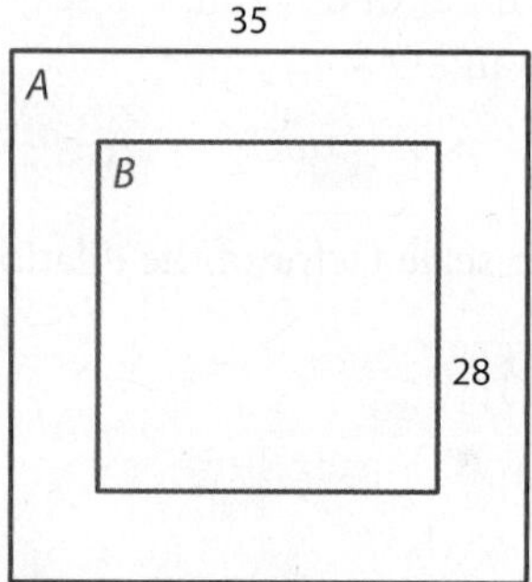

6. Copy each figure. Then apply a dilation to $\overline{AC}$ with a scale factor of 2 and center at the point O.

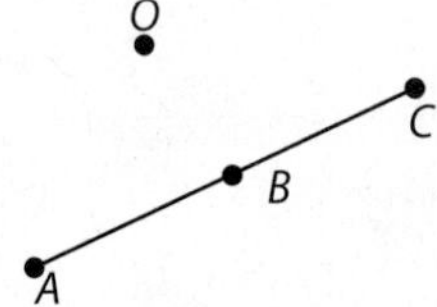

7. Copy each figure. Then apply a dilation to $\overline{AC}$ with a scale factor of $\frac{1}{3}$ and center at the point O.

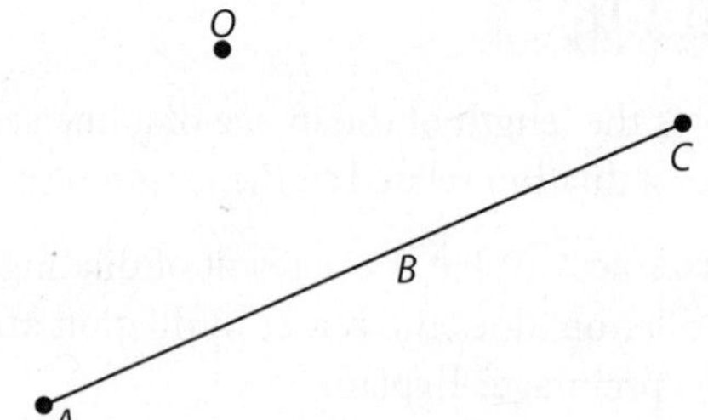

8. What happens when a triangle is dilated using one of the vertices as the center of dilation?

9. Draw $WXYZ$ and its image under a dilation. The center of the dilation is O, and the scale factor is 2.

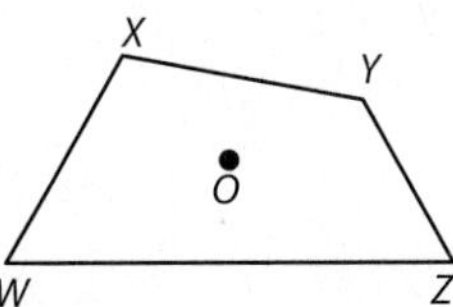

10. Draw $\triangle ABC$ and its image under a dilation. The center of dilation is C, and the scale factor is 1.5.

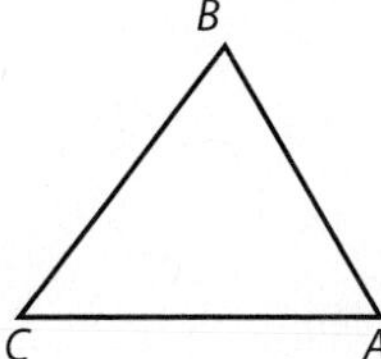

11. Compare dilations to rigid motions. How are they similar? How are they different?

Determine if the transformation of figure *A* to figure *B* on the coordinate plane is a dilation. Verify ratios of corresponding side lengths for a dilation.

12.

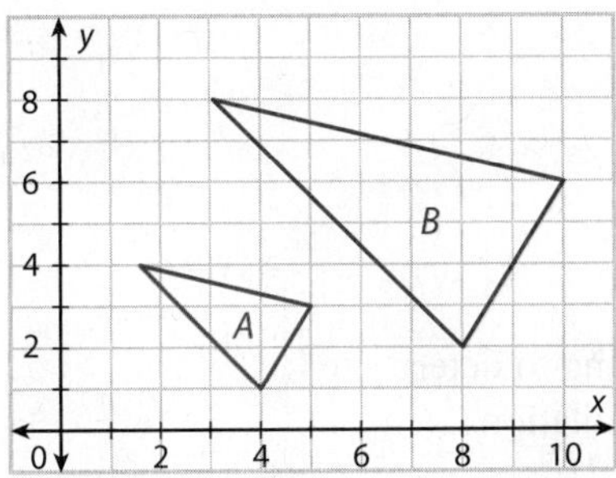

13.

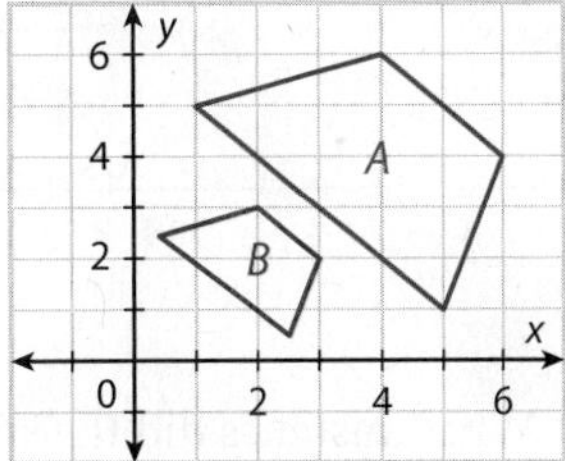

Copy each figure. Then determine the center of dilation and the scale factor of the dilation.

14.

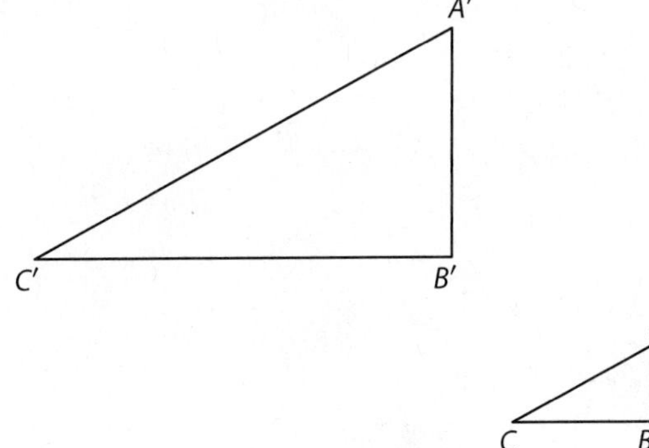

15.

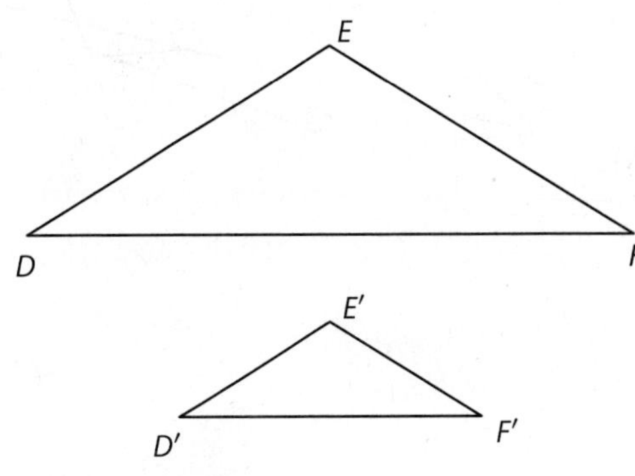

16. You work at a photography store. A customer has a picture that is 4.5 inches tall. The customer wants a reduced copy of the picture to fit a space of 1.8 inches tall on a postcard. What scale factor should you use to reduce the picture to the correct size?

17. Computer Graphics An artist uses a computer program to enlarge a design, as shown. What is the scale factor of the dilation?

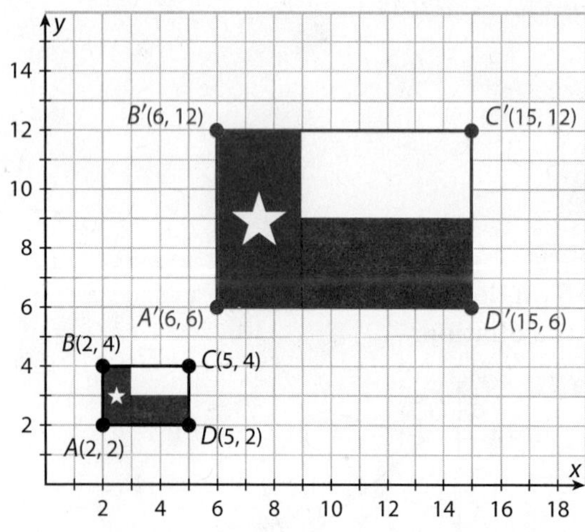

18. Explain the Error What mistakes did the student make when trying to determine the center of dilation? Copy the figure and determine the center of dilation.

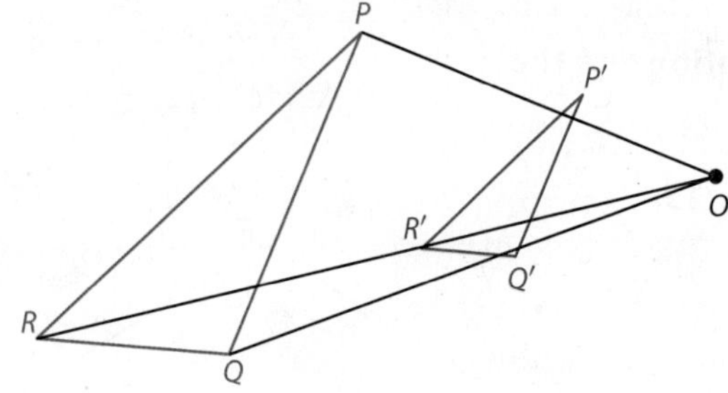

H.O.T. Focus on Higher Order Thinking

19. Draw $\triangle DEF$ with vertices $D(3, 1)$, $E(3,5)$, and $F(0, 5)$.

a. Determine the perimeter and the area of $\triangle DEF$.

b. Draw an image of $\triangle DEF$ after a dilation having a scale factor of 3, with the center of dilation at the origin $(0, 0)$. Determine the perimeter and area of the image.

c. How is the scale factor related to the ratios $\frac{\text{perimeter } \triangle D'E'F'}{\text{perimeter } \triangle DEF}$ and $\frac{\text{area } \triangle D'E'F'}{\text{area } \triangle DEF}$?

20. Draw $\triangle WXY$ with vertices $(4, 0)$, $(4, 8)$, and $(-2, 8)$.

a. Dilate $\triangle WXY$ using a factor of $\frac{1}{4}$ and the origin as the center. Then dilate its image using a scale factor of 2 and the origin as the center. Draw the final image.

b. Use the scale factors given in part (a) to determine the scale factor you could use to dilate $\triangle WXY$ with the origin as the center to the final image in one step.

c. Do you get the same final image if you switch the order of the dilations in part (a)? Explain your reasoning.

Lesson Performance Task

You've hung a sheet on a wall and lit a candle. Now you move your hands into position between the candle and the sheet and, to the great amusement of your audience, create an image of an animal on the sheet.

Compare and contrast what you're doing with what happens when you draw a dilation of a triangle on a coordinate plane. Point out ways that dilations and hand puppets are alike and ways they are different. Discuss measures that are preserved in hand-puppet projections and those that are not. Some terms you might like to discuss:

- pre-image
- image
- center of dilation
- scale factor
- transformation
- input
- output

16.2 Proving Figures are Similar Using Transformations

Essential Question: How can similarity transformations be used to show two figures are similar?

Explore Confirming Similarity

A **similarity transformation** is a transformation in which an image has the same shape as its pre-image. Similarity transformations include reflections, translations, rotations, and dilations. Two plane figures are **similar** if and only if one figure can be mapped to the other through one or more similarity transformations.

A grid shows a map of the city park. Use tracing paper to confirm that the park elements are similar.

(A) Trace patio *EFHG*. Turn the paper so that patio *EFHG* is mapped onto patio *LMON*. Describe the transformation. What does this confirm about the patios?

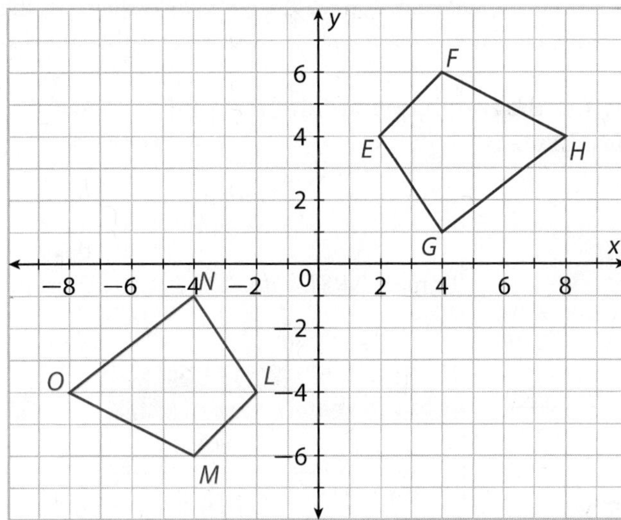

(B) Trace statues *ABCDEF* and *JKLMNO*. Fold the paper so that statue *ABCDEF* is mapped onto statue *JKLMNO*. Describe the transformation. What does this confirm about the statues?

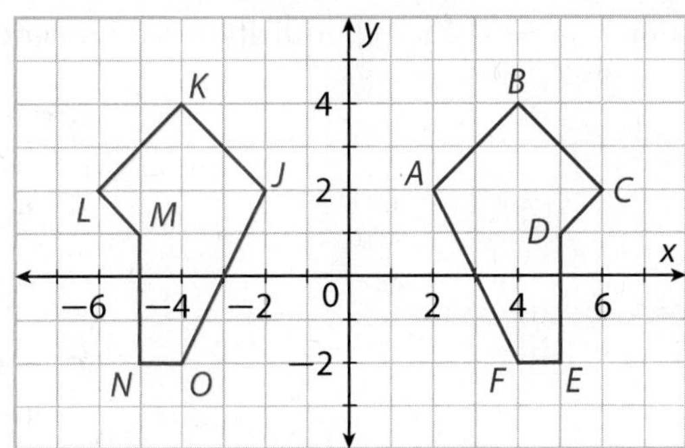

(C) Describe the transformation you can use to map vertices of garden *RST* to corresponding vertices of garden *DEF*. What does this confirm about the gardens?

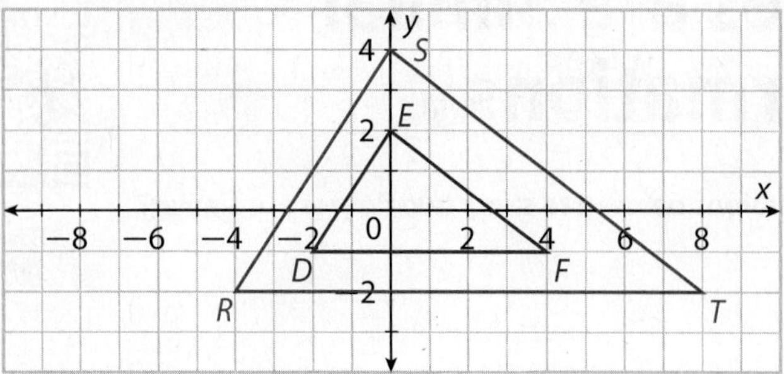

Reflect

1. Look back at all the steps. Were any of the images congruent to the pre-images? If so, what types of similarity transformations were performed with these figures? What does this tell you about the relationship between similar and congruent figures?
2. If two figures are similar, can you conclude that corresponding angles are congruent? Why or why not?

Explain 1 Determining If Figures are Similar

You can represent dilations using the coordinate notation $(x, y) \rightarrow (kx, ky)$, where k is the scale factor and the center of dilation is the origin. If $0 < k < 1$, the dilation is a reduction. If $k > 1$, the dilation is an enlargement.

Example 1 **Determine whether the two figures are similar using similarity transformations. Explain.**

(A) $\triangle RST$ and $\triangle XYZ$

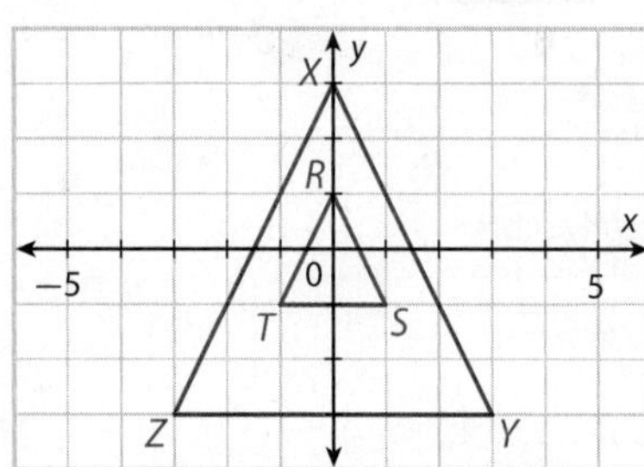

To map $\triangle RST$ onto $\triangle XYZ$, there must be some factor k that dilates $\triangle RST$.

Pre-image	Image
$R(0, 1)$	$X(0, 3)$
$S(1, -1)$	$Y(3, -3)$
$T(-1, -1)$	$Z(-3, -3)$

You can see that each coordinate of the pre-image is multiplied by 3 to get the image, so this is a dilation with scale factor 3. Therefore, $\triangle RST$ can be mapped onto $\triangle XYZ$ by a dilation with center at the origin, which is represented by the coordinate notation $(x, y) \rightarrow (3x, 3y)$. A dilation is a similarity transformation, so $\triangle RST$ is similar to $\triangle XYZ$.

Ⓑ *PQRS* and *WXYZ*

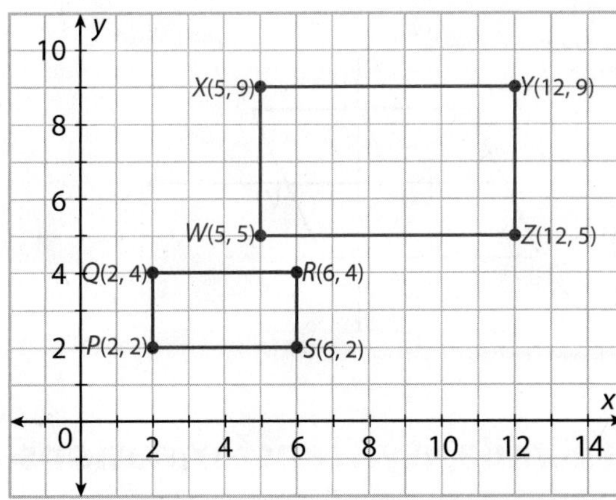

To map *PQRS* onto *WXYZ*, there must be some factor *k* that enlarges *PQRS*.

Pre-image	Image
$P(2, 2)$	$W(5, 5)$
$Q(2, 4)$	$X(5, 9)$
$R(6, 4)$	$Y(12, 9)$
$S(6, 2)$	$Z(12, 5)$

Find each distance: $PQ = 2$, $QR =$ 4 , $WX =$ 4 , and $XY = 7$

If $kPQ = WX$, then $k = 2$. However. $2QR \neq XY$.

No value of *k* can be determined that will map *PQRS* to *WXYZ*.

So, the figures are not similar.

Your Turn

Determine whether the two figures are similar using similarity transformations. Explain.

3. *LMNO* and *GHJK*

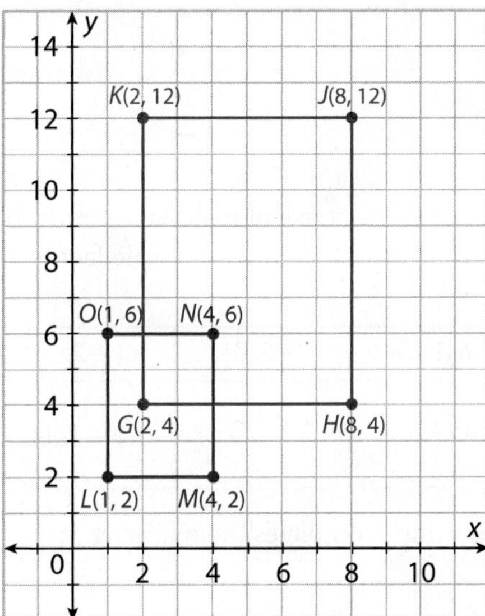

4. $\triangle JKL$ and $\triangle MNP$

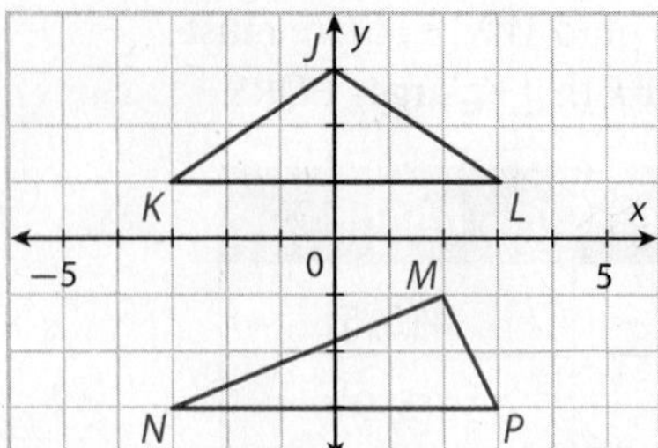

5. *CDEF* and *TUVF*

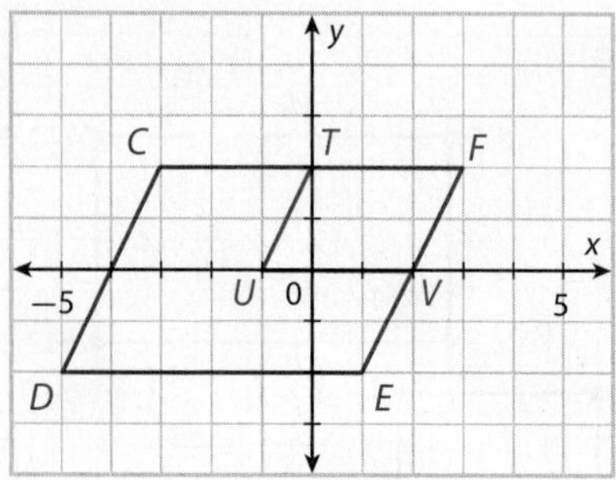

Explain 2 Finding a Sequence of Similarity Transformations

In order for two figures to be similar, there has to be some sequence of similarity transformations that maps one figure to the other. Sometimes there will be a single similarity transformation in the sequence. Sometimes you must identify more than one transformation to describe a mapping.

Example 2 **Find a sequence of similarity transformations that maps the first figure to the second figure. Write the coordinate notation for each transformation.**

(A) *ABDC* to *EFHG*

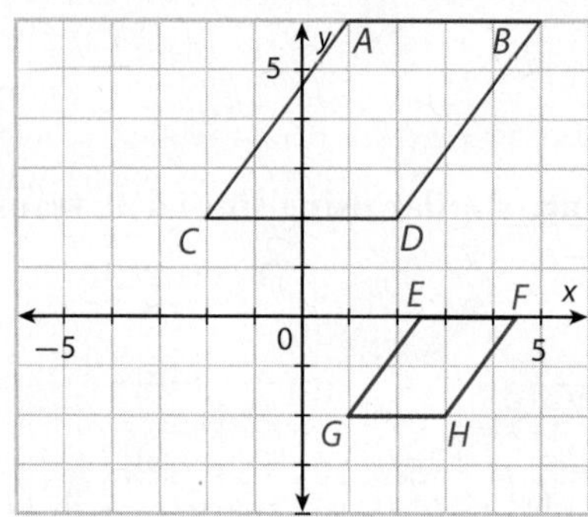

Since *EFHG* is smaller than *ABDC*, the scale factor *k* of the dilation must be between 0 and 1. The length of $\overline{AB}$ is 4 and the length of $\overline{EF}$ is 2; therefore, the scale factor is $\frac{1}{2}$. Write the new coordinates after the dilation:

Original Coordinates	$A(1, 6)$	$B(5, 6)$	$C(-2, 2)$	$D(2, 2)$
Coordinates after dilation $k = \frac{1}{2}$	$A'\left(\frac{1}{2}, 3\right)$	$B'\left(\frac{5}{2}, 3\right)$	$C'(-1, 1)$	$D'(1, 1)$

A translation right 2 units and down 3 units completes the mapping.

Coordinates after dilation	$A'\left(\frac{1}{2}, 3\right)$	$B'\left(\frac{5}{2}, 3\right)$	$C'(-1, 1)$	$D'(1, 1)$
Coordinates after translation $(x + 2, y - 3)$	$E\left(\frac{5}{2}, 0\right)$	$F\left(\frac{9}{2}, 0\right)$	$G(1, -2)$	$H(3, -2)$

The coordinates after translation are the same as the coordinates of *EFGH*, so you can map *ABDC* to *EFHG* by the dilation $(x, y) \rightarrow \left(\frac{1}{2}x, \frac{1}{2}y\right)$ followed by a translation $(x, y) \rightarrow (x + 2, y - 3)$.

Ⓑ $\triangle JKL$ to $\triangle PQR$

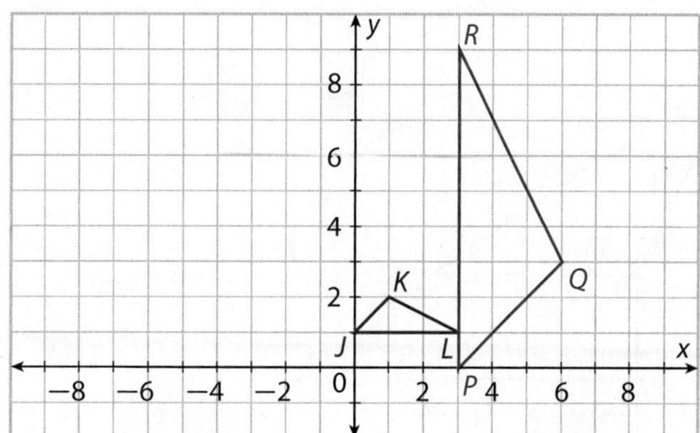

You can map $\triangle JKL$ to $\triangle PQR$ with a reflection across the x-axis followed by a dilation followed by a

90 ° counterclockwise rotation about the origin.

Reflection: $(x, y) \rightarrow (x, -y)$ Dilation: $(x, y) \rightarrow (3x, 3y)$

90 ° counterclockwise rotation: $(x, y) \rightarrow (-y, x)$

Reflect

6. Using the figure in Example 3A, describe a single dilation that maps *ABDC* to *EFHG*.

7. Using the figure in Example 3B, describe a different sequence of transformations that will map $\triangle JKL$ to $\triangle PQR$.

Your Turn

For each pair of similar figures, find a sequence of similarity transformations that maps one figure to the other. Use coordinate notation to describe the transformations.

8. *PQRS* to *TUVW*

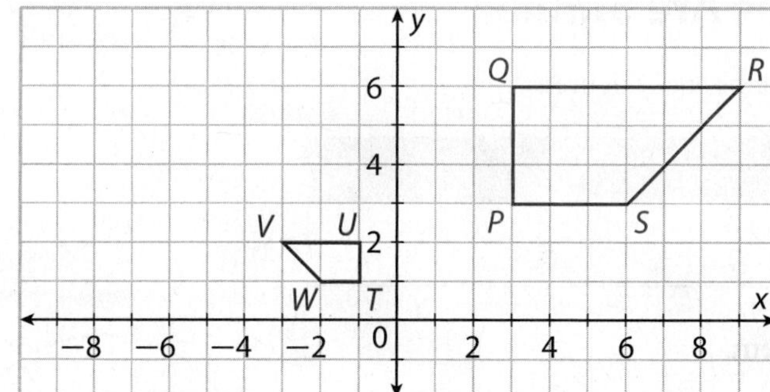

9. $\triangle ABC$ to $\triangle DEF$

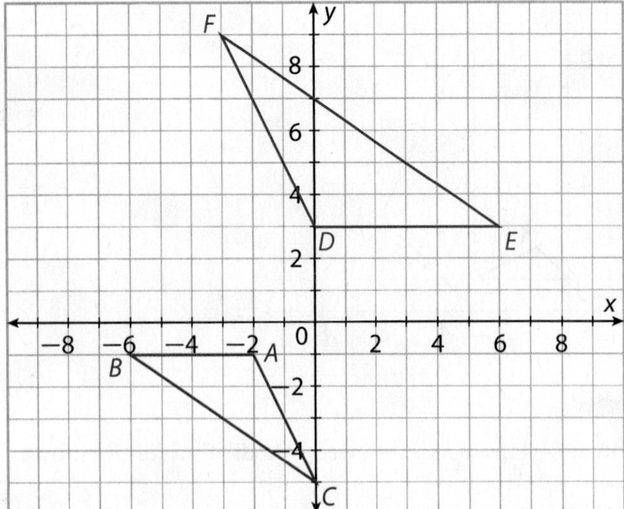

10. Describe a sequence of similarity transformations that maps *JKLMN* to *VWXYZ*.

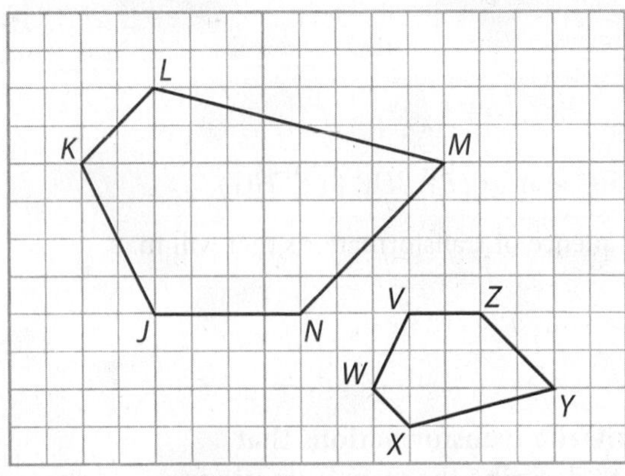

Explain 3 Proving All Circles Are Similar

You can use the definition of similarity to prove theorems about figures.

Circle Similarity Theorem

All circles are similar.

Example 3 **Prove the Circle Similarity Theorem.**

Given: Circle *C* with center *C* and radius *r*.
Circle *D* with center *D* and radius *s*.

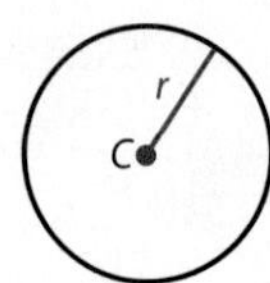

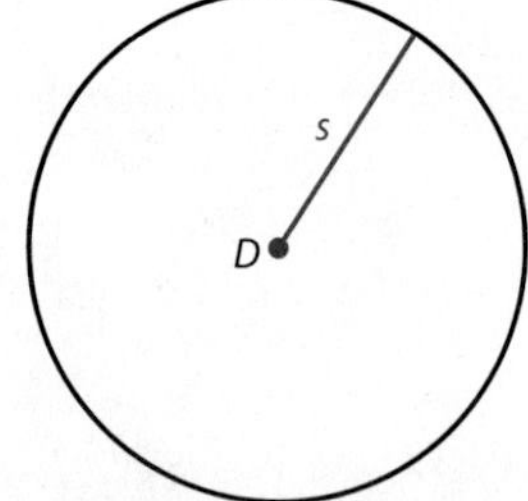

Prove: Circle *C* is similar to circle *D*.

To prove similarity, you must show that there is a sequence of similarity transformations that maps circle *C* to circle *D*.

(A) Start by transforming circle C with a translation along the vector $\overrightarrow{CD}$.

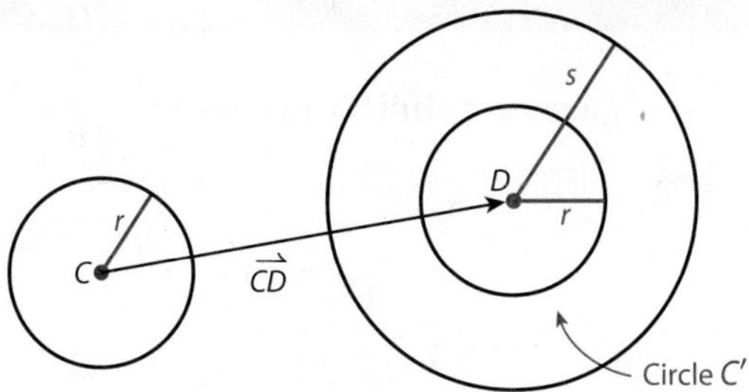

Through this translation, the image of point C is point D.

Let the image of circle C be circle C'. The center of circle C' coincides with point D.

(B) Transform circle C' with the dilation with center of dilation D and scale factor $\frac{s}{r}$.

Circle C' is made up of all the points at distance r from point D.

After the dilation, the image of circle C' will consist of all the points at distance $\frac{s}{r} \times r = s$ from point D.

These are the same points that form circle D. Therefore, the translation followed by the dilation maps circle C to circle D. Because translations and dilations are similarity transformations, you can conclude that circle C is similar to circle D.

Reflect

11. Can you show that circle C and circle D are similar through another sequence of similarity transformations? Explain.

12. Discussion Is it possible that circle C and circle D are congruent? If so, does the proof of the similarity of the circles still work? Explain.

Elaborate

13. Translations, reflections, and rotations are rigid motions. What unique characteristic keeps dilations from being considered a rigid motion?

14. Essential Question Check-In Two squares in the coordinate plane have horizontal and vertical sides. Explain how they are similar using similarity transformations.

Evaluate: Homework and Practice

- Online Homework
- Hints and Help
- Extra Practice

In Exercises 1–4, determine if the two figures are similar using similarity transformations. Explain.

1. *EFGH* and *ABCD*

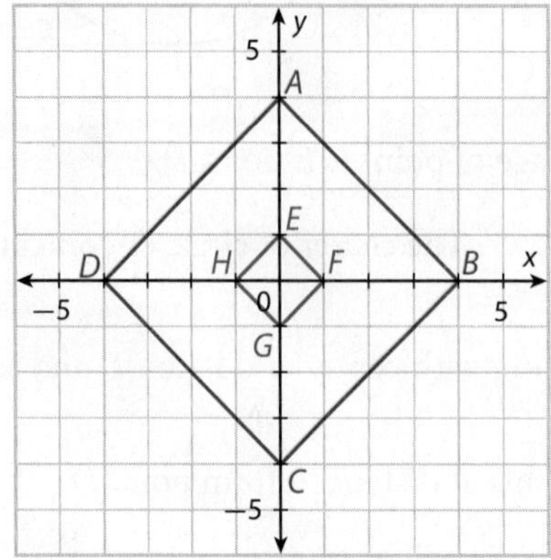

2. $\triangle PQR$ and $\triangle STU$

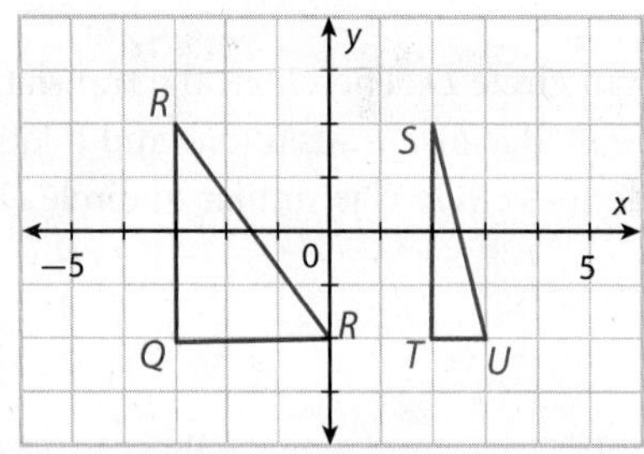

3. *JKLMN* and *JPQRS*

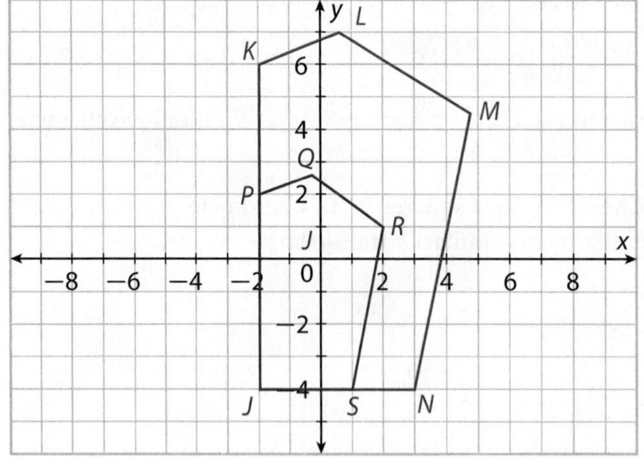

4. $\triangle UVW$ and $\triangle GHI$

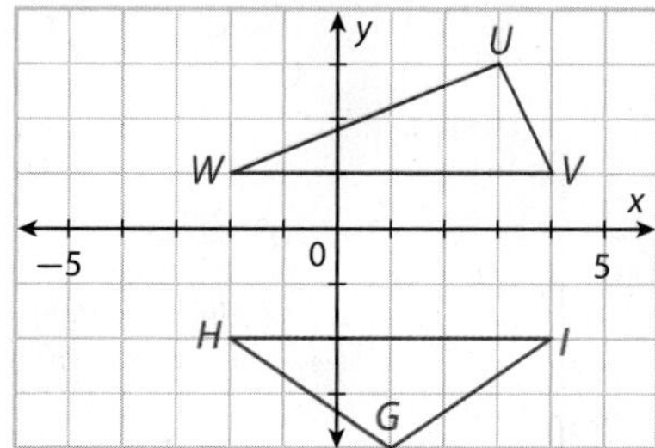

For the pair of similar figures in each of Exercises 5–10, find a sequence of similarity transformations that maps one figure to the other. Provide the coordinate notation for each transformation.

5. Map $\triangle ABC$ to $\triangle PQR$.

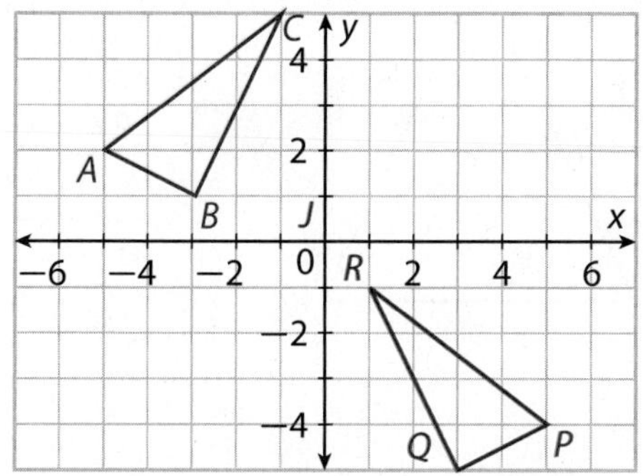

6. Map $ABCD$ to $EFGH$.

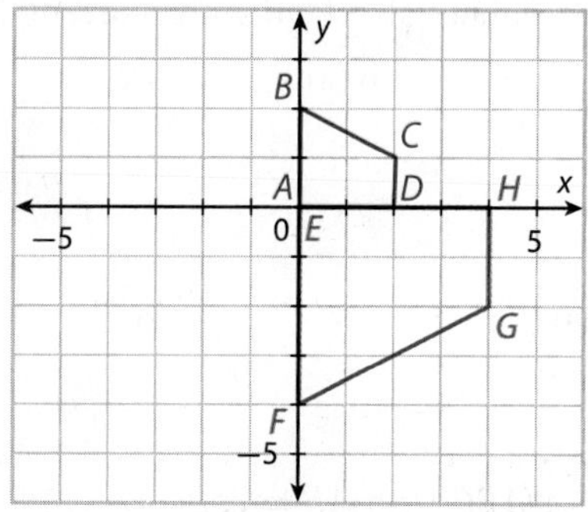

7. Map $\triangle CED$ to $\triangle CBA$.

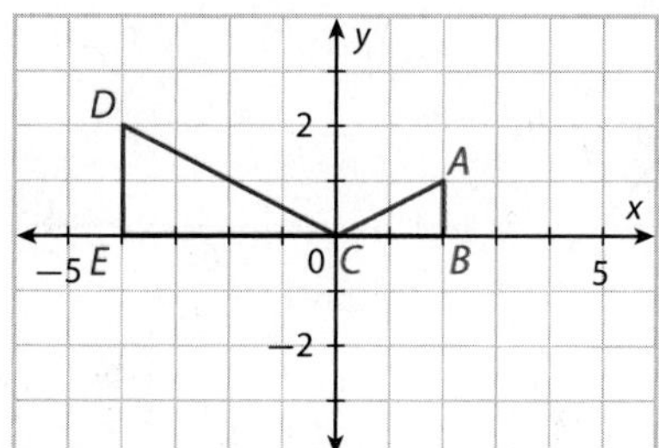

8. Map $ABCDE$ to $JKLMN$.

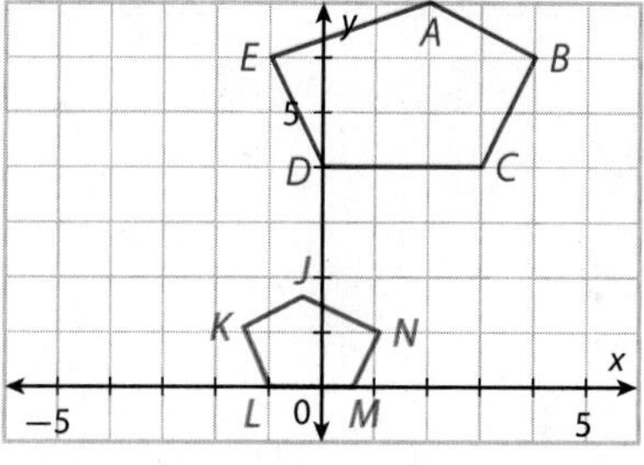

9. Map $ABCD$ to $JKLM$.

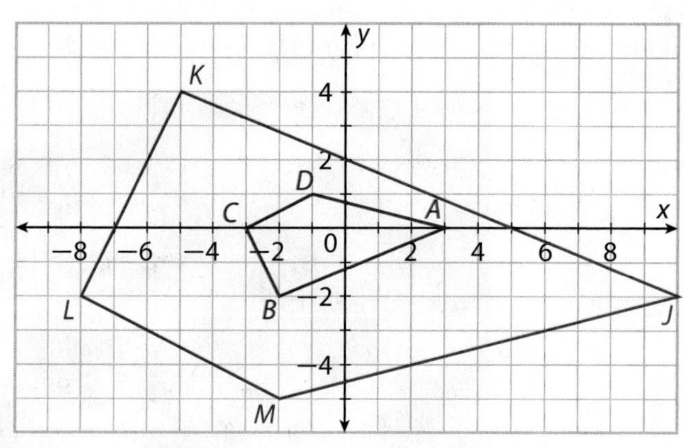

10. Map $\triangle JKL$ to $\triangle PQR$.

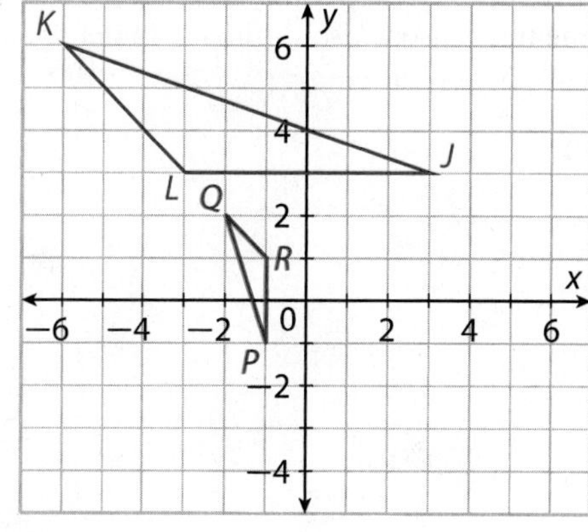

Complete the proof.

11. Given: Square $ABCD$ with side length x.
Square $EFGH$ with side length y.

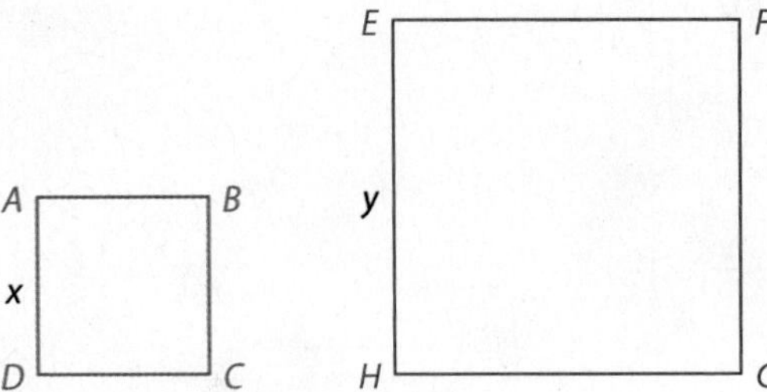

Prove: Square $ABCD$ is similar to square $EFGH$.

12. Given: Equilateral $\triangle JKL$ with side length j.
Equilateral $\triangle PQR$ with side length p

Prove: $\triangle JKL$ is similar to $\triangle PQR$.

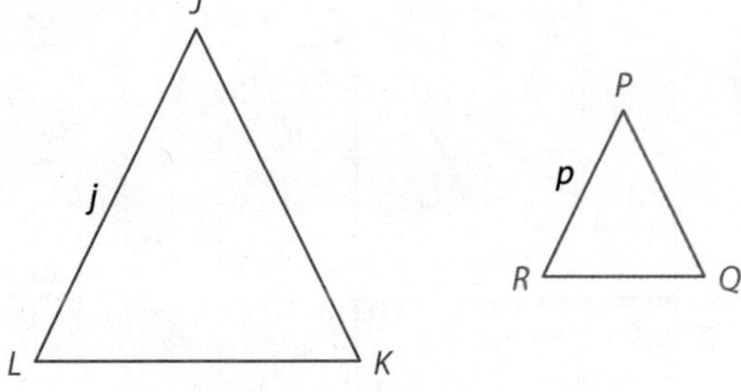

13. Given: $\triangle ABC$ with $AB = c$, $BC = a$, $AC = b$
$\triangle XYZ$ with $YZ = x$, $XY = \frac{cx}{a}$, $XZ = \frac{bx}{a}$

Prove: $\triangle ABC$ is similar to $\triangle XYZ$.

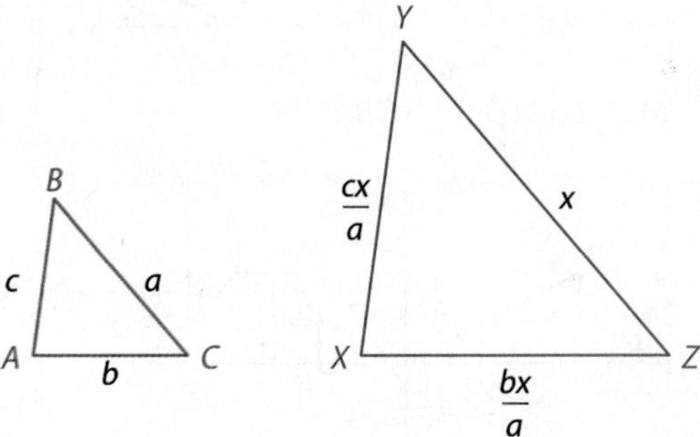

14. The dimensions of a standard tennis court are 36 feet × 78 feet with a net that is 3 feet high in the center. The court is modified for players aged 10 and under such that the dimensions are 27 feet × 60 feet, and the same net is used. Use similarity to determine if the modified court is similar to the standard court.

15. Represent Real-World Problems A scuba flag is used to indicate there is a diver below. In North America, scuba flags are red with a white stripe from the upper left corner to the lower right corner. Justify the triangles formed on the scuba flag are similar triangles.

16. The most common picture size is 4 inches $\times 6$ inches. Other common pictures sizes (in inches) are 5×7, 8×10, 9×12, 11×14, 14×18, and 16×20.

a. Are any of these picture sizes similar? Explain using similarity transformations.

b. What does your conclusion indicate about resizing pictures?

17. Nicole wants to know the height of the snow sculpture but it is too tall to measure. Nicole measured the shadow of the snow sculpture's highest point to be 10 feet long. At the same time of day Nicole's shadow was 40 inches long. If Nicole is 5 feet tall, what is the height of the snow sculpture?

18. Which of the following is a dilation?

A. $(x, y) \rightarrow (x, 3y)$

B. $(x, y) \rightarrow (3x, -y)$

C. $(x, y) \rightarrow (3x, 3y)$

D. $(x, y) \rightarrow (x, y - 3)$

E. $(x, y) \rightarrow (x - 3, y - 3)$

19. What is not preserved under dilation? Determine all that apply.

A. Angle measure

B. Betweenness

C. Collinearity

D. Distance

E. Proportionality

H.O.T. Focus on Higher Order Thinking

20. Analyze Relationships Consider the transformations below.

I. Translation **II.** Reflection **III.** Rotation **IV.** Dilation

a. Which transformations preserve distance?

b. Which transformations preserve angle measure?

c. Use your knowledge of rigid transformations to compare and contrast congruency and similarity.

Justify Reasoning For Exercises 21–23, use the figure shown. Determine whether the given assumptions are enough to prove that the two triangles are similar. Write the correct correspondence of the vertices. If the two triangles must be similar, describe a sequence of similarity transformations that maps one triangle to the other. If the triangles are not necessarily similar, explain why.

21. The lengths AX, BX, CX, and DX satisfy the equation $\frac{AX}{BX} = \frac{DX}{CX}$.

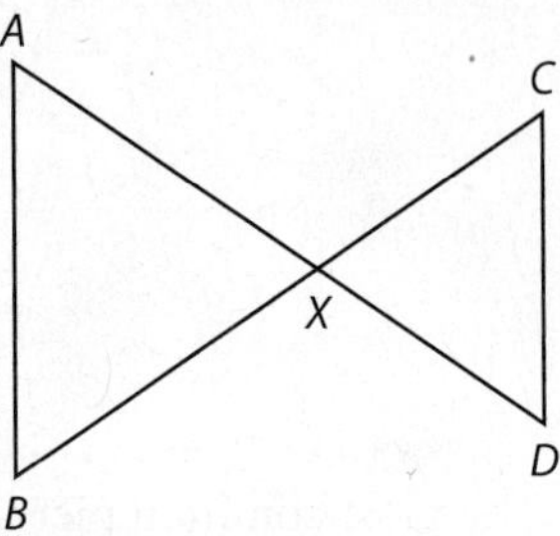

22. Lines AB and CD are parallel.

23. $\angle XAB$ is congruent to $\angle XCD$.

Lesson Performance Task

Answer the following questions about the dartboard pictured here.

1. Are the circles similar? Explain, using the concept of a dilation in your explanation.
2. You throw a dart and it sticks in a random location on the board. What is the probability that it sticks in Circle A? Circle B? Circle C? Circle D? Explain how you found your answers.

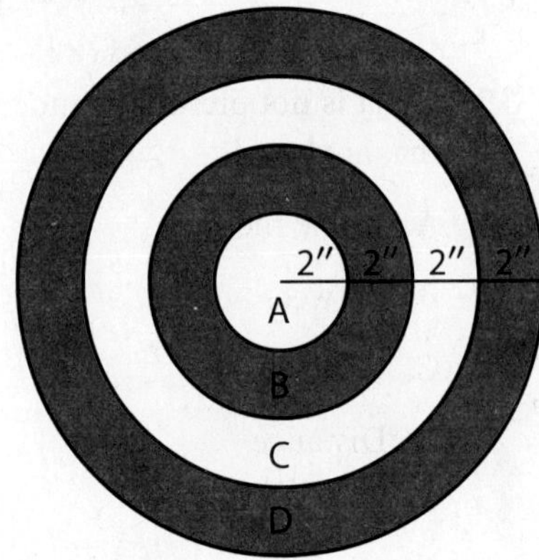

16.3 Corresponding Parts of Similar Figures

Essential Question: **If you know two figures are similar, what can you determine about measures of corresponding angles and lengths?**

Resource Locker

Explore Connecting Angles and Sides of Figures

You know that if figures are similar, the side lengths are proportional and the angle measures are equal. If you have two figures with proportional side lengths and congruent angles, can you conclude that they are similar?

(A) Consider the graph of $ABCD$ and $KLMN$.

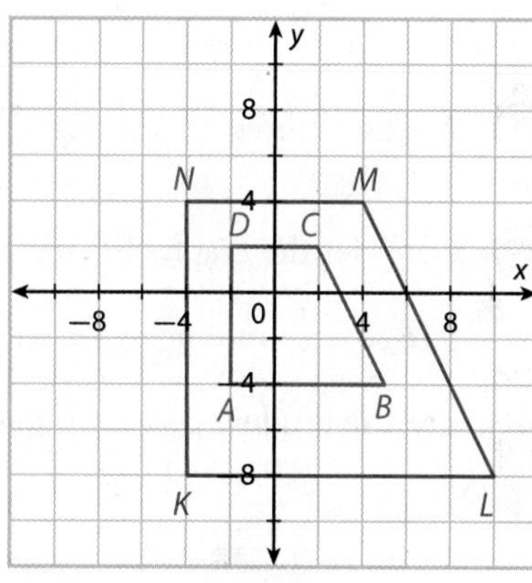

Are corresponding angles congruent?

Measure the angles.

$m\angle A =$ ▭ $m\angle K =$ ▭

$m\angle B =$ ▭ $m\angle L =$ ▭

$m\angle C =$ ▭ $m\angle M =$ ▭

$m\angle D =$ ▭ $m\angle N =$ ▭

(B) Are the ratios of corresponding side lengths equal?

$\frac{AB}{KL} = \frac{▭}{▭}$ $\frac{BC}{LM} = \frac{▭}{▭}$ $\frac{CD}{MN} = \frac{▭}{▭}$ $\frac{AD}{KN} = \frac{▭}{▭}$

(C) Are the figures similar? Describe how you know using similarity transformations.

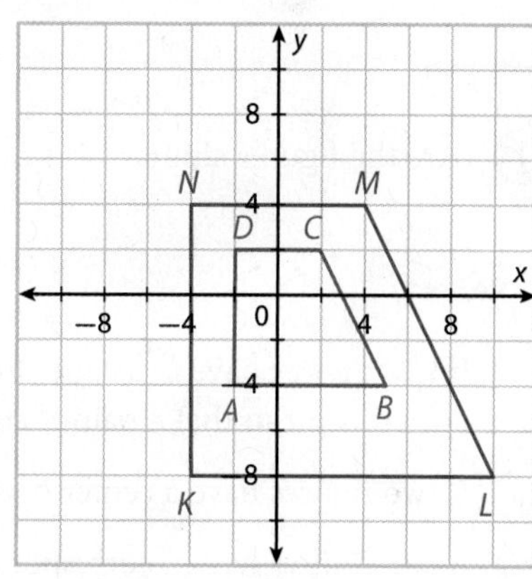

Ⓓ Consider the graph of *ABCD* and *EFGH*.

Are corresponding angles congruent? Explain.

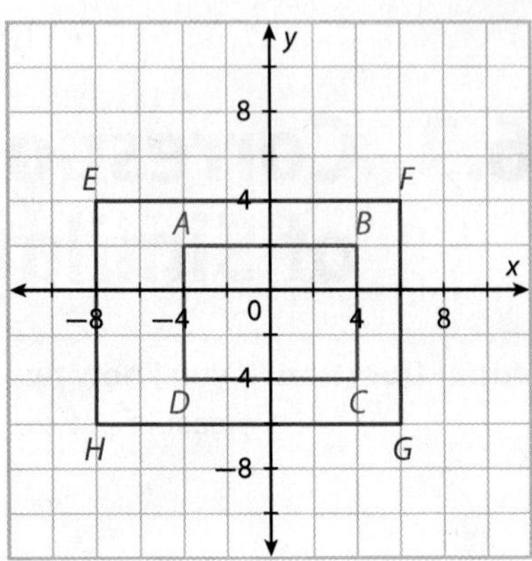

Ⓔ Are the ratios of corresponding side lengths equal?

$\frac{AB}{EF} =$ $\frac{BC}{FG} =$ $\frac{CD}{GH} =$ $\frac{AD}{EH} =$

Ⓕ Are the figures similar? Describe how you know using similarity transformations.

Ⓖ Consider the graph of *PQRS* and *WXYZ*.

Are corresponding angles congruent?

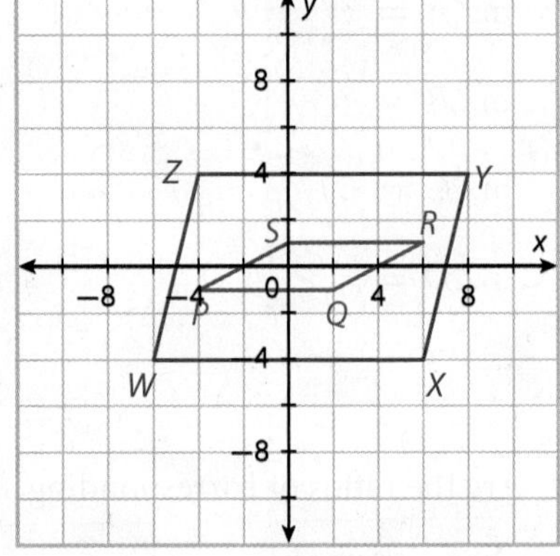

Measure the angles.

$m\angle P =$ $m\angle W =$

$m\angle Q =$ $m\angle X =$

$m\angle R =$ $m\angle Y =$

$m\angle S =$ $m\angle Z =$

Ⓗ Are the ratios of corresponding side lengths equal?

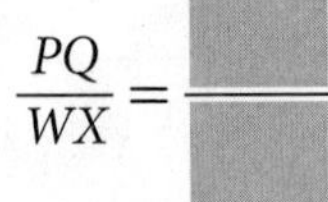

$\frac{PQ}{WX} =$ $\frac{QR}{XY} =$ $\frac{RS}{YZ} =$ $\frac{PS}{WZ} =$

Ⓘ Are the figures similar? Describe how you know using similarity transformations.

Reflect

1. If two figures have the same number of sides and the corresponding angles are congruent, does this mean that a pair of corresponding sides are either congruent or proportional?
2. If two figures have a center of dilation, is a corresponding pair of sides necessarily proportional?
3. If two figures have a correspondence of proportional sides, do the figures necessarily have a center of dilation?

Explain 1 Justifying Properties of Similar Figures Using Transformations

Two figures that can be mapped to each other by similarity transformations (dilations and rigid motions) are similar. Similar figures have certain properties.

Properties of Similar Figures

Corresponding angles of similar figures are congruent.

Corresponding sides of similar figures are proportional.

If $\triangle ABC \sim \triangle XYZ$, then

$\angle A \cong \angle X \quad \angle B \cong \angle Y \quad \angle C \cong \angle Z$

$\frac{AB}{XY} = \frac{BC}{YZ} = \frac{AC}{XZ}$

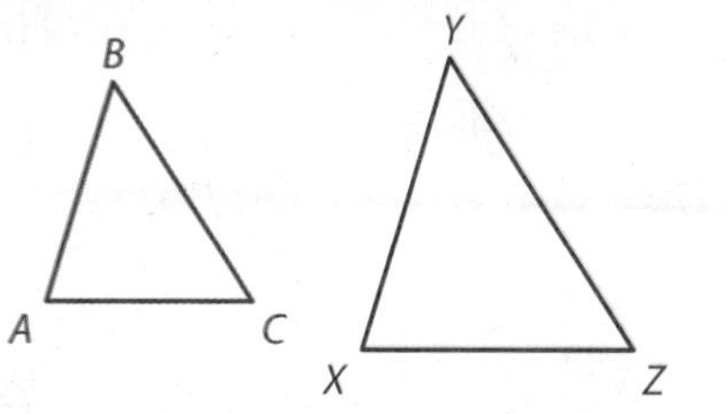

To show that two figures with all pairs of corresponding sides having equal ratio k and all pairs of corresponding angles congruent are similar, you can use similarity transformations.

Dilate one figure using k. The dilated figure is congruent to the second figure by the definition of congruence. So, there is a sequence of rigid motions (which are also similarity transformations) that maps one to the other.

Example 1 **Identify properties of similar figures.**

(A) Figure $EFGH$ maps to figure $RSTU$ by a similarity transformation. Write a proportion that contains EF and RU. List any angles that must be congruent to $\angle G$ or congruent to $\angle U$.

$\frac{EF}{RS} = \frac{EH}{RU}$ $\angle T$ is congruent to $\angle G$, and $\angle H$ is congruent to $\angle U$.

(B) Figure $JKLMN$ maps to figure $TUVWX$ by a similarity transformation. Write a proportion that contains TX and LM. List any angles that must be congruent to $\angle V$ or congruent to $\angle K$.

$\frac{JN}{TX} = \frac{LM}{VW}$ $\angle L$ is congruent to $\angle V$, and $\angle U$ congruent to $\angle K$.

Reflect

4. If you know two figures are similar, what angle or side measurements must you know to find the dilation used in the transformations mapping one figure to another?

Your Turn

5. Triangles $\triangle PQR$ and $\triangle LMN$ are similar. If $QR = 6$ and $MN = 9$, what similarity transformation (in coordinate notation) maps $\triangle PQR$ to $\triangle LMN$?

6. **Error Analysis** Triangles $\triangle DEF$ and $\triangle UVW$ are similar. $\frac{DE}{UV} = \frac{VW}{EF}$ Is the statement true?

Explain 2 Applying Properties of Similar Figures

The properties of similar figures can be used to find the measures of corresponding parts.

Example 2 **Given that the figures are similar, find the values of x and y.**

(A)

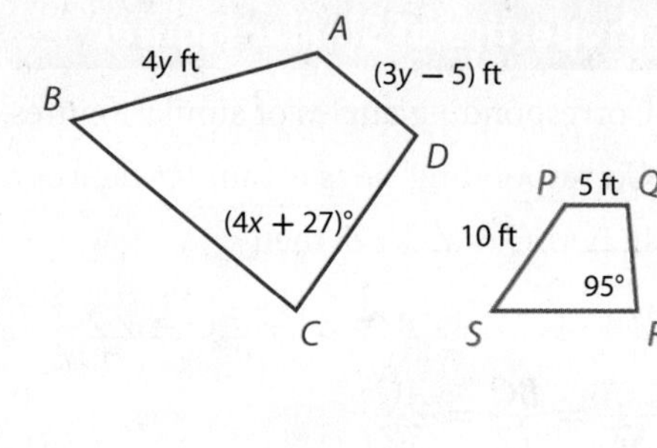

Find the value of x.

$\angle C \cong \angle R$, so $m\angle C = m\angle R$

$4x + 27 = 95$

$4x = 68$

$x = 17$

Find the value of y.

$$\frac{AB}{PS} = \frac{AD}{PQ}$$

$$\frac{4y}{10} = \frac{3y - 5}{5}$$

$$\frac{4y}{10} \cdot 10 = \frac{3y - 5}{5} \cdot 10$$

$$4y = 6y - 10$$

$$y = 5$$

(B)

K, L, M, N, J; (2y – 8) cm; 5(x – 5)°; 1.5 cm

Z, V, Y, X, W; 1 cm; 4x°; 4 cm

Find the value of x.

$m\angle LMN = m\angle XYZ$

$5(x - 5) = 4$

$5x - 25 = 4x$

$x = 25$

Find the value of y.

$$\frac{JK}{VW} = \frac{MN}{YZ}$$

$$\frac{2x - 8}{4} = \frac{1.5}{1}$$

$$2x - 8 = 1.5(4)$$

$$2x - 8 = 6$$

$$2x = 14$$

$$x = 7$$

Reflect

7. **Discussion** What are some things you need to be careful about when solving problems involving finding the values of variables in similar figures?

Your Turn

Use the diagram, in which $\triangle ABE \sim \triangle ACD$.

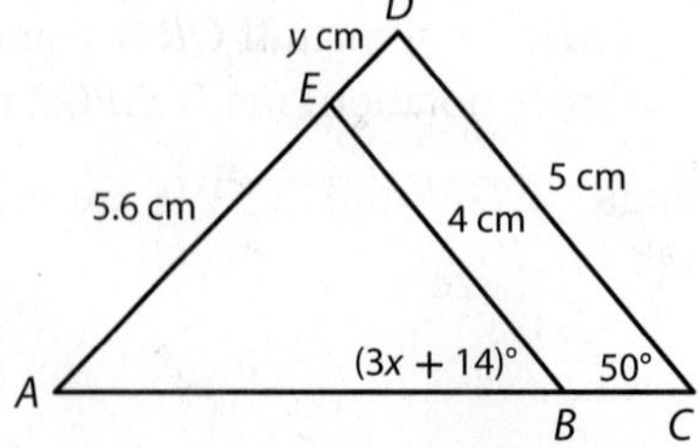

8. Find the value of x.

9. Find the value of y.

Elaborate

10. Consider two similar triangles $\triangle ABC$ and $\triangle A'B'C'$. If both $m\angle A' = m\angle C$ and $m\angle B' = m\angle A$, what can you conclude about triangle $\triangle ABC$? Explain your reasoning.

11. Rectangle $JKLM$ maps to rectangle $RSTU$ by the transformation $(x, y) \rightarrow (4x, 4y)$. If the perimeter of $RSTU$ is x, what is the perimeter of $JKLM$ in terms of x?

12. **Essential Question Check-In** If two figures are similar, what can we conclude about their corresponding parts?

Evaluate: Homework and Practice

- Online Homework
- Hints and Help
- Extra Practice

In the figures, are corresponding angles congruent? Are corresponding sides proportional? Are the figures similar? Describe how you know using similarity transformations.

1.

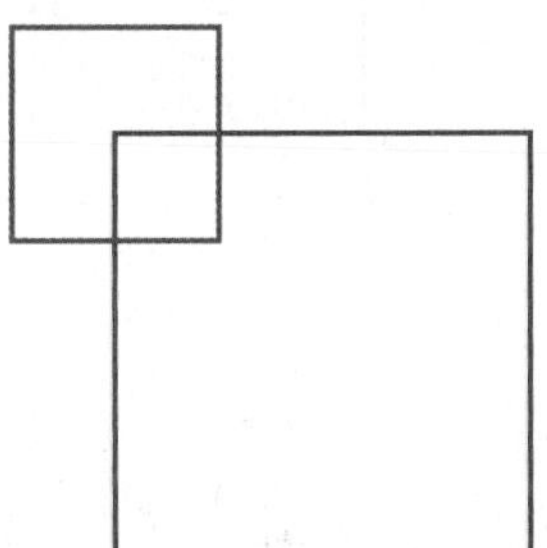

2.

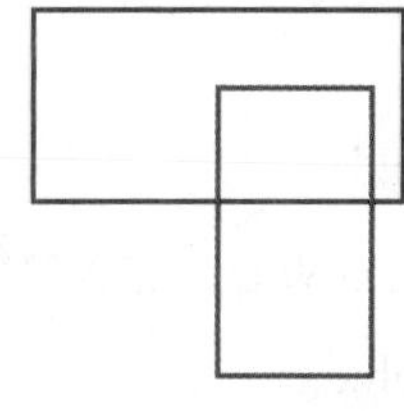

3.

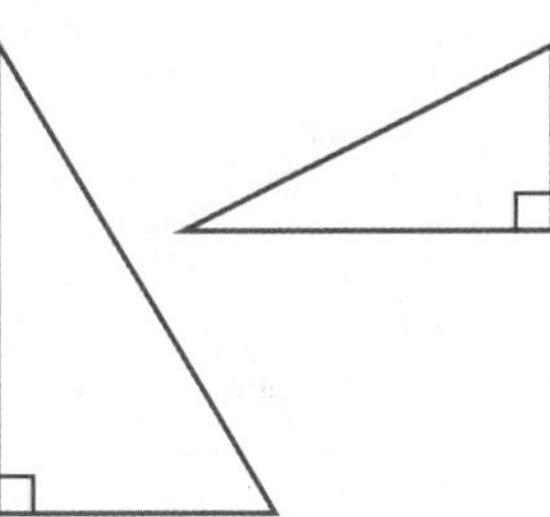

4.

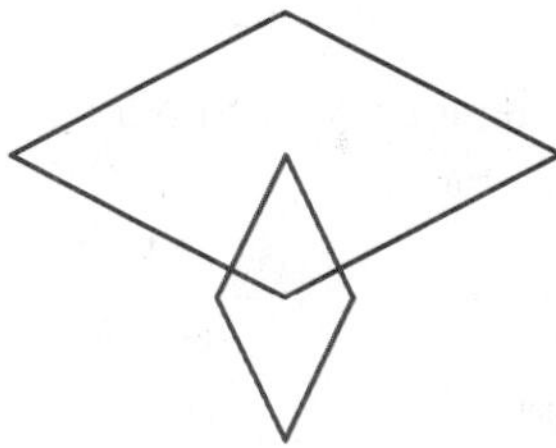

5. Figure $ABCD$ is similar to figure $MNKL$. Write a proportion that contains BC and KL.

6. $\triangle DEF$ is similar to $\triangle STU$. Write a proportion that contains ST and SU.

7. $\triangle XYZ$ is similar to $\triangle XVW$. Write the congruence statements that must be true.

8. $\triangle MNP$ is similar to $\triangle HJK$, and both triangles are isosceles. If $m\angle P > 90°$, name all angles that are congruent to $\angle H$.

9. $CDEF$ maps to $JKLM$ with the transformations $(x, y) \rightarrow (5x, 5y) \rightarrow (x - 4, y - 4)$. What is the value of $\frac{EF}{LM}$?

10. $\triangle PQR$ maps to $\triangle VWX$ with the transformation $(x, y) \rightarrow (x + 3, y - 1) \rightarrow (2x, 2y)$. If $WX = 12$, what does QR equal?

11. $\triangle QRS$ maps to $\triangle XYZ$ with the transformation $(x, y) \rightarrow (6x, 6y)$. If $QS = 7$, what is the length of XZ?

12. **Algebra** Two similar figures are similar based on the transformation $(x, y) \rightarrow (12x, 3a^2y)$. What is/are the value(s) of a?

13. Algebra $\triangle PQR$ is similar to $\triangle XYZ$. If $PQ = n + 2$, $QR = n - 2$, and $XY = n^2 - 4$, what is the value of YZ, in terms of n?

14. Which transformations will not produce similar figures? Determine all that apply and explain your choices.

A. $(x, y) \rightarrow (x - 4, y) \rightarrow (-x, -y) \rightarrow (8x, 8y)$

B. $(x, y) \rightarrow (x + 1, y + 1) \rightarrow (3x, 2y) \rightarrow (-x, -y)$

C. $(x, y) \rightarrow (5x, 5y) \rightarrow (x, -y) \rightarrow (x + 3, y - 3)$

D. $(x, y) \rightarrow (x, 2y) \rightarrow (x + 6, y - 2) \rightarrow (2x, y)$

E. $(x, y) \rightarrow (x, 3y) \rightarrow (2x, y) \rightarrow (x - 3, y - 2)$

15. The figures in the picture are similar to each other. Find the value of x.

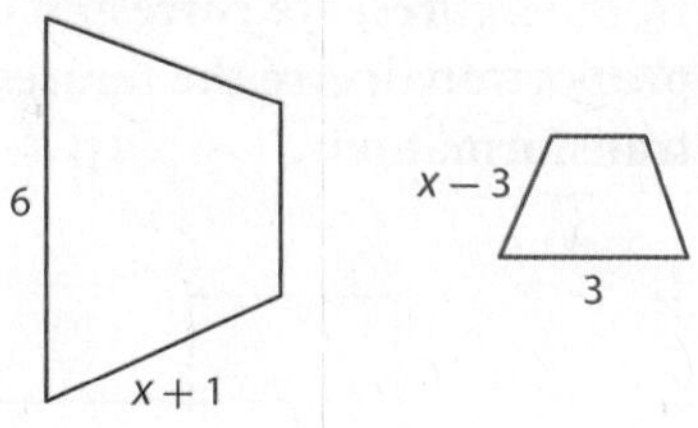

16. In the diagram, $\triangle NPQ \sim \triangle NLM$ and $PL = 5$.

a. Find the value of x.

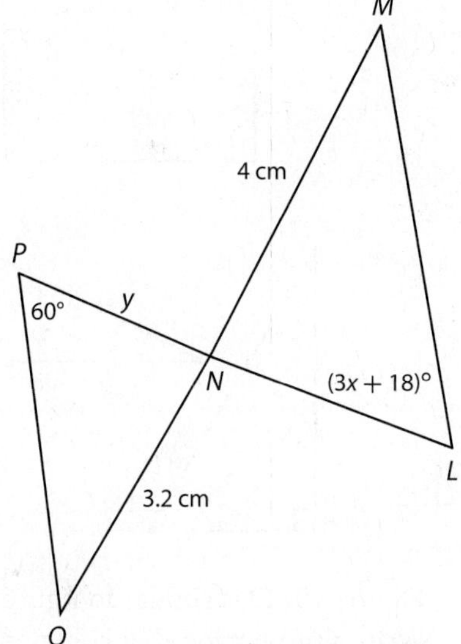

b. Find the lengths NP and NL.

17. $\triangle CDE$ maps to $\triangle STU$ with the transformations $(x, y) \rightarrow (x - 2, y - 2) \rightarrow (3x, 3y) \rightarrow (x, -y)$.
If $CD = a + 1$, $DE = 2a - 1$, $ST = 2b + 3$, and $TU = b + 6$, find the values of a and b.

18. If a sequence of transformations contains the transformation (ax, by), with $a \neq b$, could the pre-image and image represent congruent figures? Could they represent similar, non-congruent figures? Justify your answers with examples.

19. Is any pair of equilateral triangles similar to each other? Why or why not?

20. Figure $CDEF$ is similar to figure $KLMN$. Which statements are false? Determine all that apply and explain why.

A. $\frac{CD}{KL} = \frac{EF}{MN}$ B. $\frac{CF}{KN} = \frac{EF}{MN}$ C. $\frac{DE}{LM} = \frac{CF}{KN}$ D. $\frac{LM}{DE} = \frac{KL}{CD}$ E. $\frac{LM}{DE} = \frac{KN}{CD}$

Consider this model of a train locomotive when answering the next two questions.

21. If the model is 18 inches long and the actual locomotive is 72 feet long, what is the similarity transformation to map from the model to the actual locomotive? Express the answer using the notation $x \longrightarrow ax$, where x is a measurement on the model and ax is the corresponding measurement on the actual locomotive.

22. If the diameter of the front wheels on the locomotive is 4 feet, what is the diameter of the front wheels on the model? Express the answer in inches.

Use the following graph to answer the next two problems.

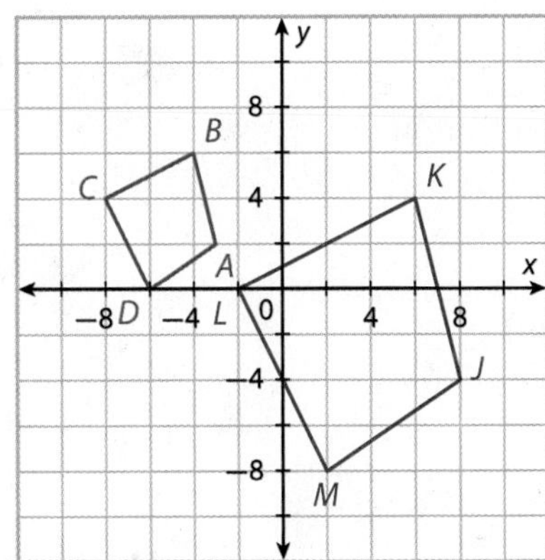

23. Specify a sequence of two transformations that will map $ABCD$ onto $JKLM$.

24. Find the value of $\frac{AC + BD}{JL + KM}$.

H.O.T. Focus on Higher Order Thinking

25. Counterexamples Consider the statement "All rectangles are similar." Is this statement true or false? If true, explain why. If false, provide a counterexample.

26. Justify Reasoning If $ABCD$ is similar to $KLMN$ and $MNKL$, what special type of quadrilateral is $KLMN$? Justify your reasoning.

27. Critique Reasoning Consider the statement "If $\triangle PQR$ is similar to $\triangle QPR$, then $\triangle PQR$ is similar to $\triangle RPQ$." Explain whether or not this statement is true.

Lesson Performance Task

You've hired an architect to design your dream house and now the house has been built. Before moving in, you've decided to wander through the house with a tape measure to see how well the builders have followed the architect's floor plan. Describe in as much detail as you can how you could accomplish your goal. Then discuss how you can decide whether the room shapes and other features of the house are similar to the corresponding shapes on the floor plan.

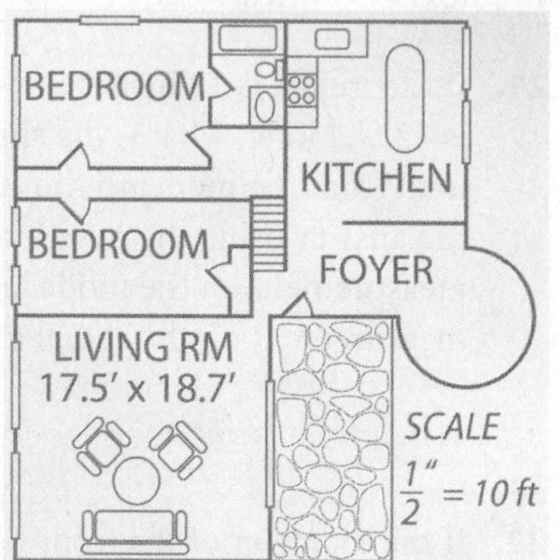

16.4 AA Similarity of Triangles

Resource Locker

Essential Question: How can you show that two triangles are similar?

Explore Exploring Angle-Angle Similarity for Triangles

Two triangles are similar when their corresponding sides are proportional and their corresponding angles are congruent. There are several shortcuts for proving triangles are similar.

(A) Draw a triangle and label it $\triangle ABC$. Elsewhere on your page, draw a segment longer than $\overline{AB}$ and label the endpoints *D* and *E*.

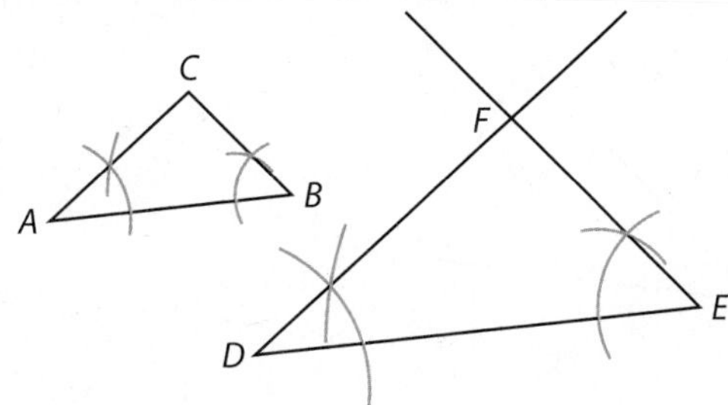

(B) Copy $\angle CAB$ and $\angle ABC$ to points *D* and *E*, respectively. Extend the rays of your copied angles, if necessary, and label their intersection point *F*. You have constructed $\triangle DEF$.

(C) You constructed angles *D* and *E* to be congruent to angles *A* and *B*, respectively. Therefore, angles *C* and *F* must also be ____ because of the ____ Theorem.

(D) Check the proportionality of the corresponding sides.

$\frac{AB}{DE} = \frac{\square}{\square} = \square \qquad \frac{AC}{DF} = \frac{\square}{\square} = \square \qquad \frac{BC}{EF} = \frac{\square}{\square} = \square$

Since the ratios are ____ the sides of the triangles are ____.

Reflect

1. **Discussion** Compare your results with your classmates. What conjecture can you make about two triangles that have two corresponding congruent angles?

Explain 1 Proving Angle-Angle Triangle Similarity

The Explore suggests the following theorem for determining whether two triangles are similar.

Angle-Angle (AA) Triangle Similarity Theorem

If two angles of one triangle are congruent to two angles of another triangle, then the two triangles are similar.

Example 1 **Prove the Angle-Angle Triangle Similarity Theorem.**

Given: $\angle A \cong \angle X$ and $\angle B \cong \angle Y$

Prove: $\triangle ABC \sim \triangle XYZ$

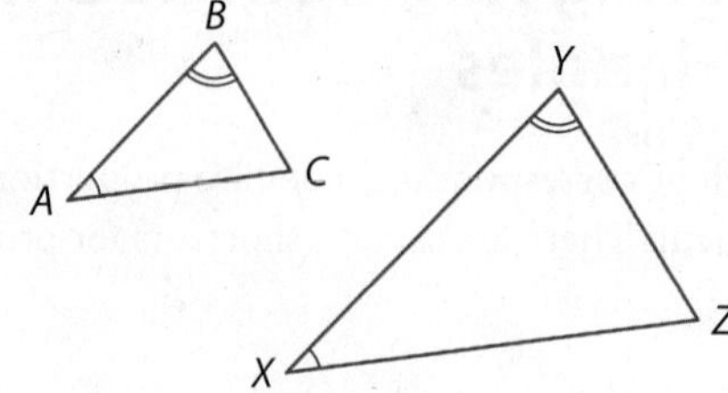

(1) Apply a dilation to $\triangle ABC$ with scale factor $k = \frac{XY}{AB}$. Let the image of $\triangle ABC$ be $\triangle A'B'C$.

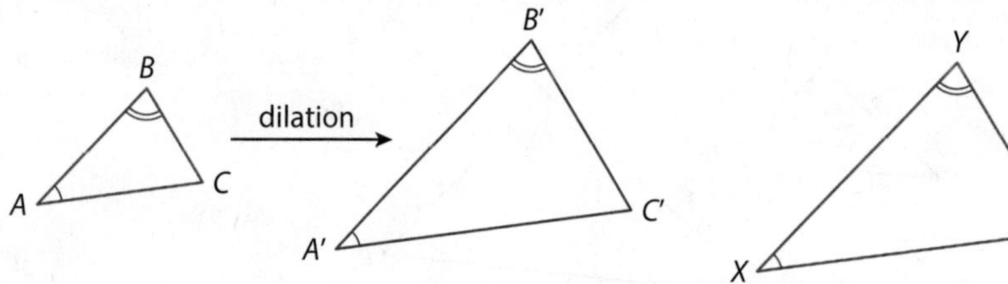

$\triangle A'B'C$ is similar to $\triangle ABC$, and $\angle A' \cong \angle A$ and $\angle B' \cong \angle B$ because corresponding angles of similar triangles are congruent.

Also, $A'B' = k \cdot AB = \frac{XY}{AB} \cdot AB = XY$.

(2) It is given that $\angle A \cong \angle X$ and $\angle B \cong \angle Y$

By the Transitive Property of Congruence, $\angle A' \cong \angle X$ and $\angle B' \cong \angle Y$.

So, $\triangle A'B'C' \cong \triangle XYZ$ by the ASA Triangle Congruence Theorem.

This means there is a sequence of rigid motions that maps $\triangle A'B'C'$ *to* $\triangle YYZ$.

The dilation followed by this sequence of rigid motions shows that there is a sequence of similarity transformations that maps $\triangle ABC$ to $\triangle XYZ$. Therefore, $\triangle ABC \sim \triangle XYZ$.

Reflect

2. **Discussion** Compare and contrast the AA Similarity Theorem with the ASA Congruence Theorem.

3. In $\triangle JKL$, $m\angle J = 40°$ and $m\angle K = 55°$. In $\triangle MNP$, $m\angle M = 40°$ and $m\angle P = 85°$. A student concludes that the triangles are not similar. Do you agree or disagree? Why?

Explain 2 Applying Angle-Angle Similarity

Architects and contractors use the properties of similar figures to find any unknown dimensions, like the proper height of a triangular roof. They can use a bevel angle tool to check that the angles of construction are congruent to the angles in their plans.

Example 2 **Find the indicated length, if possible.**

Ⓐ *BE*

First, determine whether $\triangle ABC \sim \triangle DBE$.

By the Alternate Interior Angles Theorem, $\angle A \cong \angle D$ and $\angle C \cong \angle E$, so $\triangle ABC \sim \triangle DBE$ by the AA Triangle Similarity Theorem.

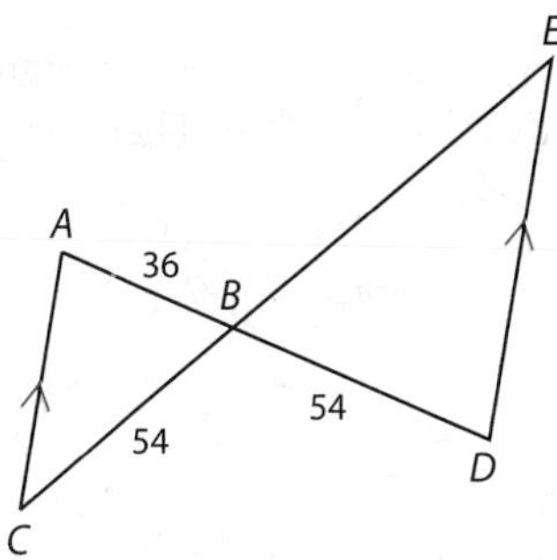

Find *BE* by solving a proportion.

$$\frac{BD}{BA} = \frac{BE}{BC}$$

$$\frac{54}{36} = \frac{BE}{54}$$

$$\frac{54}{36} \cdot 54 = \frac{BE}{54} \cdot 54$$

$$BE = 81$$

Ⓑ *RT*

Check whether $\triangle RSV \sim \triangle RTU$:

It is given in the diagram that $\angle$ RSV $\cong \angle$ T . $\angle R$ is shared by both triangles,

so $\angle R \cong \angle R$ by the Reflexive Property of Congruence.

So, by the AA Triangle Similarity Theorem, $\triangle RST \sim \triangle RTU$.

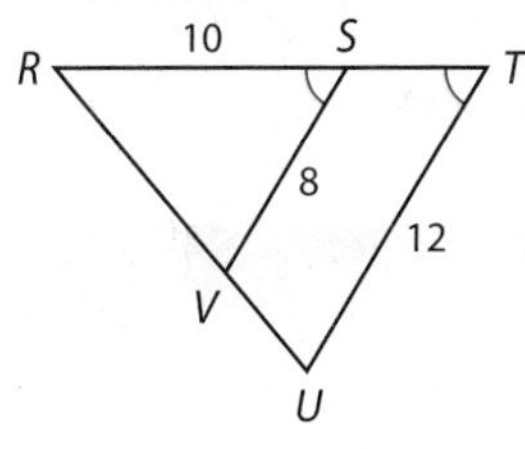

Find *RT* by solving a proportion.

$$\frac{RT}{RS} = \frac{TU}{SV}$$

$$\frac{RT}{10} = \frac{12}{8}$$

$$RT = 15$$

Reflect

4. In Example 2A, is there another way you can set up the proportion to solve for *BE*?

5. **Discussion** When asked to solve for *y*, a student sets up the proportion as shown. Explain why the proportion is wrong. How should you adjust the proportion so that it will give the correct result?

$\frac{y}{8} = \frac{14}{10}$

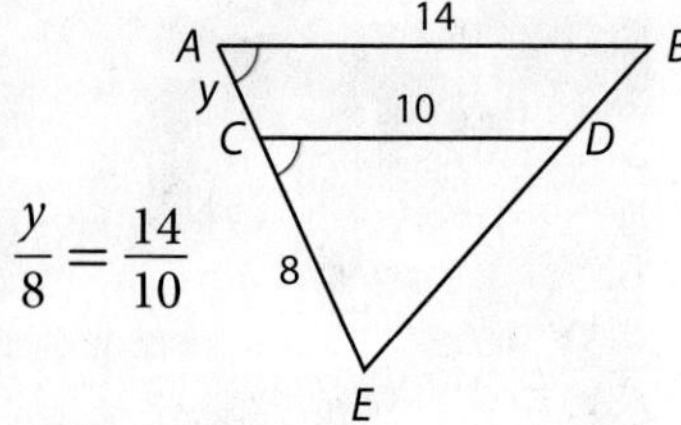

Your Turn

6. A builder was given a design plan for a triangular roof as shown. Explain how he knows that $\triangle AED \sim \triangle ACB$. Then find *AB*.

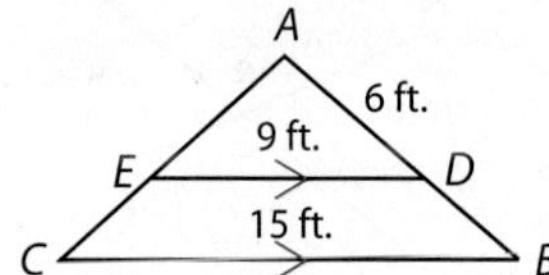

7. Find *PQ*, if possible.

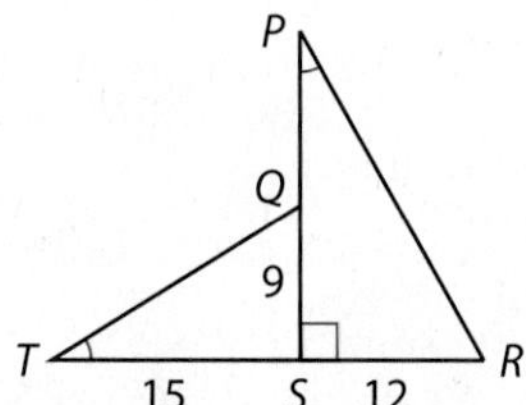

Explain 3 Applying SSS and SAS Triangle Similarity

In addition to Angle-Angle Triangle Similarity, there are two additional shortcuts for proving two triangles are similar.

Side-Side-Side (SSS) Triangle Similarity Theorem

If the three sides of one triangle are proportional to the corresponding sides of another triangle, then the triangles are similar.

Side-Angle-Side (SAS) Triangle Similarity Theorem

If two sides of one triangle are proportional to the corresponding sides of another triangle and their included angles are congruent, then the triangles are similar.

Example 3 **Determine whether the given triangles are similar. Justify your answer.**

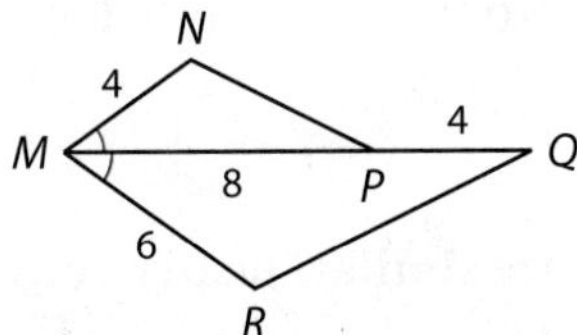

You are given two pairs of corresponding side lengths and one pair of congruent corresponding angles, so try using SAS.

Check that the ratios of corresponding sides are equal.

$\frac{MN}{MR} = \frac{4}{6} = \frac{2}{3}$ $\qquad$ $\frac{MP}{MQ} = \frac{8}{8+4} = \frac{8}{12} = \frac{2}{3}$

Check that the included angles are congruent: $\angle NMP \cong \angle QMR$ is given in the diagram.

Therefore $\triangle NMP \sim \triangle RMQ$ by the SAS Triangle Similarity Theorem.

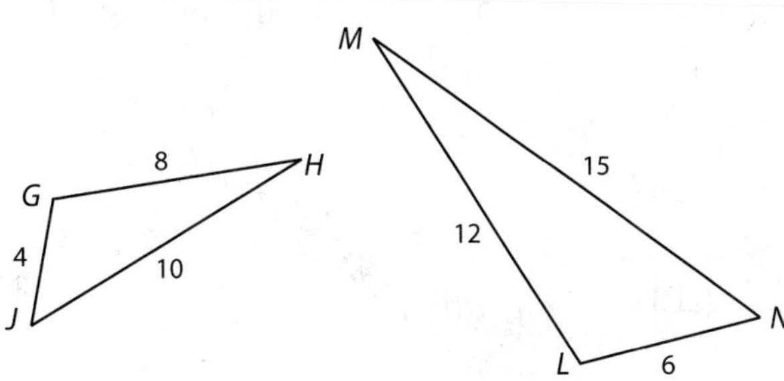

You are given three pairs of corresponding side lengths and zero congruent corresponding angles, so try using the SSS Triangle Similarity Theorem.

Check that the ratios of corresponding sides are equal.

$\frac{LM}{GH} = \frac{12}{8} = \frac{3}{2}$ $\qquad$ $\frac{MN}{HJ} = \frac{15}{10} = \frac{3}{2}$ $\qquad$ $\frac{GJ}{LN} = \frac{6}{4} = \frac{3}{2}$

Therefore $\triangle$ GHJ $\sim \triangle$ LMN by SSS Triangle Similarity Theorem.

Since you are given all three pairs of sides, you don't need to check for congruent angles.

Reflect

8. Are all isosceles right triangles similar? Explain why or why not.

9. Why isn't Angle-Side-Angle (ASA) used to prove two triangles similar?

Your Turn

If possible, determine whether the given triangles are similar. Justify your answer.

10.

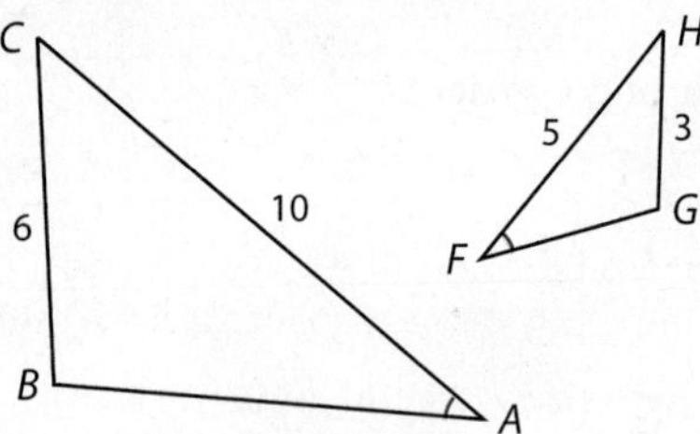

11.

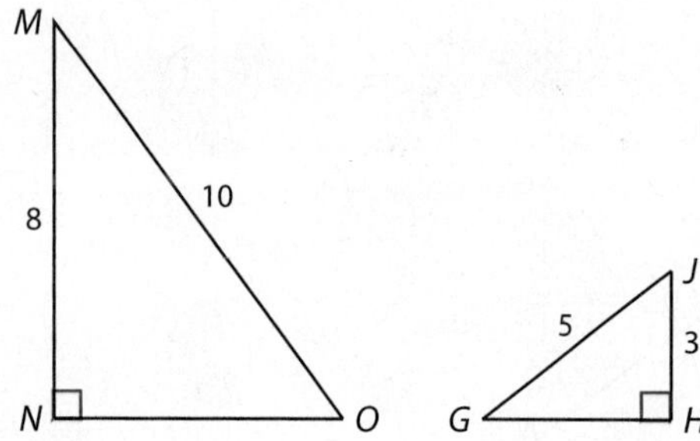

Elaborate

12. Is triangle similarity transitive? If you know $\triangle ABC \sim \triangle DEF$ and $\triangle DEF \sim \triangle GHJ$, is $\triangle ABC \sim \triangle GHJ$? Explain.

13. The AA Similarity Theorem applies to triangles. Is there an AAA Similarity Theorem for quadrilaterals? Use your geometry software to test your conjecture or create a counterexample.

14. **Essential Question Check-In** How can you prove triangles are similar?

Evaluate: Homework and Practice

- Online Homework
- Hints and Help
- Extra Practice

Show that the triangles are similar by measuring the lengths of their sides and comparing the ratios of the corresponding sides.

1.

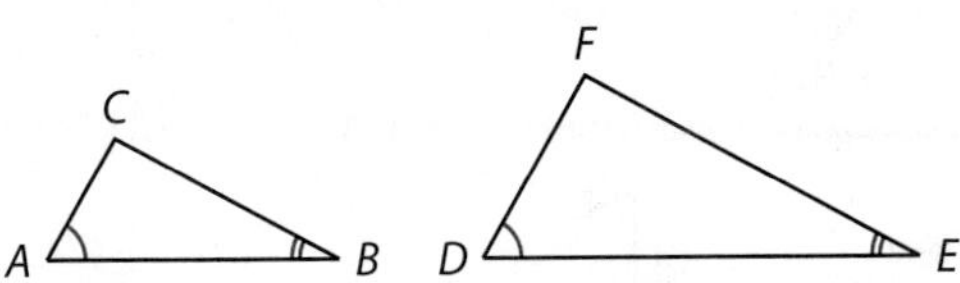

$\frac{DE}{AB} = \frac{\square}{\square} = \square$

$\frac{DF}{AC} = \frac{\square}{\square} = \square$

$\frac{EF}{BC} = \frac{\square}{\square} = \square$

2.

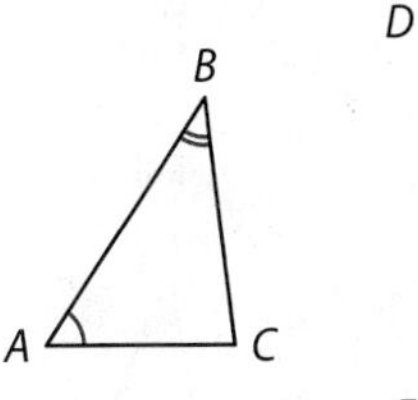

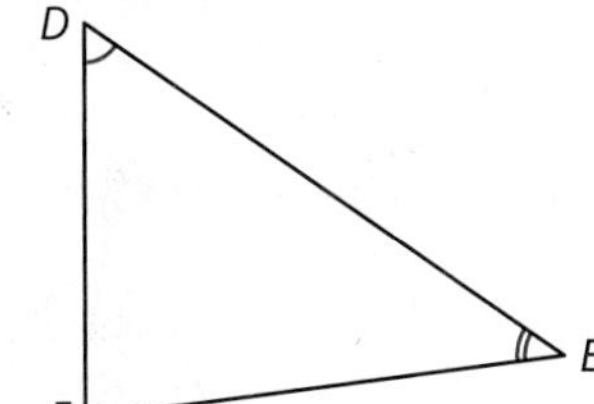

$\frac{AB}{DE} = \frac{\square}{\square} = \square$

$\frac{AC}{DF} = \frac{\square}{\square} = \square$

$\frac{BC}{EF} = \frac{\square}{\square} = \square$

Determine whether the two triangles are similar. If they are similar, write the similarity statement.

3.

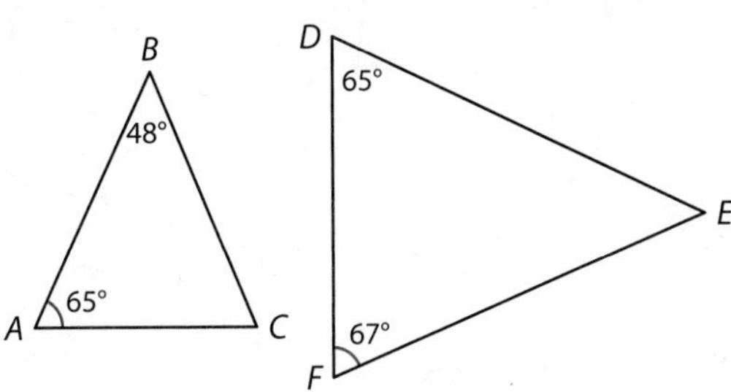

4.

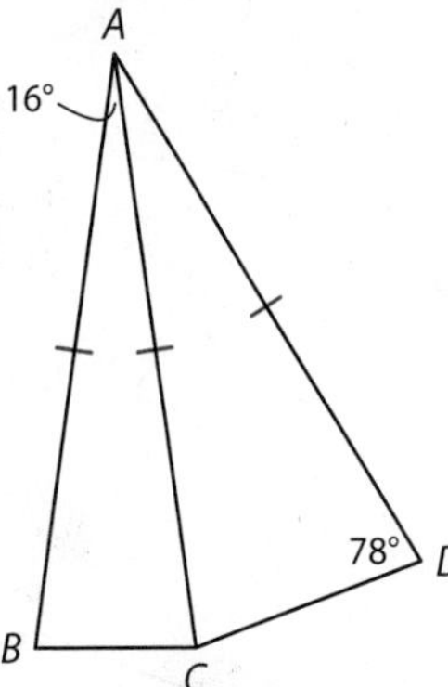

Determine whether the two triangles are similar. If they are similar, write the similarity statement.

5.

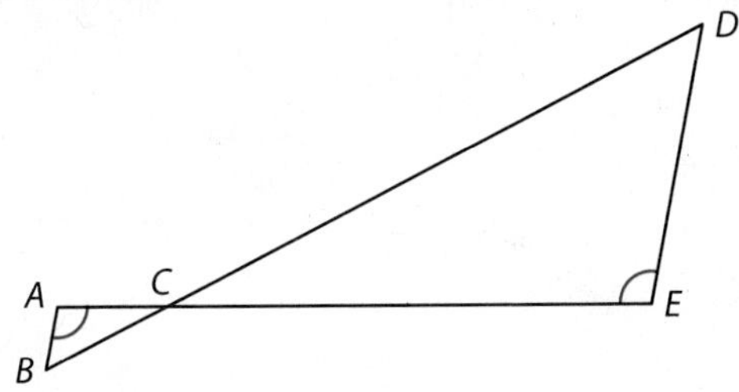

6.

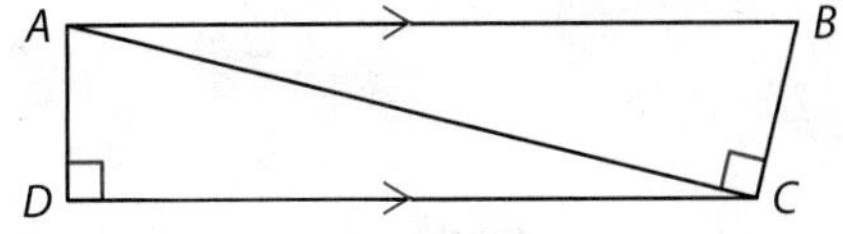

Explain how you know whether the triangles are similar. If possible, find the indicated length.

7. AC

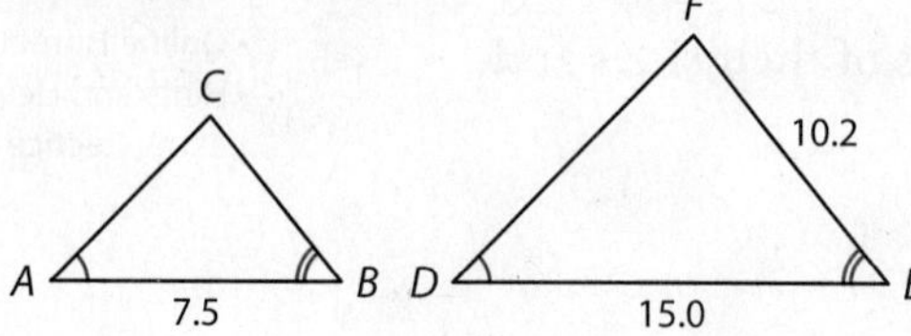

8. AD

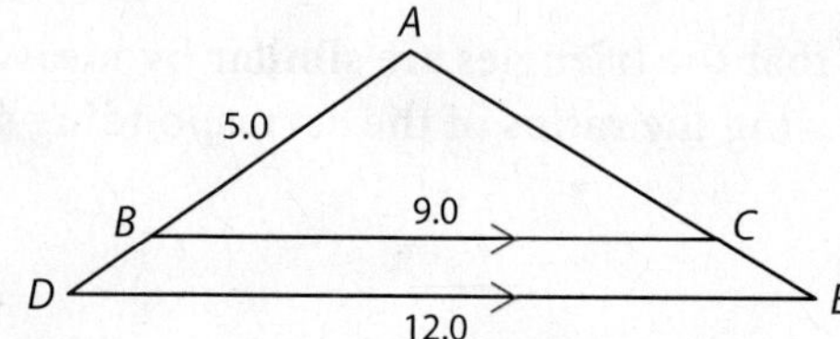

9. QR

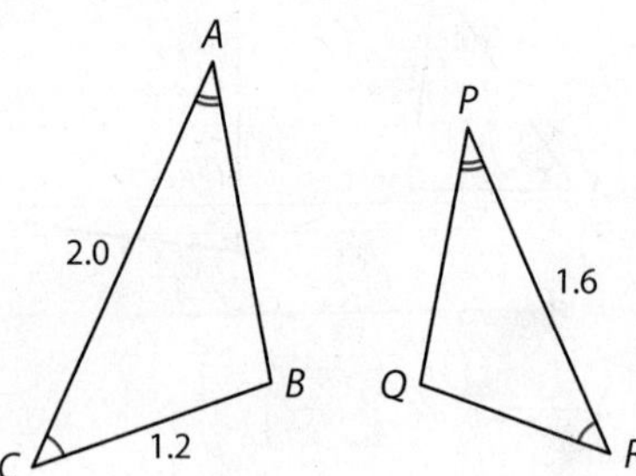

10. Find BD.

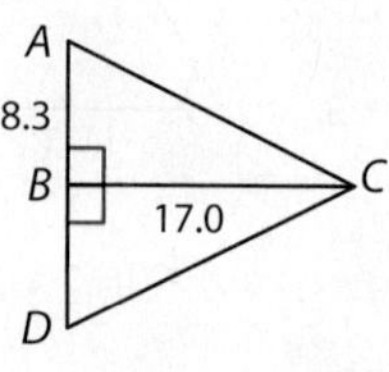

Show whether or not each pair of triangles are similar, if possible. Justify your answer, and write a similarity statement when the triangles are similar.

11.

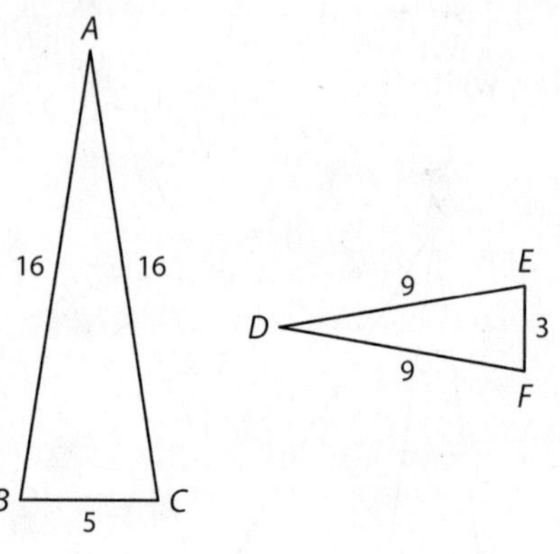

12.

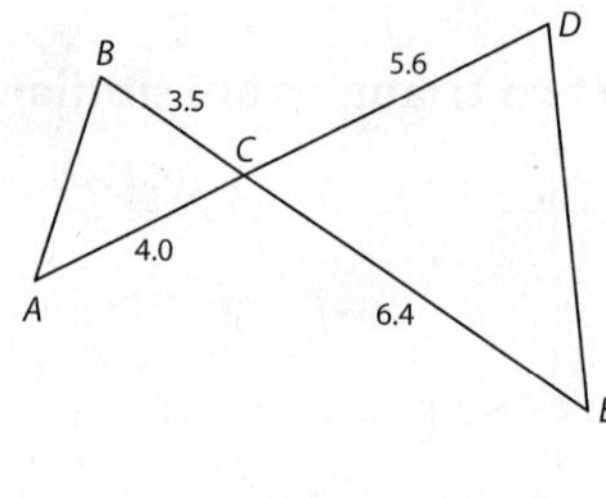

13.

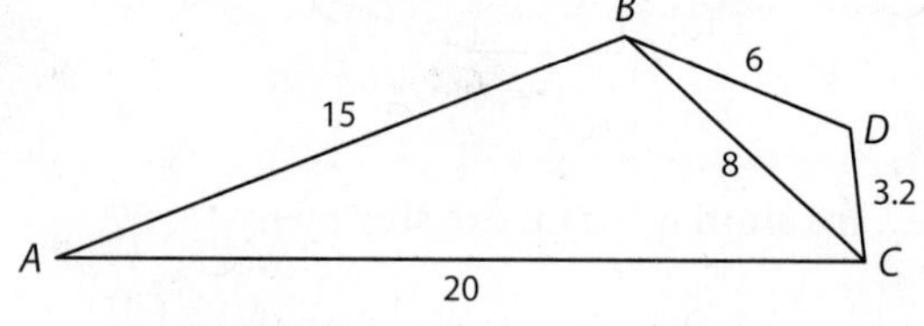

14.

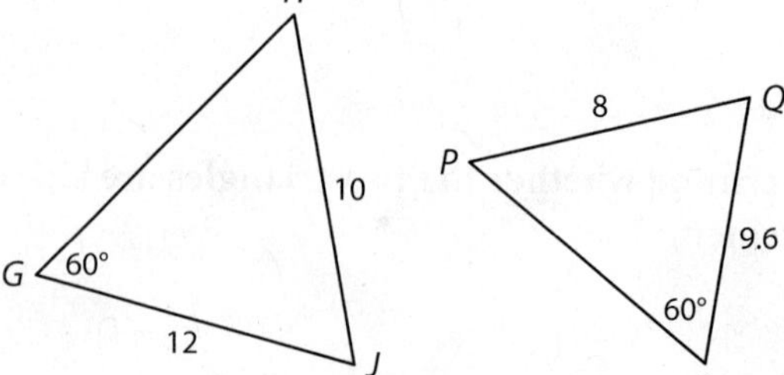

15. Explain the Error A student analyzes the two triangles shown below. Explain the error that the student makes.

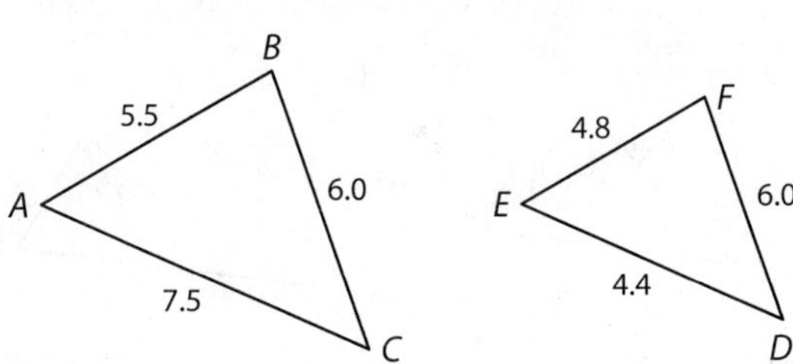

$\frac{AB}{EF} = \frac{5.5}{4.8} = 1.15$, and $\frac{BC}{DF} = \frac{6}{6} = 1$

Because the two ratios are not equal, the two triangles are not similar.

16. Algebra Find all possible values of x for which these two triangles are similar.

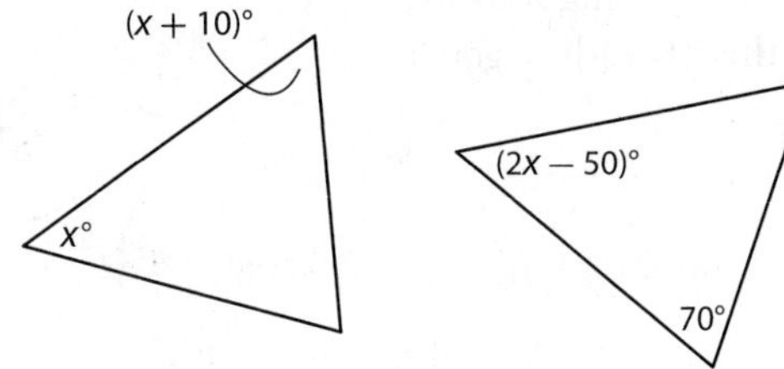

17. Multi-Step Identify two similar triangles in the figure, and explain why they are similar. Then find AB.

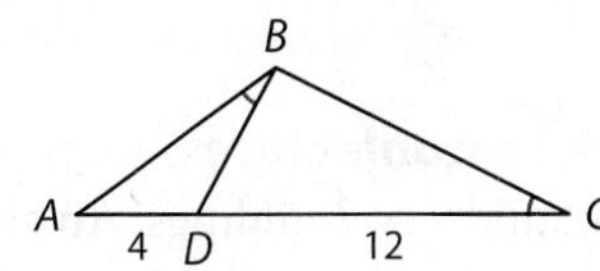

18. The picture shows a person taking a pinhole photograph of himself. Light entering the opening reflects his image on the wall, forming similar triangles. What is the height of the image to the nearest inch?

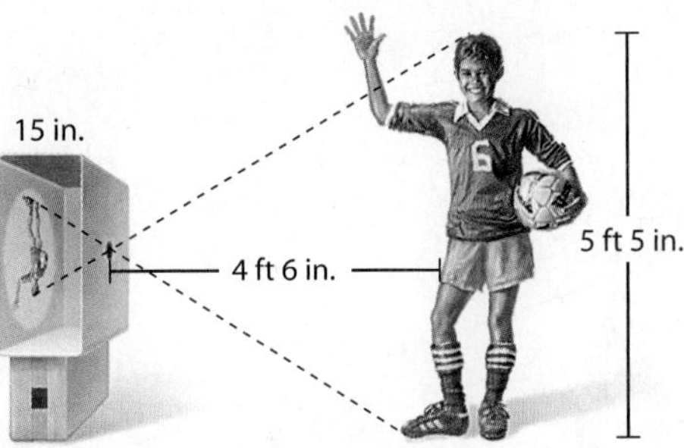

H.O.T. Focus on Higher Order Thinking

19. Analyze Relationships Prove the SAS Triangle Similarity Theorem.

Given: $\frac{XY}{AB} = \frac{XZ}{AC}$ and $\angle A \cong \angle X$

Prove: $\triangle ABC \sim \triangle XYZ$

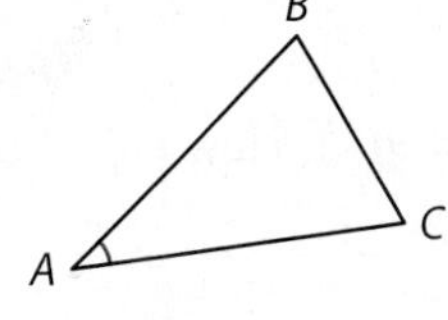

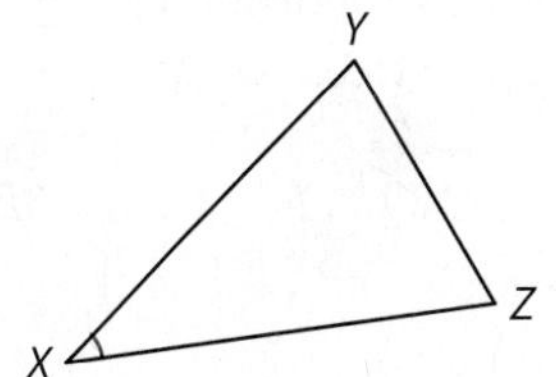

20. Analyze Relationships Prove the SSS Triangle Similarity Theorem.

Given: $\frac{XY}{AB} = \frac{XZ}{AC} = \frac{YZ}{BC}$

Prove: $\triangle ABC \sim \triangle XYZ$

(Hint: The main steps of the proof are similar to those of the proof of the AA Triangle Similarity Theorem.)

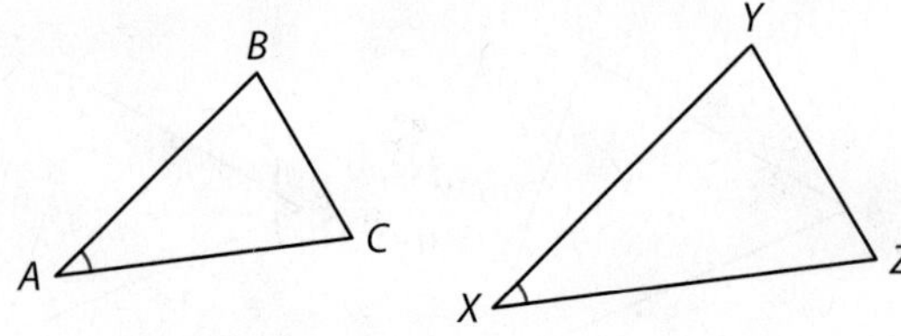

21. Communicate Mathematical Ideas A student is asked to find point X on $\overleftrightarrow{BC}$ such that $\triangle ABC \sim \triangle XBA$ and XB is as small as possible. The student does so by constructing a perpendicular line to $\overleftrightarrow{AC}$ at point A, and then labeling X as the intersection of the perpendicular line with $\overleftrightarrow{BC}$. Explain why this procedure generates the similar triangle that the student was requested to construct.

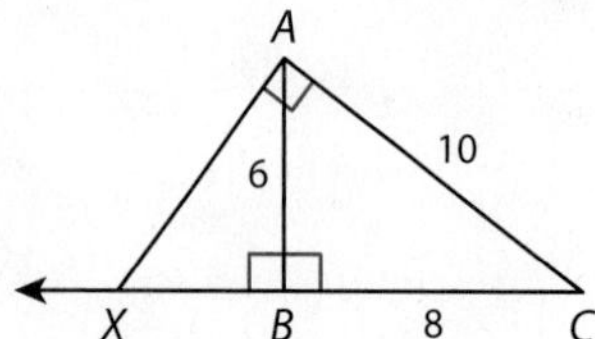

22. Make a Conjecture Builders and architects use scale models to help them design and build new buildings. An architecture student builds a model of an office building in which the height of the model is $\frac{1}{400}$ of the height of the actual building, while the width and length of the model are each $\frac{1}{200}$ of the corresponding dimensions of the actual building. The model includes several triangles. Describe how a triangle in this model could be similar to the corresponding triangle in the actual building, then describe how a triangle in this model might not be similar to the corresponding triangle in the actual building. Use a similarity theorem to support each answer.

Lesson Performance Task

The figure shows a camera obscura and the object being "photographed." Answer the following questions about the figure:

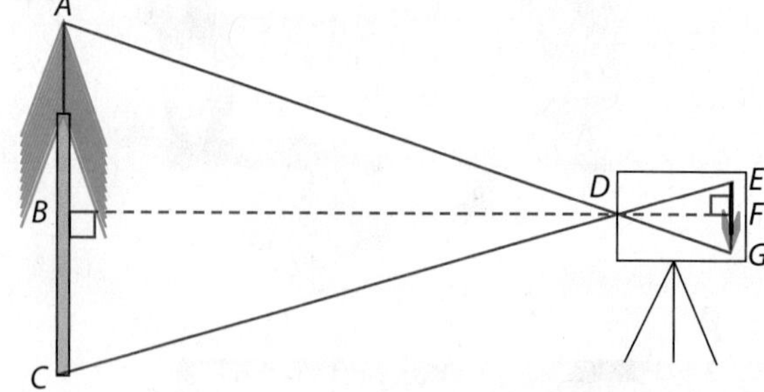

1. Explain how the image of the object would be affected if the camera were moved closer to the object. How would that limit the height of objects that could be photographed?

2. How do you know that $\triangle ADC$ is similar to $\triangle GDE$?

3. Write a proportion you could use to find the height of the pine tree.

4. $DF = 12$ in., $EG = 8$ in., $BD = 96$ ft. How tall is the pine tree?

STUDY GUIDE REVIEW

Similarity and Transformations

MODULE 16

Essential Question: How can you use similarity and transformations to solve real-world problems?

Key Vocabulary

center of dilation *(centro de dilatación)*
dilation *(dilatación)*
scale factor *(factor de escala)*
Side-Side-Side Similarity *(Similitud Lado -Lado -Lado)*
Side-Angle-Side Similarity *(Similitud Lado-Ángulo-Lado)*
similar *(semejantes)*
similarity transformation *(transformación de semejanza)*

KEY EXAMPLE *(Lesson 16.1)*

Determine the center of dilation and the scale factor of the dilation.

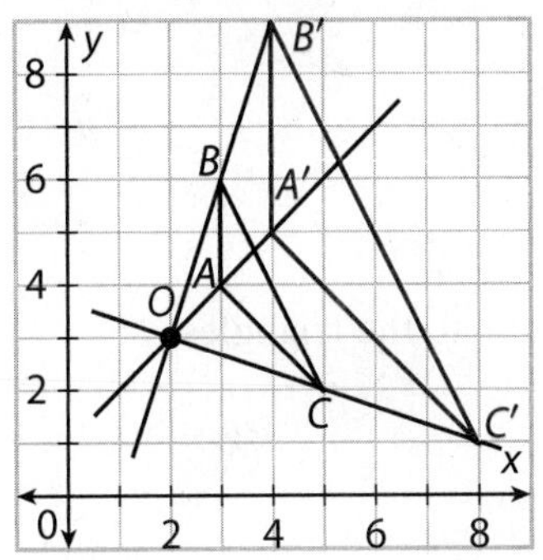

Draw a line through A and A'. Draw a line through B and B'. Draw a line through C and C'.

The three lines intersect at point $O(2, 3)$.

Find the distance from point O to points A and A'.

$d_A = \sqrt{(2-3)^2 + (3-4)^2} = \sqrt{2}$ Find the distance to point ***A***.

$d_{A'} = \sqrt{(2-4)^2 + (3-5)^2} = 2\sqrt{2}$ Find the distance to point ***A'***.

The distance from point O to point A' is twice the distance from point O to point A. The scale factor of dilation is 2 to 1.

KEY EXAMPLE *(Lesson 16.3)*

$\triangle ABCD$ maps to $\triangle EFGH$ by a similarity transformation. Write a proportion that contains $\overline{BC}$ and $\overline{EH}$. Then list any angles that are congruent to $\angle D$ or $\angle E$.

Corresponding sides of similar figures are proportional.

$\overline{BC} \cong \overline{FG}$ and $\overline{EH} \cong \overline{AD}$, so $\frac{\overline{BC}}{\overline{FG}} = \frac{\overline{AD}}{\overline{EH}}$.

Corresponding angles of similar figures are congruent.

$\angle D \cong \angle H$ and $\angle E \cong \angle A$.

KEY EXAMPLE *(Lesson 16.4)*

Determine whether $\triangle ABC$ and $\triangle DEF$ are similar. If so, justify by SSS Similarity or SAS Similarity.

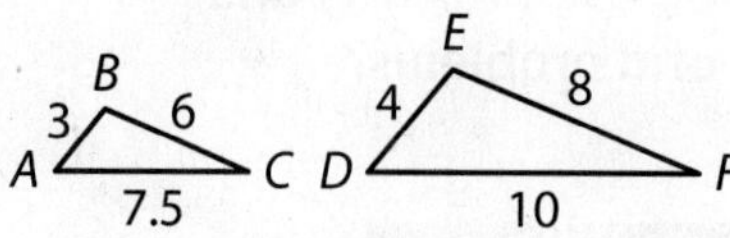

Check that the ratios of the lengths of corresponding sides are equal.

$\frac{3}{4}$

$\frac{6}{8} = \frac{3}{4}$

$\frac{7.5}{10} = \frac{3}{4}$

Since all the ratios of the lengths of corresponding sides are equal, the triangles are similar by SSS Similarity.

EXERCISES

Copy the trapezoids on a coordinate grid. Then determine the following for the dilation. *(Lesson 16.1)*

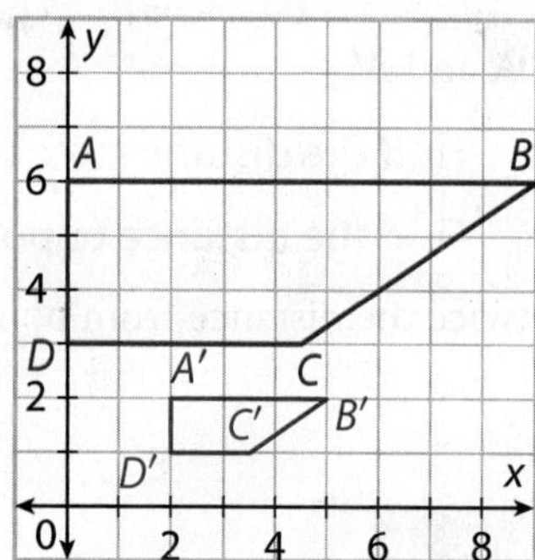

1. center ___?___

2. scale factor ___?___

Determine whether the two figures are similar using similarity transformations.
(Lesson 16.2)

3. $\triangle ABC$ to $\triangle DEF$

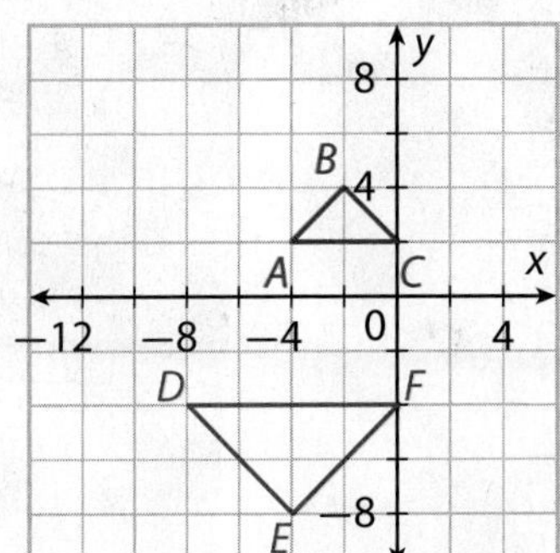

4. $\triangle ABCD$ to $\triangle EFGH$

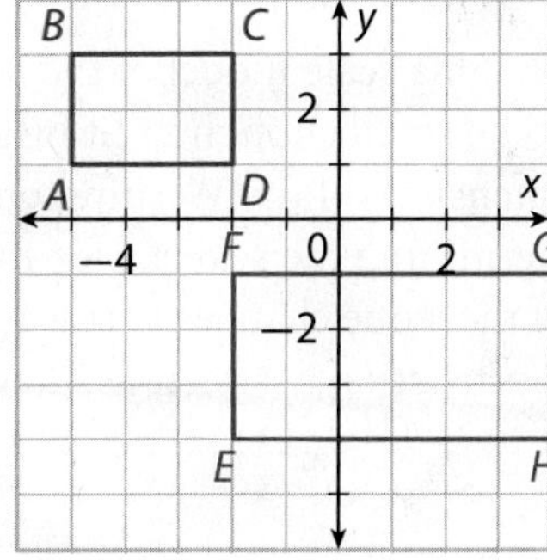

$\triangle ABC$ maps to $\triangle DEF$ by a similarity transformation. *(Lesson 16.3)*

5. Write a proportion that contains $\overline{AB}$ and $\overline{EF}$.

6. Write a proportion that contains $\overline{BC}$ and $\overline{DF}$.

7. List any angles that are congruent to $\angle A$ or $\angle E$.

Determine whether $\triangle ABC$ and $\triangle DEF$ are similar. If so, justify by SSS or *SAS*.
(Lesson 16.4)

8.

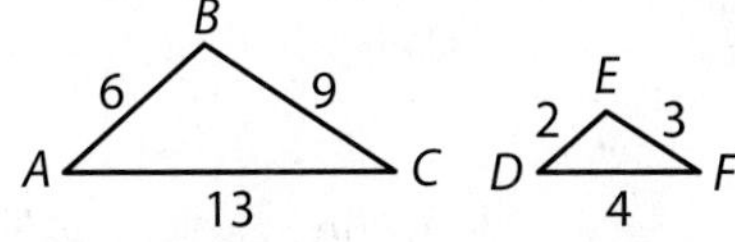

9.

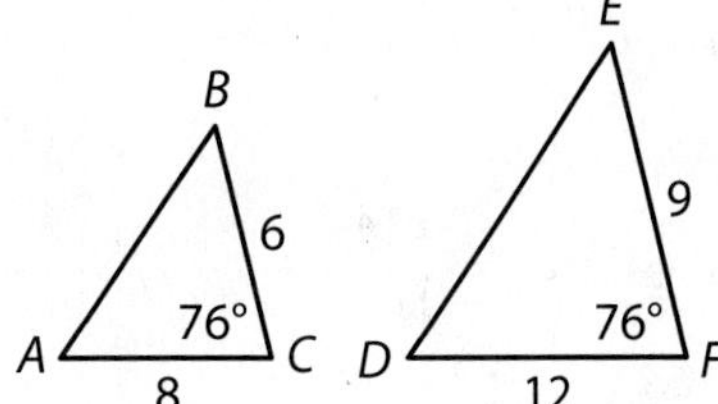

Designing a Model of the Washington Monument

Your challenge is to design a scale model of the Washington Monument that would be small enough to fit inside your classroom. Here are some key dimensions of the Washington Monument for you to consider in determining the scale factor for your model. (Note that the color of the stone changes part way up the monument because of a halt in construction between 1854 and 1877.)

Key Dimension	Measurement
Total height	555 ft 5 in.
Height to top of trapezoidal side	500 ft
Width at base	55 ft 1 in.
Width at top of trapezoidal side	34 ft 5 in.
Height at which stone color changes	151 ft

What scale factor will you use for your model? What are the key dimensions of your model?

Begin by making some notes about your strategy for designing the model. Then complete the task. Present your plan using diagrams, words, and/or numbers.

Ready to Go On?

16.1–16.4 Similarity and Transformations

- Online Homework
- Hints and Help
- Extra Practice

Answer each problem about the image. (Lesson 16.1)

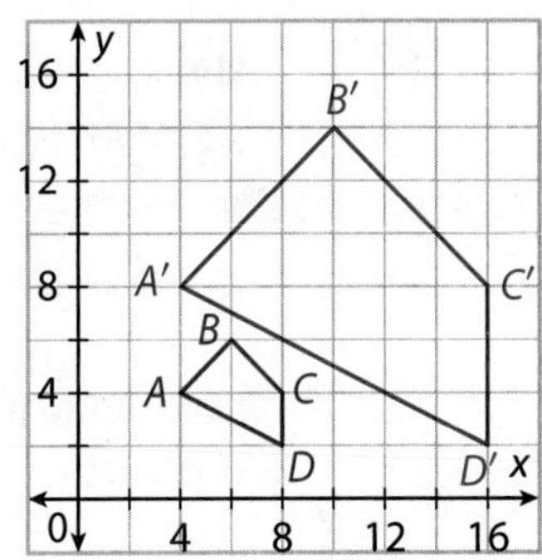

1. Are the two shapes similar?

2. Find the scale factor k.

3. Find the center of dilation.

4. Compare k to the ratio $\frac{\text{area } \triangle A'D'C'}{\text{area } \triangle ADC}$.

Determine which of the following transformations are dilations. (Lesson 16.1)

5. $(x, y) \rightarrow (4x, 4y)$

6. $(x, y) \rightarrow (-x, 3y)$

7. $(x, y) \rightarrow (x - 2, y - 2)$

8. $(x, y) \rightarrow \left(\frac{1}{3}x, \frac{1}{3}y\right)$

Find the missing length. (Lesson 16.3)

9. $\triangle XYZ$ maps to $\triangle MNO$ with the transformation $(x, y) \rightarrow (7x, 7y)$. If $XY = 3$, what is the length of MN?

Find the appropriate statements about the triangles. (Lesson 16.4)

10. $\triangle ABC$ is similar to $\triangle RTS$. Write a proportion that contains AC and RT. Also write the congruence statements that must be true.

ESSENTIAL QUESTION

11. How can you determine whether a shape is similar to another shape?

MODULE 16
MIXED REVIEW

Assessment Readiness

1. Consider each transformation. Does the transformation preserve distance? Write Yes or No for A–C.

A. Dilations

B. Reflections

C. Rotations

2. $\triangle MNO$ maps to $\triangle RST$ with the transformation $(x, y) \rightarrow \left(\frac{1}{3}x, \frac{1}{3}y\right)$. Determine if each statement is True or False.

A. If $RT = 3$, $MO = 9$.

B. If $RT = 12$, $MO = 4$.

C. If $RT = 9$, $MO = 27$.

3. Determine if the triangles are similar. If so, explain how. Note that $\overline{AC} \parallel \overline{BD}$.

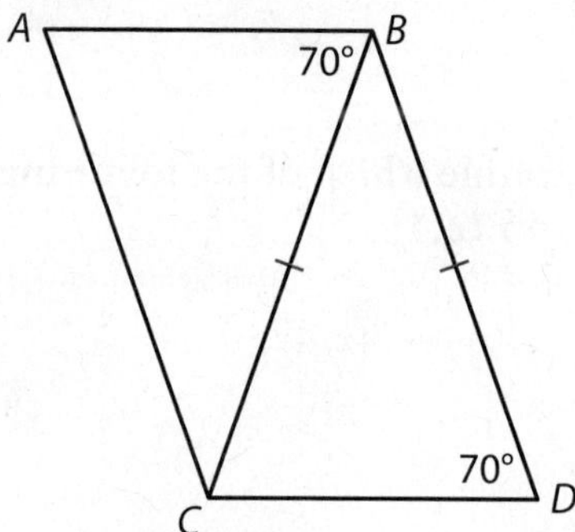

4. If $\triangle ABC$ is similar to $\triangle XYZ$ and $\triangle YZX$, what special type of triangle is $\triangle ABC$? Justify your reasoning.

MODULE 17

Using Similar Triangles

Essential Question: How can you use similar triangles to solve real-world problems?

REAL WORLD VIDEO
Check out how properties of similar triangles can be used to determine real-world areas of geographic regions like the Bermuda Triangle.

MODULE PERFORMANCE TASK PREVIEW

How Large Is the Bermuda Triangle?

In this module, you will be asked to determine the area of the Bermuda Triangle from a map. How can indirect measurement and the properties of similar triangles help you find the answer? Let's get started on solving this "mystery" of the Bermuda Triangle!

Are YOU Ready?

Complete these exercises to review skills you will need for this module.

- Online Homework
- Hints and Help
- Extra Practice

Scale Factor and Scale Drawings

Example 1

Determine the length of the segment $A'B'$ given $AB = 4$, $BC = 3$, and $B'C' = 6$.

The image of $\triangle ABC$ is created as a result of a scale drawing, so the transformation is a dilation.

$2BC = B'C'$, so $2AB = A'B'$.

$A'B' = 2(4) = 8$

A
A′
C B
C′ B′

Give the side length.

1. BC, given $AC = 5$, $A'C' = 15$, and $B'C' = 18$

Similar Figures

Example 2

The figures $PQRS$ and $KLMN$ are similar. Determine the angle in figure $KLMN$ that is congruent to $\angle Q$ and find its measure if $m\angle Q = 45°$.

$\angle Q \cong \angle L$ — Corresponding angles of similar figures are congruent.

$m\angle Q = m\angle L = 45°$ — Definition of congruency of angle.

Give each angle measure.

2. $m\angle A$, given $\triangle ABC \cong \triangle DEF$ and $m\angle D = 67°$

3. $m\angle E$, given $\triangle PQR \cong \triangle DEF$, $m\angle R = 13°$, and $m\angle D = 67°$

The Pythagorean Theorem

Example 3

A right triangle $\triangle ABC$ has side lengths $AB = 3$ and $BC = 4$. Find the length of the hypotenuse $\overline{AC}$.

$\triangle ABC$ is a right triangle, so the Pythagorean Theorem can be used.

$AC = \sqrt{(AB)^2 + (BC)^2}$ — Write the Pythagorean Theorem.

$AC = \sqrt{3^2 + 4^2} = \sqrt{9 + 16}$ — Substitute and simplify.

$AC = 5$ — Simplify.

Find the side length for each right triangle.

4. DE, given $DF = 5$, $EF = 12$, and $\overline{DE}$ is the hypotenuse

5. BC, given $AB = 15$, $AC = 17$, and $\overline{AC}$ is the hypotenuse

17.1 Triangle Proportionality Theorem

Resource Locker

Essential Question: When a line parallel to one side of a triangle intersects the other two sides, how does it divide those sides?

Explore Constructing Similar Triangles

In the following activity you will see one way to construct a triangle similar to a given triangle.

(A) Draw a triangle. Label it ABC as shown.

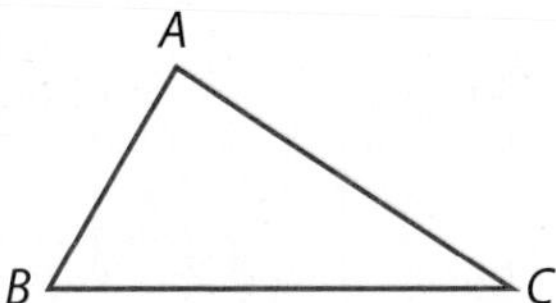

(B) Select a point on $\overline{AB}$. Label it E.

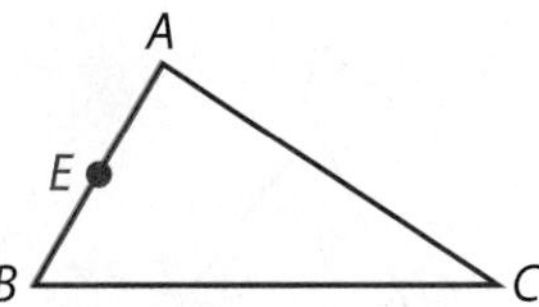

(C) Construct an angle with vertex E that is congruent to $\angle B$. Label the point where the side of the angle you constructed intersects $\overline{AC}$ as F.

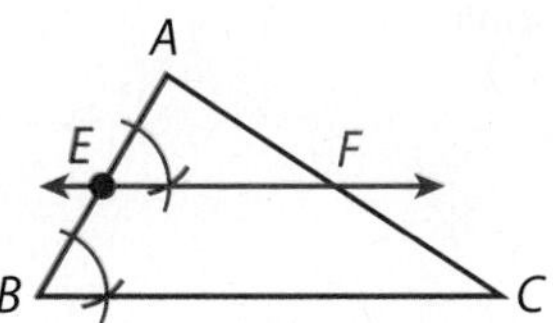

(D) Why are $\overleftrightarrow{EF}$ and $\overline{BC}$ parallel?

(E) Use a ruler to measure $\overline{AE}$, $\overline{EB}$, $\overline{AF}$, and $\overline{FC}$. Then compare the ratios $\frac{AE}{EB}$ and $\frac{AF}{FC}$.

Reflect

1. **Discussion** How can you show that $\triangle AEF \sim \triangle ABC$? Explain.
2. What do you know about the ratios $\frac{AE}{AB}$ and $\frac{AF}{AC}$? Explain.
3. **Make a Conjecture** Use your answer to Step E to make a conjecture about the line segments produced when a line parallel to one side of a triangle intersects the other two sides.

Explain 1 Proving the Triangle Proportionality Theorem

As you saw in the Explore, when a line parallel to one side of a triangle intersects the other two sides of the triangle, the lengths of the segments are proportional.

Triangle Proportionality Theorem

Theorem	Hypothesis	Conclusion
If a line parallel to a side of a triangle intersects the other two sides, then it divides those sides proportionally.	$\overline{EF} \parallel \overline{BC}$	$\frac{AE}{EB} = \frac{AF}{FC}$

Example 1 **Prove the Triangle Proportionality Theorem**

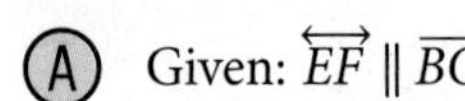

(A) Given: $\overleftrightarrow{EF} \parallel \overline{BC}$

Prove: $\frac{AE}{EB} = \frac{AF}{FC}$

Step 1 Show that $\triangle AEF \sim \triangle ABC$.

Because $\overleftrightarrow{EF} \parallel \overline{BC}$, you can conclude that $\angle 1 \cong \angle 2$ and $\angle 3 \cong \angle 4$ by the Corresponding Angles Theorem.

So, $\triangle AEF \sim \triangle ABC$ by the AA Similarity Criterion.

Step 2 Use the fact that corresponding sides of similar triangles are proportional to prove that $\frac{AE}{EB} = \frac{AF}{FC}$.

$$\frac{AB}{AE} = \frac{AC}{AF}$$ Corresponding sides are proportional.

$$\frac{AE + EB}{AE} = \frac{AF + FC}{AF}$$ Segment Addition Postulate

$$1 + \frac{EB}{AB} = 1 + \frac{FC}{AF}$$ Use the property that $\frac{a+b}{c} = \frac{a}{c} + \frac{b}{c}$.

$$\frac{EB}{AE} = \frac{FC}{AF}$$ Subtract 1 from both sides.

$$\frac{AE}{EB} = \frac{AF}{FC}$$ Take the reciprocal of both sides.

Reflect

4. Explain how you conclude that $\triangle AEF \sim \triangle ABC$ without using $\angle 3$ and $\angle 4$.

Explain 2 Applying the Triangle Proportionality Theorem

Example 2 **Find the length of each segment.**

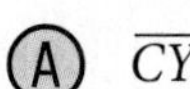

Ⓐ $\overline{CY}$

It is given that $\overline{XY} \parallel \overline{BC}$ so $\frac{AX}{XB} = \frac{AY}{YC}$ by the Triangle Proportionality Theorem.

Substitute 9 for AX, 4 for XB, and 10 for AY.

Then solve for CY.

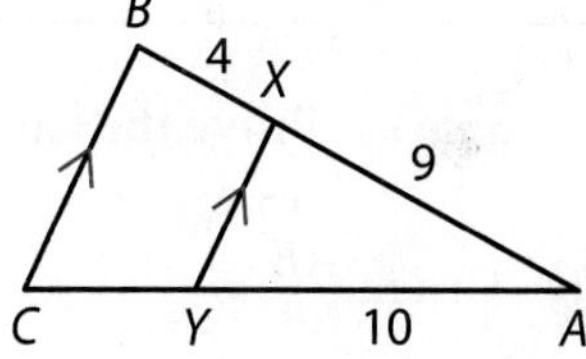

$$\frac{9}{4} = \frac{10}{CY}$$

Take the reciprocal of both sides.

$$\frac{4}{9} = \frac{CY}{10}$$

Next, multiply both sides by 10.

$$10\left(\frac{4}{9}\right) = \left(\frac{CY}{10}\right)10 \quad \rightarrow \quad \frac{40}{9} = CY, \text{ or } 4\frac{4}{9} = CY$$

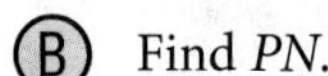

Ⓑ Find PN.

It is given that $\overline{PQ} \parallel \overline{LM}$, so $\frac{NQ}{QM} = \frac{NP}{PL}$ by the Triangle Proportionality Theorem.

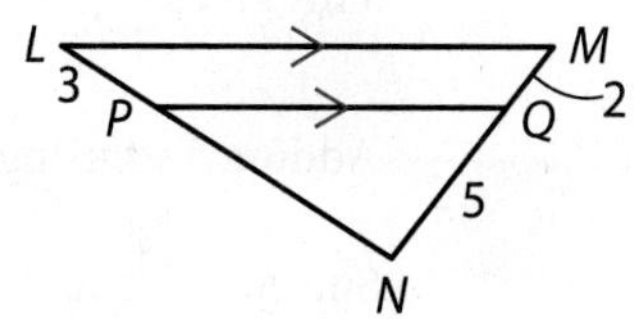

Substitute 5 for NQ, 2 for QM, and 3 for PL.

$$\frac{5}{2} = \frac{NP}{3}$$

Multiply both sides by 3: $\boxed{3}\left(\frac{5}{2}\right) = \boxed{3}\left(\frac{NP}{3}\right) \rightarrow \frac{15}{2}$ or $7\frac{1}{2} = NP$

Your Turn

Find the length of each segment.

5. $\overline{DG}$

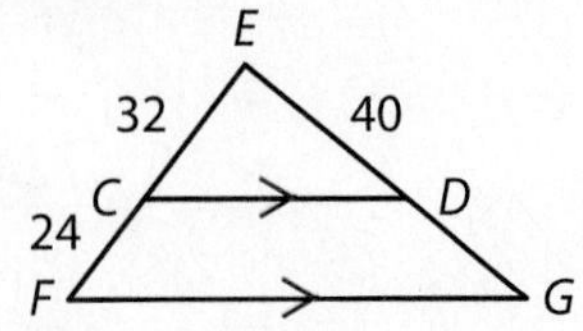

6. $\overline{RN}$

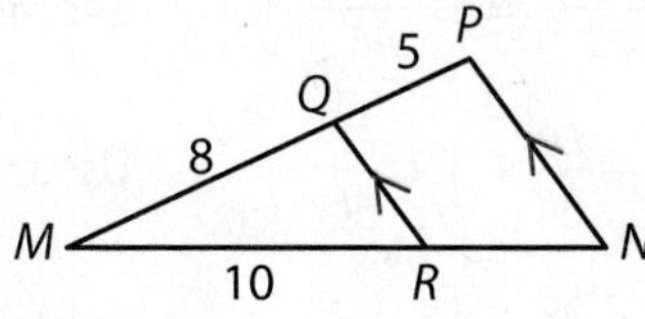

Explain 3 Proving the Converse of the Triangle Proportionality Theorem

The converse of the Triangle Proportionality Theorem is also true.

Converse of the Triangle Proportionality Theorem		
Theorem	**Hypothesis**	**Conclusion**
If a line divides two sides of a triangle proportionally, then it is parallel to the third side.	$\frac{AE}{EB} = \frac{AF}{FC}$	$\overleftrightarrow{EF} \parallel \overline{BC}$

Example 3 **Prove the Converse of the Triangle Proportionality Theorem**

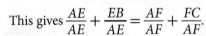

(A) Given: $\frac{AE}{EB} = \frac{AF}{FC}$

Prove: $\overleftrightarrow{EF} \parallel \overline{BC}$

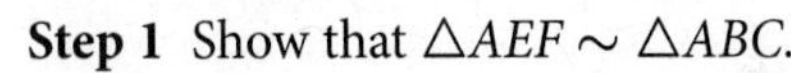

Step 1 Show that $\triangle AEF \sim \triangle ABC$.

It is given that $\frac{AE}{EB} = \frac{AF}{FC}$, and taking the reciprocal of both sides shows that $\frac{EB}{AE} = \frac{FC}{AF}$. Now add 1 to both sides by adding $\frac{AE}{AE}$ to the left side and $\frac{AF}{AF}$ to the right side.

This gives $\frac{AE}{AE} + \frac{EB}{AE} = \frac{AF}{AF} + \frac{FC}{AF}$.

Adding and using the Segment Addition Postulate gives $\frac{AB}{AE} = \frac{AC}{AF}$.

Since $\angle A \cong \angle A$, $\triangle AEF \sim \triangle ABC$ by the SAS Similarity Criterion.

Step 2 Use corresponding angles of similar triangles to show that $\overleftrightarrow{EF} \parallel \overline{BC}$.

$\angle AEF \cong \angle ABC$ and are corresponding angles.

So, $\overleftrightarrow{EF} \parallel \overline{BC}$ by the Converse of the Corresponding Angles Theorem.

Reflect

7. **Critique Reasoning** A student states that $\overline{UV}$ must be parallel to $\overline{ST}$. Do you agree? Why or why not?

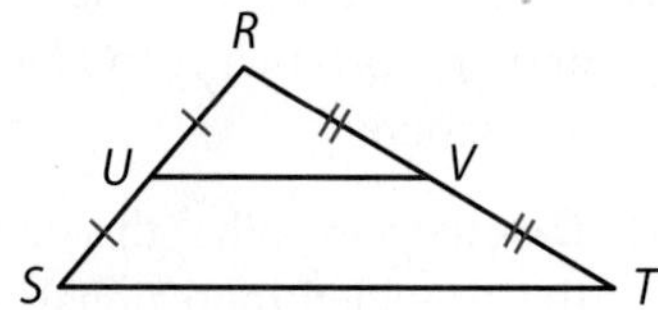

Explain 4 Applying the Converse of the Triangle Proportionality Theorem

You can use the Converse of the Triangle Proportionality Theorem to verify that a line is parallel to a side of a triangle.

Example 4 **Verify that the line segments are parallel.**

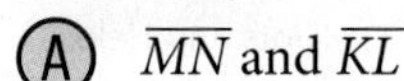

(A) $\overline{MN}$ and $\overline{KL}$

$\frac{JM}{MK} = \frac{42}{21} = 2$ $\qquad$ $\frac{JN}{NL} = \frac{30}{15} = 2$

Since $\frac{JM}{MK} = \frac{JN}{NL}$, $\overline{MN} \| \overline{KL}$ by the Converse of the Triangle Proportionality Theorem.

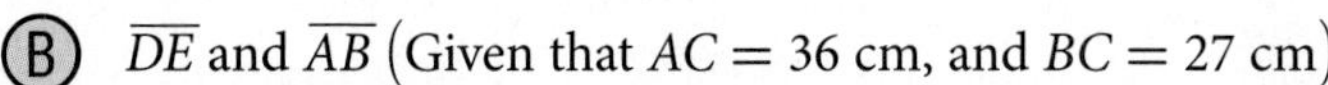

(B) $\overline{DE}$ and $\overline{AB}$ (Given that $AC = 36$ cm, and $BC = 27$ cm)

$AD = AC - DC = 36 - 20 = 16$

$BE = BC - \boxed{EC} = \boxed{27} - \boxed{15} = \boxed{12}$

$\frac{CD}{DA} = \frac{\boxed{20}}{\boxed{16}} = \frac{\boxed{5}}{\boxed{4}}$ $\qquad$ $\frac{CE}{EB} = \frac{\boxed{15}}{\boxed{12}} = \boxed{\frac{5}{4}}$

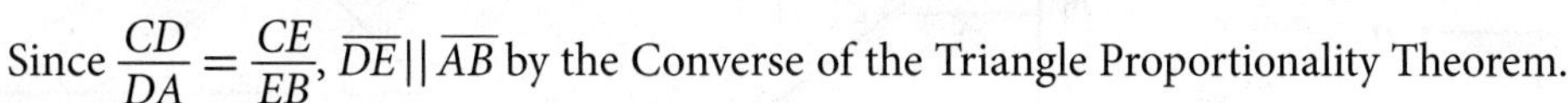

Since $\frac{CD}{DA} = \frac{CE}{EB}$, $\overline{DE} \| \overline{AB}$ by the Converse of the Triangle Proportionality Theorem.

Reflect

8. **Communicate Mathematical Ideas** In $\triangle ABC$, in the example, what is the value of $\frac{AB}{DE}$? Explain how you know.

Your Turn

9. Verify that $\overline{TU}$ and $\overline{RS}$ are parallel.

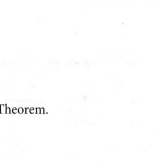

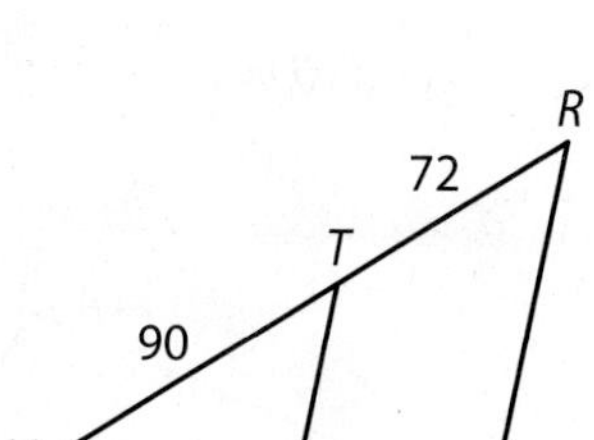

Elaborate

10. In $\triangle ABC$, $\overline{XY} \parallel \overline{BC}$. Use what you know about similarity and proportionality to identify as many different proportions as possible.

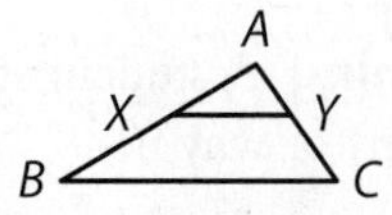

11. **Discussion** What theorems, properties, or strategies are common to the proof of the Triangle Proportionality Theorem and the proof of Converse of the Triangle Proportionality Theorem?

12. **Essential Question Check-In** Suppose a line parallel to side $\overline{BC}$ of $\triangle ABC$ intersects sides $\overline{AB}$ and $\overline{AC}$ at points X and Y, respectively, and $\frac{AX}{XB} = 1$. What do you know about X and Y? Explain.

Evaluate: Homework and Practice

- Online Homework
- Hints and Help
- Extra Practice

1. Copy the triangle ABC that you drew for the Explore activity. Construct a line $\overleftrightarrow{FG}$ parallel to $\overline{AB}$ using the same method you used in the Explore activity.

2. $\overline{ZY} \parallel \overleftrightarrow{MN}$. Write a paragraph proof to show that $\frac{XM}{MZ} = \frac{XN}{NY}$.

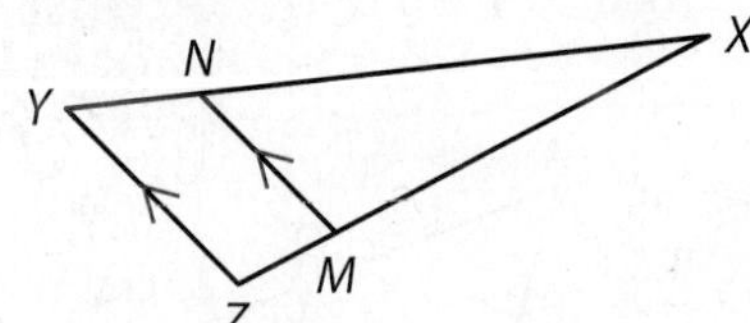

Find the length of each segment.

3.  $\overline{KL}$

4. 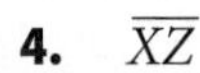 $\overline{XZ}$

5. $\overline{VM}$

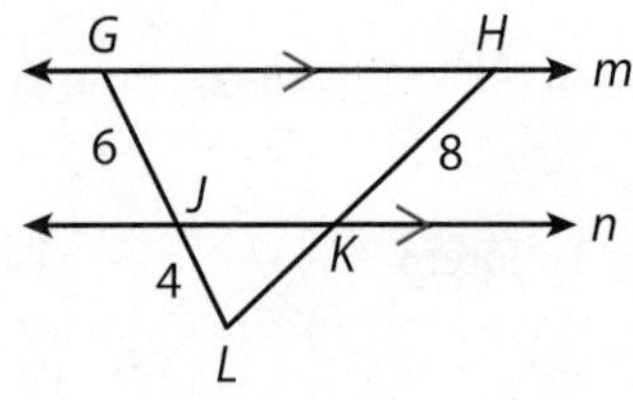

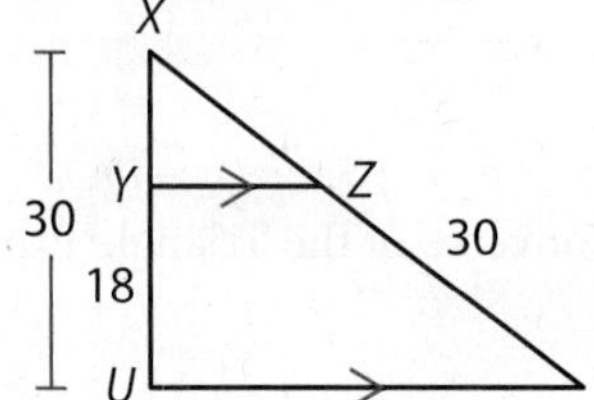

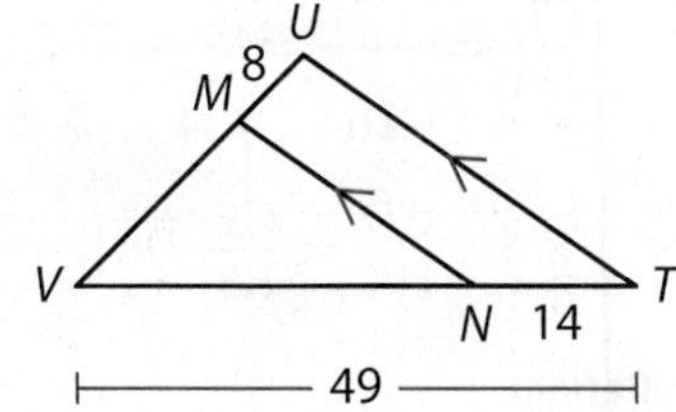

6. $\overline{AB}$ and $\overline{CD}$

7. $\overline{MN}$ and $\overline{QR}$

8. $\overline{WX}$ and $\overline{DE}$

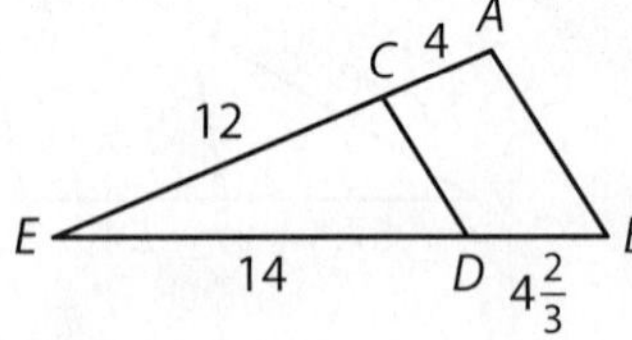

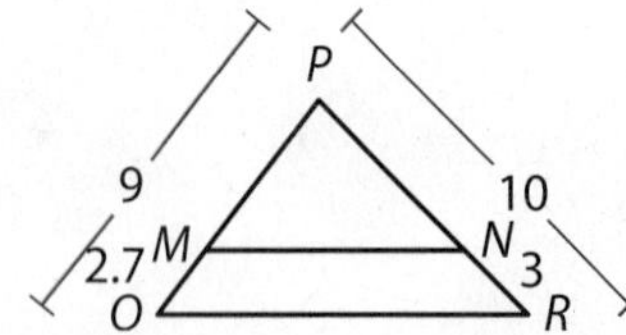

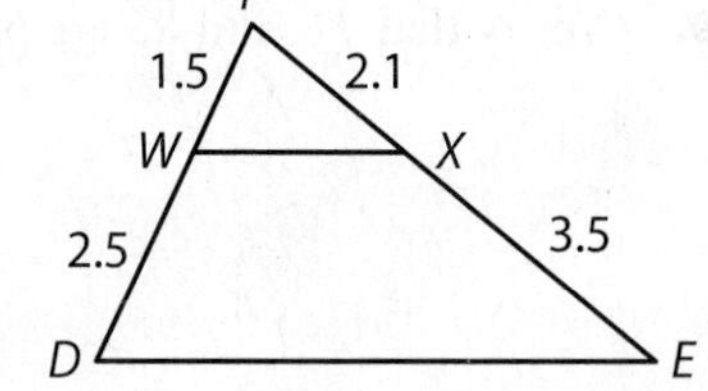

9. Use the Converse of the Triangle Proportionality Theorem to identify parallel lines in the figure.

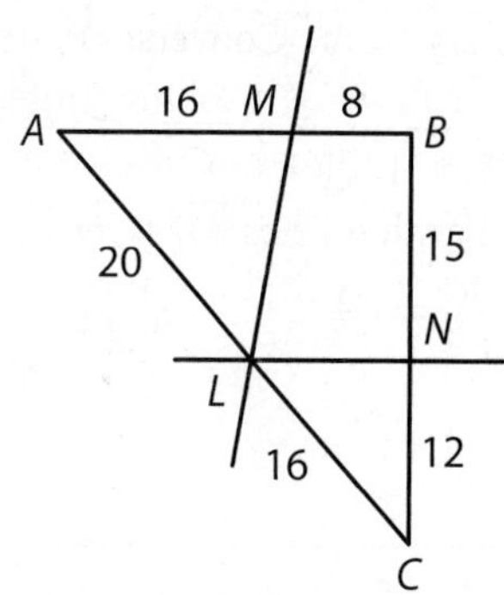

10. On the map, 1st Street and 2nd Street are parallel. What is the distance from City Hall to 2nd Street along Cedar Road?

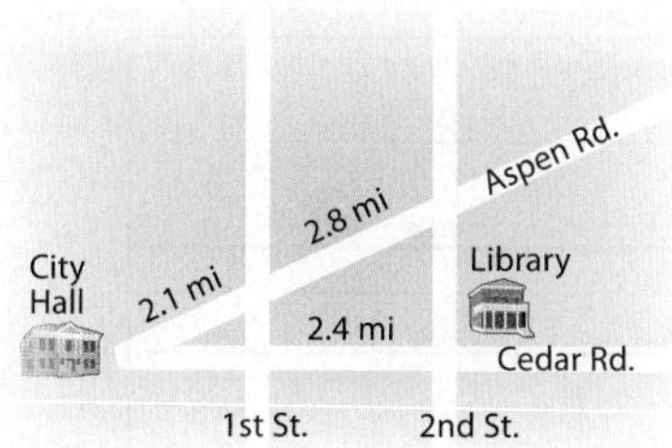

11. On the map, 5th Avenue, 6th Avenue, and 7th Avenue are parallel. What is the length of Main Street between 5th Avenue and 6th Avenue?

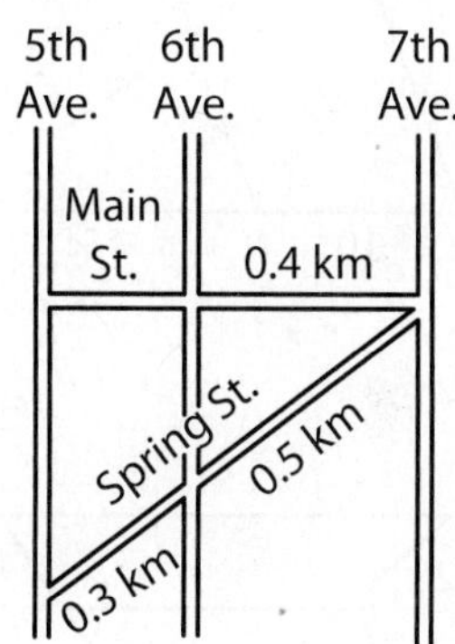

12. Multi-Step The storage unit has horizontal siding that is parallel to the base.

a. Find LM.

b. Find GM.

c. Find MN to the nearest tenth of a foot.

d. Make a Conjecture Write the ratios $\frac{LM}{MN}$ and $\frac{HJ}{JK}$ as decimals to the nearest hundredth and compare them. Make a conjecture about the relationship between parallel lines $\overleftrightarrow{LD}$, $\overleftrightarrow{ME}$, and $\overleftrightarrow{NF}$ and transversals $\overleftrightarrow{GN}$ and $\overleftrightarrow{GK}$.

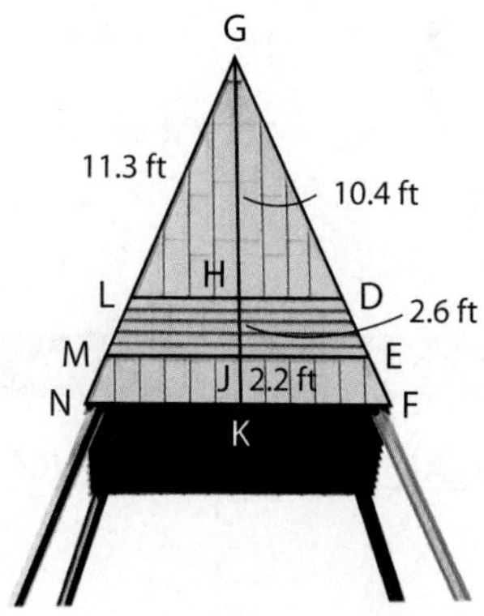

13. A corollary to the Converse of the Triangle Proportionality Theorem states that if three or more parallel lines intersect two transversals, then they divide the transversals proportionally. Complete the proof of the corollary.

Given: Parallel lines $\overleftrightarrow{AB} \parallel \overleftrightarrow{CD}, \overleftrightarrow{CD} \parallel \overleftrightarrow{EF}$

Prove: $\frac{AC}{CE} = \frac{BX}{XE}, \frac{BX}{XE} = \frac{BD}{DF}, \frac{AC}{CE} = \frac{BD}{DF}$

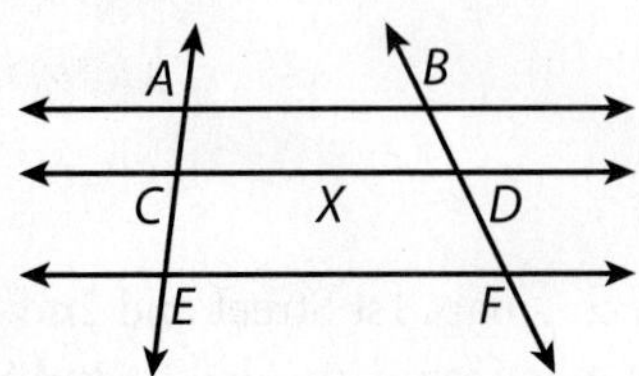

Statements	Reasons
1. $\overleftrightarrow{AB} \parallel \overleftrightarrow{CD}$, $\overleftrightarrow{CD} \parallel \overleftrightarrow{AF}$	1. Given
2. Draw $\overleftrightarrow{EB}$ intersecting $\overleftrightarrow{CD}$ at *X*.	2. Two points ___?___
3. $\frac{AC}{CE} = \frac{BX}{XE}$	3. ___?___
4. $\frac{BX}{XE} = \frac{BD}{DF}$	4. ___?___
5. $\frac{AC}{CE} = \frac{BD}{DF}$	5. ___?___ Property of Equality

14. Suppose that $LM = 24$. Use the Triangle Proportionality Theorem to find *PM*.

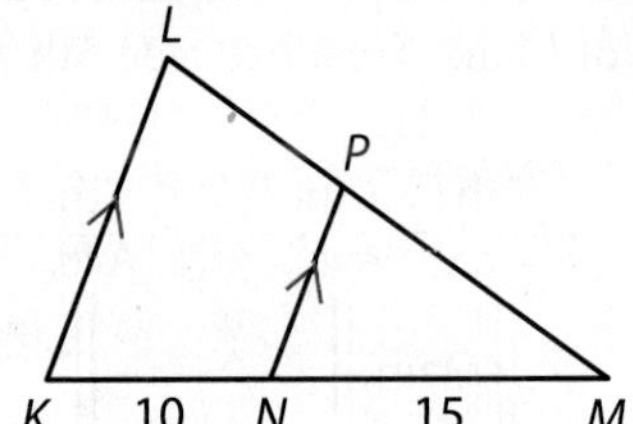

15. Which of the given measures allow you to conclude that $\overline{UV} \parallel \overline{ST}$? Determine all that apply.

A. $SR = 12, TR = 9$

B. $SR = 16, TR = 20$

C. $SR = 35, TR = 28$

D. $SR = 50, TR = 48$

E. $SR = 25, TR = 20$

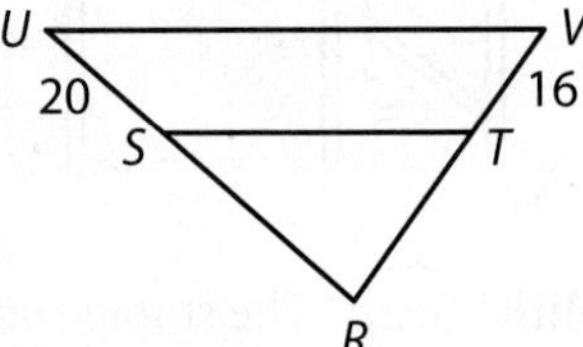

H.O.T. Focus on Higher Order Thinking

16. Algebra For what value of *x* is $\overline{GF} \parallel \overline{HJ}$?

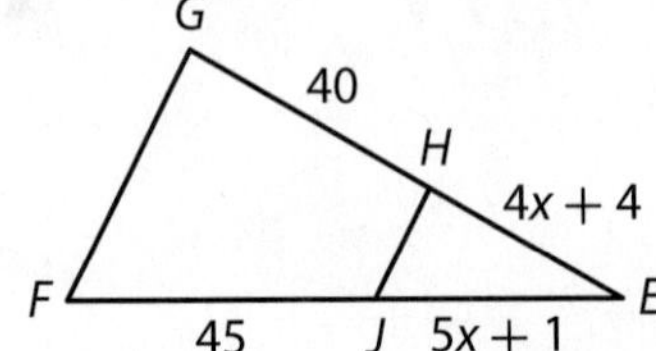

17. Communicate Mathematical Ideas John used $\triangle ABC$ to write a proof of the Centroid Theorem. He began by drawing medians $\overline{AK}$ and $\overline{CL}$, intersecting at Z. Next he drew midsegments $\overline{LM}$ and $\overline{NP}$, both parallel to median $\overline{AK}$.

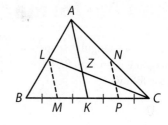

Given: $\triangle ABC$ with medians $\overline{AK}$ and $\overline{CL}$, and midsegments $\overline{LM}$ and $\overline{NP}$

Prove: Z is located $\frac{2}{3}$ of the distance from each vertex of $\triangle ABC$ to the midpoint of the opposite site.

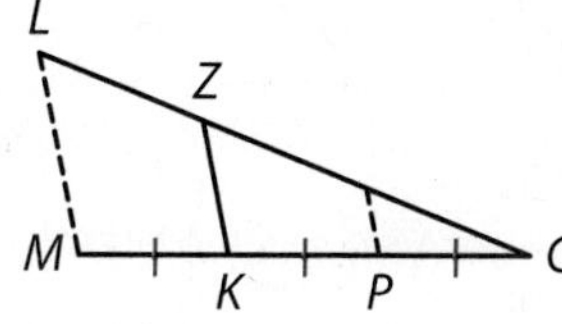

a. Complete each statement to justify the first part of John's proof.

By the definition of __?__, $MK = \frac{1}{2}BK$. By the definition of __?__, $BK = KC$. So, by __?__, $MK = \frac{1}{2}KC$, or $\frac{KC}{MK} = 2$. Consider $\triangle LMC$. $\overline{LM} \| \overline{AK}$, so $\frac{ZC}{LZ} = \frac{KC}{MK}$ by the __?__ Theorem, and $ZC = 2LZ$. Because $LC = 3LZ$, $\frac{ZC}{LC} = \frac{2LZ}{3LZ} = \frac{2}{3}$, and Z is located $\frac{2}{3}$ of the distance from vertex C of $\triangle ABC$ to the midpoint of the opposite side.

b. Explain how John can complete his proof.

18. Persevere in Problem Solving Given $\triangle ABC$ with $FC = 5$, you want to find BF. First, find the value that y must have for the Triangle Proportionality Theorem to apply. Then describe more than one way to find BF, and find BF.

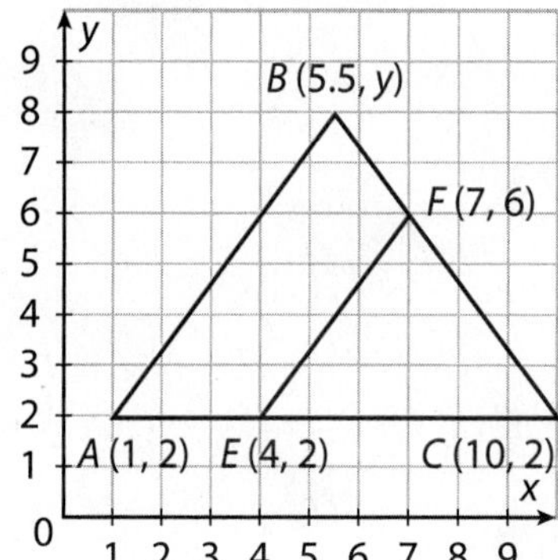

Lesson Performance Task

Shown here is a triangular striped sail, together with some of its dimensions. In the diagram, segments *BJ*, *CI*, and *DH* are all parallel to segment EG. Find each of the following:

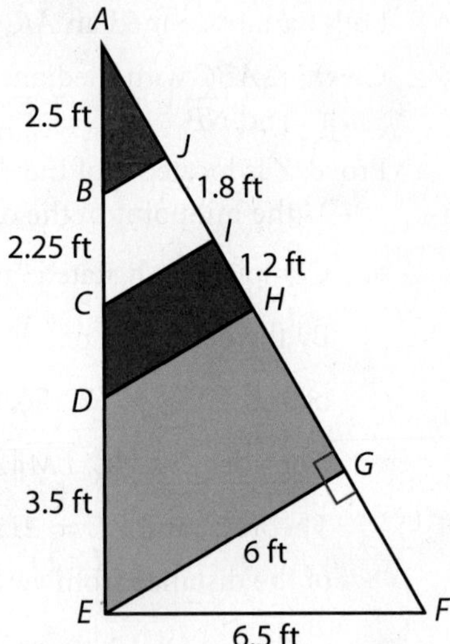

1. *AJ*

2. *CD*

3. *HG*

4. *GF*

5. the perimeter of $\triangle AEF$

6. the area of $\triangle AEF$

7. the number of sails you could make for $10,000 if the sail material costs $30 per square yard

17.2 Subdividing a Segment in a Given Ratio

Resource Locker

Essential Question: How do you find the point on a directed line segment that partitions the given segment in a given ratio?

Explore Partitioning a Segment in a One-Dimensional Coordinate System

It takes just one number to specify an exact location on a number line. For this reason, a number line is sometimes called a one-dimensional coordinate system. The mile markers on a straight stretch of a highway turn that part of the highway into a one-dimensional coordinate system.

On a straight highway, the exit for Arthur Avenue is at mile marker 14. The exit for Collingwood Road is at mile marker 44. The state highway administration plans to put an exit for Briar Street at a point that is $\frac{2}{3}$ of the distance from Arthur Avenue to Collingwood Road. Follow these steps to determine where the new exit should be placed.

(A) Draw a number line from 10 to 50 marked in units of 1. Mark Arthur Avenue (point A) and Collingwood Road (point C) on the number line.

(B) What is the distance from Arthur Avenue to Collingwood Road? Explain.

(C) How far will the Briar Street exit be from Arthur Avenue? Explain.

(D) What is the mile marker number for the Briar Street exit? Why?

(E) Plot and label the Briar Street exit (point B) on the number line.

(F) The highway administration also plans to put an exit for Dakota Lane at a point that divides the highway from Arthur Avenue to Collingwood Road in a ratio of 2 to 3. What is the mile marker number for Dakota Lane? Why? (*Hint*: Let the distance from Arthur Avenue to Dakota Lane be $2x$ and let the distance from Dakota Lane to Collingwood Road be $3x$.)

(G) Plot and label the Dakota Lane exit (point D) on the number line.

Reflect

1. How can you tell that the location at which you plotted point *B* is reasonable?
2. Would your answer in Step F be different if the exit for Dakota Lane divided the highway from Arthur Avenue to Collingwood Road in a ratio of 3 to 2? Explain.

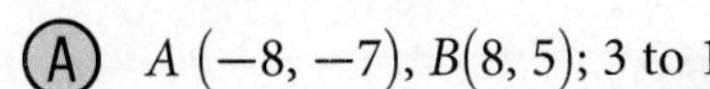

Explain 1 Partitioning a Segment in a Two-Dimensional Coordinate System

A *directed line segment* is a segment between two points *A* and *B* with a specified direction, from *A* to *B* or from *B* to *A*. To partition a directed line segment is to divide it into two segments with a given ratio.

Example 1 **Find the coordinates of the point *P* that divides the directed line segment from *A* to *B* in the given ratio.**

(A) $A(-8, -7)$, $B(8, 5)$; 3 to 1

Step 1 Write a ratio that expresses the distance of point *P* along the segment from *A* to *B*.

Point *P* is $\frac{3}{3+1} = \frac{3}{4}$ of the distance from *A* to *B*.

Step 2 Find the run and the rise of the directed line segment.

run $= 8 - (-8) = 16$

rise $= 5 - (-7) = 12$

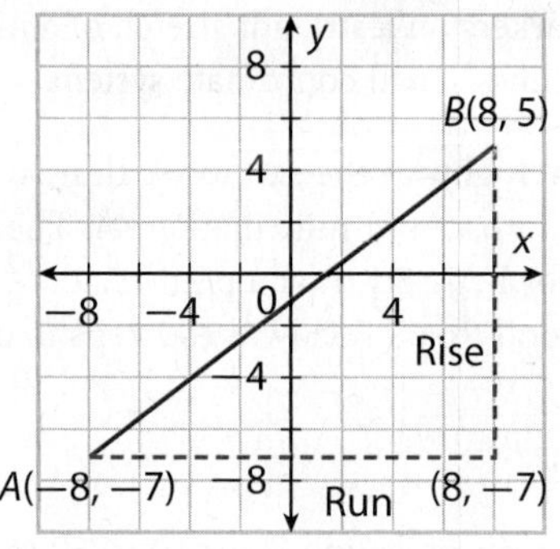

Step 3 Point *P* is $\frac{3}{4}$ of the distance from point *A* to point *B*, so find $\frac{3}{4}$ of both the rise and the run.

$\frac{3}{4}$ of run $= \frac{3}{4}(16) = 12$

$\frac{3}{4}$ of rise $= \frac{3}{4}(12) = 9$

Step 4 To find the coordinates of point *P*, add the values from Step 3 to the coordinates of point *A*.

x-coordinate of point $P = -8 + 12 = 4$

y-coordinate of point $P = -7 + 9 = 2$

The coordinates of point *P* are $(4, 2)$.

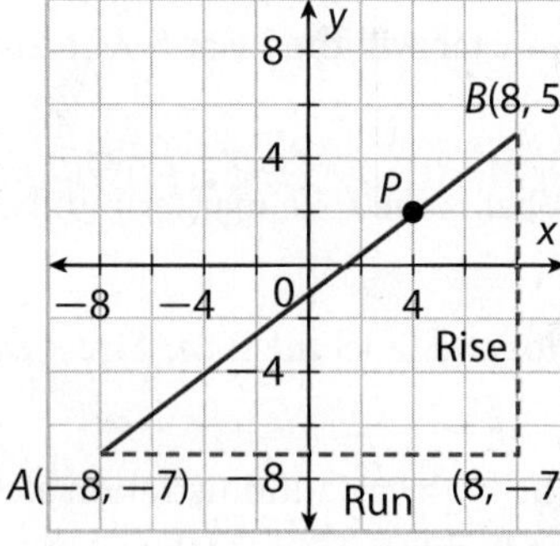

(B) $A(-4, 4)$, $B(2, 1)$; 1 to 2

Step 1 Write a ratio that expresses the distance of point *P* along the segment from *A* to *B*.

Point *P* is $\frac{1}{1+2} = \frac{1}{3}$ of the distance from *A* to *B*.

Step 2 Graph the directed line segment. Find the run and the rise of the directed line segment.

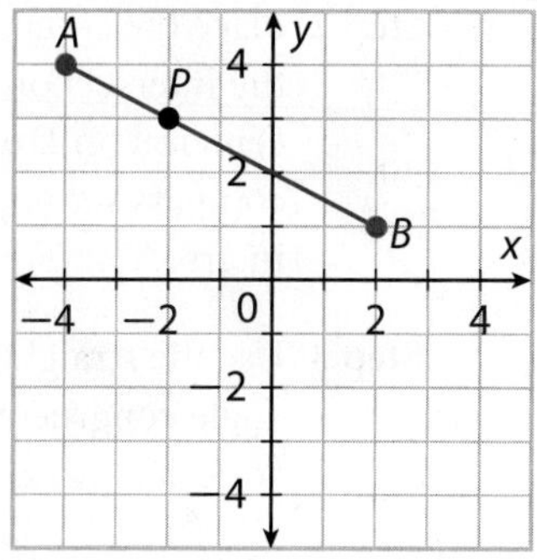

run $= 2 - (-4) = 6$

rise $= \boxed{1} - \boxed{4} = \boxed{-3}$

Step 3 Point P is $\dfrac{\boxed{1}}{\boxed{3}}$ of the distance from point A to point B.

$\dfrac{\boxed{1}}{\boxed{3}}$ of run $= \dfrac{\boxed{1}}{\boxed{3}}(6) = \boxed{2}$ $\qquad$ $\dfrac{\boxed{1}}{\boxed{3}}$ of rise $= \dfrac{\boxed{1}}{\boxed{3}}\left(\boxed{-3}\right) = \boxed{-1}$

Step 4 To find the coordinates of point P, add the values from Step 3 to the coordinates of point A.

x-coordinate of point $P = -4 + \boxed{2} = \boxed{-2}$ $\qquad$ y-coordinate of point $P = 4 + \boxed{-1} = \boxed{3}$

The coordinates of point P are $\left(\boxed{-2}, \boxed{3}\right)$. Plot point P on the above graph.

Reflect

3. In Part A, show how you can use the Distance Formula to check that point P partitions the directed line segment in the correct ratio.

4. **Discussion** What can you conclude about a point that partitions a segment in the ratio 1 to 1? How can you find the coordinates of such a point?

Your Turn

Find the coordinates of the point P that divides the directed line segment from A to B in the given ratio.

5. $A(-6, 5)$, $B(2, -3)$; 5 to 3

6. $A(4, 2)$, $B(-6, -13)$; 3 to 2

Explain 2 Constructing a Partition of a Segment

Example 2 **Given the directed line segment from A to B, construct the point P that divides the segment in the given ratio from A to B.**

Ⓐ 2 to 1

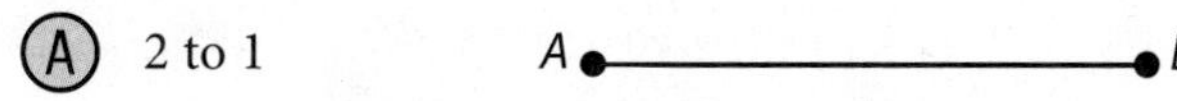

Step 1 Use a straightedge to draw $\overrightarrow{AC}$. The exact measure of the angle is not important, but the construction is easiest for angles from about 30° to 60°.

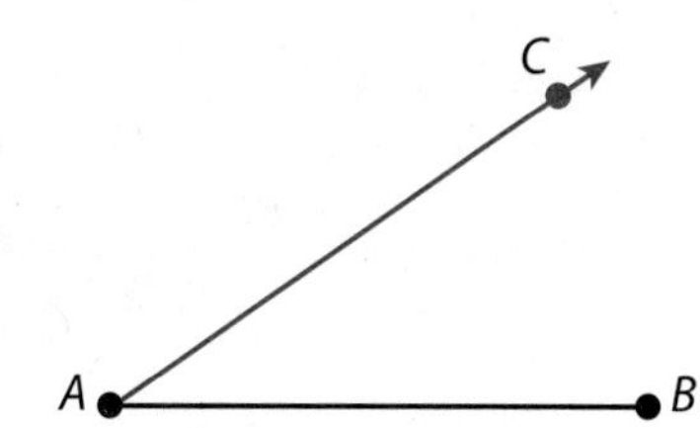

Step 2 Place the compass point on A and draw an arc through $\overrightarrow{AC}$. Label the intersection D. Using the same compass setting, draw an arc centered on D and label the intersection E. Using the same compass setting, draw an arc centered on E and label the intersection F.

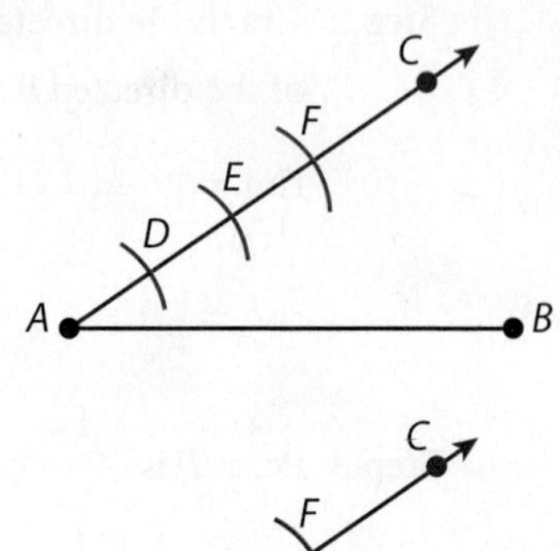

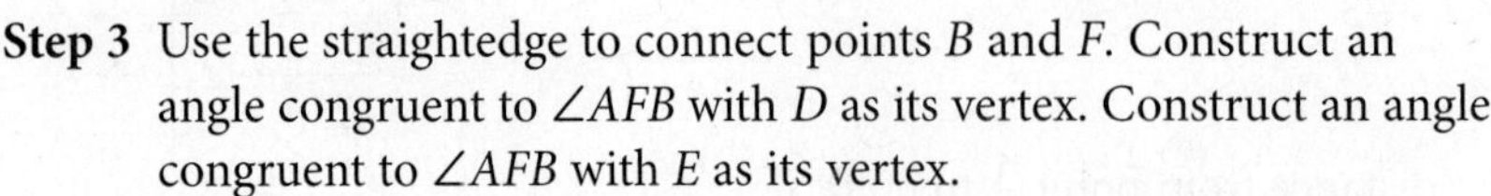

Step 3 Use the straightedge to connect points B and F. Construct an angle congruent to $\angle AFB$ with D as its vertex. Construct an angle congruent to $\angle AFB$ with E as its vertex.

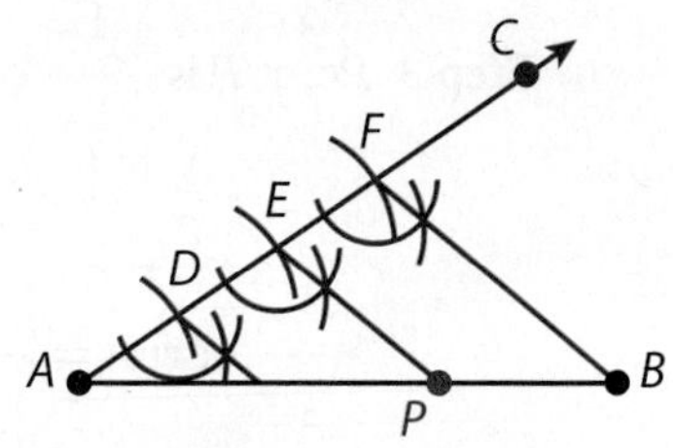

Step 4 The construction partitions $\overline{AB}$ into 3 equal parts. Label point P at the point that divides the segment in the ratio 2 to 1 from A to B.

(B) 1 to 3

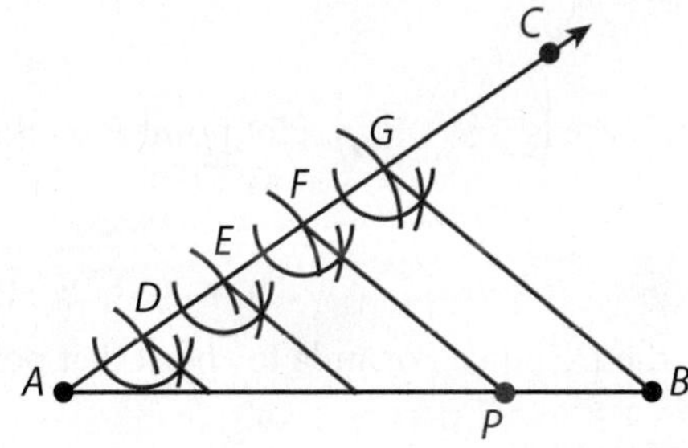

Step 1 Use a straightedge to draw $\overline{AC}$.

Step 2 Place the compass point on A and draw an arc through $\overline{AC}$. Label the intersection D. Using the same compass setting, draw an arc centered on D and label the intersection E. Using the same compass setting, draw an arc centered on E and label the intersection F. Using the same compass setting, draw an arc centered on F and label the intersection G.

Step 3 Use the straightedge to connect points B and G. Construct angles congruent to $\angle AGB$ with D, E, and F as the vertices.

Step 4 The construction partitions $\overline{AB}$ into [4] equal parts. Label point P at the point that divides the segment in the ratio [1] to [3] from A to B.

Reflect

7. In Part A, why is $\overline{EP}$ is parallel to $\overline{FB}$?

8. How can you use the Triangle Proportionality Theorem to explain why this construction method works?

Your Turn

Copy the directed line segment from A to B. Construct the point P that divides the segment in the given ratio from A to B.

9. 1 to 2

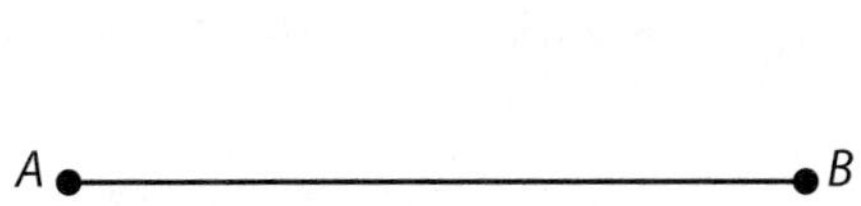

10. 3 to 2

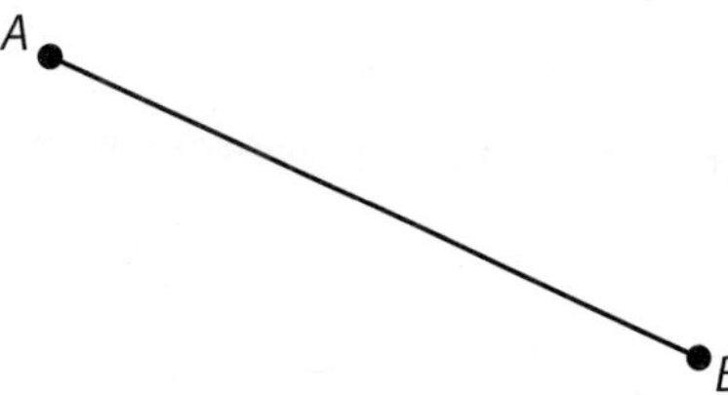

Elaborate

11. How is a one-dimensional coordinate system similar to a two-dimensional coordinate system? How is it different?

12. Is finding a point that is $\frac{4}{5}$ of the distance from point A to point B the same as finding a point that divides $\overline{AB}$ in the ratio 4 to 5? Explain.

13. **Essential Question Check-In** What are some different ways to divide a segment in the ratio 2 to 1?

Evaluate: Homework and Practice

- Online Homework
- Hints and Help
- Extra Practice

A choreographer uses a number line to position dancers for a ballet. Dancers A and B have coordinates 5 and 23, respectively. In Exercises 1–4, find the coordinate for each of the following dancers based on the given locations.

1. Dancer C stands at a point that is $\frac{5}{6}$ of the distance from Dancer A to Dancer B.

2. Dancer D stands at a point that is $\frac{1}{3}$ of the distance from Dancer A to Dancer B.

3. Dancer E stands at a point that divides the line segment from Dancer A to Dancer B in a ratio of 2 to 1.

4. Dancer F stands at a point that divides the line segment from Dancer A to Dancer B in a ratio of 1 to 5.

Find the coordinates of the point P that divides the directed line segment from A to B in the given ratio.

5. $A(-3, -2), B(12, 3)$; 3 to 2

6. $A(-1, 5), B(7, -3)$; 7 to 1

7. $A(-1, 4), (B-9, 0)$; 1 to 3

8. $A(7, -3), B(-7, 4)$; 3 to 4

Copy the directed line segment from A to B. Construct the point P that divides the segment in the given ratio from A to B.

9. 3 to 1

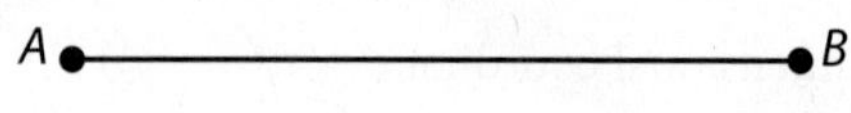

10. 2 to 3

A
B

11. 1 to 4

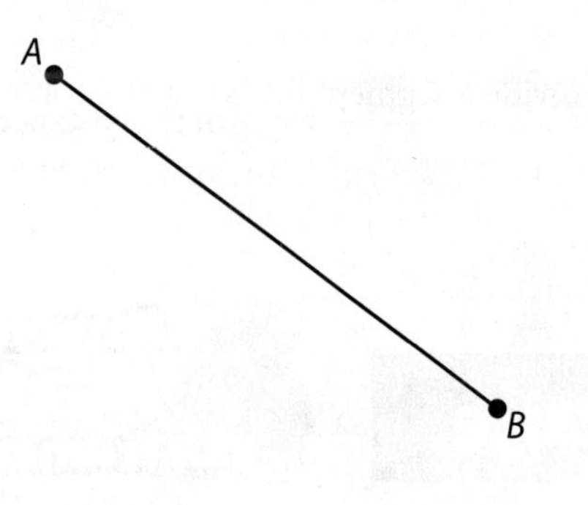

12. 4 to 1

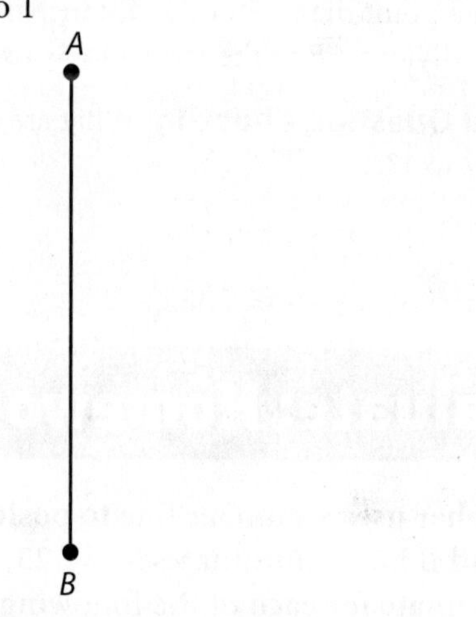

Find the coordinate of the point P that divides each directed line segment in the given ratio.

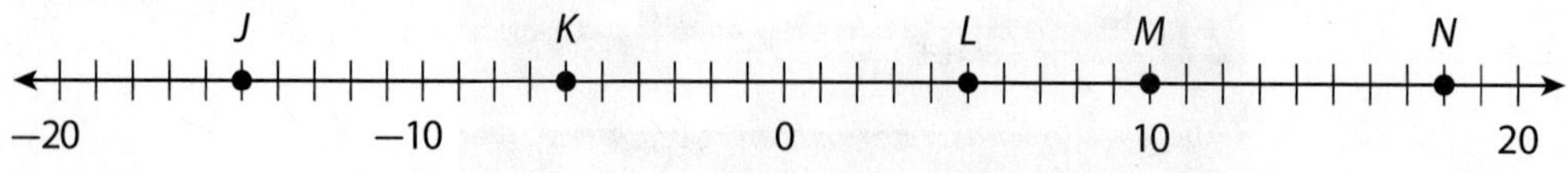

13. from J to M; 1 to 9

14. from K to L; 1 to 1

15. from N to K; 3 to 5

16. from K to J; 7 to 11

17. Communicate Mathematical Ideas Leon constructed a point P that divides the directed segment from A to B in the ratio 2 to 1. Chelsea constructed a point Q that divides the directed segment from B to A in the ratio 1 to 2. How are points P and Q related? Explain.

18. City planners use a number line to place landmarks along a new street. Each unit of the number line represents 100 feet. A fountain F is located at coordinate -3 and a plaza P is located at coordinate 21. The city planners place two benches along the street at points that divide the segment from F to P in the ratios 1 to 2 and 3 to 1. What is the distance between the benches?

19. The course for a marathon includes a straight segment from city hall to the main library. The planning committee wants to put water stations along this part of the course so that the stations divide the segment into three equal parts. Find the coordinates of the points at the which the water stations should be placed.

20. Multi-Step Carlos is driving on a straight section of highway from Ashford to Lincoln. Ashford is at mile marker 433 and Lincoln is at mile marker 553. A rest stop is located along the highway $\frac{2}{3}$ of the distance from Ashford to Lincoln. Assuming Carlos drives at a constant rate of 60 miles per hour, how long will it take him to drive from Ashford to the rest stop?

21. The directed segment from J to K is shown in the figure.

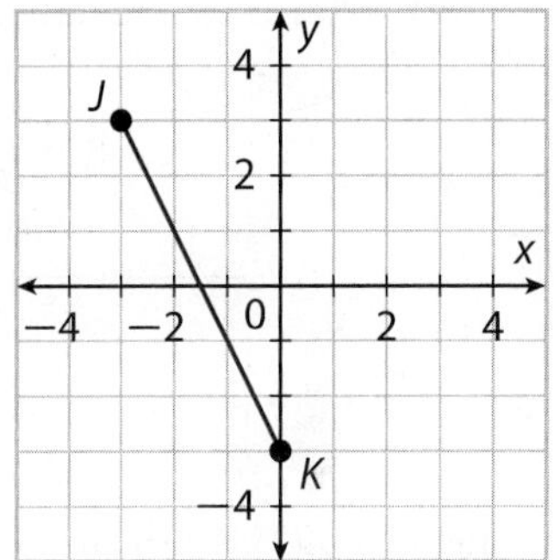

Points divide the segment from J to K in the each of the following ratios. Which points have integer coordinates? Determine all that apply.

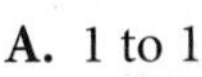

A. 1 to 1

B. 2 to 1

C. 2 to 3

D. 1 to 3

E. 1 to 2

H.O.T. Focus on Higher Order Thinking

22. Critique Reasoning Jeffrey was given a directed line segment and was asked to use a compass and straightedge to construct the point that divides the segment in the ratio 4 to 2. He said he would have to draw a ray and then construct 6 congruent segments along the ray. Tamara said it is not necessary to construct 6 congruent segments along the ray. Do you agree? If so, explain Tamara's shortcut. If not, explain why not.

23. Explain the Error Point A has coordinate -9 and point B has coordinate 9. A student was asked to find the coordinate of the point P that is $\frac{2}{3}$ of the distance from A to B. The student said the coordinate of point P is -3.

a. Without doing any calculations, how can you tell that the student made an error?

b. What error do you think the student made?

24. Analyze Relationships Point P divides the directed segment from A to B in the ratio 3 to 2. The coordinates of point A are $(-4, -2)$ and the coordinates of point P are $(2, 1)$. Find the coordinates of point B.

25. Critical Thinking $\overline{RS}$ passes through $R(-3, 1)$ and $S(4, 3)$. Find a point P on $\overline{RS}$ such that the ratio of RP to SP is 5 to 4. Is there more than one possibility? Explain.

Lesson Performance Task

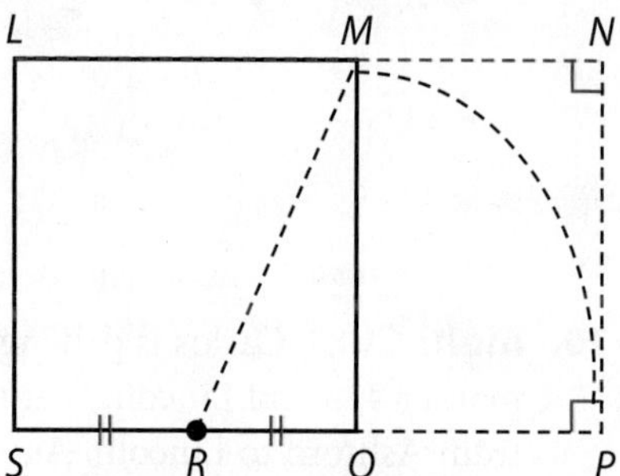

In this lesson you will subdivide line segments in given ratios. The diagram shows a line segment divided into two parts in such a way that the longer part divided by the shorter part equals the entire length divided by the longer part:

$$\frac{a}{b} = \frac{a + b}{a}$$

Each of these ratios is called the Golden Ratio. To find the point on a line segment that divides the segment this way, study this figure:

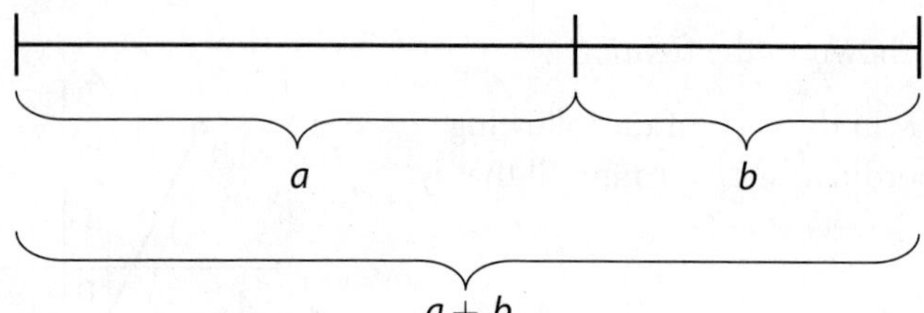

In the figure, $LMQS$ is a square. $\frac{LN}{LM}$ equals the Golden Ratio (the entire segment length divided by the longer part).

1. Describe how, starting with line segment $\overline{LM}$, you can find the location of point N.

2. Letting LM equal 1, find $\frac{LN}{LM} = \frac{LN}{1} = LN$, the Golden Ratio. Describe your method.

17.3 Using Proportional Relationships

Resource Locker

Essential Question: How can you use similar triangles to solve problems?

Explore Exploring Indirect Measurement

In this Explore, you will consider how to find heights, lengths, or distances that are too great to be measured directly, that is, with measuring tools like rulers. **Indirect measurement** involves using the properties of similar triangles to measure such heights or distances.

(A) During the day sunlight creates shadows, as shown in the figure below. The dashed segment represents the ray of sunlight. What kind of triangle is formed by the flagpole, its shadow, and the ray of sunlight?

(B) Suppose the sun is shining, and you are standing near a flagpole, but out of its shadow. You will cast a shadow as well. You can assume that the rays of the sun are parallel. What do you know about the two triangles formed? Explain your reasoning.

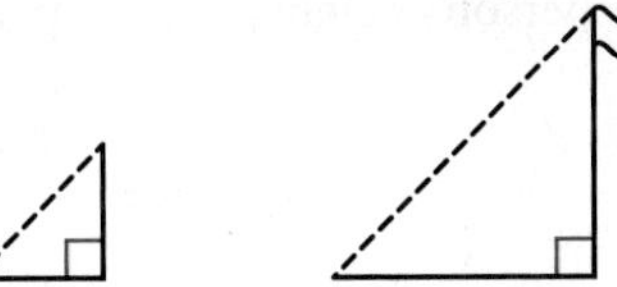

(C) In the diagram, what heights or lengths do you already know?

(D) What heights or lengths can be measured directly?

Reflect

1. How could you use similar triangles to measure the height of the flagpole indirectly?

Explain 1 Finding an Unknown Height

Example 1 **Find the indicated dimension using the measurements shown in the figure and the properties of similar triangles.**

Ⓐ In order to find the height of a palm tree, you measure the tree's shadow and, at the same time of day, you measure the shadow cast by a meter stick that you hold at a right angle to the ground. Find the height h of the tree.

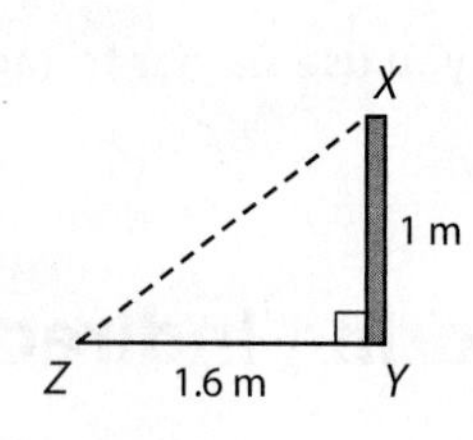

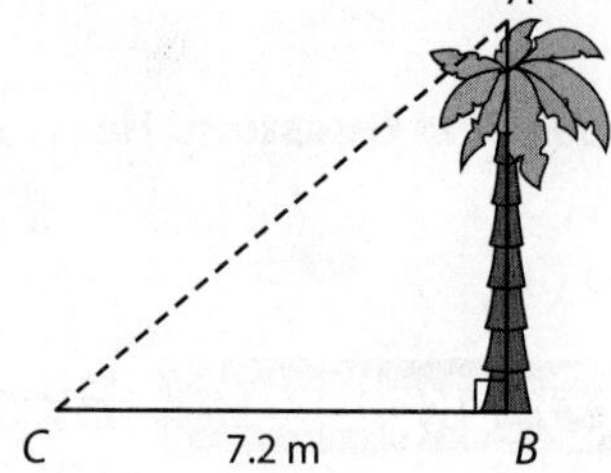

Because $\overline{ZX} \parallel \overline{CA}$, $\angle Z \cong \angle C$. All right angles are congruent, so $\angle Y \cong \angle B$. So $\triangle XYZ \cong \triangle ABC$.

Set up proportion. $\frac{AB}{XY} = \frac{BC}{YZ}$

Substitute. $\frac{h}{7.2} = \frac{1}{1.6}$

Multiply each side by 7.2. $h = 7.2\left(\frac{1}{1.6}\right)$

Simplify. $h = 4.5$

The tree is 4.5 meters high.

Ⓑ Sid is 72 inches tall. To measure a flagpole, Sid stands near the flag. Sid's friend Miranda measures the lengths of Sid's shadow and the flagpole's shadow. Find the height h of the flagpole.

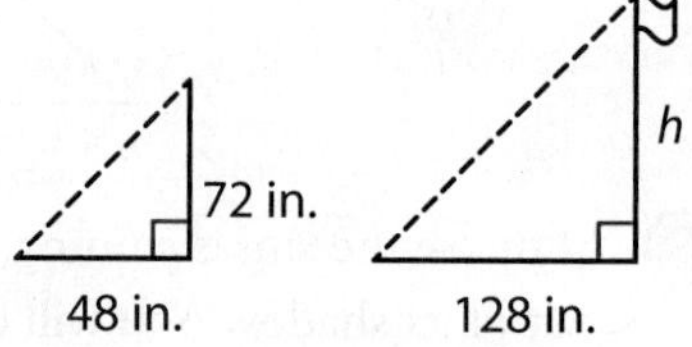

The triangles are similar by the AA Similarity Criterion.

Set up proportion. $\frac{\text{flagpole's height}}{\text{person's height}} = \frac{\text{flagpole's shadow}}{\text{person's shadow}}$

Substitute. $\frac{h}{72} = \frac{\boxed{128}}{48}$

Multiply each side by 72. $h = 72\left(\frac{\boxed{128}}{48}\right)$

Simplify. $x = \boxed{192}$

The flagpole is 192 inches tall.

Reflect

2. In the tree example, how can you check that your answer is reasonable?

Your Turn

3. Liam is 6 feet tall. To find the height of a tree, he measures his shadow and the tree's shadow. The measurements of the two shadows are shown. Find the height h of the tree.

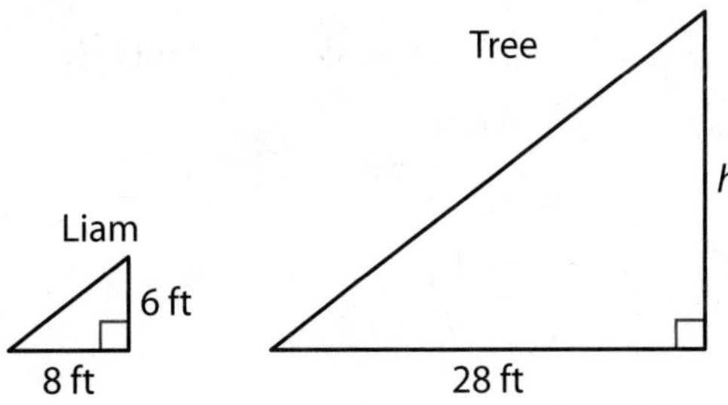

Explain 2 Finding an Unknown Distance

In real-world situations, you may not be able to measure an object directly because there is a physical barrier separating you from the object. You can use similar triangles in these situations as well.

Example 2 **Explain how to use the information in the figure to find the indicated distance.**

(A) A hiker wants to find the distance d across a canyon. She locates points as described.

1. She identifies a landmark at X. She places a marker (Y) directly across the canyon from X.
2. At Y, she turns 90° away from X and walks 400 feet in a straight line. She places a marker (Z) at this location.
3. She continues walking another 600 feet, and places a marker (W) at this location.
4. She turns 90° away from the canyon and walks until the marker Z aligns with X. She places a marker (V) at this location and measures $\overline{WV}$.

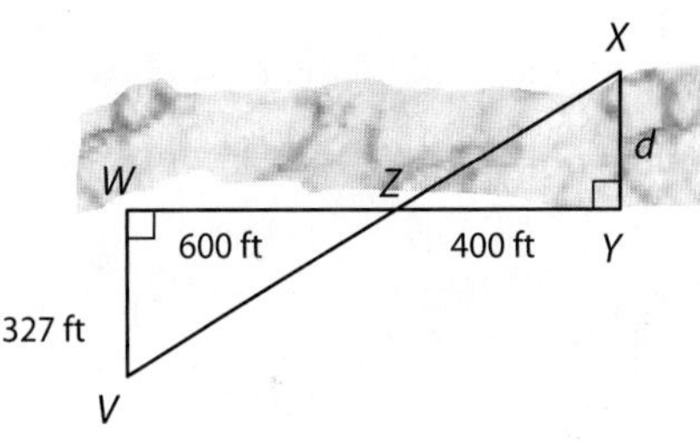

$\angle VWZ \cong \angle XYZ$ (All right angles are congruent) and

$\angle VZW \cong \angle XZY$ (Vertical angles are congruent). So,

$\triangle VWZ \sim \triangle XYZ$ by the AA Similarity Criterion.

$\frac{XY}{VW} = \frac{YZ}{WZ}$, So $\frac{d}{327} = \frac{400}{600}$, or $\frac{d}{327} = \frac{2}{3}$

Then $d = 327\left(\frac{2}{3}\right) = 218$.

The distance across the canyon is 218 feet.

(B) To find the distance d across the gorge, a student identifies points as shown in the figure. Find d.

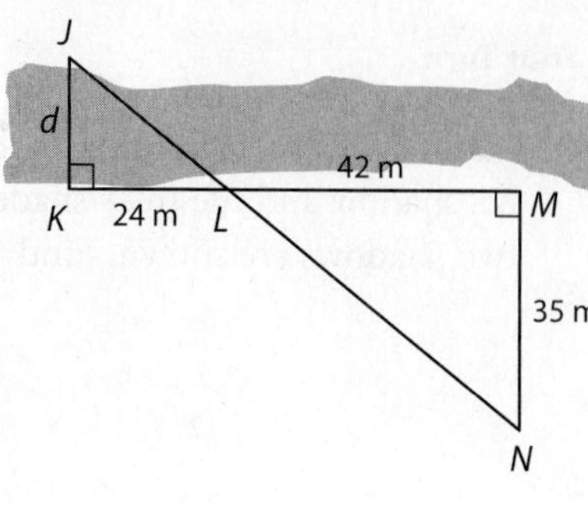

$\triangle JKL \sim \triangle NML$ by the AA Similarity Criterion.

$$\frac{JK}{NM} = \frac{KL}{\boxed{ML}}$$

$$\frac{d}{35} = \frac{24}{\boxed{42}}$$

$$d = \boxed{35} \cdot \frac{\boxed{24}}{42} = \boxed{35} \cdot \frac{\boxed{4}}{7}$$

$$d = \frac{\boxed{140}}{7}$$

$$d = \boxed{20}$$

The distance across the gorge is 20 meters.

Reflect

4. In the example, why is $\angle JLK \cong \angle NLM$?

Your Turn

5. To find the distance d across a stream, Levi located points as shown in the figure. Use the given information to find d.

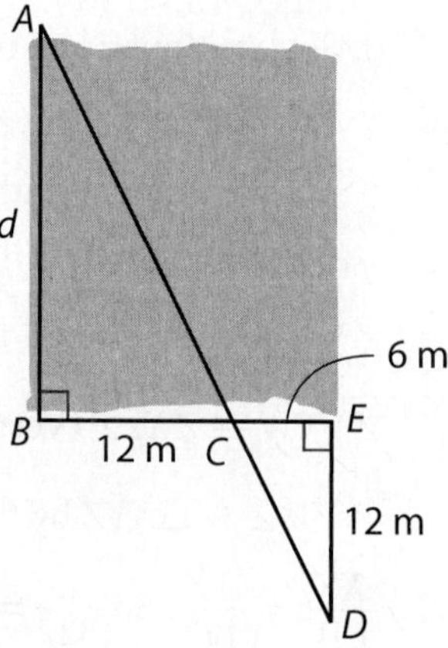

Elaborate

6. Discussion Suppose you want to help a friend prepare for solving indirect measurement problems. What topics would you suggest that your friend review?

7. Essential Question Check-In You are given a figure including triangles that represent a real-world situation. What is the first step you should take to find an unknown measurement?

✪ Evaluate: Homework and Practice

- Online Homework
- Hints and Help
- Extra Practice

1. Finding distances using similar triangles is called ___?___.

Use similar triangles $\triangle ABC$ and $\triangle XYZ$ to find the missing height h.

2. 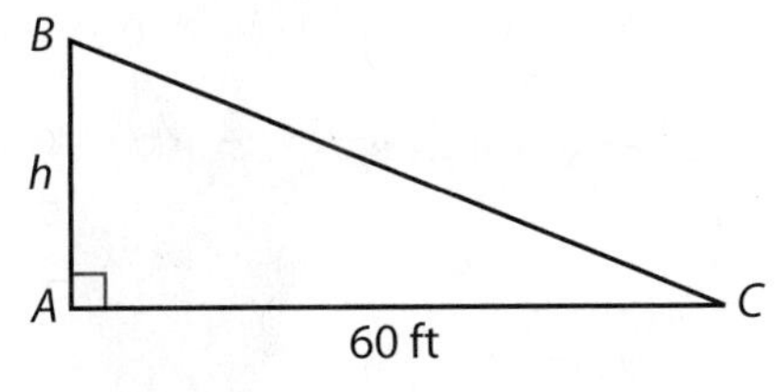

3. 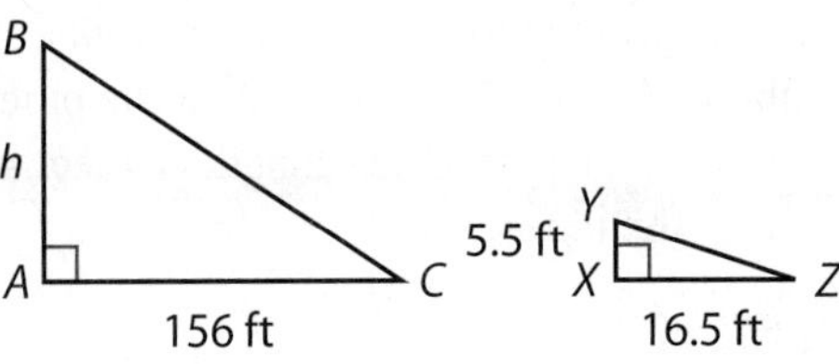

4. 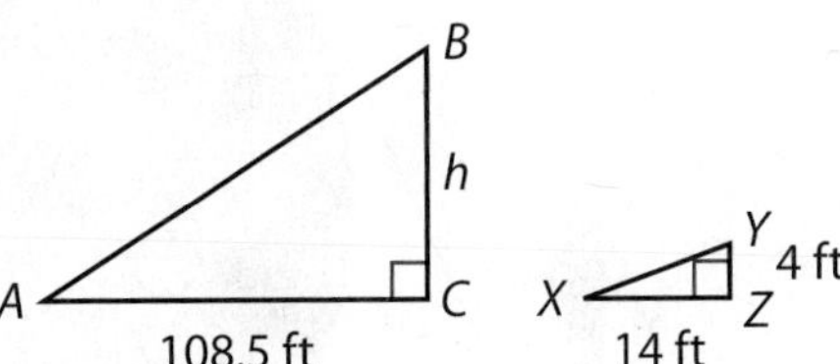

5. 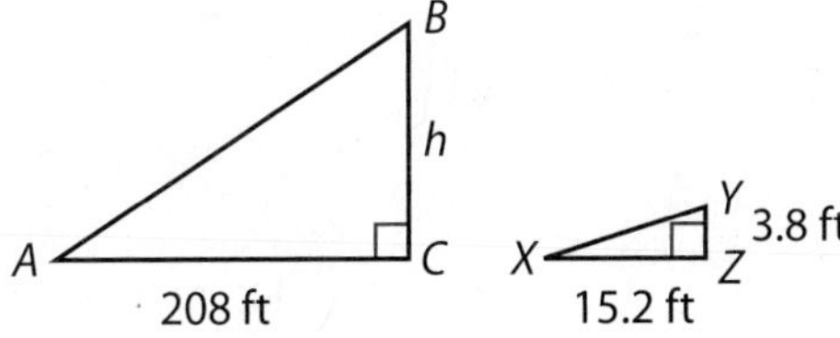

Use similar triangles $\triangle EFG$ and $\triangle IHG$ to find the missing distance d.

6. 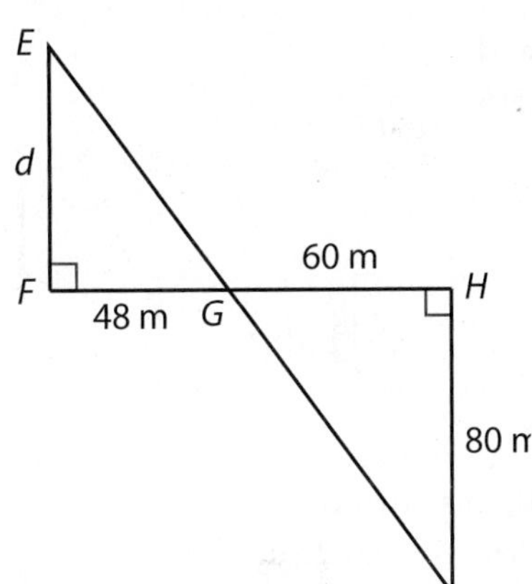

7. 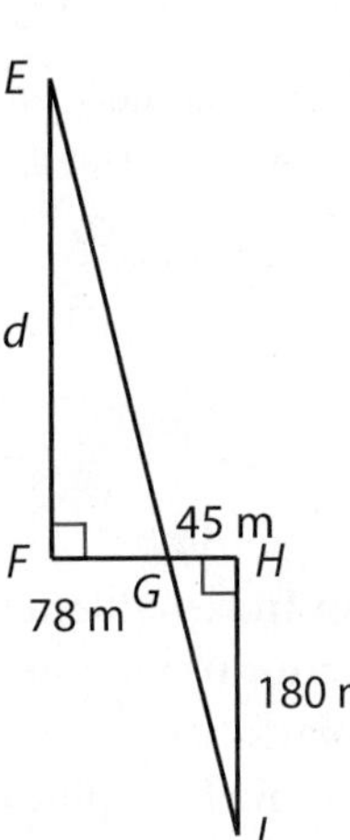

8. 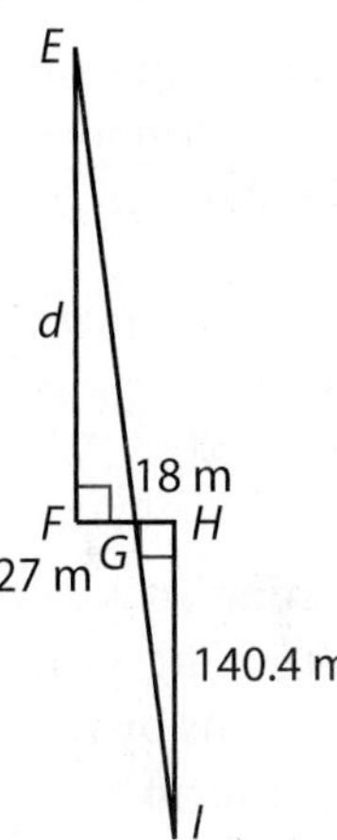

9. 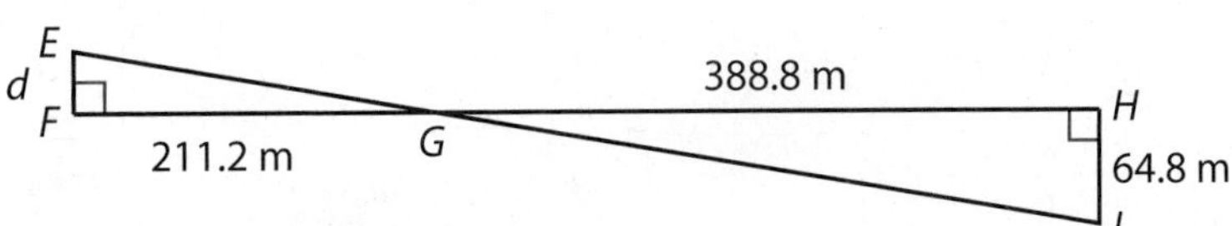

10. To find the height h of a dinosaur in a museum, Amir placed a mirror on the ground 40 feet from its base. Then he stepped back 4 feet so that he could see the top of the dinosaur in the mirror. Amir's eyes were approximately 5 feet 6 inches above the ground. What is the height of the dinosaur?

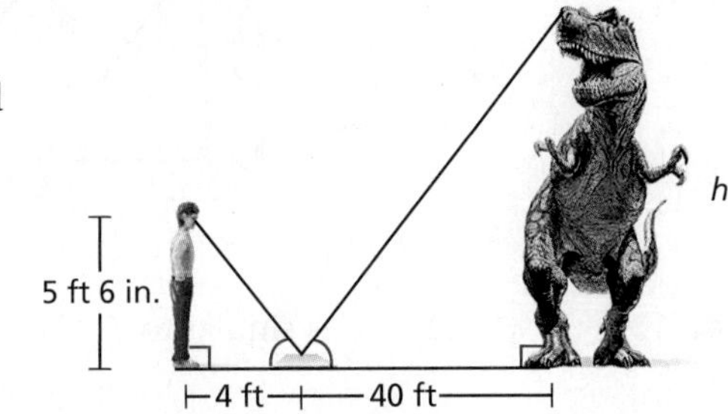

11. Jenny is 5 feet 2 inches tall. To find the height h of a light pole, she measured her shadow and the pole's shadow. What is the height of the pole?

h

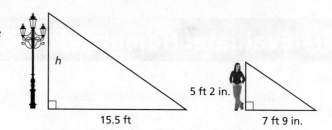

5 ft 2 in.

15.5 ft

7 ft 9 in.

12. A student wanted to find the height h of a statue of a pineapple in Nambour, Australia. She measured the pineapple's shadow and her own shadow. The student's height is 5 feet 4 inches. What is the height of the pineapple?

13. To find the height h of a flagpole, Casey measured her own shadow and the flagpole's shadow. Given that Casey's height is 5 feet 4 inches, what is the height of the flagpole?

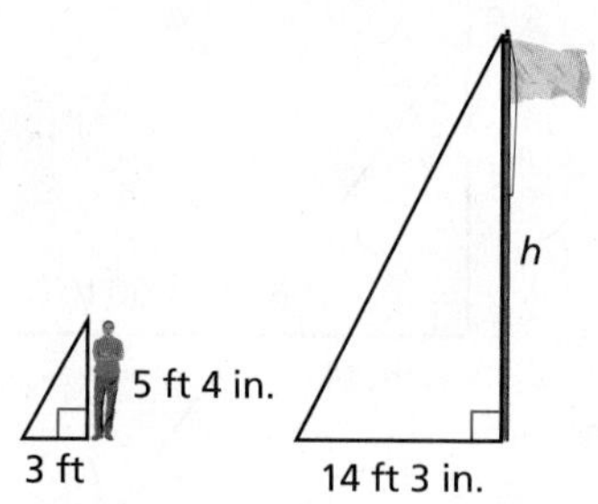

A city is planning an outdoor concert for an Independence Day celebration. To hold speakers and lights, a crew of technicians sets up a scaffold with two platforms by the stage. The first platform is 8 feet 2 inches off the ground. The second platform is 7 feet 6 inches above the first platform. The shadow of the first platform stretches 6 feet 3 inches across the ground.

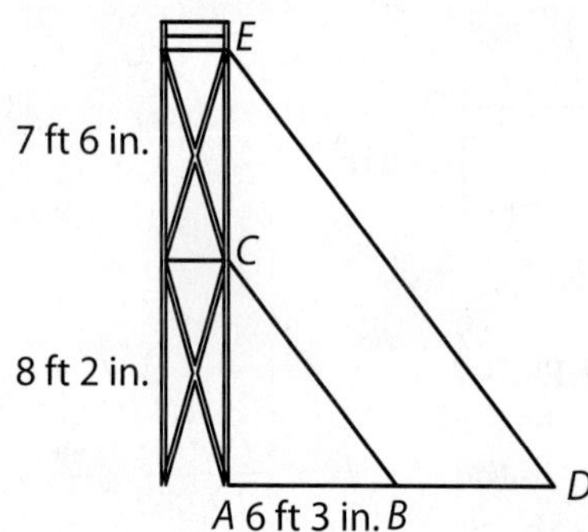

14. Explain why $\triangle ABC$ is similar to $\triangle ADE$. (*Hint*: rays of light are parallel.)

15. Find the length of the shadow of the second platform in feet and inches to the nearest inch.

16. A technician is 5 feet 8 inches tall. The technician is standing on top of the second platform. Find the length *s* of the shadow that is cast by the scaffold and the technician to the nearest inch.

17. To find the distance *XY* across a lake, you locate points as shown in the figure. Explain how to use this information to find *XY*.

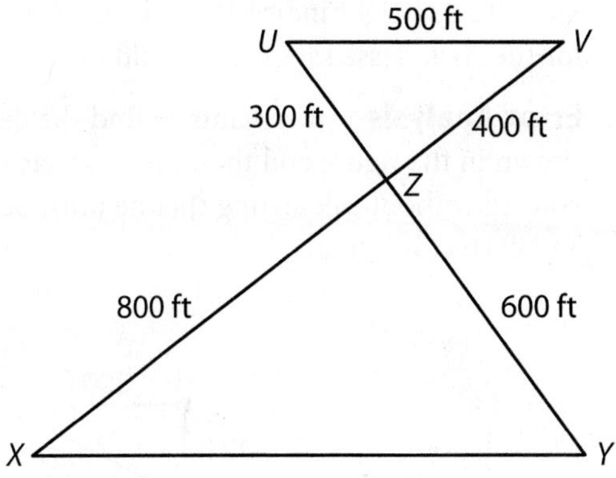

18. In order to find the height of a cliff, you stand at the bottom of the cliff, walk 60 feet from the base, and place a mirror on the ground. Then you face the cliff and step back 5 feet so that can see the top of the cliff in the mirror. Assuming your eyes are 6 feet above the ground, explain how to use this information to find the height of the cliff. (The angles marked congruent are congruent because of the nature of the reflection of light in a mirror.)

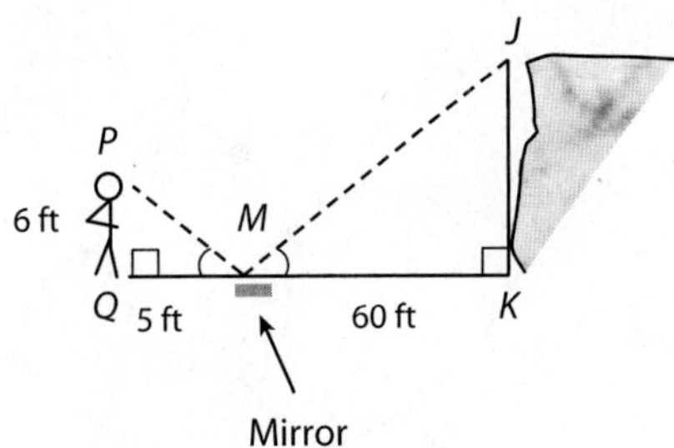

19. To find the height of a tree, Adrian measures the tree's shadow and then his shadow. Which proportion could Adrian use to find the height of the tree? Determine all that apply.

A. $\frac{AC}{DF} = \frac{BC}{EF}$

B. $\frac{DF}{AC} = \frac{EF}{BC}$

C. $\frac{AB}{DF} = \frac{BC}{EF}$

D. $\frac{DF}{BC} = \frac{EF}{AC}$

E. $\frac{BC}{EF} = \frac{AC}{DF}$

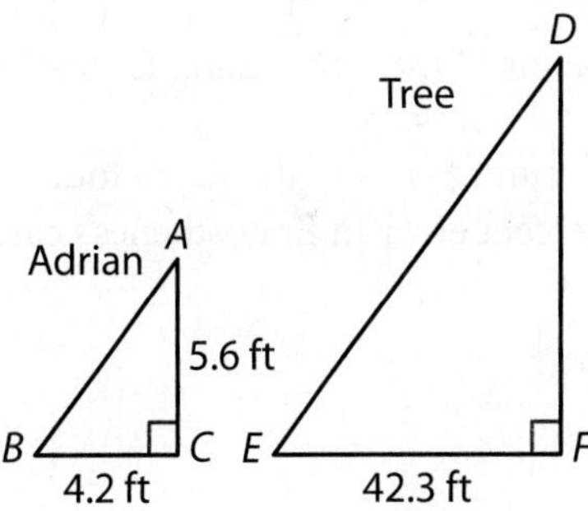

H.O.T. Focus on Higher Order Thinking

20. **Critique Reasoning** Jesse and Kyle are hiking. Jesse is carrying a walking stick. They spot a tall tree and use the walking stick as a vertical marker to create similar triangles and measure the tree indirectly. Later in the day they come upon a rock formation. They measure the rock formation's shadow and again want to use similar triangles to measure its height indirectly. Kyle wants to use the shadow length they measured earlier for the stick. Jesse says they should measure it again. Who do you think is right?

21. **Error Analysis** Andy wants to find the distance d across a river. He located points as shown in the figure and then used similar triangles to find that $d = 220.5$ feet. How can you tell without calculating that he must be wrong? Tell what you think he did wrong and correct his error.

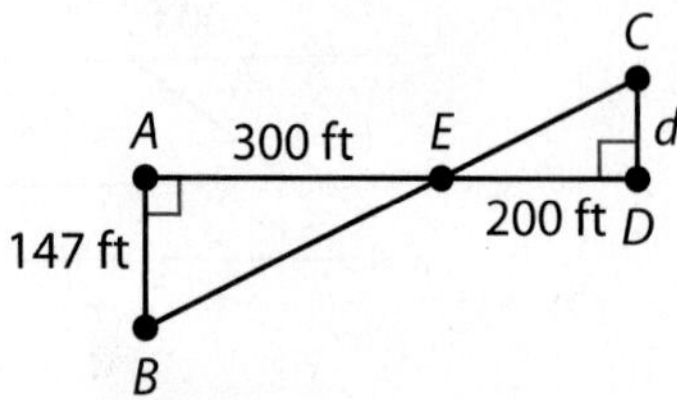

Lesson Performance Task

Around 240 B.C., the Greek astronomer Eratosthenes was residing in Alexandria, Egypt. He believed that the Earth was spherical and conceived of an experiment to measure its circumference. At noon in the town of Syene, the sun was directly overhead. A stick stuck vertically in the ground cast no shadow. At the same moment in Alexandria, 490 miles from Syene, a vertical stick cast a shadow that veered 7.2° from the vertical.

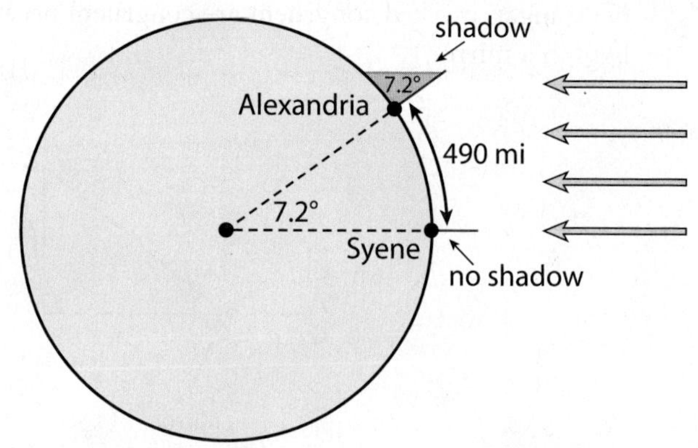

1. Refer to the diagram. Explain why Eratosthenes reasoned that the angle at the center of the Earth that intercepted a 490-mile arc measured 7.2 degrees.

2. Calculate the circumference of the Earth using Eratosthenes's figures. Explain how you got your answer.

3. Calculate the radius of the Earth using Eratosthenes's figures.

4. The accepted circumference of the Earth today is 24,901 miles. Calculate the percent error in Eratosthenes's calculations.

17.4 Similarity in Right Triangles

Essential Question: How does the altitude to the hypotenuse of a right triangle help you use similar right triangles to solve problems?

Resource Locker

Explore Identifying Similarity in Right Triangles

(A) Make two copies of the right triangle on a piece of paper and cut them out.

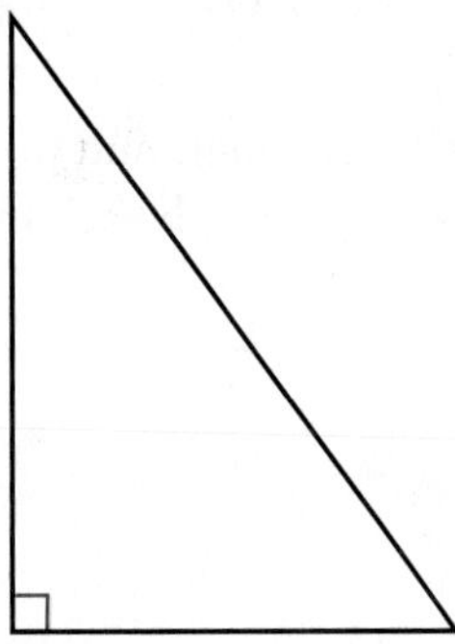

(B) Choose one of the triangles. Fold the paper to find the altitude to the hypotenuse.

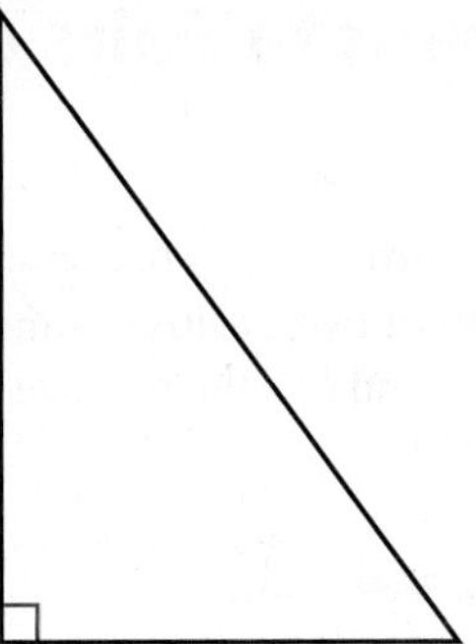

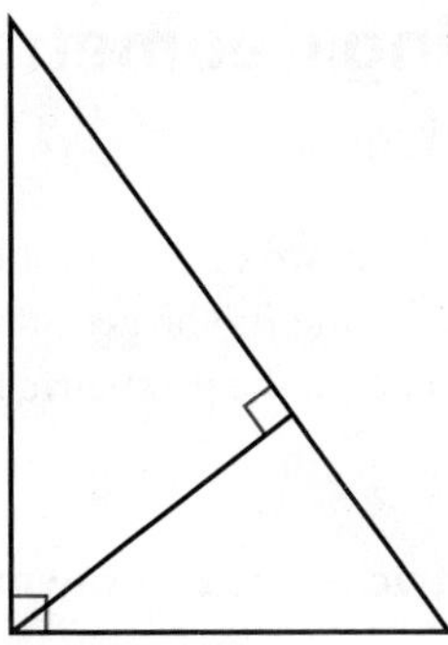

(C) Cut the second triangle along the altitude. Label the triangles as shown.

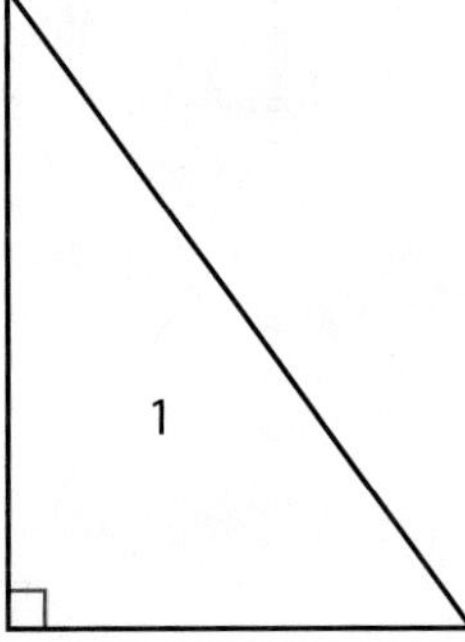

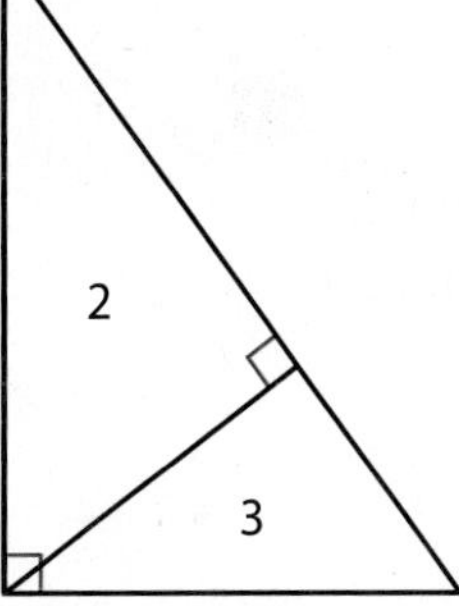

Ⓓ Place triangle 2 on top of triangle 1. What do you notice about the angles?

Ⓔ What is true of triangles 1 and 2? How do you know?

Ⓕ Repeat Steps 1 and 2 for triangles 1 and 3. Does the same relationship hold true for triangles 1 and 3?

Reflect

1. How are the hypotenuses of the triangles 2 and 3 related to triangle 1?
2. What is the relationship between triangles 2 and 3? Explain.
3. When you draw the altitude to the hypotenuse of a right triangle, what kinds of figures are produced?
4. Suppose you draw $\triangle ABC$ such that $\angle B$ is a right angle and the altitude to the hypotenuse intersects hypotenuse $\overline{AC}$ at point P. Match each triangle to a similar triangle. Explain your reasoning.

A. $\triangle ABC$ **a.** __?__ $\triangle PAB$

B. $\triangle PBC$ **b.** __?__ $\triangle CAB$

C. $\triangle BAP$ **c.** __?__ $\triangle BPC$

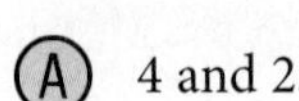

Explain 1 Finding Geometric Means of Pairs of Numbers

Consider the proportion $\frac{a}{x} = \frac{x}{b}$ where two of the numbers in the proportion are the same. The number x is the *geometric mean* of a and b. The **geometric mean** of two positive numbers is the positive square root of their product. So the geometric mean of a and b is the positive number x such that $x = \sqrt{ab}$ or $x^2 = ab$.

Example 1 **Find the geometric mean x of the numbers.**

Ⓐ 4 and 25

Write proportion.	$\frac{4}{x} = \frac{x}{25}$
Multiply both sides by the product of the denominators.	$25x \cdot \frac{4}{x} = 25x \cdot \frac{x}{25}$
Multiply.	$\frac{100x}{x} = \frac{25x^2}{25}$
Simplify.	$100 = x^2$
Take the square root of both sides.	$\sqrt{100} = \sqrt{x^2}$
Simplify.	$10 = x$

(B) 9 and 20

Write proportion. $\frac{9}{x} = \frac{x}{20}$

Multiply both sides by the product of the denominators. $20x \cdot \frac{9}{x} = 20x \cdot \frac{x}{20}$

Multiply. $\frac{180x}{x} = \frac{20x^2}{20}$

Simplify. $180 = x^2$

Take the square root of both sides. $\sqrt{180} = \sqrt{x^2}$

Simplify. $6\sqrt{5} = x$

Reflect

5. How can you show that if positive numbers a and b are such that $\frac{a}{x} = \frac{x}{b}$, then $x = \sqrt{ab}$?

Your Turn

Find the geometric mean of the numbers. If necessary, give the answer in simplest radical form.

6. 6 and 24

7. 5 and 12

Explain 2 Proving the Geometric Means Theorems

In the Explore activity, you discovered a theorem about right triangles and similarity.

The altitude to the hypotenuse of a right triangle forms two triangles that are similar to each other and to the original triangle.

That theorem leads to two additional theorems about right triangles. Both of the theorems involve geometric means.

Geometric Means Theorems

Theorem	Example	Diagram
The length of the altitude to the hypotenuse of a right triangle is the geometric mean of the lengths of the segments of the hypotenuse.	$h^2 = xy$ or $h = \sqrt{xy}$	x, c, y, a, h, b
The length of a leg of a right triangle is the geometric mean of the lengths of the hypotenuse and the segment of the hypotenuse adjacent to that leg.	$a^2 = xc$ or $a = \sqrt{xc}$ $b^2 = yc$ or $b = \sqrt{yc}$	

Example 2 **Prove the first Geometric Means Theorem.**

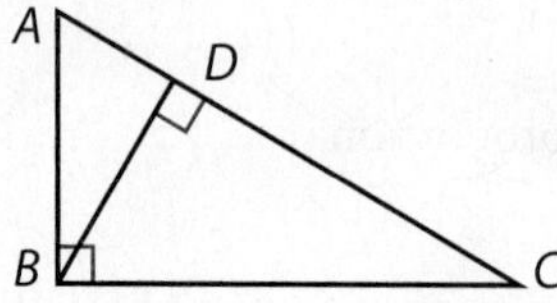

Given: Right triangle ABC with altitude $\overline{BD}$

Prove: $\frac{CD}{BD} = \frac{BD}{AD}$

Statements	Reasons
1. $\triangle ABC$ with altitude $\overline{BD}$	**1.** Given
2. $\triangle CBD \sim \triangle BAD$	**2.** The altitude to the hypotenuse of a right triangle forms two triangles that are similar to the original triangle and to each other.
3. $\frac{CD}{BD} = \frac{BD}{AD}$	**3.** Corresponding sides of similar triangles are proportional.

Reflect

8. Discussion How can you prove the second Geometric Means Theorem?

Explain 3 Using the Geometric Means Theorems

You can use the Geometric Means Theorems to find unknown segment lengths in a right triangle.

Example 3 **Find the indicated value.**

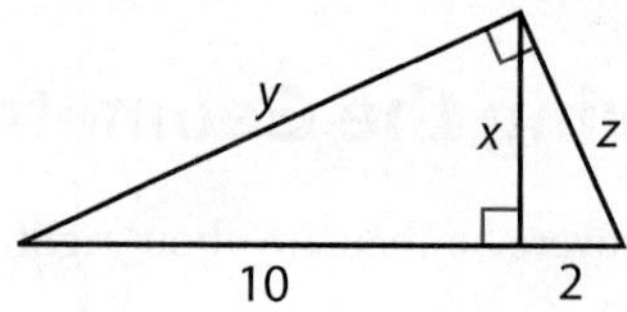

 x

Write proportion. $\frac{2}{x} = \frac{x}{10}$

Multiply both sides by the product of the denominators. $10x \cdot \frac{2}{x} = 10x \cdot \frac{x}{10}$

Multiply. $\frac{20x}{x} = \frac{10x^2}{10}$

Simplify. $20 = x^2$

Take the square root of both sides. $\sqrt{20} = \sqrt{x^2}$

Simplify. $2\sqrt{5} = x$

Ⓑ y

Write proportion.	$\frac{10}{y} = \frac{y}{12}$
Multiply both sides by the product of the denominators.	$\boxed{12y}\,\frac{10}{y} = \boxed{12y}\,\frac{y}{12}$
Multiply.	$\frac{\boxed{120y}}{y} = \frac{\boxed{12y^2}}{12}$
Simplify.	$\boxed{120} = \boxed{y^2}$
Take the square root of both sides.	$\sqrt{\boxed{120}} = \sqrt{\boxed{y^2}}$
Simplify.	$\boxed{2\sqrt{30}} = y$

Reflect

9. Discussion How can you check your answers?

Your Turn

10. Find x.

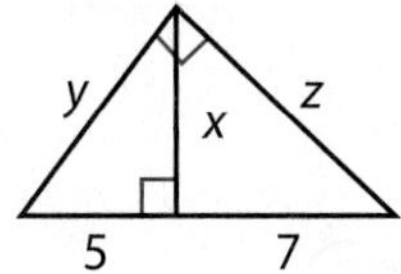

Explain 4 Proving the Pythagorean Theorem using Similarity

You have used the Pythagorean Theorem in earlier courses as well as in this one. There are many, many proofs of the Pythagorean Theorem. You will prove it now using similar right triangles.

The Pythagorean Theorem

In a right triangle, the square of the sum of the lengths of the legs is equal to the square of the length of the hypotenuse.

Example 4 **Complete the proof of the Pythagorean Theorem.**

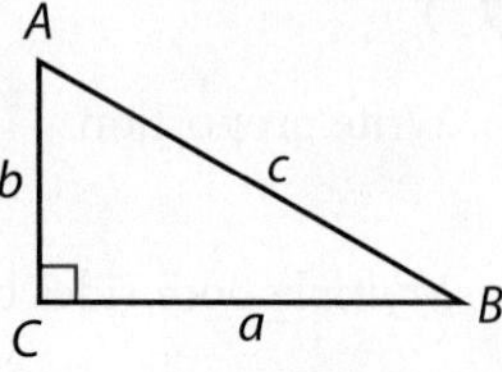

Given: Right $\triangle ABC$

Prove: $a^2 + b^2 = c^2$

Part 1

Draw the altitude to the hypotenuse.
Label the point of intersection X.

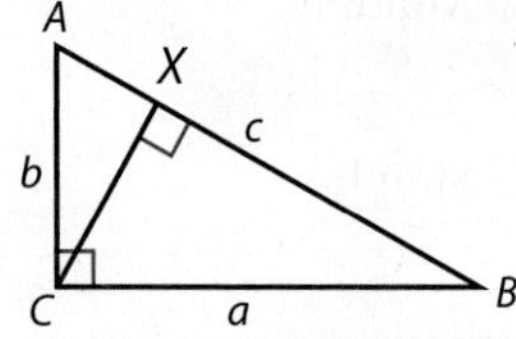

$\angle BXC \cong \angle BCA$ because all right angles are congruent.

$\angle B \cong \angle B$ by the Reflexive Property of Congruence.

So, $\triangle BXC \sim \triangle BCA$ by the AA Similarity Criterion.

$\angle AXC \cong \angle ACB$ because all right angles are congruent.

$\angle A \cong \angle A$ by the Reflexive Property of Congruence.

So, $\triangle AXC \sim \triangle ACB$ by the AA Similarity Criterion.

Part 2

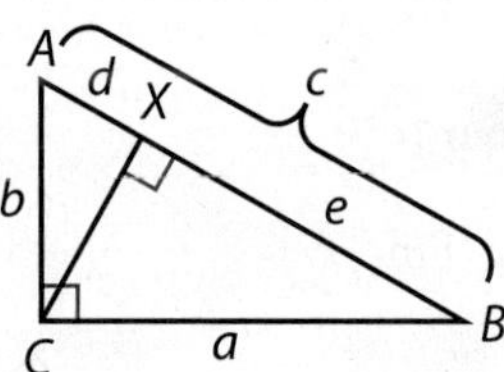

Let the lengths of the segments of the hypotenuse be d and e, as shown in the figure.

Use the fact that corresponding sides of similar triangles are proportional to write two proportions.

Proportion 1: $\triangle BXC \sim \triangle BCA$, so $\frac{a}{c} = \frac{e}{a}$.

Proportion 2: $\triangle AXC \sim \triangle ACB$, so $\frac{b}{c} = \frac{d}{b}$.

Part 3

Now perform some algebra to complete the proof as follows.

Multiply both sides of Proportion 1 by ac. Write the resulting equation. $a^2 = ce$

Multiply both sides of Proportion 12 by bc. Write the resulting equation. $b^2 = cd$

Adding the two resulting equations give this: $a^2 + b^2 = ce + cd$

Factor the right side of the equation: $a^2 + b^2 = c(e + d)$

Finally, use the fact that $e + d = c$ by the Segment Addition Postulate to rewrite the equation as $a^2 + b^2 = c^2$.

Reflect

11. **Error Analysis** A student used the figure in Part 2 of the example, and wrote the following incorrect proof of the Pythagorean Theorem. Critique the student's proof. $\triangle BXC \sim \triangle BCA$ and $\triangle BCA \sim \triangle CXA$, so $\triangle BXC \sim \triangle CXA$ by transitivity of similarity. Let $CX = f$. Since corresponding sides of similar triangles are proportional, $\frac{e}{f} = \frac{f}{d}$ and $f^2 = ed$. Because $\triangle BXC \sim$ and $\triangle CXA$ are right triangles, $a^2 = e^2 + f^2$ and $b^2 = f^2 + d^2$.

Add the equations.	$a^2 + b^2 = e^2 + 2f^2 + d^2$
Substitute.	$= e^2 + 2ed + d^2$
Factor.	$= (e + d)^2$
Segment Addition Postulate	$= c^2$

Elaborate

12. How would you explain to a friend how to find the geometric mean of two numbers?

13. $\triangle XYZ$ is an isosceles right triangle and the right angle is $\angle Y$. Suppose the altitude to hypotenuse $\overline{XZ}$ intersects $\overline{XZ}$ at point P. Describe the relationships among triangles $\triangle XYZ$, $\triangle YPZ$ and $\triangle XPY$.

14. Can two different pairs of numbers have the same geometric mean? If so, give an example. If not, explain why not.

15. **Essential Question Check-In** How is the altitude to the hypotenuse of a right triangle related to the segments of the hypotenuse it creates?

Evaluate: Homework and Practice

- Online Homework
- Hints and Help
- Extra Practice

Write a similarity statement comparing the three triangles to each diagram.

1.

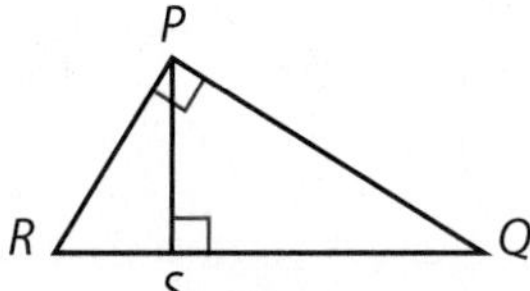

2.

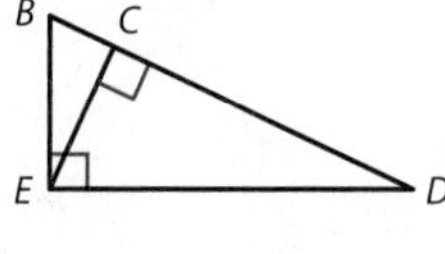

3.

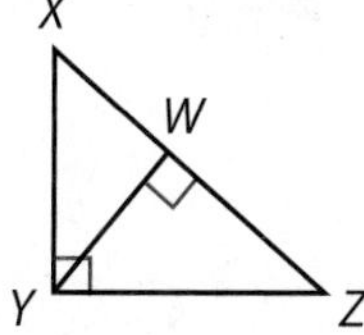

Find the geometric mean x of each pair of numbers. If necessary, give the answer in simplest radical form.

4. 5 and 20

5. 3 and 12

6. 8 and 13

7. 3.5 and 20

8. 1.5 and 84

9. $\frac{2}{3}$ and $\frac{27}{40}$

Find *x*, *y*, and *z*.

10.

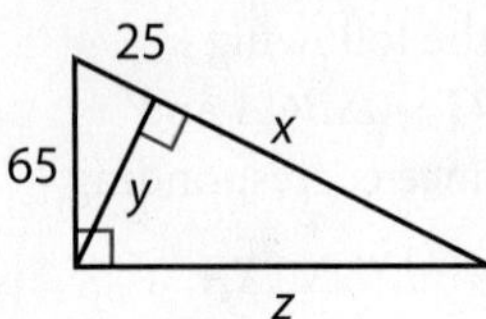

11.

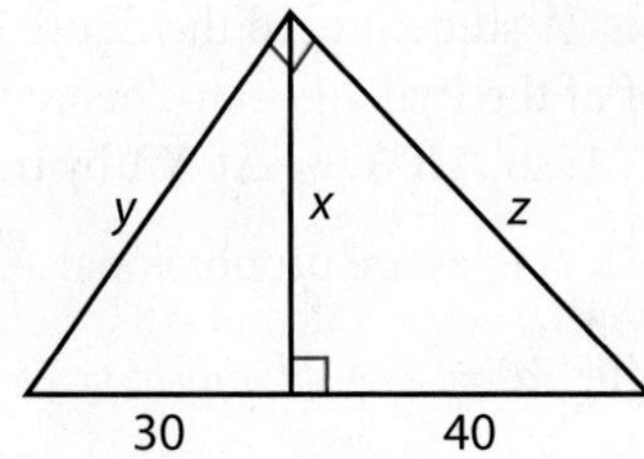

12.

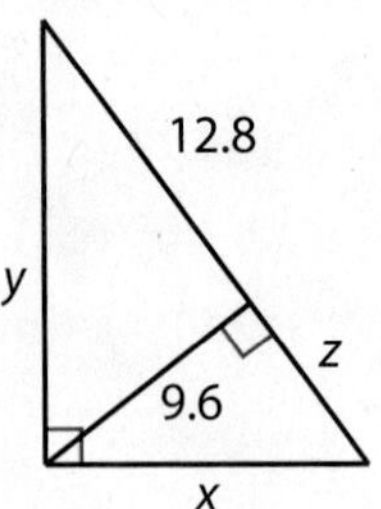

Use the diagram to complete each equation.

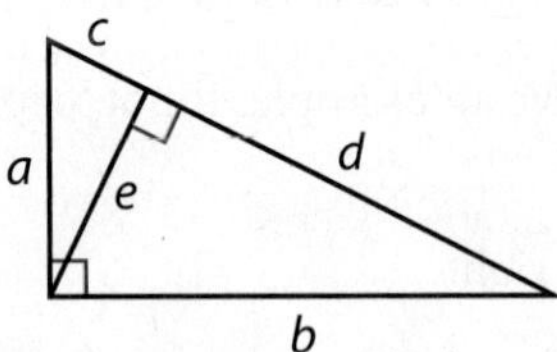

13. $\frac{c}{e} = \frac{\square}{d}$

14. $\frac{c}{a} = \frac{a}{\square}$

15. $\frac{c+d}{b} = \frac{b}{\square}$

16. $\frac{d}{\square} = \frac{e}{c}$

17. $c(c+d) = \square^2$

18. $\square^2 = cd$

Find the length of the altitude to the hypotenuse under the given conditions.

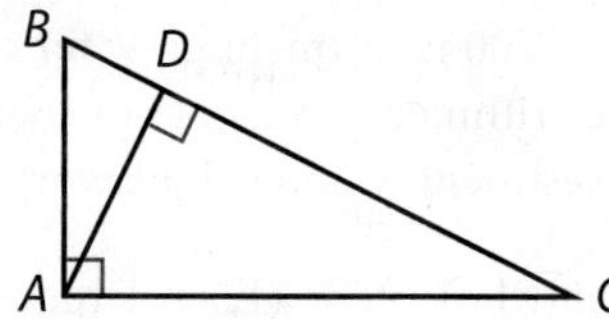

19. $BC = 5$
$AC = 4$

20. $BC = 17$
$AC = 15$

21. $BC = 13$
$AC = 12$

22. Communicate Mathematical Ideas The area of a rectangle with a length of ℓ and a width of w has the same area as a square. Show that the side length of the square is the geometric mean of the length and width of the rectangle.

H.O.T. Focus on Higher Order Thinking

23. Algebra An 8-inch-long altitude of a right triangle divides the hypotenuse into two segments. One segment is 4 times as long as the other. What are the lengths of the segments of the hypotenuse?

24. Error Analysis Cecile and Amelia both found a value for EF in $\triangle DEF$. Both students work are shown. Which student's solution is correct? What mistake did the other student make?

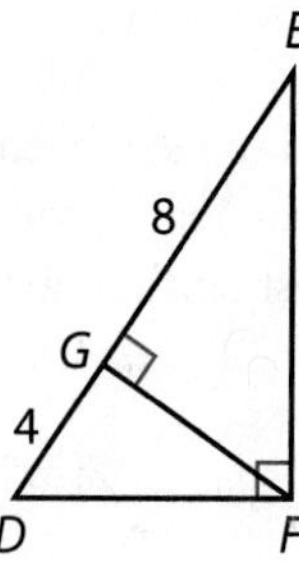

Cecile: $\frac{12}{EF} = \frac{EF}{8}$

So $EF^2 = 12(8) = 96$.

Then $EF = \sqrt{96} = 4\sqrt{6}$.

Amelia: $\frac{8}{EF} = \frac{EF}{4}$

So $EF^2 = 8(4) = 32$.

Then $EF = \sqrt{32} = 4\sqrt{2}$.

Lesson Performance Task

In the example at the beginning of the lesson, a \$100 investment grew for one year at the rate of 50%, to \$150, then fell for one year at the rate of 50%, to \$75. The arithmetic mean of +50% and −50%, which is 0%, was not a good predictor of the change, for it predicted the investment would still be worth \$100 after two years, not \$75.

1. Find the geometric mean of $1 + 50\%$ and $1 - 50\%$. (Each 1 represents the fact that at the beginning of each year, an investment is worth 100% of itself.) Round to the nearest thousandth.

2. It is the geometric mean, not the arithmetic mean, that tells you what the interest rate would have had to have been over an entire investment period to achieve the end result. You can use your answer to Exercise 1 to check this claim. Find the value of a \$100 investment after it increased or decreased at the rate you found in Exercise 1 for two years. Show your work.

3. Copy the right triangle shown here. Write the terms "Year 1 Rate", "Year 2 Rate", and "Average Rate" to show geometrically how the three investment rates relate to each other.

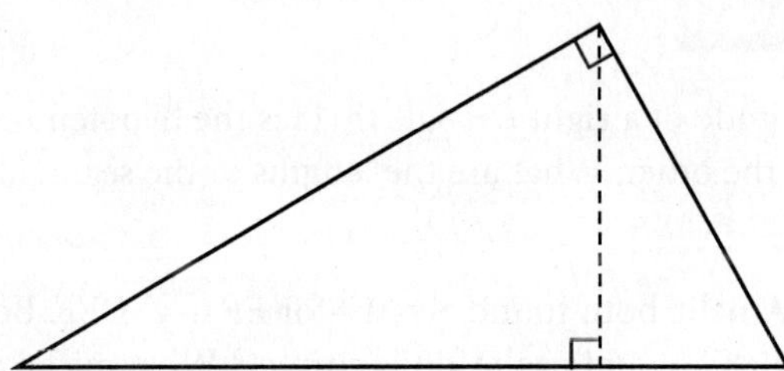

4. The geometric mean of n numbers is the nth root of the product of the numbers. Find what the interest rate would have had to have been over 4 years to achieve the result of a \$100 investment that grew 20% in Year 1 and 30% in Year 2, then lost 20% in Year 3 and 30% in Year 4. Show your work. Round your answer to the nearest tenth of a percent.

Using Similar Triangles

Essential Question: How can you use similar triangles to solve real-world problems?

Key Vocabulary
indirect measurement *(medición indirecta)*
geometric mean *(media geométrica)*

KEY EXAMPLE *(Lesson 17.1)*

Find the missing length x.

$\frac{ZU}{UX} = \frac{ZV}{VY}$ Write a proportion.

$\frac{x}{10} = \frac{16}{9}$ Substitute.

$x = \left(\frac{16}{9}\right)(10)$ Multiply both sides by 10.

$x \approx 17.8$ Simplify.

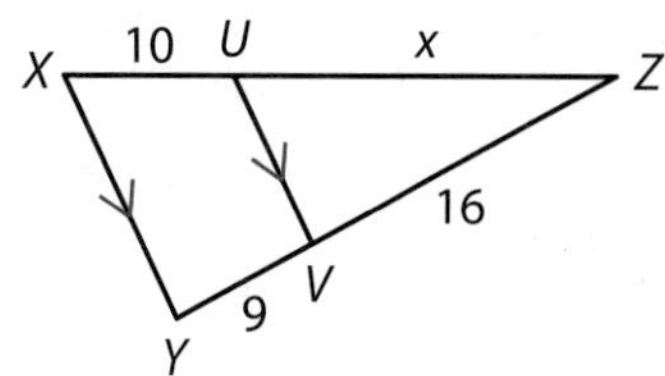

KEY EXAMPLE *(Lesson 17.2)*

Given the directed line segment from A to B, construct the point P that divides the segment in the ratio 2 to 3 from A to B.

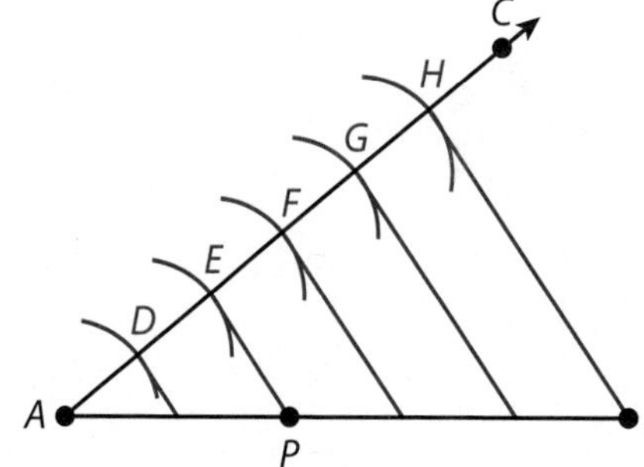

Use a straightedge to draw $\overrightarrow{AC}$.

Place a compass on point A and draw an arc through $\overrightarrow{AC}$. Label the intersection D. Continue this for intersections D through H.

Use a straightedge to connect points B and H.

Construct angles congruent to $\angle AHB$ with points D through G.

$\overline{AB}$ is partitioned into five equal parts. Label point P at the point that divides the segment in the ratio 2 to 3 from A to B.

KEY EXAMPLE *(Lesson 17.3)*

A 5.8-foot-tall man is standing next to a basketball hoop that casts an 11.2-foot shadow. The man's shadow is 6.5 feet long. How tall is the basketball hoop?

Let x be the height of the basketball hoop.

$\frac{x}{11.2} = \frac{5.8}{6.5}$ Write a proportion.

$x = \left(\frac{5.8}{6.5}\right)(11.2)$ Multiply both sides by 11.2.

$x \approx 10$

EXERCISES

Find the missing lengths. (Lesson 17.1)

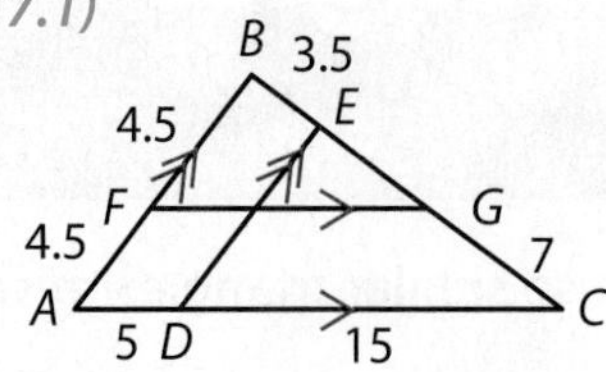

1. BG

2. CE

Copy the directed line segment from A to B. Construct the point P that divides the segment in the ratio 3 to 1 from A to B. (Lesson 17.2)

3.

A ———————— B

Find the unknown length. (Lesson 17.3)

4. A 5.9-foot-tall-man stands near a 12-foot statue. The man places a mirror on the ground a certain distance from the base of the statue, and then stands another 7 feet from the mirror to see the top of the statue in it. How far is the mirror from the base of the statue?

5. A 45-foot flagpole casts a 22-foot shadow. At the same time of day, a woman casts a 2.7-foot shadow. How tall is the woman?

Find the lengths. (Lesson 17.4)

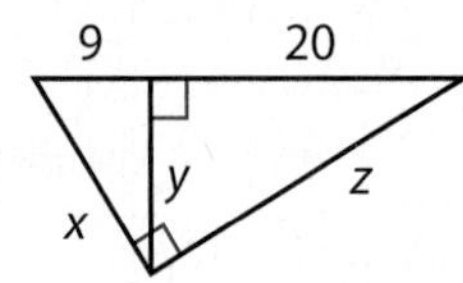

6. x

7. y

8. z

MODULE PERFORMANCE TASK

How Large Is the Bermuda Triangle?

The boundaries of the Bermuda Triangle are not well defined, but the region is often represented as a triangle with vertices at Miami, Florida; San Juan, Puerto Rico; and Hamilton, Bermuda. The distance between Miami and San Juan is about 1,034 miles. What is the approximate area of this region? One tool that you may find helpful in solving this problem is the similar triangle shown here with angle measures labeled.

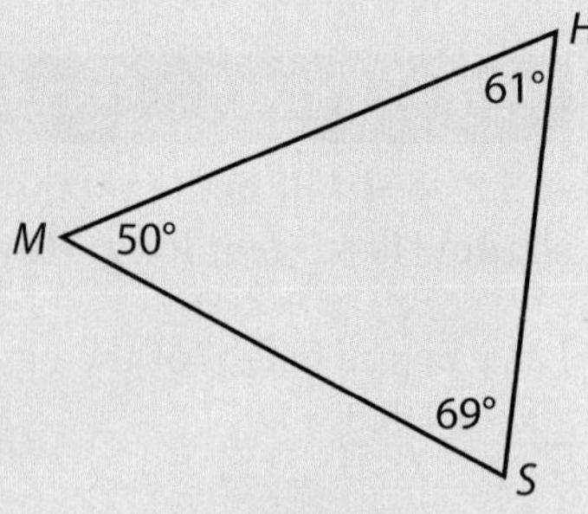

Be sure to record all your data and assumptions. Then use graphs, diagrams, words, or numbers to explain how you reached your conclusion.

Ready to Go On?

17.1–17.4 Using Similar Triangles

- Online Homework
- Hints and Help
- Extra Practice

Find the missing lengths. *(Lessons 17.1, 17.4)*

1. 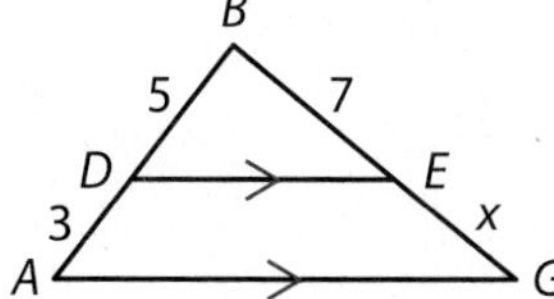

2. 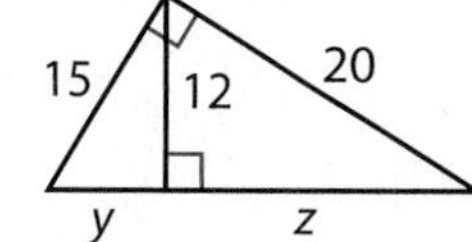

Copy the directed line segment from *A* to *B*. Construct the point *P* that divides the segment in the given ratio from *A* to *B*. *(Lesson 17.2)*

3. 3 to 4

Find the missing height. *(Lesson 17.3)*

4. The height of a street light is 25 feet. It casts a 12-foot shadow. At the same time, a man standing next to the street light casts a 3-foot shadow. How tall is the man?

ESSENTIAL QUESTION

5. How can you use similar triangles to find the missing parts of a triangle?

MODULE 17
MIXED REVIEW

Assessment Readiness

SELECTED RESPONSE

1. $\triangle XYZ$ is given by the points $X(-1, -1)$, $Y(3, 5)$, and $Z(5, 1)$. Consider each of the points below. Is each point a vertex of the image under the transformation $(x, y) \rightarrow (x + 3, y - 2) \rightarrow \left(\frac{1}{2}x, y\right) \rightarrow (y, -x)$?

Write Yes or No for A–C.

A. $X'''(-3, -1)$
B. $Y'''(3, -3)$
C. $Z'''(-1, -4)$

2. Which of the following statements are true about the triangle at the right? Determine if each statement is True or False.

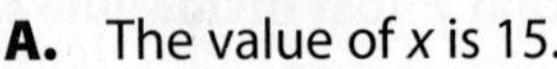

A. The value of x is 15.
B. The value of y is 12.
C. The value of y is 16.

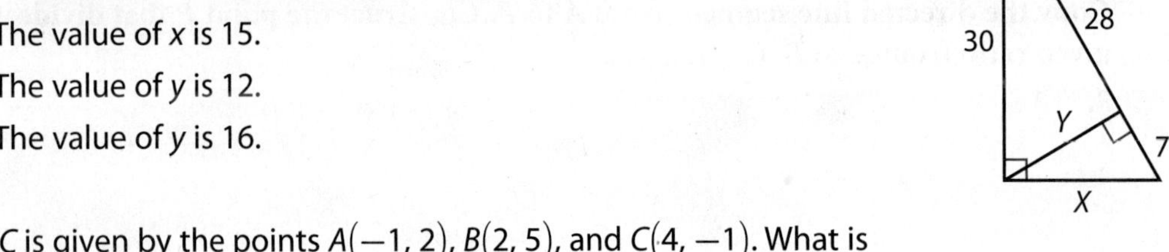

3. $\triangle ABC$ is given by the points $A(-1, 2)$, $B(2, 5)$, and $C(4, -1)$. What is the point $\left(\frac{1}{2}, \frac{5}{2}\right)$? Explain what this means.

4. Copy the directed segment from A to B. Construct the point P that divides the segment in the ratio 1 to 5 from A to B. Explain your process and how it relates to similar triangles.

Trigonometry with Right Triangles

MODULE 18

Essential Question: How can you use trigonometry with right triangles to solve real-world problems?

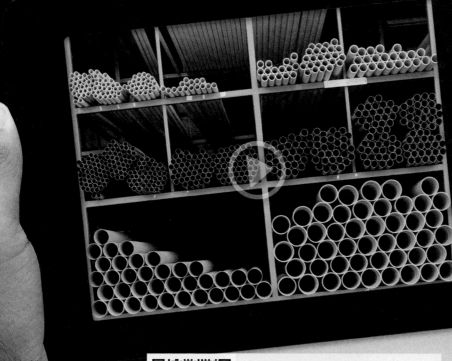

REAL WORLD VIDEO
Check out how right triangle trigonometry is used in real-world warehouses to minimize the space needed for items being shipped or stored.

MODULE PERFORMANCE TASK PREVIEW

How Much Shorter Are Staggered Pipe Stacks?

In this module, you will investigate how much space can be saved by stacking pipes in a staggered pattern rather than directly on top of each other. How can trigonometry help you find the answer to this problem? Get prepared to discover the "staggering" results!

Complete these exercises to review skills you will need for this module.

- Online Homework
- Hints and Help
- Extra Practice

Angle Relationships

Example 1 Find the angle complementary to the given angle. 75°

$x + 75° = 90°$ Write as an equation.

$x = 90° - 75°$ Solve for x.

$x = 15°$

Find the complementary angle.

1. 20°

2. 35°

3. 67°

Find the supplementary angle.

4. 80°

5. 65°

6. 34°

Find the remaining angle or angles for △ABC.

7. $m\angle A = 50°$, $m\angle B = 40°$

8. $m\angle A = 60°$, $m\angle C = 20°$

9. $m\angle B = 70°$ and $\angle A \cong \angle C$

10. $\angle A \cong \angle B \cong \angle C$

11. $m\angle B = 30°$ and $m\angle A = \frac{1}{2}m\angle C$

12. $\triangle ABC$ is similar to $\triangle DEF$ and $m\angle D = 70°$ and $m\angle F = 50°$

13. $\triangle ABC$ is similar to $\triangle PQR$ and $m\angle R = 50°$ and $\angle P \cong \angle Q$

14. $m\angle A = 45°$ and $m\angle B = m\angle C$

15. $m\angle B = 105°$ and $m\angle A = 2 \cdot m\angle C$

16. $m\angle A = 5°$ and $m\angle B = 9 \cdot m\angle C$

18.1 Tangent Ratio

Essential Question: How do you find the tangent ratio for an acute angle?

Explore Investigating a Ratio in a Right Triangle

In a given a right triangle, $\triangle ABC$, with a right angle at vertex C, there are three sides. The side **adjacent** to $\angle A$ is the leg that forms one side of $\angle A$. The side **opposite** $\angle A$ is the leg that does not form a side of $\angle A$. The side that connects the adjacent and opposite legs is the hypotenuse.

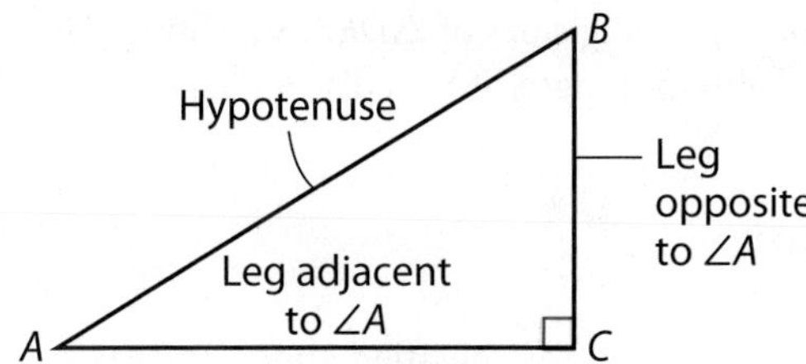

Ⓐ In $\triangle DEF$, label the legs opposite and adjacent to $\angle D$ are labeled. Measure the lengths of the legs in centimeters and record their values.

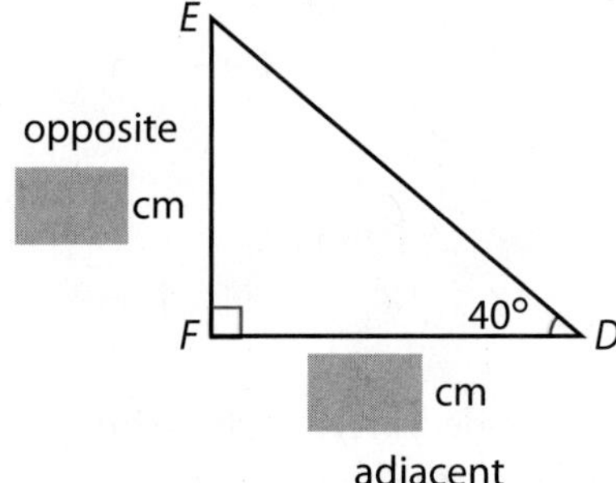

Ⓑ What is the ratio of the opposite leg length to the adjacent leg length, rounded to the nearest hundredth?

$\frac{EF}{DF} \approx$ ______

Ⓒ Using a protractor and ruler, draw right triangle $\triangle JKL$ with a right angle at vertex L and $\angle J = 40°$ so that $\triangle JKL \sim \triangle DEF$. Label the opposite and adjacent legs to $\angle J$ and include their measurements.

Ⓓ What is the ratio of the opposite leg length to the adjacent leg length, rounded to the nearest hundredth?

$\frac{KL}{JL} \approx$ ______

Reflect

1. **Discussion** Compare your work with that of other students. Do all the triangles have the same angles? Do they all have the same side lengths? Do they all have the same leg ratios? Summarize your findings.

2. If you repeated Steps A–D with a right triangle having a 30° angle, how would your results be similar? How would they be different?

Explain 1 Finding the Tangent of an Angle

The ratio you calculated in the Explore section is called the *tangent* of an angle. The **tangent** of acute angle A, written $\tan \angle A$, is defined as follows:

$$\tan A = \frac{\text{length of leg opposite } \angle A}{\text{length of leg adjacent to } \angle A}$$

You can use what you know about similarity to show why the tangent of an angle is constant. By the AA Similarity Theorem, given $\angle D \cong \angle J$ and also $\angle F \cong \angle L$, then $\triangle DEF \sim \triangle JKL$. This means the lengths of the sides of $\triangle JKL$ are each the same multiple, k, of the lengths of the corresponding sides of $\triangle DEF$. Substituting into the tangent equation shows that the ratio of the length of the opposite leg to the length of the adjacent leg is always the same value for a given acute angle.

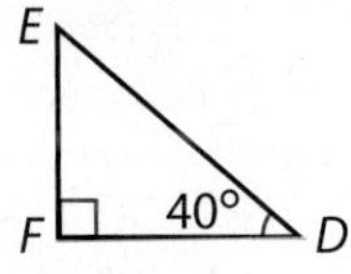

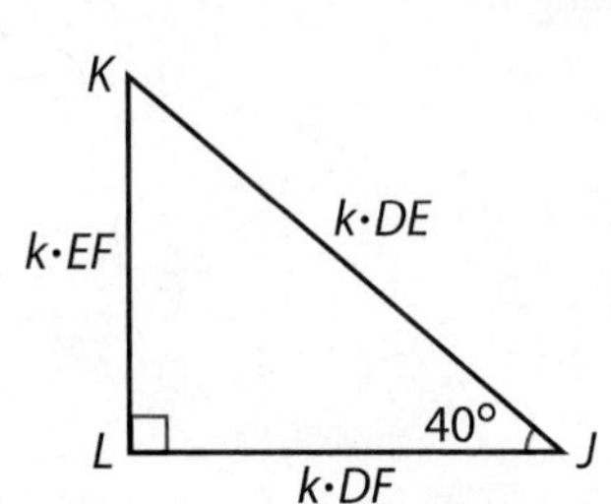

tangent defined for specified angle $\triangle DEF$ $\triangle JKL$

$$\tan 40° = \frac{\text{leg opposite } \angle 40°}{\text{leg adjacent to } \angle 40°} = \frac{EF}{DF} = \frac{KL}{JL} = \frac{K \cdot EF}{K \cdot DF} = \frac{EF}{DF}$$

Example 1 **Find the tangent of each specified angle. Write each ratio as a fraction and as a decimal rounded to the nearest hundredth.**

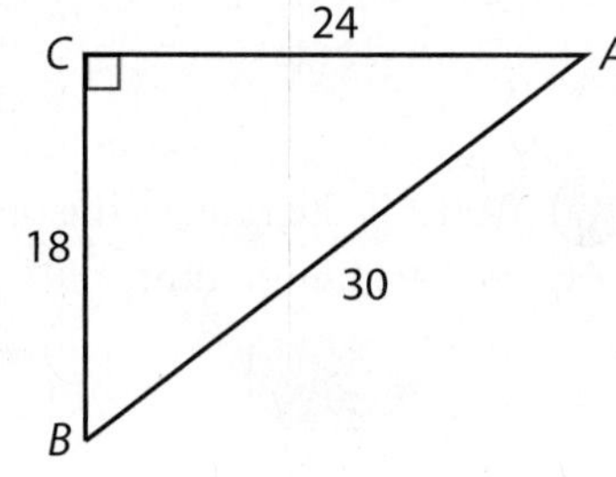

(A) $\angle A$

$$\tan A = \frac{\text{length of leg opposite } \angle A}{\text{length of leg adjacent to } \angle A} = \frac{18}{24} = \frac{3}{4} = 0.75$$

(B) $\angle B$

$$\tan B = \frac{\text{length of leg } \boxed{\text{opposite}} \ \angle B}{\text{length of leg } \boxed{\text{adjacent}} \text{ to } \angle B} = \frac{\boxed{24}}{\boxed{18}} = \frac{\boxed{4}}{3} \approx \boxed{1.33}$$

Reflect

3. What is the relationship between the ratios for tan A and tan B? Do you believe this relationship will be true for acute angles in other right triangles? Explain.

4. Why does it not make sense to ask for the value of tan L?

Your Turn

Find the tangent of each specified angle. Write each ratio as a fraction and as a decimal rounded to the nearest hundredth.

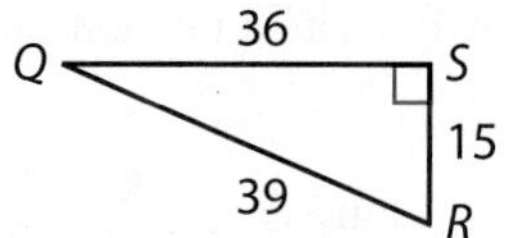

5. $\angle Q$

6. $\angle R$

Explain 2 Finding a Side Length using Tangent

When you know the length of a leg of a right triangle and the measure of one of the acute angles, you can use the tangent to find the length of the other leg. This is especially useful in real-world problems.

Example 2 **Apply the tangent ratio to find unknown lengths.**

In order to meet safety guidelines, a roof contractor determines that she must place the base of her ladder 6 feet away from the house, making an angle of 76° with the ground. To the nearest tenth of a foot, how far above the ground is the eave of the roof?

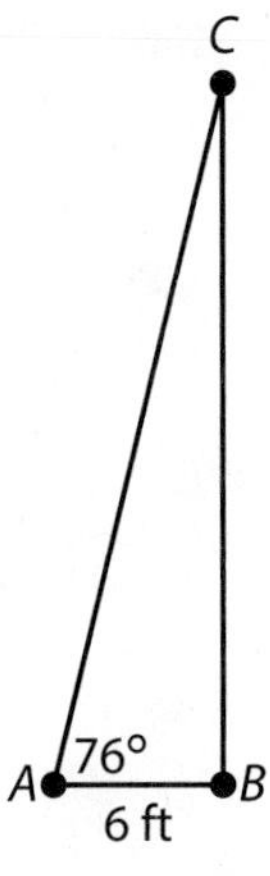

Step 1 Write a tangent ratio that involves the unknown length.

$$\tan A = \frac{\text{length of leg opposite } \angle A}{\text{length of leg adjacent to } \angle A} = \frac{BC}{BA}$$

Step 2 Identify the given values and substitute into the tangent equation.

Given: $BA = 6$ ft and $m\angle A = 76°$

Substitute: $\tan 76° = \frac{BC}{6}$

Step 3 Solve for the unknown leg length. Be sure the calculator is in degree mode and do not round until the final step of the solution.

Multiply each side by 6.	$6 \cdot \tan 76° = \frac{6}{1} \cdot \frac{BC}{6}$
Use a calculator to find $\tan 76°$.	$6 \cdot \tan 76° = BC$
Substitute this value in for $\tan 76°$.	$6(4.010780934) = BC$
Multiply. Round to the nearest tenth.	$24.1 \approx BC$

So, the eave of the roof is about 24.1 feet above the ground.

(B) For right triangle $\triangle STU$, what is the length of the leg adjacent to $\angle S$?

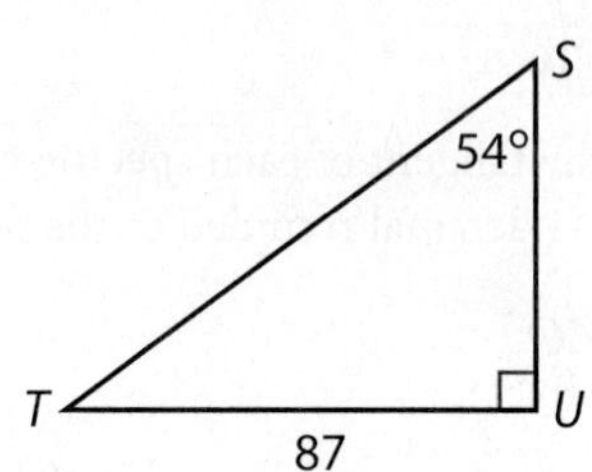

Step 1 Write a tangent ratio that involves the unknown length.

$$\tan S = \frac{\text{length of leg opposite } \angle S}{\text{length of leg adjacent to } \angle S} = \frac{\boxed{TU}}{\boxed{SU}}$$

Step 2 Identify the given values and substitute into the tangent equation.

Given: $TU = \boxed{87}$ and $m\angle S = \boxed{54}°$

Substitute: $\tan \boxed{54}° = \frac{\boxed{87}}{SU}$

Step 3 Solve for the unknown leg length.

Multiply both sides by SU, then divide both sides by 54°. $SU = \frac{\boxed{87}}{\tan \boxed{54}°}$

Use a calculator to find 54° and substitute. $SU \approx \frac{\boxed{87}}{\boxed{1.37638192}}$

Divide. Round to the nearest tenth. $SU \approx \boxed{63.2}$

Your Turn

7. A ladder needs to reach the second story window, which is 10 feet above the ground, and make an angle with the ground of 70°. How far out from the building does the base of the ladder need to be positioned?

Explain 3 Finding an Angle Measure using Tangent

In the previous section you used a given angle measure and leg measure with the tangent ratio to solve for an unknown leg. What if you are given the leg measures and want to find the measures of the acute angles? If you know the tan A, read as "tangent of $\angle A$," then you can use the **$\tan^{-1} A$**, read as "**inverse tangent of $\angle A$,**" to find $m\angle A$. So, given an acute angle $\angle A$, if $\tan A = x$, then $\tan^{-1} x = m\angle A$.

Example 3 **Find the measure of the indicated angle. Round to the nearest degree.**

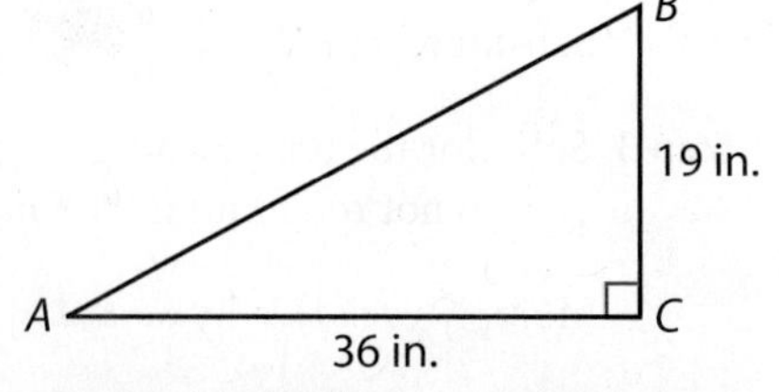

(A) What is $m\angle A$?

Step 1 Write the tangent ratio for $\angle A$ using the known values.	Step 2 Write the inverse tangent equation.	Step 3 Evaluate using a calculator and round as indicated.
$\tan A = \frac{19}{36}$	$\tan^{-1} \frac{19}{36} = m\angle A$	$m\angle A \approx 27.82409638 \approx 28°$

(B) What is m∠B?

Step 1 Write the tangent ratio for ∠B using the known values.	Step 2 Write the inverse tangent equation.	Step 3 Evaluate using a calculator and round as indicated.
$\tan B = \frac{36}{19}$	$\tan^{-1}\frac{36}{19} = m\angle B$	$m\angle B \approx$ 62.17590362° ≈ 62°

Your Turn

8. Find m∠J.

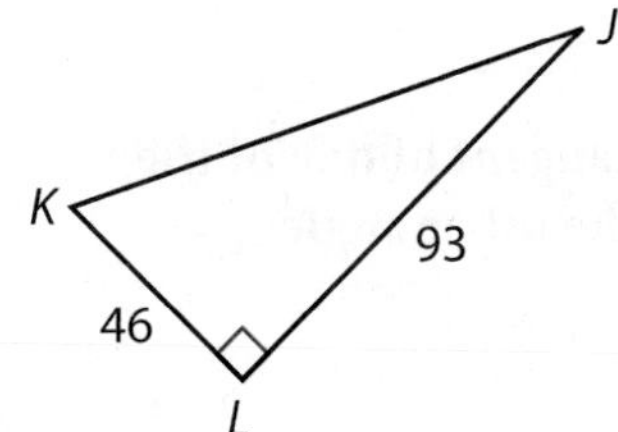

Elaborate

9. Explain how to identify the opposite and adjacent legs of a given acute angle.

10. **Discussion** How does tan *A* change as m∠*A* increases? Explain the basis for the identified relationship.

11. **Essential Question Check-In** Compare and contrast the use of the tangent and inverse tangent ratios for solving problems.

Evaluate: Homework and Practice

- Online Homework
- Hints and Help
- Extra Practice

1. In each triangle, measure the length of the adjacent side and the opposite side of the 22° angle. Then calculate and compare the ratios.

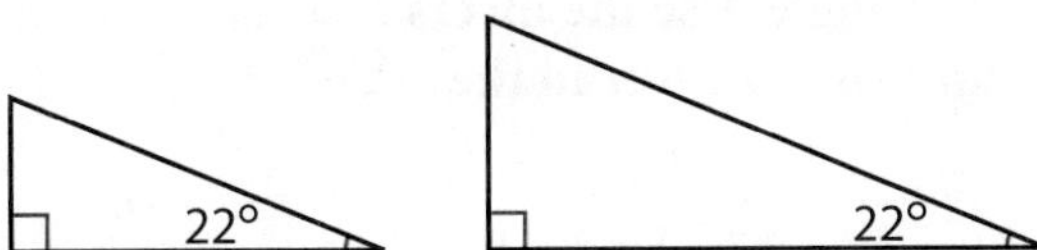

In each right triangle, find the tangent of each angle that is not the right angle.

2.

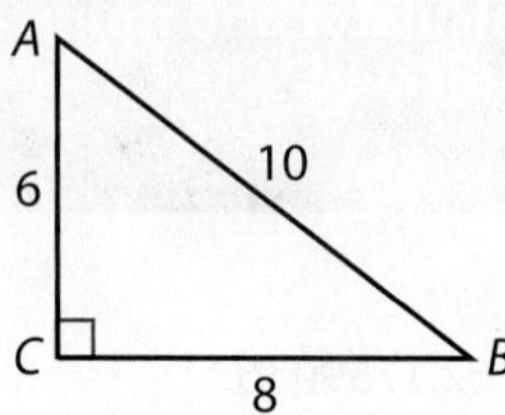

3.

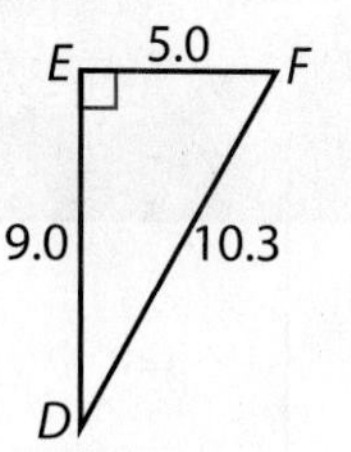

4.

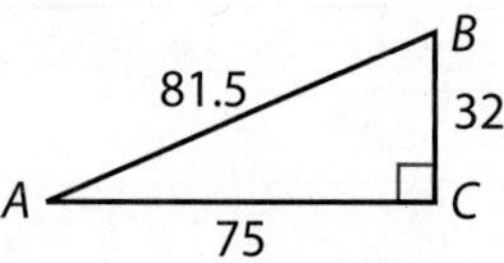

5.

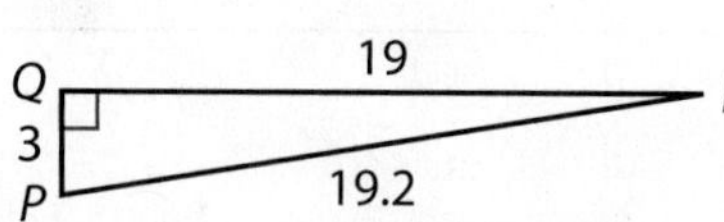

Let $\triangle ABC$ be a right triangle, with $m\angle C = 90°$. Given the tangent of one of the complementary angles of the triangle, find the tangent of the other angle.

6. $\tan \angle A = 1.25$

7. $\tan \angle B = 0.50$

8. $\tan \angle B = 1.0$

Use the tangent to find the unknown side length.

9. Find *QR*.

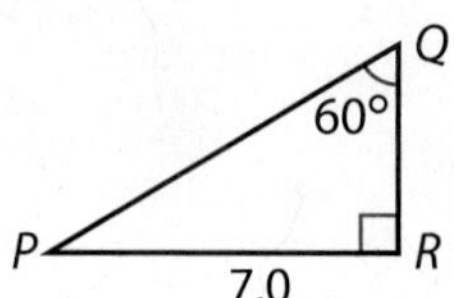

10. Find *AC*.

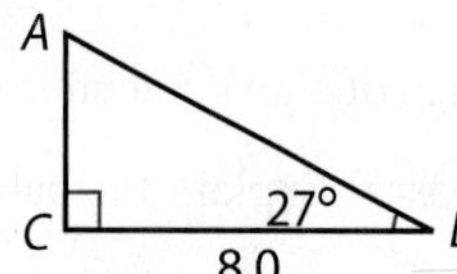

11. Find *PQ*.

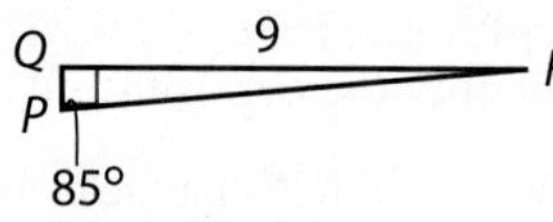

12. Find *DE*.

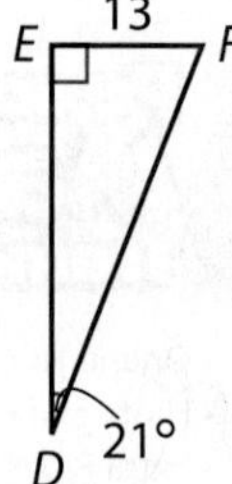

13. Find *AB*.

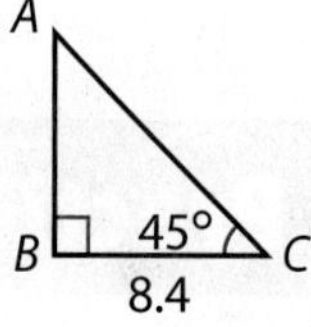

14. Find *PR*.

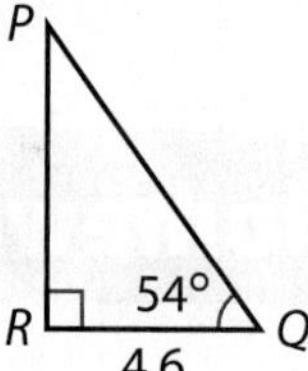

Find the measure of the angle specified for each triangle. Use the inverse tangent ($\tan^{-1}$) function of your calculator. Round your answer to the nearest degree.

15. Find $\angle A$.

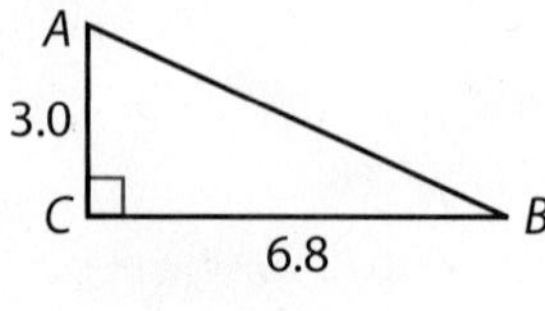

16. Find $\angle R$.

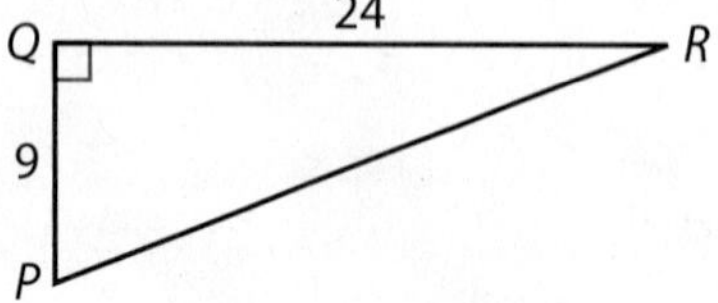

17. Find $\angle B$.

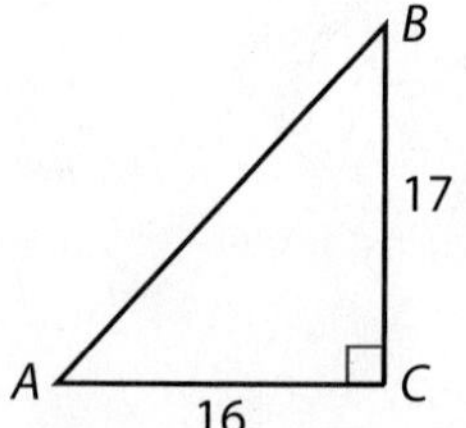

Write an equation using either tan or $\tan^{-1}$ to express the measure of the angle or side. Then solve the equation.

18. Find BC.

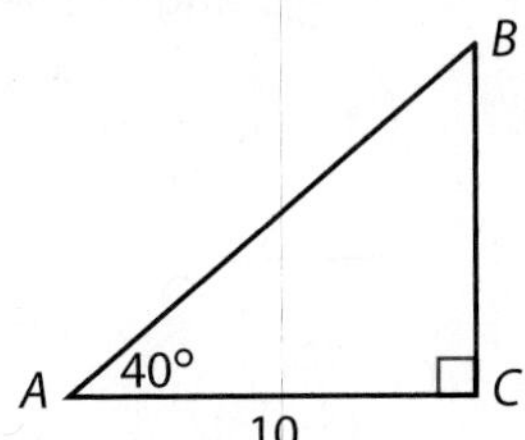

19. Find PQ.

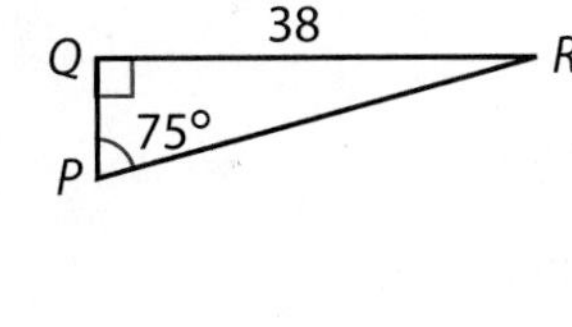

20. Find $\angle A$ and $\angle C$.

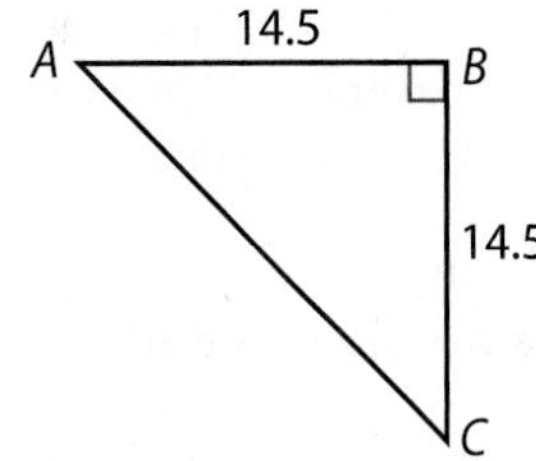

21. Multi-Step Find the measure of angle D. Show your work.

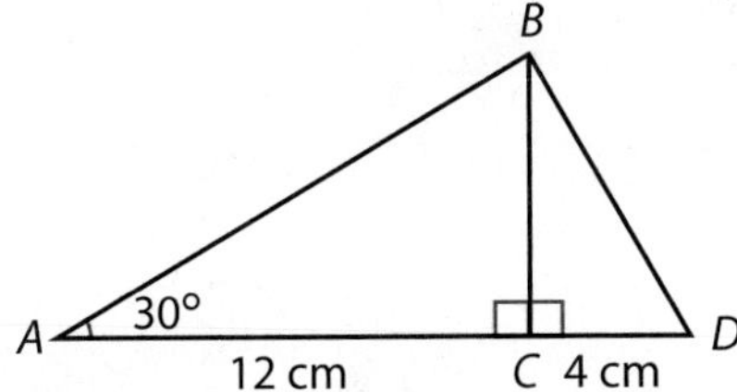

22. Engineering A client wants to build a ramp that carries people to a height of 1.4 meters, as shown in the diagram. What additional information is necessary to identify the measure of angle a, the angle the ramp forms with the horizontal? After the additional measurement is made, describe how to find the measure of the angle.

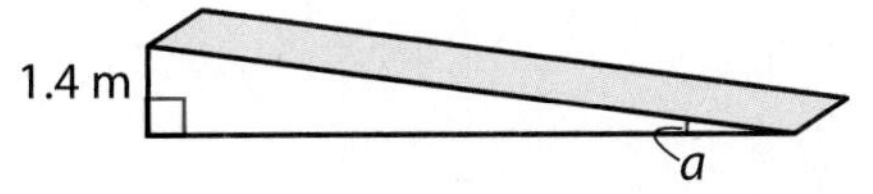

23. Explain the Error A student uses the triangle shown to calculate a. Find and explain the student's error.

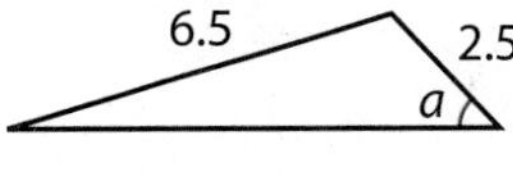

$$a = \tan^{-1}\left(\frac{6.5}{2.5}\right) = \tan^{-1}(2.6)$$

$$a = 69.0°$$

24. When $m\angle A + m\angle B = 90°$, what relationship is formed by $\tan \angle A$ and $\tan \angle B$? Determine all that apply.

A. $\tan\angle A = \dfrac{1}{\tan B}$

B. $\tan\angle A + \tan\angle B = 1$

C. $(\tan\angle A)(\tan\angle B) = 1$

D. $(\tan\angle A)(\tan\angle B) = -1$

H.O.T. Focus on Higher Order Thinking

25. Analyze Relationships To travel from Pottstown to Cogsville, a man drives his car 83 miles due east on one road, and then 15 miles due north on another road. Describe the path that a bird could fly in a straight line from Pottstown to Cogsville. What angle does the line make with the two roads that the man used?

26. Critical Thinking A right triangle has only one 90° angle. Both of its other angles have measures greater than 0° and less than 90°. Why is it useful to define the tangent of 90° to equal 1, and the tangent of 0° to equal 0?

Lesson Performance Task

When they form conical piles, granular materials such as salt, gravel, and sand settle at different "angles of repose," depending on the shapes of the grains. One particular 13-foot tall cone of dry sand has a base diameter of 38.6 feet.

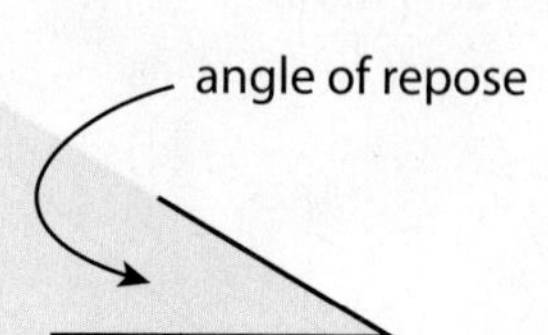

1. To the nearest tenth of a degree, what is the angle of repose of this type of dry sand?

2. A different conical pile of the same type of sand is 10 feet tall. What is the diameter of the cone's base?

3. Henley Landscaping Supply sells a type of sand with a 30° angle of repose for $32 per cubic yard. Find the cost of an 11-foot-tall cone of this type of sand. Show your work.

18.2 Sine and Cosine Ratios

Resource Locker

Essential Question: How can you use the sine and cosine ratios, and their inverses, in calculations involving right triangles?

Explore Investigating Ratios in a Right Triangle

You can use geometry software or an online tool to explore ratios of side lengths in right triangles.

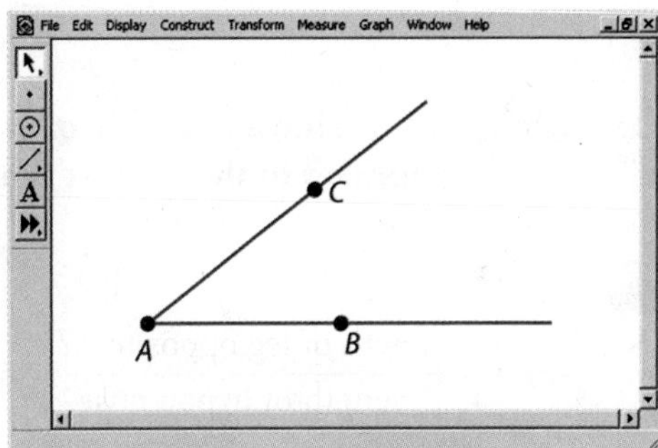

(A) Construct three points A, B, and C. Construct rays $\overrightarrow{AB}$ and $\overrightarrow{AC}$. Move C so that $\angle A$ is acute.

(B) Construct point D on $\overline{AC}$. Construct a line through D perpendicular to $\overline{AB}$. Construct point E as the intersection of the perpendicular line and $\overline{AB}$.

(C) Measure $\angle A$. Measure the side lengths DE, AE, and AD of $\triangle ADE$.

(D) Calculate the ratios $\frac{DE}{AD}$ and $\frac{AE}{AD}$.

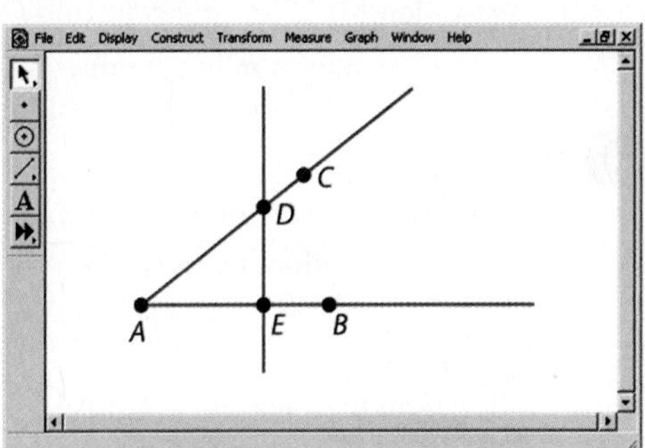

Reflect

1. Drag D along $\overrightarrow{AC}$. What happens to $m\angle A$ as D moves along $\overrightarrow{AC}$? What postulate or theorem guarantees that the different triangles formed are similar to each other?

2. As you move D along $\overrightarrow{AC}$, what happens to the values of the ratios $\frac{DE}{AD}$ and $\frac{AE}{AD}$? Use the properties of similar triangles to explain this result.

3. Move C. What happens to $m\angle A$? With a new value of $m\angle A$, note the values of the two ratios. What happens to the ratios if you drag D along $\overrightarrow{AC}$?

Explain 1 Finding the Sine and Cosine of an Angle

Trigonometric Ratios

A **trigonometric ratio** is a ratio of two sides of a right triangle. You have already seen one trigonometric ratio, the tangent. There are two additional trigonometric ratios, the sine and the cosine, that involve the hypotenuse of a right triangle.

The **sine** of $\angle A$, written $\sin A$, is defined as follows:

$$\sin A = \frac{\text{length of leg opposite } \angle A}{\text{length of hypotenuse}} = \frac{BC}{AB}$$

The **cosine** of $\angle A$, written $\cos A$, is defined as follows:

$$\cos A = \frac{\text{length of leg adjacent to } \angle A}{\text{length of hypotenuse}} = \frac{AC}{AB}$$

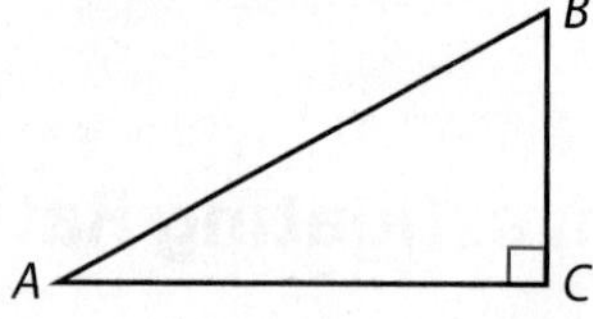

You can use these definitions to calculate trigonometric ratios.

Example 1 **Write sine and cosine of each angle as a fraction and as a decimal rounded to the nearest thousandth.**

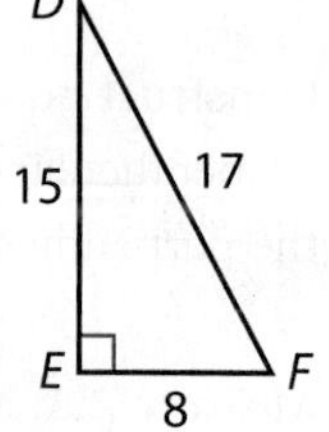

(A) $\angle D$

$$\sin D = \frac{\text{length of leg opposite } \angle D}{\text{length of hypotenuse}} = \frac{EF}{DF} = \frac{8}{17} \approx 0.471$$

$$\cos D = \frac{\text{length of leg adjacent to } \angle D}{\text{length of hypotenuse}} = \frac{DE}{DF} = \frac{15}{17} \approx 0.882$$

(B) $\angle F$

$$\sin F = \frac{\text{length of leg opposite to } \angle F}{\text{length of hypotenuse}} = \frac{DE}{DF} = \frac{15}{17} \approx 0.882$$

$$\cos F = \frac{\text{length of leg adjacent to } \angle F}{\text{length of hypotenuse}} = \frac{8}{17} \approx 0.471$$

Reflect

4. What do you notice about the sines and cosines you found? Do you think this relationship will be true for any pair of acute angles in a right triangle? Explain.

5. In a right triangle $\triangle PQR$ with hypotenuse 5, $m\angle Q = 90°$, and $PQ > QR$, what are the values of $\sin P$ and $\cos P$?

Explain 2 Using Complementary Angles

The acute angles of a right triangle are complementary. Their trigonometric ratios are related to each other as shown in the following relationship.

Trigonometric Ratios of Complementary Angles

If $\angle A$ and $\angle B$ are the acute angles in a right triangle, then $\sin A = \cos B$ and $\cos A = \sin B$.

Therefore, if θ ("theta") is the measure of an acute angle, then $\sin \theta = \cos(90° - \theta)$ and $\cos \theta = \sin(90° - \theta)$.

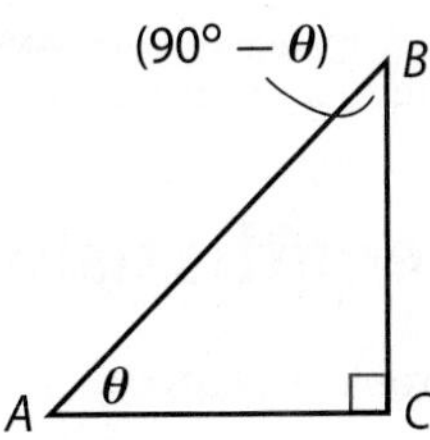

You can use these relationships to write equivalent expressions.

Example 2 **Write each trigonometric expression.**

(A) Given that $\sin 38° \approx 0.616$, write the cosine of a complementary angle in terms of the sine of 38°. Then find the cosine of the complementary angle.

Use an expression relating trigonometric ratios of complementary angles.

$$\sin \theta = \cos(90° - \theta)$$

Substitute 38 into both sides. $\sin 38° = \cos(90° - 38°)$

Simplify. $\sin 38° = \cos 52°$

Substitute for sin 38°. $0.616 \approx \cos 52°$

So, the cosine of the complementary angle is about 0.616.

(B) Given that $\cos 60° = 0.5$, write the sine of a complementary angle in terms of the cosine of 60°. Then find the sine of the complementary angle.

Use an expression relating trigonometric ratios of complementary angles.

$$\cos \theta = \sin(90° - \theta)$$

Substitute 60 into both sides. $\cos 60° = \sin(90° - 60°)$

Simplify the right side. $\cos 60° = \sin 30°$

Substitute for the cosine of 60°. $0.5 = \sin 30°$

So, the sine of the complementary angle is 0.5.

Reflect

6. What can you conclude about the sine and cosine of 45°? Explain.
7. **Discussion** Is it possible for the sine or cosine of an acute angle to equal 1? Explain.

Your Turn

Write each trigonometric expression.

8. Given that $\cos 73° \approx 0.292$, write the sine of a complementary angle.

9. Given that $\sin 45° \approx 0.707$, write the cosine of a complementary angle.

Explain 3 Finding Side Lengths using Sine and Cosine

You can use sine and cosine to solve real-world problems.

Example 3 **A 12-ft ramp is installed alongside some steps to provide wheelchair access to a library. The ramp makes an angle of 11° with the ground. Find each dimension, to the nearest tenth of a foot.**

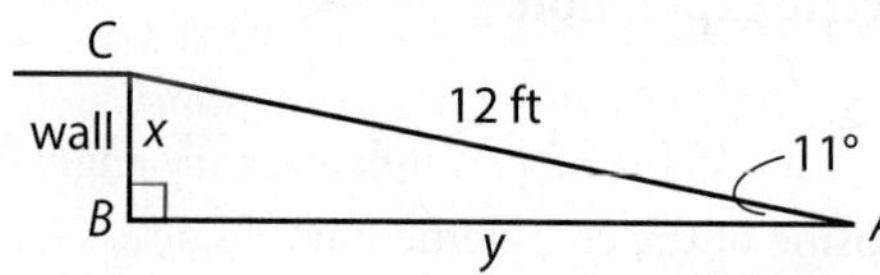

(A) Find the height x of the wall.

Use the definition of sine. $\sin A = \frac{\text{length of leg opposite } \angle A}{\text{length of hypotenuse}} = \frac{AB}{AC}$

Substitute 11° for A, x for BC, and 12 for AC. $\sin 11° = \frac{x}{12}$

Multiply both sides by 12. $12 \sin 11° = x$

Use a calculator to evaluate the expression. $x \approx 2.3$

So, the height of the wall is about 2.3 feet.

(B) Find the distance y that the ramp extends in front of the wall.

Use the definition of cosine. $\cos A = \frac{\text{length of leg adjacent to } \angle A}{\text{length of hypotenuse}} = \frac{AB}{AC}$

Substitute 11 ° for A, y for AB, and 12 for AC. $\cos 11° = \frac{y}{12}$

Multiply both sides by 12. $12 \cos 11° = y$

Use a calculator to evaluate the expression. $y \approx 11.8$

So, the ramp extends in front of the wall about 11.8 feet.

Reflect

10. Could you find the height of the wall using the cosine? Explain.

Your Turn

11. Suppose a new regulation states that the maximum angle of a ramp for wheelchairs is 8°. At least how long must the new ramp be? Round to the nearest tenth of a foot.

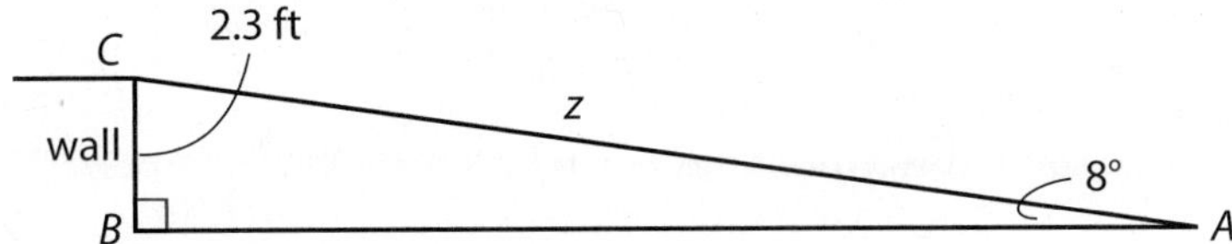

Explain 4 Finding Angle Measures using Sine and Cosine

In the triangle, $\sin A = \frac{5}{10} = \frac{1}{2}$. However, you already know that $\sin 30° = \frac{1}{2}$. So you can conclude that $m\angle A = 30°$, and write $\sin^{-1}\left(\frac{1}{2}\right) = 30°$.

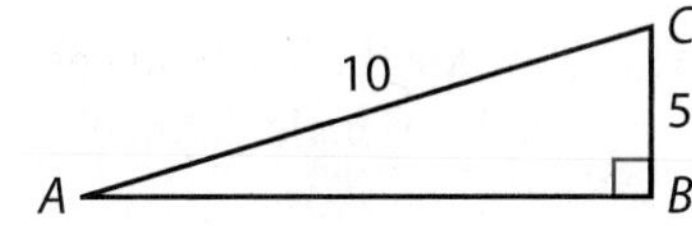

Extending this idea, the **inverse trigonometric ratios** for sine and cosine are defined as follows:

Given an acute angle, $\angle A$,

- if $\sin A = x$, then $\sin^{-1} x = m\angle A$, read as "inverse sine of x"
- if $\cos A = x$, then $\cos^{-1} x = m\angle A$, read as "inverse cosine of x"

You can use a calculator to evaluate inverse trigonometric expressions.

Example 4 **Find the acute angle measures in $\triangle PQR$, to the nearest degree.**

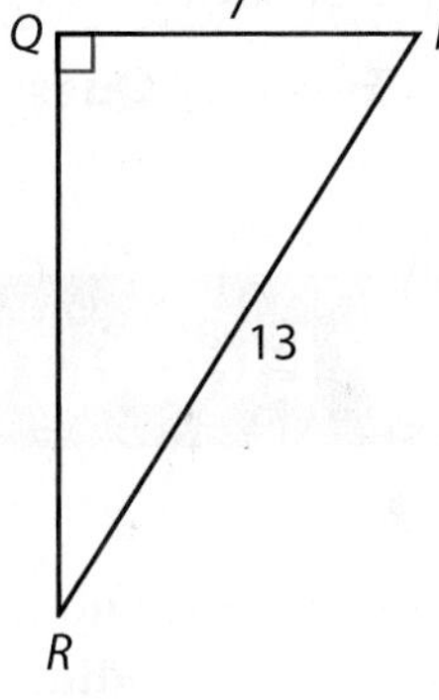

(A) Write a trigonometric ratio for $\angle R$.

Since the lengths of the hypotenuse and the opposite leg are given, use the sine ratio. $\sin R = \frac{PQ}{PR}$

Substitute 7 for PQ and 13 for PR. $\sin R = \frac{7}{13}$

(B) Write and evaluate an inverse trigonometric ratio to find $m\angle R$ and $m\angle P$.

Start with the trigonometric ratio for $\angle R$. $\sin R = \frac{7}{13}$

Use the definition of the inverse sine ratio. $m\angle R = \sin^{-1} \frac{7}{13}$

Use a calculator to evaluate the inverse sine ratio. $m\angle R = 33°$

Write a cosine ratio for $\angle P$. $\cos P = \frac{PQ}{PR}$

Substitute 7 for PQ and 13 for PR. $\cos P = \frac{7}{13}$

Use the definition of the inverse cosine ratio. $m\angle P = \cos^{-1} \frac{7}{13}$

Use a calculator to evaluate the inverse cosine ratio. $m\angle P = 57°$

Reflect

12. How else could you have determined $m\angle P$?

Your Turn

Find the acute angle measures in $\triangle XYZ$, to the nearest degree.

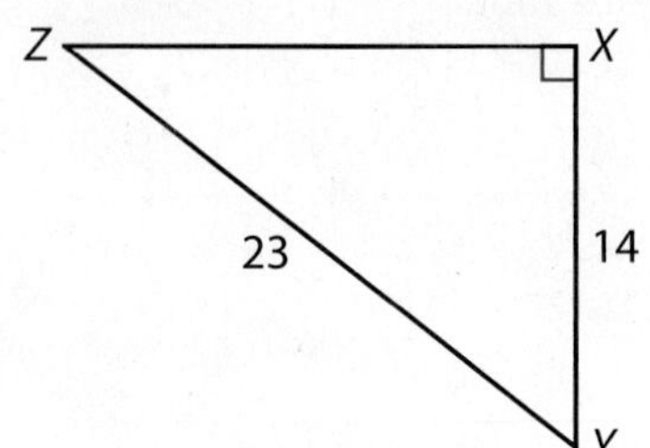

13. $m\angle Y$

14. $m\angle Z$

Elaborate

15. How are the sine and cosine ratios for an acute angle of a right triangle defined?

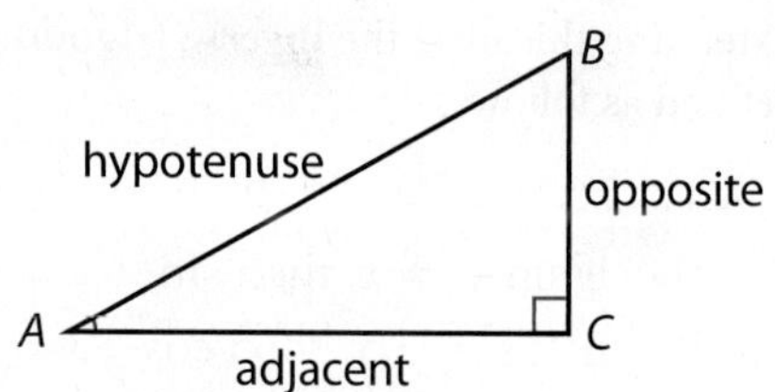

16. How are the inverse sine and cosine ratios for an acute angle of a right triangle defined?

17. **Essential Question Check-In** How do you find an unknown angle measure in a right triangle?

Evaluate: Homework and Practice

- Online Homework
- Hints and Help
- Extra Practice

Write each trigonometric expression. Round trigonometric ratios to the nearest thousandth.

1. Given that $\sin 60° \approx 0.866$, write the cosine of a complementary angle.

2. Given that $\cos 26° \approx 0.899$, write the sine of a complementary angle.

Write each trigonometric ratio as a fraction and as a decimal, rounded (if necessary) to the nearest thousandth.

3. $\sin A$

4. $\cos A$

5. $\cos B$

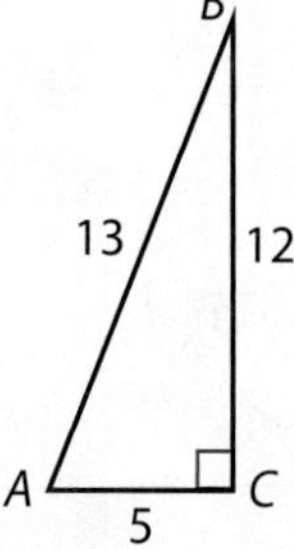

6. sin D

7. cos F

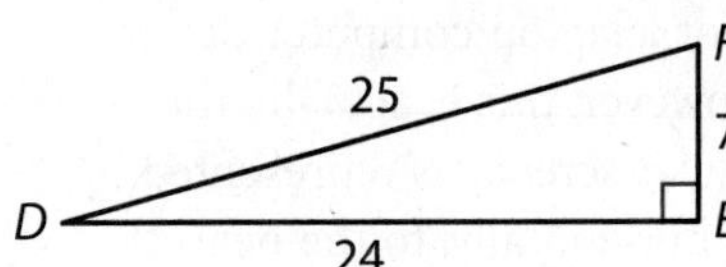

8. sin F

Find the unknown length x in each right triangle, to the nearest tenth.

9.

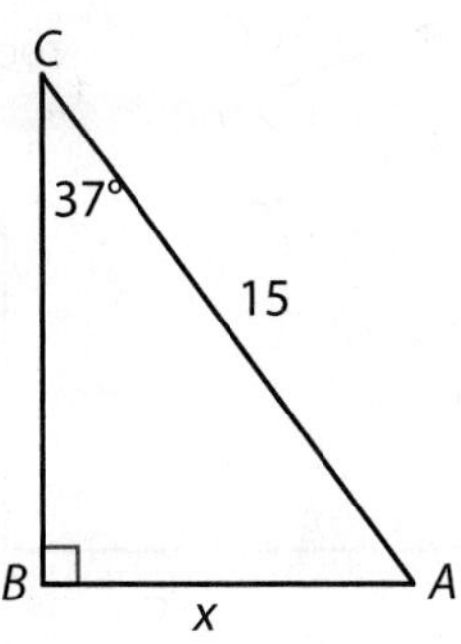

10.

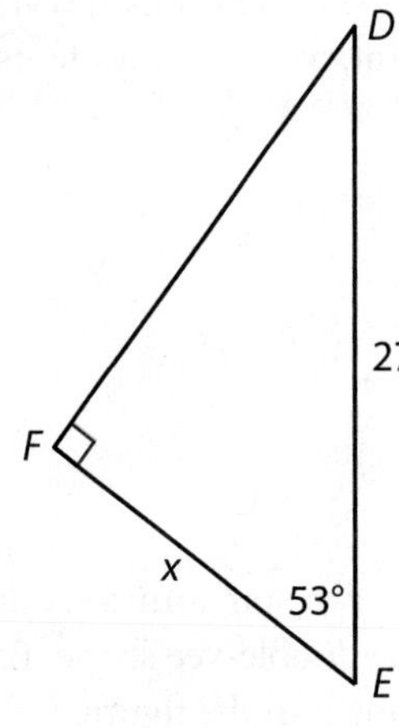

11.

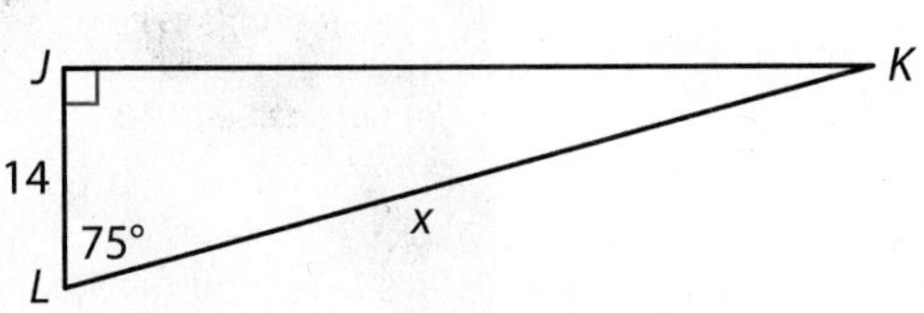

12.

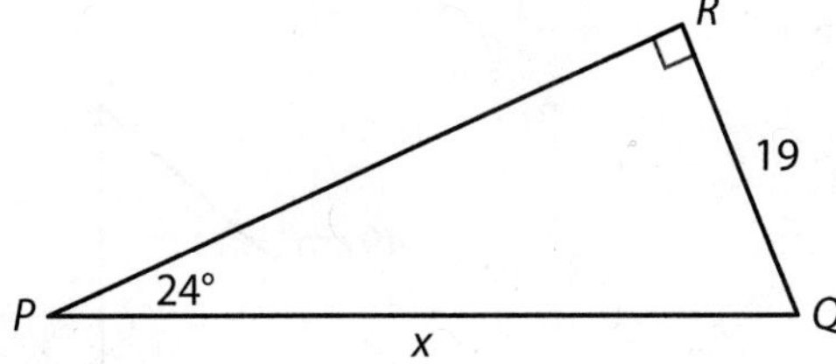

Find each acute angle measure, to the nearest degree.

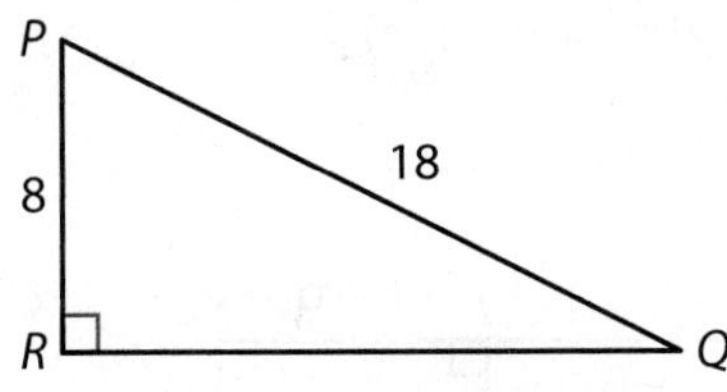

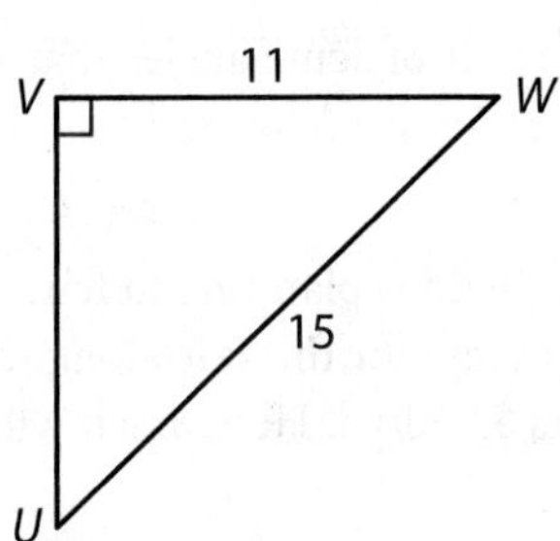

13. m$\angle P$

14. m$\angle Q$

15. m$\angle U$

16. m$\angle W$

17. Use the property that corresponding sides of similar triangles are proportional to explain why the trigonometric ratio sin A is the same when calculated in $\triangle ADE$ as in $\triangle ABC$.

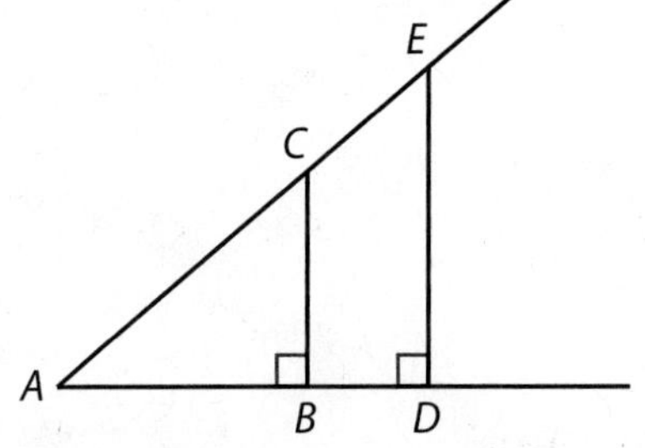

18. Technology The specifications for a laptop computer describe its screen as measuring 15.6 in. However, this is actually the length of a diagonal of the rectangular screen, as represented in the figure. How wide is the screen horizontally, to the nearest tenth of an inch?

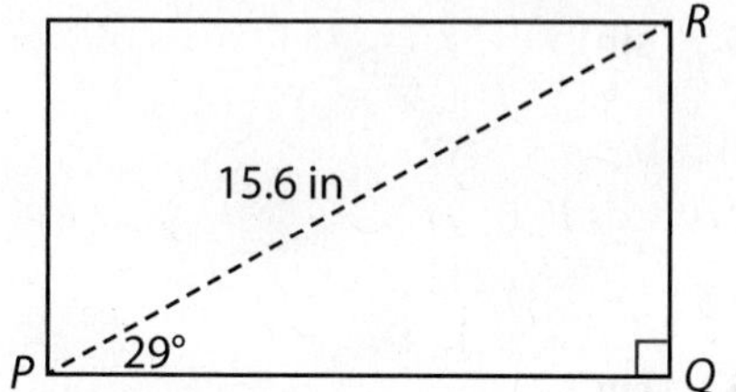

19. Building Sharla's bedroom is directly under the roof of her house. Given the dimensions shown, how high is the ceiling at its highest point, to the nearest tenth of a foot?

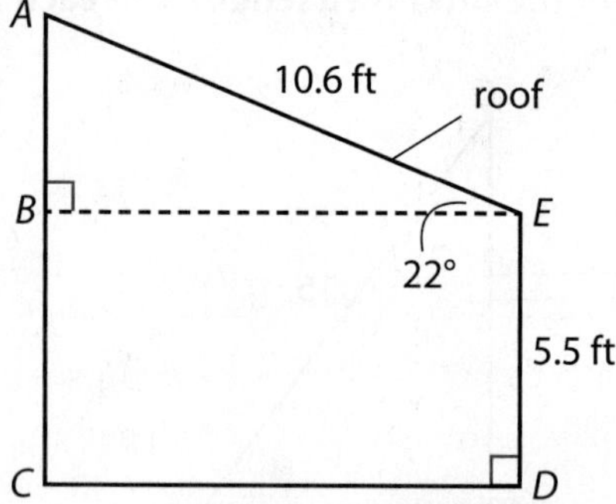

20. Zoology You can sometimes see an eagle gliding with its wings flexed in a characteristic double-vee shape. Each wing can be modeled as two right triangles as shown in the figure. Find the measure of the angle in the middle of the wing, $\angle DHG$ to the nearest degree.

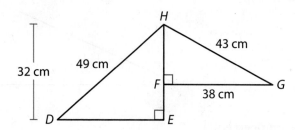

21. Algebra Find a pair of acute angles that satisfy the equation $\sin(3x + 9) = \cos(x + 5)$. Check that your answers make sense.

22. Multi-Step Reginald is planning to fence his back yard. Every side of the yard except for the side along the house is to be fenced, and fencing costs \$3.50/yd. How much will the fencing cost?

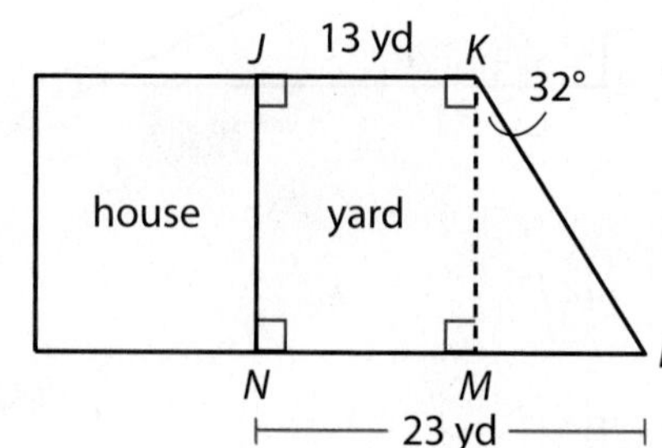

23. Architecture The sides of One World Trade Center in New York City form eight isosceles triangles, four of which are 200 ft long at their base BC. The length AC of each sloping side is approximately 1185 ft.

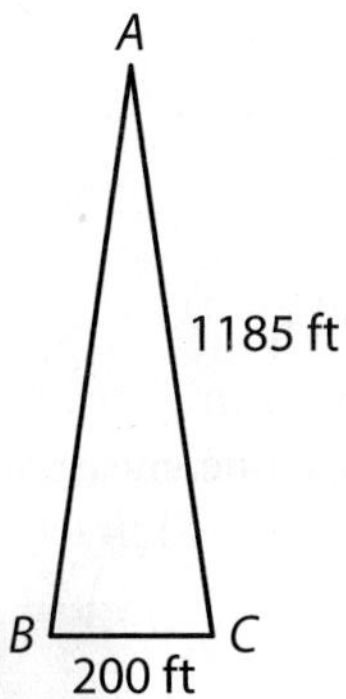

Find the measure of the apex angle BAC of each isosceles triangle, to the nearest tenth of a degree. (*Hint:* Use the midpoint D of $\overline{BC}$ to create two right triangles.)

H.O.T. Focus on Higher Order Thinking

24. Explain the Error Melissa has calculated the length of $\overline{XZ}$ in $\triangle XYZ$. Explain why Melissa's answer must be incorrect, and identify and correct her error.

Melissa's solution:

$$\cos X = \frac{XZ}{XY}$$

$$XZ = \frac{XY}{\cos X}$$

$$XZ = 27 \cos 42° \approx 20.1$$

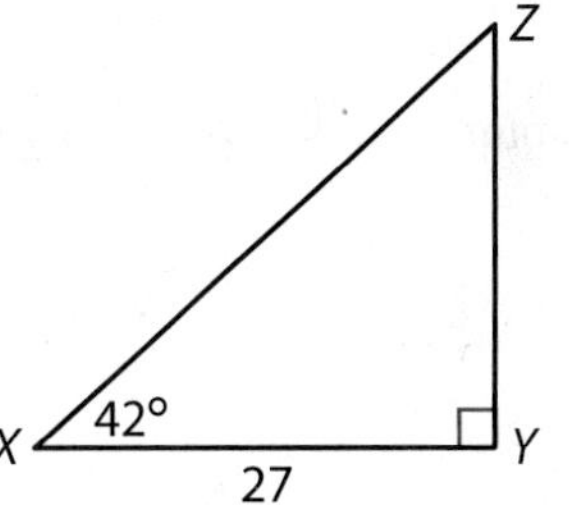

25. Communicate Mathematical Ideas Explain why the sine and cosine of an acute angle are always between 0 and 1.

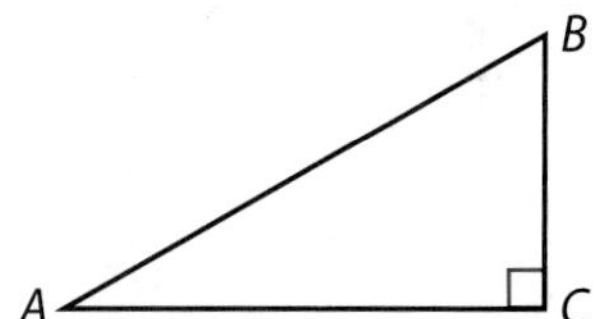

26. Look for a Pattern In $\triangle ABC$, the hypotenuse $\overline{AB}$ has a length of 1. Use the Pythagorean Theorem to explore the relationship between the squares of the sine and cosine of $\angle A$, written $\sin^2 A$ and $\cos^2 A$. Could you derive this relationship using a right triangle without any lengths specified? Explain.

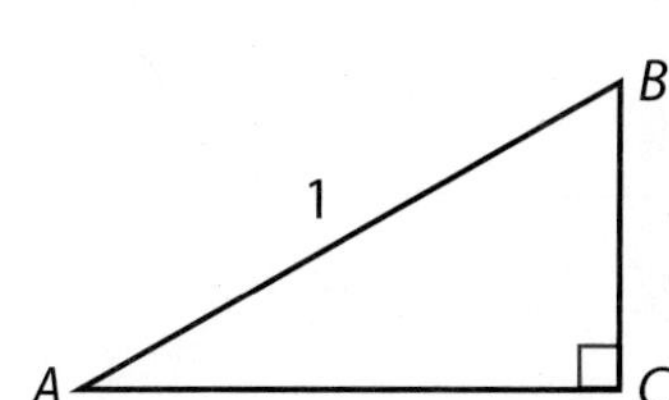

27. Justify Reasoning Use the Triangle Proportionality Theorem to explain why the trigonometric ratio $\cos A$ is the same when calculated in $\triangle ADE$ as in $\triangle ABC$.

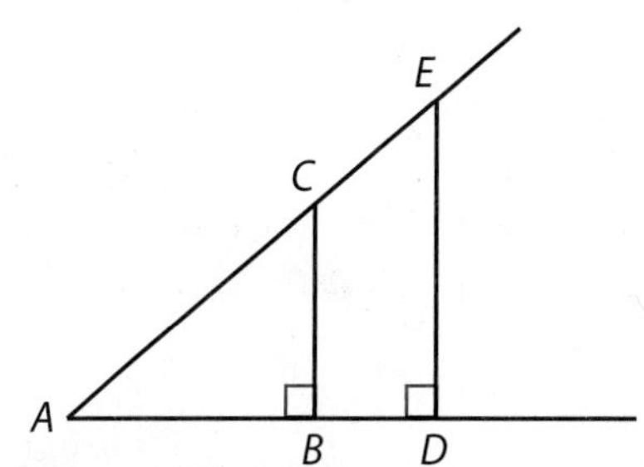

Lesson Performance Task

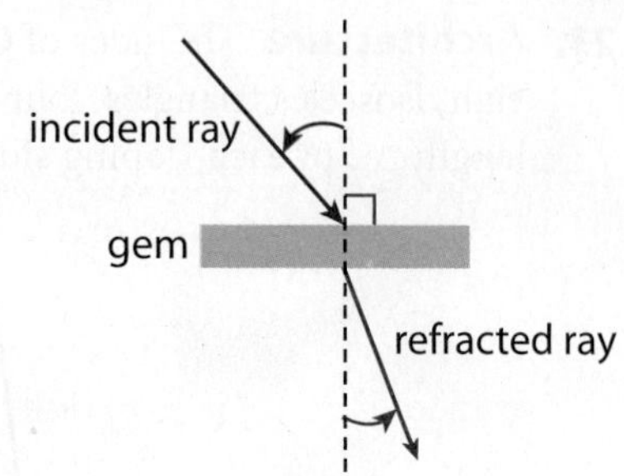

As light passes from a vacuum into another medium, it is *refracted*—that is, its direction changes. The ratio of the sine of the angle of the incoming *incident* ray, *I*, to the sine of the angle of the outgoing *refracted* ray, *r*, is called the *index of refraction*:

$n = \frac{\sin I}{\sin r}$, where n is the index of refraction.

This relationship is important in many fields, including gemology, the study of precious stones. A gemologist can place an unidentified gem into an instrument called a refractometer, direct an incident ray of light at a particular angle into the stone, measure the angle of the refracted ray, and calculate the index of refraction. Because the indices of refraction of thousands of gems are known, the gemologist can then identify the gem.

Gem	Index of Refraction
Hematite	2.94
Diamond	2.42
Zircon	1.95
Azurite	1.85
Sapphire	1.77
Tourmaline	1.62
Serpentine	1.56
Coral	1.49
Opal	1.39

1. Identify the gem, given these angles obtained from a refractometer:

a. $I = 71°, r = 29°$

b. $I = 51°, r = 34°$

c. $I = 45°, r = 17°$

2. A thin slice of sapphire is placed in a refractometer. The angle of the incident ray is 56°. Find the angle of the refracted ray to the nearest degree.

3. An incident ray of light struck a slice of serpentine. The resulting angle of refraction measured 21°. Find the angle of incidence to the nearest degree.

4. Describe the error(s) in a student's solution and explain why they were error(s):

$$n = \frac{\sin I}{\sin r}$$
$$= \frac{\sin 51°}{\sin 34°}$$
$$= \frac{51°}{34°}$$
$$= 1.5 \rightarrow \text{coral}$$

18.3 Special Right Triangles

Essential Question: What do you know about the side lengths and the trigonometric ratios in special right triangles?

Resource Locker

Explore 1 Investigating an Isosceles Right Triangle

Discover relationships that always apply in an isosceles right triangle.

(A) The figure shows an isosceles right triangle. Identify the base angles, and use the fact that they are complementary to write an equation relating their measures.

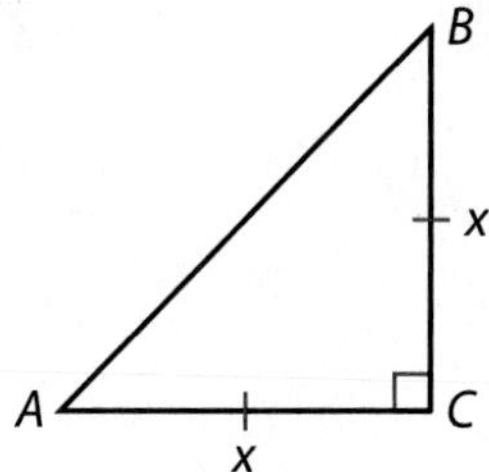

(B) Use the Isosceles Triangle Theorem to write a different equation relating the base angle measures.

(C) What must the measures of the base angles be? Why?

(D) Use the Pythagorean Theorem to find the length of the hypotenuse in terms of the length of each leg, x.

Reflect

1. Is it true that if you know one side length of an isosceles right triangle, then you know all the side lengths? Explain.

2. **What if?** Suppose you draw the perpendicular from C to $\overline{AB}$. Explain how to find the length of $\overline{CD}$.

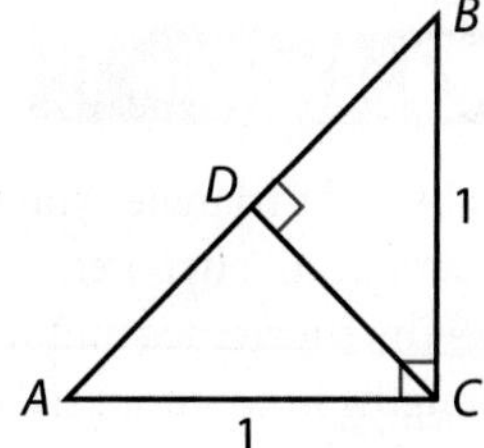

Explore 2 Investigating Another Special Right Triangle

Discover relationships that always apply in a right triangle formed as half of an equilateral triangle.

(A) $\triangle ABD$ is an equilateral triangle and $\overline{BC}$ is a perpendicular from B to $\overline{AD}$. Determine all three angle measures in $\triangle ABC$.

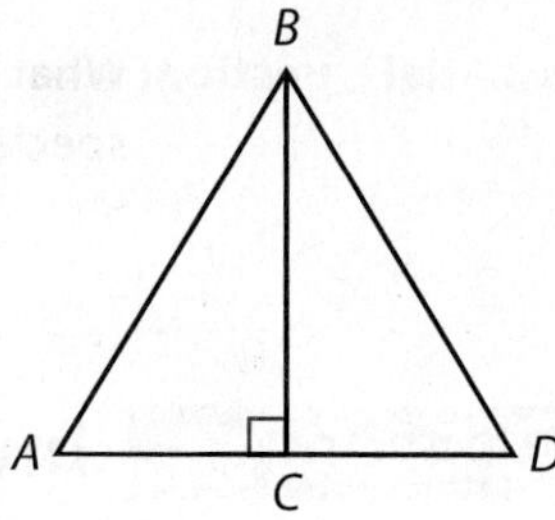

(B) Explain why $\triangle ABC \cong \triangle DBC$.

(C) Let the length of $\overline{AC}$ be x. What is the length of $\overline{AB}$, and why?

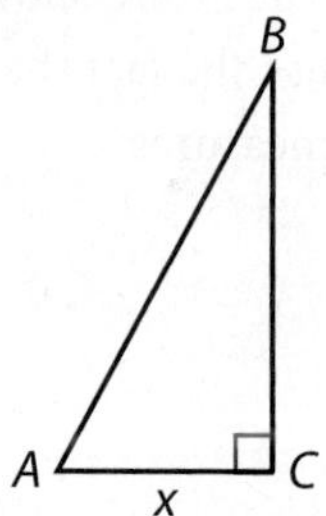

(D) Using the Pythagorean Theorem, find the length of $\overline{BC}$.

Reflect

3. What is the numerical ratio of the side lengths in a right triangle with acute angles that measure 30° and 60°? Explain.

4. **Explain the Error** A student has drawn a right triangle with a 60° angle and a hypotenuse of 6. He has labeled the other side lengths as shown. Explain how you can tell at a glance that he has made an error and how to correct it.

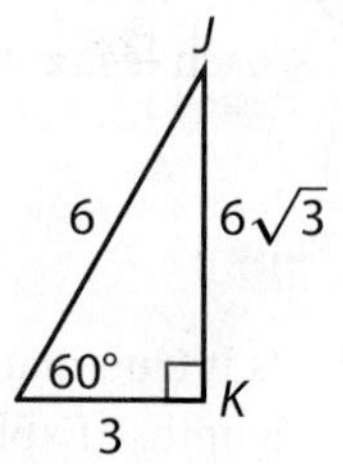

Explain 1 Applying Relationships in Special Right Triangles

The right triangles you explored are sometimes called 45°—45°—90° and 30°—60°—90° triangles. In a 45°—45°—90° triangle, the hypotenuse is $\sqrt{2}$ times as long as each leg. In a 30°—60°—90° triangle, the hypotenuse is twice as long as the shorter leg and the longer leg is $\sqrt{3}$ times as long as the shorter leg. You can use these relationships to find side lengths in these special types of right triangles.

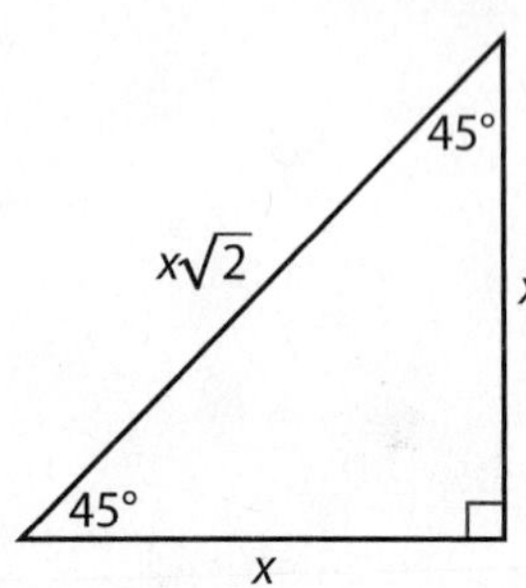

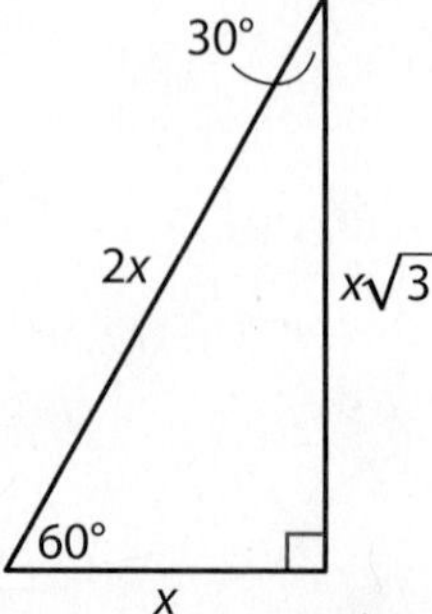

Example 1 **Find the unknown side lengths in each right triangle.**

(A) Find the unknown side lengths in $\triangle ABC$.

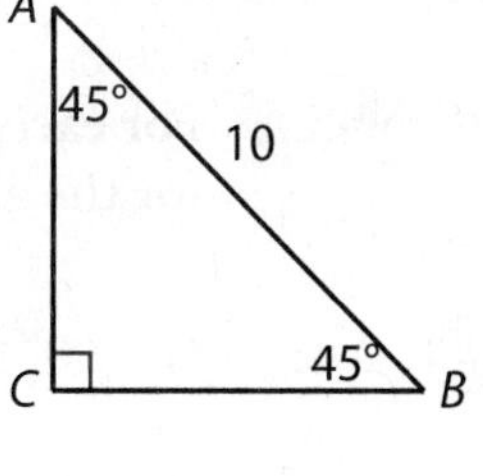

The hypotenuse is $\sqrt{2}$ times as long as each leg.	$AB = AC\sqrt{2} = BC\sqrt{2}$
Substitute 10 for AB.	$10 = AC\sqrt{2} = BC\sqrt{2}$
Multiply by $\sqrt{2}$.	$10\sqrt{2} = 2AC = 2BC$
Divide by 2.	$5\sqrt{2} = AC = BC$

(B) In right $\triangle DEF$, $m\angle D = 30°$ and $m\angle E = 60°$. The shorter leg measures $5\sqrt{3}$. Find the remaining side lengths.

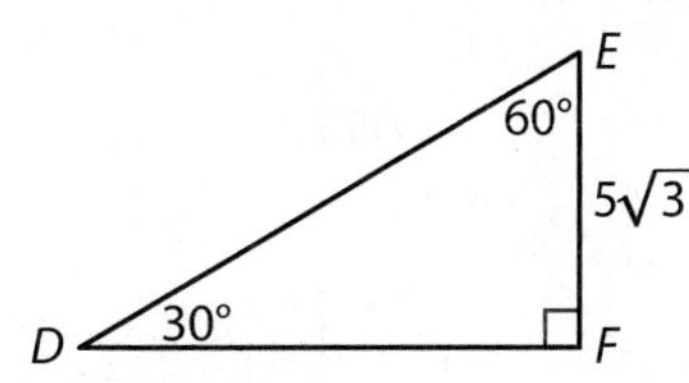

The hypotenuse is twice as long as the shorter leg.	$DE = 2\ EF$
Substitute $5\sqrt{3}$ for EF.	$DE = 2(5\sqrt{3})$
Simplify.	$DE = 10\sqrt{3}$
The longer leg is $\sqrt{3}$ times as long as the shorter leg.	$DF = EF\sqrt{3}$
Substitute $5\sqrt{3}$ for EF.	$DF = 5\sqrt{3}\sqrt{3}$
Simplify.	$DF = 15$

Your Turn

Find the unknown side lengths in each right triangle.

5.

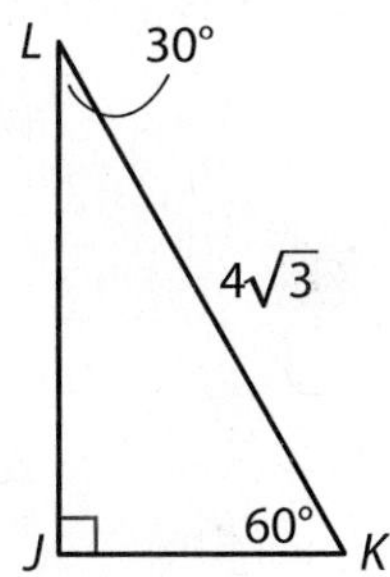

6.

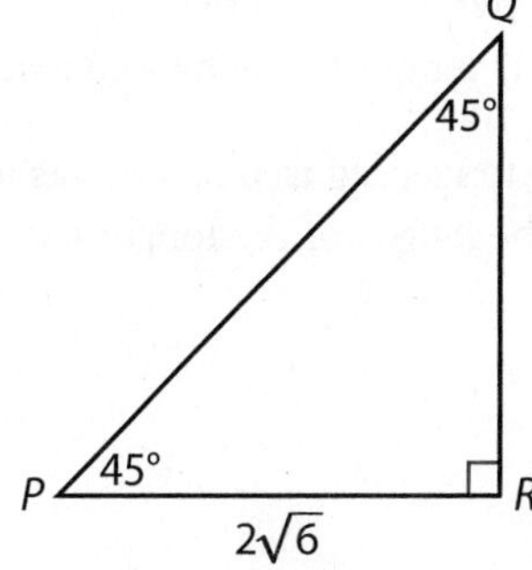

Explain 2 Trigonometric Ratios of Special Right Triangles

You can use the relationships you found in special right triangles to find trigonometric ratios for the angles 45°, 30°, and 60°.

Example 2 **For each triangle, find the unknown side lengths and trigonometric ratios for the angles.**

(A) A 45°—45°—90° triangle with a leg length of 1

Step 1

Since the lengths of the sides opposite the 45° angles are congruent, they are both 1. The length of the hypotenuse is $\sqrt{2}$ times as long as each leg, so it is $1(\sqrt{2})$, or $\sqrt{2}$.

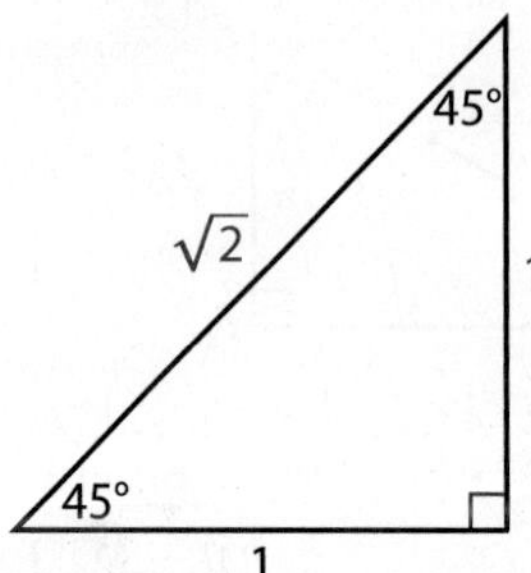

Step 2

Use the triangle to find the trigonometric ratios for 45°. Write each ratio as a simplified fraction.

Angle	Sine $= \frac{\text{opp}}{\text{hyp}}$	Cosine $= \frac{\text{adj}}{\text{hyp}}$	Tangent $= \frac{\text{opp}}{\text{adj}}$
45°	$\frac{\sqrt{2}}{2}$	$\frac{\sqrt{2}}{2}$	1

(B) A 30°—60°—90° triangle with a shorter leg of 1

Step 1

The hypotenuse is twice as long as the shorter leg, so the length of the hypotenuse is 2.

The longer leg is $\sqrt{3}$ times as long as the shorter leg, so the length of the longer leg is $\sqrt{3}$.

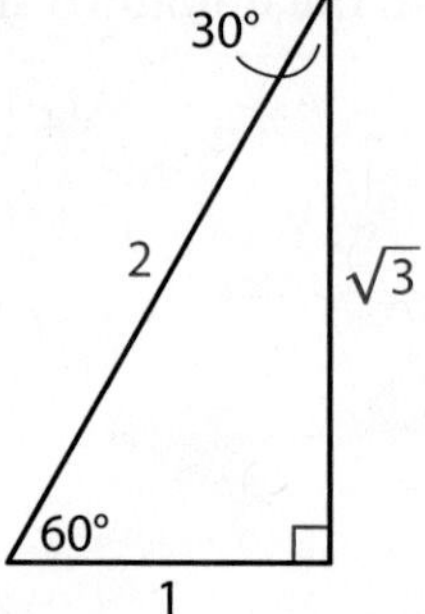

Step 2

Use the triangle to complete the table. Write each ratio as a simplified fraction.

Angle	Sine $= \frac{\text{opp}}{\text{hyp}}$	Cosine $= \frac{\text{adj}}{\text{hyp}}$	Tangent $= \frac{\text{opp}}{\text{adj}}$
30°	$\frac{1}{2}$	$\frac{\sqrt{3}}{2}$	$\frac{\sqrt{3}}{3}$
60°	$\frac{\sqrt{3}}{2}$	$\frac{1}{2}$	$\sqrt{3}$

Reflect

7. Write any patterns or relationships you see in the tables in Part A and Part B as equations. Why do these patterns or relationships make sense?

8. For which acute angle measure θ, is $\tan\theta$ less than 1? equal to 1? greater than 1?

Your Turn

Find the unknown side lengths and trigonometric ratios for the 45° angles.

9.

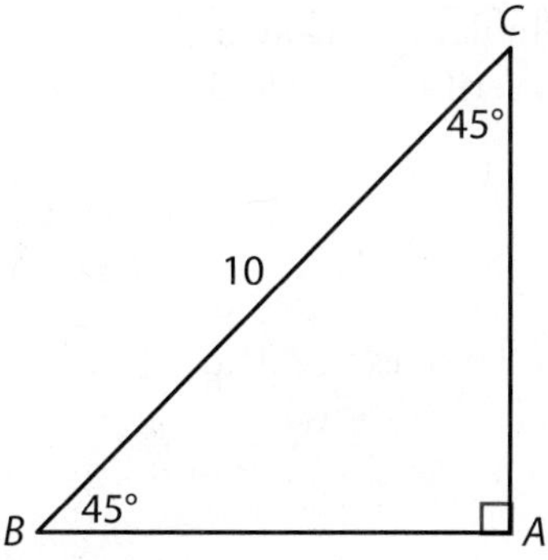

Explain 3 Investigating Pythagorean Triples

Pythagorean Triples

A **Pythagorean triple** is a set of positive integers a, b, and c that satisfy the equation $a^2 + b^2 = c^2$. This means that a, b, and c are the legs and hypotenuse of a right triangle. Right triangles that have non-integer sides will not form Pythagorean triples.

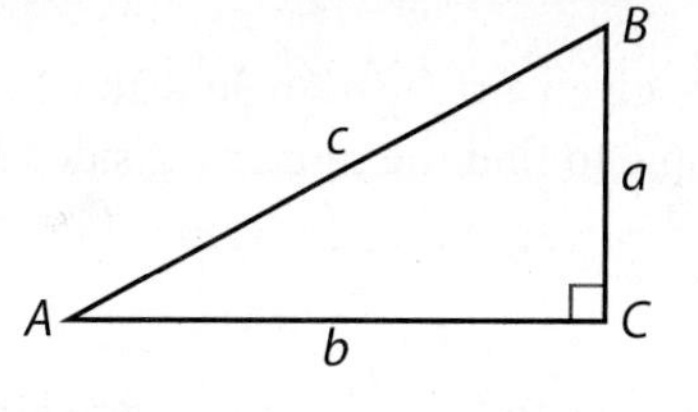

Examples of Pythagorean triples include 3, 4, and 5; 5, 12, and 13; 7, 24, and 25; and 8, 15, and 17.

Example 3 **Use Pythagorean triples to find side lengths in right triangles.**

Ⓐ Verify that the side lengths 3, 4, and 5; 5, 12, and 13; 7, 24, and 25; and 8, 15, and 17 are Pythagorean triples.

$3^2 + 4^2 = 9 + 16 = 25 = 5^2$ ✓ $5^2 + 12^2 = 25 + 144 = 169 = 13^2$ ✓

$7^2 + 24^2 = 49 + 576 = 625 = 25^2$ ✓ $8^2 + 15^2 = 64 + 225 = 289 = 17^2$ ✓

The numbers in Step A are not the only Pythagorean triples. In the following steps you will discover that multiples of known Pythagorean triples are also Pythagorean triples.

Ⓑ In right triangles *DEF* and *JKL*, *a*, *b*, and *c* form a Pythagorean triple, and *k* is a positive integer greater than 1. Explain how the two triangles are related.

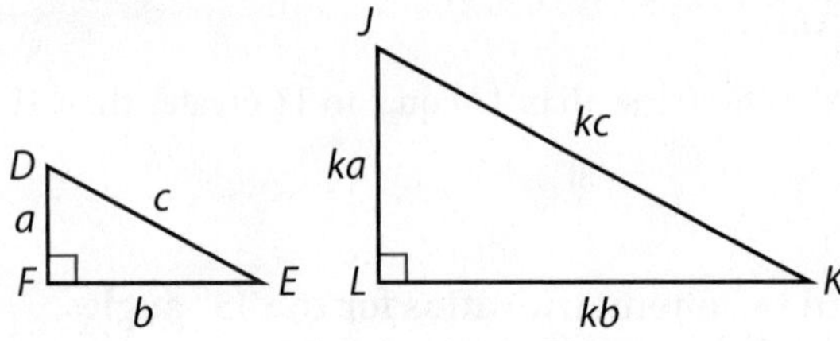

$\triangle DEF$ is similar to $\triangle JKL$ by the Side-Side-Side (SSS) Triangle Similarity Theorem because the corresponding sides are proportional. Complete the ratios to verify Side-Side-Side (SSS) Triangle Similarity.

$a : b : c = ka : kb : kc$

Ⓒ You can use the Pythagorean Theorem to compare the lengths of the sides of $\triangle JKL$. What must be true of the set of numbers *ka*, *kb*, and *kc*?

$$(ka^2) + (kb^2) = k^2a^2 + k^2b^2$$
$$= k^2(a^2 + b^2)$$
$$= k^2(c^2) = (kc)^2$$

The set of numbers *ka*, *kb*, and *kc* form a Pythagorean triple.

Reflect

10. Suppose you are given a right triangle with two side lengths. What would have to be true for you to use a Pythagorean triple to find the remaining side length?

Your Turn

Use Pythagorean triples to find the unknown side length.

11.

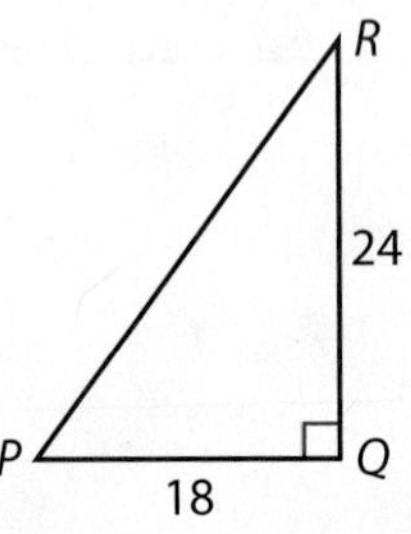

12. In $\triangle XYZ$, the hypotenuse $\overline{XY}$ has length 68, and the shorter leg $\overline{XZ}$ has length 32.

Elaborate

13. Describe the type of problems involving special right triangles you can solve.

14. How can you use Pythagorean triples to solve right triangles?

15. **Discussion** How many Pythagorean triples are there?

16. **Essential Question Check-In** What is the ratio of the length of the hypotenuse to the length of the shorter leg in any 30°-60°-90° triangle?

Evaluate: Homework and Practice

- Online Homework
- Hints and Help
- Extra Practice

For each triangle, state whether the side lengths shown are possible. Explain why or why not.

1.

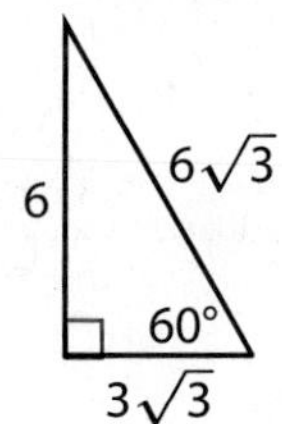

2.

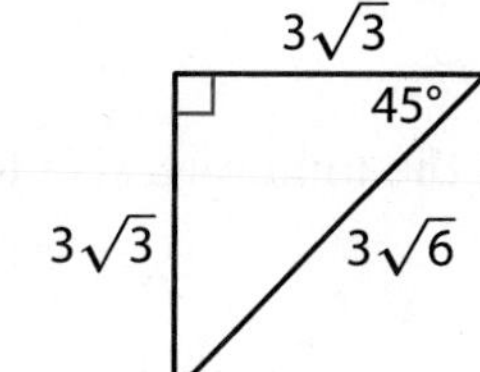

3.

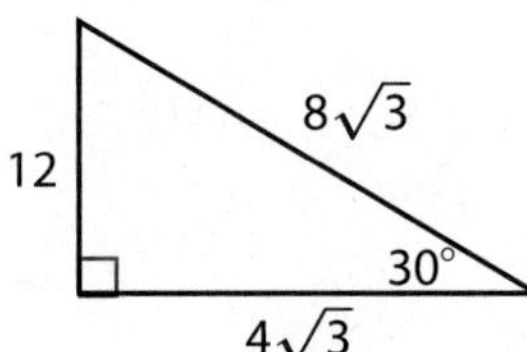

4.

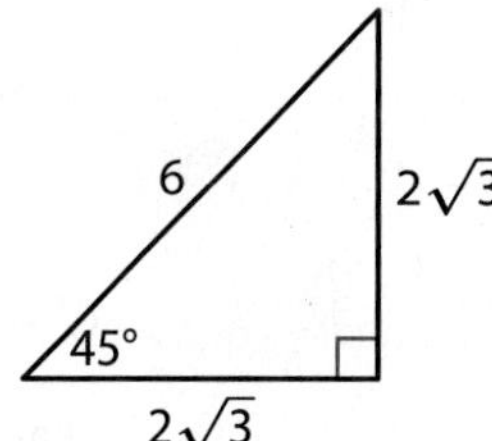

Find the unknown side lengths in each right triangle.

5.

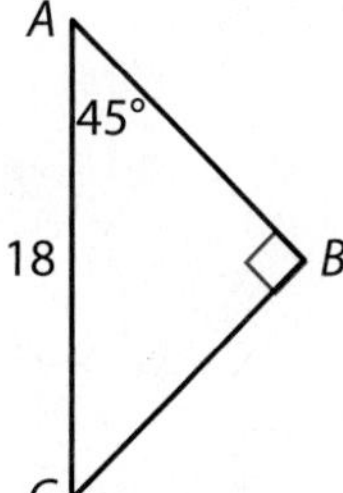

6.

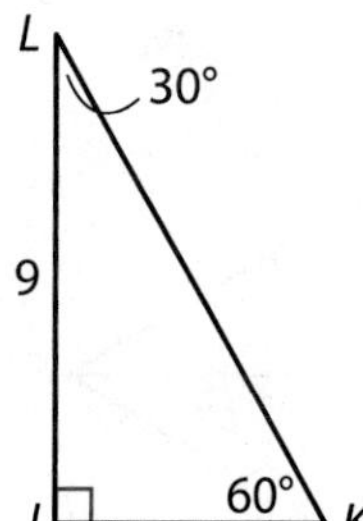

7. Right triangle *UVW* has acute angles *U* measuring 30° and *W* measuring 60°. Hypotenuse $\overline{UW}$ measures 12. (You may want to draw the triangle in your answer.)

8. Right triangle *PQR* has acute angles *P* and *Q* measuring 45°. Leg $\overline{PR}$ measures $5\sqrt{10}$. (You may want to draw the triangle in your answer.)

Use trigonometric ratios to solve each right triangle.

9.

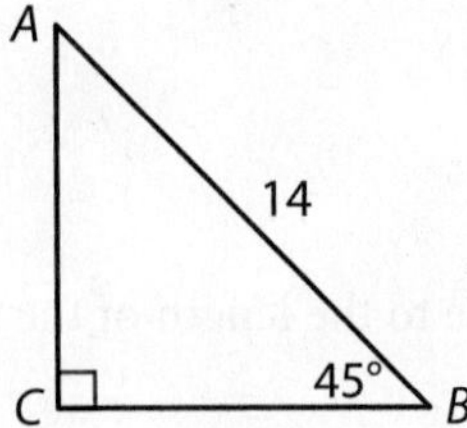

10.

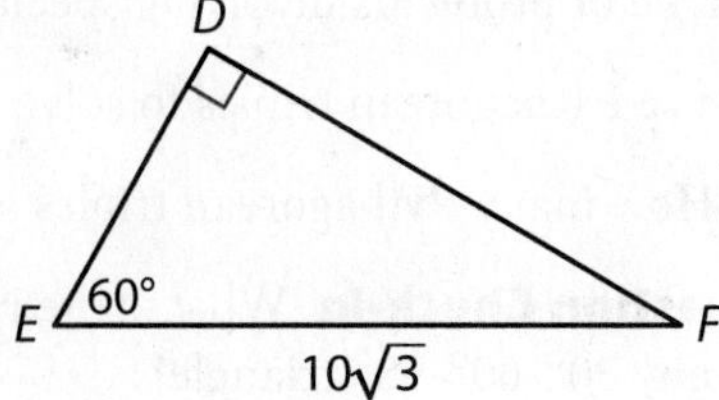

11. Right $\triangle KLM$ with $m\angle J = 45°$, leg $JK = 4\sqrt{3}$

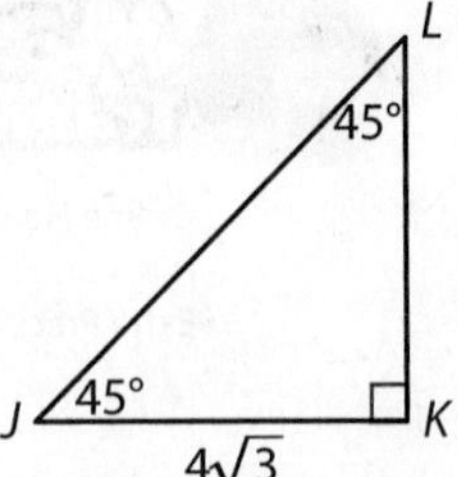

12. Right $\triangle PQR$ with $m\angle Q = 30°$, leg $QR = 15$

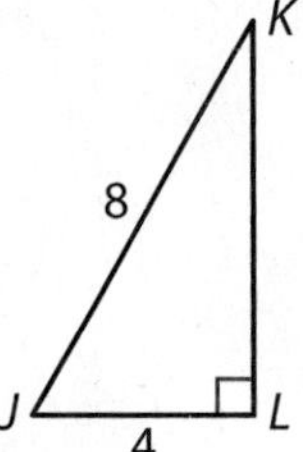

For each right triangle, find the unknown side length using a Pythagorean triple. If it is not possible, state why.

13.

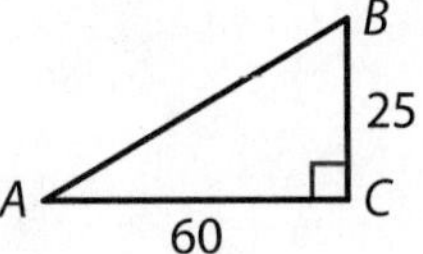

14.

15. In right $\triangle PQR$, the legs have lengths $PQ = 9$ and $QR = 21$.

16. In right $\triangle XYZ$, the hypotenuse $\overline{XY}$ has length 35, and the shorter leg $\overline{YZ}$ has length 21.

17. Solve for x.

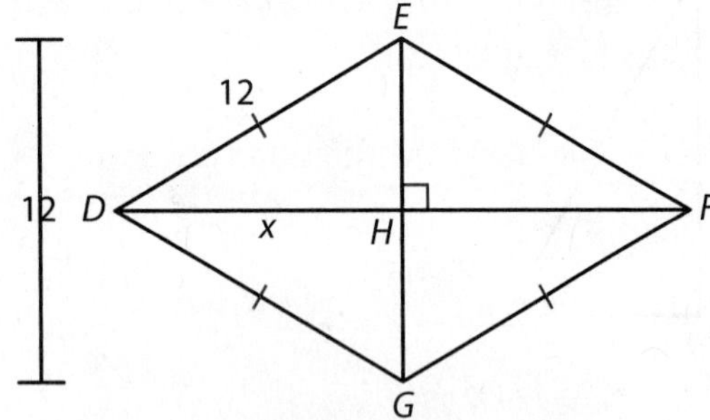

18. Represent Real-World Problems A baseball "diamond" actually forms a square, each side measuring 30 yards. How far, to the nearest yard, must the third baseman throw the ball to reach first base?

19. In a right triangle, the longer leg is exactly $\sqrt{3}$ times the length of the shorter leg. Use the inverse tangent trigonometric ratio to prove that the acute angles of the triangle measure 30° and 60°.

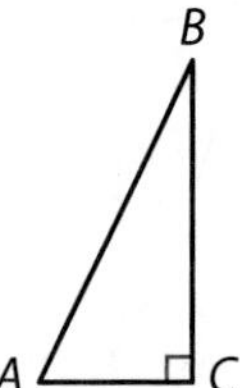

Algebra **Find the value of x in each right triangle.**

20.

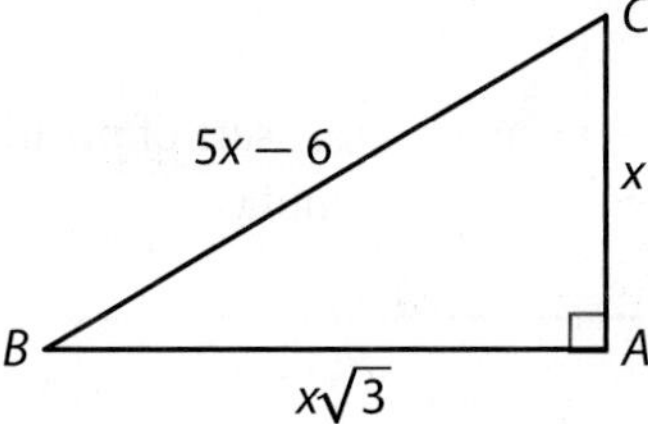

21.

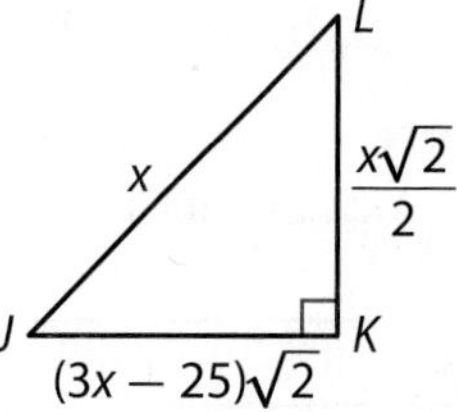

22. **Explain the Error** Charlene is trying to find the unknown sides of a right triangle with a 30° acute angle, whose hypotenuse measures $12\sqrt{2}$. Identify, explain, and correct Charlene's error.

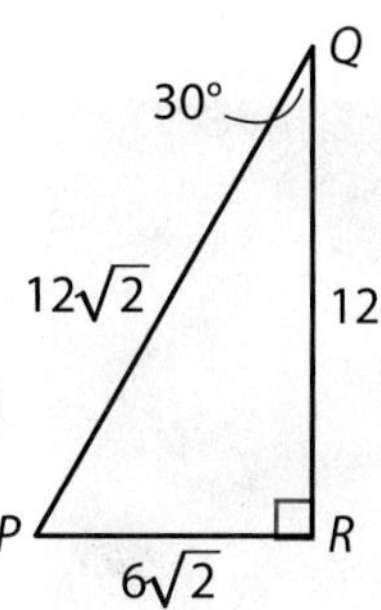

23. **Represent Real-World Problems** Honeycomb blinds form a string of almost-regular hexagons when viewed end-on. Approximately how much material, to the nearest ten square centimeters, is needed for each 3.2-cm deep cell of a honeycomb blind that is 125 cm wide? (*Hint: Draw a picture.* A regular hexagon can be divided into 6 equilateral triangles.)

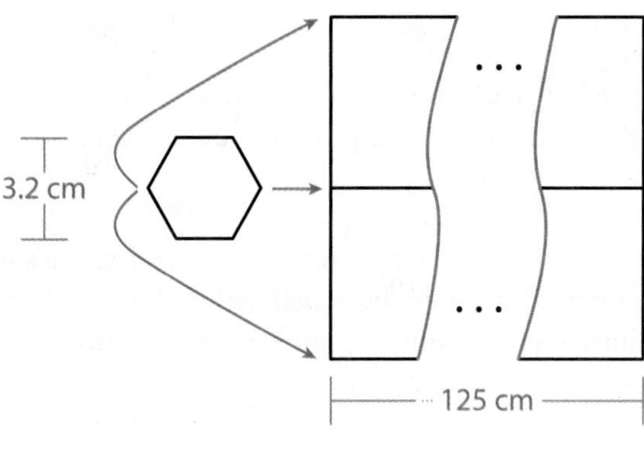

24. Which of these pairs of numbers are two out of three integer-valued side lengths of a right triangle? (*Hint:* for positive integers *a, b, c*, and *k*, *ka, kb*, and *kc* are side lengths of a right triangle if and only if *a, b*, and *c* are side lengths of a right triangle.) Write True or False for each pair.

A. 15, 18

B. 15, 30

C. 15, 51

D. 16, 20

E. 16, 24

H.O.T. Focus on Higher Order Thinking

25. Communicate Mathematical Ideas Is it possible for the three side lengths of a right triangle to be odd integers? Explain.

26. Make a Conjecture Use spreadsheet software to investigate this question: are there sets of positive integers *a, b*, and *c* such that $a^3 + b^3 = c^3$? You may choose to begin with these formulas:

	A	B	C	D
1	1	=A1+1	=A1^3+B1^3	=C1^(1/3)
2	=A1	=B1+1	=A2^3+B2^3	=C2^(1/3)

Lesson Performance Task

Kate and her dog are longtime flying disc players. Kate has decided to start a small business making circles of soft material that dogs can catch without injuring their teeth. Since she also likes math, she's decided to see whether she can apply Pythagorean principles to her designs. She used the of her first three designs.

$r = 3$ in.
small

$r = 4$ in.
medium

$r = 5$ in.
large

1. Is it true that the (small area) + (medium area) = (large area)? Explain.

2. If the circles had radii based on the Pythagorean triple 5—12—13, would the above equation be true? Explain.

3. Three of Kate's circles have radii of *a, b*, and *c*, where *a, b*, and *c* form a Pythagorean triple $(a^2 + b^2 = c^2)$. Show that the sum of the areas of the small and medium circles equals the area of the large circle.

4. Kate has decided to go into the beach ball business. Sticking to her Pythagorean principles, she starts with three spherical beach balls--a small ball with radius 3 in., a medium ball with radius 4 in., and a large ball with radius 5 in. Is it true that (small volume) + (medium volume) = (large volume)? Show your work.

5. Explain the discrepancy between your results in Exercises 3 and 4.

18.4 Problem Solving with Trigonometry

Essential Question: How can you solve a right triangle?

Explore Deriving an Area Formula

You can use trigonometry to find the area of a triangle without knowing its height.

(A) Suppose you draw an altitude $\overline{AD}$ to side $\overline{BC}$ of $\triangle ABC$. Then write an equation using a trigonometric ratio in terms of $\angle C$, the height h of $\triangle ABC$, and the length of one of its sides.

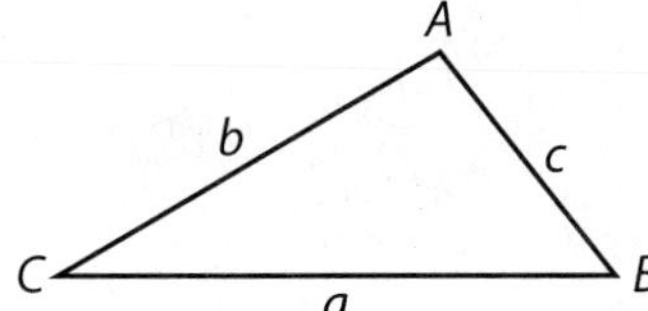

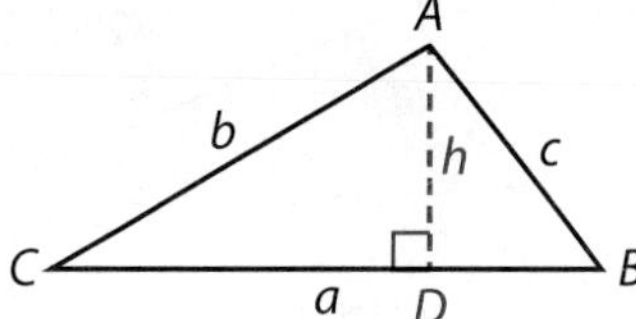

(B) Solve your equation from Step A for h.

(C) Complete this formula for the area of $\triangle ABC$ in terms of h and another of its side lengths: Area $= \frac{1}{2}$ ____

(D) Substitute your expression for h from Step B into your formula from Step C.

Reflect

1. Does the area formula you found work if $\angle C$ is a right angle? Explain.
2. Suppose you used a trigonometric ratio in terms of $\angle B$, h, and a different side length. How would this change your findings? What does this tell you about the choice of sides and included angle?

Explain 1 Using the Area Formula

Area Formula for a Triangle in Terms of its Side Lengths

The area of $\triangle ABC$ with sides a, b, and c can be found using the lengths of two of its sides and the sine of the included angle: Area $= \frac{1}{2}bc \sin A$, Area $= \frac{1}{2}ac \sin B$, or Area $= \frac{1}{2}\, ab \sin C$.

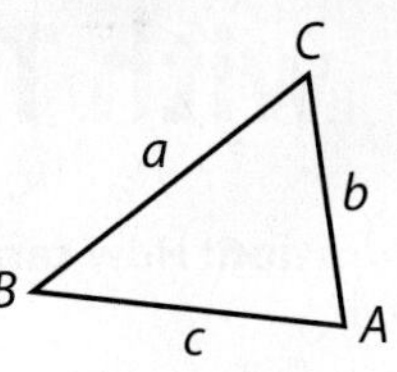

You can use any form of the area formula to find the area of a triangle, given two side lengths and the measure of the included angle.

Example 1 **Find the area of each triangle to the nearest tenth.**

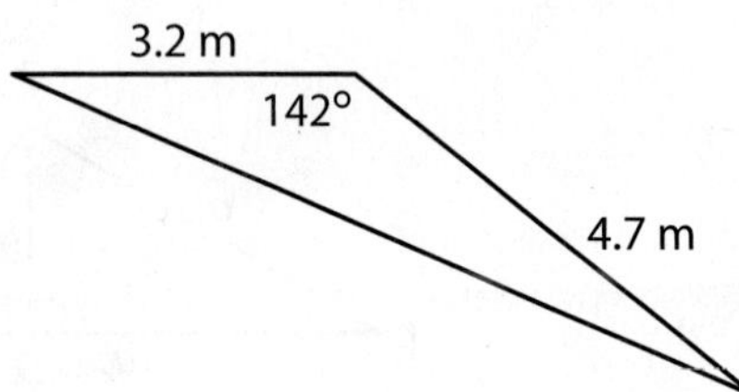

Let the known side lengths be a and b.	$a = 3.2$ m and $b = 4.7$ m
Let the known angle be $\angle C$.	$m\angle C = 142°$
Substitute in the formula Area $= \frac{1}{2}ab \sin C$.	Area $= \frac{1}{2}(3.2)(4.7)\sin 142°$
Evaluate, rounding to the nearest tenth.	Area $\approx 4.6\ \text{m}^2$

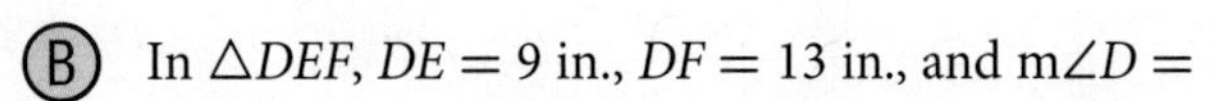

(B) In $\triangle DEF$, $DE = 9$ in., $DF = 13$ in., and $m\angle D = 57°$.

Sketch $\triangle DEF$ and check that $\angle D$ is the included angle.

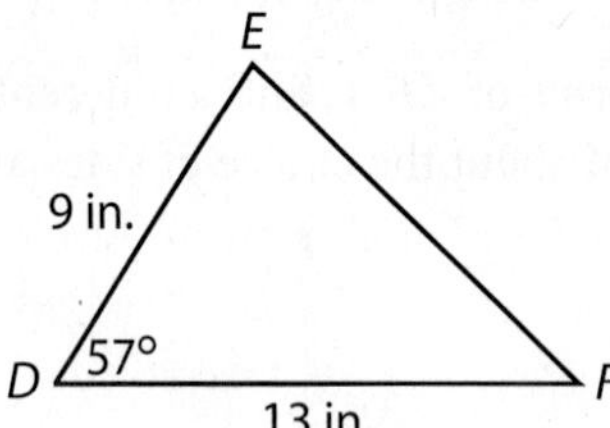

Write the area formula in terms of $\triangle DEF$.	Area $= \frac{1}{2}(DE)(\boxed{DF})\sin \boxed{D}$
Substitute in the area formula.	Area $= \frac{1}{2}(\boxed{9})(\boxed{13})\sin \boxed{57}°$
Evaluate, rounding to the nearest tenth.	Area $\approx \boxed{49.1}\ \text{in.}^2$

Your Turn

Find the area of each triangle to the nearest tenth.

3.

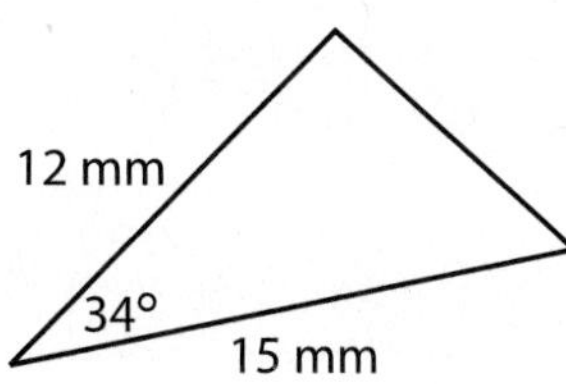

4. In $\triangle PQR$, $PQ = 3$ cm, $QR = 6$ cm, and $m\angle Q = 108°$.

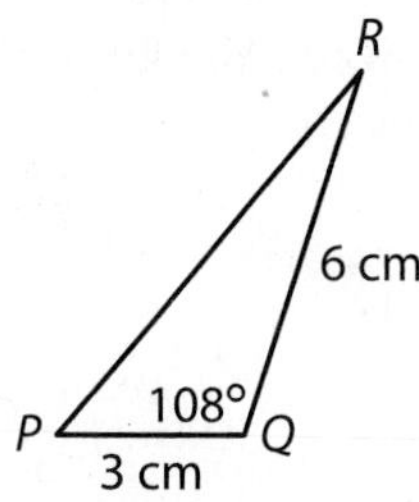

Explain 2 Solving a Right Triangle

Solving a right triangle means finding the lengths of all its sides and the measures of all its angles. To solve a right triangle you need to know two side lengths or one side length and an acute angle measure. Based on the given information, choose among trigonometric ratios, inverse trigonometric ratios, and the Pythagorean Theorem to help you solve the right triangle.

A shelf extends perpendicularly 7 in. from a wall. You want to place a 9-in. brace under the shelf, as shown. To the nearest tenth of an inch, how far below the shelf will the brace be attached to the wall? To the nearest degree, what angle will the brace make with the shelf and with the wall?

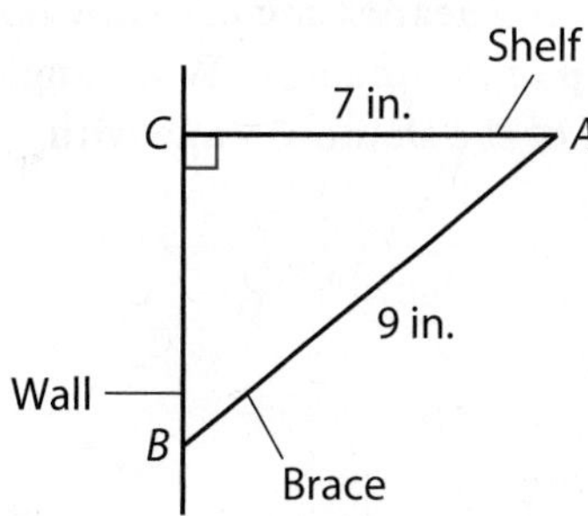

(A) Find BC.

Use the Pythagorean Theorem to find the length of the third side.	$AC^2 + BC^2 = AB^2$
Substitute 7 for AC and 9 for AB.	$7^2 + BC^2 = 9^2$
Find the squares.	$49 + BC^2 = 81$
Subtract 49 from both sides.	$BC^2 = 32$
Find the square root and root.	$BC \approx 5.7$

(B) Find m$\angle A$ and m$\angle B$.

Use an inverse trigonometric ratio to find m$\angle A$. You know the lengths of the adjacent side and the hypotenuse, so use the cosine ratio.

Write a cosine ratio for $\angle A$.	$\cos A = \boxed{\frac{7}{9}}$
Write an inverse cosine ratio.	$m\angle A = \cos^{-1}\left(\boxed{\frac{7}{9}}\right)$
Evaluate the inverse cosine ratio and round.	$m\angle A \approx \boxed{39}°$
$\angle$ [A] and $\angle B$ are complementary.	$m\angle \boxed{A} + m\angle B = 90°$
Substitute [39]° for m$\angle$ [A].	$\boxed{39}° + m\angle B \approx 90°$
Subtract [39]° from both sides.	$m\angle B \approx \boxed{51}°$

Reflect

5. Is it possible to find m$\angle B$ before you find m$\angle A$? Explain.

Your Turn

A building casts a 33-m shadow when the Sun is at an angle of 27° to the vertical. How tall is the building, to the nearest meter? How far is it from the top of the building to the tip of the shadow? What angle does a ray from the Sun along the edge of the shadow make with the ground?

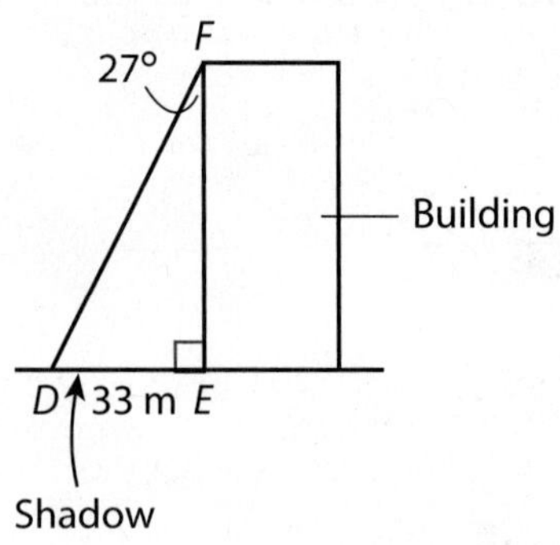

6. Use a trigonometric ratio to find the distance EF.

7. Use another trigonometric ratio to find the distance DF.

8. Use the fact that acute angles of a right triangle are complementary to find m$\angle D$.

Explain 3 Solving a Right Triangle in the Coordinate Plane

You can use the distance formula as well as trigonometric tools to solve right triangles in the coordinate plane.

Example 3 **Solve each triangle.**

(A) Triangle ABC has vertices $A(-3, 3)$, $B(-3, -1)$, and $C(4, -1)$. Find the side lengths to the nearest hundredth and the angle measures to the nearest degree.

Plot points A, B, and C, and draw $\triangle ABC$.

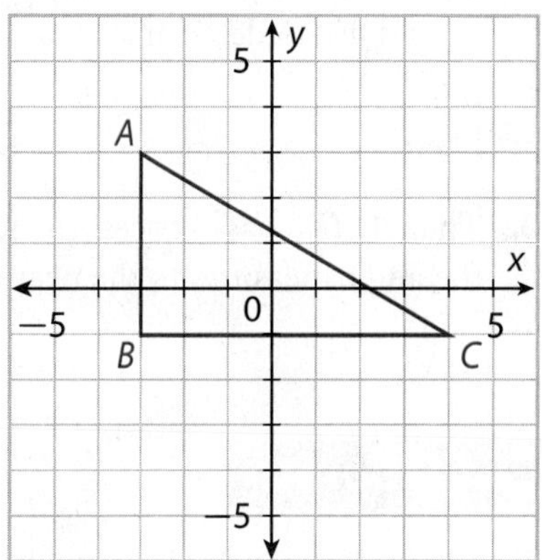

Find the side lengths: $AB = 4$, $BC = 7$

Use the distance formula to find the length of $\overline{AC}$.

$AC = \sqrt{(4 - (-3))^2 + (-1 - 3)^2} = \sqrt{65} \approx 8.06$

Find the angle measures: $\overline{AB} \perp \overline{BC}$, so $m\angle B = 90°$.

Use an inverse tangent ratio to find

$m\angle C = \tan^{-1}\left(\frac{AB}{BC}\right) = \tan^{-1}\left(\frac{4}{7}\right) \approx 30°$.

$\angle A$ and $\angle C$ are complementary, so $m\angle A \approx 90° - 30° = 60°$.

(B) Triangle DEF has vertices $D(-4, 3)$, $E(3, 4)$, and $F(0, 0)$. Find the side lengths to the nearest hundredth and the angle measures to the nearest degree.

Plot points D, E, and F, and draw $\triangle DEF$.

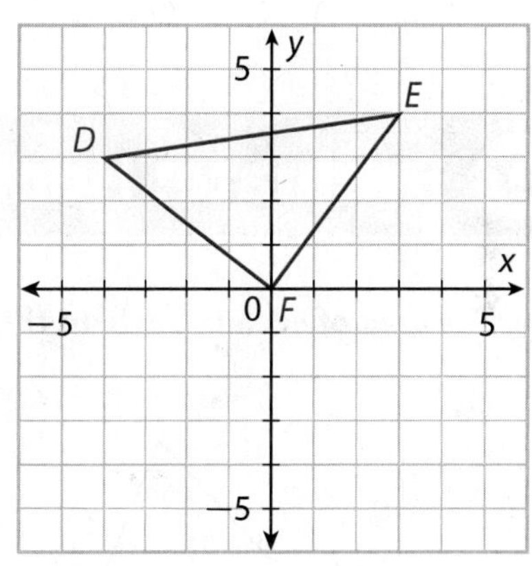

$\angle F$ appears to be a right angle. To check, find the slope

of $\overline{DF}$: $\frac{\boxed{0} - 3}{0 - \boxed{-4}} = \frac{\boxed{-3}}{\boxed{4}} = \boxed{-\frac{3}{4}}$;

slope of $\boxed{\overline{EF}}$: $\frac{\boxed{0} - \boxed{4}}{\boxed{0} - 3} = \frac{\boxed{-4}}{\boxed{-3}} = \frac{\boxed{4}}{\boxed{3}}$;

so $m\angle F = \boxed{90}°$.

Find the side lengths using the distance formula:

$DE = \sqrt{\left(3 - \boxed{-4}\right)^2 + \left(\boxed{4} - 3\right)^2} = \sqrt{\boxed{50}} = \boxed{5}\sqrt{\boxed{2}} \approx \boxed{7.07}$,

$DF = \sqrt{\left(\boxed{0} - \boxed{-4}\right)^2 + \left(\boxed{0} - 3\right)^2} = \sqrt{\boxed{25}} = \boxed{5}$,

$\boxed{EF} = \sqrt{\left(\boxed{0} - \boxed{3}\right)^2 + \left(\boxed{0} - 4\right)^2} = \sqrt{\boxed{25}} = \boxed{5}$

Use an inverse sine ratio to find m∠D.

$$m\angle D = \sin^{-1}\left(\frac{EF}{DE}\right) = \sin^{-1}\left(\frac{5}{5\sqrt{2}}\right) = 45°$$

∠D and ∠ E are complementary, so m∠ E = 90° − 45 ° = 45 °.

Reflect

9. How does the given information determine which inverse trigonometric ratio you should use to determine an acute angle measure?

Your Turn

10. Triangle *JKL* has vertices $J(3, 5)$, $K(-3, 2)$, and $L(5, 1)$. Find the side lengths to the nearest hundredth and the angle measures to the nearest degree.

Elaborate

11. Would you use the area formula you determined in this lesson for a right triangle? Explain.

12. Discussion How does the process of solving a right triangle change when its vertices are located in the coordinate plane?

13. Essential Question Check-In How do you find the unknown angle measures in a right triangle?

Evaluate: Homework and Practice

- Online Homework
- Hints and Help
- Extra Practice

Find the area of each triangle to the nearest tenth.

1.

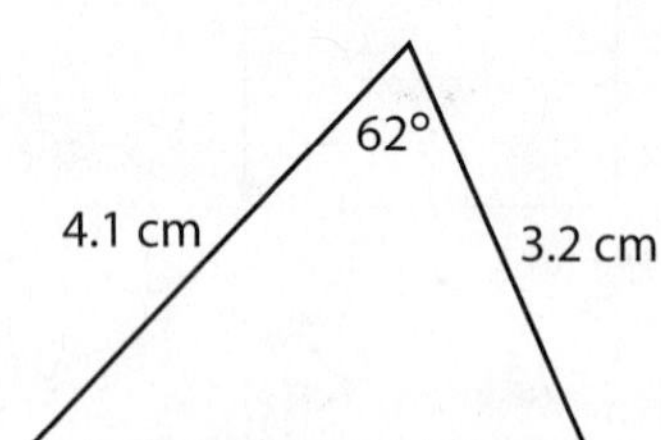

2. In △*PQR*, *PR* = 23 mm, *QR* = 39 mm, and m∠*R* = 163°.

Solve each right triangle. Round lengths to the nearest tenth and angles to the nearest degree.

3.

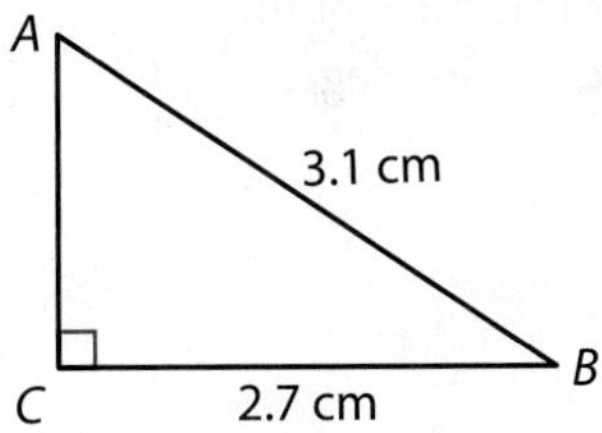

4.

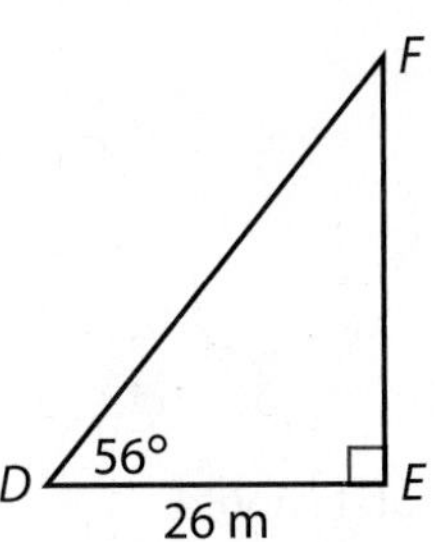

5. Right $\triangle PQR$ with $\overline{PQ} \perp \overline{PR}$, $QR = 47$ mm, and $m\angle Q = 52°$

Solve each triangle. Find the side lengths to the nearest hundredth and the angle measures to the nearest degree.

6. Triangle ABC with vertices $A(-4, 4)$, $B(3, 4)$, and $C(3, -2)$

7. Triangle JKL with vertices $J(-3, 1)$, $K(-1, 4)$, and $L(6, -5)$

8. Triangle PQR with vertices $P(5, 5)$, $Q(-5, 3)$, and $R(-4, -2)$

9. **Surveying** A plot of land is in the shape of a triangle, as shown. Find the area of the plot, to the nearest hundred square yards.

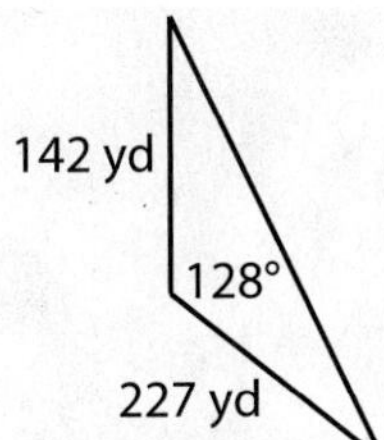

10. History A drawbridge at the entrance to an ancient castle is raised and lowered by a pair of chains. The figure represents the drawbridge when flat. Find the height of the suspension point of the chain, to the nearest tenth of a meter, and the measures of the acute angles the chain makes with the wall and the drawbridge, to the nearest degree.

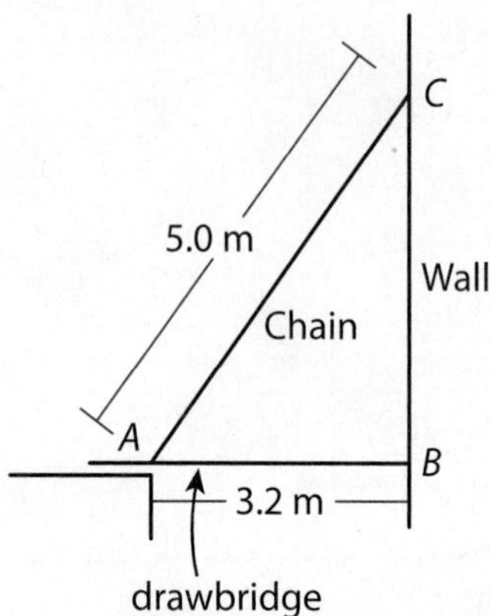

11. Building For safety, the angle a wheelchair ramp makes with the horizontal should be no more than 3.5°. What is the maximum height of a ramp of length 30 ft? What distance along the ground would this ramp cover? Round to the nearest tenth of a foot.

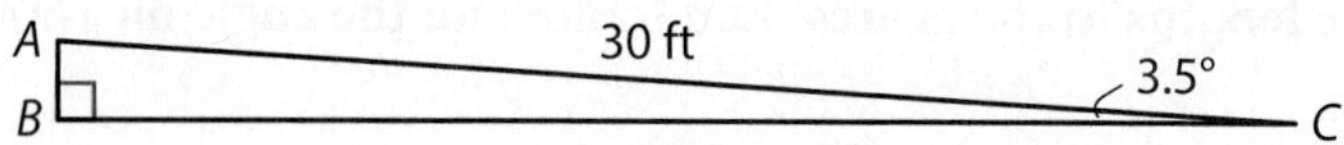

12. Multi-Step The figure shows an origami crane as well as a stage of its construction. The area of each wing is shown by the shaded part of the figure, which is symmetric about its vertical center line. Use the information in the figure to find the total wing area of the crane, to the nearest tenth of a square inch.

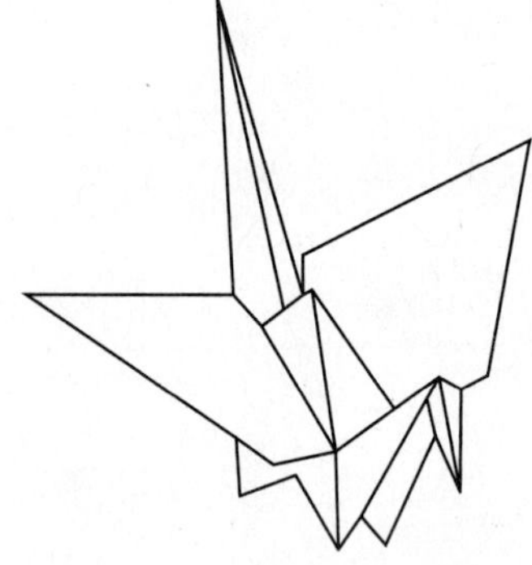

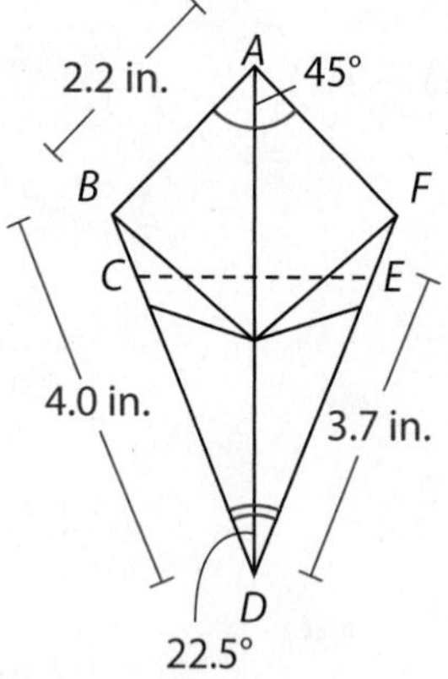

13. Right triangle $\triangle XYZ$ has vertices $X(1, 4)$ and $Y(2, -3)$. The vertex Z has positive integer coordinates, and $XZ = 5$. Find the coordinates of Z and solve $\triangle XYZ$; give exact answers.

14. Critique Reasoning Shania and Pedro are discussing whether it is always possible to solve a right triangle, given enough information, without using the Pythagorean Theorem. Pedro says that it is always possible, but Shania thinks that when two side lengths and no angle measures are given, the Pythagorean Theorem is needed. Who is correct, and why?

15. Design The logo shown is symmetrical about one of its diagonals. Find the angle measures in $\triangle CAE$, to the nearest degree. (*Hint:* First find an angle in $\triangle ABC$, $\triangle CDE$ or $\triangle AEF$) Then, find the area of $\triangle CAE$, without first finding the areas of the other triangles.

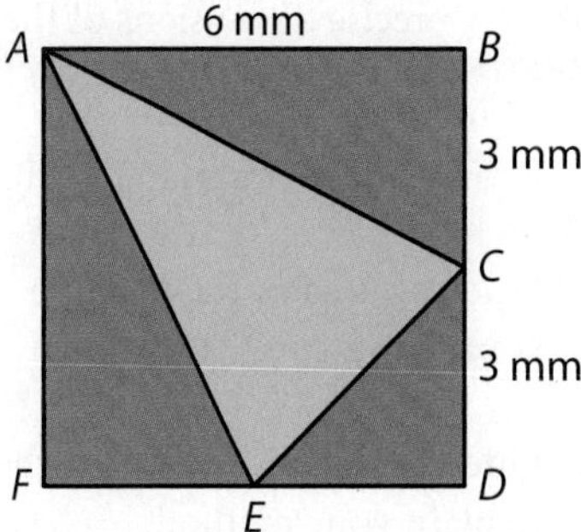

16. Use the area formula for obtuse $\angle B$ in the diagram to show that if an acute angle and an obtuse angle are supplementary, then their sines are equal.

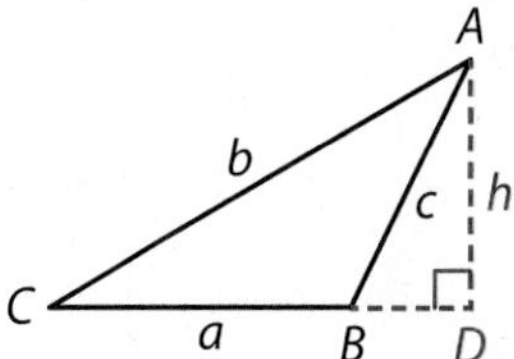

H.O.T. Focus on Higher Order Thinking

17. Communicate Mathematical Ideas The HL Congruence Theorem states that for right triangles ABC and DEF such that $\angle A$ and $\angle D$ are right angles, $\overline{BC} \cong \overline{EF}$, and $\overline{AB} \cong \overline{DE}$, $\triangle ABC \cong \triangle DEF$.
Explain, without formal proof, how solving a right triangle with given leg lengths, or with a given side length and acute angle measure, shows that right triangles with both legs congruent, or with corresponding sides and angles congruent, must be congruent.

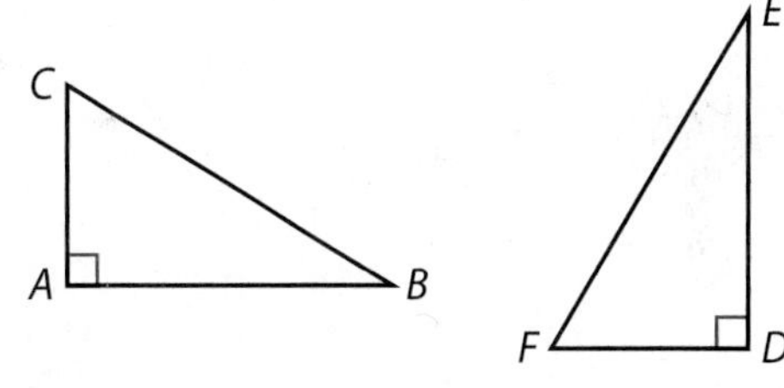

18. Persevere in Problem Solving Find the perimeter and area of $\triangle ABC$, as exact numbers. Then, find the measures of all the angles to the nearest degree.

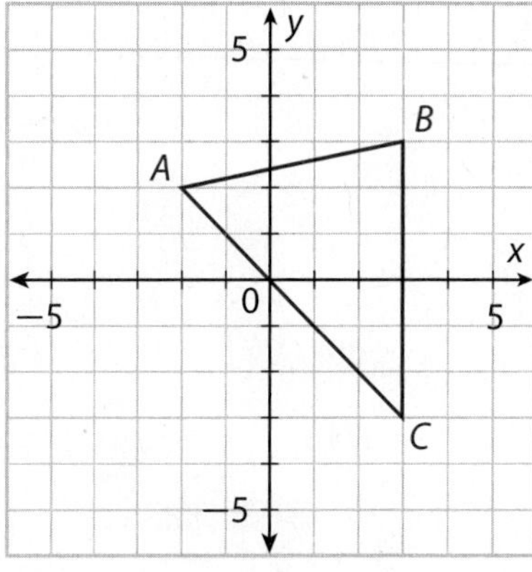

19. Analyze Relationships Find the area of the triangle using two different formulas, and deduce an expression for $\sin 2\theta$.

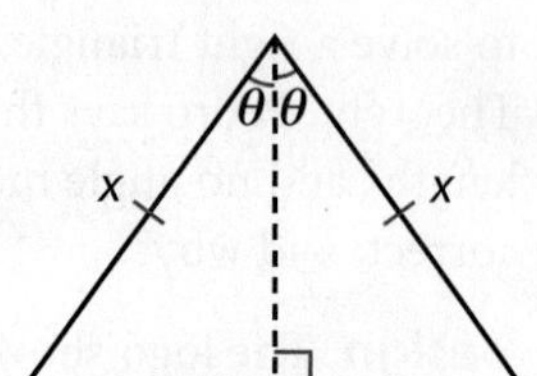

Lesson Performance Task

Every molecule of water contains two atoms of hydrogen and one atom of oxygen. The drawing shows how the atoms are arranged in a molecule of water, along with the incredibly precise dimensions of the molecule that physicists have been able to determine. (1 pm = 1 picometer = 10^{-12}m)

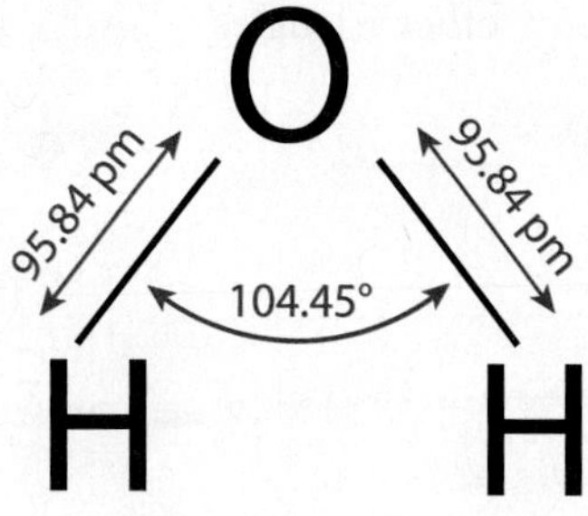

1. Draw and label a triangle with the dimensions shown.

2. Find the area of the triangle in square centimeters. Show your work.

3. Find the distance between the hydrogen atoms in centimeters. Explain your method.

18.5 Using a Pythagorean Identity

Essential Question: How can you use a given value of one of the trigonometric functions to calculate the values of the other functions?

Explore Proving a Pythagorean Identity

In the previous lesson, you learned that the coordinates of any point (x, y) that lies on the unit circle where the terminal ray of an angle θ intersects the circle are $x = \cos\theta$ and $y = \sin\theta$, and that $\tan\theta = \frac{y}{x}$. Combining these facts gives the identity $\tan\theta = \frac{\sin\theta}{\cos\theta}$, which is true for all values of θ where $\cos\theta \neq 0$. In the following Explore, you will derive another identity based on the Pythagorean theorem, which is why the identity is known as a *Pythagorean identity.*

(A) The terminal side of an angle θ intersects the unit circle at the point (a, b) as shown. Write a and b in terms of trigonometric functions involving θ.

$a =$ ▭

$b =$ ▭

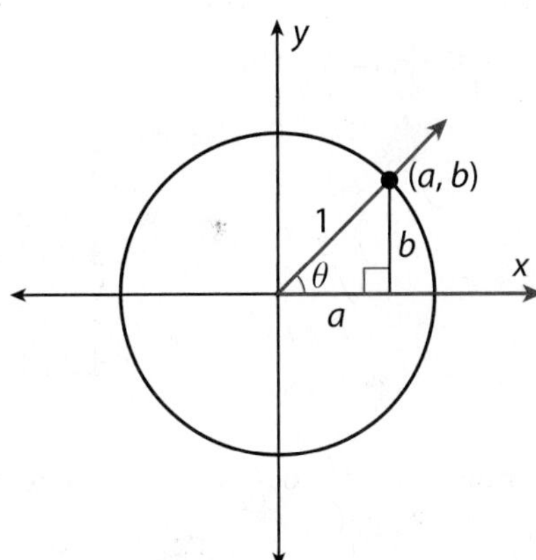

(B) Apply the Pythagorean theorem to the right triangle in the diagram. Note that when a trigonometric function is squared, the exponent is typically written immediately after the name of the function. For instance, $(\sin\theta)^2 = \sin^2\theta$.

Write the Pythagorean Theorem. $a^2 + b^2 = c^2$

Substitute for a, b, and c. $(▭)^2 + (▭)^2 = ▭^2$

Square each expression. ▭ + ▭ = ▭

Reflect

1. The identity is typically written with the sine function first. Write the identity this way, and explain why it is equivalent to the one in Step B.
2. Confirm the Pythagorean identity for $\theta = \frac{\pi}{3}$.
3. Confirm the Pythagorean identity for $\theta = \frac{3\pi}{4}$.

Explain 1 Finding the Value of the Other Trigonometric Functions Given the Value of sin θ or cos θ

You can rewrite the identity $\sin^2\theta + \cos^2\theta = 1$ to express one trigonometric function in terms of the other. As shown, each alternate version of the identity involves both positive and negative square roots. You can determine which sign to use based on knowing the quadrant in which the terminal side of θ lies.

Solve for $\sin\theta$	Solve for $\cos\theta$
$\sin^2\theta + \cos^2\theta = 1$	$\sin^2\theta + \cos^2\theta = 1$
$\cos^2\theta = 1 - \cos^2\theta$	$\sin^2\theta = 1 - \cos^2\theta$
$\cos\theta = \pm\sqrt{1 - \sin^2\theta}$	$\sin\theta = \pm\sqrt{1 - \cos^2\theta}$

Example 1 **Find the approximate value of each trigonometric function.**

(A) Given that $\sin\theta = 0.766$ where $0 < \theta < \frac{\pi}{2}$, find $\cos\theta$.

Use the identity to solve for $\cos\theta$. $\cos\theta = \pm\sqrt{1 - \sin^2\theta}$

Substitute for $\sin\theta$. $= \pm\sqrt{1 - (0.766)^2}$

Use a calculator, then round. $\approx \pm 0.643$

The terminal side of θ lies in Quadrant I, where $\cos\theta > 0$. So, $\cos\theta \approx 0.643$.

(B) Given that $\cos\theta = -0.906$ where $\pi < \theta < \frac{3\pi}{2}$, find $\sin\theta$.

Use the identity to solve for $\sin\theta$. $\sin\theta = \pm\sqrt{1 - \cos^2\theta}$

Substitute for $\cos\theta$. $= \pm\sqrt{1 - \left(\boxed{-0.906}\right)^2}$

Use a calculator, then round. $\approx \pm \boxed{0.423}$

The terminal side of θ lies in Quadrant $\boxed{\text{III}}$, where $\sin\theta \boxed{<} 0$. So, $\sin\theta \approx \boxed{-0.423}$.

Reflect

4. Suppose that $\frac{\pi}{2} < \theta < \pi$ instead of $0 < \theta < \frac{\pi}{2}$ in part A of this Example. How does this affect the value of $\sin\theta$?

5. Suppose that $\frac{3\pi}{2} < \theta < 2\pi$ instead of $\pi < \theta < \frac{3\pi}{2}$ in part B of this Example. How does this affect the value of $\sin\theta$?

6. Explain how you would use the results of part A of this Example to determine the approximate value for $\tan\theta$. Then find it.

Your Turn

7. Given that $\sin\theta = -0.644$ where $\pi < \theta < \frac{3\pi}{2}$, find $\cos\theta$.

8. Given that $\cos\theta = -0.994$ where $\frac{\pi}{2} < \theta < \pi$, find $\sin\theta$. Then find $\tan\theta$.

Explain 2 Finding the Value of Other Trigonometric Functions Given the Value of tanθ

If you multiply both sides of the identity $\tan\theta = \frac{\sin\theta}{\cos\theta}$ by $\cos\theta$, you get the identity $\cos\theta\tan\theta = \sin\theta$, or $\sin\theta = \cos\theta\tan\theta$. Also, if you divide both sides of $\sin\theta = \cos\theta\tan\theta$ by $\tan\theta$, you get the identity $\cos\theta = \frac{\sin\theta}{\tan\theta}$. You can use the first of these identities to find the sine and cosine of an angle when you know the tangent.

Example 2 **Find the approximate value of each trigonometric function.**

Ⓐ Given that $\tan\theta \approx -2.327$ where $\frac{\pi}{2} < \theta < \pi$, find the values of $\sin\theta$ and $\cos\theta$.

First, write $\sin\theta$ in terms of $\cos\theta$.

Use the identity $\sin\theta = \cos\theta\tan\theta$.	$\sin\theta = \cos\theta\tan\theta$
Substitute the value of $\tan\theta$.	$\approx -2.327\cos\theta$

Now use the Pythagorean Identity to find $\cos\theta$. Then find $\sin\theta$.

Use the Pythagorean Identity.	$\sin^2\theta + \cos^2\theta = 1$
Substitute for $\sin\theta$.	$(-2.327\cos\theta)^2 + \cos^2\theta \approx 1$
Square.	$5.415\cos^2\theta + \cos^2\theta \approx 1$
Combine like terms.	$6.415\cos^2\theta \approx 1$
Solve for $\cos^2\theta$.	$\cos^2\theta \approx 0.156$
Solve for $\cos\theta$.	$\cos\theta \approx \pm 0.395$

The terminal side of θ lies in Quadrant II, where $\cos\theta < 0$. Therefore, $\cos\theta \approx -0.395$ and $\sin\theta \approx -2.327\cos\theta \approx 0.919$.

 Given that $\tan\theta \approx -4.366$ where $\frac{3\pi}{2} < \theta < 2\pi$, find the values of $\sin\theta$ and $\cos\theta$.

First, write $\sin\theta$ in terms of $\cos\theta$.

Use the identity $\sin\theta = \cos\theta \tan\theta$. $\qquad \sin\theta = \cos\theta \tan\theta$

Substitute the value of $\tan\theta$. $\qquad \approx \boxed{-4.366} \cos\theta$

Now use the Pythagorean Identity to find $\cos\theta$. Then find $\sin\theta$.

Use the Pythagorean Identity. $\qquad \sin^2\theta + \cos^2\theta = 1$

Substitute for $\sin\theta$. $\qquad \left(\boxed{-4.366} \cos\theta\right)^2 + \cos^2\theta \approx 1$

Square. $\qquad \boxed{19.062} \cos^2\theta + \cos^2\theta \approx 1$

Combine like terms. $\qquad \boxed{20.062} \cos^2\theta \approx 1$

Solve for $\cos^2\theta$. $\qquad \cos^2\theta \approx \boxed{0.050}$

Solve for $\cos\theta$. $\qquad \cos\theta \approx \boxed{0.223}$

The terminal side of θ lies in Quadrant $\boxed{\text{IV}}$, where $\cos\theta \boxed{>} 0$. Therefore, $\cos\theta \approx \boxed{0.223}$

and $\sin\theta \approx \boxed{-4.366} \cos\theta \approx \boxed{-0.974}$.

Reflect

9. In part A of this Example, when you multiplied the given value of $\tan\theta$ by the calculated value of $\cos\theta$ in order to find the value of $\sin\theta$, was the product positive or negative? Explain why this is the result you would expect.

10. If $\tan\theta = 1$ where $0 < \theta < \frac{\pi}{2}$, show that you can solve for $\sin\theta$ and $\cos\theta$ exactly using the Pythagorean identity. Why is this so?

Your Turn

11. Given that $\tan\theta \approx 3.454$ where $\pi < \theta < \frac{3\pi}{2}$, find the values of $\sin\theta$ and $\cos\theta$.

Elaborate

12. What conclusions can you draw if you are given only the information that $\tan\theta = -1$?

13. **Discussion** Explain in what way the process of finding the sine and cosine of an angle from the tangent ratio is similar to the process of solving a linear equation in two variables by substitution.

14. **Essential Question Check-In** If you know only the sine or cosine of an angle and the quadrant in which the angle terminates, how can you find the other trigonometric ratios?

Evaluate: Homework and Practice

- Online Homework
- Hints and Help
- Extra Practice

Find the approximate value of each trigonometric function.

1. Given that $\sin\theta = 0.515$ where $0 < \theta < \frac{\pi}{2}$, find $\cos\theta$.
2. Given that $\cos\theta = 0.198$ where $\frac{3\pi}{2} < \theta < 2\pi$, find $\sin\theta$.
3. Given that $\sin\theta = -0.447$ where $\frac{3\pi}{2} < \theta < 2\pi$, find $\cos\theta$.
4. Given that $\cos\theta = -0.544$ where $\frac{\pi}{2} < \theta < 2\pi$, find $\sin\theta$.
5. Given that $\sin\theta = -0.908$ where $\pi < \theta < \frac{3\pi}{2}$, find $\cos\theta$.
6. Given that $\sin\theta = 0.313$ where $\frac{\pi}{2} < \theta < \pi$, find $\cos\theta$.
7. Given that $\cos\theta = 0.678$ where $0 < \theta < \frac{\pi}{2}$, find $\sin\theta$.
8. Given that $\cos\theta = -0.489$ where $\pi < \theta < \frac{3\pi}{2}$, find $\sin\theta$.

Find the approximate value of each trigonometric function.

9. Given that $\tan\theta \approx -3.966$ where $\frac{\pi}{2} < \theta < \pi$, find the values of $\sin\theta$ and $\cos\theta$.
10. Given that $\tan\theta \approx -4.580$ where $\frac{3\pi}{2} < \theta < 2\pi$, find the values of $\sin\theta$ and $\cos\theta$.
11. Given that $\tan\theta \approx 7.549$ where $0 < \theta < \frac{\pi}{2}$, find the values of $\sin\theta$ and $\cos\theta$.
12. Given that $\tan\theta \approx 4.575$ where $\pi < \theta < \frac{3\pi}{2}$, find the values of $\sin\theta$ and $\cos\theta$.
13. Given that $\tan\theta \approx -1.237$ where $\frac{3\pi}{2}, < \theta < 2\pi$ find the values of $\sin\theta$ and $\cos\theta$.
14. Given that $\tan\theta \approx 5.632$ where $\pi < \theta < \frac{3\pi}{2}$, find the values of $\sin\theta$ and $\cos\theta$.
15. Given that $\tan\theta \approx 6.653$ where $0 < \theta < \frac{\pi}{2}$, find the values of $\sin\theta$ and $\cos\theta$.
16. Given that $\tan\theta \approx -9.366$ where $\frac{\pi}{2}, < \theta < \pi$ find the values of $\sin\theta$ and $\cos\theta$.
17. Given the trigonometric function and the location of the terminal angle, state whether the function value will be positive or negative.
    A. $\cos\theta$, Quadrant I
    B. $\sin\theta$, Quadrant IV
    C. $\tan\theta$, Quadrant II
    D. $\sin\theta$, Quadrant III
    E. $\tan\theta$, Quadrant III
18. Confirm the Pythagorean identity $\sin^2\theta + \cos^2\theta = 1$ for $\theta = \frac{7\pi}{4}$.
19. Recall that the equation of a circle with radius r centered at the origin is $x^2 + y^2 = r^2$. Use this fact and the fact that the coordinates of a point on this circle are $(x, y) = (r\cos\theta, r\sin\theta)$ for a central angle θ to show that the Pythagorean identity derived above is true.

20. Sports A ski supply company is testing the friction of a new ski wax by placing a waxed block on an inclined plane covered with wet snow. The inclined plane is slowly raised until the block begins to slide. At the instant the block starts to slide, the component of the weight of the block parallel to the incline, $mg\sin\theta$, and the resistive force of friction, $\mu mg\cos\theta$, are equal, where μ is the coefficient of friction. Find the value of μ to the nearest hundredth if $\sin\theta = 0.139$ at the instant the block begins to slide.

21. Driving Tires and roads are designed so that the coefficient of friction between the rubber of the tires and the asphalt of the roads is very high, which gives plenty of traction for starting, stopping, and turning. For a particular road surface and tire, the steepest angle for which a car could rest on the slope without starting to slide has a sine of 0.643. This value satisfies the equation $mg\sin\theta = \mu mg\cos\theta$ where μ is the coefficient of friction. Find the value of μ to the nearest hundredth.

H.O.T. Focus on Higher Order Thinking

22. Explain the Error Julian was given that $\sin\theta = -0.555$ where $\frac{3\pi}{2} < \theta < 2\pi$ and told to find $\cos\theta$. He produced the following work:

$$\cos\theta = \pm\sqrt{1 - \sin^2\theta}$$
$$= \pm\sqrt{1 - \left(-0.555^2\right)}$$
$$\approx \pm 1.144$$

Since $\cos\theta > 0$ when $\frac{3\pi}{2} < \theta < 2\pi$, $\cos\theta \approx 1.144$.

Explain his error and state the correct answer.

Critical Thinking **Rewrite each trigonometric expression in terms of $\cos\theta$ and simplify.**

23. $\dfrac{\sin^2\theta}{1 - \cos\theta}$

24. $\cos\theta + \sin\theta\cos\theta - \tan\theta + \tan\theta\sin^2\theta$ (Hint: Begin by factoring $\tan\theta$ from the last two terms.)

25. Critical Thinking To what trigonometric function does the expression $\dfrac{\sqrt{1 - \cos^2\theta}}{\sqrt{1 - \sin^2\theta}}$ simplify? Explain your answer.

Lesson Performance Task

A tower casts a shadow that is 160 feet long at a particular time one morning. With the base of the tower as the origin, east as the positive x-axis, and north as the positive y-axis, the shadow at this time is in the northwest quadrant formed by the axes. Also at this time, the tangent of the angle of rotation measured so that the shadow lies on the terminal ray is $\tan\theta = -2.545$. What are the coordinates of the tip of the shadow to the nearest foot, and what do they indicate?

STUDY GUIDE REVIEW

Trigonometry with Right Triangles

MODULE 18

Essential Question: How can you use trigonometry with right triangles to solve real-world problems?

Key Vocabulary

adjacent *(adyacente)*
opposite *(opuesto)*
tangent *(tangente)*
$tan^{-1} A$ *($tan^{-1} A$)*
inverse tangent of ∠A *(tangente inversa de ∠A)*
trigonometric ratio *(proporción trigonométrica)*
sine *(seno)*
cosine *(coseno)*
inverse trigonometric ratios *(proporción inversa trigonométrica)*
Pythagorean triple *(terna pitagórica)*

KEY EXAMPLE *(Lesson 18.1)*

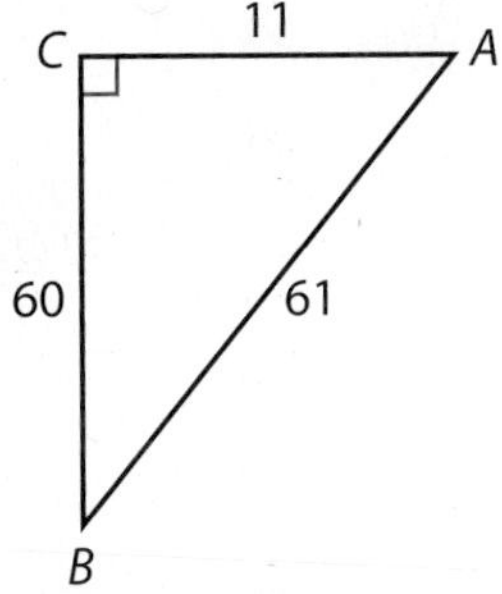

Find the tangent of angle A.

$\tan A = \dfrac{\text{length of leg opposite } \angle A}{\text{length of leg adjacent to } \angle A}$ Definition of tangent

$\tan A = \dfrac{60}{11} \approx 5.45$ Substitute and simplify

KEY EXAMPLE *(Lesson 18.2)*

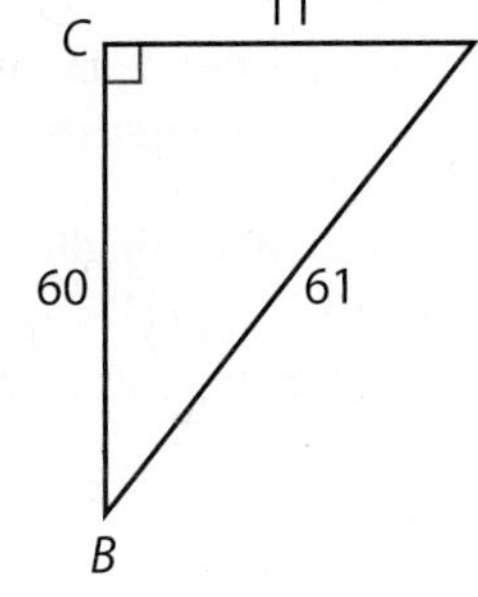

Find the sine and cosine of angle A.

$\sin A = \dfrac{\text{length of leg opposite } \angle A}{\text{length of hypotenuse}}$ Definition of sine

$\sin A = \dfrac{60}{61} \approx .98$ Simplify.

$\cos A = \dfrac{\text{length of leg adjacent to } \angle A}{\text{length of hypotenuse}}$ Definition of cosine

$\cos A = \dfrac{11}{61} \approx .18$ Simplify.

KEY EXAMPLE *(Lesson 18.3)*

Given an isosceles right triangle ∠DEF with ∠F = 90° and DE = 7, find the length of the other two sides.

$DE = DF\sqrt{2}$ Apply the relationship of 45°-45°-90° triangles.

$7 = DF\sqrt{2}$ Substitute.

$\dfrac{7}{\sqrt{2}} = DF$ Simplify.

$DF = EF = \dfrac{7}{\sqrt{2}} = \dfrac{7\sqrt{2}}{2}$ Apply properties of isosceles triangles.

EXERCISES

Given a right triangle $\triangle XYZ$ where $\angle Z$ is a right angle, $XY = 53$, $YZ = 28$, and $XZ = 45$, find the following rounded to the nearest hundredth. *(Lessons 18.1, 18.2)*

1. $\sin X$ **2.** $\cos X$ **3.** $\tan X$

Find the area of the following triangle, rounding to the nearest tenth.

4. triangle $\triangle ABC$, where $C = 127°$, $AC = 5$, and $BC = 9$

Find the other two sides of the following triangle. Find exact answers in order of least to greatest. *(Lesson 18.3)*

5. 30°-60°-90° triangle with a hypotenuse of 14

MODULE PERFORMANCE TASK

How Much Shorter Are Staggered Pipe Stacks?

How much space can be saved by stacking pipe in a staggered pattern? The illustration shows you the difference between layers of pipe stacked directly on top of each other (left) and in a staggered pattern (right). Suppose you have pipes that are 2 inches in diameter. How much shorter will a staggered stack of 10 layers be than a non-staggered stack with the same number of layers? In general, how much shorter are n layers of staggered pipe?

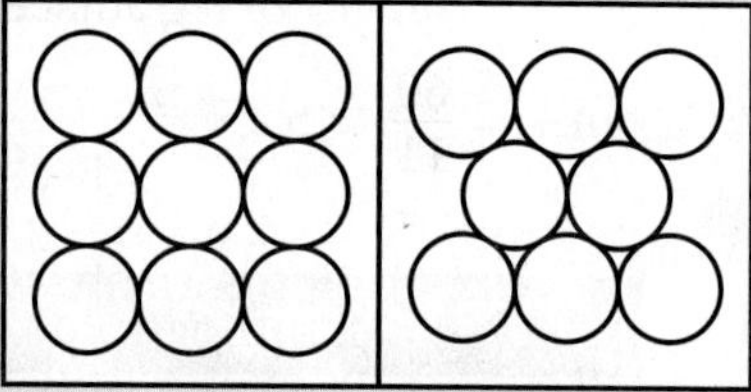

Start by writing how you plan to tackle the problem. Then complete the task. Be sure to write down all your data and assumptions. Then use numbers, graphs, diagrams, or algebraic equations to explain how you reached your conclusion.

Ready to Go On?

18.1–18.5 Trigonometry with Right Triangles

- Online Homework
- Hints and Help
- Extra Practice

Solve the problem. *(Lesson 18.1)*

1. A painter is placing a ladder to reach the third story window, which is 20 feet above the ground and makes an angle with the ground of 70°. How far out from the building does the base of the ladder need to be positioned?

2. Given the value of $\cos 30° = \frac{\sqrt{3}}{2}$, write the sine of a complementary angle. Use an expression relating trigonometric ratios of complementary angles. *(Lesson 18.2)*

Find the area of the regular polygon. *(Lessons 18.3, 18.4)*

3. What is the area of a regular hexagon with a distance from its center to a vertex of 1 cm? (Hint: A regular hexagon can be divided into six equilateral triangles.)

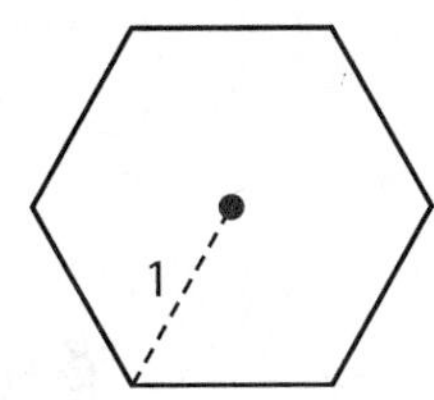

ESSENTIAL QUESTION

4. How would you go about finding the area of a regular pentagon given the distance from its center to the vertices?

MODULE 18
MIXED REVIEW

Assessment Readiness

1. Julia is standing 2 feet away from a lamppost. She casts a shadow of 5 feet and the light makes a 20° angle relative to the ground from the top of her shadow. Consider each expression. Does the expression give you the height of the lamppost?

Write Yes or No for A–C.

A. $7 \sin 20°$

B. $7 \tan 20°$

C. $7 \tan 70°$

2. A right triangle has two sides with lengths 10 and 10. Determine if each statement is True or False.

A. The triangle has two angles that measure 45° each.

B. The triangle is equilateral.

C. The length of the third side is $10\sqrt{2}$.

3. The measure of angle 1 is 125° and the measure of angle 2 is 55°. State two different relationships that can be used to prove $m\angle 3 = 125°$.

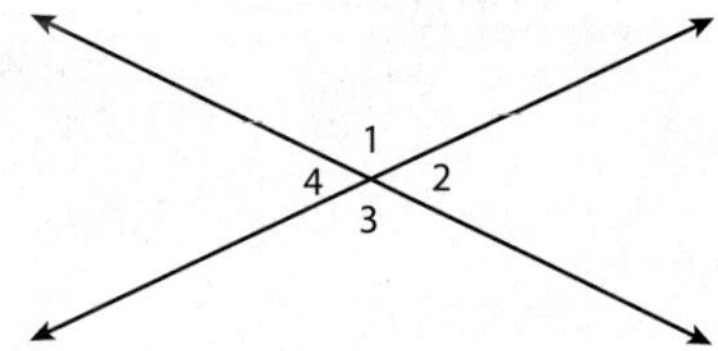

4. For the rhombus, specify how to find its area using the four congruent right triangles with variable angle θ.

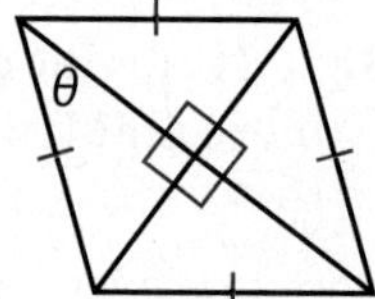

Assessment Readiness

- Online Homework
- Hints and Help
- Extra Practice

1. Determine if each statement is True or False.

A. Dilations preserve angle measure.

B. Dilations preserve distance.

C. Dilations preserve collinearity.

D. Dilations preserve orientation.

2. Was the given transformation used to map *ABCD* to *QRST*? Write Yes or No for A–C.

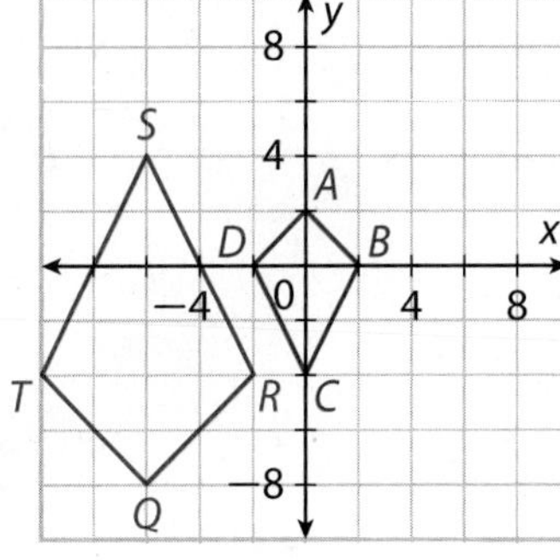

A. Reflection across the *y*-axis

B. Reflection across the *x*-axis

C. Dilation

D. Translation

3. The vertices of quadrilateral *JKLM* are $J(-2, 0)$, $K(-1, 2)$, $L(1, 3)$, and $M(0, 1)$. Can you use slopes and/or the distance formula to prove each statement?

Write Yes or No for A–C.

A. Quadrilateral *JKLM* is a parallelogram.

B. Quadrilateral *JKLM* is a rhombus.

C. Quadrilateral *JKLM* is a rectangle.

4. Will the transformation produce similar figures?

Tell whether each statement is correct.

A. $(x, y) \rightarrow (x - 5, y + 5) \rightarrow (-x, -y) \rightarrow (3x, 3y)$

B. $(x, y) \rightarrow (3x, y + 5) \rightarrow (x, 3y) \rightarrow (x - 1, y - 1)$

C. $(x, y) \rightarrow (x, y + 5) \rightarrow (2x, y) \rightarrow (x + 5, y)$

5. Is *ABC* similar to *DEF*? Tell whether each statement is correct.

A. $A(-1, -3)$, $B(1, 3)$, $C(3, -5)$ $D(2, -6)$, $E(3, 0)$, $F(6, -8)$

B. $A(-1, -3)$, $B(1, 3)$, $C(3, -5)$ $D(-5, -1)$, $E(-4, 2)$, $F(-3, -2)$

C. $A(-1, -3)$, $B(1, 3)$, $C(3, -5)$ $D(-2, -2)$, $E(2, 4)$, $F(2, -4)$

6. Are the triangles similar? Write Yes or No for each pair.

A.

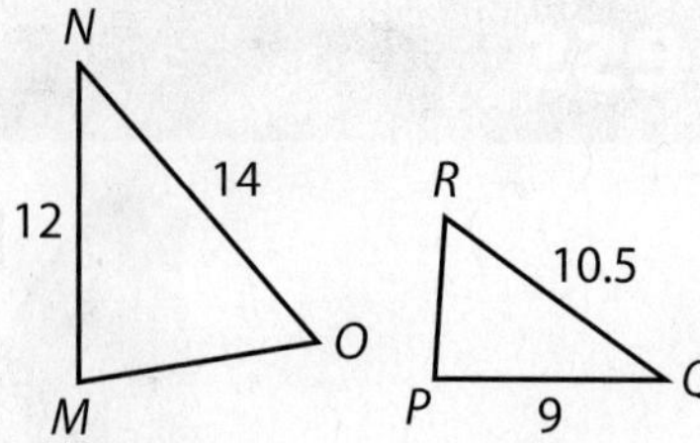

B.

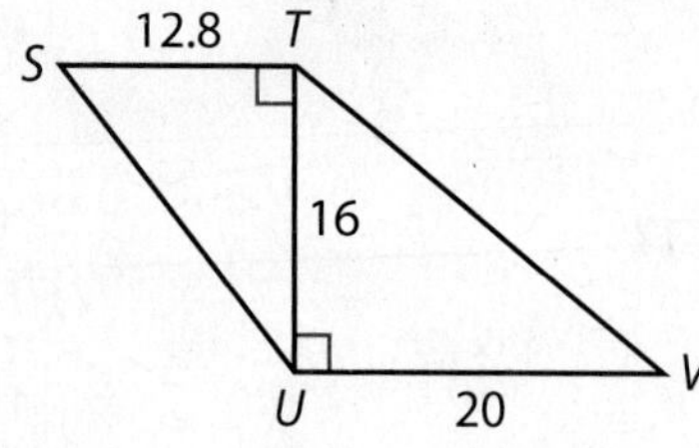

C.

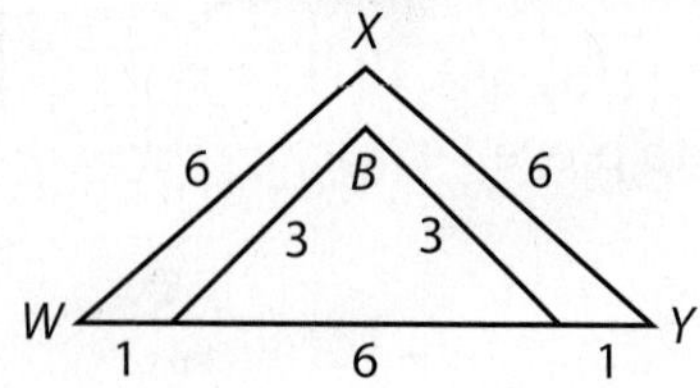

7. Find the missing lengths.

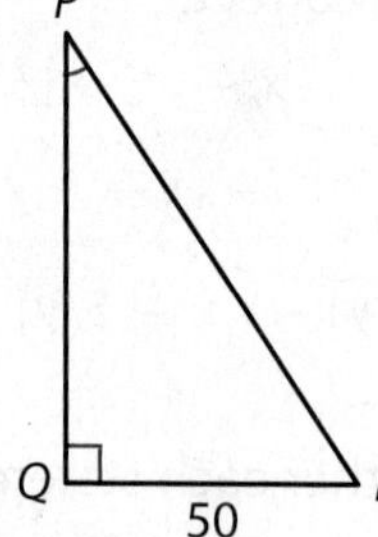

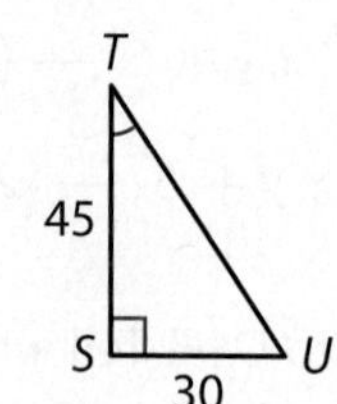

Performance Tasks

★ **8.** The map shows that A Street and B Street are parallel. Find the distance on 6th Ave between A Street and the library. Name any theorems that come into play here.

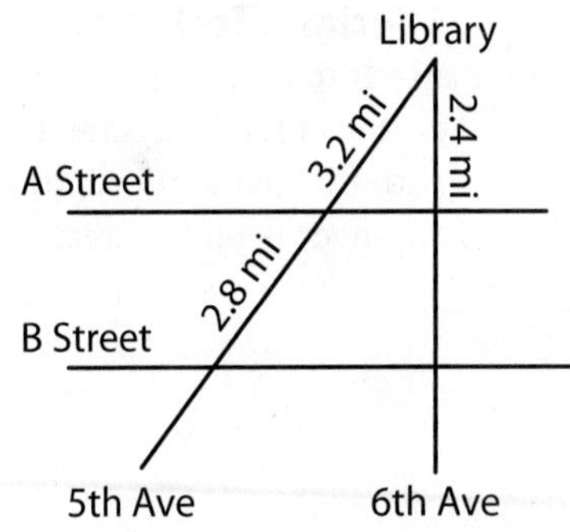

★★ **9.** A city has a walkway between the middle school and the library that can be represented in the image given. The city decides it wants to place three trash cans, equally spaced along the walkway, to help reduce any littering. Find the coordinates of the points at which the trash cans should be placed, and then plot them on the graph.

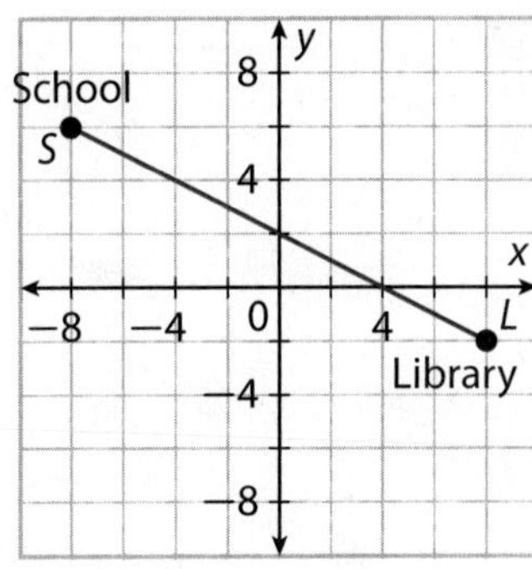

★★★**10.** Sam is planning to fence his backyard. Every side of the yard except for the side along the house is to be fenced, and fencing costs \$3/yd and can only be bought in whole yards. (Note that $m\angle NPM = 28°$, and the side of his yard opposite the house measures 35 yd.) How much will the fencing cost? Explain how you found your answer.

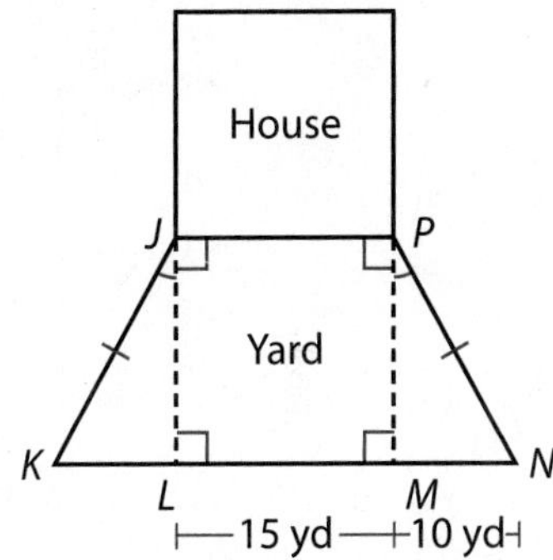

MATH IN CAREERS

Special Effects Engineers A special effects engineer is helping create a movie and needs to add a shadow to a tall totem pole that is next to a 6-foot-tall man. The totem pole is 48 feet tall and is next to the man, who has a shadow that is 2.5 feet long. Create an image with the given information and then use the image to find the length of the shadow that the engineer needs to create for the totem pole.

UNIT 8

Properties of Circles

MODULE 19

Angles and Segments in Circles

MODULE 20

Arc Length and Sector Area

MATH IN CAREERS

Astronomer An astronomer uses advanced technology and mathematics to study outer space. Astronomers apply mathematics to study the positions, movement, and energy of celestial objects.

If you're interested in a career as an astronomer, you should study these mathematical subjects:

- Algebra
- Geometry
- Trigonometry
- Calculus

Research other careers that require the use of physics to understand real-world scenarios. See the related Career Activity at the end of this unit.

Reading Start-Up

Visualize Vocabulary

Use the ✔ words to complete the sequence diagram.

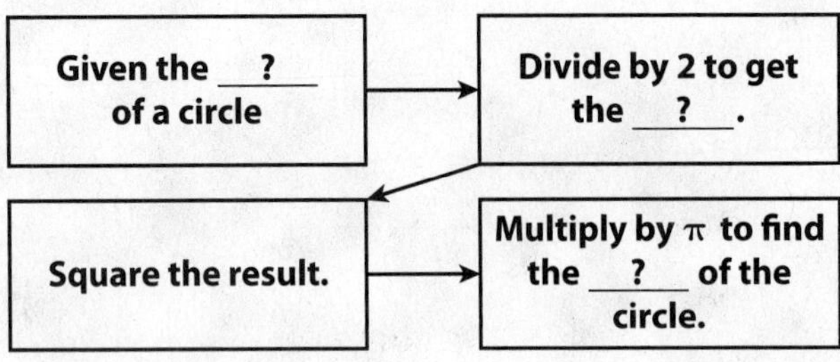

Given the ? of a circle
Divide by 2 to get the ? .
Square the result.
Multiply by π to find the ? of the circle.

Understand Vocabulary

Complete the sentences using the preview words.

1. An angle with a vertex on a circle formed by two rays that intersect other points on the circle is called a(n) ___?___.

2. A radius of a circle is perpendicular to a tangent line at ___?___.

3. A ___?___ of a circle is a line segment with both endpoints on the circle.

Vocabulary

Review Words

✔ area *(área)*
✔ circumference *(circunferencia)*
✔ diameter *(diámetro)*
✔ perpendicular *(perpendicular)*
✔ radius *(radio)*
✔ vertical angles *(ángulos verticales)*

Preview Words

adjacent arcs *(arcos adyacentes)*
arc *(arco)*
arc length *(longitud de arco)*
central angle *(ángulo central)*
chord *(acorde)*
circumscribed *(circunscrito)*
inscribed angle *(ángulo apuntado)*
point of tangency *(punto de tangencia)*
radian measure *(radianes)*
secant *(secante)*
sector *(sector)*
semicircle *(semicírculo)*
tangent *(tangente)*

Active Reading

Four-Corner Fold Create a Four-Corner Fold with flaps for segments, angles, arcs, and sectors. Add relevant vocabulary terms while reading the modules. Emphasize using the written words when discussing these topics with teachers and classmates.

Angles and Segments in Circles

MODULE 19

Essential Question: How can you use angles and segments in circles to solve real-world problems?

REAL WORLD VIDEO
Check out how package designers make use of the mathematics of angles and segments to design efficient and attractive packages and containers.

MODULE PERFORMANCE TASK PREVIEW

How Many Marbles Will Fit?

In this module, you will be challenged to determine the size of the largest marble that can fit into a triangular package. How can an understanding of segment and angle relationships in circles help you to solve this problem? Don't "lose your marbles" before you get a chance to find out!

Are YOU Ready?

Complete these exercises to review skills you will need for this module.

Personal Math Trainer

- Online Homework
- Hints and Help
- Extra Practice

Angle Relationships

Example 1 Find m$\angle ABD$ given that m$\angle CBE = 40°$ and the angles are formed by the intersection of the lines $\overleftrightarrow{AC}$ and $\overleftrightarrow{DE}$ at point B.

When two lines intersect, they form two pairs of vertical angles at their intersection. Note that $\angle ABD$ and $\angle CBE$ are vertical angles and $\angle DBC$ and $\angle ABE$ are vertical angles.

$\angle ABD \cong \angle CBE$ — Theorem: Vertical Angles are Congruent

m$\angle ABD$ = m$\angle CBE = 40°$ — Definition of congruence of angles

Find the measure of the complementary or supplementary angle.

1. Complementary to 40°

2. Complementary to 67°

3. Supplementary to 80°

4. Supplementary to 65°

Use the figure to find the angles or their measures, assuming $\overleftrightarrow{CD}$ is parallel to $\overleftrightarrow{EF}$.

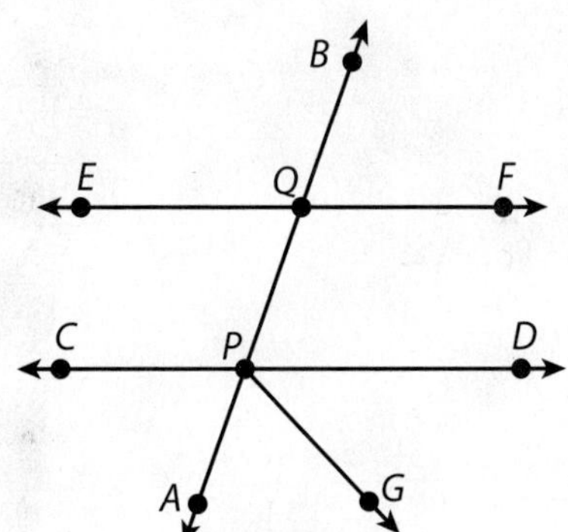

5. All angles congruent to $\angle APD$

6. m$\angle BPD$ when m$\angle BQE = 165°$

7. m$\angle APG$ when m$\angle DPG = 55°$ and m$\angle BPC = 110°$

8. All angles congruent to $\angle GPC$

Determine whether the lines $\overleftrightarrow{CD}$ and $\overleftrightarrow{EF}$ in the above figure are parallel for the given angle measures.

9. m$\angle BPG = 135°$, m$\angle GPC = 95°$, and m$\angle BQF = 110°$

10. m$\angle BPD = 35°$, m$\angle APG = 115°$, and m$\angle EQA = 35°$

19.1 Central Angles and Inscribed Angles

Resource Locker

Essential Question: How can you determine the measures of central angles and inscribed angles of a circle?

Explore Investigating Central Angles and Inscribed Angles

A **chord** is a segment whose endpoints lie on a circle.

A **central angle** is an angle less than 180° whose vertex lies at the center of a circle.

An **inscribed angle** is an angle whose vertex lies on a circle and whose sides contain chords of the circle.

The diagram shows two examples of an inscribed angle and the corresponding central angle.

Chords
$\overline{AB}$ and $\overline{BD}$
Central Angle
$\angle ACD$
Inscribed Angle
$\angle ABD$

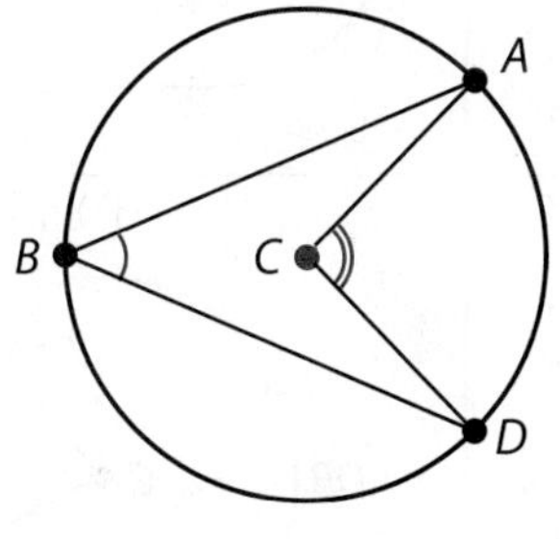

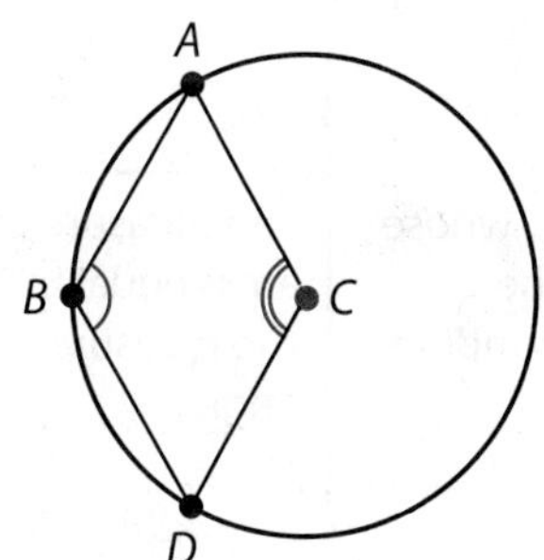

(A) Use a compass to draw a circle. Label the center C.

(B) Use a straightedge to draw an acute inscribed angle on your circle from Step A. Label the angle as $\angle DEF$.

(C) Use a straightedge to draw the corresponding central angle, $\angle DCF$.

(D) Use a protractor to measure the inscribed angle and the central angle. Record the measure of the inscribed angle, the measure of the central angle, and 360° minus the measure of the central angle. List your results in a table.

Angle Measure	Circle C	Circle 2	Circle 3	Circle 4	Circle 5	Circle 6	Circle 7
$m\angle DEF$							
$m\angle DCF$							
$360° - m\angle DCF$							

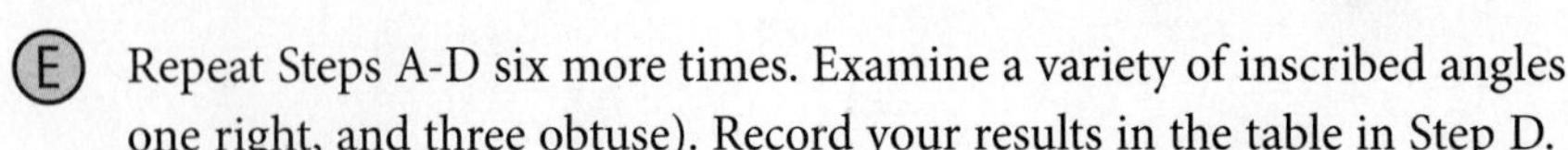

(E) Repeat Steps A-D six more times. Examine a variety of inscribed angles (two more acute, one right, and three obtuse). Record your results in the table in Step D.

Reflect

1. Examine the values in the first and second rows of the table. Is there a mathematical relationship that exists for some or all of the values? Make a conjecture that summarizes your observation.
2. Examine the values in the first and third rows of the table. Is there a mathematical relationship that exists for some or all of the values? Make a conjecture that summarizes your observation.

Explain 1 Understanding Arcs and Arc Measure

An **arc** is a continuous portion of a circle consisting of two points (called the endpoints of the arc) and all the points on the circle between them.

Arc	Measure	Figure
A **minor arc** is an arc whose points are on or in the interior of a corresponding central angle.	The measure of a minor arc is equal to the measure of the central angle. $m\overset{\frown}{AB} = m\angle ACB$	
A **major arc** is an arc whose points are on or in the exterior of a corresponding central angle.	The measure of a major arc is equal to 360° minus the measure of the central angle. $m\overset{\frown}{ADB} = 360° - m\angle ACB$	
A **semicircle** is an arc whose endpoints are the endpoints of a diameter.	The measure of a semicircle is 180°.	

Adjacent arcs are arcs of the same circle that intersect in exactly one point. $\overset{\frown}{DE}$ and $\overset{\frown}{EF}$ are adjacent arcs.

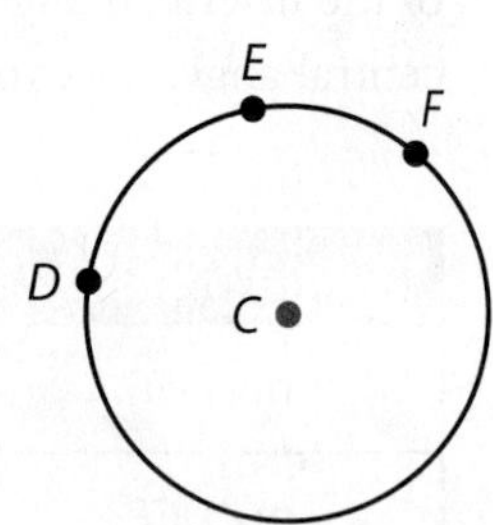

Arc Addition Postulate

The measure of an arc formed by two adjacent arcs is the sum of the measures of the two arcs.

$m\widehat{ADB} = m\widehat{AD} + m\widehat{DB}$

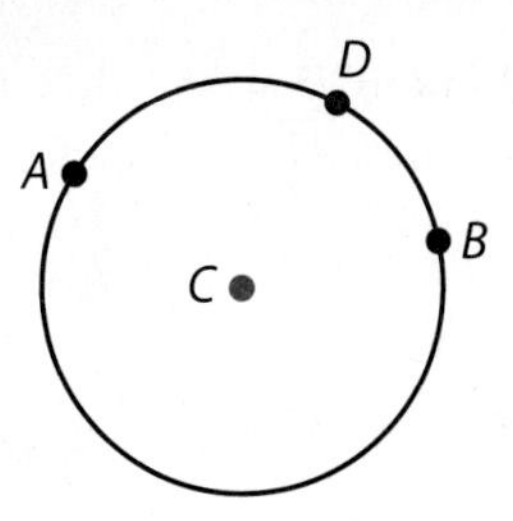

Example 1

Ⓐ If $m\angle BCD = 18°$ and $m\widehat{EF} = 33°$, determine $m\widehat{ABD}$ using the appropriate theorems and postulates. $\overleftrightarrow{AF}$ and $\overleftrightarrow{BE}$ intersect at Point C.

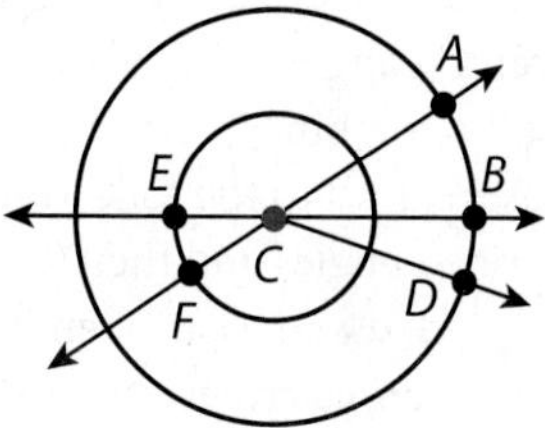

If $m\widehat{EF} = 33°$, then $m\angle ECF = 33°$. If $m\angle ECF = 33°$, then $m\angle ACB = 33°$ by the Vertical Angles Theorem. If $m\angle ACB = 33°$ and $m\angle BCD = 18°$, then $m\widehat{AB} = 33°$ and $m\widehat{BD} = 18°$. By the Arc Addition Postulate, $m\widehat{ABD} = m\widehat{AB} + m\widehat{BD}$, and so $m\widehat{ABD} = 51°$.

Ⓑ If $m\widehat{JK} = 27°$, determine $m\widehat{NP}$ using the appropriate theorems and postulates. $\overleftrightarrow{MK}$ and $\overleftrightarrow{NJ}$ intersect at Point C.

If $m\widehat{JK} = 27°$, then $m\angle JCK = 27°$. If $m\angle JCK = 27°$, then

$m\angle$ MCN $= 27°$ by the Vertical Angles Theorem.

If $m\angle MCN = 27°$ and $m\angle MCP =$ 90 °, then $m\widehat{MN} = 27°$

and $m\widehat{MNP} =$ 90 °. By the Arc Addition Postulate,

$m\widehat{MNP} = m\widehat{MN} + m\widehat{NP}$, and so $m\widehat{NP} = m$ $\widehat{MNP}$ $- m\widehat{MN} =$ 63 °

Reflect

3. The minute hand of a clock sweeps out an arc as time moves forward. From 3:10 p.m. to 3:30 p.m., what is the measure of this arc? Explain your reasoning.

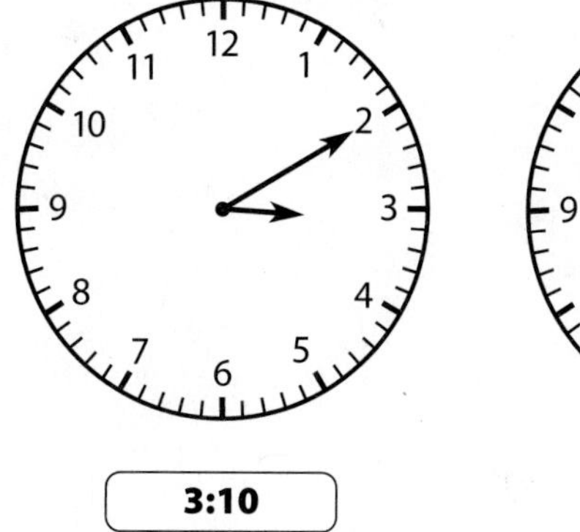

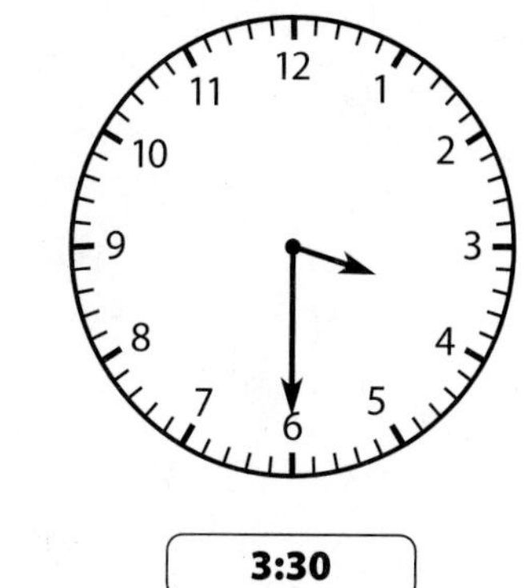

Your Turn

4. If $m\widehat{EF} = 45°$ and $m\angle ACD = 56°$, determine $m\widehat{BD}$ using the appropriate theorems and postulates. $\overleftrightarrow{AE}$, $\overleftrightarrow{BF}$, and $\overleftrightarrow{DC}$ intersect at Point C.

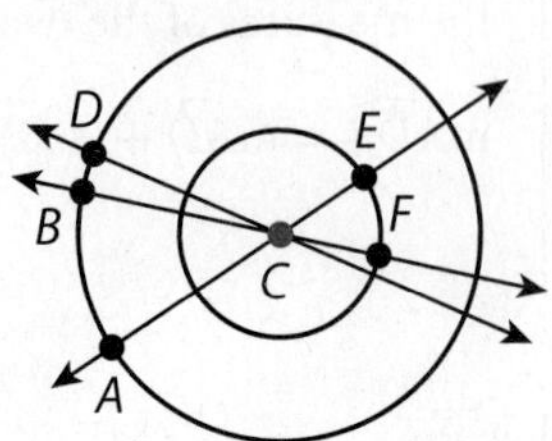

Explain 2 Using the Inscribed Angle Theorem

In the Explore you looked at the relationship between central angles and inscribed angles. Those results, combined with the definitions of arc measure, lead to the following theorem about inscribed angles and their *intercepted arcs*. An **intercepted arc** consists of endpoints that lie on the sides of an inscribed angle and all the points of the circle between them.

Inscribed Angle Theorem

The measure of an inscribed angle is equal to half the measure of its intercepted arc.

$m\angle ADB = \frac{1}{2} m\widehat{AB}$

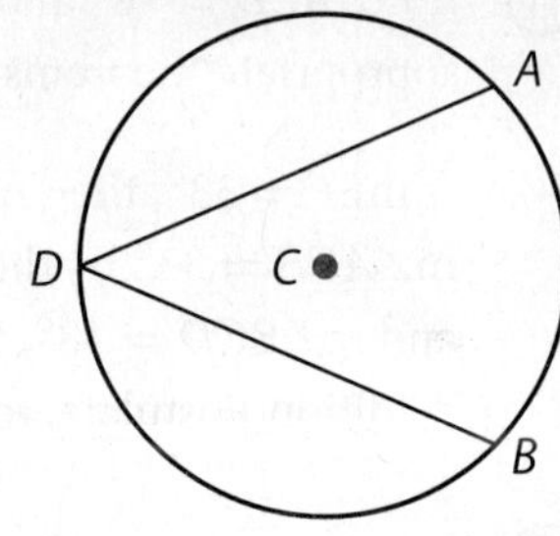

Example 2 Use the Inscribed Angle Theorem to find inscribed angle measures.

(A) Determine $m\widehat{DE}$, $m\widehat{BD}$, $m\angle DAB$, and $m\angle ADE$ using the appropriate theorems and postulates.

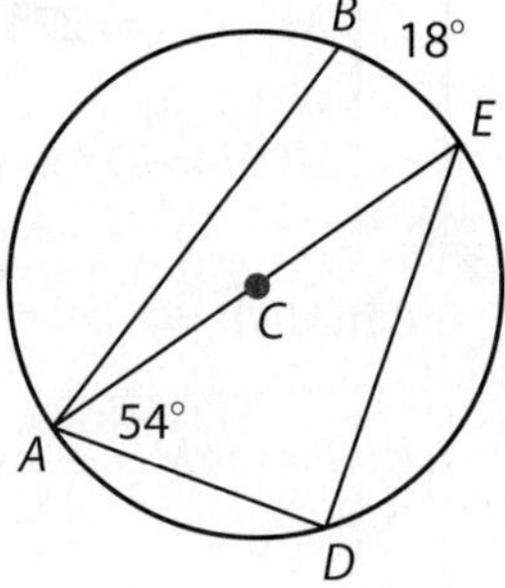

By the Inscribed Angle Theorem, $m\angle DAE = \frac{1}{2}m\widehat{DE}$, and so $m\widehat{DE} = 2 \times 54° = 108°$. By the Arc Addition Postulate, $m\widehat{BD} = m\widehat{BE} + m\widehat{ED} = 18° + 108° = 126°$. By the Inscribed Angle Theorem, $m\angle DAB = \frac{1}{2}m\widehat{BD} = \frac{1}{2} \times 126° = 63°$. Note that $\widehat{ABE}$ is a semicircle, and so $m\widehat{ABE} = 180°$. By the Inscribed Angle Theorem, $m\angle ADE = \frac{1}{2}m\widehat{ABE} = \frac{1}{2} \times 180° = 90°$.

Ⓑ Determine m$\widehat{WX}$, m$\widehat{XZ}$, m$\angle XWZ$, and m$\angle WXZ$ using the appropriate theorems and postulates.

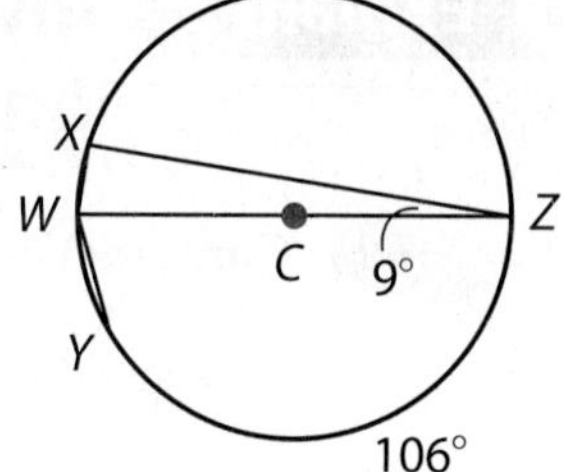

By the Inscribed Angle Theorem, m$\angle WZX = \frac{1}{2}$ m$\widehat{WX}$,

and so m$\widehat{WX} = 2 \times 9° = 18°$. Note that $\widehat{WXZ}$ is a semicircle and,

therefore, m$\widehat{WXZ} = 180°$. By the Arc Addition Postulate,

m$\widehat{WXZ}$ = m$\widehat{WX}$ + m$\widehat{XZ}$ and then m$\widehat{XZ} = 180° - 18° = 162°$

By the Inscribed Angle Theorem, m$\angle XWZ = \frac{1}{2}$m$\widehat{XZ} = \frac{1}{2} \times 162° = 81°$.

Note that $\widehat{WYZ}$ is a semicircle, and so m$\widehat{WYZ} = 180°$. By the Inscribed Angle Theorem, m$\angle WXZ = \frac{1}{2}$m $\widehat{WYZ} = \frac{1}{2} \times 180° = 90°$.

Reflect

5. Discussion Explain an alternative method for determining m$\angle \widehat{XZ}$ in Example 2B.

6. Justify Reasoning How does the measure of $\angle ABD$ compare to the measure of $\angle ACD$? Explain your reasoning.

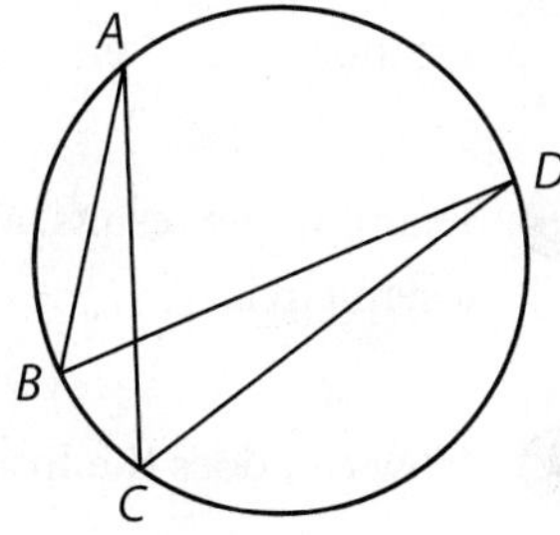

Your Turn

7. If m$\angle EDF = 15°$, determine m$\angle ABE$ using the appropriate theorems and postulates.

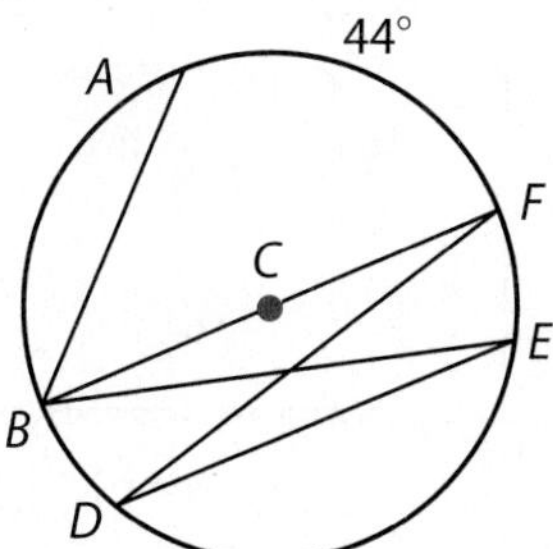

Explain 3 Investigating Inscribed Angles on Diameters

Example 3 **Construct and analyze an angle inscribed in a semicircle.**

You can examine angles that are inscribed in a semicircle.

(A) Use a compass to draw a circle with center *C*. Use a straightedge to draw a diameter of the circle. Label the diameter $\overline{DF}$.

(B) Use a straightedge to draw an inscribed angle ∠*DEF* on your circle from Step A whose sides contain the endpoints of the diameter.

(C) Use a protractor to determine the measure of ∠*DEF* (to the nearest degree). Copy the table and record the results in the table.

Angle Measure	Circle C	Circle 2	Circle 3	Circle 4
m∠*DEF*				

(D) Repeat the process three more times. Make sure to vary the size of the circle, and the location of the vertex of the inscribed angle. Record the results in the table in Part C.

(E) Examine the results, and make a conjecture about the measure of an angle inscribed in a semicircle.

(F) How can does the Inscribed Angle Theorem justify your conjecture?

Inscribed Angle of a Diameter Theorem

The endpoints of a diameter lie on an inscribed angle if and only if the inscribed angle is a right angle.

Reflect

8. A right angle is inscribed in a circle. If the endpoints of its intercepted arc are connected by a segment, must the segment pass through the center of the circle?

Elaborate

9. An equilateral triangle is inscribed in a circle. How does the relationship between the measures of the inscribed angles and intercepted arcs help determine the measure of each angle of the triangle?

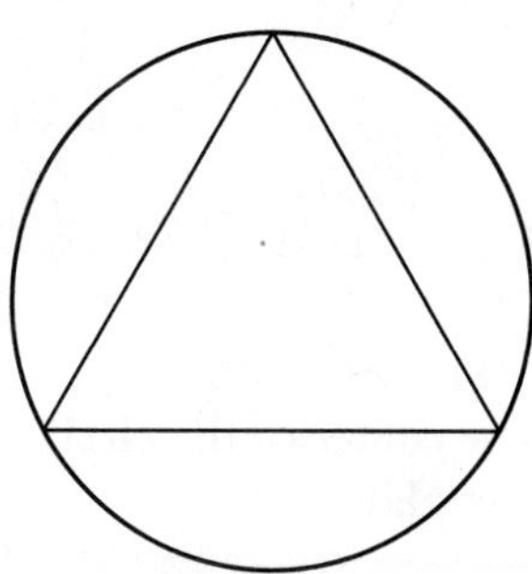

10. **Essential Question Check-In** What is the relationship between inscribed angles and central angles in a circle?

- Online Homework
- Hints and Help
- Extra Practice

Evaluate: Homework and Practice

Identify the chord(s), inscribed angle(s), and central angle(s) in the figure. The center of the circles in Exercises 1, 2, and 4 is *C*.

1.

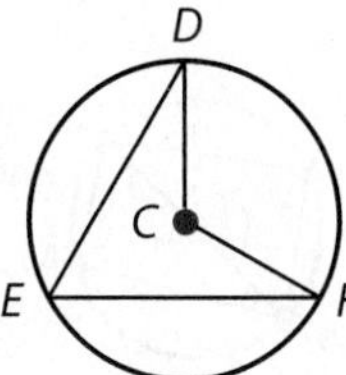

2.

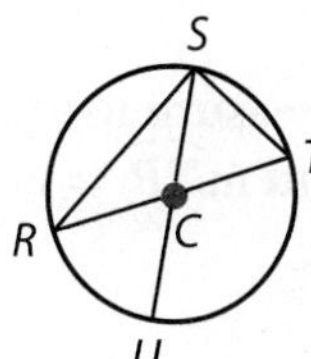

3.

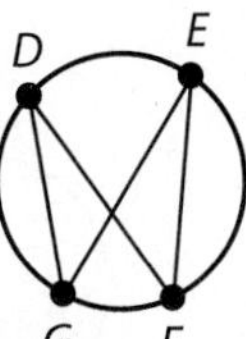

4.

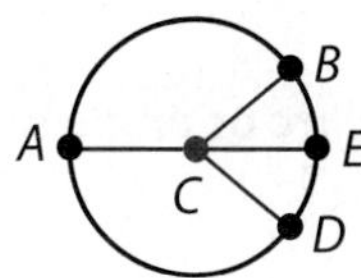

In circle C, $m\widehat{DE} = 84°$. Find each measure.

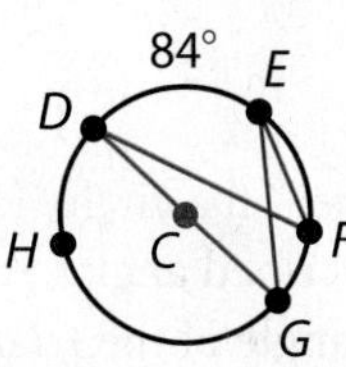

5. $m\angle DGE$

6. $m\angle EFD$

The center of the circle is A. Find each measure using the appropriate theorems and postulates.

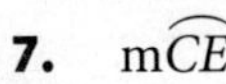

7. $m\widehat{CE}$

8. $m\widehat{DF}$

9. $m\widehat{BEC}$

Find each measure using the appropriate theorems and postulates. $m\widehat{AC} = 116°$

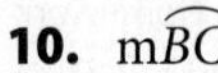

10. $m\widehat{BC}$

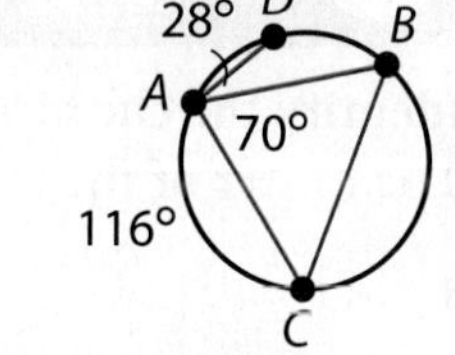

11. $m\widehat{AD}$

The center of the circle is C. Find each measure using the appropriate theorems and postulates. $m\widehat{LM} = 70°$ and $m\widehat{NP} = 60°$.

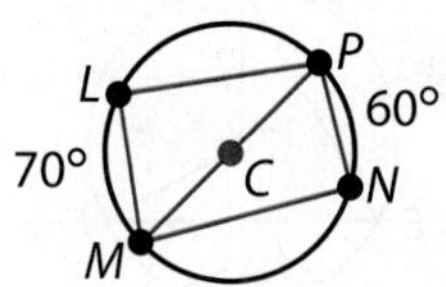

12. $m\angle MNP$

13. $m\angle LMN$

The center of the circle is O. Find each arc or angle measure using the appropriate theorems and postulates.

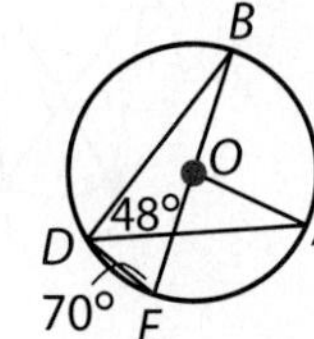

14. $m\angle BDE$

15. $m\widehat{ABD}$

16. $m\widehat{ED}$

17. $m\angle DBE$

Represent Real-World Problems **The circle graph shows how a typical household spends money on energy. Use the graph to find the measure of each arc.**

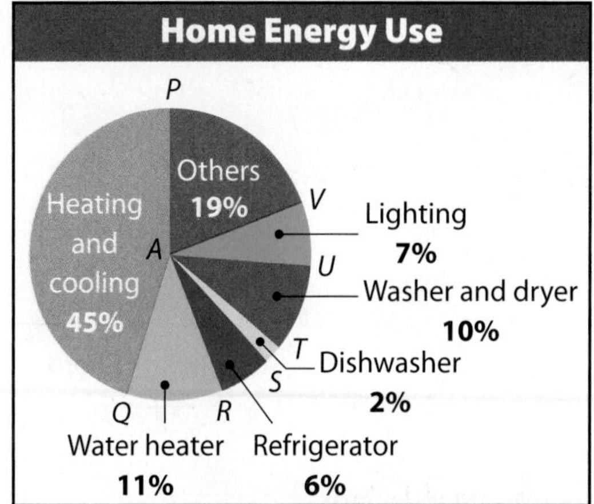

18. m$\widehat{PQ}$

19. m$\widehat{UPT}$

20. Communicate Mathematical Ideas A carpenter's square is a tool that is used to draw right angles. Suppose you are building a toy car and you have four small circles of wood that will serve as the wheels. You need to drill a hole in the center of each wheel for the axle. Explain how you can use the carpenter's square to find the center of each wheel.

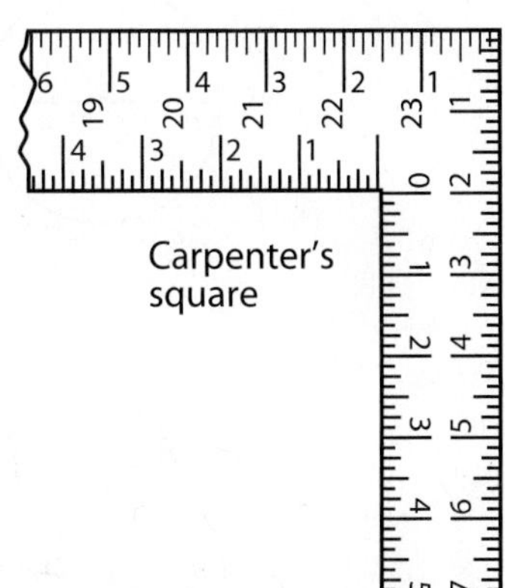

21. Choose the expressions that are equivalent to m∠*AOB*.

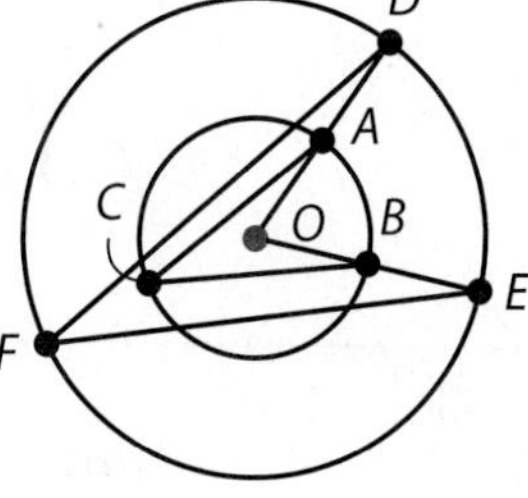

A. $\frac{1}{2}$m∠*ACB*

B. m∠*ACB*

C. 2m∠*ACB*

D. m$\widehat{AB}$

E. m∠*DOE*

F. m∠*DFE*

G. 2m∠*DFE*

H. m$\widehat{DE}$

22. Analyze Relationships Copy the diagram. Draw arrows to connect the concepts shown in the boxes. Then explain how the terms shown in the concept map are related.

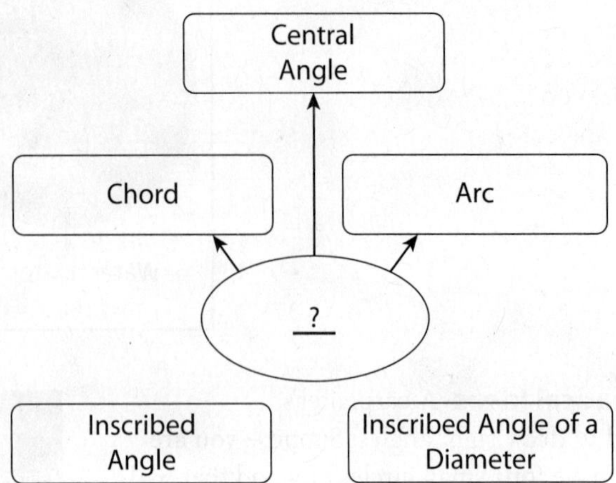

23. In circle E, the measures of $\angle DEC$, $\angle CEB$, and $\angle BEA$ are in the ratio 3:4:5. Find $m\overset{\frown}{AC}$.

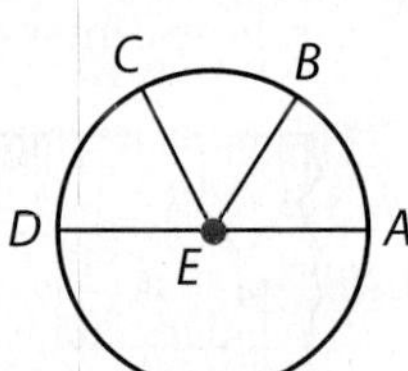

H.O.T. Focus on Higher Order Thinking

24. Explain the Error The center of the circle is G. Below is a student's work to find the value of x. Explain the error and find the correct value of x.

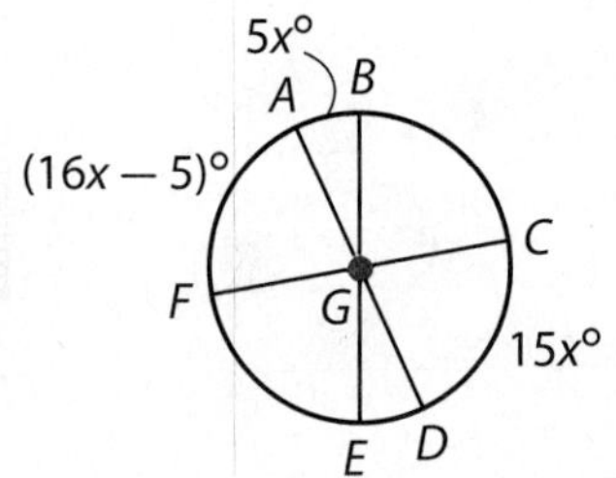

$\overline{AD}$ is a diameter, so $m\overset{\frown}{ACD} = 180°$.

Since $m\overset{\frown}{ACD} = m\overset{\frown}{AB} + m\overset{\frown}{BC} + m\overset{\frown}{CD}$, $m\overset{\frown}{AB} + m\overset{\frown}{BC} + m\overset{\frown}{CD} = 180°$.

$5x + 90 + 15x = 180$

$20x = 90$

$x = 4.5$

25. Multi-Step An inscribed angle with a diameter as a side has measure $x°$. If the ratio of $m\widehat{AD}$ to $m\widehat{DB}$ is 1:4, what is $m\widehat{DB}$?

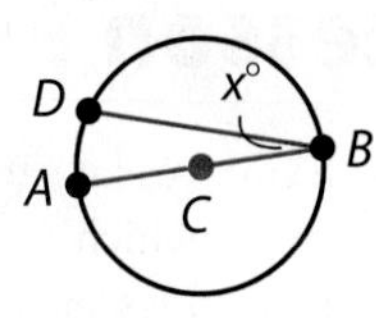

26. Justify Reasoning To prove the Inscribed Angle Theorem you need to prove three cases. In Case 1, the center of the circle is on a side of the inscribed angle. In Case 2, the center the circle is in the interior of the inscribed angle. In Case 3, the center the circle is in the exterior of the inscribed angle.

a. Complete the proof for Case 1 to show that $m\angle DAB = \frac{1}{2}\ m\widehat{DB}$.

Given: $\angle DAB$ is inscribed in circle C.

Prove: $m\angle DAB = \frac{1}{2} m\widehat{DB}$

Proof: Let $m\angle A = x°$. Draw $\overline{DC}$.

$\triangle ADC$ is ______ So $m\angle A = m\angle$ ______ by the Isosceles Triangle Theorem.

Then ______ $= 2x°$ by the Exterior Angle Theorem. So, $m\widehat{DB} =$ ______ by the definition of the measure of an arc of a circle.

Since $m\widehat{DB} =$ ______ and $m\widehat{DAB} =$ ______, $m\widehat{DAB} = \frac{1}{2}\widehat{DB}$.

b. Draw and label a diagram for Case 2. Then use a paragraph proof to prove that the inscribed angle is one-half the intercepted arc.

c. Draw and label a diagram for Case 3. Then use a paragraph proof to prove that the inscribed angle is one-half the intercepted arc.

Lesson Performance Task

Diana arrives late at the theater for a play. Her ticket entitles her to sit anywhere in Circle G. She had hoped to sit in Seat D, which she thought would give her the widest viewing angle of the stage. But Seat D is taken, as are all the other nearby seats in Circle G. The seating chart for the theater is shown.

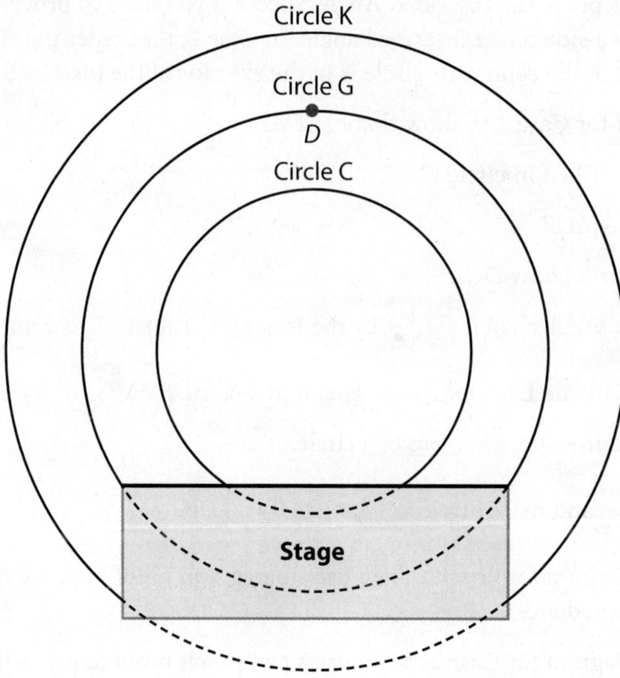

Identify two other spots where Diana can sit that will give her the same viewing angle she would have had in Seat D. Explain how you know how your points would provide the same viewing angle, and support your claim by showing the viewing angles on the drawing.

19.2 Angles in Inscribed Quadrilaterals

Essential Question: What can you conclude about the angles of a quadrilateral inscribed in a circle?

Explore Investigating Inscribed Quadrilaterals

There is a relationship among the angles of a quadrilateral that is inscribed in a circle. You can use a protractor and compass to explore the angle measures of a quadrilateral inscribed in a circle.

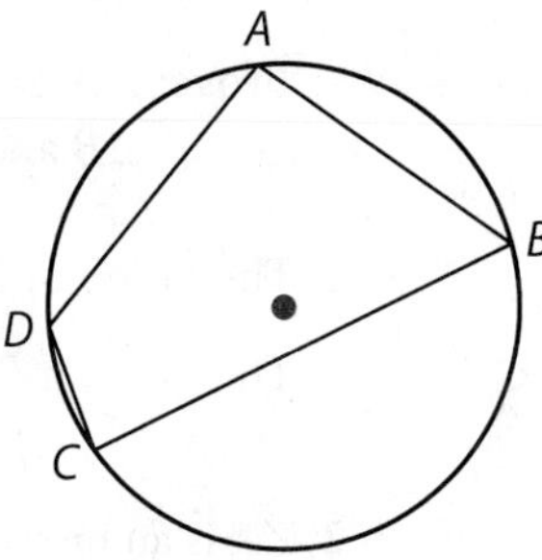

(A) Measure the four angles of quadrilateral *ABCD* and record their values to the nearest degree.

(B) Find the sums of the indicated angles.

$m\angle DAB + m\angle ABC =$ ___ ° $m\angle ABC + m\angle BCD =$ ___ °

$m\angle DAB + m\angle BCD =$ ___ ° $m\angle ABC + m\angle CDA =$ ___ °

$m\angle DAB + m\angle CDA =$ ___ ° $m\angle BCD + m\angle CDA =$ ___ °

(C) Use a compass to draw a circle with a diameter greater than the circle in Step A. Plot points *E*, *F*, *G*, and *H* consecutively around the circumference of the circle so that the center of the circle is not inside quadrilateral *EFGH*. Use a straightedge to connect each pair of consecutive points to draw quadrilateral *EFGH*.

(D) Measure the four angles of *EFGH* to the nearest degree and record their values.

(E) Find the sums of the indicated angles.

$m\angle HEF + m\angle EFG =$ ___ ° $m\angle EFG + m\angle FGH =$ ___ °

$m\angle HEF + m\angle FGH =$ ___ ° $m\angle EFG + m\angle GHE =$ ___ °

$m\angle HEF + m\angle GHE =$ ___ ° $m\angle FGH + m\angle GHE =$ ___ °

Reflect

1. **Discussion** Compare your work with that of other students. What conclusions can you make about the angles of a quadrilateral inscribed in a circle?

2. Based on your observations, does it matter if the center of the circle is inside or outside the inscribed quadrilateral for the relationship between the angles to hold? Explain.

Explain 1 Proving the Inscribed Quadrilateral Theorem

The result from the Explore can be formalized in the Inscribed Quadrilateral Theorem.

Inscribed Quadrilateral Theorem
If a quadrilateral is inscribed in a circle, then its opposite angles are supplementary.

Example 1 **Prove the Inscribed Quadrilateral Theorem.**

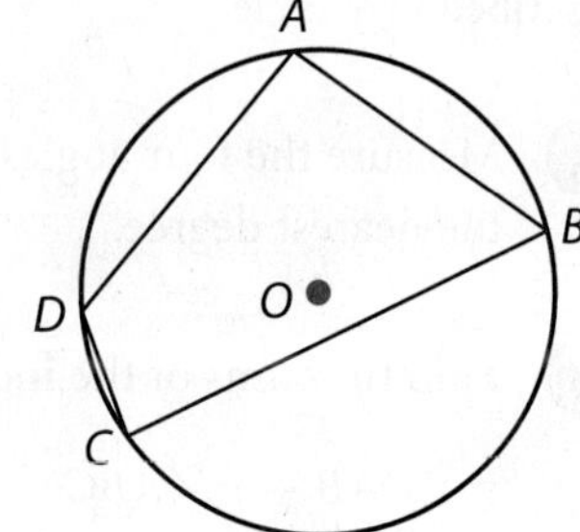

Given: Quadrilateral $ABCD$ is inscribed in circle O.

Prove: $\angle A$ and $\angle C$ are supplementary.
$\angle B$ and $\angle D$ are supplementary.

Step 1 The union of $\widehat{BCD}$ and $\widehat{DAB}$ is circle O.

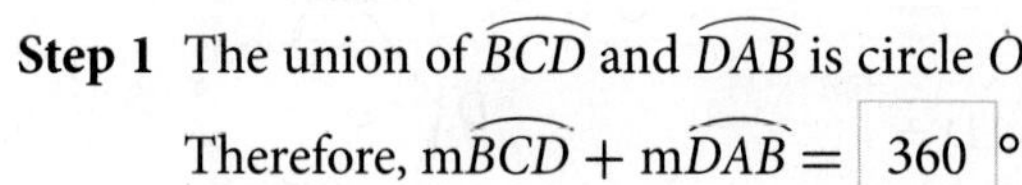

Therefore, $m\widehat{BCD} + m\widehat{DAB} =$ 360 °

Step 2 $\angle A$ is an inscribed angle and its intercepted arc is $\widehat{BCD}$.

$\angle$ C is an inscribed angle and its intercepted arc is $\widehat{DAB}$.

By the Inscribed Angle Theorem, $m\angle A = \frac{1}{2}\, m\widehat{BCD}$ and

$m\angle C = \frac{1}{2}\, m\widehat{DAB}$.

Step 3 So, $m\angle A + m\angle C = \frac{1}{2}m\widehat{BCD} + \frac{1}{2}m\widehat{DAB}$ Substitution Property of Equality

$= \frac{1}{2}\left(m\widehat{BCD} + m\widehat{DAB}\right)$ Distributive Property

$= \frac{1}{2}(360°)$ Substitution Property of Equality

$= 180°$ Simplify.

So, $\angle A$ and $\angle C$ are supplementary, by the definition of supplementary. Similar reasoning shows that $\angle B$ and $\angle D$ are also supplementary.

The converse of the Inscribed Quadrilateral Theorem is also true. That is, if the opposite angles of a quadrilateral are supplementary, it can be inscribed in a circle. Taken together, these statements can be stated as the following biconditional statement. A quadrilateral can be inscribed in a circle *if and only if* its opposite angles are supplementary.

Reflect

3. What must be true about a parallelogram that is inscribed in a circle? Explain.
4. Quadrilateral $PQRS$ is inscribed in a circle and $m\angle P = 57°$. Is it possible to find the measure of some or all of the other angles? Explain.

Explain 2 Applying the Inscribed Quadrilateral Theorem

Example 2 **Find the angle measures of each inscribed quadrilateral.**

(A) $PQRS$

$(y^2 + 53)°$ Q, R $(15y + 17)°$, P $(5y + 3)°$, S

Find the value of y.

$m\angle P + m\angle R = 180°$	$PQRS$ is inscribed in a circle.
$(5y + 3) + (15y + 17) = 180$	Substitute.
$20y + 20 = 180$	Simplify.
$y = 8$	Solve for y.

Find the measure of each angle.

$m\angle P = 5(8) + 3 = 43°$	Substitute the value of y into each angle expression and evaluate.
$m\angle R = 15(8) + 17 = 137°$	
$m\angle Q = 8^2 + 53 = 117°$	
$m\angle S + m\angle Q = 180°$	Definition of supplementary
$m\angle S + 117° = 180°$	Substitute.
$m\angle S = 63°$	Subtract 117 from both sides.

So, $m\angle P = 43°$, $m\angle R = 137°$, $m\angle Q = 117°$, and $m\angle S = 63°$.

(B) $JKLM$

$(39 + 7x)°$ J, $\left[\frac{20x}{3}\right]°$ K, M, L, $(6x - 15)°$

Find the value of x.

$m\angle J + m\angle$ L = 180 °	$JKLM$ is inscribed in a circle.
$(39 + 7x) + (6x - 15) = 180$	Substitute.
$13x + 24 = 180$	Simplify.
$13x = 156$	Subtract 24 from both sides.
$x = 12$	Divide both sides by 13.

Find the measure of each angle.

$m\angle J = 39 + 7\left(\boxed{12}\right) = \boxed{123}°$ Substitute the value of x into each angle expression and evaluate.

$m\angle L = 6\left(\boxed{12}\right) - 15 = \boxed{57}°$

$m\angle K = \dfrac{20\left(\boxed{12}\right)}{3} = \boxed{80}°$

$m\angle M + m\angle \boxed{K} = \boxed{180}°$ Definition of supplementary

$m\angle M + \boxed{80}° = \boxed{180}°$ Substitute.

$m\angle M = \boxed{100}°$ Subtract 80 from both sides.

So, $m\angle J = \boxed{123}°$, $m\angle L = \boxed{57}°$, $m\angle K = \boxed{80}°$, and $m\angle M = \boxed{100}°$.

Your Turn

5. Find the measure of each angle of inscribed quadrilateral *TUVW*.

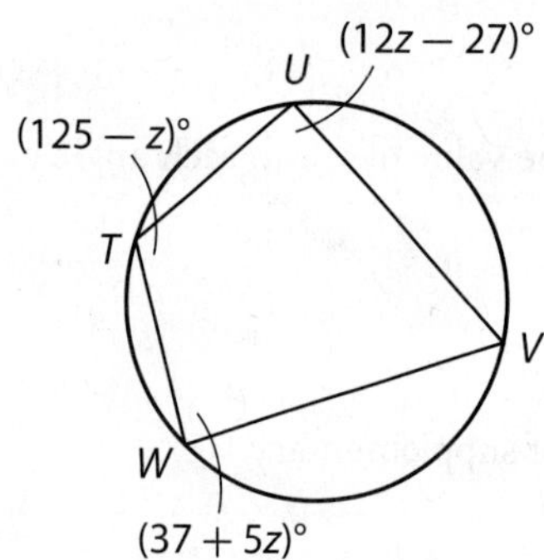

Explain 3 Constructing an Inscribed Square

Many designs are based on a square inscribed in a circle. Follow the steps to construct rectangle *ACBD* inscribed in a circle. Then show *ACBD* is a square.

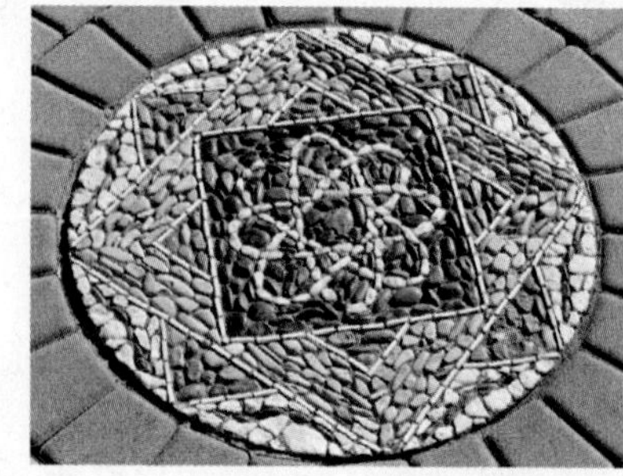

Example 3 **Construct an inscribed square.**

Step 1 Use your compass to draw a circle. Mark the center, *O*. Draw diameter $\overline{AB}$ using a straightedge.

Step 2 Use your compass to construct the perpendicular bisector of $\overline{AB}$. Label the points where the bisector intersects the circle as C and D. See Step 1 answer.

Step 3 Use your straightedge to draw $\overline{AC}$, $\overline{CB}$, $\overline{BD}$, and $\overline{DA}$. See Step 1 answer.

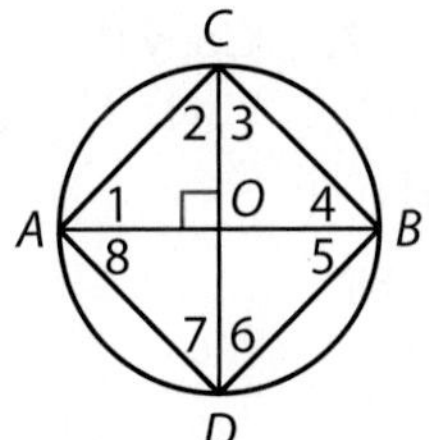

Step 4 To show that $ACBD$ is a square, you need to show that it has 4 congruent sides and 4 right angles.

Step 5 Complete the two-column proof to prove that $ACBD$ has four congruent sides.

Statements	Reasons
$\overline{OA} \cong \overline{OC} \cong \overline{OB} \cong \overline{OD}$	Radii of the circle O
$m\angle AOC = m\angle COB = m\angle BOD = m\angle DOA = 90°$	$\overline{CD}$ is the perpendicular bisector of $\overline{AB}$.
$\triangle AOC \cong \triangle COB \cong \triangle BOD \cong \triangle DOA$	SAS
$\overline{AC} \cong \overline{CB} \cong \overline{BD} \cong \overline{DA}$	CPCTC

Use the diagram to complete the paragraph proof in Steps 6 and 7 that $ACBD$ has four right angles.

Step 6 Since $\triangle AOC \cong \triangle COB$, then $\angle 1 \cong \angle 3$ by CPCTC. By reasoning similar to that in the previous proof, it can be shown that $\triangle BOC \cong \triangle COB$. Therefore, by the Transitive Property of Congruence, $\triangle AOC \cong \triangle BOC$, and $\angle 1 \cong \angle 4$ by CPCTC. Also by the Transitive Property of Congruence, $\angle 3 \cong \angle 4$. Similar arguments show that $\angle 1 \cong \angle 2$, $\angle 5 \cong \angle 6$, and $\angle 7 \cong \angle 8$.

Step 7 The sum of all the angle measures in a triangle is 180°, so $m\angle 1 + m\angle 2 + m\angle AOC = 180°$. Since $m\angle AOC = 90°$, $m\angle 1 + m\angle 2 + 90° = 180°$. This means that $m\angle 1 + m\angle 2 = 90°$. Since $m\angle 1 = m\angle 2$, it can be concluded that $m\angle 1 = m\angle 2 = 45°$. By similar reasoning, it is shown that the measure of each of the congruent numbered angles is 45°. Therefore, the measure of each of the four angles of quadrilateral $ACBD$ is the sum of the measures of two of the adjacent numbered angles, which is 90°.

Reflect

6. How could reflections be used to construct an inscribed square?

Your Turn

7. Copy the quilt block pattern. Finish the pattern by inscribing a square in the circle. Shade in your square.

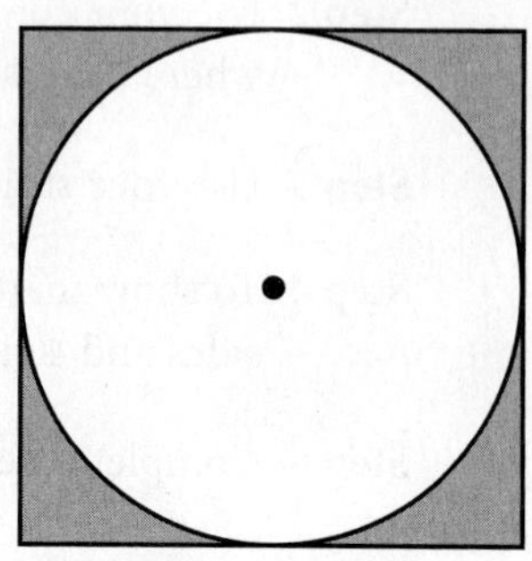

Elaborate

8. **Critique Reasoning** Marcus said he thought some information was missing from one of his homework problems because it was impossible to answer the question based on the given information. The question and his work are shown. Critique Marcus's work and reasoning.

Homework Problem

Find the measures of the angles of quadrialatral *ABCD*, which can be inscribed in a circle.

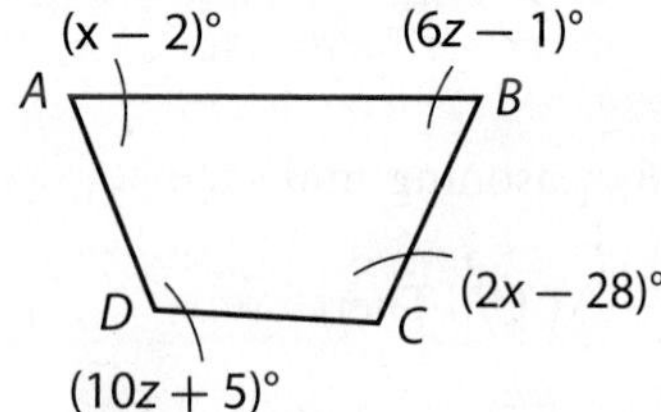

Marcus's Work

$x - 2 + 6z - 1 + 2x - 28 + 10z + 5 = 360$

$3x + 16z - 26 = 360$

$3x + 16z = 386$

Cannot solve for two different variables!

9. What must be true about a rhombus that is inscribed in a circle? Explain.

10. **Essential Question Check-In** Can all types of quadrilaterals be inscribed in a circle? Explain.

Evaluate: Homework and Practice

- Online Homework
- Hints and Help
- Extra Practice

You use geometry software to inscribe quadrilaterals *ABCD* and *GHIJ* in a circle as shown in the figures. You then measure the angle at each vertex.

Use the figure for Exercises 1–2.

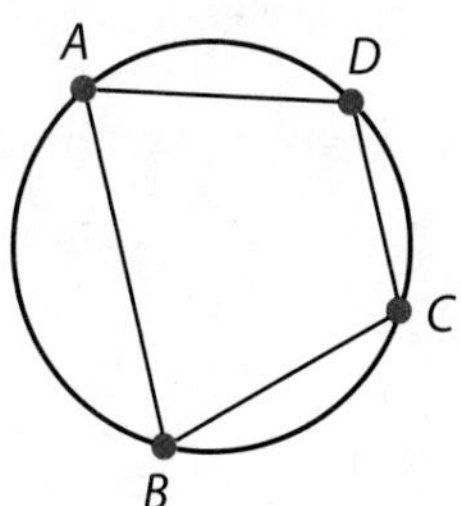

Use the figure for Exercises 3–4.

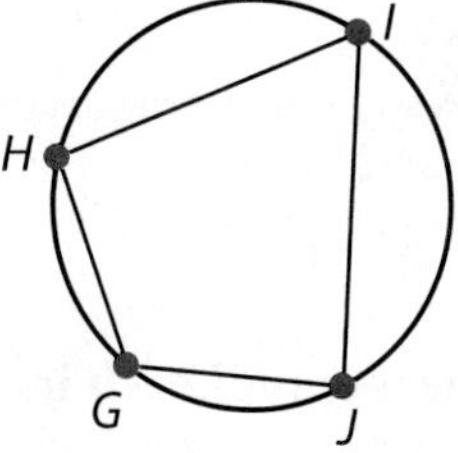

1. Suppose you drag the vertices of $\angle A$ and $\angle C$ to new positions on the circle and then measure $\angle A$ and $\angle C$ again. Does the relationship between $\angle A$ and $\angle C$ change? Explain.

2. Suppose you know that $m\angle B$ is 74°. Is $m\angle D = 74°$? Explain.

3. Suppose $m\angle HIJ = 65°$ and that $m\angle H = m\angle J$. Can you find the measures of all the angles? Explain.

4. **Justify Reasoning** You have found that $m\angle H = m\angle J$, but then you drag the vertex of $\angle H$ so that $m\angle H$ changes. Is the statement $m\angle H = m\angle J$ still true? Justify your reasoning.

Use the figure for Exercices 5–6. Find each measure using the appropriate theorems and postulates.

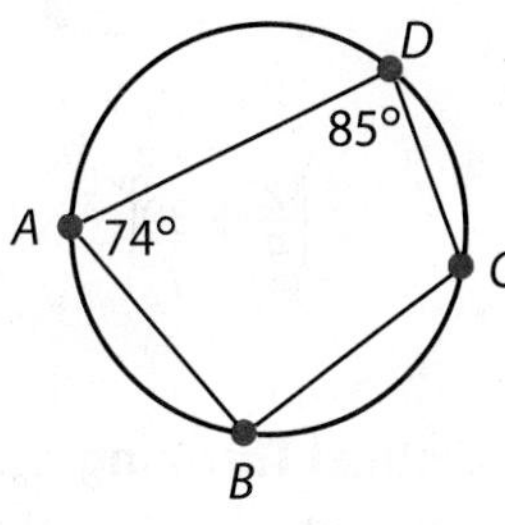

5. $m\angle B$

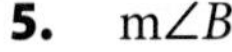

6. $m\overset{\frown}{DAB}$

7. *GHIJ* is a quadrilateral. If $m\angle HIJ + m\angle HGJ = 180°$ and $m\angle H + m\angle J = 180°$, could the points *G, H, I,* and *J* points of a circle? Explain.

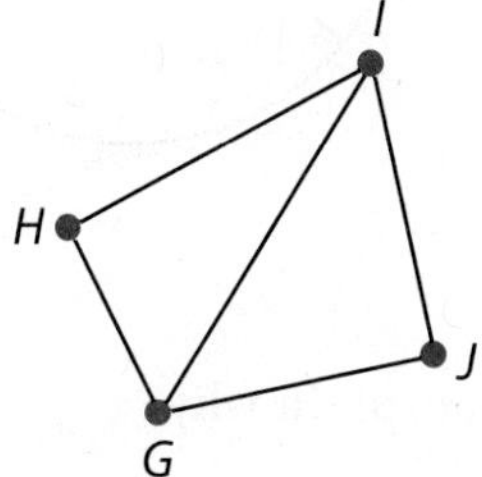

8. *LMNP* is a quadrilateral inscribed in a circle. If $m\angle L = m\angle N$, is $\overline{MP}$ a diameter of the circle? Explain.

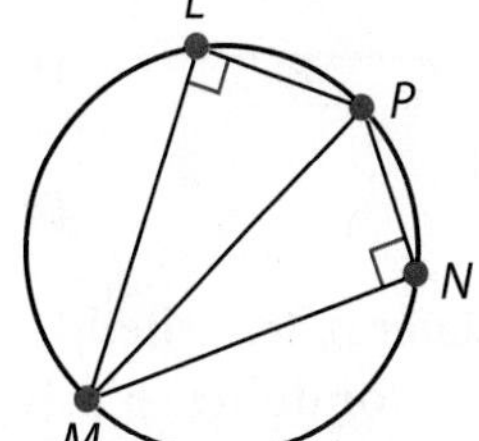

9. Rafael was asked to construct a square inscribed in a circle. He drew a circle and a diameter of the circle. Describe how to complete his construction. Then, copy the circle and complete the construction.

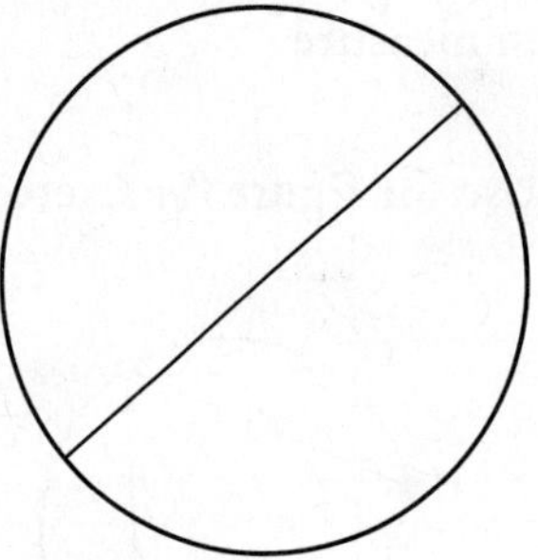

Multi-Step **Find the angle measures of each inscribed quadrilateral.**

10.

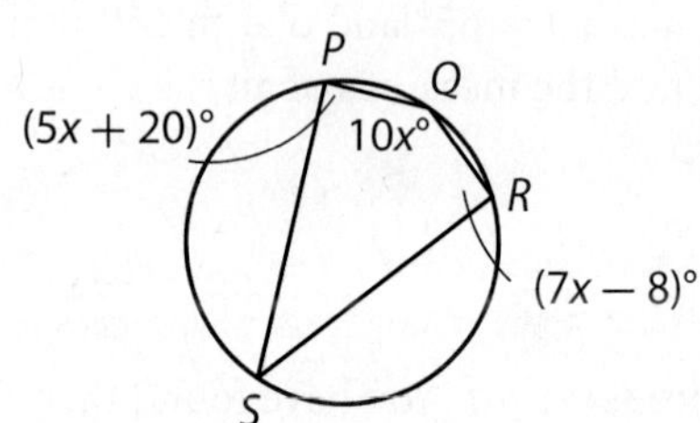

11.

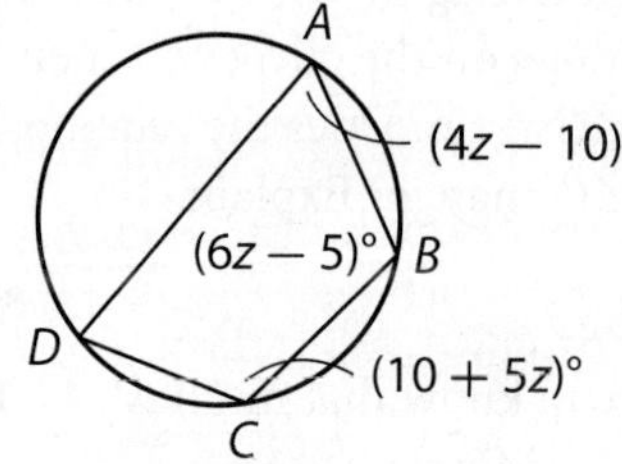

12.

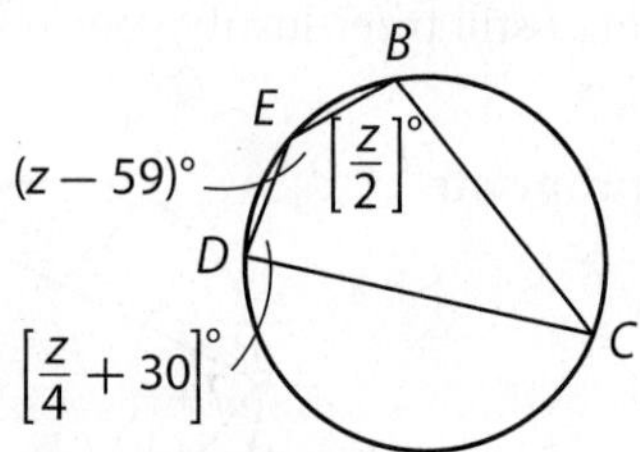

13.

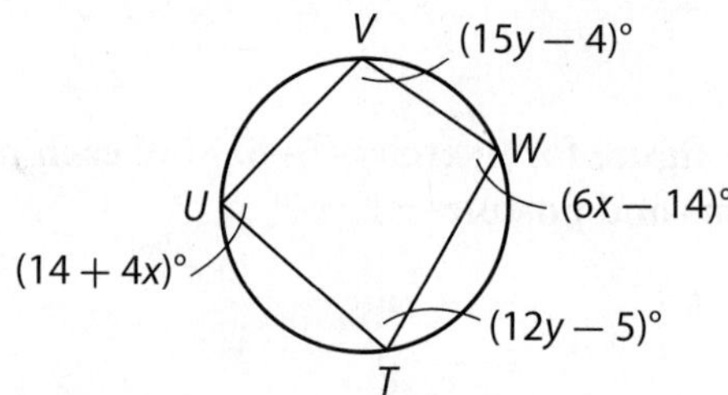

14. Critical Thinking Haruki is designing a fountain that consists of a square pool inscribed in a circular base represented by circle O. He wants to construct the square so that one of its vertices is point X. Copy the figure. Then construct the square and explain your method.

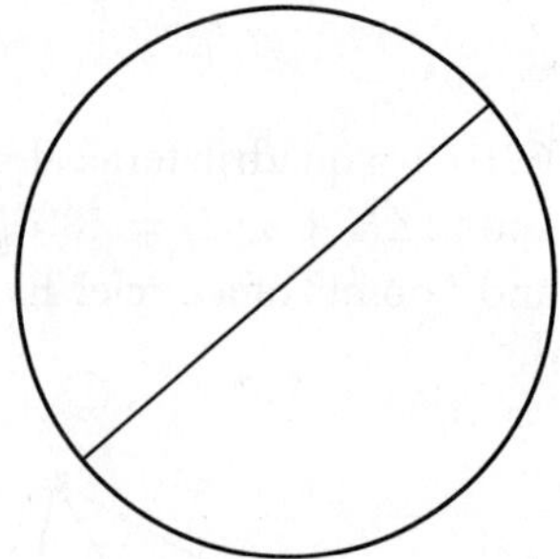

For each quadrilateral, tell whether it can be inscribed in a circle. If so, describe a method for doing so using a compass and straightedge. If not, explain why not.

15. a parallelogram that is not a rectangle

16. a kite with two right angles

17. Represent Real-World Problems Lisa has not yet learned how to stop on ice skates, so she just skates straight across the circular rink until she reaches a wall. If she starts at P, turns 75° at Q, and turns 100° at R, find how many degrees she must turn at S to go back to her starting point.

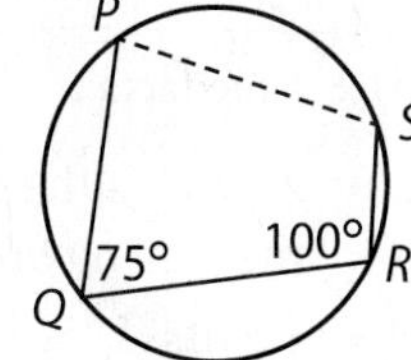

18. In the diagram, C is the center of the circle and $\angle YXZ$ is inscribed in the circle. Classify each statement as true, false, or cannot be determined.

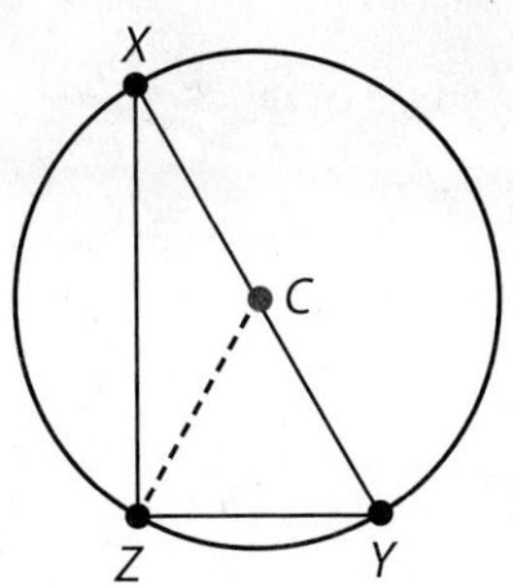

a. $\overline{CX} \cong \overline{CY}$

b. $\overline{CZ} \cong \overline{XY}$

c. $\triangle CXZ$ is isosceles.

d. $\triangle CYZ$ is equilateral.

e. $\overline{XY}$ is a diameter of circle C.

H.O.T. Focus on Higher Order Thinking

19. Multi-Step In the diagram, $m\widehat{JKL} = 198°$ and $m\widehat{KLM} = 216°$. Find the measures of the angles of quadrilateral $JKLM$.

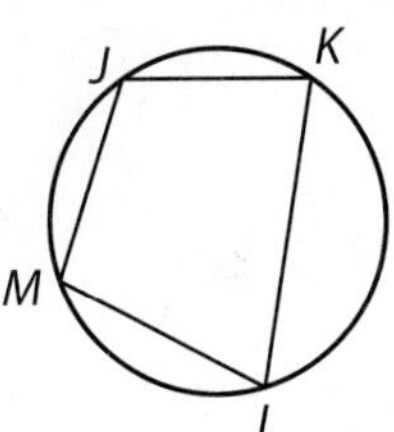

20. Critical Thinking Explain how you can construct a regular octagon inscribed in a circle.

21. Represent Real-World Problems A patio tile design is constructed from a square inscribed in a circle. The circle has radius $5\sqrt{2}$ feet.

a. Find the area of the square.

b. Find the area of the shaded region outside the square.

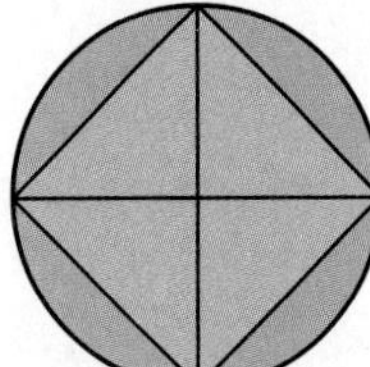

Lesson Performance Task

Here are some facts about the baseball field shown here:

- *ABCD* is the baseball "diamond," a square measuring 90 feet on a side.
- Points *A, B, E, H* are collinear.
- The distance from third base (Point *B*) to the left field fence (Point *E*) equals the distance from first base (point *D*) to the right field fence (Point *G*).

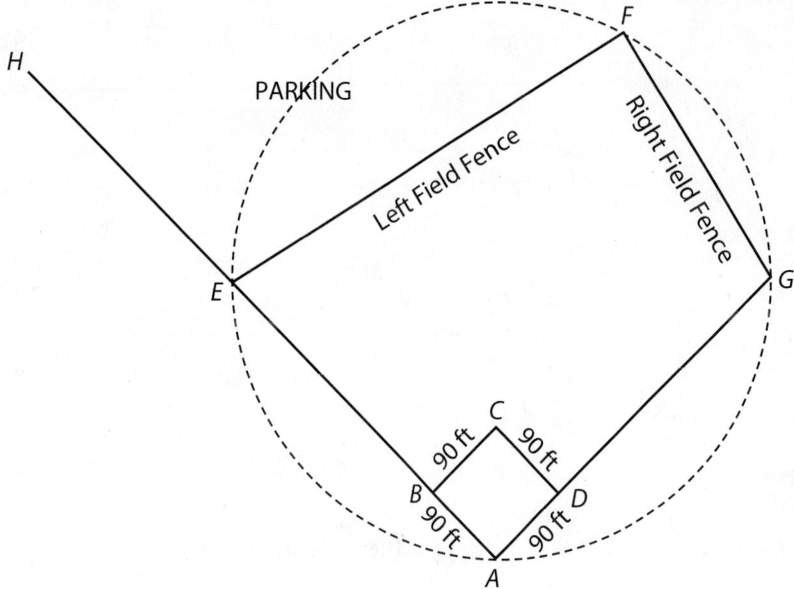

a. Is $\overset{\frown}{EA}$ congruent to $\overset{\frown}{AG}$? Explain why or why not.

b. Find m∠*F*. Explain your reasoning.

c. Identify an angle congruent to ∠*HEF*. Explain your reasoning.

19.3 Tangents and Circumscribed Angles

Essential Question: What are the key theorems about tangents to a circle?

Explore Investigating the Tangent-Radius Theorem

A **tangent** is a line in the same plane as a circle that intersects the circle in exactly one point. The point where a tangent and a circle intersect is the **point of tangency**.

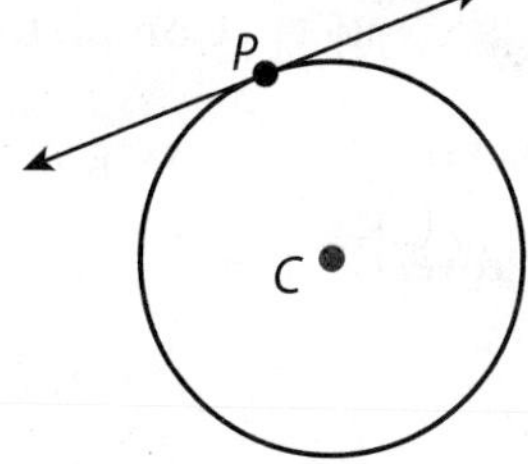

In the figure, the line is tangent to circle *C*, and point *P* is the point of tangency. You can use a compass and straightedge to construct a circle and a line tangent to it.

(A) Use a compass to draw a circle. Label the center *C*.

(B) Mark a point *P* on the circle. Using a straightedge, draw a tangent to the circle through point *P*. Mark a point *Q* at a different position on the tangent line.

(C) Use a straightedge to draw the radius $\overline{CP}$.

(D) Use a protractor to measure $\angle CPQ$. Record the result. Repeat the process two more times. Make sure to vary the size of the circle and the location of the point of tangency.

Reflect

1. **Make a Conjecture** Examine your results. Make a conjecture about the relationship between a tangent line and the radius to the point of tangency.

2. **Discussion** Describe any possible inaccuracies related to the tools you used in this Explore.

Explain 1 Proving the Tangent-Radius Theorem

The Explore illustrates the Tangent-Radius Theorem.

Tangent-Radius Theorem

If a line is tangent to a circle, then it is perpendicular to a radius drawn to the point of tangency.

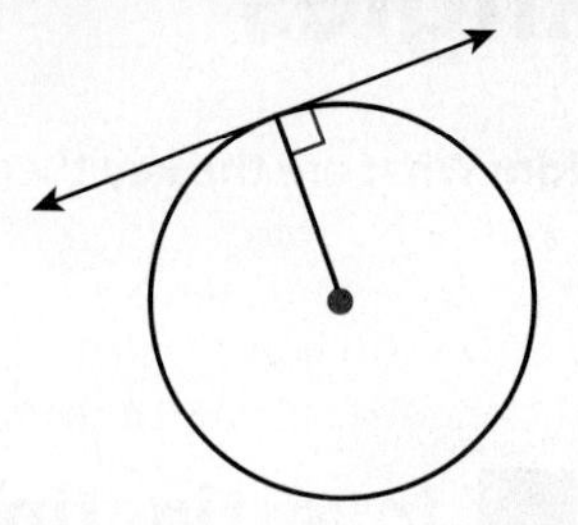

Example 1 **Complete the proof of the Tangent–Radius Theorem.**

Given: Line m is tangent to circle C at point P.

Prove: $\overline{CP} \perp m$

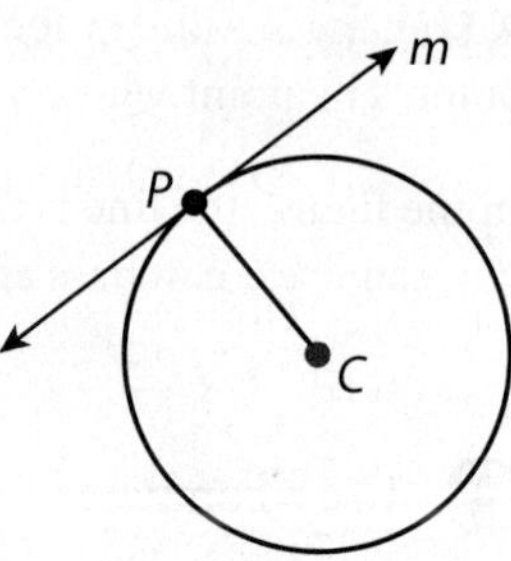

(A) Use an indirect proof. Assume that $\overline{CP}$ is not perpendicular to line m. There must be a point Q on line m such that $\overline{CQ} \perp m$.

If $\overline{CQ} \perp m$, then $\triangle CQP$ is a right triangle, and $CP > CQ$ because $\overline{CP}$ is the hypotenuse of the right triangle.

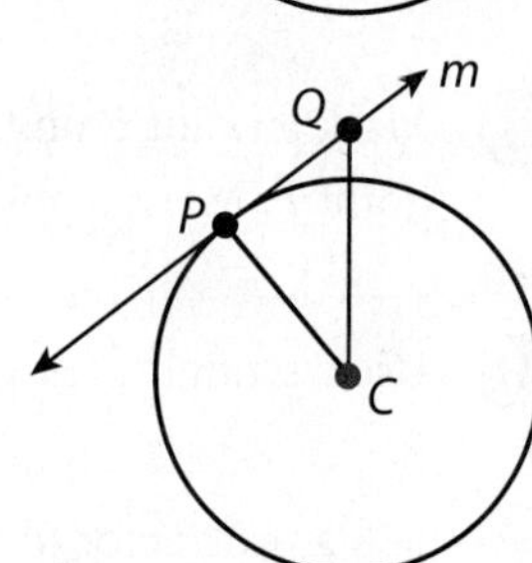

(B) Since line m is a tangent line, it can intersect circle C at only point P, and all other points of line m are in the exterior of the circle.

(C) This means point Q is in the exterior of the circle. You can conclude that $CP < CQ$ because $\overline{CP}$ is a radius of circle C.

(D) This contradicts the initial assumption that a point Q exists such that $\overline{CQ} \perp m$, because that meant that $CP > CQ$. Therefore, the assumption is false and $\overline{CP}$ must be perpendicular to line m.

Reflect

3. Both lines in the figure are tangent to the circle, and $\overline{AB}$ is a diameter. What can you conclude about the tangent lines?

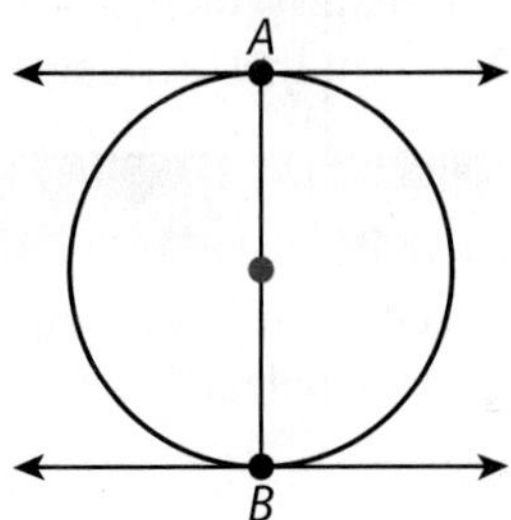

The converse of the Tangent-Radius Theorem is also true. You will be asked to prove this theorem as an exercise.

Converse of the Tangent-Radius Theorem

If a line is perpendicular to a radius of a circle at a point on the circle, then it is tangent to the circle at that point on the circle.

Explain 2 Constructing Tangents to a Circle

From a point outside a circle, two tangent lines can be drawn to the circle.

Example 2 **Use the steps to construct two tangent lines from a point outside a circle.**

(A) Use a compass to draw a circle. Label the center *C*.

(B) Mark a point *X* outside the circle and use a straightedge to draw $\overline{CX}$.

(C) Use a compass and straightedge to construct the midpoint of $\overline{CX}$ and label the midpoint *M*.

(D) Use a compass to construct a circle with center *M* and radius *CM*.

(E) Label the points of intersection of circle *C* and circle *M* as *A* and *B*.
Use a straightedge to draw $\overleftrightarrow{XA}$ and $\overleftrightarrow{XB}$. Both lines are tangent to circle *C*.

Reflect

4. How can you justify that $\overleftrightarrow{XA}$ (or $\overleftrightarrow{XB}$) is a tangent line? (Hint: Draw $\overline{CA}$ on your diagram.)

5. Draw $\overline{CA}$ and $\overline{CB}$ on your diagram. Consider quadrilateral *CAXB*. State any conclusions you can reach about the measures of the angles of quadrilateral *CAXB*.

Explain 3 Proving the Circumscribed Angle Theorem

A **circumscribed angle** is an angle formed by two rays from a common endpoint that are tangent to a circle.

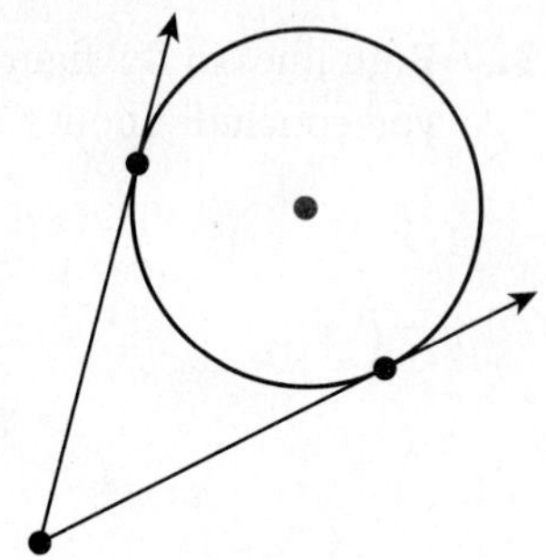

Circumscribed Angle Theorem

A circumscribed angle of a circle and its associated central angle are supplementary.

Example 3 **Prove the Circumscribed Angle Theorem.**

Given: $\angle AXB$ is a circumscribed angle of circle C.

Prove: $\angle AXB$ and $\angle ACB$ are supplementary.

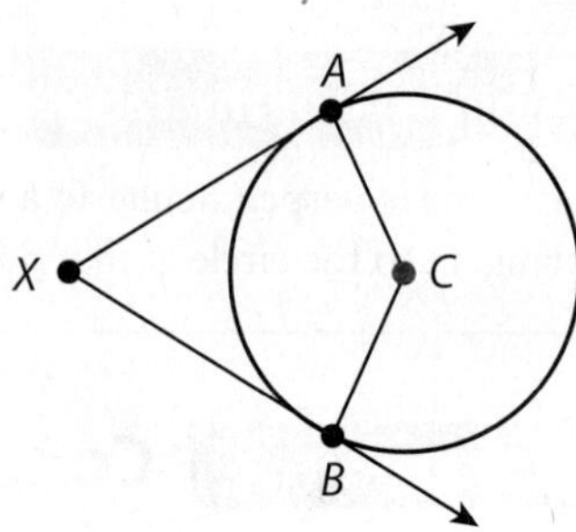

Since $\angle AXB$ is a circumscribed angle of circle C, $\overline{XA}$ and $\overline{XB}$ are tangents to the circle. Therefore, $\angle XAC$ and $\angle XBC$ are right angles by the Tangent-Radius Theorem.

In quadrilateral $XACB$, the sum of the measures of its four angles is 360°.

Since $m\angle XAC + m\angle XBC =$ 180°, this means $m\angle AXB + m\angle ACB = 360° - 180° =$ 180°.

So, $\angle AXB$ and $\angle ACB$ are supplementary by the definition of supplementary angles.

Reflect

6. Is it possible for quadrilateral $AXBC$ to be a parallelogram? If so, what type of parallelogram must it be? If not, why not?

Elaborate

7. $\overrightarrow{KM}$ and $\overrightarrow{KN}$ are tangent to circle C. Explain how to show that $\overline{KM} \cong \overline{KN}$, using congruent triangles.

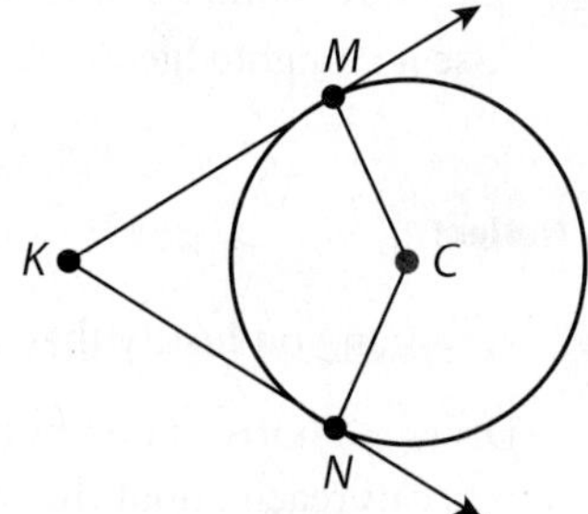

8. **Essential Question Check-In** What are the key theorems regarding tangent lines to a circle?

Evaluate: Homework and Practice

- Online Homework
- Hints and Help
- Extra Practice

Use the figure for Exercises 1–2. You use geometry software to construct a tangent to circle O at point X on the circle, as shown in the diagram.

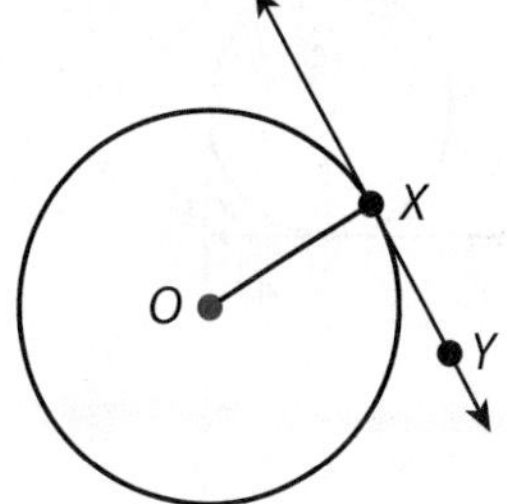

1. What do you expect to be the measure of $\angle OXY$? Explain.

2. Suppose you drag point X so that is in a different position on the circle. Does the measure of $\angle OXY$ change? Explain.

3. **Make a Conjecture** You use geometry software to construct circle A, diameters $\overline{AB}$ and $\overline{AD}$, and lines m and n which are tangent to circle A at points D and B, respectively. Make a conjecture about the relationship of the two tangents. Explain your conjecture.

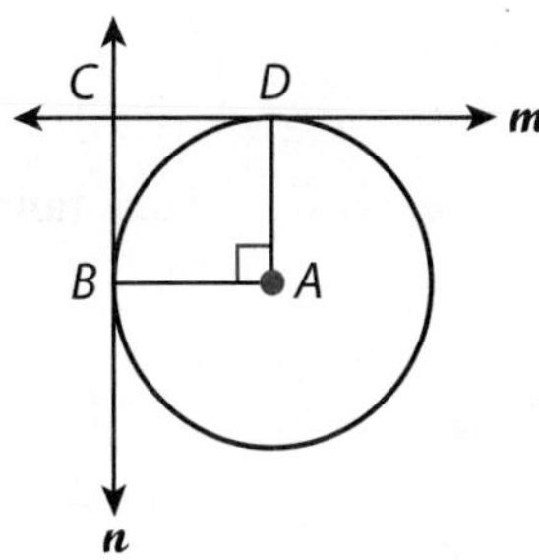

4. In the figure, $\overline{RQ}$ is tangent to circle P at point Q. What is m$\angle PRQ$? Explain your reasoning.

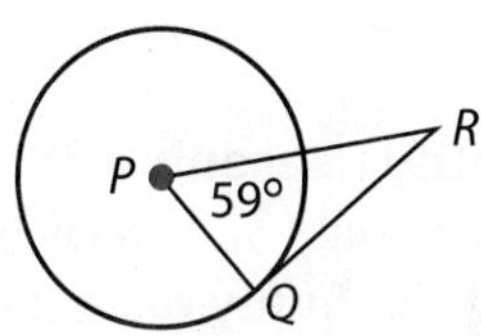

5. **Represent Real-World Problems** The International Space Station orbits Earth at an altitude of about 240 miles. In the diagram, the Space Station is at point E. The radius of Earth is approximately 3960 miles. To the nearest ten miles, what is EH, the distance from the space station to the horizon?

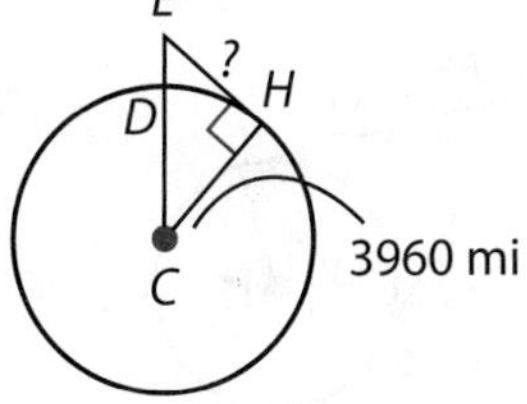

Multi-Step Find the length of each radius. Identify the point of tangency, and write the equation of the tangent line at that point.

6.

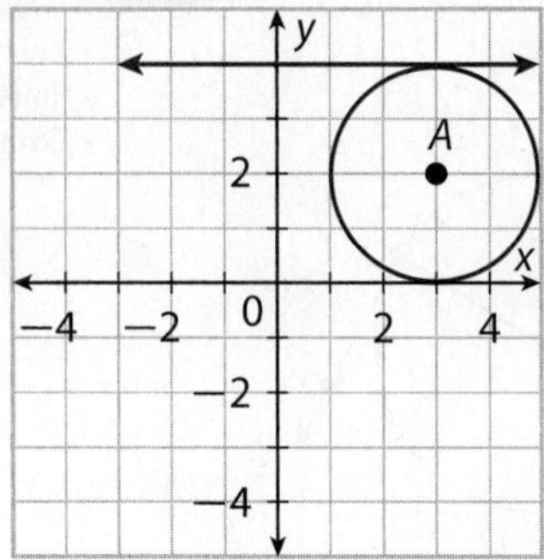

7.

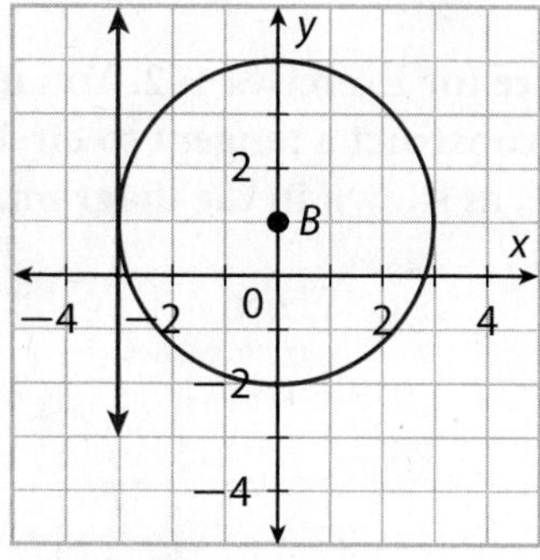

8. In the figure, $QS = 5$, $RT = 12$, and $\overleftrightarrow{RT}$ is tangent to radius $\overline{QR}$ with the point of tangency at R. Find QT.

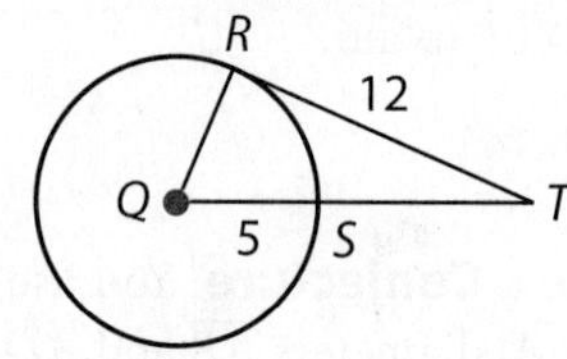

The segments in each figure are tangent to the circle at the points shown. Find each length.

9.

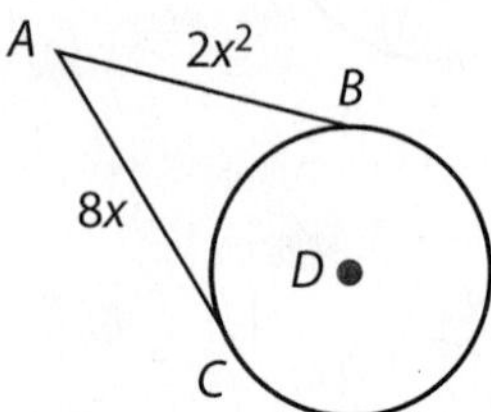

10.

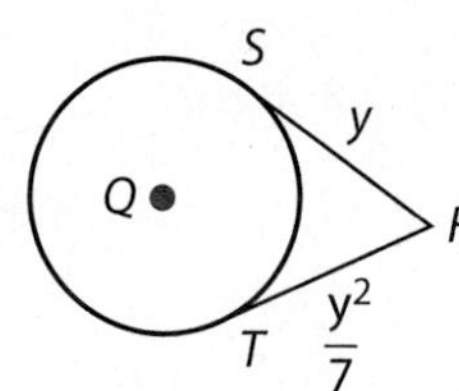

11. Justify Reasoning Suppose you construct a figure with $\overline{PR}$ tangent to circle Q at R and $\overline{PS}$ tangent to circle Q at S. Make a conjecture about $\angle P$ and $\angle Q$. Justify your reasoning.

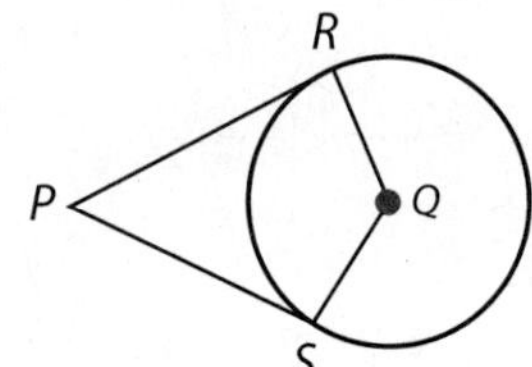

12. $\overline{PR}$ is tangent to circle Q at R and $\overline{PS}$ is tangent to circle Q at S. Find $m\angle Q$.

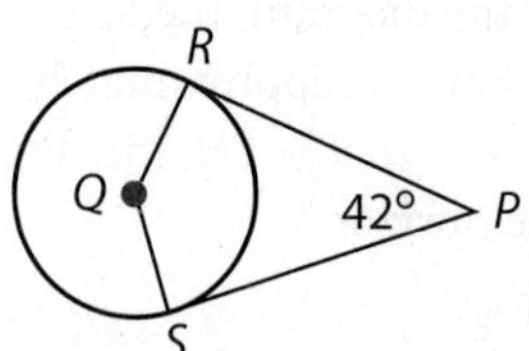

13. $\overline{PR}$ is tangent to circle Q at R and $\overline{PS}$ is tangent to circle Q at S. Find $m\angle P$.

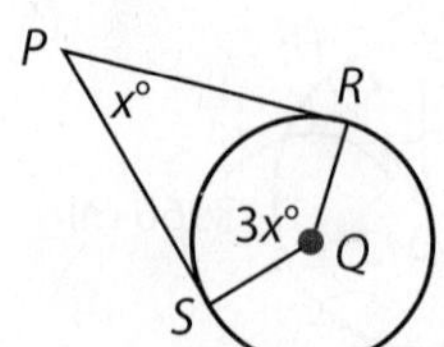

$\overline{PA}$ is tangent to circle O at A and $\overline{PB}$ is tangent to circle O at B, and $m\angle P = 56°$. Use the figure to find each measure.

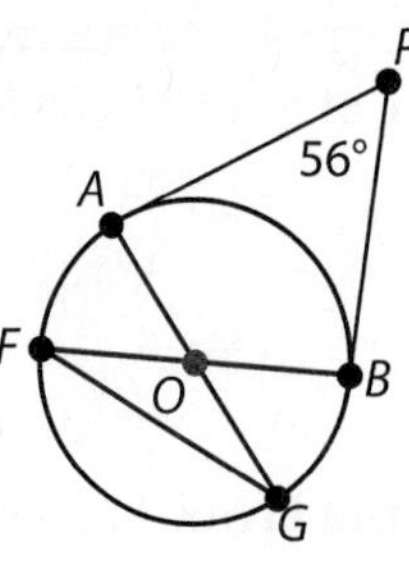

14. $m\angle AOB$

15. $m\angle OGF$

16. Which statements correctly relate $\angle BDC$ and $\angle BAC$? Determine all that apply.

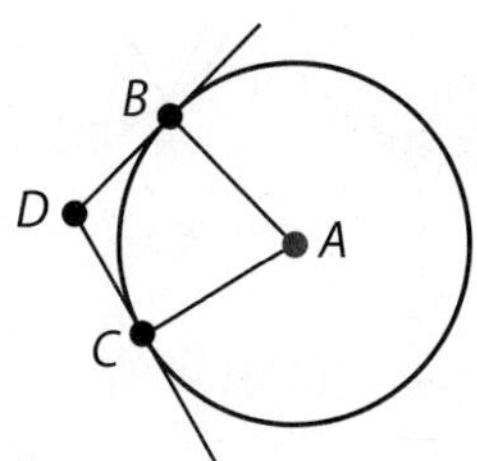

A. $\angle BDC$ and $\angle BAC$ are complementary.

B. $\angle BDC$ and $\angle BAC$ are supplementary.

C. $\angle BDC$ and $\angle BAC$ are congruent.

D. $\angle BDC$ and $\angle BAC$ are right angles.

E. The sum of the measures of $\angle BDC$ and $\angle BAC$ is 180°.

F. It is impossible to determine a relationship between $\angle BDC$ and $\angle BAC$.

17. Critical Thinking Given a circle with diameter $\overline{BC}$, is it possible to construct tangents to B and C from an external point X? If so, make a construction. If not, explain why it is not possible.

$\overrightarrow{KJ}$ is tangent to circle C at J, $\overrightarrow{KL}$ is tangent to circle C at L, and $m\overset{\frown}{ML} = 138°$.

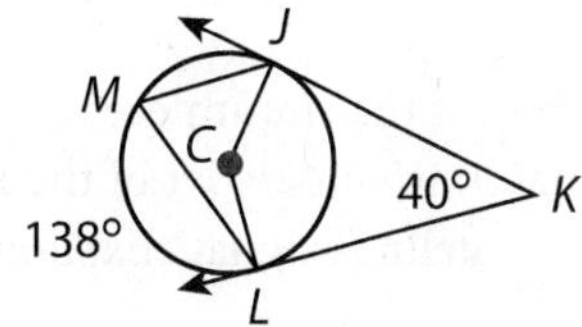

18. Find $m\angle M$.

19. Find $m\overset{\frown}{MJ}$.

H.O.T. Focus on Higher Order Thinking

20. Justify Reasoning Prove the converse of the Tangent-Radius Theorem. Given: Line m is in the plane of circle C, P is a point of circle C, and $\overline{CP} \perp m$ Prove: m is tangent to circle C at P.

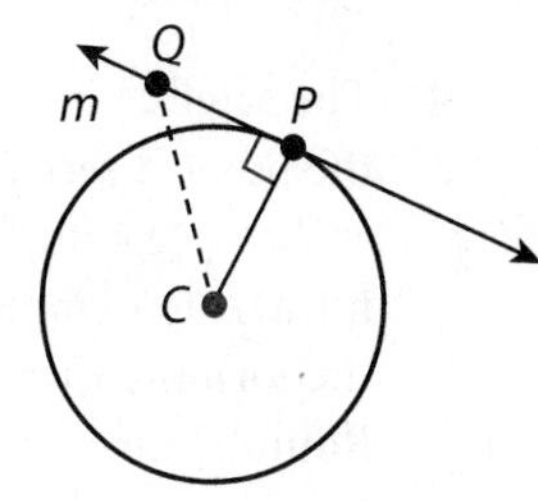

21. Draw Conclusions A grapic designer created a preliminary sketch for a company logo. In the figure, $\overleftrightarrow{BC}$ and $\overleftrightarrow{CD}$ are tangent to circle A and $BC > BA$. What type of quadrilateral is figure $ABCD$ that she created? Explain.

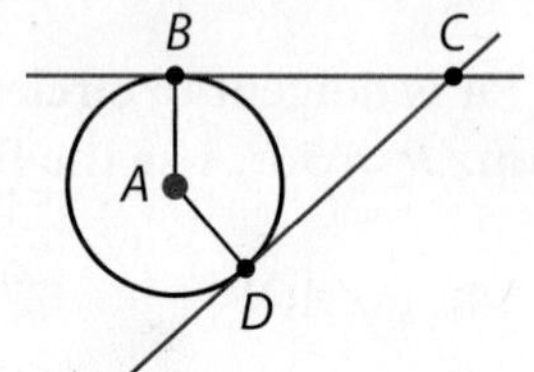

22. Explain the Error In the given figure, $\overleftrightarrow{QP}$ and $\overleftrightarrow{QR}$ are tangents. A student was asked to find m$\angle PSR$. Critique the student's work and correct any errors.

Since $\angle PQR$ is a circumscribed angle, $\angle PQR$ and $\angle PCR$ are supplementary. So m$\angle PCR = 110°$. Since $\angle PSR = \angle PQR$, m$\angle PCR = 110°$.

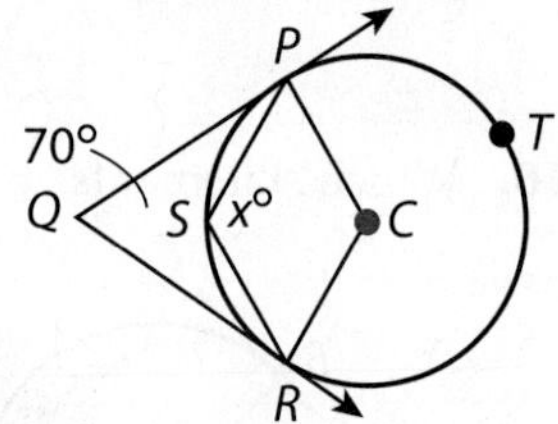

23. Copy circle O and points B and C. Construct a triangle that is circumscribed around the circle.

Lesson Performance Task

A communications satellite is in a synchronous orbit 22,000 miles above Earth's surface. Points B and D in the figure are points of tangency of the satellite signal with the Earth. They represent the greatest distance from the satellite at which the signal can be received directly. Point C is the center of the Earth.

1. Find distance AB. Round to the nearest mile. Explain your reasoning.
2. m$\angle BAC = 9°$. If the circumference of the circle represents the Earth's equator, what percent of the Earth's equator is within range of the satellite's signal? Explain your reasoning.
3. How much longer does it take a satellite signal to reach point B than it takes to reach point E? Use 186,000 mi/sec as the speed of a satellite signal. Round your answer to the nearest hundredth.
4. The satellite is in orbit above the Earth's equator. Along with the point directly below it on the Earth's surface, the satellite makes one complete revolution every 24 hours. How fast must it travel to complete a revolution in that time? You can use the formula $C = 2\pi r$ to find the circumference of the orbit. Round your answer to the nearest whole number.

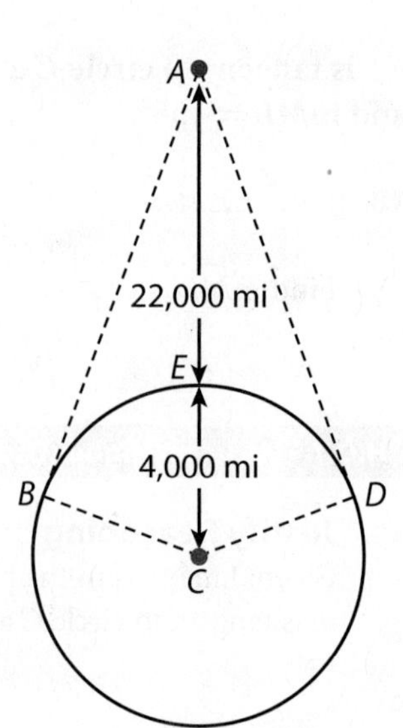

19.4 Segment Relationships in Circles

Resource Locker

Essential Question: What are the relationships between the segments in circles?

Explore — Exploring Segment Length Relationships in Circles

Any segment connecting two points on a circle is a chord. In some cases, two chords drawn inside the same circle will intersect, creating four segments. In the following activity, you will look for a pattern in how these segments are related and form a conjecture.

(A) Using geometry software or a compass and straightedge, construct circle A with two chords $\overline{CD}$ and $\overline{EF}$ that intersect inside the circle. Label the intersection point G.

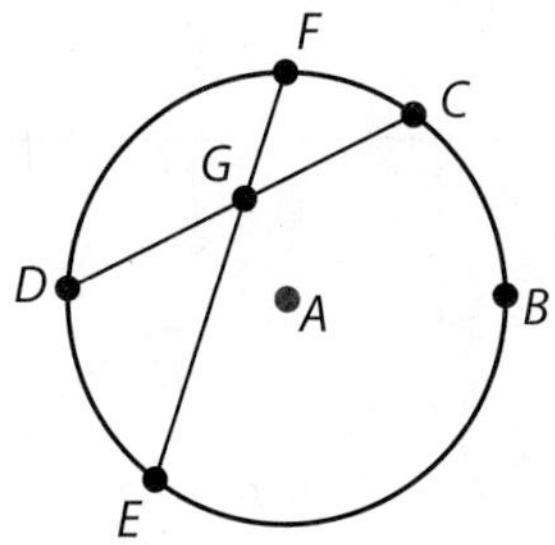

(B) Repeat your construction with two more circles. Vary the size of the circles and where you put the intersecting chords inside them.

(C) Copy the table, insert the lengths of the segments measured to the nearest millimeter, and calculate their products.

	DG	GC	EG	GF	$DG \cdot GC$	$EG \cdot GF$
Circle 1						
Circle 2						
Circle 3						

(D) Look for a pattern among the measurements and calculations of the segments. From the table, it appears that ______ will always equal ______.

Reflect

1. **Discussion** Compare your results with those of your classmates. What do you notice?
2. What conjecture can you make about the products of the segments of two chords that intersect inside a circle?

Explain 1 Applying the Chord-Chord Product Theorem

In the Explore, you discovered a pattern in the relationship between the parts of two chords that intersect inside a circle. In this Example, you will apply the following theorem to solve problems.

Chord-Chord Product Theorem

If two chords intersect inside a circle, then the products of the lengths of the segments of the chords are equal.

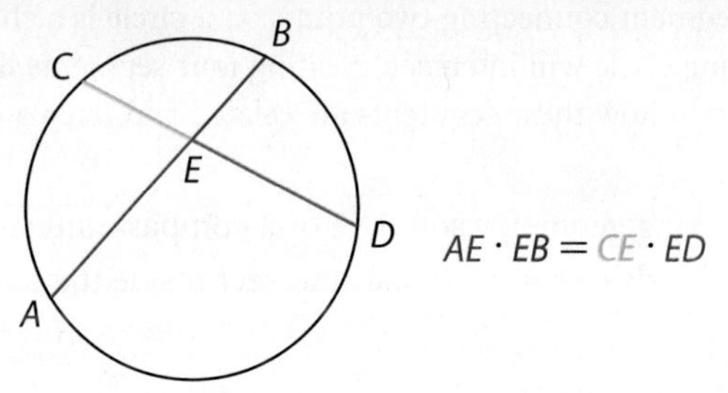

$AE \cdot EB = CE \cdot ED$

Example 1 **Find the value of x and the length of each chord.**

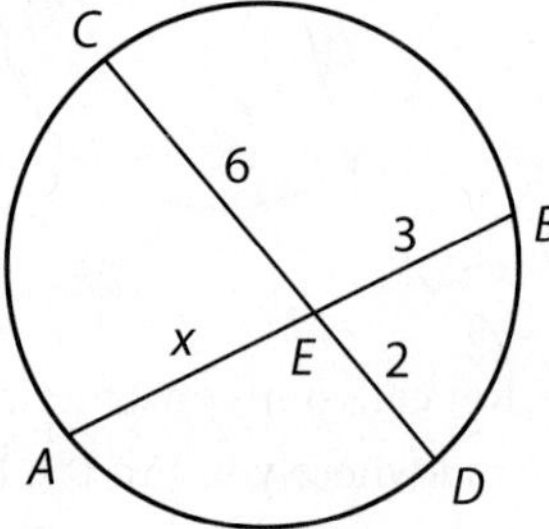

(A) Set up an equation according to the Chord-Chord Product Theorem and solve for x.

$CE \cdot ED = AE \cdot EB$

$6(2) = 3(x)$

$12 = 3x$

$4 = x$

Add the segment lengths to find the length of each chord.

$CD = CE + ED = 6 + 2 = 8$

$AB = AE + EB = 4 + 3 = 7$

(B) Set up an equation according to the Chord-Chord Product Theorem and solve for x:

$HG \cdot GJ = KG \cdot GI$

$\boxed{9}\left(\boxed{8}\right) = \boxed{6}\left(\boxed{x}\right)$

$\boxed{72} = 6x$

$\boxed{12} = x$

Add the segment lengths together to find the lengths of each chord:

$HJ = HG + GJ = \boxed{9} + 8 = \boxed{17}$

$KI = \boxed{KG} + GI = 6 + \boxed{12} = \boxed{18}$

Your Turn

3. Given $AD = 12$. Find the value of x and the length of each chord.

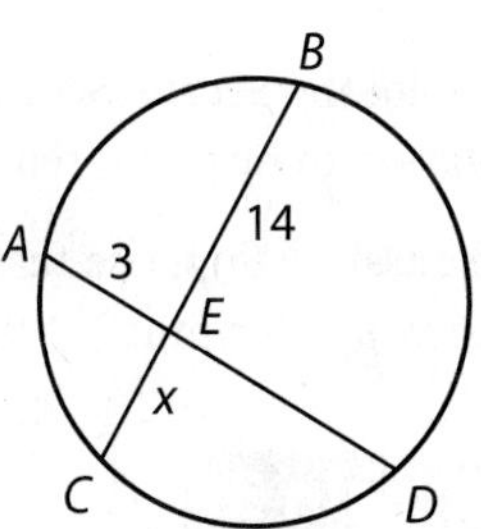

Explain 2 Proving the Secant-Secant Product Theorem

A **secant** is any line that intersects a circle at exactly two points. A **secant segment** is part of a secant line with at least one point on the circle. A secant segment that lies in the exterior of the circle with one point on the circle is called an **external secant segment**. Secant segments drawn from the same point in the exterior of a circle maintain a certain relationship that can be stated as a theorem.

Secant-Secant Product Theorem

If two secants intersect in the exterior of a circle, then the product of the lengths of one secant segment and its external segment equals the product of the lengths of the other secant segment and its external segment.

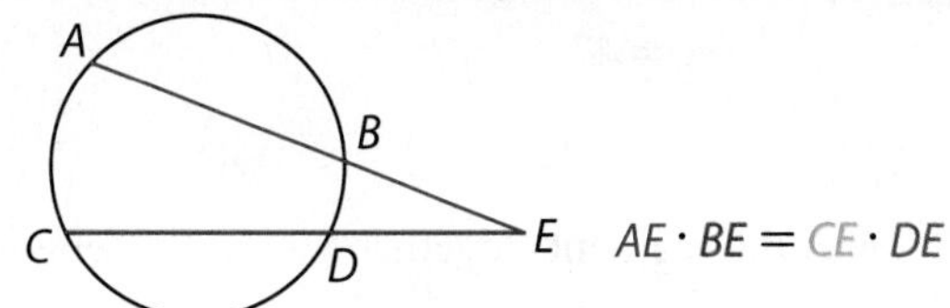

Example 2 **Use similar triangles to prove the Secant-Secant Product Theorem.**

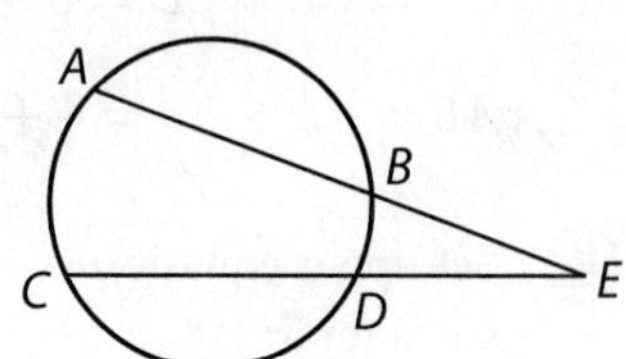

Step 1 Identify the segments in the diagram. The whole secant segments in this diagram are $\overline{AE}$ and $\overline{CE}$.
The external secant segments in this diagram are $\overline{BE}$ and $\overline{DE}$.

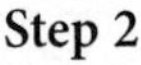

Step 2

Given the diagram as shown, prove that $AE \cdot BE = CE \cdot DE$.

Prove: $AE \cdot BE = CE \cdot DE$

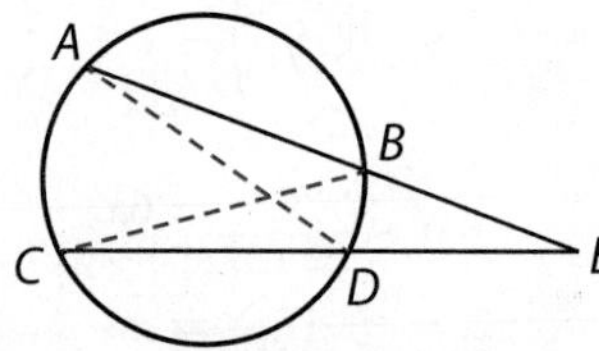

Proof: Draw auxiliary line segments $\overline{AD}$ and $\overline{CB}$. $\angle EAD$ and $\angle ECB$ both intercept $\widehat{BD}$, so $\angle$ EAD $\cong \angle$ ECB . $\angle E \cong \angle E$ by the Reflexive Property. Thus, $\triangle EAD \sim \triangle ECB$ by the AA Triangle Similarity Theorem. Therefore, corresponding sides are proportional,

so $\dfrac{AE}{CE} = \dfrac{DE}{BE}$. By the Multiplication Property of Equality,

$BE(CE) \cdot \frac{AE}{CE} = \frac{DE}{BE} \cdot BE(CE)$, and thus $AE \cdot BE = CE \cdot DE$.

Reflect

4. Rewrite the Secant-Secant Theorem in your own words. Use a diagram or shortcut notation to help you remember what it means.

5. **Discussion**: Suppose that two secants are drawn so that they intersect on the circle. Can you determine anything about the lengths of the segments formed? Explain.

Explain 3 Applying the Secant-Secant Product Theorem

You can use the Secant-Secant Product Theorem to find unknown measures of secants and secant segments by setting up an equation.

Example 3 **Find the value of x and the length of each secant segment.**

Ⓐ Set up an equation according to the Secant-Secant Product Theorem and solve for x.

$$AC \cdot AB = AE \cdot AD$$
$$(5 + x)(5) = (12)(6)$$
$$5x + 25 = 72$$
$$5x = 47$$
$$x = 9.4$$

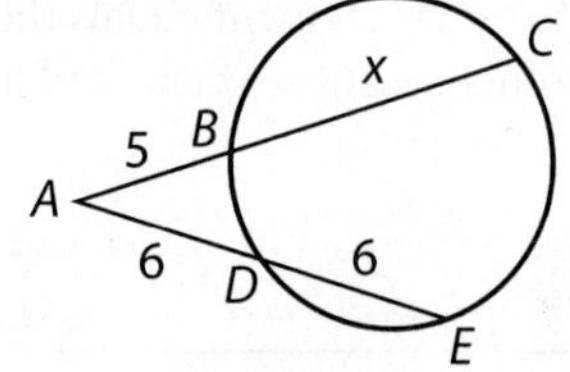

Add the segments together to find the lengths of each secant segment.

$AC = 5 + 9.4 = 14.4$; $AE = 6 + 6 = 12$

(B) Set up an equation according to the Secant-Secant Product Theorem and solve for x.

$UP \cdot TP = SP \cdot RP$

$(x + 7)(7) = (14)(6)$

$7x + 49 = 84$

$7x = 35$

$x = 5$

Add the segments together to find the lengths of each secant segment.

$UP = 7 + 5 = 12$; $SP = 8 + 6 = 14$

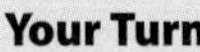

Your Turn

Find the value of x and the length of each secant segment.

6.

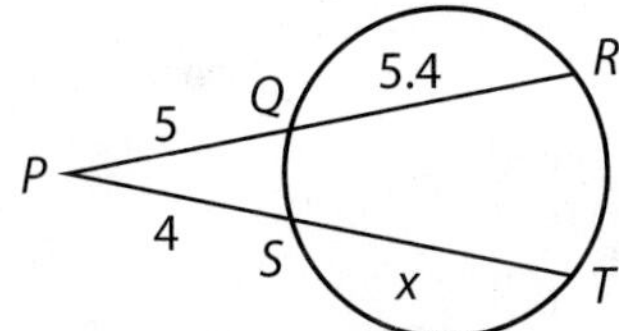

7.

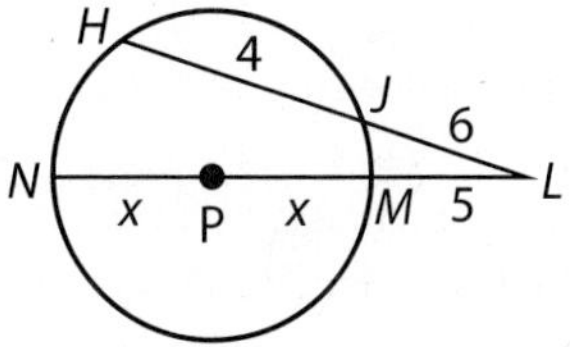

Explain 4 Applying the Secant-Tangent Product Theorem

A similar theorem applies when both a secant segment and tangent segment are drawn to a circle from the same exterior point. A **tangent segment** is a segment of a tangent line with exactly one endpoint on the circle.

Secant-Tangent Product Theorem

If a secant and a tangent intersect in the exterior of a circle, then the product of the lengths of the secant segment and its external segment equals the length of the tangent segment squared.

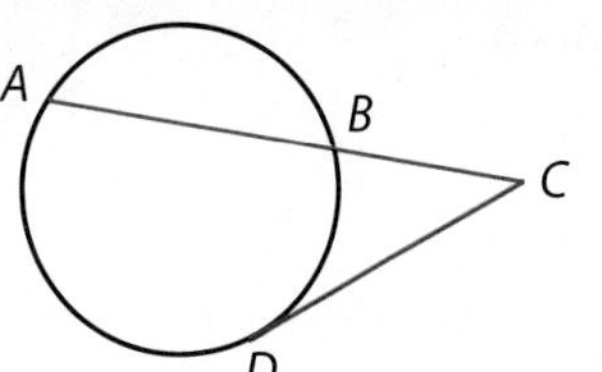

$AC \cdot BC = DC^2$

Example 4 **Find the value of *x*.**

Ⓐ Given the diameter of the Earth as 8,000 miles, a satellite's orbit is 6,400 miles above the Earth. Its range, shown by $\overline{SP}$, is a tangent segment.

Set up an equation according to the Secant-Tangent Product Theorem and solve for *x*:

$$SA \cdot SE = SP^2$$

$$(8000 + 6400)(6400) = x^2$$

$$(14400)(6400) = x^2$$

$$92{,}160{,}000 = x^2$$

$$\pm 9600 = x$$

Since distance must be positive, the value of *x* must be 9600 miles.

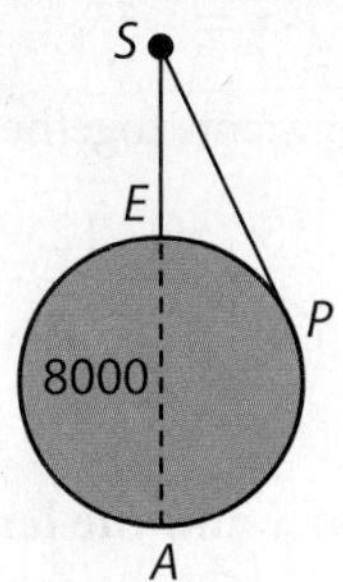

Ⓑ Set up an equation according to the Secant-Tangent Product Theorem and solve for *x*:

$$BD \cdot BC = BA^2$$

$$\left(\boxed{x + 2}\right)(2) = 5^2$$

$$\boxed{2}\,x + \boxed{4} = \boxed{25}$$

$$\boxed{2}\,x = \boxed{21}$$

$$x = \boxed{10.5}$$

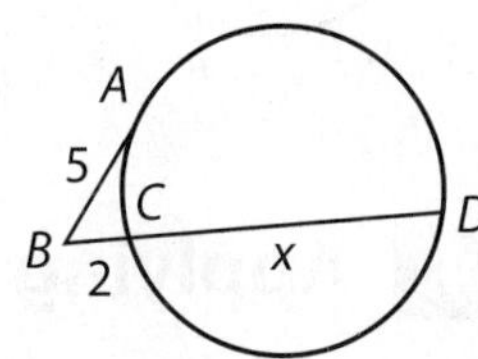

Reflect

8. Compare and contrast the Secant-Secant Product Theorem with the Secant-Tangent Product Theorem.

Your Turn

Find the value of *x*.

9. On a bird-watching trip, you travel along a path tangent to a circular pond to a lookout station that faces a hawk's nest. Given the measurements in the diagram on your bird-watching map, how far is the nest from the lookout station?

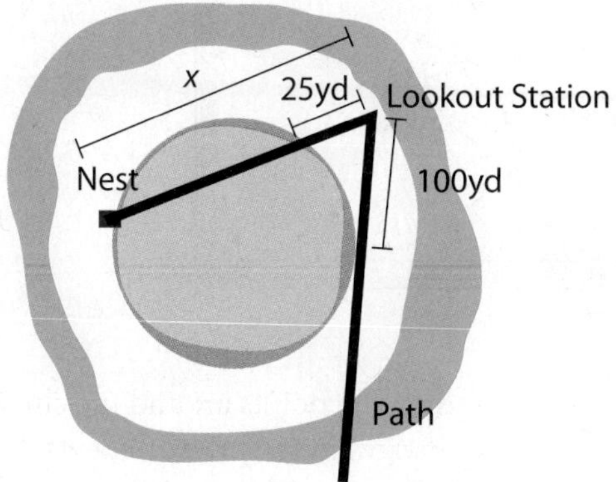

10.

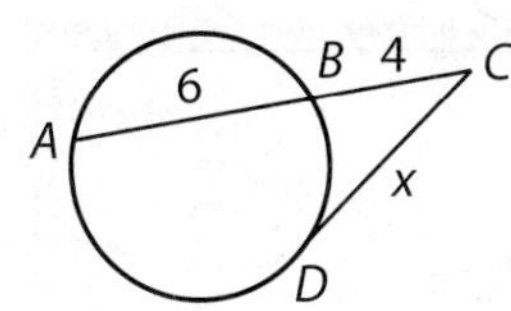

Elaborate

11. How is solving for y in the following diagram different from Example 3?

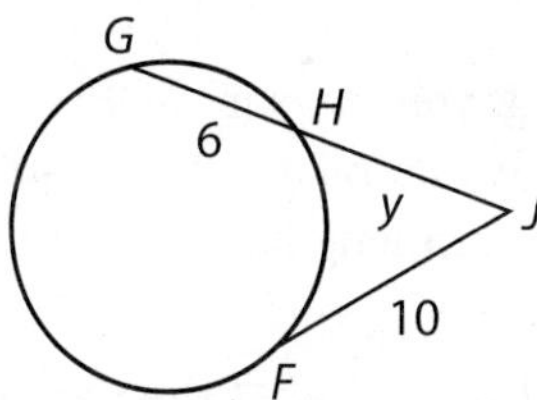

12. A circle is constructed with two secant segments that intersect outside the circle. If both external secant segments are equal, is it reasonable to conclude that both secant segments are equal? Explain.

13. Essential Question Check-In How are the theorems in this lesson related?

Evaluate: Homework and Practice

• Online Homework
• Hints and Help
• Extra Practice

Use the figure for Exercises 1–2.

Suppose you use geometry software to construct two chords $\overline{RS}$ and $\overline{TU}$ that intersect inside a circle at V.

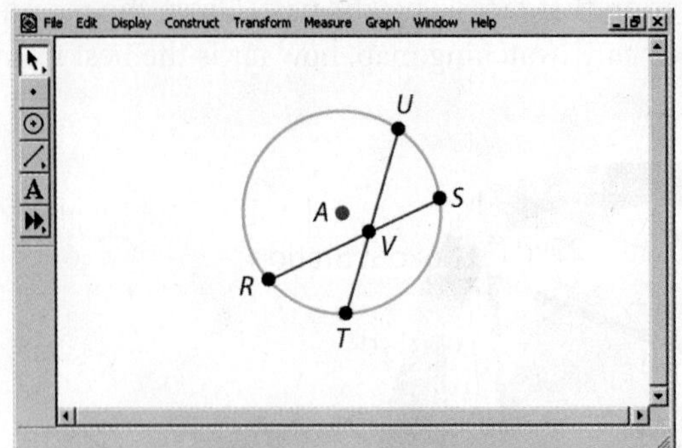

1. If you measured $\overline{RV}$, $\overline{VS}$, $\overline{TV}$, and $\overline{VU}$, what would be true about the relationship between their lengths?

2. Suppose you drag the points around the circle and examine the changes in the measurements. Would your answer to Exercise 1 change? Explain.

Use the figure for Exercises 3–4.

Suppose you use geometry software to construct two secants $\overleftrightarrow{DC}$ and $\overleftrightarrow{BE}$ that intersect outside a circle at F.

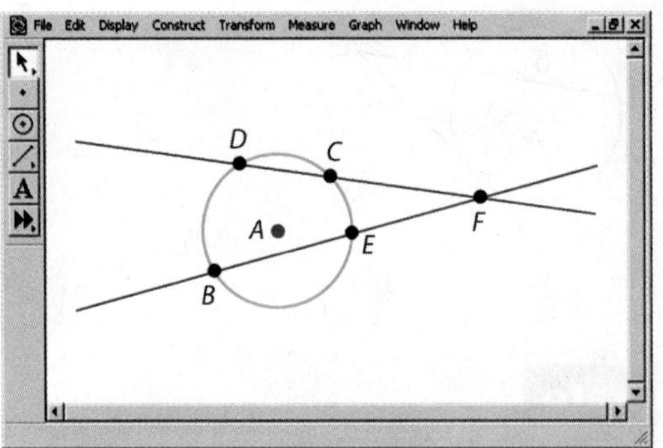

3. If you measured $\overline{DF}$, $\overline{CF}$, $\overline{BF}$, and $\overline{EF}$, what would be true about the relationship between their lengths?

4. Suppose you drag F and examine the changes in the measurements. Would your answer to Exercise 3 change? Explain.

Find the value of the variable and the length of each chord.

5.

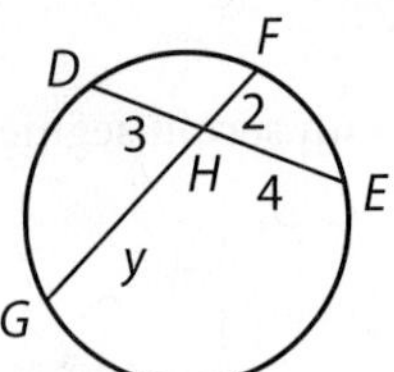

6.

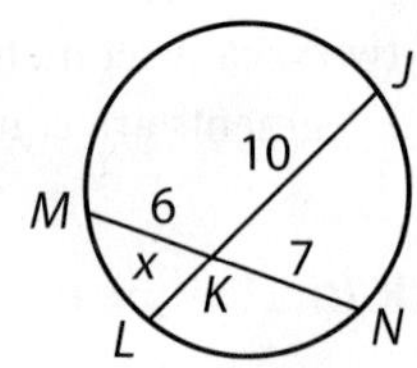

7. M is the midpoint of $\overline{PQ}$, The diameter of circle O is 13 in. and $RM = 4$ in.

a. Find PM.

b. Find PQ.

8. Representing a Real-World Problem A broken pottery shard found at archaeological dig has a curved edge. Find the diameter of the original plate. (Use the fact that the diameter $\overline{PR}$ is the perpendicular bisector of chord $\overline{AB}$.)

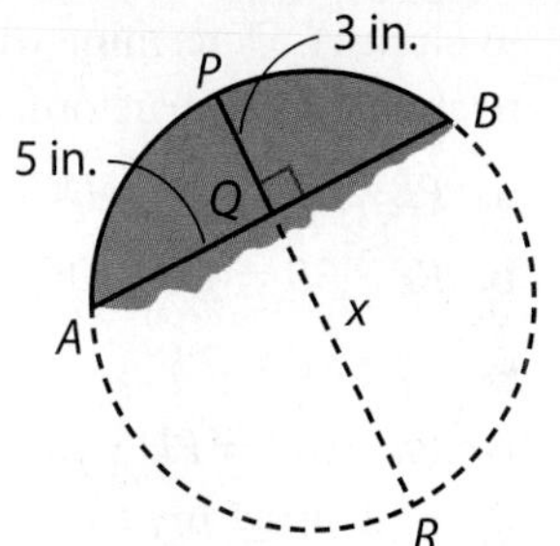

9. Critique Reasoning A student drew a circle and two secant segments. He concluded that if $\overline{PQ} \cong \overline{PS}$, then $\overline{QR} \cong \overline{ST}$. Do you agree with the student's conclusion? Why or why not?

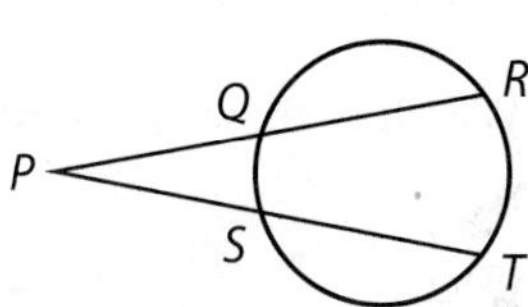

Find the value of the variable and the length of each secant segment.

10.

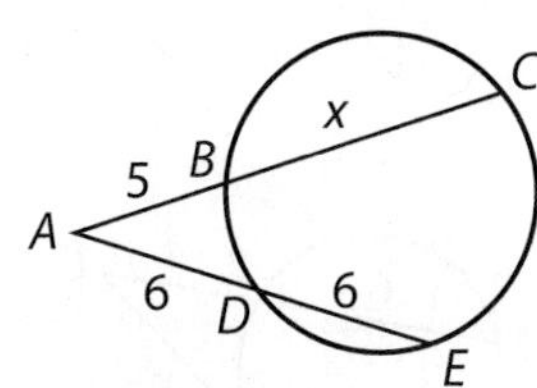

11.

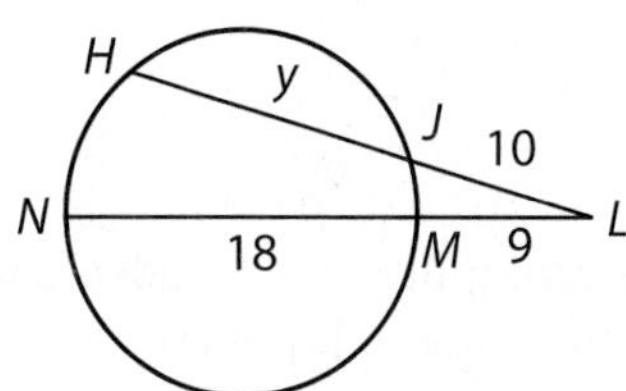

12. Find the value of x.

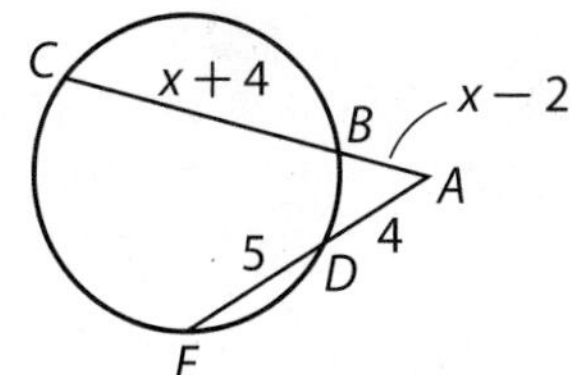

Find the value of the variable.

13.

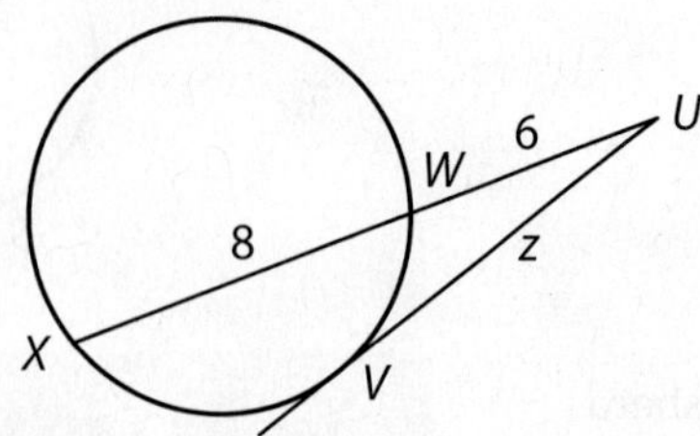

14.

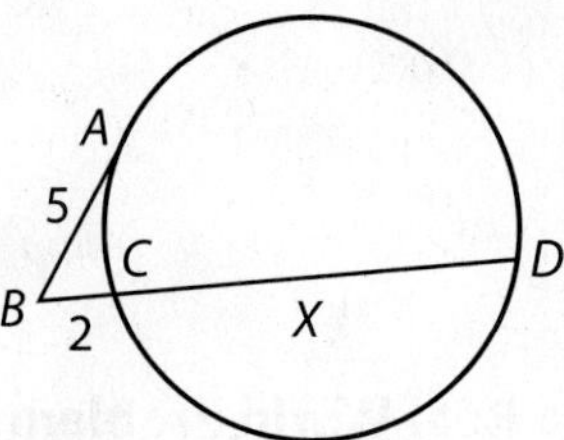

15.

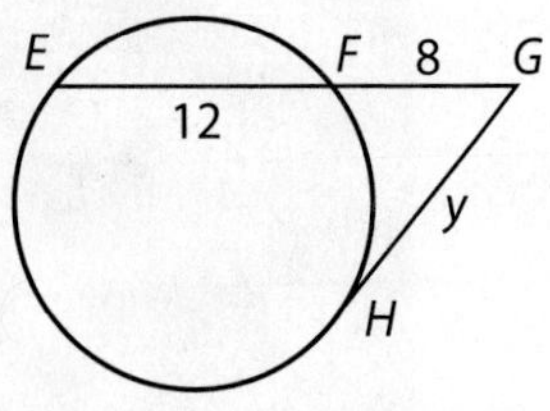

16. Tangent $\overleftrightarrow{PF}$ and secants $\overleftrightarrow{PD}$ and $\overleftrightarrow{PB}$ are drawn to circle A. Determine whether each of the following relationships is true or false.

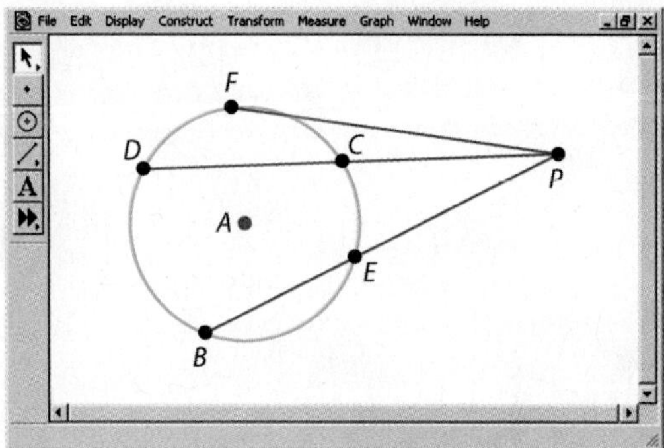

a. $PB \cdot EB = PD \cdot DC$

b. $PE \cdot EB = PC \cdot DC$

c. $PB \cdot PE = PF^2$

d. $PB \cdot DC = PD \cdot EB$

e. $PB \cdot PE = PD \cdot PC$

f. $PB \cdot PE = PF \cdot PC$

17. Which of these is closest to the length of tangent segment $\overline{PQ}$?

A. 6.9 **B.** 9.2

C. 9.9 **D.** 10.6

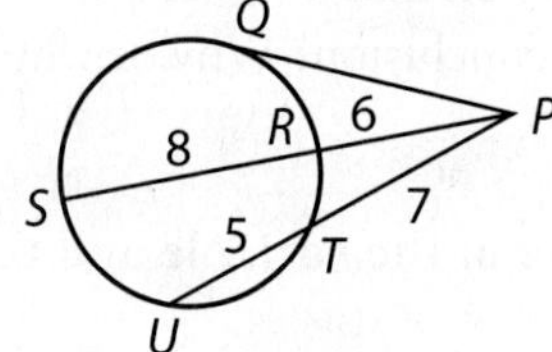

18. Explain the Error Below is a student's work to find the value of x. Explain the error and find the correct value of x.

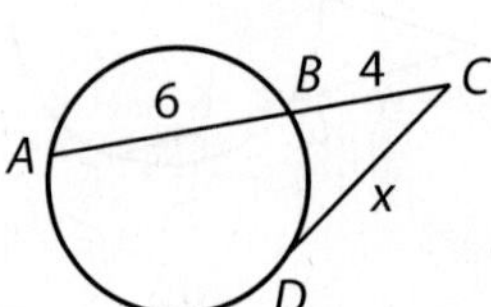

$AB \cdot BC = DC^2$

$6(4) = x^2$

$x^2 = 24$

$x = \pm\sqrt{24} = \pm 2\sqrt{6}$

19. Represent Real-World Problems Molokini is a small, crescent-shaped island $2\frac{1}{2}$ miles from the Maui, Hawaii, coast. It is all that remains of an extinct volcano. To approximate the diameter of the mouth of the volcano, a geologist used a diagram like the one shown. The geologist assumed that the mouth of the volcano was a circle. What was the approximate diameter of the volcano's mouth to the nearest ten feet?

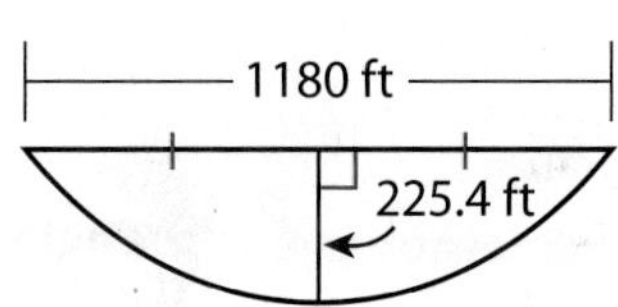

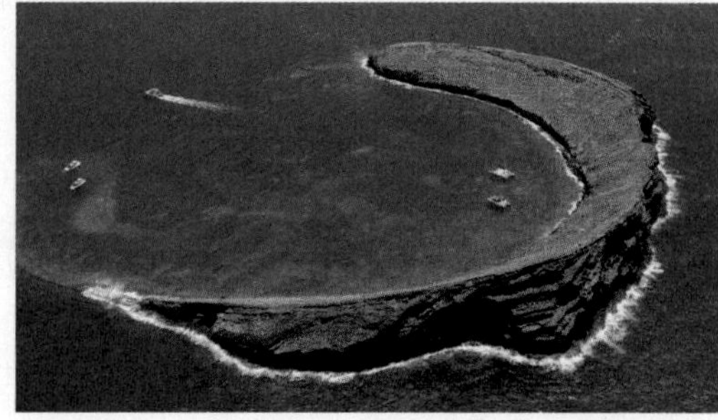

20. Multi-step Find the value of both variables in the figure.

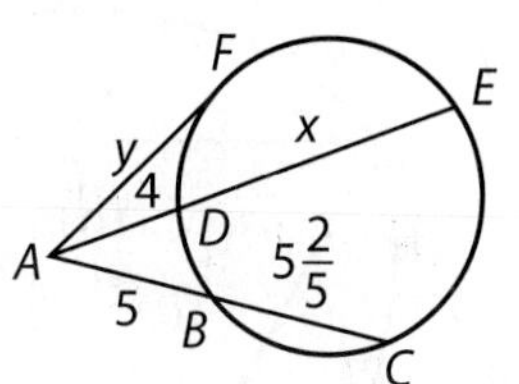

21. $\overline{KL}$ is a tangent segment of circle N and $\overline{KM}$ and $\overline{LM}$ are secants of the circle. Find the value of x.

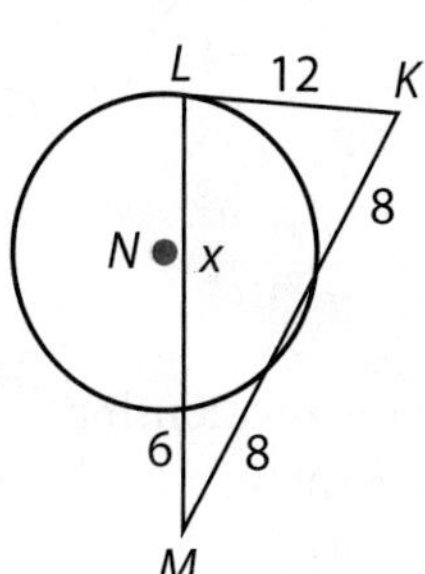

H.O.T. Focus on Higher Order Thinking

22. Justify Reasoning Prove the Chord-Chord Product Theorem

Given: Chords $\overline{AB}$ and $\overline{CD}$ intersect at point E.

Prove: $AE \cdot EB = CE \cdot ED$ (*Hint*: Draw $\overline{AC}$ and $\overline{BD}$.)

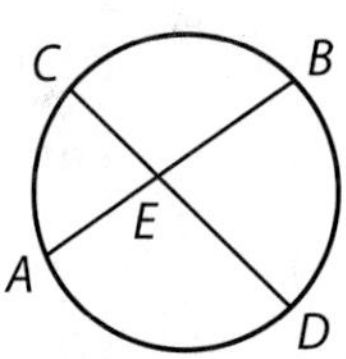

23. Justify Reasoning $\overline{PQ}$ is a tangent segment of a circle with radius 4 in. Q lies on the circle, and $PQ = 6$ in. Make a sketch and find the distance from P to the circle. Round to the nearest tenth of an inch. Explain your reasoning.

24. Justify Reasoning The circle in the diagram has radius c. Use this diagram and the Chord-Chord Product Theorem to prove the Pythagorean Theorem.

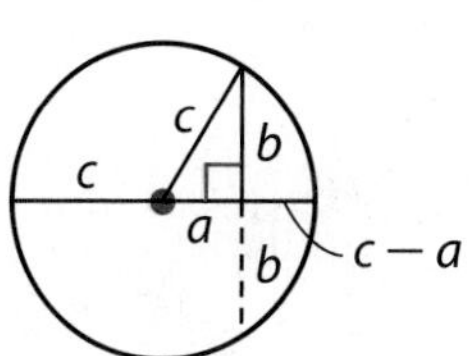

25. Critical Thinking The radius of circle A is 4. $CD = 4$, and $\overline{CB}$ is a tangent segment. Describe two different methods you can use to find BC.

Lesson Performance Task

The figure shows the basic design of a Wankel rotary engine. The triangle is equilateral, with sides measuring 10 inches. An arc on each side of the triangle has as its center the vertex on the opposite side of the triangle. In the figure, the arc ADB is an arc of a circle with its center at C.

a. Use the sketch of the engine. What is the measure of each arc along the side of the triangle?

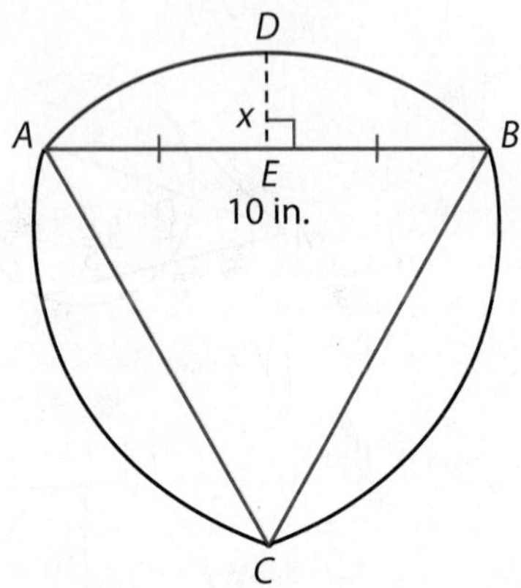

b. Use the relationships in an equilateral triangle to find the value of x. Explain.

c. Use the Chord-Chord Product Theorem to find the value of x. Explain.

19.5 Angle Relationships in Circles

Resource Locker

Essential Question: What are the relationships between angles formed by lines that intersect a circle?

Explore Exploring Angle Measures in Circles

The sundial is one of many instruments that use angles created in circles for practical applications, such as telling time.

In this lesson, you will observe the relationships between angles created by various line segments and their intercepted arcs.

Ⓐ Using geometry software, construct a circle with two secants $\overleftrightarrow{CD}$ and $\overleftrightarrow{EF}$ that intersect inside the circle at G, as shown in the figure.

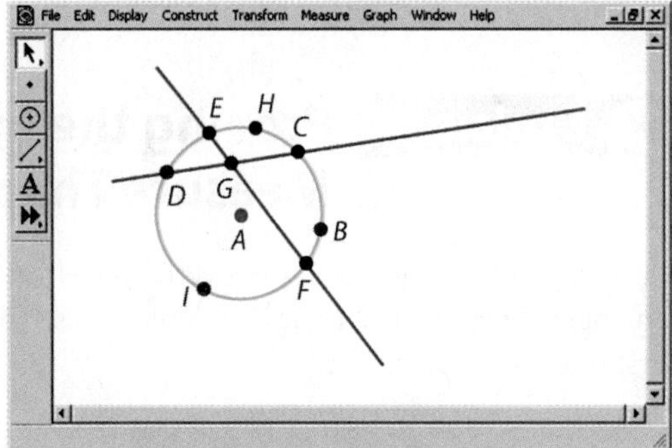

Ⓑ Create two new points H and I that are on the circle as shown. These will be used to measure the arcs. Hide B if desired.

Ⓒ Measure $\angle DGF$ formed by the secant lines, and measure $\overset{\frown}{CHE}$ and $\overset{\frown}{DIF}$. Copy the table and record the angle and arc measurements in the first column.

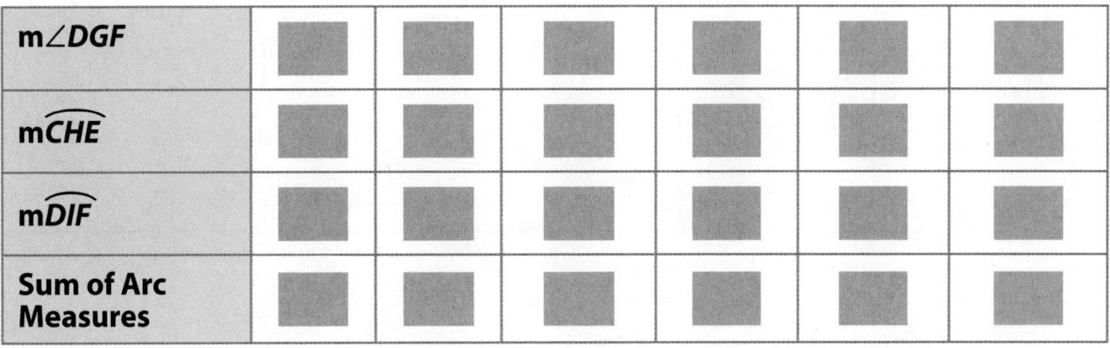

$m\angle DGF$						
$m\overset{\frown}{CHE}$						
$m\overset{\frown}{DIF}$						
Sum of Arc Measures						

Ⓓ Drag F around the circle and record the changes in measures in the table in Part C. Try to create acute, right, and obtuse angles. Be sure to keep H between C and E and I between D and F for accurate arc measurement. Move them if necessary.

Reflect

1. Can you make a conjecture about the relationship between the angle measure and the two arc measures?

2. Using the same circle you created in step A, drag points around the circle so that the intersection is outside the circle, as shown. Measure $\angle FGC$ formed by the secant lines and measure $\overset{\frown}{CIF}$ and $\overset{\frown}{DHE}$. Drag points around the circle and observe the changes in measures. Copy the table and record some of your measurements.

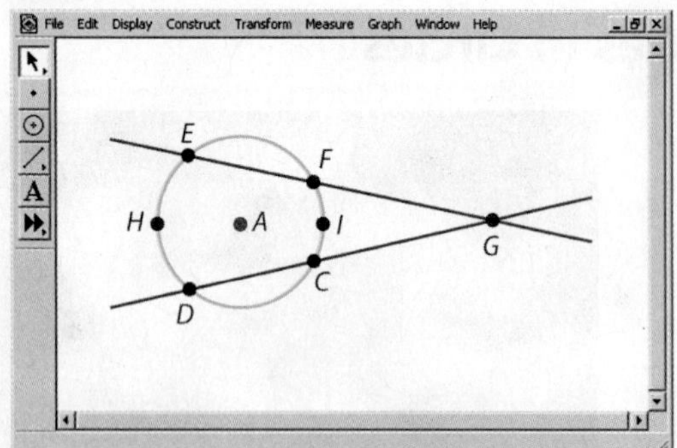

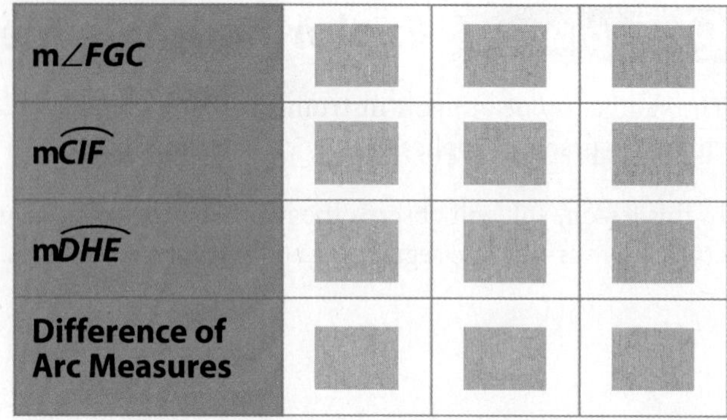

$m\angle FGC$			
$m\overset{\frown}{CIF}$			
$m\overset{\frown}{DHE}$			
Difference of Arc Measures			

What is similar and different about the relationships between the angle measure and the arc measures when the secants intersect outside the circle?

Explain 1 Proving the Intersecting Chords Angle Measure Theorem

In the Explore section, you discovered the effects that line segments, such as chords and secants, have on angle measures and their intercepted arcs. These relationships can be stated as theorems, with the first one about chords.

The Intersecting Chords Angle Measure Theorem

If two secants or chords intersect in the interior of a circle, then the measure of each angle formed is half the sum of the measures of its intercepted arcs.

Chords $\overline{AD}$ and $\overline{BC}$ intersect at E.

$m\angle 1 = \frac{1}{2}\left(m\overset{\frown}{AB} + m\overset{\frown}{CD}\right)$

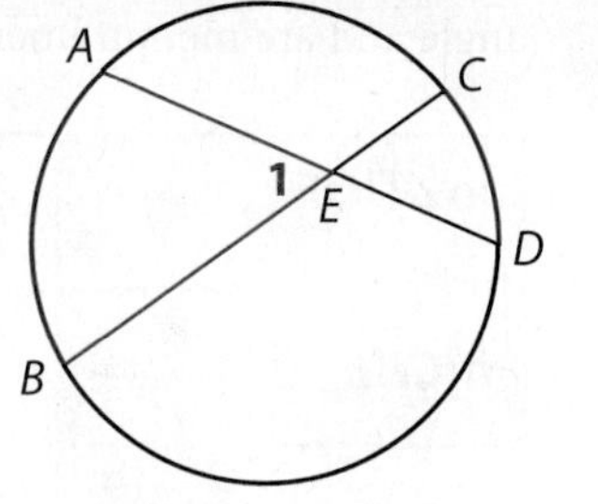

Example 1 Prove the Intersecting Chords Angle Measure Theorem

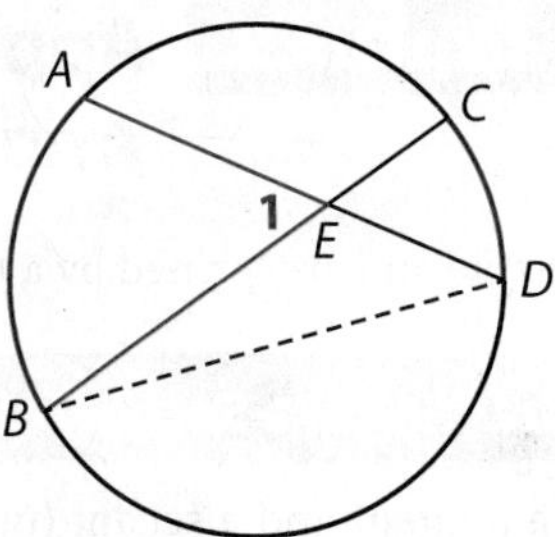

Given: $\overline{AD}$ and $\overline{BC}$ intersect at E.

Prove: $m\angle 1 = \frac{1}{2}\left(m\widehat{AB} + m\widehat{CD}\right)$

Statements	Reasons
1. $\overline{AD}$ and $\overline{BC}$ intersect at E.	1. Given
2. Draw $\overline{BD}$.	2. Through any two points, there is exactly one line.
3. $m\angle 1 = m\angle EDB + m\angle EBD$	3. Exterior Angle Theorem
4. $m\angle EDB = \frac{1}{2}m\widehat{AB}$, $m\angle EBD$ Property	4. Inscribed Angle Theorem
5. $m\angle 1 = \frac{1}{2}m\widehat{AB} + \frac{1}{2}m\widehat{CD}$	5. Substitution Property
6. $m\angle 1 = \frac{1}{2}\left(m\widehat{AB} + m\widehat{CD}\right)$	6. Distributive Property

Reflect

3. Discusssion Explain how an auxiliary segment and the Exterior Angle Theorem are used in the proof of the Intersecting Chords Angle Measure Theorem.

Your Turn

Find each unknown measure.

4. $m\angle MPK$

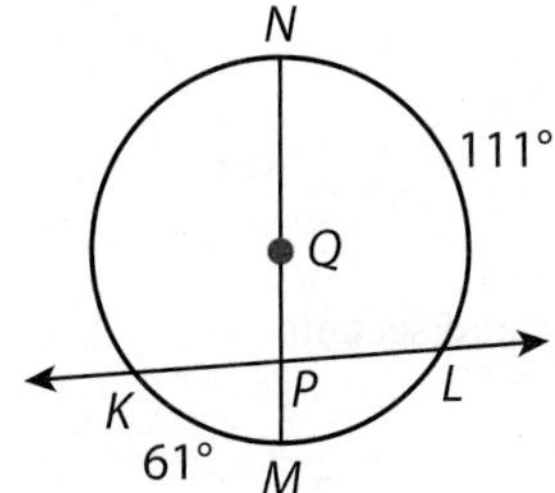

5. $m\widehat{PR}$

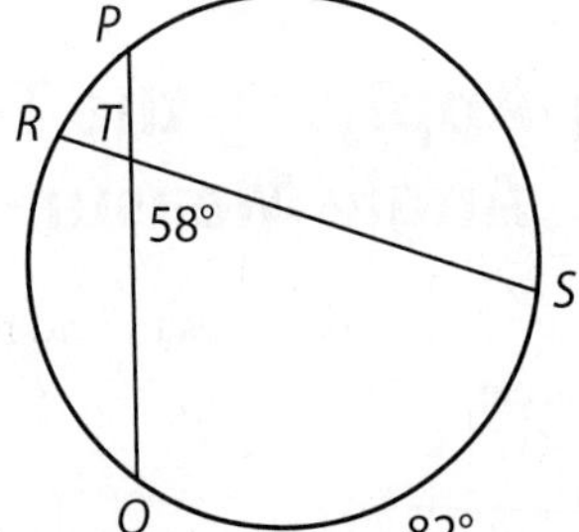

Explain 2 Applying the Tangent-Secant Interior Angle Measure Theorem

The angle and arc formed by a tangent and secant intersecting *on* a circle also have a special relationship.

The Tangent-Secant Interior Angle Measure Theorem

If a tangent and a secant (or a chord) intersect on a circle at the point of tangency, then the measure of the angle formed is half the measure of its intercepted arc.

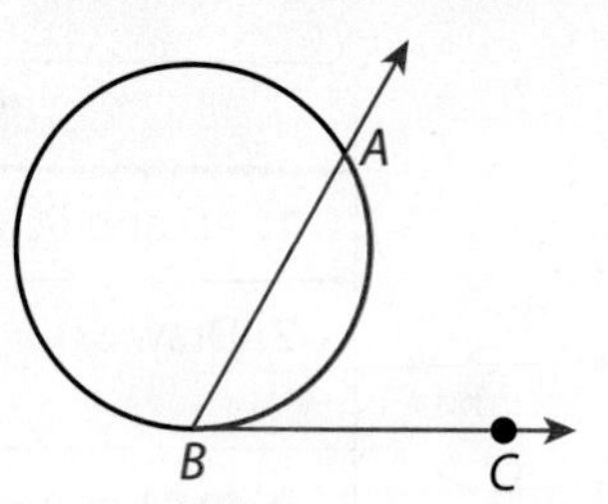

Tangent $\overrightarrow{BC}$ and secant $\overrightarrow{BA}$ intersect at B.

$$m\angle ABC = \frac{1}{2}\, m\widehat{AB}$$

Example 2 **Find each unknown measure.**

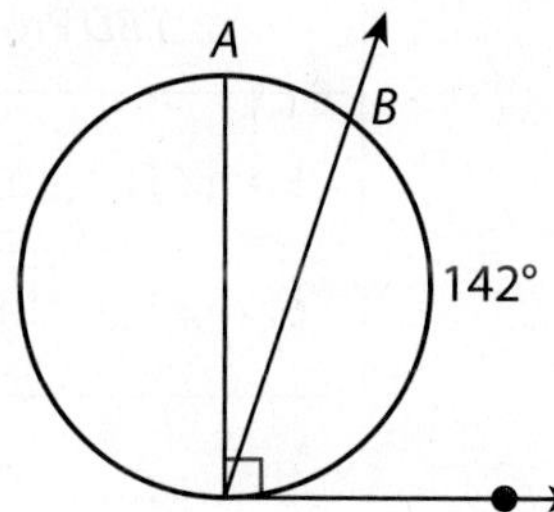

 $m\angle BCD$

$$m\angle BCD = \frac{1}{2} m\widehat{BC}$$
$$= \frac{1}{2}(142°)$$
$$= 71°$$

 $m\widehat{ABC}$

$$m\angle ACD = \frac{1}{2}\left(m\widehat{ABC}\right)$$
$$\boxed{90°} = \frac{1}{2}\left(m\widehat{ABC}\right)$$
$$\boxed{180°} = m\widehat{ABC}$$

Your Turn

Find the measure.

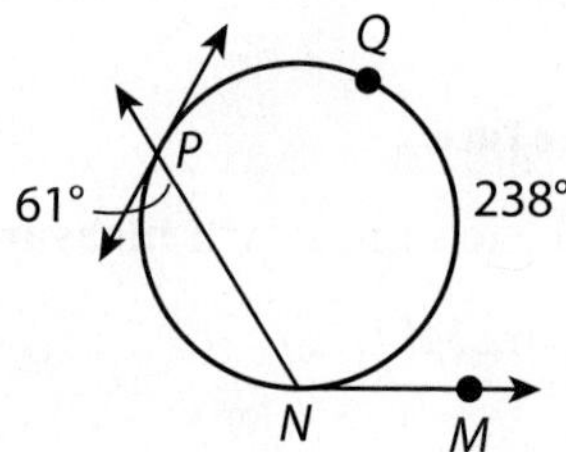

6. $m\widehat{PN}$

7. $m\angle MNP$

Explain 3 Applying the Tangent-Secant Exterior Angle Measure Theorem

You can use the *difference* in arc measures to find measures of angles formed by tangents and secants intersecting *outside* a circle.

The Tangent-Secant Exterior Angle Measure Theorem

If a tangent and a secant, two tangents, or two secants intersect in the exterior of a circle, then the measure of the angle formed is half the difference of the measures of its intercepted arcs.

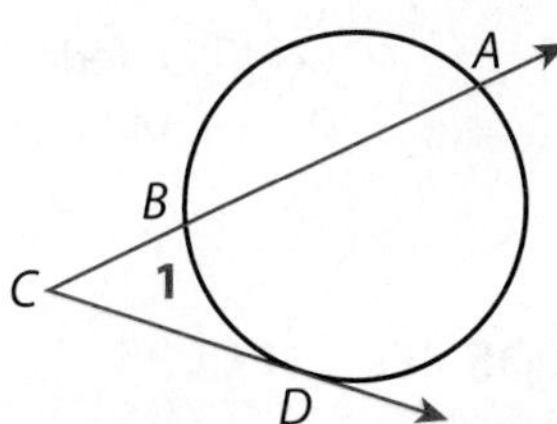

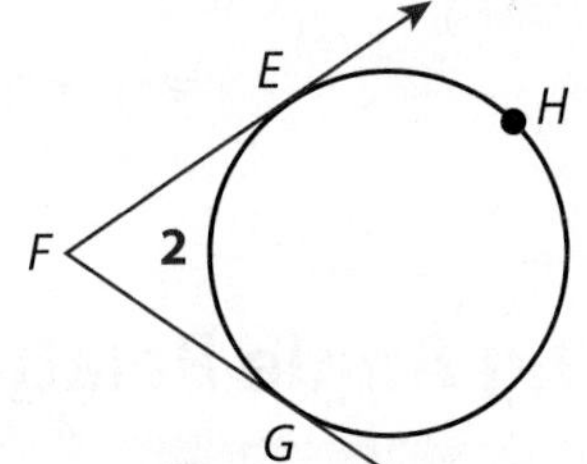

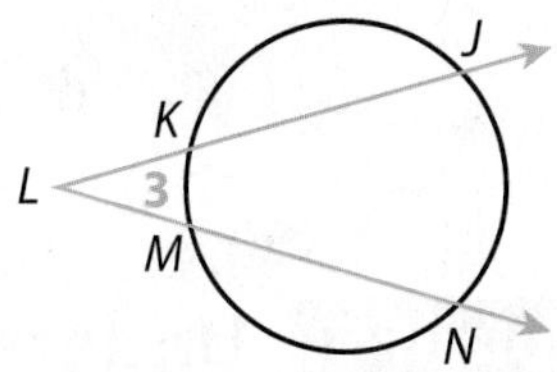

$m\angle 1 = \frac{1}{2}\left(m\widehat{AD} - m\widehat{BD}\right)$ $m\angle 2 = \frac{1}{2}\left(m\widehat{EHG} - m\widehat{EG}\right)$ $m\angle 3 = \frac{1}{2}\left(m\widehat{JN} - m\widehat{KM}\right)$

Example 3 Find the value of x.

(A)

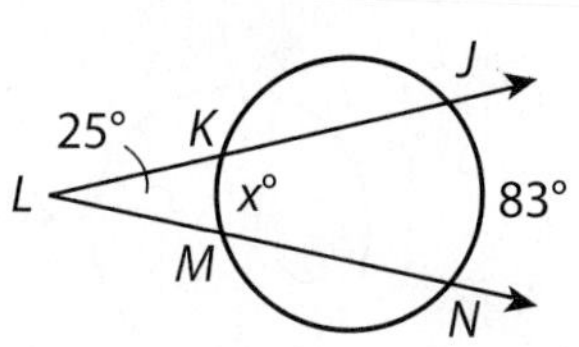

$$m\angle L = \frac{1}{2}\left(m\widehat{JN} - m\widehat{KM}\right)$$
$$25° = \frac{1}{2}(83° - x°)$$
$$50 = 83 - x$$
$$-33 = -x$$
$$33 = x$$

(B)

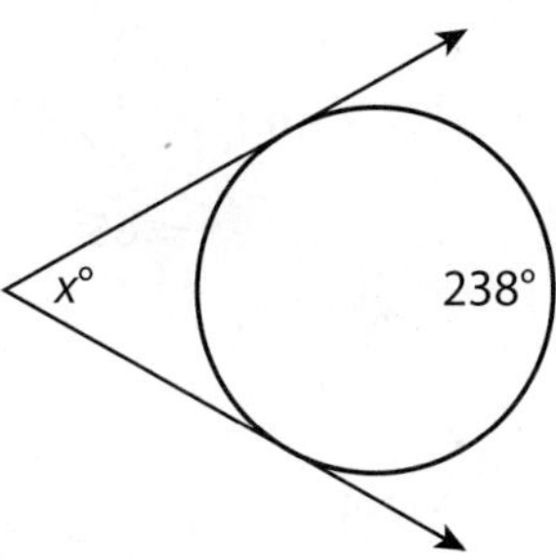

$$x° = \frac{1}{2}\left(238° - \left(360° - \boxed{238°}\right)\right)$$
$$x = \frac{1}{2}\left(\left(238 - \boxed{122}\right)\right)$$
$$x = \frac{1}{2}\left(\boxed{116}\right)$$
$$x = \boxed{58}$$

Your Turn

Find the value of x.

8.

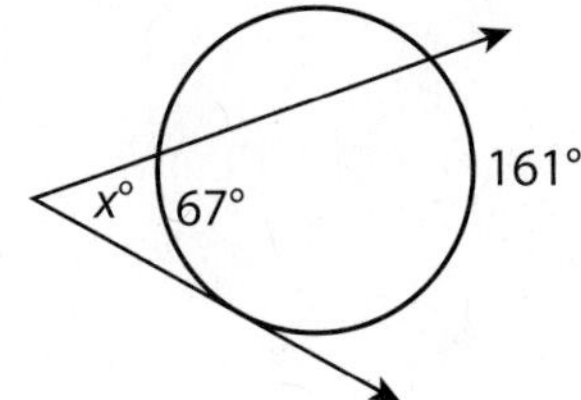

9. The superior oblique and inferior oblique are two muscles that help control eye movement. They intersect behind the eye to create an angle, as shown. If $m\widehat{AEB} = 225°$, what is $m\angle ACB$?

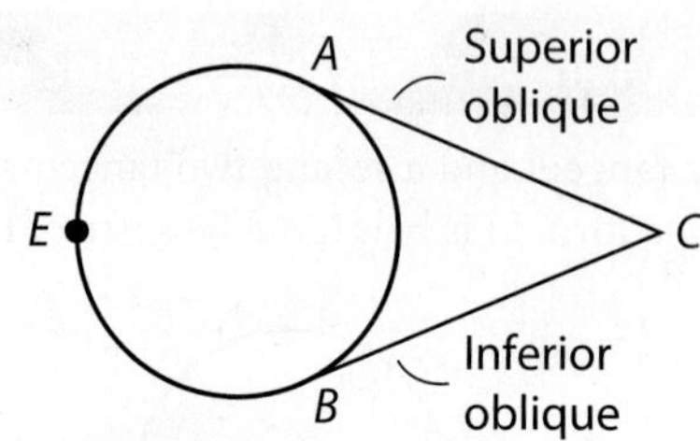

Explain 4 Understanding Angle Relationships in Circles

You can summarize angle relationships in circles by looking at where the vertex of the angle lies: on the circle, inside the circle, or outside the circle.

Angle Relationships in Circles

Vertex of the Angle	Measure of Angle	Diagrams	
On a circle	Half the measure of its intercepted arc	1, 120° $m\angle 1 = 60°$	200°, 2 $m\angle 2 = 100°$
Inside a circle	Half the sum of the measures of its intercepted arcs	44°, 1, 86°	$m\angle 1 = \frac{1}{2}(44° + 86°)$ $= 65°$
Outside a circle	Half the difference of the measures of its intercepted arcs	1, 78°, 202° $m\angle 1 = \frac{1}{2}(202° - 78°)$ $= 62°$	2, 45°, 125° $m\angle 2 = \frac{1}{2}(125° - 45°)$ $= 40°$

Example 4 **Find the unknown arc measures.**

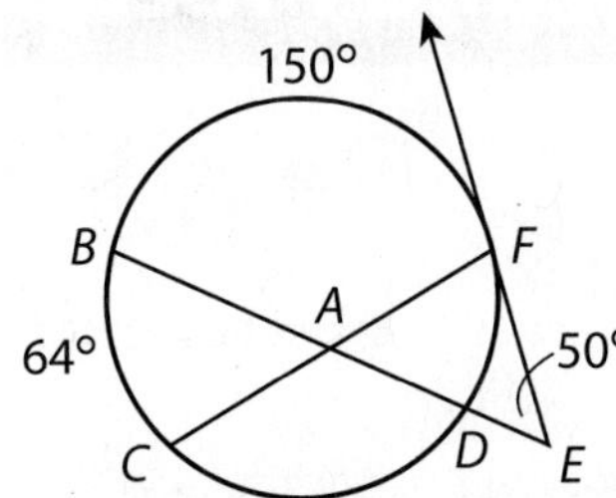

Ⓐ Find $m\widehat{FD}$.

$$m\angle E = \frac{1}{2}\left(m\widehat{BF} - m\widehat{FD}\right)$$

$$50° = \frac{1}{2}\left(150° - m\widehat{FD}\right)$$

$$100° = \left(50° - m\widehat{FD}\right)$$

$$-50° = -m\widehat{FD}$$

$$50° = m\widehat{FD}$$

Ⓑ Find $m\widehat{CD}$.

$$m\widehat{CD} = \boxed{360°} - \left(m\widehat{BC} + m\widehat{BF} + m\widehat{FD}\right)$$

$$= \boxed{360°} - \left(\boxed{64°} + \boxed{150°} + \boxed{50°}\right)$$

$$= \boxed{360°} - \boxed{264°}$$

$$= \boxed{96°}$$

Your Turn

10. Find $m\widehat{KN}$.

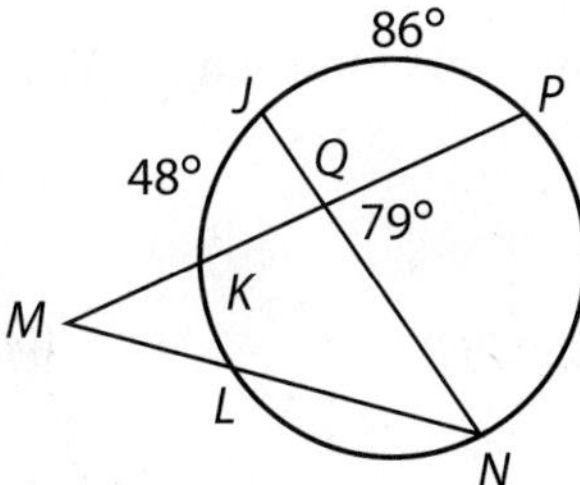

Elaborate

11. Copy and complete the graphic organizer that shows the relationship between the angle measurement and the location of its vertex.

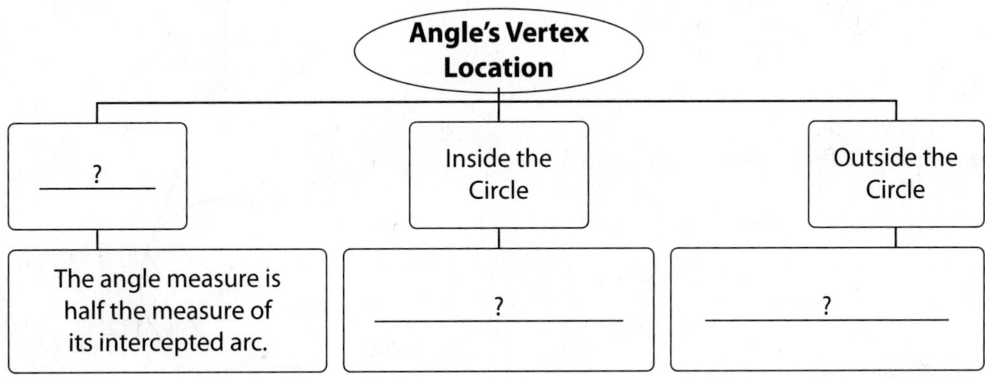

12. Essential Question Check-In What is similar about all the relationships between angle measures and their intercepted arcs?

Evaluate: Homework and Practice

- Online Homework
- Hints and Help
- Extra Practice

Use the figure for Exercises 1–2.

Suppose you use geometry software to construct a secant $\overleftrightarrow{CE}$ and tangent $\overleftrightarrow{CD}$ that intersect on a circle at point C.

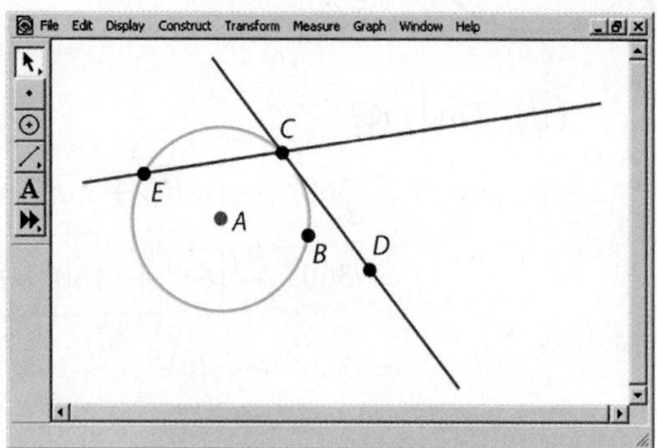

1. Suppose you measure $\angle DCE$ and you measure $\widehat{CBE}$. Then you drag the points around the circle and measure the angle and arc three more times. What would you expect to find each time? Which theorem from the lesson would you be demonstrating?

2. When the measure of the intercepted arc is 180°, what is the measure of the angle? What does that tell you about the secant?

Find each measure.

3. $m\angle QPR$

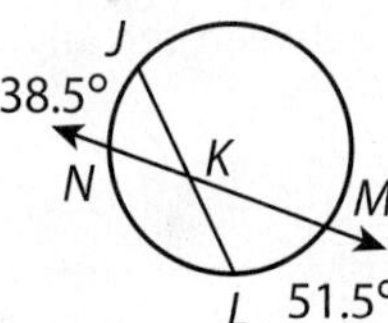

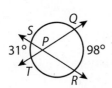

4. $m\angle ABC$

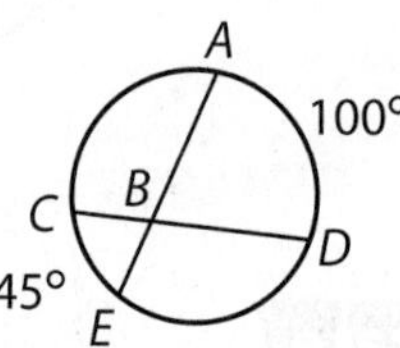

5. $m\angle MKJ$

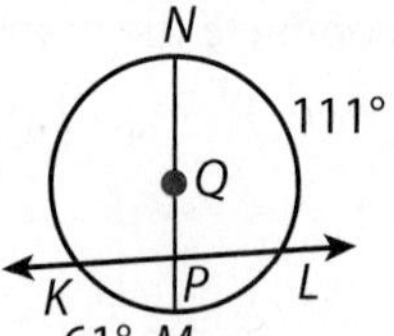

6. $m\angle NPK$

Find each measure. Use the figure for Exercises 7–8.

7. $m\angle BCD$

8. $m\angle ABC$

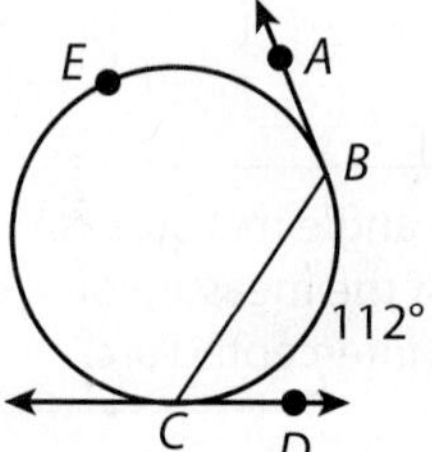

Find each measure. Use the figure for Exercises 9–10.

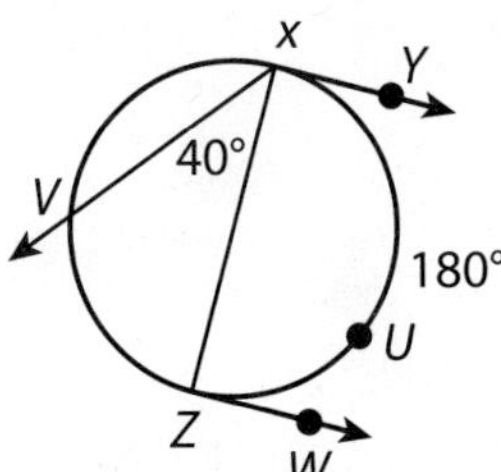

9. m$\angle XZW$

10. m$\angle YXZ$

Find the value of *x*.

11.

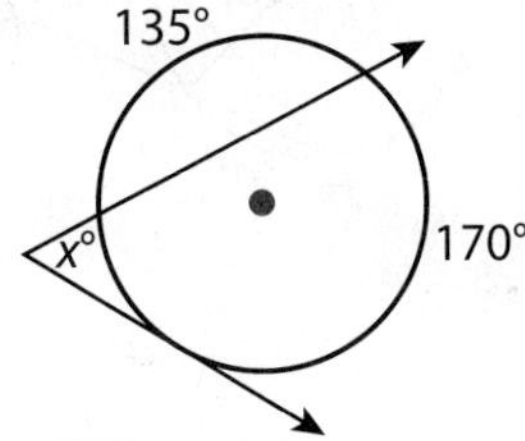

12.

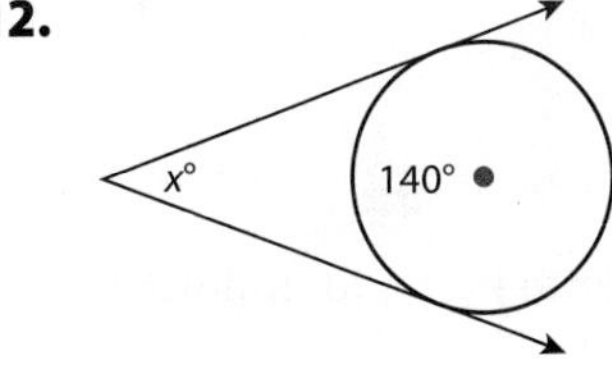

13.

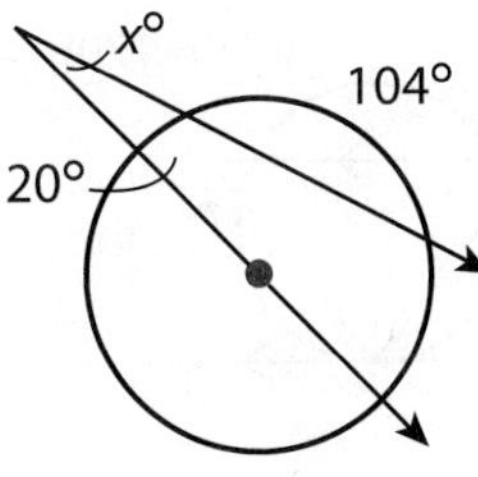

14. Represent Real-World Problems Stonehenge is a circular arrangement of massive stones near Salisbury, England. A viewer at V observes the monument from a point where two of the stones A and B are aligned with stones at the endpoints of a diameter of the circular shape. Given that m$\overparen{AB} = 48°$, what is m$\angle AVB$?

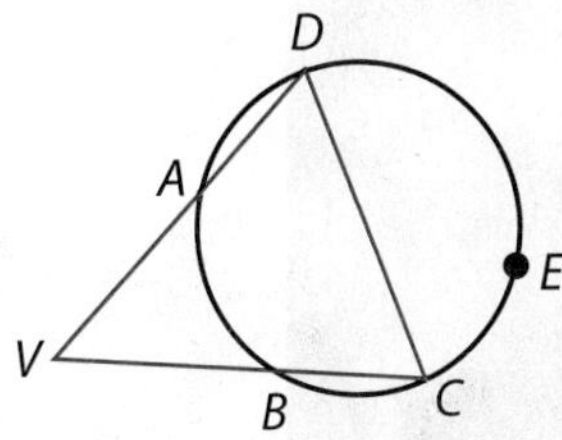

15. Multi-Step Find each measure.

a. Find m$\widehat{PN}$.

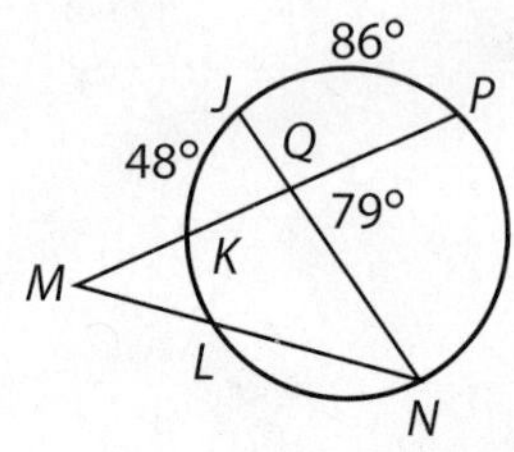

b. Use your answer to part a to find m$\widehat{KN}$.

16. Multi-Step Find each measure.

a. Find m$\widehat{DE}$.

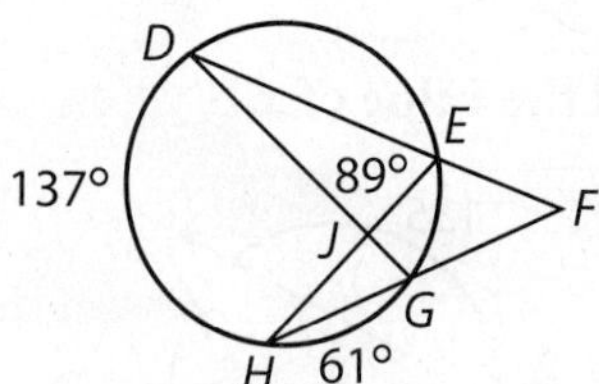

b. Use your answer to part a to find m$\angle F$.

$\overleftrightarrow{MS} \parallel \overleftrightarrow{PQ}$ and m$\angle PNS = 50°$. Find each measure.

17. m$\widehat{PR}$

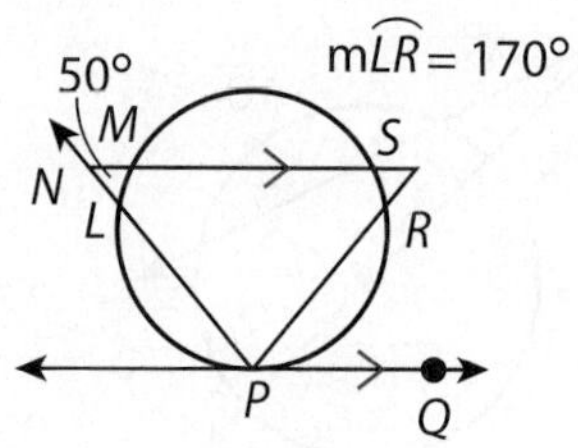

18. m$\widehat{LP}$

19. Represent Real-World Problems A satellite orbits Mars. When it reaches *S* it is about 12,000 km above the planet. What is $x°$, the measure of the arc that is visible to a camera in the satellite?

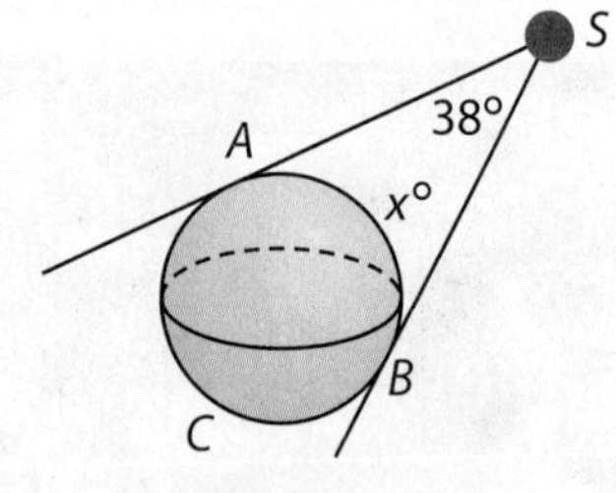

20. Use the circle with center J. Match each angle or arc on the left with its measure on the right.

A. $\angle BAE$ **a.** ___?___ $41°$

B. $\angle ACD$ **b.** ___?___ $180°$

C. $\overset{\frown}{AF}$ **c.** ___?___ $101°$

D. $\angle AED$ **d.** ___?___ $90°$

E. $\overset{\frown}{ADE}$ **e.** ___?___ $60°$

21. Use the Plan for Proof to write a proof for one case of the Tangent-Secant Exterior Angle Measure Theorem.

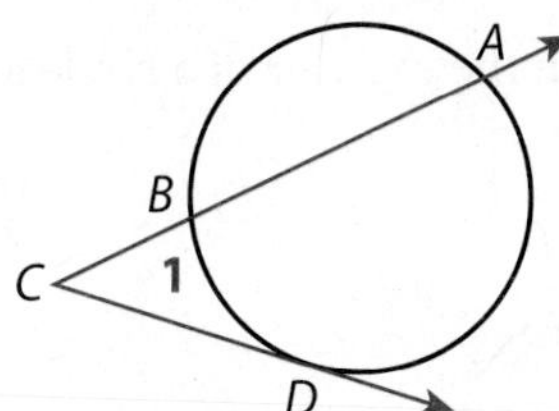

Given: Tangent $\overrightarrow{CD}$ and secant $\overrightarrow{CA}$

Prove: $m\angle ACD = \frac{1}{2}\left(m\overset{\frown}{AD} - m\overset{\frown}{BD}\right)$

Plan: Draw auxiliary line segment $\overline{BD}$. Use the Exterior Angle Theorem to show that $m\angle ACD = m\angle ABD - m\angle BDC$. Then use the Inscribed Angle Theorem and the Tangent-Secant Interior Angle Measure Theorem.

22. Justify Reasoning Write a proof that the figure shown is a square.

Given: $\overline{YZ}$ and $\overline{WZ}$ are tangent to circle X, $m\overset{\frown}{WY} = 90°$

Prove: $WXYZ$ is a square.

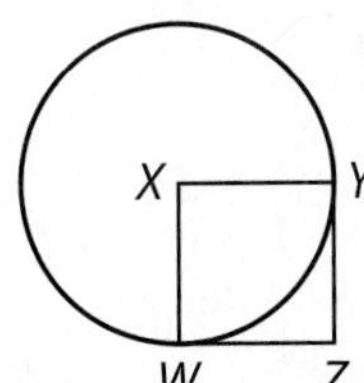

H.O.T. Focus on Higher Order Thinking

23. Justify Reasoning Prove the Tangent-Secant Interior Angle Theorem.

Given: Tangent $\overrightarrow{BC}$ and secant $\overrightarrow{BA}$

Prove: $m\angle ABC = \frac{1}{2}m\widehat{AB}$

$\left(\textit{Hint}\text{: Consider two cases, one where } \overline{AB} \text{ is a diameter and one where } \overline{AB} \text{ is not a diameter.}\right)$

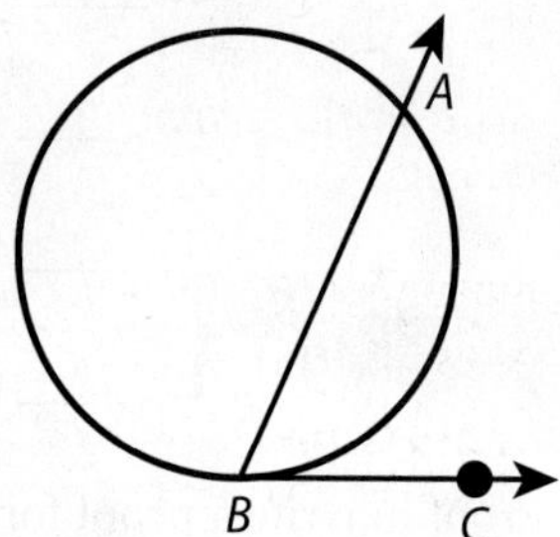

24. Critical Thinking Suppose two secants intersect in the exterior of a circle as shown. Which is greater, $m\angle 1$ or $m\angle 2$? Justify your answer.

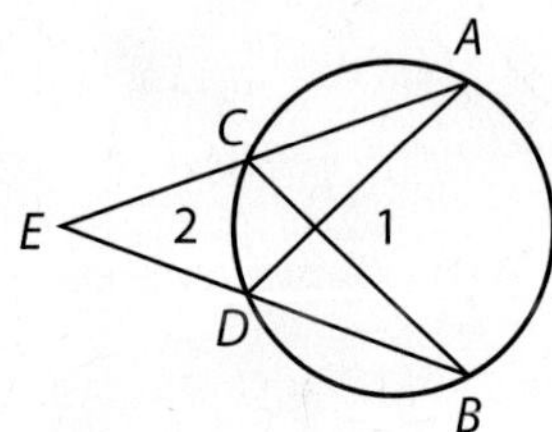

Lesson Performance Task

The diameter of the Moon is about 2160 miles. From Earth, the portion of the Moon's surface that an observer can see is from a circumscribed angle of approximately 0.5°.

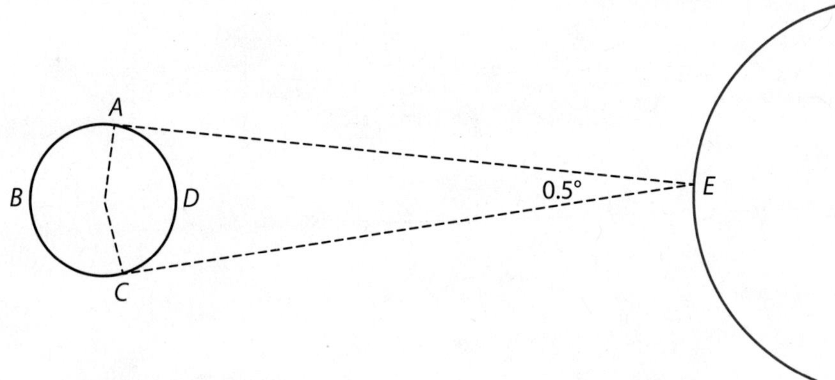

a. Find the measure of $\widehat{ADC}$. Explain how you found the measure.

b. What fraction of the circumference of the Moon is represented by $\widehat{ADC}$?

c. Find the length of $\widehat{ADC}$. You can use the formula $C = 2\pi r$ to find the circumference of the Moon.

STUDY GUIDE REVIEW

Angles and Segments in Circles

MODULE 19

Essential Question: How can you use angles and segments in circles to solve real-world problems?

KEY EXAMPLE (Lesson 19.1)

Determine $m\widehat{DE}$, $m\widehat{BD}$, $m\widehat{DAB}$, and $m\angle ADE$.

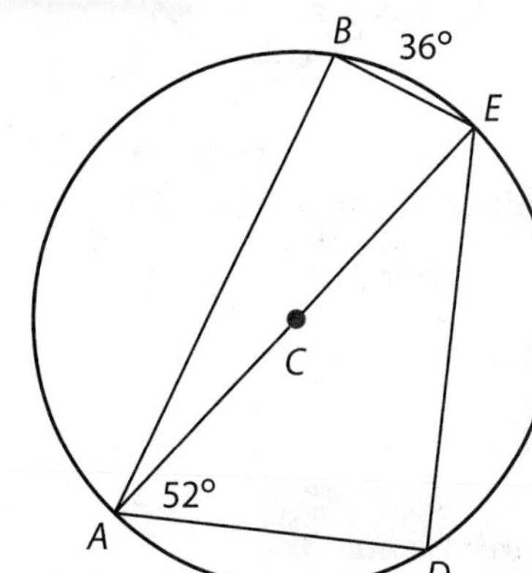

Since chord AE passes through the center of the circle at C, the chord AE is a diameter of the circle. $\widehat{ABE}$ is then a semicircle, and $m\widehat{ABE} = 180°$.

But $m\angle ADE = \frac{1}{2}m\widehat{ABE} = 90°$. $\triangle ADE$ is a right triangle with $m\angle AED = 36°$.

Also, $m\angle DAE = \frac{1}{2}m\widehat{DE}$, which implies that $m\widehat{DE} = 2m\angle DAE = 108°$. Since $m\widehat{BD} = m\widehat{BE} + m\widehat{DE}$, $m\widehat{BD} = 18° + 108° = 126°$. Finally, $m\angle DAB = \frac{1}{2}m\widehat{BD} = 63°$.

KEY EXAMPLE (Lesson 19.2)

Determine the angles J, K, L, and M in the given quadrilateral.

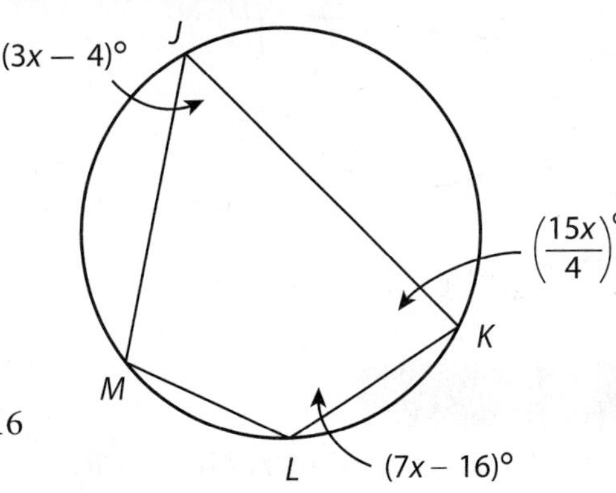

$(40 + 8x) + (5x - 16) = 180$. $24 + 13x = 180$. $13x = 156$. $x = 12$.

$m\angle J = 40 + 8x = 40 + 8(12) = 136°$

$m\angle L = 5x - 16 = 5(12) - 16 = 60 - 16 = 44°$

$m\angle K = \dfrac{20(12)}{4} = 60°$. $m\angle M + m\angle K = 180°$.

$m\angle M = 180° - 60° = 120°$

Key Vocabulary

chord *(cuerda)*
central angle *(ángulo central)*
inscribed angle *(ángulo inscrito)*
arc *(arco)*
minor arc *(arco menor)*
major arc *(arco principal)*
semicircle *(semicirculo)*
adjacent arcs *(arcos adyacentes)*
Inscribed Angle Theorem *(teorema del ángulo inscrito)*
Inscribed Quadrilateral Theorem *(teorema del ángulo inscrito)*
tangent *(tangent)*
point of tangency *(punto de tangencia)*
Tangent-Radius Theorem *(teorema de la tangente-radio)*
Chord-Chord Product Theorem *(teorema del producto de la cuerda de la cuerda)*
secant *(secante)*
secant segment *(segmente secante)*
external secant segment *(segmento externo secante)*
Secant-Secant Theorem *(Teorema de la secante-secante)*
tangent segment *(segmento tangente)*
Intersecting Chords Angle Measure Theorem *(teorema de medida de ángulo de intersección acordes)*
Tangent-Secant Interior Angle Measure Theorem *(teorema de la medida de ángulo interior tangente-secante)*
Tangent-Secant Exterior Angle Measure Theorem *(teorema de la medida de ángulo exterior tangente-secante)*

KEY EXAMPLE *(Lesson 19.3)*

Two tangent lines are drawn to a circle from point K intersecting the circle at points M and N. If m major $\widehat{MPN}$ = 210°, what is m$\angle MKN$?

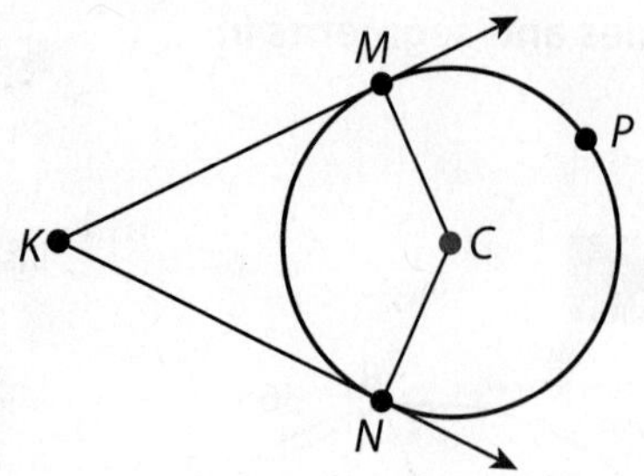

If m major $\widehat{MN} = 210°$, then m minor $\widehat{MN} = 360° - 210°, = 150°$.

$$m\angle MKN = \frac{1}{2}\left(\text{m major } \widehat{MPN} - \text{ m minor } \widehat{MPN}\right)$$

$$m\angle MKN = \frac{1}{2}(210° - 150°) = \frac{1}{2}(60°) = 30°$$

KEY EXAMPLE *(Lesson 19.4)*

A tangent and a secant are drawn to a circle from the external point B. The point of tangency is at point A, and the secant intersects the circle at points C and D. Find x.

From the Secant-Tangent Product Theorem, we can say that $BD \cdot BC = AB^2$. So $(2 + x) \cdot 2 = 8^2$.

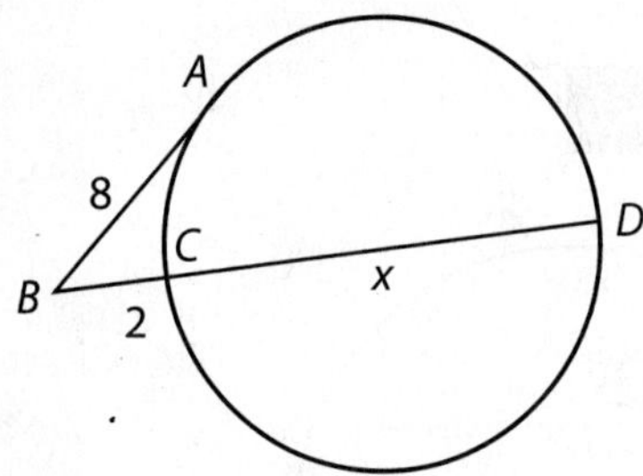

So $4 + 2x = 64$. $2x = 60$ and $x = 30$.

KEY EXAMPLE *(Lesson 19.5)*

Two chords intersect the interior of a circle at point T. Find m$\widehat{PR}$.

By the Intersecting Chords Angle Measure Theorem we can say the following:

$$m\angle QTS = \frac{1}{2}\left(m\widehat{QS} + m\widehat{PR}\right)$$

$$60° = \frac{1}{2}\left(80° + m\widehat{PR}\right)$$

$$120° = \left(80° + m\widehat{PR}\right)$$

$$120° - 80° = m\widehat{PR}$$

$$40° = m\widehat{PR}$$

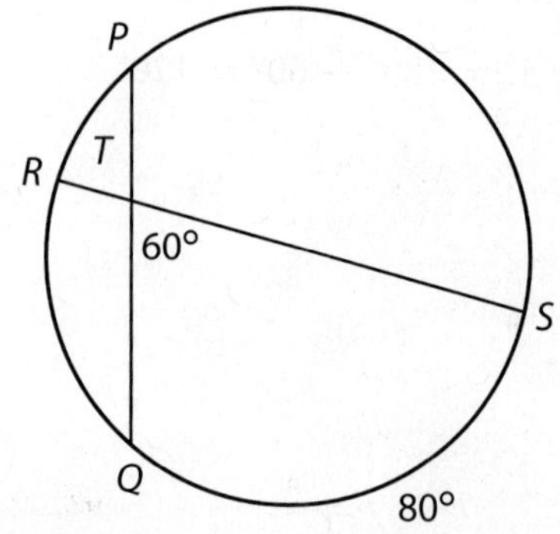

EXERCISES

Use the Inscribed Angle Theorem. *(Lesson 19.1)*

1. Find the measure of the intercepted arc for an inscribed angle of 50°.

Use the Inscribed Quadrilateral Theorem. *(Lesson 19.2)*

2. If one angle of a quadrilateral inscribed in a circle is 50°, what is the measure of its opposite angle?

Use the Circumscribed Angle Theorem. *(Lesson 19.3)*

3. Two tangents are drawn from an external point A to a circle. If one of the intercepted arcs on the circle is 120°, what must be the measure of the other intercepted arc?

Use the Chord-Chord Product Theorem. *(Lesson 19.4)*

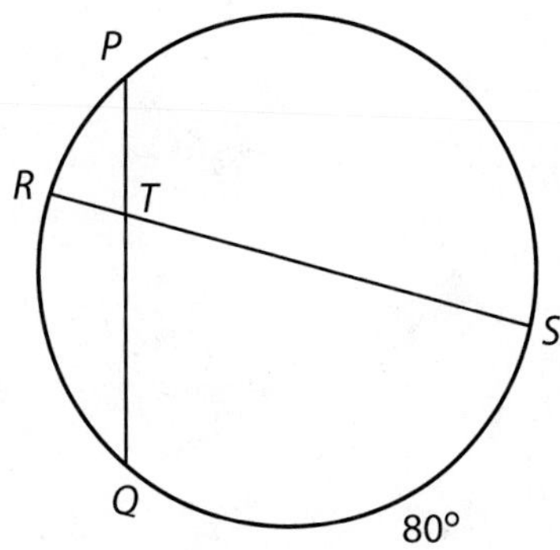

4. Given $RT = 2$, $TS = 6$, and $PT = 3$. Find TQ

Use the Tangent-Secant Exterior Angle Measure Theorem. *(Lesson 19.5)*

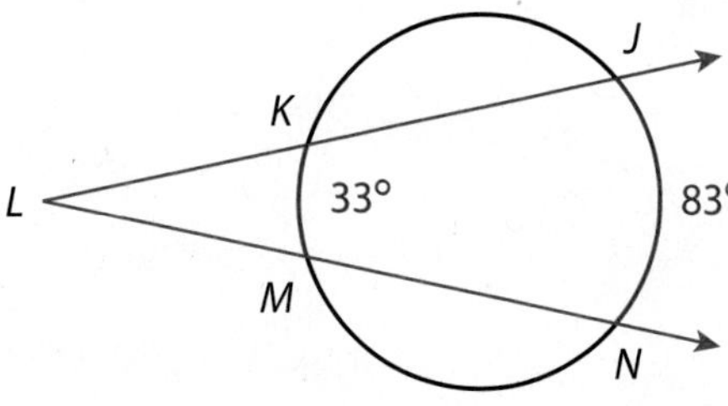

5. Find m$\angle L$ in the diagram given the m$\widehat{KM}$ and m$\widehat{JN}$.

MODULE PERFORMANCE TASK

How Many Marbles Will Fit?

Consider a package of marbles in the shape of a triangular prism. The cross-section of the package is an equilateral triangle with a side length of 1.5 inches, and the length of the package is 10 inches. What is the diameter of the largest marble that will fit inside the package? How many such marbles can fit within the package?

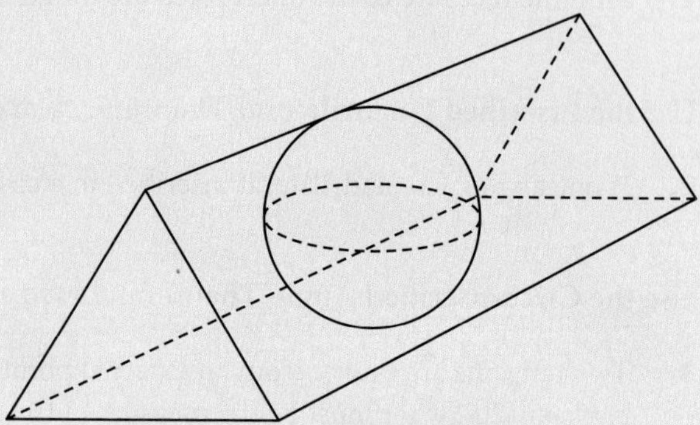

Start by listing how you plan to tackle the problem. Then complete the task. Be sure to write down all your data and assumptions. Then use words, numbers, diagrams, or algebra to explain how you reached your conclusion.

Ready to Go On?

19.1–19.5 Angles and Segments in Circles

- Online Homework
- Hints and Help
- Extra Practice

1. If $m\angle BCD = 20°$ and $m\widehat{EF} = 34°$, determine $m\widehat{ABD}$ using the appropriate theorems and postulates. *(Lessons 19.1, 19.5)*

If $m\widehat{EF} = 34°$, then $m\angle ECF =$ __?__. If $m\angle ECF = 34°$, then $m\angle ACB =$ __?__ by the __?__ Theorem. If $m\angle ACB = 34°$ and $m\angle BCD = 20°$, then $m\widehat{AB} =$ __?__ and __?__. By the __?__, $m\widehat{ABD} = m\widehat{AB} + m\widehat{BD}$, and so $m\widehat{ABD} =$ __?__.

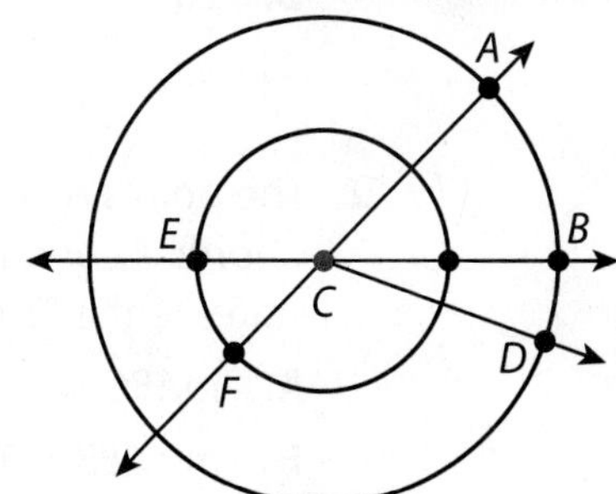

2. Find the measures of each angle in the inscribed quadrilateral. *(Lesson 19.2)*

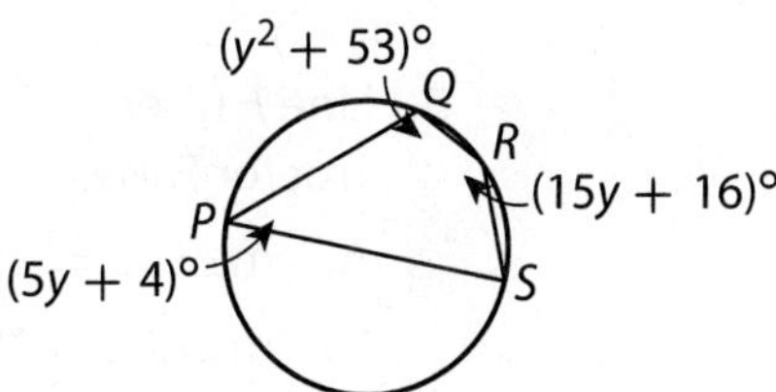

Fill in the proper conclusions based on known theorems and relationships. *(Lesson 19.3)*

3. Use the given figure where $\overline{KM}$ and $\overline{KN}$ are tangent to the circle at M and N respectively.

a. What angles are right angles?

b. Suppose that $m\angle MKN = 80°$. What is $m\angle MCN$?

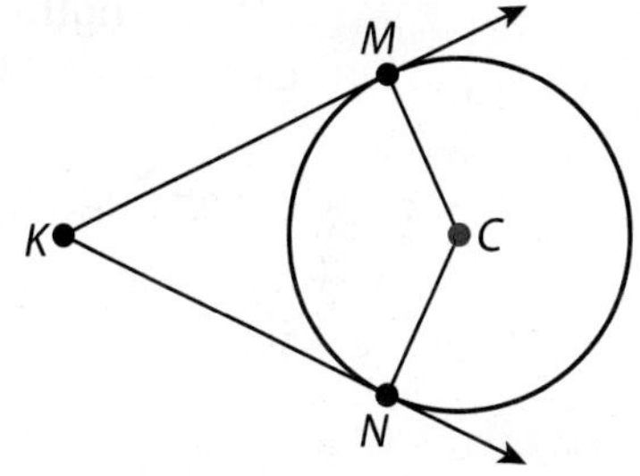

ESSENTIAL QUESTION

4. What are the major theorems that allow you to determine the relationships between angles formed by lines that intersect a circle?

MODULE 19
MIXED REVIEW

Assessment Readiness

SELECTED RESPONSE

1. An angle of 20° is inscribed in a circle. Could the given value be the measure of the arc intercepted by this angle? Write Yes or No for A–C.

A. 10°

B. 20°

C. 40°

2. The points *A, B, C,* and *D* are taken in order on the circumference of a circle. Chords *AC* and *BD* intersect at point *E*. $m\overset{\frown}{AB} = 76°$ and $m\overset{\frown}{CD} = 80°$. Determine if each statement is True or False.

A. $m\overset{\frown}{ABC} = 156°$

B. $m\angle AEB = 78°$

C. $m\angle AED = 72°$

3. Line *F* bisects $\angle ABC$, $\angle ABF = 6x$, and $\angle FBC = 2x + 60$. Determine if each statement is True or False.

A. $m\angle FBC = 45°$

B. $m\angle ABC = 180°$

C. $\angle ABF$ is a right angle.

4. If two chords intersect inside a circle, then what do you know about the products of the lengths of the segments of the chords? How can you determine whether two circles are similar?

5. $\triangle ABC$ is inscribed in a circle such that vertices *A* and *B* lie on a diameter of the circle. If the length of the diameter of the circle is 13 and the length of chord *BC* is 5, find side *AC*.

Arc Length and Sector Area

MODULE 20

Essential Question: How can the arc length and sector area of a circle be used to solve real-world problems? How are they related?

REAL WORLD VIDEO
Check out how you can use sector areas to help you order wisely the next time you're buying pizza.

MODULE PERFORMANCE TASK PREVIEW

What's the Better Deal on Pizza?

In this module, you will use geometry to figure out which pizza order gets you more pizza for your money. How can calculating sector area help you to solve this problem? Let's find out.

Are YOU Ready?

Complete these exercises to review skills you will need for this module.

- Online Homework
- Hints and Help
- Extra Practice

Area of a Circle

Example 1 Find the area of a circle with radius equal to 5.

$A = \pi r^2$ — Write the equation for the area of a circle of radius *r*.

$A = \pi(5)^2$ — Substitute the radius.

$A = 25\pi$ — Simplify.

Find each area.

1. A circle with radius 3

2. A circle with radius 6

3. A circle with radius 2π

4. A circle with radius $\frac{5}{\pi}$

Circumference

Example 2 Find the circumference of a circle with radius equal to 6.

$C = 2\pi r$ — Write the equation for the circumference of a circle with radius *r*.

$C = 2\pi(6)$ — Substitute the radius.

$C = 12\pi$ — Simplify.

Find each circumference.

5. A circle with radius 4

6. A circle with radius 3π

7. A circle with diameter 2

8. A circle with diameter $\frac{6}{\pi}$

Quadratic Functions

Example 3 Write x in terms of y. $10yx^2 = 60$

$10yx^2 = 60$ — Write the equation.

$yx^2 = 6$ — Divide both sides by 10.

$x^2 = \frac{6}{y}$ — Divide both sides by *y*.

$x = \sqrt{\frac{6}{y}}, x = -\sqrt{\frac{6}{y}}$ — Find the square root and its negative.

Solve each equation for *x*.

9. $4x^2 + 8x + 4 = 100$

10. $5y^2x^2 = 125$

20.1 Justifying Circumference and Area of a Circle

Essential Question: How can you justify and use the formulas for the circumference and area of a circle?

Explore Justifying the Circumference Formula

To find the circumference of a given circle, consider a regular polygon that is inscribed in the circle. As you increase the number of sides of the polygon, the perimeter of the polygon gets closer to the circumference of the circle.

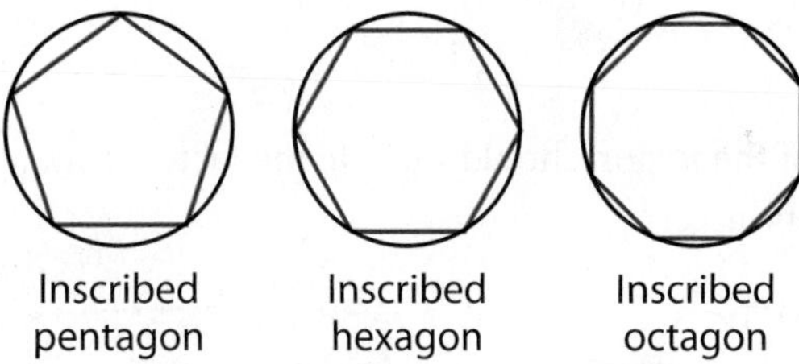

Let circle O be a circle with center O and radius r. Inscribe a regular n–gon in circle O and draw radii from O to the vertices of the n-gon.

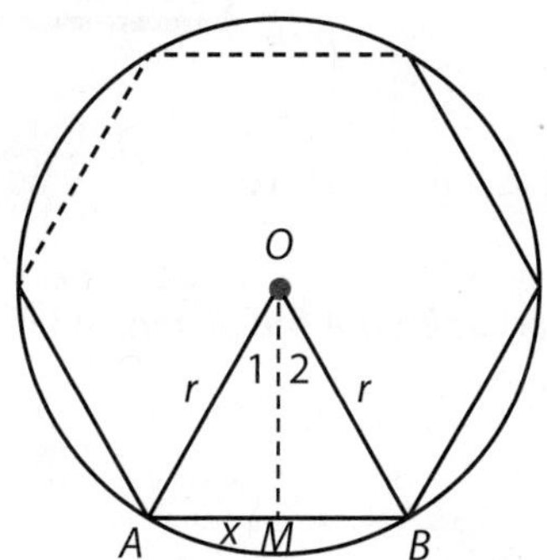

Let $\overline{AB}$ be one side of the n-gon. Draw $\overline{OM}$, the segment from O to the midpoint of $\overline{AB}$.

(A) Then $\triangle AOM \cong \triangle BOM$ by ______.

(B) So, $\angle 1 \cong \angle 2$ by ______.

(C) There are n triangles, all congruent to $\triangle AOB$, that surround point O and fill the n-gon.

Therefore, $m\angle AOB =$ ______ and $m\angle 1 =$ ______.

(D) Since $\angle OMA \cong \angle OMB$ by CPCTC, and $\angle OMA$ and $\angle OMB$ form a linear pair, these angles are supplementary and must have measures of 90°. So $\triangle AOM$ and $\triangle BOM$ are right triangles.

In $\triangle AOM$, $\sin\angle 1 = \dfrac{\text{length of opposite leg}}{\text{length of hypotenuse}} = \dfrac{x}{r}$.

So, $x = r\sin\angle 1$ and substituting the expression for $m\angle 1$ from above gives

$x = r\sin$ ______.

(E) Now express the perimeter of the n-gon in terms of x.

The length of $\overline{AB}$ is $2x$, because ______.

This means the perimeter of the n-gon is ______.

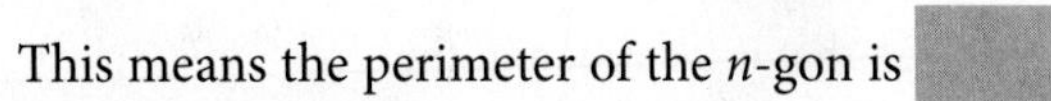

Substitute the expression for x in Step D.

The perimeter of the n-gon in terms of x is ______.

(F) Your expression for the perimeter of the n-gon should include the factor $n\sin\left(\frac{180°}{n}\right)$. What happens to this factor as n gets larger?

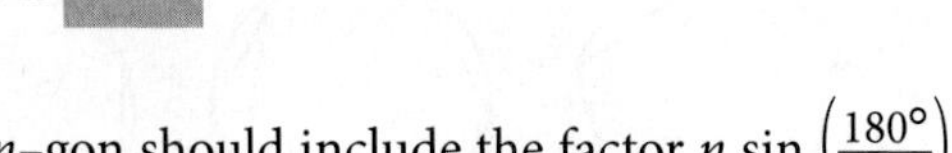

Use your calculator to do the following.

- Enter the expression $x\sin\left(\frac{180}{x}\right)$ as Y_1.
- Go to the Table Setup menu and enter the values shown.
- View a table for the function.
- Use arrow keys to scroll down.

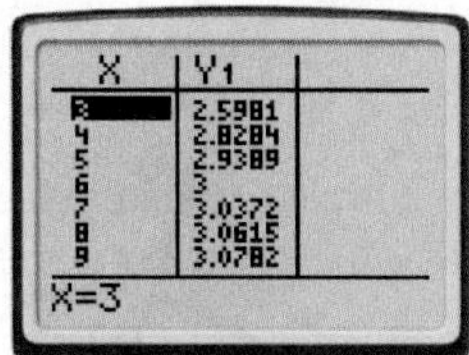

What happens to the value of $x\sin\left(\frac{180°}{x}\right)$ as x gets larger?

(G) Look at the expression you wrote for the perimeter of the n-gon. What happens to the value of this expression, as n gets larger?

Reflect

1. When n is very large, does the perimeter of the n-gon ever equal the circumference of the circle? Why or why not?
2. How does the above argument justify the formula $C = 2\pi r$?

Explain 1 Applying the Circumference Formula

Example 1 **Find the circumference indicated.**

(A) A Ferris wheel has a diameter of 40 feet. What is its circumference? Use 3.14 for π.

Diameter $= 2r$

$40 = 2r$

$20 = r$

Use the formula $C = 2\pi r$ to find the circumference.

$C = 2\pi r$

$C = 2\pi(20)$

$C = 2(3.14)(20)$

$C \approx 125.6$

The circumference is about 125.6 feet.

(B) A pottery wheel has a diameter of 2 feet. What is its circumference? Use 3.14 for π.

The diameter is 2 feet, so the radius in inches is $r =$ 12.

$C = 2\pi r$

$C =$ 2 · 3.14 · 12

$C \approx$ 75.36 in.

The circumference is about 75.36 inches.

Reflect

3. **Discussion** Suppose you double the radius of a circle. How does the circumference of this larger circle compare with the circumference of the smaller circle? Explain.

Your Turn

4. The circumference of a tree is 20 feet. What is its diameter? Round to the nearest tenth of a foot. Use 3.14 for π.

5. The circumference of a circular fountain is 32 feet. What is its diameter? Round to the nearest tenth of a foot. Use 3.14 for π.

Explain 2 Justifying the Area Formula

To find the area of a given circle, consider a regular polygon that is inscribed in the circle. As you increase the number of sides of the polygon, the area of the polygon gets closer to the area of the circle.

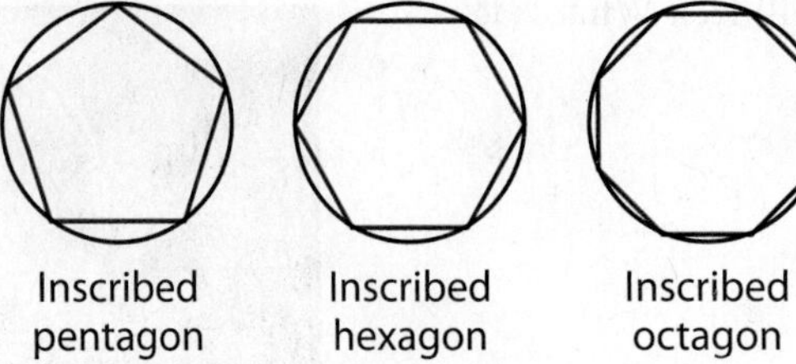

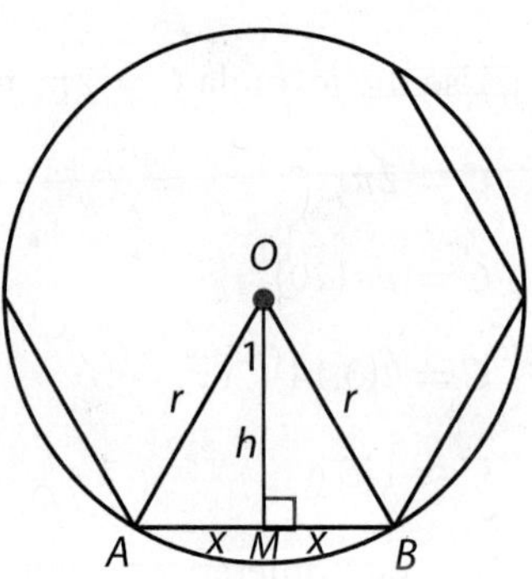

Let circle O be a circle with center O and radius r. Inscribe a regular n–gon in circle O and draw radii from O to the vertices of the n-gon.

Let $\overline{AB}$ be one side of the n–gon. Draw $\overline{OM}$, the segment from O to the midpoint of $\overline{AB}$.

We know that $\overline{OM}$ is perpendicular to $\overline{AB}$ because triangle AOM is congruent to triangle BOM.

Let the length of $\overline{OM}$ be h.

Example 2 **Justify the formula for the area of a circle.**

(A) There are n triangles, all congruent to $\triangle AOB$, that surround point O and fill the n-gon.

Therefore, the measure of $\angle AOB$ is $\frac{360°}{n}$, and the measure of $\angle 1$ is $\frac{180°}{n}$.

We know that $x = r\sin\left(\frac{180°}{n}\right)$. Write a similar expression for h.

$h = r\cos\left(\frac{180°}{n}\right)$

(B) The area of $\triangle AOB$ is $\frac{1}{2}(2x)(h) = xh = r\sin\left(\frac{180°}{n}\right)h$.

Substitute your value for h to get area $\triangle AOB = r^2\sin\left(\frac{180°}{n}\right)\cos\left(\frac{180°}{n}\right)$.

(C) There are n of these triangles, so the area of the n-gon is $nr^2\sin\left(\frac{180°}{n}\right)\cos\frac{(180°)}{n}$.

(D) Your expression for the area of the n–gon includes the factor $n\ \sin\left(\frac{180°}{n}\right)\cos\left(\frac{180°}{n}\right)$. What happens to this expression as n gets larger?

Use your graphing calculator to do the following.

- Enter the expression $x\ \sin\left(\frac{180°}{x}\right)\cos\left(\frac{180°}{x}\right)$ as Y_1.
- View a table for the function.
- Use arrow keys to scroll down.

What happens to the value of $x\ \sin\left(\frac{180°}{x}\right)\cos\left(\frac{180°}{x}\right)$ as x gets larger? The value gets closer to π.

(E) Look at the expression you wrote for the area of the n–gon. What happens to the value of this expression as n gets larger? The expression gets closer to πr^2.

Reflect

6. When n is very large, does the area of the n-gon ever equal the area of the circle? Why or why not?

7. How does the above argument justify the formula $A = \pi r^2$?

Explain 3 Applying the Area Formula

Example 3 **Find the area indicated.**

(A) A rectangular piece of cloth is 3 ft by 6 ft. What is the area of the largest circle that can be cut from the cloth? Round the nearest square inch.

The diameter of the largest circle is 3 feet, or 36 inches. The radius of the circle is 18 inches.

$A = \pi r^2$

$A = \pi(18)^2$

$A = 324\pi$

$A \approx 1{,}017.9 \text{ in}^2$

So, the area is about 1,018 square inches.

(B) A slice of a circular pizza measures 9 inches in length. What is the area of the entire pizza? Use 3.14 for π.

The 9-in. side of the pizza is also the length of the radius of the circle. So, $r = \boxed{9}$.

$A = \pi r^2$

$A = \pi \boxed{9}^2$

$A = \boxed{81} \pi \approx \boxed{254.34}$

To the nearest square inch, the area of the pizza is 255 in^2.

Reflect

8. Suppose the slice of pizza represents $\frac{1}{6}$ of the whole pizza. Does this affect your answer to Example 3B? What additional information can you determine with this fact?

Your Turn

9. A circular swimming pool has a diameter of 18 feet. To the nearest square foot, what is the smallest amount of material needed to cover the surface of the pool? Use 3.14 for π.

Elaborate

10. If the radius of a circle is doubled, is the area doubled? Explain.

11. **Essential Question Check-In** How do you justify and use the formula for the circumference of a circle?

☆ Evaluate: Homework and Practice

- Online Homework
- Hints and Help
- Extra Practice

1. Which inscribed figure has a perimeter closer to the circumference of a circle, a regular polygon with 20 sides or a regular polygon with 40 sides? Explain.

Find the circumference of each circle with the given radius or diameter. Round to the nearest tenth. Use 3.14 for π.

2. $r = 9$ cm

3. $r = 24$ in.

4. $d = 14.2$ mm

5. A basketball rim has a radius of 9 inches. Find the circumference of the rim. Round to the nearest tenth. Use 3.14 for π.

6. The diameter of a circular swimming pool is 12 feet. Find its circumference. Use 3.14 for π.

7. The diameter of the U.S. Capitol Building's dome is 96 feet at its widest point. Find its circumference. Use 3.14 for π.

Find the area of each circle with the given radius or diameter. Use 3.14 for π.

8. $r = 7$ yd

9. $d = 5$ m

10. $d = 16$ ft

11. A drum has a diameter of 10 inches. Find the area of the top of the drum. Use 3.14 for π.

12. The circumference of a quarter is about 76 mm. What is the area? Round to the nearest tenth.

Algebra Find the area of the circle with the given circumference C. Use 3.14 for π.

13. $C = 31.4$ ft

14. $C = 21.98$ ft

15. $C = 69.08$ ft

16. A Ferris wheel has a diameter of 56 ft. How far will a rider travel during a 4-minute ride if the wheel rotates once every 20 seconds?
Use $\frac{22}{7}$ for π.

17. A giant water lily pad is shaped like a circle with a diameter of up to 5 feet. Find the circumference and area of the pad. Round to the nearest tenth.

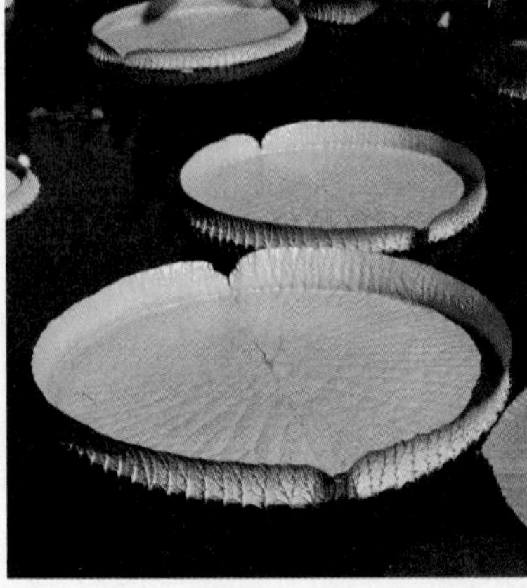

18. A pizza parlor offers pizzas with diameters of 8 in., 10 in., and 12 in. Find the area of each size pizza. Round to the nearest tenth. If the pizzas cost \$9, \$12, and \$18 respectively, which is the better buy?

19. Critical Thinking Which do you think would seat more people, a 4 ft by 6 ft rectangular table or a circular table with a diameter of 6 ft? How many people would you sit at each table? Explain your reasoning.

20. You can estimate a tree's age in years by using the formula $a = \frac{r}{w}$, where r is the tree's radius without bark and w is the average thickness of the tree's rings. The circumference of a white oak tree is 100 inches. The bark is 0.5 in. thick, and the average thickness of a ring is 0.2 in. Estimate the tree's age and the area enclosed by the outer circumference of the widest ring.

21. Multi-Step A circular track for a model train has a diameter of 8.5 feet. The train moves around the track at a constant speed of 0.7 ft/s.

a. To the nearest foot, how far does the train travel when it goes completely around the track 10 times?

b. To the nearest minute, how long does it take the train to go completely around the track 10 times?

22. The Parthenon is a Greek temple dating to about 445 BCE. The temple features 46 Doric columns, which are roughly cylindrical. The circumference of each column at the base is about 5.65 meters. What is the approximate diameter of each column? Round to the nearest tenth.

23. Explain the Error A circle has a diameter of 2π in. Which calculation of the area is incorrect? Explain.

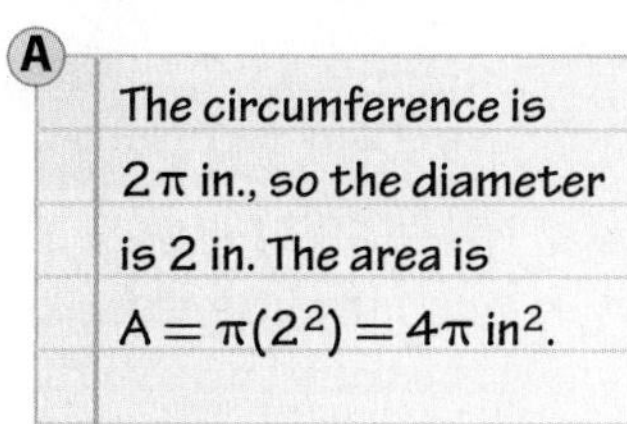

A
The circumference is
2π in., so the diameter
is 2 in. The area is
A = π(2²) = 4π in².

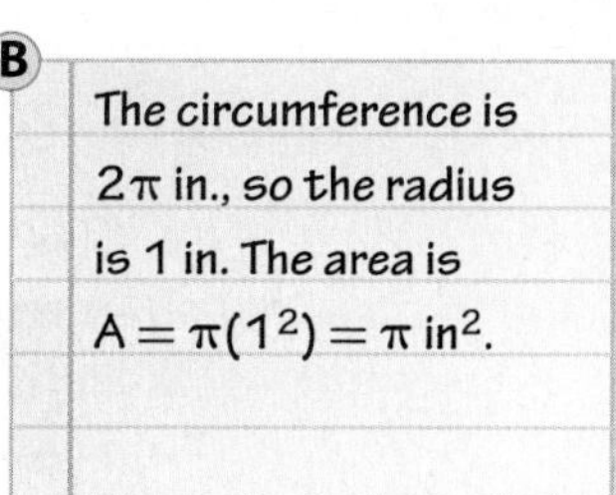

24. Write About It The center of each circle in the figure lies on the number line. Describe the relationship between the circumference of the largest circle and the circumferences of the four smaller circles.

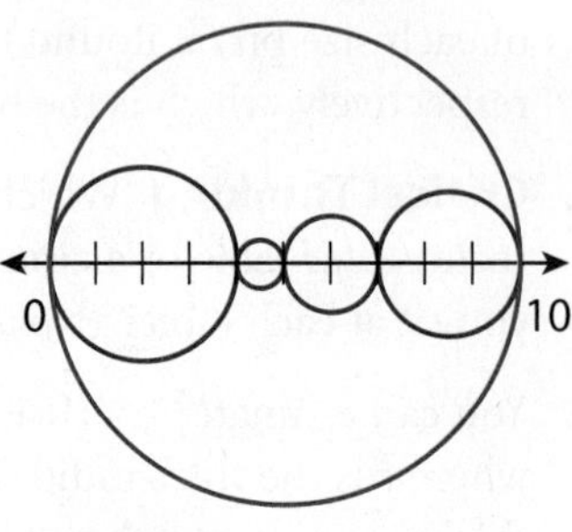

25. Find the diameter of a data storage disk with an area 113.1 cm^2.

26. Which of the following ratios can be derived from the formula for the circumference of a circle? Determine all that apply.

A. $\frac{C}{d}$

B. $\frac{C}{2r}$

C. $\frac{C}{\pi}$

D. $\frac{C}{2\pi}$

E. $\frac{C}{2c}$

27. A meteorologist measured the eyes of hurricanes to be 15 to 20 miles in diameter during one season. What is the range of areas of the land underneath the eyes of the hurricanes?

28. A circle with a 6 in. diameter is stamped out of a rectangular piece of metal as shown. Find the area of the remaining piece of metal. Use 3.14 for π.

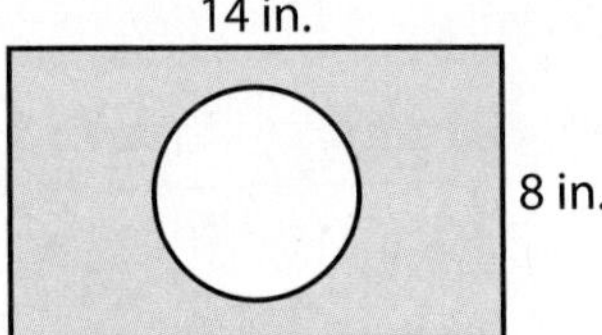

H.O.T. Focus on Higher Order Thinking

29. Critique Reasoning A standard bicycle wheel has a diameter of 26 inches. A student claims that during a one-mile bike ride the wheel makes more than 1000 complete revolutions. Do you agree or disagree? Explain. (*Hint:* 1 mile = 5280 feet)

30. Algebra A graphic artist created a company logo from two tangent circles whose diameters are in the ratio 3:2. What percent of the total logo is the area of the region outside of the smaller circle?

31. Communicate Mathematical Ideas In the figure, $\overline{AB}$ is a diameter of circle C, D is the midpoint of $\overline{AC}$, and E is the midpoint of $\overline{AD}$. How does the circumference of circle E compare to the circumference of circle C? Explain.

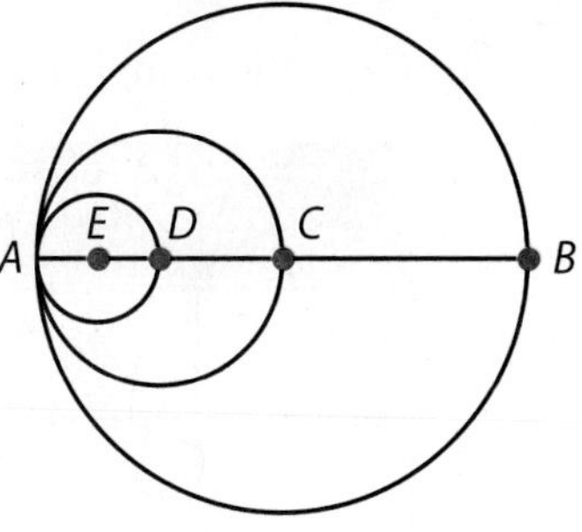

32. Critical Thinking Evelyn divides the circle and rearranges the pieces to make a shape that resembles a parallelogram.

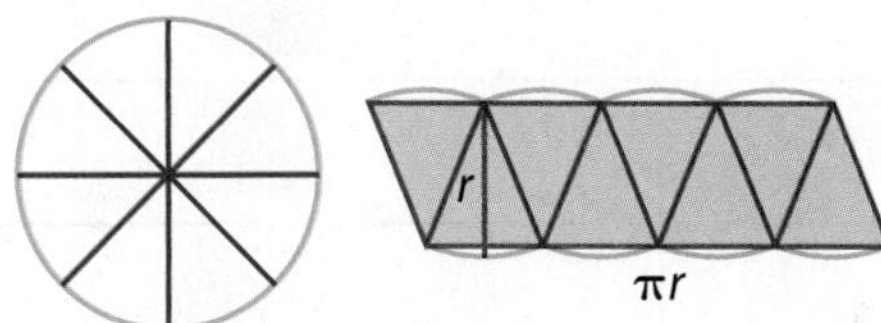

She then divides the circle into more pieces and rearranges them into a shape that resembles a parallelogram. She thinks that the area of the new parallelogram will be closer to the area of a circle. Is she correct? Explain.

Lesson Performance Task

In the lesson, you saw that the more wedges into which you divide a circle, the more closely each wedge resembles a triangle, and the closer to the area of a circle the area of the reassembled wedges becomes. In the branch of mathematics called calculus, this process is called finding a *limit.* Even though you can't cut a circle into millions of tiny wedges to calculate the actual area of the circle, you can see what the area is going to be long before that, by spotting a pattern. You can apply this method in many ways, some of them unexpected.

Mac is a race walker. He is training for a race. He has decided that in the weeks leading up to the race, he'll walk a total of 150 kilometers. His plan is to walk 72 kilometers the first day of training, and then increase each day's distance by half the previous day's increase, until he reaches his goal.

1. Copy and complete the table for Mac's first 8 days of training.

Day	Previous Total Distance + New Distance	Total Distance
1	$0 + 72$	72
2	$72 + 36$	108
3		
4		
5		
6		
7		
8		

2. Describe your results in relation to Mac's plan to walk a total of 150 kilometers.

3. Suppose Mac continues his plan for a month year. Predict his total mileage. Explain how you made your prediction. Will Mac ever reach his goal?

20.2 Arc Length and Radian Measure

Resource Locker

Essential Question: How do you find the length of an arc?

Explore Deriving the Formula for Arc Length

An **arc** is an unbroken part of a circle consisting of two points called the endpoints and all the points on the circle between them. **Arc length** is understood to be the distance along a circular arc measured in linear units (such as feet or centimeters). You can use proportional reasoning to find arc length.

Find the arc length of $\widehat{AB}$. Express your answer in terms of π and rounded to the nearest tenth.

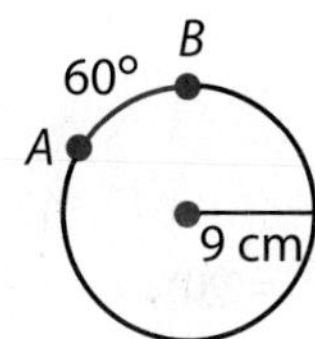

(A) First find the circumference of the circle.

$C = 2\pi r$ — Substitute the radius, 9, for r.

$C =$ ____

(B) The entire circle has 360°. Therefore, the arc's length is $\frac{60}{360}$ or $\frac{1}{6}$ of the circumference.

Arc length of $\widehat{AB} = \frac{1}{6} \cdot$ ____ — Arc length is $\frac{1}{6}$ of the circumference.

$=$ ____ — Multiply.

$\approx$  — Use a calculator to evaluate. Then round.

So, the arc length of $\widehat{AB}$ is ____ or ____.

Reflect

1. How could you use the reasoning process you used above to find the length of an arc of the circle that measures $m°$?

Explain 1 Applying the Formula for Arc Length

You were able to find an arc length using concepts of circumference. Using the same reasoning results in the formula for finding arc length.

Arc Length

The arc length, s, of an arc with measure $m°$ and radius r is given by the formula $s = \frac{m}{360} \cdot 2\pi r$.

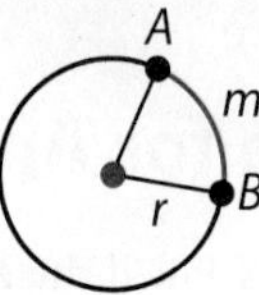

Example 1 **Find the arc length.**

(A) On a clock face, the minute hand of a clock is 10 inches long. To the nearest tenth of an inch, how far does the tip of the minute hand travel as the time progresses from 12:00 to 12:15?

The minute hand moves 15 minutes.

$\frac{15 \text{ minutes}}{60 \text{ minutes}} = \frac{1}{4}$ so the central angle formed is $\frac{1}{4} \cdot 360° = 90°$.

$s = \frac{m}{360} \cdot 2\pi r$	Use the formula for arc length.
$= \frac{90}{360} \cdot 2\pi(10)$	Substitute 10 for r and 90 for m.
$= 5\pi$	Simplify.
≈ 15.7 in.	Simplify.

(B) The minute hand of a clock is 6 inches long. To the nearest tenth of an inch, how far does the tip of the minute hand travel as the time progresses from 12:00 to 12:30?

The minute hand moves 30 minutes.

$\frac{30 \text{ minutes}}{60 \text{ minutes}} = \boxed{\frac{1}{2}}$, so the central angle formed is $\frac{1}{2} \cdot \boxed{360°} = \boxed{180°}$.

$s = \frac{m}{360} \cdot 2\pi r$	Use the formula for arc length.
$= \frac{\boxed{180}}{360} \cdot 2\pi\left(\boxed{6}\right)$	Substitute 6 for r and 180 for m.
$= \boxed{6\pi}$	Simplify.
$\approx \boxed{18.8}$ in.	Simplify.

The length of the arc is $\boxed{18.8}$ inches.

Reflect

2. **Discussion** Why does the formula represent the length of an arc of a circle?

Your Turn

3. The minute hand of a clock is 8 inches long. To the nearest tenth of an inch, how far does the tip of the minute hand travel as the time progresses from 12:00 to 12:45?

Explain 2 Investigating Arc Lengths in Concentric Circles

Consider a set of concentric circles with center O and radius 1, 2, and 3, and so on. The central angle shown in the figure is a right angle and it cuts off arcs that measure 90°.

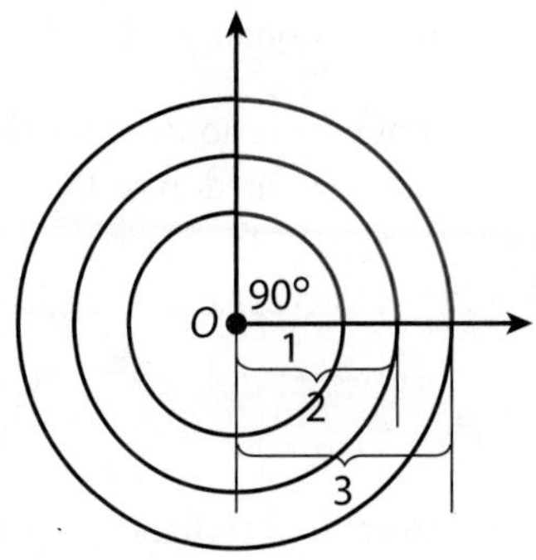

Example 2 **Find and graph arc lengths for different radii.**

(A) For each value of the radius r listed in the table below, find the corresponding arc length. Write the length in terms of π and rounded to the nearest hundredth.

For example, when $r = 1$, the arc length is $\frac{90}{360} \cdot 2\pi(1) = \frac{1}{2}\pi \approx 1.57$.

Radius r	1	2	3	4	5
Arc length s in terms of π	$\frac{1}{2}\pi$	π	$\frac{3}{2}\pi$	2π	$\frac{5}{2}\pi$
Arc length s to the nearest hundredth	1.57	3.14	4.71	6.28	7.58

(B) Plot the ordered pairs from the table on a coordinate plane.

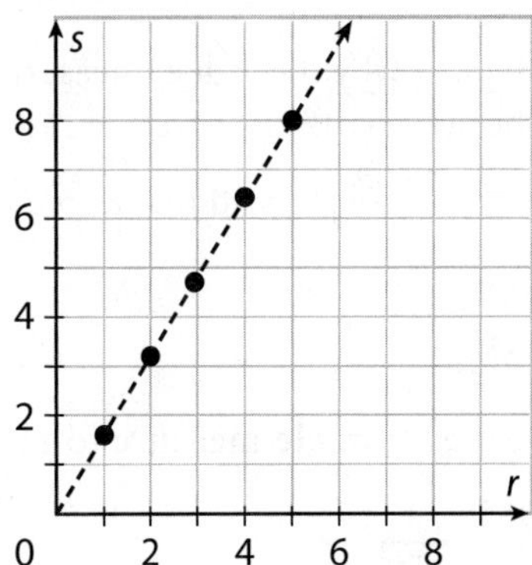

What do you notice about the points?

What type of relationship is the relationship between arc length and radius? The relationship is proportional (direct variation).

What is the constant of proportionality for this relationship?

The constant of proportionality is $\frac{1}{2}\pi$.

Reflect

4. What happens to the arc length when you double the radius? How is this connected to the idea that all circles are similar?

Explain 3 Converting Radian Measure

As you discovered in Explain 2, when the central angle is fixed at $m°$, the length of the arc cut off by a central angle is proportional to (or varies directly with) the radius. In fact, you can see that the formula for arc length is a proportional relationship when m is fixed.

$$s = \underbrace{\frac{m}{360} \cdot 2\pi}r$$

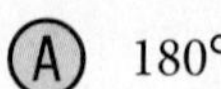

constant of proportionality

The constant of proportionality for the proportional relationship is $\frac{m}{360} \cdot 2\pi$. This constant of proportionality is defined to be the **radian measure** of the angle.

Example 3 **Convert each angle measure to radian measure.**

(A) 180°

To convert to a radian measure, let $m = 180$ in the expression $\frac{m}{360} \cdot 2\pi$.

$180° = \frac{180}{360} \cdot 2\pi$ Substitute 180 for m.

$= \pi$ radians Simplify.

(B) 60°

To convert to a radian measure, let $m = 60$ in the expression $\frac{m}{360} \cdot 2\pi$.

$60° = \frac{\boxed{60}}{360} \cdot 2\pi$ Substitute 60 for m.

$= \boxed{\frac{\pi}{3}}$ radians Simplify.

Reflect

5. Explain why the radian measure for an angle $m°$ is sometimes defined as the length of the arc cut off on a circle of radius 1 by a central angle of $m°$.

6. Explain how to find the degree measure of an angle whose radian measure is $\frac{\pi}{4}$.

Your Turn

Convert each angle measure to radian measure.

7. 90°

8. 45°

Elaborate

9. You know that 360° is the degree measure that corresponds to a full circle. What is the radian measure that corresponds to a full circle?

10. Suppose you are given that the measure in radians of an arc of a circle with radius r is θ. How can you find the length of the arc in radians?

11. **Essential Question Check-In** What two pieces of information do you need to calculate arc length?

 Evaluate: Homework and Practice

- Online Homework
- Hints and Help
- Extra Practice

Use the formula, $s = \frac{m}{360} \cdot 2\pi r$, to answer the questions.

1. What part of the circle does the expression $2\pi r$ represent?
2. What part of the circle does $\frac{m}{360}$ represent?
3. What part of the circle does the expression $2r$ represent?
4. **Critical Thinking** Suppose an arc were intercepted by a central angle measuring 15°. The diameter of the circle is 9 cm. Can both of these values be substituted into the arc length formula? Explain.

Find the arc length of $\overparen{AB}$ to the nearest tenth.

5.

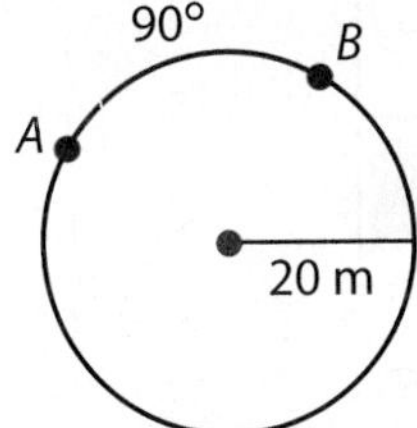

6.

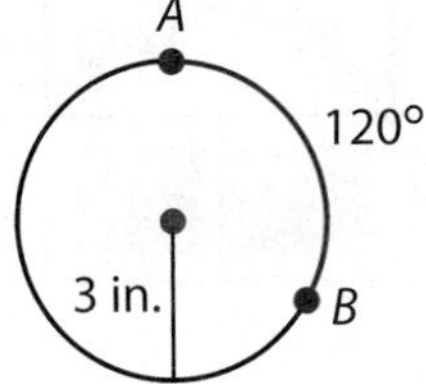

7.

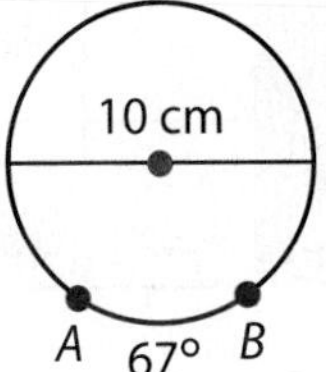

8. The minute hand of a clock is 5 inches long. To the nearest tenth of an inch, how far does the tip of the minute hand travel as the time progresses from 12:00 to 12:25?

9. The circles are concentric. Find the length of the intercepted arc in the larger circle.

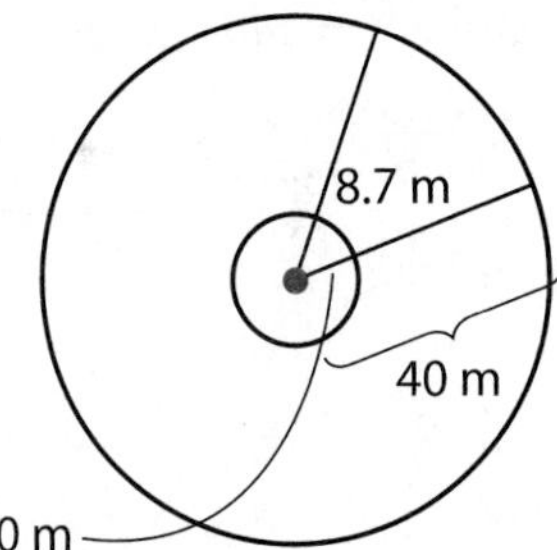

10. The circles are concentric. Find the length of $\overparen{PQ}$.

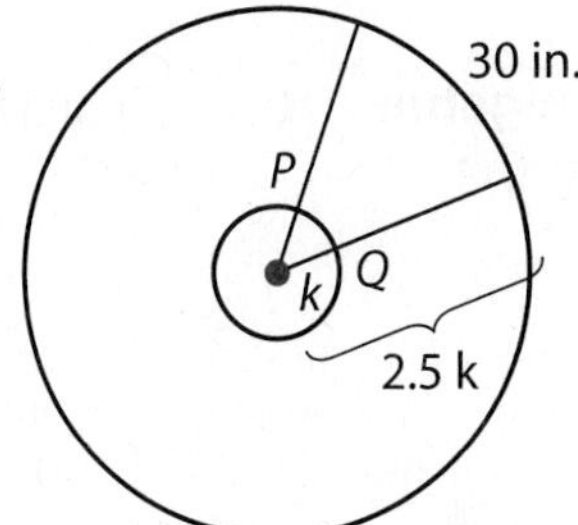

11. Two arcs of concentric circles are intercepted by the same central angle. The resulting arc length of the arc of the larger circle is 16 m and the radius of the larger circle is 12 m. The radius of the smaller circle is 7.5 m. Find the length of the corresponding arc of the smaller circle.

12. Two arcs of concentric circles are intercepted by the same central angle. The resulting arc length of the arc of the smaller circle is 36 ft and its radius is 30 ft. The radius of the larger circle is 45 ft. Find the length of the corresponding arc of the larger circle.

Convert each angle measure to radian measure.

13. 40°

14. 80°

15. 100°

16. 12°

17. It is convenient to know the radian measure for benchmark angles such as 0°, 30°, 45°, and so on. Copy and complete the table by finding the radian measure for each of the given benchmark angles.

Benchmark Angles									
Degree Measure	0°	30°	45°	60°	90°	120°	135°	150°	180°
Radian Measure									

Convert each radian measure to degree measure.

18. $\frac{5\pi}{8}$

19. $\frac{8\pi}{9}$

20. In the diagram, $\overline{WY}$, and $\overline{XZ}$ are diameters of $\odot T$, and $WY = XZ = 6$. If $m\overset{\frown}{XY} = 140°$, what is the length of $\overset{\frown}{YZ}$? Determine all that apply.

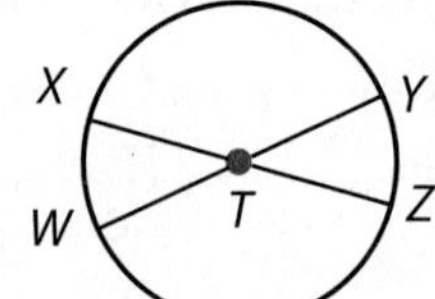

A. $\frac{4\pi}{6}$

B. $\frac{4\pi}{3}$

C. $\frac{2}{3}\pi$

D. 4π

E. 6π

21. Algebra The length of $\overset{\frown}{TS}$ is 12 in. Find the length of $\overset{\frown}{RS}$.

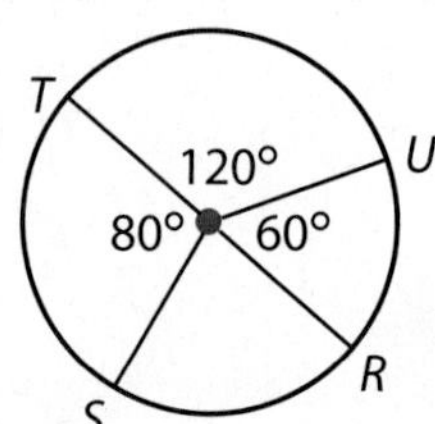

22. Multi-Step The diagram shows the plan for a putting a decorative trim around a corner desk. The trim will be 4-inch high around the perimeter of the desk. The curve is one quarter of the circumference of a circle. Find the length of trim needed to the nearest half foot.

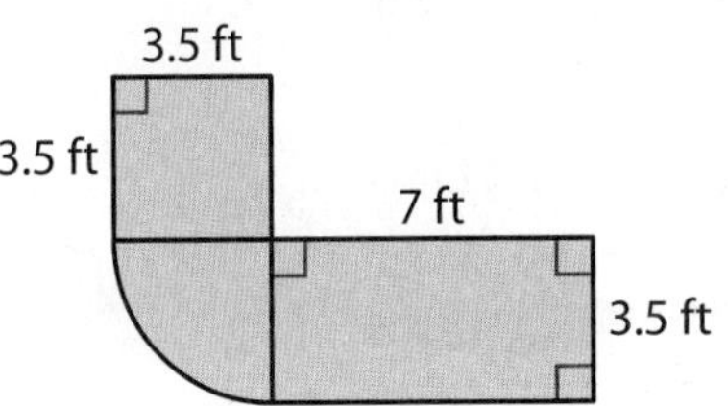

23. Explain the Error A student was asked to find the arc length of $\widehat{PQ}$. The student's work is shown. Explain the student's error and give the correct arc length.

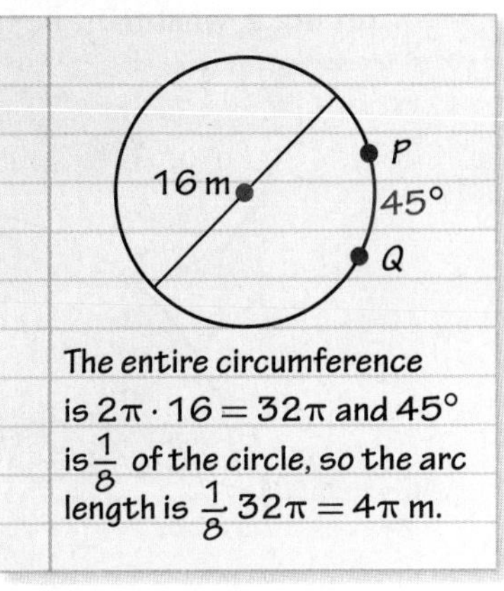

16 m
P
45°
Q
The entire circumference is $2\pi \cdot 16 = 32\pi$ and 45° is $\frac{1}{8}$ of the circle, so the arc length is $\frac{1}{8} 32\pi = 4\pi$ m.

H.O.T. Focus on Higher Order Thinking

24. Critique Reasoning A friend tells you two arcs from different circles have the same arc length if their central angles are equal. Is your friend correct? Explain your reasoning.

25. Multi-Step A carpenter is making a tray to fit between two circular pillars in the shape of the shaded area as shown. She is using a jigsaw to cut along the edge of the tray. What is the length of the cut encompassing the tray? Round to the nearest half foot.

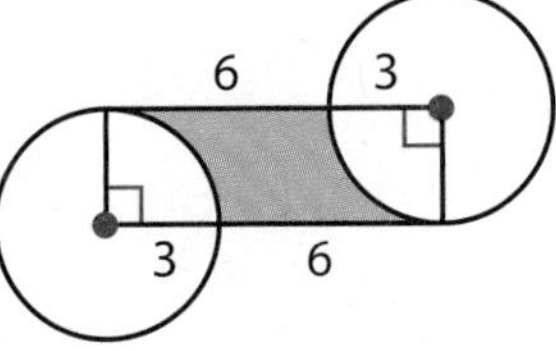

26. Critical Thinking The pedals of a penny-farthing Bicycle are directly connected to the front wheel.

a. Suppose a penny-farthing bicycle has a front wheel with a diameter of 5 ft. To the nearest tenth of a foot, how far does the bike move when you turn the pedals through an angle of 90°?

b. Through what angle should you turn the pedals in order to move forward by a distance of 4.5 ft? Round to the nearest degree.

Lesson Performance Task

The latitude of a point is a measure of its position north or south on the Earth's surface. Latitudes North (N) are measured from 0° N at the equator to 90° N at the North Pole. Latitudes South (S) are measured from 0° S at the equator to 90° S at the South Pole.

The figure shows the latitudes of Washington, D.C. and Lima, Peru. The radius of the Earth is approximately 6,370 kilometers.

1. Find the angle at the Earth's center between radii drawn to Washington and Lima.

2. Find the distance between Washington and Lima. Show your work.

3. A point's longitude is a measure of its position east or west on the Earth's surface. In order for your calculation of the distance between Washington and Lima to be accurate, what must be true about the longitudes of the two cities?

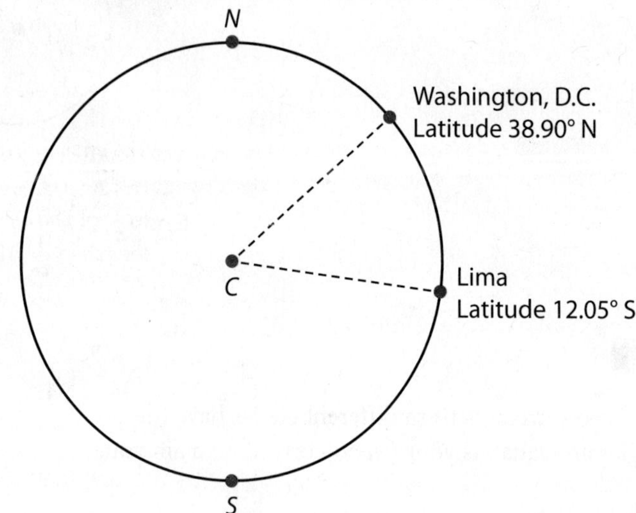

20.3 Sector Area

Essential Question: How do you find the area of a sector of a circle?

Explore Derive the Formula for the Area of a Sector

A **sector** of a circle is a region bounded by two radii and their intercepted arc. A sector is named by the endpoints of the arc and the center of the circle. For example, the figure shows sector *POQ*.

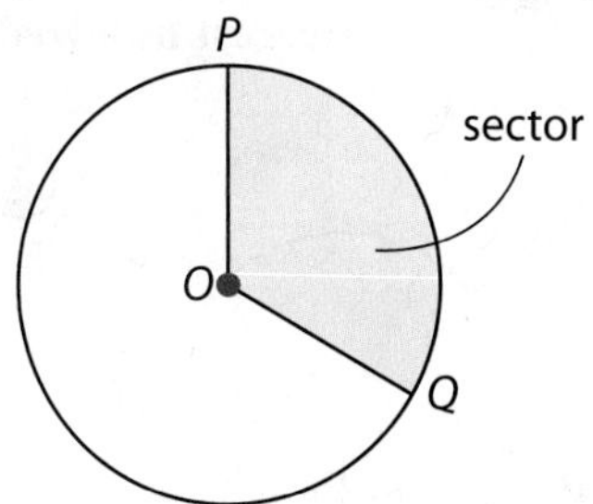

In the same way that you used proportional reasoning to find the length of an arc, you can use proportional reasoning to find the area of a sector.

Find the area of sector *AOB*. Express your answer in terms of π and rounded to the nearest tenth.

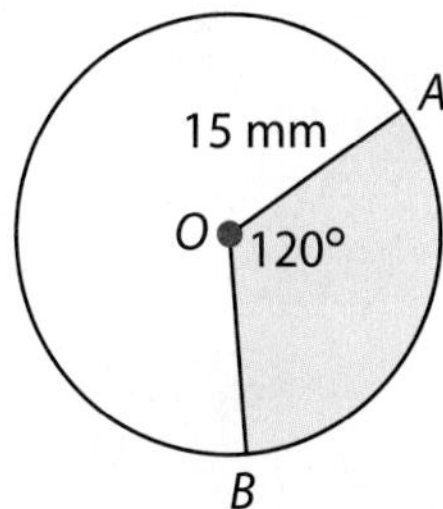

(A) First find the area of the circle.

$A = \pi r^2 = \pi\left(\boxed{}\right)^2$

$= \boxed{}$

(B) The entire circle is 360°, but $\angle AOB$ measures 120°. Therefore, the sector's area is $\frac{120}{360}$ or $\frac{1}{3}$ of the circle's area.

Area of sector $AOB = \frac{1}{3} \cdot \boxed{}$ — The area is $\frac{1}{3}$ of the circle's area.

$= \boxed{}$ — Simplify.

$= \boxed{}$ — Use a calculator to evaluate. Then round.

So, the area of sector *AOB* is $\boxed{}$ or $\boxed{}$.

Reflect

1. How could you use the above process to find the area of a sector of the circle whose central angle measures $m°$?

2. **Make a Conjecture** What do you think is the formula for the area of a sector with a central angle of $m°$ and radius r?

Explain 1 Using the Formula for the Area of a Sector

The proportional reasoning process you used in the Explore can be generalized. Given a sector with a central angle of $m°$ and radius r, the area of the entire circle is πr^2 and the area of the sector is $\frac{m}{360}$ times the circle's area. This gives the following formula.

Area of a Sector

The area A of a sector with a central angle of $m°$ of a circle with radius r is given by $A = \frac{m}{360} \cdot \pi r^2$

Example 1 **Find the area of each sector, as a multiple of π and to the nearest hundredth.**

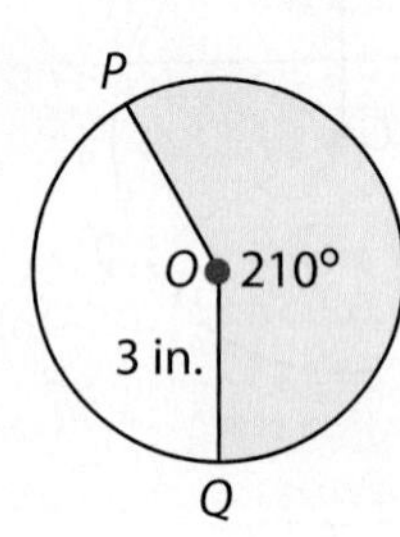

(A) sector POQ

$$A = \frac{m}{360} \cdot \pi r^2$$
$$= \frac{210}{360} \cdot \pi (3)^2$$
$$= \frac{7}{12} \cdot 9\pi$$
$$= \frac{21}{4}\pi$$
$$\approx 16.49 \text{ in}^2$$

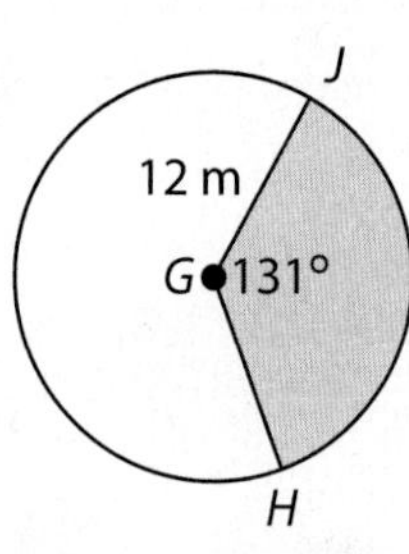

(B) sector HGJ

$$A = \frac{m}{360} \cdot \pi r^2$$
$$= \frac{131}{360} \cdot \pi (12)^2$$
$$= \frac{131}{360} \cdot 144\pi$$
$$= 52.4\pi$$
$$\approx 164.62 \text{ m}^2$$

Reflect

3. **Discussion** Your friend said that the value of $m°$ in the formula for the area of a sector can never be larger than 360°. Do you agree or disagree? Explain your reasoning.

Your Turn

Find the area of each sector, as a multiple of π and to the nearest hundredth.

4. sector AOB

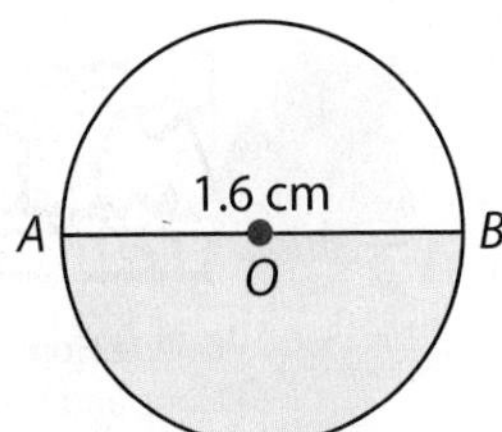

5. sector POQ

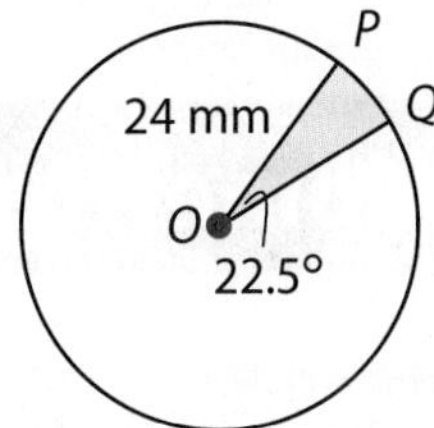

Explain 2 Applying the Formula for the Area of a Sector

You can apply the formula for the area of a sector to real-world problems.

Example 2 **Find each area.**

Ⓐ A beam from a lighthouse is visible for a distance of 3 mi. To the nearest square mile, what is the area covered by the beam as it sweeps in an arc of 150°?

$A = \frac{m}{360} \cdot \pi r^2$

$= \frac{150}{360} \cdot \pi(3)^2$

$= \frac{5}{12} \cdot 9\pi$

$= 3.75\pi$

$\approx 12 \text{ mi}^2$

Ⓑ A circular plot with a 180-foot diameter is watered by a spray irrigation system. To the nearest square foot, what is the area that is watered as the sprinkler rotates through an angle of 50°?

$d = 180$ ft, so $r = 90$ ft

$A = \frac{m}{360} \cdot \pi r^2$

$= \frac{50}{360} \cdot \pi(90)^2$

$= \frac{5}{36} \cdot 8100\pi$

$= 1125\pi$

$= 3{,}534 \text{ ft}^2$

Your Turn

6. To the nearest square foot, what is the area watered in Example 2B as the sprinkler rotates through a semicircle?

Elaborate

7. **Discussion** When can you use proportional reasoning to find the area of a sector without knowing or finding its central angle? Explain your reasoning by giving an example.

8. **Essential Question Check-In** What information do you need to find the area of a sector?

Evaluate: Homework and Practice

- Online Homework
- Hints and Help
- Extra Practice

1. The region within a circle that is bounded by two radii and an arc is called a ___?___.

2. Suppose you know the area and the measure of the central angle of a sector. Describe the process of finding the area of the sector.

3. What is the formula for the area of a circle? Define all variables in the formula.

4. If the angle of a sector measures 45°, what fraction of the circle is the sector?

Find the area of sector *AOB*. Express your answer in terms of π and rounded to the nearest tenth.

5.
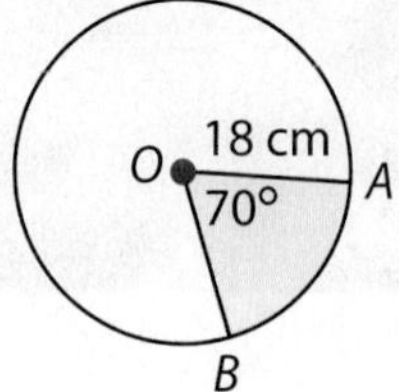

6.
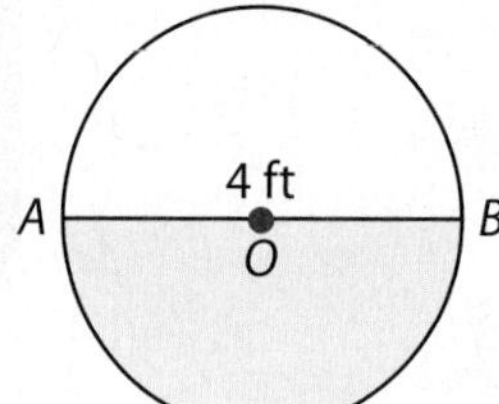

7.
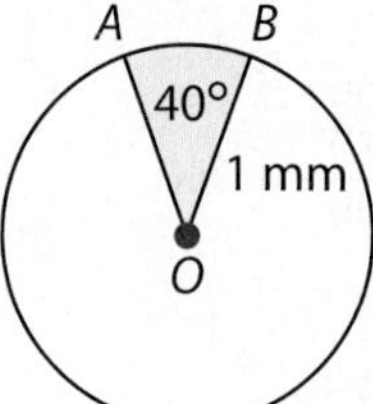

8.
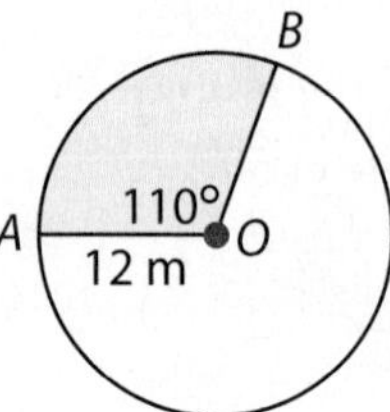

9.
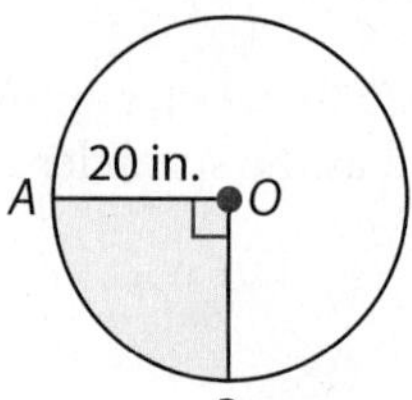

10.
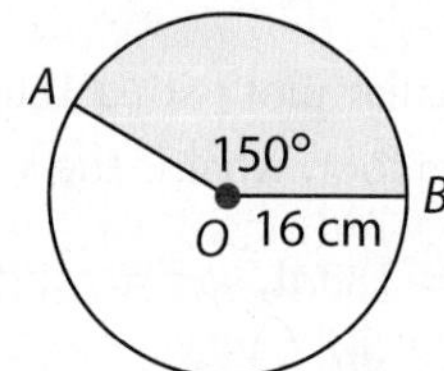

11. A round pizza is cut into congruent sectors. If the angle measure of the pizza slice is 20°, how many pieces are in the whole pizza?

12. The area of a piece of pie in the shape of a sector is 7.1 in^2. The angle of the sector is 40°.

    a. What is the area of the entire pie?

    b. What is the diameter of the pie?

13. A *lunette* is a semicircular window that is sometimes placed above a doorway or above a rectangular window. The diameter of the lunette is 40 inches. To the nearest square inch, what is the area of the lunette?

Find the area of each sector. Give your answer in terms of π and rounded to the nearest hundredth.

14. sector *PQR*

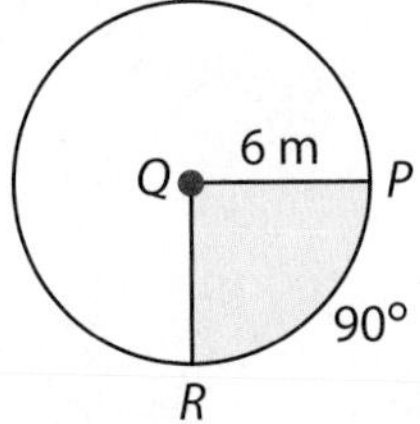

15. sector *JKL*

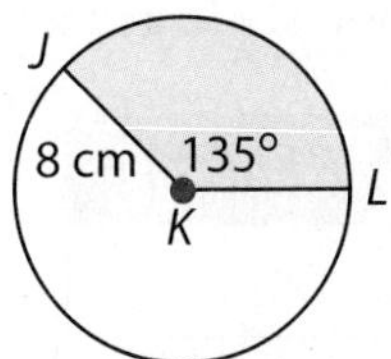

16. sector *ABC*

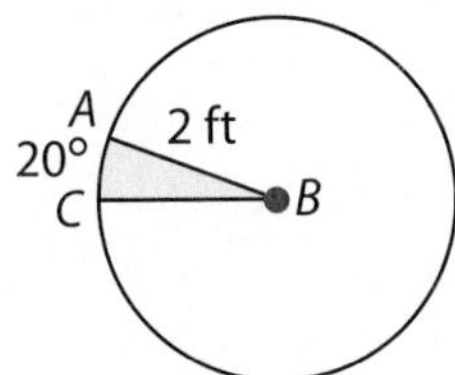

17. sector *RST*

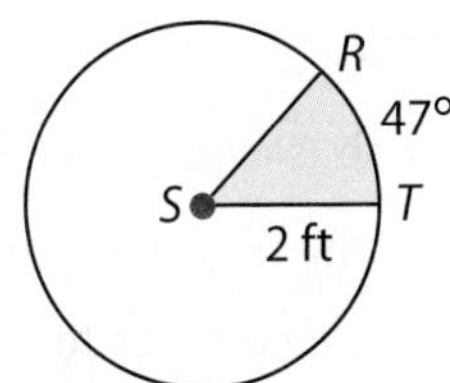

18. The beam from a lighthouse is visible for a distance of 15 mi. To the nearest square mile, what is the area covered by the beam as it sweeps in an arc of 270°?

19. The radius of circle *O* is 6 mm. The area of sector *AOB* is $\frac{9}{2}\pi$. Explain how to find m∠*AOB*.

The Artisan Pizza Co sells take-out pizza in two shapes: an "individual" 6-in. square slice and a circular "party" wheel with an 18 in. diameter. The party wheel is cut into 8 slices/sectors for the customer. An individual slice of the party wheel costs $2.95 and the entire party wheel costs $15.95.

20. Which is larger, the square slice or one sector of the wheel?

21. Which option is the better value, buying by the slice or buying the entire wheel?

22. Greek mathematicians studied the *salinon*, a figure bounded by four semicircles. What is the area of this salinon to the nearest tenth of a square inch?

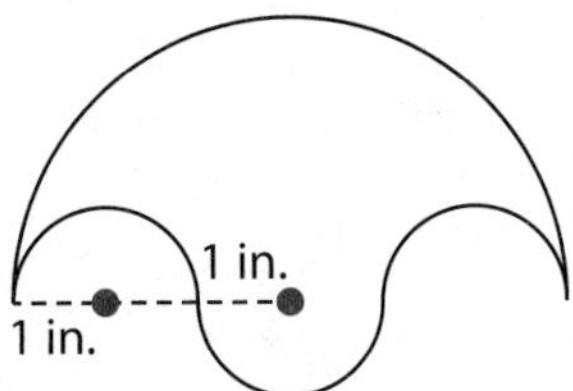

23. Which of the following express the measure of the angle of a sector, m, as a ratio between the area of the sector and the radius of the circle?

A. $\frac{360\pi}{Ar^2}$

B. $\frac{360\,A}{\pi r^2}$

C. $360r^2 \cdot \frac{A}{\pi}$

D. $\frac{A\pi r^2}{360}$

E. $\frac{Ar^2}{360\pi}$

F. $360A \cdot \frac{1}{\pi r^2}$

24. Algebra The table shows how students get to school.

Methods	% of Students
Bus	65%
Walk	25%
Other	10%

a. Explain why a circle graph is appropriate for the data.

b. Use a proportion to find the measure of the central angle for each sector. Then use a protractor and a compass to draw the circle graph.

c. Find the area of each sector. Use a radius of 2 inches.

Multi-Step A *segment of a circle* is a region bounded by an arc and its chord. Find the area of each segment to the nearest hundredth.

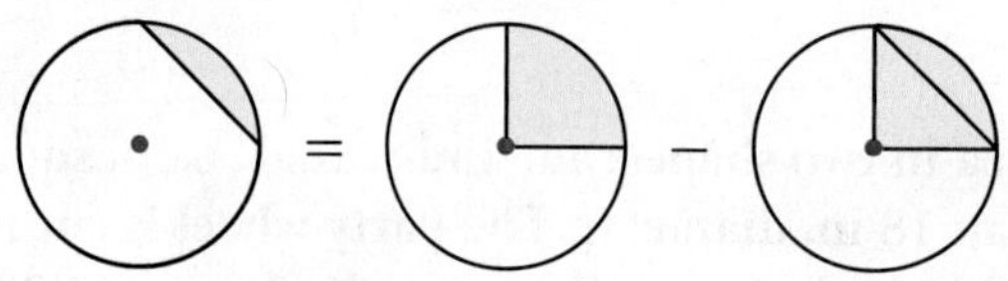

area of segment = area of sector − area of triangle

25. 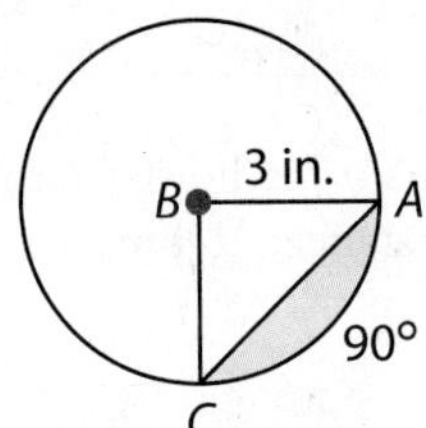

26. 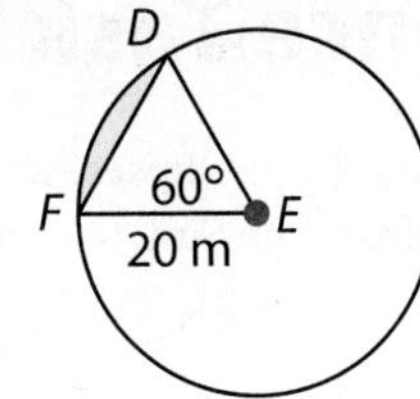

H.O.T. Focus on Higher Order Thinking

27. Critique Reasoning A student claims that when you double the radius of a sector while keeping the measure of the central angle constant, you double the area of the sector. Do you agree or disagree? Explain.

28. Multi-Step The exclamation point (!) on a billboard consists of a circle sector and circle. The radius of the sector is 9 ft, and the radius of the circle is 1.5 ft. The angle of the sector is 24°. What is the total area of the exclamation point on the billboard? Round to the nearest tenth.

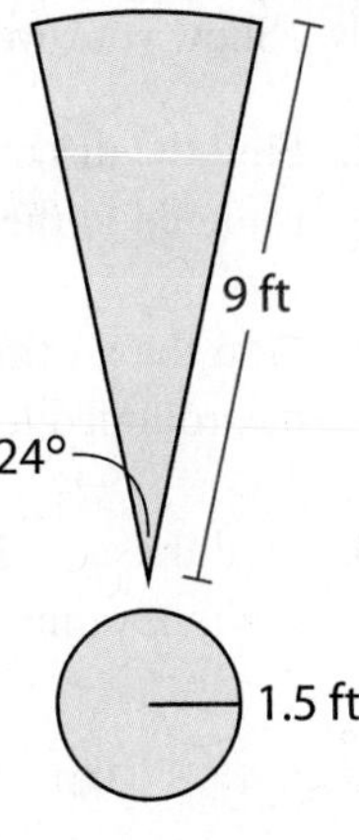

29. Analyze Relationships Compare finding arc length to finding the area of a sector. Name any common and different processes.

30. Critique Reasoning Melody says that she needs only to know the length of an arc and radius of a circle to find the area of the corresponding sector. If arc length is L and sector area is A, then $A = \frac{2L}{r}$. Is she correct? Justify your answer.

Lesson Performance Task

The planets orbit the Sun not in circles but in ellipses, which are "flattened" circles. The Earth's orbit, however, isn't flattened much. Its greatest distance from the Sun, 94.5 million miles, differs from its least distance, 91.4 million miles, by only about 3%.

To answer the following questions, make the following assumptions:

a. Summer includes all of the days from June 21 through September 21. During that time Earth travels in a circular orbit with a radius of 94.5 million miles. A year lasts 365 days.

b. Winter includes all of the days from December 21 through March 20. During that time Earth travels in a circular orbit with a radius of 91.4 million miles. The year you will consider lasts 365 days and is not a leap year.

Solve. Show your work. Use 3.14 for π.

1. Find the distances that the Earth travels in summer and in winter. Give your answers in millions of miles rounded to the nearest tenth.

2. Find the Earth's average rate of speed in summer and in winter. Give your answers in millions of miles per day rounded to the nearest hundredth.

3. Find the areas of the sectors that the Earth traverses in summer and in winter. Give your answers in millions of miles squared rounded to the nearest tenth.

Arc Length and Sector Area

Essential Question: How can the arc length and sector area of a circle be used to solve a real-world problem? How are they related?

KEY EXAMPLE *(Lesson 20.1)*

The circumference of a tire is 90 inches. What is its radius? Round to the nearest inch.

$C = 2\pi r$	Write the circumference formula.
$90 = 2\pi r$	Substitute the circumference.
$\frac{90}{2\pi} = r$	Simplify.
$14 \text{ in} \approx r$	Substitute 3.14 for π to approximate the solution.

KEY EXAMPLE *(Lesson 20.2)*

Find the arc length of an arc that measures 150° in a circle with a radius of 8 meters. Give your answer in terms of π.

$A = \frac{m}{360} \cdot 2\pi r$	Write the arc length formula.
$A = \frac{150}{360} \cdot 2\pi 8$	Substitute the angle measure and radius.
$A = \frac{20}{3}\pi$	Simplify.

KEY EXAMPLE *(Lesson 20.3)*

A sandwich shop sells sandwiches on two types of bread: a 9-inch square flatbread and a round roll with a 4-inch radius. Which type of bread is larger?

$A = s^2$	Write the area of a square.
$A = (9 \text{ in})^2$	Substitute the side length of the flatbread.
$A = 81 \text{ in}^2$	Simplify.
$A = \pi r^2$	Write the area of a circle.
$A = \pi(4)^2 \text{ in}^2$	Substitute the radius of the roll.
$A = 16\pi \text{ in}^2$	Simplify.
$A \approx 50.24 \text{ in}^2$	Substitute 3.14 for π to approximate the solution.

The flatbread is larger than the roll.

EXERCISES

Find the radius of the circle with the given circumference. *(Lesson 20.1)*

1. $C = 15$ in

2. $C = \pi$ cm

Find the arc length given the angle measure and radius of the circle. Give your answer in terms of π. *(Lesson 20.2)*

3. $m = 180°$, $r = 4$ inches

Apply the formula for the area of a sector to solve the real-world problem. *(Lesson 20.3)*

4. A paper airplane can be made out of two different pieces of paper: a circular piece 10 inches wide and a square piece 11 inches wide. Which piece of paper will provide the greater area for flight?

MODULE PERFORMANCE TASK

What's the Better Deal on Pizza?

You are ordering pizza and you have two choices: a slice of pizza from a large pizza with a diameter of 22 inches or an entire personal-size pizza that has a diameter of 6 inches. The slice costs $4.95, and the smaller pizza costs $3.75. Assuming that the large pizza is cut into 8 slices, will you get more pizza for your money by buying one slice of the larger pizza or by buying the personal-size pizza?

Be sure to write down all of your assumptions and data. Then use words, diagrams, numbers, or geometry to explain how you came to your conclusion.

Ready to Go On?

20.1–20.3 Arc Length and Sector Area

- Online Homework
- Hints and Help
- Extra Practice

Apply the appropriate area formula. *(Lesson 20.1)*

1. At a campground, the area of a rectangular fire pit is 5 feet by 4 feet. What is the area of the largest circular fire than can be made in this fire pit? Round to the nearest square inch.

Find the arc length. Give your answer in terms of π and round to the nearest hundredth. *(Lesson 20.2)*

2. $\widehat{AB}$

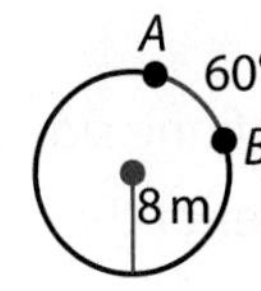

Apply the formula for the area of a sector to solve the real-world problem. *(Lesson 20.3)*

3. A Mexican restaurant sells quesadillas in two sizes: a "large" 10–inch round quesadilla and a "small" 6–inch round quesadilla. Which is larger, half of the 10-inch quesadilla or the entire 6-inch quesadilla?

ESSENTIAL QUESTION

4. What is the relationship between the arc length and sector area of a circle?

MODULE 20
MIXED REVIEW

Assessment Readiness

SELECTED RESPONSE

1. Consider each equation. Does it show a true relationship between degree measure and radian measure? Write Yes or No for A–C.

A. $\frac{5\pi}{12}$ radians $= 75°$

B. $\frac{\pi}{2}$ radians $= 180°$

C. $\frac{\pi}{3}$ radians $= 60°$

2. Consider a circle with a radius of 2 meters that has an arc angle of 90°. Determine if each statement is True or False.

A. The arc measure is 90°.

B. The circumference and the area of this circle, taking away the units, are equal.

C. The arc length is π meters.

3. $\triangle ABC$ is an equilateral triangle, $\overline{AB} = 3x + 27$, and $\overline{BC} = 5x - 9$. Determine if each statement is True or False.

A. $x = 18$

B. The length of one side of the triangle is 162 units.

C. The perimeter of the triangle is 243 units.

4. Write an equation that represents the circumference of a circle with a radius of 6 feet. What is the diameter of the circle?

5. Given the sector area, how can the radius be determined? From the radius, how can the arc length be determined?

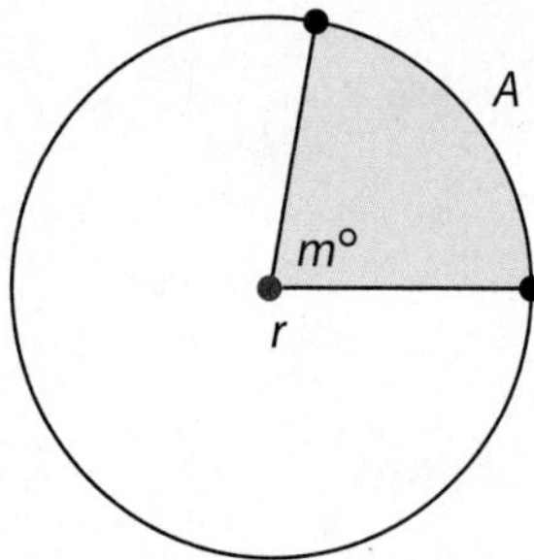

UNIT 8 MIXED REVIEW

Assessment Readiness

- Online Homework
- Hints and Help
- Extra Practice

1. Determine whether each arc is a minor arc, a major arc, or a semicircle.

A. $\overset{\frown}{AB}$

B. $\overset{\frown}{ABE}$

C. $\overset{\frown}{ADB}$

2. Quadrilateral *ABCD* is inscribed in a circle with angle measures $m\angle A = (11x - 8)°$, $m\angle B = (3x^2 + 1)°$, $m\angle C = (15x + 32)°$, and $m\angle D = (2x^2 - 1)°$. Are each of the following measures of the quadrilateral's angles? Write Yes or No.

A. $m\angle A = 135°$

B. $m\angle B = 109°$

C. $m\angle C = 227°$

D. $m\angle D = 71°$

3. $\triangle ABC$ and $\triangle DEF$ are congruent.

Determine if each statement is True or False.

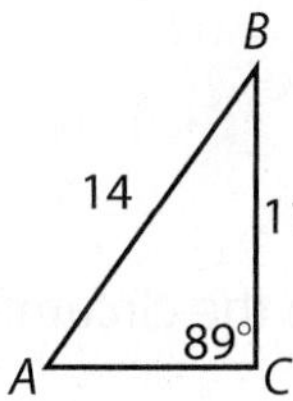

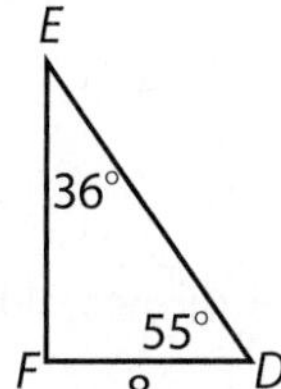

A. $m\angle F = 91°$

B. $m\angle A = 55°$

C. $\overline{EF} = 11$

4. Determine whether the vertex of $\angle 1$ is on the circle, inside the circle, or outside the circle, given its measure and the measure of its intercepted arc(s).

A. $m\angle 1 = 58°, m\angle 2 = 85°, m\angle 3 = 31°$

B. $m\angle 1 = 52°, m\angle 2 = 104°$

C. $m\angle 1 = 27°, m\angle 2 = 85°, m\angle 3 = 31°$

5. Are each of the following lengths of chords in the circle? Write Yes or No.

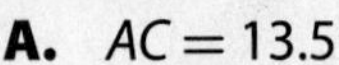

A. $AC = 13.5$

B. $EF = 7.1$

C. $BF = 2.9$

6. Are each of the following lengths of the segments in the triangle? Write Yes or No.

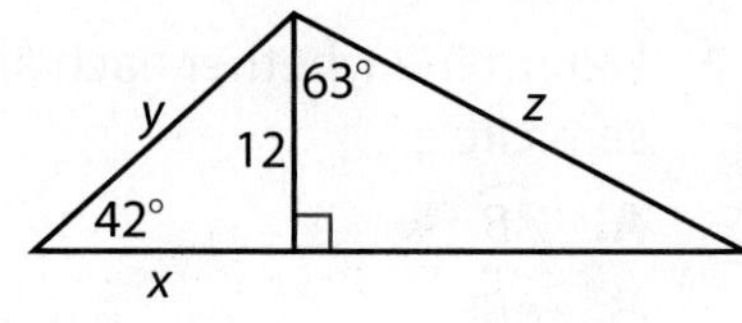

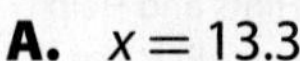

A. $x = 13.3$

B. $y = 16.1$

C. $z = 13.5$

7. Given that $\triangle ABC$ is a right triangle, determine if it is a special right triangle.

A. $AC = BC = 3\sqrt{2}$ and $AB = 6$

B. $AC = BC = 5\sqrt{2}$ and $AB = 10$

C. $m\angle A = 30°$

8. Renee is designing a logo for an airline. She starts by making a figure with angle measures as shown. She measures $\overline{AB}$ and finds that the length of the segment is 5 inches. Can she determine the length of $\overline{DB}$ without measuring? If so, explain how. If not, explain why not.

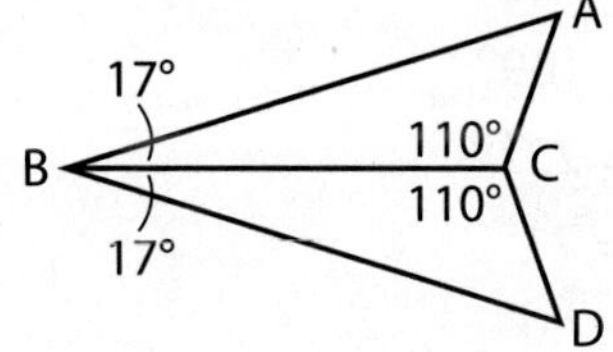

9. A car tire has a diameter of 21.3 inches. What are the circumference and the area of the tire?

Performance Tasks

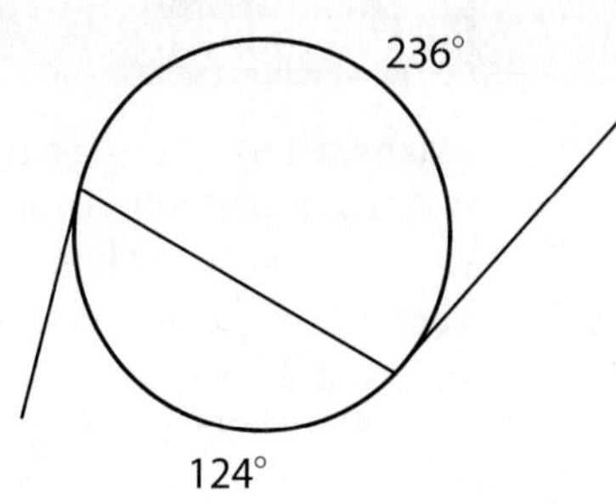

★10. A city planner is designing a bridge to cross a circular lake in the park. There will be two footpaths, both tangent to the lake, that connect to each side of the bridge. At what angles do the footpaths connect with the bridge?

★★11. Nestor cuts a cake with a 12-inch diameter. One of the pieces he cuts has a central angle of 24°. What is the area of the slice of cake? What fraction of the entire cake is this? Explain.

★★★12. Jeanine's swimming pool has a diameter of 27 feet. Surrounding the pool is a deck that extends 5 feet from the edges of the pool. Jeanine wants to paint the deck and then put a fence around it. Paint costs $0.85 per square foot and fencing costs $8.25 per foot. How much will it cost Jeanine to paint the deck and add fencing? Explain how you found your answer.

MATH IN CAREERS

Astronomer During a partial solar eclipse, the moon aligns with the sun and Earth such that it partially covers the sun from view on a circular area on Earth's surface with a radius of 130 kilometers (km). The lines tangent to both the moon and this area meet at a 144° angle. What is the measure and length of the arc on the area in which a person on Earth will be able to witness a partial eclipse?

UNIT 9

Volume

MODULE 21

Volume Formulas

MATH IN CAREERS

Jewelry Maker A jewelry maker designs and creates jewelry. Jewelry makers often employ geometric designs and shapes in their work, and so they need a good understanding of geometry. For example, they must calculate volume and surface area to determine the amount of materials needed. They can also use computer designing programs to help them with their design specifications. Jewelry makers often need to calculate costs of materials and labor to determine production costs for their designs.

If you are interested in a career as a jewelry maker, you should study these mathematical subjects:

- Algebra
- Geometry
- Business Math

Research other careers that require knowing the geometry of three-dimensional objects. Check out the career activity at the end of the unit to find out how **jewelry makers** use math.

Reading Start-Up

Vocabulary

Review Words

area (*área*)
composite figure (*figura compuesta*)
✔ cone (*cono*)
✔ cylinder (*cilindro*)
✔ pyramid (*pirámide*)
✔ sphere (*esfera*)
volume (*volume*)

Preview Words

apothem (*apotema*)
oblique cylinder (*cilindro oblicuo*)
oblique prism (*prisma oblicuo*)
regular pyramid (*pirámide regular*)
right cone (*cono recto*)
right cylinder (*cilindro recto*)
right prism (*prisma recto*)

Visualize Vocabulary

Copy and complete the chart. Use four of the ✔ words and draw an example of each.

Object	Example
?	?
?	?
?	?
?	?

Understand Vocabulary

Complete the sentences using the preview words.

1. A cone whose axis is perpendicular to its base is called a(n) __?__.

2. A prism that has at least one nonrectangular lateral face is called a(n) __?__.

Active Reading

Pyramid Create a pyramid and organize the adjectives used to describe different objects—right, regular, oblique—on each of its faces. When listening to descriptions of objects, look for these words and associate them with the object that follows.

Volume Formulas

MODULE 21

Essential Question: How can you use volume formulas to solve real-world problems?

REAL WORLD VIDEO
Check out how volume formulas can be used to find the volumes of real-world objects, including sinkholes.

MODULE PERFORMANCE TASK PREVIEW

How Big Is That Sinkhole?

In 2010, a giant sinkhole opened up in a neighborhood in Guatemala and swallowed up the three-story building that stood above it. In this module, you will choose and apply an appropriate formula to determine the volume of this giant sinkhole.

Complete these exercises to review skills you will need for this module.

Personal Math Trainer

- Online Homework
- Hints and Help
- Extra Practice

Area of a Circle

Example 1 Find the area of a circle with radius equal to 5.

$A = \pi r^2$ Write the equation for the area of a circle of radius *r*.

$A = \pi(5)^2$ Substitute the radius.

$A = 25\pi$ Simplify.

Find each area.

1. A circle with radius 4

2. A circle with radius 6

3. A circle with radius 3π

4. A circle with radius $\frac{2}{\pi}$

Volume Properties

Example 2 Find the number of cubes that are 1 cm^3 in size that fit into a cube of size 1 m^3.

Notice that the base has a length and width of 1 m or 100 cm, so its area is 1 m^2 or 10,000 cm^2.

The 1 m^3 cube is 1 m or 100 cm high, so multiply the area of the base by the height to find the volume of 1,000,000 cm^3.

Find the volume.

5. The volume of a 1 km^3 body of water in m^3

6. The volume of a 1 ft^3 box in $in.^3$

Volume of Rectangular Prisms

Example 3 Find the volume of a rectangular prism with height 4 cm, length 3 cm, and width 5 cm.

$V = Bh$ Write the equation for the volume of a rectangular prism.

$V = (3)(5)(4)$ The volume of a rectangular prism is the area of the base times the height.

$V = 60\ cm^3$ Simplify.

Find each volume.

7. A rectangular prism with length 3 m, width 4 m, and height 7 m

8. A rectangular prism with length 2 cm, width 5 cm, and height 12 cm

21.1 Volume of Prisms and Cylinders

Resource Locker

Essential Question: How do the formulas for the volume of a prism and cylinder relate to area formulas that you already know?

Explore Developing a Basic Volume Formula

The volume of a three-dimensional figure is the number of nonoverlapping cubic units contained in the interior of the figure. This prism is made up of 8 cubes, each with a volume of 1 cubic centimeter, so it has a volume of 8 cubic centimeters. You can use this idea to develop volume formulas.

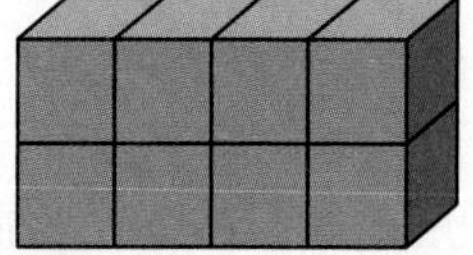

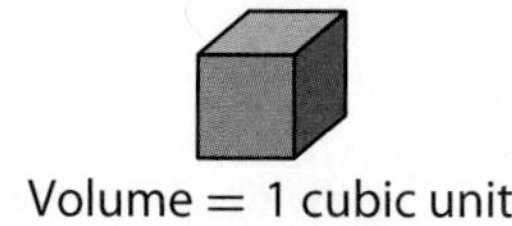

Volume = 1 cubic unit

In this activity you'll explore how to develop a volume formula for a right prism and a right cylinder.

A **right prism** has lateral edges that are perpendicular to the bases, with faces that are all rectangles.	A **right cylinder** has bases that are perpendicular to its center axis.
right prism	axis right cylinder

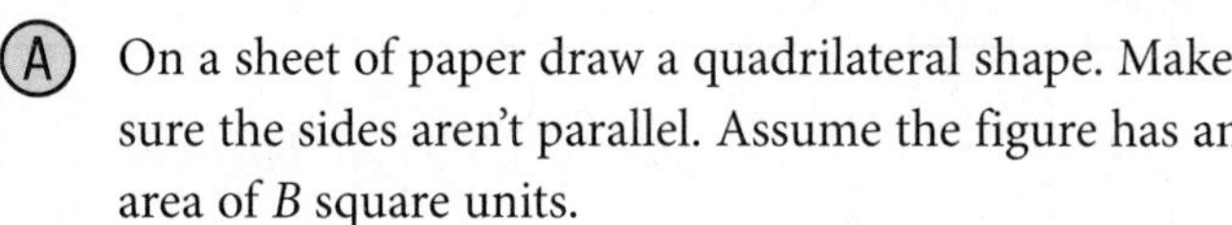

(A) On a sheet of paper draw a quadrilateral shape. Make sure the sides aren't parallel. Assume the figure has an area of B square units.

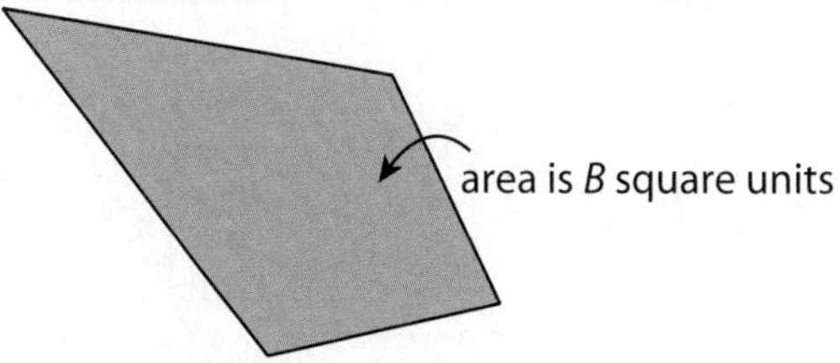

(B) Use it as the base for a prism. Take a block of Styrofoam and cut to the shape of the base. Assume the prism has a height of 1 unit.

How would changing the area of the base change the volume of the prism?

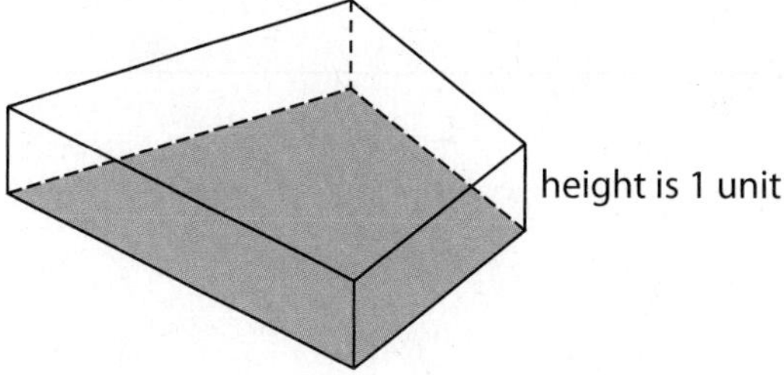

(C) If the base has an area of B square units, how many cubic units does the prism contain?

 Now use the base to build a prism with a height of h units.

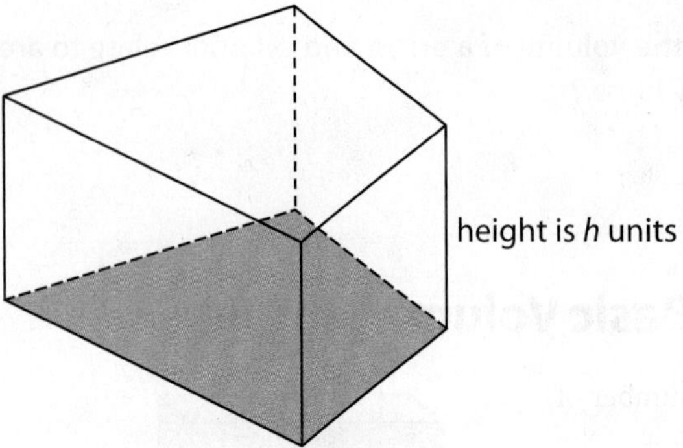

How much greater is the volume of this prism compared to the one with a height of 1?

Reflect

1. Suppose the base of the prism was a rectangle of sides l and w. Write a formula for the volume of the prism using l, w, and h.
2. A cylinder has a circular base. Use the results of the Explore to write a formula for the volume of a cylinder. Explain what you did.

Explain 1 Finding the Volume of a Prism

The general formula for the volume of a prism is $V = B \cdot h$. With certain prisms the volume formula can include the formula for the area of the base.

Volume of a Prism	
The formula for the volume of a right rectangular prism with length ℓ, width w, and height h is $V = \ell wh$.	The formula for the volume of a cube with edge length s is $V = s^3$.
h, ℓ, w	s, s, s

Example 1 **Use volume formulas to solve real world problems.**

(A) A shark and ray tank at the aquarium has the dimensions shown. Estimate the volume of water in gallons. Use the conversion 1 gallon $= 0.134$ ft^3.

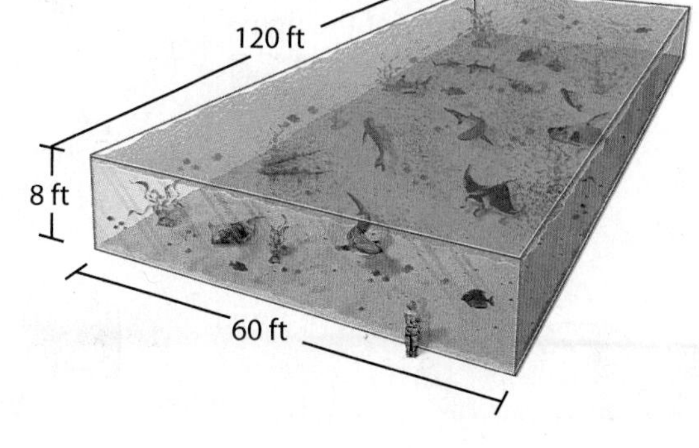

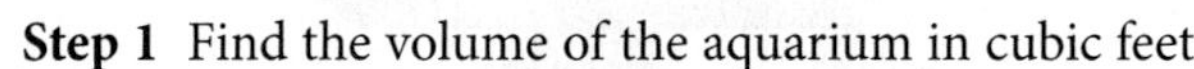

Step 1 Find the volume of the aquarium in cubic feet.

$$V = \ell wh = (120)(60)(8) = 57{,}600 \text{ ft}^3$$

Step 2 Use the conversion factor $\dfrac{1 \text{ gallon}}{0.134 \text{ ft}^3}$ to estimate the volume of the aquarium in gallons.

$$57{,}600 \text{ ft}^3 \cdot \frac{1 \text{ gallon}}{0.134 \text{ ft}^3} \approx 429{,}851 \text{ gallons} \qquad \frac{1 \text{ gallon}}{0.134 \text{ ft}^3} = 1$$

Step 3 Use the conversion factor $\dfrac{1 \text{ gallon}}{8.33 \text{ pounds}}$ to estimate the weight of the water.

$$429{,}851 \text{ gallons} \cdot \frac{8.33 \text{ pounds}}{1 \text{ gallon}} \approx 3{,}580{,}659 \text{ pounds} \qquad \frac{8.33 \text{ pounds}}{1 \text{ gallon}} = 1$$

The aquarium holds about 429,851 in gallons. The water in the aquarium weighs about 3,580,659 pounds.

(B) **Chemistry** Ice takes up more volume than water. This cubic container is filled to the brim with ice. Estimate the volume of water once the ice melts.

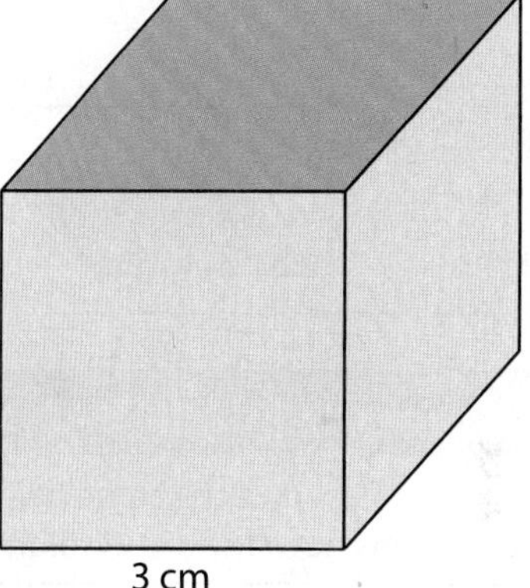

Density of ice: 0.9167 g/cm^3 Density of water: 1 g/cm^3

Step 1 Find the volume of the cube of ice.

$$V = s^3 = \boxed{3^3} = \boxed{27} \text{ cm}^3$$

Step 2 Convert the volume to mass using the conversion factor

$\boxed{0.9167} \dfrac{\text{g}}{\text{cm}^3}$.

$$\boxed{27} \text{ cm}^3 \cdot \boxed{0.9167} \frac{\text{g}}{\text{cm}^3} \approx \boxed{24.8} \text{ g}$$

Step 3 Use the mass of ice to find the volume of water. Use the conversion factor $\boxed{\dfrac{1\text{cm}^3}{\text{g}}}$.

$$24.8 \text{ g} \cdot \boxed{\frac{1\text{cm}^3}{\text{g}}} \approx \boxed{24.8} \text{ cm}^3$$

Reflect

3. The general formula for the volume of a prism is $V = B \cdot h$. Suppose the base of a prism is a parallelogram of length l and altitude h. Use H as the variable to represent the height of the prism. Write a volume formula for this prism.

Your Turn

4. Find the volume of the figure.

Volume = 8 cubic units

5. Find the volume of the figure.

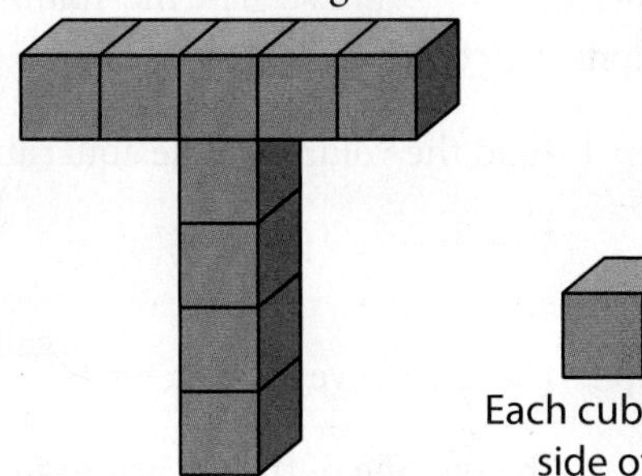

Each cube has a side of $2k$.

Explain 2 Finding the Volume of a Cylinder

You can also find the volume of prisms and cylinders whose edges are not perpendicular to the base.

Oblique Prism	Oblique Cylinder
An **oblique prism** is a prism that has at least one non-rectangular lateral face.	An **oblique cylinder** is a cylinder whose axis is not perpendicular to the bases.

Cavalieri's Principle

If two solids have the same height and the same cross-sectional area at every level, then the two solids have the same volume.

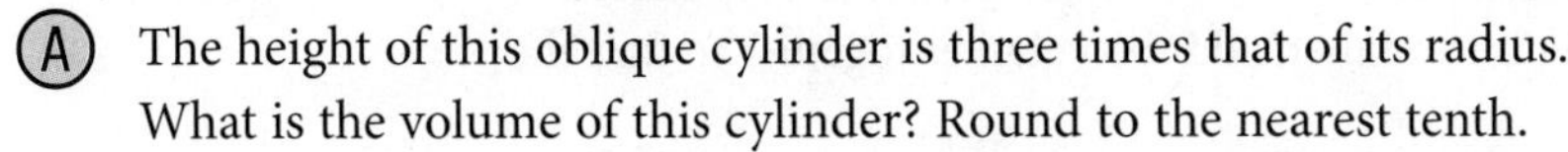

Example 2 **To find the volume of an oblique cylinder or oblique prism, use Cavalieri's Principle to find the volume of a comparable right cylinder or prism.**

Ⓐ The height of this oblique cylinder is three times that of its radius. What is the volume of this cylinder? Round to the nearest tenth.

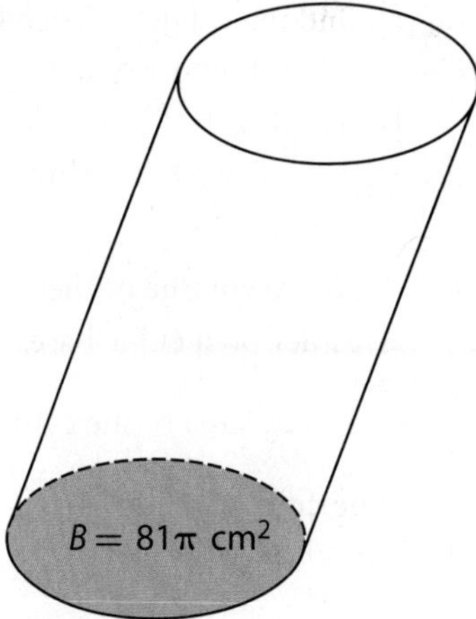

Use Cavalieri's Principle to find the volume of a comparable right cylinder.

Represent the height of the oblique cylinder: $h = 3r$

Use the area of the base to find r: $\pi r^2 = 81\pi$ cm^2, so $r = 9$.

Calculate the height: $h = 3r = 27$ cm

Calculate the volume: $V = Bh = (81\pi)27 \approx 6870.7$

The volume is about 6870.7 cubic centimeters.

Ⓑ The height of this oblique square-based prism is four times that of side length of the base. What is the volume of this prism? Round to the nearest tenth.

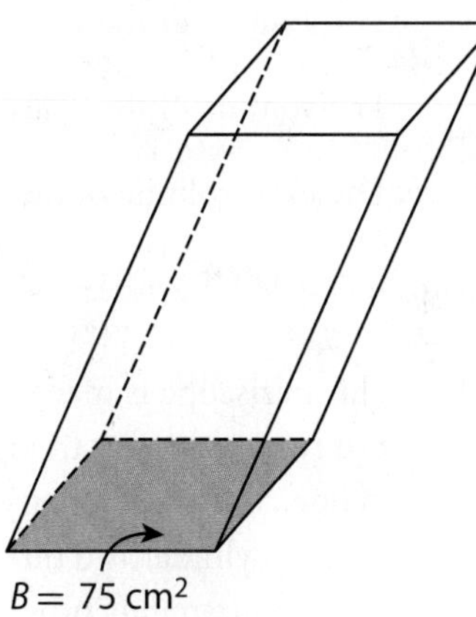

Calculate the height of the oblique prism:

$h = 4s$, where s is the length of the square base.

Use the area of the base to find s.

$s^2 = \boxed{75}$ cm^2

$s = \sqrt{\boxed{75}}$ cm

Calculate the height.

$h = 4s = 4\boxed{\sqrt{75}}$ cm

Calculate the volume.

$V = Bh$

$= (75 \text{ cm}^2)\left(\boxed{4\sqrt{75}} \text{ cm}\right)$

$= \boxed{2598.1}$ cm^3

Your Turn

Find the volume.

6.

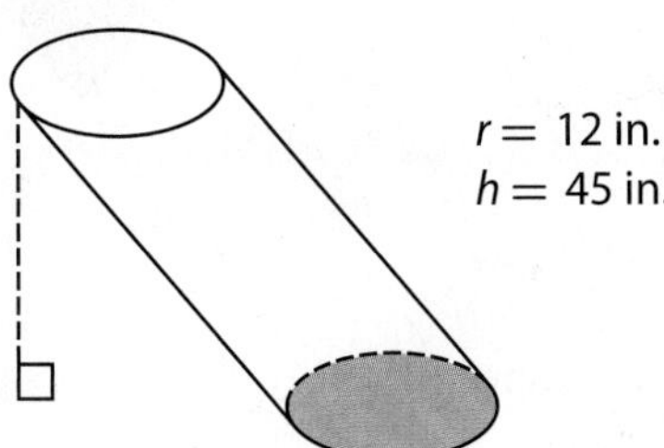

7.

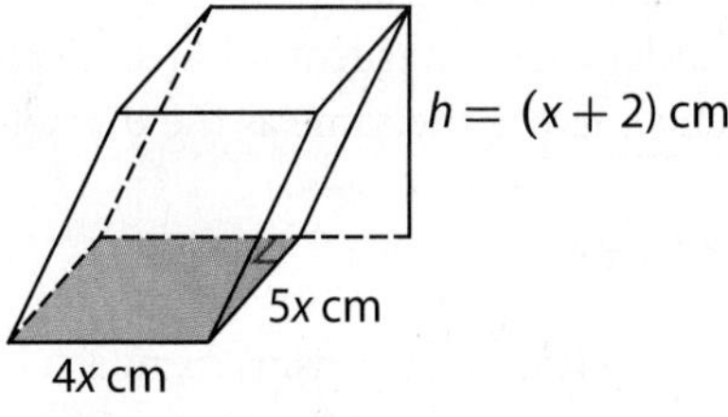

Explain 3 Finding the Volume of a Composite Figure

Recall that a composite figure is made up of simple shapes that combine to create a more complex shape. A composite three-dimensional figure is formed from prisms and cylinders. You can find the volume of each separate figure and then add the volumes together to find the volume of the composite figure.

Example 3 **Find the volume of each composite figure.**

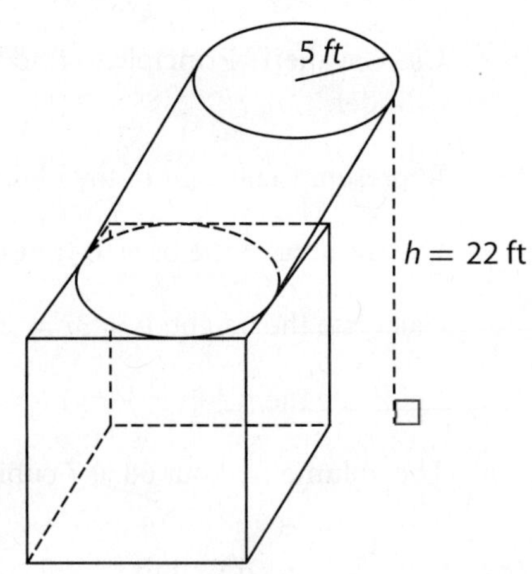

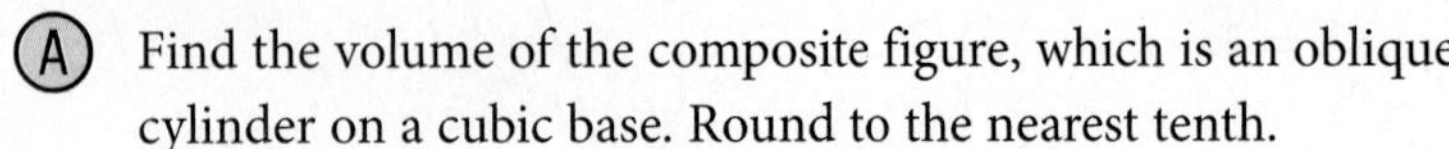

(A) Find the volume of the composite figure, which is an oblique cylinder on a cubic base. Round to the nearest tenth.

The base area of the cylinder is $B = \pi r^2 = \pi(5)^2 = 25\pi \text{ ft}^2$.

The cube has side lengths equal to the diameter of the cylinder's circular base: $s = 10$.

The height of the cylinder is $h = 22 - 10 = 12$ ft.

The volume of the cube is $V = s^3 = 10^3 = 1000 \text{ ft}^3$.

The volume of the cylinder is $V = Bh = (25\pi \text{ ft}^2)(12 \text{ ft}) \approx 942.5 \text{ ft}^3$.

The total volume of the composite figure is the sum of the individual volumes.

$V = 1000 \text{ ft}^3 + 942.5 \text{ ft}^3 = 1942.5 \text{ ft}^3$

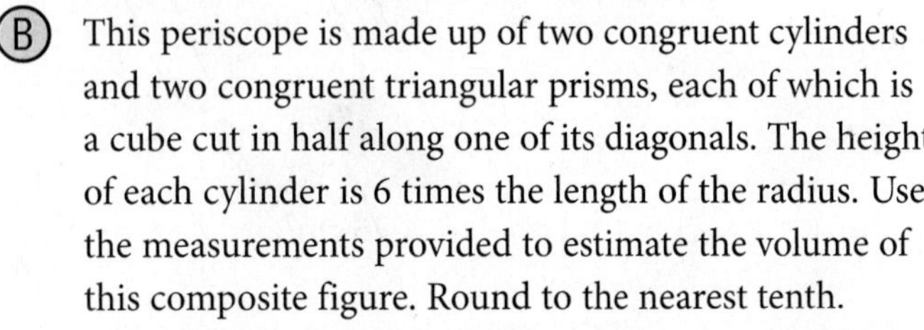

(B) This periscope is made up of two congruent cylinders and two congruent triangular prisms, each of which is a cube cut in half along one of its diagonals. The height of each cylinder is 6 times the length of the radius. Use the measurements provided to estimate the volume of this composite figure. Round to the nearest tenth.

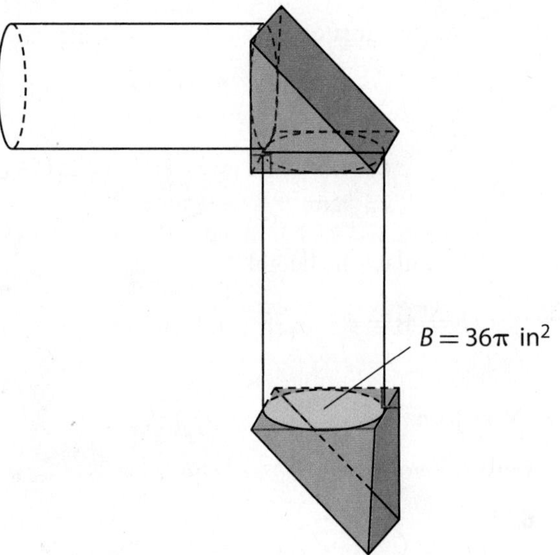

Use the area of the base to find the radius. $B = \pi r^2$

$\pi r^2 =$ [36] π, so $r =$ [6] in.

Calculate the height each cylinder:

$h = 6r = 6 \cdot$ [6] $=$ [36] in.

The faces of the triangular prism that intersect the cylinders are congruent squares. The side length s of each square is the same as the diameter of the circle.

$s = d = 2 \cdot$ [6] $=$ [12] in.

The two triangular prisms form a cube. What is the volume of this cube?

$V = s^3 =$ [12]^3 $=$ [1728] in^3

Find the volume of the two cylinders: $V = 2 \cdot 36\pi \cdot$ [6] $=$ [432π] in^3

The total volume of the composite figure is the sum of the individual volumes.

$V =$ [1728] $\text{in}^3 +$ [432π] $\text{in}^3 \approx$ [3085.17] in^3

Reflect

8. A pipe consists of two concentric cylinders, with the inner cylinder hollowed out. Describe how you could calculate the volume of the solid pipe. Write a formula for the volume.

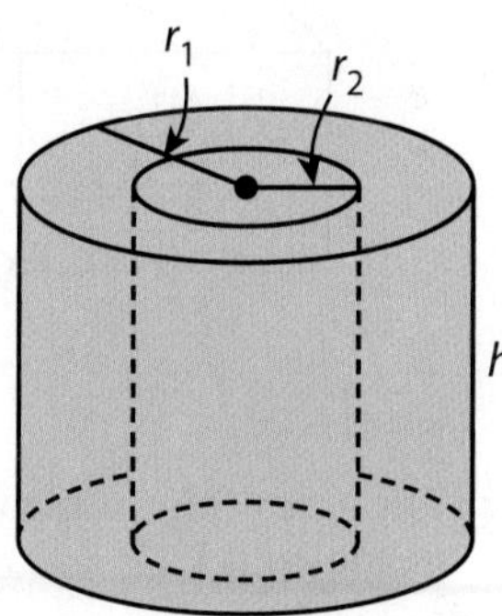

Your Turn

9. This robotic arm is made up of two cylinders with equal volume and two triangular prisms for a hand. The volume of each prism is $\frac{1}{2}r \times \frac{1}{3}r \times 2r$, where r is the radius of the cylinder's base. What fraction of the total volume does the hand take up?

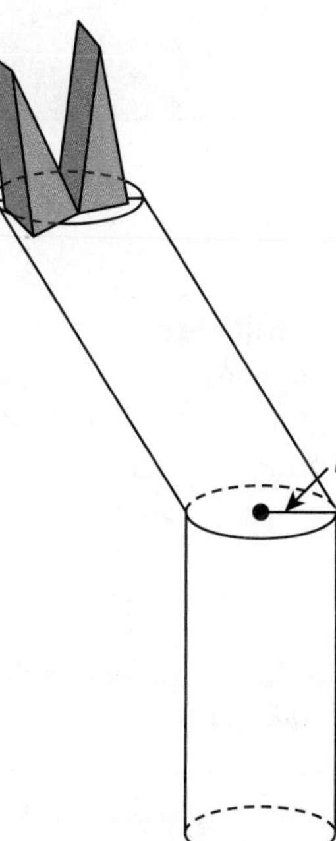

Elaborate

10. If an oblique cylinder and a right cylinder have the same height but not the same volume, what can you conclude about the cylinders?

11. A right square prism and a right cylinder have the same height and volume. What can you conclude about the radius of the cylinder and side lengths of the square base?

12. **Essential Question Check-In** How does the formula for the area of a circle relate to the formula for the volume of a cylinder?

Evaluate: Homework and Practice

- Online Homework
- Hints and Help
- Extra Practice

1. The volume of prisms and cylinders can be represented with Bh, where B represents the area of the base. Identify the type of figure shown and match the prism or cylinder with the appropriate volume formula.

a. ___?___ $V = (\pi r^2)h$ b. ___?___ $V = \left(\frac{1}{2}bh\right)h$ c. ___?___ $V = \ell wh$

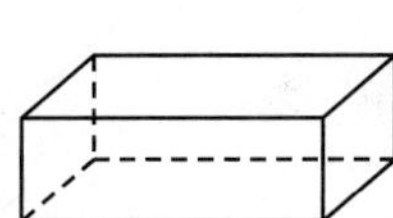

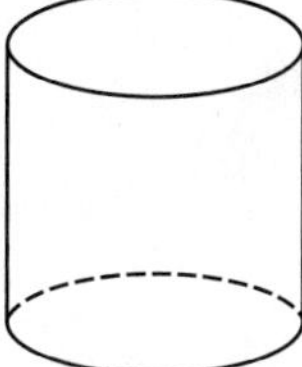

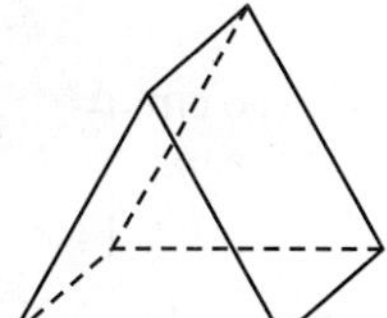

Find the volume of each prism or cylinder. Round to the nearest hundredth.

2.

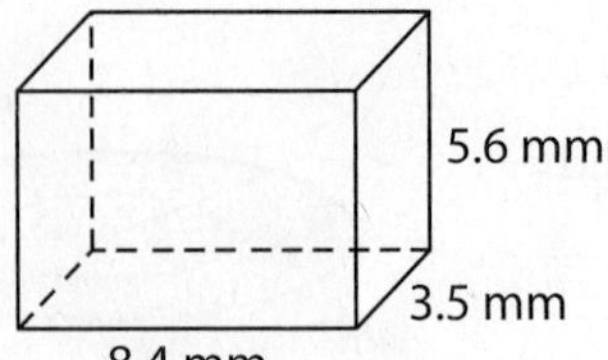

3.

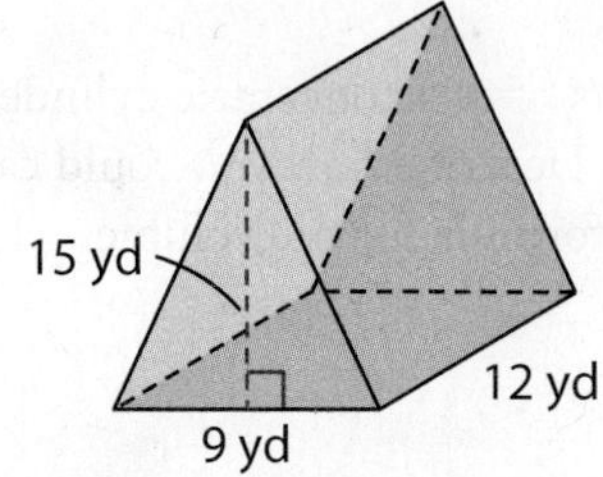

4. The area of the hexagonal base is $\left(\frac{54}{\tan 30°}\right)$ m². Its height is 8 m.

5. The area of the pentagonal base is $\left(\frac{125}{\tan 36°}\right)$ m². Its height is 15 m.

6.

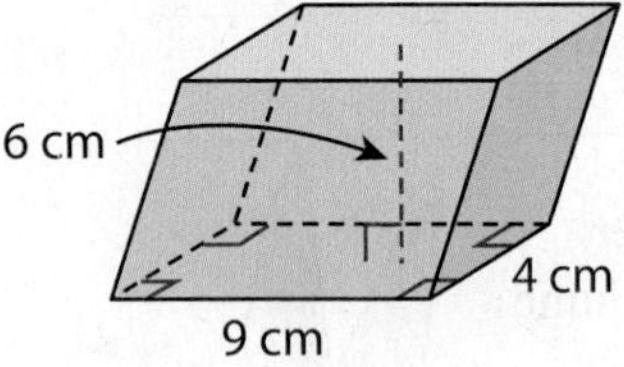

7.

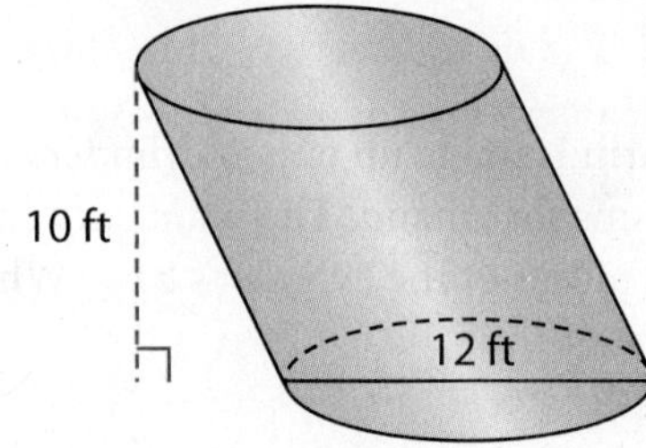

8. **Multi-Step** A vase in the shape of an oblique cylinder has the dimensions shown. What is the volume of the vase in liters? Round to the nearest thundredth. (*Hint:* Use the right triangle in the cylinder to find its height.)

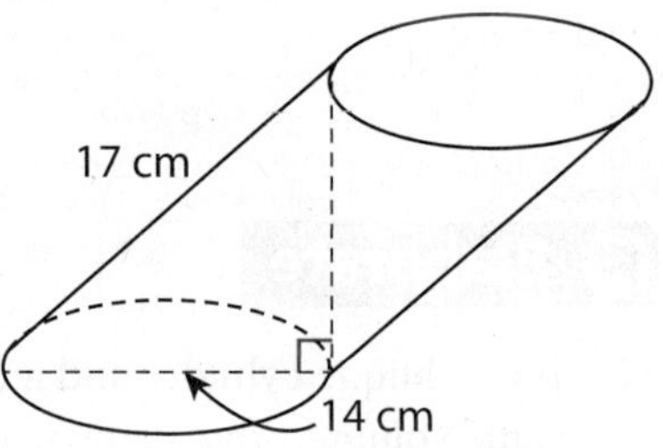

Find the volume of each composite figure. Round to the nearest tenth.

9.

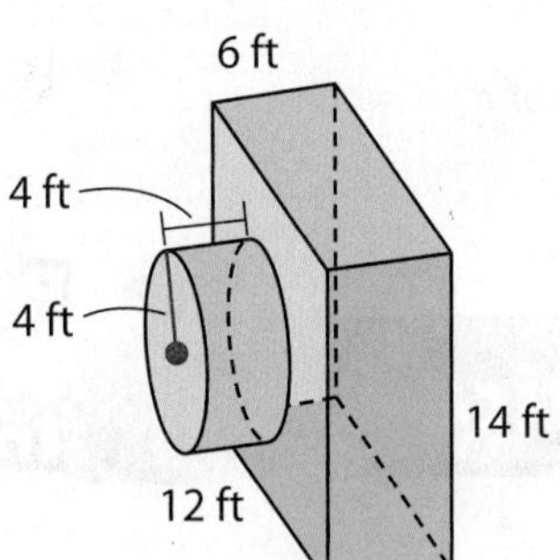

10.

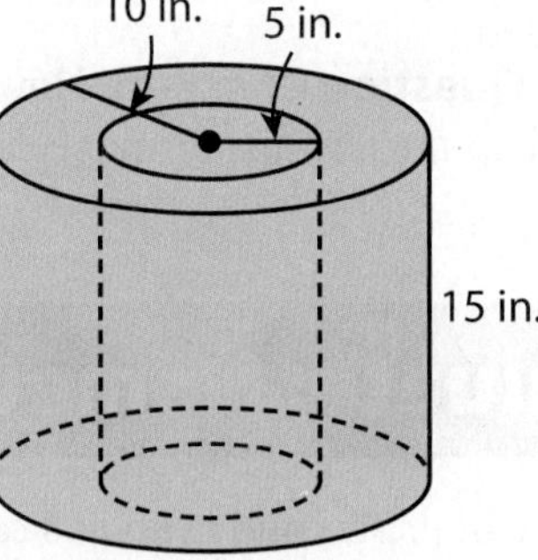

11.

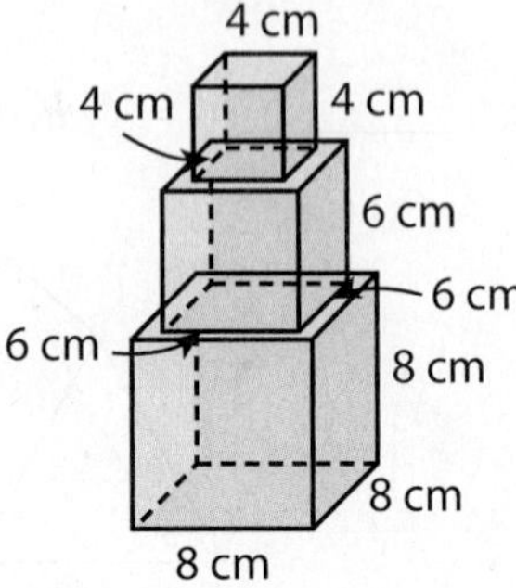

12. The two figures on each end combine to form a right cylinder.

2 ft

4 ft

4 ft

2 ft

12 ft

13. Colin is buying dirt to fill a garden bed that is a 9 ft by 16 ft rectangle. If he wants to fill it to a depth of 4 in., how many cubic yards of dirt does he need? Round to the nearest cubic yard. If dirt costs $25 per yd^3, how much will the project cost?

14. **Persevere in Problem Solving** A cylindrical juice container with a 3 in. diameter has a hole for a straw that is 1 in. from the side. Up to 5 in. of a straw can be inserted.

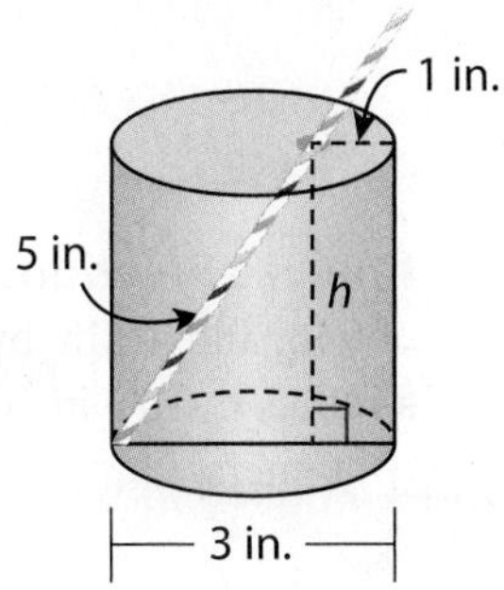

a. Find the height h of the container to the nearest tenth.

b. Find the volume of the container to the nearest tenth.

c. How many ounces of juice does the container hold? (*Hint*: $1 \text{ in}^3 \approx 0.55$ oz)

15. Abigail has a cylindrical candle mold with the dimensions shown. If Abigail has a rectangular block of wax measuring 15 cm by 12 cm by 18 cm, about how many candles can she make after melting the block of wax? Round to the nearest tenth.

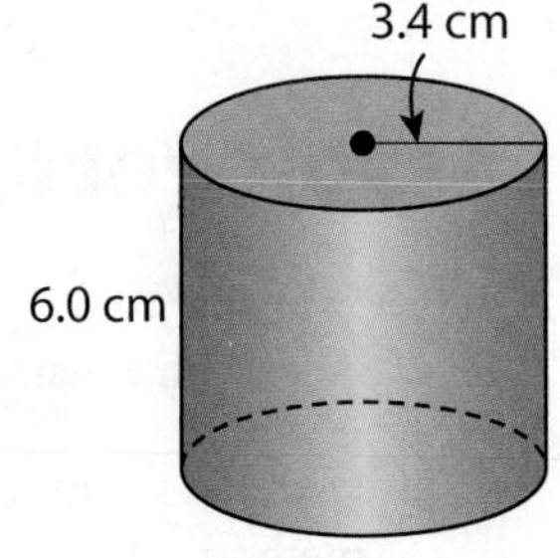

16. **Algebra** Find the volume of the three-dimensional figure in terms of x.

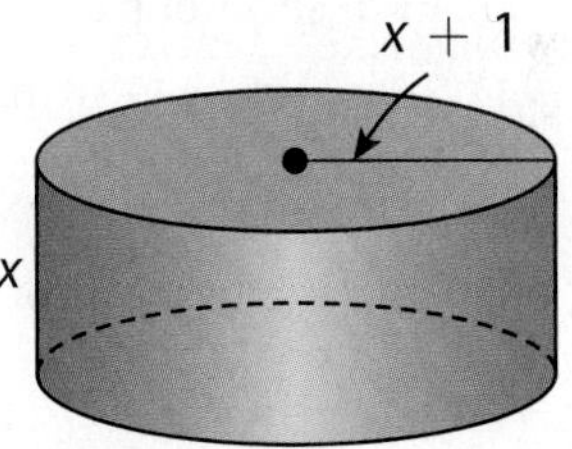

17. One cup is equal to 14.4375 in^3. If a 1-cup measuring cylinder has a radius of 2 in., what is its height? If the radius is 1.5 in., what is its height? Round to the nearest tenth.

18. **Make a Prediction** A cake is a cylinder with a diameter of 10 in. and a height of 3 in. For a party, a coin has been mixed into the batter and baked inside the cake. The person who gets the piece with the coin wins a prize.

a. Find the volume of the cake. Round to the nearest tenth.

b. Keka gets a piece of cake that is a right rectangular prism with a 3 in. by 1 in. base. What is the probability that the coin is in her piece? Round to the nearest hundredth.

H.O.T. Focus on Higher Order Thinking

19. **Multi-Step** What is the volume of the three-dimensional object with the dimensions shown in the three views?

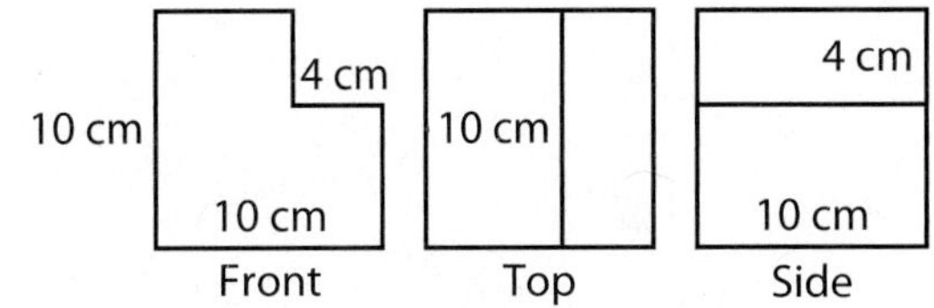

20. Draw Conclusions You can use *displacement* to find the volume of an irregular object, such as a stone. Suppose a 2 foot by 1 foot tank is filled with water to a depth of 8 in. A stone is placed in the tank so that it is completely covered, causing the water level to rise by 2 in. Find the volume of the stone.

21. Analyze Relationships One juice container is a rectangular prism with a height of 9 in. and a 3 in. by 3 in. square base. Another juice container is a cylinder with a radius of 1.75 in. and a height of 9 in. Describe the relationship between the two containers.

Lesson Performance Task

A full roll of paper towels is a cylinder with a diameter of 6 inches and a hollow inner cylinder with a diameter of 2 inches.

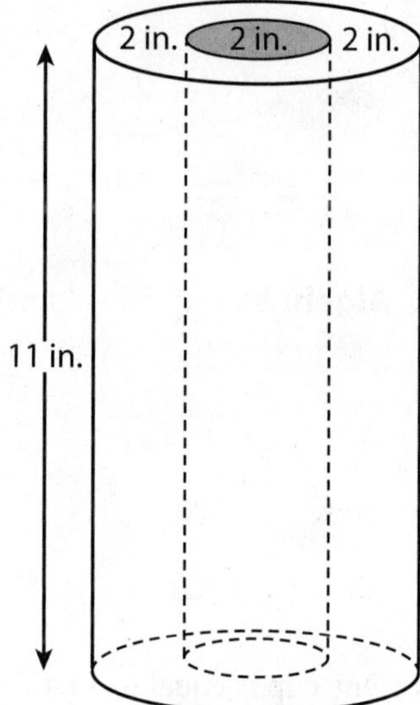

1. Find the volume of the paper on the roll. Explain your method.

2. Each sheet of paper on the roll measures 11 inches by 11 inches by $\frac{1}{32}$ inch. Find the volume of one sheet. Explain how you found the volume.

3. How many sheets of paper are on the roll? Explain.

21.2 Volume of Pyramids

Essential Question: How do you find the volume of a pyramid?

Explore Developing a Volume Formula

You can think of irregular pyramids as parts of a rectangular prism. This cube can be divided into three square pyramids.

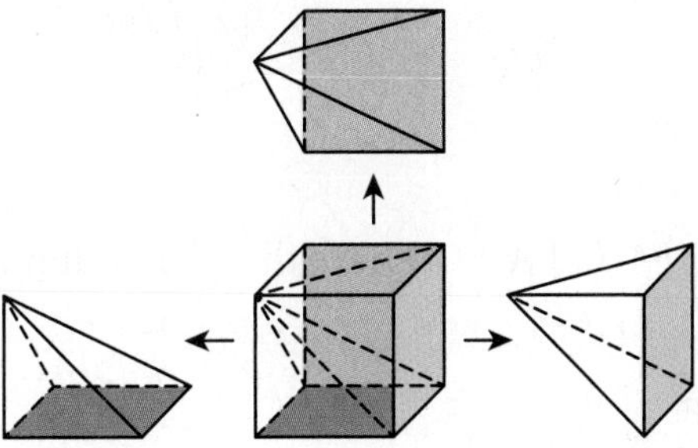

The volume of a pyramid is related to the volume of a prism with the same base and height. This triangular pyramid can be thought of as part of a triangular prism.

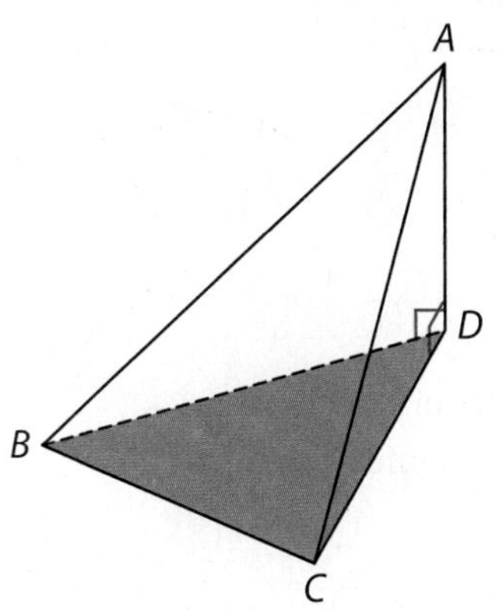

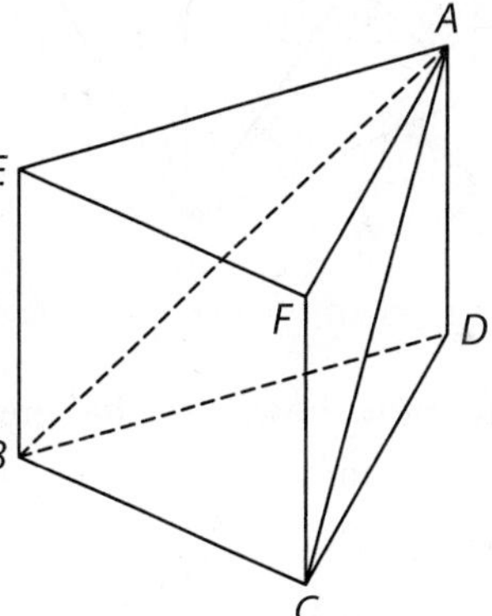

To find the volume of the first pyramid, A-BCD, first let the area of the base of $\triangle BCD$ be B, and let the height of the pyramid, AD, be h. The edges $\overline{EB}$ and $\overline{FC}$ are congruent to $\overline{AD}$ and parallel to $\overline{AD}$. The bases of the prism, $\triangle EFA$ and $\triangle BCD$, are congruent.

(A) What is the volume of the triangular prism in terms of B and h?

(B) You will now compare the volume of pyramid *A-BCD* and the volume of the triangular prism.

- Draw $\overline{EC}$. This is the diagonal of a rectangle, so $\triangle$ ______ $\cong \triangle$ ______ .
- Explain why pyramids *A-EBC* and *A-CFE* have the same volume.

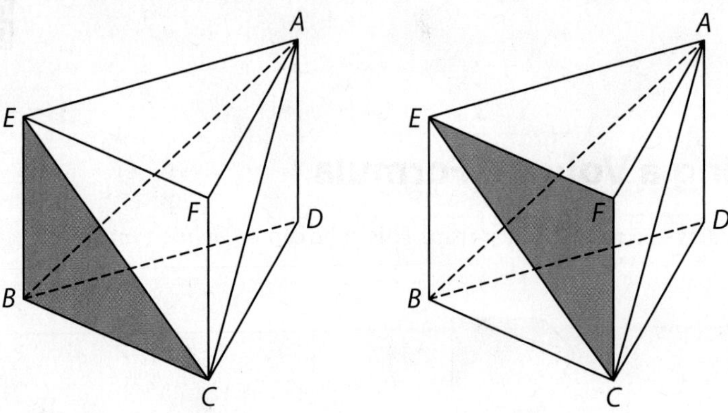

- Explain why pyramids *C-EFA* and *A-BCD* have the same volume.

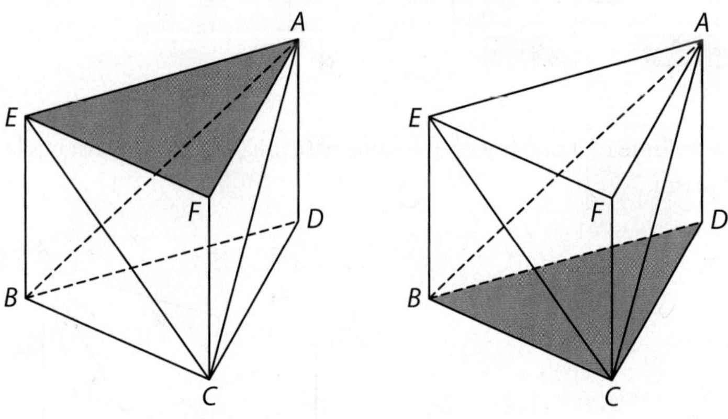

(C) You have now shown that the three pyramids that form the triangular prism all have the same volume. Compare the volume of pyramid *A-BCD* and the volume of the triangular prism.

(D) Write the volume of pyramid *A-BCD* in terms of *B* and *h*.

Reflect

1. Explain how you know that the three pyramids that form that triangular prism all have the same volume.

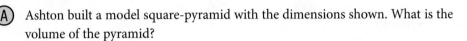

Explain 1 Finding the Volume of a Pyramid

Since the volume of any triangular or rectangular pyramid can be shown to compose one third the volume of a rectangular prism, the formula for the volume of a triangular prism can be generalized.

Volume of a Pyramid

The volume V of a pyramid with base area B and height h is given by $V = \frac{1}{3}Bh$.

Example 1 **Solve a volume problem.**

(A) Ashton built a model square-pyramid with the dimensions shown. What is the volume of the pyramid?

The pyramid is composed of wooden blocks that are in the shape of cubes. A block has the dimensions 4 cm by 4 by 4 cm. How many wooden blocks did Ashton use to build the pyramid?

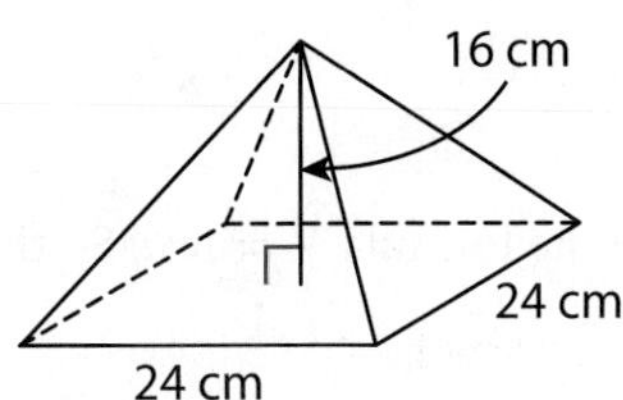

- Find the volume of the pyramid.

  The area of the base B is the area of the square with sides of length 24 cm. So, $B = 576\ \text{cm}^2$.

  The volume V of the pyramid is $\frac{1}{3}Bh = \frac{1}{3} \cdot 576 \cdot 16$.

  So $V = 3072\ \text{cm}^3$.

- Find the volume of an average block.

  The volume of a cube is given by the formula $V = s^3$. So the volume W of a wooden block is $64\ \text{cm}^3$.

- Find the approximate number of stone blocks in the pyramid, divide V by W. So the number of blocks that Ashton used is 144.

Ⓑ The Great Pyramid in Giza, Egypt, is approximately a square pyramid with the dimensions shown. The pyramid is composed of stone blocks that are rectangular prisms. An average block has dimensions 1.3 m by 1.3 m by 0.7 m. Approximately how many stone blocks were used to build the pyramid? Round to the nearest hundred thousand.

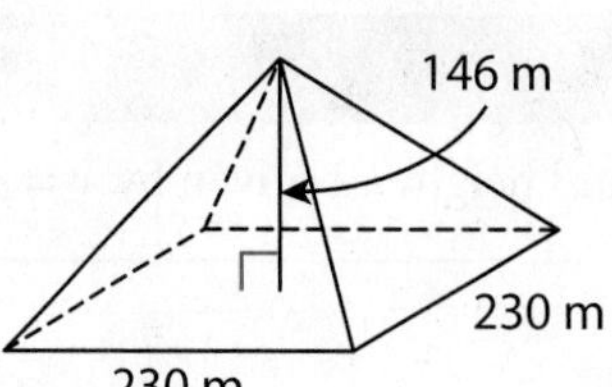

- Find the volume of the pyramid.

  The area of the base B is the area of the square with sides of length 230 m. So, $B = 52{,}900 \text{ m}^2$.

  The volume V of the pyramid is $\frac{1}{3}Bh = \frac{1}{3} \cdot 52{,}900 \cdot 146$.

  So $V \approx 2{,}574{,}466.7\text{m}^3$.

- Find the volume of an average block.

  The volume of a rectangular prism is given by the formula $V = lwh$. So the volume W of an average block is 1.183 m^3.

- Find the approximate number of stone blocks in the pyramid, divide V by W. So the approximate number of blocks is 2,200,00.

Reflect

2. What aspects of the model in Part B may lead to inaccuracies in your estimate?

3. Suppose you are told that the average height of a stone block 0.69 m rather than 0.7 m. Would the increase or decrease your estimate of the total number of blocks in the pyramid? Explain.

Your Turn

4. A piece of pure silver in the shape of a rectangular pyramid with the dimensions shown has a mass of 19.7 grams. What is the density of silver? Round to the nearest tenth.
(Hint: $density = \frac{mass}{volume}$.)

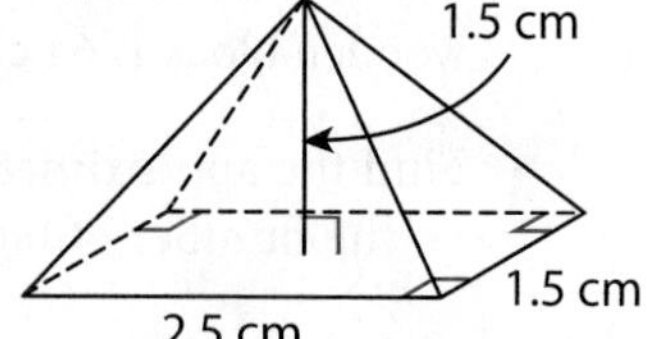

Explain 2 Finding the Volume of a Composite Figure

You can add or subtract to find the volume of composite figures.

Example 2 **Find the volume of the composite figure formed by a pyramid removed from a prism. Round to the nearest tenth.**

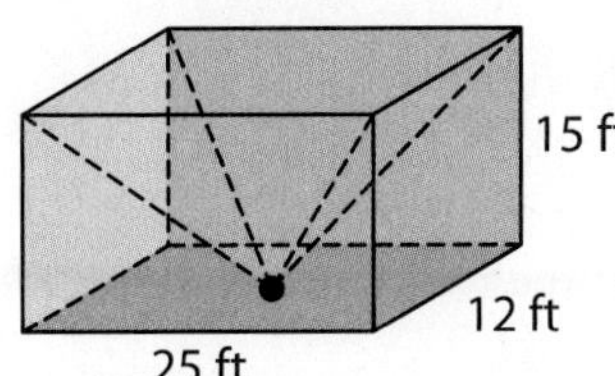

- Find the volume of the prism.
  $V = lwh = (25)(12)(15) = 4500 \text{ ft}^3$
- Find the volume of pyramid.
  Area of base: $B = (25)(12) = 300 \text{ ft}^2$
  Volume of pyramid: $V = \frac{1}{3}(300)(15) = 1500 \text{ ft}^3$
- Subtract the volume of the pyramid from volume of the prism to find the volume of the composite figure.
  $4500 - 1500 = 3000$
  So the volume of the composite figure is 3000 ft^3.

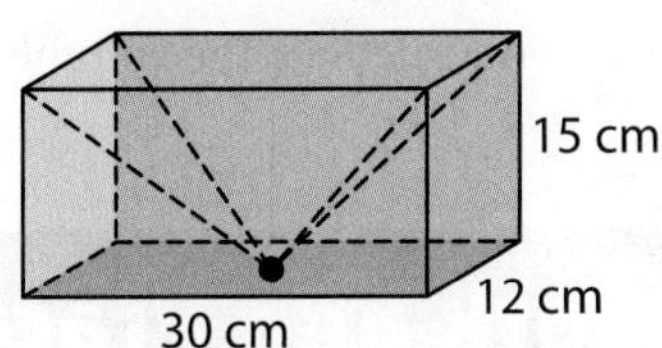

- Find the volume of the prism.
  $V = lwh = (30)(12)(15) = (5400) \text{ cm}^3$
- Find the volume of the pyramid.
  Area of base: $B = (30)(12) = 360\text{cm}^2$
  Volume of pyramid: $V = \frac{1}{3}(360)(15) = (1800) \text{ cm}^3$
- Subtract volume of pyramid from volume of prism to find volume of composite figure.
  $5400 - 1800 = 3600$
  So the volume of the composite figure is 3600 cm^3.

Your Turn

Find the volume of the composite figure. Round to the nearest tenth.

5. The composite figure is formed from two pyramids. The base of each pyramid is a square with a side length of 6 inches and each pyramid has a height of 8 inches.

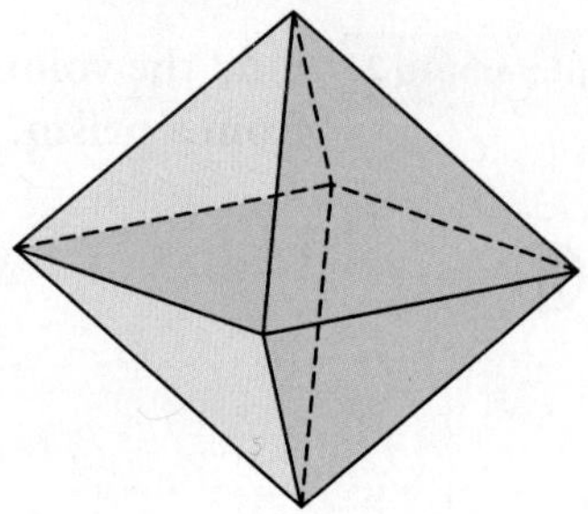

6. The composite figure is formed by a rectangular prism with two square pyramids on top of it.

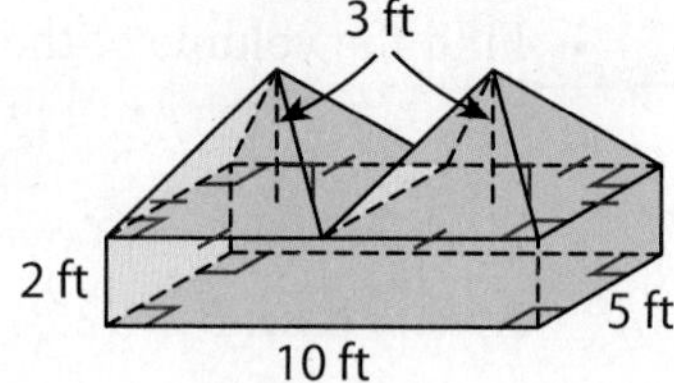

Elaborate

7. Explain how the volume of a pyramid is related to the volume of a prism with the same base and height.

8. If the length and width of a rectangular pyramid are doubled and the height stays the same, how does the volume of the pyramid change? Explain.

9. **Essential Question Check-In** How do you calculate the volume of a pyramid?

Evaluate: Homework and Practice

- Online Homework
- Hints and Help
- Extra Practice

1. Compare the volume of a square pyramid to the volume of a square prism with the same base and height as the pyramid.

2. Which of the following equations could describe a square pyramid? Determine all that apply.

A. $3Vh = B$

B. $V = \frac{1}{3}\ell wB$

C. $w = \frac{3V}{\ell h}$

D. $\frac{V}{B} = \frac{h}{3}$

E. $V = \frac{w^2h}{3}$

F. $\frac{1}{3} = VBh$

3. **Justify Reasoning** As shown in the figure, polyhedron *ABCDEFGH* is a cube and *P* is any point on face *EFGH*. Compare the volume of the pyramid *PABCD* and the volume of the cube. Demonstrate how you came to your answer.

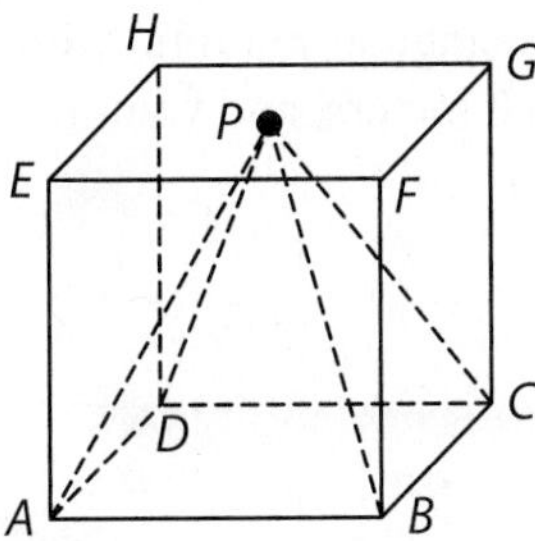

Find the volume of the pyramid. Round your answer to the nearest tenth.

4.

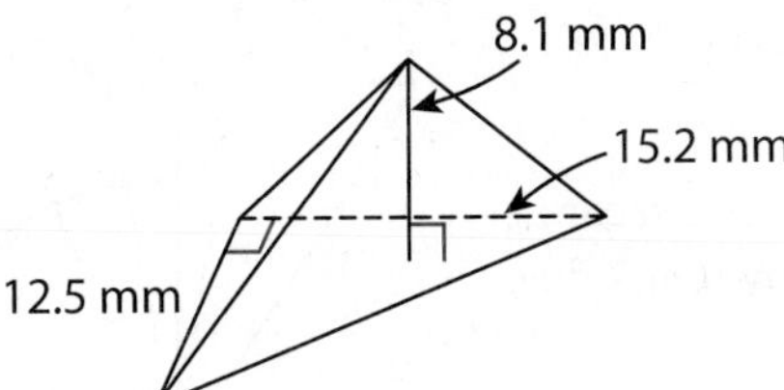

5.

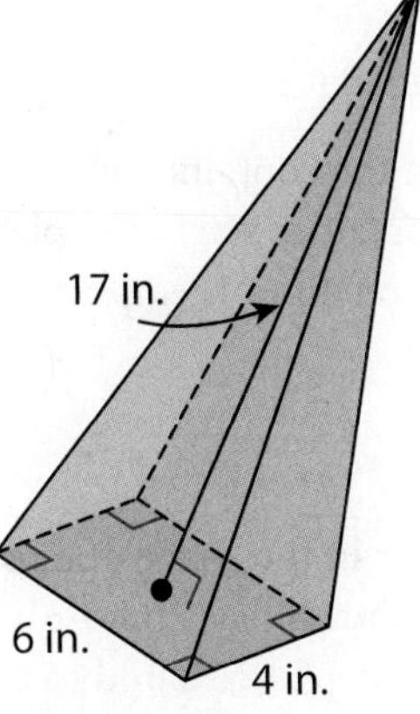

6. Find the volume of a hexagonal pyramid with a base area of 25 ft^2 and a height of 9 ft.

7. The area of the base of a hexagonal pyramid is $\frac{24}{\tan 30°}$ cm^2. Find its volume.

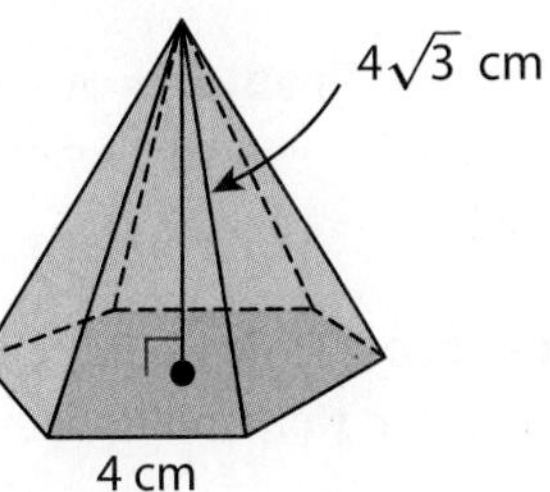

Find the volume of the composite figure. Round to the nearest tenth.

8.

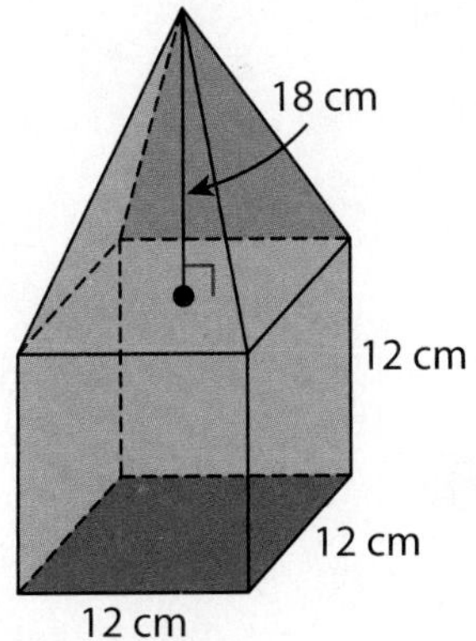

9.

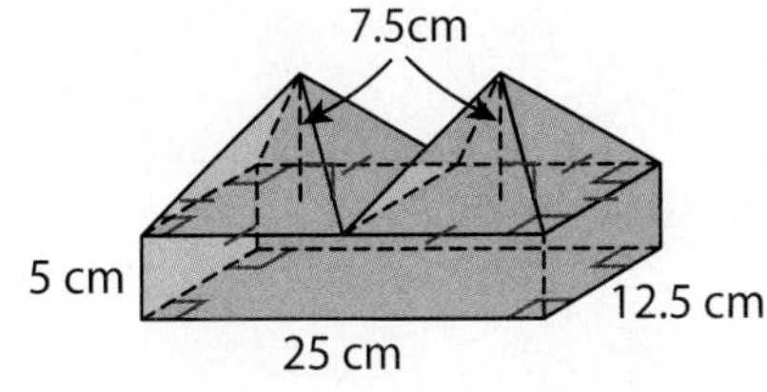

10. Given a square pyramid with a height of 21 ft and a volume of 3969 cubic feet, find the length of one side of the square base. Round to the nearest tenth.

11. Consider a pyramid with height 10 feet and a square base with side length of 7 feet. How does the volume of the pyramid change if the base stays the same and the height is doubled?

12. Algebra Find the value of x if the volume of the pyramid shown is 200 cubic centimeters.

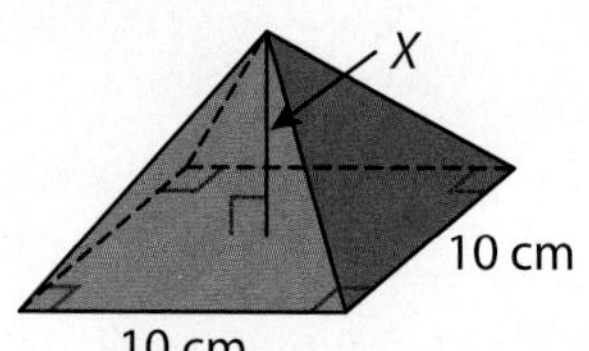

13. Find the height of a rectangular pyramid with length 3 meters, width 8 meters, and volume 112 cubic meters.

14. A storage container for grain is in the shape of a square pyramid with the dimensions shown.

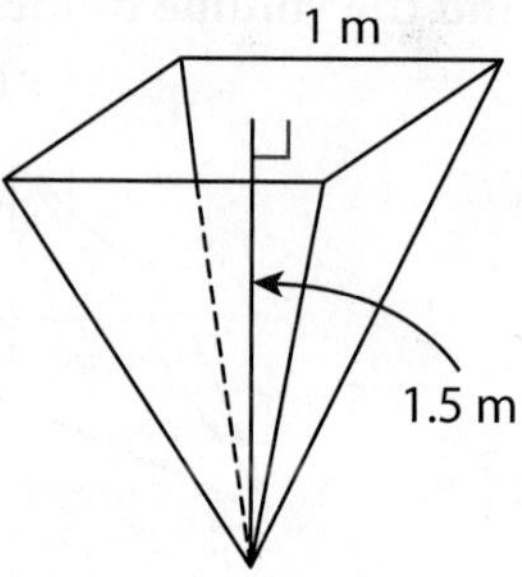

a. What is the volume of the container in cubic centimeters?

b. Grain leaks from the container at a rate of 4 cubic centimeters per second. Assuming the container starts completely full, about how many hours does it take until the container is empty?

15. A piece of pure copper in the shape of a rectangular pyramid with the dimensions shown has a mass of 16.76 grams. What is the density of copper? Round to the nearest hundredth. $\left(\text{Hint: } density = \frac{mass}{volume}.\right)$

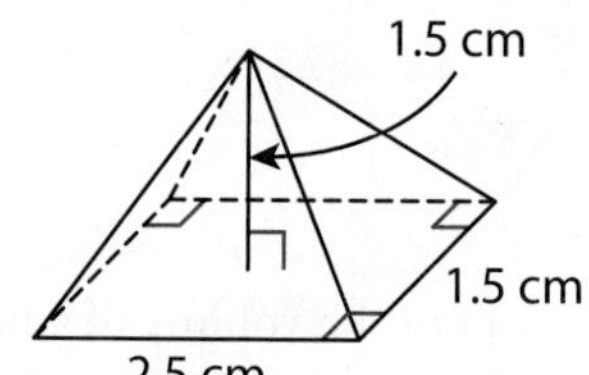

16. Represent Real World Problems An art gallery is a 6 story square pyramid with base area $\frac{1}{2}$ acre (1 acre $= 4840$ yd^2, 1 story ≈ 10 ft). Estimate the volume in cubic yards and cubic feet.

17. Analyze Relationships How would the volume of the pyramid shown change if each dimension were multiplied by 6? Explain how you found your answer.

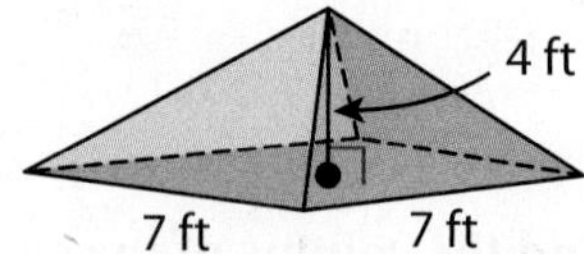

18. Geology A crystal is cut into a shape formed by two square pyramids joined at the base. Each pyramid has a base edge length of 5.7 mm and a height of 3 mm. What is the volume of the crystal to the nearest cubic millimeter?

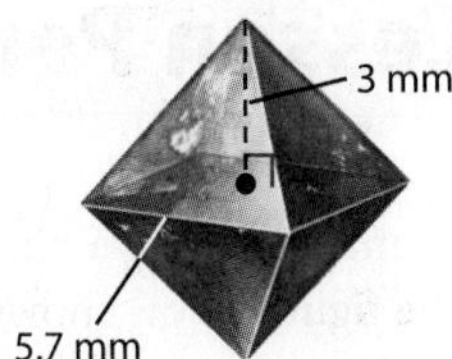

19. A roof that encloses an attic is a square pyramid with a base edge length of 45 feet and a height of 5 yards. What is the volume of the attic in cubic feet? In cubic yards?

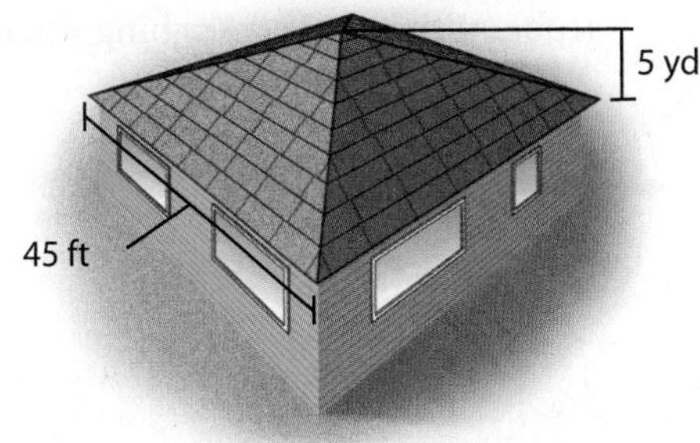

H.O.T. Focus on Higher Order Thinking

20. Explain the Error Describe and correct the error in finding the volume of the pyramid.

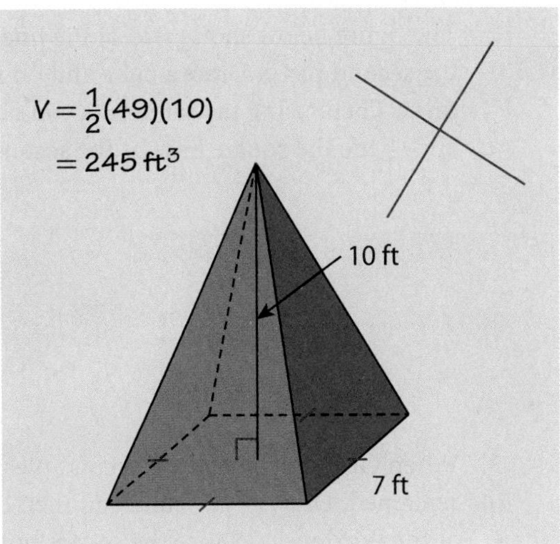

21. Communicate Mathematical Ideas A pyramid has a square base and a height of 5 ft. The volume of the pyramid is 60 ft^3. Explain how to find the length of a side of the pyramid's base.

22. Critical Thinking A triangular pyramid has a length of 2, a width of x, and a height of $3x$. Its volume is 512 cm^3. What is the area of the base?

Lesson Performance Task

Genna is making a puzzle using a wooden cube. She's going to cut the cube into three pieces. The figure below shows the lines along which she plans to cut away the first piece. The result will be a piece with four triangular sides and a square side (shaded).

1. Each cut Genna makes will begin at the upper left corner of the cube. Write a rule describing where she drew the lines for the first piece.

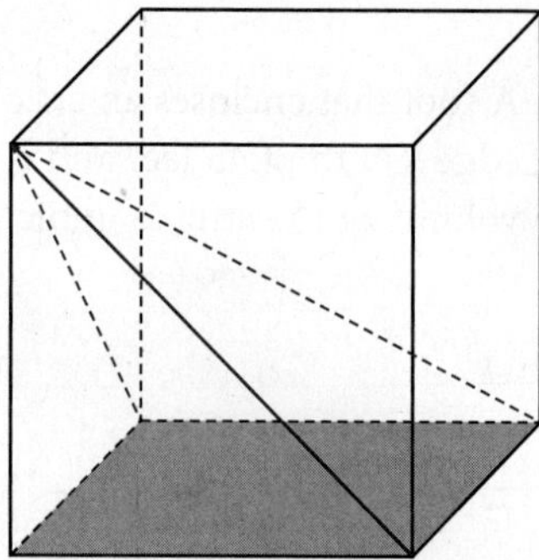

2. The figure below shows two of the lines along which Genna will cut the second piece. Draw a cube and on it, draw the two lines Genna drew. Then, using the same rule you used above, draw the third line and shade the square base of the second piece.

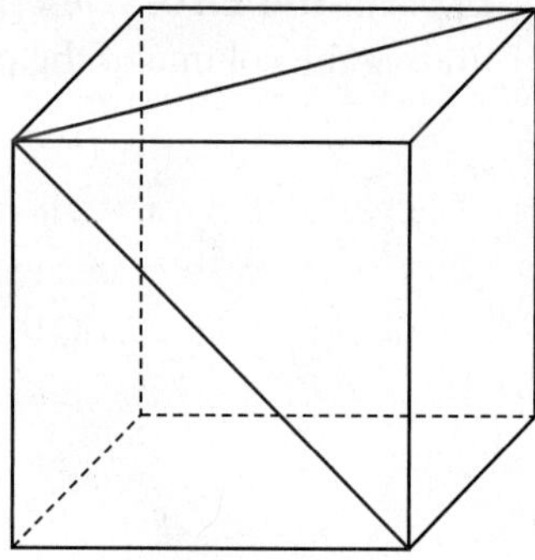

3. When Genna cut away the second piece of the puzzle, the third piece remained. Draw a new cube and then draw the lines that mark the edges of the third piece. Shade the square bottom of the third piece.

4. Compare the volumes of the three pieces. Explain your reasoning.

5. Explain how the model confirms the formula for the volume of a pyramid.

21.3 Volume of Cones

Resource Locker

Essential Question: How do you calculate the volumes of composite figures that include cones?

Explore Developing a Volume Formula

You can approximate the volume of a cone by finding the volumes of inscribed pyramids.

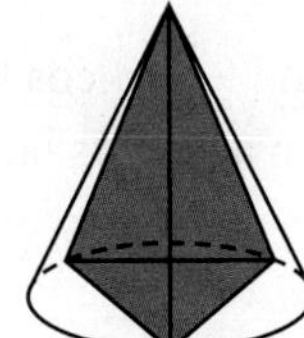

Base of inscribed pyramid has 3 sides

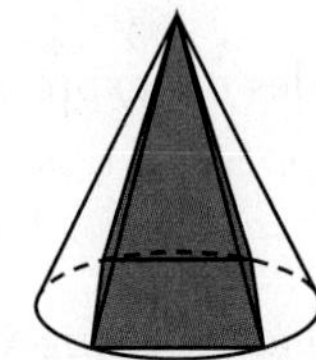

Base of inscribed pyramid has 4 sides

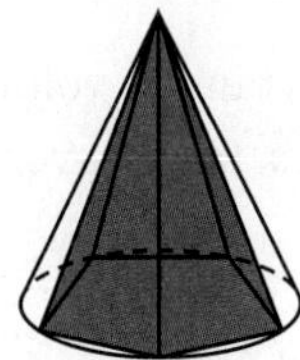

Base of inscribed pyramid has 5 sides

(A) The base of a pyramid is inscribed in the circular base of the cone and is a regular n-gon. Let O be the center of the cone's base, let r be the radius of the cone, and let h be the height of the cone. Draw radii from O to the vertices of the n-gon.

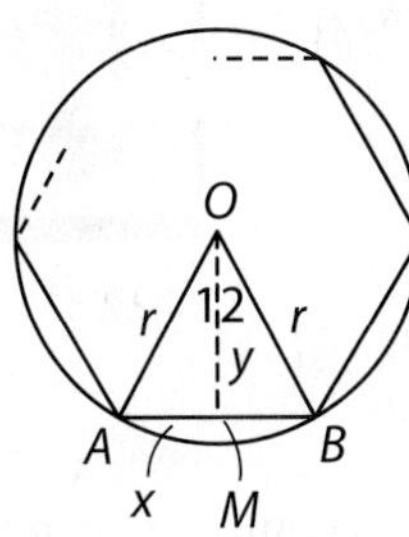

Construct segment $\overline{OM}$ from O to the midpoint M of $\overline{AB}$. How can you prove that $\triangle AOM \cong \triangle BOM$?

(B) How is $\angle 1 \cong \angle 2$?

(C) How many triangles congruent to $\triangle AOB$ surround point O to make up the n-gon that is the base of the pyramid? How can this be used to find the angle measures of $\triangle AOM$ and $\triangle BOM$?

(D) In $\triangle AOM$, $\sin \angle 1 = \frac{x}{r}$, so $x = r\sin \angle 1$. In $\triangle AOM$, $\cos \angle 1 = \frac{y}{r}$, so $y = r\cos \angle 1$. Since $\angle 1$ has a known value, rewrite x and y using substitution.

Ⓔ To write an expression for the area of the base of the pyramid, first write an expression for the area of $\triangle AOB$.

$$\text{Area of } \triangle AOB = \frac{1}{2} \cdot base \cdot height$$
$$= \frac{1}{2} \cdot 2x \cdot y$$
$$= xy$$

What is the area of $\triangle AOB$, substituting the new values for x and y? What is the area of the n triangles that make up the base of the pyramid?

Ⓕ Use the area of the base of the pyramid to find an equation for the volume of the pyramid.

Ⓖ Your expression for the pyramid's volume includes the expression $n \sin\left(\frac{180°}{n}\right) \cos\left(\frac{180°}{n}\right)$. Use a calculator, as follows, to discover what happens to this expression as n gets larger and larger.

- Enter the expression $n \sin\left(\frac{180°}{n}\right) \cos\left(\frac{180°}{n}\right)$ as Y_1, using x for n.
- Go to the Table Setup menu and enter the values shown.
- View a table for the function and scroll down.

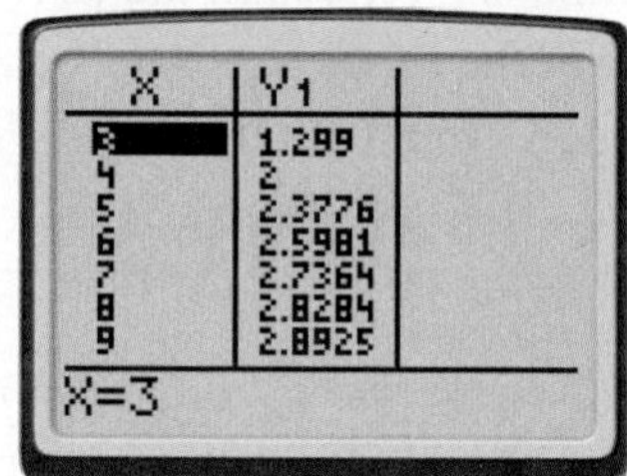

What happens to the expression as n gets very large?

Ⓗ If $n \sin\left(\frac{180°}{n}\right) \cos\left(\frac{180°}{n}\right)$ gets closer to π as n becomes greater, what happens to the entire expression for the volume of the inscribed pyramid? How is the area of the circle related to the expression for the base?

Reflect

1. How is the formula for the volume of a cone related to the formula for the volume of a pyramid?

Explain 1 Finding the Volume of a Cone

The volume relationship for cones that you found in the Explore can be stated as the following formula.

Volume of a Cone

The volume of a cone with base radius r and base area $B = \pi r^2$ and height h is given by $V = \frac{1}{3}Bh$ or by $V = \frac{1}{3}\pi r^2 h$.

You can use a formula for the volume of a cone to solve problems involving volume and capacity.

Example 1 **The figure represents a conical paper cup. How many fluid ounces of liquid can the cup hold? Round to the nearest tenth. (*Hint*: $1 \text{ in}^3 \approx 0.554$ fl oz.)**

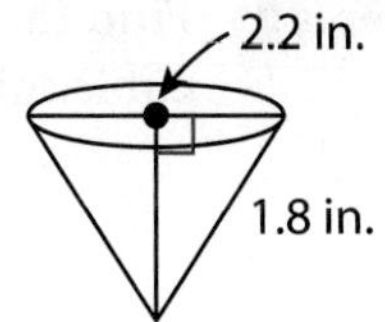

(A) Find the radius and height of the cone to the nearest hundredth.

The radius is half of the diameter, so $r = \frac{1}{2}(2.2 \text{ in.}) = 1.1$ in.

To find the height of the cone, use the Pythagorean Theorem:

$$r^2 + h^2 = (1.8)^2$$

$$(1.1)^2 + h^2 = (1.8)^2$$

$$1.21 + h^2 = 3.24$$

$$h^2 = 2.03, \text{ so } h \approx 1.42 \text{ in.}$$

(B) Find the volume of the cone in cubic inches.

$$V = \frac{1}{3}\pi r^2 h \approx \frac{1}{3}\pi\left(\boxed{1.1}\right)^2\left(\boxed{1.42}\right) \approx \boxed{1.80} \text{ in}^3$$

(C) Find the capacity of the cone to the nearest tenth of a fluid ounce.

$$\boxed{1.80} \text{ in}^3 \approx \boxed{1.80} \text{ in}^3 \times \frac{0.554 \text{ fl oz}}{1 \text{ in}^3} \approx \boxed{1.00} \text{ fl oz}$$

Your Turn

Right after Cindy buys a frozen yogurt cone, her friend Maria calls her, and they talk for so long that the frozen yogurt melts before Cindy can eat it. The cone has a slant height of 3.9 in. and a diameter of 2.4 in. If the frozen yogurt has the same volume before and after melting, and when melted just fills the cone, how much frozen yogurt did Cindy have before she talked to Maria, to the nearest tenth of a fluid ounce?

2. Find the radius. Then use the Pythagorean Theorem to find the height of the cone.

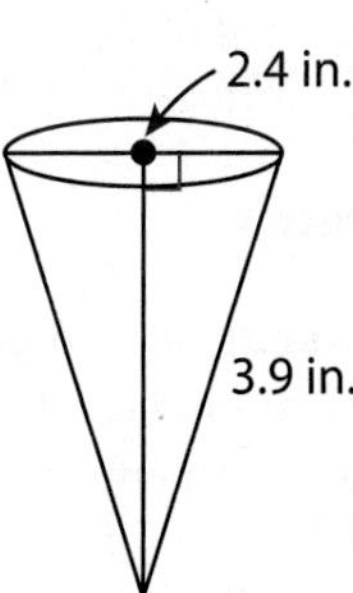

3. Find the volume of the cone in cubic inches.

4. Find the capacity of the cone to the nearest fluid ounce.

Explain 2 Finding the Volume of a Composite Figure

You can find the volume of a composite figure using appropriate volume formulas for the different parts of the figure.

Example 2 **Find the volume of the composite figure. Round to the nearest cubic millimeter.**

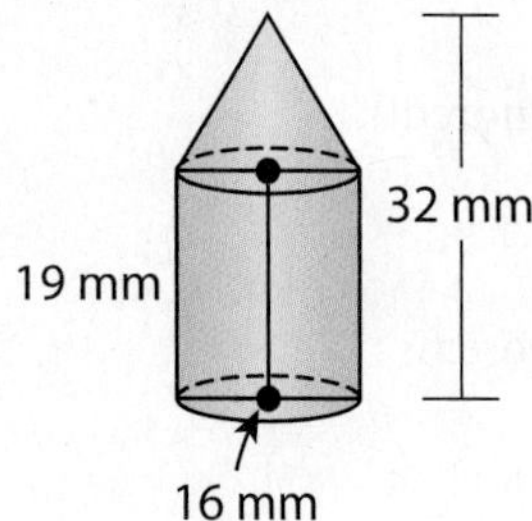

(A) Find the volume of the cylinder.

First, find the radius: $r = \frac{1}{2}(16 \text{ mm}) = 8 \text{ mm}$

$V = \pi r^2 h = \pi(8)^2(19) = 3{,}820.176 \ldots \text{ mm}^3$

(B) Find the volume of the cone.

The height of the cone is $h =$ 32 mm − 19 mm = 13 mm.

It has the same radius as the cylinder, $r =$ 8 mm.

$V = \frac{1}{3}\pi r^2 h = \frac{1}{3}\pi\left(8\right)^2\left(13\right) \approx 871.268 \text{ mm}^3$

(C) Find the total volume.

Total volume = volume of cylinder + volume of cone

= 3,820.177 mm³ + 871.268 mm³

≈ 4,691 mm³

Reflect

5. **Discussion** A composite figure is formed from a cone and a cylinder with the same base radius, and its volume can be calculated by multiplying the volume of the cylinder by a rational number, $\frac{a}{b}$. What arrangements of the cylinder and cone could explain this?

Your Turn

Making a cone-shaped hole in the top of a cylinder forms a composite figure, so that the apex of the cone is at the base of the cylinder. Find the volume of the figure, to the nearest tenth.

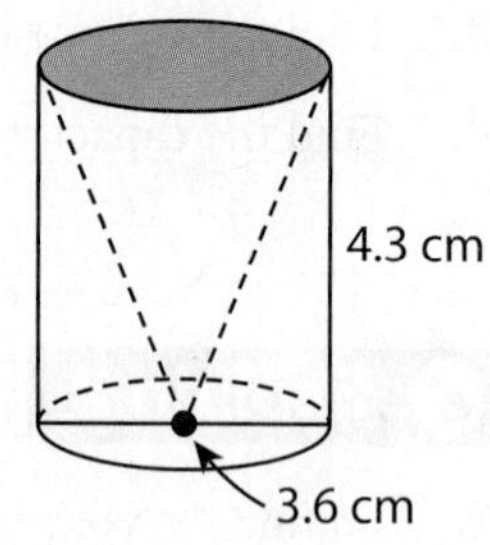

6. Find the volume of the cylinder.
7. Find the volume of the figure.

Elaborate

8. Could you use a circumscribed regular n-gon as the base of a pyramid to derive the formula for the volume of a cone? Explain.

9. **Essential Question Check-In** How do you calculate the volumes of composite figures that include cones?

Evaluate: Homework and Practice

Personal Math Trainer
- Online Homework
- Hints and Help
- Extra Practice

1. **Interpret the Answer** Katherine is using a cone to fill a cylinder with sand. If the radii and height are equal on both objects, and Katherine fills the cone to the very top, how many cones will it take to fill the cylinder with sand? Explain your answer.

Find the volume of the cone. Round the answer to the nearest tenth.

2.

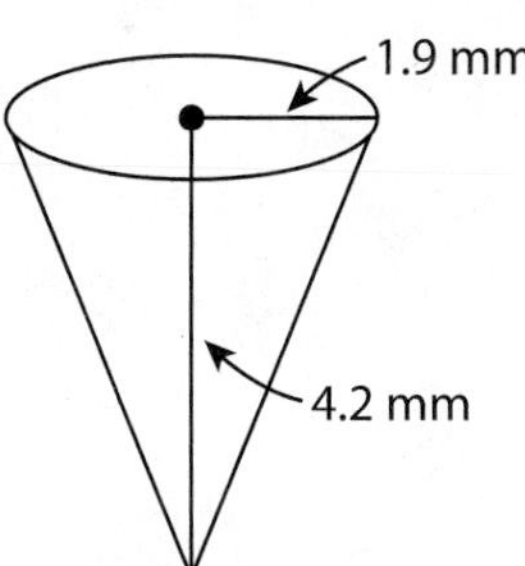

3.

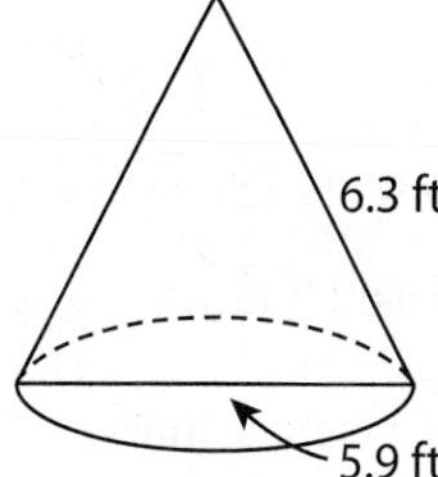

4.

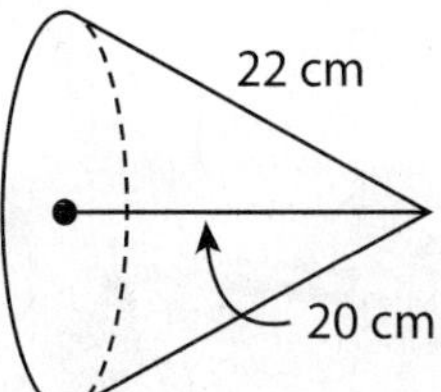

Find the volume of the cone. Leave the answer in terms of π.

5.

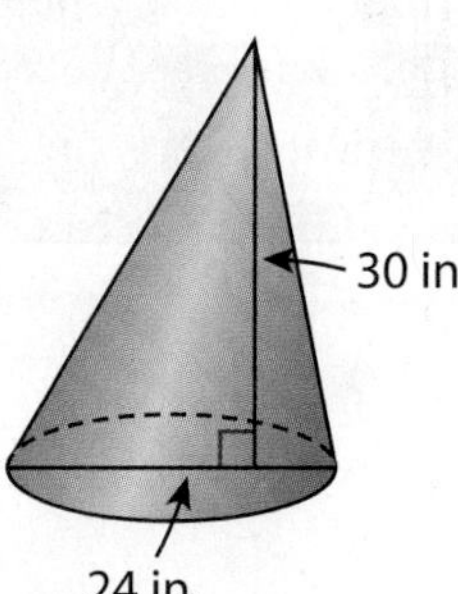

6.

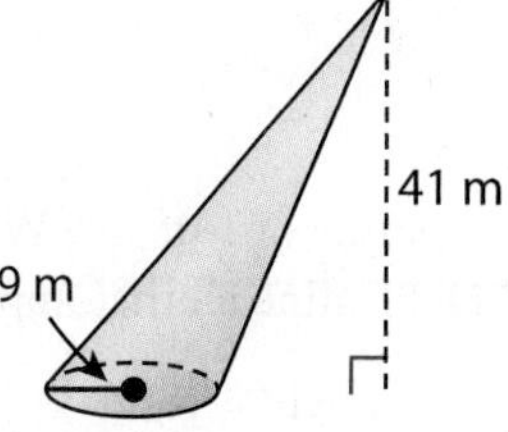

Find the volume of the composite figures. Round the answer to the nearest tenth.

7.

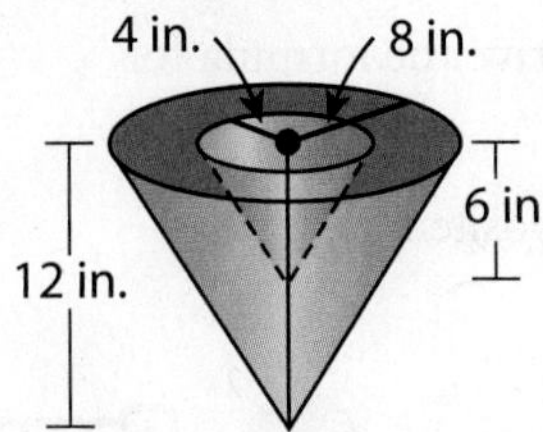

8.

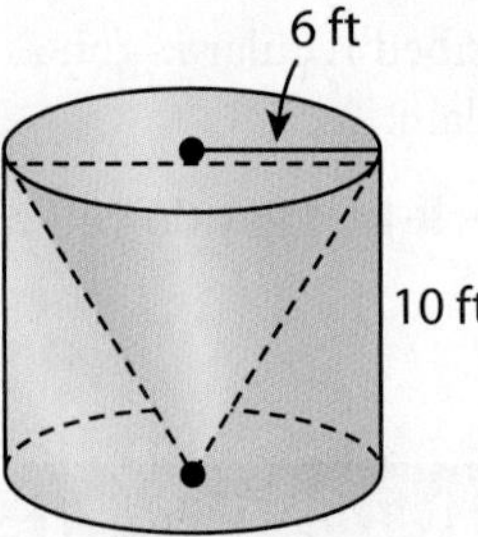

9.

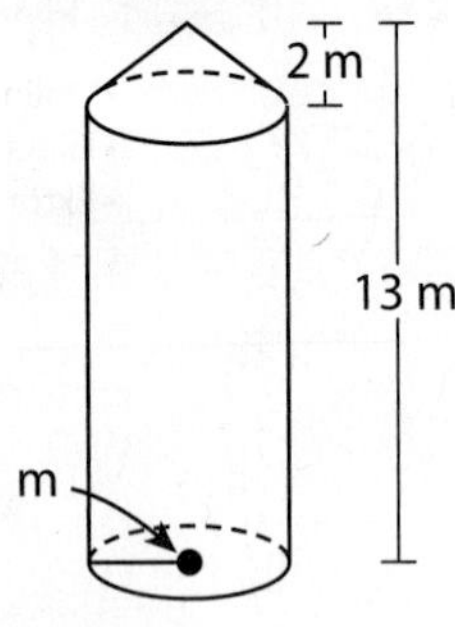

10.

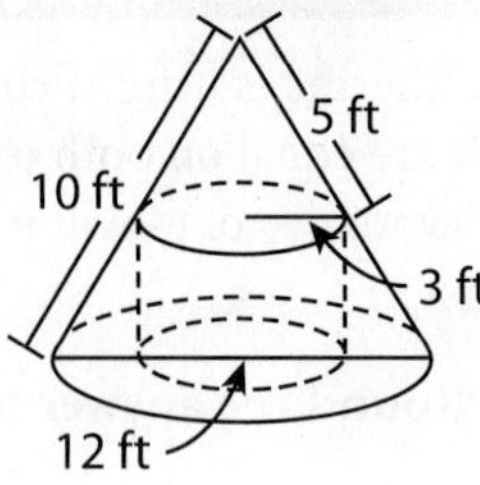

11. Match the dimensions of each cone with its volume.

A. radius 3 units, height 7 units — **a.** __?__ $\frac{25\pi}{6}$ units^3

B. diameter 5 units, height 2 units — **b.** __?__ 240π units^3

C. radius 28 units, slant height 53 units — **c.** __?__ $11{,}760\pi$ units^3

D. diameter 24 units, slant height 13 units. — **d.** __?__ 21π units^3

12. The roof of a grain silo is in the shape of a cone. The inside radius is 20 feet, and the roof is 10 feet tall. Below the cone is a cylinder 30 feet tall, with the same radius.

a. What is the volume of the silo?

b. If one cubic foot of wheat is approximately 48 pounds, and the farmer's crop consists of approximately 2 million pounds of wheat, will all of the wheat fit in the silo?

13. A cone has a volume of 18π in^3. Which are possible dimensions of the cone? Determine all that apply.

A. diameter 1 in., height 18 in.

B. diameter 6 in., height 6 in.

C. diameter 3 in., height 6 in.

D. diameter 6 in., height 3 in.

E. diameter 4 in., height 13.5 in.

F. diameter 13.5 in., height 4 in.

14. The figure shows a water tank that consists of a cylinder and a cone. How many gallons of water does the tank hold? Round to the nearest gallon. (Hint: 1 ft^3 = 7.48 gal)

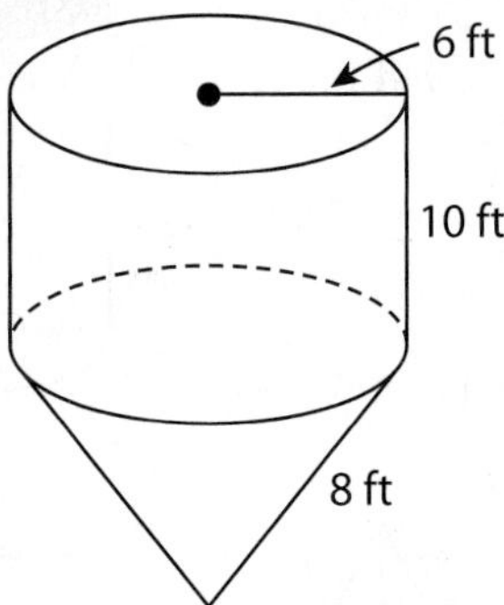

15. Roland is using a special machine to cut cones out of cylindrical pieces of wood. The machine is set to cut out two congruent cones from each piece of wood, leaving no gap in between the vertices of the cones. What is the volume of material left over after two cones are cut out?

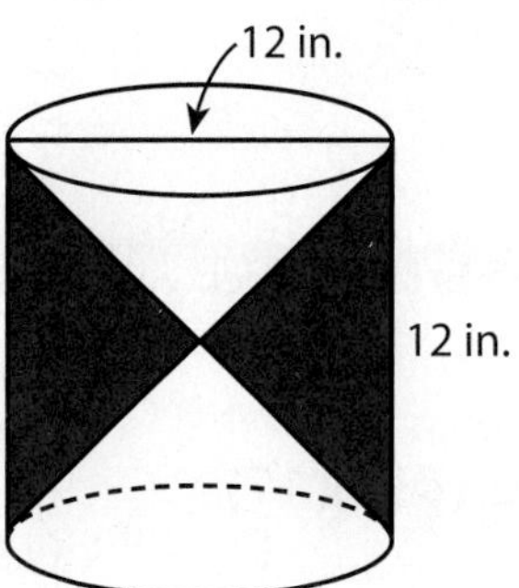

16. **Algebra** Develop an expression that could be used to solve for the volume of this solid for any value of x.

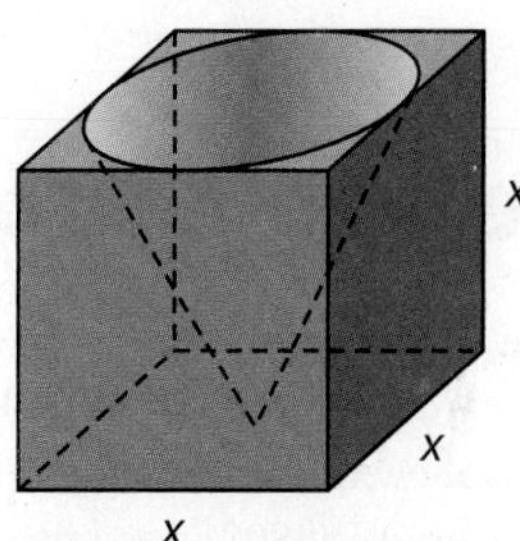

17. **Persevere in Problem Solving** A juice stand sells smoothies in cone-shaped cups that are 8 in. tall. The regular size has a 4 in. diameter. The jumbo size has an 8 in. diameter.

a. Find the volume of the regular size to the nearest tenth.

b. Find the volume of the jumbo size to the nearest tenth.

c. The regular size costs $1.25. What would be a reasonable price for the jumbo size? Explain your reasoning.

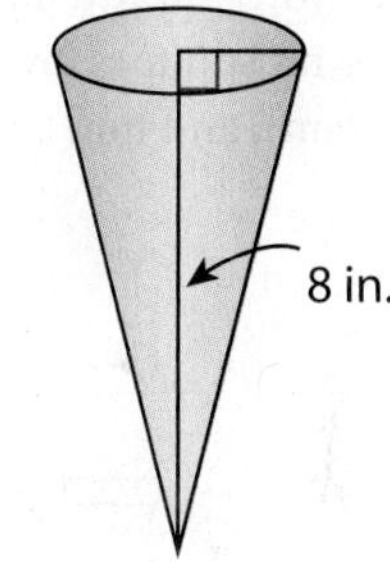

18. Find the volume of a cone with base area 36π ft^2 and a height equal to twice the radius.

19. Find the base circumference of a cone with height 5 cm and volume 125π cm^3.

H.O.T. Focus on Higher Order Thinking

20. **Analyze Relationships** Popcorn is available in two cups: a square pyramid or a cone, as shown. The price of each cup of popcorn is the same. Which cup is the better deal? Explain.

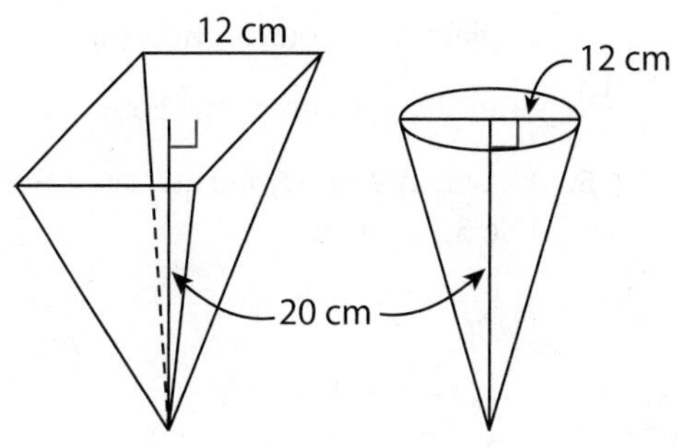

21. Make a Conjecture A cylinder has a radius of 5 in. and a height of 3 in. Without calculating the volumes, find the height of a cone with the same base and the same volume as the cylinder. Explain your reasoning.

22. Analyze Relationships A sculptor removes a cone from a cylindrical block of wood so that the vertex of the cone is the center of the cylinder's base, as shown. Explain how the volume of the remaining solid compares with the volume of the original cylindrical block of wood.

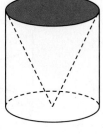

23. Explain the Error Which volume is incorrect? Explain the error.

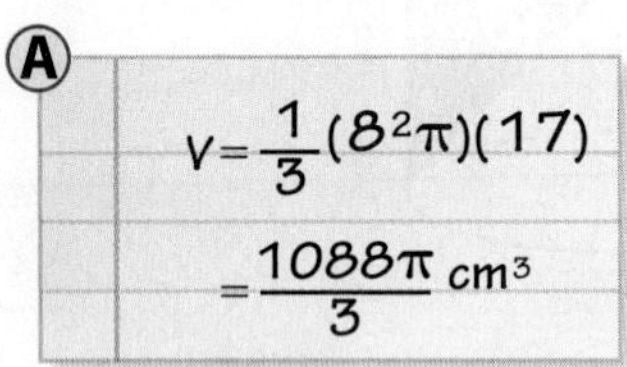

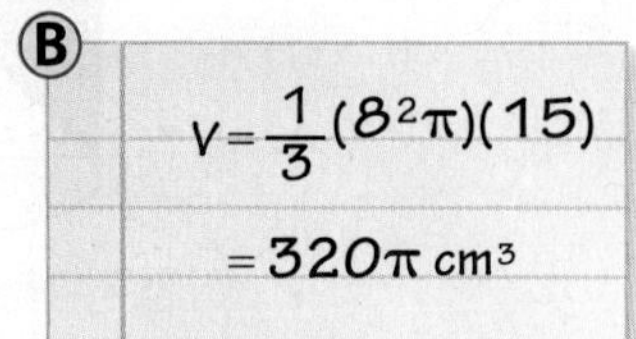

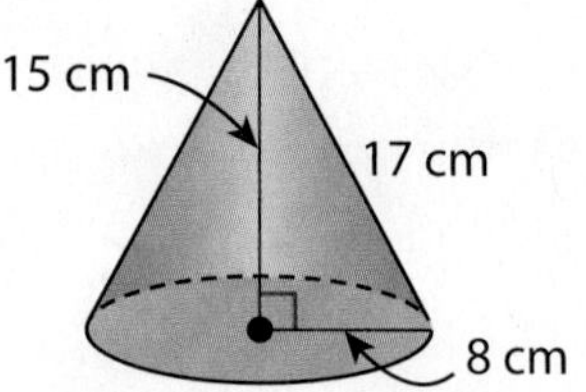

Lesson Performance Task

You've just set up your tent on the first night of a camping trip that you've been looking forward to for a long time. Unfortunately, mosquitoes have been looking forward to your arrival even more than you have. When you turn on your flashlight you see swarms of them—an average of 800 mosquitos per square meter, in fact.

Since you're always looking for a way to use geometry, you decide to solve a problem: How many mosquitoes are in the first three meters of the cone of your flashlight (Zone 1 in the diagram), and how many are in the second three meters (Zone 2)?

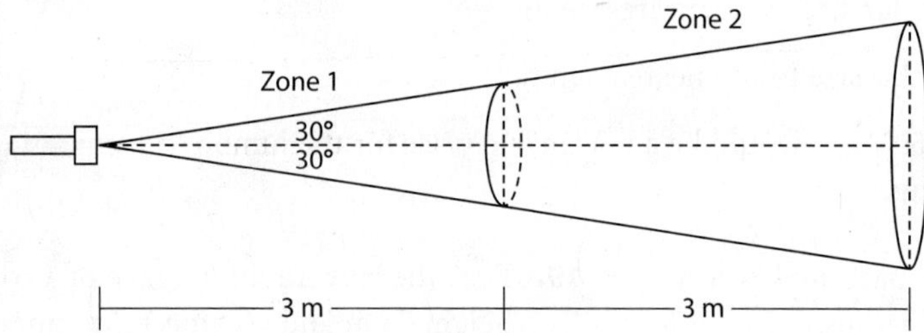

1. Explain how you can find the volume of the Zone 1 cone.
2. Find the volume of the Zone 1 cone. Write your answer in terms of π.
3. Explain how you can find the volume of the Zone 2 cone.
4. Find the volume of the Zone 2 cone. Write your answer in terms of π.
5. How many more mosquitoes are there in Zone 2 than there are in Zone 1? Use 3.14 for π.

21.4 Volume of Spheres

Essential Question: How can you use the formula for the volume of a sphere to calculate the volumes of composite figures?

Resource Locker

Explore Developing a Volume Formula

To find the volume of a sphere, compare one of its hemispheres to a cylinder of the same height and radius from which a cone has been removed.

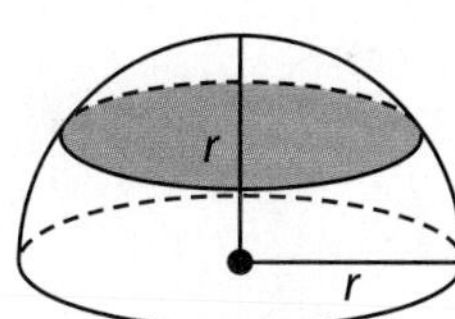

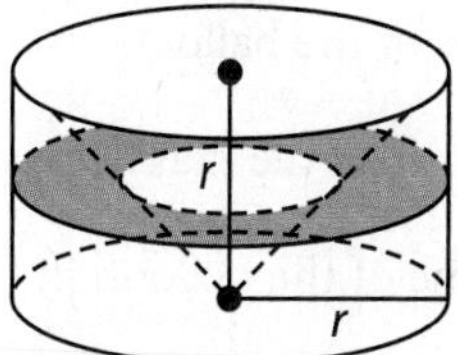

(A) The region of a plane that intersects a solid figure is called a **cross section**. To show that cross sections have the same area at every level, use the Pythagorean Theorem to find a relationship between r, x, and R.

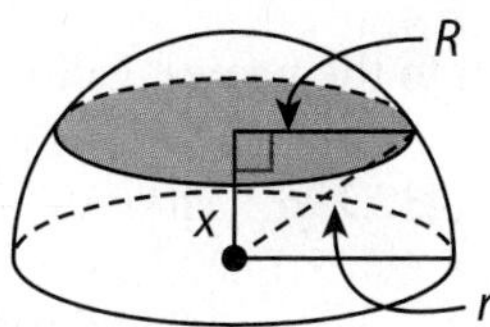

(B) A cross section of the cylinder with the cone removed is a ring.

To find the area of the ring, find the area of the outer circle and of the inner circle. Then subtract the area of the inner circle from the outer circle.

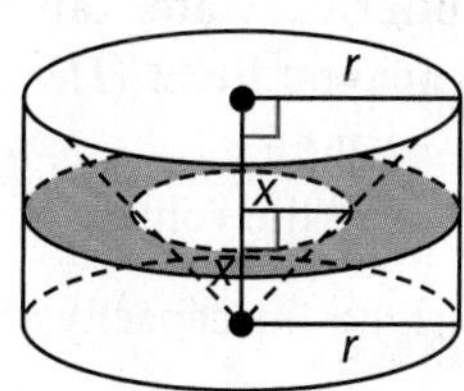

(C) Find an expression for the volume of the cylinder with the cone removed.

(D) Use Cavalieri's principle to deduce the volume of a sphere with radius r.

Reflect

1. How do you know that the height h of the cylinder with the cone removed is equal to the radius r?

2. What happens to the cross-sectional areas when $x = 0$? when $x = r$?

Explain 1 Finding the Volume of a Sphere

The relationship you discovered in the Explore can be stated as a volume formula.

Volume of a Sphere

The volume of a sphere with radius r is given by $V = \frac{4}{3}\pi r^3$.

You can use a formula for the volume of a sphere to solve problems involving volume and capacity.

Example 1 **The figure represents a spherical helium-filled balloon. This tourist attraction allows up to 28 passengers at a time to ride in a gondola suspended underneath the balloon, as it cruises at an altitude of 500 ft. How much helium, to the nearest hundred gallons, does the balloon hold? Round to the nearest tenth. (*Hint:* 1 gal $\approx$ 0.1337 ft^3)**

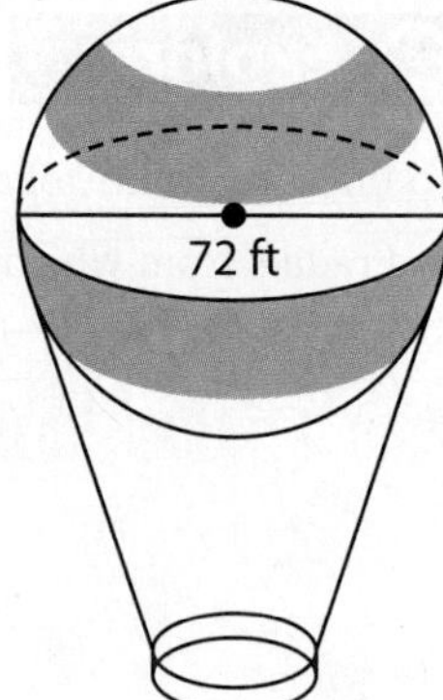

Step 1 Find the radius of the balloon.

The radius is half of the diameter, so $r = \frac{1}{2}(72 \text{ ft}) = 36$ ft.

Step 2 Find the volume of the balloon in cubic feet.

$$V = \frac{4}{3}\pi r^3$$

$$= \frac{4}{3}\pi\left(\boxed{36}\right)^3$$

$$\approx \boxed{195{,}432.196} \text{ ft}^3$$

Step 3 Find the capacity of the balloon to the nearest gallon.

$$\boxed{195{,}432.196} \text{ ft}^3 \approx \boxed{195{,}432.196} \text{ ft}^3 \times \frac{1 \text{ gal}}{0.1337 \text{ ft}^3} \approx \boxed{1{,}462{,}000} \text{ gal}$$

Your Turn

A spherical water tank has a diameter of 27 m. How much water can the tank hold, to the nearest liter? (*Hint:* 1,000 L = 1 m^3)

3. Find the volume of the tank in cubic meters.

4. Find the capacity of the tank to the nearest liter.

Explain 2 Finding the Volume of a Composite Figure

You can find the volume of a composite figure using appropriate volume formulas for the different parts of the figure.

Example 2 **Find the volume of the composite figure. Round to the nearest cubic centimeter.**

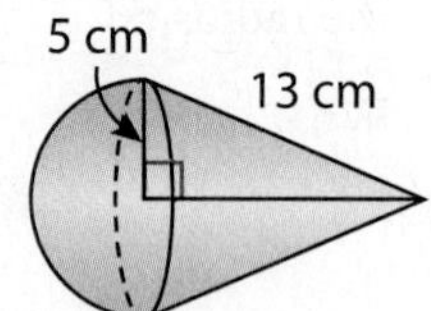

Step 1 Find the volume of the hemisphere.

$$V = \frac{2}{3}\pi r^3 = \frac{2}{3}\pi(5)^3 \approx 261.799 \text{ cm}^3$$

Step 2 Find the height of the cone.

$$h^2 + (5)^2 = (13)^2$$
$$h^2 + 25 = 169$$
$$h^2 = 144$$
$$h = 12$$

Step 3 Find the volume of the cone.

The cone has the same radius as the hemisphere, $r = 5$ cm.

$$V = \frac{1}{3}\pi r^2 h$$
$$= \frac{1}{3}\pi(5)^2(12)$$
$$= 314.159 \text{ cm}^3$$

Step 4 Find the total volume.

Total volume = volume of hemisphere + volume of cone

$$= 261.799 \text{ cm}^3 + 314.159 \text{ cm}^3$$
$$\approx 576 \text{ cm}^3$$

Reflect

5. Is it possible to create a figure by taking a cone and removing from it a hemisphere with the same radius?

Your Turn

6. A composite figure is a cylinder with a hemispherical hole in the top. The bottom of the hemisphere is tangent to the base of the cylinder. Find the volume of the figure, to the nearest tenth.

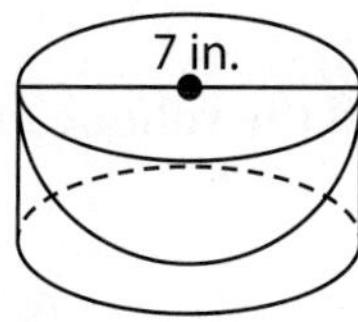

Elaborate

7. **Discussion** Could you use an inscribed prism to derive the volume of a hemisphere? Why or why not? Are there any other ways you could approximate a hemisphere, and what problems would you encounter in finding its volume?

8. **Essential Question Check-In** A gumball is in the shape of a sphere, with a spherical hole in the center. How might you calculate the volume of the gumball? What measurements are needed?

Evaluate: Homework and Practice

Personal Math Trainer

- Online Homework
- Hints and Help
- Extra Practice

1. **Analyze Relationships** Use the diagram of a sphere inscribed in a cylinder to describe the relationship between the volume of a sphere and the volume of a cylinder.

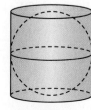

Find the volume of the sphere. Round the answer to the nearest tenth.

2.

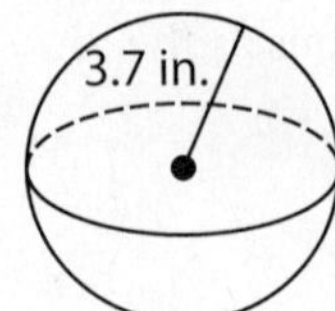

3.

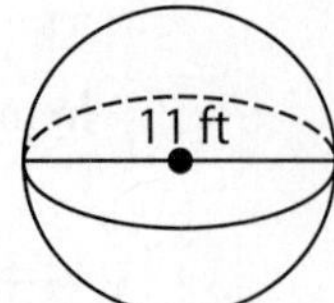

4.

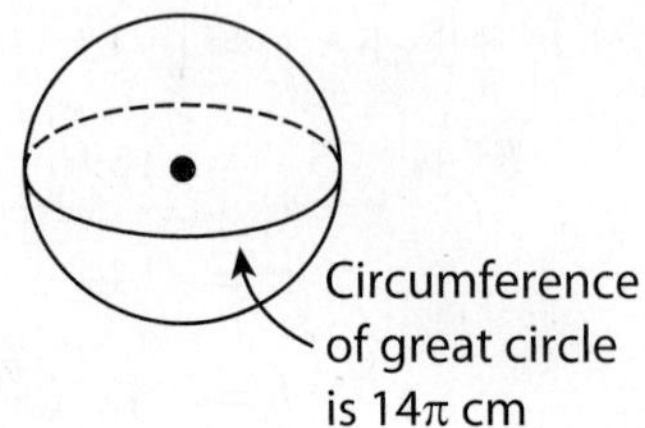

Find the volume of the sphere. Leave the answer in terms of π.

5.

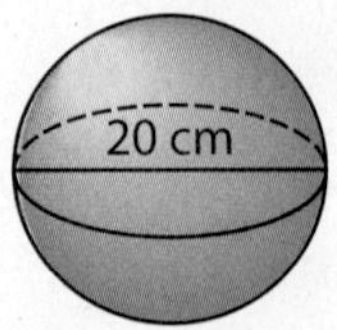

6.

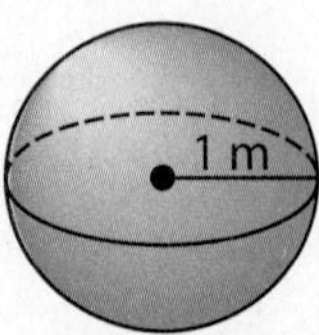

7.

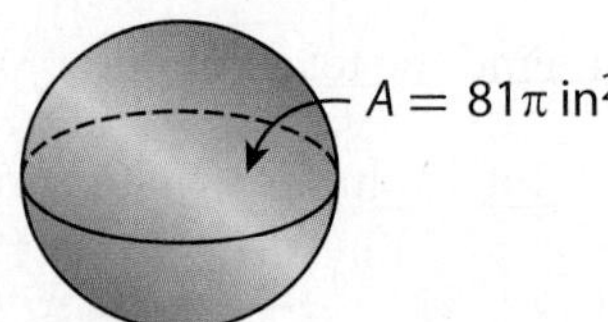

Find the volume of the composite figure. Leave the answer in terms of π.

8.

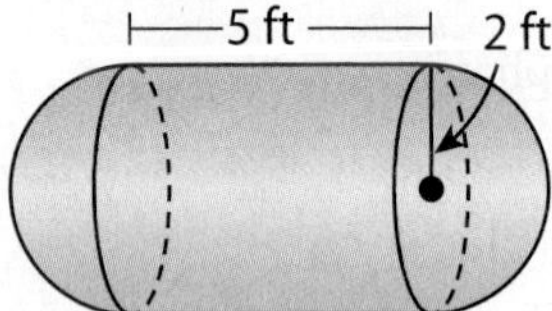

9.

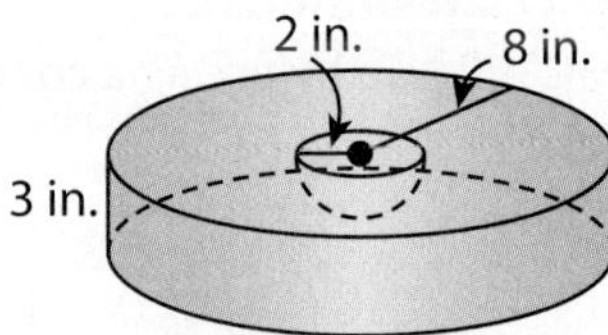

Find the volume of the composite figure. Round the answer to the nearest tenth.

10.

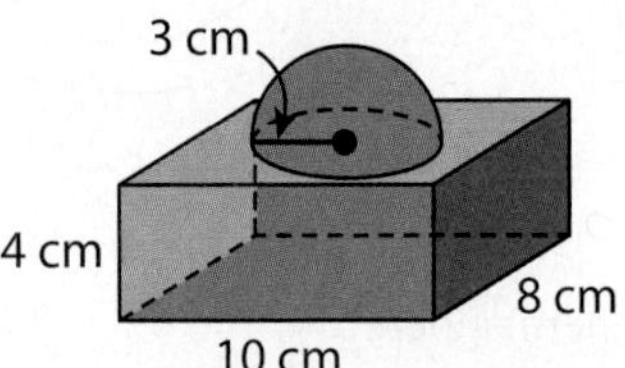

11.

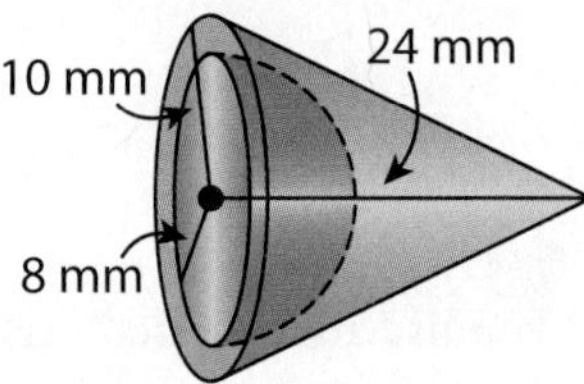

12. Analyze Relationships Approximately how many times as great is the volume of a grapefruit with diameter 10 cm as the volume of a lime with diameter 5 cm?

13. A bead is formed by drilling a cylindrical hole with a 2-mm diameter through a sphere with an 8-mm diameter. Estimate the volume of the bead to the nearest whole.

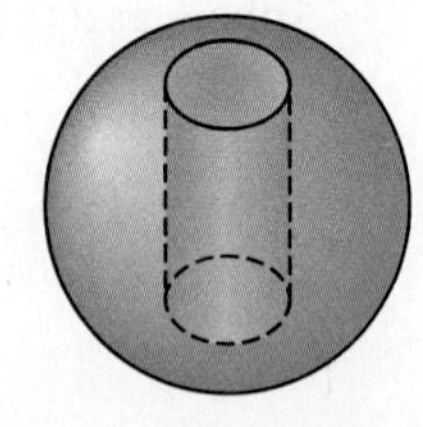

14. Algebra Write an expression representing the volume of the composite figure formed by a hemisphere with radius r and a cube with side length $2r$.

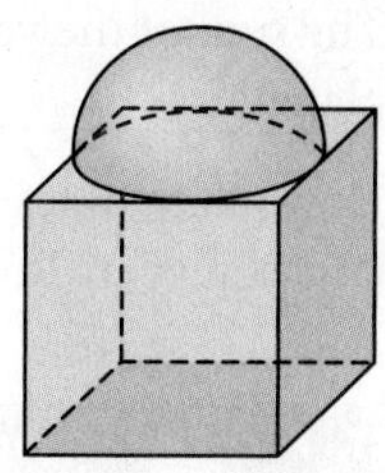

15. One gallon of propane yields approximately 91,500 BTU. About how many BTUs does the spherical storage tank shown provide? Round to the nearest billion BTUs. (*Hint:* $1 \text{ ft}^3 \approx 7.48$ gal)

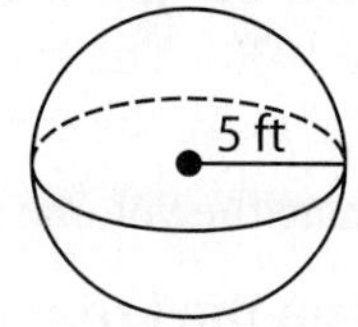

16. The aquarium shown is a rectangular prism that is filled with water. You drop a spherical ball with a diameter of 6 inches into the aquarium. The ball sinks, causing the water to spill from the tank. How much water is left in the tank? Express your answer to the nearest tenth. (*Hint:* $1 \text{ in.}^3 \approx 0.00433$ gal)

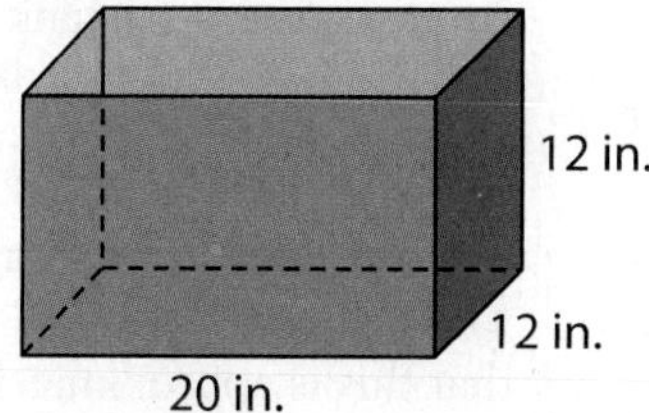

17. A sphere with diameter 8 cm is inscribed in a cube. Find the ratio of the volume of the cube to the volume of the sphere.

A. $\frac{6}{\pi}$

B. $\frac{2}{3\pi}$

C. $\frac{3\pi}{4}$

D. $\frac{3\pi}{2}$

For Exercises 18–20, use the table. Round each volume to the nearest billion π.

Planet	Diameter (mi)
Mercury	3,032
Venus	7,521
Earth	7,926
Mars	4,222
Jupiter	88,846
Saturn	74,898
Uranus	31,763
Neptune	30,775

18. Explain the Error Margaret used the mathematics shown to find the volume of Saturn.

$V = \frac{4}{3}\pi r^2 = \frac{4}{3}\pi(74{,}898)^2 \approx \frac{4}{3}\pi(6{,}000{,}000{,}000) \approx 8{,}000{,}000{,}000\pi$

Explain the two errors Margaret made, then give the correct answer.

19. The sum of the volumes of Venus and Mars is about equal to the volume of which planet?

20. How many times as great as the volume of the smallest planet is the volume of the largest planet? Round to the nearest thousand.

H.O.T. Focus on Higher Order Thinking

21. **Make a Conjecture** The *bathysphere* was an early version of a submarine, invented in the 1930s. The inside diameter of the bathysphere was 54 inches, and the steel used to make the sphere was 1.5 inches thick. It had three 8-inch diameter windows. Estimate the volume of steel used to make the bathysphere.

22. **Explain the Error** A student solved the problem shown. Explain the student's error and give the correct answer to the problem.

A spherical gasoline tank has a radius of 0.5 ft. When filled, the tank provides 446,483 BTU. How many BTUs does one gallon of gasoline yield? Round to the nearest thousand BTUs and use the fact that 1 $ft^3 \approx 7.48$ gal.

The volume of the tank is $\frac{4}{3}\pi r^3 = \frac{4}{3}\pi(0.5)^3$ ft^3. Multiplying by 7.48 shows that this is approximately 3.92 gal. So the number of BTUs in one gallon of gasoline is approximately $446{,}483 \times 3.92 \approx 1{,}750{,}000$ BTU.

23. **Persevere in Problem Solving** The top of a gumball machine is an 18 in. sphere. The machine holds a maximum of 3300 gumballs, which leaves about 43% of the space in the machine empty. Estimate the diameter of each gumball.

Lesson Performance Task

For his science project, Bizbo has decided to build a scale model of the solar system. He starts with a grapefruit with a radius of 2 inches to represent Earth. His "Earth" weighs 0.5 pounds.

Find each of the following for Bizbo's model. Use the rounded figures in the table. Round your answers to two significant figures. Use 3.14 for π.

1. the scale of Bizbo's model: 1 inch = ___?___ miles
2. Earth's distance from the Sun, in inches and in miles
3. Neptune's distance from the Sun, in inches and in miles
4. the Sun's volume, in cubic inches and cubic feet
5. the Sun's weight, in pounds and in tons (Note: the Sun's density is 0.26 times the Earth's density.)

21.5 Scale Factor

Essential Question: How does multiplying one or more of the dimensions of a figure affect its attributes?

Resource Locker

Explore Exploring Effects of Changing Dimensions on Perimeter and Area

Changes made to the dimensions of a figure can affect the perimeter and the area.

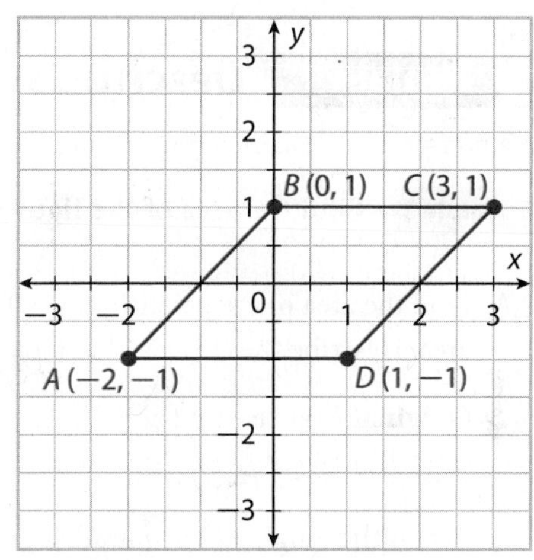

Use the figure to investigate how changing one or more dimensions of the figure affect its perimeter and area.

Ⓐ Apply the transformation $(x, y) \rightarrow (3x, y)$. Find the perimeter and the area.

Original Dimensions	Dimensions after $(x, y) \rightarrow (3x, y)$
$P = 6 + 4\sqrt{2}$	$P =$
$A = 6$	$A =$

Ⓑ Apply the transformation $(x, y) \rightarrow (x, 3y)$. Find the perimeter and the area.

Original Dimensions	Dimensions after $(x, y) \rightarrow (x, 3y)$
$P = 6 + 4\sqrt{2}$	$P =$
$A = 6$	$A =$

Ⓒ Apply the transformation $(x, y) \to (3x, 3y)$. Find the perimeter and the area.

Original Dimensions	Dimensions after $(x, y) \to (3x, 3y)$
$P = 6 + 4\sqrt{2}$	$P =$ ▢
$A = 6$	$A =$ ▢

Reflect

1. Describe the changes that occurred in Steps A and B. Did the perimeter or area change by a constant factor?

2. Describe the changes that occurred in Step C. Did the perimeter or area change by a constant factor?

Explain 1 Describe a Non-Proportional Dimension Change

In a non-proportional dimension change, you do not use the same factor to change each dimension of a figure.

Example 1 **Find the area of the figure.**

Ⓐ Find the area of the parallelogram. Then multiply the length by 2 and determine the new area. Describe the changes that took place.

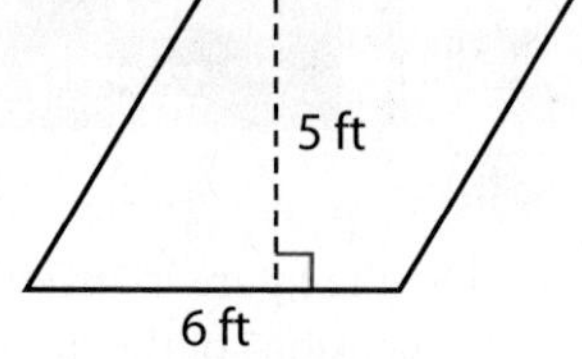

Original Figure

$A = bh = 6 \cdot 5 = 30 \text{ ft}^2$

Transformed Figure

$A = bh = 12 \cdot 5 = 60 \text{ ft}^2$

When the length of the parallelogram changes by a factor of 2, the area changes by a factor of 2.

Ⓑ Find the area of the trapezoid. Then multiply the height by 0.5 and determine the new area. Describe the changes that took place.

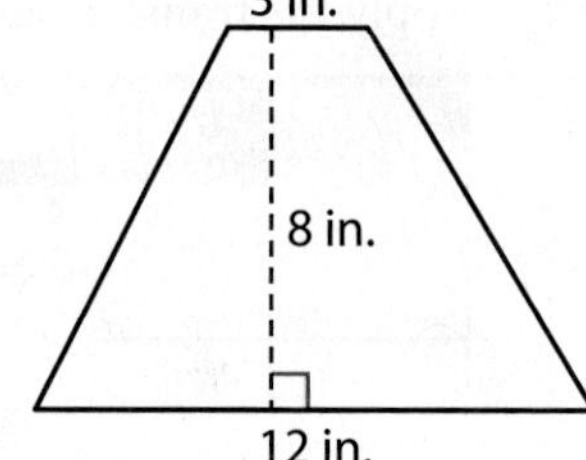

Original Figure $A = \frac{1}{2}(b_1 + b_2)h = \frac{1}{2}(3 + 12)8 = 60$

Transformed Figure $A = \frac{1}{2}(b_1 + b_2)h = \frac{1}{2}(3 + 12)4 = 30$

When the height of the trapezoid changes by a factor of 0.5, the area of the trapezoid changes by a factor of 0.5.

Reflect

3. **Discussion** When a non-proportional change is applied to the dimensions of a figure, does the perimeter change in a predictable way?

Your Turn

4. Find the area of a triangle with vertices $(-5, -2)$, $(-5, 7)$, and $(3, 1)$. Then apply the transformation $(x, y) \rightarrow (x, 4y)$ and determine the new area. Describe the changes that took place.

5. Find the area of the figure. Then multiply the width by 5 and determine the new area. Describe the changes that took place.

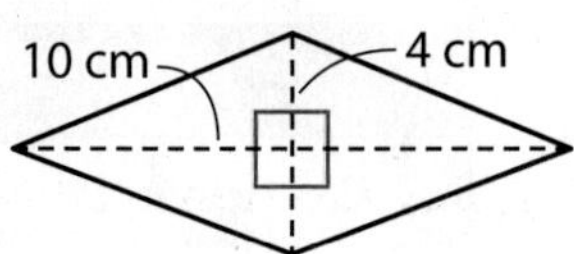

Explain 2 Describe a Proportional Dimension Change

In a proportional dimension change, you use the same factor to change each dimension of a figure.

Example 2 **Find the area and perimeter of a circle.**

(A) Find the circumference and area of the circle. Then multiply the radius by 3 and find the new circumference and area. Describe the changes that took place.

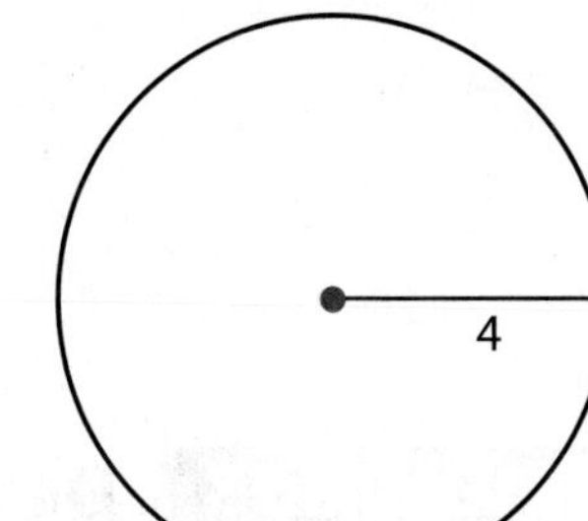

Original Figure $C = 2\pi(4) = 8\pi$

$A = \pi(4)^2 = 16\pi$

Transformed Figure $C = 2\pi(12) = 24\pi$

$A = \pi(12)^2 = 144\pi$

The circumference changes by a factor of 3, and the area changes by a factor of 9 or 3^2.

(B) Find the perimeter and area of the figure. Then multiply the length and height by $\frac{1}{3}$ and find the new perimeter and area. Describe the changes that took place.

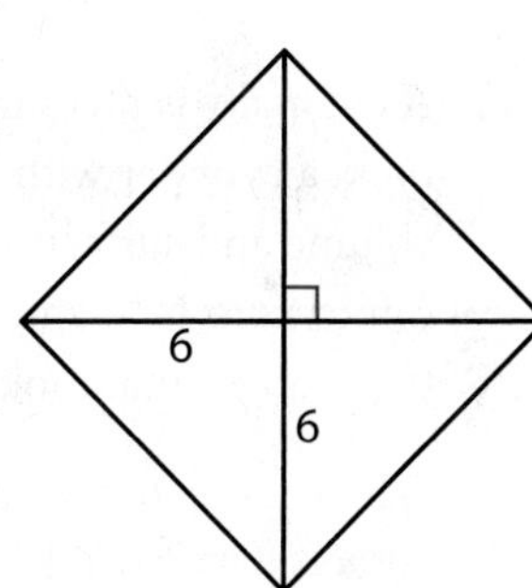

Original Figure	Transformed Figure
$P = 4(6\sqrt{2}) = 24\sqrt{2}$	$P = 4(2\sqrt{2}) = 8\sqrt{2}$
$A = \frac{1}{2}d_1d_2 = \frac{1}{2}(12 \cdot 12) = 72$	$A = \frac{1}{2}d_1d_2 = \frac{1}{2}(4 \cdot 4) = 8$

The perimeter changes by a factor of $\frac{1}{3}$, and the area changes by a factor of $\frac{1}{9}$ or $\frac{1}{3^2}$.

Reflect

6. Describe the effect on perimeter (or circumference) and area when the dimensions of a figure are changed proportionally.

Effects of Changing Dimensions Proportionally		
Change in Dimensions	**Perimeter or Circumference**	**Area**
All dimensions multiplied by *a*		

Your Turn

7. Find the circumference and area of the circle. Then multiply the radius by 0.25 and find the new circumference and area. Describe the changes that took place.

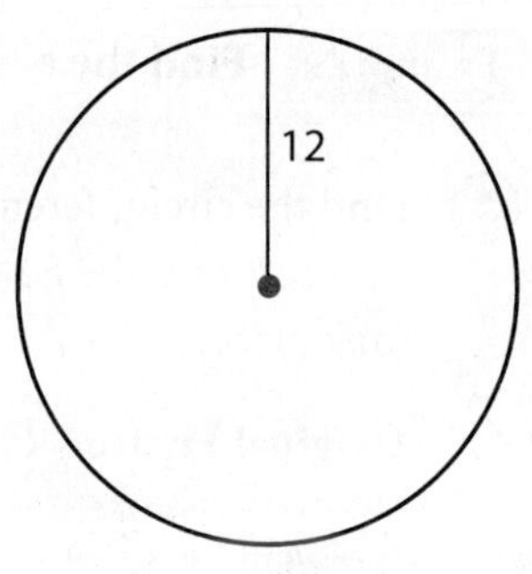

Explain 3 Describe a Proportional Dimension Change for a Solid

In a proportional dimension change to a solid, you use the same factor to change each dimension of a figure.

Example 3 **Find the volume of the composite solid.**

Ⓐ A company is planning to create a similar version of this storage tank, a cylinder with hemispherical caps at each end. Find the volume and surface area of the original tank. Then multiply all the dimensions by 2 and find the new volume and surface area. Describe the changes that took place.

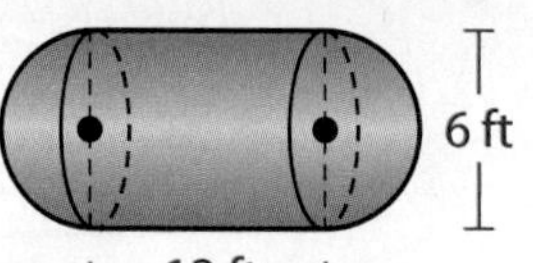

The volume of the solid is $V = \pi r^2 h + \frac{4}{3}\pi r^3$, and the surface area is $S = 2\pi rh + 4\pi r^2$.

Original Solid

$V = \pi(3)^2(12) + \frac{4}{3}\pi(3)^3 = 144\pi$ cu. ft.

$S = 2\pi(3 \cdot 12) + 4\pi(3)^2 = 108\pi$ sq. ft.

Transformed Solid

$V = \pi(6)^2(24) + \frac{4}{3}\pi(6)^3 = 1152\pi$ cu. ft.

$S = 2\pi(6 \cdot 24) + 4\pi(6)^2 = 432\pi$ sq. ft.

The volume changes by a factor of 8, and the surface area changes by a factor of 4.

(B) A children's toy is shaped like a hemisphere with a conical top. A company decides to create a smaller version of the toy. Find the volume and surface area of the original toy. Then multiply all dimensions by $\frac{2}{3}$ and find the new volume and surface area. Describe the changes that took place.

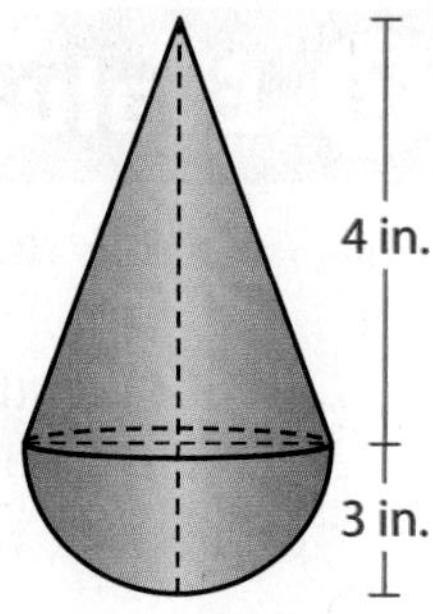

The volume of the solid is $V = \frac{1}{3}\pi r^2 h + \frac{2}{3}\pi r^3$,

and the surface area is $S = \pi r\sqrt{r^2 + h^2} + 2\pi r^2$.

Original Solid

$V = \boxed{\frac{1}{3}\pi(3)^2 4 + \frac{2}{3}\pi(3)^3 = 30\pi}$ cu. in.

$S = \boxed{\pi(3)\sqrt{3^2 + 4^2} + 2\pi(3)^2 = 33\pi}$ sq. in.

Transformed Solid

$V = \boxed{\frac{1}{3}\pi(2)^2\left(\frac{8}{3}\right) + \frac{2}{3}\pi(2)^3 = \frac{80}{9}\pi}$ cu. in.

$S = \boxed{\pi(2)\sqrt{(2)^2 + \left(\frac{8}{3}\right)^2} + 2\pi(2)^2 = \frac{44}{3}\pi}$ sq. in.

The volume changes by a factor of $\frac{8}{27}$, and the surface area changes by a factor of $\frac{4}{9}$.

Reflect

8. Describe the effect on surface area and volume when the dimensions of a figure are changed proportionally.

Effects of Changing Dimensions Proportionally		
Change in Dimensions	**Surface Area**	**Volume**
All dimensions multiplied by *a*		

Your Turn

9. A farmer has made a scale model of a new grain silo. Find the volume and surface area of the model. Use the scale ratio 1 : 36 to find the volume and surface area of the silo. Compare the volumes and surface areas relative to the scale ratio. Be consistent with units of measurement.

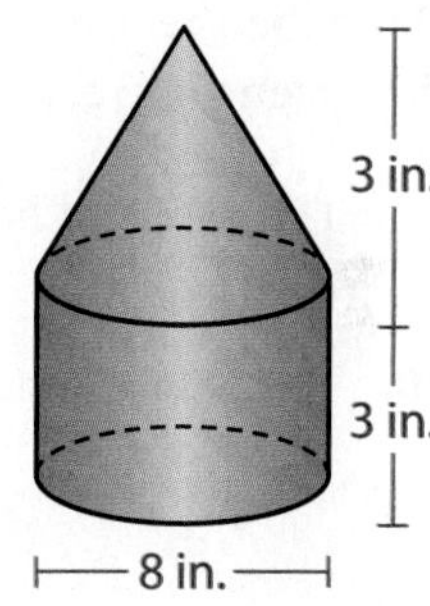

Elaborate

10. Two square pyramids are similar. If the ratio of a pair of corresponding edges is $a : b$, what is the ratio of their volumes? What is the ratio of their surface areas?

11. Essential Question Check-In How is a non-proportional dimension change different from a proportional dimension change?

Evaluate: Homework and Practice

- Online Homework
- Hints and Help
- Extra Practice

A trapezoid has the vertices (0, 0), (4, 0), (4, 4), and (−3, 4).

1. Describe the effect on the area if only the x-coordinates of the vertices are multiplied by $\frac{1}{2}$.

2. Describe the effect on the area if only the y-coordinates of the vertices are multiplied by $\frac{1}{2}$.

3. Describe the effect on the area if both the x- and y-coordinates of the vertices are multiplied by $\frac{1}{2}$.

4. Describe the effect on the area if the x-coordinates are multiplied by 2 and y-coordinates are multiplied by $\frac{1}{2}$.

Describe the effect of the change on the area of the given figure.

5. The height of the triangle is doubled.

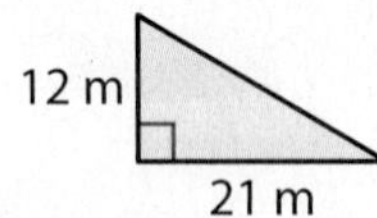

6. The height of a trapezoid with base lengths 12 cm and 8 cm and height 5 cm is multiplied by $\frac{1}{3}$.

7. The base of the parallelogram is multiplied by $\frac{2}{3}$.

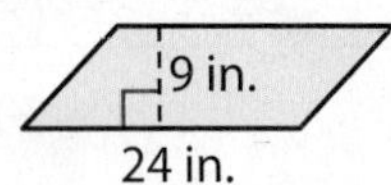

8. Communicate Mathematical Ideas A triangle has vertices (1, 5), (2, 3), and (−1, −6). Find the effect that multiplying the height of the triangle by 4 has on the area of the triangle, without doing any calculations. Explain.

Describe the effect of each change on the perimeter or circumference and the area of the given figure.

9. The base and height of an isosceles triangle with base 12 in. and height 6 in. are both tripled.

10. The base and height of the rectangle are both multiplied by $\frac{1}{2}$.

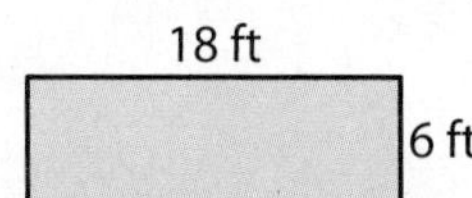

11. The dimensions are multiplied by 5.

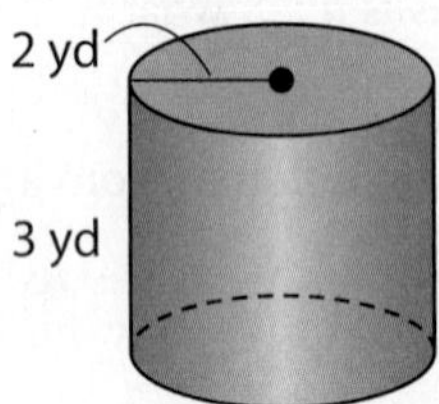

12. The dimensions are multiplied by $\frac{3}{5}$.

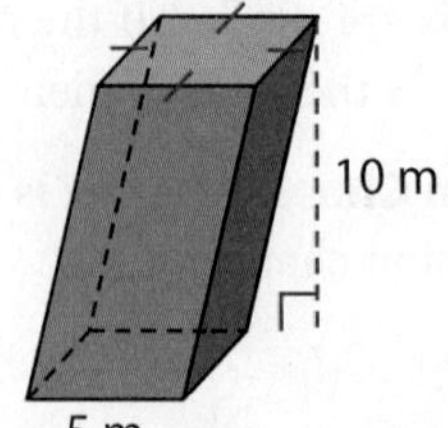

13. For each change, determine whether the change is non-proportional or proportional.

A. The height of a triangle is doubled.

B. All sides of a square are quadrupled.

C. The length of a rectangle is multiplied by $\frac{3}{4}$.

D. The height of a triangular prism is tripled.

E. The radius of a sphere is multiplied by $\sqrt{5}$.

14. Tina and Kleu built rectangular play areas for their dogs. The play area for Tina's dog is 1.5 times as long and 1.5 times as wide as the play area for Kleu's dog. If the play area for Kleu's dog is 60 square feet, how big is the play area for Tina's dog?

15. A map has the scale 1 inch = 10 miles. On the map, the area of Big Bend National Park in Texas is about 12.5 square inches. Estimate the actual area of the park in acres. (*Hint:* 1 square mile = 640 acres)

16. A restaurant has a weekly ad in a local newspaper that is 2 inches wide and 4 inches high and costs $36.75 per week. The cost of each ad is based on its area. If the owner of the restaurant decided to double the width and height of the ad, how much will the new ad cost?

17. Suppose the dimensions of a triangle with a perimeter of 18 inches are doubled. Find the perimeter of the new triangle in inches.

A rectangular prism has vertices (0, 0, 0), (0, 3, 0), (7, 0, 0), (7, 3, 0), (0, 0, 6), (0, 3, 6), (7, 0, 6) and (7, 3, 6).

18. Suppose all the dimensions are tripled. Find the new vertices.

19. Find the effect of the change on the volume of the prism.

20. How would the effect of the change be different if only the height had been tripled?

21. **Analyze Relationships** How could you change the dimensions of a parallelogram to increase the area by a factor of 5 if the parallelogram does not have to be similar to the original parallelogram? if the parallelogram does have to be similar to the original parallelogram?

H.O.T. Focus on Higher Order Thinking

22. **Algebra** A square has a side length of $(2x + 5)$ cm.

a. If the side length is mulitplied by 5, what is the area of the new square?

b. Use your answer to part (a) to find the area of the original square without using the area formula. Justify your answer.

23. **Algebra** A circle has a diameter of 6 in. If the circumference is multiplied by $(x + 3)$, what is the area of the new circle? Justify your answer.

24. **Communicate Mathematical Ideas** The dimensions of a prism with volume V and surface area S are multiplied by a scale factor of k to form a similar prism. Make a conjecture about the ratio of the surface area of the new prism to its volume. Test your conjecture using a cube with an edge length of 1 and a scale factor of 2.

Lesson Performance Task

On a computer screen, lengths and widths are measured not in inches or millimeters but in **pixels**. A pixel is the smallest visual element that a computer is capable of processing. A common size for a large computer screen is 1024 × 768 pixels. (Widths rather than heights are conventionally listed first.) For the following, assume you're working on a 1024 × 768 screen.

1024 pixels

768 pixels

1. You have a photo measuring 640 × 300 pixels and you want to enlarge it proportionally so that it is as wide as the computer screen. Find the measurements of the photo after it has been scaled up. Explain how you found the answer.

2. **a.** Explain why you can't enlarge the photo proportionally so that it is as tall as the computer screen.

   b. Why can't you correct the difficulty in (a) by scaling the width of the photo by a factor of 1024 ÷ 640 and the height by a factor of 768 ÷ 300?

3. You have some square photos and you would like to fill the screen with them, so there is no overlap and there are no gaps between photos. Find the dimensions of the largest such photos you can use (all of them the same size), and find the number of photos. Explain your reasoning.

Volume Formulas

Essential Question: How can you use volume formulas to solve real-world problems?

Key Vocabulary

right prism *(prisma recto)*
right cylinder *(cilindro recto)*
oblique prism *(prisma oblicuo)*
oblique cylinder *(cilindro oblicuo)*
cross section *(sección transversal)*

KEY EXAMPLE *(Lesson 21.1)*

Find the volume of a cylinder with a base radius of 3 centimeters and a height of 5 centimeters. Write an exact answer.

$V = \pi r^2 h$ Write the formula for the volume of a cylinder.

$= \pi(3)^2(5)$ Substitute.

$= 45\pi \text{ cm}^3$ Simplify.

KEY EXAMPLE *(Lesson 21.2)*

Find the volume of a square pyramid with a base side length of 12 inches and a height of 7 inches.

$V = \frac{1}{3}Bh$ Write the formula for the volume of a pyramid.

$= \frac{1}{3}(12)^2(7)$ Substitute.

$= 336 \text{ in}^3$ Simplify.

KEY EXAMPLE *(Lesson 21.3)*

Find the volume of a cone with a base diameter of 16 feet and a height of 18 feet. Write an exact answer.

$r = \frac{1}{2}(16 \text{ ft})$ Find the radius.

$= 8 \text{ ft}$ Simplify.

$V = \frac{1}{3}\pi r^2 h$ Write the formula for the volume of a cone.

$= \frac{1}{3}\pi(8)^2(18)$ Substitute.

$= 384\pi \text{ ft}^3$ Simplify.

KEY EXAMPLE *(Lesson 21.4)*

Find the volume of a sphere with a radius of 30 miles. Write an exact answer.

$V = \frac{4}{3}\pi r^3$ Write the formula for the volume of a sphere.

$= \frac{4}{3}\pi(30)^3$ Substitute.

$= 36{,}000\pi \text{ mi}^3$ Simplify.

EXERCISES

Find the volume of each figure. Write an exact answer. *(Lessons 21.1–21.4)*

1.

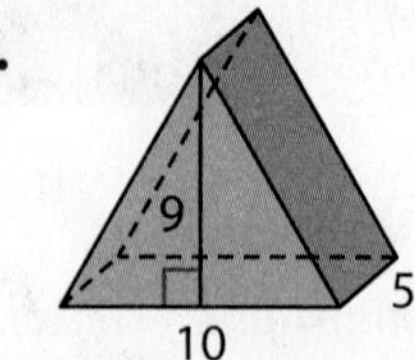

2.

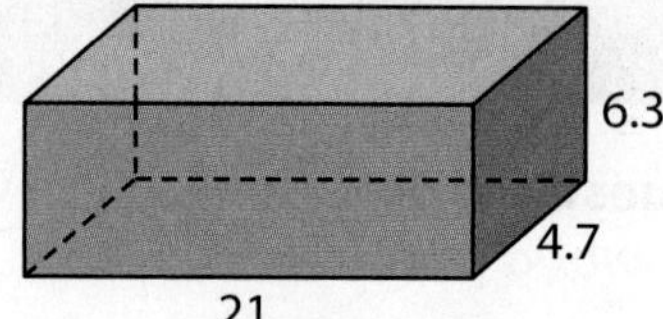

3.

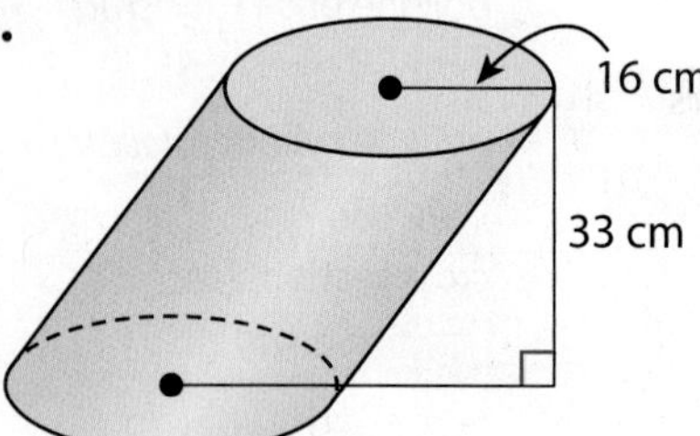

4.

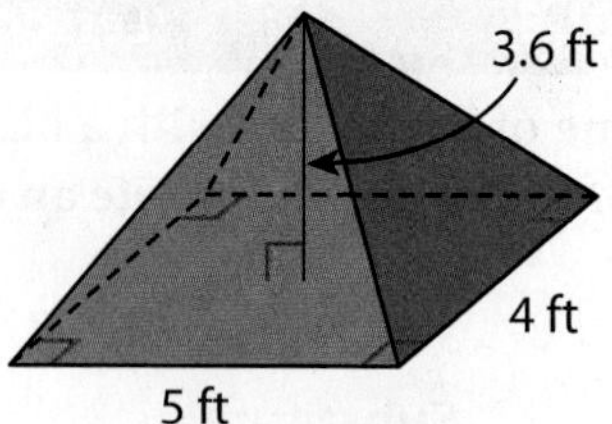

5.

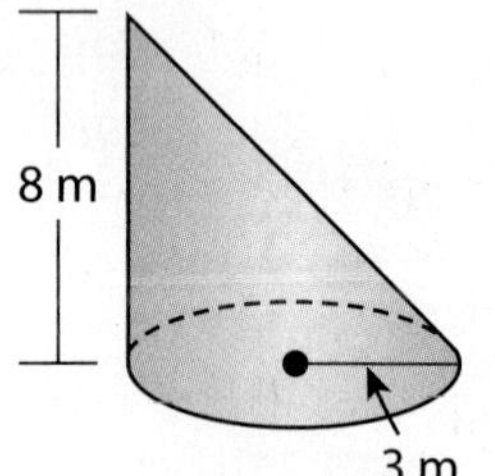

6.

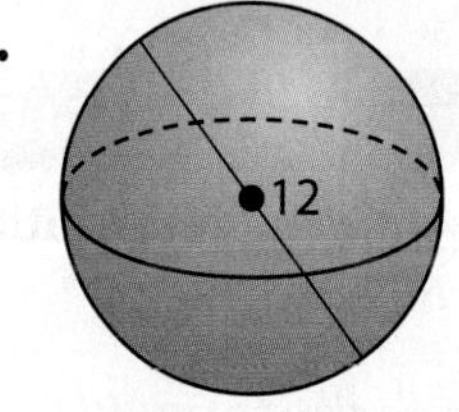

7. One side of a rhombus measures 12 inches. Two angles measure 60°. Find the perimeter and area of the rhombus. Then multiply the side lengths by 3. Find the new perimeter and area. Describe the changes that took place. *(Lesson 21.5)*

MODULE PERFORMANCE TASK

How Big Is That Sinkhole?

In 2010 an enormous sinkhole suddenly appeared in the middle of a Guatemalan neighborhood and swallowed a three-story building above it. The sinkhole has an estimated depth of about 100 feet.

How much material is needed to fill the sinkhole? Determine what information is needed to answer the question. Do you think your estimate is more likely to be too high or too low?

What are some material options for filling the sinkhole, and how much would they cost? Which material do you think would be the best choice?

Ready to Go On?

21.1–21.5 Volume Formulas

- Online Homework
- Hints and Help
- Extra Practice

Find the volume of the figure. *(Lessons 21.1–21.4)*

1. An oblique cylinder next to a cube

10 ft

44 ft

2. A prism of volume 3 with a pyramid of the same height cut out

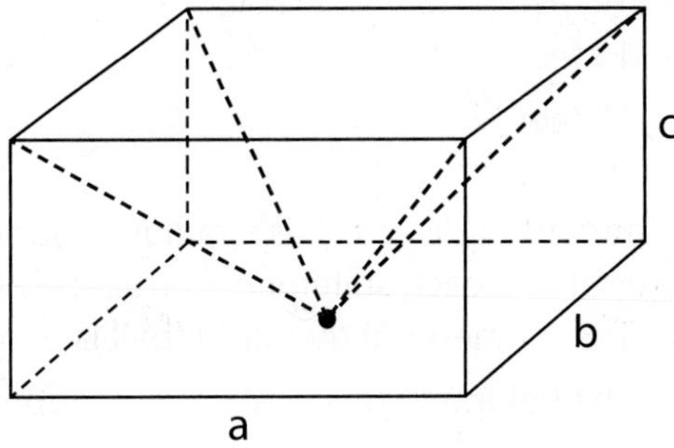

3. A cone with a square pyramid of the same height cut out. The pyramid has height l, and its square base has area l^2.

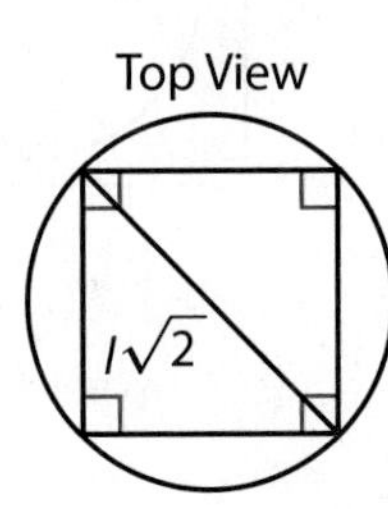

4. A cube with sides of length s with the biggest sphere that fits in it cut out.

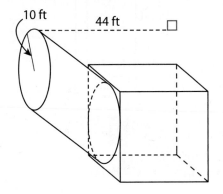

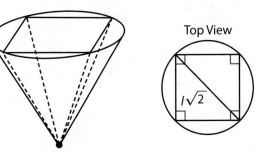

ESSENTIAL QUESTION

5. How would you find the volume of an ice-cream cone with a sphere-shaped scoop of ice cream in it? What measurements would you need?

MODULE 21
MIXED REVIEW

Assessment Readiness

1. A simplified model of a particular monument is a rectangular pyramid placed on top of a rectangular prism, as shown. The volume of the monument is 66 cubic feet. Determine whether the given measurement could be the height of the monument.
Write Yes or No for A–C.

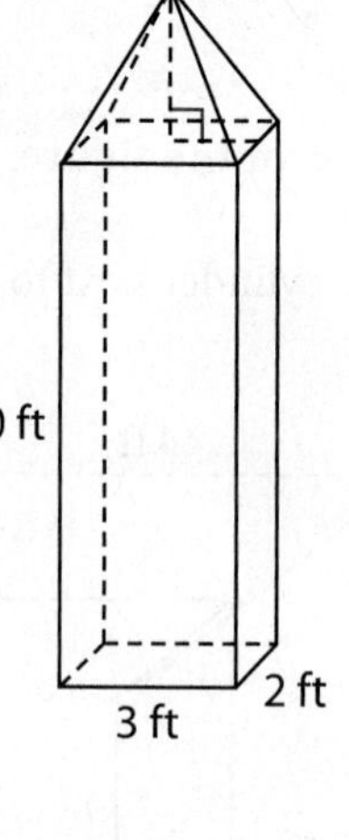

A. 10 feet

B. 13 feet

C. 15 feet

2. A standard basketball has a radius of about 4.7 inches. Determine if each statement is True or False.

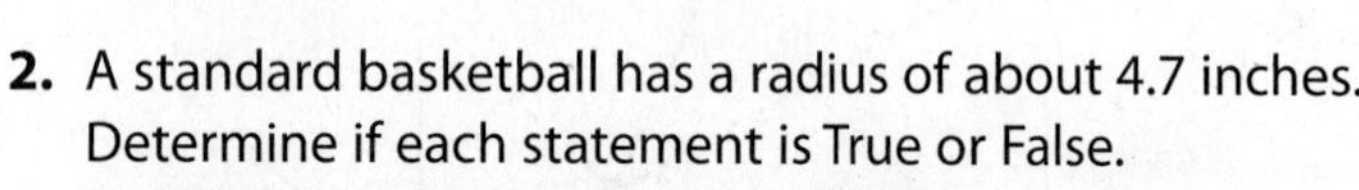

A. The diameter of the basketball is about 25 inches.

B. The volume of the basketball is approximately 277.6 in^3.

C. The volume of the basketball is approximately 434.9 in^3.

3. A triangle has a side of length 8, a second side of length 17, and a third side of length x. Find the range of possible values for x.

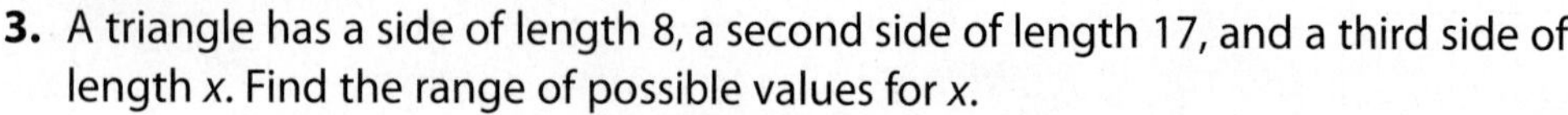

4. Find the approximate volume of the figure at right, composed of a cone, a cylinder, and a hemisphere. Explain how you found the values needed to compute the volume.

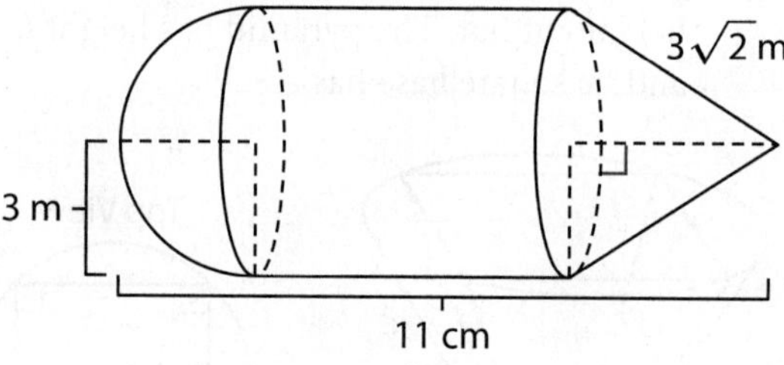

Assessment Readiness

- Online Homework
- Hints and Help
- Extra Practice

1. Consider each congruence theorem below.
Can you use the theorem to determine whether $\triangle ABC \cong \triangle ABD$?

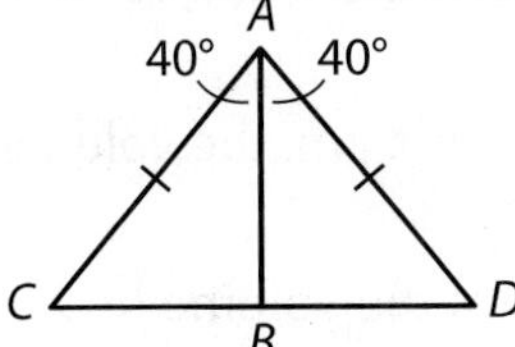

Write Yes or No for A–C.

A. ASA Triangle Congruence Theorem

B. SAS Triangle Congruence Theorem

C. SSS Triangle Congruence Theorem

2. Determine if each statement is True or False.

A. A rectangular pyramid with $\ell = 3$ m, $w = 4$ m, $h = 7$ m has volume 84 m^3.

B. A triangular pyramid with base $B = 14$ ft^2 and $h = 5$ ft has volume 60 ft^2.

C. A pyramid with the same base and height of a prism has less volume.

3. Determine if each statement is True or False.

A. A cone with base radius $r = 5$ in. and $h = 12$ in. has volume 100π in^3.

B. A sphere with radius $r = \frac{6}{\pi}$ m has volume $\frac{8}{\pi^2}$ m^3.

C. A sphere is composed of multiple cones with the same radius.

4. DeMarcus draws $\triangle ABC$. Then he translates it along the vector $(-4, -3)$, rotates it 180°, and reflects it across the x-axis.

Determine if each statement is True or False.

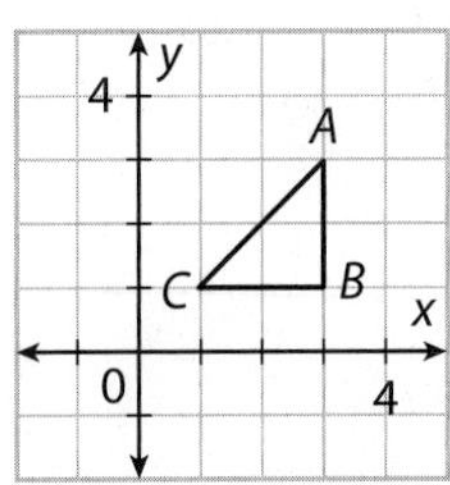

A. The final image of $\triangle ABC$ is in Quadrant IV.

B. The final image of $\triangle ABC$ is a right triangle.

C. DeMarcus will get the same result if he performs the reflection followed by the translation and rotation.

5. A volleyball has a radius of about 8 inches. A soccer ball has a radius of about 4.25 inches. Determine if each statement is True or False.

A. The volume of the volleyball is about 682.7π in^3

B. The volume of the soccer ball is about 76.8π in^3

C. The volume of the volleyball is about 3.75π times the volume of the soccer ball.

6. A cone and a cylinder have the same height and base diameter. Determine if each statement is True or False.

A. If the height is 8 cm and the base diameter is 6 cm, the volume of the cone is 72π cm^3.

B. If the height is 6 cm and the base diameter is 4 cm, the volume of the cylinder is 24π cm^3.

C. The volume of the cylinder is always 3 times the volume of the cone.

7. A vase is in the shape of a cylinder with a height of 15 feet. The vase holds 375π in^3 of water. What is the diameter of the base of the vase? Show your work.

8. A salt shaker is a cylinder with half a sphere on top. The radius of the base of the salt shaker is 3 cm and the height of the cylindrical bottom is 9 cm as shown in the diagram.

What is the volume of the salt shaker? Explain how you got your answer.

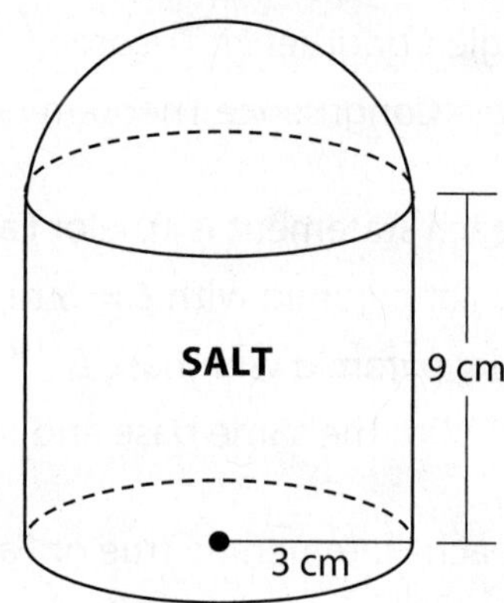

9. A cube is dilated by a factor of 4. By what factor does its volume increase? Explain your reasoning.

Performance Tasks

★10. A scientist wants to compare the volumes of two cylinders. One is twice as high and has a diameter two times as long as the other. If the volume of the smaller cylinder is 30 cm^3, what is the volume of the larger cylinder?

★★11. You are trying to pack in preparation for a trip and need to fit a collection of children's toys in a box. Each individual toy is a composite figure of four cubes, and all of the toys are shown in the figure. Arrange the toys in an orderly fashion so that they will fit in the smallest box possible. Draw the arrangement. What is the volume of the box if each of the cubes have side lengths of 10 cm?

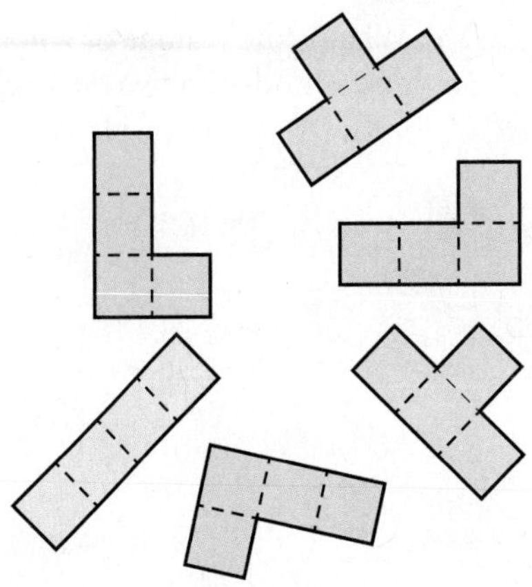

★★★12. A carpenter has a wooden cone with a slant height of 16 inches and a diameter of 12 inches. The vertex of the cone is directly above the center of its base. He measures halfway down the slant height and makes a cut parallel to the base. He now has a truncated cone and a cone half the height of the original.

A. He expected the two parts to weigh about the same, but they don't. Which is heavier? Why?

B. Find the ratio of the weight of the small cone to that of the truncated cone. Show your work.

MATH IN CAREERS

Model Maker A jewelry maker creates a pendant out of glass by attaching two square-based pyramids at their bases to form an octahedron. Each triangular face of the octahedron is an equilateral triangle.

a. Derive a formula for the volume of the pendant, if the side length is a. Show your work.

b. The jewelry maker wants to package the pendant in a cylindrical box. What should be the smallest dimensions of the box if the pendant just fits inside, in terms of a? Explain how you determined your answer.

c. What is the volume of empty space inside the box? Your answer should be in terms of a, and rounded to two decimal places. Show your work.

UNIT 10

Understanding Probability

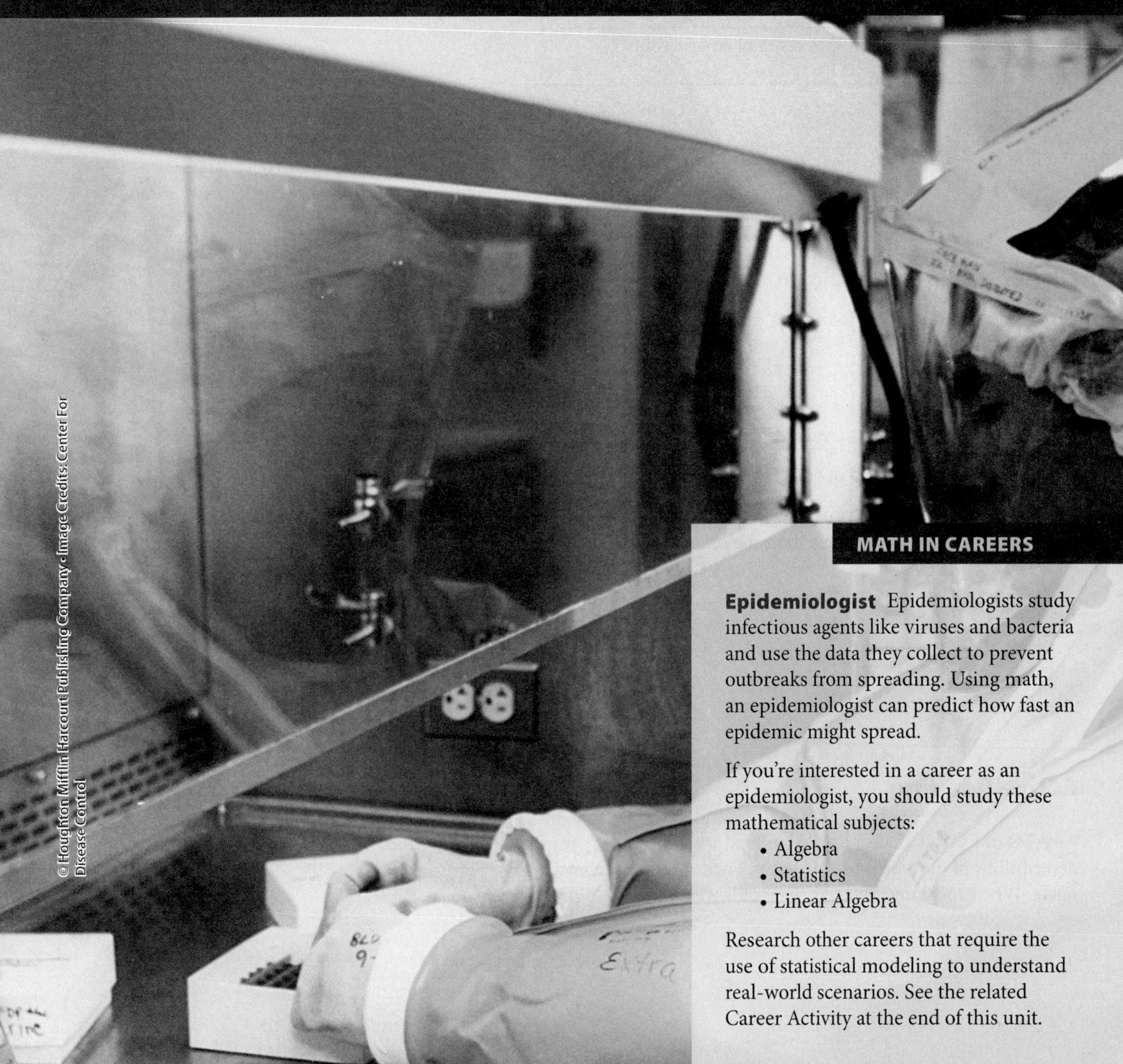

MATH IN CAREERS

Epidemiologist Epidemiologists study infectious agents like viruses and bacteria and use the data they collect to prevent outbreaks from spreading. Using math, an epidemiologist can predict how fast an epidemic might spread.

If you're interested in a career as an epidemiologist, you should study these mathematical subjects:

- Algebra
- Statistics
- Linear Algebra

Research other careers that require the use of statistical modeling to understand real-world scenarios. See the related Career Activity at the end of this unit.

Reading Start-Up

Vocabulary

Review Words

✔ event (*evento*)

✔ geometric probability (*probabilidad geométrica*)

✔ outcome (*resultado*)

✔ sample space (*muestra de espacio*)

Preview Words

combination (*combinación*)
complement (*complementar*)
conditional probability (*probabilidad condicional*)
dependent events (*eventos dependientes*)
element (*elemento*)
empty set (*conjunto vacío*)
factorial (*factorial*)
independent events (*eventos independientes*)
intersection (*intersección*)
permutation (*permutación*)
set (*conjunto*)
subset (*subconjunto*)
union (*unión*)

Visualize Vocabulary

Match the ✔ words to their descriptions to complete the chart.

Word	Description
	The use of geometric measures to represent probability
	All possible outcomes of an experiment
	Any set of outcomes
	A result of an experiment

Understand Vocabulary

Complete the sentences using the preview words.

1. The __?__ contains no elements.
2. If the occurrence of one event does not affect the occurrence of another event, then the events are called __?__.
3. A(n) __?__ is a group of objects in a particular order.
4. To find the __?__ of a positive integer, find the product of the number and all of the positive integers less than the number.

Active Reading

Key-Term Fold Create a Key-Term Fold with vocabulary words on the flaps and descriptions of the words behind them. Focus on how the vocabulary words for the unit relate. When speaking, describe the words when needed to make sure your ideas clear.

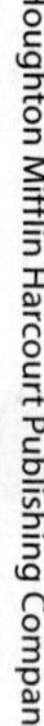

Introduction to Probability

MODULE 22

Essential Question: How can you use probability to solve real-world problems?

REAL WORLD VIDEO
Check out how principles of statistics and probability are used to derive and interpret baseball players' statistics.

MODULE PERFORMANCE TASK PREVIEW
Baseball Probability

In this module, you will use concepts of probability to determine the chances of various outcomes for a baseball player at bat. To successfully complete this task, you'll need to calculate a theoretical probability for a real-world situation. Batter up!

Are YOU Ready?

Complete these exercises to review skills you will need for this module.

- Online Homework
- Hints and Help
- Extra Practice

Probability of Simple Events

Example 1 Find the probability of rolling a 4 when using a normal six-sided die with each side having equal probability.

Each of the six faces has equal probability, so the probability of any face being rolled is $\frac{1}{6}$.

There is only one face with a four on it, so the probability of rolling a four is also $\frac{1}{6}$.

Find each probability.

1. The probability of flipping a coin and getting a heads, given that the probability of getting a tails is the same, and there is no chance that the coin lands on its side

2. The probability of drawing a jack of hearts from a 52-card deck given the deck is properly shuffled

3. The probability of any particular day being Sunday

Probability of Compound Events

Example 2 Find the probability of drawing a red card or a black card when the probability of either is $\frac{1}{4}$ and you only draw one card.

Only one card is drawn and either card has a $\frac{1}{4}$ probability, so the probability of drawing one or the other is the sum of their probabilities.

Probability of drawing a red card or black card $\frac{1}{4} + \frac{1}{4} = \frac{1}{2}$.

Find each probability.

4. The probability of rolling a twelve-sided die and getting a 4 or a 6 given the probability of getting a 4 is $\frac{1}{12}$ and is equal to the probability of getting a 6

5. The probability of pulling a red or a blue marble from a jar given the probability of drawing a red marble is $\frac{1}{4}$ and the probability of pulling a blue marble is $\frac{1}{2}$ and you only pull one marble

22.1 Probability and Set Theory

Essential Question: How are sets and their relationships used to calculate probabilities?

Resource Locker

Explore Working with Sets

A **set** is a collection of distinct objects. Each object in a set is called an **element** of the set. A set is often denoted by writing the elements in braces.

The set with no elements is the **empty set**, denoted by ∅ or { }.

The set of all elements under consideration is the **universal set**, denoted by U.

Identifying the number of elements in a set is important for calculating probabilities.

(A) Use set notation to identify each set described in the table and identify the number of elements in each set.

Set	Set Notation	Number of Elements in the Set
Set A is the set of prime numbers less than 10.	$A = \{2, 3, \_\_, 7\}$	$n(A) = 4$
Set B is the set of even natural numbers less than 10.	$B = \{\_\_, \_\_, \_\_, \_\_\}$	$n(B) = \_\_$
Set C is the set of natural numbers less than 10 that are multiples of 4.	$\_\_ = \{4, \_\_\}$	$n(C) = \_\_$
The universal set is all natural numbers less than 10.	$U = \_\_$	$\_\_(\_\_) = 9$

The following table identifies terms used to describe relationships among sets. Use sets A, B, C, and U from the previous table. Copy the Example column of the table. Then draw Venn diagrams in each of the four empty cells of your Example column by completing Steps B–I below.

Term	Notation	Venn Diagram	Example
Set C is a **subset** of set B if every element of C is also an element of B.	$C \subset B$	U, B, C	
The **intersection** of sets A and B is the set of all elements that are in both A *and* B.	$A \cap B$	U, A, B $A \cap B$ is the double-shaded region.	
The **union** of sets A and B is the set of all elements that are in A *or* B.	$A \cup B$	U, A, B $A \cup B$ is the entire shaded region.	
The **complement** of set A is the set of all elements in the universal set U that are *not* in A.	A^C or $\sim A$	U, A A^c is the shaded region.	

Ⓑ Since C is a subset of B, every element of set C, which consists of the numbers ▭ and ▭, is located not only in oval C, but also within oval B. Set B includes the elements of C as well as the additional elements ▭ and ▭, which are located in oval B outside of oval C. The universal set includes the elements of sets B and C as well as the additional elements ▭, ▭, ▭, ▭, and ▭, which are located in region U outside of ovals B and C.

Ⓒ In the top cell of your Example column, draw the corresponding Venn diagram that includes the elements of B, C, and U.

Ⓓ To determine the intersection of A and B, first define the elements of set A and set B separately, then identify all the elements found in both sets A *and* B.

$A = \{\square, \square, \square, \square\}$

$B = \{\square, \square, \square, \square\}$

$A \cap B = \{\square\}$

(E) In the second cell of your Example column, draw the Venn diagram for $A \cap B$ that includes the elements of A, B, and U and the double-shaded intersection region.

(F) To determine the union of sets A and B, identify all the elements found in either set A or set B by combining all the elements of the two sets into the union set.

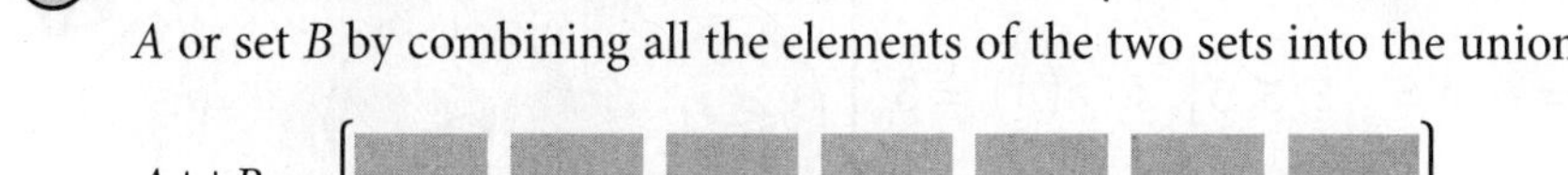

(G) In the third cell of your Example column, draw the Venn diagram for $A \cup B$ that includes the elements of A, B, and U and the shaded union region.

(H) To determine the complement of set A, first identify the elements of set A and universal set U separately, then identify all the elements in the universal set that are *not* in set A.

$A = \{\ ,\ ,\ ,\ \}$

$U = \{\ ,\ ,\ ,\ ,\ ,\ ,\ ,\ ,\ \}$

$A^C = \{\ ,\ ,\ ,\ ,\ \}$

(I) In the bottom cell of your Example column, draw the Venn diagram for A^c that includes the elements of A and U and the shaded region that represents the complement of A.

Reflect

1. **Draw Conclusions** Do sets always have an intersection that is not the empty set? Provide an example to support your conclusion.

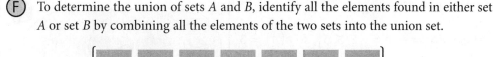

Explain 1 Calculating Theoretical Probabilities

A *probability experiment* is an activity involving chance. Each repetition of the experiment is called a *trial* and each possible result of the experiment is termed an *outcome.* A set of outcomes is known as an *event,* and the set of all possible outcomes is called the *sample space.*

Probability measures how likely an event is to occur. An event that is impossible has a probability of 0, while an event that is certain has a probability of 1. All other events have a probability between 0 and 1. When all the outcomes of a probability experiment are equally likely, the **theoretical probability** of an event A in the sample space S is given by

$$P(A) = \frac{\text{number of outcomes in the event}}{\text{number of outcomes in the sample space}} = \frac{n(A)}{n(S)}.$$

Example 1 Calculate $P(A)$, $P(A \cup B)$, $P(A \cap B)$, and $P(A^C)$ for each situation.

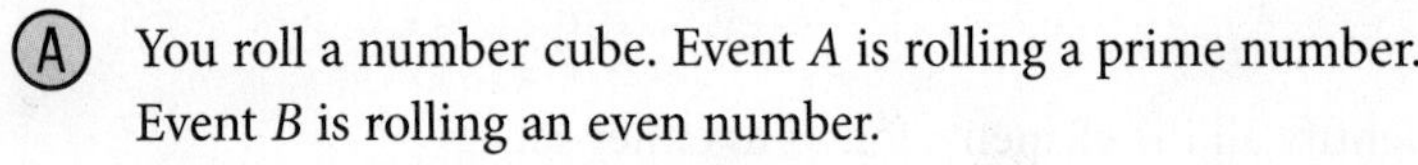

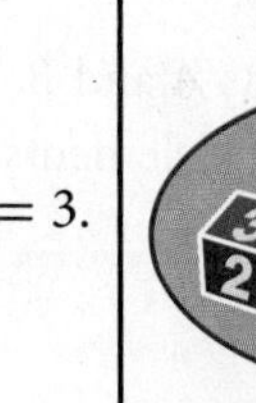

Ⓐ You roll a number cube. Event A is rolling a prime number. Event B is rolling an even number.

$S = \{1, 2, 3, 4, 5, 6\}$, so $n(S) = 6$. $A = \{2, 3, 5\}$, so $n(A) = 3$.

So, $P(A) = \dfrac{n(A)}{n(S)} = \dfrac{3}{6} = \dfrac{1}{2}$.

$A \cup B = \{2, 3, 4, 5, 6\}$, so $n(A \cup B) = 5$. So, $P(A \cup B) = \dfrac{n(A \cup B)}{n(S)} = \dfrac{5}{6}$.

$A \cap B = \{2\}$, so $n(A \cap B) = 1$. So, $P(A \cap B) = \dfrac{n(A \cap B)}{n(S)} = \dfrac{1}{6}$.

$A^C = \{1, 4, 6\}$, so $n(A^C) = 3$. So, $P(A^C) = \dfrac{n(A^C)}{n(S)} = \dfrac{3}{6} = \dfrac{1}{2}$.

Ⓑ Your grocery basket contains one bag of each of the following items: oranges, green apples, green grapes, green broccoli, white cauliflower, orange carrots, and green spinach. You are getting ready to transfer your items from your cart to the conveyer belt for check-out. Event A is picking a bag containing a vegetable first. Event B is picking a bag containing a green food first. All bags have an equal chance of being picked first.

$S = \{$orange, apple, grape, broccoli, cauliflower, carrot, spinach$\}$, so $n(S) = \boxed{7}$.

$A = \{$broccoli, cauliflower, carrot, spinach$\}$, so $n(A) = \boxed{4}$. So $P(A) = \dfrac{n\left(\boxed{A}\right)}{n\left(\boxed{S}\right)} = \dfrac{\boxed{4}}{\boxed{7}}$.

$A \cup B = \{$broccoli, cauliflower, carrot, spinach, apple, grape$\}$, so $n(A \cup B) = \boxed{6}$.

$$P(A \cup B) = \frac{\boxed{n}\left(\boxed{A}\boxed{\cup}\boxed{B}\right)}{\boxed{n}\left(\boxed{S}\right)} = \frac{\boxed{6}}{\boxed{7}}$$

$A \cap B = \{$broccoli, spinach$\}$, so $n(A \cap B) = \boxed{2}$

$$P(A \cap B) = \frac{\boxed{n}\left(\boxed{A}\boxed{\cap}\boxed{B}\right)}{\boxed{n}\left(\boxed{S}\right)} = \frac{\boxed{2}}{\boxed{7}}$$

$$P\left(\boxed{A^c}\right) = \frac{\boxed{n}\left(\boxed{A^c}\right)}{\boxed{n}\left(\boxed{S}\right)} = \frac{\boxed{3}}{\boxed{7}}$$

Reflect

2. **Discussion** In Example 1B, which is greater, $P(A \cup B)$ or $P(A \cap B)$? Do you think this result is true in general? Explain.

Your Turn

The numbers 1 through 30 are written on slips of paper that are then placed in a hat. Students draw a slip to determine the order in which they will give an oral report. Event *A* is being one of the first 10 students to give their report. Event *B* is picking a multiple of 6. If you pick first, calculate each of the indicated probabilities.

3. $P(A)$

4. $P(A \cup B)$

5. $P(A \cap B)$

6. $P(A^c)$

Explain 2 Using the Complement of an Event

You may have noticed in the previous examples that the probability of an event occurring and the probability of the event not occurring (i.e., the probability of the complement of the event) have a sum of 1. This relationship can be useful when it is more convenient to calculate the probability of the complement of an event than it is to calculate the probability of the event

Probabilities of an Event and Its Complement	
$P(A) + P(A^c) = 1$	The sum of the probability of an event and the probability of its complement is 1.
$P(A) = 1 - P(A^c)$	The probability of an event is 1 minus the probability of its complement.
$P(A^c) = 1 - P(A)$	The probability of the complement of an event is 1 minus the probability of the event.

Example 2 **Use the complement to calculate the indicated probabilities.**

Ⓐ You roll a blue number cube and a white number cube at the same time. What is the probability that you do not roll doubles?

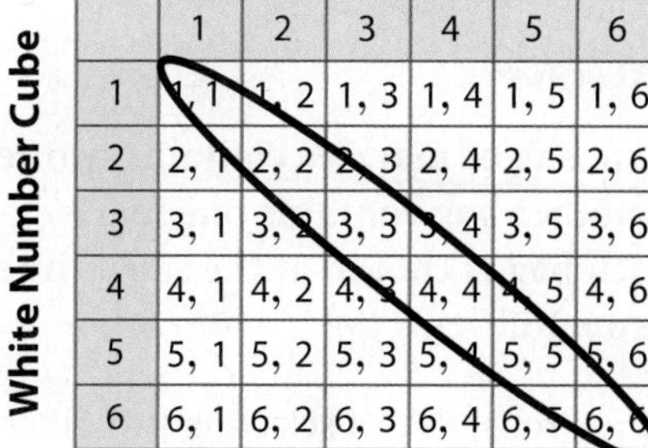

Blue Number Cube (columns); White Number Cube (rows)

	1	2	3	4	5	6
1	1, 1	1, 2	1, 3	1, 4	1, 5	1, 6
2	2, 1	2, 2	2, 3	2, 4	2, 5	2, 6
3	3, 1	3, 2	3, 3	3, 4	3, 5	3, 6
4	4, 1	4, 2	4, 3	4, 4	4, 5	4, 6
5	5, 1	5, 2	5, 3	5, 4	5, 5	5, 6
6	6, 1	6, 2	6, 3	6, 4	6, 5	6, 6

Step 1 **Define the events.** Let *A* be that you do not roll doubles and A^c that you do roll doubles.

Step 2 **Make a diagram.** A two-way table is one helpful way to identify all the possible outcomes in the sample space.

Step 3 **Determine $P(A^c)$.** Since there are fewer outcomes for rolling doubles, it is more convenient to determine the probability of rolling doubles, which is $P(A^c)$. To determine $n(A^c)$, draw a loop around the outcomes in the table that correspond to A^c and then calculate $P(A^c)$.

$$P(A^c) = \frac{n(A^c)}{n(S)} = \frac{6}{36} = \frac{1}{6}$$

Step 4 Determine $P(A)$. Use the relationship between the probability of an event and its complement to determine $P(A)$.

$$P(A) = 1 - P(A^c) = 1 - \frac{1}{6} = \frac{5}{6}$$

So, the probability of not rolling doubles is $\frac{5}{6}$.

(B) One pile of cards contains the numbers 2 through 6 in red hearts. A second pile of cards contains the numbers 4 through 8 in black spades. Each pile of cards has been randomly shuffled. If one card from each pile is chosen at the same time, what is the probability that the sum will be less than 12?

Step 1 Define the events. Let A be the event that the sum is less than 12 and A^c be the event that the sum is not less than 12.

Step 2 Make a diagram. Copy and complete the table to show all the outcomes in the sample space.

Step 3 Determine $P(A^c)$. Circle the outcomes in your table that correspond to A^c, then determine $P(A^c)$.

		Red Hearts ♥				
		2	3	4	5	6
Black Spades ♠	4	4+2	4+3	4+4	4+5	4+6
	5	5+2	5+3	5+4	5+5	5+6
	6	6+2	6+3	6+4	6+5	(6+6)
	7	7+2	7+3	7+4	(7+5)	(7+6)
	8	8+2	8+3	(8+4)	(8+5)	(8+6)

$$P(A^c) = \frac{n(A^c)}{n(S)} = \frac{6}{25}$$

Step 4 Determine $P(A)$. Use the relationship between the probability of an event and its complement to determine $P(A^c)$.

$$P(A) = 1 - P(A^c) = 1 - \frac{6}{25} = \frac{19}{25}$$

So, the probability that the sum of the two cards is less than 12 is $\frac{19}{25}$.

Reflect

7. Describe a different way to calculate the probability that the sum of the two cards will be less than 12.

Your Turn

One bag of marbles contains two red, one yellow, one green, and one blue marble. Another bag contains one marble of each of the same four colors. One marble from each bag is chosen at the same time. Use the complement to calculate the indicated probabilities.

8. Probability of selecting two different colors

9. Probability of not selecting a yellow marble

Elaborate

10. Can a subset of A contain elements of A^C? Why or why not?

11. For any set A, what does $A \cap \emptyset$ equal? What does $A \cup \emptyset$ equal? Explain.

12. **Essential Question Check-In** How do the terms *set*, *element*, and *universal set* correlate to the terms used to calculate theoretical probability?

Evaluate: Homework and Practice

- Online Homework
- Hints and Help
- Extra Practice

Set A is the set of factors of 12, set B is the set of even natural numbers less than 13, set C is the set of odd natural numbers less than 13, and set D is the set of even natural numbers less than 7. The universal set for these questions is the set of natural numbers less than 13.

So, $A = \{1, 2, 3, 4, 6, 12\}$, $B = \{2, 4, 6, 8, 10, 12\}$, $C = \{1, 3, 5, 7, 9, 11\}$, $D = \{2, 4, 6\}$, and $U = \{1, 2, 3, 4, 5, 6, 7, 8, 9, 10, 11, 12\}$.

Answer each question.

1. Is $D \subset A$? Explain why or why not.

2. Is $B \subset A$? Explain why or why not.

3. What is $A \cap B$?

4. What is $A \cap C$?

5. What is $A \cup B$?

6. What is $A \cup C$?

7. What is A^C?

8. What is B^C?

You have a set of 10 cards numbered 1 to 10. You choose a card at random. Event A is choosing a number less than 7. Event B is choosing an odd number. Calculate the probability.

9. $P(A)$

10. $P(B)$

11. $P(A \cup B)$

12. $P(A \cap B)$

13. $P(A^C)$

14. $P(B^C)$

Use the complement of the event to find the probability.

15. You roll a 6-sided number cube. What is the probability that you do not roll a 2?

16. You choose a card at random from a standard deck of cards. What is the probability that you do not choose a red king?

17. You spin the spinner shown. The spinner is divided into 12 equal sectors. What is the probability of not spinning a 2?

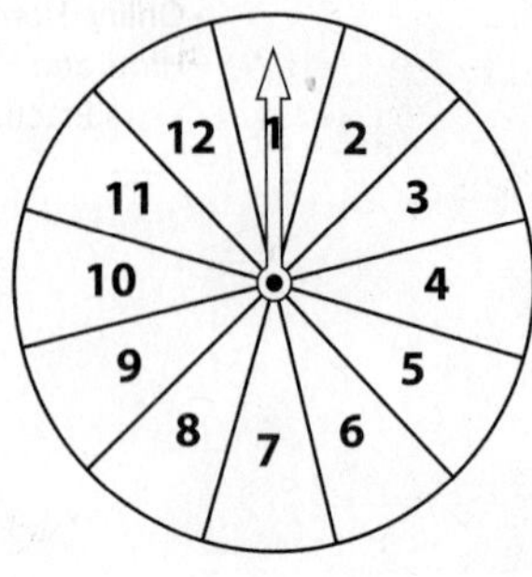

18. A bag contains 2 red, 5 blue, and 3 green balls. A ball is chosen at random. What is the probability of not choosing a red ball?

19. Cards numbered 1–12 are placed in a bag. A ball is chosen at random. What is the probability of not choosing a number less than 5?

20. Slips of paper numbered 1–20 are folded and placed into a hat, and then a slip of paper is drawn at random. What is the probability the slip drawn has a number which is not a multiple of 4 or 5?

21. You are going to roll two number cubes, a white number cube and a red number cube, and find the sum of the two numbers that come up.

a. What is the probability that the sum will be 6?

b. What is the probability that the sum will not be 6?

22. You have cards with the letters A, B, C, D, E, F, G, H, I, J, K, L, M, N, O, P. Event U is choosing the cards A, B, C or D. Event V is choosing a vowel. Event W is choosing a letter in the word "APPLE". Find $P(U \cap V \cap W)$.

A standard deck of cards has 13 cards (2, 3, 4, 5, 6, 7, 8, 9, 10, jack, queen, king, ace) in each of 4 suits (hearts, clubs, diamonds, spades). The hearts and diamonds cards are red. The clubs and spades cards are black. Answer each question.

23. You choose a card from a standard deck of cards at random. What is the probability that you do not choose an ace? Explain.

24. You choose a card from a standard deck of cards at random. What is the probability that you do not choose a club? Explain.

25. You choose a card from a standard deck of cards at random. Event A is choosing a red card. Event B is choosing an even number. Event C is choosing a black card. Find $P(A \cap B \cap C)$. Explain.

26. You are selecting a card at random from a standard deck of cards. Match each event with the correct probability.

A. Picking a card that is both red and a heart.	**a.** ___?___	$\frac{1}{52}$
B. Picking a card that is both a heart and an ace.	**b.** ___?___	$\frac{1}{4}$
C. Picking a card that is not both a heart and an ace.	**c.** ___?___	$\frac{51}{52}$

H.O.T. Focus on Higher Order Thinking

27. Critique Reasoning A bag contains white tiles, black tiles, and gray tiles. Someone is going to choose a tile at random. $P(W)$, the probability of choosing a white tile, is $\frac{1}{4}$. A student claims that the probability of choosing a black tile, $P(B)$, is $\frac{3}{4}$ since $P(B) = 1 - P(W) = 1 - \frac{1}{4} = \frac{3}{4}$. Do you agree? Explain.

28. Communicate Mathematical Ideas A bag contains 5 red marbles and 10 blue marbles. You are going to choose a marble at random. Event A is choosing a red marble. Event B is choosing a blue marble. What is $P(A \cap B)$? Explain.

29. Critical Thinking Jeffery states that for a sample space S where all outcomes are equally likely, $0 \le P(A) \le 1$ for any subset A of S. Create an argument that will justify his statement or state a counterexample.

Lesson Performance Task

For the sets you've worked with in this lesson, membership in a set is binary: Either something belongs to the set or it doesn't. For instance, 5 is an element of the set of odd numbers, but 6 isn't.

In 1965, Lofti Zadeh developed the idea of "fuzzy" sets to deal with sets for which membership is not binary. He defined a *degree* of membership that can vary from 0 to 1. For instance, a membership function $m_L(w)$ for the set L of large dogs where the degree of membership m is determined by the weight w of a dog might be defined as follows:

- A dog is a full member of the set L if it weighs 80 pounds or more. This can be written as $m_L(w) = 1$ for $w \geq 80$.
- A dog is not a member of the set L if it weighs 60 pounds or less. This can be written as $m_L(w) = 0$ for $w \leq 60$.
- A dog is a partial member of the set L if it weighs between 60 and 80 pounds. This can be written as $0 < m_L(w) < 1$ for $60 < w < 80$.

The "large dogs" portion of the graph shown displays the membership criteria listed above. Note that the graph shows only values of $m(w)$ that are positive.

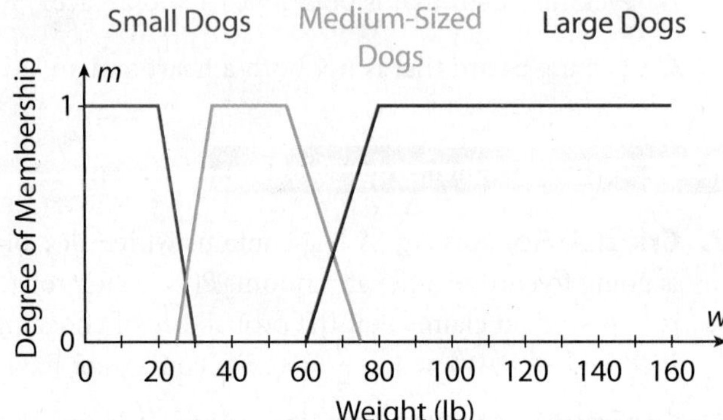

1. Using the graph, give the approximate weights for which a dog is considered a full member, a partial member, and not a member of the set S of small dogs.

2. The union of two "fuzzy" sets A and B is given by the membership rule $m_{A \cup B}(x) = \text{maximum}\left(m_A(x), m_B(x)\right)$. So, for a dog of a given size, the degree of its membership in the set of small or medium-sized dogs $(S \cup M)$ is the greater of its degree of membership in the set of small dogs and its degree of membership in the set of medium-sized dogs.

The intersection of A and B is given by the membership rule $m_{A \cap B}(x) = \text{minimum}\left(m_A(x), m_B(x)\right)$. So, for a dog of a given size, the degree of its membership in the set of dogs that are both small and medium-sized $(S \cap M)$ is the lesser of its degree of membership in the set of small dogs and its degree of membership in the set of medium-sized dogs.

Using the graph above and letting S be the set of small dogs, M be the set of medium-sized dogs, and L be the set of large dogs, draw the graph of each set.

a. $S \cup M$

b. $M \cap L$

22.2 Permutations and Probability

Essential Question: When are permutations useful in calculating probability?

Resource Locker

Explore Finding the Number of Permutations

A **permutation** is a selection of objects from a group in which order is important. For example, there are 6 permutations of the letters A, B, and C.

ABC	ACB	BAC	BCA	CAB	CBA

You can find the number of permutations with the **Fundamental Counting Principle**.

Fundamental Counting Principle

If there are n items and a_1 ways to choose the first item, a_2 ways to select the second item after the first item has been chosen, and so on, there are $a_1 \times a_2 \times \ldots \times a_n$ ways to choose n items.

There are 7 members in a club. Each year the club elects a president, a vice president, and a treasurer.

(A) What is the number of permutations of all 7 members of the club?

There are ____ different ways to make the first selection.

Once the first person has been chosen, there are ____ different ways to make the second selection.

Once the first two people have been chosen, there are ____ different ways to make the third selection.

Continuing this pattern, there are ____ permutations of all the members of the club.

(B) The club is holding elections for a president, a vice president, and a treasurer. How many different ways can these positions be filled?

There are ____ different ways the position of president can be filled.

Once the president has been chosen, there are ____ different ways the position of vice president can be filled. Once the president and vice president have been chosen, there are ____ different ways the position of treasurer can be filled.

So, there are ____ different ways that the positions can be filled.

Ⓒ What is the number of permutations of the members of the club who were not elected as officers?

After the officers have been elected, there are ☐ members remaining. So there are ☐ different ways to make the first selection.

Once the first person has been chosen, there are ☐ different ways to make the second selection.

Continuing this pattern, there are ☐ permutations of the unelected members of the club.

Ⓓ Divide the number of permutations of all the members by the number of permutations of the unelected members.

There are ☐ permutations of all the members of the club.

There are ☐ permutations of the unelected members of the club.

The quotient of these two values is ☐.

Reflect

1. How does the answer to Step D compare to the answer to Step B?

2. **Discussion** Explain the effect of dividing the total number of permutations by the number of permutations of items not selected.

Explain 1 Finding a Probability Using Permutations

The results of the Explore can be generalized to give a formula for permutations. To do so, it is helpful to use *factorials*. For a positive integer *n*, ***n* factorial,** written *n*!, is defined as follows.

$$n! = n \times (n-1) \times (n-2) \times \ldots \times 3 \times 2 \times 1$$

That is, *n*! is the product of *n* and all the positive integers less than *n*. Note that 0! is defined to be 1.

In the Explore, the number of permutations of the 7 objects taken 3 at a time is

$$7 \times 6 \times 5 = \frac{7 \times 6 \times 5 \times \cancel{4} \times \cancel{3} \times \cancel{2} \times \cancel{1}}{\cancel{4} \times \cancel{3} \times \cancel{2} \times \cancel{1}} = \frac{7!}{4!} = \frac{7!}{(7-3)!}$$

This can be generalized as follows.

Permutations

The number of permutations of *n* objects taken *r* at a time is given by ${}_nP_r = \frac{n!}{(n-r)!}$.

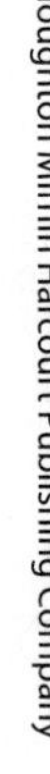

Example 1 **Use permutations to find the probabilities.**

(A) A research laboratory requires a four-digit security code to gain access to the facility. A security code can contain any of the digits 0, 1, 2, 3, 4, 5, 6, 7, 8, and 9, but no digit is repeated. What is the probability that a scientist is randomly assigned a code with the digits 1, 2, 3, and 4 in any order?

The sample space S consists of permutations of 4 digits selected from 10 digits.

$$n(S) = {}_{10}P_4 = \frac{10!}{(10-4)!} = \frac{10!}{6!} = 5040$$

Event A consists of permutations of a security code with the digits 1, 2, 3, and 4.

$$n(A) = {}_4P_4 = \frac{4!}{(4-4)!} = \frac{4!}{0!} = 24$$

The probability of getting a security code with the digits 1, 2, 3, and 4 is

$$P(A) = \frac{n(A)}{n(S)} = \frac{24}{5040} = \frac{1}{210}.$$

(B) A certain motorcycle license plate consists of 5 digits that are randomly selected. No digit is repeated. What is the probability of getting a license plate consisting of all even digits?

The sample space S consists of permutations of 5 digits selected from 10 digits.

$$n(S) = {}_{\boxed{10}}P_{\boxed{5}} = \frac{\boxed{10!}}{\boxed{5!}} = \boxed{30,240}$$

Event A consists of permutations of a license plate with all even digits.

$$n(A) = {}_{\boxed{5}}P_{\boxed{5}} \frac{\boxed{5!}}{\boxed{0!}} = \boxed{120}$$

The probability of getting a license plate withall even digits is

$$P(A) = \frac{n(A)}{n(S)} = \frac{\boxed{120}}{\boxed{30,240}} = \frac{\boxed{1}}{\boxed{252}}.$$

Your Turn

There are 8 finalists in the 100-meter dash at the Olympic Games. Suppose 3 of the finalists are from the United States, and that all finalists are equally likely to win.

3. What is the probability that the United States will win all 3 medals in this event?

4. What is the probability that the United States will win no medals in this event?

Explain 2 Finding the Number of Permutations with Repetition

Up to this point, the problems have focused on finding the permutations of distinct objects. If some of the objects are repeated, this will reduce the number of permutations that are distinguishable.

For example, here are the permutations of the letters A, B, and C.

ABC	ACB	BAC	BCA	CAB	CBA

Next, here are the permutations of the letters M, O, and M. Bold type is used to show the different positions of the repeated letter.

MOM	MO**M**	**M**MO	M**M**O	O**M**M	OM**M**

Shown without the bold type, here are the permutations of the letters M, O, and M.

MOM	MOM	MMO	MMO	OMM	OMM

Notice that since the letter M is repeated, there are only 3 distinguishable permutations of the letters. This can be generalized with a formula for permutations with repetition.

Permutations with Repetition

The number of different permutations of n objects where one object repeats a times, a second object repeats b times, and so on is

$$\frac{n!}{a! \times b! \times \ldots}$$

Example 2 **Find the number of permutations.**

(A) How many different permutations are there of the letters in the word ARKANSAS?

There are 8 letters in the word, and there are 3 A's and 2 S's, so the number of permutations of the letters in ARKANSAS is $\frac{8!}{3!2!} = 3360$.

(B) One of the zip codes for Anchorage, Alaska, is 99522. How many permutations are there of the numbers in this zip code?

There are 5 digits in the zip code, and there are 2 nines, and 2 twos in the zip code, so the number of permutations of the zip code is

$$\frac{5!}{2!2!} = 30.$$

Your Turn

5. How many different permutations can be formed using all the letters in MISSISSIPPI?

6. One of the standard telephone numbers for directory assistance is 555–1212. How many different permutations of this telephone number are possible?

Explain 3 Finding a Probability Using Permutations with Repetition

Permutations with repetition can be used to find probablilities.

Example 3 **The school jazz band has 4 boys and 4 girls, and they are randomly lined up for a yearbook photo.**

(A) Find the probability of getting an alternating boy-girl arrangement.

The sample space S consists of permutations of 8 objects, with 4 boys and 4 girls.

$n(S)\ \dfrac{8!}{4!4!} = 70$

Event A consists of permutations that alternate boy-girl or girl-boy. The possible permutations are BGBGBGBG and GBGBGBGB.

$n(A) = 2$

The probability of getting an alternating boy-girl arrangement is $P(A) = \dfrac{n(A)}{n(S)} = \dfrac{2}{70} = \dfrac{1}{35}$.

(B) Find the probability of getting all of the boys grouped together.

The sample space S consists of permutations of 8 students, with 4 boys and 4 girls.

$n(S) = \dfrac{8!}{4!4!} = 70$

Event A consists of permutations with all 4 boys in a row. The possible permutations are BBBBGGGG, GBBBBGGG, GGBBBBGG, GGGBBBBG, and GGGGBBBB.$n(A) = 5$

The probability of getting all the boys grouped together is $P(A) = \dfrac{n(A)}{n(S)} = \dfrac{5}{70} = \dfrac{1}{14}$.

Your Turn

7. There are 2 mystery books, 2 romance books, and 2 poetry books to be randomly placed on a shelf. What is the probability that the mystery books are next to each other, the romance books are next to each other, and the poetry books are next to each other?

8. What is the probability that a random arrangement of the letters in the word APPLE will have the two P's next to each other?

Elaborate

9. If ${}_nP_a = {}_nP_b$, what is the relationship between a and b? Explain your answer.

10. It was observed that there are 6 permutations of the letters A, B, and C. They are ABC, ACB, BAC, BCA, CAB, and CBA. If the conditions are changed so that the order of selection does not matter, what happens to these 6 different groups?

11. **Essential Question Check-In** How do you determine whether choosing a group of objects involves permutations?

Evaluate: Homework and Practice

- Online Homework
- Hints and Help
- Extra Practice

1. An MP3 player has a playlist with 12 songs. You select the shuffle option, which plays each song in a random order without repetition, for the playlist. In how many different orders can the songs be played?

2. There are 10 runners in a race. Medals are awarded for 1st, 2nd, and 3rd place. In how many different ways can the medals be awarded?

3. There are 9 players on a baseball team. In how many different ways can the coach choose players for first base, second base, third base, and shortstop?

4. A bag contains 9 tiles, each with a different number from 1 to 9. You choose a tile without looking, put it aside, choose a second tile without looking, put it aside, then choose a third tile without looking. What is the probability that you choose tiles with the numbers 1, 2, and 3 in that order?

5. There are 11 students on a committee. To decide which 3 of these students will attend a conference, 3 names are chosen at random by pulling names one at a time from a hat. What is the probability that Sarah, Jamal, and Mai are chosen in any order?

6. A clerk has 4 different letters that need to go in 4 different envelopes. The clerk places one letter in each envelope at random. What is the probability that all 4 letters are placed in the correct envelopes?

7. A swim coach randomly selects 3 swimmers from a team of 8 to swim in a heat. What is the probability that she will choose the three strongest swimmers?

8. How many different sequences of letters can be formed using all the letters in ENVELOPE?

9. Yolanda has 3 each of red, blue, and green marbles. How many possible ways can the 9 marbles be arranged in a row?

10. Jane has 16 cards. Ten of the cards look exactly the same and have the number 1 on them. The other 6 cards look exactly the same and have the number 2 on them. Jane is going to make a row containing all 16 cards. How many different ways can she order the row?

11. Ramon has 10 cards, each with one number on it. The numbers are 1, 2, 3, 4, 4, 6, 6, 6, 6, 6. Ramon is going to make a row containing all 10 cards. How many different ways can he order the row?

12. A grocer has 5 apples and 5 oranges for a window display. The grocer makes a row of the 10 pieces of fruit by choosing one piece of fruit at random, making it the first piece in the row, choosing a second piece of fruit at random, making it the second piece in the row, and so on. What is the probability that the grocer arranges the fruits in alternating order? (Assume that the apples are not distinguishable and that the oranges are not distinguishable.)

13. The letters G, E, O, M, E, T, R, Y are on 8 tiles in a bag, one letter on each tile. If you select tiles randomly from the bag and place them in a row from left to right, what is the probability the tiles will spell out GEOMETRY?

14. There are 11 boys and 10 girls in a classroom. A teacher chooses a student at random and puts that student at the head of a line, chooses a second student at random and makes that student second in the line, and so on, until all 21 students are in the line. What is the probability that the teacher puts them in a line alternating boys and girls, where no two of the same gender stand together?

15. There are 4 female and 4 male kittens are sleeping together in a row. Assuming that the arrangement is a random arrangement, what is the probability that all the female kittens are together, and all the male kittens are together?

16. If a ski club with 12 members votes to choose 3 group leaders, what is the probability that Marsha, Kevin, and Nicola will be chosen in any order for President, Treasurer, and Secretary?

17. There are 7 books numbered 1–7 on the summer reading list. Peter randomly chooses 2 books. What is the probability that Peter chooses books numbered 1 and 2, in either order?

18. On an exam, students are asked to list 5 historical events in the order in which they occurred. A student randomly orders the events. What is the probability that the student chooses the correct order?

19. A fan makes 6 posters to hold up at a basketball game. Each poster has a letter of the word TIGERS. Six friends sit next to each other in a row. The posters are distributed at random. What is the probability that TIGERS is spelled correctly when the friends hold up the posters?

20. The 10 letter tiles S, A, C, D, E, E, M, I, I, and O are in a bag. What is the probability that the letters S-A-M-E will be drawn from the bag at random, in that order?

21. If three cards are drawn at random from a standard deck of 52 cards, what is the probability that they will all be 7s? (There are four 7s in a standard deck of 52 cards.)

22. A shop classroom has ten desks in a row. If there are 6 students in shop class and they choose their desks at random, what is the probability they will sit in the first six desks?

23. Match each event with its probability. All orders are chosen randomly.

A. There are 15 floats that will be in a town parade. Event A: The mascot float is chosen to be first and the football team float is chosen to be second.

a. __?__ $\frac{1}{1092}$

B. Beth is one of 10 students performing in a school talent show. Event B: Beth is chosen to be the fifth performer and her best friend is chosen to be fourth.

b. __?__ $\frac{1}{210}$

C. Sylvester is in a music competition with 14 other musicians. Event C: Sylvester is chosen to be last, and his two best friends are chosen to be first and second.

c. __?__ $\frac{1}{90}$

H.O.T. Focus on Higher Order Thinking

24. Explain the Error Describe and correct the error in evaluating the expression.

$$_5P_3 = \frac{5!}{3!} = \frac{5 \times 4 \times 3!}{3!} = 20$$

25. Make a Conjecture If you are going to draw four cards from a deck of cards, does drawing four aces from the deck have the same probability as drawing four 3s? Explain.

26. Communicate Mathematical Ideas Nolan has Algebra, Biology, and World History homework. Assume that he chooses the order that he does his homework at random. Explain how to find the probability of his doing his Algebra homework first.

27. Explain the Error A student solved the problem shown. The student's work is also shown. Explain the error and provide the correct answer.

A bag contains 6 tiles with the letters A, B, C, D, E, and F, one letter on each tile. You choose 4 tiles one at a time without looking and line them up from left to right as you choose them. What is the probability that your tiles spell BEAD?

Let S be the sample space and let A be the event that the tiles spell BEAD.

$$n(S) = {}_6P_4 = \frac{6!}{(6-4)!} = \frac{6!}{2!} = 360$$

$$n(A) = {}_4P_4 = \frac{4!}{(4-4)!} = \frac{4!}{0!} = 24$$

$$P(A) = \frac{n(A)}{n(S)} = \frac{24}{360} = \frac{1}{5}$$

Lesson Performance Task

How many different ways can a blue card, a red card, and a green card be arranged? The diagram shows that the answer is six.

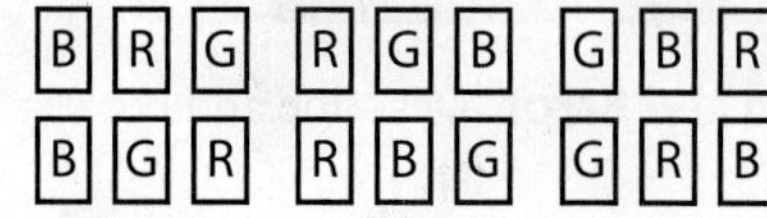

1. Now solve this problem: What is the least number of colors needed to color the pattern shown here, so that no two squares with a common boundary have the same color? Draw a sketch to show your answer.

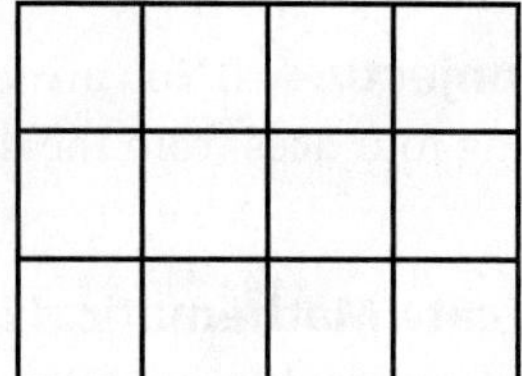

2. Now try this one. Again, find the least number of colors needed to color the pattern so that no two regions with a common boundary have the same color. Draw a sketch to show your answer.

3. In 1974, Kenneth Appel and Wolfgang Haken solved a problem that had confounded mathematicians for more than a century. They proved that no matter how complex a map is, it can be colored in a maximum of four colors, so that no two regions with a common boundary have the same color. Sketch the figure shown here. Can you color it in four colors? Can you color it in three colors?

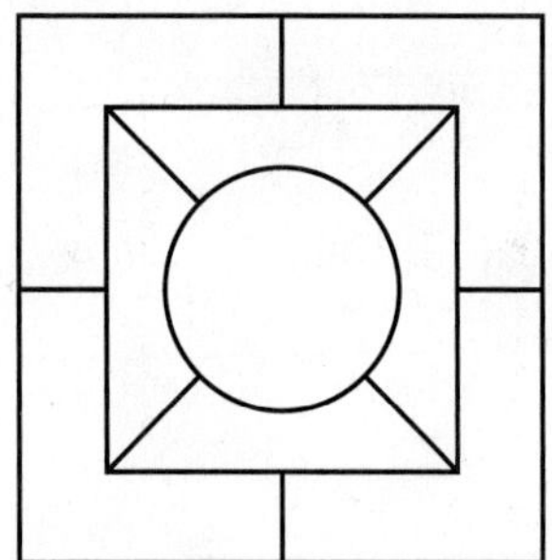

22.3 Combinations and Probability

Essential Question: What is the difference between a permutaion and a combination?

Explore Finding the Number of Combinations

A **combination** is a selection of objects from a group in which order is unimportant. For example, if 3 letters are chosen from the group of letters A, B, C, and D, there are 4 different combinations.

ABC	ABD	ACD	BCD

A restaurant has 8 different appetizers on the menu, as shown in the table. They also offer an appetizer sampler, which contains any 3 of the appetizers served on a single plate. How many different appetizer samplers can be created? The order in which the appetizers are selected does not matter.

Appetizers	
Nachos	Chicken Wings
Chicken Quesadilla	Vegetarian Egg Rolls
Potato Skins	Soft Pretzels
Beef Chili	Guacamole Dip

(A) Find the number appetizer samplers that are possible if the order of selection does matter. This is the number of permutations of 8 objects taken 3 at a time.

$$_8P_3 = \frac{\square}{(\square - \square)!} = \frac{\square}{\square} = \square$$

(B) Find the number of different ways to select a particular group of appetizers. This is the number of permutations of 3 objects.

$$_3P_3 = \frac{\square}{(\square - \square)!} = \frac{\square}{\square} = \square$$

(C) To find the number of possible appetizer samplers if the order of selection does not matter, divide the answer to part A by the answer to part B.

So the number of appetizer samplers that can be created is $\frac{\square}{\square} = \square$.

Reflect

1. Explain why the answer to Part A was divided by the answer to Part B.
2. On Mondays and Tuesdays, the restaurant offers an appetizer sampler that contains any 4 of the appetizers listed. How many different appetizer samplers can be created?
3. In general, are there more ways or fewer ways to select objects when the order does not matter? Why?

Explain 1 Finding a Probability Using Combinations

The results of the Explore can be generalized to give a formula for combinations. In the Explore, the number of combinations of the 8 objects taken 3 at a time is

$$_8P_3 \div {_3P_3} = \frac{8!}{(8-3)!} \div \frac{3!}{(3-3)!} = \frac{8!}{(8-3)!} \cdot \frac{0!}{3!} = \frac{8!}{(8-3)!} \cdot \frac{1!}{3!} = \frac{8!}{3!(8-3)!}$$

This can be generalized as follows.

Combinations

The number of combinations of n objects taken r at a time is given by

$$_nC_r = \frac{n!}{r!(n-r)!}$$

Example 1 Find each probability.

(A) There are 4 boys and 8 girls on the debate team. The coach randomly chooses 3 of the students to participate in a competition. What is the probability that the coach chooses all girls?

The sample space S consists of combinations of 3 students taken from the group of 12 students.

$n(S) = {_{12}C_3} = \frac{12!}{3!9!} = 220$

Event A consists of combinations of 3 girls taken from the set of 8 girls.

$n(A) = {_8C_3} = \frac{8!}{3!5!} = 56$

The probability that the coach chooses all girls is $P(A) = \frac{n(A)}{n(S)} = \frac{56}{220} = \frac{14}{55}$.

(B) There are 52 cards in a standard deck, 13 in each of 4 suits: clubs, diamonds, hearts, and spades. Five cards are randomly drawn from the deck. What is the probability that all five cards are diamonds?

The sample space S consists of combinations of 5 cards drawn from 52 cards.

$n(S) = {_{52}C_5} = \frac{52!}{5!47!} = 2,598,960$

Event A consists of combinations of 5 cards drawn from the 13 diamonds.

$n(A) = {_{13}C_5} = \frac{13!}{5!8!} = 1287$

The probability of randomly selecting 5 cards that are diamonds is

$$P(A) = \frac{n(A)}{n(S)} = \frac{\boxed{1287}}{\boxed{2{,}598{,}960}} = \frac{\boxed{33}}{\boxed{66{,}640}}.$$

Your Turn

4. A coin is tossed 4 times. What is the probability of getting exactly 3 heads?

5. A standard deck of cards is divided in half, with the red cards (diamonds and hearts) separated from the black cards (spades and clubs). Four cards are randomly drawn from the red half. What is the probability they are all diamonds?

Explain 2 Finding a Probability Using Combinations and Addition

Sometimes, counting problems involve the phrases "at least" or "at most." For these problems, combinations must be added.

For example, suppose a coin is flipped 3 times. The coin could show heads 0, 1, 2, or 3 times. To find the number of combinations with at least 2 heads, add the number of combinations with 2 heads and the number of combinations with 3 heads $\left({}_3C_2 + {}_3C_3\right)$.

Example 2 Find each probability.

(A) A coin is flipped 5 times. What is the probability that the result is heads at least 4 of the 5 times?

The number of outcomes in the sample space S can be found by using the Fundamental Counting Principle since each flip can result in heads or tails.

$n(S) = 2 \cdot 2 \cdot 2 \cdot 2 \cdot 2 = 2^5 = 32$

Let A be the event that the coin shows heads at least 4 times. This is the sum of 2 events, the coin showing heads 4 times and the coin showing heads 5 times. Find the sum of the combinations with 4 heads from 5 coins and with 5 heads from 5 coins.

$n(A) = {}_5C_4 + {}_5C_5 = \frac{5!}{4!1!} + \frac{5!}{5!0!} = 5 + 1 = 6$

The probability that the coin shows at least 4 heads is $P(A) = \frac{n(A)}{n(S)} = \frac{6}{32} = \frac{3}{16}$.

(B) Three number cubes are rolled and the result is recorded. What is the probability that at least 2 of the number cubes show 6?

The number of outcomes in the sample space S can be found by using the Fundamental Counting Principle since each roll can result in 1, 2, 3, 4, 5, or 6.

$n(S) = \boxed{6^3} = \boxed{216}$

Let A be the event that at least 2 number cubes show 6. This is the sum of 2 events, 2 number cubes showing 6 or 3 number cubes showing 6. The event of getting 6 on 2 number cubes occurs 5 times since there are 5 possibilities for the other number cube.

$$n(A) = \boxed{5 \cdot {}_3C_2} + \boxed{{}_3C_3} = \boxed{5 \cdot \frac{3!}{2!1!}} + \boxed{\frac{3!}{3!0!}} = \boxed{15} + \boxed{1} = \boxed{16}$$

The probability of getting a 6 at least twice in 3 rolls is $P(A) = \frac{n(A)}{n(S)} = \frac{\boxed{16}}{\boxed{216}} = \frac{\boxed{2}}{\boxed{27}}$.

Your Turn

6. A math department has a large database of true-false questions, half of which are true and half of which are false, that are used to create future exams. A new test is created by randomly selecting 6 questions from the database. What is the probability the new test contains at most 2 questions where the correct answer is "true"?

7. There are equally many boys and girls in the senior class. If 5 seniors are randomly selected to form the student council, what is the probability the council will contain at least 3 girls?

Elaborate

8. Discussion A coin is flipped 5 times, and the result of heads or tails is recorded. To find the probability of getting tails at least once, the events of 1, 2, 3, 4, or 5 tails can be added together. Is there a faster way to calculate this probability?

9. If ${}_nC_a = {}_nC_b$, what is the relationship between a and b? Explain your answer.

10. Essential Question Check-In How do you determine whether choosing a group of objects involves combinations?

Evaluate: Homework and Practice

• Online Homework
• Hints and Help
• Extra Practice

1. A cat has a litter of 6 kittens. You plan to adopt 2 of the kittens. In how many ways can you choose 2 of the kittens from the litter?

2. An amusement park has 11 roller coasters. In how many ways can you choose 4 of the roller coasters to ride during your visit to the park?

3. Four students from 30-member math club will be selected to organize a fundraiser. How many groups of 4 students are possible?

4. A school has 5 Spanish teachers and 4 French teachers. The school's principal randomly chooses 2 of the teachers to attend a conference. What is the probability that the principal chooses 2 Spanish teachers?

5. There are 6 fiction books and 8 nonfiction books on a reading list. Your teacher randomly assigns you 4 books to read over the summer. What is the probability that you are assigned all nonfiction books?

6. A bag contains 26 tiles, each with a different letter of the alphabet written on it. You choose 3 tiles from the bag without looking. What is the probability that you choose the tiles with the letters A, B, and C?

7. You are randomly assigned a password consisting of 6 different characters chosen from the digits 0 to 9 and the letters A to Z. As a percent, what is the probability that you are assigned a password consisting of only letters? Round you answer to the nearest tenth of a percent.

8. A bouquet of 6 flowers is made up by randomly choosing between roses and carnations. What is the probability the bouquet will have at most 2 roses?

9. A bag of fruit contains 10 pieces of fruit, chosen randomly from bins of apples and oranges. What is the probability the bag contains at least 6 oranges?

10. You flip a coin 10 times. What is the probability that you get at most 3 heads?

11. You flip a coin 8 times. What is the probability you will get at least 5 heads?

12. You flip a coin 5 times. What is the probability that every result will be tails?

13. There are 12 balloons in a bag: 3 each of blue, green, red, and yellow. Three balloons are chosen at random. Find the probability that all 3 balloons are green.

14. There are 6 female and 3 male kittens at an adoption center. Four kittens are chosen at random. What is the probability that all 4 kittens are female?

There are 21 students in your class. The teacher wants to send 4 students to the library each day. The teacher will choose the students to go to the library at random each day for the first four days from the list of students who have not already gone. Answer each question.

15. What is the probability you will be chosen to go on the first day?

16. If you have not yet been chosen to go on days 1–3, what is the probability you will be chosen to go on the fourth day?

17. Your teacher chooses 2 students at random to represent your homeroom. The homeroom has a total of 30 students, including your best friend. What is the probability that you and your best friend are chosen?

There are 12 peaches and 8 bananas in a fruit basket. You get a snack for yourself and three of your friends by choosing four of the pieces of fruit at random. Answer each question.

18. What is the probability that all 4 are peaches?

19. What is the probability that all 4 are bananas?

20. There are 30 students in your class. Your science teacher will choose 5 students at random to create a group to do a project. Find the probability that you and your 2 best friends in the science class will be chosen to be in the group.

21. On a television game show, 9 members of the studio audience are randomly selected to be eligible contestants.

    a. Six of the 9 eligible contestants are randomly chosen to play a game on the stage. How many combinations of 6 players from the group of eligible contestants are possible?

    b. You and your two friends are part of the group of 9 eligible contestants. What is the probability that all three of you are chosen to play the game on stage? Explain how you found your answer.

22. Determine whether you should use permutations or combinations to find the number of possibilities in each of the following situations.

a. Selecting a group of 5 people from a group of 8 people

b. Finding the number of combinations for a combination lock

c. Awarding first and second place ribbons in a contest

d. Choosing 3 books to read in any order from a list of 7 books

H.O.T. Focus on Higher Order Thinking

23. Communicate Mathematical Ideas Using the letters *A*, *B*, and *C*, explain the difference between a permutation and a combination.

24. a. Draw Conclusions Calculate ${}_{10}C_6$ and ${}_{10}C_4$.

b. What do you notice about these values? Explain why this makes sense.

c. Use your observations to help you state a generalization about combinations.

25. Justify Reasoning Use the formula for combinations to make a generalization about ${}_nC_n$. Explain why this makes sense.

26. Explain the Error Describe and correct the error in evaluating ${}_9C_4$.

$${}_9C_4 = \frac{9!}{(9-4)!} = \frac{9!}{5!} = 3024$$

Lesson Performance Task

1. In the 2012 elections, there were six candidates for the United States Senate in Vermont. In how many different orders, from first through sixth, could the candidates have finished?

2. The winner of the Vermont Senatorial election received 208,253 votes, 71.1% of the total votes cast. The candidate coming in second received 24.8% of the vote. How many votes did the second-place candidate receive? Round to the nearest ten.

3. Following the 2012 election there were 53 Democratic, 45 Republican, and 2 Independent senators in Congress.

   a. How many committees of 5 Democratic senators could be formed?

   b. How many committees of 48 Democratic senators could be formed?

   c. Explain how a clever person who knew nothing about combinations could guess the answer to (b) if the person knew the answer to (a).

4. Following the election, a newspaper printed a circle graph showing the make-up of the Senate. How many degrees were allotted to the sector representing Democrats, how many to Republicans, and how many to Independents?

22.4 Mutually Exclusive and Overlapping Events

Essential Question: How are probabilities affected when events are mutually exclusive or overlapping?

Resource Locker

Explore 1 Finding the Probability of Mutually Exclusive Events

Two events are **mutually exclusive events** if they cannot both occur in the same trial of an experiment. For example, if you flip a coin it cannot land heads up and tails up in the same trial. Therefore, the events are mutually exclusive.

A number dodecahedron has 12 sides numbered 1 through 12. What is the probability that you roll the cube and the result is an even number or a 7?

(A) Let A be the event that you roll an even number. Let B be the event that you roll a 7. Let S be the sample space.

Copy and complete the Venn diagram by writing all outcomes in the sample space in the appropriate region.

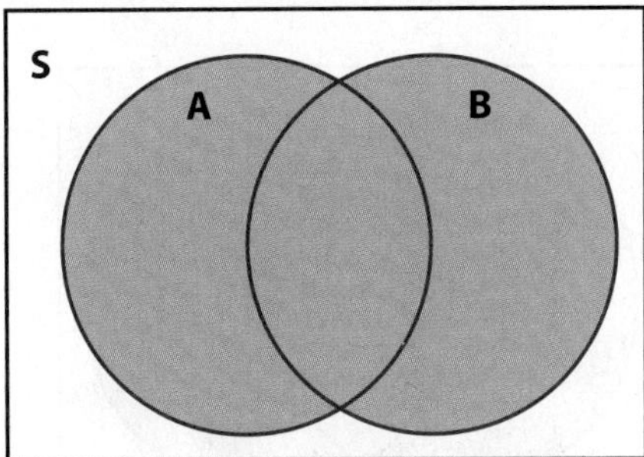

(B) Calculate $P(A)$.

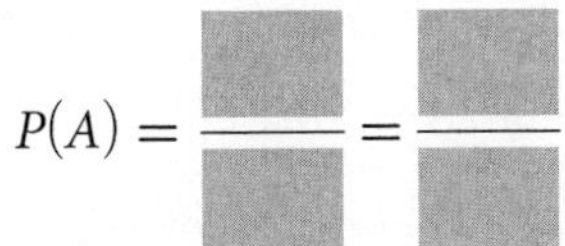

$P(A) = \frac{\square}{\square} = \frac{\square}{\square}$

(C) Calculate $P(B)$.

$P(B) = \frac{\square}{\square}$

(D) Calculate $P(A \text{ or } B)$.

$n(S) = \square$

$n(A \text{ or } B) = n(A) + n(B)$

$= \square + \square = \square$

So, $P(A \text{ or } B) = \frac{n(A \text{ or } B)}{n(S)} = \frac{\square}{\square}$.

(E) Calculate $P(A) + P(B)$. Compare the answer to Step D.

$P(A) + P(B) = \frac{\square}{\square} + \frac{\square}{\square} = \frac{\square}{\square}$

$P(A) + P(B)$ $\square$ $P(A \text{ or } B)$.

Reflect

1. **Discussion** How would you describe mutually exclusive events to another student in your own words? How could you use a Venn diagram to assist in your explanation?

2. Look back over the steps. What can you conjecture about the probability of the union of events that are mutually exclusive?

Explore 2 Finding the Probability of Overlapping Events

The process used in the previous Explore can be generalized to give the formula for the probability of mutually exclusive events.

Mutually Exclusive Events
If A and B are mutually exclusive events, then $P(A \text{ or } B) = P(A) + P(B)$.

Two events are **overlapping events** (or inclusive events) if they have one or more outcomes in common.

What is the probability that you roll a number dodecahedron cube and the result is an even number or a number greater than 7?

(A) Let A be the event that you roll an even number. Let B be the event that you roll a number greater than 7. Let S be the sample space.

Copy and complete the Venn diagram by writing all outcomes in the sample space in the appropriate region.

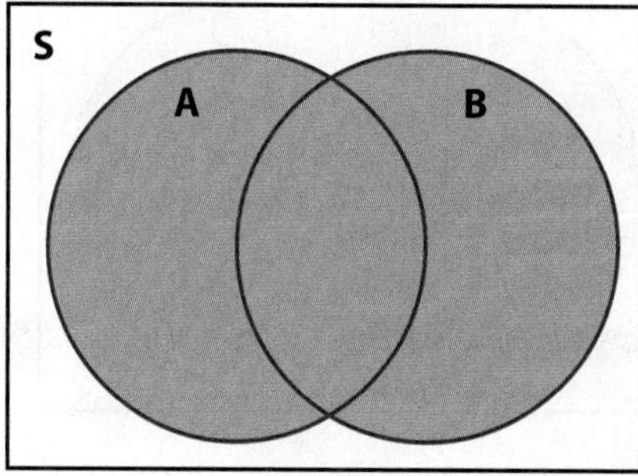

(B) Calculate $P(A)$.

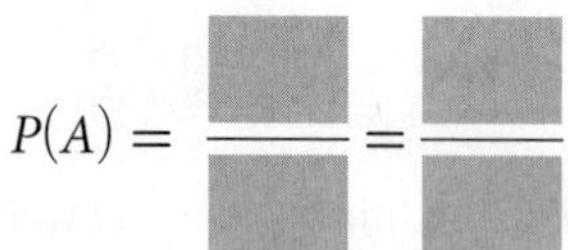

(C) Calculate $P(B)$.

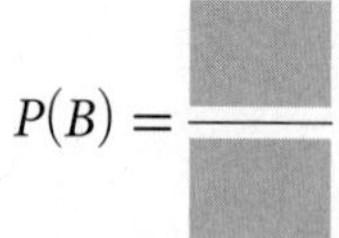

(D) Calculate $P(A \text{ and } B)$.

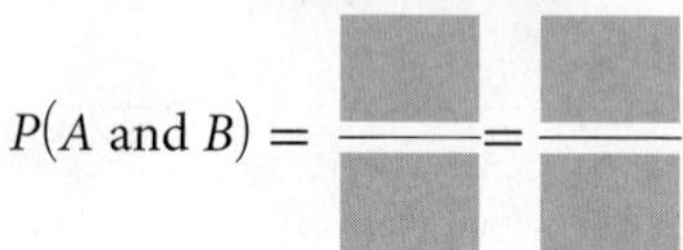

(E) Use the Venn diagram to find $P(A \text{ or } B)$.

$P(A \text{ or } B) =$

Ⓕ Now, use $P(A)$, $P(B)$, and $P(A \text{ and } B)$ to calculate $P(A \text{ or } B)$.

$P(A) = \square$ $P(B) = \square$ $P(A \text{ and } B) = \square$

$P(A) + P(B) - P(A \text{ and } B) = \square + \square - \square = \square$

Reflect

3. Why must you subtract $P(A \text{ and } B)$ from $P(A) + P(B)$ to determine $P(A \text{ or } B)$?

4. Look back over the steps. What can you conjecture about the probability of the union of two events that are overlapping?

Explain 1 Finding a Probability From a Two-Way Table of Data

The previous Explore leads to the following rule.

The Addition Rule

$P(A \text{ or } B) = P(A) + P(B) - P(A \text{ and } B)$

Example 1 **Use the given two-way tables to determine the probabilities.**

Ⓐ $P(\text{senior or girl})$

	Freshman	Sophomore	Junior	Senior	TOTAL
Boy	98	104	100	94	396
Girl	102	106	96	108	412
Total	200	210	196	202	808

To determine $P(\text{senior or girl})$, first calculate $P(\text{senior})$, $P(\text{girl})$, and $P(\text{senior and girl})$.

$P(\text{senior}) = \frac{202}{808} = \frac{1}{4}$; $P(\text{girl}) = \frac{412}{808} = \frac{103}{202}$ $P(\text{senior and girl}) = \frac{108}{808} = \frac{27}{202}$

Use the addition rule to determine $P(\text{senior or girl})$.

$$P(\text{senior or girl}) = P(\text{senior}) + P(\text{girl}) - P(\text{senior and girl})$$

$$= \frac{1}{4} + \frac{103}{202} - \frac{27}{202}$$

$$= \frac{253}{404}$$

Therefore, the probability that a student is a senior or a girl is $\frac{253}{404}$.

Ⓑ $P\left((\text{domestic or late})^c\right)$

	Late	On Time	Total
Domestic Flights	12	108	120
International Flights	6	54	60
Total	18	162	180

To determine $P\left((\text{domestic or late})^c\right)$, first calculate $P(\text{domestic or late})$.

$P(\text{domestic}) = \frac{120}{180} = \frac{2}{3}$; $P(\text{late}) = \frac{18}{180} = \frac{1}{10}$; $P(\text{domestic and late}) = \frac{12}{180} = \frac{1}{15}$

Use the addition rule to determine $P(\text{domestic or late})$.

$P(\text{domestic or late}) = P(\text{domestic}) + P(\text{late}) - P(\text{domestic and late})$

$$= \frac{2}{3} + \frac{1}{10} - \frac{1}{15} = \frac{7}{10}$$

Therefore, $P\left((\text{domestic or late})^c\right) = 1 - P(\text{domestic or late})$

$$= 1 - \frac{7}{10}$$

$$= \frac{3}{10}$$

Your Turn

5. Use the table to determine $P(\text{headache or no medicine})$.

	Took Medicine	No Medicine	TOTAL
Headache	12	15	27
No Headache	48	25	73
TOTAL	60	40	100

Elaborate

6. Give an example of mutually exclusive events and an example of overlapping events.

7. **Essential Question Check-In** How do you determine the probability of mutually exclusive events and overlapping events?

Evaluate: Homework and Practice

- Online Homework
- Hints and Help
- Extra Practice

1. A bag contains 3 blue marbles, 5 red marbles, and 4 green marbles. You choose one without looking. What is the probability that it is red or green?

2. A number icosahedron has 20 sides numbered 1 through 20. What is the probability that the result of a roll is a number less than 4 or greater than 11?

3. A bag contains 26 tiles, each with a different letter of the alphabet written on it. You choose a tile without looking. What is the probability that you choose a vowel (a, e, i, o, or u) or a letter in the word GEOMETRY?

4. **Persevere in Problem Solving** You roll two number cubes at the same time. Each cube has sides numbered 1 through 6. What is the probability that the sum of the numbers rolled is even or greater than 9? (*Hint:* Create and fill out a probability chart.)

The table shows the data for car insurance quotes for 125 drivers made by an insurance company in one week.

	Teen	Adult (20 or over)	Total
0 accidents	15	53	68
1 accident	4	32	36
2+ accidents	9	12	21
Total	28	97	125

You randomly choose one of the drivers. Find the probability of each event.

5. The driver is an adult.

6. The driver is a teen with 0 or 1 accident.

7. The driver is a teen.

8. The driver has 2+ accidents.

9. The driver is a teen and has 2+ accidents.

10. The driver is a teen or a driver with 2+ accidents.

Use the following information for Exercises 11–16. The table shown shows the results of a customer satisfaction survey for a cellular service provider, by location of the customer. In the survey, customers were asked whether they would recommend a plan with the provider to a friend.

	Arlington	Towson	Parkville	Total
Yes	40	35	41	116
No	18	10	6	34
Total	58	45	47	150

One of the customers that was surveyed was chosen at random. Find the probability of each event.

11. The customer was from Towson and said No.

12. The customer was from Parkville.

13. The customer said Yes.

14. The customer was from Parkville and said Yes.

15. The customer was from Parkville or said Yes.

16. Explain why you cannot use the rule $P(A \text{ or } B) = P(A) + P(B)$ in Exercise 15.

Use the following information for Exercises 17–21. Roberto is the owner of a car dealership. He is assessing the success rate of his top three salespeople in order to offer one of them a promotion. Over two months, for each attempted sale, he records whether the salesperson made a successful sale or not. The results are shown in the chart.

	Successful	Unsuccessful	Total
Becky	6	6	12
Raul	4	5	9
Darrell	6	9	15
Total	16	20	36

Roberto randomly chooses one of the attempted sales.

17. Find the probability that the sale was one of Becky's or Raul's successful sales.

18. Find the probability that the sale was one of the unsuccessful sales or one of Raul's successful sales.

19. Find the probability that the sale was one of Darrell's unsuccessful sales or one of Raul's unsuccessful sales.

20. Find the probability that the sale was an unsuccessful sale or one of Becky's attempted sales.

21. Find the probability that the sale was a successful sale or one of Raul's attempted sales.

22. You are going to draw one card at random from a standard deck of cards. A standard deck of cards has 13 cards (2, 3, 4, 5, 6, 7, 8, 9, 10, jack, queen, king, ace) in each of 4 suits (hearts, clubs, diamonds, spades). The hearts and diamonds cards are red. The clubs and spades cards are black. Which of the following have a probability of less than $\frac{1}{4}$? Choose all that apply.

a. Drawing a card that is a spade and an ace

b. Drawing a card that is a club or an ace

c. Drawing a card that is a face card or a club

d. Drawing a card that is black and a heart

e. Drawing a red card and a number card from 2–9

H.O.T. Focus on Higher Order Thinking

23. Draw Conclusions A survey of 1108 employees at a software company finds that 621 employees take a bus to work and 445 employees take a train to work. Some employees take both a bus and a train, and 321 employees take only a train. To the nearest percent, find the probability that a randomly chosen employee takes a bus or a train to work. Explain.

24. Communicate Mathematical Ideas Explain how to use a Venn diagram to find the probability of randomly choosing a multiple of 3 or a multiple of 4 from the set of numbers from 1 to 25. Then find the probability.

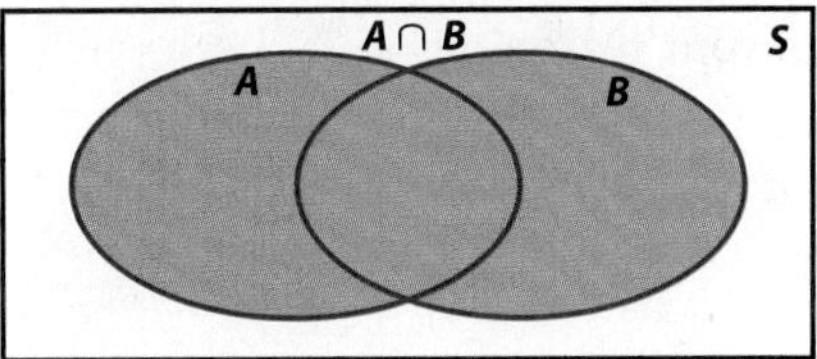

25. Explain the Error Sanderson attempted to find the probability of randomly choosing a 10 or a diamond from a standard deck of playing cards. He used the following logic:

Let S be the sample space, A be the event that the card is a 10, and B be the event that the card is a diamond.

There are 52 cards in the deck, so $n(S) = 52$.

There are four 10s in the deck, so $n(A) = 4$.

There are 13 diamonds in the deck, so $n(B) = 13$.

One 10 is a diamond, so $n(A \cap B) = 1$.

$$P(A \cup B) = \frac{n(A \cup B)}{n(S)} = \frac{n(A) \cdot n(B) - n(A \cap B)}{n(S)} = \frac{4 \cdot 13 - 1}{52} = \frac{51}{52}$$

Describe and correct Sanderson's mistake.

Lesson Performance Task

What is the smallest number of randomly chosen people that are needed in order for there to be a better than 50% probability that at least two of them will have the same birthday? The astonishing answer is 23. Follow these steps to find why.

1. Can a person have a birthday on two different days? Use the vocabulary of this lesson to explain your answer.

Looking for the probability that two or more people in a group of 23 have matching birthdays is a challenge. Maybe there is one match but maybe there are five matches or seven or fourteen. A much easier way is to look for the probability that there are *no* matches in a group of 23. In other words, all 23 have different birthdays. Then use that number to find the answer.

2. There are 365 days in a non-leap year.

a. Write an expression for the number of ways can you assign different birthdays to 23 people. (Hint: Think of the people as standing in a line, and you are going to assign a different number from 1 to 365 to each person.)

b. Write an expression for the number ways can you assign any birthday to 23 people. (Hint: Now think about assigning any number from 1 to 365 to each of 23 people.)

c. How can you use your answers to (a) and (b) to find the probability that no people in a group of 23 have the same birthday? Use a calculator to find the probability to the nearest ten-thousandth.

d. What is the probability that at least two people in a group of 23 have the same birthday? Explain your reasoning.

STUDY GUIDE REVIEW

Introduction to Probability

MODULE 22

Essential Question: How can you use probability to solve real-world problems?

Key Vocabulary

set *(conjunto, juego)*
element *(elemento)*
empty set *(conjunto vacío)*
universal set *(conjunto universal)*
subset *(subconjunto)*
intersection *(intersección)*
union *(unión)*
complement *(complemento)*
theoretical probability *(probabilidad teórica)*
permutation *(permutación)*
Fundamental Counting Principle *(principio fundamental de conteo)*
factorial *(factorial)*
combination *(combinación)*

KEY EXAMPLE (Lesson 22.1)

When rolling two fair number cubes, what is the probability that the sum of the two cubes will not be even or prime?

The sum of two number cubes can be any integer from 2 through 12. Of these, the only possible sum that is not even or prime is 9. There are 36 possible outcomes for rolling two number cubes. Of these, the only ones that sum to 9 are (3, 6), (6, 3), (4, 5), and (5, 4). So, $P(\text{sum is not even or prime}) = \frac{4}{36} = \frac{1}{9}$.

KEY EXAMPLE (Lesson 22.2)

Ten marbles are placed in a jar. Of those 10 3 marbles are blue, 2 are red, 3 are green, 1 is orange, and 1 is yellow. The 10 marbles are randomly placed in a line. What is the probability that all marbles of the same color are next to each other?

Marbles of the same color are indistinguishable objects. The sample space S consists of permutations of 10 objects, with 3 of one type, 3 of another type, and 2 of a third type.

$$n(S) = \frac{10!}{3!3!2!} = 50{,}400$$

Event A consists of permutations that have all marbles of the same color next to each other, so it is the number of ways of ordering the 5 colors.

$$n(A) = 5! = 120$$

The probability that all marbles of the same color are next to each other is

$$P(A) = \frac{n(A)}{n(S)} = \frac{120}{50{,}400} = \frac{1}{420}.$$

KEY EXAMPLE (Lesson 22.3)

A class of 15 boys and 15 girls is putting together a random group of 3 students to do classroom chores. What is the probability that at least 2 of the students are boys?

The sample space S consists is the number of combinations of three student groups.

$$n(S) = \frac{30!}{3!27!} = 4060$$

Event A consists of combinations that have 2 boys or 3 boys in the group.
The event of getting 2 boys in the group occurs 15 times, once for each individual girl in the class.

$$n(A) = 15 \cdot {}_{15}C_2 + {}_{15}C_3 = 15 \cdot \frac{15!}{2!13!} + \frac{15!}{3!12!} = 2030$$

The probability that there will be at least 2 boys in the group is $P(A) = \frac{n(A)}{n(S)} = \frac{2030}{4060} = \frac{1}{2}$.

EXERCISES

Use the sets below to find the indicated set for problems 1–4. *(Lesson 22.1)*

U = {1, 2, 3, 4, 5, 6, 7, 8, 9}

A = {1, 3, 5, 7, 9}

B = {2, 4, 6, 8}

C = {1, 2, 4, 5, 7, 9}

1. $A \cup C$

2. $B \cap C$

3. A^C

4. $A \cap B$

5. A computer password can use all digits (0–9) and all letters (*a–z*) that are case sensitive (upper and lower). How many different permutations of 5-figure passwords are there if there is no repeated input? *(Lesson 22.2)*

6. Brandon is rolling a 10-sided number cube 5 times. What is the probability that he will roll at least two 7s? *(Lesson 22.3)*

Determine if the given events are mutually exclusive. If not, explain why. *(Lesson 22.4)*

7. Rolling a 3 or a 4 on a regular number cube

8. Drawing a queen or a red card from a standard deck of 52 cards

9. Flipping a coin and having it land on heads or tails

10. Rolling an even number or a prime number on a number cube

MODULE PERFORMANCE TASK

Baseball Probability

A baseball player will be batting three times during today's game. So far this season, the player has gotten an average of 1 hit in every 3 times times at bat. Based on this data, what is the probability that the player will get exactly one hit in today's game? Is that outcome more or less likely than getting no hits?

Start by making notes about your plan for solving the problem. Then complete the task, using words, numbers, or diagrams to explain how your reached your conclusions.

Ready to Go On?

22.1–22.4 Introduction to Probability

- Online Homework
- Hints and Help
- Extra Practice

Find the probabilities. *(Lesson 22.3)*

1. Twenty-six tiles with the letters A through Z are placed face down on a table and mixed. (For the purpose of this exercise assume that the letter Y is a vowel.) Five tiles are drawn in order. Compute the probability that only consonants are selected.

2. The two-way table shows the results of a poll in a certain country that asked voters, sorted by political party, whether they supported or opposed a proposed government initiative. Find the given probabilities.

	Party A	Party B	Other Party	No Party	Total
Support	97	68	8	19	192
Oppose	32	81	16	11	140
Undecided	9	23	10	26	68
Total	138	172	34	56	400

a. $P(\text{no party or undecided})$

b. $P\left((\text{party A or support})^c\right)$

ESSENTIAL QUESTION

3. A teacher is assigning 32 presentation topics to 9 students at random. Each student will get 3 topics, and no topic will be repeated. Somil is very interested in 5 topics. What is the probability that Somil will be assigned at least one of his preferred topics? Explain how you arrived at your answer.

MODULE 22
MIXED REVIEW

Assessment Readiness

1. Jonah is arranging books on a shelf. The order of the books matters to him. There are 336 ways he can arrange the books. Determine whether each statement is correct.

A. He might be arranging 3 books from a selection of 8 different books.

B. He might be arranging 4 books from a selection of 8 different books.

C. He might be arranging 5 books from a selection of 8 different books.

2. Decide whether the probability of tossing the given sum with two dice is $\frac{3}{36}$. Write Yes or No for A–C.

A. A sum of 6

B. A sum of 7

C. A sum of 8

3. Let H be the event that a coin flip lands with heads showing, and let T be the event that a flip lands with tails showing. (Note that $P(H) = P(T) = 0.5$.) What is the probability that you will get heads at least once if you flip the coin ten times? Explain your reasoning.

4. There are 8 girls and 6 boys on the student council. How many committees of 3 girls and 2 boys can be formed? Show your work.

Conditional Probability and Independence of Events

MODULE 23

Essential Question: How can you use conditional probability and independence of events to solve real-world problems?

REAL WORLD VIDEO
Check out how principles of conditional probability are used to understand the chances of events in playing cards.

MODULE PERFORMANCE TASK PREVIEW

Playing Cards

In this module, you will use concepts of conditional probability to determine the chance of drawing a hand of cards with a certain property. To successfully complete this task, you'll need to master these skills:

- Distinguish between independent and dependent events.
- Apply the conditional probability formula to a real-world situation.
- Use the Multiplication Rule appropriately.

Complete these exercises to review skills you will need for this module.

Personal Math Trainer

- Online Homework
- Hints and Help
- Extra Practice

Probability of Compound Events

Example 1 Find the probability of rolling a pair of six-sided dice and the sum of their faces being even or equal to 3.

Three is not even, so the two probabilities are mutually exclusive. The probability is equal to the sums of the probabilities of rolling an even sum or rolling a sum of 3.

Probability of rolling an even sum $= \frac{18}{36}$ Count the number of outcomes for the first event.

Probability of rolling a sum of 3 $= \frac{2}{36}$ Count the number of outcomes for the second event.

Probability of rolling an even sum or a sum of 3 $= \frac{18}{36} + \frac{2}{36} = \frac{20}{36} = \frac{5}{9}$

Find each probability.

1. The probability of rolling two number cubes at the same time and getting a 4 with either die or the sum of the dice is 6

2. The probability of rolling two number cubes at the same time and getting a 4 with either die and the sum of the dice is 6

3. The probability of pulling red or blue s (or both) from a jar when you pull out two marbles given that pulling red and pulling blue are equally likely events

4. The probability of pulling a red marble and a blue marble from a jar when you pull out two marbles given that pulling red and pulling blue are equally likely events

5. The probability of flipping a coin three times and getting exactly two heads or at least one tails given the probability of getting a heads is $\frac{1}{2}$ and the probability of getting a tails is $\frac{1}{2}$

6. The probability of flipping a coin three times and getting exactly two heads and at least one tails given the probability of getting a heads is $\frac{1}{2}$ and the probability of getting a tails is $\frac{1}{2}$

7. The probability of flipping a coin three times and getting at least two heads or at least one tails given the probability of getting a heads is $\frac{1}{2}$ and the probability of getting a tails is $\frac{1}{2}$

23.1 Conditional Probability

Essential Question: How do you calculate a conditional probability?

Explore 1 Finding Conditional Probabilities from a Two-Way Frequency Table

The probability that event A occurs given that event B has already occurred is called the **conditional probability** of A given B and is written $P(A \mid B)$.

One hundred migraine headache sufferers participated in a study of a new medicine. Some were given the new medicine, and others were not. After one week, participants were asked if they had experienced a headache during the week. The two-way frequency table shows the results.

	Took medicine	No medicine	Total
Headache	11	13	24
No headache	54	22	76
Total	65	35	100

Let event A be the event that a participant did not get a headache. Let event B be the event that a participant took the medicine.

(A) To the nearest percent, what is the probability that a participant who took the medicine did not get a headache?

[ ] participants took the medicine. So, $P(A \mid B) = \frac{[\ ]}{[\ ]} \approx$ [ ] %.

Of these, [ ] did not get a headache.

(B) To the nearest percent, what is the probability that a participant who did not get a headache took the medicine?

[ ] participants did not get a headache. So, $P(B \mid A) = \frac{[\ ]}{[\ ]} \approx$ [ ] %.

Of these, [ ] took the medicine.

(C) Let $n(A)$ be the number of participants who did not get a headache, $n(B)$ be the number of participants who took the medicine, and $n(A \cap B)$ be the number of participants who took the medicine and did not get a headache.

$n(A) =$ [ ] $n(B) =$ [ ] $n(A \cap B) =$ [ ]

Express $P(A \mid B)$ and $P(B \mid A)$ in terms of $n(A)$, $n(B)$, and $n(A \cap B)$.

$P(A \mid B) = \frac{[\ ]}{[\ ]}$ $P(B \mid A) = \frac{[\ ]}{[\ ]}$

Reflect

1. For the question "What is the probability that a participant who did not get a headache took the medicine?", what event is assumed to have already occurred?

2. In general, does it appear that $P(A|B) = P(B|A)$? Why or why not?

Explore 2 Finding Conditional Probabilities from a Two-Way Relative Frequency Table

You can develop a formula for $P(A|B)$ that uses relative frequencies (which are probabilities) rather than frequencies (which are counts).

	Took medicine	No medicine	Total
Headache	11	13	24
No headache	54	22	76
Total	65	35	100

(A) To obtain relative frequencies, divide every number in the table by 100, the total number of participants in the study. Copy the table below and enter the quotients in the appropriate spaces.

	Took medicine	No medicine	Total
Headache			
No headache			
Total			1

(B) Recall that event A is the event that a participant did not get a headache and that event B is the event that a participant took the medicine. Use the relative frequency table from Step A to find $P(A)$, $P(B)$, and $P(A \cap B)$.

(C) In the first Explore, you found the conditional probabilities $P(A|B) \approx 83\%$ and $P(B|A) \approx 71\%$ by using the frequencies in the two-way frequency table. Use the relative frequencies from the table in Step A to find the equivalent conditional probabilities.

$$P(A|B) = \frac{P(A \cap B)}{P(B)} = \frac{\square}{\square} \approx \square\%$$

$$P(B|A) = \frac{P(A \cap B)}{P(A)} = \frac{\square}{\square} \approx \square\%$$

(D) Generalize the results by using $n(S)$ as the number of elements in the sample space (in this case, the number of participants in the study). For instance, you can write $P(A) = \frac{n(A)}{n(S)}$. Write each of the following probabilities in a similar way.

$$P(B) = \frac{\square}{\square} \qquad P(A \cap B) = \frac{\square}{\square} \qquad P(A|B) = \frac{\frac{n(A \cap B)}{\square}}{\frac{n(B)}{\square}} = \frac{P(A \cap B)}{\square}$$

Reflect

3. Why are the two forms of $P(A \cap B)$, $\frac{n(A \cap B)}{n(B)}$ and $\frac{P(A \cap B)}{P(B)}$, equivalent?

4. What is a formula for $P(B|A)$ that involves probabilities rather than counts? How do you obtain this formula from the fact that $P(B|A) = \frac{n(A \cap B)}{n(A)}$?

Explain 1 Using the Conditional Probability Formula

In the previous Explore, you discovered the following formula for conditional probability.

Conditional Probability

The conditional probability of A given B (that is, the probability that event A occurs given that event B occurs) is as follows:

$$P(A|B) = \frac{P(A \cap B)}{P(A)}$$

Example 1 **Find the specified probability.**

(A) For a standard deck of playing cards, find the probability that a red card randomly drawn from the deck is a jack.

Step 1 Find $P(R)$, the probability that a red card is drawn from the deck.

There are 26 red cards in the deck of 52 cards, so $P(R) = \frac{26}{52}$.

Step 2 Find $P(J \cap R)$, the probability that a red jack is drawn from the deck.

There are 2 red jacks in the deck, so $P(J \cap R) = \frac{2}{52}$.

Step 3 Substitute the probabilities from Steps 1 and 2 into the formula for conditional probability.

$$P(J|R) = \frac{P(J \cap R)}{P(R)} = \frac{\frac{2}{52}}{\frac{26}{52}}$$

Step 4 Simplify the result.

$$P(J|R) = \frac{\frac{2}{52} \cdot 52}{\frac{26}{52} \cdot 52} = \frac{2}{26} = \frac{1}{13}$$

(B) For a standard deck of playing cards, find the probability that a jack randomly drawn from the deck is a red card.

Step 1 Find $P(J)$, the probability that a jack is drawn from the deck.

There are 4 jacks in the deck of 52 cards, so $P(J) = \frac{\boxed{4}}{52}$.

Step 2 Find $P(J \cap R)$, the probability that a red jack is drawn from the deck.

There are 2 red jacks in the deck, so $P(J \cap R) = \frac{\boxed{2}}{52}$.

Step 3 Substitute the probabilities from Steps 1 and 2 into the formula for conditional probability.

$$P(R|J) = \frac{P(J \cap R)}{P(R)} = \frac{\frac{\boxed{2}}{52}}{\frac{\boxed{4}}{52}}$$

Step 4 Simplify the result.

$$P(R|J) = \frac{\frac{\boxed{2}}{52} \cdot 52}{\frac{\boxed{4}}{52} \cdot 52} = \frac{\boxed{2}}{\boxed{4}} = \frac{1}{\boxed{2}}$$

Your Turn

5. For a standard deck of playing cards, find the probability that a face card randomly drawn from the deck is a king. (The ace is *not* a face card.)

6. For a standard deck of playing cards, find the probability that a queen randomly drawn from the deck is a diamond.

Elaborate

7. When calculating a conditional probability from a two-way table, explain why it doesn't matter whether the table gives frequencies or relative frequencies.

8. **Discussion** Is it possible to have $P(B|A) = P(A|B)$ for some events A and B? What conditions would need to exist?

9. **Essential Question Check-In** In a two-way frequency table, suppose event A represents a row of the table and event B represents a column of the table. Describe how to find the conditional probability $P(A|B)$ using the frequencies in the table.

Evaluate: Homework and Practice

- Online Homework
- Hints and Help
- Extra Practice

In order to study the relationship between the amount of sleep a student gets and his or her school performance, a researcher collected data from 120 students. The two-way frequency table shows the number of students who passed and failed an exam and the number of students who got more or less than 6 hours of sleep the night before. Use the table to answer the questions in Exercises 1–3.

	Passed exam	Failed exam	Total
Less than 6 hours of sleep	12	10	22
More than 6 hours of sleep	90	8	98
Total	102	18	120

1. To the nearest percent, what is the probability that a student who failed the exam got less than 6 hours of sleep?

2. To the nearest percent, what is the probability that a student who got less than 6 hours of sleep failed the exam?

3. To the nearest percent, what is the probability that a student got less than 6 hours of sleep and failed the exam?

4. You have a standard deck of playing cards from which you randomly select a card. Event D is getting a diamond, and event F is getting a face card (a jack, queen, or king). Show that $P(D|F) = \frac{n(D \cap F)}{n(F)}$ and $P(D|F) = \frac{P(D \cap F)}{P(F)}$ are equal.

The table shows data in the previous table as relative frequencies (rounded to the nearest thousandth when necessary). Use the table for Exercises 5–7.

	Passed exam	Failed exam	Total
Less than 6 hours of sleep	0.100	0.083	0.183
More than 6 hours of sleep	0.750	0.067	0.817
Total	0.850	0.150	1.000

5. To the nearest percent, what is the probability that a student who passed the exam got more than 6 hours of sleep?

6. To the nearest percent, what is the probability that a student who got more than 6 hours of sleep passed the exam?

7. Which is greater, the probability that a student who got less than 6 hours of sleep passed the exam or the probability that a student who got more than 6 hours of sleep failed the exam? Explain.

You randomly draw a card from a standard deck of playing cards. Let A be the event that the card is an ace, let B be the event that the card is black, and let C be the event that the card is a club. Find the specified probability as a fraction.

8. $P(A|B)$

9. $P(B|A)$

10. $P(A|C)$

11. $P(C|A)$

12. $P(B|C)$

13. $P(C|B)$

14. A botanist studied the effect of a new fertilizer by choosing 100 orchids and giving 70% of these plants the fertilizer. Of the plants that got the fertilizer, 40% produced flowers within a month. Of the plants that did not get the fertilizer, 10% produced flowers within a month.

a. Use the given information to complete a two-way frequency table.

	Received fertilizer	Did not receive fertilizer	Total
Did not flower in one month			
Flowered in one month			
Total			

b. To the nearest percent, what is the probability that an orchid that produced flowers got fertilizer?

c. To the nearest percent, what is the probability that an orchid that got fertilizer produced flowers?

15. At a school fair, a box contains 24 yellow balls and 76 red balls. One-fourth of the balls of each color are labeled "Win a prize." Match each description of a probability with its value as a percent.

A. The probability that a randomly selected ball labeled "Win a prize" is yellow

B. The probability that a randomly selected ball labeled "Win a prize" is red

C. The probability that a randomly selected ball is labeled "Win a prize" and is red

D. The probability that a randomly selected yellow ball is labeled "Win a prize"

a. __?__ 76%

b. __?__ 25%

c. __?__ 24%

d. __?__ 19%

16. A teacher gave her students two tests. If 45% of the students passed both tests and 60% passed the first test, what is the probability that a student who passed the first test also passed the second?

17. You randomly select two marbles, one at a time, from a pouch containing blue and green marbles. The probability of selecting a blue marble on the first draw and a green marble on the second draw is 25%, and the probability of selecting a blue marble on the first draw is 56%. To the nearest percent, what is the probability of selecting a green marble on the second draw, given that the first marble was blue?

You roll two number cubes, one red and one blue. The table shows the probabilities for events based on whether or not a 1 is rolled on each number cube. Use the table to find the specified conditional probability, expressed as a fraction. Then show that the conditional probability is correct by listing the possible outcomes as ordered pairs of the form (number on red cube, number on blue cube) and identifying the successful outcomes.

	Rolling a 1 on the red cube	Not rolling a 1 on the red cube	Total
Rolling a 1 on the blue cube	$\frac{1}{36}$	$\frac{5}{36}$	$\frac{1}{6}$
Not rolling a 1 on the blue cube	$\frac{5}{36}$	$\frac{25}{36}$	$\frac{5}{6}$
Total	$\frac{1}{6}$	$\frac{5}{6}$	1

18. P(not rolling a 1 on the blue cube | rolling a 1 on the red cube)

19. P(not rolling a 1 on the blue cube | not rolling a 1 on the red cube)

20. The table shows the results of a quality-control study at a computer factory.

	Shipped	Not shipped	Total
Defective	3	7	10
Not defective	89	1	90
Total	92	8	100

a. To the nearest tenth of a percent, what is the probability that a shipped computer is not defective?

b. To the nearest tenth of a percent, what is the probability that a defective computer is shipped?

H.O.T. Focus on Higher Order Thinking

21. Analyze Relationships In the Venn diagram, the circles representing events A and B divide the sample space S into four regions: the overlap of the circles, the part of A not in the overlap, the part of B not in the overlap, and the part of S not in A or B. Suppose that the area of each region is proportional to the number of outcomes that fall within the region. Which conditional probability is greater: $P(A \mid B)$ or $P(B \mid A)$? Explain.

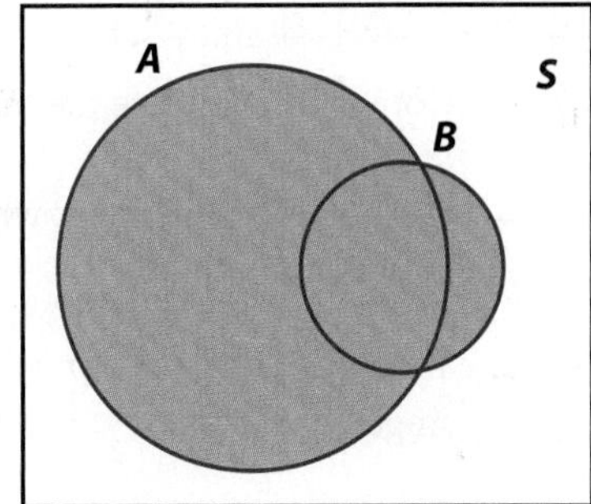

22. Explain the Error A student was asked to use the table shown to find the probability, to nearest percent, that a participant in a study of a new medicine for migraine headaches did not take the medicine, given that the participant reported no headaches.

	Took medicine	No medicine	Total
Headache	11	13	24
No headache	54	22	76
Total	65	35	100

The student made the following calculation.

$P(\text{no medicine} \mid \text{no headache}) = \frac{22}{35} \approx 0.63 = 63\%$

Explain the student's error, and find the correct probability.

23. Communicate Mathematical Ideas Explain how a conditional probability based on a two-way frequency table effectively reduces it to a one-way table. In your explanation, refer to the two-way table shown, which lists frequencies for events A, B, and their complements. Identify the part of the table that supports your explanation.

	A	Not A	Total
B	$n(A \cap B)$	$n(\text{not } A \cap B)$	$n(B)$
Not B	$n(A \cap \text{not } B)$	$n(\text{not } A \cap \text{not } B)$	$n(\text{not } B)$
Total	$n(A)$	$n(\text{not } A)$	$n(S)$

Lesson Performance Task

The two-way frequency table gives the results of a survey that asked students this question: Which of these would you most like to meet: a famous singer, a movie star, or a sports star?

	Famous singer	Movie star	Sports star	Total
Boys	20	15	55	
Girls	40	50	20	
Total				

a. Copy and complete the table by finding the row totals, column totals, and grand total.

b. To the nearest percent, what is the probability that a student who chose "movie star" is a girl?

c. To the nearest percent, what is the probability that a student who chose "famous singer" is a boy?

d. To the nearest percent, what is the probability that a boy chose "sports star"?

e. To the nearest percent, what is the probability that a girl chose "famous singer"?

f. To the nearest percent, what is the probability that a student who chose either "famous singer" or "movie star" is a boy?

g. To the nearest percent, what is the probability that a girl did not choose "sports star"?

23.2 Independent Events

Essential Question: What does it mean for two events to be independent?

Resource Locker

Explore Understanding the Independence of Events

Suppose you flip a coin and roll a number cube. You would expect the probability of getting heads on the coin to be $\frac{1}{2}$ regardless of what number you get from rolling the number cube. Likewise, you would expect the probability of rolling a 3 on the number cube to be $\frac{1}{6}$ regardless of whether of the coin flip results in heads or tails.

When the occurrence of one event has no effect on the occurrence of another event, the two events are called **independent events**.

(A) A jar contains 15 red marbles and 17 yellow marbles. You randomly draw a marble from the jar. Let R be the event that you get a red marble, and let Y be the event that you get a yellow marble.

Since the jar has a total of ☐ marbles, $P(R) = \frac{☐}{☐}$ and $P(Y) = \frac{☐}{☐}$.

(B) Suppose the first marble you draw is a red marble, and you put that marble back in the jar before randomly drawing a second marble. Find $P(Y|R)$, the probability that you get a yellow marble on the second draw after getting a red marble on the first draw. Explain your reasoning.

Since the jar still has a total of ☐ marbles and ☐ of them are yellow, $P(Y|R) = \frac{☐}{☐}$.

(C) Suppose you *don't* put the red marble back in the jar before randomly drawing a second marble. Find $P(Y|R)$, the probability that you get a yellow marble on the second draw after getting a red marble on the first draw. Explain your reasoning.

Since the jar now has a total of ☐ marbles and ☐ of them are yellow, $P(Y|R) = \frac{☐}{☐}$.

Reflect

1. In one case you replaced the first marble before drawing the second, and in the other case you didn't. For which case was $P(Y|R)$ equal to $P(Y)$? Why?

2. In which of the two cases would you say the events of getting a red marble on the first draw and getting a yellow marble on the second draw are independent? What is true about $P(Y|R)$ and $P(Y)$ in this case?

Explain 1 Determining if Events are Independent

To determine the independence of two events A and B, you can check to see whether $P(A|B) = P(A)$ since the occurrence of event A is unaffected by the occurrence of event B if and only if the events are independent.

Example 1 **The two-way frequency table gives data about 180 randomly selected flights that arrive at an airport. Use the table to answer the question.**

	Late Arrival	On Time	Total
Domestic Flights	12	108	120
International Flights	6	54	60
Total	18	162	180

(A) Is the event that a flight is on time independent of the event that a flight is domestic?

Let O be the event that a flight is on time. Let D be the event that a flight is domestic. Find $P(O)$ and $P(O|D)$. To find $P(O)$, note that the total number of flights is 180, and of those flights, there are 162 on-time flights. So, $P(O) = \frac{162}{180} = 90\%$.

To find $P(O|D)$, note that there are 120 domestic flights, and of those flights, there are 108 on-time flights. So, $P(O|D), = \frac{108}{120} = 90\%$.

Since $P(O|D) = P(O)$, the event that a flight is on time is independent of the event that a flight is domestic.

(B) Is the event that a flight is international independent of the event that a flight arrives late?

Let I be the event that a flight is international. Let L be the event that a flight arrives late. Find $P(I)$ and $P(I|L)$. To find $P(I)$, note that the total number of flights is 180, and of those flights, there are 60 international flights. So, $P(I) = \frac{60}{180} = 33\frac{1}{3}\%$.

To find $P(I|L)$, note that there are 18 flights that arrive late, and of those flights, there are 6 international flights. So, $P(I|L) = \frac{6}{18} = 33\frac{1}{3}\%$.

Since $P(I|L) = P(I)$, the event that a flight is international is independent of the event that a flight arrives late.

Your Turn

The two-way frequency table gives data about 200 randomly selected apartments in a city. Use the table to answer the question.

	1 Bedroom	2+ Bedrooms	Total
Single Occupant	64	12	76
Multiple Occupants	26	98	124
Total	90	110	200

3. Is the event that an apartment has a single occupant independent of the event that an apartment has 1 bedroom?

4. Is the event that an apartment has 2 or more bedrooms independent of the event that an apartment has multiple occupants?

Explain 2 Finding the Probability of Independent Events

From the definition of conditional probability you know that $P(A|B) = \frac{P(A \cap B)}{P(B)}$ for any events A and B. If those events happen to be independent, you can replace $P(A|B)$ with $P(A)$ and get $P(A) = \frac{P(A \cap B)}{P(B)}$. Solving the last equation for $P(A \cap B)$ gives the following result.

Probability of Independent Events

Events A and B are independent if and only if $P(A \cap B) = P(A) \cdot P(B)$.

Example 2 **Find the specified probability.**

(A) Recall the jar with 15 red marbles and 17 yellow marbles from the Explore. Suppose you randomly draw one marble from the jar. After you put that marble back in the jar, you randomly draw a second marble. What is the probability that you draw a yellow marble first and a red marble second?

Let Y be the event of drawing a yellow marble first. Let R be the event of drawing a red marble second. Then $P(Y) = \frac{17}{32}$ and, because the first marble drawn is replaced before the second marble is drawn, $P(R|Y) = P(R) = \frac{15}{32}$. Since the events are independent, you can multiply their probabilities: $P(Y \cap R) = P(Y) \cdot P(R) = \frac{17}{32} \cdot \frac{15}{32} = \frac{255}{1024} \approx 25\%$.

(B) You spin the spinner shown two times. What is the probability that the spinner stops on an even number on the first spin, followed by an odd number on the second spin?

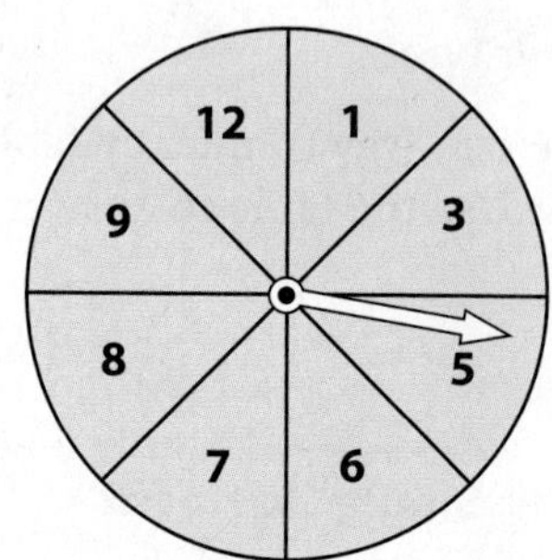

Let E be the event of getting an even number on the first spin. Let O be the event of getting an odd

number on the second spin. Then $P(E) = \frac{3}{8}$ and, because the first spin has no effect on the second spin, $P(O|E) = P(O) = \frac{5}{8}$. Since the events are independent, you can multiply their probabilities:

$P(E \cap O) = P(E) \cdot P(O) = \frac{3}{8} \cdot \frac{5}{8} = \frac{15}{64} \approx 23\%$.

Reflect

5. In Part B, what is the probability that the spinner stops on an odd number on the first spin, followed by an even number on the second spin? What do you observe? What does this tell you?

Your Turn

6. You spin a spinner with 4 red sections, 3 blue sections, 2 green sections, and 1 yellow section. If all the sections are of equal size, what is the probability that the spinner stops on green first and blue second?

7. A number cube has the numbers 3, 5, 6, 8, 10, and 12 on its faces. You roll the number cube twice. What is the probability that you roll an odd number on both rolls?

Explain 3 Showing That Events Are Independent

So far, you have used the formula $P(A \cap B) = P(A) \cdot P(B)$ when you knew that events A and B are independent. You can also use the formula to determine whether two events are independent.

Example 3 **Determine if the events are independent.**

(A) The two-way frequency table shows data for 120 randomly selected patients who have the same doctor. Determine whether a patient who takes vitamins and a patient who exercises regularly are independent events.

	Takes Vitamins	No Vitamins	Total
Regular Exercise	48	28	76
No regular Exercise	12	32	44
Total	60	60	120

Let V be the event that a patient takes vitamins. Let E be the event that a patient exercises regularly.

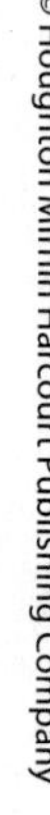

Step 1 Find $P(V)$, $P(E)$, and $P(V \cap E)$. The total number of patients is 120.

There are 60 patients who take vitamins, so $P(V) = \frac{60}{120} = \frac{1}{2}$.

There are 76 patients who exercise regularly, so $P(B) = \frac{76}{120} = \frac{19}{30}$.

There are 48 patients who take vitamins and exercise regularly, so $P(V \cap E) = \frac{48}{120} = 40\%$.

Step 2 Compare $P(V \cap E)$ and $P(V) \cdot P(E)$.

$P(V) \cdot P(E) = \frac{1}{2} \cdot \frac{19}{30} = \frac{19}{60} \approx 32\%$

Because $P(V \cap E) \neq P(V) \cdot P(E)$, the events are not independent.

(B) The two-way frequency table shows data for 60 randomly selected children at an elementary school. Determine whether a child who knows how to ride a bike and a child who knows how to swim are independent events.

	Knows how to Ride a Bike	**Doesn't Know how to Ride a Bike**	**Total**
Knows how to Swim	30	10	40
Doesn't Know how to Swim	15	5	20
Total	45	15	60

Let B be the event a child knows how to ride a bike. Let S be the event that a child knows how to swim.

Step 1 Find $P(B)$, $P(S)$, and $P(B \cap S)$. The total number of children is 60.

There are 45 children who know how to ride a bike, so $P(B) = \frac{\boxed{45}}{60} = \frac{\boxed{3}}{4}$.

There are 40 children who know how to swim, so $P(S) = \frac{\boxed{40}}{60} = \frac{\boxed{2}}{3}$.

There are 30 children who know how to ride a bike and swim, so $P(B \cap S) = \frac{\boxed{30}}{60} = \frac{\boxed{1}}{2}$.

Step 2 Compare $P(B \cap S)$ and $P(B) \cdot P(S)$.

$P(B) \cdot P(S) = \frac{\boxed{3}}{4} \cdot \frac{\boxed{2}}{3} = \frac{\boxed{1}}{2}$

Because $P(B \cap S)$ $\boxed{=}$ $P(B) \cdot P(S)$, the events are independent.

Your Turn

8. A farmer wants to know if an insecticide is effective in preventing small insects called aphids from damaging tomato plants. The farmer experiments with 80 plants and records the results in the two-way frequency table. Determine whether a plant that was sprayed with insecticide and a plant that has aphids are independent events.

	Has Aphids	No Aphids	Total
Sprayed with Insecticide	12	40	52
Not Sprayed with Insecticide	14	14	28
Total	26	54	80

9. A student wants to know if right-handed people are more or less likely to play a musical instrument than left-handed people. The student collects data from 250 people, as shown in the two-way frequency table. Determine whether being right-handed and playing a musical instrument are independent events.

	Right-Handed	Left-Handed	Total
Plays a Musical Instrument	44	6	50
Does not Play a Musical Instrument	176	24	200
Total	220	30	250

Elaborate

10. What are the ways that you can show that two events A and B are independent?

11. How can you find the probability that two independent events A and B both occur?

12. **Essential Question Check-In** Give an example of two independent events and explain why they are independent.

Evaluate: Homework and Practice

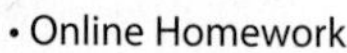

Personal Math Trainer

• Online Homework
• Hints and Help
• Extra Practice

1. A bag contains 12 red and 8 blue chips. Two chips are separately drawn at random from the bag.

   a. Suppose that a single chip is drawn at random from the bag. Find the probability that the chip is red and the probability that the chip is blue.

   b. Suppose that two chips are separately drawn at random from the bag and that the first chip is returned to the bag before the second chip is drawn. Find the probability that the second chip drawn is blue given the first chip drawn was red.

c. Suppose that two chips are separately drawn at random from the bag and that the first chip is not returned to the bag before the second chip is drawn. Find the probability that the second chip drawn is blue given the first chip drawn was red.

d. In which situation—the first chip is returned to the bag or not returned to the bag—are the events that the first chip is red and the second chip is blue independent? Explain.

2. Determine whether the events are independent or not independent.

a. Flip a coin twice and get tails both times.

b. Roll a number cube and get 1 on the first roll and 6 on the second.

c. Draw an ace from a shuffled deck, put the card back and reshuffle the deck, and then draw an 8.

d. Rotate a bingo cage and draw the ball labeled B-4, set it aside, and then rotate the cage again and draw the ball labled N-38.

Answer the question using the fact that $P(A|B) = P(A)$ only when events A and B are independent.

3. The two-way frequency table shows data for 80 randomly selected people who live in a metropolitan area. Is the event that a person prefers public transportation independent of the event that a person lives in the city?

	Prefers to Drive	Prefers Public Transportation	Total
Lives in the City	12	24	36
Lives in the Suburbs	33	11	44
Total	45	35	80

4. The two-way frequency table shows data for 120 randomly selected people who take vacations. Is the event that a person prefers vacationing out of state independent of the event that a person is a woman?

	Prefers Vacationing Out of State	Prefers Vacationing in State	Total
Men	48	32	80
Women	24	16	40
Total	72	48	120

A jar contains marbles of various colors as listed in the table. Suppose you randomly draw one marble from the jar. After you put that marble back in the jar, you randomly draw a second marble. Use this information to answer the question, giving a probability as a percent and rounding to the nearest tenth of percent when necessary.

Color of Marble	Number of Marbles
Red	20
Yellow	18
Green	12
Blue	10

5. What is the probability that you draw a blue marble first and a red marble second?

6. What is the probability that you draw a yellow marble first and a green marble second?

7. What is the probability that you draw a yellow marble both times?

8. What color marble for the first draw and what color marble for the second draw have the greatest probability of occurring together? What is that probability?

You spin the spinner shown two times. Each section of the spinner is the same size. Use this information to answer the question, giving a probability as a percent and rounding to the nearest tenth of a percent when necessary.

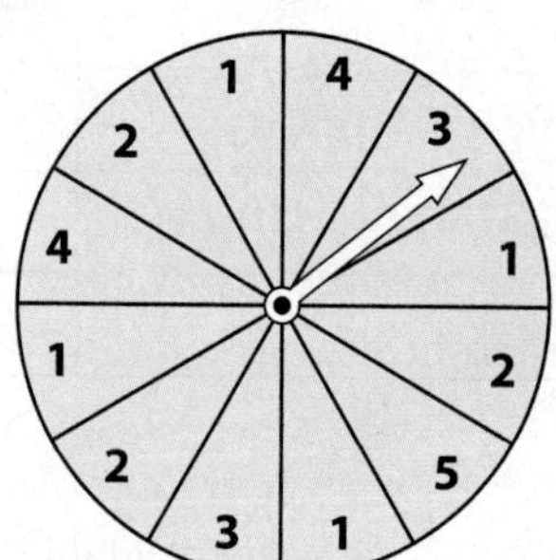

9. What is the probability that the spinner stops on 1 first and 2 second?

10. What is the probability that the spinner stops on 4 first and 3 second?

11. What is the probability that the spinner stops on an odd number first and an even number second?

12. What first number and what second number have the least probability of occurring together? What is that probability?

13. Find the probability of getting heads on every toss of a coin when the coin is tossed 3 times.

14. You are randomly choosing cards, one at a time and with replacement, from a standard deck of cards. Find the probability that you choose an ace, then a red card, and then a face card. (Remember that face cards are jacks, queens, and kings.)

Determine whether the given events are independent using the fact that $P(A \cap B) = P(A) \cdot P(B)$ only when events A and B are independent.

15. The manager of a produce stand wants to find out whether there is a connection between people who buy fresh vegetables and people who buy fresh fruit. The manager collects data on 200 randomly chosen shoppers, as shown in the two-way frequency table. Determine whether buying fresh vegetables and buying fresh fruit are independent events.

	Bought Vegetables	No Vegetables	Total
Bought Fruit	56	20	76
No Fruit	49	75	124
Total	105	95	200

16. The owner of a bookstore collects data about the reading preferences of 60 randomly chosen customers, as shown in the two-way frequency table. Determine whether being a female and preferring fiction are independent events.

	Prefers Fiction	Prefers Nonfiction	Total
Female	15	10	25
Male	21	14	35
Total	36	24	60

17. The psychology department at a college collects data about whether there is a relationship between a student's intended career and the student's like or dislike for solving puzzles. The two-way frequency table shows the collected data for 80 randomly chosen students. Determine whether planning for a career in a field involving math or science and a like for solving puzzles are independent events.

	Plans a Career in a Math/Science Field	Plans a Career in a Non-Math/Science Field	Total
Likes Solving Puzzles	35	15	50
Dislikes Solving Puzzles	9	21	30
Total	44	36	80

18. A local television station surveys some of its viewers to determine the primary reason they watch the station. The two-way frequency table gives the survey data. Determine whether a viewer is a man and a viewer primarily watches the station for entertainment are independent events.

	Primarily Watches for Information (News, Weather, Sports)	Primarily Watches for Entertainment (Comedies, Dramas)	Total
Men	28	12	40
Women	35	15	50
Total	63	27	90

19. Copy and complete the two-way frequency table in such a way that any event from a column will be independent of any event from a row. Give an example using the table to demonstrate the independence of two events.

	Women	Men	Total
Prefers Writing with a Pen	▒	▒	100
Prefers Writing with a Pencil	▒	▒	50
Total	60	90	150

H.O.T. Focus on Higher Order Thinking

20. Make a Prediction A box contains 100 balloons. The balloons come in two colors: 80 are yellow and 20 are green. The balloons are also either marked or unmarked: 50 are marked "Happy Birthday!" and 50 are not. A balloon is randomly chosen from the box. How many yellow "Happy Birthday!" balloons must be in the box if the event that a balloon is yellow and the event that a balloon is marked "Happy Birthday!" are independent? Explain.

21. Construct Arguments Given that events A and B are independent, prove that the complement of event A, A^c, is also independent of event B.

22. Multi-Step The two-way frequency table shows two events, A and B, and their complements, A^c and B^c. Let $P(A) = a$ and $P(B) = b$. Using a, b, and the grand total T, form the products listed in the table to find the number of elements in $A \cap B$, $A \cap B^c$, $A^c \cap B$, and $A^c \cap B^c$.

	A	**A^c**	**Total**
B	abT	$(1-a)bT$	
B^c	$a(1-b)T$	$(1-a)(1-b)T$	
Total			T

a. Copy and complete the table, showing the table's missing row and column totals in simplest form.

b. Show that events A and B are independent using the fact that $P(A \mid B) = P(A)$ only when events A and B are independent.

c. Show that events A and B^c are independent.

d. Show that events A^c and B are independent.

e. Show that events A^c and B^c are independent.

Lesson Performance Task

Before the mid-1800s, little was known about the way that plants pass along characteristics such as color and height to their offspring. From painstaking observations of garden peas, the Austrian monk Gregor Mendel discovered the basic laws of heredity. The table shows the results of three of Mendel's experiments. In each experiment, he looked at a particular characteristic of garden peas by planting seeds exclusively of one type.

Characteristic	Type Planted	Results in Second Generation
Flower color	100% violet	705 violet, 224 white
Seed texture	100% round	5474 round, 1850 wrinkled
Seed color	100% yellow	6022 yellow, 2011 green

1. Suppose you plant garden peas with violet flowers and round, yellow seeds. Estimate the probability of obtaining second-generation plants with violet flowers, the probability of obtaining second-generation plants with round seeds, and the probability of obtaining second-generation plants with yellow seeds. Explain how you made your estimates.

Mendel saw that certain traits, such as violet flowers and round seeds, seemed stronger than others, such white flowers and wrinkled seeds. He called the stronger traits "dominant" and the weaker traits "recessive." Both traits can be carried in the genes of a plant, because a gene consists of two *alleles*, one received from the mother and one from the father. (For plants, the "father" is the plant from which the pollen comes, and the "mother" is the plant whose pistil receives the pollen.) When at least one of the alleles has the dominant trait, the plant exhibits the dominant trait. Only when both alleles have the recessive trait does the plant exhibit the recessive trait.

You can use a 2 × 2 Punnett square, like the one shown, to see the results of crossing the genes of two parent plants. In this Punnett square, *V* represents the dominant flower color violet and *v* represents the recessive flower color white. If each parent's genes contain both *V* and *v* alleles, the offspring may receive, independently and with equal probability, either a *V* allele or a *v* allele from each parent.

	V	v
V	VV	Vv
v	vV	vv

2. After planting a first generation of plants exhibiting only dominant traits, Mendel observed that the second generation consisted of plants with a ratio of about 3:1 dominant-to-recessive traits. Does the Punnett square support or refute Mendel's observation? Explain.

3. Draw a 4 × 4 Punnett square for finding the results of crossing two violet-flower-and-round-seed parent plants. Let *V* and *R* represent the dominant traits violet flowers and round seeds, respectively. Let *v* and *r* represent the recessive traits white flowers and wrinkled seeds, respectively. Each column heading and row heading of your Punnett square should contain a two-letter combination of *V* or *v* and *R* or *r*. Each cell of your Punnett square will then contain four letters. Use the Punnett square to find the probability that a second-generation plant will have white flowers and round seeds. Explain your reasoning.

23.3 Dependent Events

Essential Question: How do you find the probability of dependent events?

Resource Locker

Explore Finding a Way to Calculate the Probability of Dependent Events

You know two tests for the independence of events A and B:

1. If $P(A|B) = P(A)$, then A and B are independent.
2. If $P(A \cap B) = P(A) \cdot P(B)$, then A and B are independent.

Two events that fail either of these tests are **dependent events** because the occurrence of one event affects the occurrence of the other event.

(A) The two-way frequency table shows the results of a survey of 100 people who regularly walk for exercise. Let O be the event that a person prefers walking outdoors. Let M be the event that a person is male. Find $P(O)$, $P(M)$, and $P(O \cap M)$ as fractions. Then determine whether events O and M are independent or dependent.

	Prefers walking outdoors	Prefers walking on a treadmill	Total
Male	40	10	50
Female	20	30	50
Total	60	40	100

(B) Calculate the conditional probabilities $P(O|M)$ and $P(M|O)$.

$$P(O|M) = \frac{n(O \cap M)}{n(M)} = \frac{\square}{\square} = \frac{\square}{5}$$

$$P(M|O) = \frac{n(O \cap M)}{n(O)} = \frac{\square}{\square} = \frac{\square}{3}$$

(C) Copy and complete the multiplication table using the fractions for $P(O)$ and $P(M)$ from Step A and the fractions for $P(O|M)$ and $P(M|O)$ from Step B.

×	$P(O)$	$P(M)$
$P(O\|M)$		
$P(M\|O)$		

(D) Do any of the four products in Step C equal $P(O \cap M)$, calculated in Step A? If so, which of the four products?

Reflect

1. In a previous lesson you learned the conditional probability formula $P(B|A) = \frac{P(A \cap B)}{P(A)}$. How does this formula explain the results you obtained in Step D?

2. Let F be the event that a person is female. Let T be the event that a person prefers walking on a treadmill. Write two formulas you can use to calculate $P(F \cap T)$. Use either one to find the value of $P(F \cap T)$, and then confirm the result by finding $P(F \cap T)$ directly from the two-way frequency table.

Explain 1 Finding the Probability of Two Dependent Events

You can use the Multiplication Rule to find the probability of dependent events.

Multiplication Rule

$P(A \cap B) = P(A) \cdot P(B|A)$ where $P(B|A)$ is the conditional probability of event B, given that event A has occurred.

Example 1 **There are 5 tiles with the letters A, B, C, D, and E in a bag. You choose a tile without looking, put it aside, and then choose another tile without looking. Use the Multiplication Rule to find the specified probability, writing it as a fraction.**

(A) Find the probability that you choose a vowel followed by a consonant.

Let V be the event that the first tile is a vowel. Let C be the event that the second tile is a consonant. Of the 5 tiles, there are 2 vowels, so $P(V) = \frac{2}{5}$.

Of the 4 remaining tiles, there are 3 consonants, so $P(C|V) = \frac{3}{4}$.

By the Multiplication Rule, $P(V \cap C) = P(V) \cdot P(V|C) = \frac{2}{5} \cdot \frac{3}{4} = \frac{6}{20} = \frac{3}{10}$.

(B) Find the probability that you choose a vowel followed by another vowel.

Let $V1$ be the event that the first tile is a vowel. Let $V2$ be the event that the second tile is also a vowel. Of the 5 tiles, there are 2 vowels, so $P(V1) = \frac{2}{5}$.

Of the 4 remaining tiles, there is 1 vowel, so $P(V2|V1) = \frac{1}{4}$.

By the Multiplication Rule, $P(V1 \cap V2) = P(V1) \cdot P(V2|V1) = \frac{2}{5} \cdot \frac{1}{4} = \frac{2}{20} = \frac{1}{10}$.

Your Turn

A bag holds 4 white marbles and 2 blue marbles. You choose a marble without looking, put it aside, and choose another marble without looking. Use the Multiplication Rule to find the specified probability, writing it as a fraction.

3. Find the probability that you choose a white marble followed by a blue marble.

4. Find the probability that you choose a white marble followed by another white marble.

Explain 2 Finding the Probability of Three or More Dependent Events

You can extend the Multiplication Rule to three or more events. For instance, for three events A, B, and C, the rule becomes $P(A \cap B \cap C) = P(A) \cdot P(B|A) \cdot P(C|A \cap B)$.

Example 2 **You have a key ring with 7 different keys. You're attempting to unlock a door in the dark, so you try keys one at a time and keep track of which ones you try.**

(A) Find the probability that the third key you try is the right one.

Let $W1$ be the event that the first key you try is wrong. Let $W2$ be the event that the second key you try is also wrong. Let R be the event that the third key you try is right.

On the first try, there are 6 wrong keys among the 7 keys, so $P(W1) = \frac{6}{7}$.

On the second try, there are 5 wrong keys among the 6 remaining keys, so $P(W2|W1) = \frac{5}{6}$.

On the third try, there is 1 right key among the 5 remaining keys, so $P(R|W2 \cap W1) = \frac{1}{5}$.

By the Multiplication Rule, $P(W1 \cap W2 \cap R) = P(W1) \cdot P(W2|W1) \cdot P(R|W1 \cap W2) = \frac{6}{7} \cdot \frac{5}{6} \cdot \frac{1}{5} = \frac{1}{7}$.

(B) Find the probability that one of the first three keys you try is right.

There are two ways to approach this problem:

1. You can break the problem into three cases: (1) the first key you try is right; (2) the first key is wrong, but the second key is right; and (3) the first two keys are wrong, but the third key is right.

2. You can use the complement: The complement of the event that one of the first three keys is right is the event that *none* of the first three keys is right.

Use the second approach.

Let $W1$, $W2$, and $W3$ be the events that the first, second, and third keys, respectively, are wrong.

From Part A, you already know that $P(W1) = \frac{\boxed{6}}{7}$ and $P(W2|W1) = \frac{\boxed{5}}{6}$.

On the third try, there are 4 wrong keys among the 5 remaining keys, so $P(W3|W2 \cap W1) = \frac{\boxed{4}}{5}$.

By the Multiplication Rule,

$$P(W1 \cap W2 \cap W3) = P(W1) \cdot P(W2|W1) \cdot P(W3|W1 \cap W2) = \frac{\boxed{6}}{7} \cdot \frac{\boxed{5}}{6} \cdot \frac{\boxed{4}}{5} = \frac{\boxed{4}}{\boxed{7}}$$

The event $W1 \cap W2 \cap W3$ is the complement of the one you want. So, the probability that one of the first three keys you try is right is $1 - P(W1 \cap W2 \cap W3) = 1 - \frac{\boxed{4}}{\boxed{7}} = \frac{\boxed{3}}{\boxed{7}}$.

Reflect

5. In Part B, show that the first approach to solving the problem gives the same result.

6. In Part A, suppose you don't keep track of the keys as you try them. How does the probability change? Explain.

Your Turn

Three people are standing in line at a car rental agency at an airport. Each person is willing to take whatever rental car is offered. The agency has 4 white cars and 2 silver ones available and offers them to customers on a random basis.

7. Find the probability that all three customers get white cars.

8. Find the probability that two of the customers get the silver cars and one gets a white car.

Elaborate

9. When are two events dependent?

10. Suppose you are given a bag with 3 blue marbles and 2 red marbles, and you are asked to find the probability of drawing 2 blue marbles by drawing one marble at a time and not replacing the first marble drawn. Why does not replacing the first marble make these events dependent? What would make these events independent? Explain.

11. **Essential Question Check-In** According to the Multiplication Rule, when finding $P(A \cap B)$ for dependent events A and B, you multiply $P(A)$ by what?

Evaluate: Homework and Practice

- Online Homework
- Hints and Help
- Extra Practice

1. Town officials are considering a property tax increase to finance the building of a new school. The two-way frequency table shows the results of a survey of 110 town residents.

	Supports a property tax increase	Does not support a property tax increase	Total
Lives in a household with children	50	20	70
Lives in a household without children	10	30	40
Total	60	50	110

a. Let C be the event that a person lives in a household with children. Let S be the event that a person supports a property tax increase. Are the events C and S independent or dependent? Explain.

b. Find $P(C|S)$ and $P(S|C)$. Which of these two conditional probabilities can you multiply with $P(C)$ to get $P(C \cap S)$? Which of the two can you multiply with $P(S)$ to get $P(C \cap S)$?

2. A mall surveyed 120 shoppers to find out whether they typically wait for a sale to get a better price or make purchases on the spur of the moment regardless of price. The two-way frequency table shows the results of the survey.

	Waits for a Sale	Buys on Impulse	Total
Woman	40	10	50
Man	50	20	70
Total	90	30	120

a. Let W be the event that a shopper is a woman. Let S be the event that a shopper typically waits for a sale. Are the events W and S independent or dependent? Explain.

b. Find $P(W|S)$ and $P(S|W)$. Which of these two conditional probabilities can you multiply with $P(W)$ to get $P(W \cap S)$? Which of the two can you multiply with $P(S)$ to get $P(W \cap S)$?

There are 4 green, 10 red, and 6 yellow marbles in a bag. Each time you randomly choose a marble, you put it aside before choosing another marble at random. Use the Multiplication Rule to find the specified probability, writing it as a fraction.

3. Find the probability that you choose a red marble followed by a yellow marble.

4. Find the probabilty that you choose one yellow marble followed by another yellow marble.

5. Find the probability that you choose a red marble, followed by a yellow marble, followed by a green marble.

6. Find the probability that you choose three red marbles.

The table shows the sums that are possible when you roll two number cubes and add the numbers. Use this information to answer the questions.

+	1	2	3	4	5	6
1	2	3	4	5	6	7
2	3	4	5	6	7	8
3	4	5	6	7	8	9
4	5	6	7	8	9	10
5	6	7	8	9	10	11
6	7	8	9	10	11	12

7. Let A be the event that you roll a 2 on the number cubes represented by the row labeled 2. Let B be the event that the sum of the numbers on the cubes is 7.

a. Are these events independent or dependent? Explain.

b. What is $P(A \cap B)$?

8. Let A be the event that you roll a 3 on the number cubes represented by the row labeled 3. Let B be the event that the sum of the numbers on the cubes is 5.

a. Are these events independent or dependent? Explain.

b. What is $P(A \cap B)$?

9. A cooler contains 6 bottles of apple juice and 8 bottles of grape juice. You choose a bottle without looking, put it aside, and then choose another bottle without looking. Match each situation with its probability. More than one situation can have the same probability.

A. Choose apple juice and then grape juice. **a.** ___?___ $\frac{4}{13}$

B. Choose apple juice and then apple juice. **b.** ___?___ $\frac{24}{91}$

C. Choose grape juice and then apple juice. **c.** ___?___ $\frac{15}{91}$

D. Choose grape juice and then grape juice.

10. Jorge plays all tracks on a playlist with no repeats. The playlist he's listening to has 12 songs, 4 of which are his favorites.

a. What is the probability that the first song played is one of his favorites, but the next two songs are not?

b. What is the probability that the first three songs played are all his favorites?

c. Jorge can also play the tracks on his playlist in a random order with repeats possible. If he does this, how does your answer to part b change? Explain why.

11. You are playing a game of bingo with friends. In this game, balls are labeled with one of the letters of the word BINGO and a number. Some of these letter-number combinations are written on a bingo card in a 5×5 array, and as balls are randomly drawn and announced, players mark their cards if the ball's letter-number combination appears on the cards. The first player to complete a row, column, or diagonal on a card says "Bingo!" and wins the game. In the game you're playing, there are 20 balls left. To complete a row on your card, you need N-32 called. To complete a column, you need G-51 called. To complete a diagonal, you need B-6 called.

a. What is the probability that the next two balls drawn do not have a letter-number combination you need, but the third ball does?

b. What is the probability that none of the letter-number combinations you need is called from the next three balls?

H.O.T. Focus on Higher Order Thinking

12. You are talking with 3 friends, and the conversation turns to birthdays.

a. What is the probability that no two people in your group were born in the same month?

b. Is the probability that at least two people in your group were born in the same month greater or less than $\frac{1}{2}$? Explain.

c. How many people in a group would it take for the probability that at least two people were born in the same month to be greater than $\frac{1}{2}$? Explain.

13. Construct Arguments Show how to extend the Multiplication Rule to three events *A*, *B*, and *C*.

14. Make a Prediction A bag contains the same number of red marbles and blue marbles. You choose a marble without looking, put it aside, and then choose another marble. Is there a greater-than-50% chance or a less-than-50% chance that you choose two marbles with different colors? Explain.

Lesson Performance Task

To prepare for an accuracy landing competition, a team of skydivers has laid out targets in a large open field. During practice sessions, team members attempt to land inside a target.

Two rectangular targets are shown on each field. Assuming a skydiver lands at random in the field, find the probabilities that the skydiver lands inside the specified target(s).

1. Calculate the probabilities using the targets shown here.

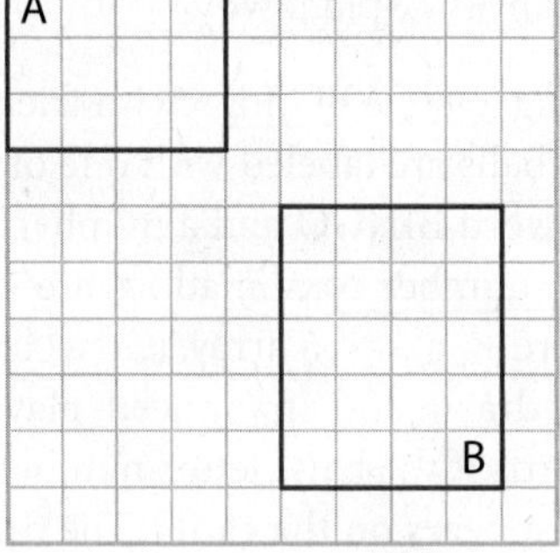

a. $P(A)$
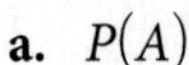

b. $P(B)$

c. $P(A \cap B)$

d. $P(A \cup B)$

e. $P(A|B)$

f. $P(B|A)$

2. Calculate the probabilities using the targets shown here.

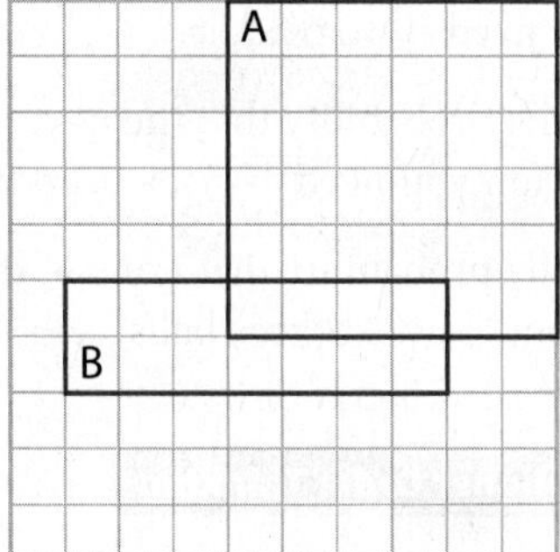

a. $P(A)$

b. $P(B)$

c. $P(A \cap B)$

d. $P(A \cup B)$

e. $P(A|B)$

f. $P(B|A)$

3. Calculate the probabilities using the targets shown here.

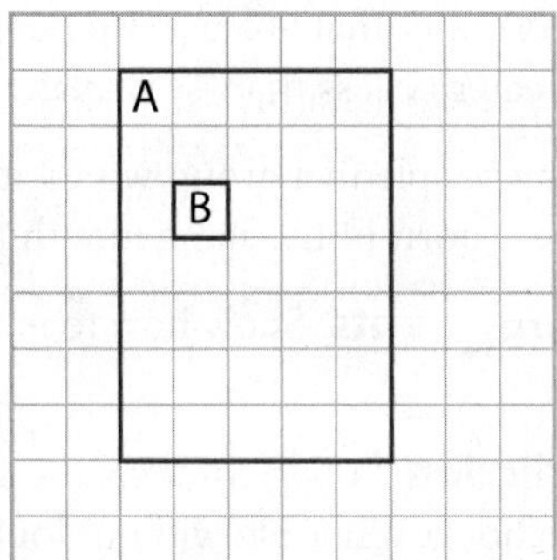

a. $P(A)$

b. $P(B)$

c. $P(A \cap B)$

d. $P(A \cup B)$

e. $P(A|B)$

f. $P(B|A)$

STUDY GUIDE REVIEW

Conditional Probability and Independence of Events

MODULE 23

Essential Question: How can you use conditional probability and independence of events to solve real-world problems?

Key Vocabulary
conditional probability *(probabilidad condicional)*
independent events *(eventos independientes)*
dependent events *(eventos dependientes)*

KEY EXAMPLE *(Lesson 23.1)*

Find the probability that a black card drawn from the deck is a queen. (The deck is a standard one of 52 cards.)

The deck has 52 cards and 26 of them are black, so the probability of drawing a black card is $P(B) = \frac{26}{52}$.

There are 2 black queens in the deck, so the probability of drawing one of them from the deck is $P(Q \cap B) = \frac{2}{52} = \frac{1}{26}$.

Using the formula for conditional probability, $P(Q \mid B) = \frac{P(Q \cap B)}{P(B)} = \frac{\frac{2}{52}}{\frac{26}{52}} = \frac{1}{13}$.

KEY EXAMPLE *(Lesson 23.2)*

Jim rolled a set of two number cubes. If these are standard 6-sided number cubes, what is the probability of obtaining 12? (That means the values of the top faces add up to 12.)

The only way to get 12 is for both of the top sides of the number cubes to be 6. The events of obtaining 6s are independent. Each of these events has the probability of $\frac{1}{6}$ (1 out of 6 options), so the probability of getting 12 is $\frac{1}{6} \cdot \frac{1}{6} = \frac{1}{36}$ by the multiplication rule.

KEY EXAMPLE *(Lesson 23.3)*

What is the probability of selecting 2 blue marbles out of a jar of 20, half of them blue? How did you obtain it?

Let event A be selecting a blue marble on the first pick. Let event B be selecting a blue marble on the second one. The first marble is not replaced, so these are dependent events. Of the 20 marbles, half of them are blue, so $P(A) = \frac{1}{2}$. Of the remaining 19 marbles, 9 of them are blue, so the probability of selecting one is $P(B) = \frac{9}{19}$. Thus, the probability of selecting 2 blue marbles is $P(A \text{ and } B) = \frac{1}{2} \cdot \frac{9}{19} = \frac{9}{38}$, using the multiplication rule.

Exercises

Determine the conditional probability. *(Lesson 23.1)*

1. What is the probability that a diamond that is drawn from the deck is a queen?

2. What is the probability that a queen drawn is a diamond?

Show that the following situation refers to independent events. *(Lesson 23.2)*

3. Isabelle believes that right- and left-footed soccer players are equally likely to score goals. She collected data from 260 players from a local soccer league. Using the following two-way frequency table, show that being right-footed and scoring goals are independent events.

	Right-Footed	Left-Footed	Total
Has scored a goal	39	13	52
Has not scored a goal	156	52	208
TOTAL	195	65	260

Identify whether a situation involves independent or dependent events. *(Lesson 23.3)*

4. Jim has 2 blue, 2 green, and 2 black socks in his drawer. He picks out 2 socks, one after the other.

MODULE PERFORMANCE TASK

Drawing Aces

You have a standard deck of 52 playing cards. You pick three cards in a row without replacement. What is the probability that all three are aces?

Now you replace the three cards, shuffle, and pick four cards in a row without replacement. What is the probability that none are aces?

Begin by making notes about your plan for approaching this problem. Then complete the task, using words, numbers, or diagrams to explain how you reached your conclusions.

23.1–23.3 Conditional Probability and Independence of Events

- Online Homework
- Hints and Help
- Extra Practice

Compute the requested probability and explain how you obtained it.

1. A farmer wants to know if a particular fertilizer can cause blackberry shrubs to produce fruit early. Using the following two-way table, compute the probability of a plant producing fruit early without receiving fertilizer. *(Lesson 23.1)*

	Early Fruit	No Fruit	Total
Received fertilizer	37	3	40
Did not receive fertilizer	19	21	40
TOTAL	56	24	80

2. Lisa flipped the same coin twice. Determine the probability of the coin landing on tails on the second try. *(Lesson 23.2)*

3. Lisa flipped the same coin three times. What is the probability she obtained all tails? *(Lesson 23.2)*

ESSENTIAL QUESTION

4. A jar contains 12 pennies, 5 nickels, and 18 quarters. You select 2 coins at random, one after the other. Does selecting a nickel affect the probability of selecting another nickel? Does not selecting a dime affect the probability of selecting a nickel? Describe how you would find the probability of selecting 2 nickels.

MODULE 23
MIXED REVIEW

Assessment Readiness

1. Are the events independent? Determine if each statement is True or False.
   A. Picking a penny and a marble out of a jar of pennies and marbles.
   B. Drawing cards from a deck to form a 4-card hand.
   C. Choosing a color for a new shirt from a choice of red, yellow, or purple

2. Of the boys running for School President, 2 are juniors and 3 are seniors. Of the girls who are running, 4 are juniors and 1 is a senior. Decide whether the situation has a probability of $\frac{2}{5}$. Write Yes or No for A–C.
   A. A girl wins.
   B. A candidate who is a boy is a junior.
   C. A candidate who is a junior is a boy.

3. You shuffle a standard deck of playing cards and deal one card. What is the probability that you deal an ace or a club? Explain your reasoning.

4. Claude has 2 jars of marbles. Each jar has 10 blue marbles and 10 green marbles. He selects 2 marbles from each jar. What is the probability they are all blue? Explain your reasoning.

MODULE 24

Probability and Decision Making

Essential Question: How can you use probability to solve real-world problems?

REAL WORLD VIDEO
Physicians today use many sophisticated tests and technologies to help diagnose illnesses, but they must still consider probability in their diagnoses and decisions about treatment.

MODULE PERFORMANCE TASK PREVIEW

What's the Diagnosis?

The science of medicine has come a long way since surgeries were performed by the neighborhood barber and leeches were used to treat just about every ailment. Nevertheless, modern medicine isn't perfect, and widely used tests for diagnosing illnesses aren't always 100 percent accurate. In this module, you'll learn how probability can be used to measure the reliability of tests and then use what you learned to evaluate decisions about a diagnosis.

Are YOU Ready?

Complete these exercises to review skills you will need for this module.

- Online Homework
- Hints and Help
- Extra Practice

Probability of Simple Events

Example 1 Two 6-sided conventional number cubes are tossed. What is the probability that their sum is greater than 8?

+	1	2	3	4	5	6
1	2	3	4	5	6	7
2	3	4	5	6	7	8
3	4	5	6	7	8	9
4	5	6	7	8	9	10
5	6	7	8	9	10	11
6	7	8	9	10	11	12

There are 10 values greater than 8 and a total number of 36 values.

$$\frac{\text{number of favorable outcomes}}{\text{total number of outcomes}} = \frac{10}{36} = \frac{5}{18}$$

The probability that the sum of the two number cubes is greater than 8 is $\frac{5}{18}$.

Two number cubes are tossed. Find each probability.

1. The sum is prime.

2. The product is prime.

3. The product is a perfect square.

Making Predictions with Probability

Example 2 A fly lands on the target shown. What is the probability that the fly landed on red?

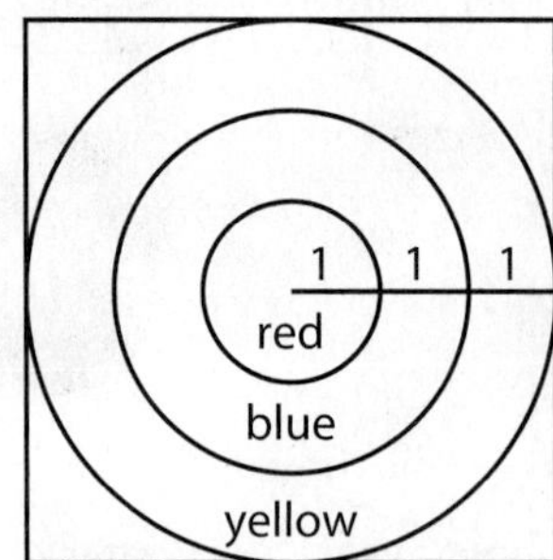

The area of the entire target is 6^2, or 36 units^2.

Red area is: $A = \pi r^2 = \pi(1)^2 = \pi$.

$$\frac{\text{number of favorable outcomes}}{\text{total number of outcomes}} = \frac{\pi}{36} \approx 8.7\%$$

Use the target to find the percent probability, to the nearest tenth.

4. Blue

5. Yellow or red

6. Not within a circle

24.1 Using Probability to Make Fair Decisions

Resource Locker

Essential Question: How can you use probability to help you make fair decisions?

Explore Using Probabilities When Drawing at Random

You are sharing a veggie supreme pizza with friends. There is one slice left and you and a friend both want it. Both of you have already had two slices. What is a fair way to solve this problem?

Ⓐ Suppose you both decide to have the same amount of pizza. This means that the last slice will be cut into two pieces. Describe a fair way to split this last piece.

Ⓑ Suppose instead you decide that one of you will get the whole slice. Copy and complete the table so that the result of each option gives a fair chance for each of you to get the last slice. Why do each of these possibilities give a fair chance?

Option	Result (you get last slice)	Result (friend gets last slice)
Flip a coin	Heads	
Roll a standard die		1, 3, 5
Play Rock, Paper, Scissors	You win.	You ___.
Draw lots using two straws of different lengths		Short straw

Reflect

1. Suppose, when down to the last piece, you tell your friend, "I will cut the last piece, and I will choose which piece you get." Why is this method unfair?

2. Your friend suggests that you shoot free throws to decide who gets the last piece. Use probability to explain why this might not be a fair way to decide.

Explain 1 Awarding a Prize to a Random Winner

Suppose you have to decide how to award a prize to a person at an event. You might want every person attending to have the same chance of winning, or you might want people to do something to improve their chance of winning. How can you award the prize fairly?

Example 1 **Explain whether each method of awarding a prize is fair.**

(A) The sponsor of an event wants to award a door prize to one attendee. Each person in attendance is given a ticket with a unique number on it. All of the numbers are placed in a bowl, and one is drawn at random. The person with the matching number wins the prize.

The method of awarding a door prize is fair. Each number has the same chance of being chosen, so each attendee has an equal probability of winning the prize. If n attendees are at the event, then the probability of winning the prize is $\frac{1}{n}$ for each attendee.

(B) A fundraiser includes a raffle in which half of the money collected goes to a charity, and the other half goes to one winner. Tickets are sold for $5 each. Copies of all the tickets are placed in a box, and one ticket is drawn at random. The person with the matching ticket wins the raffle.

The method of choosing a raffle winner is fair because each ticket has an equal probability of being drawn.

Reflect

3. In Example 1B, the probability may not be the same for each person to win the raffle. Explain why the method is still fair.

Your Turn

4. Each month, a company wants to award a special parking space to an employee at random. Describe a fair way to do this. Include a way to ensure that a person doesn't win a second time before each employee has won once.

Explain 2 Solving Real-World Problems Fairly

You can use a random number generator to choose a winner of a prize.

Example 2 **Use a problem solving plan.**

A class of 24 students sold 65 magazine subscriptions to raise money for a trip. As an incentive to participate, you will award a prize to one student in the class. Describe a method of awarding the prize fairly. Use probabilities to explain why your method is fair for the students listed.

Student	Subscriptions Sold
Miri	5
Liam	2
Madison	0

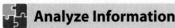

Analyze Information

Identify the important information.

- There are 24 students.
- They sold 65 magazine subscriptions.
- There is one prize, so there will be one winner.

Formulate a Plan

To be fair, students who sold more subscriptions should have a better chance of winning the prize than the students who sold fewer.

Find a method of assigning and choosing chances to win so that the chance of winning is proportional to the number of subscriptions sold.

Solve

The class sold 65 subscriptions, so assign the numbers 1–65 to the students. Each student gets as many numbers as the number of subscriptions he or she sold.

Student	Subscriptions Sold	Numbers Assigned	Probability of Winning
Miri	5	1–5	$\frac{5}{65} \approx$ 0.077
Liam	2	6, 7	$\frac{2}{65} \approx$ 0.031
Madison	0	none	$\frac{0}{65} =$ 0

Then use a calculator to find a random integer from 1 to 65. If the result is 7, then Liam wins the prize.

Justify and Evaluate

This method seems fair because it gives everyone who sold subscriptions a chance of winning. You could award a prize to the student who sold the most subscriptions, but this might not be possible if multiple students all sold the same number, and it might not seem fair if some students have better access to buyers than others.

Reflect

5. A student suggests that it would be better to assign the numbers to students randomly rather than in numerical order. Would doing this affect the probability of winning?

6. A charity is giving a movie ticket for every 10 coats donated. Jacob collected 8 coats, Ben collected 6, and Ryan and Zak each collected 3. They decide to donate the coats together so that they will get 2 movie tickets. Describe how to use a random number generator to decide which 2 boys get a ticket.

Explain 3 Solving the Problem of Points

The decision-making situation that you will apply in this example is based on the "Problem of Points" that was studied by the French mathematicians Blaise Pascal and Pierre de Fermat in the 17th century. Their work on the problem launched the branch of mathematics now known as probability.

Example 3 **Two students, Lee and Rory, find a box containing 100 baseball cards. To determine who should get the cards, they decide to play a game with the rules shown.**

Game Rules

- One of the students repeatedly tosses a coin.
- When the coin lands heads up, Lee gets a point.
- When the coin lands tails up, Rory gets a point.
- The first student to reach 20 points wins the game and gets the baseball cards.

As Lee and Rory are playing the game they are interrupted and are unable to continue. How should the 100 baseball cards be divided between the students given that the game was interrupted at the described moment?

(A) When they are interrupted, Lee has 19 points and Rory has 17 points.

At most, 3 coin tosses would have been needed for someone to win the game.

Make a list of all possible results using H for heads and T for tails. Box the outcomes in which Lee wins the game.

0T, 3H	1T, 2H	2T, 1H	3T, 0H
HHH	THH	TTH	TTT
	HTH	THT	
	HHT	HTT	

There are 8 possible results. Lee wins in 7 of them and Rory wins in 1 of them.

The probability of Lee winning is $\frac{7}{8}$, so he should get $\frac{7}{8}$ of the cards which is 87.5 cards. The probability of Rory winning is $\frac{1}{8}$, so he should get $\frac{1}{8}$ of the cards which is 12.5 cards. Rather than split a card into two, they might decide to flip a coin for that card or to let Lee have it because he was more likely to win it.

(B) When they are interrupted, Lee has 18 points and Rory has 17 points.

At most, four more coin tosses would have been needed.

List all possible results. Box the outcomes in which Lee wins.

0T, 4H	1T, 3H	2T, 2H	3T, 1H	4T, 0H
[HHHH]	[THHH]	[TTHH]	TTTH	TTTT
	[HTHH]	[THTH]	TTHT	
	[HHTH]	[THHT]	THTT	
	[HHHT]	[HTTH]	HTTT	
		[HTHT]		
		[HHTT]		

There are 16 possible results. Lee wins in 11 of them and Rory wins in 5 of them.

The probability of Lee winning is $\frac{11}{16}$, so he should get 69 cards.

The probability of Rory winning is $\frac{5}{16}$, so he should get 31 cards.

Reflect

7. **Discussion** A student suggests that a better way to divide the cards in Example 3B would be to split the cards based on the number of points earned so far. Which method do you think is better?

Your Turn

8. Describe a situation where the game is interrupted, resulting in the cards needing to be divided evenly between the two players.

Elaborate

9. **Discussion** In the situation described in the Explore, suppose you like the crust and your friend does not. Is there a fair way to cut the slice of pizza that might not result in two equal size pieces?

10. How would the solution to Example 2 need to change if there were two prizes to award? Assume that you do not want one student to win both prizes.

11. **Essential Question Check-In** Describe a way to use probability to make a fair choice of a raffle winner.

Evaluate: Homework and Practice

- Online Homework
- Hints and Help
- Extra Practice

1. You and a friend split the cost of a package of five passes to a climbing gym. Describe a way that you could fairly decide who gets to use the fifth pass.

2. In addition to prizes for first, second, and third place, the organizers of a race have a prize that they want each participant to have an equal chance of winning. Describe a fair method of choosing a winner for this prize.

Decide whether each method is a fair way to choose a winner if each person should have an equal chance of winning. Explain your answer by evaluating each probability.

3. Roll a standard die. Meri wins if the result is less than 3. Riley wins if the result is greater than 3.

4. Draw a card from a standard deck of cards. Meri wins if the card is red. Riley wins if the card is black.

5. Flip a coin. Meri wins if it lands heads. Riley wins if it lands tails.

6. Meri and Riley both jump as high as they can. Whoever jumps higher wins.

7. Roll a standard die. Meri wins if the result is even. Riley wins if the result is odd.

8. Draw a stone from a box that contains 5 black stones and 4 white stones. Meri wins if the stone is black. Riley wins if the stone is white.

9. A chess club has received a chess set to give to one of its members. The club decides that everyone should have chance of winning the set based on how many games they have won this season. Describe a fair method to decide who wins the set. Find the probability that each member will win it.

Member	Games Won	Probability of Winning	Member	Games Won	Probability of Winning
Kayla	30		Hailey	12	
Noah	23		Gabe	12	
Ava	18		Concour	5	

10. Owen, Diego, and Cody often play a game during lunch. When they can't finish, they calculate the probability that each will win given the current state of the game and assign partial wins. Today, when they had to stop, it would have taken at most 56 more moves for one of them to win. Owen would have won 23 of the moves, Diego would have won 18 of them, and Cody would have won 15. To 2 decimal places, how should they assign partial wins?

Represent Real-World Problems Twenty students, including Paige, volunteer to work at the school banquet. Each volunteer worked at least 1 hour. Paige worked 4 hours. The students worked a total of 45 hours. The organizers would like to award a prize to 1 of the volunteers.

11. Describe a process for awarding the prize so that each volunteer has an equal chance of winning. Find the probability of Paige winning.

12. Describe a process for awarding the prize so that each volunteer's chance of winning is proportional to how many hours the volunteer worked. Find the probability of Paige winning.

There are 10,000 seats available in a sports stadium. Each seat has a package beneath it, and 20 of the seats have an additional prize winning package with a family pass for the entire season.

13. Is this method of choosing a winner for the family passes fair?

14. What is the probability of winning a family pass if you attend the game?

15. What is the probability of not winning a family pass if you attend the game?

A teacher tells students, "For each puzzle problem you complete, I will assign you a prize entry." In all, 10 students complete 53 puzzle problems. Leon completed 7. To award the prize, the teacher sets a calculator to generate a random integer from 1 to 53. Leon is assigned 18 to 24 as "winners".

16. What is the probability that a specific number is chosen?

17. What is the probability that one of Leon's numbers will be chosen?

18. What is the probability that one of Leon's numbers will not be chosen?

19. Is this fair to Leon according to the original instructions? Explain.

H.O.T. Focus on Higher Order Thinking

20. **Make a Conjecture** Two teams are playing a game against one another in class to earn 10 extra points on an assignment. The teacher said that the points will be split fairly between the two teams, depending on the results of the game. If Team A earned 1300 points, and Team B earned 2200 points, describe one way the teacher could split up the 10 extra points. Explain.

21. **Persevere in Problem Solving** Alexa and Sofia are at a yard sale, and they find a box of 20 collectible toys that they both want. They can't agree about who saw it first, so they flip a coin until Alexa gets 10 heads or Sofia gets 10 tails. When Alexa has 3 heads and Sofia has 6 tails, they decide to divide the toys proportionally based on the probability each has of winning under the original rules. How should they divide the toys?

Lesson Performance Task

Three games are described below. For each game, tell whether it is fair (all players are equally likely to win) or unfair (one player has an advantage). Explain how you reached your decision, being sure to discuss how probability entered into your decision.

1. You and your friend each toss a quarter. If two heads turn up, you win. If a head and a tail turn up, your friend wins. If two tails turn up, you play again.
2. You and your friend each roll a die. If the sum of the numbers is odd, you get 1 point. If the sum is even, your friend gets 1 point.
3. You and your friend each roll a die. If the product of the numbers is odd, you get 1 point. If the product is even, your friend gets 1 point.

24.2 Analyzing Decisions

Resource Locker

Essential Question: How can conditional probability help you make real-world decisions?

Explore 1 Analyzing a Decision Using Probability

Suppose scientists have developed a test that can be used at birth to determine whether a baby is right-handed or left-handed. The test uses a drop of the baby's saliva and instantly gives the result. The test has been in development, long enough for the scientists to track the babies as they grow into toddlers and to see whether their test is accurate. About 10% of babies turn out to be left-handed.

The scientists have learned that when children are left-handed, the test correctly identifies them as left-handed 92% of the time. Also when children are right-handed, the test correctly identifies them as right-handed 95% of the time.

(A) In the first year on the market, the test is used on 1,000,000 babies. Complete the table starting with the Totals. Then use the given information to determine the expected number in each category.

	Tests Left-handed	Tests Right-handed	Total
Truly Left-handed			
Truly Right-handed			
Total			1,000,000

(B) What is the probability that a baby who tests left-handed actually is left-handed?

(C) What is the probability that a baby who tests right-handed actually is right-handed?

Reflect

1. Is the test a good test of right-handedness?
2. A baby is tested, and the test shows the baby will be left-handed. The parents decide to buy a left-handed baseball glove for the baby. Is this a reasonable decision?
3. **Discussion** Describe two ways in which the test can become a more reliable indicator of left-handedness.

Explore 2 Deriving Bayes' Theorem

You can generalize your results so that they are applicable to other situations in which you want to analyze decisions. Now, you will derive a formula known as Bayes' Theorem.

(A) Complete the steps to derive Bayes' Theorem.

Write the formula for $P(B|A)$.

Solve for $P(A \text{ and } B)$.

Write the formula for $P(A|B)$.

Substitute the expression for $P(A \text{ and } B)$.

(B) Explain how you can use a table giving the number of results for each case to find $P(B)$.

	B	B^c	Total
A	n	p	$n+p$
A^c	m	q	$m+q$
Total	$n+m$	$p+q$	$n+m+p+q$

(C) Explain how you can use the tree diagram to find $P(B)$.

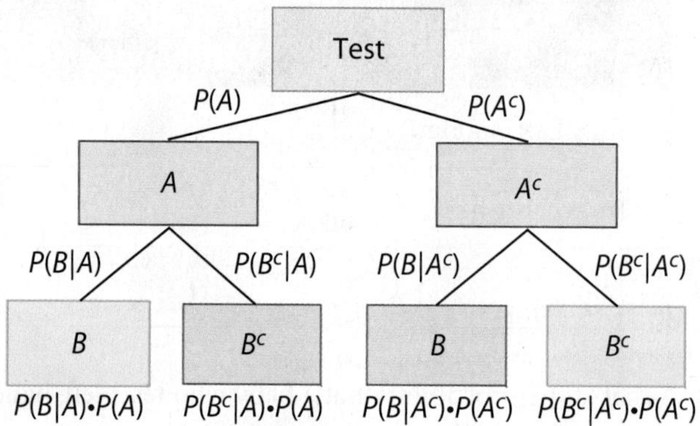

(D) Use your result from Step C to rewrite your final expression from Step A to get another form of Bayes' Theorem.

Reflect

5. Explain in words what each expression means in the context of Explore 1.

$P(A)$ is the probability of actually being left-handed.

$P(B)$ is the probability of testing left-handed.

$P(A|B)$ is ______.

$P(B|A)$ is ______.

6. Use Bayes' Theorem to calculate the probability that a baby actually is left-handed, given that the baby tests left-handed. Explain what this probability means.

Explain 1 Using Bayes' Theorem

Bayes' Theorem is a useful tool when you need to analyze decisions.

Bayes' Theorem

Given two events A and B with $P(B) \neq 0$, $P(A|B) = \dfrac{P(B|A) \cdot P(A)}{P(B)}$.

Another form is $P(A|B) = \dfrac{P(B|A) \cdot P(A)}{P(B|A) \cdot P(A) + P(B|A^c) \cdot P(A^c)}$.

Example 1 **Suppose Walter operates an order-filling machine that has an error rate of 0.5%. He installs a new order-filling machine that has an error rate of only 0.1%. The new machine takes over 80% of the order-filling tasks.**

(A) One day, Walter gets a call from a customer complaining that her order wasn't filled properly. Walter blames the problem on the old machine. Was he correct in doing so?

First, find the probability that the order was filled by the old machine given that there was an error in filling the order, P(old | error).

$$P(\text{old}|\text{error}) = \frac{P(\text{error}|\text{old}) \cdot P(\text{old})}{P(\text{error})}$$

$$= \frac{0.005 \cdot (0.20)}{0.001 + 0.0008} = \frac{0.001}{0.0018} = \frac{5}{9} \approx 0.56$$

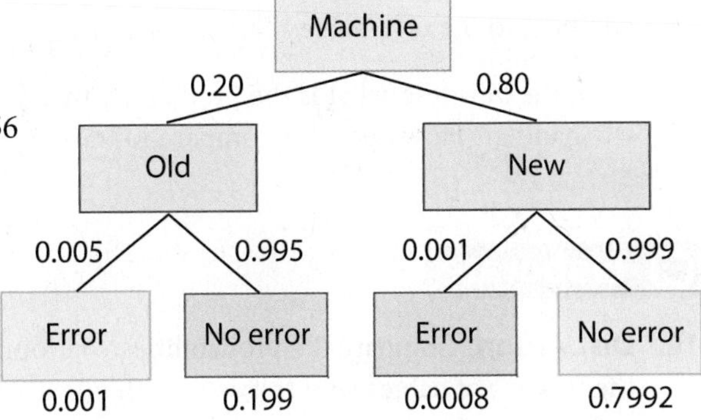

Given that there is a mistake, the probability is about 56% that the old machine filled the order. The probability that the new machine filled the order is $1 - 0.56 = 0.44 = 44\%$. The old machine is only slightly more likely than the new machine to have filled the order. Walter shouldn't blame the old machine.

(B) Walter needs to increase capacity for filling orders, so he increases the number of orders being filled by the old machine to 30% of the total orders. What percent of errors in filled orders are made by the old machine? Is Walter unreasonably increasing the risk of shipping incorrectly filled orders?

Find the probability that the order was filled by the old machine given that there is an error in filling the package,

P(old | error).

Use Bayes' Theorem.

$$P(A|B) = \frac{P(B|A) \cdot P(A)}{P(B)} = \frac{0.005(0.30)}{0.0015 + 0.0007}$$

$$= \frac{0.0015}{0.0022} = \frac{15}{22} \approx 0.68$$

Machine
0.30 0.70
Old New
0.005 0.995 0.001 0.999
Error No error Error No error
0.0015 0.2985 0.0007 0.6993

Describe the result of making this change.

Given that there is a mistake, the probability is about 68% that the old machine filled the package. Making this change increases the number of errors by 4 orders for every 10,000 orders. This seems like a worthwhile risk.

Reflect

8. The old machine fills so few orders. How can it be responsible for more than half of the errors?

Your Turn

In the situation described in the Explore, suppose the scientists have changed the test so that now it correctly identifies left-handed children 100% of the time, and still correctly identifies right-handed children 95% of the time.

7. Copy and complete the tree diagram.

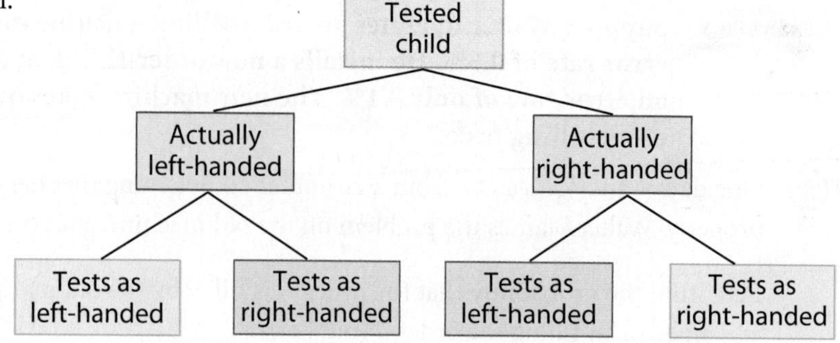

8. With the new test, what is the probability that a child who tests as left-handed will be left-handed? How does this compare to the original test?

9. With the new test, what is the probability that a child who tests as right-handed will be left-handed? How does this compare to the original test?

Elaborate

10. Discussion Compare the probabilities you found in the Explore and Your Turn 8 and 9. Why did the percent of babies who test as right-handed and are actually left-handed increase?

11. Essential Question Check-In How can you use probability to help you analyze decisions?

Evaluate: Homework and Practice

- Online Homework
- Hints and Help
- Extra Practice

1. A factory manager is assessing the work of two assembly-line workers. Helen has been on the job longer than Kyle. Their production rates for the last month are in the table. Based on comparing the number of defective products, the manager is considering putting Helen on probation. Is this a good decision? Why or why not?

	Helen	Kyle	Total
Defective	50	20	70
Not defective	965	350	1,315
Total	1,015	370	1,385

2. **Multiple Step** A reporter asked 150 voters if they plan to vote in favor of a new library and a new arena. The table shows the results. If you are given that a voter plans to vote ***no*** to the new arena, what is the probability that the voter also plans to vote no to the new library?

		Library		
		Yes	No	**Total**
Arena	Yes	21	30	51
	No	57	42	99
	Total	78	72	**150**

3. You want to hand out coupons for a local restaurant to students who live off campus at a rural college with a population of 10,000 students. You know that 10% of the students live off campus and that 98% of those students ride a bike. Also, 62% of the students who live on campus do not have a bike. You decide to give a coupon to any student you see who is riding a bike. Copy and complete the table. Then explain whether this a good decision.

	bike	no bike	Total
on campus			
off campus			
Total			

4. A test for a virus correctly identifies someone who has the virus (by returning a positive result) 99% of the time. The test correctly identifies someone who does not have the virus (by returning a negative result) 99% of the time. It is known that 0.5% of the population has the virus. A doctor decides to treat anyone who tests positive for the virus. Copy and complete the two-way table assuming a total population of 1,000,000 people have been tested. Is this a good decision?

	Tests Positive	Tests Negative	Total
Virus			
No virus			
Total			1,000,000

5. It is known that 2% of the population has a certain allergy. A test correctly identifies people who have the allergy 98% of the time. The test correctly identifies people who do not have the allergy 95% of the time. A website recommends that anyone who tests positive for the allergy should begin taking medication. Copy and complete the two-way table. Do you think this is a good recommendation? Why or why not?

	Test Positive	Test Negative	Total
Total			10,000

6. Use the tree diagram shown.

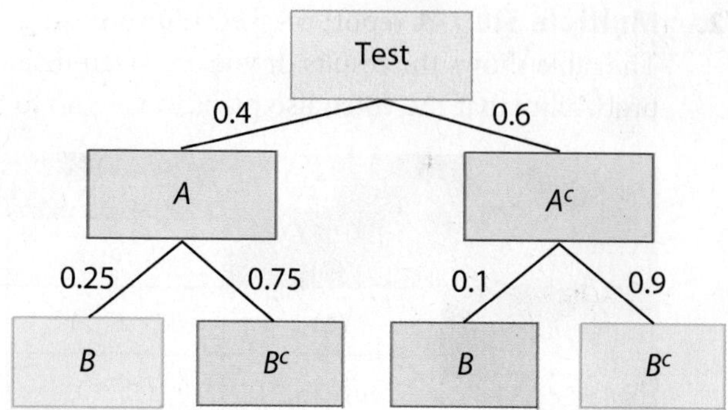

a. Find $P(B|A^c) \cdot P(A^c)$.

b. Find $P(B)$.

c. Use Bayes Theorem to find $P(A^c|B)$.

7. The probabilities of drawing lemons and limes from a bag are shown in the tree diagram. Find the probability of drawing the two pieces of fruit randomly from the bag.

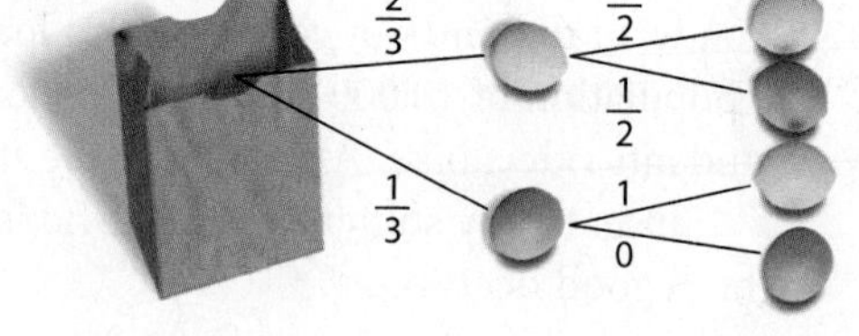

a. two lemons

b. two limes

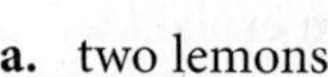

c. lime, then lemon

d. lemon, then lime

8. **Multiple Step** A school principal plans a school picnic for June 2. A few days before the event, the weather forecast predicts rain for June 2, so the principal decides to cancel the picnic. Consider the following information.

- In the school's town, the probability that it rains on any day in June is 3%.
- When it rains, the forecast correctly predicts rain 90% of the time.
- When it does not rain, the forecast incorrectly predicts rain 5% of the time.

a. Find $P(\text{prediction of rain} \mid \text{rains})$ and $P(\text{rains})$.

b. Copy and complete the tree diagram, and find $P(\text{Prediction of rain})$.

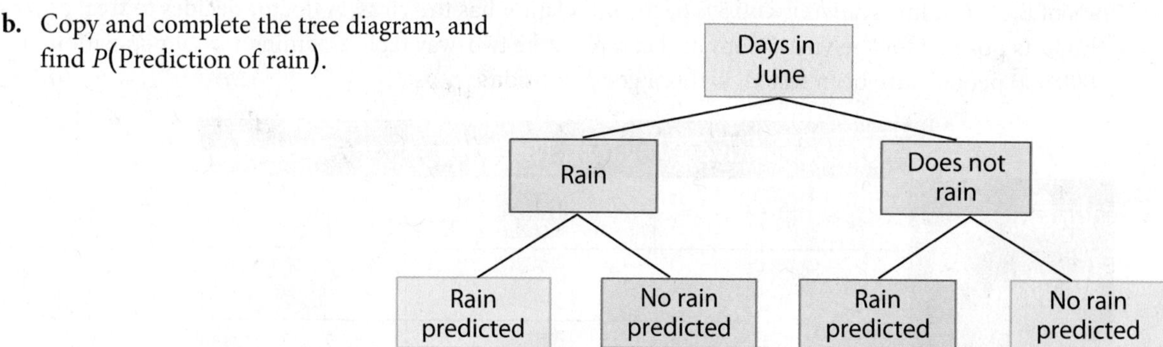

c. Find $P(\text{rains} \mid \text{prediction of rain})$.

d. Is the decision to cancel the picnic reasonable?

9. Pamela has collected data on the number of students in the sophomore class who play a sport or play a musical instrument. She has learned the following.

- 42.5% of all students in her school play a musical instrument.
- 20% of those who play a musical instrument also play a sport.
- 40% of those who play no instrument also play no sport.

Copy and complete the tree diagram. Would it be reasonable to conclude that a student who doesn't play a sport plays a musical instrument?

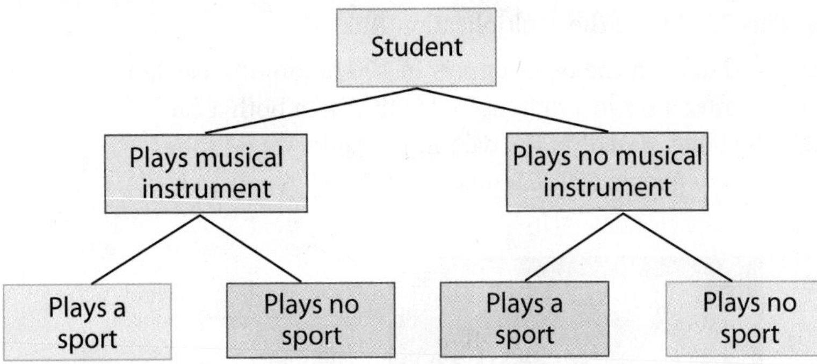

10. Interpret the Answer Company X supplies 35% of the phones to an electronics store and Company Y supplies the remainder. The manager of the store knows that 25% of the phones in the last shipment from Company X were defective, while only 5% of the phones from Company Y were defective. The manager chooses a phone at random and finds that it is defective. The manager decides that the phone must have come from Company X. Do you think this is a reasonable conclusion? Why or why not?

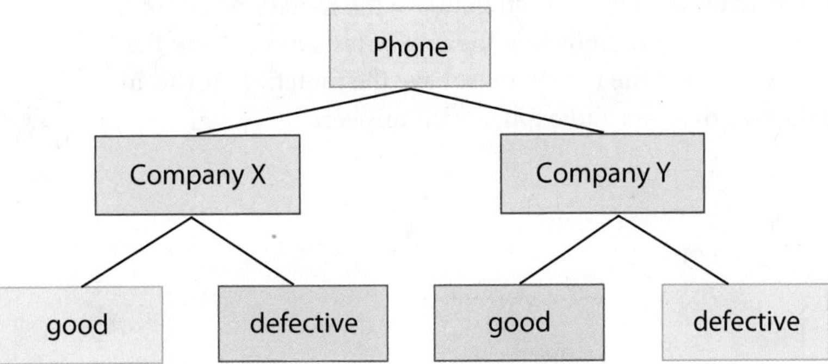

11. Suppose that strep throat affects 2% of the population and a test to detect it produces an accurate result 99% of the time. Create a tree diagram and use Bayes, Theorem to find the probability that someone who tests positive actually has strep throat.

12. A hand-made quilt is first prize in a fund-raiser raffle. The table shows information about all the ticket buyers. Copy and complete the table. Given that the winner of the quilt is a man, what is the probability that he resides in Sharonville?

	Men	Women	Total
Forestview	35	45	80
Sharonville	15	25	40
■	■	■	■

13. Explain how to derive Bayes' Theorem using the Multiplication Rule.

14. **Sociology** A sociologist collected data on the types of pets in 100 randomly selected households. Suppose you want to offer a service to households that own both a cat and a dog. Copy and complete the table. Based on the data in the table, would it be more effective to hand information to people walking dogs or to people buying cat food?

		Owns a Cat		
		Yes	No	■
Owns a Dog	Yes	15	24	■
	No	18	43	■
	■	■	■	■

15. **Interpret the Answer** It is known that 1% of all mice in a laboratory have a genetic mutation. A test for the mutation correctly identifies mice that have the mutation 98% of the time. The test correctly identifies mice that do not have the mutation 96% of the time. A lab assistant tests a mouse and finds that the mouse tests positive for the mutation. The lab assistant decides that the mouse must have the mutation. Is this a good decision? Complete the tree diagram and explain your answer.

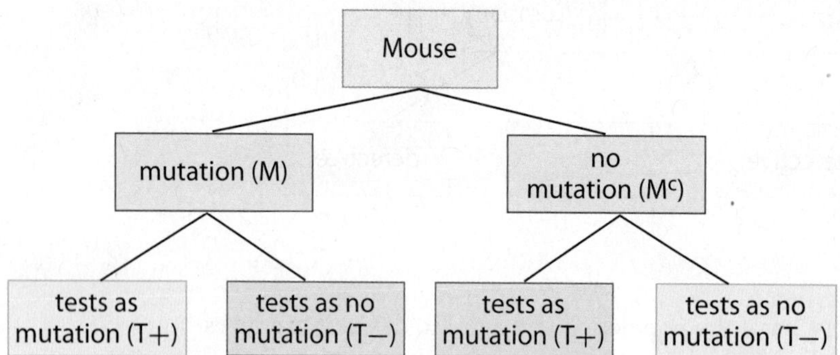

16. **Interpret the Answer** It is known that 96% of all dogs do not get trained. One professional trainer claims that 54% of trained dogs will sit on one of the first four commands and that no other dogs will sit on command. A condominium community wants to impose a restriction on dogs that are not trained. They want each dog owner to show that his or her dog will sit on one of the first four commands. Assuming that the professional trainer's claim is correct, is this a fair way to identify dogs that have not been trained? Explain.

17. Multiple Steps Tomas has a choice of three possible routes to work. On each day, he randomly selects a route and keeps track of whether he is late. Based on this 40-day trial, which route makes Tomas least likely to be late for work?

	Late	Not Late
Route A	IIII	𝍸 𝍸
Route B	III	𝍸 II
Route C	IIII	𝍸 𝍸 II

H.O.T. Focus on Higher Order Thinking

18. Critique Reasoning When Elisabeth saw this tree diagram, she said that the calculations must be incorrect. Do you agree? Justify your answer.

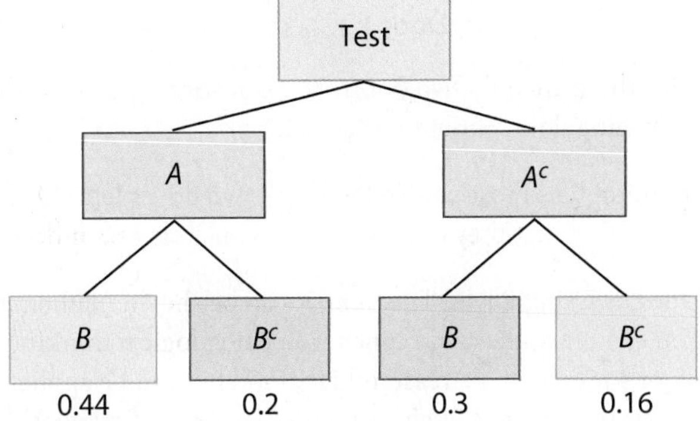

19. Multiple Representations The Venn diagram shows how many of the first 100 customers of a new bakery bought either bread or cookies, both, or neither. Taryn claims that the data indicate that a customer who bought cookies is more likely to have bought bread than a customer who bought bread is likely to have bought cookies. Is she correct?

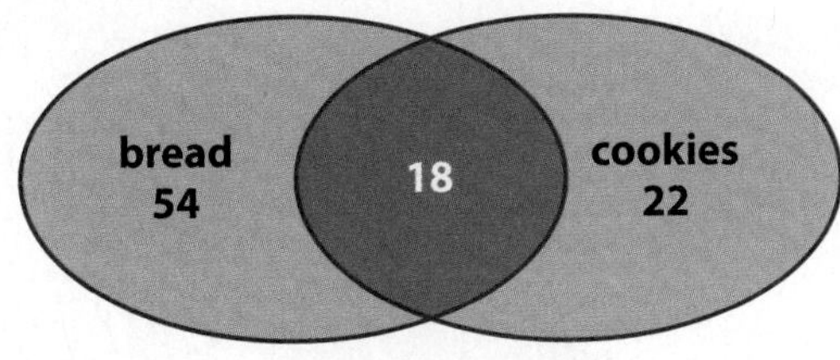

20. Persevere in Problem Solving At one high school, the probability that a student is absent today, given that the student was absent yesterday, is 0.12. The probability that a student is absent today, given that the student was present yesterday, is 0.05. The probability that a student was absent yesterday is 0.1. A teacher forgot to take attendance in several classes yesterday, so he assumed that attendance in his class today is the same as yesterday. If there were 40 students in these classes, how many errors would you expect by doing this?

Lesson Performance Task

You're a contestant on a TV quiz show. Before you are three doors. Behind two of the doors, there's a goat. Behind one of the doors, there's a new car. You are asked to pick a door. After you make your choice, the quizmaster opens one of the doors you *didn't* choose, revealing a goat.

Door 1

Door 2

Door 3

Now there are only two doors. You can stick with your original choice or you can switch to the one remaining door. Should you switch?

Intuition tells most people that, with two doors left, there's a 50% probability that they're right and a 50% probability that they're wrong. They conclude that it doesn't matter whether they switch or not.

Does it? Using Bayes' Theorem, it can be shown mathematically that you're much better off switching! You can reach the same conclusion using logical thinking skills. Assume that the car is behind Door #1. (The same reasoning that follows can be applied if the car is behind one of the other doors.) You've decided to switch your choice after the first goat is revealed. There are three possibilities.

STUDY GUIDE REVIEW

Probability and Decision Making

MODULE 24

Essential Question: How can you use probability to solve real-world problems?

KEY EXAMPLE *(Lesson 24.1)*

Determine whether the method of awarding a prize is fair. Explain.

A festival has a baked goods fundraising raffle in which tickets are drawn for winners. The tickets are sold for $2 each, and the purchaser of the ticket places his or her name on the ticket before placing the ticket into a fishbowl on a table. There are 20 cakes for prizes. A ticket is drawn at random from the fishbowl for each cake.

The method of awarding the prize is fair. This is because each ticket has an equal probability of being drawn. For each of n tickets bought, that ticket has a $\frac{1}{n}$ chance of being drawn. The more tickets someone buys, the better chance they have of winning a cake.

KEY EXAMPLE *(Lesson 24.2)*

Suppose Rhonda's Block Warehouse operates a block-making machine that has an error rate of 0.7%. Then Rhonda installs a new block-making machine that has an error rate of only 0.3%. The new machine takes over 75% of the block-making tasks. One day, Rhonda gets a call from a customer complaining that his block is not made properly. Rhonda blames the problem on the old machine. Was she correct in doing so?

Find Event A, Event B, $P(A|B)$, $P(B)$, and $P(A)$.

Event A is the error making the block, Event B is that the old machine made the block, $P(A|B)$ is the error rate of the old machine (0.007), $P(B)$ is the probability the old machine made the block (0.25), and $P(A)$ is $0.75 \cdot 0.003 + 0.25 \cdot 0.007 = 0.004$.

$$P(B|A) = \frac{P(A|B)P(B)}{P(A)}$$ Bayes' Theorem

$$P(\text{old machine}|\text{bad block}) = \frac{0.007 \cdot 0.25}{0.004}$$ Substitute known probabilities

$$P(\text{old machine}|\text{bad block}) = 0.4375 = 43.75\%$$

Given that the probability that a bad block is made by the old machine is less than 50%, Rhonda should not blame the old machine for the bad block.

EXERCISES

Determine whether the method of awarding a prize is fair. Explain. If it is not fair, describe a way that would be fair. *(Lesson 24.1)*

1. A teacher gives a ticket to each student who earns a 90 or above on any homework assignment. At the end of each week, the teacher draws from the ticket jar and gives the winning student a free homework pass for the next week.

Suppose that a card dealing machine has a probability of 23% for pulling a face card. An older machine has a 14% chance of pulling a face card. Use Bayes' Theorem to find the probability. *(Lesson 24.2)*

2. If each machine is used 50% of the time, and a face card is the next card drawn, what is the probability the new machine drew the card?

MODULE PERFORMANCE TASK

What's the Diagnosis?

Lenny works in a factory that makes cleaning products. Lately he has been suffering from headaches. He asks his doctor if the chemicals used in the factory might be responsible for his headaches. The doctor performs a blood test that is routinely used to diagnose the kind of illness Lenny is concerned about.

Use the following facts to gauge the probability that Lenny has the illness if he tests positive:

1. The test has a reliability rate of 85 percent.
2. The test has a false positive rate of 8 percent.
3. The illness affects 3 percent of people who are Lenny's age and who work in conditions similar to those he works in.

Start by listing the information you will need to solve the problem. Then complete the task. Use numbers, words, or algebra to explain how you reached your conclusion.

Ready to Go On?

24.1–24.2 Probability and Decision Making

- Online Homework
- Hints and Help
- Extra Practice

Determine whether the method of awarding a prize is fair. Explain briefly. *(Lesson 24.1)*

1. Prize to every 500th customer

2. Ticket to every customer; drawing

3. Choose number 1–10; draw number

4. Ticket to all cars; two to red cars

Rodney's Repair Service has a lug nut tightening machine that works well 89% of the time. They got a new machine that works well 98% of the time. Each machine is used 50% of the time. Use Bayes' Theorem to find each probability. *(Lesson 24.2)*

5. new machine malfunctioned

6. old machine malfunctioned

7. old machine worked well

8. new machine worked well

ESSENTIAL QUESTION

9. How can probability and decision making help the organizer of a raffle?

MODULE 24
MIXED REVIEW

Assessment Readiness

1. Consider the situation. Is the method of awarding the prize fair? Write Yes or No for A–C.

A. Ticket for every \$10 spent

B. Coupon every 10 guests

C. Entry for every mile driven

2. Consider the situation of having four tiles in a bag spelling M–A–T–H drawn randomly without replacement. Write True or False for each statement.

A. There is one way to draw all 4 tiles from the bag, if order doesn't matter.

B. There are six ways to draw 2 tiles from the bag, if order matters.

C. There are twenty four ways to draw 3 tiles from the bag if order matters.

3. The band class has two trumpet players. Of the two, the first trumpet player plays a wrong note 4% of the time, and the second trumpet player plays a wrong note 9% of the time. If one song has the first trumpet player playing 75% of the song, and the second trumpet player playing the rest, use Bayes' Theorem to find the probability that a wrong note was played by the second trumpet. Explain whether your answer makes sense.

4. Given a triangle with a side of length 11 and another side of length 6, find the range of possible values for x, the length of the third side. Explain your reasoning.

UNIT 10 MIXED REVIEW

Assessment Readiness

- Online Homework
- Hints and Help
- Extra Practice

1. Figure *ABCDE* is similar to figure *LMNOP*. Write True or False for each mathematical statement.

A. $\frac{BC}{AE} = \frac{MN}{OP}$

B. $\frac{AB}{DE} = \frac{LM}{OP}$

C. $\frac{BD}{AE} = \frac{MN}{LP}$

2. The transformation $(x, y) \rightarrow (x - 2, y + 1)$ is applied to $\triangle XYZ$. Determine if each statement is True or False.

A. The area of $\triangle X'Y'Z'$ is the same as the area of $\triangle XYZ$.

B. The distance from X to X' is equal to the distance from Z to Z'.

C. The transformation is a rotation.

3. Does each scenario describe independent events? Write Yes or No for each situation.

A. Drawing two cards from a standard deck of cards that are both aces

B. Rolling a fair number cube twice and getting 6 on both rolls

C. Rolling a 3 on a fair number cube and flipping tails on a fair coin

4. Each student in a class has been assigned at random to draw a parallelogram, a rectangle, a rhombus, or a square. Write True or False for each statement about the likelihood that a student will draw a parallelogram.

A. It is unlikely because the probability is less than 0.5.

B. It is likely because the probability is between 0.5 and 0.75.

C. It is impossible for it not to happen because the probability is 1.

5. The events A and B are independent. Determine if each statement is True or False.

A. $P(A \mid B) = P(B \mid A)$

B. $P(A \text{ and } B) = P(B)P(A)$

C. $P(A) = P(B)$

6. Vera needs to place 15 student volunteers at a local fire station. Five students will wash fire trucks, 7 will be assigned to paint, and 3 will be assigned to wash windows. What is the number of possible job assignments expressed using factorials and as a simplified number?

7. The table below shows the number of days that a meteorologist predicted it would be sunny and the number of days it was sunny. Based on the data in the table, what is the conditional probability that it will be sunny on a day when the meteorologist predicts it will be sunny? Show your work.

	Sunny	Not Sunny	Total
Predicts Sunny	570	20	590
Does Not Predict Sunny	63	347	410
Total	633	367	1000

8. Copy and complete the two-way table below. Then find the fraction of red cards in a standard 52-card deck that have a number on them and find the fraction of numbered cards that are red.

	Red	Black	Total
Number			
No Number			
Total			

Performance Tasks

★ **9.** Sixteen cards numbered 1 through 16 are placed face down, and Stephanie chooses one at random. What is the probability that the number on Stephanie's card is less than 5 or greater than 10? Show your work.

★★**10.** Students in 4 different classes are surveyed about their favorite movie type. What is the probability that a randomly selected student in class B prefers comedies? What is the probability that a randomly selected student who prefers comedies is in class B? Explain why the two probabilities are not the same. Show your work.

	A	B	C	D
Action	12	9	8	11
Comedy	13	11	15	4
Drama	6	11	7	18

★★★**11.** A Chinese restaurant has a buffet that includes ice cream for dessert. The table shows the selections made last week.

	Chocolate	Vanilla	Strawberry
Cone	24	18	12
Dish	12	21	15

A. Which flavor is the most popular? Which serving method? Is the combination of the most popular flavor and serving method the most popular dessert choice overall? Explain.

B. Which of the following is more likely? Explain.

- A customer chooses vanilla, given that the customer chose a cone.
- A customer chooses a cone, given that the customer chose vanilla.

C. A class of 24 students gets the buffet for lunch. If all the students get ice cream, about how many will get a cone or vanilla? Explain.

MATH IN CAREERS

Epidemiologist An epidemiologist is aiding in the treatment of a community plagued by two different infectious agents, X and Z. Each infectious agent must be treated differently with a new treatment if the patient has been infected by both agents. The community has a total population of 15,000 people, where 5% are not affected by either agent and 60% are afflicted by the X infection. 39% of the population is afflicted by X but not by Z. Unfortunately, the treatment for the X infection fails 35% of the time. The same incident happened to 10 other communities with similar results as the first. What is the probability that people will be healthy? have the X affliction? have the Z affliction? have both afflictions?

9. 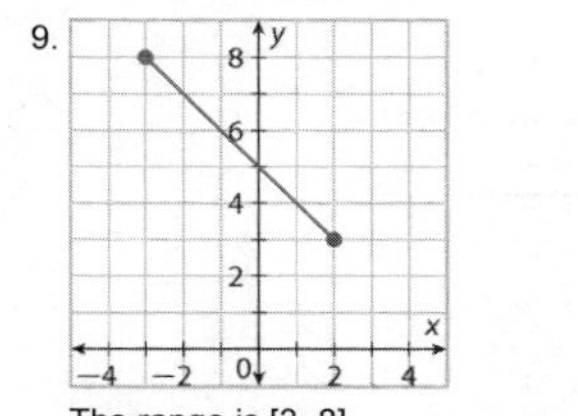

The range is [3, 8].

11. $d(t) = 12t$. The domain is $\{t \mid 0 \le t \le 0.75\}$.
The range is $\{d \mid 0 \le d \le 9\}$.

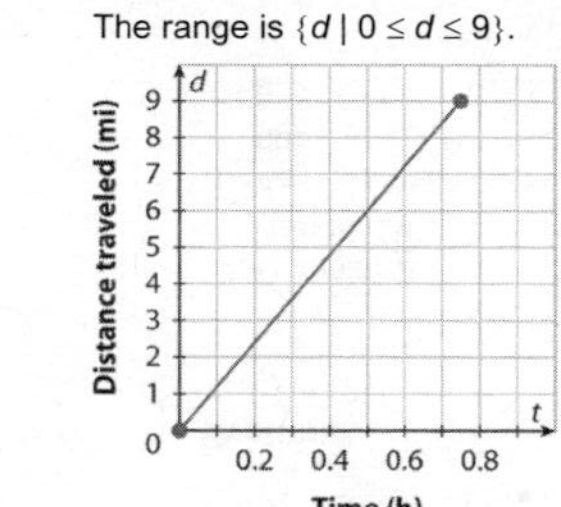

13. Cameron's function is correct, but the domain and range are incorrect. The domain should be $0 \le t \le 6$. The range should be $0 \le n \le 150$.

15. $y = -0.46x + 500$.
Domain: $0 \le x \le 1091$, $\{x \mid 0 \le x \le 1091\}$, [0, 1091]
Range: $0 \le y \le 500$, $\{y \mid 0 \le y \le 500\}$, [0, 500]

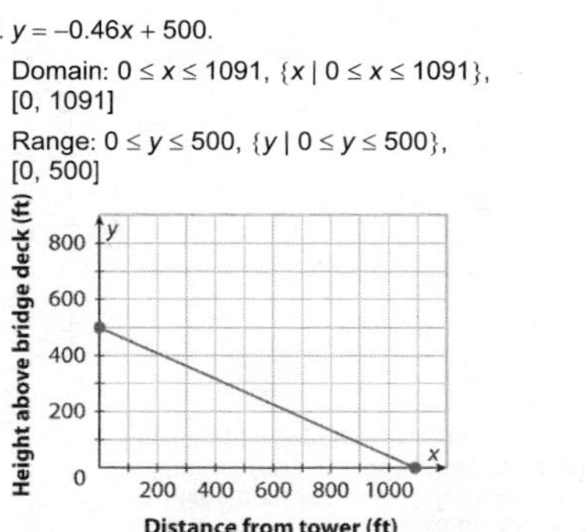

9.

The range is [3, 8].

11. $d(t) = 12t$. The domain is $\{t \mid 0 \le t \le 0.75\}$.
The range is $\{d \mid 0 \le d \le 9\}$.

Distance traveled (mi)
Time (h)

13. Cameron's function is correct, but the domain and range are incorrect. The domain should be $0 \le t \le 6$. The range should be $0 \le n \le 150$.

15. $y = -0.46x + 500$.
Domain: $0 \le x \le 1091$, $\{x \mid 0 \le x \le 1091\}$, [0, 1091]
Range: $0 \le y \le 500$, $\{y \mid 0 \le y \le 500\}$, [0, 500]

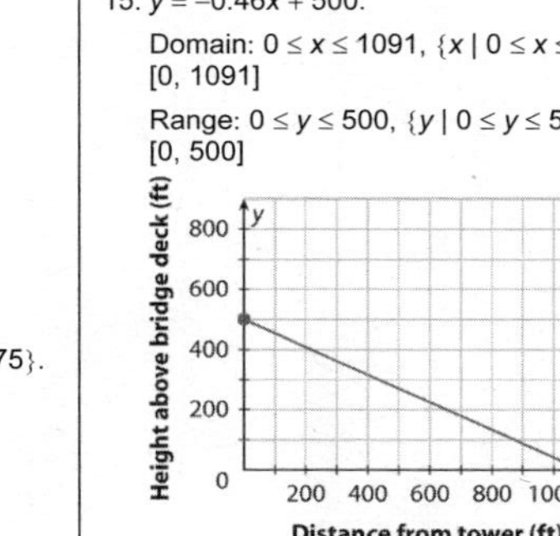

Original content Copyright © by Houghton Mifflin Harcourt. Additions and changes to the original content are the responsibility of the instructor.

2

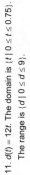

UNIT 1 Selected Answers

MODULE 1

Lesson 1.2 Characteristics of Function Graphs

Your Turn

4. Strawberries on Shelves

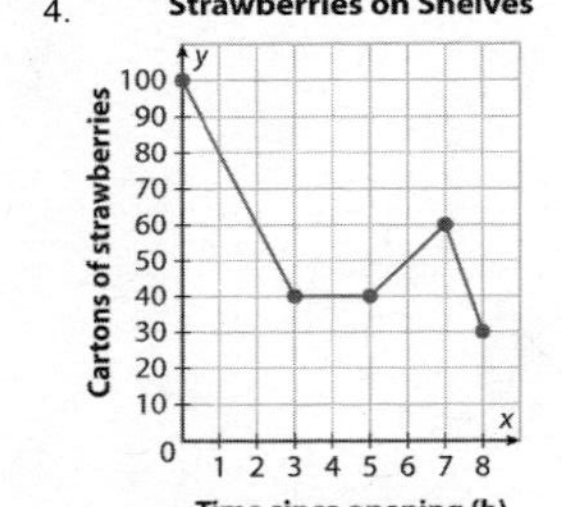

6. The linear regression model is $y = 2.4x + 11$ where x represents the day and y represents the number of hits. The model predicts that on day 15 there will be $y = 2.4(15) + 11 = 47$ hits.

Evaluate

1. $\{t \mid 3 \le t \le 13\}$

   $\{t \mid 0 \le t \le 3\}$ and $\{t \mid 13 \le t \le 18\}$

3. Domain: $\{t \mid 0 \le t \le 18\}$;
   Range: $\{V(t) \mid 0.75 \le V(t) \le 3\}$.

5. As n increases without bound, $P(n)$ approaches 0.

7. a. 2; b. –2; c. –1; d. 4; e. –3; f. 0

9. $\{x \mid x < -3\}$ and $\{x \mid -1 < x < 2\}$.

11.

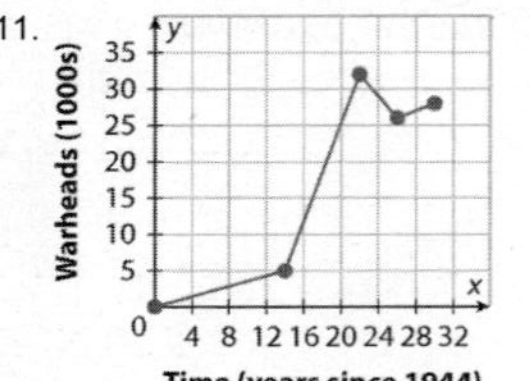
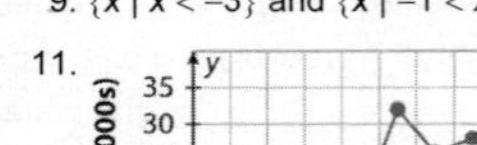
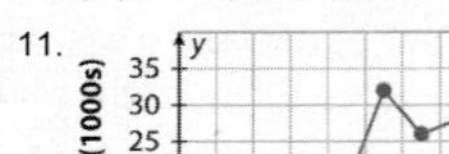

13.

15. a.

b. The ball reaches a maximum height of 64 feet in 2 seconds.

c. The height is increasing on the interval $\{t \mid 0 \le t < 2\}$.

d. The height is decreasing on the interval $\{t \mid 2 < t \le 4\}$.

17. The linear regression model is $h = 2.75\ell + 71.97$ where ℓ is the length of a woman's humerus (in centimeters) and h is her overall height (in centimeters).
The woman's height would be about 160 centimeters. Because 32 is in the domain of the regression model, the prediction is an interpolation.

19. The average rate of change on an interval uses only the endpoints of the interval in the calculation. If the endpoints happen to have the same y-coordinate, the average rate of change will be 0, but that doesn't mean the function remains constant throughout the interval. For example, the average rate of change for $f(x) = x^2$ on the interval $\{x \mid -1 \le x \le 1\}$ is $\frac{f(1) - f(-1)}{1 - (-1)} = \frac{1 - 1}{1 - (-1)} = \frac{0}{2} = 0$, but the function is decreasing from (–1, 1) to (0, 0) and then increasing from (0, 0) to (1, 1), so the function is clearly not constant on the interval.

UNIT 1 Selected Answers

MODULE 1

Lesson 1.3 Inverses of Functions

Your Turn

5. $f^{-1}(x) = \frac{-x+3}{2}$

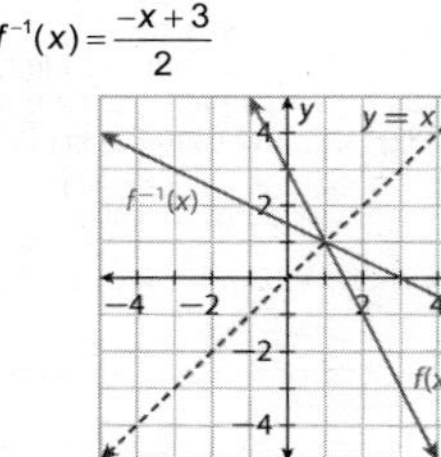

6. $\{w \mid 0 \le w \le 600\}$

   $-\frac{1}{20}w + 30 = t$

   The inverse function gives the time (in hours) the pool has been draining as a function of the amount of water (in thousands of gallons) remaining in the pool.

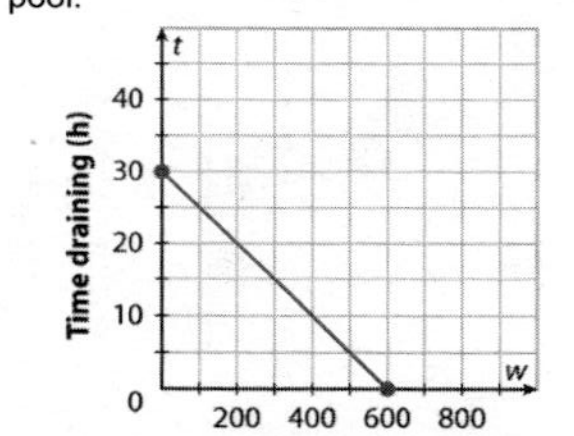

Evaluate

1. 16; 12; 18

   The inverse is a function, because for each input there is only one output.

3. Inverse of function:

   $\{(-3, -4), (-4, -2), (-2, 0), (0, 1), (3, 2)\}$

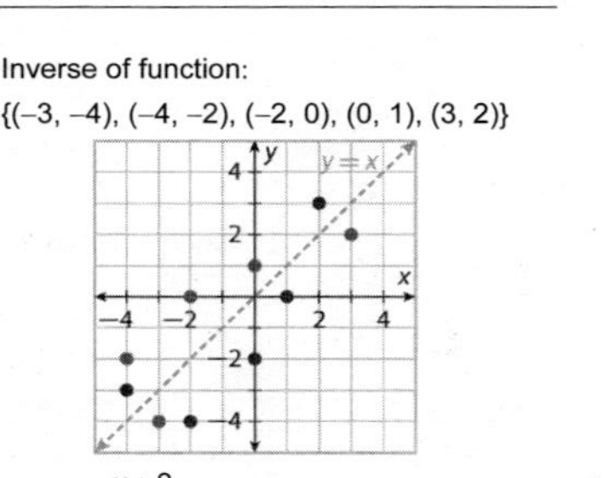

5. $f^{-1}(x) = \frac{x+8}{4}$

7. $f^{-1}(x) = 6x - 1$

9. $f^{-1}(x) = -\frac{1}{3}x + 1$

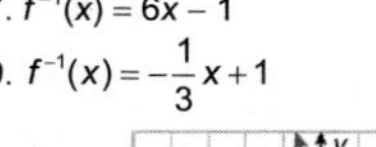

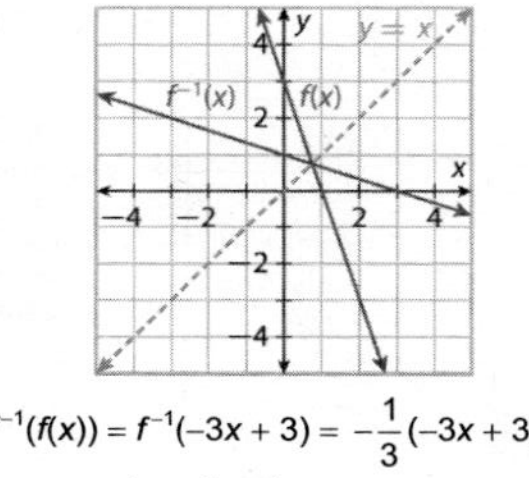

$f^{-1}(f(x)) = f^{-1}(-3x+3) = -\frac{1}{3}(-3x+3) + 1$

$= (x-1) + 1 = x$

$f(f^{-1}(x)) = f\left(-\frac{1}{3}x+1\right) = -3\left(-\frac{1}{3}x+1\right) + 3$

$= (x-3) + 3 = x$

11. The domain of the function $A = \frac{1}{2}(20)h$ is restricted.

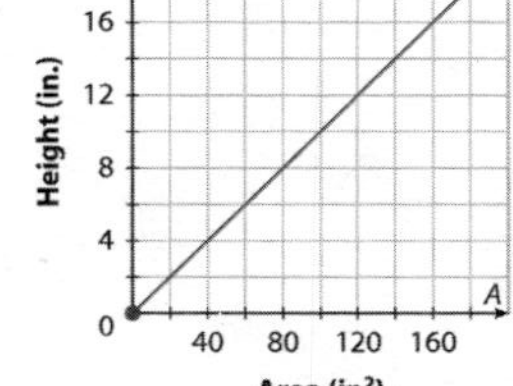

   The inverse function is $h = \frac{A}{10}$.

   The inverse function gives the height (in inches) of a triangle with a base of 20 inches as a function of the area (in square inches) of the triangle.

13. The function's inverse is not a function, because the function is many-to-one. If the domain is restricted to $\{x|x \le 0\}$, $\{x|x \ge 0\}$, or some subset of these sets, the function becomes one-to-one, and the inverse is a function.

15. A, B, F, G and H.

17. You have to restrict the domains of quadratic functions and absolute value functions, because these functions are many-to-one functions. For instance, the quadratic function $f(x) = x^2$ pairs both -2 and 2 with 4, and the absolute value function $f(x) = |x|$ pairs both -2 and 2 with 2. On the other hand, linear functions (excluding constant functions) and exponential functions are one-to-one functions, so their domains do not need to be restricted.

UNIT 1 Selected Answers

MODULE 2

Lesson 2.1 Graphing Absolute Value Functions

Your Turn

2. Vertex: $(h, k) = (-6, 4)$
   $(4, 2)$
   $(-16, 2)$

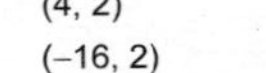

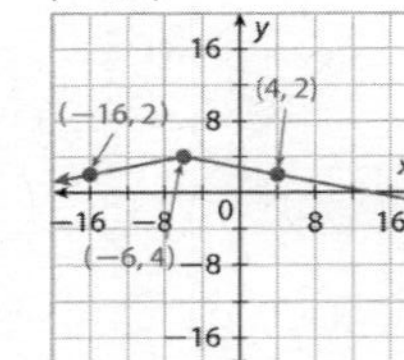

3. $g(x) = |2(x+5)| - 1$
4. The second student should stand 5.57 meters away from the first student.

Evaluate

1.

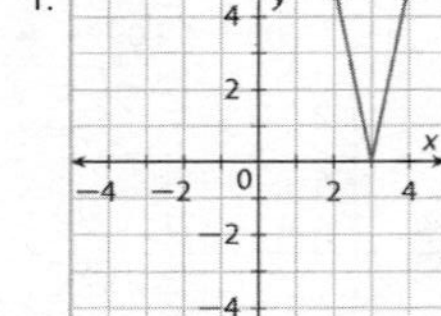

$g(x)$ is the graph of $f(x) = |x|$ vertically stretched by a factor of 5 and shifted 3 units to the right.

3.

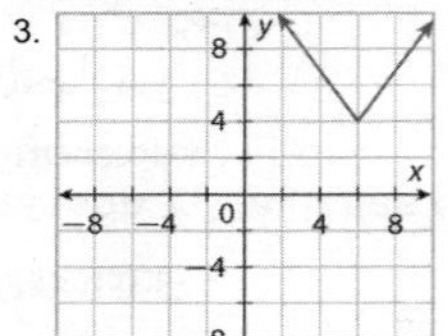

$g(x)$ is the graph of $f(x) = |x|$ horizontally compressed by a factor of $\frac{5}{7}$, shifted 6 units to the right and 4 units up.

5. $g(x)$ is the graph of $f(x) = |x|$ vertically stretched by a factor of $\frac{7}{4}$, shifted 2 units to the right, and 3 units down.

7.

D: all real numbers; R: $y \geq 7$

9.

D: all real numbers; R: $y \geq -7$

11.

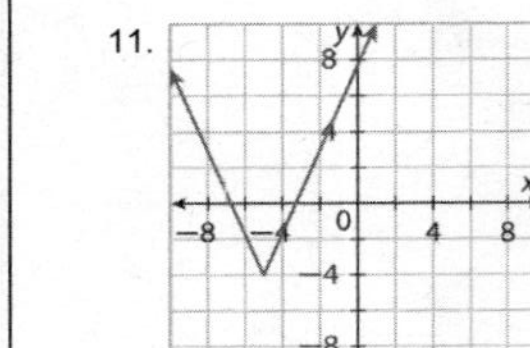

D: all real numbers; R: $y \geq -4$

13. $g(x) = -\frac{1}{4}|(x-4)| + 3$
15. a. An equation for the path of the ball is $y = \frac{5}{4}|x - 6|$.
    b. The point (10, 5) satisfies the equation, so the player does make the shot.
17. $y = -\frac{1706}{145}|x - 72.5| + 853$
19. The graph shown cannot be the graph of $y = |x+3| + 2$ because the +3 inside of the absolute value symbols means the parent graph should be shifted to the left 3 units. The graph shown is shifted to the right 3 units, so it represents $y = |x-3| + 2$.

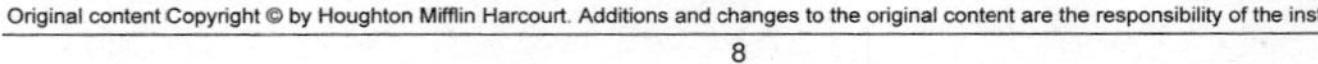

UNIT 1 Selected Answers

MODULE 2

Lesson 2.2 Solving Absolute Value Equations

Your Turn

3. $x = 18$ or $x = -22$

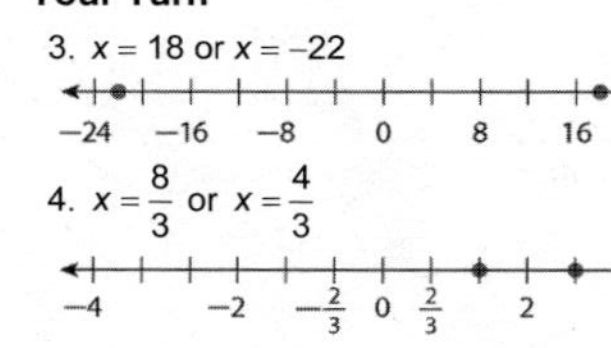

–24 –16 –8 0 8 16 24

4. $x = \frac{8}{3}$ or $x = \frac{4}{3}$

–4 –2 $-\frac{2}{3}$ 0 $\frac{2}{3}$ 2 4

5. $\left|\frac{1}{2}x + 5\right| = -\frac{2}{3}$

No solution

6. $\left|\frac{4}{3}x - 2\right| = 0$

$x = \frac{3}{2}$

Evaluate

1.

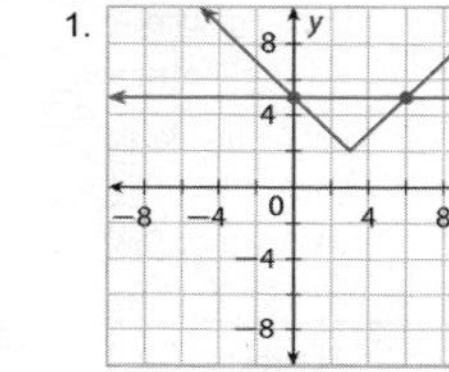

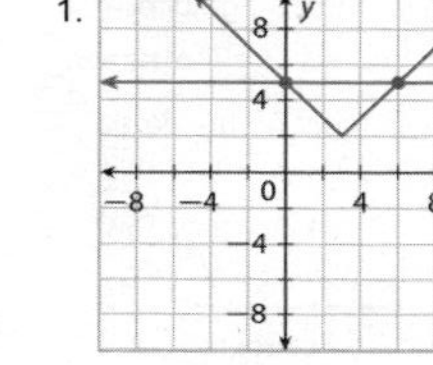

$x = 0$ or $x = 6$

3.

$x = -4$ or $x = -6$

5.

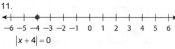

–3 –2 –1 0 1 2 3

$x = \frac{3}{2}$ or $x = -\frac{3}{2}$

7.

0 1 2 3 4

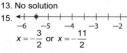

$x = \frac{5}{3}$ or $x = \frac{4}{3}$

9. No solution

11.

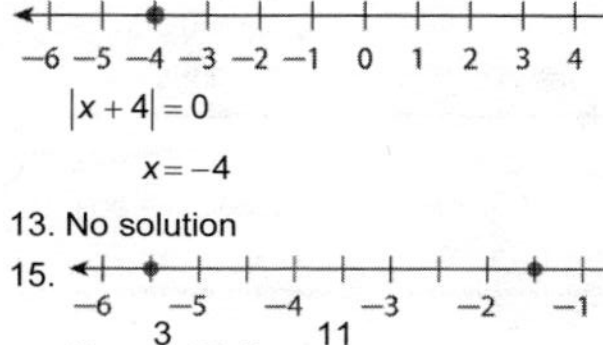

–6 –5 –4 –3 –2 –1 0 1 2 3 4 5 6

$|x + 4| = 0$

$x = -4$

13. No solution

15.

–6 –5 –4 –3 –2 –1 0

$x = -\frac{3}{2}$ or $x = -\frac{11}{2}$

17. The buoys should be placed at either 150 ft or 330 ft from the left-hand shore.

19. The points are (–2, 0) and (8, 0).

21. No Solution. Terry does not have a spot on his roof that is 30 feet high.

23. $3|x - 2| - 5|x - 2| = -7$ Subtraction Property of Equality

$(3 - 5)|x - 2| = -7$ Distributive Property

$|x - 2| = \frac{7}{2}$ Division Property of Equality

$x - 2 = \frac{7}{2}$ or $x - 2 = -\frac{7}{2}$ Definition of absolute value

$x = \frac{11}{2}$ or $x = -\frac{3}{2}$ Addition Property of Equality

25. Answers will vary. Sample answer: time, distance, height, length, speed.

UNIT 1 Selected Answers

MODULE 2

Lesson 2.3 Solving Absolute Value Inequalities

Your Turn

6. $x \geq -3$ and $x \leq 1$

9. The solution is $x \leq 4$ and $x \geq 10$.

−4 −2 0 2 4 6 8 10 12 14 16 18

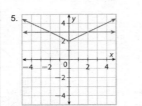

10. The solution is $-4 < x < 1$.

−5 −4 −3 −2 −1 0 1 2 3 4 5

11. $|w - 13.8| \leq 0.1$

The range of acceptable weights of the cereal (in ounces) is $13.7 \leq w \leq 13.9$.

Evaluate

1. The integers from −5 to 5 that satisfy the inequality are −5, −4, −3, −2, −1, 3, 4, and 5.

−5 −4 −3 −2 −1 0 1 2 3 4 5

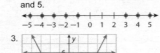

3.

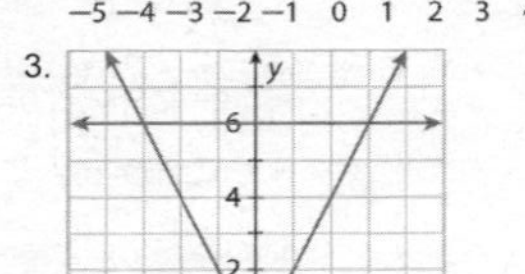

The solution is $-3 \leq x \leq 3$.

5.

The solution is $-2 < x < 2$.

7. C. The solution is $x < -2$ or $x > 2$.

9. B. The solution is $-\frac{5}{2} < x < \frac{1}{2}$.

11. −2 −1 0 1 2 3 4 5 6 7 8 9

The solution is $x < 3$ or $x > 4$.

13. The solution is $x \leq -5$ or $x \geq -3$.

−9 −8 −7 −6 −5 −4 −3 −2 −1 0 1

15. all real numbers.

17. The range of house temperatures (in degrees Fahrenheit) is $66 \leq T \leq 70$.

19. The range of ages (in years) that a squirrel lives is $5 \leq a \leq 8$.

21. The range of typical speeds (in miles per hour) is $25 \leq s \leq 35$.

23. The student identified where the graph of $g(x)$ lies above the graph of $f(x)$, but the student should have identified where the graph of $f(x)$ lies above the graph of $g(x)$ because the inequality has the form $f(x) > g(x)$. So, the solution of the inequality is $x < -3$ or $x > 5$.

UNIT 2 Selected Answers

MODULE 3

Lesson 3.1 Understanding Rational Exponents and Radicals

Your Turn

3. 2
4. 7
5. 8
6. 24

Evaluate

1. $\frac{1}{100}$

3. $\frac{1}{16}$

5. 1

7. 9

9. 5

11. 343

13. 89

15. $\frac{1}{5}$

17. 1

19. $1\frac{2}{3}$

21. 8

23. 1000 cm^3

25. It needs to be moving at about 1400 miles per hour.

27. No, he is not correct. It is only even numbers in the denominator of an exponent that cannot be evaluated with a negative base. With an odd denominator and an even numerator in the exponent, there is no problem. The correct answer is:

$$(-8)^{\frac{2}{3}} = \left(\sqrt[3]{-8}\right)^2 = \left(\sqrt[3]{(-2)^3}\right)^2 = (-2)^2 = 4$$

29. In the first line, the exponential terms should be added, not multiplied. Compounding the first error, the exponential term in the second line implies the product of 2 and $\frac{1}{2}$ is 0, not 1.

UNIT 2 Selected Answers

MODULE 3

Lesson 3.2 Simplifying Expressions with Rational Exponents and Radicals

Your Turn

5. $x^4 y^3$
6. $\sqrt{x}$
8. $\frac{2}{x^4}$
9. $\frac{1}{3x^4}$
10. a. $3 \times 10^8 = fw \Rightarrow f = \frac{3 \times 10^8}{w}$
    b. $f = \frac{3 \times 10^8}{w} = (3 \times 10^8)w^{-1}$
    c. The frequency of violet light with a wavelength of 400 nanometers is 7.5×10^{14} cycles per second.
11. 36π
    The sphere has surface area of 36π cm squared. While the units are different, the number is the same.

Evaluate

1. Addition and multiplication are commutative. A subtraction table would not be symmetric because subtraction is not commutative.
3. $81x^4$
5. $64y^6$
7. $32x^5$
9. 0
11. $\frac{5}{x^4}$
13. $8x^3$
15. x^6y^5
17. xy^2z^4
19. $\frac{1}{x^2}$
21. $x^8y^{\frac{17}{4}}$
23. The brain of the mouse has an approximate mass of 2 grams.
25. They should plan on buying approximately 1.59*a* liters of paint.
27. a. Rational
    b. Irrational
    c. Rational
    d. Irrational
    e. Irrational
    f. Rational
    g. Rational
29. a. No
    b. No
31.

$\left(\sqrt[3]{x}\right)^3 = x$	Definition of cube root
$\left(x^k\right)^3 = x$	Substitute x^k for $\sqrt[3]{x}$.
$x^{3k} = x^1$	Power of a Power Property
$3k = 1$	Equate the exponents.
$k = \frac{1}{3}$	Solve for *k*.

UNIT 2 Selected Answers

MODULE 4

Lesson 4.1 Understanding Polynomial Expressions

Your Turn

5. 4th degree trinomial
6. 3rd degree binomial
7. $x^5 + 4x^3 - 3x^2 + 10$, 1
8. $-3y^8 + 18y^5 + 10y$, -3
9. $-5x + 13$, -5
10. $9b^2 + 8b$, 9
12. $-q^3p^2 + pq$
13. $11a - 3b - 14c$
14. $2a^2 - 4ab + 26$
15. The area of the kitchen is 486 square feet.
16. The rocket will rise 564 feet.

Evaluate

1. $(5 + 4x^0)\,2x$ is a monomial, but $(5 + 4x^2)\,2x$ is a binomial.
3. 3rd degree binomial
5. 7th degree trinomial
7. 1st degree trinomial
9. $-40x^3 - 2x^2 + 2x$; -40
11. $4b^2 - 2b$; 4
13. $-y^3$
15. $xyz\left(\sqrt[3]{2} + 2^5\right) + 2^{10}xy$
    or
    $\left(32 + \sqrt[3]{2}\right)xyz + 1024xy$
17. The well is 190 feet deep.
19.

Evaluate for $t = 20°C$	Evaluate for $t = 30°C$
$t^2 + 4t + 4$	$t^2 + 3t + 4$
$(1)^2 + 4(1) + 4$	$(1)^2 + 3(1) + 4$
$1 + 4 + 4$	$1 + 3 + 4$
9	8

21. Enrique treated the numbers like variables, but their degree is 0. The degree of the polynomial is 2 from the exponent of 2 over the *x* in the term 2^2x^2.
23. By counterexample, $x + y$ is not a monomial, although it is a sum of monomials.
25. $\frac{1}{2}h(h + 8)$; area = 192 cm^2

UNIT 2 Selected Answers

MODULE 4

Lesson 4.2 Adding Polynomial Expressions

Your Turn

3. $3x^2 - x - 1$
4. $z^3 - z^2 - 1$
5. $5x - 7$
6. $-10x^2 + 2$
7. $-5x^3 + x + y + 2$
8. $4y + 11$
10. $(t^2 + 4t + 4) + (t^2 + 2t + 4)$
    The total number of cells is $2t^2 + 6t + 8$ for time t.
11. $(3x^2 + 7x - 5) + (5x^2 - 4x + 11)$
    $8x^2 + 3x + 6$

Evaluate

1. This is a lot like the horizontal method, but you can make an argument for either. The algebra in the Explore is written using the horizontal method.
3. 0
5. $x^2 + 2x + 2$
7. $x^2 + y$
9. -1
11. $-2cab^2 + ab^2 + 2b^2$
13. $\left(2 + \sqrt[3]{2}\right)ab$
15. $(8g^2 + 3g - 4) + (6g^2 + 2g - 1)$
    $14g^2 + 5g - 5$
17. $14a + 2b$
    170
19. $-x$
21. Jane is correct. Jill distributed the 2 incorrectly. She should have written
    $= (2x^2 + x) + 2(-x^2 + x)$
    $= \cancel{2x^2} + x - \cancel{2x^2} + 2x$
    $= 3x$
23. Sample answer: $\frac{1}{x}$ is the quotient of two monomials but is not a monomial.
25. Sample answers:
    $(3m^2 + m) + (m^2 + m) = 4m^2 + 2m$
    $= 5(m^2 + m) - (m^2 + 3m)$
    $= (5m^2 - m^2) + (5m - 3m) = 4m^2 + 2m$

UNIT 2 Selected Answers

MODULE 4

Lesson 4.3 Subtracting Polynomial Expressions

Your Turn

3. $5x^2 - x + 1$
4. $-4z - 2$
5. $11y - 8$
6. $y^2 - 2x$
7. $7z + 17$
9. The 25 °C culture has 4t more cells at time t. There are 60 more cells in the 25 °C culture after 15 minutes.
10. $-g^2 + 5g + 1$
    At a rate of 5 gallons per minute, the change of the volume will be 1 gallon per minute.

Evaluate

1. $(x^2 + x - 3) + (-x^2 - 2x - 1)$
   $x^2 + (-x^2) + x + (-2x) - 3 + (-1)$
   $-x - 4$
3. $-3x^4 + 3x^2$
5. $-x^2 - 2x + 2$
7. $m + 2z + y$
9. $-4x^2 + 2x + 2$
11. $-2cab^2 + ab^2 + 2b^2$
13. $-ab$
15. $y^2 - 99{,}500$
    If the company can only make 300 bicycles, they will lose money.
17. $\ell^2\left(1 - \frac{\pi}{4}\right)$
19. The volume of the cube is $(6c)^3 = 216c^3$.
21. c is incorrect because the −1 was distributed incorrectly. e is correct in the case that the number of units sold, x, is not the same number of units, y produced. a, b and d are also correct and are algebraicially equivalent.
23. You can write $(3y^2 + 8y - 16) - P_1 = y^2 - 4$ for some polynomial P_1. Just rewrite the equation and solve for P_1. By the Subtraction Property of Equality, $(3y^2 + 8y - 16) - P_1 = y^2 - 4$ is equivalent to $(3y^2 + 8y - 16) - (y^2 - 4) = P_1$.
    Simplify the left side.
    $(3y^2 + 8y - 16) - (y^2 - 4) = P_1$
    $(3y^2 + 8y - 16) + (-y^2 + 4) = P_1$
    $(3y^2 - y^2) + 8y + (-16 + 4) = P_1$
    $2y^2 + 8y - 12 = P_1$
    Hallie subtracted the quantity $2y^2 + 8y - 12$.
25. −b; c; b; c

UNIT 2 Selected Answers

MODULE 5

Lesson 5.1 Multiplying Polynomial Expressions by Monomials

Your Turn

4. $54x^{11}y^8z^5$
6. $10a^2b^2 + 6a^3b + 12a^3 + 2a^2$
7. $x = 5$ inches is the closest possible answer. $x + 4 = 5 + 4 = 9$

   The width should be 5 inches and the length should be 9 inches.

Evaluate

1. $6x^3$
3. $18x^{10}$
5. $21x^3y^4$
7. $32xy^7z^2$
9. $x^5 + x^4$
11. $x^5 + 2x^4 + 5x^3$
13. $4x^5y + 8x^2y^3 + 12x^3y^2$
15. $6x^5y^2 + 18x^4y^3 + 18x^2y^5$
17. When $x = 10$, the area is 130 square feet.
19. $x = 15$ feet is the closest possible answer.
21. $-x^2 + 3x - 2$
23. Sandy multiplied the exponents for x^2 and x^3 instead of adding them.

UNIT 2 Selected Answers

MODULE 5

Lesson 5.2 Multiplying Polynomial Expressions

Your Turn

3. $x^2 - x - 2$
6. $x^3 + 6x^2 + 3x + 18$
10. The area, including the walkway, is $(4x^2 + 70x + 300)\text{ft}^2$.

Evaluate

1. $x^2 + 2x - 24$
3. $x^2 - 5x - 6$
5. $x^3 + 6x^2 + 11x + 66$
7. $x^2 + 10x + 21$
9. $6x^2 + 19x + 10$
11. $x^3 - 3x^2 + 9x - 27$
13. $x^3 - x^2 - 5x - 3$
15. $x^5 + 4x^4 + x^3 + 4x^2 + x + 4$
17. $x^5 + 2x^3 + x^2 + 4x + 12$
19. Let y represent the area of Cameron's garden. Then the equation for this situation is $y = (x + 6)(x + 2)$.

    The area of Cameron's garden is 77 ft^2.
21. Let x be the width of the frame. $(12 + 2x)(10 + 2x)$

    The area of the framed photograph is $(4x^2 + 44x + 120)$ in^2.
23. a. $6x^2$

    b. $3x^{12}$

    c. x^2

    d. $6x^4$

    e. x^6
25. $n^3 + 6n^2 + 8n$
27. Bill added the constants in the binomials. He should have multiplied the constant of each binomial together instead.

UNIT 2 Selected Answers

MODULE 5

Lesson 5.3 Special Products of Binomials

Your Turn

5. $16 + 8x^2 + x^4$
6. $x^2 - 6x + 9$
8. $16x^2 - 24xy + 9y^2$
9. $9 - 6x^2 + x^4$
11. $49 - x^2$
13. Total area
    $(x + 3)^2 = x^2 + 2(x)(3) + 3^2 = x^2 + 6(x) + 9$
    Area of patio
    $(x - 3)\ 2 = x^2 - 2(x)(3) + 3^2 = x^2 - 6(x) + 9$
    Area of flower garden = total area − area of patio
    $= x^2 + 6x + 9 - (x^2 - 6x + 9)$
    $12x$

Evaluate

1. $x^2 + 16x + 64$
3. $36 + 12x^2 + x^4$
5. $x^2 + 22x + 121$
7. $x^2 - 6x + 9$
9. $(36x^2) - 84xy + 49y^2$
11. $25x^2 - 40xy + 16y^2$
13. $x^2 - 16$
15. $81 - x^2$
17. $9x^4 - 64y^2$
19. Area of walkway = Total area − area of pool
    $= (x + 1)^2 - (x - 2)^2$
    $6x - 3$
    When $x = 7$ feet, the area of the walkway is $6(7) - 3 = 39$ square feet.
21. $3x^2 - 40x - 28$
    \$8.
23. b, c, and d are true.
25. a. $(a + b)^2 = a^2 + ab + ab + b^2 = a^2 + 2ab + b^2$
    b. $(a - b)^2 = a^2 - ab - ab - b^2 = a^2 - 2ab + b^2$
    c. $(a + b)(a - b) = a^2 + ab - ab - b^2 = a^2 - b^2$

UNIT 3 Selected Answers

MODULE 6

Lesson 6.1 Understanding Quadratic Functions

Your Turn

4. D: all real; R: $y \geq 0$
5. D: all real; R: $y \geq 0$
7. D: all real; R: $y \leq 0$
8. D: all real; R: $y \leq 0$
9. $g(x) = 4x^2$
10. $g(x) = -x^2$
11. The y-intercept occurs at the left end-point, which is also the vertex, and represents the height $h = 0$ at which the rock was released at ground level.
    The right end point represents the height $h = -64$ feet at which the rock hits the bottom of the well $t = 2$ seconds after it was released.
    $d(t) = -16t^2$

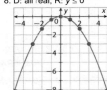

Evaluate

1. 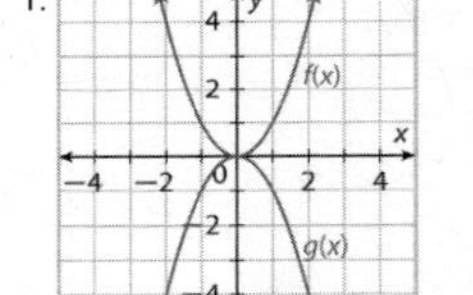

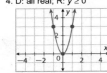

   Domain, vertex, and axis of symmetry are the same. Range, maximum, and minimum are different. ($f(x)$ doesn't have a maximum, and $g(x)$ doesn't have a minimum.)
3. 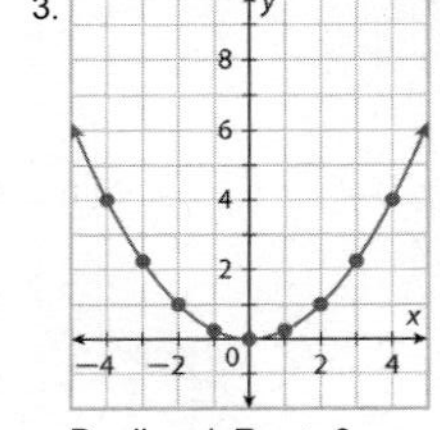

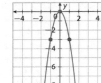

   D: all real; R: $y \geq 0$
5. D: all real; R: $y \geq 0$

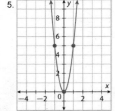

7.

D: all real; R: $y \le 0$

9. D: all real; R: $y \le 0$

11. $g(x) = -\frac{1}{2}x^2$

13. $g(x) = \frac{5}{4}x^2$

15. $h(d) = -31.25d^2$

17. $E(d) = \frac{1}{2}d^2$

19. $E(r) = 0.001r^2$

21. $E(\ell) = 0.06\ell^2$

23. When a is negative, the y values cannot be positive. Since the y-value is positive, a must be positive.

25. When $f(x)$ has a minimum value, it means $a > 0$. When it has a maximum value, $a < 0$. In either case, the minimum or the maximum value will be 0.

UNIT 3 Selected Answers

MODULE 6

Lesson 6.2 Transforming Quadratic Functions

Your Turn

5. The function $g(x) = x^2 + 4$ has a minimum value of 4.

   The axis of symmetry for $g(x) = x^2 + 4$ is $x = 0$.

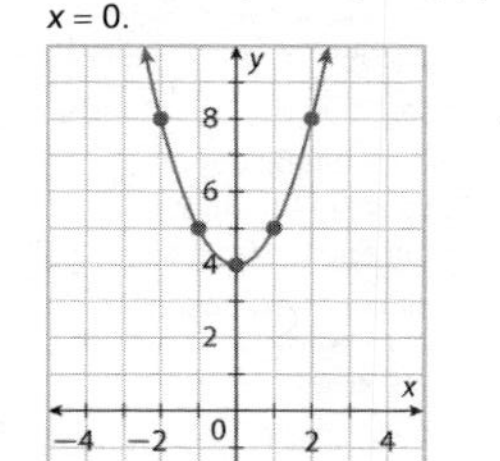

6. The function $g(x) = x^2 - 7$ has a minimum value of -7.

   The axis of symmetry for $g(x) = x^2 - 7$ is $x = 0$.

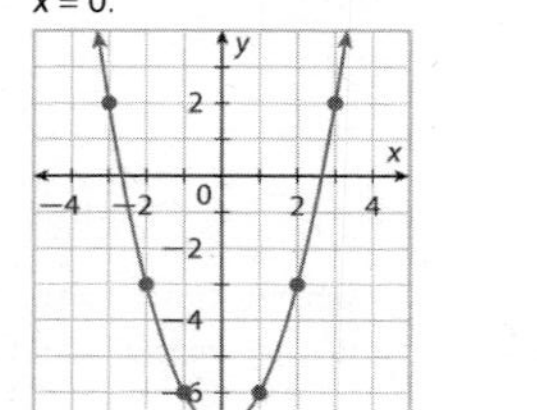

9.

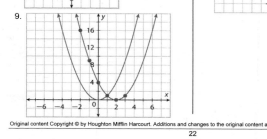

10.

12.

13.

Evaluate

1\.

The parent function has been translated 2 units right and 5 units up. It has been stretched vertically by a factor of 2.

3\.

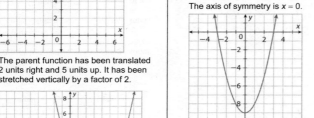

The parent function has been translated 3 units right and 4 units down. It has been vertically compressed by a factor of $\frac{1}{2}$.

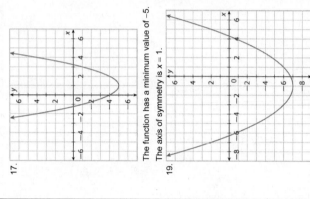

5\.

7\.

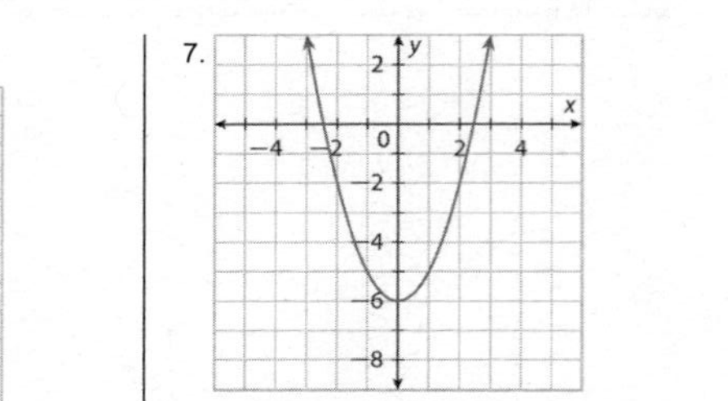

9\. The function has a minimum value of –9.

The axis of symmetry is $x = 0$.

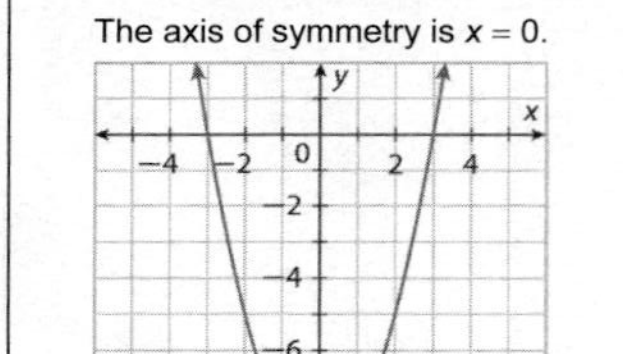

11\.

The function has a minimum value of 0.

The axis of symmetry is $x = 3$.

13\. The graph of $g(x) = (x + 12)^2$ is the graph of $f(x) = x^2$ translated 12 units left.

15\. Translate the graph of the parent function 2 units *to the* right.

17\.

The function has a minimum value of –5.

The axis of symmetry is $x = 1$.

19\.

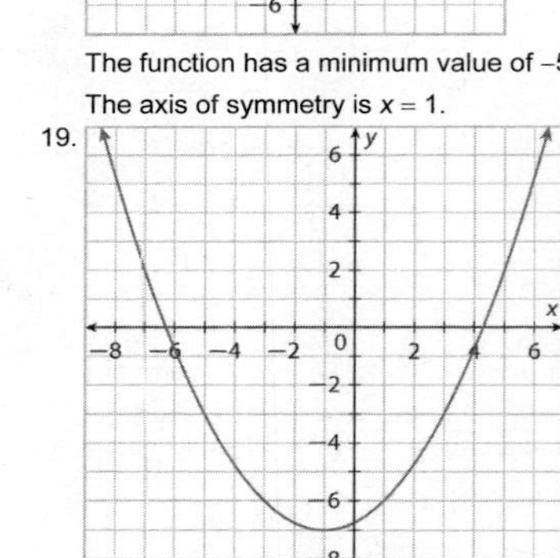

The function has a minimum value of –7.

The axis of symmetry is $x = -1$.

21\. Translate the graph of the parent function 3 units to the right and 2 units up.

23\. When $b > 1$, the graph of $y = (bx)^2$ is compressed horizontally by a factor of $\frac{1}{b}$.

25\. Nina should have subtracted 4 from x in the equation instead of adding it.

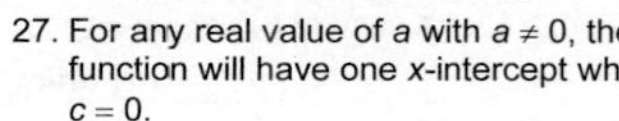

27\. For any real value of a with $a \neq 0$, the function will have one x-intercept when $c = 0$.

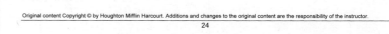

UNIT 3 Selected Answers

MODULE 6

Lesson 6.3 Interpreting Vertex Form and Standard Form

Your Turn

6. $y - 4x + x^2 = 0$ is a quadratic function.
7. This is not a quadratic function because $a = 0$.
9. The standard form of $y = 2(x + 5)^2 + 3$ is $y = 2x^2 + 20x + 53$.
10. The standard form of $y = -3(x - 7)^2 + 2 + 3$ is $y = -3x^2 + 42x - 145$.
12. Vertex form $y = 6(x - 2)^2 + 5$

    Standard form $y = 6x^2 - 24x + 29$
13. Vertex form $y = -5(x + 2)^2 - 7$

    Standard form $y = -5x^2 - 20x - 27$
16. The equation for the function is $f(x) = -(x - 1)^2 + 1$.
17. The equation for the function is $f(t) = -16t^2 + 45$.

Evaluate

1. The graph is a parabola. It is quadratic.
3. The graph is a parabola. It is quadratic.
5. No, $a = 0$
7. Yes, $a \neq 0$, b, and c are real numbers.
9. b, d
11. The axis of symmetry is the y-axis, or $x = 0$.
13. The standard form of $y = -2(x + 4)^2 - 11$ is $y = -2x^2 - 16x - 43$.
15. The standard form of $y = -4(x - 3)^2 - 9$ is $y = -4x^2 + 24x - 45$.
17. Sample answer: Expand the squared term. Then distribute the a-value. Finally, combine like terms.
19. Vertex form $y = -\frac{1}{2}(x - 4)^2 + 7$.

    Standard form $y = -\frac{1}{2}x^2 + 4x - 1$.
21. Vertex form $y = -4(x + 3)^2 + 10$.

    Standard form $y = -4x^2 - 24x - 26$.
23. The equation for the function is $f(t) = -16t^2 + 20$.
25. The equation for the function is $f(t) = -16(t - 1.5)^2 - 40$.

    The curve appears to intersect the x-axis at 3.1.

    So, evaluate the function $f(t)$ at 3.1;

    $f(3.1) = -16(3.1 - 1.5)^2 + 40 = -0.96$

    -0.96 is close to the expected value of 0, so the equation is reasonable.

UNIT 3 Selected Answers

MODULE 7

Lesson 7.1 Connecting Intercepts and Zeroes

Your Turn

3. The related function is $y = x^2 - 1$.

   The zeros of the function are 1 and -1, so the solutions of the equation are $x = -1$ and $x = 1$.
5. The graphs intersect at two locations: (1, 3) and (3, 3).

   This means $f(x) = g(x)$ when $x = 1$ and $x = 3$.

   So the solutions of $3(x - 2)^2 - 3 = 0$ are 1 and 3.
7. The egg will hit the plant after about 1.12 seconds.
8. The fish is out of the water for 0.3125 second.

Evaluate

1.

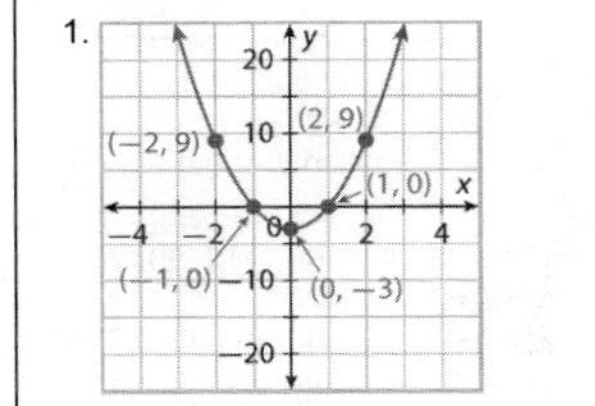

The zeros of $y = 3x^2 - 3$ are 1 and -1, so $x = -1$ or $x = 1$.

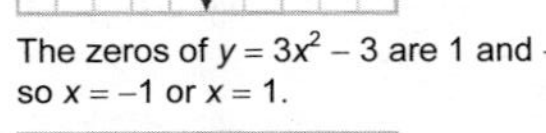

3.

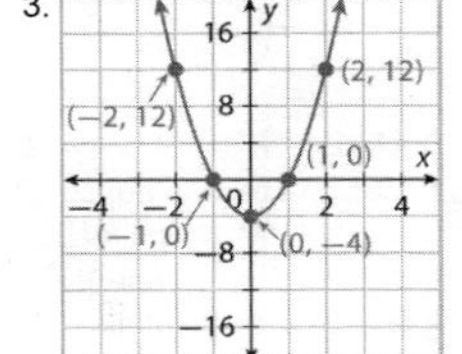

The zeros of $y = 4x^2 - 4$ are 1 and -1, so $x = -1$ or $x = 1$.

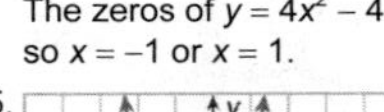

5.

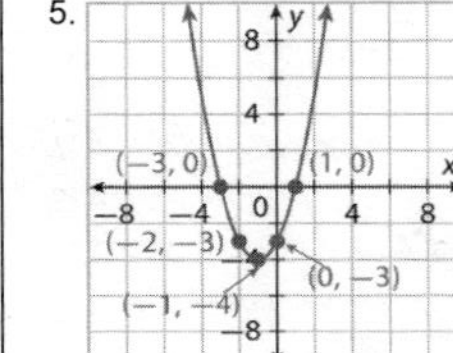

The zeros of $y = x^2 + 2x - 3$ are -3 and -1, so $x = -3$ or $x = 1$.

7.

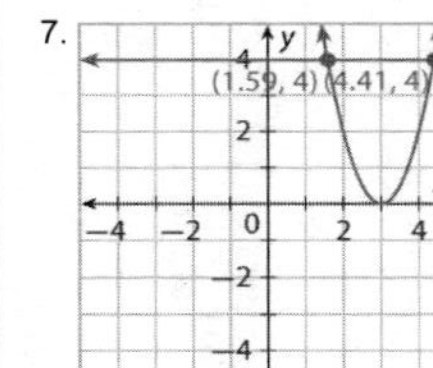

The graphs of $f(x) = 2(x - 3)^2$ and $g(x) = 4$ intersect at (1.59, 4) and (4.41, 4). So $x = 1.59$ or $x = 4.41$.

9.

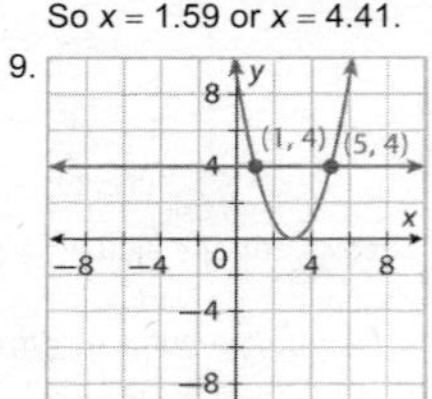

The graphs of $f(x) = (x - 3)^2$ and $g(x) = 4$ intersect at (5, 4) and (1, 4). So $x = 5$ or $x = 1$.

11.

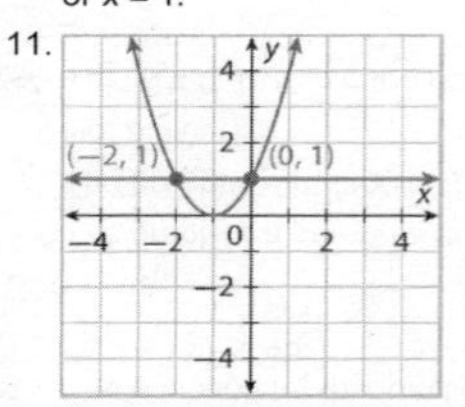

The graphs of $f(x) = (x + 1)^2$ and $g(x) = 1$ intersect at (−2, 1) and (0, 1). So $x = -2$ or $x = 0$.

13. The graphs of $y = -16x^2 + 30$ and $y = 5$ intersect at about (1.25, 5). The twig will hit the rosebush after about 1.25 seconds.

15. The graphs of $y = -16x^2 + 60$ and $y = 58$ intersect at about (0.4, 58). The trampolinist will land back on the trampoline after about 0.4 seconds.

17. The graph of $f(x) = -16x^2 + 18x$ shows a zero of about 1.125. The shark is out of the water for about 1.125 seconds.

19. The graph of $f(x) = -16x^2 + 11x$ shows a zero of about 0.7. The fish is in the air for about 0.7 seconds.

21. a. $a = 3$, $b = 2$, $c = 4$

b. $a = 0$, $b = 2$, $c = 1$

c. $a = 1$, $b = 0$, $c = 0$

d. $a = 0$, $b = 0$, $c = 5$

e. $a = 3$, $b = 8$, $c = 11$

23. Sample answer: The graph of $f(x) = x^2$ opens upward, but the related equation, $x^2 = 0$, has only one solution.

25. Jamie could create an equation of the graph by knowing only the zeros if she rewrote the zeros as factors of the polynomial and then solved by inserting the values from the random point to find *a*.

UNIT 3 Selected Answers

MODULE 7

Lesson 7.2 Connecting Intercepts and Linear Factors

Your Turn

5. $y = x^2 - 8x + 7$

6. $y = 4x^2 + 8x - 12$

9. $y = -2x^2 - 12x - 10$

The factored form shows that *x*-intercepts are −5 and −1.; the zeros are −5 and −1.

10. $y = 5x^2 - 20x + 15$

The factored form shows that *x*-intercepts are 1 and 3; the zeros are 1 and 3.

12. $k = 1$:
$f(x) = x^2 - 9x + 8$

$k = -4$:
$f(x) = -4x^2 + 36x - 32$

$k = 5$:
$f(x) = 5x^2 - 45x + 40$

13. $k = 1$:
$f(x) = x^2 + 4x - 21$

$k = -5$:
$f(x) = -5x^2 - 20x + 105$

$k = 7$:
$f(x) = 7x^2 + 28x - 147$

Evaluate

1.

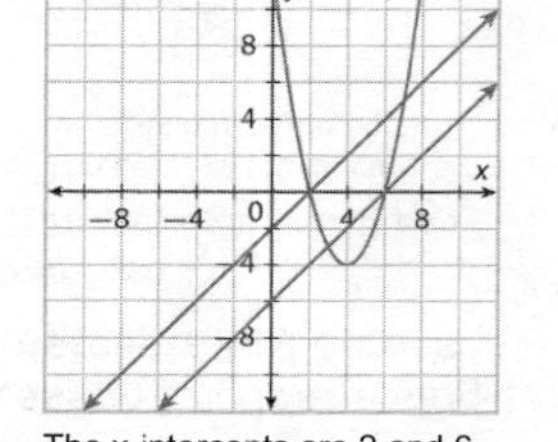

The x-intercepts are 2 and 6.

The axis of symmetry is $x = 4$.

3.

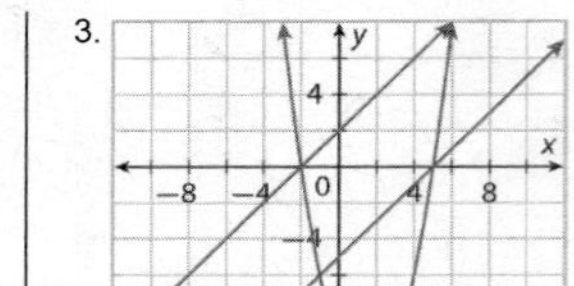

The *x*-intercepts are −2 and 5.

The axis of symmetry is $x = 1.5$.

5. $y = 5x^2 - 5x - 10$

7. $y = -2x^2 + 2x + 40$

9. c

11. $y = -2x^2 + 12x - 16$

x-intercepts are 2 and 4. The zeros are 2 and 4.

13. $y = -3x^2 + 6x + 9$

x-intercepts are −1 and 3. The zeros are −1 and 3.

15. The *x*-intercepts are 0 and 2. The ball will hit the ground in 2 seconds

17. $k = 1$: $f(x) = 1(x + 5)(x - 3)$

$f(x) = x^2 + 2x - 15$

$k = -2$: $f(x) = -2(x + 5)(x - 3)$

$f(x) = -2x^2 - 4x + 30$

$k = 5$: $f(x) = 5(x + 5)(x - 3)$

$f(x) = 5x^2 + 10x - 75$

19. The factored form is $f(x) = 4(x - 3)(x - 9)$ and the standard form is $f(x) = -4x^2 - 48x + 108$. Kelly substituted negative values for the *x*-intercepts.

21. Find the product $(x - (-3))\ (x - 1)$, or $(x + 3)(x - 1)$. Then write a quadratic function using this product. So a possible quadratic function is $y = x^2 + 2x - 3$.

UNIT 3 Selected Answers

MODULE 7

Lesson 7.3 Applying the Zero Product Property to Solve Equations

Your Turn

5. The zeros are 10 and 6.
6. The zeros are 13 and –12.
8. $x = \frac{2}{7}$ $x = 11$
9. $x = \frac{3}{8}$ $x = -6$
11. The ball is in the air for 2 seconds.

Evaluate

1. $x = 15$ $x = 22$
3. $x = -15$ $x = -17$
5. $x = 1.9$ $x = 3.5$
7. $x = \frac{3}{4}$
9. $x = -12$ $x = -\frac{15}{6}$
11. $x = -\frac{2}{3}$ $x = -\frac{1}{5}$
13. $9 = x$ $x = -\frac{1}{21}$
15. $-\frac{1}{2} = t$ $t = \frac{5}{2}$
17. The solutions are $t = -0.5$ and $t = 5$. Since time cannot be negative, the flare is in the air for 5 seconds.
19. The solutions are $t = -0.125$ and $t = 1$. Since time cannot be negative, the time it takes for the beanbag to reach the ground is 1 second.
21. A. E
    B. A, D
    C. C
    D. B
23. a. Since the ball starts at $d = 0$, it will hit the ground at $d = 4$. Since the curve is symmetric, the ball will be at its maximum height at half this distance, or 2 meters.
    b. The maximum height is 8 meters. The point $(2, h)$, or $(2, 8)$, is the vertex of the graph of the function.
25. First number: x
    Second number: $x + 3$
    Third number: $4(x + 3)$
    $4(x + 3) + x(x + 3) = 0$
    $x = -4$, or $x = -3$
    The three numbers are either –4, –1, and –4, or –3, 0, and 0.

UNIT 4 Selected Answers

MODULE 8

Lesson 8.1 Solving Equations by Factoring $x^2 + bx + c$

Your Turn

9. $x = -6$ or $x = -9$
10. $x = 12$ or $x = 1$
11. $x = -7$ or $x = 8$

Evaluate

1. 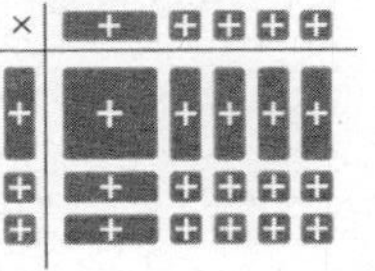

+4 +2

3. $(x - 4)(x - 11)$
5. $(x - 2)(x + 16)$
7. $(x + 4)(x + 6)$
9. $x = -7$ or $x = -12$
11. $x = 3$ or $x = 9$
13. $x = 9$ or $x = -15$
15. $x = 11$ or $x = -12$
17. The dimensions of the outside border of the walkway are $(x + 6)$ feet and $(x + 14)$ feet.
19. Rug:
    Length: 25 feet
    Width: 16 feet
    Wall:
    Width: 22 ft
    Length: 35 ft
21. b
    d
    c
    a
23. There are no other values where $b = c$ that make the expression factorable. The expression $x^2 + 4x + 4$ is factorable because $2 + 2 = 4$ and $2 \cdot 2 = 4$. The only number that has equal factors which sum to the number itself is 4, so no other factorable expressions exist where $b = c$.
25. The possible values of b are the sums of the factors of 64: ±65, ±34, ±20, and ±16.

UNIT 4 Selected Answers

MODULE 8

Lesson 8.2 Solving Equations by Factoring $ax^2 + bx + c$

Your Turn

5. $-1(x - 2)(5x + 2)$
7. $x = -\frac{3}{2}$ and $x = -\frac{5}{2}$
8. The rock lands 3 seconds after it is thrown.

Evaluate

1. $(3x + 1)(2x + 1)$
3. $(2x - 1)(2x - 3)$
5. $(x + 1)(3x - 5)$
7. $2(2x - 1)(3x + 7)$
9. $x = -3$ or $x = -\frac{3}{5}$
11. $x = -4$ or $x = -\frac{1}{3}$
13. $x = \frac{3}{2}$ or $x = -\frac{1}{4}$
15. $x = -2$ or $x = \frac{1}{8}$
17. It takes the ball $2\frac{1}{2}$ seconds to land.
19. It takes $\frac{1}{3}$ second to travel 30 more feet.
21. length = $(6x - 1)$, width = $(x + 3)$
23. b. $5(3x + 1)(x - 2)$
    d. $5(x - 2)(3x + 1)$
25. $(2x + 5)^2$

UNIT 4 Selected Answers

MODULE 8

Lesson 8.3 Using Special Factors to Solve Equations

Your Turn

3. $2y(y + 3)^2$
4. $(10z - 1)^2$
6. $(x + 12)(x - 12)$
7. $9y^2(3y + 1)(3y - 1)$
8. $x = \frac{1}{5}$
9. $x = 0$
   $x = -\frac{1}{2}$ $x = \frac{1}{2}$
10. $t = \frac{1}{4}$ $t = \frac{1}{2}$
    At 0.25 second or 0.5 second the ball will be 8 ft high. There are two solutions because both occur after $t = 0$, when the ball is set.
11. $t = \pm 1$
    After one second, the rocket will have descended a distance of 490 centimeters. The negative time cannot be used in this context.

Evaluate

1. 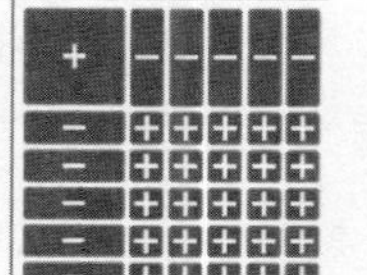

   $(x - 5)(x - 5)$
3. $(2x + 1)^2$
5. $x(4x + 1)^2$
7. $(x + 13)(x - 13)$
9. $8x^2(2x + 1)(2x - 1)$
11. $x = -\frac{2}{5}$
13. $x = 0$ $x = -1$
15. $x = -9$ $x = 9$
17. $q = -\frac{9}{4}$ $x = \frac{9}{4}$
19. After $t = \frac{8}{7} \approx 1.14$ seconds, the rocket will have reached a height of 640 centimeters.
21. After $t = \frac{10}{7} \approx 1.43$ seconds, the rocket will have descended a distance of 1000 centimeters. The negative value of t cannot be used in this context.
23. After $t = \frac{7}{4} = 1.75$ seconds, the diver will have reached the water.
25. He factored out a 2 from both $(12x + 10)$ and $(12x + 10)$, which is the same as factoring out a 4 from the whole expression. It should be $4(6x + 5)(6x - 5)$.
    $144x^2 - 100 = (12x + 10)(12x - 10)$
    $= 2(6x + 5) \cdot 2(6x - 5)$
    $= 4(6x + 5)(6x - 5)$
27. The area of the frame is $4(2x + y)(2x - y)$.
29. She can factor each side of the equation, and then subtract the right side from both sides so one side of the equation is 0. She can then simplify the equation and set the factors equal to 0 to solve for x.
    The solutions are 0 and -1.

UNIT 4 Selected Answers

MODULE 9

Lesson 9.1 Solving Equations by Taking Square Roots

Your Turn

4. $x = \pm\sqrt{9}$

   The solutions are 3 and –3.

   The graph intersects the x-axis at (3, 0) and (–3, 0).

5. $x = \pm\sqrt{2.2}$

   The approximate solutions are 1.48 and –1.48.

   The graph intersects the x-axis at approximately (1.48, 0) and (–1.48, 0).

7. $x = -\sqrt{6} - 10$ or $x = \sqrt{6} - 10$

   $x \approx -12.45$ $\quad x \approx -7.55$

8. $x = 1$ $\quad x = 17$

9. The zookeeper should buy 95 + 95, or 190, feet of fencing.

Evaluate

1. ± 0.09
3. $\pm 4\sqrt{6}$
5. $x = \pm\sqrt{100}$

   $x = \pm 10$

   The graph intersects the x-axis at (10, 0) and (–10, 0).

7. $x = \pm\sqrt{78}$

   $x \approx \pm 8.83$

   The graph intersects the x-axis at approximately (8.83, 0) and (–8.83, 0).

9. $x = \pm\sqrt{\frac{8}{7}}$

   $x \approx \pm 1.07$

   The graph intersects the x-axis at approximately (1.07, 0) and (–1.07, 0).

11. $x = -24$ $\quad x = -6$
13. $x = 34$ $\quad x = 46$
15. $x = -\frac{\sqrt{7}}{2} - 5.4$ or $x = \frac{\sqrt{7}}{2} - 5.4$

    $x \approx -6.72$ $\quad x \approx -4.08$

17. The x-intercepts are 6.8 units from the origin. So, they are located at (–6.8, 0) and (6.8, 0).
19. It will take the sack approximately 6.12 seconds to reach the ground.
21. The ball will hit the ground after approximately 0.7 second.
23. Lisa's solution is correct. By the definition of a square root of a, $x^2 = a$, so the square of a real number is always non-negative. So, a must be non-negative. In the equation $x^2 = -225$, a is negative. So, there are no real solutions of the equation.
25. When $b > 0$, the solution of $x^2 + b = 0$ is the square root of a negative number, which is not real; but the solution of $x^2 - b = 0$ is the square root of a positive number, which has 2 possible values.

UNIT 4 Selected Answers

MODULE 9

Lesson 9.2 Solving Equations by Completing the Square

Your Turn

4. $x^2 + 12x + 36$
5. $x = 11$ $\quad x = -1$
6. $x = -3 + \sqrt{11}$ $\quad x = -3 - \sqrt{11}$
8. $x = \frac{5}{4}$ $\quad x = -\frac{1}{4}$
9. $x = \frac{-3 + \sqrt{14}}{2}$ $\quad x = \frac{-3 - \sqrt{14}}{2}$
11. $x = -3 + \sqrt{37}$ $\quad x = -3 - \sqrt{37}$
12. $x = 4$ $\quad x = -2$
13. 49 feet; after 2 seconds

Evaluate

1. $x^2 + 26x + 169$
3. $x^2 - 2x + 1$
5. $x = 3$ $\quad x = -11$
7. $x = -6 + \sqrt{41}$ $\quad x = -6 - \sqrt{41}$
9. $x = \frac{4}{3}$ $\quad x = -\frac{8}{3}$
11. $x = \frac{13}{4}$ $\quad x = -\frac{5}{4}$
13. $x = 2$ $\quad x = -10$
15. $x = \frac{-7 + \sqrt{57}}{2}$ $\quad x = \frac{-7 - \sqrt{57}}{2}$
17. $h = -16t^2 + 8t$

    $h = -16\left(t - \frac{1}{4}\right)^2 + 1$

    The ball will be at its highest when it is at its vertex, or at 1 foot.

    The graph of the function confirms the vertex at (0.25, 1). The x-intercept at 0.5 indicates that the ball will hit the ground after 0.5 second.

19. The vertex is $\left(\frac{1}{2}, 9\right)$, so the maximum height is 9 feet.

    The volleyball will hit the ground after 1.25 seconds.

21. $a = 11$

    $a = 4$

    $a = 0$

    $a = 5$

    $a = 3$

23. The student forgot that the square root of 81 has two solutions:
    –9 and 9. The correct solution is $x + 2 = \pm 9$, or $x = 7$ and $x = -11$.
25. When solving a quadratic model, some solutions are considered extraneous because they have a negative value, which is not useful in a real-world context. However, this is not always the case, as some quadratic models will have two valid solutions.

UNIT 4 Selected Answers

MODULE 9

Lesson 9.3 Using the quadratic formula to Solve Equations

Your Turn

3. two real solutions
4. no real solutions
5. one real solution
7. The solutions are 7 and –1.
8. The solutions are $2 + \frac{\sqrt{2}}{2}$ and $2 - \frac{\sqrt{2}}{2}$
9. The soccer ball reached the ground after about $t \approx 1.33$ seconds.
10. The ball was in the air for $t \approx 0.94$ second.

Evaluate

1. Since $b^2 - 4ac = 0$, the equation has one real solution.
3. Since $b^2 - 4ac > 0$, the equation has two real solutions.
5. Since $b^2 - 4ac > 0$, the equation has two real solutions.
7. Since $b^2 - 4ac = 0$, the equation has one real solution.
9. The solutions are 2 and $-\frac{1}{3}$.
11. The solutions are $\frac{-1+\sqrt{65}}{8}$ and $\frac{-1-\sqrt{65}}{8}$.
13. The solutions are $-\frac{1}{4}$ and $-\frac{3}{2}$.
15. Since $b^2 - 4ac > 0$, the equation has two real solutions.

    $t \approx -1.19$ or $t \approx 0.17$

    Disregard the negative solution because there is no negative time in this context. The soccer ball reached the goal after about $t \approx 0.17$ seconds.
17. There is an equal number of both types of bacteria at $t \approx 15.18$ minutes.
19. a. d. e.

    The letters A, D, and E are possible heights of the gymnast
21. Because every positive number has two square roots, a positive discriminant results in two solutions to a quadratic equation.

UNIT 4 Selected Answers

MODULE 9

Lesson 9.4 Choosing a Method for Solving Quadratic Equations

Your Turn

Sample explanations given.

6. Take the square roots because $b = 0$.

   $x = \pm\frac{10}{3}$
7. Complete the square, because it is not factorable, but the coefficients are small and will not lead to a lot of fractional terms

   $x = -2 \pm \sqrt{11}$
8. $0 = -16t^2 + 24t + 40$

   The wheel will not hit the ground before it falls off, so the answer must be the positive, and the time is 2.5 seconds. I chose to solve by factoring because after 8 was factored out, the quadratic was easy to factor.
9. The ball reaches the same height as the kite at about 1.20 seconds, and then again on the way back down at 1.92 seconds.

Evaluate

1. This formula is expressed with two digit decimal coefficients. Factoring and completing the squares could be attempted by multiplying the equation by 100 to get to integer coefficients, but the amount of work in either method would be unreasonable. The quadratic formula, on the other hand, can be used easily with a calculator to evaluate the coefficients without any further manipulation.
3. Taking square roots, because $b = 0$.

   $x = \pm\frac{4}{3}$
5. Factoring, because there are not many factors to check, and in this case, it works.

   $x = -\frac{1}{8}$ or $x = -1$
7. The quadratic formula, because the equation cannot be factored and completing the square will be complicated.

   $x = 1.27$ or $x = -0.56$
9. Completing the square, because it is not factorable, but the coefficients are small and will not lead to a lot of fractional terms.

   $x = -1 \pm \frac{\sqrt{10}}{2}$
11. Factoring, because there are not too many factors to check, and in this case, it works.

    $x = 1$ or $x = \frac{1}{4}$
13. Completing the square, because it is not factorable, but the coefficients are small and will not lead to a lot of fractional terms.

    $x = 2 \pm \frac{\sqrt{7}}{2}$
15. Completing the square, because it is not factorable, but the coefficients are small and will not lead to a lot of fractional terms.

    $x = -1 \pm \frac{\sqrt{3}}{3}$
17. The quadratic formula, because factoring and completing the square may be time-consuming.

    $x = 1$ or $x = -\frac{19}{6}$
19. The quadratic formula, because the equation cannot be factored and completing the square will be complicated.

    1.54 seconds after it is headed.
21. The quadratic formula, because the equation cannot be factored and completing the square will be complicated.

    1.06 seconds.

23. Equations that can be solved by taking square roots or by factoring are usually solved that way because there is less computation involved in both of those methods. The answer will usually be found in less time and with fewer errors. If an equation cannot be factored, but can be solved by completing the square without large or fractional terms, it will probably be easier to solve by completing the square rather than using the quadratic formula.

25. The second statement is false. Some quadratic equations cannot be solved for a real value of x. If there are real solutions, then the quadratic formula can be used to find them. Either way, the first statement is true.

UNIT 4 Selected Answers

MODULE 9

Lesson 9.5 Solving Nonlinear Systems

Your Turn

2. Solution: (−4, 0) or (−2, 8)

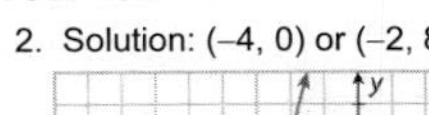

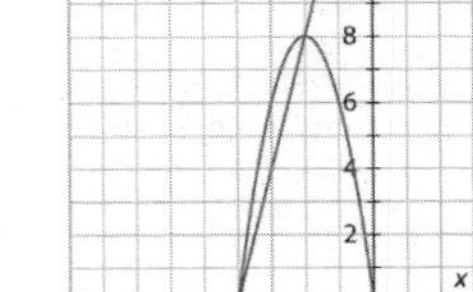

3. Solution: (2, 0)

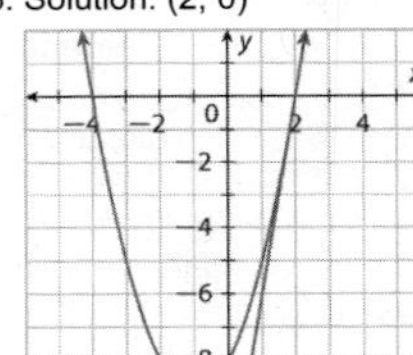

5. The discriminant is negative, so there are no real solutions.
7. The paint brush passes by the can about 7.3 seconds after the painter starts hoisting it up or about 2.3 seconds after the paintbrush starts to fall.

Evaluate

1. 2; 1; 0

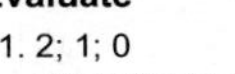

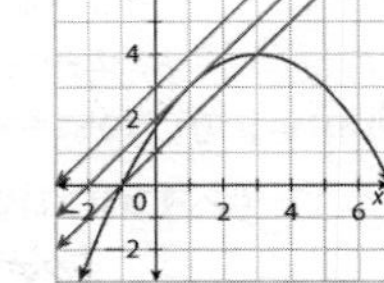

3. No Solutions

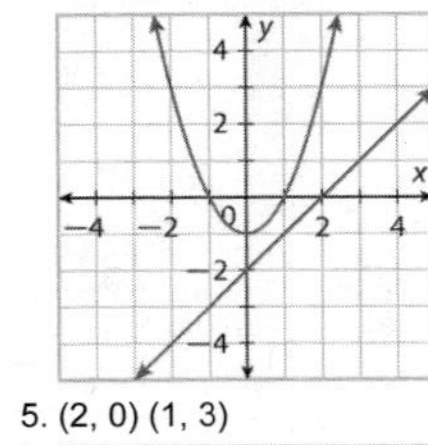

5. (2, 0) (1, 3)

7. No Solution

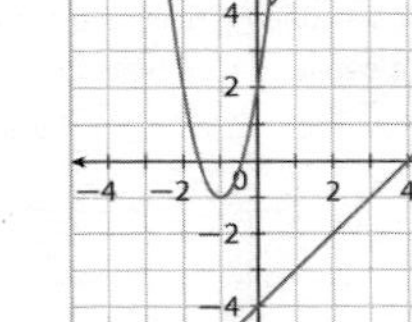

9. (2, 0) (5, 12)
11. (2, 4) (1, 3)
13. (2, 11) (−11, 128)
15. There are no real solutions.
17. The wildebeest escapes.
19. The jumper hears the tire blow-out at a height of about 79.2 meters.
21. One solution has a negative value of *t*, which would mean the bolt hit the elevator before it began to fall.

23. The second intersection point at 22.18 seconds corresponds to a height −5654.74 feet, or under the ground. The second intersection point is outside the range of the model even though it has a positive time, and it cannot be a valid solution.

25. The two solutions are points on the line and can be used to solve for the line.

$$m = \frac{10-7}{5-2} = 1 \qquad \begin{aligned} y &= mx = b \\ 10 &= 1(5) + b \\ b &= 5 \end{aligned}$$

The line is $y = x + 5$. Two points define a line, so there is no need to use the quadratic equation.

UNIT 4 Selected Answers

MODULE 10

Lesson 10.1 Fitting a Linear Model to Data

Your Turn

7.

x	y (Actual)	y Predicted by $y = x + 4$	Residual for $y = x + 4$	y Predicted by $y = x + 4.2$	Residual for $y = x + 4.2$
1	4	5	−1	5.2	−1.2
2	7	6	1	6.2	0.8
3	8	7	1	7.2	0.8
4	6	8	−2	8.2	−2.2

$y = x + 4$: $(-1)^2 + (1)^2 + (1)^2 + (-2)^2 = 7$

$y = x + 4.2$: $(-1.2)^2 + (0.8)^2 + (0.8)^2 + (-2.2)^2 = 7.56$

The sum of the squared residuals for $y = x + 4$ is smaller, so it provides a better fit.

10. The temperature in Trenton, New Jersey, should be around 40 degrees Fahrenheit. The correlation coefficient is about −0.99, which indicates a very strong correlation. Therefore, the line of best fit is reliable for estimating temperatures within the same range of latitudes.

Evaluate

1. $y = x + 5$: $(-6)^2 + (-6)^2 + (-6)^2 + (-6)^2 = 36 + 36 + 36 + 36 = 144$

   $y = x + 4.9$: $(-5.9)^2 + (-5.9)^2 + (-5.9)^2 + (-5.9)^2 = 139.24$

   The sum of the squared residuals for $y = x + 4.9$ is smaller, so it provides a better fit for the data.

3. $y = 3x + 4$: $(-8)^2 + (-8)^2 + (-18)^2 + (-22)^2 = 936$

   $y = 3x + 4.1$: $(-8.1)^2 + (-8.1)^2 + (-18.1)^2 + (-22.1)^2 = 947.24$

   The sum of the squared residuals for $y = 3x + 4$ is smaller, so it provides a better fit.

5. $y = 3x + 1.2$: $(-6.2)^2 + (-8.2)^2 + (-15.2)^2 + (-22.2)^2 = 829.56$

   $y = 3x + 1$: $(-6)^2 + (-8)^2 + (-15)^2 + (-22)^2 = 809$

   The sum of the squared residuals for $y = 3x + 1$ is smaller, so it provides a better fit.

7. $y = 2x + 1$: $(-2)^2 + (-3)^2 + (-9)^2 + (-12)^2 = 238$

   $y = 2x + 1.4$: $(-2.4)^2 + (-3.4)^2 + (-9.4)^2 + (-12.4)^2 = 259.44$

   The sum of the squared residuals for $y = 2x + 1$ is smaller, so it provides a better fit.

9. $y = x + 3$: $(-4)^2 + (-2)^2 + (-2)^2 + (-8)^2 = 88$

   $y = x + 2.6$: $(-3.6)^2 + (-1.6)^2 + (-1.6)^2 + (-7.6)^2 = 75.84$

   The sum of the squared residuals for $y = x + 2.6$ is smaller, so it provides a better fit.

11. $y = 2x + 3.1$: $(-3.1)^2 + (1.9)^2 + (-2.1)^2 + (0.9)^2 = 18.44$

   $y = 2x + 3.5$: $(-3.5)^2 + (1.5)^2 + (-2.5)^2 + (0.5)^2 = 21$

   The sum of the squared residuals for $y = 2x + 3.1$ is smaller, so it provides a better fit.

13. $y = x + 5$: $(1)^2 + (-2)^2 + (3)^2 + (-1)^2 = 15$
    $y = 1.3x + 5$: $(0.7)^2 + (-2.6)^2 + (2.1)^2 + (-2.2)^2 = 16.5$
    The sum of the squared residuals for $y = x + 5$ is smaller, so it provides a better fit.
15. $y = -0.95x + 71.13$

    The correlation coefficient is about –0.99, which indicates a very strong correlation. Therefore, the line of best fit is reliable for estimating temperatures within the same range of latitudes.

    The temperature in Panama City should be around 63 degrees Fahrenheit.
17. $y = -0.87x + 85.19$

    The correlation coefficient is about –0.99, which indicates a very strong correlation. Therefore, the line of best fit is reliable for estimating temperatures within the same range of latitudes.

    The temperature in Jerusalem should be around 58 degrees Fahrenheit.
19. Since the residuals are large, the line $y = 0.5x + 20$ is not a good fit.
21. 2, 2.3, –2.6, 3.6
23. This means that either all of the residuals are either the same as each other or the opposite of each other.

UNIT 4 Selected Answers

MODULE 10

Lesson 10.2 Graphing Exponential Functions

Your Turn

5. $a = 2$
   $b = 2$
   y-intercept: (0, 2)
   End Behavior: As $x \to \infty$, $y \to \infty$ and as $x \to -\infty$, $y \to 0$.

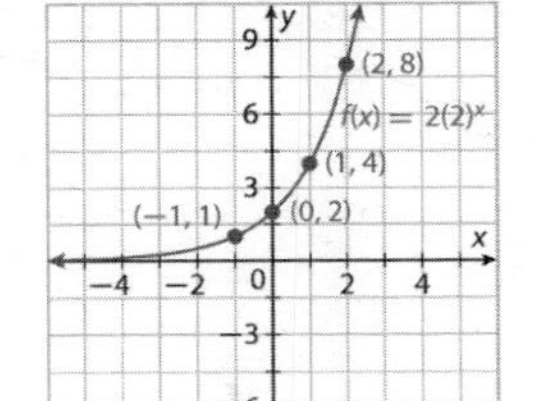

7. $a = -3$
   $b = 3$
   y-intercept: (0, –3)
   End Behavior: As $x \to \infty$, $y \to -\infty$ and as $x \to -\infty$, $y \to 0$.

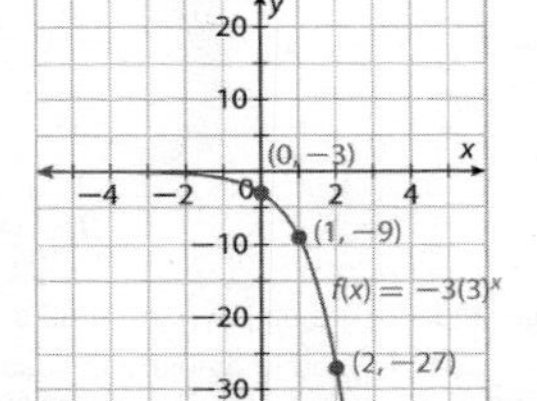

9. $a = 3$
   $b = 0.5$
   y-intercept: (0, 3)
   End Behavior: As $x \to \infty$, $y \to 0$ and as $x \to -\infty$, $y \to \infty$.

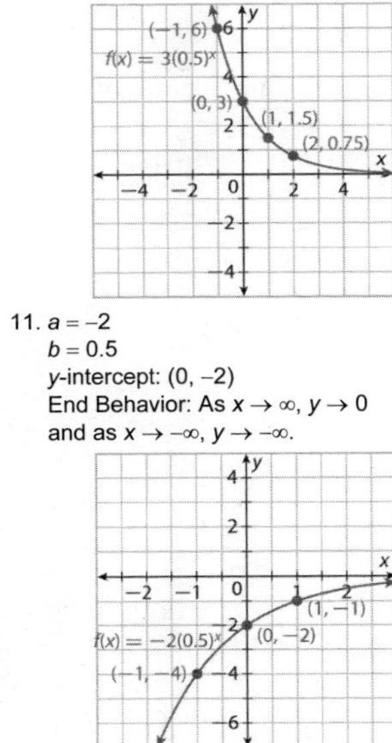

11. $a = -2$
    $b = 0.5$
    y-intercept: (0, –2)
    End Behavior: As $x \to \infty$, $y \to 0$ and as $x \to -\infty$, $y \to -\infty$.

Evaluate

1. $a = 2$
   $b = 3$
   y-intercept: (0, 2)
3. $a = -5$
   $b = 0.5$
   y-intercept: (0, –5)

5. $a = 6$
$b = 3$
y-intercept: (0, 6)

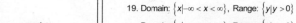

7. $a = 7$
$b = 0.9$
y-intercept: (0, 7)

9. $a = 3$
$b = 3$
y-intercept: (0, 3)
End Behavior: As $x \to \infty$, $y \to \infty$ and as $x \to -\infty$, $y \to 0$.

11. $a = -6$; $b = 0.7$
y-intercept: (0, –6)
End Behavior: As $x \to \infty$, $y \to 0$ and as $x \to -\infty$, $y \to -\infty$.

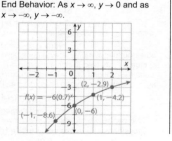

13. $a = 5$; $b = 2$
y-intercept: (0, 5)
End Behavior: As $x \to \infty$, $y \to \infty$ and as $x \to -\infty$, $y \to 0$.

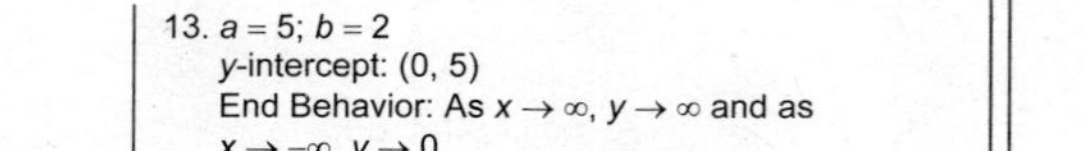

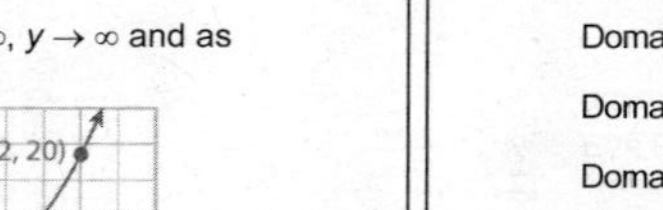

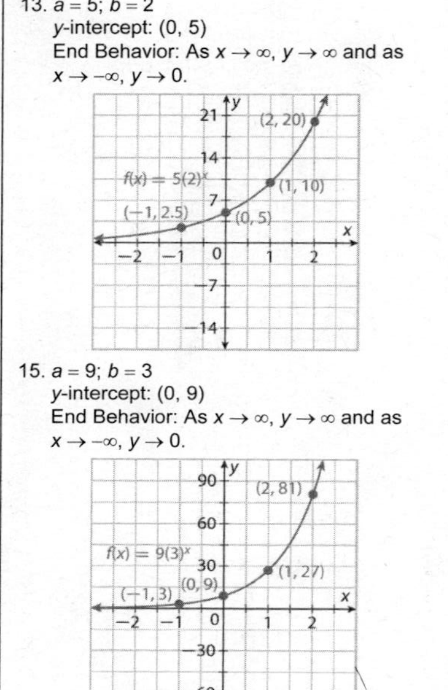

15. $a = 9$; $b = 3$
y-intercept: (0, 9)
End Behavior: As $x \to \infty$, $y \to \infty$ and as $x \to -\infty$, $y \to 0$.

17. $a = 7$; $b = 0.4$
y-intercept: (0, 7)
End Behavior: As $x \to \infty$, $y \to 0$ and as $x \to -\infty$, $y \to \infty$.

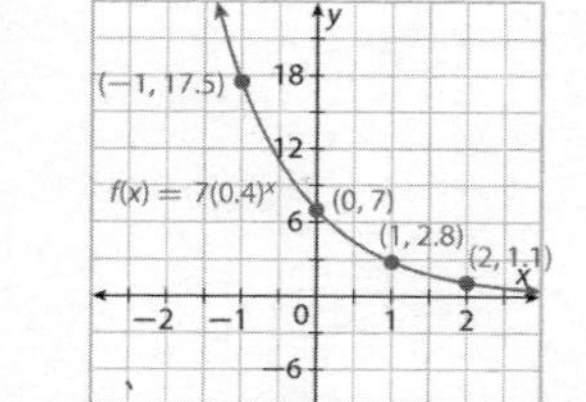

19. Domain: $\{x \mid -\infty < x < \infty\}$, Range: $\{y \mid y > 0\}$
Domain: $\{x \mid -\infty < x < \infty\}$, Range: $\{y \mid y > 0\}$
Domain: $\{x \mid -\infty < x < \infty\}$, Range: $\{y \mid y < 0\}$
Domain: $\{x \mid -\infty < x < \infty\}$, Range: $\{y \mid y < 0\}$
Domain: $\{x \mid -\infty < x < \infty\}$, Range: $\{y \mid y > 0\}$

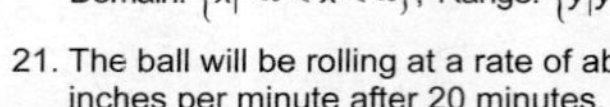

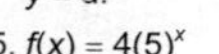

21. The ball will be rolling at a rate of about 10 inches per minute after 20 minutes.
23. The graph of b will be a horizontal line at $y = a$.
25. $f(x) = 4(5)^x$

UNIT 4 Selected Answers

MODULE 10

Lesson 10.3 Modeling Exponential Growth and Decay

Your Turn

10. After 8 years, the coin will be worth approximately $3.51.
    The domain is the set of real numbers t such that $t \geq 0$.
    The range is the set of real numbers y such that $y \geq 3$.
    The y-intercept is the value of y when $t = 0$, which is the value of the coin when it was sold.

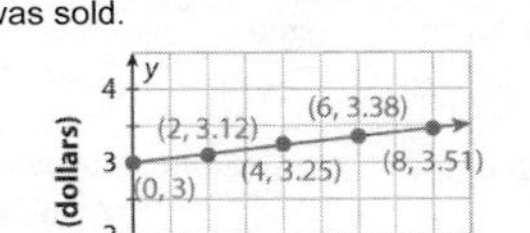

13. After 7 years, the boat will be worth approximately $9,198.35. The domain is the set of real numbers t such that $t \geq 0$. The range is the set of real numbers y such that $0 \leq y \leq 17,800$. The y-intercept is 17,800, the value of y when $t = 0$, which is the original value of the boat.

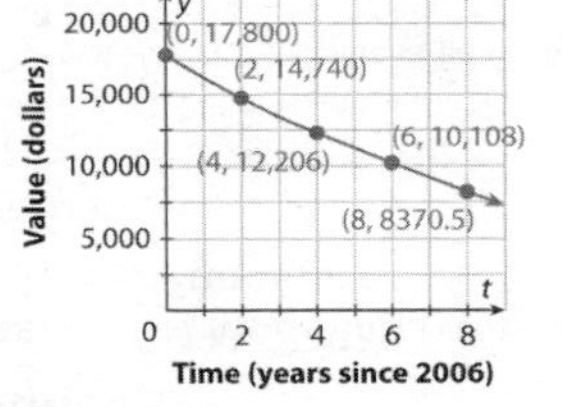

15. $A(t) = 150(0.3)^t$
    $B(t) = 5(3)^t$

The value of Stock A is going down over time. The value of Stock B is going up over time. The initial value of Stock A is greater than the initial value of Stock B. However, after about 1.5 years, the value of Stock B becomes greater than the value of Stock A.

Evaluate

1. Domain: $\{x \mid -\infty < x < \infty\}$ Range: $\{y \mid y > 0\}$
   End behavior: As $x \to -\infty$, $y \to 0$ and as $x \to \infty$, $y \to \infty$ Asymptote: $y = 0$
3. Domain: $\{x \mid -\infty < x < \infty\}$ Range: $\{y \mid y > 0\}$
   End behavior: As $x \to -\infty$, $y \to 0$ and as $x \to \infty$, $y \to \infty$ Asymptote: $y = 0$
5. $309,845.72
7. $349.47
9. $59,068.21
11. 28,584
13. $y = a(1 - r)^t = 192,000\ (0.93)^t$
    $y = 192,000(0.93)^9 \approx 99,918,93$
    After 9 years, the boat will be worth approximately $99,918.93.
    Domain: $\{x \mid 0 < x < \infty\}$ Range: $\{y \mid y > 0\}$
    The y-intercept is 192,000, the original value of the boat in 2004.

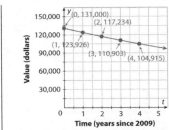

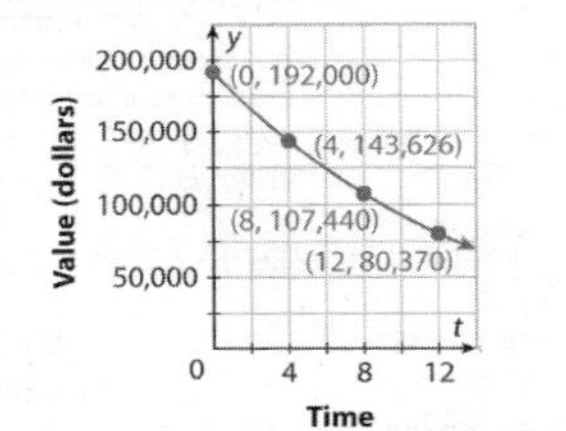

15. $y = a(1 - r)^t = 51.5(0.93)^t$
    $y = 51.5(0.93)^9 \approx 26.8$
    After 9 years, the airplane will be worth approximately $26.8 million.
    Domain: $\{x \mid 0 < x < \infty\}$ Range: $\{y \mid y > 0\}$
    The y-intercept is 51.5, the original value of the airplane in 2004.

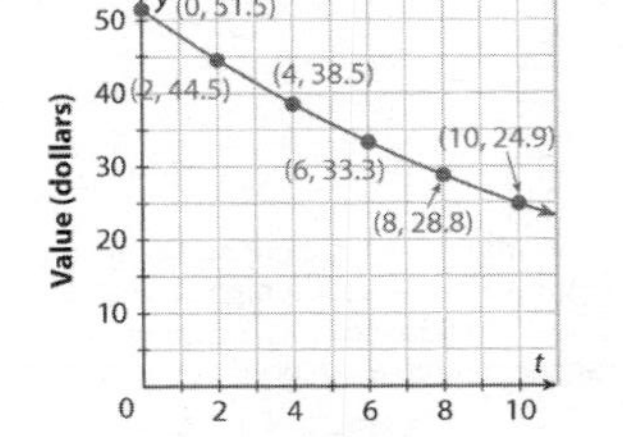

17. $y = a(1 - r)^t = 1232(0.938)^t$
    $y = 1232(0.938)^7 \approx 787.10$
    After 7 years, the couch will be worth approximately $787.10.
    Domain: $\{x \mid 0 < x < \infty\}$ Range: $\{y \mid y > 0\}$
    The y-intercept is 1232, the original value of the couch in 2007.

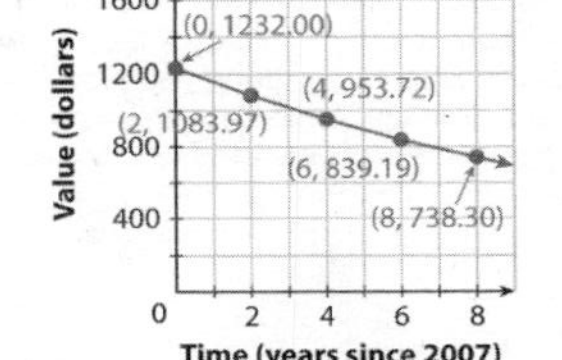

19. $y = a(1 - r)^t = 131,000(0.946)^t$
    $y = 131,000(0.946)^{10} \approx 75,194$
    After 10 years, the house will be worth about $75,194.
    Domain: $\{x \mid 0 < x < \infty\}$ Range: $\{y \mid y > 0\}$
    The y-intercept is 131,000, the original value of the house in 2009.

21. The value of $A(t)$ is decreasing. The value of $B(t)$ is increasing. The initial value of $A(t)$ is greater than the initial value of $B(t)$. However, after about .7 units, the value of $B(t)$ becomes greater than the value of $A(t)$.
23. The value of $A(t)$ is decreasing. The value of $B(t)$ is increasing. The initial value of $A(t)$ is greater than the initial value of $B(t)$. However, for t greater than about 2.7 units, the value of $B(t)$ becomes greater than the value of $A(t)$.
25. a. (0, 3123)
    b. (0, 0)
    c. (0, 45)
    d. (0, 76)
    e. (0, 1)
27. The value of the function will never be 0 because the right side of the function is a product of positive numbers. Although the value can become extremely close to 0, it can never equal 0.

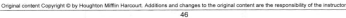

UNIT 4 Selected Answers

MODULE 10

Lesson 10.4 Modeling with Quadratic Functions

Your Turn

4. $y \approx -16.8x^2 + 120.6x - 1.143$
5. $y \approx -2x^2 + 2.286x - 6.081$
6. The first size with the surcharge will be size 11.
   The function represents the cost of specific sizes so the domain will be integer values of x with $x > 0$ and the range will be $y > 0$.
7. A clock with diameter of $15\frac{1}{4}$ inches can be made for $4.00.
   The function represents the cost of different sizes of clocks, so the domain will be $x > 0$ and the range will be $y > 0$.

Evaluate

1. is not
3. is not
5. Second Difference: 4, 5, 3, 3, 5, 3, 5, 3, 6, 3
   $y \approx 0.0531x^2 + 1.990x + 90.67 \quad R^2 = 1$
7. Second Difference: 20, 19, 16, 16, 18, 19, 17, 17, 16, 15
   $y \approx 0.0423x^2 - 19.03x + 2012 \quad R^2 = 1$
9. Second Difference: −16, −17, −16, −14, −17, −17, −15, −17, −17, −16
   $y \approx -0.8172x^2 - 28.73x - 747.5 \quad R^2 = 1$
11. Second Difference: 103, 87, 102, 67
   $y \approx 11.39x^2 - 122.8x - 353.6 \quad R^2 = 0.9999$
13. $y \approx -4.645x^2 + 50.89x + 113.4$
15. If the company sells its product for $5.19, it will maximize its revenue.
   The model is for selling price and profit, so the domain will be $x > 0$ and the range will be $-\infty < y < 413.57$.
17. The skier was in the air for 6.6 seconds. The function models height based on a reference point after an event begins, and the skier does not go above the maximum height or below the landing point, so the domain will be $0 < x \le 6.6$ and the range is $-30 \le y \le 21.06$
19. Full Set: $y \approx 13.84x^2 - 86.13x + 104.6$
   $R^2 = 0.9493$
   Four points: $y \approx 0.632x^2 + 0.0788x + 1.290$
   $R^2 = 1$
   The value of R^2 for the full set reflects the entire graph, so even though a model could be very close for small values of x, any model over a large domain will not be close at all.

UNIT 4 Selected Answers

MODULE 10

Lesson 10.5 Comparing Linear, Exponential, and Quadratic Models

Your Turn

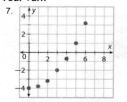

7. The function appears to be quadratic based on the curvature, although the apparent end behavior is not consistent with either a linear or a quadratic function. The function has increasing first differences and constant second differences so it is a quadratic function.

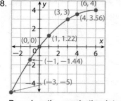

8. Based on the graph, the data could be either quadratic or exponential.
   The second differences are constant. Therefore, the function is quadratic.

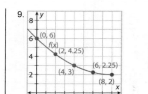

9. Based on the graph, the data could be either quadratic or exponential.
   The second differences are constant. Therefore, the function is quadratic.

10. 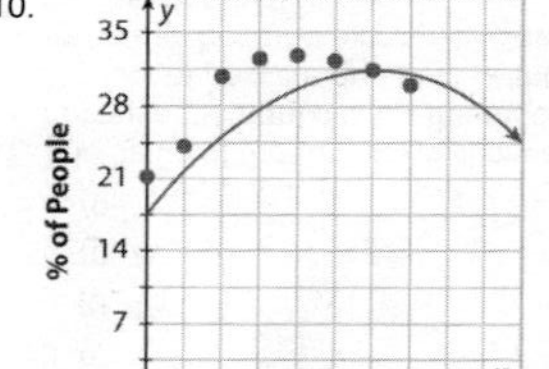

The function appears to best fit a quadratic function.
The end behavior of the data is as x approaches infinity, $f(x)$ approaches negative infinity.
Since the ratios increase quickly and then decrease quickly, a quadratic function should probably be used for this data set.
The quadratic regression is a good fit for the data set.
By the year 2000, 20.62% of people were be living in central cities in the United States.

11.

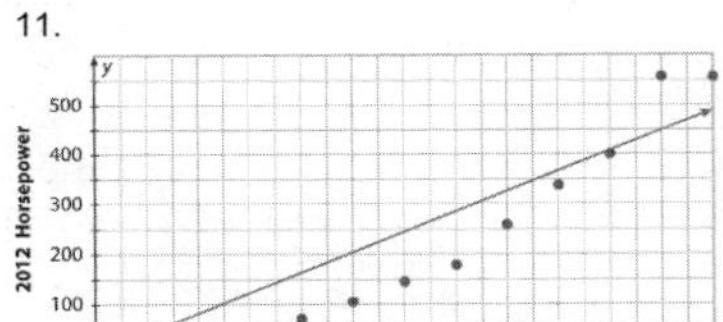

The data set appears to best fit a linear function.
The end behavior of the data is that as x approaches infinity, $f(x)$ approaches infinity.
The changing ratios suggest that the data set is best described by a quadratic or linear function. However, the average of the second difference is close to 0, so a linear regression should be used.
The linear regression is a good fit for the data set.
A car weighing 6500 pounds will have 606 horsepower in 2012.

Evaluate

1. $f(x)$ increases faster from 0 to 1.
$g(x)$ increases faster from 2 to 3.

3.

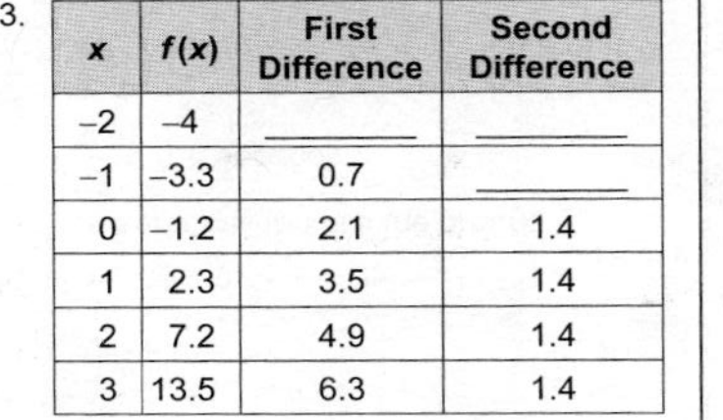

x	$f(x)$	First Difference	Second Difference
−2	−4	______	______
−1	−3.3	0.7	______
0	−1.2	2.1	1.4
1	2.3	3.5	1.4
2	7.2	4.9	1.4
3	13.5	6.3	1.4

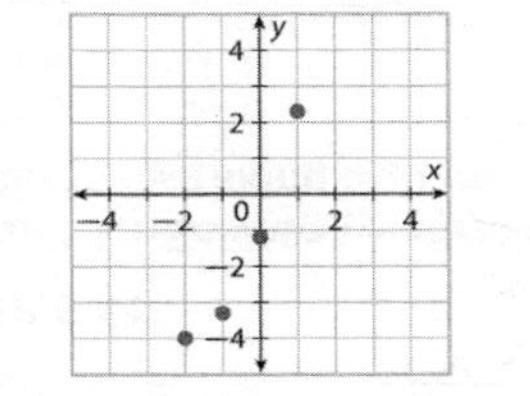

The shape appears slightly curved upward.
$f(x)$ appears to increase without end as x approaches infinity and to decrease without end as x approaches negative infinity.
The function appears to be quadratic because of the curvature, but the observable end behavior is not consistent with a quadratic function.
The function has constant second differences and decreasing first differences, so it is quadratic.

5.

x	$f(x)$	First Difference	Second Difference
1	−7.2	______	______
2	−3.8	3.4	______
3	0	3.8	0.4
4	4.2	4.2	0.4
5	8.8	4.6	0.4

The shape appears straight.
$f(x)$ appears to increase without end as x increases and to decrease as x decreases.
The function appears to be linear.
The function has constant second differences and increasing first differences, so it is quadratic.

7.

x	$f(x)$	First Difference	Second Difference	Ratio
−2	9	______	______	______
0	5.5	−3.5	______	0.61
2	3	−2.5	1	0.55
4	1.5	−1.5	1	0.5
6	1	−0.5	1	0.67

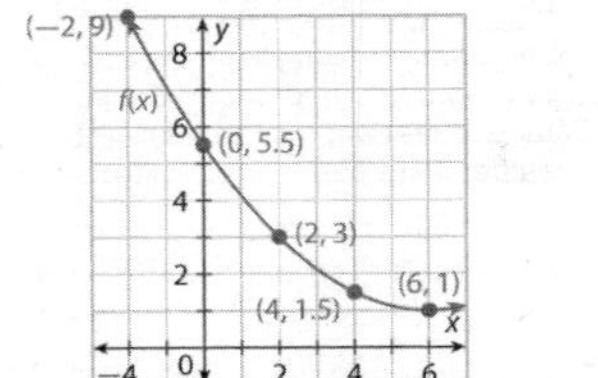

Based on the graph, the data could be either quadratic or exponential.
Since $f(x)$ has not been defined for $x > 6$, the end behavior of the function as x approaches infinity cannot be determined.
As x approaches negative infinity, $f(x)$ appears to increase without end.
No conclusions can be drawn about $f(x)$ from the graph.
The second differences are constant. Therefore, the function is quadratic.

9. If a quadratic, linear, and exponential regression model were to produce the same answer, the linear model should be used since it is preferable to use the simplest answer that fits the data. There is no evidence that a quadratic or exponential is a better fit than the linear.
11. Since all three types of regression models have insignificant r^2-values, none of them should be chosen for this data set.

UNIT 5 Selected Answers

MODULE 11

Lesson 11.1 Solving Quadratic Equations by Taking Square Roots

Your Turn

3. $x = \pm 2\sqrt{6}$
4. $x = \pm -\dfrac{\sqrt{13}}{2}$
6. $50 - 16t^2 = 0$

   The water balloon hits the ground in $\dfrac{5\sqrt{2}}{4} \approx 1.8$ seconds.
7. $\dfrac{8}{3}t^2 = 4$

   The tool falls 4 feet in $\dfrac{\sqrt{6}}{2} \approx 1.2$ seconds.
9. $= -4$
10. $= -\dfrac{1}{3}$
11. $x = \pm 6i$
12. $x = \pm \dfrac{\sqrt{35}}{5} i$

Evaluate

1. a. $x = -3$ and $x = 3$.

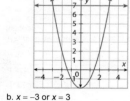

   b. $x = -3$ or $x = 3$

   c. $x = \pm 3$
3. $x = \pm \sqrt{6}$
5. $x = \pm \dfrac{\sqrt{2}}{2}$
7. $16t^2 = 20$

   The acorn falls 20 feet in $\dfrac{\sqrt{5}}{2} \approx 1.1$ seconds.
9. So, the width of the rectangle is $\sqrt{15} \approx 3.9$ cm, and the length is $3\sqrt{15} \approx 11.6$ cm.
11. -9
13. $-\dfrac{1}{2}$
15. $x = \pm 4i$

    The solutions are imaginary.
17. $x = \pm 9i$
19. $x = \pm \dfrac{2\sqrt{5}}{5} i$
21. The smaller square has a side length of $\sqrt{14} \approx 3.7$ cm, and the larger square has a side length of $2\sqrt{14} \approx 7.5$ cm.
23. a. Imaginary

    b. Real

    c. Real

    d. Real

    e. Imaginary

    f. Real
25. The width of the screen is $16\sqrt{6} \approx 39.2$ inches, and the height of the screen is $9\sqrt{6} \approx 22.0$ inches.

UNIT 5 Selected Answers

MODULE 11

Lesson 11.2 Complex Numbers

Your Turn

4. The real part of 11 is 11, and the imaginary part is 0. Because the imaginary part is 0, the number belongs to these sets: real numbers and complex numbers.
5. The real part of $-1 + i$ is -1, and the imaginary part is 1. Because both the real and imaginary parts of $-1 + i$ are nonzero, the number belongs only to the set of complex numbers.
7. $8 - 16i$
8. $8 + 5i$
10. $-32 - 75i$
11. $73 + 173i$
13. Total impedance $= 6 - 2i$

    Voltage for the first resistor $= 72 + 24i$

    Voltage for the second resistor $= 36 + 12i$

    Voltage for the inductor $= -18 + 54i$

    Voltage for the capacitor $= 30 - 90i$

Evaluate

1. $7 - 3x$

   Replacing x with the imaginary unit i gives this result: $(3 + 2i) + (4 - 5i) = 7 - 3i$.
3. The real part is 5, and the imaginary part is 1. Because both the real and imaginary parts are nonzero, the number belongs only to the set of complex numbers.
5. The real part is 25, and the imaginary part is 0. Because the imaginary part is 0, the number belongs to these sets: real numbers and complex numbers.
7. $10 + 15i$
9. $-11 + 2i$
11. $-5 - 3i$
13. $1 + 2i$
15. $-9 + 19i$
17. $108 - 23i$
19. Total impedance $= 1 - 3i$

    Voltage for the resistor $= 12 + 36i$

    Voltage for the capacitor $= 108 - 36i$
21. Total impedance $= 6 - 8i$

    Voltage for the inductor $= -19.2 + 14.4i$

    Voltage for the capacitor $= 96 - 72i$
23. A. B

    B. D

    C. A

    D. C
25. Show that the square of each number is $6i$.

    $$\left(\sqrt{3} + i\sqrt{3}\right)\left(\sqrt{3} + i\sqrt{3}\right) = 3 + 3i + 3i + 3i^2 = 3 + 3i + 3i + 3(-1) = 6i$$

    $$\left(-\sqrt{3} - i\sqrt{3}\right)\left(-\sqrt{3} - i\sqrt{3}\right) = 3 + 3i + 3i + 3i^2 = 3 + 3i + 3i + 3(-1) = 6i$$

UNIT 5 Selected Answers

MODULE 11

Lesson 11.3 Finding Complex Solutions of Quadratic Equations

Your Turn

5. There are two non-real solutions:

   $-4 + i$ and $-4 - i$.

6. There are two real solutions:

   $-5 + 4\sqrt{2}$ and $-5 - 4\sqrt{2}$.

7. Write the area A of the sail as a function of b. $A = \frac{1}{2}b(2b) = b^2$

   Substitute 10 for A. $10 = b^2$

   Subtract 10 from both sides. $0 = b^2 - 10$

   Find the discriminant. $0^2 - 4(1)(-10) = 0 + 40 = 40$

   Because the discriminant is positive, the equation has two real solutions, so the area of the sail can be 10 in^2.

8. The solutions are $\frac{4}{3}$ and $-\frac{1}{2}$.

   Check

   $$6\left(\frac{4}{3}\right)^2 - 5\left(\frac{4}{3}\right) - 4 \stackrel{?}{=} 0$$
   $$\frac{32}{3} - \frac{20}{3} - 4 \stackrel{?}{=} 0$$
   $$0 = 0$$

9. The solution are $-3 + i\sqrt{3}$ and $-3 - i\sqrt{3}$.

   $$\left(-3 + i\sqrt{3}\right)^2 + 8\left(-3 + i\sqrt{3}\right) + 12 \stackrel{?}{=} 2\left(-3 + i\sqrt{3}\right)$$
   $$6 - 6i\sqrt{3} - 24 + 8i + 12 \stackrel{?}{=} -6 + 2i\sqrt{3}$$
   $$-6 + 2i\sqrt{3} = -6 + 2i\sqrt{3}$$

Evaluate

1. The graph of $g(x) = -6$ intersects the graph of $f(x)$ twice, so the equation $x^2 + 6x + 6 = 0$ has two real solutions. The graph of $g(x) = -9$ intersects the graph of $f(x)$ once, so the equation $x^2 + 6x + 9 = 0$ has one real solution. The graph of $g(x) = -12$ doesn't intersect the graph of $f(x)$, so the equation $x^2 + 6x + 12 = 0$ has no real solutions.

3. Two real solutions:

   $-2 + \sqrt{3}$ and $-2 - \sqrt{3}$.

5. Two non–real solutions:

   $\frac{5}{2} + \frac{i\sqrt{55}}{2}$ and $\frac{5}{2} - \frac{i\sqrt{55}}{2}$.

7. Two real solutions:

   $\frac{-13 + \sqrt{309}}{14}$ and $\frac{-13 - \sqrt{309}}{14}$.

9. The equation has two real solutions.

11. The equation has two non-real solutions.

13. $70w - w^2 = 1300$ the equation has two non-real solutions, so the gardener does not have enough fencing.

15. $x(5 - x) = 6.5$ the equation has two non-real solutions, so a student who is 6 feet 6 inches tall cannot walk through the arch without ducking.

17. The solutions are $4 + i\sqrt{11}$ and $4 - i\sqrt{11}$.

   $$\left(4 + i\sqrt{11}\right)^2 - 8\left(4 + i\sqrt{11}\right) + 27 \stackrel{?}{=} 0$$
   $$5 + 8i\sqrt{11} - 8\left(4 + i\sqrt{11}\right) + 27 \stackrel{?}{=} 0$$
   $$5 + 8i\sqrt{11} - 32 - 8i\sqrt{11} + 27 \stackrel{?}{=} 0$$
   $$5 - 32 + 27 \stackrel{?}{=} 0$$
   $$0 = 0$$

19. The two solutions are $\frac{1 + \sqrt{13}}{2}$ and $\frac{1 - \sqrt{13}}{2}$.

   Check

   $$\left(\frac{1 + \sqrt{13}}{2}\right)^2 - \left(\frac{1 + \sqrt{13}}{2}\right) - 3 \stackrel{?}{=} 0$$
   $$\frac{14 + 2 + \sqrt{13}}{4} - \left(\frac{1 + \sqrt{13}}{2}\right) - 3 \stackrel{?}{=} 0$$
   $$\frac{14 + 2 + \sqrt{13}}{4} - \left(\frac{2 + 2 + \sqrt{13}}{4}\right) - 3 \stackrel{?}{=} 0$$
   $$\frac{12}{4} - 3 \stackrel{?}{=} 0$$
   $$0 \stackrel{?}{=} 0$$

21.

Equation	Two Real Solutions	One Real Solution	Two Non-Real Solutions
$x^2 - 3x + 1 = 0$			
$x^2 - 2x + 1 = 0$			
$x^2 - x + 1 = 0$			
$x^2 + 1 = 0$			
$x^2 - x + 1 = 0$			
$x^2 + 2x + 1 = 0$			
$x^2 + 3x + 1 = 0$			

23. The equation has two real solutions when $c < 16$. The equation has one real solution when $c = 16$. The equation has two non–real solutions when $c > 16$.

UNIT 5 Selected Answers

MODULE 12

Lesson 12.1 Circles

Your Turn

3. $(x-1)^2+(y+4)^2=4$
4. $(x+2)^2+(y-5)^2=36$
5. $(x+2)^2+(y+3)^2=9$

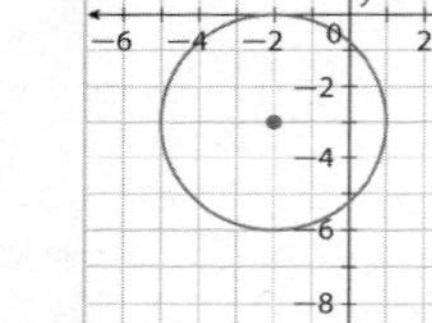

6. $(x-3)^2+(y-4)^2=\frac{16}{9}$

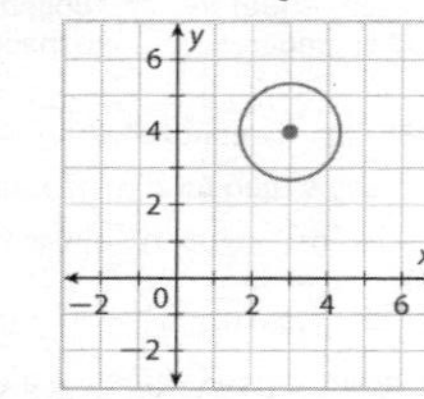

8. The inequality $x^2+(y+1)^2<16$ represents the situation.
   Sasha delivers to the houses located at points *B*, *D*, and *E*.

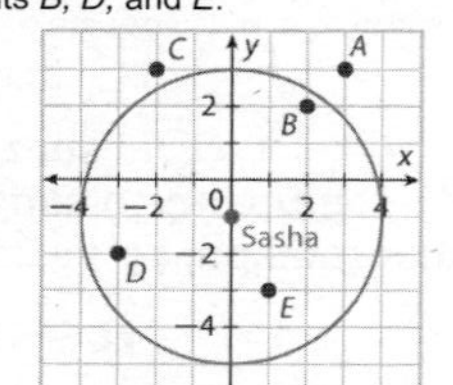

Evaluate

1. $(x-4)^2+(y+11)^2=256$
3. $(x+8)^2+(y-2)^2=65$
5. $(x-1)^2+(y-4)^2=4$

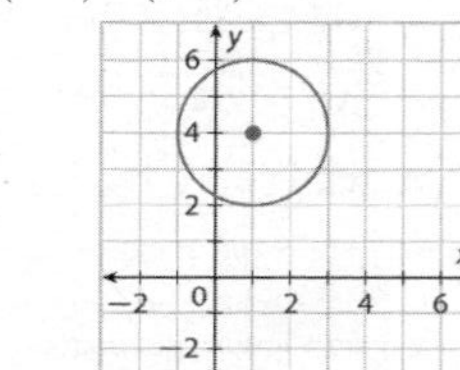

7. $(x+2)^2+(y+6)^2=1$

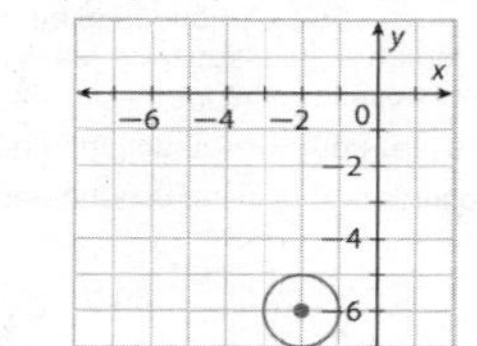

9. $(x-1)^2+(y-2)^2=16$

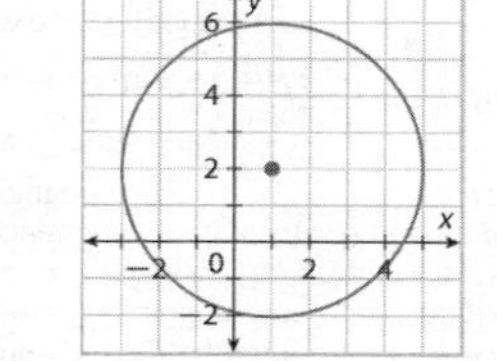

11. $(x-4)^2+(y-1)^2=\frac{1}{4}$

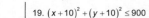

13. $(x-30)^2+(y-30)^2\le 1225$

15. $(x-30)^2+(y-40)^2\le 625$

17. $(x-5)^2+y^2>100$

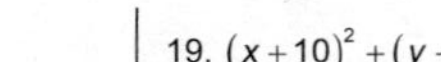

19. $(x+10)^2+(y+10)^2\le 900$

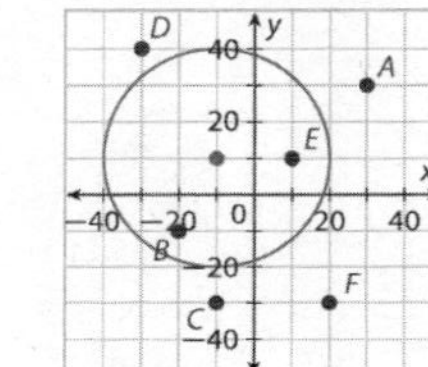

21. B, C, A, D
23. $x^2+y^2=4489$, Venus is approximately 67 million miles from the Sun.
25. Let the center of the sphere be *C* (*h*, *k*, *j*), the radius be *r*, and an arbitrary point on the sphere be *P* (*x*, *y*, *z*). The plane $z=j$ includes the points *C* (*h*, *k*, *j*) and *P'* (*x*, *y*, *j*), which is the perpendicular projection of *P* (*x*, *y*, *z*) onto the plane. Because *C* and *P'* are both in the plane $z=j$, $CP'=\sqrt{(x-h)^2+(y-k)^2}$. Applying the Pythagorean Theorem to $\triangle CP'P$, which is a right triangle, gives the following:

$$(CP')^2+(P'P)^2=(CP)^2$$
$$\left(\sqrt{(x-h)^2+(y-k)^2}\right)^2+(z-j)^2=r^2$$
$$(x-h)^2+(y-k)^2+(z-j)^2=r^2$$

UNIT 5 Selected Answers

MODULE 12

Lesson 12.2 Parabolas

Your Turn

3.

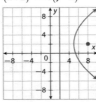

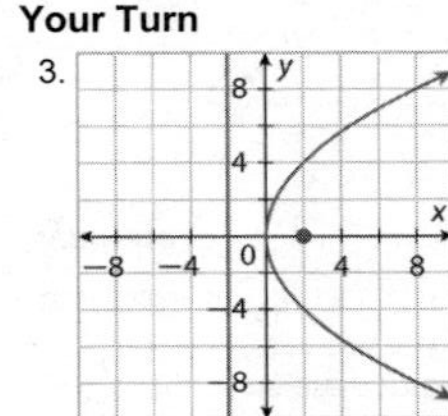

$y^2 = 8x$

4.

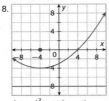

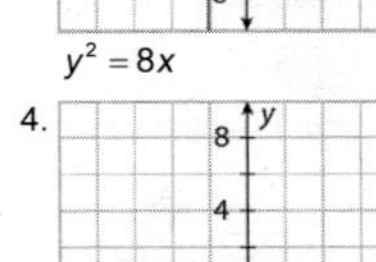

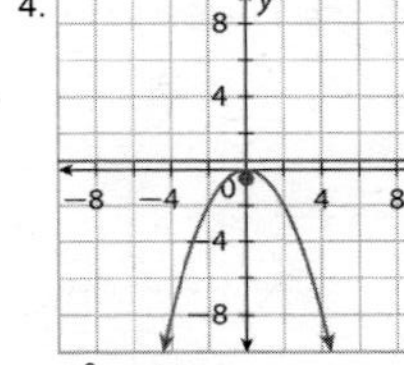

$x^2 = -2y$

5.

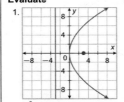

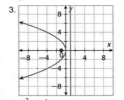

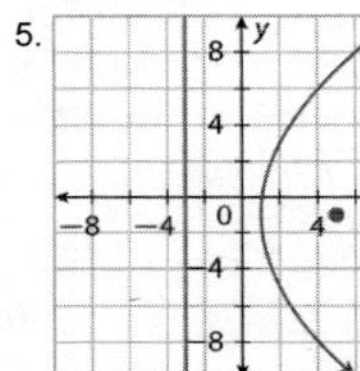

$(y+1)^2 = 16(x-1)$

6.

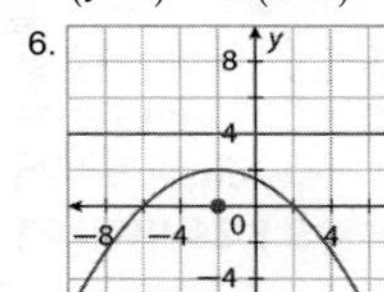

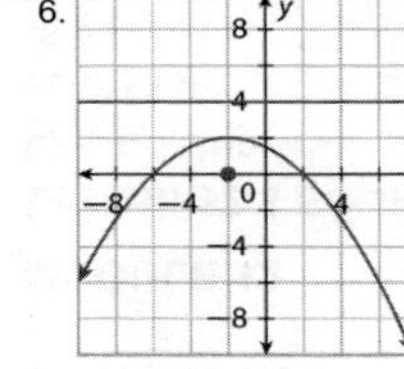

$(x+2)^2 = -8(y-2)$

7.

$(y-2)^2 = 12(x-5)$

8.

$(x+4)^2 = 16(y+4)$

9. The team wins the game.

Evaluate

1.

$y^2 = 12x$

3.

$y^2 = -4x$

5. $(y-6)^2 = -5(x+3)$

7.

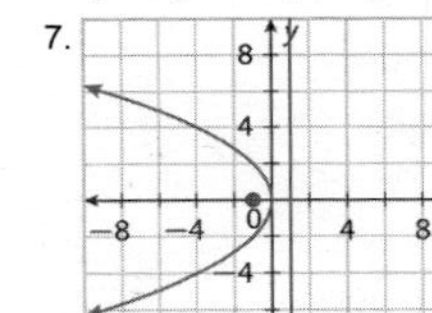

$(x-5)^2 = -8(y-5)$

9.

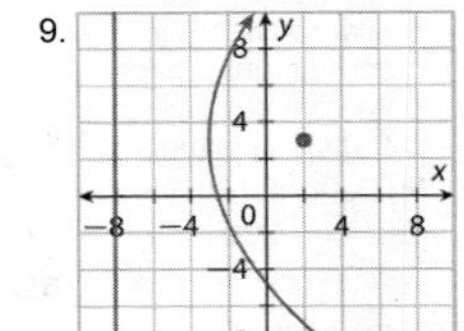

$(y-3)^2 = 20(x+3)$

11. The focus is 12.5 in. from the vertex of the cross section.

13. The ball travels 40 feet before it hits the ground.

15. B; C; A

17. $y^2 = -4px$

19. The parabola has the equation: $y^2 = 4px$. The axis of symmetry of this parabola is the x-axis. The line containing the latus rectum is perpendicular to the x-axis and goes through the focus so it has an equation of $x = p$. Setting $x = p$ in the equation above and solving for y we obtain the coordinates of the endpoints of the latus rectum. Their coordinates are $(p, 2p)$ and $(p, -2p)$. The length of this segment is $2p - (-2p) = 4p$ as expected for a vertical segment with those endpoints.

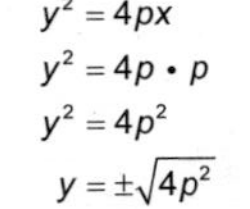

$y^2 = 4px$

$y^2 = 4p \cdot p$

$y^2 = 4p^2$

$y = \pm\sqrt{4p^2}$

$y = \pm 2p$

UNIT 5 Selected Answers

MODULE 12

Lesson 12.3 Solving Linear-Quadratic Systems

Your Turn

3. 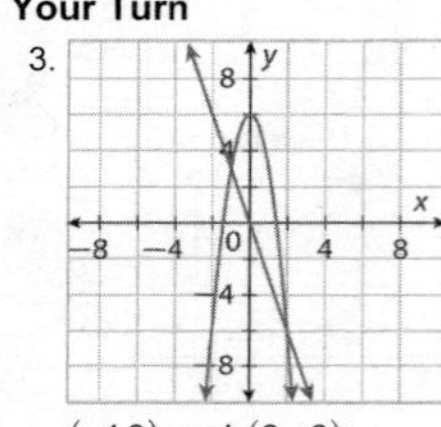

$(-1, 3)$ and $(2, -6)$

4. 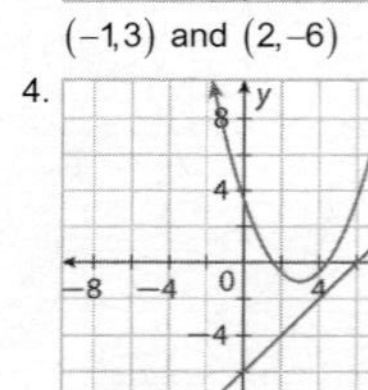

No solution

6. The solutions are $(0, 6)$ and $\left(\frac{9}{2}, -3\right)$.
7. The solutions are $(0, -7)$ and $(1, -6)$.
8. The solutions are approximately $(-1.117, -7.04)$ and $(1.65, -6.94)$.
9. (4, 20)

Evaluate

1. 1
3. 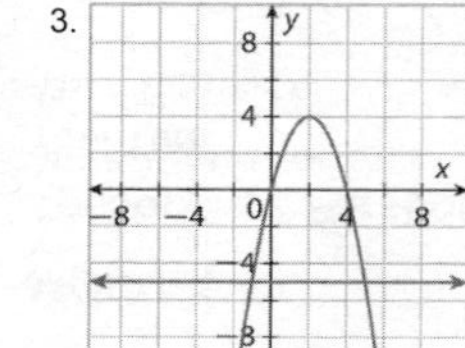

$(-1, -5)$ and $(5, -5)$

5. No solution
7. No solution
9. $(-3, 2)$
11. $(1, -5)$ and $(5, -1)$
13. $(0, 1)$ and $(1, 2)$
15. It takes $\frac{1}{60}$ of an hour, or 1 minute, to catch up.
17. The quarter and the balloon will pass after 4 seconds.
19. B; D; A; C
21. The student did not give a linear equation. The first equation is a circle, and the second equation is a parabola.
23. Because the graphs are both parabolas that share a vertex, any line that goes through the vertex but is not horizontal or vertical will go through some other point on each parabola.

UNIT 5 Selected Answers

MODULE 13

Lesson 13.1 Graphing Polynomial Functions

Your Turn

3. Odd degree, negative leading coefficient
4. Even degree, positive leading coefficient
5. odd function; the leading coefficient is negative
6. even function; the leading coefficient is negative

Evaluate

1. There are two turning points.
   As $x \to -\infty$, $f(x) \to -\infty$.
   As $x \to +\infty$, $f(x) \to +\infty$.
3. even degree, positive leading coefficient
5. even degree, negative leading coefficient
7. even degree, positive leading coefficient
9. odd degree, negative leading coefficient
11. odd degree, negative leading coefficient
13. even function; negative leading coefficient
15. odd function, positive leading coefficient
17. even function, positive leading coefficient
19. As $x \to -\infty$, $f(x) \to +\infty$.
    As $x \to +\infty$, $f(x) \to -\infty$.
21. Rhonda is correct. The end behavior of a polynomial is entirely determined by the term with the highest degree. Carlos missed a turning point because he did not adjust the graph window from the default settings. (To see all of the important features of the graph, adjust Ymax to 80 and Xmin to –20).

UNIT 5 Selected Answers

MODULE 13

Lesson 13.2 Understanding Inverse Functions

Your Turn

4.

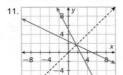

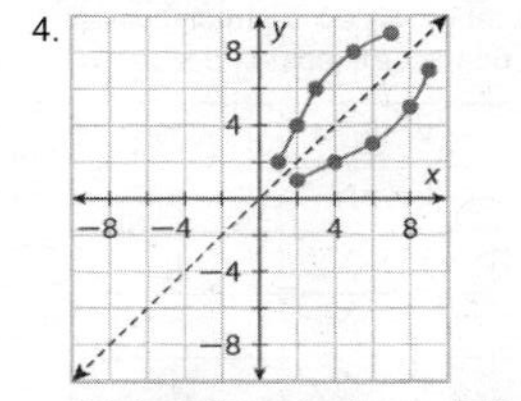

Original: Domain: $1 \le x \le 7$ Range: $2 \le y \le 9$
Inverse: Domain: $2 \le x \le 9$ Range: $1 \le y \le 7$

5. $f^{-1}(x) = \frac{x+7}{5}$

Sample check: $f(5) = 5(5) - 7 = 25 - 7 = 18$

$f^{-1}(18) = \frac{18+7}{5} = \frac{25}{5} = 5$

6.

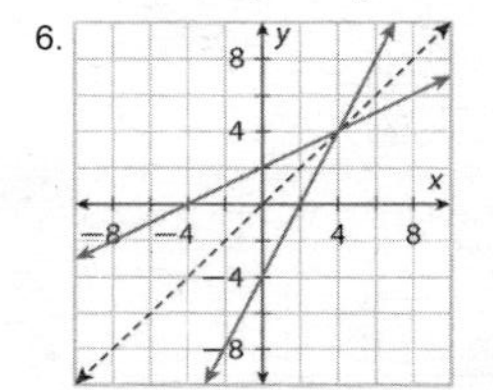

$f^{-1}(x) = \frac{1}{2}x + 2$

8. For 7 teaspoons, 36 ounces of water are needed.

Check: $t = \frac{1}{6}(36) + 1 = 7$

Evaluate

1. 3.

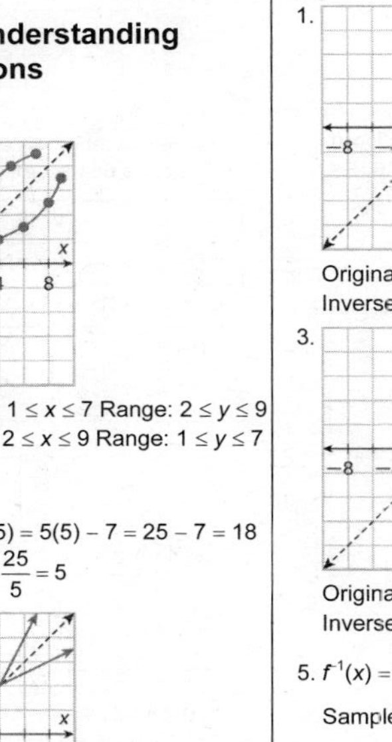

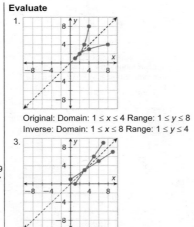

1. Original: Domain: $1 \le x \le 4$ Range: $1 \le y \le 8$
Inverse: Domain: $1 \le x \le 8$ Range: $1 \le y \le 4$

3. Original: Domain: $1 \le x \le 7$ Range: $0 \le y \le 9$
Inverse: Domain: $0 \le x \le 9$ Range: $1 \le y \le 7$

5. $f^{-1}(x) = \frac{x+1}{5}$

Sample check: $f(4) = 5(4) - 1 = 19$ and

$f^{-1}(19) = \frac{19+1}{5} = 4$

7. $f^{-1}(x) = -2(x - 3)$
Sample check:

$f(8) = 3 - \frac{1}{8}(8) = -1$ and

$f^{-1}(-1) = -2(-1 - 3) = 8$

9. $f^{-1}(x) = \frac{x-4}{4}$

Sample check: $f(3) = 4(3 + 1) = 4 \cdot 4 = 16$

and $f^{-1}(16) = \frac{16-4}{4} = \frac{12}{4} = 3$

11.

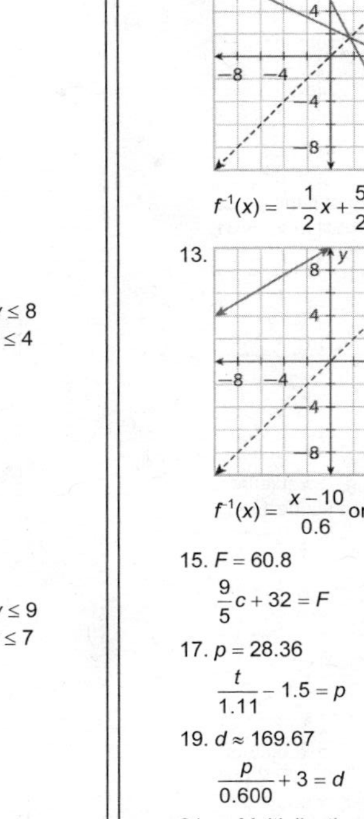

$f^{-1}(x) = -\frac{1}{2}x + \frac{5}{2}$

13.

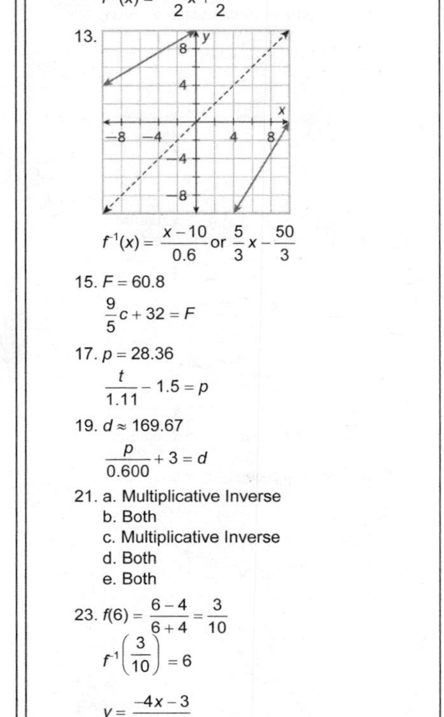

$f^{-1}(x) = \frac{x-10}{0.6}$ or $\frac{5}{3}x - \frac{50}{3}$

15. $F = 60.8$

$\frac{9}{5}c + 32 = F$

17. $p = 28.36$

$\frac{t}{1.11} - 1.5 = p$

19. $d \approx 169.67$

$\frac{p}{0.600} + 3 = d$

21. a. Multiplicative Inverse
b. Both
c. Multiplicative Inverse
d. Both
e. Both

23. $f(6) = \frac{6-4}{6+4} = \frac{3}{10}$

$f^{-1}\left(\frac{3}{10}\right) = 6$

$y = \frac{-4x-3}{x-1}$

UNIT 5 Selected Answers

MODULE 13

Lesson 13.3 Graphing Square Root Functions

Your Turn

3.

x	$y=\sqrt{x+1}$	(x, y)
−1	$\sqrt{-1+1}$	(−1, 0)
0	$\sqrt{0+1}$	(0, 1)
3	$\sqrt{3+1}$	(3, 2)
8	$\sqrt{8+1}$	(8, 3)

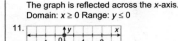

There is a horizontal translation 1 unit to the left. Domain: $x \geq -1$ Range: $y \geq 0$

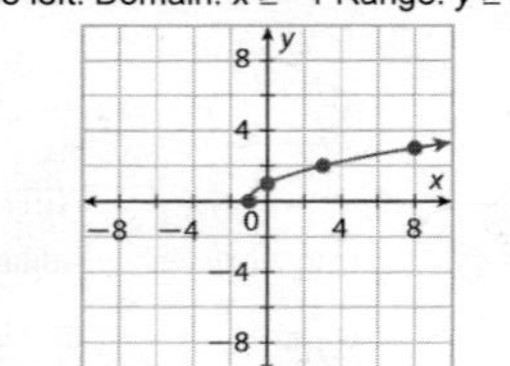

4.

x	$y=\sqrt{x}-4$	(x, y)
0	$\sqrt{0}-4$	(0, −4)
1	$\sqrt{1}-4$	(1, −3)
4	$\sqrt{4}-4$	(4, −2)
9	$\sqrt{9}-4$	(9, −1)

There is a vertical translation 4 units down. Domain: $x \geq 0$ Range: $y \geq -4$

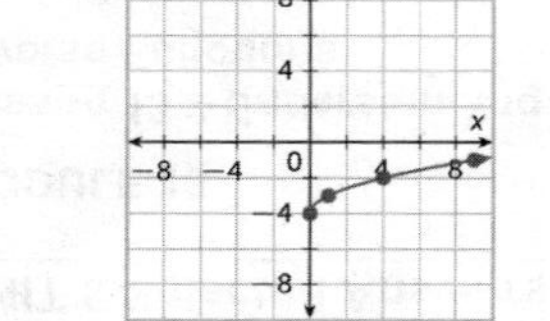

5.

x	$y=3\sqrt{x}$	(x, y)
0	$3\sqrt{0}$	(0, 0)
1	$3\sqrt{1}$	(1, 3)
4	$3\sqrt{4}$	(4, 6)
9	$3\sqrt{9}$	(9, 9)

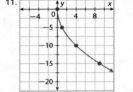

There is a vertical stretch by a factor of 3, and there is no reflection across the x-axis. Domain: $x \geq 0$ Range: $y \geq 0$

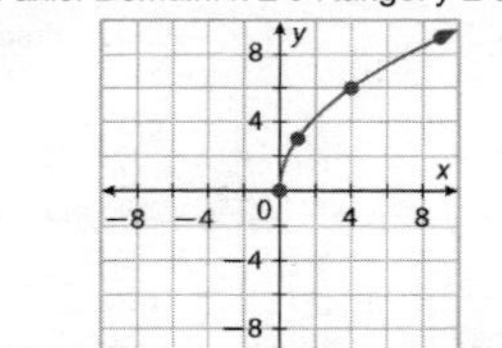

6.

x	$y=-\frac{1}{4}\sqrt{x}$	(x, y)
0	$-\frac{1}{4}\sqrt{0}$	(0, 0)
1	$-\frac{1}{4}\sqrt{1}$	$\left(1, -\frac{1}{4}\right)$
4	$-\frac{1}{4}\sqrt{4}$	$\left(4, -\frac{1}{2}\right)$
9	$-\frac{1}{4}\sqrt{9}$	$\left(9, -\frac{3}{4}\right)$

Vertical compression by a factor of $\frac{1}{4}$, and the graph is reflected across the x-axis. Domain: $x \geq 0$ Range: $y \leq 0$

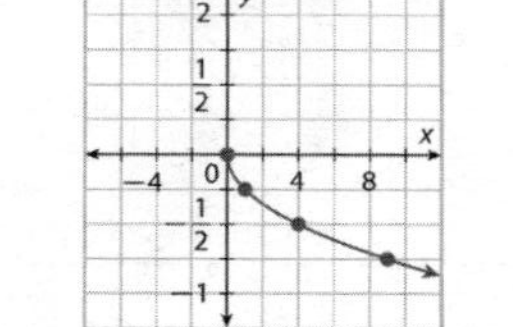

7. $g(x) = \frac{2\sqrt{5}}{5}\sqrt{x}$

$g(6.2) \approx 2.2$ miles

8. $g(5.5) \approx 2.1$ miles

Evaluate

1. B

3.

The graph is translated 4 units down and 1 unit to the left.
Domain: $x \geq -1$ Range: $y \geq -4$

5.

The graph is translated to the left 8 units.
Domain: $x \geq -8$ Range: $y \geq 0$

7.

The graph is translated 7 down units and 5 units to the left.
Domain: $x \geq -5$ Range: $y \geq -7$.

9.

The graph is reflected across the x-axis.
Domain: $x \geq 0$ Range: $y \leq 0$

11.

The graph is stretched by a factor of 5 and is reflected across the x-axis.
Domain: $x \geq 0$ Range: $y \leq 0$

13.

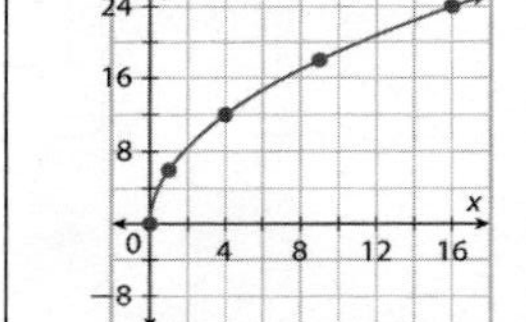

The graph is stretched by a factor of 6.
Domain: $x \geq 0$ Range: $y \geq 0$

15. The speed of the tsunami is about 149.5 mph.

17. ≈ 8 samples

19. $y = -\sqrt{x+3} + 4$

The graph is translated 3 units to the left, reflected across the x-axis, and translated 4 units up.

21. Both the domain and range are incorrect. The correct domain is $x \geq -10$ and the correct range is $y \geq -7$.

23. Possible Answer: A horizontal translation affects the domain, but not the range. The domain of the translated function is $x \geq h$, where h is the number of units the function is translated horizontally. A vertical translation affects the range, but not the domain. The range of the translated function is $f(x) \geq k$, where k is the number of units the function is translated vertically.

UNIT 5 Selected Answers

MODULE 13

Lesson 13.4 Graphing Cube Root Functions

Your Turn

3.

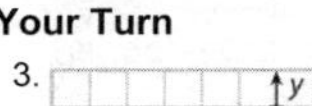

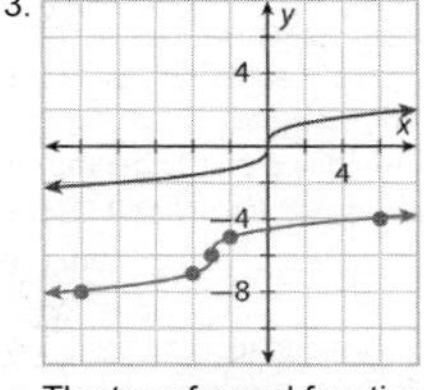

The transformed function was shifted left by 3 units and down by 6 units.

Domain: $-\infty < x < \infty$

Range: $-\infty < y < \infty$

4.

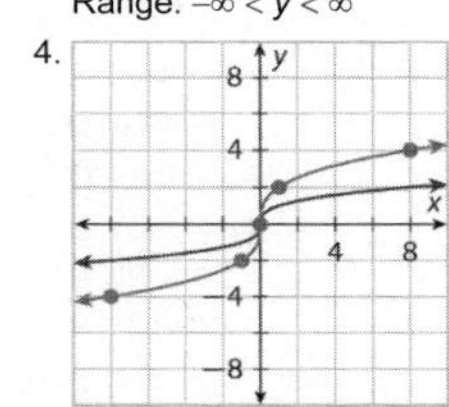

The transformed plot was stretched by a factor of 2 and is not reflected across the x-axis.

Domain: $-\infty < x < \infty$

Range: $-\infty < y < \infty$

Evaluate

1. The inverse of $y = 8x^3$ is $y = \frac{\sqrt[3]{x}}{2}$ or

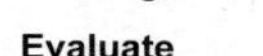

$y = \frac{1}{2}\sqrt[3]{x}$.

3.

5.

7.

9.

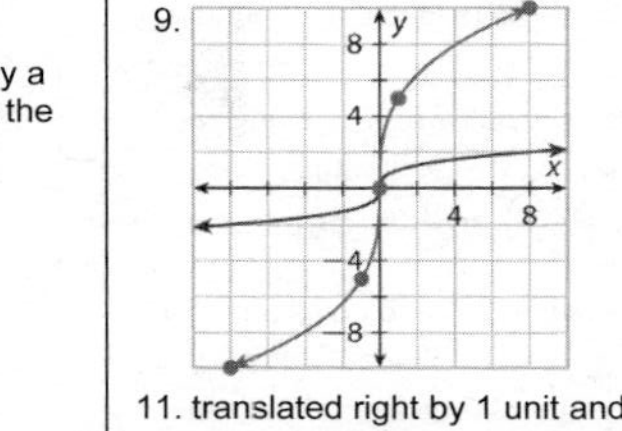

11. translated right by 1 unit and up by 5 units
13. translated right by 3 units and down by 3 units
15. stretched vertically by a factor of 3
17. compressed vertically by a factor of $\frac{1}{5}$, and reflected across the x-axis

19.

21.

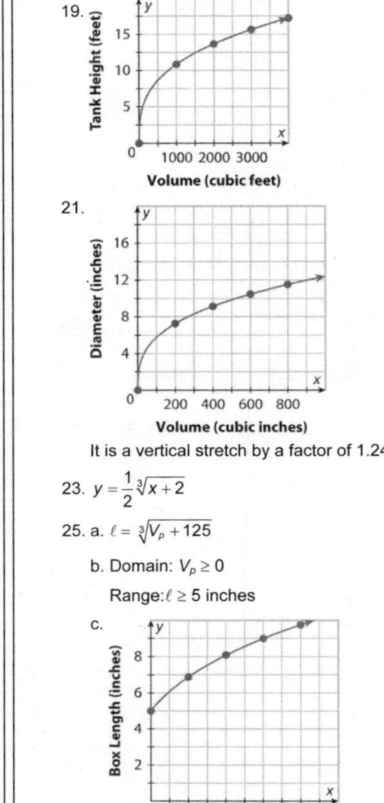

It is a vertical stretch by a factor of 1.24.

23. $y = \frac{1}{2}\sqrt[3]{x+2}$

25. a. $\ell = \sqrt[3]{V_p + 125}$

b. Domain: $V_p \geq 0$

Range: $\ell \geq 5$ inches

c.

UNIT 6 Selected Answers

MODULE 14

Lesson 14.1 Angles Formed by Intersecting Lines

Your Turn

6. $18 = x$
7. $10 = x$

   The measure of each angle is 13°.
9. The measure of the angle is 45°.
   The measure of its complement is 45°.
10. The measure of the angle is 120°.
    The measure of its supplement is 60°.

Evaluate

1. A. Vertical
   B. Neither
   C. Linear Pair
   D. Linear Pair
   E. Vertical
   F. Neither
3. 130°
5. $m\angle 2 = 47.5°$
   $m\angle 3 = 42.5°$
   $m\angle 4 = 42.5°$
7. False. Vertical angles do not share a common side.
9. True
11. The measure of the angle is 45°, the measure of its complement is 45°, and the measure of its supplement is 135°.
13. Plan for Proof: If $\angle ABC \cong \angle DEF$, then $m\angle ABC = m\angle DEF$.

    The measure of the complement of $\angle ABC = 90° - m\angle ABC$.

    The measure of the complement of $\angle DEF = 90° - m\angle DEF$.

    Since $m\angle ABC = m\angle DEF$, the measure of the complement of $\angle DEF = 90° - m\angle ABC$.

    Therefore, the measure of the complement of $\angle ABC$ = the measure of the complements of $\angle DEF$.

    The measures of the complements of the angles are equal, so the complements of the angles are congruent.
15. 2. supplement
    3. Definition of the supplement of an angle.
    4. $m\angle ABC = m\angle DEF$
    5. Equality
    6. Substitution Property of Equality
    7. $\angle DEF$
17. In the diagram of intersecting lines, $\angle 2$ and $\angle 4$ are vertical angles. Also, $\angle 2$ and $\angle 3$ are a linear pair and $\angle 3$ and $\angle 4$ are a linear pair. By the Linear Pair Theorem, $\angle 2$ and $\angle 3$ are supplementary and $\angle 3$ and $\angle 4$ are supplementary. Then $m\angle 2 + m\angle 3 = 180°$ and $m\angle 3 + m\angle 4 = 180°$ by the definition of supplementary angles. By the Transitive Property of Equality, $m\angle 2 + m\angle 3 = m\angle 3 + m\angle 4$. Using the Subtraction Property of Equality, $m\angle 2 = m\angle 4$. So, $\angle 2 \cong \angle 4$ by the definition of congruence.
19. Yes; 90°: the measure of its complement is 0°, and the measure of its supplement is 90°, so $0° + 90° = 90°$.

UNIT 2 Selected Answers

MODULE 14

Lesson 14.2 Transversals and Parallel Lines

Your Turn

7. $x = 10$, $y = 3$; the Corresponding Angles Postulate and the Alternate Interior Angles Theorem.

Evaluate

1. A. C
   B. A
   C. D
   D. B
3. $m\angle 5 = 98°$
5. $m\angle 5 = 122°$
7. $m\angle 1 = 109°$
9. $m\angle 10 = 69°$
11. $m\angle 7 = 118°$
13. $m\angle 14 = 66°$
15. $y = 40$
    $x = 15$
17. $y = 15$
19.

Statements	Reasons
1. $p \parallel q$	1. Given
2. $m\angle 3 = m\angle 5$	2. Alternate Interior Angles Theorem
3. $m\angle 1 = m\angle 3$	3. Vertical Angles Theorem
4. $m\angle 1 = m\angle 5$	4. Substitution Property of Equality

21. A possible diagram is shown, with two nonparallel lines cut by a transversal.
    I can measure the angles in my drawing with a protractor as a counterexample. $\angle 4$ and $\angle 5$ are alternate interior angles, but $m\angle 4 = 90°$ and $m\angle 5 = 130°$, so the measures are not the same when the lines are not parallel.
23. B

UNIT 6 Selected Answers

MODULE 14

Lesson 14.3 Proving Lines are Parallel

Your Turn

4. m∠1 = 120° and m∠2 = 120°. They are congruent alternate interior angles. The lines are parallel because of the Converse of the Alternate Interior Angles Theorem.
5. m∠1 = 120° and m∠2 = 60°. The angles are supplementary. The lines are parallel because of the Converse of the Same-Side Interior Angles Postulate.
7.

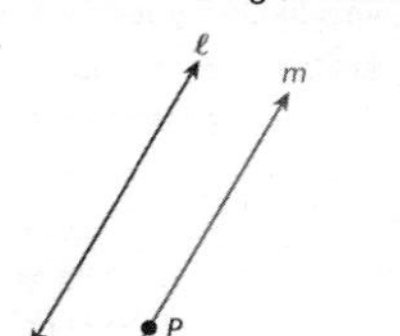

8. Same side interior angles; by the Converse of the Same Side Interior Angles Postulate.
9. Corresponding angles; by the Converse of the Corresponding Angles Theorem.

Evaluate

1. lines ℓ and *m* are parallel; 5.

   If ∠1 ≅ ∠5, then lines ℓ and *m* are parallel.
3. lines ℓ and *m* are parallel; 3.

   If ∠3 ≅ ∠6, then lines ℓ and *m* are parallel.
5. ∠7 ≅ ∠3; Converse of the Corresponding Angles Theorem
7. m∠4 = 65° and m∠5 = 115°, so m∠4 + m∠5 = 180°. Yes, the lines are parallel by the Converse of the Same-Side Interior Angles Postulate.
9. When $x = 25$, $x + 25 = 2x = 50$; the alternate interior angles are congruent and the horizontal parts of the letter Z are parallel.
11. $x = 28$
13. *m* *P*

15.

Statements	Reasons
1. lines ℓ and m are cut by a transversal; ∠1 ≅ ∠2	1. Given
2. m∠1 = m∠2	2. Definition of congruence
3. ∠2 and ∠3 are supplementary.	3. Linear Pair Theorem
4. m∠2 + m∠3 = 180°	4. Definition of supplementary angles
5. m∠1 + m∠3 = 180°	5. Substitution Property of Equality
6. ∠1 and ∠3 are supplementary.	6. Definition of supplementary angles
7. ℓ ∥ m	7. Converse of Same-Side Interior Angles Postulate

UNIT 6 Selected Answers

MODULE 14

Lesson 14.4 Perpendicular Lines

Your Turn

4. $DC = 20$ cm
5. $BC = 25$ cm
7. $AC = 16$ in.
9. m∠4 = 40°

Evaluate

1. Fold line ℓ onto itself so that the crease passes through point *P*. The crease is the required perpendicular line.
3. The midpoint of the segment is the point on the perpendicular bisector that is closest to the endpoints of the segment.
5. $PC = 5$ cm
7. 8 cm
9. 52°
11. 90°
13. 180°
15. $x = 45$; $y = 5$.
17. The valve pistons are lines that are perpendicular to the same line (the lead pipe), so they form right angles with the same line. By the corresponding angles theorem, all the congruent right angles mean the valve pistons are parallel to each other.
19. are both obtuse

    90°

    the definition of obtuse angles

    180°

    m∠1 + m∠2 = 180°

    false

    ∠1 and ∠2 cannot both be obtuse

UNIT 6 Selected Answers

MODULE 15

Lesson 15.1 Interior and Exterior Angles

Your Turn

6. Each unknown angle measure is 135°.
7. 87°
8. 68° and 136°
11. 100°
12. 37°

Evaluate

1. They must be complementary.
3. 1980°
5. 103°
7. 146°
9. 120°
11. $w = 136$
13. 59°
15. A. A; B. B; C. D; D. E; E. C
17. 135°
19. 1440°

    144°; 36°
21. $x = 20°$; $y = 45°$; $z = 115°$
23. A regular hexagon; if the construction continues and the sides are kept congruent, the polygon will include six 120° angles and six congruent sides, so it is a regular hexagon.
25. 360°; 360°; 72°, 72°(5) = 360°; 720°, 60°, 60°(6) = 360°

    It appears from the table that the sum of the measures of the exterior angles of any polygon is always 360°.
27. By the Triangle Sum Theorem, $m\angle L + m\angle M + m\angle N = 180°$ and $m\angle R + m\angle S + m\angle T = 180°$. Since each set of angle measures total 180°, they are equal using the substitution property of equality. So, $m\angle L + m\angle M + m\angle N = m\angle R + m\angle S + m\angle T$. Since $\angle L \cong \angle R$ and $\angle M \cong \angle S$, then $m\angle L = m\angle R$ and $m\angle M = m\angle S$ by the definition of congruence. Subtracting equals from both sides gives $m\angle N = m\angle T$. Then $\angle N \cong \angle T$ by the definition of congruence.
29.

Number of Sides, n	3	4	5	6	7	8
Number of Diagonals, d	0	2	5	9	14	20

The number of diagonals increases by 2, then 3, 4, 5, etc. A formula relating n and d is $d = \frac{n(n-3)}{2}$.

UNIT 6 Selected Answers

MODULE 15

Lesson 15.2 Isosceles and Equilateral Triangles

Your Turn

5. 51°
6. 15 cm

Evaluate

1. A C B

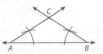

$\angle CAB \cong \angle CBA$, so opposite sides $\overline{CA}$ and $\overline{CB}$ are congruent. Therefore, it is an isosceles triangle.

3.

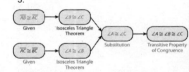

$\overline{AB} \cong \overline{AC}$ (Given) → $\angle B \cong \angle C$ (Isosceles Triangle Theorem)

$\overline{AC} \cong \overline{BC}$ (Given) → $\angle A \cong \angle B$ (Isosceles Triangle Theorem)

→ $\angle A \cong \angle C$ (Substitution) → $\angle A \cong \angle B \cong \angle C$ (Transitive Property of Congruence)

5. 76°
7. 57°
9. $KL = 33$
11. $BC = \frac{2}{13}$
13. $x°$ will equal 112°
15. By the Angle Addition Postulate, $m\angle ATB = 80° - 40° = 40°$. $m\angle BAT = 40°$ by Alt. Int. ∠ Thm. $\angle ATB \cong \angle BAT$ by the definition of congruence and $\overline{BA} \cong \overline{BT}$ by the Converse of the Isosceles Triangle Theorem. Then $BA = BT = 2.4$ mi.
17. 48°
19.

Statements	Reasons
1. M is the midpoint of $\overline{BC}$.	1. Given
2. $\overline{BM} \cong \overline{CM}$	2. Definition of midpoint
3. $\overline{AB} \cong \overline{AC}$	3. Given
4. $\overline{AM} \cong \overline{AM}$	4. Reflexive Property of Congruence
5. $\Delta AMB \cong \Delta AMC$	5. SSS Triangle Congruence Theorem
6. $\angle B \cong \angle C$	6. CPCTC

21. Triangles ABD and CBD are congruent by ASA.
23.

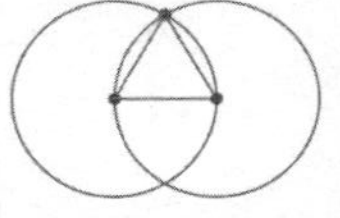

The three line segments drawn are radii, which have the same length in both circles, since the circles are the same size. Therefore, all of the line segments are congruent and form the three sides of an equilateral triangle.

UNIT 6 Selected Answers

MODULE 15

Lesson 15.3 Triangle Inequalities

Your Turn

6. No; $12 + 4 \not> 17$
7. Yes; $24 + 8 > 30$, $8 + 30 > 24$, and $24 + 30 > 8$
9. $7 < x < 35$
10. $9 < x < 27$
11. $m\angle A, m\angle B, m\angle C$
12. $m\angle B, m\angle C, m\angle A$
13. CB, AC, AB
14. AC, BC, AB

Evaluate

1. No
3. No
5. No
7. Yes
9. $5 < x < 11$
11. $5.3 < x < 49.9$
13. $m\angle A, m\angle B, m\angle C$
15. $m\angle P, m\angle R, m\angle Q$
17. DE, EF, DF
19. PR, PQ, QR
21. The safest route is to avoid sailing between the islands at X and Y.
23. The towers at Q and R are closest together.
25. $AB + BC > x$

    $AB + x > BC$

    $x > BC - AB$

    $BC + x > AB$

    $x > AB - BC$

    Since $AB > BC$, $BC - AB < 0$, so the second inequality is not relevant. Combining the first and last inequalities gives $AB - BC < x < AB + BC$.

    The constructions show that AC approaches but is always greater than $AB - BC$, and that AC approaches but is always less than $AB + BC$.
27. B, C, D
29. Write two equations, $AD^2 + CD^2 = AC^2$ and $BD^2 + CD^2 = BC^2$. Equating expressions for CD^2, $AC^2 - AD^2 = BC^2 - BD^2$ and therefore $AC^2 - BC^2 = AD^2 - BD^2$. Since the right side is positive, so is the left side, which leads to $BC < AC$.

UNIT 6 Selected Answers

MODULE 15

Lesson 15.4 Perpendicular Bisectors of Triangles

Your Turn

5. $ZJ = 65$

   $HJ = 126$
6. $GM = 60$

   $ZG = 65$
8. 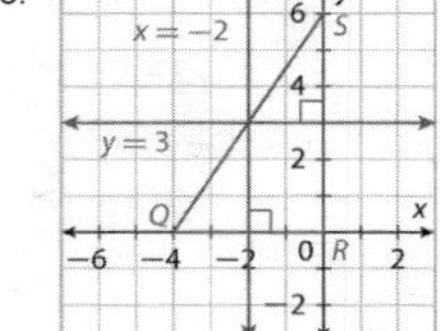

   (−2, 3)
9. 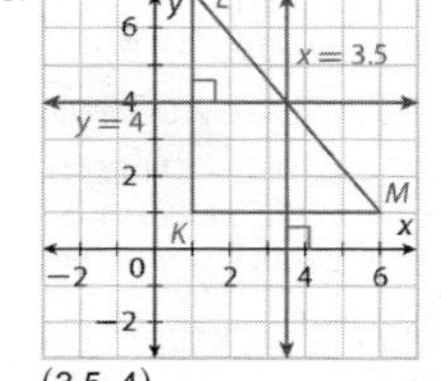

   (3.5, 4)

Evaluate

1. 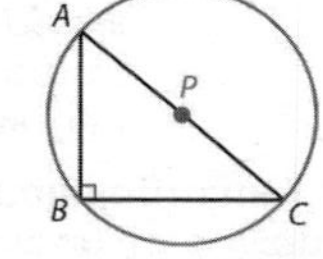

3. 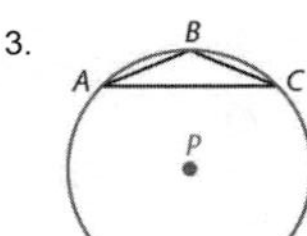

5. $ZC = 85$

   $AC = 154$
7. $BC = 136$
9. 1. Given; 2. Given; 3. PB; 4. PB; 5. PB PC; Transitive Property of Equality
11. (−2.5, 3.5)
13. Let the three towns be vertices of a triangle. By the Circumcenter Theorem, the circumcenter of the triangle is equidistant from the vertices. Trace the outline of the lake. Draw the triangle formed by the towns. To find the circumcenter, find the perpendicular bisectors of each side. The position of the boat is the circumcenter, F.
15. a. To find AB, note that $\overline{DB}$ is a leg of right triangle $\triangle ZBD$ and $\overline{ZB}$ is the hypotenuse. Use the Pythagorean Theorem to find DB and multiply by 2 because D is the midpoint of $\overline{AB}$. To find AC, use the same method, noting first that $ZC = ZB$ because C is the circumcenter of ABC. Also, $\overline{ZF}$ is a leg of right triangle $\triangle ZCF$ and $\overline{ZC}$ is the hypotenuse.

    b. $AB = 210; AC = 288$

    c. No; the only information given about isosceles $\triangle ZBC$ is the length of two sides, which is insufficient for finding BC.

UNIT 6 Selected Answers

MODULE 15

Lesson 15.5 Angle Bisectors of Triangles

Your Turn

4. $QS = 14.7$
5. $m\angle LJM = 58°$
8. 19.2
9. $m\angle PQX = 52°$

Evaluate

1. Use the compass to measure both perpendicular segments from P to the sides of of $\angle A$
3. $m\angle LKM = 31.5°$
5. $m\angle HFJ = 90°$
7.

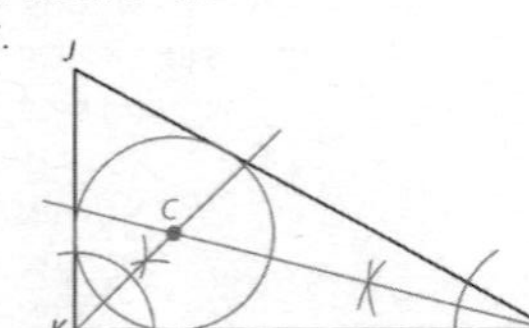

9. $m\angle FED = 46°$
11. $m\angle RTJ = 55°$
13. $VY = 17$
15. $m\angle GDF = 39°$
17. 1. Given; 2. Definition of perpendicular; 3. Reflexive Property of Congruence; 4. HL Triangle Congruence Theorem; 5. Corresponding parts of congruent triangles are congruent.; 6. $\overline{YV}$ bisects $\angle XYZ$; 8. Definition of angle bisector
19.

Fillmore Street
Polk Street
Buchanan Street

Draw the bisectors of two angles of the triangular park. The monument should be at the intersection of the bisectors. This point is the incenter of the triangle. By the Incenter Theorem, it is equidistant from the sides of the triangle.

21. a. False b. True c. False d. True e. False
23. The circle will not necessarily pass through the points where the angle bisectors intersect the sides of the triangle. Instead, the student should have used S as the center of the circle and made a circle that just touches the three sides of the triangle.

UNIT 6 Selected Answers

MODULE 15

Lesson 15.6 Properties of Parallelograms

Your Turn

8. $QR = 20$
9. $PR = 28$

Evaluate

1. Possible answer: He can use the ruler to draw $\overline{JL}$ and $\overline{KM}$, label their intersection as point N, and use the ruler to find that $JN = LN$ and $KN = MN$. His conjecture would be that the diagonals of a parallelogram bisect each other.
3. $ABCD$ is a parallelogram.

   $\overline{AB} \parallel \overline{DC}, \overline{AD} \parallel \overline{BC}$; Draw $\overline{DB}$.

   $\angle ADB \cong \angle CBD$, $\angle ABD \cong \angle CDB$; $\overline{DB} \cong \overline{DB}$

   $\Delta ABD \cong \Delta CDB$

   $\overline{AB} \cong \overline{CB}$ and $\overline{AD} \cong \overline{CB}$
5. 1. $ABCD$ is a parallelogram
   2. $\overline{AB} \parallel \overline{DC}$
   3. $\angle ABE \cong \angle CDE$, $\angle BAE \cong \angle DCE$
   4. $\overline{AB} \cong \overline{DC}$
   5. $\Delta ABE \cong \Delta CDE$
   6. $\overline{AE} \cong \overline{CE}$ and $\overline{BE} \cong \overline{DE}$

   1. Given
   2. Definition of parallelogram
   3. Alt. Int. Angles Thm.
   4. Opposite sides of a parallelogram are congruent
   5. ASA Triangle Cong. Thm.
   6. CPCTC
7. 80
9. 23
11. The diag. of $PRQS$ bisect each other, so $QT = ST = 18$.
13. Opp. angles of $PRQS$ are congruent, so $m\angle SPQ \cong m\angle QRS = 110°$.
15. 1. $PSTV$ is a parallelogram
    2. $\angle STV \cong \angle P$
    3. $\overline{PQ} \cong \overline{RQ}$
    4. ΔPQR is isosceles
    5. $\angle P \cong \angle R$
    6. $\angle STV \cong \angle R$

    1. Given
    2. Opp. angles of a ▱ are congruent
    3. Given
    4. Definition of isosceles triangle
    5. Isosceles Triangle Theorem
    6. Transitive Property of Congruence
17. Sometimes; opposite sides of a parallelogram are congruent, but consecutive sides, such as $\overline{RS}$ and $\overline{ST}$, may or may not be congruent.
19. Always; opposite sides of a parallelogram are congruent.
21. Never; diagonals of a parallelogram bisect each other.
23. a. $\angle 3$, $\angle 6$, $\angle 8$;

    b. $\angle 1$ is supplementary to $\angle 2$, $\angle 4$, $\angle 5$, and $\angle 7$.
25. The side lengths of the tile are 6 inches and 8.5 inches.
27. $y = 2x$

UNIT 6 Selected Answers

MODULE 15

Lesson 15.7 Conditions for Rectangles, Rhombuses, and Squares

Your Turn

4. Yes; the figure is a parallelogram because of congruent opposite sides, and it is a rectangle because it is a parallelogram with congruent diagonals.
5. No; by the Angle Addition Postulate, $m\angle FEH = 45° + 50° = 95°$, so $\angle FEH$ is not a right angle and *EFGH* is not a rectangle.
6. It is given that $\overline{JK} \cong \overline{KL}$. Because opposite sides of a parallelogram are congruent, $\overline{KL} \cong \overline{MJ}$ and $\overline{JK} \cong \overline{LM}$. By substituting the sides $\overline{JK}$ for $\overline{KL}$ and visa versa, $\overline{JK} \cong \overline{MJ}$ and $\overline{KL} \cong \overline{LM}$. So, $\overline{JK} \cong \overline{KL} \cong \overline{LM} \cong \overline{MJ}$, making *JKLM* a rhombus.
8. The conclusion is not valid. You must also first be given that ABCD is a parallelogram.

Evaluate

1. Square; because the diagonals are congruent, it is a rectangle and because the diagonals are perpendicular, it is a rhombus. A figure that is both a rectangle and a rhombus must be a square.
3. No information is known about its sides or angles, so it may not be a parallelogram. So, it cannot be determined if it is a rectangle
5. Rhombus
7. You need to know that *JKLM* is a parallelogram.
9. The conclusion is valid.
11. 6.5
13. parallelogram, rhombus, rectangle, square
15. parallelogram, rhombus
17. Since both pairs of opposite sides are congruent, *PQRS* is a parallelogram. Since *PZ*, *QZ*, *RZ*, and *SZ* are all equal lengths, $PZ + RZ = QZ + SZ$. So $\overline{QS} \cong \overline{PR}$ Since the diagonals are congruent, *PQRS* is a rectangle.
19. parallelogram

    rhombus
21. $\angle ABC$ is a right angle. And since $\overline{DE} \perp \overline{EF}$, $\angle DEF$ is a right angle. By the Hypotenuse-Leg (HL) Triangle Congruence Theorem, $\Delta ABC \cong \Delta DEF$.

    By CPCTC, $\overline{BC} \cong \overline{EF}$. Since the opposite sides of *EBCF* are parallel and congruent, it is a parallelogram. Since $\overline{BE} \perp \overline{EF}$, then $\angle BEF$ is a right angle, which makes *EBCF* a rectangle.

UNIT 7 Selected Answers

MODULE 16

Lesson 16.1 Dilations

Your Turn

5. It is a dilation. The scale factor is $\frac{3}{2}$.
6. This is not a dilation.
8.

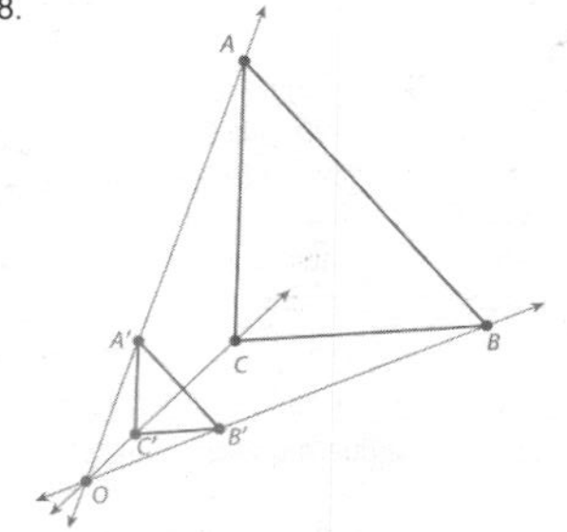

1 to 3.

Evaluate

1. The ratios of the lengths of the corresponding sides are equal.
3. No, this is not a dilation.
5. (c)
7.

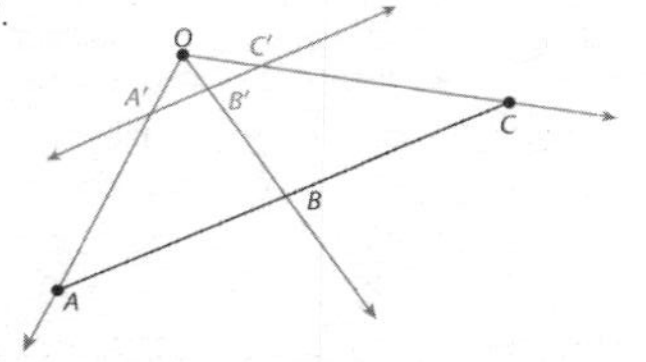

9.

11. Rigid motions preserve angle measure, betweenness, and collinearity. Dilations preserve all of these except distance.
13. It is a dilation $\frac{1}{2}$.
15.

    1 to 2.
17. 3 to 1.
19.

    a. Perimeter is 12 units, Area is 6 square units

    b. Perimeter is 36 units, Area is 54 square units

    c. $\frac{\text{perimeter}}{\text{perimeter}} = \frac{3}{1} = \text{scale factor}$

    $\frac{\text{area}}{\text{area}} = \frac{9}{1} = \text{scale factor squared}$

UNIT 7 Selected Answers

MODULE 16

Lesson 16.2 Proving Figures are Similar Using Transformations

Your Turn

3. Yes
4. No, the angles are different.
5. Yes
8. Reflection: $(x, y) \to (-x, y)$

   Dilation: $(x, y) \to \left(\frac{1}{3}x, \frac{1}{3}y\right)$
9. Rotation: $(x, y) \to (-x, -y)$

   Dilation: $(x, y) \to \left(\frac{3}{2}x, \frac{3}{2}y\right)$

   Translation: (x, y) $(x - 3, y + 1.5)$
10. Translate *JKLMN* right 7 units so that *J* maps to *V*.

    Reflect *JKLMN* across $\overline{JN}$.

    Dilate *JKLMN* with center *J* and scale factor $\frac{1}{2}$.

Evaluate

1. *EFGH* can be mapped onto *ABCD* with a dilation of 4 with center at the origin.
3. *JKLMN* is similar to *JPQRS*.
5. Reflection: $(x, y) \to (-x, y)$

   Translation: $(x, y) \to (x, y - 6)$
7. Reflection: $(x, y) \to (-x, y)$

   Dilation: $(x, y) \to \left(\frac{1}{2}x, \frac{1}{2}y\right)$
9. Reflection: $(x, y) \to (x, -y)$

   Dilation: $(x, y) \to (3x, 3y)$

   Translation: $(x, y) \to (x + 1, y - 2)$
11. Step A: Dilate *ABCD* with center of dilation *A* and scale factor $\frac{y}{x}$, producing square $A'B'C'D'$. Square *ABCD* has four sides of length *x*. Square $A'B'C'D'$ will have four sides of length $\frac{y}{x}(x) = y$. These are the same side lengths as *EFGH*. The angles are all 90° in each square, so $A'B'C'D'$ is congruent to *EFGH*.

    Step B: Translate $A'B'C'D'$ with a translation along the vector $\overline{A'E}$, producing $A''B''C''D''$. Through this translation, A'' is mapped to *E*. It may be true that B'' is mapped to *F*, C'' is mapped to *G*, and D'' is mapped to *H*. If not, rotate $A''B''C''D''$ about *E* so *that* B''' *is mapped to F.* Then, C''' lands on *G* and D''' lands on *H*.
13. Step A: Dilate $\triangle ABC$ with center of dilation *B* and scale factor $k\frac{x}{a}$, producing $\triangle A'B'C'$. After the dilation $\triangle A'B'C'$ will have sides of length $B'C' = ka = \frac{x}{a}(a) = x$,

    $A'C' = kb = \frac{x}{a}(b) = \frac{bx}{a}$, and

    $A'B' = kc = \frac{x}{a}(c) = \frac{cx}{a}$. These are the same side lengths of $\triangle XYZ$. By SSS Triangle Congruence, $\triangle A'B'C'$ is congruent to $\triangle XYZ$.

    Step B: Translate $\triangle A'B'C'$ along the vector $\overline{B'Y}$, producing $\triangle A''B''C''$. Through this translation, B'' is mapped to *Y*. It may be true that A'' and C'' are mapped to *X* and *Z*. If not, rotate $\triangle A''B''C''$ about *Y* so that *B* is mapped to *Y*. Then, *C* is mapped to *Z*.

15. Since the base and the height of the triangles are equal, no dilation has occurred. The triangles are 180° reflections of each other. The triangles are similar to each other.
17. 180 in., or 15 ft
19. D
21. Step A: Rearrange $\frac{AX}{BX} = \frac{DX}{CX}$ into $\frac{AX}{DX} = \frac{BX}{CX}$. Let $K = \frac{AX}{DX}$.

    Step B: Rotate $\triangle DXC$ 180° around point X so that $\angle DXC$ coincides with $\angle AXB$.

    Step C: Dilate $\angle DXC$ by a factor of k about the center X. This dilation moves the point *D* to *A*, since $k(DX) = AX$, and moves *C* to *B*, since $k(CX) = BX$. Since the dilation is through point X and dilations take line segments to line segments, $\triangle DXC$ is mapped to $\triangle AXB$. So $\triangle DXC$ is similar to $\triangle AXB$.
23. Step A: Draw the bisector of $\angle AXC$.

    Step B: Reflect $\triangle CXD$ across the angle bisector. This maps $\overline{XC}$ onto $\overline{XA}$. Since reflections preserve angles, it also maps $\overline{XD}$ onto $\overline{XB}$. Since $\triangle XCD \cong \triangle XAB$, the image of $\overline{CD}$ is parallel to $\overline{AB}$.

    Step C: Dilate $\triangle XCD$ about point *X*. This moves the new point C to A. Since $\overline{AB}$ is parallel to $\overline{CD}$, the new $\overline{CD}$, moves onto $\overline{AB}$. Therefore, the new point *D* is mapped to *B* and $\triangle XCD$ is mapped to $\triangle XAB$. So $\triangle XCD$ is similar to $\triangle XAB$.

UNIT 7 Selected Answers

MODULE 16

Lesson 16.3 Corresponding Parts of Similar Figures

Your Turn

5. The similarity transformation is $(x, y) \to (1.5x, 1.5y)$.
6. No
8. $12 = x$
9. $y = 1.4$

Evaluate

1. Yes; yes; yes
3. No; no; no
5. $\frac{BC}{NK} = \frac{CD}{KL}$
7. $\angle X \cong \angle X$, $\angle Y \cong \angle V$, and $\angle Z \cong \angle W$
9. $\frac{1}{5}$
11. $XZ = 42$
13. $YZ = n^2 - 4n + 4$
15. $x = 7$
17. $a = 2$; $b = 3$
19. Yes, corresponding angles are congruent. The ratio of corresponding sides is constant.
21. $x \to 48x$
23. Possible answer: $(x, y) \to (2x, 2y) \to (x + 14, y - 8)$ or $(x, y) \to (x + 7, y - 4) \to (2x, 2y)$
25. The statement is false. A rectangle measuring 5 units by 2 units is not similar to a rectangle measuring 4 units by 3 units.
27. The statement is false.

UNIT 7 Selected Answers

MODULE 16

Lesson 16.4 AA Similarity of Triangles

Your Turn

6. $AB = 10$ feet
7. $PQ = 11$
10. The two triangles cannot be proven similar. Although the two given sides are in proportion, there is not a pair of included congruent angles.
11. By the Pythagorean Theorem, $NO = 6$ and $GH = 4$, so $\frac{HJ}{NO} = \frac{GH}{MN} = \frac{GJ}{MO} = \frac{1}{2}$. $\triangle MNO \sim \triangle GHI$ by the SSS Triangle Similarity Theorem

Evaluate

1. $\frac{4.5}{3} = \frac{3}{2}$ or 1.5

   $\frac{2.1}{1.4} = \frac{3}{2}$ or 1.5

   $\frac{3.9}{2.6} = \frac{3}{2}$ or 1.5
3. By the AA Triangle Similarity Theorem, $\triangle ABC \sim \triangle DEF$.
5. $\triangle ABC \sim \triangle EDC$ by the AA Triangle Similarity Theorem.
7. The triangles are similar by the AA Triangle Similarity Theorem. It is not possible to find the indicated length.
9. The triangles are similar by AA Similarity. $QR = 0.96$
11. The ratios are not equal, so the two triangles are not similar.
13. $\triangle ABC \sim \triangle BDC$ by SSS Similarity.
15. The student did not compare corresponding sides of the two triangles. $\overline{AB}$ is the shortest side of $\triangle ABC$, so its corresponding side is $\overline{DE}$ the shortest side of $\triangle DEF$. The ratios $\frac{AB}{DE}$, $\frac{BC}{EF}$ and $\frac{AC}{DF}$ are equal, so the triangles are similar by SSS Similarity.
17. $\triangle ABD \approx \triangle ACB$ by the AA Triangle Similarity Theorem. $AB = 8$
19. Apply a dilation to $\triangle ABC$ with scale factor $k = \frac{XY}{AB}$ and let the image of $\triangle ABC$ be $\triangle A'B'C'$. Then $\angle A' \cong \angle A$. It is given that $\angle A \cong \angle X$, so by transitivity $\angle A' \cong \angle X$. Also $A'B' = k \cdot AB = \frac{XY}{AB} \cdot AB = XY$ and

    $A'C' = k \cdot AC = \frac{XY}{AB} \cdot AC = \frac{XZ}{AC} \cdot AC = XZ$.

    Therefore, $\triangle A'B'C \cong \triangle XYZ$ by SAS Congruence. So a sequence of rigid motions maps $\triangle A'B'C$ to $\triangle XYZ$. The dilation followed by this sequence of rigid motions shows that there is a sequence of similarity transformations that maps $\triangle ABC$ to $\triangle XYZ$. So $\triangle ABC \sim \triangle XYZ$.
21. Possible Answer: For XB to be as small as possible, it should correspond to the shortest side of $\triangle ABC$, which is $\overline{AB}$. Thus, X corresponds to A.

UNIT 7 Selected Answers

MODULE 17

Lesson 17.1 Triangle Proportionality Theorem

Your Turn

5. $DG = \frac{960}{32} = 30$

6. $RN = 6\frac{1}{4}$

9. $\frac{VT}{TR} = \frac{90}{72} = \frac{5}{4}$, $\frac{VU}{US} = \frac{67.5}{54} = \frac{135}{108} = \frac{5}{4}$
$\frac{VT}{TR} = \frac{VU}{US}$, so $\overline{RS} \parallel \overline{TU}$.

Evaluate

3. $5\frac{1}{3}$

5. 20

7. $\overline{MN} \parallel \overline{QR}$

9. $\overline{LN} \parallel \overline{AB}$

11. 0.24 kilometer

13. Determine a line
Triangle Proportionality Theorem
Triangle Proportionality Theorem
Transitive

15. C and E

17. a. midsegment
median
substitution
Triangle Proportionality
b. Can repeat the same process twice to show that Z is also located $\frac{2}{3}$ of the distance from vertices A and B of $\triangle ABC$ to the midpoints of their opposite sides.

UNIT 7 Selected Answers

MODULE 17

Lesson 17.2 Subdividing a Segment in a Given Ratio

Your Turn

5. (–1, 0)

6. (–2, –7)

9.

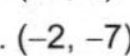
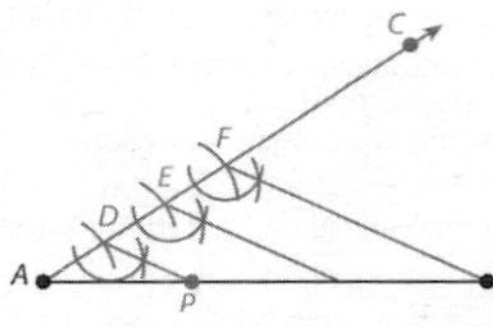

10.

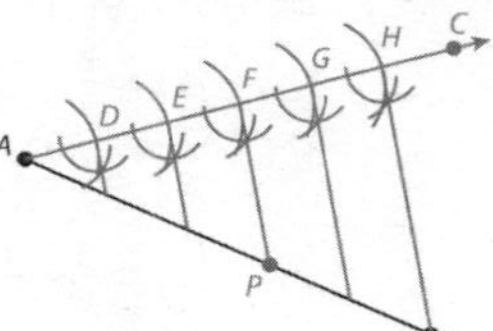

Evaluate

1. 20

3. 17

5. (6, 1)

7. (–3, 3)

9.

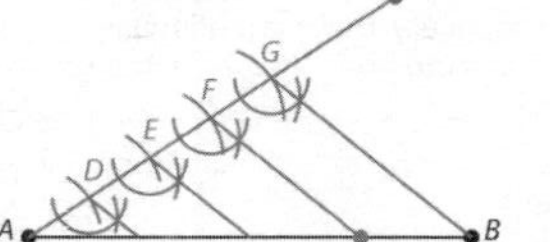

11.

13. –12.5

15. 9

17. Points P and Q are the same point.
Sample explanation: Point P is $\frac{2}{3}$ of the distance from A to B. Point Q is $\frac{1}{3}$ of the distance from B to A. This means the points lie at the same location along the line segment.

19. $\left(-1, -\frac{1}{3}\right)$ and $\left(1, 1\frac{1}{3}\right)$

21. B
E

23. Point P must be closer to point B than to point A, so the coordinate of point P should be positive.
Sample answer: The student found the coordinate of the point that is $\frac{2}{3}$ of the distance from B to A.

25. If point P is on $\overline{RS}$, $\left(\frac{8}{9}, 2\frac{1}{9}\right)$. There is also a point P, not on $\overline{RS}$, that lies beyond point S (32, 11).

UNIT 7 Selected Answers

MODULE 17

Lesson 17.3 Using Proportional Relationships

Your Turn

3. The tree is 21 feet tall.
5. 24 meters

Evaluate

1. Indirect measurement
3. 52 ft
5. 52
7. 312 meters
9. 35.2 meters
11. $10\frac{1}{3}$ or 10 feet 4 inches
13. 304 inches or 25 feet 4 inches
15. 69 inches or 5 feet 9 inches
17. $\triangle XYZ \sim \triangle VUZ$ by the SAS Similarity Criterion, so $\frac{XY}{VU} = \frac{XZ}{VZ}$. Then $\frac{XY}{500} = \frac{800}{400}$, so $XY = 1{,}000$ ft.
19. A
    B
    E
21. $\overline{AB}$ is the shortest side of right $\triangle ABE$, so corresponding side $\overline{DC}$ of $\triangle DCE$ must be shorter than $\overline{DE}$, that is, $DE < 200$. The triangles are similar, but Andy must have used the wrong proportion. The correct proportion is $\frac{d}{147} = \frac{200}{300}$, so $d = 147\left(\frac{200}{300}\right) = 98$. The distance across the river is 98 ft.

UNIT 7 Selected Answers

MODULE 17

Lesson 17.4 Similarity in Right Triangles

Your Turn

6. 12
7. $2\sqrt{15}$
10. $\sqrt{35}$

Evaluate

1. $\triangle PQR \sim \triangle SPR \sim \triangle SQP$
3. $\triangle XYZ \sim \triangle XWY \sim \triangle YWZ$
5. 6
7. $\sqrt{70}$
9. $\frac{3\sqrt{5}}{10}$
11. $x = 20\sqrt{3}$
    $y = 10\sqrt{21}$
    $z = 20\sqrt{7}$
13. *e*
15. *d*
17. *a*
19. 2.4
21. ≈ 4.62
23. 4 inches and 16 inches

UNIT 7 Selected Answers

MODULE 18

Lesson 18.1 Tangent Ratio

Your Turn

5. $\frac{5}{12} \approx 0.42$
6. $\frac{12}{5} = 2.4$
7. 3.6 ft
8. 26°

Evaluate

1. 0.40
   0.40; The ratios are the same.
3. $\tan\angle F = 1.8$
   $\tan\angle D = 0.56$
5. $\tan\angle R = 0.16$
   $\tan\angle P = 6.33$
7. $\tan\angle A = 2.0$
9. $QR = 4.0$
11. $PQ = 0.79$
13. $AB = 8.4$
15. $m\angle A = 66°$
17. $m\angle B = 43°$
19. $PQ = \frac{38}{\tan 75°} = 10.2$
21. 60°
23. The student's calculations are correct only if the triangle is a right triangle.
25. 10.2° with the first road and 79.8° with the second road.

UNIT 7 Selected Answers

MODULE 18

Lesson 18.2 Sine and Cosine Ratios

Your Turn

8. $\sin 17° \approx 0.292$
9. $\cos 45° \approx 0.707$
11. ≈ 16.5
13. $m\angle Y \approx 37°$
14. $m\angle Z \approx 53°$

Evaluate

1. $0.866 \approx \cos 30°$
3. $\frac{12}{13} \approx 0.923$
5. $\frac{12}{13} \approx 0.9231$
7. $\frac{7}{25} \approx 0.28$
9. $9.0 \approx x$
11. ≈ 54.1
13. $\approx 64°$
15. $\approx 47°$
17. $\angle A \cong \angle A$ and $\angle ABC \cong \angle ADE$, since both are right angles.
   By AA~, $\triangle ABC \sim \triangle ADE$, so corresponding sides are proportional:
   $\frac{AC}{AE} = \frac{BC}{DE} \Rightarrow AC = \frac{(BC)(AE)}{DE} \Rightarrow \frac{AC}{BC} = \frac{AE}{DE}$
   These ratios determine sin *A*, and since they are equal, sin *A* is the same when calculated in either right triangle.
19. 9.5 ft
21. 66° and 24°
   Check: $66° + 24° = 90°$
23. $\approx 9.7°$
25. $0 < BC < AB \Rightarrow \frac{0}{AB} < \frac{BC}{AB} < \frac{AB}{AB} \Rightarrow 0$
   $< \sin A < 1$
   The same argument shows that $0 < \cos A < 1$.
27. Two segments ⊥ to the same line are ∥ to each other, so $\overline{BC} \parallel \overline{DE}$. By the Triangle Proportionality Theorem, $\overline{BC}$ divides sides $\overline{AD}$ and $\overline{AE}$ of $\triangle ADE$ proportionally:
   $\frac{BD}{AB} = \frac{CE}{AC} \Rightarrow 1 + \frac{BD}{AB} = 1 + \frac{CE}{AC} \Rightarrow \frac{AB+BD}{AB}$
   $= \frac{AC+CE}{AC} \Rightarrow \frac{AD}{AB} = \frac{AE}{AC} \Rightarrow \frac{AD}{AE} = \frac{AB}{AC}$
   These ratios determine cos *A*, and since they are equal, cos *A* is the same when calculated in either triangle.

UNIT 7 Selected Answers

MODULE 18

Lesson 18.3 Special Right Triangles

Your Turn

5. $2\sqrt{3} = JK$

   $JL = 6$

6. $PR = 2\sqrt{6}$

   $PQ = 4\sqrt{3}$

9. $AB = 5\sqrt{2}$

   $AC = 5\sqrt{2}$

   $\sin 45° = \cos 45° = \frac{5\sqrt{2}}{10} = \frac{\sqrt{2}}{2}$;

   $\tan 45° = 1$

11. $PR = 30$

12. $YZ = 60$

Evaluate

1. No; $3\sqrt{3} : 6 : 6\sqrt{3} \neq 1 : \sqrt{3} : 2$

3. Yes; $4\sqrt{3} : 12 : 8\sqrt{3} = 1 : \sqrt{3} : 2$

5. $9\sqrt{2} = AB = BC$

7. $UV = 6\sqrt{3}$

   $6 = VW$

9. $7\sqrt{2} = AC \quad 7\sqrt{2} = BC$

11. $JL = 4\sqrt{6} \quad KL = 4\sqrt{3}$

13. $AB = 65$

15. Not possible: $9^2 + 21^2 = 522$; 522 is not a perfect square.

17. $x = 6\sqrt{3}$

19. Given: $BC = AC\sqrt{3}$. Since $\tan A = \frac{BC}{AC}$, use an inverse tangent ratio:

    $\tan A = \frac{BC}{AC} = \frac{AC\sqrt{3}}{AC} = \sqrt{3}$

    $m\angle A = \tan^{-1}\sqrt{3} = 60°$

    $\angle A$ and $\angle B$ are complementary, so $m\angle B = 90° - m\angle A = 90° - 60° = 30°$.

21. $10 = x$

23. $\approx 4{,}150 \text{ cm}^2$

25. No; if the two shorter side lengths are odd, then their squares are odd, because the square of an odd number is always odd. But the sum of their squares is even, because the sum of two odd numbers is always even. Therefore the sum of the squares of the two shorter side lengths cannot itself be the square of an odd number.

UNIT 7 Selected Answers

MODULE 13

Lesson 18.4 Problem Solving with Trigonometry

Your Turn

3. $\approx 50.3 \text{ mm}^2$

4. $\approx 8.6 \text{ cm}^2$

6. ≈ 65 m

7. ≈ 73 m

8. 63°

10. $JK \approx 6.71$; $JL \approx 4.47$; $KL \approx 8.06$

    $m\angle J = 90°$.

    $m\angle K \approx 34°$.

    $m\angle L \approx 66°$

Evaluate

1. $\approx 5.8 \text{ cm}^2$

3. $AC \approx 1.5$ cm

   $m\angle A \approx 61°$

   $m\angle B \approx 29°$

5. $m\angle R = 38°$

   $37.0 \text{ mm} \approx PR \quad 28.9 \text{ mm} \approx PQ$

7. $m\angle J = 90°$; $JK \approx 3.6$; $JL \approx 10.8$; $KL \approx 11.4$; $m\angle L \approx 18°$; $m\angle K \approx 72°$

9. $\approx 12{,}700 \text{ yd}^2$

11. $1.8 \text{ ft} \approx AB \quad 29.9 \text{ ft} \approx BC$

13. $Z(5, 1)$

    $m\angle Z = 90°$

    $XY = 5\sqrt{2}$, $XZ = 5$, $YZ = 5$

    $m\angle X = m\angle Y = 45°$.

15. $m\angle CAE \approx 37°$; $m\angle AEC \approx 27°$; $m\angle ACE \approx 27°$

    Area $\approx 13.5 \text{ mm}^2$

17. Suppose $\overline{AB} \cong \overline{DE}$ and $\overline{AC} \cong \overline{DF}$. Solving either of these right triangles determines the length of the hypotenuse in the same way, e.g., using the Pythagorean Theorem, so $BC = EF$ and therefore, by SSS $\cong$, $\triangle ABC \cong \triangle DEF$.

    Suppose $\angle B \cong \angle E$. The given corresponding side lengths allow the unknown sides to be calculated in the same way using trigonometric ratios, so that all corresponding side lengths are equal and therefore all corresponding sides are congruent. Again, by SSS $\cong$, $\triangle ABC \cong \triangle DEF$.

19. $\sin 2\theta = 2\sin\theta\cos\theta$

UNIT 7 Selected Answers

MODULE 18

Lesson 18.5 Using a Pythagorean Identity

Your Turn

7. $\cos\theta \approx -0.765$
8. $\tan\theta \approx -0.110$
11. $\sin\theta \approx -0.960$; $\cos\theta \approx -0.278$

Evaluate

1. $\cos\theta \approx 0.857$
3. $\cos\theta \approx 0.895$
5. $\cos\theta \approx -0.419$
7. $\sin\theta \approx 0.735$
9. $\cos\theta \approx -0.245$ and $\sin\theta \approx 0.972$
11. $\cos\theta \approx 0.130$ and $\sin\theta \approx 0.981$
13. $\cos\theta \approx 0.628$ and $\sin\theta \approx -0.777$
15. $\cos\theta \approx 0.148$ and $\sin\theta \approx 0.985$
17. A. Positive
    B. Negative
    C. Negative
    D. Negative
    E. Positive
19. $x^2 + y^2 = r^2 \Rightarrow (r\cos\theta)^2 + (r\sin\theta)^2 = r^2$
    $r^2\cos^2\theta + r^2\sin^2\theta = r^2 \Rightarrow \cos^2\theta + \sin^2\theta = 1$
21. $\mu \approx 0.84$
23. $1 + \cos\theta$
25. The expression $\frac{\sqrt{1-\cos^2\theta}}{\sqrt{1-\sin^2\theta}}$ simplifies to $\tan\theta$. If you rewrite $\frac{\sqrt{1-\cos^2\theta}}{\sqrt{1-\sin^2\theta}}$ using the Pythagorean Identity, you get the result $\frac{\sqrt{\sin^2\theta}}{\sqrt{\cos^2\theta}}$. Taking the square root results in the expression $\frac{\sin\theta}{\cos\theta}$, which is equivalent to $\tan\theta$.

UNIT 8 Selected Answers

MODULE 19

Lesson 19.1 Central Angles and Inscribed Angles

Your Turn

4. $m\widehat{BD} = 11°$
7. $m\angle ABE = 37°$

Evaluate

1. $\overline{DE}$, $\overline{EF}$; $\angle DEF$; $\angle DCF$
3. $\overline{DF}$, $\overline{DG}$, $\overline{EF}$, $\overline{EG}$; $\angle DGE$, $\angle DFE$, $\angle FDG$, $\angle FEG$; none
5. 42°
7. 141°
9. 321°
11. 48°
13. 85°
15. 236°
17. 20°
19. 324°
21. C, D, E, G, H
23. 135°
25. 144°

MODULE 19

Lesson 19.2 Angles in Inscribed Quadrilaterals

Your Turn

7. 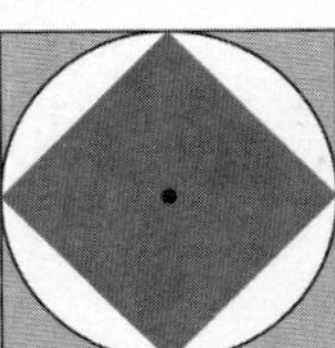

Evaluate

1. No. $\angle A$ and $\angle C$ are still supplementary. Opposite angles of an inscribed quadrilateral are always supplementary.
3. Yes; m$\angle HGJ = 115°$; $\angle H$ and $\angle J$ measure 90°
5. 95°
7. Yes. Since the opposite angles of quadrilateral *GHIJ* are supplementary, the quadrilateral can be inscribed in a circle.
9. 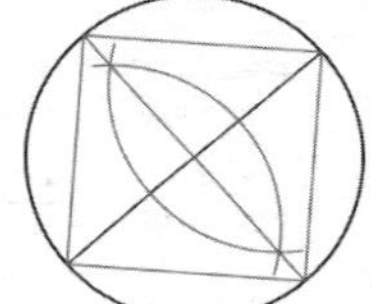

   Construct the perpendicular bisector of the diameter. Connect the points where the perpendicular bisector and the diameter intersect the circle.
11. m$\angle A = 70°$; m$\angle B = 115°$; m$\angle C = 110°$; m$\angle D = 65°$
13. m$\angle V = 101°$; m$\angle T = 79°$; m$\angle U = 86°$; m$\angle W = 94°$
15. Cannot be inscribed in a circle.
17. 105°
19. m$\angle M = 99°$; m$\angle J = 108°$; m$\angle K = 81°$; m$\angle L = 72°$.
21. a. 100 square feet

    b. $(50\pi - 100)$ square feet

MODULE 19

Lesson 19.3 Tangents and Circumscribed Angles

Evaluate

1. 90°
3. The tangents are perpendicular.
5. approximately 1400 mi
7. 3 units

   (–3, 1)

   $x = -3$
9. $AC = 32$

   $AB = 32$
11. $\angle P$ and $\angle Q$ are supplementary angles.
13. m$\angle P = 45°$
15. 28°
17. It is not possible.
19. $m\overset{\frown}{MJ} = 82$
21. *ABCD* is a kite.
23. From point *B*, construct two tangents to circle *O*. From point *C*, construct two tangents to circle *O*. Label the point of intersection of the tangent from *B* and the tangent from *C* as point *D*. Triangle *DEB* is circumscribed about circle *O*.

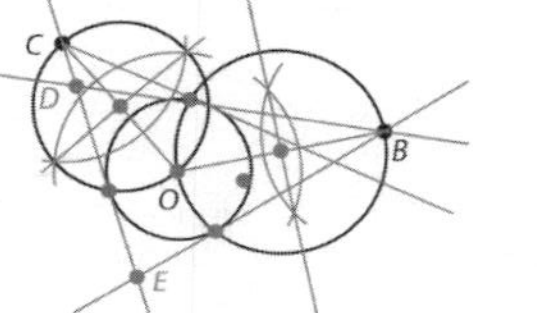

UNIT 8 Selected Answers

MODULE 19

Lesson 19.4 Segment Relationships in Circles

Your Turn

3. $1.93 \approx x$
   $CB \approx 15.93$
   $AD = 12$ (given)
6. $x = 9$
   $PT = 13$; $PR = 10.4$
7. $x = 3.5$
   HL = 10; NL = 12
9. 400 yards

Evaluate

1. The product of the lengths of the segments on one chord will equal the product of the lengths of the segments on the other chord: $RV \cdot VS = TV \cdot VU$.
3. $DF \cdot CF = BF \cdot EF$
5. $y = 6$. $DE = 7$; $FG = 8$.
7. a. $PM = 6$ in.
   b. $PQ = 12$ in.
9. I agree.
11. $y = 14.3$; $HL = 24.3$; $NL = 27$
13. $z = 2\sqrt{21}$
15. $y = 4\sqrt{10}$
17. B
19. 1770 feet
21. $x = 18$
23. about 3.2 in
25. Method 1: By the Secant-Tangent Product Theorem, $BC^2 = 12 \cdot 4$ and so $BC = \sqrt{48} = 4\sqrt{3}$.
   Method 2: Because a line tangent to a circle is a line ⊥ to the radius, $\angle ABC$ is a right angle. By the Pythagorean Theorem, $BC^2 + 4^2 = 8^2$. Thus $BC^2 = 64 - 16 = 48$ and $BC = \sqrt{48} = 4\sqrt{3}$.

UNIT 8 Selected Answers

MODULE 19

Lesson 19.5 Angle Relationships in Circles

Your Turn

4. 86°
5. 34°
6. 122°
7. 119°
8. 47
9. 45°
10. 116°

Evaluate

1. The measure of the angle will be half the measure of its intercepted arc; the Tangent-Secant Interior Angle Theorem.
3. 64.5°
5. 135°
7. 56°
9. 90°
11. 57.5°
13. 18°
15. a. 110°
    b. 116°
17. 90°
19. 142°
21. Since though any two points, there exists exactly one line, then $\overline{BD}$ can be drawn. By the Exterior Angle Theorem, $m\angle ABD = m\angle ACD + m\angle BDC$, so $m\angle ACD = m\angle ABD - m\angle BDC$. $m\angle ABD = \frac{1}{2}m\widehat{AD}$ by the Inscribed Angle Theorem, and $m\angle BCD = \frac{1}{2}m\widehat{BD}$ because the measure of an angle formed by a tangent and a secant intersecting on a circle at the point of tangency is half the measure of the intercepted arc. By subst., $m\angle ACD = \frac{1}{2}m\widehat{AD} - \frac{1}{2}m\widehat{BD}$. Thus by the Distributive Property, $m\angle ACD = \frac{1}{2}\left(m\widehat{AD} - m\widehat{BD}\right)$.
23. Case 1: Assume $\overline{AB}$ is a diameter of the circle. Then $m\widehat{AB} = 180°$, and $\angle ABC$ is a right angle, because a diameter is perpendicular to a tangent at the point of tangency. Thus $m\angle ABC = \frac{1}{2}m\widehat{AB}$.
    Case 2: Assume $\overline{AB}$ is not a diameter of the circle. Let X be the center of the circle and draw radii $\overline{XA}$ and $\overline{XB}$. Since they are radii, $\overline{XA} \cong \overline{XB}$ so ΔAXB is isosceles. Thus $\angle XAB \cong \angle XBA$, and $2m\angle XBA + m\angle AXB = 180°$. This means that $m\angle XBA = 90° - \frac{1}{2}m\angle AXB$. Because a line tangent to a circle is perpendicular to the radius at the point of tangency, $\angle XBC$ is a right angle, so $m\angle XBA + m\angle ABC = 90°$ or $m\angle ABC = 90° - m\angle XBA$. By substitution, $m\angle ABC = 90° - \left(90° - \frac{1}{2}m\angle AXB\right)$.
    Simplifying gives $m\angle ABC = \frac{1}{2}m\angle AXB$.
    $m\angle AXB = m\widehat{AB}$ because $\angle AXB$ is a central angle. Thus $m\angle ABC = \frac{1}{2}m\widehat{AB}$.

MODULE 20

Lesson 20.1 Justifying Circumference and Area of a Circle

Your Turn

4. about 6.4 feet
5. about 10.2 feet
9. 254 ft^2

Evaluate

1. A regular polygon with 40 sides.
3. $\approx$ 150.7 cm
5. $\approx$ 56.5 in.
7. $\approx$ 301.4 ft
9. 19.625 m^2
11. 78.5 in^2.
13. $5 = r$; $A = 78.5$ ft^2
15. $11 = r$; $A \approx 379.9$ ft^2
17. $C \approx 15.7$ ft.
    $A \approx 19.6$ ft^2
19. Possible answer: The circular table would fit at least as many people as the rectangular table. At the rectangular table, 2 people would fit at each of the 4 ft sides and 3 people would fit at each of the 6 ft sides, for a total of 10 people. Each person would have 2 ft of space. The circumference of the circular table is $C = \pi d = \pi(6) \approx 18.8$ ft. If 11 people sat at the circular table, each person would have $\frac{18.8}{11} \approx 1.7$ ft, or about 1 ft 8 in. of space.
21. a. 267 ft
    b. $\approx$ 6 min
23. The calculation shown in A is incorrect because the diameter, instead of the radius, is used to find the area.
25. about 12 cm
27. The range of areas is about 177 square miles to about 314 square miles.
29. Disagree; the total distance is 5280 • 12 = 63,360 inches and the number of revolutions equals the total distance divided by the circumference, which is $\frac{63{,}360}{26\pi} \approx 775.7$ revolutions.
31. The circumference of circle E is $\frac{1}{4}$ the circumference of circle C because the radius of circle E is $\frac{1}{4}$ the radius of circle C.

MODULE 20

Lesson 20.2 Arc Length and Radian Measure

Your Turn

3. $\approx$ 37.7 in.
7. $\frac{\pi}{2}$ radians
8. $\frac{\pi}{4}$ radians

Evaluate

1. The circumference of the circle.
3. The diameter of the circle.
5. $\approx$ 31.4 m
7. $\approx$ 5.8 cm
9. 34.8 m
11. 10 m
13. $\frac{2}{9}\pi$
15. $\frac{5\pi}{9}$
17. For 0°: 0
    For 30°: $\frac{\pi}{6}$
    For 45°: $\frac{\pi}{4}$
    For 60°: $\frac{\pi}{3}$
    For 90°: $\frac{\pi}{2}$
    For 120°: $\frac{2\pi}{3}$
    For 135°: $\frac{3\pi}{4}$
    For 150°: $\frac{5\pi}{6}$
    For 180°: π
19. 160°
21. 15 in.
23. The student used the diameter instead of the radius in the circumference formula. 2π m.
25. $\approx$ 21.4 ft

UNIT 8 Selected Answers

MODULE 20

Lesson 20.3 Sector Area

Your Turn

4. $\approx 0.32\pi$

   $\approx 1.01\ \text{cm}^2$

5. $= 36\pi$

   $\approx 113.10\ \text{mm}^2$

6. $\approx$ 12, 723 mi^2

Evaluate

1. sector
3. $A = \pi r^2$, where A represents the area and r represents the length of the radius.
5. $A = 63\pi \approx 197.7\ \text{cm}^2$
7. $A = \frac{\pi}{9} \approx 0.3\ \text{mm}^2$
9. $A = 100\pi \approx 314.2\ \text{in}^2$
11. 18 pieces
13. $\approx 628.3\ \text{in}^2$
15. $= 24\pi$

    $\approx 75.40\ \text{cm}^2$

17. $= \frac{47}{4}\pi$

    $\approx 1.64\ \text{ft}^2$

19. Let $m\angle AOB = m°$, then $\frac{m}{360} \cdot \pi(6)^2 = \frac{9}{2}\pi$.
    Solving for m shows that $m\angle AOB = 45°$.
21. Buying an entire wheel is the better value.
23. B, F
25. $2.57\ \text{in}^2$
27. Disagree; the original area is $\frac{m}{360} \cdot \pi r^2$ and the new area is $\frac{m}{360} \cdot \pi(2r)^2$ or $4 \cdot \frac{m}{360} \cdot \pi r^2$, so the area becomes 4 times greater.
29. Arc length requires using the circumference of the circle, whereas area requires the circle's area. In each, the central angle is used to find the fraction of the circumference or area of the circle.

UNIT 9 Selected Answers

MODULE 21

Lesson 21.1 Volume of Prisms and Cylinders

Your Turn

4. 88 cubic units
5. $72k^3$ cubic units
6. 20,357.5 in.^3
7. $20x^2(x + 2)$
9. $\frac{r}{3\pi h + r}$

Evaluate

1. A. rectangular prism; C

   B. cylinder; A

   C. triangular prism; B

3. $810\ \text{yd}^3$
5. $\approx 2580.72\ \text{m}^3$
7. $\approx 1130.97\ \text{ft}^3$
9. $\approx 1209.1\ \text{ft}^3$
11. $792\ \text{cm}^3$
13. $\approx 2\ \text{yd}^3$; \$50
15. ≈ 14.9

    Because 0.9 of a candle would not make an entire candle, 14 candles.

17. 2 in. radius $h \approx 1.2$ in.

    1.5 in. radius $h \approx 2.0$ in.

19. $V = 840\ \text{cm}^3$
21. The cylinder's volume is greater than the rectangular prism's volume by $5.6\ \text{in}^3$.

UNIT 9 Selected Answers

MODULE 21

Lesson 21.2 Volume of Pyramids

Your Turn

4. $D = 10.5$
5. 192 in^3
6. 150 ft^2

Evaluate

1. The volume of the square pyramid is $\frac{1}{3}$ the volume of the square prism.
3. The volume of *PABCD* is $\frac{1}{3}$ the volume of the cube.
5. 136 in^3
7. 96 cm^3
9. 2343.8 cm^3
11. The volume doubles.
13. $h = 14$ m
15. $\approx 10.5 \frac{g}{cm^3}$
17. The volume would be 216 times larger; dividing the volume of the enlarged pyramid by the volume of the original pyramid gives 216.
19. 10, 125 ft^3
    375 ft^3
21. Let s be the length of a side of the pyramid's base. Then the area of the base is s^2, and $\frac{1}{3}s^2(5) = 60$. Solving shows that $s = 6$ ft.

UNIT 9 Selected Answers

MODULE 21

Lesson 21.3 Volume of Cones

Your Turn

2. $r = 1.2$ in.
   $h \approx 3.711$ in.
3. 5.596 in^3
4. ≈ 3.1 fl oz
6. 43.769 cm^3
7. ≈ 29.2 cm^3

Evaluate

1. It will take three cones to fill the cylinder with sand. Because the volume formula for a cylinder is $V = \pi r^2 h$, and the volume formula for a cone is $V = \frac{1}{3}\pi r^2 h$, the volume of a cone is $\frac{1}{3}$ the volume of the cylinder.
3. ≈ 51.0 ft^3
5. 1440π in^3
7. ≈ 703.7 in^3
9. ≈ 42.9 m^3
11. A. B
    B. D
    C. C
    D. A
13. B; E
15. 904.8 in^3
17. a. ≈ 33.5 in^3
    b. ≈ 134.0 in^3
    c. $5; the large size holds 4 times as much.
19. $10\pi\sqrt{3}$ cm
21. $h = 9$ in.
23. The calculation show in A is incorrect because it uses the slant height of the cone instead of the height.

UNIT 9 Selected Answers

MODULE 21

Lesson 21.4 Volume of Spheres

Your Turn

3. 10,305.9947... m^3
4. ≈ 10,305,995 L
6. ≈ 44.9 in^3

Evaluate

1. The volume of the cylinder is 1.5 times the volume of the sphere.
3. 696.9 ft^3
5. $1333.\overline{3}\pi$ cm^3
7. 972π in^3
9. $\frac{560\pi}{3}$ in^3
11. ≈ 1441 mm^3
13. 243 mm^3
15. ≈ 358,000,000 BTU
17. A
19. Volume of Venus + Volume of Mars = Volume of Earth
21. 14,294 in^3
23. approximately 1 in.

UNIT 9 Selected Answers

MODULE 21

Lesson 21.5 Scale Factor

Your Turn

4. Possible answer: The original area is 36. After the transformation the area is 144. When the base length changes by a factor of 4, the area changes by a factor of 4.
5. Original area is 20. After the transformation the area is 100. When the width changes by a factor of 5, the area changes by a factor of 5.
7. Possible answer: The original circumference is 24π, the original area is 144π. After the transformation, the circumference is 6π, and the area is 9π. The circumference changes by a factor of 0.25, and the area changes by a factor of $(0.25)^2 = 0.0625$.
9. For the model, the volume is 64π cu. in., and the surface area is 60π sq. in. For the silo, the volume is 2985984π cu. in. and the surface area is 77760π sq. in. The volume changes by a factor of 36^3, and the surface area changes by a factor of 36^2.

Evaluate

1. The area is multiplied by $\frac{1}{2}$.
3. The area is multiplied by $\frac{1}{4}$.
5. The area is doubled.
7. The area is multiplied by $\frac{2}{3}$.
9. The perimeter is tripled. The area is multiplied by 9.
11. Volume is multiplied by 125.
13. A. non-proportional; B. proportional; C. non-proportional; D. non-proportional; E. proportional
15. ≈ 800,000 acres
17. 36 in.
19. The volume is multiplied by 27.
21. Multiply the base or height by 5; Multiply the base and height by $\sqrt{5}$.
23. $(9\pi x^2 + 54\pi x + 81\pi)$ in^2

UNIT 10 Selected Answers

MODULE 22

Lesson 22.1 Probability and Set Theory

Your Turn

3. $\frac{1}{3}$
4. $\frac{14}{30}$
5. $\frac{1}{30}$
6. $\frac{2}{3}$
8. $\frac{3}{4}$
9. $\frac{3}{5}$

Evaluate

1. Yes, because every element of *D* is also an element of *A*.
3. $\{2, 4, 6, 12\}$
5. $\{1, 2, 3, 4, 6, 8, 10, 12\}$
7. $\{5, 7, 9, 10, 11\}$
9. $\frac{3}{5}$
11. $\frac{4}{5}$
13. $\frac{2}{5}$
15. $\frac{5}{6}$
17. $\frac{11}{12}$
19. $\frac{2}{3}$
21. a. $\frac{5}{36}$
    b. $\frac{31}{36}$
23. $\frac{12}{13}$
25. 0
27. No; choosing a black tile is not the complement of choosing a white tile since the bag also contains gray tiles.
29. Assume *A* is a subset of *S*. Then $0 \le n(A) \le n(S)$. For example, if *S* has 10 elements, the number of elements of *A* is greater than or equal to 0 and less than or equal to 10. No subset of *S* can have fewer than 0 elements or more than 10 elements. So $0 \le \frac{n(A)}{n(S)} \le 1$. When all the outcomes are equally likely, $P(A) = \frac{n(A)}{n(S)}$. Therefore $0 \le P(A) \le 1$.

UNIT 10 Selected Answers

MODULE 22

Lesson 22.2 Permutations and Probability

Your Turn

3. $\frac{1}{56}$
4. $\frac{5}{28}$
5. 34,650
6. 210
7. $\frac{1}{15}$
8. $\frac{2}{5}$

Evaluate

1. 479,001,600 different orders
3. 3024 ways
5. $\frac{1}{165}$
7. $\frac{1}{56}$
9. 1680
11. 15,120
13. $\frac{1}{20,160}$
15. $\frac{1}{35}$
17. $\frac{1}{21}$
19. $\frac{1}{720}$
21. $\frac{1}{5525}$
23. A. C
    B. A
    C. B
25. Yes
27. $n(A)$ should be 1 since the tiles must appear in the order B-E-A-D. The correct probability is $\frac{1}{360}$.

UNIT 10 Selected Answers

MODULE 22

Lesson 22.3 Combinations and Probability

Your Turn

4. $\frac{1}{4}$
5. $\frac{11}{230}$
6. $\frac{11}{32}$
7. $\frac{1}{2}$

Evaluate

1. 15 ways
3. 27,405 groups
5. $\frac{10}{143}$
7. ≈ 11.8%
9. $\frac{193}{512}$
11. $\frac{93}{256}$
13. $\frac{1}{220}$
15. $\frac{4}{21}$
17. $\frac{1}{435}$
19. $\frac{14}{969}$
21. a. 84

    b. $\frac{5}{21}$
23. In permutations, order matters. In combinations, order does not matter. In a permutation of *A*, *B*, and *C*, *ABC* is different from *CBA*, so they would be counted as two different permutations. In a combination, *ABC* is the same as *CBA*, and would not be counted again.

    a. 210; 210

    b. ${}_{10}C_6 = {}_{10}C_4 = 210$

    c. In general, ${}_nC_r = {}_cC_{n-r}$.
25. ${}_nC_n = 1$

UNIT 10 Selected Answers

MODULE 22

Lesson 22.4 Mutually Exclusive and Overlapping Events

Your Turn

5. $\frac{13}{25}$

Evaluate

1. $\frac{3}{4}$
3. $\frac{5}{13}$
5. $\frac{97}{125}$
7. $\frac{28}{125}$
9. $\frac{9}{125}$
11. $\frac{1}{15}$
13. $\frac{58}{75}$
15. $\frac{61}{75}$
17. $\frac{5}{18}$
19. $\frac{7}{18}$
21. $\frac{7}{12}$
23. 85%
25. When finding $n(A \cup B)$, $n(A)$ should be added to $n(B)$, not multiplied.

    $\frac{4}{13}$

UNIT 10 Selected Answers

MODULE 23

Lesson 23.1 Conditional Probability

Your Turn

5. $\frac{1}{3}$

6. $\frac{1}{4}$

Evaluate

1. ≈ 56%
3. ≈ 8%
5. ≈ 88%
7. $P(Pa|L)$; ≈ 55%, and $P(F|M)$
   ≈ 8%, so the probability that a student who got less than 6 hours of sleep passed the exam is greater.
9. $\frac{1}{2}$
11. $\frac{1}{4}$
13. $\frac{1}{2}$
15. A. B
    B. D
    C. A
    D. C
17. 45%
19. $\frac{5}{6}$
    Given that not rolling a 1 on the red number cube has occurred, there are 30 possible outcomes:
    (2, 1), (2, 2), (2, 3), (2, 4), (2, 5), (2, 6), (3, 1), (3, 2), (3, 3), (3, 4), (3, 5), (3, 6), (4, 1), (4, 2), (4, 3), (4, 4), (4, 5), (4, 6), (5, 1), (5, 2), (5, 3), (5, 4), (5, 5), (5, 6), (6, 1), (6, 2), (6, 3), (6, 4), (6, 5), and (6, 6).
    all but 5 outcomes—(2, 1), (3, 1), (4, 1), (5, 1), and (6, 1)—are successful
21. $P(A|B) > \frac{1}{2} > P(B|A)$
23. $n(A \cap B)$; $n(\text{not } A \cap B)$; $n(B)$
    The conditional probability $P(A|B) = \frac{n(A \cap B)}{n(B)}$ restricts the discussion to event B because that event is assumed to have occurred. The numbers used to calculate $P(A|B)$ both come from the highlighted row in the table: $n(A \cap B)$ is the number of outcomes in event B that are also in event A, while $n(B)$ is the number of all outcomes in event B. The rest of the table is irrelevant.

UNIT 10 Selected Answers

MODULE 23

Lesson 23.2 Independent Events

Your Turn

3. The events are not independent.
4. The events are not independent.
6. 6%
7. ≈ 11%
8. The events are not independent.
9. The events are independent.

Evaluate

1. a. $P(R) = \frac{3}{5}$ and $P(B) = \frac{2}{5}$
   b. $\frac{2}{5}$
   c. $\frac{8}{19}$
   d. Events R and B are independent when the first chip is returned to the bag because $P(B|R) = P(B)$ in that case
3. The events are not independent.
5. ≈ 5.6%
7. 9%
9. ≈ 8.3%
11. ≈ 24.3%
13. $\frac{1}{8}$
15. The events are not independent.
17. The events are not independent.
19. 40; 60
    20; 30
    Sample answer: Let W be the event that a person is a woman. Let Pe be the event that a person prefers writing with a pen.
    $P(W) = \frac{60}{150} = \frac{2}{5}$, $P(Pe) = \frac{100}{150} = \frac{2}{5}$, and
    $P(W) \cdot P(Pe) = \frac{2}{5} \cdot \frac{2}{3} = \frac{4}{15}$. Since
    $P(W \cap Pe) = \frac{40}{150} = \frac{4}{15}$ and
    $P(W \cap Pe) = P(W) \cdot P(Pe)$, the events are independent.
21. $P(A^c|B) = 1 - P(A|B)$ Definition of complementary events
    $= 1 - P(A)$ Definition of independent events
    $= P(A^c)$ Definition of complementary events
    So, events A^c and B are also independent.

UNIT 10 Selected Answers

MODULE 23

Lesson 23.3 Dependent Events

Your Turn

3. $\frac{4}{15}$
4. $\frac{2}{5}$
7. $\frac{1}{5}$
8. $\frac{1}{5}$

Evaluate

1. a. The events C and S are dependent.

   b. $P(C|S) = \frac{5}{6}$ and $P(S|C) = \frac{5}{7}$.

   Multiplying $P(C)$ and $P(S|C)$ gives $P(C \cap S)$.

   Multiplying $P(S)$ and $P(C|S)$ gives $P(C \cap S)$.

3. $\frac{3}{19}$
5. $\frac{2}{57}$
7. Events A and B are independent.
9. a. D

   b. A, C

   c. B
11. a. $\frac{68}{285}$

    b. $\frac{34}{57}$

13. $P(A \cap B \cap C) = P((A \cap B) \cap C)$ Group events A and B as one event.

    $= P(A \cap B) \cdot P(C|A \cap B)$ Apply the Multiplication Rule to $A \cap B$ and C.

    $= P(A) \cdot P(B|A) \cdot P(C|A \cap B)$ Apply the Multiplication Rule to A and B.

UNIT 10 Selected Answers

MODULE 24

Lesson 24.1 Using Probability to Make Fair Decisions

Your Turn

4. Possible answer: Choose an employee's name at random from a list of all employees. Each month, remove the previous winners from the list. Once every employee has won once, begin again with the list of all employees.
8. Possible answer: If the game is interrupted when the players are tied, they each have a probability of winning equal to $\frac{1}{2}$.

Evaluate

1. Possible answer: You could split the cost of a sixth pass to the climbing gym so that you each get a third visit for half of the price of an additional pass. Or you could toss a coin and the winner gets the fifth pass. Tossing a coin gives each of you a 50% (or equal) chance of winning the last pass.
3. Not fair; $P(\text{Meri wins}) = \frac{1}{3}$;

   $P(\text{Riley wins}) = \frac{1}{2}$
5. Fair; $P(\text{Meri wins}) = \frac{1}{2}$; $P(\text{Riley wins}) = \frac{1}{2}$
7. Fair; $P(\text{Meri wins}) = \frac{1}{2}$; $P(\text{Riley wins}) = \frac{1}{2}$
9. 0.30; 0.12

   0.23; 0.12

   0.18; 0.05

   Find the total number of games won: $30 + 23 + 18 + 12 + 12 + 5 = 100$. Assign numbers from 1–100 to the members so each has as many numbers assigned as the number of games won. Then use a random number generator to choose an integer from 1 to 100.
11. Possible answer: Write the names on slips of paper, but for each hour that a student worked, write his or her name on an extra slip. Then draw a slip at random. The probability of Paige winning is 4 out of 45, or about 0.089.
13. $\frac{1}{500}$
15. $\approx 1.89\%$
17. $\approx 86.79\%$
19. Possible answer: Team A should receive 3.7 points. Team B should receive 6.3 points.

UNIT 10 Selected Answers

MODULE 24

Lesson 24.2 Analyzing Decisions

Your Turn

7.

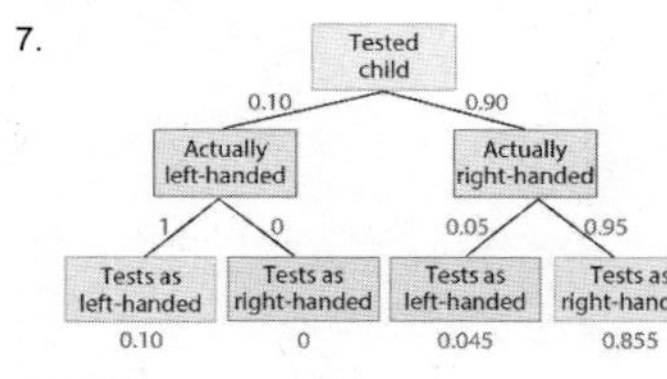

8. 69%

   The probability of the test being correct in this case increases about 2%.

9. 31%

   The probability of the test being correct in this case increases about 30%.

Evaluate

1. No; Of the 1,015 products that Helen completed, 50 were defective, which is about 4.9%. Of the 370 products that Kyle completed, 20 were defective, which is about 5.5%.

3. 9,000(0.38) = 3,420

   1,000(0.98) = 980

   4,400

   9,000(0.62) = 5,580

   1,000(0.02) = 20

   5,600

   10,000(0.90) = 9,000

   10,000(0.10) = 1,000

   10,000

   Only 22% of the coupons will go to the intended target of students living off campus. Therefore, this is not a good decision.

5. Allergy 196; 4; 200

   No allergy 490; 9,310; 9,800

   686; 9,314

   No; Only 196 people out of the 686 who tested positive actually have the allergy. This is about 29% of those who test positive.

7. $\frac{1}{3}$; 0

   $\frac{1}{3}$; $\frac{2}{3}$

9. Student; 0.425 Plays musical instrument; 0.575 Plays no musical instrument; 0.2 Plays a sport 0.085; 0.8 Plays no sport 0.340; 0.6 Plays a sport 0.345; 0.4 Plays no sport 0.230

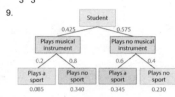

   It would not be reasonable to assume that this is true.

11. Person; 0.02 has strep (S); 0.98 does not have strep(S^c); 0.99 tests positive (+) 0.0198; 0.01 tests negative (−) 0.0002; 0.01 tests positive (+) 0.0098; 0.99 tests negative (−) 0.9702

    About 67%

13. $P(B) \cdot P(A|B) = P(A) \cdot P(B|A)$ — $P(B) \cdot P(A|B)$ and $P(A) \cdot P(B|A)$ are equal

    $\frac{P(B) \cdot P(A|B)}{P(B)} = \frac{P(A) \cdot P(B|A)}{P(B)}$ — Divide each side by $P(B)$

    $P(A|B) = \frac{P(A) \cdot P(B|A)}{P(B)}$ — *Bayes' Theorem*

15. Mouse; 0.01 mutation (M); 0.99 no mutation (M^c); 0.98 tests as mutation (T+); 0.02 tests as no mutation (T−); 0.04 tests as mutation (T+); 0.96 tests as no mutation (T−)

    It is not a good decision, because there is only a 19.8% probability that a mouse that tests positive for the mutation actually has the mutation.

17. Tomas is least likely to be late if he takes Route *C*.

19. Yes, because $P(B|C) = 0.45$, while $P(C|B) = 0.25$.

Glossary/Glosario

A

ENGLISH	SPANISH	EXAMPLES
absolute value The absolute value of x is the distance from zero to x on a number line, denoted $\|x\|$. $\|x\| = \begin{cases} x & \text{if } x \geq 0 \\ -x & \text{if } x < 0 \end{cases}$	**valor absoluto** El valor absoluto de x es la distancia de cero a x en una recta numérica, y se expresa $\|x\|$. $\|x\| = \begin{cases} x & \text{si } x \geq 0 \\ -x & \text{si } x < 0 \end{cases}$	$\|3\| = 3$ $\|-3\| = 3$
absolute-value equation An equation that contains absolute-value expressions.	**ecuación de valor absoluto** Ecuación que contiene expresiones de valor absoluto.	$\|x + 4\| = 7$
absolute-value function A function whose rule contains absolute-value expressions.	**función de valor absoluto** Función cuya regla contiene expresiones de valor absoluto.	$y = \|x + 4\|$
absolute-value inequality An inequality that contains absolute-value expressions.	**desigualdad de valor absoluto** Desigualdad que contiene expresiones de valor absoluto.	$\|x + 4\| > 7$
acute angle An angle that measures greater than 0° and less than 90°.	**ángulo agudo** Ángulo que mide más de 0° y menos de 90°.	
acute triangle A triangle with three acute angles.	**triángulo acutángulo** Triángulo con tres ángulos agudos.	
adjacent angles Two angles in the same plane with a common vertex and a common side, but no common interior points.	**ángulos adyacentes** Dos ángulos en el mismo plano que tienen un vértice y un lado común pero no comparten puntos internos.	1 2 $\angle 1$ and $\angle 2$ are adjacent angles.
adjacent arcs Two arcs of the same circle that intersect at exactly one point.	**arcos adyacentes** Dos arcos del mismo círculo que se cruzan en un punto exacto.	R S T $\widehat{RS}$ and $\widehat{ST}$ are adjacent arcs.

Glossary/Glosario

ENGLISH	SPANISH	EXAMPLES

alternate exterior angles For two lines intersected by a transversal, a pair of angles that lie on opposite sides of the transversal and outside the other two lines.

ángulos alternos externos Dadas dos líneas cortadas por una transversal, par de ángulos no adyacentes ubicados en los lados opuestos de la transversal y fuera de las otras dos líneas.

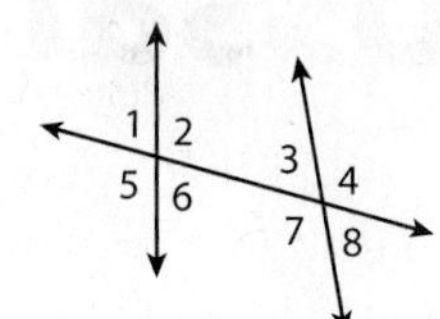

$\angle 4$ and $\angle 5$ are alternate exterior angles.

alternate interior angles For two lines intersected by a transversal, a pair of nonadjacent angles that lie on opposite sides of the transversal and between the other two lines.

ángulos alternos internos Dadas dos líneas cortadas por una transversal, par de ángulos no adyacentes ubicados en los lados opuestos de la transversal y entre las otras dos líneas.

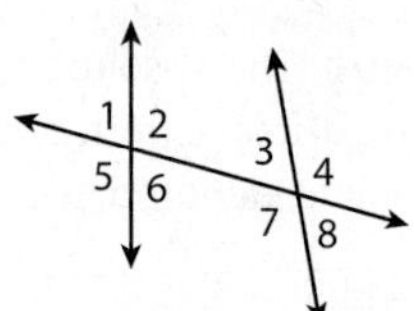

$\angle 3$ and $\angle 6$ are alternate interior angles.

altitude of a cone A segment from the vertex to the plane of the base that is perpendicular to the plane of the base.

altura de un cono Segmento que se extiende desde el vértice hasta el plano de la base y es perpendicular al plano de la base.

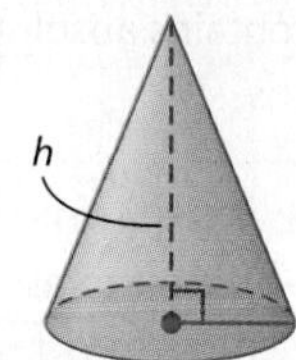

altitude of a cylinder A segment with its endpoints on the planes of the bases that is perpendicular to the planes of the bases.

altura de un cilindro Segmento con sus extremos en los planos de las bases que es perpendicular a los planos de las bases.

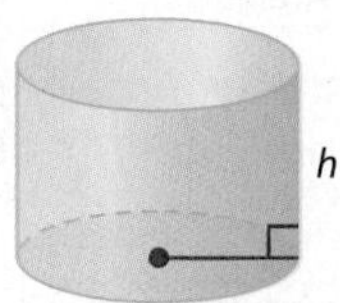

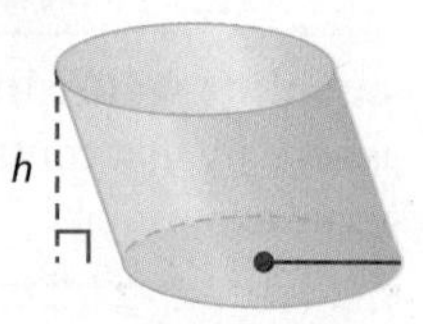

altitude of a prism A segment with its endpoints on the planes of the bases that is perpendicular to the planes of the bases.

altura de un prisma Segmento con sus extremos en los planos de las bases que es perpendicular a los planos de las bases.

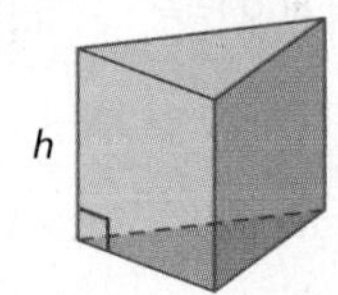

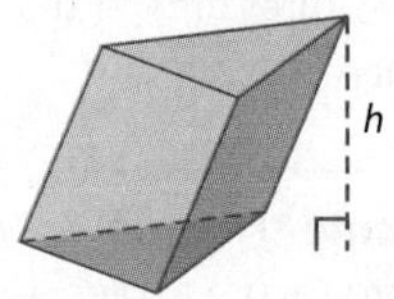

altitude of a pyramid A segment from the vertex to the plane of the base that is perpendicular to the plane of the base.

altura de una pirámide Segmento que se extiende desde el vértice hasta el plano de la base y es perpendicular al plano de la base.

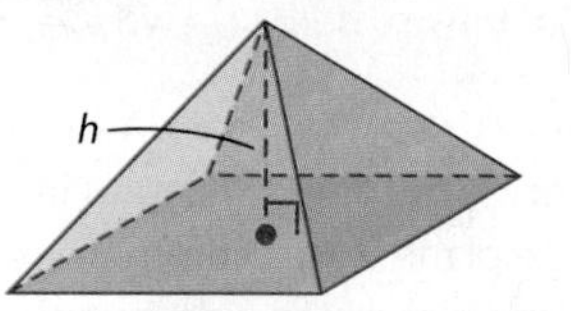

altitude of a triangle A perpendicular segment from a vertex to the line containing the opposite side.

altura de un triángulo Segmento perpendicular que se extiende desde un vértice hasta la línea que forma el lado opuesto.

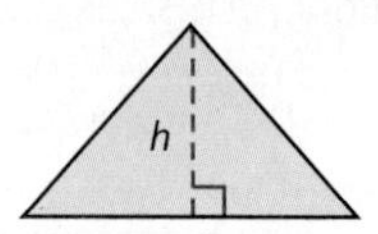

angle bisector A ray that divides an angle into two congruent angles.

bisectriz de un ángulo Rayo que divide un ángulo en dos ángulos congruentes.

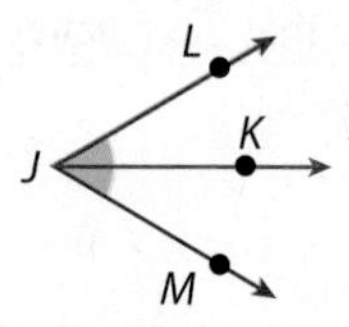

$\overrightarrow{JK}$ is an angle bisector of $\angle LJM$.

Glossary/Glosario

ENGLISH	SPANISH	EXAMPLES
angle of rotation An angle formed by a rotating ray, called the terminal side, and a stationary reference ray, called the initial side.	**ángulo de rotación** Ángulo formado por un rayo rotativo, denominado lado terminal, y un rayo de referencia estático, denominado lado inicial.	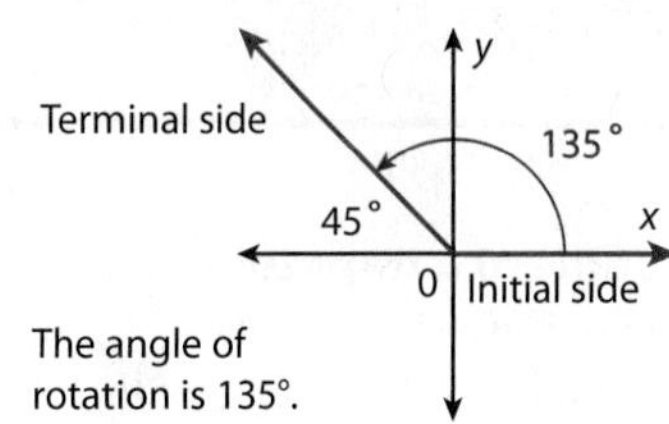
angle of rotational symmetry The smallest angle through which a figure with rotational symmetry can be rotated to coincide with itself.	**ángulo de simetría de rotación** El ángulo más pequeño alrededor del cual se puede rotar una figura con simetría de rotación para que coincida consigo misma.	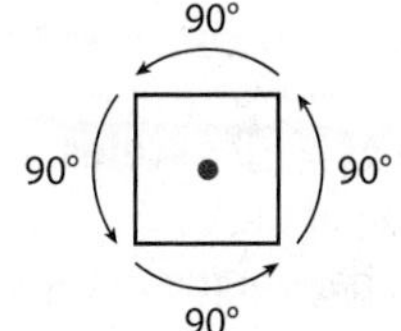
arc An unbroken part of a circle consisting of two points on the circle, called the endpoints, and all the points on the circle between them.	**arco** Parte continua de una circunferencia formada por dos puntos de la circunferencia denominados extremos y todos los puntos de la circunferencia comprendidos entre éstos.	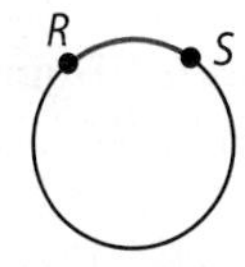
arc length The distance along an arc measured in linear units.	**longitud de arco** Distancia a lo largo de un arco medida en unidades lineales.	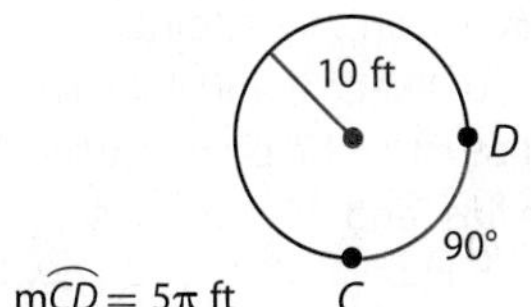
arc marks Marks used on a figure to indicate congruent angles.	**marcas de arco** Marcas utilizadas en una figura para indicar ángulos congruentes.	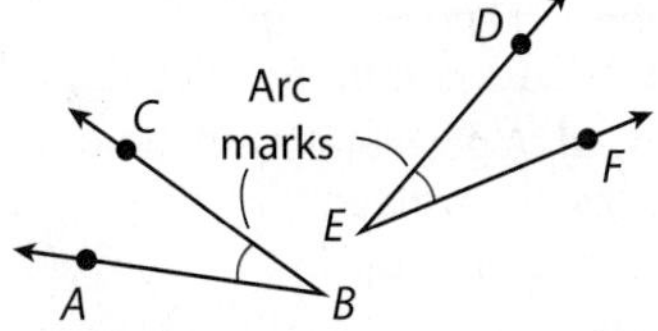
auxiliary line A line drawn in a figure to aid in a proof.	**línea auxiliar** Línea dibujada en una figura como ayuda en una demostración.	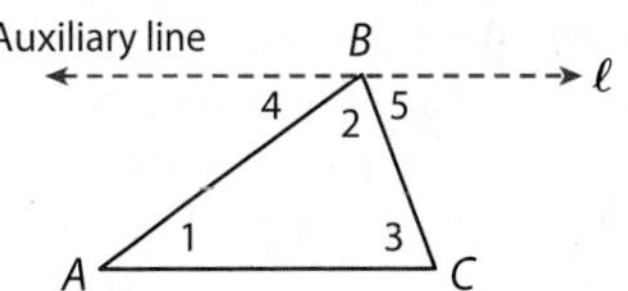
axiom *See* postulate.	**axioma** *Ver* postulado.	
axis of symmetry A line that divides a plane figure or a graph into two congruent reflected halves.	**eje de simetría** Línea que divide una figura plana o una gráfica en dos mitades reflejadas congruentes.	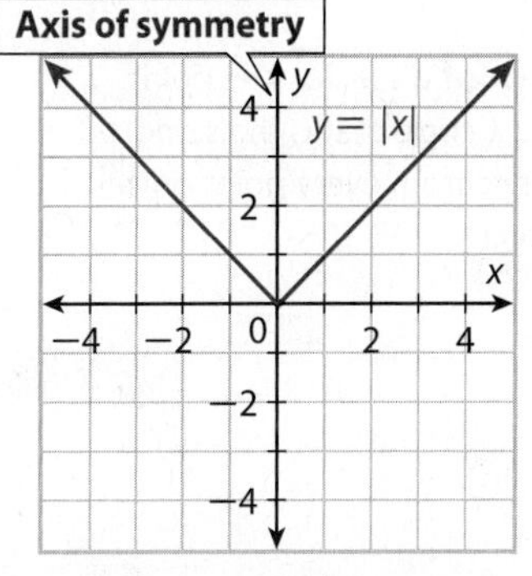

Glossary/Glosario

ENGLISH | **SPANISH** | **EXAMPLES**

B

base angle of a trapezoid One of a pair of consecutive angles whose common side is a base of the trapezoid.

ángulo base de un trapecio Uno de los dos ángulos consecutivos cuyo lado en común es la base del trapecio.

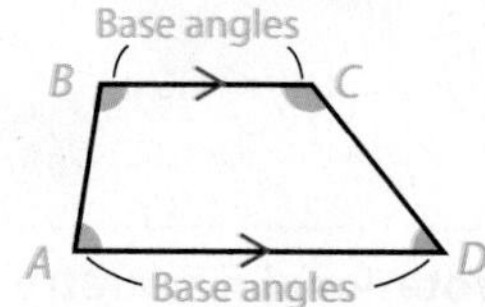

base angle of an isosceles triangle One of the two angles that have the base of the triangle as a side.

ángulo base de un triángulo isósceles Uno de los dos ángulos que tienen como lado la base del triángulo.

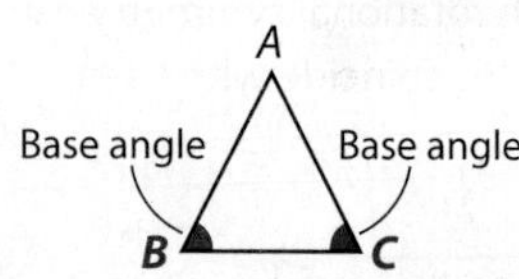

base of a geometric figure A side of a polygon; a face of a three-dimensional figure by which the figure is measured or classified.

base de una figura geométrica Lado de un polígono; cara de una figura tridimensional por la cual se mide o clasifica la figura.

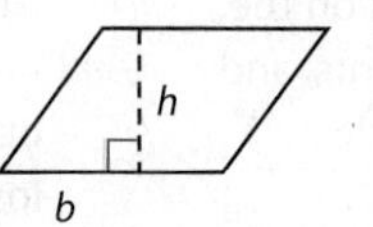

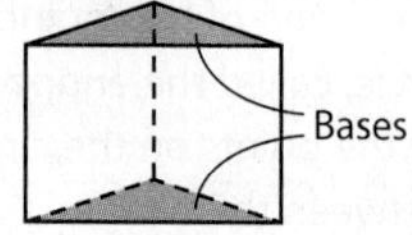

between Given three points A, B, and C, B is between A and C if and only if all three of the points lie on the same line, and $AB + BC = AC$.

entre Dados tres puntos A, B y C, B está entre A y C si y sólo si los tres puntos se encuentran en la misma línea y $AB + BC = AC$.

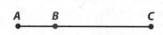

biconditional statement A statement that can be written in the form "*p* if and only if *q*."

enunciado bicondicional Enunciado que puede expresarse en la forma "*p* si y sólo si *q*".

A figure is a triangle if and only if it is a three-sided polygon.

binomial A polynomial with two terms.

binomio Polinomio con dos términos.

$x + y$

$2a^2 + 3$

$4m^3n^2 + 6mn^4$

bisect To divide into two congruent parts.

trazar una bisectriz Dividir en dos partes congruentes.

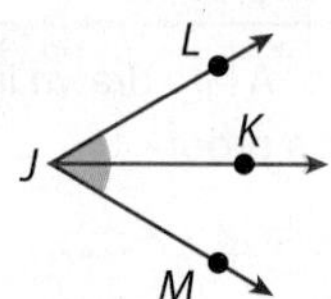

$\overrightarrow{JK}$ bisects $\angle LJM$.

C

center of a circle The point inside a circle that is the same distance from every point on the circle.

centro de un círculo Punto dentro de un círculo que se encuentra a la misma distancia de todos los puntos del círculo.

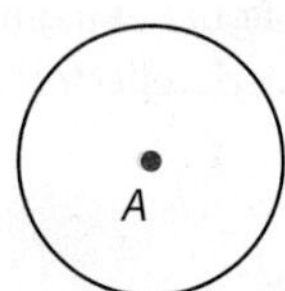

ENGLISH	SPANISH	EXAMPLES
center of a sphere The point inside a sphere that is the same distance from every point on the sphere.	**centro de una esfera** Punto dentro de una esfera que está a la misma distancia de cualquier punto de la esfera.	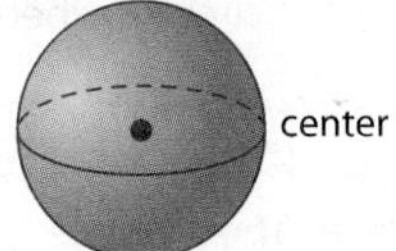
center of dilation The intersection of the lines that connect each point of the image with the corresponding point of the preimage.	**centro de dilatación** Intersección de las líneas que conectan cada punto de la imagen con el punto correspondiente de la imagen original.	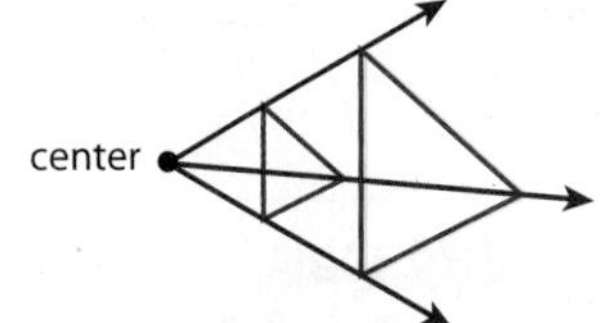
center of rotation The point around which a figure is rotated.	**centro de rotación** Punto alrededor del cual rota una figura.	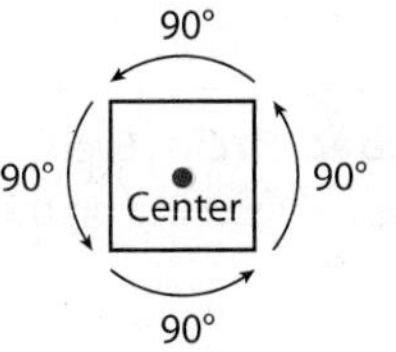
central angle of a circle An angle whose vertex is the center of a circle.	**ángulo central de un círculo** Ángulo cuyo vértice es el centro de un círculo.	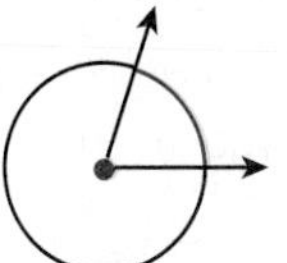
centroid of a triangle The point of concurrency of the three medians of a triangle. Also known as the *center of gravity*.	**centroide de un triángulo** Punto donde se encuentran las tres medianas de un triángulo. También conocido como *centro de gravedad*.	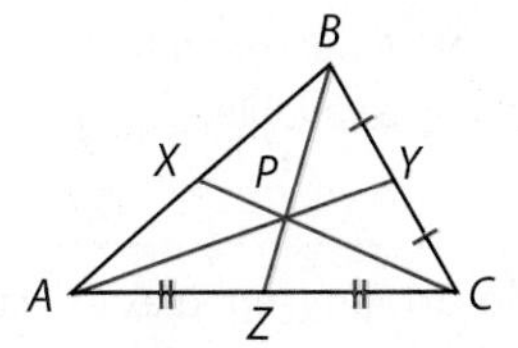 The centroid is *P*.
chord A segment whose endpoints lie on a circle.	**cuerda** Segmento cuyos extremos se encuentran en un círculo.	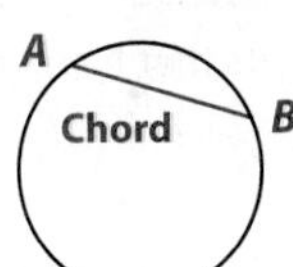
circle The set of points in a plane that are a fixed distance from a given point called the center of the circle.	**círculo** Conjunto de puntos en un plano que se encuentran a una distancia fija de un punto determinado denominado centro del círculo.	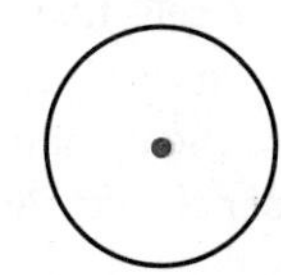
circumcenter of a triangle The point of concurrency of the three perpendicular bisectors of a triangle.	**circuncentro de un triángulo** Punto donde se cortan las tres mediatrices de un triángulo.	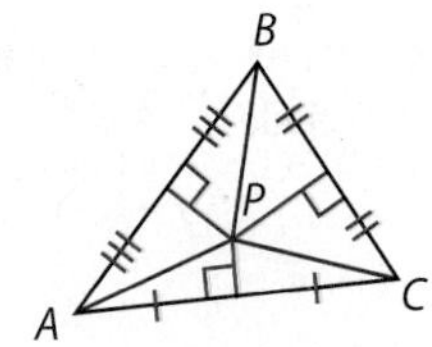 The circumcenter is *P*.

ENGLISH	SPANISH	EXAMPLES
circumcircle *See* circumscribed circle.	**circuncírculo** *Véase* círculo circunscrito.	
circumference The distance around the circle.	**circunferencia** Distancia alrededor del círculo.	Circumference
circumscribed angle An angle formed by two rays from a common endpoint that are tangent to a circle	**ángulo circunscrito** Ángulo formado por dos semirrectas tangentes a un círculo que parten desde un extremo común.	
circumscribed circle Every vertex of the polygon lies on the circle.	**círculo circunscrito** Todos los vértices del polígono se encuentran sobre el círculo.	
circumscribed polygon Each side of the polygon is tangent to the circle.	**polígono circunscrito** Todos los lados del polígono son tangentes al círculo.	
coefficient A number that is multiplied by a variable.	**coeficiente** Número que se multiplica por una variable.	In the expression $2x + 3y$, 2 is the coefficient of x and 3 is the coefficient of y.
coincide To correspond exactly; to be identical.	**coincidir** Corresponder exactamente, ser idéntico.	
collinear Points that lie on the same line.	**colineal** Puntos que se encuentran sobre la misma línea.	*K* *L* *M* *K*, *L*, and *M* are collinear points.
combination A selection of a group of objects in which order is *not* important. The number of combinations of *r* objects chosen from a group of *n* objects is denoted ${}_nC_r$.	**combinación** Selección de un grupo de objetos en la cual el orden *no* es importante. El número de combinaciones de *r* objetos elegidos de un grupo de *n* objetos se expresa así: ${}_nC_r$.	For 4 objects *A*, *B*, *C*, and *D*, there are ${}_4C_2 = 6$ different combinations of 2 objects: *AB*, *AC*, *AD*, *BC*, *BD*, *CD*.
common tangent A line that is tangent to two circles.	**tangente común** Línea que es tangente a dos círculos.	*A* *B* *ℓ* *m* *p* *q* *A* *B*

ENGLISH	SPANISH	EXAMPLES
complement of an angle The sum of the measures of an angle and its complement is 90°.	**complemento de un ángulo** La suma de las medidas de un ángulo y su complemento es 90°.	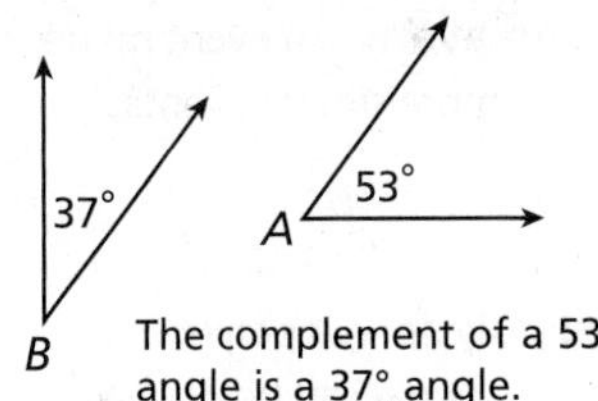 The complement of a 53° angle is a 37° angle.
complement of an event All outcomes in the sample space that are not in an event E, denoted $\bar{E}$.	**complemento de un suceso** Todos los resultados en el espacio muestral que no están en el suceso E y se expresan $\bar{E}$.	In the experiment of rolling a number cube, the complement of rolling a 3 is rolling a 1, 2, 4, 5, or 6.
complementary angles Two angles whose measures have a sum of 90°.	**ángulos complementarios** Dos ángulos cuyas medidas suman 90°.	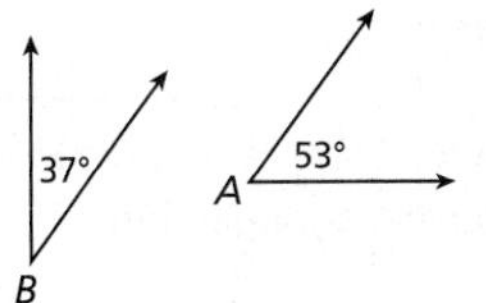
completing the square A process used to form a perfect-square trinomial. To complete the square of $x^2 + bx$, add $\left(\frac{b}{2}\right)^2$.	**completar el cuadrado** Proceso utilizado para formar un trinomio cuadrado perfecto. Para completar el cuadrado de $x^2 + bx$, hay que sumar $\left(\frac{b}{2}\right)^2$.	$x^2 + 6x + \blacksquare$ Add $\left(\frac{6}{2}\right)^2 = 9$. $x^2 + 6x + 9$
complex number Any number that can be written as $a + bi$, where a and b are real numbers and $i = \sqrt{-1}$.	**número complejo** Todo número que se puede expresar como $a + bi$, donde a y b son números reales e $i = \sqrt{-1}$.	$4 + 2i$ $5 + 0i = 5$ $0 - 7i = -7i$
component form The form of a vector that lists the vertical and horizontal change from the initial point to the terminal point.	**forma de componente** Forma de un vector que muestra el cambio horizontal y vertical desde el punto inicial hasta el punto terminal.	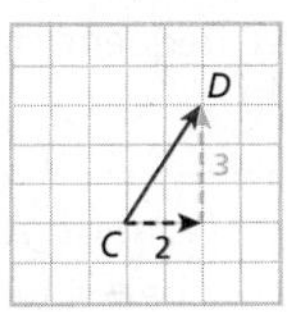 The component form of $\overrightarrow{CD}$ is $\langle 2, 3 \rangle$.
composite figure A plane figure made up of triangles, rectangles, trapezoids, circles, and other simple shapes, or a three-dimensional figure made up of prisms, cones, pyramids, cylinders, and other simple three-dimensional figures.	**figura compuesta** Figura plana compuesta por triángulos, rectángulos, trapecios, círculos y otras figuras simples, o figura tridimensional compuesta por prismas, conos, pirámides, cilindros y otras figuras tridimensionales simples.	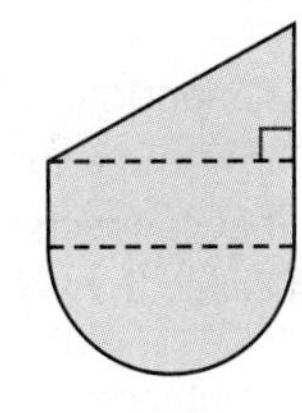
composition of transformations One transformation followed by another transformation.	**composición de transformaciones** Una transformación seguida de otra transformación.	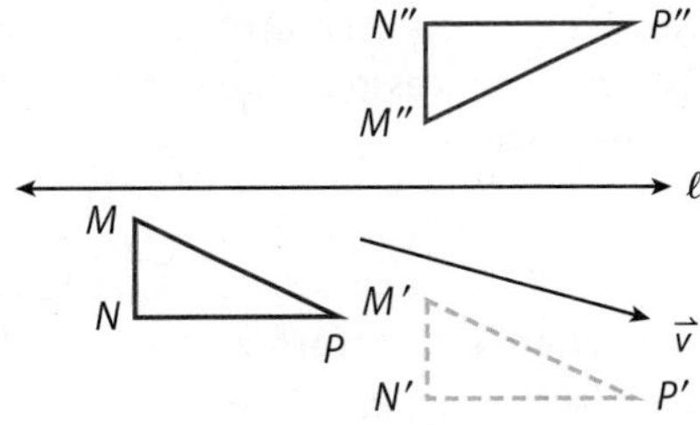

Glossary/Glosario

ENGLISH	SPANISH	EXAMPLES
compound event An event made up of two or more simple events.	**suceso compuesto** Suceso formado por dos o más sucesos simples.	In the experiment of tossing a coin and rolling a number cube, the event of the coin landing heads and the number cube landing on 3.
concave polygon A polygon in which a diagonal can be drawn such that part of the diagonal contains points in the exterior of the polygon.	**polígono cóncavo** Polígono en el cual se puede trazar una diagonal tal que parte de la diagonal contiene puntos ubicados fuera del polígono.	Concave quadrilateral
conclusion The part of a conditional statement following the word *then*.	**conclusión** Parte de un enunciado condicional que sigue a la palabra *entonces*.	If $x + 1 = 5$, then $\underbrace{x = 4.}_{\text{Conclusion}}$
concurrent Three or more lines that intersect at one point.	**concurrente** Tres o más líneas que se cortan en un punto.	
conditional probability The probability of event *B*, given that event *A* has already occurred or is certain to occur, denoted $P(B \mid A)$; used to find probability of dependent events.	**probabilidad condicional** Probabilidad del suceso *B*, dado que el suceso *A* ya ha ocurrido o es seguro que ocurrirá, expresada como $P(B \mid A)$; se utiliza para calcular la probabilidad de sucesos dependientes.	
conditional relative frequency The ratio of a joint relative frequency to a related marginal relative frequency in a two-way table.	**frecuencia relativa condicional** Razón de una frecuencia relativa conjunta a una frecuencia relativa marginal en una tabla de doble entrada.	
conditional statement A statement that can be written in the form "if *p*, then *q*," where *p* is the hypothesis and *q* is the conclusion.	**enunciado condicional** Enunciado que se puede expresar como "si *p*, entonces *q*", donde *p* es la hipótesis y *q* es la conclusión.	If $\underbrace{x + 1 = 5,}_{\text{Hypothesis}}$ then $\underbrace{x = 4.}_{\text{Conclusion}}$
cone A three-dimensional figure with a circular base and a curved lateral surface that connects the base to a point called the vertex.	**cono** Figura tridimensional con una base circular y una superficie lateral curva que conecta la base con un punto denominado vértice.	
congruence statement A statement that indicates that two polygons are congruent by listing the vertices in the order of correspondence.	**enunciado de congruencia** Enunciado que indica que dos polígonos son congruentes enumerando los vértices en orden de correspondencia.	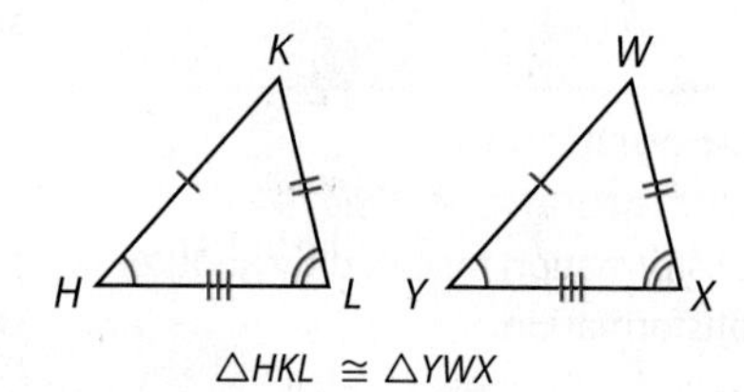 $\triangle HKL \cong \triangle YWX$
congruence transformation *See* isometry.	**transformación de congruencia** *Ver* isometría.	

ENGLISH	SPANISH	EXAMPLES

congruent Having the same size and shape, denoted by $\cong$.

congruente Que tiene el mismo tamaño y la misma forma, expresado por $\cong$.

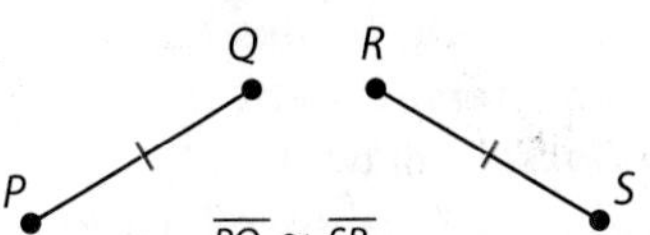

---

congruent polygons Two polygons whose corresponding sides and angles are congruent.

polígonos congruentes Dos polígonos cuyos lados y ángulos correspondientes son congruentes.

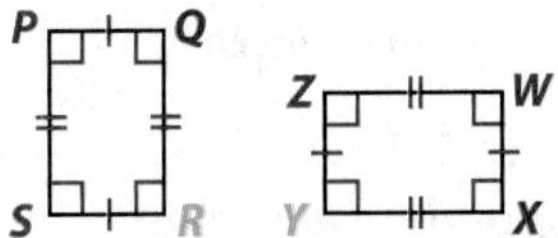

---

conjecture A statement that is believed to be true.

conjetura Enunciado que se supone verdadero.

A sequence begins with the terms 2, 4, 6, 8, 10. A reasonable conjecture is that the next term in the sequence is 12.

---

consecutive interior angles *See* same-side interior angles.

ángulos internos consecutivos *Ver* ángulos internos del mismo lado.

---

contrapositive The statement formed by both exchanging and negating the hypothesis and conclusion of a conditional statement.

contrarrecíproco Enunciado que se forma al intercambiar y negar la hipótesis y la conclusión de un enunciado condicional.

Statement: If $n + 1 = 3$, then $n = 2$.
Contrapositive: If $n \neq 2$, then $n + 1 \neq 3$.

---

converse The statement formed by exchanging the hypothesis and conclusion of a conditional statement.

recíproco Enunciado que se forma intercambiando la hipótesis y la conclusión de un enunciado condicional.

Statement: If $n + 1 = 3$, then $n = 2$.
Converse: If $n = 2$, then $n + 1 = 3$.

---

convex polygon A polygon in which no diagonal contains points in the exterior of the polygon.

polígono convexo Polígono en el cual ninguna diagonal contiene puntos fuera del polígono.

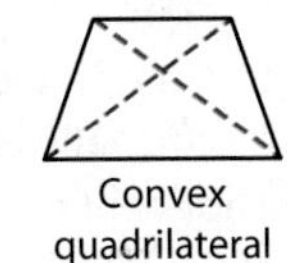

Convex quadrilateral

---

coordinate A number used to identify the location of a point. On a number line, one coordinate is used. On a coordinate plane, two coordinates are used, called the *x*-coordinate and the *y*-coordinate. In space, three coordinates are used, called the *x*-coordinate, the *y*-coordinate, and the *z*-coordinate.

coordenada Número utilizado para identificar la ubicación de un punto. En una recta numérica se utiliza una coordenada. En un plano cartesiano se utilizan dos coordenadas, denominadas coordenada *x* y coordenada *y*. En el espacio se utilizan tres coordenadas, denominadas coordenada *x*, coordenada *y* y coordenada *z*.

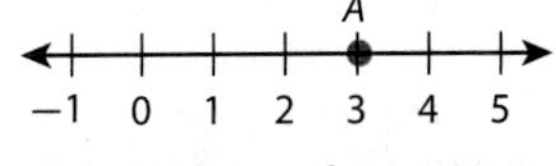

The coordinate of point *A* is 3.

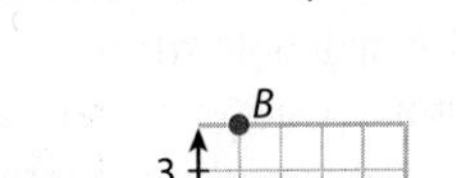

The coordinates of point *B* are (1, 4).

---

coplanar Points that lie in the same plane.

coplanar Puntos que se encuentran en el mismo plano.

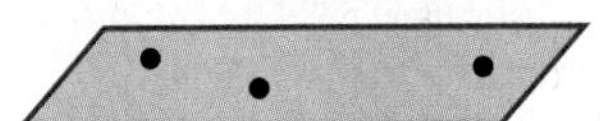

---

corollary A theorem whose proof follows directly from another theorem.

corolario Teorema cuya demostración proviene directamente de otro teorema.

ENGLISH	SPANISH	EXAMPLES

corresponding angles of lines intersected by a transversal For two lines intersected by a transversal, a pair of angles that lie on the same side of the transversal and on the same sides of the other two lines.

ángulos correspondientes de líneas cortadas por una transversal Dadas dos líneas cortadas por una transversal, el par de ángulos ubicados en el mismo lado de la transversal y en los mismos lados de las otras dos líneas.

$\angle 1$ and $\angle 3$ are corresponding.

---

corresponding angles of polygons Angles in the same position in two different polygons that have the same number of angles.

ángulos correspondientes de los polígonos Ángulos que tienen la misma posición en dos polígonos diferentes que tienen el mismo número de ángulos.

$\angle A$ and $\angle D$ are corresponding angles.

---

corresponding sides of polygons Sides in the same position in two different polygons that have the same number of sides.

lados correspondientes de los polígonos Lados que tienen la misma posición en dos polígonos diferentes que tienen el mismo número de lados.

$\overline{AB}$ and $\overline{DE}$ are corresponding sides.

---

cosecant In a right triangle, the cosecant of angle *A* is the ratio of the length of the hypotenuse to the length of the side opposite *A*. It is the reciprocal of the sine function.

cosecante En un triángulo rectángulo, la cosecante del ángulo *A* es la razón entre la longitud de la hipotenusa y la longitud del cateto opuesto a *A*. Es la inversa de la función seno.

$$\csc A = \frac{\text{hypotenuse}}{\text{opposite}} = \frac{1}{\sin A}$$

---

cosine In a right triangle, the cosine of angle *A* is the ratio of the length of the leg adjacent to angle *A* to the length of the hypotenuse. It is the reciprocal of the secant function.

coseno En un triángulo rectángulo, el coseno del ángulo *A* es la razón entre la longitud del cateto adyacente al ángulo *A* y la longitud de la hipotenusa. Es la inversa de la función secante.

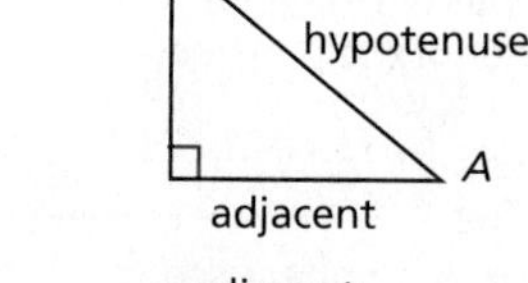

$$\cos A = \frac{\text{adjacent}}{\text{hypotenuse}} = \frac{1}{\sec A}$$

---

cotangent In a right triangle, the cotangent of angle A is the ratio of the length of the side adjacent to *A* to the length of the side opposite *A*. It is the reciprocal of the tangent function.

cotangente En un triángulo rectángulo, la cotangente del ángulo *A* es la razón entre la longitud del cateto adyacente a *A* y la longitud del cateto opuesto a *A*. Es la inversa de la función tangente.

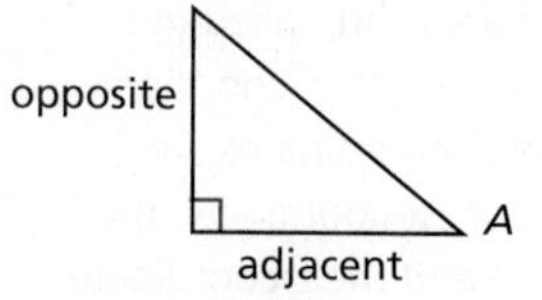

$$\cot A = \frac{\text{adjacent}}{\text{opposite}} = \frac{1}{\tan A}$$

---

counterexample An example that proves that a conjecture or statement is false.

contraejemplo Ejemplo que demuestra que una conjetura o enunciado es falso.

ENGLISH	SPANISH	EXAMPLES
CPCTC An abbreviation for "Corresponding Parts of Congruent Triangles are Congruent," which can be used as a justification in a proof after two triangles are proven congruent.	**PCTCC** Abreviatura que significa "Las partes correspondientes de los triángulos congruentes son congruentes", que se puede utilizar para justificar una demostración después de demostrar que dos triángulos son congruentes (CPCTC, por sus siglas en inglés).	
cross section The intersection of a three-dimensional figure and a plane.	**sección transversal** Intersección de una figura tridimensional y un plano.	
cube A prism with six square faces.	**cubo** Prisma con seis caras cuadradas.	
cylinder A three-dimensional figure with two parallel congruent circular bases and a curved lateral surface that connects the bases.	**cilindro** Figura tridimensional con dos bases circulares congruentes y paralelas y una superficie lateral curva que conecta las bases.	

D

ENGLISH	SPANISH	EXAMPLES
decagon A ten-sided polygon.	**decágono** Polígono de diez lados.	
deductive reasoning The process of using logic to draw conclusions.	**razonamiento deductivo** Proceso en el que se utiliza la lógica para sacar conclusiones.	
definition A statement that describes a mathematical object and can be written as a true biconditional statement.	**definición** Enunciado que describe un objeto matemático y se puede expresar como un enunciado bicondicional verdadero.	
degree A unit of angle measure; one degree is $\frac{1}{360}$ of a circle.	**grado** Unidad de medida de los ángulos; un grado es $\frac{1}{360}$ de un círculo.	
degree of a polynomial The degree of the term of the polynomial with the greatest degree.	**grado de un polinomio** Grado del término del polinomio con el grado máximo.	$3x^2y^2 + 4xy^5 - 12x^3y^2$ (Degree 4, Degree 6, Degree 5)
dependent events Events for which the occurrence or nonoccurrence of one event affects the probability of the other event.	**sucesos dependientes** Dos sucesos son dependientes si el hecho de que uno de ellos se cumpla o no afecta la probabilidad del otro.	From a bag containing 3 red marbles and 2 blue marbles, drawing a red marble, and then drawing a blue marble without replacing the first marble.

Glossary/Glosario

ENGLISH	SPANISH	EXAMPLES
diagonal of a polygon A segment connecting two nonconsecutive vertices of a polygon.	**diagonal de un polígono** Segmento que conecta dos vértices no consecutivos de un polígono.	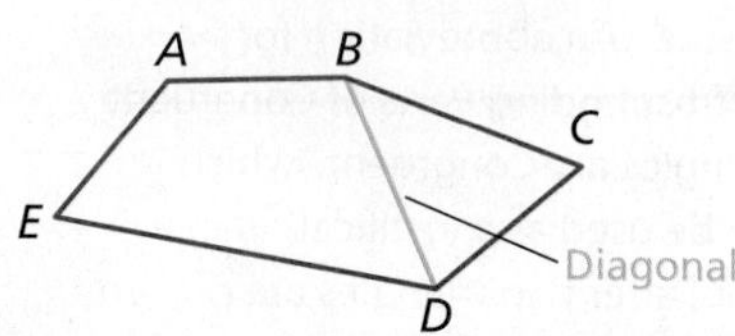
diameter A segment that has endpoints on the circle and that passes through the center of the circle; also the length of that segment.	**diámetro** Segmento que atraviesa el centro de un círculo y cuyos extremos están sobre la circunferencia; longitud de dicho segmento.	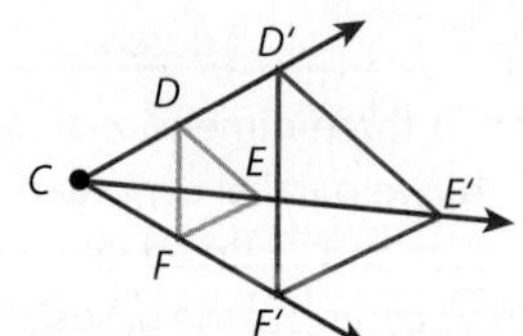
difference of two squares A polynomial of the form $a^2 - b^2$, which may be written as the product $(a + b)(a - b)$.	**diferencia de dos cuadrados** Polinomio del tipo $a^2 - b^2$, que se puede expresar como el producto $(a + b)(a - b)$.	$x^2 - 4 = (x + 2)(x - 2)$
dilation A transformation in which the lines connecting every point P with its preimage P' all intersect at a point C known as the center of dilation, and $\frac{CP'}{CP}$ is the same for every point P; a transformation that changes the size of a figure but not its shape.	**dilatación** Transformación en la cual las líneas que conectan cada punto P con su imagen original P' se cruzan en un punto C conocido como centro de dilatación, y $\frac{CP'}{CP}$ es igual para cada punto P; transformación que cambia el tamaño de una figura pero no su forma.	
directed line segment A segment between two points A and B with a specified direction, from A to B or from B to A.	**segmento de una línea con dirección** Un segmento entro dos puntos con una dirección especificada.	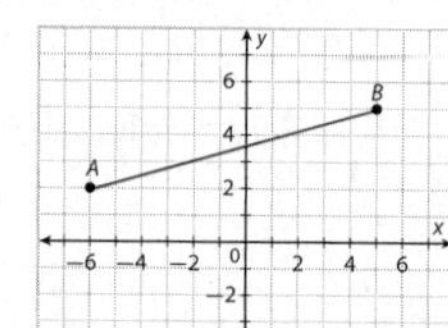
directrix A fixed line used to define a *parabola*. Every point on the parabola is equidistant from the directrix and a fixed point called the *focus*.	**directriz** Línea fija utilizada para definir una *parábola*. Cada punto de la parábola es equidistante de la directriz y de un punto fijo denominado *foco*.	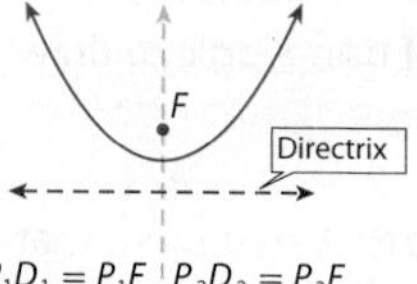 $P_1D_1 = P_1F$ $P_2D_2 = P_2F$
direction of a vector The orientation of a vector, which is determined by the angle the vector makes with a horizontal line.	**dirección de un vector** Orientación de un vector, determinada por el ángulo que forma el vector con una línea horizontal.	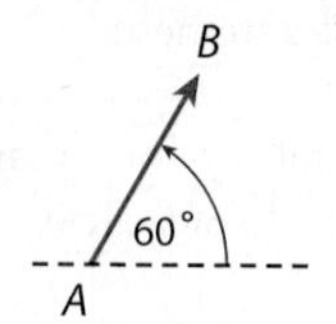
discrete function A function whose graph is made up of unconnected points.	**función discreta** Función cuya gráfica compuesta de puntos no conectados.	
discriminant The discriminant of the quadratic equation $ax^2 + bx + c = 0$ is $b^2 - 4ac$.	**discriminante** El discriminante de la ecuación cuadrática $ax^2 + bx + c = 0$ es $b^2 - 4ac$.	The discriminant of $2x^2 - 5x - 3 = 0$ is $(-5)^2 - 4(2)(-3)$ or 49.

Glossary/Glosario

ENGLISH	SPANISH	EXAMPLES
distance between two points The absolute value of the difference of the coordinates of the points.	**distancia entre dos puntos** Valor absoluto de la diferencia entre las coordenadas de los puntos.	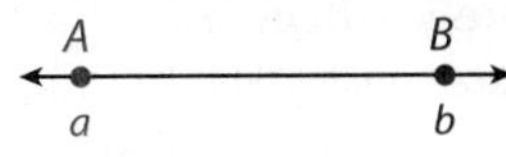 $AB = \|a - b\| = \|b - a\|$
distance from a point to a line The length of the perpendicular segment from the point to the line.	**distancia desde un punto hasta una línea** Longitud del segmento perpendicular desde el punto hasta la línea.	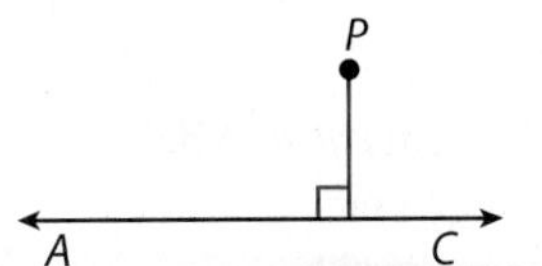 The distance from P to $\overleftrightarrow{AC}$ is 5 units.
dodecagon A 12-sided polygon.	**dodecágono** Polígono de 12 lados.	
domain The set of all possible input values of a relation or function.	**dominio** Conjunto de todos los posibles valores de entrada de una función o relación.	The domain of the function $f(x) = \sqrt{x}$ is $\{x \mid x \geq 0\}$.

E

ENGLISH	SPANISH	EXAMPLES
element of a set An item in a set.	**elemento de un conjunto** Componente de un conjunto.	4 is an element of the set of even numbers. $4 \in \{\text{even numbers}\}$
empty set A set with no elements.	**conjunto vacío** Conjunto sin elementos.	The solution set of $\|\mathbf{x}\| < 0$ is the empty set, $\{\ \}$, or $\varnothing$.
end behavior The trends in the *y*-values of a function as the *x*-values approach positive and negative infinity.	**comportamiento extremo** Tendencia de los valores de y de una función a medida que los valores de *x* se aproximan al infinito positivo y negativo.	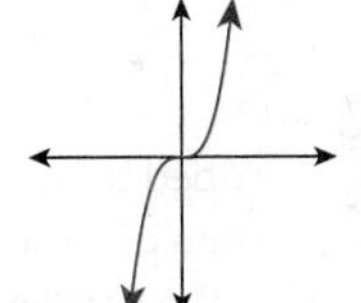 End behavior: $f(x) \to \infty$ as $x \to \infty$; $f(x) \to -\infty$ as $x \to -\infty$
endpoint A point at an end of a segment or the starting point of a ray.	**extremo** Punto en el final de un segmento o punto de inicio de un rayo.	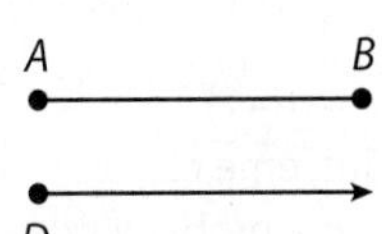
enlargement A dilation with a scale factor greater than 1. In an enlargement, the image is larger than the preimage.	**agrandamiento** Dilatación con un factor de escala mayor que 1. En un agrandamiento, la imagen es más grande que la imagen original.	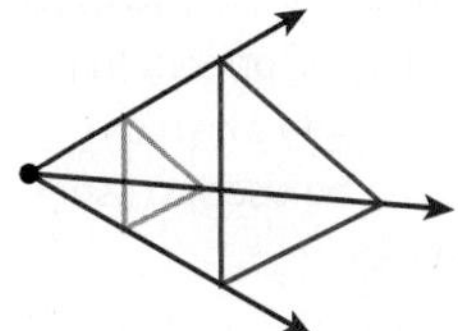

ENGLISH	SPANISH	EXAMPLES
equally likely outcomes Outcomes are equally likely if they have the same probability of occurring. If an experiment has *n* equally likely outcomes, then the probability of each outcome is $\frac{1}{n}$.	**resultados igualmente probables** Los resultados son igualmente probables si tienen la misma probabilidad de ocurrir. Si un experimento tiene *n* resultados igualmente probables, entonces la probabilidad de cada resultado es $\frac{1}{n}$.	If a coin is tossed, and heads and tails are equally likely, then $P(\text{heads}) = P(\text{tails}) = \frac{1}{2}$.
equiangular polygon A polygon in which all angles are congruent.	**polígono equiangular** Polígono cuyos ángulos son todos congruentes.	
equiangular triangle A triangle with three congruent angles.	**triángulo equiangular** Triángulo con tres ángulos congruentes.	
equidistant The same distance from two or more objects.	**equidistante** Igual distancia de dos o más objetos.	X A Y B *X* is equidistant from *A* and *B*.
equilateral polygon A polygon in which all sides are congruent.	**polígono equilátero** Polígono cuyos lados son todos congruentes.	
equilateral triangle A triangle with three congruent sides.	**triángulo equilátero** Triángulo con tres lados congruentes.	
Euclidean geometry The system of geometry described by Euclid. In particular, the system of Euclidean geometry satisfies the Parallel Postulate, which states that there is exactly one line through a given point parallel to a given line.	**geometría euclidiana** Sistema geométrico desarrollado por Euclides. Específicamente, el sistema de la geometría euclidiana cumple con el postulado de las paralelas, que establece que por un punto dado se puede trazar una única línea paralela a una línea dada.	
event An outcome or set of outcomes in a probability experiment.	**suceso** Resultado o conjunto de resultados en un experimento de probabilidad.	In the experiment of rolling a number cube, the event "an odd number" consists of the outcomes 1, 3, 5.
experiment An operation, process, or activity in which outcomes can be used to estimate probability.	**experimento** Una operación, proceso o actividad en la que se usan los resultados para estimar una probabilidad.	Tossing a coin 10 times and noting the number of heads.

ENGLISH	SPANISH	EXAMPLES
experimental probability The ratio of the number of times an event occurs to the number of trials, or times, that an activity is performed.	**probabilidad experimental** Razón entre la cantidad de veces que ocurre un suceso y la cantidad de pruebas, o veces, que se realiza una actividad.	Kendra made 6 of 10 free throws. The experimental probability that she will make her next free throw is $P(\text{free throw}) = \frac{\text{number made}}{\text{number attempted}} = \frac{6}{10}$.
exterior of a circle The set of all points outside a circle.	**exterior de un círculo** Conjunto de todos los puntos que se encuentran fuera de un círculo.	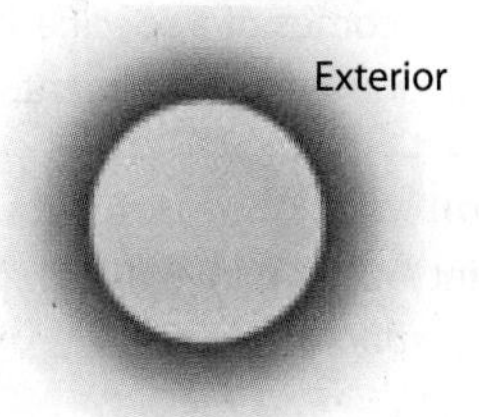
exterior of an angle The set of all points outside an angle.	**exterior de un ángulo** Conjunto de todos los puntos que se encuentran fuera de un ángulo.	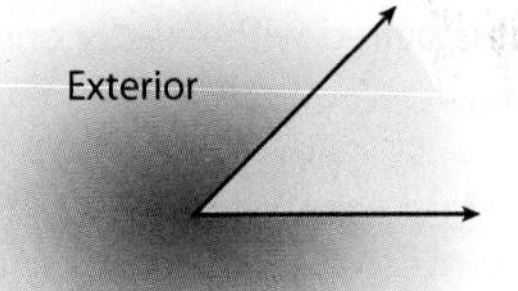
exterior of a polygon The set of all points outside a polygon.	**exterior de un polígono** Conjunto de todos los puntos que se encuentran fuera de un polígono.	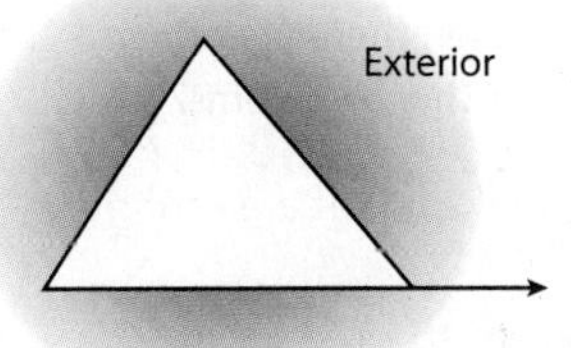
exterior angle of a polygon An angle formed by one side of a polygon and the extension of an adjacent side.	**ángulo externo de un polígono** Ángulo formado por un lado de un polígono y la prolongación del lado adyacente.	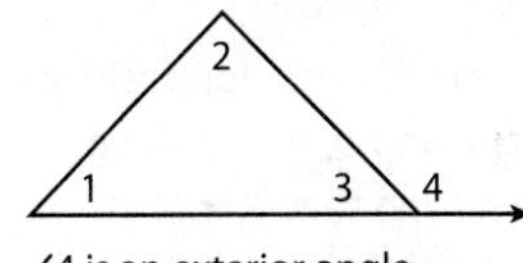 $\angle 4$ is an exterior angle.
external secant segment A segment of a secant that lies in the exterior of the circle with one endpoint on the circle.	**segmento secante externo** Segmento de una secante que se encuentra en el exterior del círculo y tiene un extremo sobre el círculo.	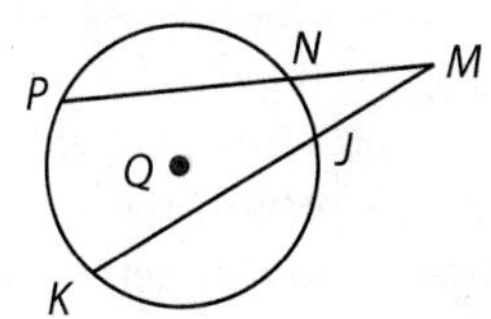 $\overline{NM}$ is an external secant segment.

F

factorial If n is a positive integer, then n factorial, written $n!$, is $n \cdot (n-1) \cdot (n-2) \cdot \ldots \cdot 2 \cdot 1$. The factorial of 0 is defined to be 1.	**factorial** Si n es un entero positivo, entonces el factorial de n, expresado como $n!$, es $n \cdot (n-1) \cdot (n-2) \cdot \ldots \cdot 2 \cdot 1$. Por definición, el factorial de 0 será 1.	$7! = 7 \cdot 6 \cdot 5 \cdot 4 \cdot 3 \cdot 2 \cdot 1 = 5040$ $0! = 1$

ENGLISH	SPANISH	EXAMPLES
fair When all outcomes of an experiment are equally likely.	**justo** Cuando todos los resultados de un experimento son igualmente probables.	When tossing a fair coin, heads and tails are equally likely. Each has a probability of $\frac{1}{2}$.
favorable outcome The occurrence of one of several possible outcomes of a specified event or probability experiment.	**resultado favorable** Cuando se produce uno de varios resultados posibles de un suceso específico o experimento de probabilidad.	In the experiment of rolling an odd number on a number cube, the favorable outcomes are 1, 3, and 5.
focus (pl. foci) of a parabola A fixed point F used with a *directrix* to define a *parabola*.	**foco de una parábola** Punto fijo F utilizado con una *directriz* para definir una *parábola*.	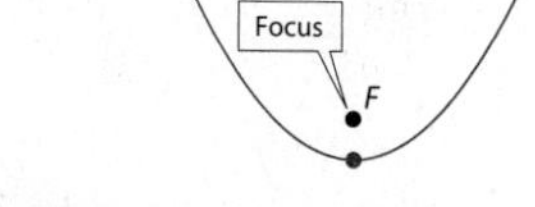
function A relation in which every input is paired with exactly one output.	**función** Una relación en la que cada entrada corresponde exactamente a una salida.	Function: $\{(0, 5), (1, 3), (2, 1), (3, 3)\}$ Not a Function: $\{(0, 1), (0, 3), (2, 1), (2, 3)\}$
Fundamental Counting Principle For n items, if there are m_1 ways to choose a first item, m_2 ways to choose a second item after the first item has been chosen, and so on, then there are $m_1 \cdot m_2 \cdot ... \cdot m_n$ ways to choose n items.	**Principio fundamental deconteo** Dados n elementos, si existen m_1 formas de elegir un primer elemento, m_2 formas de elegir un segundo elemento después de haber elegido el primero, y así sucesivamente, entonces existen $m_1 \cdot m_2 \cdot ... \cdot m_n$ formas de elegir n elementos.	If there are 4 colors of shirts, 3 colors of pants, and 2 colors of shoes, then there are $4 \cdot 3 \cdot 2 = 24$ possible outfits.

G

ENGLISH	SPANISH	EXAMPLES
geometric mean For positive numbers a and b, the positive number x such that $\frac{a}{x} = \frac{x}{b}$. In a geometric sequence, a term that comes between two given nonconsecutive terms of the sequence.	**media geométrica** Dados los números positivos a y b, el número positivo x tal que $\frac{a}{x} = \frac{x}{b}$. En una sucesión geométrica, un término que está entre dos términos no consecutivos dados de la sucesión.	$\frac{a}{x} = \frac{x}{b}$ $x^2 = ab$ $x = \sqrt{ab}$
geometric probability A form of theoretical probability determined by a ratio of geometric measures such as lengths, areas, or volumes.	**probabilidad geométrica** Una forma de la probabilidad teórica determinada por una razón de medidas geométricas, como longitud, área o volumen.	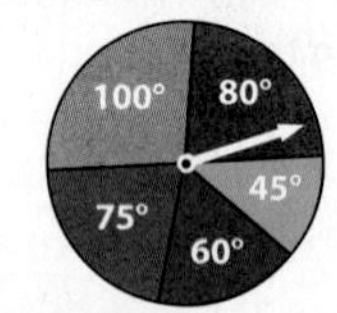 The probability of the pointer landing on 80° is $\frac{2}{9}$.
great circle A circle on a sphere that divides the sphere into two hemispheres.	**círculo máximo** En una esfera, círculo que divide la esfera en dos hemisferios.	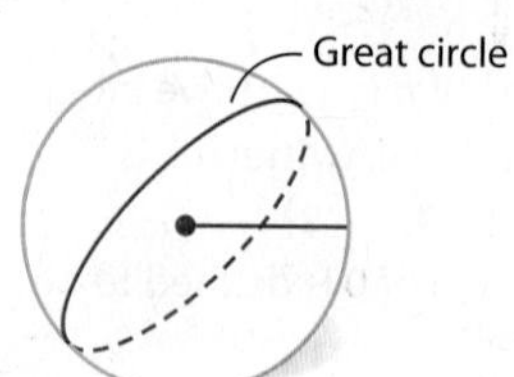

ENGLISH	SPANISH	EXAMPLES

H

ENGLISH	SPANISH	EXAMPLES
height of a figure The length of an altitude of the figure.	**altura de una figura** Longitud de la altura de la figura.	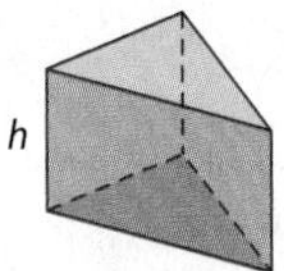 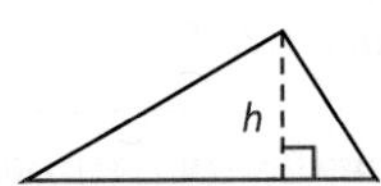
hemisphere Half of a sphere.	**hemisferio** Mitad de una esfera.	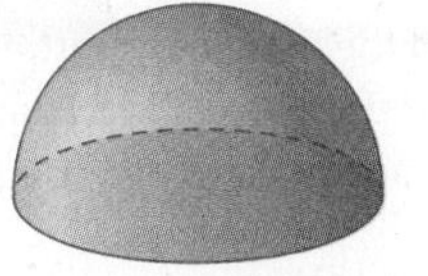
heptagon A seven-sided polygon.	**heptágono** Polígono de siete lados.	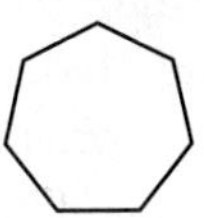
hexagon A six-sided polygon.	**hexágono** Polígono de seis lados.	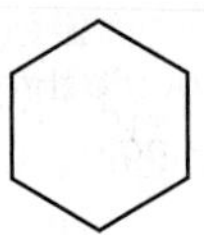
hypotenuse The side opposite the right angle in a right triangle.	**hipotenusa** Lado opuesto al ángulo recto de un triángulo rectángulo.	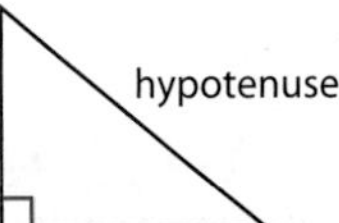
hypothesis The part of a conditional statement following the word *if.*	**hipótesis** La parte de un enunciado condicional que sigue a la palabra *si.*	If $x + 1 = 5$, then $x = 4$. Hypothesis

I

ENGLISH	SPANISH	EXAMPLES
identity An equation that is true for all values of the variables.	**identidad** Ecuación verdadera para todos los valores de las variables.	$3 = 3$ $2(x - 1) = 2x - 2$
image A shape that results from a transformation of a figure known as the preimage.	**imagen** Forma resultante de la transformación de una figura conocida como imagen original.	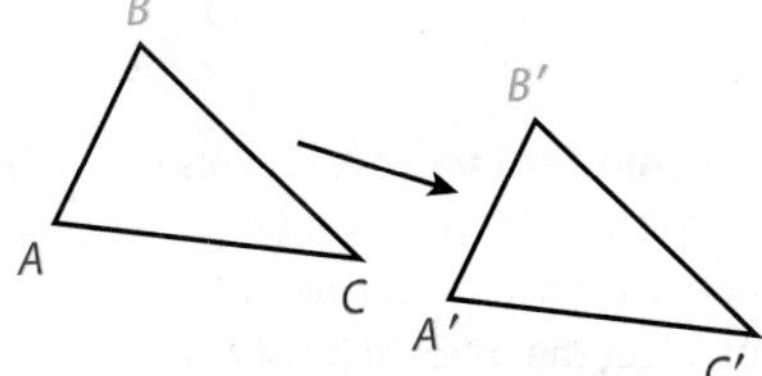

Glossary/Glosario

ENGLISH	SPANISH	EXAMPLES
imaginary number The square root of a negative number, written in the form *bi*, where *b* is a real number and *i* is the imaginary unit, $\sqrt{-1}$. Also called a *pure imaginary number.*	**número imaginario** Raíz cuadrada de un número negativo, expresado como *bi*, donde *b* es un número real e *i* es la unidad imaginaria, $\sqrt{-1}$. También se denomina *número imaginario puro.*	$\sqrt{-16} = \sqrt{16} \cdot \sqrt{-1} = 4i$
imaginary part of a complex number For a complex number of the form $a + bi$, the real number *b* is called the imaginary part, represented graphically as *b* units on the imaginary axis of a complex plane.	**parte imaginaria de un número complejo** Dado un número complejo del tipo $a + bi$, el número real *b* se denomina parte imaginaria y se representa gráficamente como *b* unidades en el eje imaginario de un plano complejo.	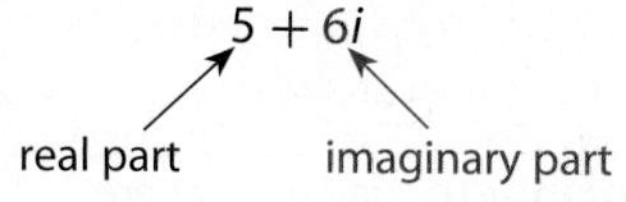
imaginary unit The unit in the imaginary number system, $\sqrt{-1}$.	**unidad imaginaria** Unidad del sistema de números imaginarios, $\sqrt{-1}$.	$\sqrt{-1} = i$
incenter of a triangle The point of concurrency of the three angle bisectors of a triangle.	**incentro de un triángulo** Punto donde se encuentran las tres bisectrices de los ángulos de un triángulo.	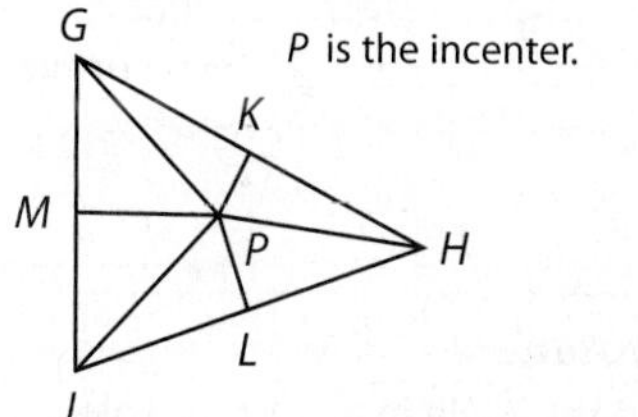
incircle *See* inscribed circle.	**incírculo** *Véase* círculo inscrito.	
included angle The angle formed by two adjacent sides of a polygon.	**ángulo incluido** Ángulo formado por dos lados adyacentes de un polígono.	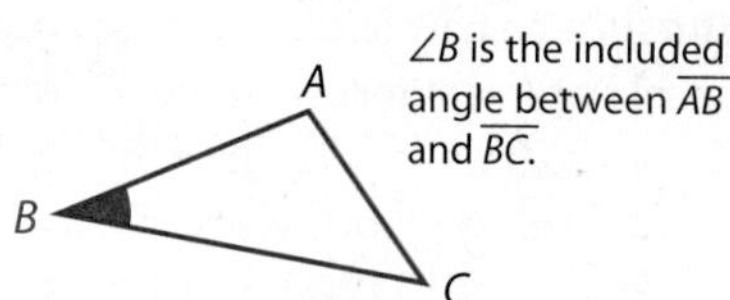 $\angle B$ is the included angle between $\overline{AB}$ and $\overline{BC}$.
included side The common side of two consecutive angles of a polygon.	**lado incluido** Lado común de dos ángulos consecutivos de un polígono.	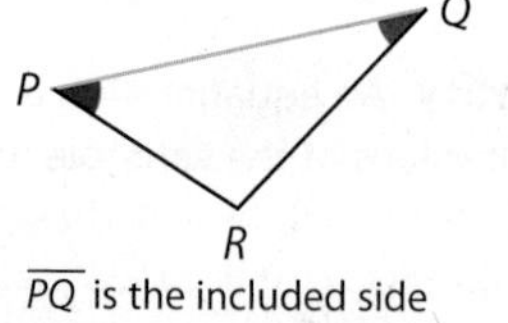 $\overline{PQ}$ is the included side between $\angle P$ and $\angle Q$.
independent events Events for which the occurrence or nonoccurrence of one event does not affect the probability of the other event.	**sucesos independientes** Dos sucesos son independientes si el hecho de que se produzca o no uno de ellos no afecta la probabilidad del otro suceso.	From a bag containing 3 red marbles and 2 blue marbles, drawing a red marble, replacing it, and then drawing a blue marble.
index In the radical $\sqrt[n]{x}$, which represents the *n*th root of *x*, *n* is the index. In the radical $\sqrt{x}$, the index is understood to be 2.	**índice** En el radical $\sqrt[n]{x}$, que representa la enésima raíz de *x*, *n* es el índice. En el radical $\sqrt{x}$, se da por sentado que el índice es 2.	The radical $\sqrt[3]{8}$ has an index of 3.

Glossary/Glosario

ENGLISH	SPANISH	EXAMPLES
indirect measurement A method of measurement that uses formulas, similar figures, and/or proportions.	**medición indirecta** Método para medir objetos mediante fórmulas, figuras semejantes y/o proporciones.	
indirect proof A proof in which the statement to be proved is assumed to be false and a contradiction is shown.	**demostración indirecta** Prueba en la que se supone que el enunciado a demostrar es falso y se muestra una contradicción.	
indirect reasoning *See* indirect proof.	**razonamiento indirecto** *Ver* demostración indirecta.	
inductive reasoning The process of reasoning that a rule or statement is true because specific cases are true.	**razonamiento inductivo** Proceso de razonamiento por el que se determina que una regla o enunciado son verdaderos porque ciertos casos específicos son verdaderos.	
inequality A statement that compares two expressions by using one of the following signs: $<$, $>$, $\leq$, $\geq$, or $\neq$.	**desigualdad** Enunciado que compara dos expresiones utilizando uno de los siguientes signos: $<$, $>$, $\leq$, $\geq$, o $\neq$.	$x \geq 2$ −4 −3 −2 −1 0 1 2 3 4 5 6
initial point of a vector The starting point of a vector.	**punto inicial de un vector** Punto donde comienza un vector.	A, B, $\vec{v}$ Initial point
initial side The ray that lies on the positive x-axis when an angle is drawn in standard position.	**lado inicial** Rayo que se encuentra sobre el eje x positivo cuando se traza un ángulo en posición estándar.	y, x, 135°, 45°, 0 Initial side
inscribed angle An angle whose vertex is on a circle and whose sides contain chords of the circle.	**ángulo inscrito** Ángulo cuyo vértice se encuentra sobre un círculo y cuyos lados contienen cuerdas del círculo.	D, E, F
inscribed circle A circle in which each side of the polygon is tangent to the circle.	**círculo inscrito** Círculo en el que cada lado del polígono es tangente al círculo.	
inscribed polygon A polygon in which every vertex of the polygon lies on the circle.	**polígono inscrito** Polígono cuyos vértices se encuentran sobre el círculo.	

ENGLISH	SPANISH	EXAMPLES
intercepted arc An arc that consists of endpoints that lie on the sides of an inscribed angle and all the points of the circle between the endpoints.	**arco abarcado** Arco cuyos extremos se encuentran en los lados de un ángulo inscrito y consta de todos los puntos del círculo ubicados entre dichos extremos.	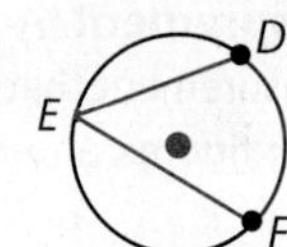 $\widehat{DF}$ is the intercepted arc.
interior angle An angle formed by two sides of a polygon with a common vertex.	**ángulo interno** Ángulo formado por dos lados de un polígono con un vértice común.	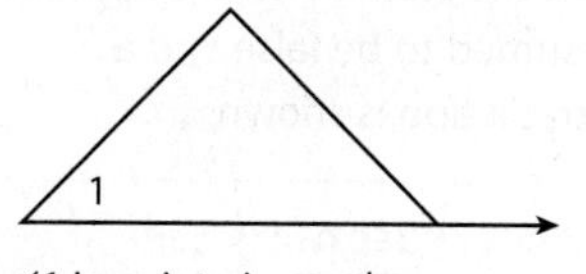 $\angle 1$ is an interior angle.
interior of a circle The set of all points inside a circle.	**interior de un círculo** Conjunto de todos los puntos que se encuentran dentro de un círculo.	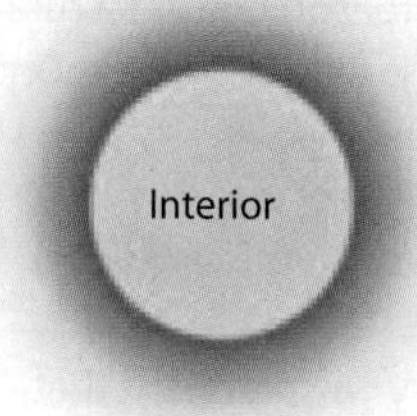
interior of an angle The set of all points between the sides of an angle.	**interior de un ángulo** Conjunto de todos los puntos entre los lados de un ángulo.	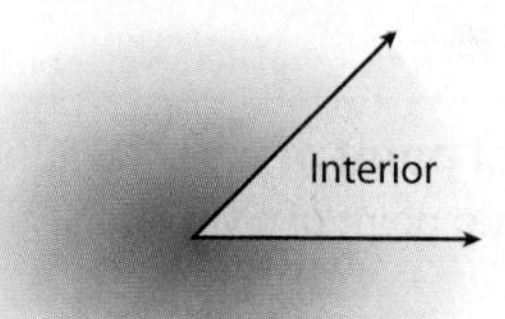
interior of a polygon The set of all points inside a polygon.	**interior de un polígono** Conjunto de todos los puntos que se encuentran dentro de un polígono.	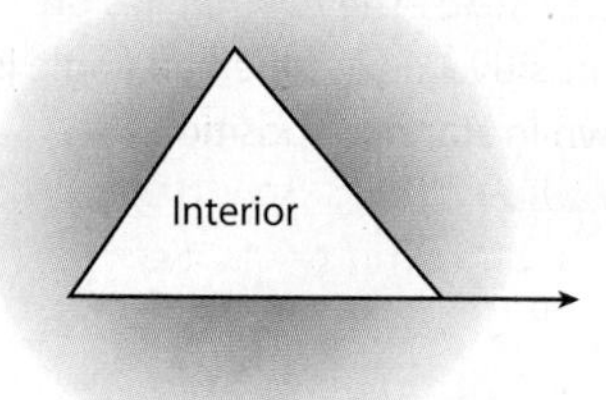
inverse The statement formed by negating the hypothesis and conclusion of a conditional statement.	**inverso** Enunciado formado al negar la hipótesis y la conclusión de un enunciado condicional.	Statement: If $n + 1 = 3$, then $n = 2$. Inverse: If $n + 1 \neq 3$, then $n \neq 2$.
inverse cosine The measure of an angle whose cosine ratio is known.	**coseno inverso** Medida de un ángulo cuya razón coseno es conocida.	If $\cos A = x$, then $\cos^{-1} x = m\angle A$.

ENGLISH	SPANISH	EXAMPLES
inverse function The function that results from exchanging the input and output values of a one-to-one function. The inverse of $f(x)$ is denoted $f^{-1}(x)$.	**función inversa** Función que resulta de intercambiar los valores de entrada y salida de una función uno a uno. La función inversa de $f(x)$ se indica $f^{-1}(x)$.	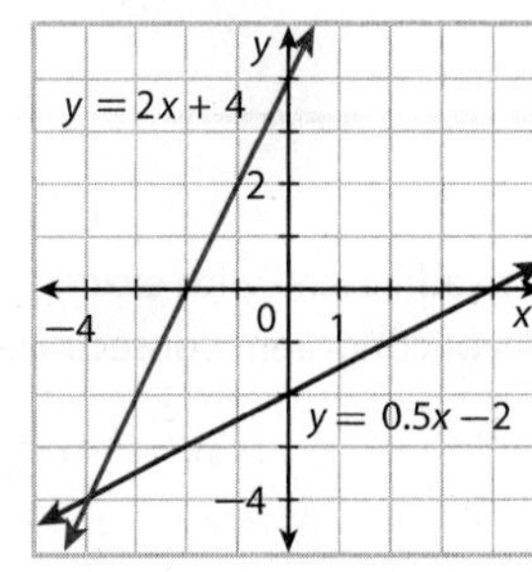 The function $y = \frac{1}{2}x - 2$ is the inverse of the function $y = 2x + 4$.
inverse sine The measure of an angle whose sine ratio is known.	**seno inverso** Medida de un ángulo cuya razón seno es conocida.	If $\sin A = x$, then $\sin^{-1}x = m\angle A$.
inverse tangent The measure of an angle whose tangent ratio is known.	**tangente inversa** Medida de un ángulo cuya razón tangente es conocida.	If $\tan A = x$, then $\tan^{-1}x = m\angle A$.
irregular polygon A polygon that is not regular.	**polígono irregular** Polígono que no es regular.	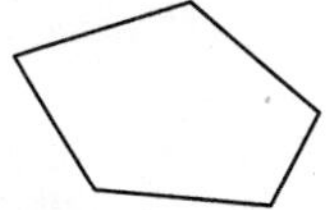
isometry A transformation that does not change the size or shape of a figure.	**isometría** Transformación que no cambia el tamaño ni la forma de una figura.	Reflections, translations, and rotations are all examples of isometries.
isosceles trapezoid A trapezoid in which the legs are congruent.	**trapecio isósceles** Trapecio cuyos lados no paralelos son congruentes.	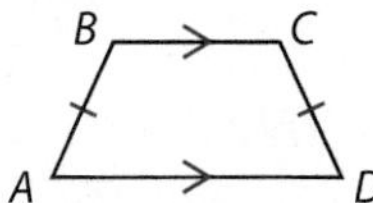
isosceles triangle A triangle with at least two congruent sides.	**triángulo isósceles** Triángulo que tiene al menos dos lados congruentes.	
iteration The repetitive application of the same rule.	**iteración** Aplicación repetitiva de la misma regla.v	  

J

ENGLISH	SPANISH	EXAMPLES
joint relative frequency The ratio of the frequency in a particular category divided by the total number of data values.	**frecuencia relativa conjunta** La razón de la frecuencia en una determinada categoría dividida entre el número total de valores.	

ENGLISH	SPANISH	EXAMPLES

K

kite A quadrilateral with exactly two pairs of congruent consecutive sides.

cometa o papalote Cuadrilátero con exactamente dos pares de lados congruentes consecutivos.

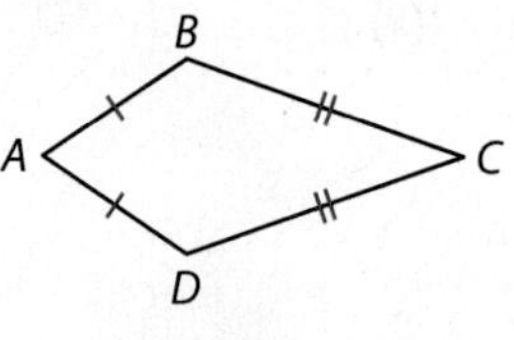

Kite *ABCD*

L

lateral area The sum of the areas of the lateral faces of a prism or pyramid, or the area of the lateral surface of a cylinder or cone.

área lateral Suma de las áreas de las caras laterales de un prisma o pirámide, o área de la superficie lateral de un cilindro o cono.

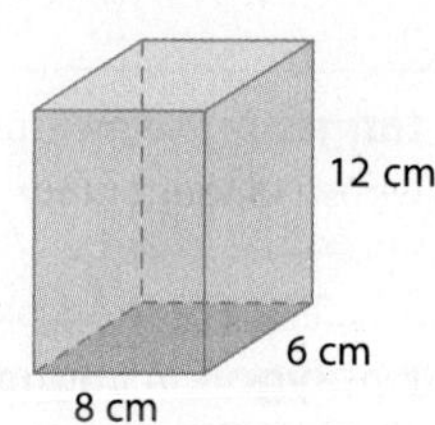

Lateral area $= 4(6)(12) = 288$ cm^2

---

lateral edge An edge of a prism or pyramid that is not an edge of a base.

arista lateral Arista de un prisma o pirámide que no es la arista de una base.

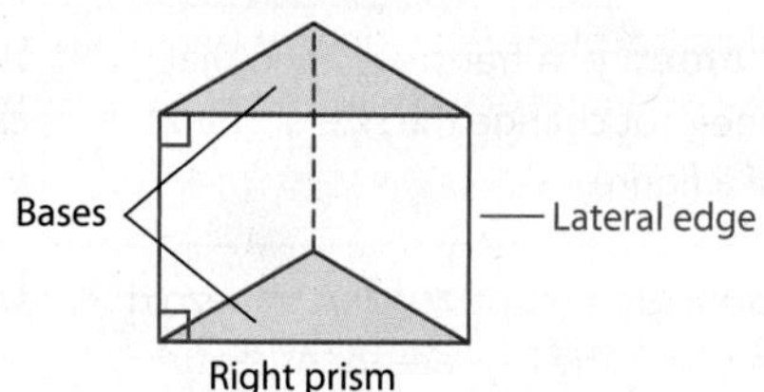

Right prism

---

lateral face A face of a prism or a pyramid that is not a base.

cara lateral Cara de un prisma o pirámide que no es la base.

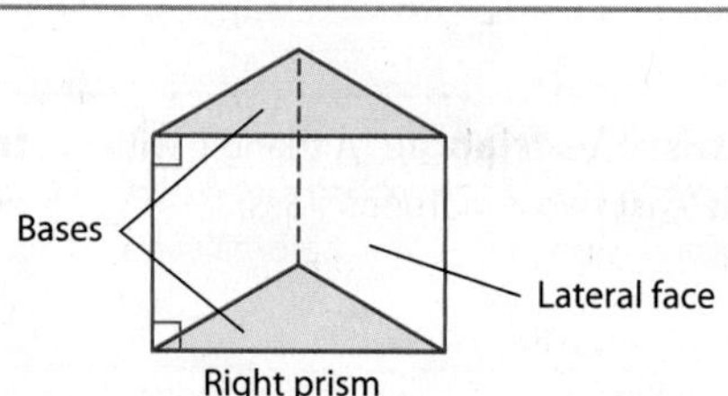

Right prism

---

lateral surface The curved surface of a cylinder or cone.

superficie lateral Superficie curva de un cilindro o cono.

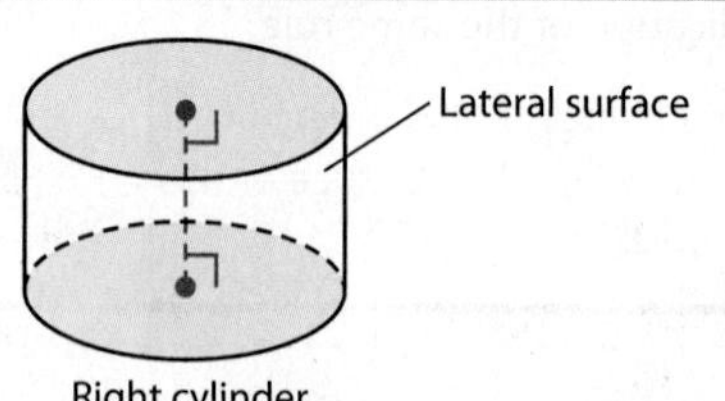

Right cylinder

---

leading coefficient The coefficient of the first term of a polynomial in standard form.

coeficiente principal Coeficiente del primer término de un polinomio en forma estándar.

$3x^2 + 7x - 2$
Leading coefficient: 3

---

leg of a right triangle One of the two sides of the right triangle that form the right angle.

cateto de un triángulo rectángulo Uno de los dos lados de un triángulo rectángulo que forman el ángulo recto.

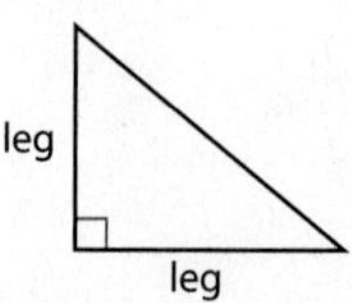

ENGLISH	SPANISH	EXAMPLES
leg of a trapezoid One of the two nonparallel sides of the trapezoid.	**cateto de un trapecio** Uno de los dos lados no paralelos del trapecio.	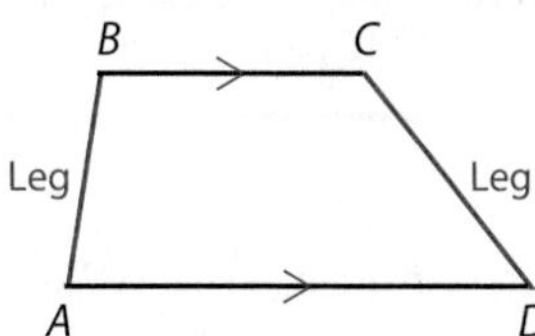
leg of an isosceles triangle One of the two congruent sides of the isosceles triangle.	**cateto de un triángulo isósceles** Uno de los dos lados congruentes del triángulo isósceles.	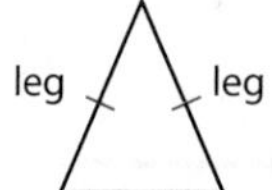
length The distance between the two endpoints of a segment.	**longitud** Distancia entre los dos extremos de un segmento.	 $AB = \|a - b\| = \|b - a\|$
line An undefined term in geometry, a line is a straight path that has no thickness and extends forever.	**línea** Término indefinido en geometría; una línea es un trazo recto que no tiene grosor y se extiende infinitamente.	ℓ
line of symmetry A line that divides a plane figure into two congruent reflected halves.	**eje de simetría** Línea que divide una figura plana en dos mitades reflejas congruentes.	
line segment *See* segment of a line.	**segmento** *Véase* segmento de recta.	
line symmetry A figure that can be reflected across a line so that the image coincides with the preimage.	**simetría axial** Figura que puede reflejarse sobre una línea de forma tal que la imagen coincida con la imagen original.	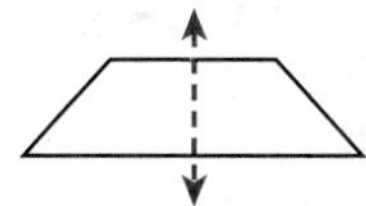
linear equation in three variables An equation with three distinct variables, each of which is either first degree or has a coefficient of zero.	**ecuación lineal en tres variables** Ecuación con tres variables diferentes, sean de primer grado o tengan un coeficiente de cero.	$5 = 3x + 2y + 6z$
linear pair A pair of adjacent angles whose noncommon sides are opposite rays.	**par lineal** Par de ángulos adyacentes cuyos lados no comunes son rayos opuestos.	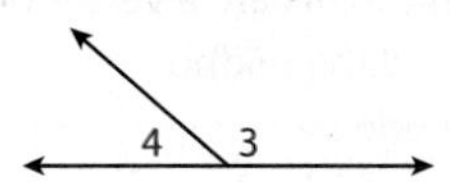 $\angle 3$ and $\angle 4$ form a linear pair.

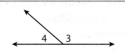

ENGLISH	SPANISH	EXAMPLES

M

major arc An arc of a circle whose points are on or in the exterior of a central angle.	**arco mayor** Arco de un círculo cuyos puntos están sobre un ángulo central o en su exterior.	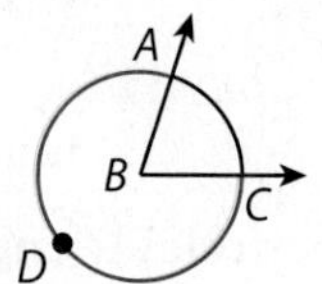 $\widehat{ADC}$ is a major arc of the circle.
mapping An operation that matches each element of a set with another element, its image, in the same set.	**correspondencia** Operación que establece una correlación entre cada elemento de un conjunto con otro elemento, su imagen, en el mismo conjunto.	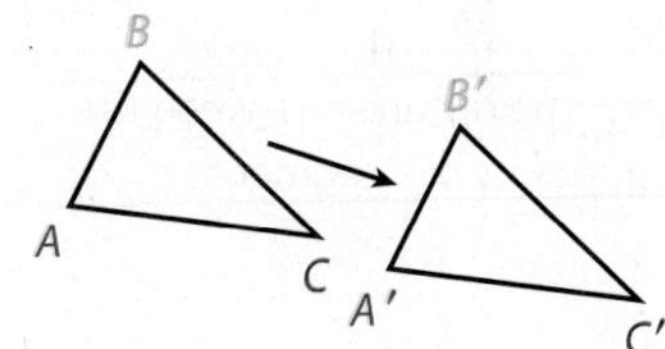
marginal relative frequency The sum of the joint relative frequencies in a row or column of a two-way table.	**frecuencia relativa marginal** La suma de las frecuencias relativas conjuntas en una fila o columna de una tabla de doble entrada.	
measure of an angle Angles are measured in degrees. A degree is $\frac{1}{360}$ of a complete circle.	**medida de un ángulo** Los ángulos se miden en grados. Un grado es $\frac{1}{360}$ de un círculo completo.	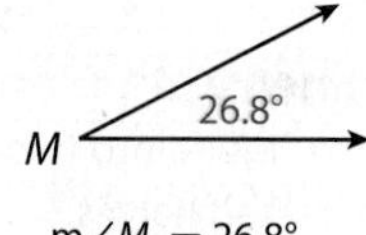 $m\angle M = 26.8°$
measure of a major arc The difference of 360° and the measure of the associated minor arc.	**medida de un arco mayor** Diferencia entre 360° y la medida del arco menor asociado.	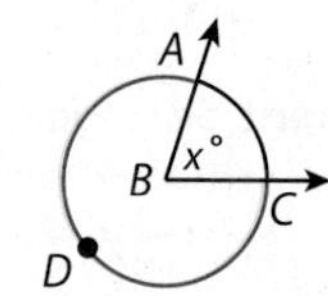 $m\widehat{ADC} = 360° - x°$
measure of a minor arc The measure of its central angle.	**medida de un arco menor** Medida de su ángulo central.	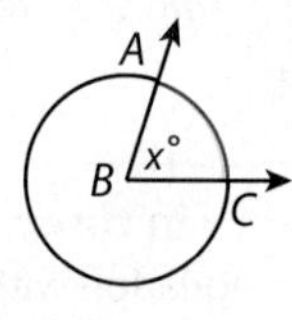 $m\widehat{AC} = x°$
median of a triangle A segment whose endpoints are a vertex of the triangle and the midpoint of the opposite side.	**mediana de un triángulo** Segmento cuyos extremos son un vértice del triángulo y el punto medio del lado opuesto.	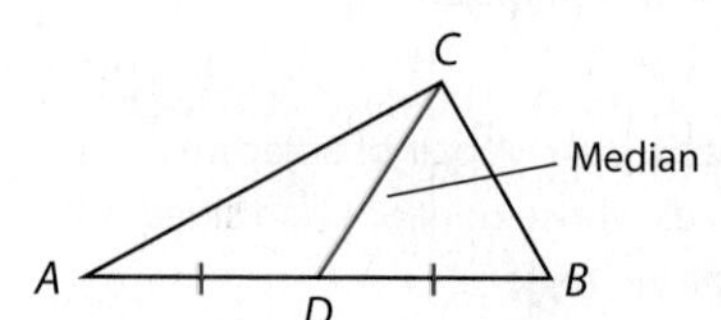
midpoint The point that divides a segment into two congruent segments.	**punto medio** Punto que divide un segmento en dos segmentos congruentes.	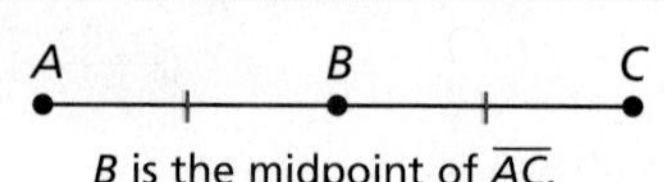 B is the midpoint of $\overline{AC}$.

Glossary/Glosario

ENGLISH	SPANISH	EXAMPLES
midsegment of a trapezoid The segment whose endpoints are the midpoints of the legs of the trapezoid.	**segmento medio de un trapecio** Segmento cuyos extremos son los puntos medios de los catetos del trapecio.	Midsegment
midsegment triangle The triangle formed by the three midsegments of a triangle.	**triángulo de segmentos medios** Triángulo formado por los tres segmentos medios de un triángulo.	Q, X, Y, P, Z, R Midsegment triangle: $\triangle XYZ$
minor arc An arc of a circle whose points are on or in the interior of a central angle.	**arco menor** Arco de un círculo cuyos puntos están sobre un ángulo central o en su interior.	A, B, C $\overset{\frown}{AC}$ is a minor arc of the circle.
monomial A number or a product of numbers and variables with whole-number exponents, or a polynomial with one term.	**monomio** Número o producto de números y variables con exponentes de números cabales, o polinomio con un término.	$3x^2y^4$
mutually exclusive events Two events are mutually exclusive if they cannot both occur in the same trial of an experiment.	**sucesos mutuamente excluyentes** Dos sucesos son mutuamente excluyentes si ambos no pueden ocurrir en la misma prueba de un experimento.	In the experiment of rolling a number cube, rolling a 3 and rolling an even number are mutually exclusive events.

N

ENGLISH	SPANISH	EXAMPLES
***n*-gon** An *n*-sided polygon.	***n*-ágono** Polígono de *n* lados.	
nonagon A nine-sided polygon.	**nonágono** Polígono de nueve lados.	
noncollinear Points that do not lie on the same line.	**no colineal** Puntos que no se encuentran sobre la misma línea.	A, B, D Points *A*, *B*, and *D* are not collinear.
noncoplanar Points that do not lie on the same plane.	**no coplanar** Puntos que no se encuentran en el mismo plano.	S, U, V, T, $\mathcal{R}$ *T*, *U*, *V*, and *S* are not coplanar.

ENGLISH	SPANISH	EXAMPLES

O

oblique cone A cone whose axis is not perpendicular to the base.

cono oblicuo Cono cuyo eje no es perpendicular a la base.

oblique cylinder A cylinder whose axis is not perpendicular to the bases.

cilindro oblicuo Cilindro cuyo eje no es perpendicular a las bases.

oblique prism A prism that has at least one nonrectangular lateral face.

prisma oblicuo Prisma que tiene por lo menos una cara lateral no rectangular.

obtuse angle An angle that measures greater than 90° and less than 180°.

ángulo obtuso Ángulo que mide más de 90° y menos de 180°.

obtuse triangle A triangle with one obtuse angle.

triángulo obtusángulo Triángulo con un ángulo obtuso.

octagon An eight-sided polygon.

octágono Polígono de ocho lados.

opposite The opposite of a number a, denoted $-a$, is the number that is the same distance from zero as a, on the opposite side of the number line. The sum of opposites is 0.

opuesto El opuesto de un número a, expresado $-a$, es el número que se encuentra a la misma distancia de cero que a, del lado opuesto de la recta numérica. La suma de los opuestos es 0.

5 units 5 units

−6 −5 −4 −3 −2 −1 0 1 2 3 4 5 6

5 and −5 are opposites.

opposite rays Two rays that have a common endpoint and form a line.

rayos opuestos Dos rayos que tienen un extremo común y forman una línea.

F E G

$\overrightarrow{EF}$ and $\overrightarrow{EG}$ are opposite rays.

orthocenter of a triangle The point of concurrency of the three altitudes of a triangle.

ortocentro de un triángulo Punto de intersección de las tres alturas de un triángulo.

P is the orthocenter.

P

Glossary/Glosario

ENGLISH	SPANISH	EXAMPLES
outcome A possible result of a probability experiment.	**resultado** Resultado posible de un experimento de probabilidad.	In the experiment of rolling a number cube, the possible outcomes are 1, 2, 3, 4, 5, and 6.
overlapping events Events that have one or more outcomes in common. Also called inclusive events.	**sucesos superpuestos** Sucesos que tienen uno o más resultados en común. También se denominan sucesos inclusivos.	Rolling an even number and rolling a prime number on a number cube are overlapping events because they both contain the outcome rolling a 2.

ENGLISH	SPANISH	EXAMPLES
parabola The shape of the graph of a quadratic function. Also, the set of points equidistant from a point *F*, called the focus, and a line *d*, called the *directrix*.	**parábola** Forma de la gráfica de una función cuadrática. También, conjunto de puntos equidistantes de un punto *F*, denominado *foco*, y una línea *d*, denominada *directriz*.	Focus Directrix
parameter One of the constants in a function or equation that may be changed. Also the third variable in a set of parametric equations.	**parámetro** Una de las constantes en una función o ecuación que se puede cambiar. También es la tercera variable en un conjunto de ecuaciones paramétricas.	$y = (x - h)^2 + k$ parameters
parallel lines Lines in the same plane that do not intersect.	**líneas paralelas** Líneas rectas en el mismo plano que no se cruzan.	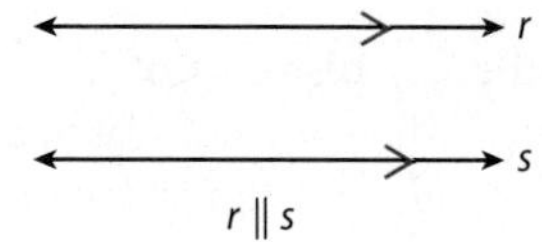 $r \parallel s$
parallel planes Planes that do not intersect.	**planos paralelos** Planos que no se cruzan.	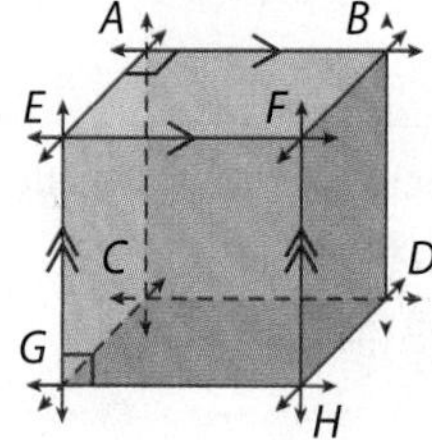 Plane *AEF* and plane *CGH* are parallel planes.
parallelogram A quadrilateral with two pairs of parallel sides.	**paralelogramo** Cuadrilátero con dos pares de lados paralelos.	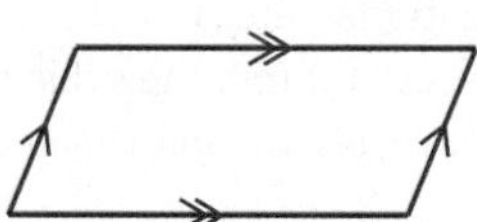
pentagon A five-sided polygon.	**diagrama** Polígono de cinco lados.	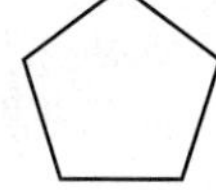

Glossary/Glosario

ENGLISH	SPANISH	EXAMPLES
perfect-square trinomial A trinomial whose factored form is the square of a binomial. A perfect-square trinomial has the form $a^2 - 2ab + b^2 = (a - b)^2$ or $a^2 + 2ab + b^2 = (a + b)^2$.	**trinomio cuadrado perfecto** Trinomio cuya forma factorizada es el cuadrado de un binomio. Un trinomio cuadrado perfecto tiene la forma $a^2 - 2ab + b^2 = (a - b)^2$ o $a^2 + 2ab + b^2 = (a + b)^2$.	$x^2 + 6x + 9$ is a perfect-square trinomial, because $x^2 + 6x + 9 = (x + 3)^2$.
perimeter The sum of the side lengths of a closed plane figure.	**perímetro** Suma de las longitudes de los lados de una figura plana cerrada.	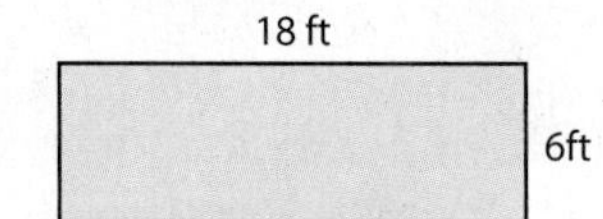 Perimeter $= 18 + 6 + 18 + 6 = 48$ ft
permutation An arrangement of a group of objects in which order is important. The number of permutations of r objects from a group of n objects is denoted ${}_nP_r$.	**permutación** Arreglo de un grupo de objetos en el cual el orden es importante. El número de permutaciones de r objetos de un grupo de n objetos se expresa ${}_nP_r$.	For 4 objects A, B, C, and D, there are ${}_4P_2 = 12$ different permutations of 2 objects: AB, AC, AD, BC, BD, CD, BA, CA, DA, CB, DB, and DC.
perpendicular Intersecting to form 90° angles, denoted by $\perp$.	**perpendicular** Que se cruza para formar ángulos de 90°, expresado por $\perp$.	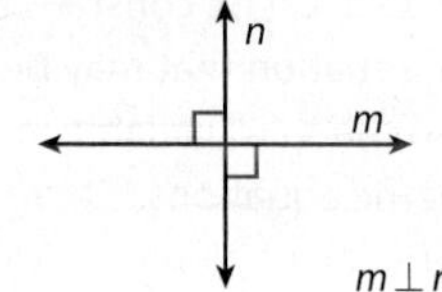 $m \perp n$
perpendicular bisector of a segment A line perpendicular to a segment at the segment's midpoint.	**mediatriz de un segmento** Línea perpendicular a un segmento en el punto medio del segmento.	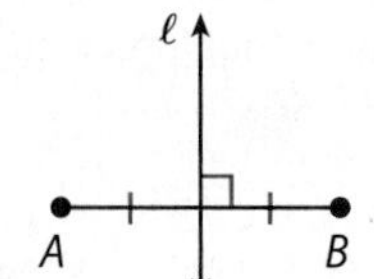 ℓ is the perpendicular bisector of $\overline{AB}$.
perpendicular lines Lines that intersect at 90° angles.	**líneas perpendiculares** Líneas que se cruzan en ángulos de 90°.	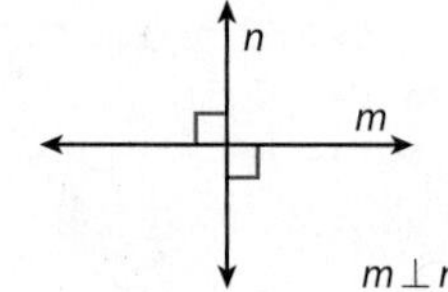 $m \perp n$
pi The ratio of the circumference of a circle to its diameter, denoted by the Greek letter π (pi). The value of π is irrational, often approximated by 3.14 or $\frac{22}{7}$.	**pi** Razón entre la circunferencia de un círculo y su diámetro, expresado por la letra griega π (pi). El valor de π es irracional y por lo general se aproxima a 3.14 ó $\frac{22}{7}$.	If a circle has a diameter of 5 inches and a circumference of C inches, then $\frac{C}{5} = \pi$, or $C = 5\pi$ inches, or about 15.7 inches.
plane An undefined term in geometry, it is a flat surface that has no thickness and extends forever.	**plano** Término indefinido en geometría; un plano es una superficie plana que no tiene grosor y se extiende infinitamente.	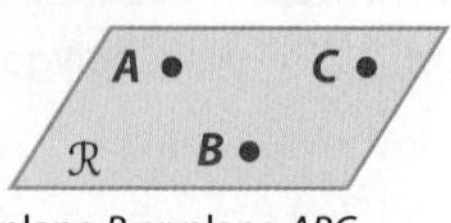 plane R or plane ABC

ENGLISH	SPANISH	EXAMPLES
plane symmetry A three-dimensional figure that can be divided into two congruent reflected halves by a plane has plane symmetry.	**simetría de plano** Una figura tridimensional que se puede dividir en dos mitades congruentes reflejadas por un plano tiene simetría de plano.	Plane symmetry
Platonic solid One of the five regular polyhedra: a tetrahedron, a cube, an octahedron, a dodecahedron, or an icosahedron.	**sólido platónico** Uno de los cinco poliedros regulares: tetraedro, cubo, octaedro, dodecaedro o icosaedro.	
point An undefined term in geometry, it names a location and has no size.	**punto** Término indefinido de la geometría que denomina una ubicación y no tiene tamaño.	*P* • point *P*
point of concurrency A point where three or more lines coincide.	**punto de concurrencia** Punto donde se cruzan tres o más líneas.	*B*
point of tangency The point of intersection of a circle or sphere with a tangent line or plane.	**punto de tangencia** Punto de intersección de un círculo o esfera con una línea o plano tangente.	*m* Tangent *C* Point of tangency
point-slope form $y - y_1 = m(x - x_1)$, where m is the slope and (x_1, y_1) is a point on the line.	**forma de punto y pendiente** $(y - y_1) = m(x - x_1)$, donde m es la pendiente y (x_1, y_1)es un punto en la línea.	
polygon A closed plane figure formed by three or more segments such that each segment intersects exactly two other segments only at their endpoints and no two segments with a common endpoint are collinear.	**polígono** Figura plana cerrada formada por tres o más segmentos tal que cada segmento se cruza únicamente con otros dos segmentos sólo en sus extremos y ningún segmento con un extremo común a otro es colineal con éste.	
polyhedron A closed three-dimensional figure formed by four or more polygons that intersect only at their edges.	**poliedro** Figura tridimensional cerrada formada por cuatro o más polígonos que se cruzan sólo en sus aristas.	
polynomial A monomial or a sum or difference of monomials.	**polinomio** Monomio o suma o diferencia de monomios.	$2x^2 + 3xy - 7y^2$

ENGLISH	SPANISH	EXAMPLES
polynomial long division A method of dividing one polynomial by another.	**división larga polinomial** Método por el que se divide un polinomio entre otro.	$\begin{array}{r} x+1 \\ x+2\overline{)\ x^2+3x+5} \\ -(x^2+2x) \\ \hline x+5 \\ -(x+2) \\ \hline 3 \end{array}$ $\frac{x^2+3x+5}{x+2}=x+1+\frac{3}{x+2}$
postulate A statement that is accepted as true without proof. Also called an *axiom*.	**postulado** Enunciado que se acepta como verdadero sin demostración. También denominado *axioma*.	
preimage The original figure in a transformation.	**imagen original** Figura original en una transformación.	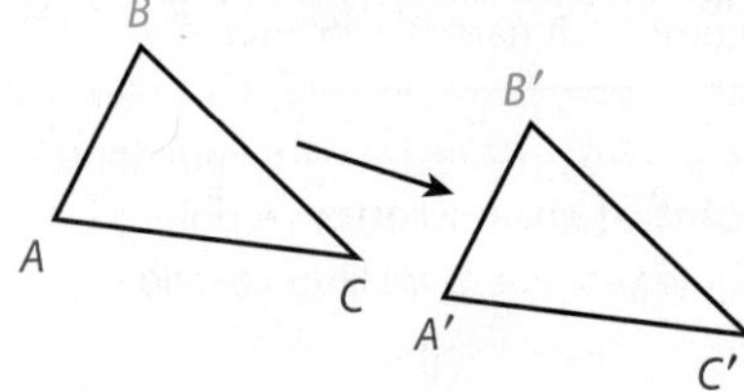
primes Symbols used to label the image in a transformation.	**apóstrofos** Símbolos utilizados para identificar la imagen en una transformación.	$A'B'C'$
prism A polyhedron formed by two parallel congruent polygonal bases connected by lateral faces that are parallelograms.	**prisma** Poliedro formado por dos bases poligonales congruentes y paralelas conectadas por caras laterales que son paralelogramos.	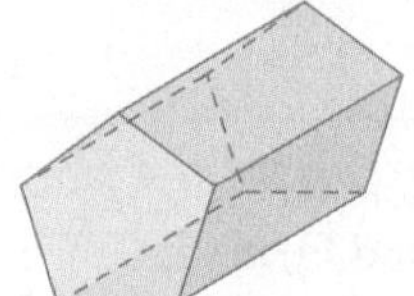
probability A number from 0 to 1 (or 0% to 100%) that is the measure of how likely an event is to occur.	**probabilidad** Número entre 0 y 1 (o entre 0% y 100%) que describe cuán probable es que ocurra un suceso.	A bag contains 3 red marbles and 4 blue marbles. The probability of randomly choosing a red marble is $\frac{3}{7}$.
proof An argument that uses logic to show that a conclusion is true.	**demostración** Argumento que se vale de la lógica para probar que una conclusión es verdadera.	
proof by contradiction *See* indirect proof.	**demostración por contradicción** *Ver* demostración indirecta.	
pure imaginary number *See* imaginary number.	**número imaginario puro** Ver número imaginario.	$3i$
pyramid A polyhedron formed by a polygonal base and triangular lateral faces that meet at a common vertex.	**pirámide** Poliedro formado por una base poligonal y caras laterales triangulares que se encuentran en un vértice común.	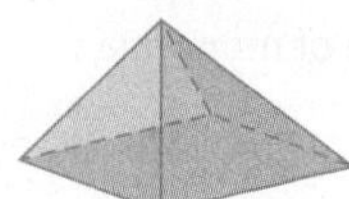

ENGLISH	SPANISH	EXAMPLES
Pythagorean Theorem If a right triangle has legs of lengths a and b and a hypotenuse of length c, then $a^2 + b^2 = c^2$.	**Teorema de Pitágoras** Dado un triángulo rectángulo con catetos de longitudes a y b y una hipotenusa de longitud c, entonces $a^2 + b^2 = c^2$.	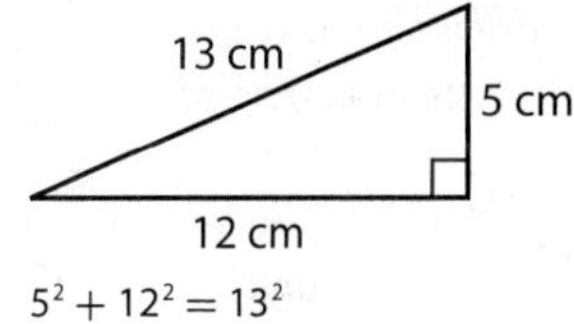 $5^2 + 12^2 = 13^2$ $25 + 144 = 169$
Pythagorean triple A set of three nonzero whole numbers a, b, and c such that $a^2 + b^2 = c^2$.	**Tripleta de Pitágoras** Conjunto de tres números cabales distintos de cero a, b y c tal que $a^2 + b^2 = c^2$.	$\{3, 4, 5\}$ $3^2 + 4^2 = 5^2$

 Q

ENGLISH	SPANISH	EXAMPLES
quadratic equation An equation that can be written in the form $ax^2 + bx + c = 0$, where a, b, and c are real numbers and $a \neq 0$.	**ecuación cuadrática** Ecuación que se puede expresar como $ax^2 + bx + c = 0$, donde a, b y c son números reales y $a \neq 0$.	$x^2 + 3x - 4 = 0$ $x^2 - 9 = 0$
Quadratic Formula The formula $x = \frac{-b \pm \sqrt{b^2 - 4ac}}{2a}$, which gives solutions, or roots, of equations in the form $ax^2 + bx + c = 0$, where $a \neq 0$.	**fórmula cuadrática** La fórmula $x = \frac{-b \pm \sqrt{b^2 - 4ac}}{2a}$, que da soluciones, o raíces, para las ecuaciones del tipo $ax^2 + bx + c = 0$, donde $a \neq 0$.	The solutions of $2x^2 - 5x - 3 = 0$ are given by $x = \frac{-(-5) \pm \sqrt{(-5)^2 - 4(2)(-3)}}{2(2)}$ $= \frac{5 \pm \sqrt{25 + 24}}{4} = \frac{5 \pm 7}{4}$ $x = 3$ or $x = -\frac{1}{2}$
quadratic function A function that can be written in the form $f(x) = ax^2 + bx + c$, where a, b, and c are real numbers and $a \neq 0$.	**función cuadrática** Función que se puede expresar como $f(x) = ax^2 + bx + c$, donde a, b y c son números reales y $a \neq 0$.	$f(x) = x^2 - 6x + 8$
quadratic polynomial A polynomial of degree 2.	**polinomio cuadrático** Polinomio de grado 2.	$x^2 - 6x + 8$
quadratic regression A statistical method used to fit a quadratic model to a given data set.	**regresión cuadrática** Método estadístico utilizado para ajustar un modelo cuadrático a un conjunto de datos determinado.	
quadrilateral A four-sided polygon.	**cuadrilátero** Polígono de cuatro lados.	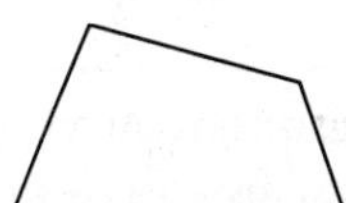

R

ENGLISH	SPANISH	EXAMPLES
radial symmetry *See* rotational symmetry.	**simetría radial** *Ver* simetría de rotación.	

ENGLISH	SPANISH	EXAMPLES
radian A unit of angle measure based on arc length. In a circle of radius *r*, if a central angle has a measure of 1 radian, then the length of the intercepted arc is *r* units. 2π radians $= 360°$ 1 radian $\approx 57°$	**radián** Unidad de medida de un ángulo basada en la longitud del arco. En un círculo de radio *r*, si un ángulo central mide 1 radián, entonces la longitud del arco abarcado es *r* unidades. 2π radians $= 360°$ 1 radian $\approx 57°$	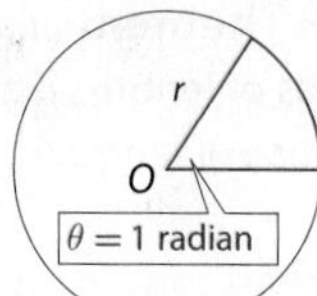
radical equation An equation that contains a variable within a radical.	**ecuación radical** Ecuación que contiene una variable dentro de un radical.	$\sqrt{x+3}+4=7$
radical expression An expression that contains a radical sign.	**expresión radical** Expresión que contiene un signo de radical.	$\sqrt{x+3}+4$
radius of a circle A segment whose endpoints are the center of a circle and a point on the circle; the distance from the center of a circle to any point on the circle.	**radio de un círculo** Segmento cuyos extremos son el centro y un punto de la circunferencia; distancia desde el centro de un círculo hasta cualquier punto de la circunferencia.	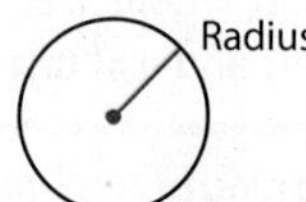
radius of a sphere A segment whose endpoints are the center of a sphere and any point on the sphere; the distance from the center of a sphere to any point on the sphere.	**radio de una esfera** Segmento cuyos extremos son el centro de una esfera y cualquier punto sobre la esfera; distancia desde el centro de una esfera hasta cualquier punto sobre la esfera.	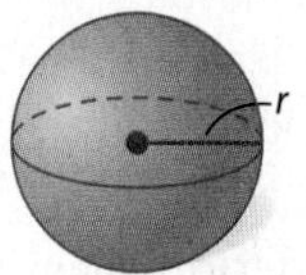
range of a data set The difference of the greatest and least values in the data set.	**rango de un conjunto de datos** La diferencia del mayor y menor valor en un conjunto de datos.	The data set $\{3, 3, 5, 7, 8, 10, 11, 11, 12\}$ has a range of $12 - 3 = 9$.
range of a function or relation The set of output values of a function or relation.	**rango de una función o relación** Conjunto de los valores desalida de una función o relación.	The range of $y = x^2$ is $\{y \mid y \geq 0\}$.
rational equation An equation that contains one or more rational expressions.	**ecuación racional** Ecuación que contiene una o más expresiones racionales.	$\frac{x+2}{x^2+3x-1}=6$
rational exponent An exponent that can be expressed as $\frac{m}{n}$ such that if *m* and *n* are integers, then $b^{\frac{m}{n}} = \sqrt[n]{b^m} = \left(\sqrt[n]{b}\right)^m$.	**exponente racional** Exponente que se puede expresar como $\frac{m}{n}$ tal que si *m* y *n* son números enteros, entonces $b^{\frac{m}{n}} = \sqrt[n]{b^m} = \left(\sqrt[n]{b}\right)^m$.	$64^{\frac{1}{6}} = \sqrt[6]{64}$
rational expression An algebraic expression whose numerator and denominator are polynomials and whose denominator has a degree ≥ 1.	**expresión racional** Expresión algebraica cuyo numerador y denominador son polinomios y cuyo denominador tiene un grado ≥ 1.	$\frac{x+2}{x^2+3x-1}$

ENGLISH	SPANISH	EXAMPLES
rational function A function whose rule can be written as a rational expression.	**función racional** Función cuya regla se puede expresar como una expresión racional.	$f(x) = \frac{x+2}{x^2+3x-1}$
rational number A number that can be written in the form $\frac{a}{b}$, where a and b are integers and $b \neq 0$.	**número racional** Número que se puede expresar como $\frac{a}{b}$, donde a y b son números enteros y $b \neq 0$.	$3, 1.75, 0.\overline{3}, -\frac{2}{3}, 0$
rationalizing the denominator A method of rewriting a fraction by multiplying by another fraction that is equivalent to 1 in order to remove radical terms from the denominator.	**racionalizar el denominador** Método que consiste en escribir nuevamente una fracción multiplicándola por otra fracción equivalente a 1 a fin de eliminar los términos radicales del denominador.	$\frac{1}{\sqrt{2}} \cdot \frac{\sqrt{2}}{\sqrt{2}} = \frac{\sqrt{2}}{2}$
ray A part of a line that starts at an endpoint and extends forever in one direction.	**rayo** Parte de una línea que comienza en un extremo y se extiende infinitamente en una dirección.	D
rectangle A quadrilateral with four right angles.	**rectángulo** Cuadrilátero con cuatro ángulos rectos.	
reduction A dilation with a scale factor greater than 0 but less than 1. In a reduction, the image is smaller than the preimage.	**reducción** Dilatación con un factor de escala mayor que 0 pero menor que 1. En una reducción, la imagen es más pequeña que la imagen original.	A, A′, C, C′, P, B′, B
reflection A transformation across a line, called the line of reflection, such that the line of reflection is the perpendicular bisector of each segment joining each point and its image.	**reflexión** Transformación sobre una línea, denominada la línea de reflexión. La línea de reflexión es la mediatriz de cada segmento que une un punto con su imagen.	B, B′, A, C, C′, A′
reflection symmetry *See* line symmetry.	**simetría de reflexión** *Ver* simetría axial.	
regular polygon A polygon that is both equilateral and equiangular.	**polígono regular** Polígono equilátero de ángulos iguales.	
regular polyhedron A polyhedron in which all faces are congruent regular polygons and the same number of faces meet at each vertex. *See also* Platonic solid.	**poliedro regular** Poliedro cuyas caras son todas polígonos regulares congruentes y en el que el mismo número de caras se encuentran en cada vértice. *Ver también* sólido platónico.	s, s, s

Glossary/Glosario

ENGLISH	SPANISH	EXAMPLES
regular pyramid A pyramid whose base is a regular polygon and whose lateral faces are congruent isosceles triangles.	**pirámide regular** Pirámide cuya base es un polígono regular y cuyas caras laterales son triángulos isósceles congruentes.	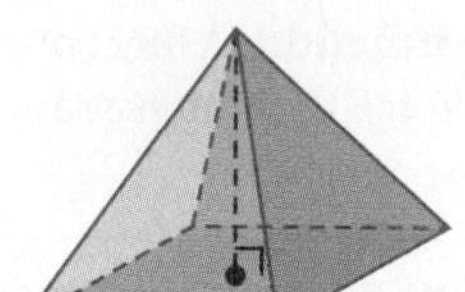
remote interior angle An interior angle of a polygon that is not adjacent to the exterior angle.	**ángulo interno remoto** Ángulo interno de un polígono que no es adyacente al ángulo externo.	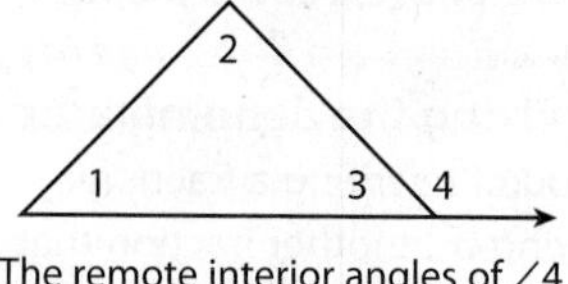 The remote interior angles of ∠4 are ∠1 and ∠2.
rhombus A quadrilateral with four congruent sides.	**rombo** Cuadrilátero con cuatro lados congruentes.	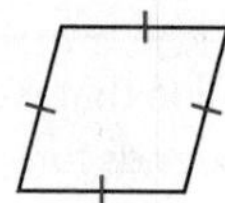
right angle An angle that measures 90°.	**ángulo recto** Ángulo que mide 90°.	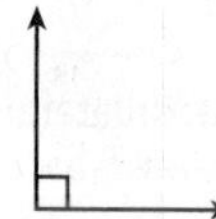
right cone A cone whose axis is perpendicular to its base.	**cono recto** Cono cuyo eje es perpendicular a su base.	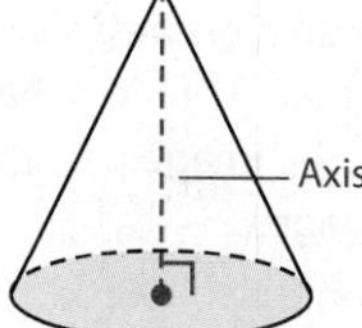
right cylinder A cylinder whose axis is perpendicular to its bases.	**cilindro recto** Cilindro cuyo eje es perpendicular a sus bases.	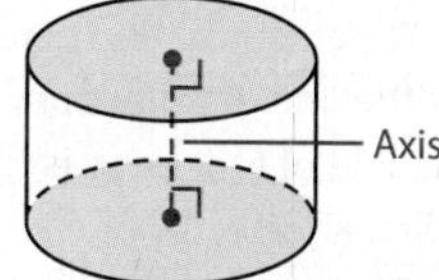
right prism A prism whose lateral faces are all rectangles.	**prisma recto** Prisma cuyas caras laterales son todas rectángulos.	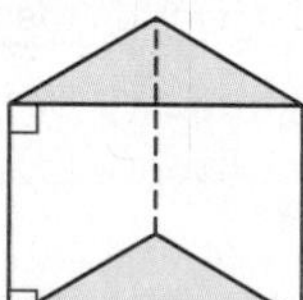
right triangle A triangle with one right angle.	**triángulo rectángulo** Triángulo con un ángulo recto.	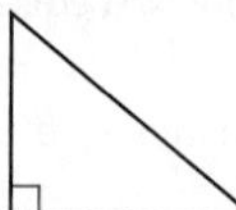
rigid motion *See* isometry.	**movimiento rígido** *Ver* isometría.	
rigid transformation A transformation that does not change the size or shape of a figure.	**transformación rígida** Transformación que no cambia el tamaño o la forma de una figura.	

ENGLISH	SPANISH	EXAMPLES
rise The difference in the y-values of two points on a line.	**distancia vertical** Diferencia entre los valores de y de dos puntos de una línea.	For the points $(3, -1)$ and $(6, 5)$, the rise is $5 - (-1) = 6$.
rotation A transformation about a point P, also known as the center of rotation, such that each point and its image are the same distance from P. All of the angles with vertex P formed by a point and its image are congruent.	**rotación** Transformación sobre un punto P, también conocido como el centro de rotación, tal que cada punto y su imagen estén a la misma distancia de P. Todos los ángulos con vértice P formados por un punto y su imagen son congruentes.	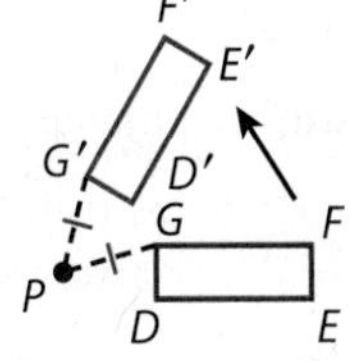
run The difference in the x-values of two points on a line.	**distancia horizontal** Diferencia entre los valores de x de dos puntos de una línea.	For the points $(3, -1)$ and $(6, 5)$, the run is $6 - 3 = 3$.

S

ENGLISH	SPANISH	EXAMPLES
same-side interior angles For two lines intersected by a transversal, a pair of angles that lie on the same side of the transversal and between the two lines.	**ángulos internos del mismo lado** Dadas dos líneas cortadas por una transversal, el par de ángulos ubicados en el mismo lado de la transversal y entre las dos líneas.	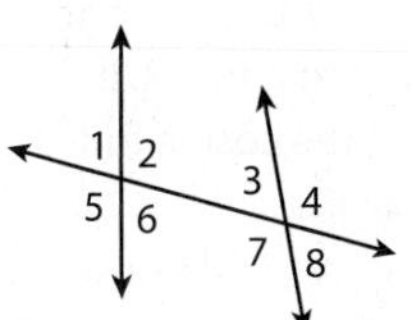 $\angle 2$ and $\angle 3$ are same-side interior angles.
sample space The set of all possible outcomes of a probability experiment.	**espacio muestral** Conjunto de todos los resultados posibles de un experimento de probabilidad.	In the experiment of rolling a number cube, the sample space is $\{1, 2, 3, 4, 5, 6\}$.
scale The ratio between two corresponding measurements.	**escala** Razón entre dos medidas correspondientes.	1 cm : 5 mi
scale drawing A drawing that uses a scale to represent an object as smaller or larger than the actual object.	**dibujo a escala** Dibujo que utiliza una escala para representar un objeto como más pequeño o más grande que el objeto original.	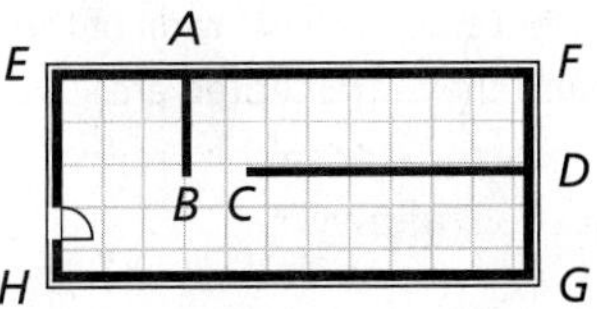 A blueprint is an example of a scale drawing.
scale factor The multiplier used on each dimension to change one figure into a similar figure.	**factor de escala** El multiplicador utilizado en cada dimensión para transformar una figura en una figura semejante.	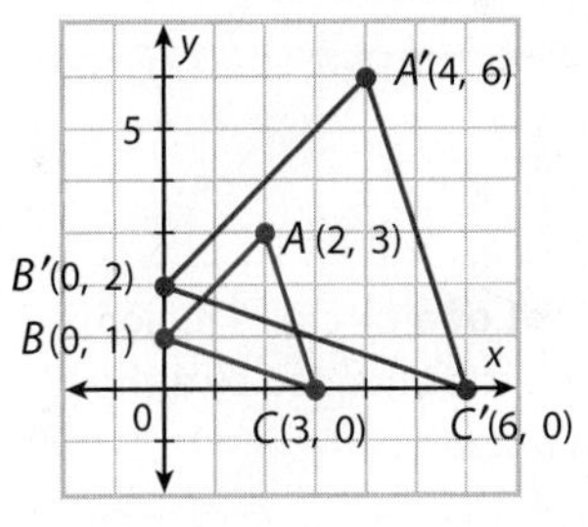 Scale factor: 2

ENGLISH	SPANISH	EXAMPLES
scale model A three-dimensional model that uses a scale to represent an object as smaller or larger than the actual object.	**modelo a escala** Modelo tridimensional que utiliza una escala para representar un objeto como más pequeño o más grande que el objeto real.	
scalene triangle A triangle with no congruent sides.	**triángulo escaleno** Triángulo sin lados congruentes.	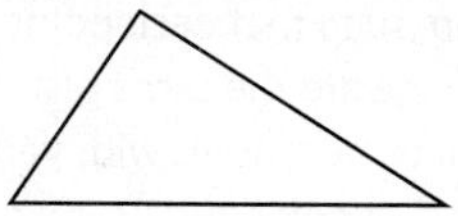
secant of a circle A line that intersects a circle at two points.	**secante de un círculo** Línea que corta un círculo en dos puntos.	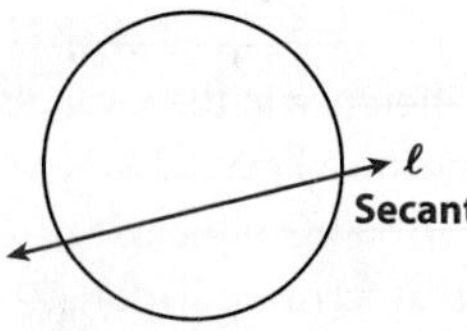 ℓ Secant
secant of an angle In a right triangle, the ratio of the length of the hypotenuse to the length of the side adjacent to angle A. It is the reciprocal of the cosine function.	**secante de un ángulo** En un triángulo rectángulo, la razón entre la longitud de la hipotenusa y la longitud del cateto adyacente al ángulo A. Es la inversa de la función coseno.	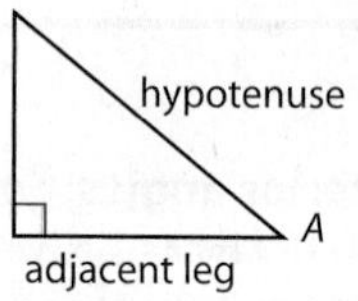 hypotenuse; adjacent leg; A $\sec A = \frac{\text{hypotenuse}}{\text{adjacent}} = \frac{1}{\cos A}$
secant segment A segment of a secant with at least one endpoint on the circle.	**segmento secante** Segmento de una secante que tiene al menos un extremo sobre el círculo.	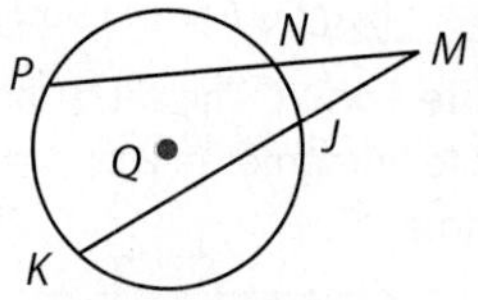 P, N, M, Q, J, K $\overline{NM}$ is an external secant segment. $\overline{JK}$ is an internal secant segment.
sector of a circle A region inside a circle bounded by two radii of the circle and their intercepted arc.	**sector de un círculo** Región dentro de un círculo delimitado por dos radios del círculo y por su arco abarcado.	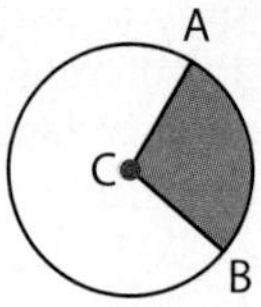 A, C, B
segment bisector A line, ray, or segment that divides a segment into two congruent segments.	**bisectriz de un segmento** Línea, rayo o segmento que divide un segmento en dos segmentos congruentes.	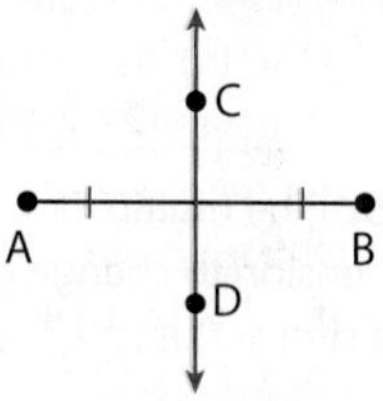 C, A, B, D
segment of a circle A region inside a circle bounded by a chord and an arc.	**segmento de un círculo** Región dentro de un círculo delimitada por una cuerda y un arco.	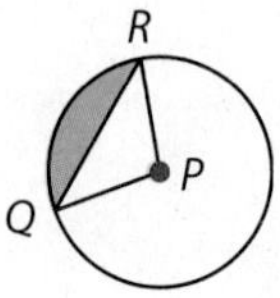 R, P, Q

ENGLISH	SPANISH	EXAMPLES
segment of a line A part of a line consisting of two endpoints and all points between them.	**segmento de una línea** Parte de una línea que consiste en dos extremos y todos los puntos entre éstos.	A B
semicircle An arc of a circle whose endpoints lie on a diameter.	**semicírculo** Arco de un círculo cuyos extremos se encuentran sobre un diámetro.	E G
set A collection of items called elements.	**conjunto** Grupo de componentes denominados elementos.	$\{1, 2, 3\}$
side of a polygon One of the segments that form a polygon.	**lado de un polígono** Uno de los segmentos que forman un polígono.	A B C D E Side
side of an angle One of the two rays that form an angle.	**lado de un ángulo** Uno de los dos rayos que forman un ángulo.	C A B $\overrightarrow{AC}$ and $\overrightarrow{AB}$ are sides of $\angle CAB$.
similar Two figures are similar if they have the same shape but not necessarily the same size.	**semejantes** Dos figuras con la misma forma pero no necesariamente del mismo tamaño.	
similar polygons Two polygons whose corresponding angles are congruent and whose corresponding side lengths are proportional.	**polígonos semejantes** Dos polígonos cuyos ángulos correspondientes son congruentes y cuyos lados correspondientes tienen longitudes proporcionales.	J 75 45 L 60 M P 24 30 N 18 S
similarity ratio The ratio of two corresponding linear measurements in a pair of similar figures.	**razón de semejanza** Razón de dos medidas lineales correspondientes en un par de figuras semejantes.	Similarity ratio: $\frac{3.5}{2.1} = \frac{5}{3}$
similarity statement A statement that indicates that two polygons are similar by listing the vertices in the order of correspondence.	**enunciado de semejanza** Enunciado que indica que dos polígonos son semejantes enumerando los vértices en orden de correspondencia.	A 6 B 5 5.4 D 4 C E 12 F 10 10.8 H 8 G quadrilateral *ABCD* ~ quadrilateral *EFGH*

ENGLISH	SPANISH	EXAMPLES
similarity transformation A transformation that produces similar figures.	**transformación de semejanza** Una transformación que resulta en figuras semejantes.	Dilations are similarity transformations.
simple event An event consisting of only one outcome.	**suceso simple** Suceso que contiene sólo un resultado.	In the experiment of rolling a number cube, the event consisting of the outcome 3 is a simple event.
sine In a right triangle, the ratio of the length of the leg opposite $\angle A$ to the length of the hypotenuse.	**seno** En un triángulo rectángulo, razón entre la longitud del cateto opuesto a $\angle A$ y la longitud de la hipotenusa.	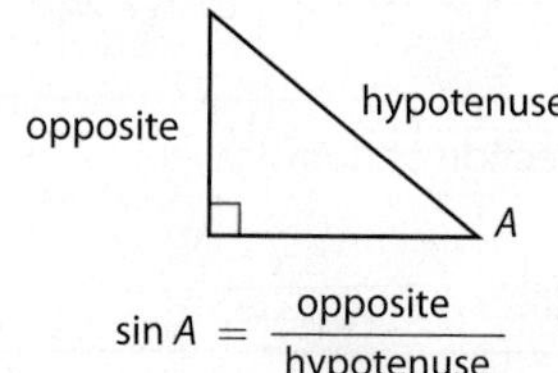 $\sin A = \frac{\text{opposite}}{\text{hypotenuse}}$
skew lines Lines that are not coplanar.	**líneas oblicuas** Líneas que no son coplanares.	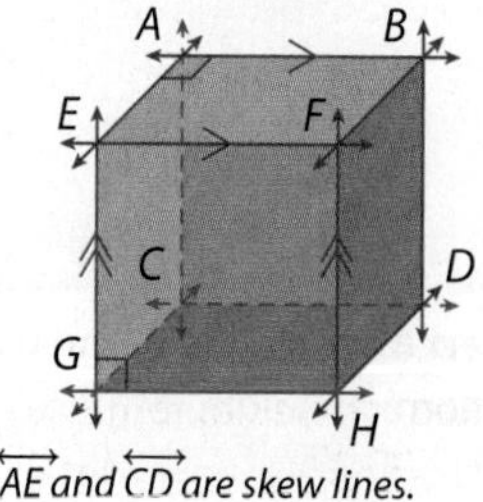 $\overleftrightarrow{AE}$ *and* $\overleftrightarrow{CD}$ *are skew lines.*
slide *See* translation.	**deslizamiento** *Ver* traslación.	
slope A measure of the steepness of a line. If (x_1, y_1) and (x_2, y_2) are any two points on the line, the slope of the line, known as m, is represented by the equation $m = \frac{y_2 - y_1}{x_2 - x_1}$.	**pendiente** Medida de la inclinación de una línea. Dados dos puntos (x_1, y_1) y (x_2, y_2) en una línea, la pendiente de la línea, denominada m, se representa con la ecuación $m = \frac{y_2 - y_1}{x_2 - x_1}$.	
slope-intercept form The slope-intercept form of a linear equation is $y = mx + b$, where m is the slope and b is the y-intercept.	**forma de pendiente-intersección** La forma de pendiente-intersección de una ecuación lineal es $y = mx + b$, donde m es la pendiente y b es la intersección con el eje y.	$y = -2x + 4$ The slope is -2. The y-intercept is 4.
solid A three-dimensional figure.	**cuerpo geométrico** Figura tridimensional.	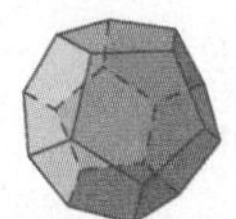 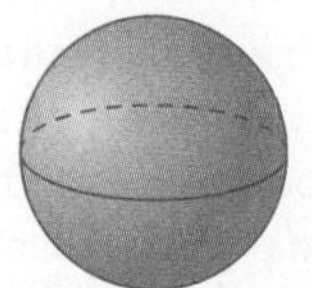
solving a triangle Using given measures to find unknown angle measures or side lengths of a triangle.	**resolución de un triángulo** Utilizar medidas dadas para hallar las medidas desconocidas de los ángulos o las longitudes de los lados de un triángulo.	

Glossary/Glosario

ENGLISH	SPANISH	EXAMPLES
special right triangle A 45°—45°—90° triangle or a 30°—60°—90° triangle.	**triángulo rectángulo especial** Triángulo de 45°—45°—90° o triángulo de 30°—60°—90°.	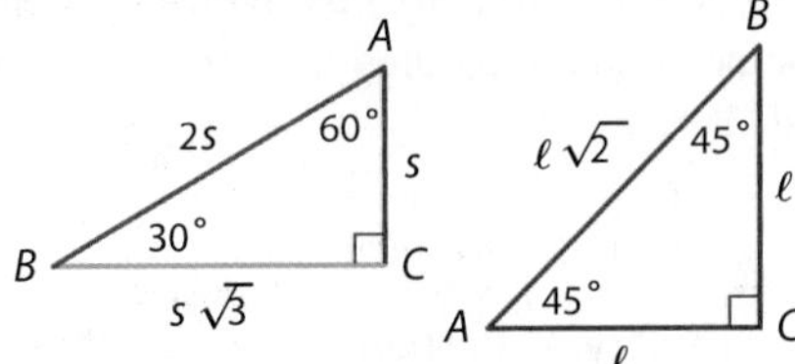
sphere The set of points in space that are a fixed distance from a given point called the center of the sphere.	**esfera** Conjunto de puntos en el espacio que se encuentran a una distancia fija de un punto determinado denominado centro de la esfera.	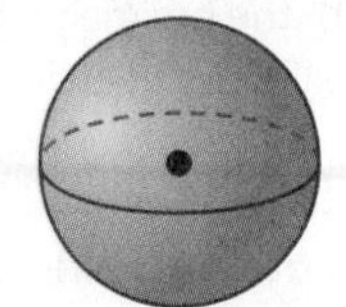
square A quadrilateral with four congruent sides and four right angles.	**cuadrado** Cuadrilátero con cuatro lados congruentes y cuatro ángulos rectos.	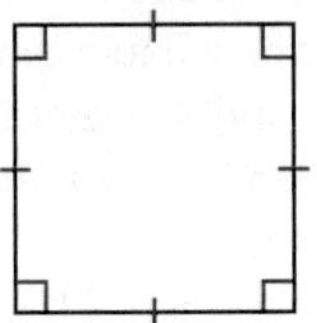
square root A number that is multiplied by itself to form a product is called a square root of that product.	**raíz cuadrada** El número que se multiplica por sí mismo para formar un producto se denomina la raíz cuadrada de ese producto.	A square root of 16 is 4, because $4^2 = 4 \cdot 4 = 16$. Another square root of 16 is −4 because $(-4)^2 = (-4)(-4) = 16$.
square root function A function whose rule contains a variable under a square root sign.	**función de raíz cuadrada** Función cuya regla contiene una variable bajo un signo de raíz cuadrada.	
standard form of a linear equation $Ax + By = C$, where A, B, and C are real numbers and A and B are not both 0.	**forma estándar de una ecuación lineal** $Ax + By = C$, donde A, B y C son números reales y A y B no son ambos cero.	$2x + 3y = 6$
standard form of a polynomial A polynomial in one variable is written in standard form when the terms are in order from greatest degree to least degree.	**forma estándar de un polinomio** Un polinomio de una variable se expresa en forma estándar cuando los términos se ordenan de mayor a menor grado.	$4x^5 - 2x^4 + x^2 - x + 1$
straight angle A 180° angle.	**ángulo llano** Ángulo que mide 180°.	
subset A set that is contained entirely within another set. Set B is a subset of set A if every element of B is contained in A, denoted $B \subset A$.	**subconjunto** Conjunto que se encuentra dentro de otro conjunto. El conjunto B es un subconjunto del conjunto A si todos los elementos de B son elementos de A; se expresa $B \subset A$.	The set of integers is a subset of the set of rational numbers.

ENGLISH	SPANISH	EXAMPLES
supplementary angles Two angles whose measures have a sum of 180°.	**ángulos suplementarios** Dos ángulos cuyas medidas suman 180°.	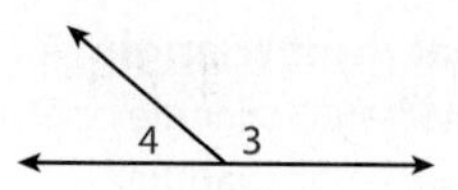 $\angle 3$ and $\angle 4$ are supplementary angles.
symmetry In the transformation of a figure such that the image coincides with the preimage, the image and preimage have symmetry.	**simetría** En la transformación de una figura tal que la imagen coincide con la imagen original, la imagen y la imagen original tienen simetría.	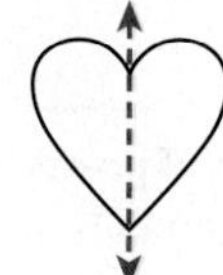
symmetry about an axis In the transformation of a figure such that there is a line about which a three-dimensional figure can be rotated by an angle greater than 0° and less than 360° so that the image coincides with the preimage, the image and preimage have symmetry about an axis.	**simetría axial** En la transformación de una figura tal que existe una línea sobre la cual se puede rotar una figura tridimensional a un ángulo mayor que 0° y menor que 360° de forma que la imagen coincida con la imagen original, la imagen y la imagen original tienen simetría axial.	
system of equations A set of two or more equations that have two or more variables.	**sistema de ecuaciones** Conjunto de dos o más ecuaciones que contienen dos o más variables.	$2x + 3y = -1$ $3x - 3y = 4$
system of linear inequalities A system of inequalities in two or more variables in which all of the inequalities are linear.	**sistema de desigualdades lineales** Sistema de desigualdades en dos o más variables en el que todas las desigualdades son lineales.	$\begin{cases} 2x + 3y \geq -1 \\ x - 3y < 4 \end{cases}$

T

ENGLISH	SPANISH	EXAMPLES
tangent circles Two coplanar circles that intersect at exactly one point. If one circle is contained inside the other, they are *internally tangent*. If not, they are *externally tangent*.	**círculos tangentes** Dos círculos coplanares que se cruzan únicamente en un punto. Si un círculo contiene a otro, son *tangentes internamente*. De lo contrario, son *tangentes externamente*.	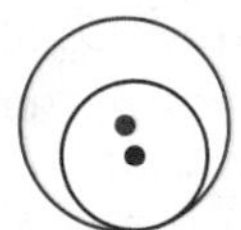 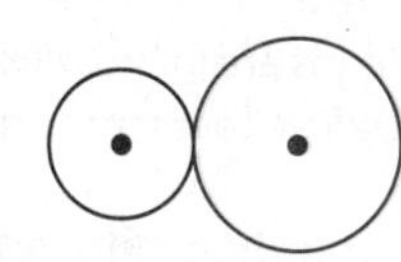
tangent of an angle In a right triangle, the ratio of the length of the leg opposite $\angle A$ to the length of the leg adjacent to $\angle A$.	**tangente de un ángulo** En un triángulo rectángulo, razón entre la longitud del cateto opuesto a $\angle A$ y la longitud del cateto adyacente a $\angle A$.	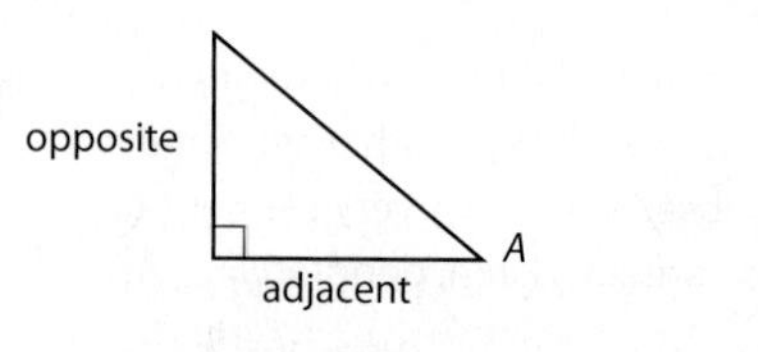 $\tan A = \frac{\text{opposite}}{\text{adjacent}}$

ENGLISH	SPANISH	EXAMPLES
tangent segment A segment of a tangent with one endpoint on the circle.	**segmento tangente** Segmento de una tangente con un extremo en el círculo.	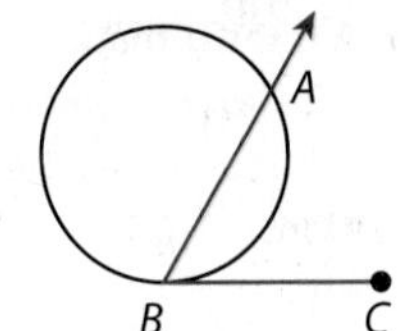 $\overline{BC}$ is a tangent segment.
tangent of a circle A line that is in the same plane as a circle and intersects the circle at exactly one point.	**tangente de un círculo** Línea que se encuentra en el mismo plano que un círculo y lo cruza únicamente en un punto.	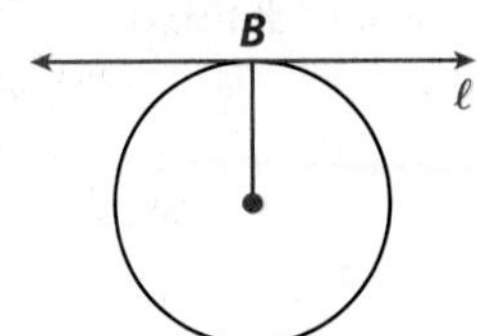
terminal point of a vector The endpoint of a vector.	**punto terminal de un vector** Extremo de un vector.	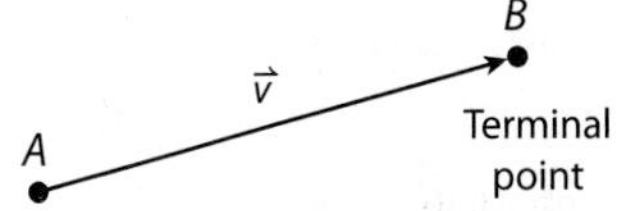
tetrahedron A polyhedron with four faces. A regular tetrahedron has equilateral triangles as faces, with three faces meeting at each vertex.	**tetraedro** Poliedro con cuatro caras. Las caras de un tetraedro regular son triángulos equiláteros y cada vértice es compartido por tres caras.	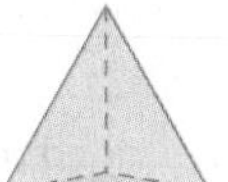
theorem A statement that has been proven.	**teorema** Enunciado que ha sido demostrado.	
theoretical probability The ratio of the number of equally likely outcomes in an event to the total number of possible outcomes.	**probabilidad teórica** Razón entre el número de resultados igualmente probables de un suceso y el número total de resultados posibles.	In the experiment of rolling a number cube, the theoretical probability of rolling an odd number is $\frac{3}{6} = \frac{1}{2}$.
three-dimensional coordinate system A space that is divided into eight regions by an *x*-axis, a *y*-axis, and a *z*-axis. The locations, or coordinates, of points are given by ordered triples	**sistema de coordenadas tridimensional** Espacio dividido en ocho regiones por un eje *x*, un eje *y* un eje *z*. Las ubicaciones, o coordenadas, de los puntos son dadas por tripletas ordenadas.	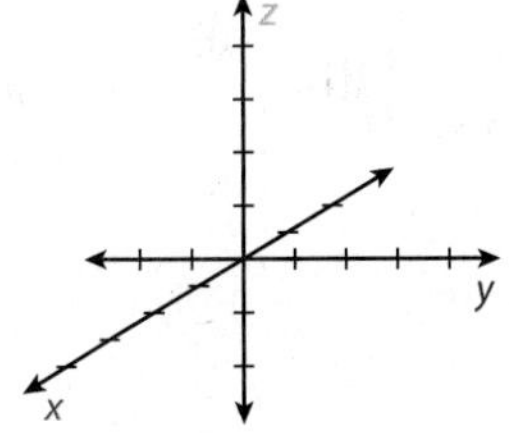
tick marks Marks used on a figure to indicate congruent segments.	**marcas "|"** Marcas utilizadas en una figura para indicar segmentos congruentes.	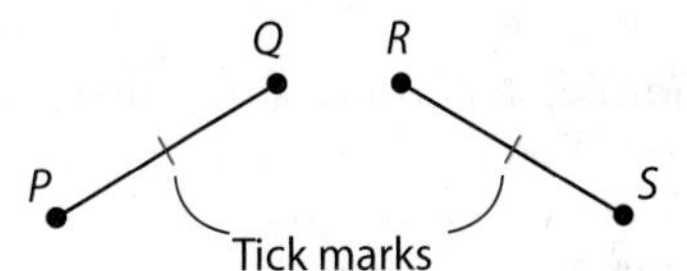
transformation A change in the position, size, or shape of a figure or graph.	**transformación** Cambio en la posición, tamaño o forma de una figura o gráfica.	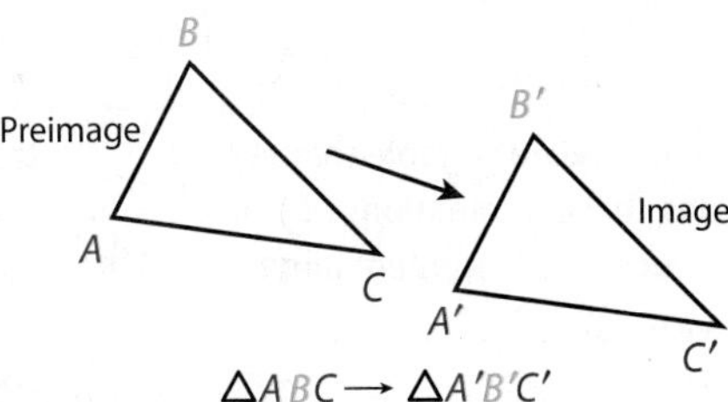

ENGLISH	SPANISH	EXAMPLES
translation A transformation that shifts or slides every point of a figure or graph the same distance in the same direction.	**traslación** Transformación en la que todos los puntos de una figura o gráfica se mueven la misma distancia en la misma dirección.	J M K L J′ M′ K′ L′
transversal A line that intersects two coplanar lines at two different points.	**transversal** Línea que corta dos líneas coplanares en dos puntos diferentes.	1 2 5 6 3 4 7 8 Transversal
trapezoid A quadrilateral with exactly one pair of parallel sides.	**trapecio** Cuadrilátero con sólo un par de lados paralelos.	B C A D
trial In probability, a single repetition or observation of an experiment.	**prueba** En probabilidad, una sola repetición u observación de un experimento.	In the experiment of rolling a number cube, each roll is one trial.
triangle A three-sided polygon.	**triángulo** Polígono de tres lados.	
triangle rigidity A property of triangles that states that if the side lengths of a triangle are fixed, the triangle can have only one shape.	**rigidez del triángulo** Propiedad de los triángulos que establece que, si las longitudes de los lados de un triángulo son fijas, el triángulo puede tener sólo una forma.	
trigonometric ratio A ratio of two sides of a right triangle.	**razón trigonométrica** Razón entre dos lados de un triángulo rectángulo.	B c a A b C $\sin A = \frac{a}{c}$; $\cos A = \frac{b}{c}$; $\tan A = \frac{a}{b}$
trigonometry The study of the measurement of triangles and of trigonometric functions and their applications.	**trigonometría** Estudio de la medición de los triángulos y de las funciones trigonométricas y sus aplicaciones.	
trinomial A polynomial with three terms.	**trinomio** Polinomio con tres términos.	$4x^2 + 3xy - 5y^2$
trisect To divide into three equal parts.	**trisecar** Dividir en tres partes iguales.	A B C D $\overline{AD}$ is trisected.
truth table A table that lists all possible combinations of truth values for a statement and its components.	**tabla de verdad** Tabla en la que se enumeran todas las combinaciones posibles de valores de verdad para un enunciado y sus componentes.	

ENGLISH	SPANISH	EXAMPLES
truth value A statement can have a truth value of true (T) or false (F).	**valor de verdad** Un enunciado puede tener un valor de verdad verdadero (V) o falso (F).	

U

undefined term A basic figure that is not defined in terms of other figures. The undefined terms in geometry are point, line, and plane.	**término indefinido** Figura básica que no está definida en función de otras figuras. Los términos indefinidos en geometría son el punto, la línea y el plano.	
union The union of two sets is the set of all elements that are in either set, denoted by ∪.	**unión** La unión de dos conjuntos es el conjunto de todos los elementos que se encuentran en ambos conjuntos, expresado por ∪.	$A = \{1, 2, 3, 4\}$ $B = \{1, 3, 5, 7, 9\}$ $A \cup B = \{1, 2, 3, 4, 5, 7, 9\}$
universal set The set of all elements in a particular context.	**conjunto universal** Conjunto de todos los elementos de un contexto determinado.	

V

vector A quantity that has both magnitude and direction.	**vector** Cantidad que tiene magnitud y dirección.	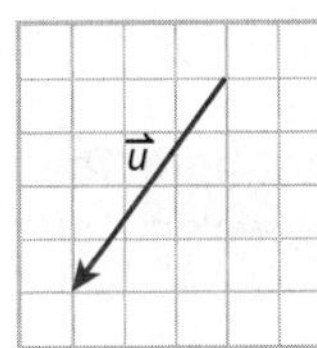
Venn diagram A diagram used to show relationships between sets.	**diagrama de Venn** Diagrama utilizado para mostrar la relación entre conjuntos.	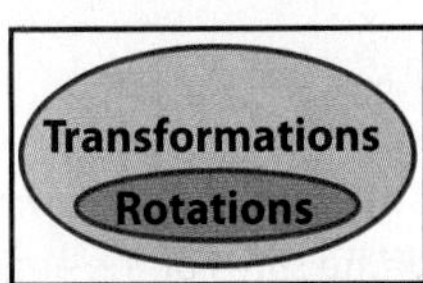
vertex angle of an isosceles triangle The angle formed by the legs of an isosceles triangle.	**ángulo del vértice de un triángulo isósceles** Ángulo formado por los catetos de un triángulo isósceles.	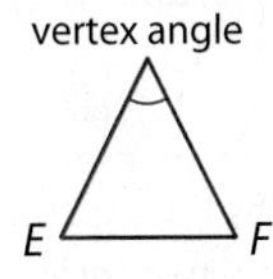
vertex form of a quadratic function A quadratic function written in the form $f(x) = a(x - h)^2 + k$, where a, h, and k are constants and (h, k) is the vertex.	**forma en vértice de una función cuadrática** Una function cuadrática expresada en la forma $f(x) = a(x - h)^2 + k$, donde a, h y k son constantes y (h, k) es el vértice.	

ENGLISH	SPANISH	EXAMPLES
vertex of a cone The point opposite the base of the cone.	**vértice de un cono** Punto opuesto a la base del cono.	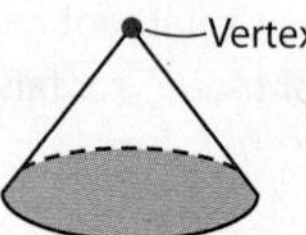
vertex of a parabola The highest or lowest point on the parabola.	**vértice de una parábola** Punto más alto o más bajo de una parábola.	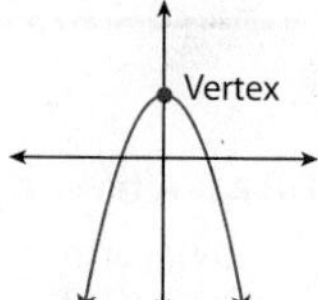
vertex of a polygon The intersection of two sides of the polygon.	**vértice de un polígono** La intersección de dos lados del polígono.	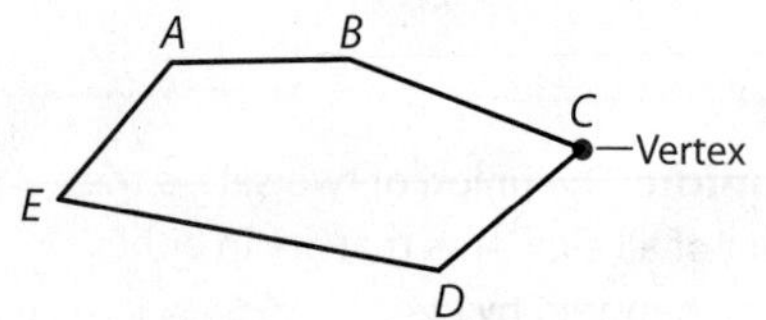 *A*, *B*, *C*, *D*, and *E* are vertices of the polygon.
vertex of a pyramid The point opposite the base of the pyramid.	**vértice de una pirámide** Punto opuesto a la base de la pirámide.	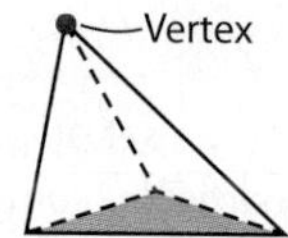
vertex of a three-dimensional figure The point that is the intersection of three or more faces of the figure.	**vértice de una figura tridimensional** Punto que representa la intersección de tres o más caras de la figura.	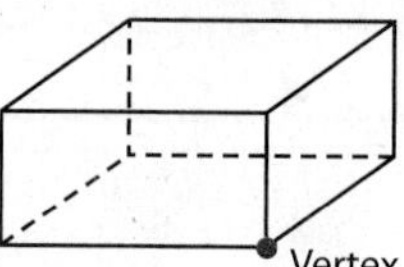
vertex of a triangle The intersection of two sides of the triangle.	**vértice de un triángulo** Intersección de dos lados del triángulo.	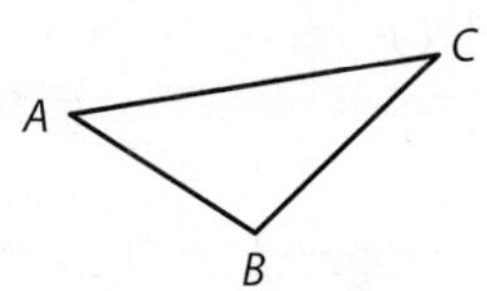 *A*, *B*, and *C* are vertices of $\triangle ABC$.
vertex of an angle The common endpoint of the sides of the angle.	**vértice de un ángulo** Extremo común de los lados del ángulo.	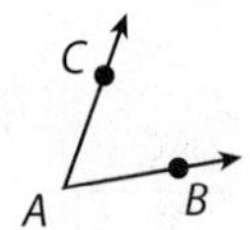 *A* is the vertex of $\angle CAB$.
vertical angles The nonadjacent angles formed by two intersecting lines.	**ángulos opuestos por el vértice** Ángulos no adyacentes formados por dos rectas que se cruzan.	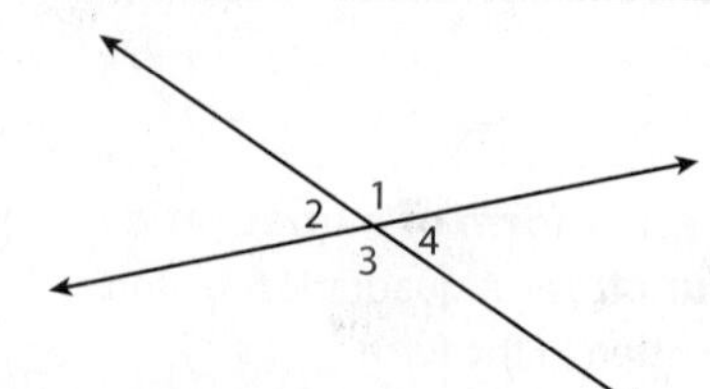 $\angle 1$ and $\angle 3$ are vertical angles. $\angle 2$ and $\angle 4$ are vertical angles.

ENGLISH	SPANISH	EXAMPLES

volume The number of nonoverlapping unit cubes of a given size that will exactly fill the interior of a three-dimensional figure.

volumen Cantidad de cubos unitarios no superpuestos de un determinado tamaño que llenan exactamente el interior de una figura tridimensional.

4 ft
3 ft
12 ft

Volume $= (3)(4)(12) = 144$ ft^3

X

***x*-axis** The horizontal axis in a coordinate plane.

eje *x* Eje horizontal en un plano cartesiano.

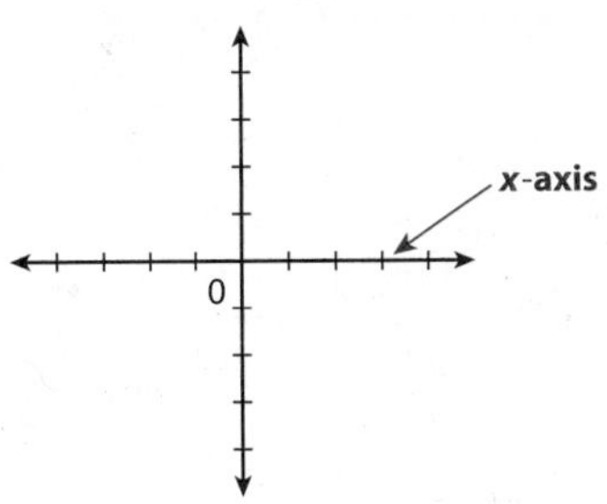

Y

***y*-axis** The vertical axis in a coordinate plane.

eje *y* Eje vertical en un plano cartesiano.

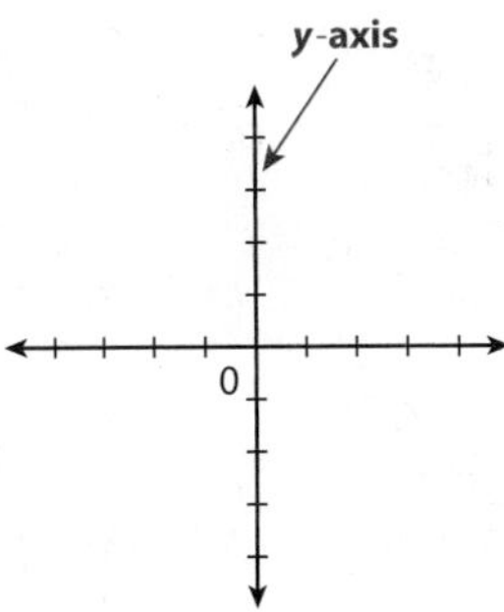

Z

zero exponent For any nonzero real number x, $x^0 = 1$.

exponente cero Dado un número real distinto de cero x, $x^0 = 1$.

$5^0 = 1$

---

zero of a function For the function f, any number x such that $f(x) = 0$.

cero de una función Dada la función f, todo número x tal que $f(x) = 0$.

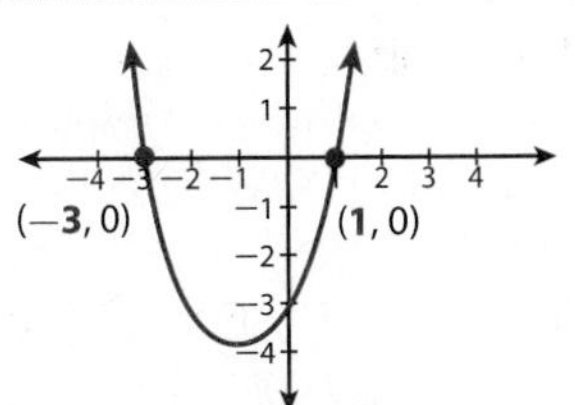

The zeros are −3 and 1.

Zero Product Property For real numbers p and q, if $pq = 0$, then $p = 0$ or $q = 0$.

Propiedad del producto cero Dados los números reales p y q, si $pq = 0$, entonces $p = 0$ o $q = 0$.

If $(x - 1)(x + 2) = 0$, then $x - 1 = 0$ or $x + 2 = 0$, so $x = 1$ or $x = -2$.

Glossary/Glosario

Index

Index locator numbers are in Module. Lesson form. For example, 2.1 indicates Module 2, Lesson 1 as listed in the Table of Contents.

A

B

C

D

E

F

G

H

I

L

M

N

O

P

Q

R

S

Index

T

U

V

X

Z

Table of Measures

LENGTH

1 inch = 2.54 centimeters
1 meter = 39.37 inches
1 mile = 5,280 feet
1 mile = 1760 yards
1 mile = 1.609 kilometers
1 kilometer = 0.62 mile

MASS/WEIGHT

1 pound = 16 ounces
1 pound = 0.454 kilograms
1 kilogram = 2.2 pounds
1 ton = 2000 pounds

CAPACITY

1 cup = 8 fluid ounces
1 pint = 2 cups
1 quart = 2 pints
1 gallon = 4 quarts
1 gallon = 3.785 liters
1 liter = 0.264 gallons
1 liter = 1000 cubic centimeters

Symbols

Symbol	Meaning
$\neq$	is not equal to
$\approx$	is approximately equal to
10^2	ten squared; ten to the second power
$2.\overline{6}$	repeating decimal 2.66666...
$\lvert -4 \rvert$	the absolute value of negative 4
$\sqrt{}$	square root
π	pi: (about 3.14)
$\perp$	is perpendicular to
$\parallel$	is parallel to
$\overleftrightarrow{AB}$	line *AB*
$\overrightarrow{AB}$	ray *AB*
$\overline{AB}$	line segment *AB*
$m\angle A$	measure of $\angle A$

Formulas

FACTORING	
Perfect square trinomials	$a^2 + 2ab + b^2 = (a+b)^2$
	$a^2 - 2ab + b^2 = (a-b)^2$
Difference of squares	$a^2 - b^2 = (a-b)(a+b)$

PROPERTIES OF EXPONENTS	
Product of powers	$a^m a^n = a^{(m+n)}$
Quotient of powers	$\frac{a^m}{a^n} = a^{(m-n)}$
Power of a power	$(a^m)^n = a^{mn}$
Rational exponent	$a^{\frac{m}{n}} = \sqrt[n]{a^m}$
Negative exponent	$a^{-n} = \frac{1}{a^n}$

QUADRATIC EQUATIONS	
Standard form	$f(x) = ax^2 + bx + c$
Vertex form	$f(x) = a(x-h)^2 + k$
Quadratic formula	$x = \frac{-b \pm \sqrt{b^2 - 4ac}}{2a}$
Axis of symmetry	$x = \frac{-b}{2a}$

VOLUME	
General Prisms	$V = Bh$
Cylinder	$V = \pi r^2 h$
Sphere	$V = \frac{4}{3}\pi r^3$
Cone	$V = \frac{1}{3}\pi r^2 h$
Pyramid	$V = \frac{1}{3}Bh$